GEORGIA QUALITY CORE CURRICULUM

correlated to

HOLT SCIENCE AND TECHNOLOGY:
Physical Science

HOLT, RINEHART AND WINSTON

A Harcourt Education Company

STAFF CREDITS

Director of Special Projects: Suzanne Thompson

Managing Editor: Joan Marie Lindsay

Senior Editor: Annie Hartnett

Product Analysts: Jan Bond and Robert Crowder

Editorial Coordinator: John Kendall

Copyright © by Holt, Rinehart and Winston

All rights reserved. No part of this publication may be reproduced or transmitted in any form or by any means, electronic or mechanical, including photocopy, recording, or any information storage and retrieval system, without permission in writing from the publisher.

Requests for permission to make copies of any part of the work should be mailed to the following address: Permissions Department, Holt, Rinehart and Winston, 10801 N. MoPac Expressway, Building 3, Austin, Texas 78759.

Printed in the United States of America

ISBN 0-03-066897-2

23 048 0302

Objective	Component Strand/Course Content Standard	Where Taught (Representative page numbers where skills are taught or assessed; *PE* refers to the Pupil's Edition and *ATE* refers to the Annotated Teacher's Edition)	
	Topic: Scientific Inquiry Process		
1.	Uses process skills of observing, classifying, communicating, measuring, predicting, inferring, identifying, and manipulating variables; recording analyzing and operationally defining, formulating models, experimenting, constructing hypotheses and drawing conclusions.	PE	5, 12, 13, 35, 59, 81, 107, 137, 161, 187, 213, 245, 279, 301, 327, 349, 373, 397, 421, 453, 481, 509, 533, 563, 593, 626, 627, 628, 629, 630, 631, 632, 633, 634, 635, 636, 637, 638, 639, 640, 641, 642, 643, 644, 645, 646, 647, 648, 649, 650, 651, 652, 653, 654, 655, 656, 657, 658, 659, 660, 661, 662, 663, 664, 665, 666, 667, 678, 679, 680, 681, 682, 683, 684, 685, 686, 687, 688, 689, 690, 691, 692, 693, 694, 695, 696, 697, 698, 699, 700, 701, 702, 706, 708, 710, 712, 713, 714, 716, 717, 718, 720, 722
	Topic: Safety Skills		
2.	Understands and applies laboratory safety rules and practices.	PE	5, 27, 49, 59, 71, 81, 87, 137, 161, 166, 187, 213, 327, 349, 357, 364, 373, 397, 442, 443, 453, 481, 509, 563, 593, 622-625, 627, 628, 629, 630, 632, 633, 634, 636, 637, 638, 640, 642, 644, 647, 650, 651, 652, 653, 654, 656, 658, 660, 664, 665, 666, 670, 671, 672, 675, 676, 680, 683, 684, 686, 688, 690, 695, 696, 698, 699, 700, 702, 706, 708, 713, 714, 716, 717, 718, 720, 722

Objective	Component Strand/Course Content Standard	Where Taught (Representative page numbers where skills are taught or assessed; *PE* refers to the Pupil's Edition and *ATE* refers to the Annotated Teacher's Edition)
	Topic: Standard International (SI) Measurements (Metric System)	
	Defines and identifies standards of measurement.	
3.1	Names the prefixes used in the SI system.	PE 24, 25, 26, 27, 729, 730
3.2	Identifies SI units and symbols for length, volume, mass, density, time, and temperature.	PE 25, 26, 27, 729, 730
3.3	Converts measurements among related SI units.	PE 26, 38, 45, 109, 113, 139, 149, 162, 170, 190, 196, 217, 249, 257, 437, 497, 519, 540, 566, 628, 630-631, 632, 638-639, 651, 658-659, 662-663, 664, 666-667, 668-669, 672-673, 675, 678, 679, 708-709, 722, 723
3.4	Uses appropriate tools for determining mass volume, temperature, density, and length.	PE 107, 161, 213, 245, 253, 373, 593, 627, 628, 629, 630-631, 632, 633, 636, 638-639, 642, 643, 644-645, 646, 650, 651, 653, 654-655, 656-657, 658-659, 662-663, 664, 666-667, 668-669, 670, 672-673, 674, 675, 678-679, 683, 684-685, 690, 692-693, 695, 706-707, 708-709, 710-711, 713, 717, 718-719, 722, 852

Objective	Component Strand/Course Content Standard	Where Taught (Representative page numbers where skills are taught or assessed; *PE* refers to the Pupil's Edition and *ATE* refers to the Annotated Teacher's Edition)	
	Topic: Reference Skills		
4.	Selects and uses multiple types of print and nonprint sources for information on science concepts.	PE	29, 53, 75, 99, 131, 155, 179, 207, 239, 271, 295, 319, 343, 367, 391, 413, 447, 475, 501, 527, 557, 587, 615, 631
	Topic: Structure of Matter		
	Explains the properties and phases of matter, using as an example the composition and properties of water.		
5.1	Distinguishes between atoms and molecules and among elements, mixtures and compounds.	PE	81, 82, 83, 84, 85, 86, 87, 88, 89, 90, 92, 93, 94, 95, 96, 97, 279, 287, 288, 289, 290, 291, 346, 347, 640, 641, 642, 643, 676, 677
		ATE	79E, 79F, 82, 83, 277F, 287, 289
5.2	Describes the structure of elements.	PE	280–283, 284, 285, 286, 287, 288, 289, 290, 291
		ATE	277E, 277F, 287, 288, 289, 676, 677
5.3	Describes the periodic table of elements and uses it to find information about an element.	PE	304, 305, 306, 307, 308, 309, 744, 745
		ATE	305, 306, 307, 308
5.4	Uses the periodic table to classify an element as a metal, nonmetal, or metalloid.	PE	304, 305, 306, 307, 308, 309, 310, 311, 312, 313, 314, 315, 316, 317
		ATE	299F, 304, 305, 306, 307, 311, 313, 316, 678, 679
5.5	Describes atomic number and atomic mass.	PE	288, 290, 742
		ATE	288, 289
5.6	Distinguishes physical and chemical properties and physical and chemical changes.	PE	34, 35, 36, 37, 38, 39, 40, 41, 43, 44, 45, 46, 630, 631, 632, 633
		ATE	33E, 33F, 34, 37, 38, 41, 42, 43, 44, 45, 46
		PE	48, 49, 50, 51, 262, 634, 635, 684, 685
		ATE	33F
5.7	Recognizes and writes common chemical symbols, chemical formulas, and chemical equations.	PE	352, 353, 354, 355, 356, 743
		ATE	347E, 354, 357

v

Objective	Component Strand/Course Content Standard	Where Taught (Representative page numbers where skills are taught or assessed; *PE* refers to the Pupil's Edition and *ATE* refers to the Annotated Teacher's Edition)
	Topic: Structure of Matter (Cont.)	
6.1	Analyzes the relationship of matter and energy. Describes how the molecular motion changes in each phase of matter.	PE 58, 59, 60, 61, 62, 63, 64, 65, 66, 67, 68, 69, 70, 71, 72, 73, 260, 261, 262, 636, 637, 638, 639 ATE 57E, 57F, 61, 62, 64, 65, 69, 70, 71, 72, 79, 260, 261
6.2	Discusses the nature of freezing, condensing, boiling, and evaporating.	PE 68, 69, 70, 71, 72, 73 ATE 57F, 69, 70, 71, 72

Objective	Component Strand/Course Content Standard	Where Taught (Representative page numbers where skills are taught or assessed; *PE* refers to the Pupil's Edition and *ATE* refers to the Annotated Teacher's Edition)
	Topic: Structure of Matter (Cont.)	
7.1	Defines acid and base. Describes the characteristic properties of acids and bases.	PE 377, 378, 379, 380, 743 ATE 371E, 378, 379
7.2	Lists the names, formulas, and uses of some common acids and bases.	PE 377, 378, 379, 380, 381, 743 ATE 371E, 378, 379, 381
7.3	Explain what a salt is and how salts form.	PE 382 ATE 371F

Objective	Component Strand/Course Content Standard	Where Taught (Representative page numbers where skills are taught or assessed; *PE* refers to the Pupil's Edition and *ATE* refers to the Annotated Teacher's Edition)
	Topic: Motion, Forces, and Energy	
8.1	Describes how energy and work are related. Distinguishes between kinetic and potential energy.	PE 215–220, 223, 224, 225, 227, 228, 232, 234, 235, 236, 242 ATE 214, 215, 216, 217, 218, 219, 220, 223, 224, 225, 227, 228, 229, 232, 234, 235, 236
8.2	Describes different forms of energy (e.g., mechanical, electrical, chemical, radiant, nuclear, etc.).	PE 215, 216, 217, 218, 219, 220, 221, 222, 223, 225, 226, 227, 232, 233, 234, 235, 236, 237 ATE 215, 217, 218, 219, 220, 223, 224, 225, 227, 228, 232, 234, 236
8.3	Describes how energy and power are related.	PE 437, 438, 439 ATE 438

Objective	Component Strand/Course Content Standard	Where Taught (Representative page numbers where skills are taught or assessed; *PE* refers to the Pupil's Edition and *ATE* refers to the Annotated Teacher's Edition)
	Topic: Motion, Forces, and Energy (Cont.)	
	Defines speed as a rate.	
9.1	Performs calculations involving speed, time, and distance to interpret distance-time graphs.	PE 107, 109, 110, 111, 112, 113, 114, 646, 748 ATE 105E, 105F, 110, 112
9.2	Compares and contrasts speed, velocity, and acceleration.	PE 109, 110, 111, 112, 113, 114 ATE 105E, 110, 111, 112
9.3	Recognizes different examples of forces.	PE 116, 117, 118, 119, 120, 121, 122, 123, 124, 125, 126, 127, 128 ATE 105E, 105F, 116, 119, 120, 121, 126, 127, 128
9.4	States and describes Newton's three laws of motion.	PE 145, 146, 147, 148, 149, 150, 151 ATE 105E, 105F, 145, 146
9.5	Gives examples of the effects of gravity.	PE 126, 127, 138, 139, 140, 141, 142, 143, 144 ATE 126, 127, 128, 139, 141, 142
9.6	Relates gravitational force to mass and distance.	PE 125, 126, 127, 128, 129, 136, 137, 138, 139, 140, 141, 142, 143, 149, 151, 651, 746 ATE 105F, 126, 127, 128, 135E, 135F, 139, 141, 653
9.7	Distinguishes between mass and weight.	PE 128, 129
9.8	Evaluates the advantages and disadvantages of passenger restraint devices as related to force and motion.	PE 146

Objective	Component Strand/Course Content Standard	Where Taught (Representative page numbers where skills are taught or assessed; *PE* refers to the Pupil's Edition and *ATE* refers to the Annotated Teacher's Edition)
	Topic: Motion, Forces, and Energy (Cont.)	
10.1	Explains the relationship among force, motion and acceleration. Explains why objects thrown or shot follow a curved path.	PE 141, 142, 143, 144 ATE 142
10.2	Compares motion in a straight line with circular motion.	PE 143, 144 ATE 143
10.3	Defines weightlessness.	PE 136, 141
10.4	Analyzes action and reaction forces.	PE 145, 146, 147, 148, 149, 150, 151, 152, 153 ATE 150, 151
10.5	Explains conservation of momentum.	PE 152, 153

Objective	Component **Strand/Course** **Content Standard**	Where Taught (Representative page numbers where skills are taught or assessed; *PE* refers to the Pupil's Edition and *ATE* refers to the Annotated Teacher's Edition)
	Topic: Motion, Forces, and Energy (Cont.)	
	Describes how particles of a fluid exert pressure.	
11.1	States Archimedes' principle.	PE 104, 168, 169, 747
11.2	States Bernoulli's principle and describes a way Bernoulli's principle is applied.	PE 173, 174, 175, 748 ATE 159F, 174, 176
11.3	Explains how a hydraulic device operates.	PE 167

Objective	Component Strand/Course Content Standard	Where Taught (Representative page numbers where skills are taught or assessed; *PE* refers to the Pupil's Edition and *ATE* refers to the Annotated Teacher's Edition)
	Topic: Motion, Forces, and Energy (Cont.)	
12.1	Explains how machines make work easier. Describes six types of simple machines.	PE 187, 198, 199, 200, 201, 202, 203, 204, 205, 211, 664, 665, 666, 667 ATE 185F, 187, 198, 199, 201, 202, 203, 211
12.2	Recognizes the simple machines that make up a compound machine.	PE 204, 205
12.3	Describes the relationship between work, power, and time.	PE 191
12.4	Explains what the science of bionics involves.	PE* 210
12.5	Contrasts two methods of using electrical signals to trigger motion of a limb or other body processes.	PE* 210

Objective	Component Strand/Course Content Standard	Where Taught (Representative page numbers where skills are taught or assessed; *PE* refers to the Pupil's Edition and *ATE* refers to the Annotated Teacher's Edition)
	Topic: Motion, Forces, and Energy (Cont.)	
13.1	Explains how satellites are placed in orbit around the earth. Gives examples of how satellites are used to improve the overall quality of life.	PE* 499
	Topic: Energy and Its Transformation: Heat	
14.1	Investigates the characteristics, movements, and measurements of heat energy. Demonstrates the difference between heat and temperature.	PE 246, 247, 248, 249, 250, 251, 252, 253, 254, 255, 256, 257, 258, 259 ATE 243, 246, 251, 253, 254, 257
14.2	Shows how heat causes matter to expand and contract.	PE 248, 250
14.3	Explains how heat is transferred by conduction, convection, and radiation.	PE 253, 254, 255 ATE 254
14.4	Identifies some causes and effects of thermal pollutions.	PE 269
14.5	Discusses some possible solutions for thermal pollution problems.	PE 269

XIII

Objective	Component Strand/Course Content Standard	Where Taught (Representative page numbers where skills are taught or assessed; *PE* refers to the Pupil's Edition and *ATE* refers to the Annotated Teacher's Edition)
	Topic: Energy and Its Transformation: Waves	
15.1	Describes how waves carry energy. Discusses the characteristics and properties of waves.	PE 510, 511, 512, 516, 517, 518, 519, 520, 521, 522, 523, 524 ATE 507E, 507F, 513, 515, 516, 517, 518, 520, 521, 522, 523
15.2	Explains how wavelength, frequency, and speed are related.	PE 517, 518, 519 ATE 517, 518
15.3	Compares transverse and compressional waves.	PE 513, 514, 515, 516 ATE 507F, 513, 514, 516
15.4	Describes how waves are refracted and reflected.	PE 520, 521 ATE 520

Objective	Component **Strand/Course** **Content Standard**	Where Taught (Representative page numbers where skills are taught or assessed; *PE* refers to the Pupil's Edition and *ATE* refers to the Annotated Teacher's Edition)
	Topic: Energy and Its Transformation: Light	
16.1	Contrasts electromagnetic waves and other kinds of waves (e.g., sound, water). Describes the electromagnetic spectrum.	PE 567, 568, 569, 570, 571, 572, 574 ATE 561E, 567, 569, 570, 572, 573, 574
16.2	Explains at least one application of each type of electromagnetic wave.	PE 567, 568, 569, 570, 571 ATE 570, 571

Objective	Component **Strand/Course** **Content Standard**	Where Taught (Representative page numbers where skills are taught or assessed; *PE* refers to the Pupil's Edition and *ATE* refers to the Annotated Teacher's Edition)
	Topic: Energy and Its Transformation: Light	
17.1	States and give an example of the law of reflection. Explains how refraction is used to separate light into the colors of the spectrum.	PE 572, 577, 578 ATE 578
17.2	Describes how diffraction and interference patterns demonstrate wave behavior.	PE 579, 580

Objective	Component Strand/Course Content Standard	Where Taught (Representative page numbers where skills are taught or assessed; *PE* refers to the Pupil's Edition and *ATE* refers to the Annotated Teacher's Edition)
	Topic: Energy and Its Transformation: Light (Cont.)	
	Investigates the relationship between light and color.	
18.1	Describes the differences among opaque, transparent, and translucent materials.	PE 582, 583 ATE 582, 583
18.2	Explains how you see color.	PE 572, 581, 582, 583, 584, 585 ATE 561F, 583
18.3	Describes the difference between light color and pigment color.	PE 584, 585

Objective	Component Strand/Course Content Standard	Where Taught (Representative page numbers where skills are taught or assessed; *PE* refers to the Pupil's Edition and *ATE* refers to the Annotated Teacher's Edition)
	Topic: Energy and Its Transformation: Light (Cont.)	
	Discusses how light interacts with mirrors and lenses to produce images.	
19.1	Explains how images are formed in mirrors.	PE 598, 599, 600, 601, 602 ATE 591F, 598, 599, 600, 601
19.2	Identifies uses of plane, concave, and convex mirrors.	PE 599, 600, 601, 602 ATE 599, 600, 601
19.3	Describes the types of images formed with convex and concave lenses.	PE 603, 604, 606 ATE 591E, 603
19.4	Compares refracting and reflecting telescopes.	PE 609
19.5	Discusses the technological advances in the use of light (e.g., fiber optics, lasers, cameras, microscopes, etc.)	PE 608, 609, 610, 611, 612, 613 ATE 591F, 609, 610, 611, 612

Objective	Component Strand/Course Content Standard	Where Taught (Representative page numbers where skills are taught or assessed; *PE* refers to the Pupil's Edition and *ATE* refers to the Annotated Teacher's Edition)
	Topic: Energy and Its Transformation: Electricity	
20.1	Lists the characteristics of electricity. Describes how static and current electricity differ.	PE 426, 427, 428 ATE 419E, 427
20.2	Describes the relationship between electrical current and circuits.	PE 433, 434, 435, 436, 437, 438, 439, 440, 441, 442, 443 ATE 419F, 434, 435, 436, 437, 441, 442, 443
20.3	Explains how a dry cell is a source of electricity.	PE 430, 431 ATE 419E
20.4	Describes, sketches and lists applications for a series and parallel circuit.	PE 441, 442, 443 ATE 419F, 441, 443
20.5	Distinguishes between conductors and insulators.	PE 426, 427
20.6	Identifies the function of circuit breakers and fuses.	PE 445 ATE 419F
20.7	Calculates the amount of electrical energy in kilowatt-hours.	PE 437, 438, 439 ATE 419F
20.8	Explains the occurrence of lightning in terms of induction and static discharge	PE 428, 429 ATE 428
20.9	Evaluates the positive and negative aspect of lightning induced forest fires.	PE* 78
20.10	Identifies safety measures when dealing with electricity and lightning.	PE 429, 445

Objective	Component Strand/Course Content Standard	Where Taught (Representative page numbers where skills are taught or assessed; *PE* refers to the Pupil's Edition and *ATE* refers to the Annotated Teacher's Edition)
	Topic: Energy and Its Transformation: Electricity and Magnetism	
	Describes the properties of magnets.	
21.1	Defines magnetic field.	PE 456 ATE 451E
21.2	Explains the magnetic effects of a current in a wire.	PE 465, 466, 467 ATE 451F, 465, 466
21.3	Compares and contrasts voltmeters and ammeters.	PE 696–697 PE* 431, 433–435, 467, 468–469, 695
21.4	Describes the function of an electric motor.	PE 466 ATE 451F, 466
21.5	Describes how a generator produces electric current.	PE 234, 470, 471 ATE 434, 471
21.6	Distinguishes between alternating and direct current.	PE 434
21.7	Explains the function of step up and step down transformers.	PE 472 ATE 472
21.8	Describes the characteristics and applications of super conductors.	PE 274, 436 ATE 436
21.9	Describes the use of magnetic resonance imaging (MRI) in medicine.	PE 479 ATE 479

Objective	Component Strand/Course Content Standard	Where Taught (Representative page numbers where skills are taught or assessed; *PE* refers to the Pupil's Edition and *ATE* refers to the Annotated Teacher's Edition)
	Topic: Energy and Its Transformation: Sound	
22.1	Describes sound as a form of energy produced by vibrations. Lists the characteristics of waves.	PE 532, 533, 539, 540, 541, 542, 543, 560, 710, 711, 713, 714, 715 ATE 531E, 531F, 539, 540, 541, 542, 543, 560
22.2	Discusses the relationship between frequency and wavelength.	PE 534, 535, 540, 541, 542 ATE 531E, 535, 541, 542
22.3	Compares and contrasts transverse and compressional waves.	PE 535

Objective	Component Strand/Course Content Standard	Where Taught (Representative page numbers where skills are taught or assessed; *PE* refers to the Pupil's Edition and *ATE* refers to the Annotated Teacher's Edition)
	Topic: Energy and Its Transformation: Sound	
23.1	Describes the transmission of sound through a medium. Identifies the relationships between intensity and loudness, and frequency and pitch.	PE 540, 541, 542 ATE 541
23.2	Illustrates the Doppler effect.	PE 542 ATE 531E, 542

Objective	Component Strand/Course Content Standard	Where Taught (Representative page numbers where skills are taught or assessed; *PE* refers to the Pupil's Edition and *ATE* refers to the Annotated Teacher's Edition)
	Topic: Energy and Its Transformation: Sound (Cont.)	
	Distinguishes between music and noise.	
24.1	Describes why instruments produce sounds of different quality.	PE 553, 554 ATE 531F, 553, 554
24.2	Explains two types of wave interference.	PE 548, 549, 550 ATE 548, 549, 550
25.1	Describes the uses of ultrasound technology in medicine.	PE 547 ATE 547

Objective	Component Strand/Course Content Standard	Where Taught (Representative page numbers where skills are taught or assessed; *PE* refers to the Pupil's Edition and *ATE* refers to the Annotated Teacher's Edition)
	Topic: Energy and Its Transformation: Alternative Energy Sources	
26.1	Recognizes the major energy sources people use today to meet their energy needs. Defines and investigates energy sources such as solar, wind, geothermal heat, nuclear, fossil fuels, and hydroelectric power.	PE 232, 233, 234, 235, 236, 237 ATE 233, 234, 236, 237
26.2	Identifies ways energy can be conserved.	PE 19, 229, 230, 231, 362 ATE 211F, 229, 230, 362
26.3	Compares and contrasts alternative energy sources.	PE 218, 219, 220, 221 ATE 211F, 218, 219
26.4	Identifies models that demonstrate how wind, sun, water, geothermal energy and waves can be used as alternative energy sources.	PE 224, 225, 226, 227, 228, 235, 236, 237 ATE 211F, 236, 237
26.5	Discusses problems associated with storing and disposal of nuclear waste.	PE 237, 409, 410, 411 ATE 408

Welcome to

Physical Science

An Overview of *Holt Science and Technology: Physical Science* T2

Components Listing T18

Correlation to the National Science Education Standards T19

**EXPECT EXCITEMENT!
EXPECT RESULTS!**

HOLT SCIENCE & TECHNOLOGY

A Text that Grabs and Holds Your Students' Attention

Pupil's Edition

Begins with a bang!
Each chapter begins with a brief introduction designed to pique your students' interest. Here they may encounter a true story or a hypothetical situation that poses prereading questions, such as **Imagine. . . .**

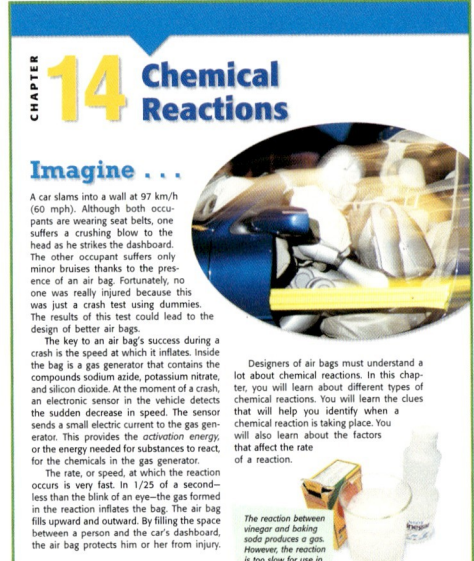

A text that motivates
Holt Science and Technology motivates your students in a variety of ways.

Visuals
- are integrated into the narrative
- clearly reveal macro-to-micro relationships
- support English-language learners and reluctant readers
- are functional, accurate, and understandable

Narrative
- contains concise, outline-style headings to help students find information easily
- presents content in a clear, logical sequence
- contains friendly language to make reading accessible and enjoyable
- incorporates analogies to help students relate concepts to the real world

HOLT SCIENCE AND TECHNOLOGY

> "I need a textbook that will **engage** and **excite** my students while they're learning."

Applies to real life

Some of your students may ask you why they are studying science. *Holt Science and Technology* provides answers with motivating features:

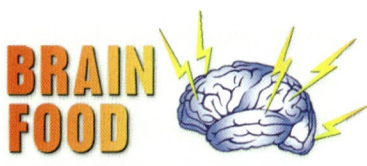

Pennies minted before 1982 are made mostly of copper and have a density of 8.85 g/cm³. In 1982, a penny's worth of copper began to cost more than one cent, so the U.S. Department of the Treasury began producing pennies using mostly zinc with a copper coating. Pennies minted after 1982 have a density of 7.14 g/cm³. Check it out for yourself!

- **Investigate!** stimulates your students' curiosity about upcoming chapter concepts with a hands-on activity.
- Tidbits to feed the mind are presented in small captions called **Brain Food**. There's nothing better than a fun fact to captivate a young audience!
- **Apply** poses real-world questions and asks your students to answer them by applying what they have just learned.
- **Activity** gives your students the opportunity to use their imaginations and to expand their learning.

Brings focus to the Internet

*sci*LINKS—a National Science Teachers Association-sponsored Web service—links you and your students to interactive activities and current information directly related to chapter content. (see page T17)

The first middle school program with sciLINKS

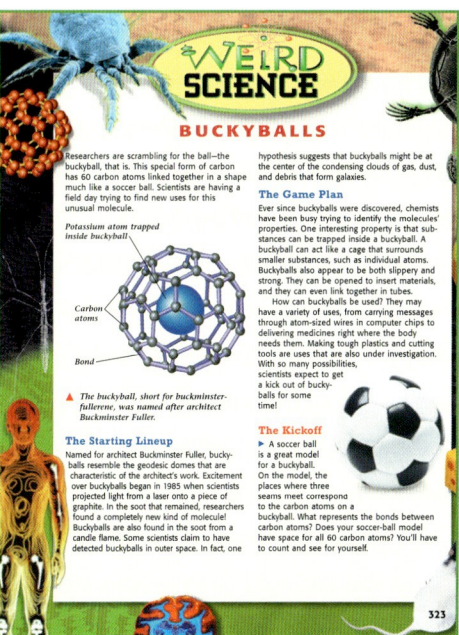

Ends with enrichment

Weird Science, **Health Watch**, **Careers**, **Scientific Debate**, and other end-of-chapter features extend chapter content with real-world examples, articles, and motivating activities.

Pupil's Edition

HOLT SCIENCE AND TECHNOLOGY

Focus on Reading and Understanding

Holt Science and Technology makes instruction accessible to all your students—English-language learners, special needs students, those having difficulty mastering content, students who need more practice or hands-on experience, and advanced learners.

Read for understanding
Each lesson gives you suggestions to help your students read for understanding.

- **What Do You Think?** assesses your students' prior knowledge and serves as a reading warm-up.

- **NOW What Do You Think?** allows students to see how their understanding has changed.

-  highlights activities that help English-language learners grasp content.

- **READING STRATEGY** emphasizes key concepts in order to guide reading and ensure comprehension.

- *Directed Reading Worksheets* makes reading an active process. A variety of strategies and fun activities help your students identify the main idea, then organize and synthesize supporting information.

- *Reinforcement & Vocabulary Review Worksheets* makes reviewing and reinforcing chapter content easy. Students have opportunities to examine issues in each section from different perspectives or to benefit from a different instructional approach.

READING STRATEGY
Prediction Guide Before students read the passage about friction...

READING STRATEGY
Writing Activity After students have read about velocity, have them write a paragraph in their ScienceLog that gives examples of when it is sufficient to know only the speed of something and when it is important to know the velocity.

NOW What Do You Think?
Take a minute to review your answers to the ScienceLog questions found on...

What Do You Think?
In your ScienceLog, try to answer the following questions based on what you already know:
1. What does it mean to do work?
2. How are machines helpful when doing work?

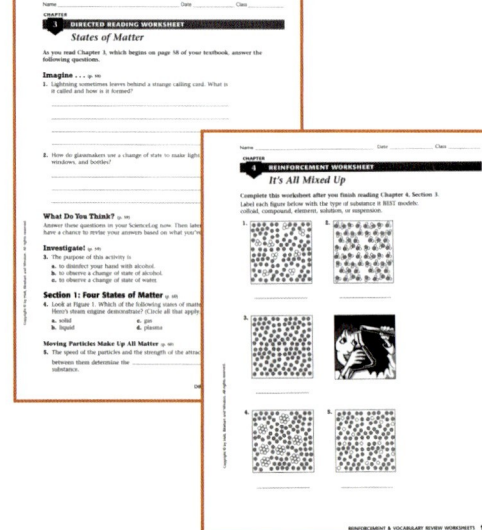

> "I need a program that helps me teach **today's students**."

Guided Reading Audio CD Program

This audio program provides students with a direct reading of each chapter using instructional visuals as guideposts. Auditory learners, students with limited reading proficiency, and Spanish-speaking students receive the explanation they need from this alternative text format.
Available in both English and Spanish.

Provide universal access

Holt Science and Technology helps all your students learn science.

- **Meeting Individual Needs** in the teacher's wrap provides engaging demonstrations and hands-on activities to help learners having difficulty and advanced learners.
- **Reteaching** gives you alternate methods of instruction for those students who need it.
- **Homework** options use a variety of teaching strategies to complement diverse learning styles.
- **Critical Thinking & Problem Solving Worksheets** provides challenging activities connecting science concepts to the "real world." Your students learn to think through a problem and to use the scientific method and other strategies to find a solution.

MEETING INDIVIDUAL NEEDS

Writing **Advanced Learners**

MEETING INDIVIDUAL NEEDS

Writing **Learners Having Difficulty**
In a given temperate region, different animals have different ways of surviving cold winters. Have students list as many behaviors or adaptations for winter survival that they can think of **Sheltered English**

Approach learning from different angles

with these in-text features and ancillaries. You can make sure your students understand science concepts no matter what their learning style.

 **Science CONNECTION**

 **Environment CONNECTION**

GROUP ACTIVITY

HOLT ANTHOLOGY OF SCIENCE FICTION

 **Multicultural CONNECTION**

REAL-WORLD CONNECTION

COOPERATIVE LEARNING

HOLT SCIENCE POSTERS

 **Teaching Transparency**

 **Science Puzzlers, Twisters & Teasers**

 **CROSS-DISCIPLINARY FOCUS**

Universal Access

Labs to Make Learning Active and Meaningful

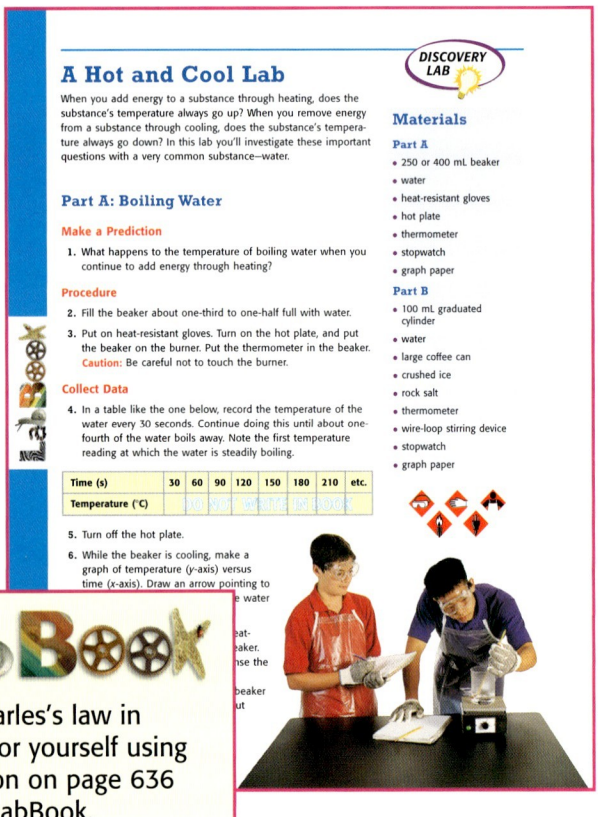

See Charles's law in action for yourself using a balloon on page 636 of the LabBook.

Holt Science and Technology provides a strong yet flexible lab program that meets lab science requirements, regardless of limited lab equipment or time restrictions. Labs include clear procedures, demonstrate scientific concepts, and develop students' understanding of scientific methods. **Using Scientific Methods**

These labs have been classroom-tested, and also reviewed by an independent laboratory, for reliability, safety, and efficiency.

Terry Rakes
Elmwood Junior High
Rogers, Arkansas

In-Text LabBook
LabBook, in the back of the *Pupil's Edition*, allows for
- more labs and activities,
- greater flexibility in lesson planning,
- a wider variety of labs,
- more detailed lab procedures and explanations,
- an uninterrupted chapter narrative, and includes
- separate *Datasheets for LabBook*.

> "I need a variety of **fun** yet **meaningful** lab activities that are **cost effective**."

Additional, in-text labs and activities

LABS AND ACTIVITES FOR EVERY LESSON

- **QuickLabs** are easy to execute and require minimal time and materials—great for quick in-class activities, teacher demonstrations, or group presentations.
- **Investigate!** stimulates your students' curiosity about scientific concepts in the upcoming chapter.
- **Activity** gives your students the opportunity to use their imaginations and expand their learning.
- **Apply** poses real-world questions and asks your students to answer them by applying what they have just learned.
- **Demonstration** and **Activity** in the teacher's edition give you options to demonstrate labs and procedures to the whole class or provide fun, hands-on activities.

QuickLab
First-Law Magic

1. On a table or desk, place a **large, empty plastic cup** on top of a **paper towel**.
2. Without touching the cup

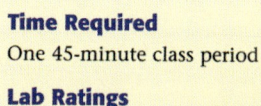

Activity

Light waves diffract around corners of buildings much less than sound waves. Imagine what would happen if light waves

Lab Ratings make choosing labs easy

Lab Ratings, for all labs, make it easy for you to determine, at a glance, which labs are most appropriate for your class.

Time Required
One 45-minute class period

Lab Ratings

EASY ———————→ HARD

TEACHER PREP △
STUDENT SET-UP △△
CONCEPT LEVEL △△
CLEAN UP △

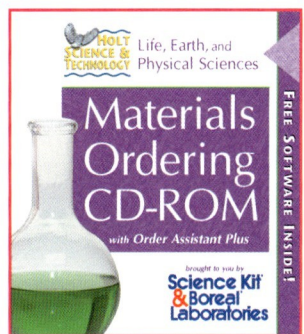

Easy-to-order lab materials

Ordering lab materials is more efficient than ever with the *Holt Science and Technology* **Materials Ordering CD-ROM**. This software, developed by Science Kit®, creates a "shopping list" of materials and their costs. The CD-ROM also lists required materials for every lab investigation in the program, including consumable and non-consumable kits.

For a complete materials list, see page xxiv in the Annotated Teacher's Edition

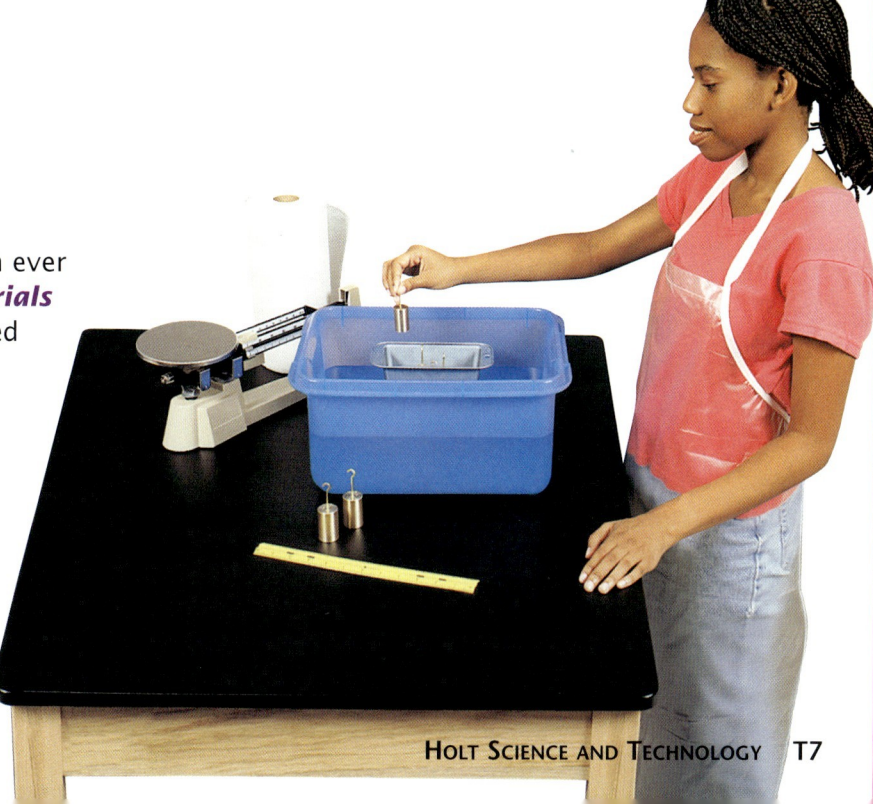

Labs

HOLT SCIENCE AND TECHNOLOGY **T7**

Lab Manuals Extend Your Options

Lab Manuals

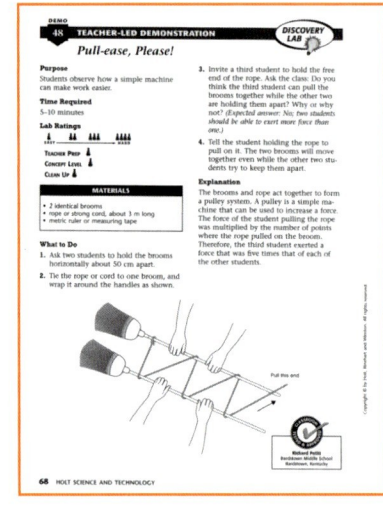

Whiz-Bang Demonstrations gives you a rousing way to get your students' attention at the beginning of a lesson. **65 labs in all!**

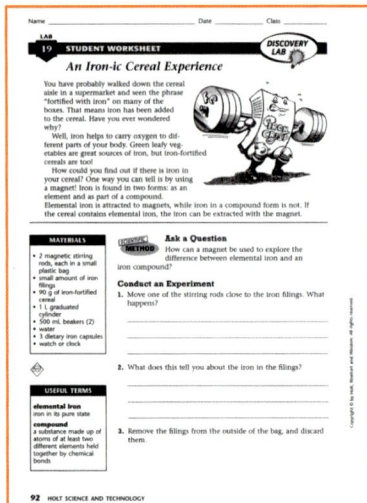

Labs You Can Eat safely incorporates food into the classroom to provide a fun inquiry-based learning tool. **25 labs in all!**

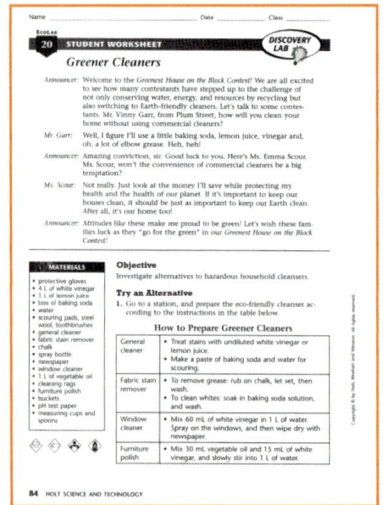

EcoLabs & Field Activities includes activities that address specific ecological questions and increase environmental awareness. **23 labs in all!**

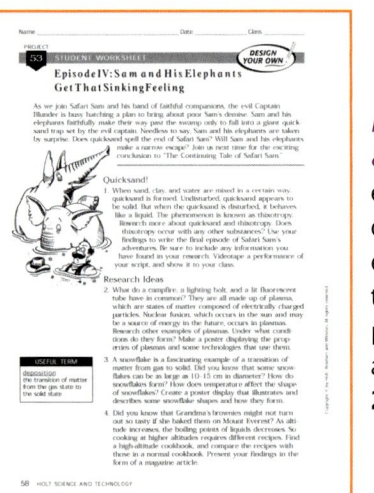

Inquiry Labs encourages your students to ask questions and investigate problems in order to find solutions. **23 labs in all!**

Long-Term Projects & Research Ideas extends and enriches chapter content with experiments, activities, inquiry-based projects, and Internet and library research. **2 for every chapter!**

T8   HOLT SCIENCE AND TECHNOLOGY

Comprehensive Skill Development

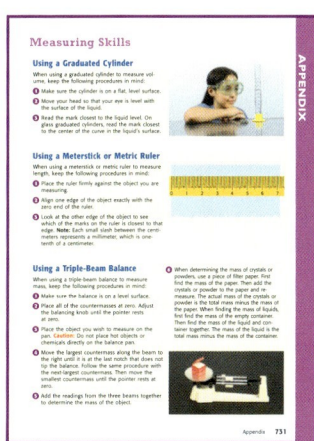

Science skills ensure future success

Holt Science and Technology gives your students ample opportunities to master the skills necessary for future success in science. Science skills are developed in a variety of ways:

- The in-text **LabBook**, activities, and lab booklets provide lots of practice using scientific methods.
- The **Appendix** helps your students refresh their measuring and data-analysis skills, as well as their understanding of the **scientific method**.
- **Apply** and **Activity** allow your students to develop science skills in fun and motivating ways.

In addition, your students can find plenty of skill-building practice in *Science Skills Worksheets*. These worksheets help your students hone important science skills, such as thinking objectively, conducting research, designing investigations, keeping accurate records, and creating and analyzing graphs.

Math is covered everywhere you look!

Holt Science and Technology also strengthens your students' math skills. From practice problems to reviews, math skills are continually developed:

- **MathBreak** provides practice with direct application to the science concepts being taught.
- **Math Concepts** reviews the math lessons presented in the chapter.
- **Math Refresher**, found in the Appendix, reviews basic math skills, such as averages, ratios, percentages, and more.

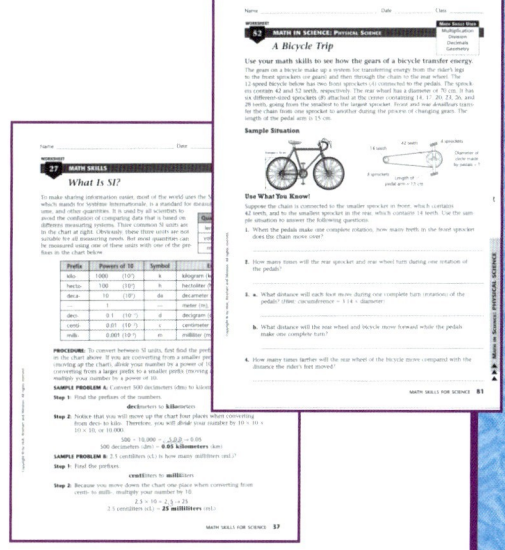

Math Skills for Science helps your students develop and apply basic math skills to scientific problems with two types of worksheets.

- **Math Skills Worksheets** provide a brief introduction to a relevant math skill, a step-by-step explanation of the math process, and example and practice problems.
- **Math in Science Worksheets** give your students practice using math in real-life science situations.

HOLT SCIENCE AND TECHNOLOGY T9

A Versatile Teacher's Edition that is Easy-to-Use

Teacher's Edition

The Chapter Organizer—your easy-to-follow road map

With such a wealth of program resources, you'll be glad to know we've included a convenient, timesaving guide suggesting how and when to use them.

The **Chapter Organizer**
- integrates all labs, technology, and print resources
- is organized according to time requirements
- includes National Standards correlated by section

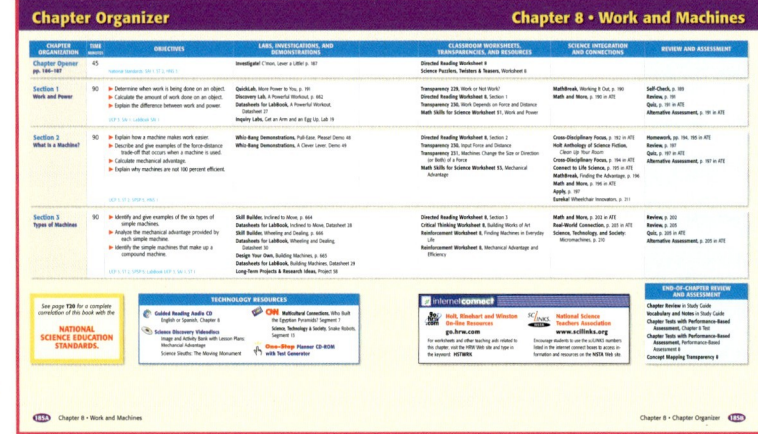

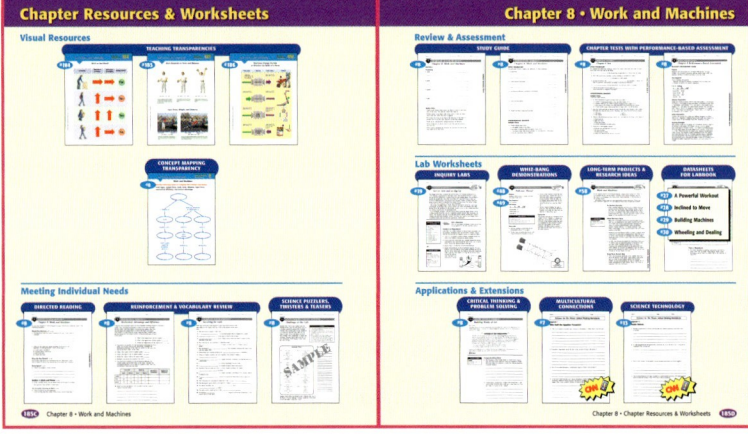

Chapter Resources & Worksheets makes choosing teaching resources easy by showing them as reduced pages. Available resources are categorized by
- Visual Resources
- Meeting Individual Needs
- Review and Assessment
- Lab Worksheets
- Applications & Extensions

The **Chapter Background** provides additional information to help you enrich upcoming lessons.

T10 HOLT SCIENCE AND TECHNOLOGY

"A teacher's edition should be **well-organized** and provide **effective** tips and techniques."

Keep the focus on the lesson

The complete lesson cycle helps you keep your students interested and involved. An array of both traditional and new teaching strategies, creative reinforcement, and thought-provoking extensions help you teach to a wide variety of learning styles, ability levels, and interests.

Fuel your presentation

Found on almost every page, fun features and intriguing stories ignite class discussion and get your students thinking.

Q: What did the compound say to the solution?
A: You're all mixed up!

IS THAT A FACT!

Some trains are too massive to be moved by one locomotive. To compensate for the larger mass, extra locomotives are added until the net force of all the locomotives is large enough to move the train.

MISCONCEPTION ALERT

Students may not understand that a gas not only will expand to fill its container but also can be compressed, or squeezed, to fill a smaller container. Scuba divers' tanks contain compressed air. A 2.24 m³ scuba tank holds enough air for an average adult to breathe underwater for 30 to 45 minutes.

Science Bloopers

In July 1983, an Air Canada Boeing 767 airliner with 69 people on board ran out of fuel in mid-flight. Before leaving their previous stop, the crew had calculated that they had enough fuel to make it to their final destination. However, the plane's crew miscalculated the mass of the fuel because they had used the wrong units; they used pounds instead of kilograms! Fortunately, the plane was able to make a safe landing at an abandoned air force base in Manitoba, Canada.

WEIRD SCIENCE

Most lightning bolts move from a cloud to the ground. However, occasionally lightning bolts travel from the ground to a cloud! They usually start from the tips of mountain peaks, antenna towers, or very tall buildings.

Teacher's Edition

HOLT SCIENCE AND TECHNOLOGY

HOLT SCIENCE & TECHNOLOGY

Teaching Support that Makes Your Job Easier

Teaching Resources

Point-and-Click Planning

One-Stop Planner CD-ROM with Test Generator

The *One-Stop Planner CD-ROM with Test Generator* is a timesaving, all-in-one planning tool that contains everything you need on a single disc!
- **customizable** lesson plans, tests, assessment checklists, and rubrics
- **powerful** test generator
- **printable** resources, including
  - worksheets
  - transparencies
  - Spanish transcripts
  - assessment materials
  - rubrics
  - National Standards Correlation
  - Science Fair Guide
  - Parent Letters
  - and much more!

Includes student worksheets

with Test Generator

> "I would love to **streamline planning** so I can spend more time on what I do best—teaching."

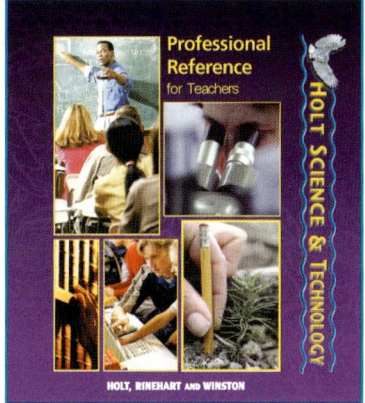

Sharpen your saw

The *Professional Reference for Teachers* (part of the *One-Stop Planner CD-ROM*) provides current information about pertinent issues in science education today. In professional articles, you can learn more about the National Science Education Standards, block scheduling, classroom management, and more. A bibliography of books, lectures, magazines, and Web sites is included.

Visualize science concepts

Teaching Transparencies, many with images taken directly from the text, reinforce important science concepts and processes.

Two *Concept Mapping Transparencies* are included for each chapter—a partial map transparency to use with your students as they progress through the chapter and a completed concept map to serve as an answer key. A correlation chart links transparencies across the sciences.

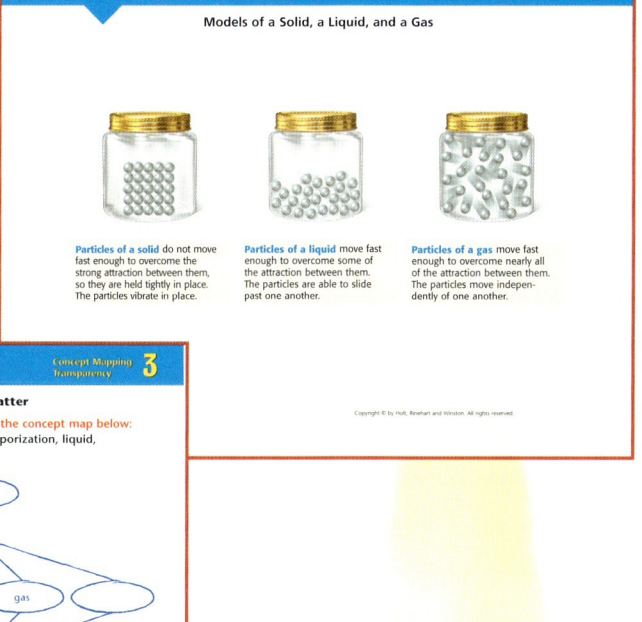

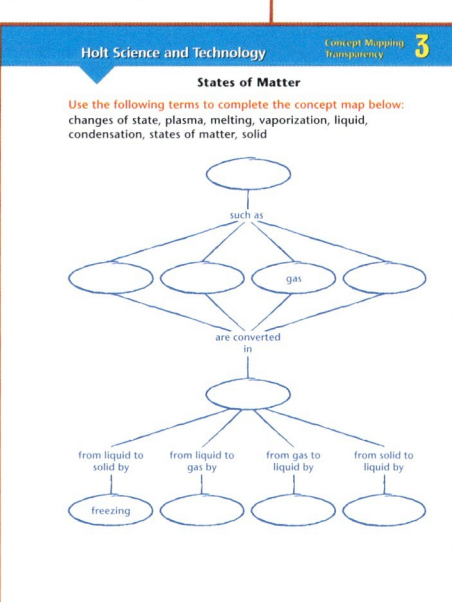

Bellringer Transparency Masters (part of the *One-Stop Planner CD-ROM*) help you focus your students' attention quickly at the beginning of class while you are dealing with administrative demands.

Assessment that Accurately Measures Mastery of Content

Check progress
Self-Check encourages your students to evaluate their own learning by answering questions found intermittently within the chapter. A page reference allows them to check their own answers. After reading each lesson, your students explore, evaluate, and extend what they've learned by answering questions in the section **Review**. In the teacher's wrap, a **Quiz** provides an objective assessment of each lesson.

> ✓ **Self-Check**
>
> How would an increase in the speed of the particles affect the pressure of gas in a metal cylinder? *(See page 724 to check your answer.)*

Chapter Highlights
lists vocabulary and provides content summaries in a concise, visual format. This helps your students organize their thoughts and synthesize information.

Study Guide contains blackline masters for Chapter Highlights and Chapter Reviews that help your students gear up for tests and quizzes.

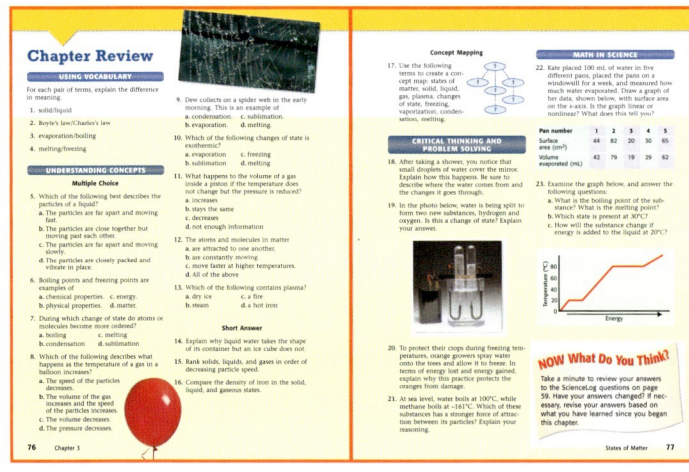

Chapter Review
question types are identical to those found on the chapter tests, making the Chapter Review an excellent resource for pretest practice.

"I want to **make sure** my students are learning the **National Standards**."

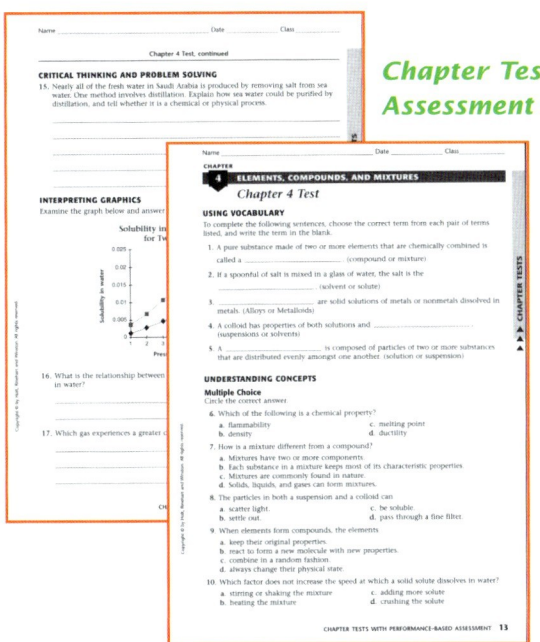

Chapter Tests with Performance-Based Assessment includes multiple-choice, concept-mapping, critical-thinking, interpreting graphics, math-in-science, and alternative assessment questions, to name a few.

Alternative Assessment in the teacher's wrap provides you with different evaluation options, such as expository writing and concept mapping, to ensure a thorough assessment.

Create your own assessments

One-Stop Planner CD-ROM

With the *One-Stop Planner CD-ROM with Test Generator*, you can create, revise, and edit quizzes, section and chapter reviews, and chapter tests, drawing from thousands of questions (including performance-based items) organized by chapter and linked to chapter objectives.

The *Test Generator: Test Item Listing* provides a printed copy of thousands of assessment items (including performance-based items) on the *Test Generator CD-ROM*. This handy guide allows you to preview test items before making selections.

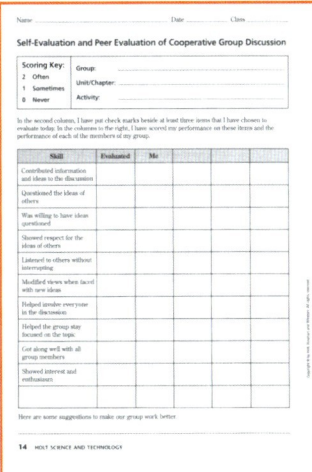

Assessment Checklists & Rubrics, available on CD-ROM or as blackline masters, gives you guidelines for evaluating your students' progress, including performance and portfolio assessment tools. You can also create a customized checklist for each class, helping you gather daily scores and determine grades.

Assessment

HOLT SCIENCE AND TECHNOLOGY

Technology

Technology that Meets Your Goals and Expands Your Options

Holt Science and Technology provides the right combination of fully integrated technology resources—including videos, CD-ROMs, and Internet connections—to make your teaching more effective, efficient, and creative.

Teacher resources

Finding, printing, and editing teaching resources is easy with the *One-Stop Planner CD-ROM with Test Generator*. You can use this cutting-edge technology to sort through thousands of pages of resources, including
- hundreds of printable worksheets
- customizable lesson plans
- a powerful test generator

(see pages T10 and T15)

One-Stop Planner CD-ROM

Classroom resources

The *CNN Presents Science in the News: Video Library* helps your students see the impact of science on their everyday lives. The CNN and CNN NEWSROOM Team brings to the classroom actual news coverage in *Scientists in Action*; *Multicultural Connections*; *Science, Technology & Society*; and *Eye on the Environment*. Each Teacher's Guide offers background information, a description of each segment, viewing questions, and teaching suggestions. In addition, a critical-thinking worksheet for each news segment enhances skill development.

Science Discovery Videodisc Programs will excite your students with visually stunning scientific images as well as provide a fun means for solving scientific problems in real-world situations. This package includes the popular *Science Sleuths* series and the *Image and Activity Bank*.

> "I don't have time to **find** and **evaluate** the **technology** resources out there."

Student interactive resources

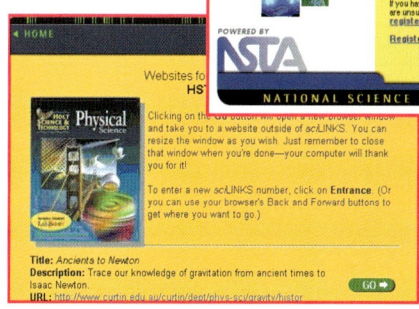

sci*LINKS* is a Web service developed and maintained by the National Science Teachers Association that links you and your students to online educational resources directly related to chapter topics in *Holt Science and Technology*.

sci*LINKS* saves you time searching for relevant Web sites. The **sci*LINKS*** staff, consisting of science educators and content experts, identifies, reviews, and monitors featured sites—so you can be assured that they contain appropriate and up-to-date information. In addition, you and your students never have to worry about a site disappearing. **sci*LINKS*** will replace an expired site with another using the same keyword.

Your students can also enrich their knowledge by exploring the Internet through the **go.hrw.com** site, which links them to online chapter activities and resources.

The **Smithsonian Institution** maintains special Web sites for use with *Holt Science and Technology*. These web sites include interactive exhibits, classroom activities, interviews with scientists, and a variety of application and extension topics.

Interactive Explorations CD-ROM Program turns a computer into a virtual laboratory where your students act as lab assistants in solving real-world problems—developing their inquiry, analysis, and decision-making skills.

The ***Interactive Science Encyclopedia CD-ROM*** gives your students instant access to more than 3,000 cross-referenced science entries, in-depth articles, science fair project ideas, interactive activities, and more.

EXPECT EXCITEMENT!
EXPECT RESULTS!

Components Listing

H51957-8	**Pupil's Edition**	
H51958-6	**Annotated Teacher's Edition**	

H52952-2 Physical Science Teaching Resources

- H54399-1 — Study Guide
- H51763-X — Study Guide Answer Key
- H54398-3 — Critical Thinking & Problem Solving Worksheets
- H55412-8 — Reinforcement & Vocabulary Review Worksheets
- H54401-7 — Science Puzzlers, Twisters & Teasers
- H54402-5 — Chapter Tests with Performance-Based Assessment
- H54397-5 — Directed Reading Worksheets
- H55409-8 — Directed Reading Worksheets Answer Key
- H54404-1 — Datasheets for LabBook
- H54408-4 — Datasheets for LabBook Answer Key
- H54403-3 — Test Generator: Test Item Listing

H54416-5 LabBank

- H54414-9 — Labs You Can Eat
- H54417-3 — Whiz-Bang Demonstrations
- H54419-X — Inquiry Labs
- H54418-1 — EcoLabs & Field Activities
- H54421-1 — Long-Term Projects & Research Ideas

H56009-8 Program Teaching Resources

- H54426-2 — Science Skills Worksheets
- H54432-7 — Math Skills for Science
- H54422-X — Professional Reference for Teachers
- H52947-6 — Holt Anthology of Science Fiction
- H55798-4 — Assessment Checklists & Rubrics
- H54424-6 — Science Fair Guide
- H54439-4 — Holt Science Posters

Technology Resources

- H54409-2 — Teaching Transparencies with Concept Mapping Transparencies
- H54406-8 — Guided Reading Audio CD Program
- H54438-6 — Guided Reading Audio CD Program, Spanish
- H54434-3 — CNN Presents Science in the News: Video Library
- H55473-X — Scientists in Action
- H55469-1 — Multicultural Connections
- H55472-1 — Science, Technology & Society
- H55474-8 — Eye on the Environment
- H56562-6 — One-Stop Planner CD-ROM with Test Generator for Mac® and Win®
- H56601-1 — Materials Ordering CD-ROM for Mac® and Win®
- H55468-3 — Interactive Explorations CD-ROM Program for Mac® and Win®
- H05569-5 — Science Discovery Videodisc Programs

Interactive Science Encyclopedia CD-ROM
- 0817239138 — Windows®
- 0817239146 — Macintosh®

HOLT SCIENCE & TECHNOLOGY Physical Science
National Science Education
STANDARDS CORRELATIONS

The following lists show the chapter correlation of **Holt Science and Technology: Earth Science** with the *National Science Education Standards* (grades 5–8).

The chapter correlations for the Life Science Content Standards begin on page T22.

UNIFYING CONCEPTS AND PROCESSES

Standard	Chapter Correlation		
Systems, order, and organization Code: UCP 1	Chapter 3 — 3.1, 3.2 Chapter 4 — 4.1, 4.2, 4.3 Chapter 5 — 5.1, 5.2, 5.4 Chapter 9 — 9.3 Chapter 10 — 10.1	Chapter 11 — 11.1, 11.2 Chapter 12 — 12.1 Chapter 13 — 13.1, 13.2 Chapter 15 — 15.2, 15.3 Chapter 16 — 16.1	Chapter 18 — 18.1 Chapter 20 — 20.1 Chapter 21 — 21.1, 21.2, 21.3, 21.4 Chapter 22 — 22.1 Chapter 23 — 23.1
Evidence, models, and explanation Code: UCP 2	Chapter 1 — 1.2, 1.3 Chapter 3 — 3.1, 3.2 Chapter 4 — 4.1, 4.2, 4.3 Chapter 7 — 7.3 Chapter 10 — 10.1, 10.2, 10.3 Chapter 11 — 11.1, 11.2	Chapter 12 — 12.2 Chapter 13 — 13.1, 13.2 Chapter 15 — 15.3 Chapter 16 — 16.1, 16.2 Chapter 17 — 17.1, 17.2, 17.4 Chapter 18 — 18.1, 18.2	Chapter 19 — 19.2 Chapter 20 — 20.1 Chapter 21 — 21.1, 21.2, 21.3, 21.4 Chapter 22 — 22.1, 22.2, 22.3, 22.4 Chapter 23 — 23.1, 23.2, 23.3
Change, constancy, and measurement Code: UCP 3	Chapter 1 — 1.4 Chapter 3 — 3.1, 3.2 Chapter 5 — 5.1, 5.3, 5.4 Chapter 6 — 6.1, 6.2 Chapter 8 — 8.1, 8.2, 8.3 Chapter 9 — 9.1, 9.3	Chapter 10 — 10.1, 10.2, 10.3 Chapter 11 — 11.3 Chapter 12 — 12.2 Chapter 13 — 13.2 Chapter 14 — 14.1, 14.2, 14.3 Chapter 15 — 15.1, 15.2, 15.3	Chapter 16 — 16.1, 16.2 Chapter 18 — 18.3 Chapter 20 — 20.2, 20.3 Chapter 21 — 21.2, 21.3 Chapter 22 — 22.4 Chapter 23 — 23.2
Evolution and equilibrium Code: UCP 4	Chapter 5 — 5.2 Chapter 6 — 6.2 Chapter 7 — 7.2 Chapter 15 — 15.3		
Form and function Code: UCP 5	Chapter 1 — 1.3 Chapter 7 — 7.3 Chapter 8 — 8.3 Chapter 15 — 15.3	Chapter 20 — 20.2 Chapter 21 — 21.4 Chapter 23 — 23.4	

SCIENCE AS INQUIRY

Standard	Chapter Correlation		
Abilities necessary to do scientific inquiry Code: SAI 1	**Chapter 1** 1.2, 1.3, 1.4 **Chapter 3** 3.1, 3.2 **Chapter 4** 4.1, 4.3 **Chapter 5** 5.1, 5.3, 5.4 **Chapter 6** 6.1, 6.2 **Chapter 7** 7.1, 7.2, 7.3	**Chapter 8** 8.1, 8.3 **Chapter 9** 9.2 **Chapter 10** 10.2 **Chapter 12** 12.1 **Chapter 14** 14.1, 14.2, 14.3 **Chapter 15** 15.2	**Chapter 16** 16.2 **Chapter 17** 17.1, 17.2, 17.4 **Chapter 18** 18.1, 18.3 **Chapter 20** 20.1, 20.2 **Chapter 21** 21.1, 21.2, 21.3 **Chapter 22** 22.2, 22.4
Understandings about scientific inquiry Code: SAI 2	**Chapter 1** 1.1, 1.2, 1.4 **Chapter 3** 3.1, 3.2 **Chapter 4** 4.2, 4.3 **Chapter 5** 5.1, 5.3 **Chapter 6** 6.2 **Chapter 7** 7.1	**Chapter 10** 10.1 **Chapter 11** 11.1 **Chapter 13** 13.1 **Chapter 14** 14.2, 14.3 **Chapter 15** 15.3 **Chapter 16** 16.1, 16.2	**Chapter 17** 17.1, 17.2, 17.4 **Chapter 20** 20.2 **Chapter 21** 21.2, 21.3 **Chapter 22** 22.2, 22.4

SCIENCE AND TECHNOLOGY

Standard	Chapter Correlation		
Abilities of technological design Code: ST 1	**Chapter 1** 1.3 **Chapter 2** 2.1 **Chapter 3** 3.2 **Chapter 6** 6.1 **Chapter 8** 8.3	**Chapter 9** 9.3 **Chapter 10** 10.2 **Chapter 16** 16.2 **Chapter 18** 18.2	
Understandings about science and technology Code: ST 2	**Chapter 1** 1.2 **Chapter 2** 2.1 **Chapter 4** 4.3 **Chapter 5** 5.4 **Chapter 7** 7.1, 7.2, 7.3 **Chapter 8** 8.2, 8.3	**Chapter 9** 9.2, 9.3, 9.4 **Chapter 11** 11.1 **Chapter 12** 12.1, 12.2 **Chapter 13** 13.1 **Chapter 14** 14.1, 14.3 **Chapter 15** 15.3	**Chapter 16** 16.1, 16.2 **Chapter 18** 18.2 **Chapter 19** 19.1, 19.2, 19.3 **Chapter 20** 20.2, 20.3 **Chapter 21** 21.1, 21.2, 21.3 **Chapter 23** 23.4

SCIENCE IN PERSONAL AND SOCIAL PERSPECTIVES

Standard	Chapter Correlation		
Personal health Code: SPSP 1	**Chapter 2** 2.1 **Chapter 4** 4.3 **Chapter 12** 12.2 **Chapter 15** 15.2, 15.3	**Chapter 16** 16.1 **Chapter 17** 17.3 **Chapter 18** 18.1 **Chapter 19** 19.2	**Chapter 21** 21.1, 21.4 **Chapter 22** 22.2 **Chapter 23** 23.3
Populations, resources, and environments Code: SPSP 2	**Chapter 10** 10.2, 10.4 **Chapter 21** 21.4 **Chapter 23** 23.4		

Science in Personal and Social Perspectives (cont'd)

Standard	Chapter Correlation		
Natural hazards Code: SPSP 3	Chapter 3 3.2 Chapter 4 4.3 Chapter 15 15.2 Chapter 16 16.2 Chapter 17 17.1	Chapter 18 18.1 Chapter 21 21.4 Chapter 22 22.2	
Risks and benefits Code: SPSP 4	Chapter 9 9.4 Chapter 15 15.2 Chapter 16 16.1, 16.2 Chapter 22 22.2		
Science and technology in society Code: SPSP 5	Chapter 1 1.1 Chapter 2 2.1 Chapter 3 3.2 Chapter 4 4.2, 4.3 Chapter 5 5.2, 5.4 Chapter 8 8.2, 8.3 Chapter 9 9.2	Chapter 10 10.1, 10.2, 10.3, 10.4 Chapter 11 11.1 Chapter 12 12.1, 12.2 Chapter 13 13.1 Chapter 14 14.1, 14.3 Chapter 15 15.3 Chapter 16 16.1, 16.2	Chapter 17 17.1, 17.2, 17.3, 17.4 Chapter 18 18.1, 18.2, 18.3 Chapter 19 19.1, 19.2, 19.3 Chapter 21 21.1, 21.2, 21.3 Chapter 22 22.1, 22.2 Chapter 23 23.1, 23.2, 23.4

History and Nature of Science

Standard	Chapter Correlation		
Science as a human endeavor Code: HNS 1	Chapter 1 1.1, 1.4 Chapter 5 5.4 Chapter 6 6.1 Chapter 8 8.2 Chapter 9 9.4 Chapter 11 11.1	Chapter 12 12.1 Chapter 13 13.1 Chapter 14 14.1, 14.3 Chapter 15 15.3 Chapter 16 16.1, 16.2 Chapter 18 18.1, 18.2, 18.3	Chapter 21 21.1, 21.2 Chapter 22 22.2 Chapter 23 23.1
Nature of science Code: HNS 2	Chapter 11 11.1, 11.2 Chapter 12 12.1 Chapter 13 13.1	Chapter 14 14.3 Chapter 16 16.1, 16.2 Chapter 20 20.2	
History of science Code: HNS 3	Chapter 3 3.2 Chapter 5 5.4 Chapter 11 11.1 Chapter 12 12.1, 12.2 Chapter 13 13.1 Chapter 14 14.1	Chapter 15 15.3 Chapter 16 16.1, 16.2 Chapter 17 17.1 Chapter 18 18.1, 18.2, 18.3 Chapter 21 21.2 Chapter 23 23.1	

Physical Science
CONTENT STANDARDS

PROPERTIES AND CHANGES OF PROPERTIES IN MATTER

Standard	Chapter Correlation	
A substance has characteristic properties, such as density, a boiling point, and solubility, all of which are independent of the amount of the sample. A mixture of substances often can be separated into the original substances using one or more of the characteristic properties. **Code: PS 1a**	**Chapter 2** 2.1, 2.2 **Chapter 3** 3.1, 3.2 **Chapter 4** 4.1, 4.3 **Chapter 10** 10.3 **Chapter 15** 15.1, 15.2	
Substances react chemically in characteristic ways with other substances to form new substances (compounds) with different characteristic properties. In chemical reactions, the total mass is conserved. Substances often are placed in categories or groups if they react in similar ways; metals is an example of such a group. **Code: PS 1b**	**Chapter 2** 2.2 **Chapter 4** 4.1, 4.2 **Chapter 10** 10.3 **Chapter 12** 12.1, 12.2 **Chapter 13** 13.1, 13.2	**Chapter 14** 14.1, 14.2, 14.3 **Chapter 15** 15.1, 15.2
Chemical elements do not break down during normal laboratory reactions involving such treatments as heating, exposure to electric current, or reaction with acids. There are more than 100 known elements that combine in a multitude of ways to produce compounds, which account for the living and nonliving substances that we encounter. **Code: PS 1c**	**Chapter 2** 2.1 **Chapter 4** 4.1, 4.2 **Chapter 13** 13.1 **Chapter 15** 15.3	

MOTIONS AND FORCES

Standard	Chapter Correlation
The motion of an object can be described by its position, direction of motion, and speed. That motion can be measured and represented on a graph. **Code: PS 2a**	**Chapter 5** 5.1
An object that is not being subjected to a force will continue to move at a constant speed and in a straight line. **Code: PS 2b**	**Chapter 5** 5.2 **Chapter 6** 6.2

MOTIONS AND FORCES (CONT'D)

Standard	Chapter Correlation
If more than one force acts on an object along a straight line, then the forces will reinforce or cancel one another, depending on their direction and magnitude. Unbalanced forces will cause changes in the speed or direction of an object's motion. Code: PS 2c	**Chapter 5** 5.2, 5.3, 5.4 **Chapter 6** 6.2 **Chapter 17** 17.1

TRANSFER OF ENERGY

Standard	Chapter Correlation	
Energy is a property of many substances and is associated with heat, light, electricity, mechanical motion, sound, nuclei, and the nature of a chemical. Energy is transferred in many ways. Code: PS 3a	**Chapter 1** 1.1 **Chapter 3** 3.2 **Chapter 9** 9.1, 9.2 **Chapter 10** 10.1, 10.2, 10.4 **Chapter 14** 14.1, 14.3 **Chapter 15** 15.1 **Chapter 16** 16.1, 16.2 **Chapter 17** 17.1, 17.2, 17.3, 17.4	**Chapter 18** 18.1, 18.2, 18.3 **Chapter 19** 19.1 **Chapter 20** 20.1, 20.2 **Chapter 21** 21.1, 21.2, 21.3 **Chapter 22** 22.1, 22.2, 22.4 **Chapter 23** 23.1
Heat moves in predictable ways, flowing from warmer objects to cooler ones, until both reach the same temperature. Code: PS 3b	**Chapter 10** 10.1, 10.2, 10.4 **Chapter 22** 22.4	
Light interacts with matter by transmission (including refraction), absorption, or scattering (including reflection). To see an object, light from that object—emitted or scattered from it—must enter the eye. Code: PS 3c	**Chapter 17** 17.1, 17.4 **Chapter 20** 20.3 **Chapter 22** 22.3, 22.4 **Chapter 23** 23.1, 23.2, 23.3, 23.4	
Electrical circuits provide a means of transferring electrical energy when heat, light, sound, and chemical changes are produced. Code: PS 3d	**Chapter 9** 9.1	
In most chemical and nuclear reactions, energy is transferred into or out of a system. Heat, light, mechanical motion, or electricity might all be involved in such transfers. Code: PS 3e	**Chapter 9** 9.1, 9.4 **Chapter 12** 12.2 **Chapter 13** 13.2 **Chapter 14** 14.1, 14.2, 14.3	**Chapter 15** 15.1 **Chapter 16** 16.1, 16.2 **Chapter 23** 23.1

Transfer of Energy (cont'd)

Standard

The sun is a major source of energy for changes on the earth's surface. The sun loses energy by emitting light. A tiny fraction of that light reaches the earth, transferring energy from the sun to the earth. The sun's energy arrives as light with a range of wavelengths, consisting of visible light, infrared, and ultraviolet radiation.

Code: PS 3f

Chapter Correlation

Chapter 1   1.1
Chapter 9   9.1, 9.2, 9.4
Chapter 10 10.2
Chapter 14 14.3
Chapter 20 20.1
Chapter 22 22.2
Chapter 23 23.1

Holt Science & Technology

Physical Science

ANNOTATED TEACHER'S EDITION

HOLT, RINEHART AND WINSTON

A Harcourt Classroom Education Company

Austin • New York • Orlando • Atlanta • San Francisco • Boston • Dallas • Toronto • London

Staff Credits

Editorial

Robert W. Todd, Executive Editor
David F. Bowman, Managing Editor
Anne Engelking, Senior Editor
Michael Mazza, Editor
Amy James, Ken Shepardson, Robin Goodman (Feature Articles)

ANNOTATED TEACHER'S EDITION
Ken Shepardson, Amy James, Michael Mazza, Kelly Rizk, Bill Burnside

ANCILLARIES
Jennifer Childers, Senior Editor
Chris Colby, Kristen Falk, Molly Frohlich, Robin Goodman, Shari Husain, Monique Mayer, Kristen McCardel, Sabelyn Pussman, Erin Roberson

COPYEDITORS
Dawn Spinozza, Copyediting Supervisor
Brooke Fugitt, Kathryn O'Shields, Cindy Foreman

EDITORIAL SUPPORT STAFF
Jeanne Graham, Rose Segrest, Tanu'e White

EDITORIAL PERMISSIONS
Cathy Paré, Permissions Manager
Jan Harrington, Permissions Editor

Art, Design, and Photo

BOOK DESIGN
Richard Metzger, Design Director
Marc Cooper, Senior Designer
Ron Bowdoin, Designer
Alicia Sullivan, Designer (ATE),
Cristina Bowerman, Design Associate (ATE), **Eric Rupprath,** Designer (Ancillaries)

IMAGE ACQUISITIONS
Joe London, Director
Elaine Tate, Art Buyer Supervisor
Sean Moynihan, Art Buyer
Tim Taylor, Photo Research Supervisor
Stephanie Morris, Assistant Photo Researcher

PHOTO STUDIO
Sam Dudgeon, Senior Staff Photographer
Victoria Smith, Photo Specialist
Lauren Eischen, Photo Coordinator

DESIGN NEW MEDIA
Susan Michael, Design Director

DESIGN MEDIA
Joe Melomo, Design Director

Production

Mimi Stockdell, Senior Production Manager
Beth Sample, Production Coordinator
Suzanne Brooks, Sara Carroll-Downs

Media Production

Kim A. Scott, Senior Production Manager
Nancy Hargis, Production Supervisor
Adriana Bardin, Production Coordinator

New Media

Jim Bruno, Senior Project Manager II
Lydia Doty, Senior Project Manager
Jessica Bega, Project Manager
Armin Gutzmer, Manager Training and Technical Support
Cathy Kuhles, Nina Degollado, Technical Assistants

Design Implementation and Production

Preface, Inc.

Copyright © 2001 by Holt, Rinehart and Winston

All rights reserved. No part of this publication may be reproduced or transmitted in any form or by any means, electronic or mechanical, including photocopy, recording, or any information storage and retrieval system, without permission in writing from the publisher.

Requests for permission to make copies of any part of the work should be mailed to the following address: Permissions Department, Holt, Rinehart and Winston, 1120 South Capital of Texas Highway, Austin, Texas 78746-6487.

For permission to reprint copyrighted material, grateful acknowledgment is made to the following source: *sci*LINKS is owned and provided by the National Science Teachers Association. All rights reserved.

Printed in the United States of America
ISBN 0-03-051958-6
4 5 6 7   048   05 04 03 02

Acknowledgments

Chapter Writers

Christie Borgford, Ph.D.
Professor of Chemistry
University of Alabama
Birmingham, Alabama

Andrew Champagne
Former Physics Teacher
Ashland High School
Ashland, Massachusetts

Mapi Cuevas, Ph.D.
Professor of Chemistry
Santa Fe Community College
Gainesville, Florida

Leila Dumas
Former Physics Teacher
LBJ Science Academy
Austin, Texas

William G. Lamb, Ph.D.
Science Teacher and Dept. Chair
Oregon Episcopal School
Portland, Oregon

Sally Ann Vonderbrink, Ph.D.
Chemistry Teacher
St. Xavier High School
Cincinnati, Ohio

Lab Writers

Phillip G. Bunce
Former Physics Teacher
Bowie High School
Austin, Texas

Kenneth E. Creese
Science Teacher
White Mountain Junior High School
Rock Springs, Wyoming

William G. Lamb, Ph.D.
Science Teacher and Dept. Chair
Oregon Episcopal School
Portland, Oregon

Alyson Mike
Science Teacher
East Valley Middle School
East Helena, Montana

Joseph W. Price
Science Teacher and Dept. Chair
H. M. Browne Junior High School
Washington, D.C.

Denice Lee Sandefur
Science Teacher and Dept. Chair
Nucla High School
Nucla, Colorado

John Spadafino
Mathematics and Physics Teacher
Hackensack High School
Hackensack, New Jersey

Walter Woolbaugh
Science Teacher
Manhattan Junior High School
Manhattan, Montana

Academic Reviewers

Paul R. Berman, Ph.D.
Professor of Physics
University of Michigan
Ann Arbor, Michigan

Russell M. Brengelman, Ph.D.
Professor of Physics
Morehead State University
Morehead, Kentucky

John A. Brockhaus, Ph.D.
Director, Mapping, Charting and Geodesy Program
Department of Geography and Environmental Engineering
United States Military Academy
West Point, New York

Walter Bron, Ph.D.
Professor of Physics
University of California
Irvine, California

Andrew J. Davis, Ph.D.
Manager, ACE Science Center
Department of Physics
California Institute of Technology
Pasadena, California

Peter E. Demmin, Ed.D.
Former Science Teacher and Department Chair
Amherst Central High School
Amherst, New York

Roger Falcone, Ph.D.
Professor of Physics and Department Chair
University of California
Berkeley, California

Cassandra A. Fraser, Ph.D.
Assistant Professor of Chemistry
University of Virginia
Charlottesville, Virginia

L. John Gagliardi, Ph.D.
Associate Professor of Physics and Department Chair
Rutgers University
Camden, New Jersey

Gabriele F. Giuliani, Ph.D.
Professor of Physics
Purdue University
West Lafayette, Indiana

Roy W. Hann, Jr., Ph.D.
Professor of Civil Engineering
Texas A&M University
College Station, Texas

John L. Hubisz, Ph.D.
Professor of Physics
North Carolina State University
Raleigh, North Carolina

Samuel P. Kounaves, Ph.D.
Professor of Chemistry
Tufts University
Medford, Massachusetts

Karol Lang, Ph.D.
Associate Professor of Physics
The University of Texas
Austin, Texas

Gloria Langer, Ph.D.
Professor of Physics
University of Colorado
Boulder, Colorado

Phillip LaRoe
Professor
Helena College of Technology
Helena, Montana

Joseph A. McClure, Ph.D.
Associate Professor of Physics
Georgetown University
Washington, D.C.

LaMoine L. Motz, Ph.D.
Coordinator of Science Education
Department of Learning Services
Oakland County Schools
Waterford, Michigan

R. Thomas Myers, Ph.D.
Professor of Chemistry, Emeritus
Kent State University
Kent, Ohio

Hillary Clement Olson, Ph.D.
Research Associate
Institute for Geophysics
The University of Texas
Austin, Texas

David P. Richardson, Ph.D.
Professor of Chemistry
Thompson Chemical Laboratory
Williams College
Williamstown, Massachusetts

John Rigden, Ph.D.
Director of Special Projects
American Institute of Physics
Colchester, Vermont

Peter Sheridan, Ph.D.
Professor of Chemistry
Colgate University
Hamilton, New York

Vederaman Sriraman, Ph.D.
Associate Professor of Technology
Southwest Texas State University
San Marcos, Texas

Jack B. Swift, Ph.D.
Professor of Physics
The University of Texas
Austin, Texas

Atiq Syed, Ph.D.
Master Instructor of Mathematics and Science
Texas State Technical College
Harlingen, Texas

Leonard Taylor, Ph.D.
Professor Emeritus
Department of Electrical Engineering
University of Maryland
College Park, Maryland

Virginia L. Trimble, Ph.D.
Professor of Physics and Astronomy
University of California
Irvine, California

Acknowledgments (cont.)

Martin VanDyke, Ph.D.
Professor of Chemistry Emeritus
Front Range Community College
Westminster, Colorado

Gabriela Waschewsky, Ph.D.
Science and Math Teacher
Emery High School
Emeryville, California

Safety Reviewer

Jack A. Gerlovich, Ph.D.
Associate Professor
School of Education
Drake University
Des Moines, Iowa

Teacher Reviewers

Barry L. Bishop
Science Teacher and Dept. Chair
San Rafael Junior High School
Ferron, Utah

Paul Boyle
Science Teacher
Perry Heights Middle School
Evansville, Indiana

Kenneth Creese
Science Teacher
White Mountain Junior High School
Rock Springs, Wyoming

Vicky Farland
Science Teacher and Dept. Chair
Centennial Middle School
Yuma, Arizona

Rebecca Ferguson
Science Teacher
North Ridge Middle School
North Richland Hills, Texas

Laura Fleet
Science Teacher
Alice B. Landrum Middle School
Ponte Vedra Beach, Florida

Jennifer Ford
Science Teacher and Dept. Chair
North Ridge Middle School
North Richland Hills, Texas

Susan Gorman
Science Teacher
North Ridge Middle School
North Richland Hills, Texas

C. John Graves
Science Teacher
Monforton Middle School
Bozeman, Montana

Dennis Hanson
Science Teacher and Dept. Chair
Big Bear Middle School
Big Bear Lake, California

David A. Harris
Science Teacher and Dept. Chair
The Thacher School
Ojai, California

Norman E. Holcomb
Science Teacher
Marion Local Schools
Maria Stein, Ohio

Kenneth J. Horn
Science Teacher and Dept. Chair
Fallston Middle School
Fallston, Maryland

Tracy Jahn
Science Teacher
Berkshire Junior-Senior High School
Canaan, New York

Kerry A. Johnson
Science Teacher
Isbell Middle School
Santa Paula, California

Drew E. Kirian
Science Teacher
Solon Middle School
Solon, Ohio

Harriet Knops
Science Teacher and Dept. Chair
Rolling Hills Middle School
El Dorado, California

Scott Mandel, Ph.D.
Director and Educational Consultant
Teachers Helping Teachers
Los Angeles, California

Thomas Manerchia
Former Science Teacher
Archmere Academy
Claymont, Delaware

Edith McAlanis
Science Teacher and Dept. Chair
Socorro Middle School
El Paso, Texas

Kevin McCurdy, Ph.D.
Science Teacher
Elmwood Junior High School
Rogers, Arkansas

Alyson Mike
Science Teacher
East Valley Middle School
East Helena, Montana

Donna Norwood
Science Teacher and Dept. Chair
Monroe Middle School
Charlotte, North Carolina

Joseph W. Price
Science Teacher and Dept. Chair
H. M. Browne Junior High School
Washington, D.C.

Terry J. Rakes
Science Teacher
Elmwood Junior High School
Rogers, Arkansas

Beth Richards
Science Teacher
North Middle School
Crystal Lake, Illinois

Elizabeth J. Rustad
Science Teacher
Crane Middle School
Yuma, Arizona

Rodney A. Sandefur
Science Teacher
Naturita Middle School
Naturita, Colorado

Helen Schiller
Science Teacher
Northwood Middle School
Taylors, South Carolina

Bert J. Sherwood
Science Teacher
Socorro Middle School
El Paso, Texas

Patricia McFarlane Soto
Science Teacher and Dept. Chair
G. W. Carver Middle School
Miami, Florida

David M. Sparks
Science Teacher
Redwater Junior High School
Redwater, Texas

Larry Tackett
Science Teacher and Dept. Chair
Andrew Jackson Middle School
Cross Lanes, West Virginia

Elsie N. Waynes
Science Teacher and Dept. Chair
R. H. Terrell Junior High School
Washington, D.C.

Sharon L. Woolf
Science Teacher
Langston Hughes Middle School
Reston, Virginia

Alexis S. Wright
Middle School Science Coordinator
Rye Country Day School
Rye, New York

Lee Yassinski
Science Teacher
Sun Valley Middle School
Sun Valley, California

John Zambo
Science Teacher
Elizabeth Ustach Middle School
Modesto, California

Contents in Brief

Unit 1 **Introduction to Matter** 2
- **Chapter 1** The World of Physical Science 4
- **Chapter 2** The Properties of Matter 34
- **Chapter 3** States of Matter 58
- **Chapter 4** Elements, Compounds, and Mixtures 80

Unit 2 **Motion and Forces** 104
- **Chapter 5** Matter in Motion 106
- **Chapter 6** Forces in Motion 136
- **Chapter 7** Forces in Fluids 160

Unit 3 **Work, Machines, and Energy** 184
- **Chapter 8** Work and Machines 186
- **Chapter 9** Energy and Energy Resources 212
- **Chapter 10** Heat and Heat Technology 244

Unit 4 **The Atom** 276
- **Chapter 11** Introduction to Atoms 278
- **Chapter 12** The Periodic Table 300

Unit 5 **Interactions of Matter** 324
- **Chapter 13** Chemical Bonding 326
- **Chapter 14** Chemical Reactions 348
- **Chapter 15** Chemical Compounds 372
- **Chapter 16** Atomic Energy 396

Unit 6 **Electricity** 418
- **Chapter 17** Introduction to Electricity 420
- **Chapter 18** Electromagnetism 452
- **Chapter 19** Electronic Technology 480

Unit 7 **Waves, Sound, and Light** 506
- **Chapter 20** The Energy of Waves 508
- **Chapter 21** The Nature of Sound 532
- **Chapter 22** The Nature of Light 562
- **Chapter 23** Light and Our World 592

LabBook 620

Contents

Master Materials List xxiv
Science & Math Skills Worksheets xxx

Unit 1 — Introduction to Matter

Timeline 2

CHAPTER 1

Chapter Organizer 3A
Chapter Resources & Worksheets 3C
Chapter Background 3E

The World of Physical Science 4

- **Section 1** Exploring Physical Science 6
- **Section 2** Using the Scientific Method 11
- **Section 3** Using Models in Physical Science 20
- **Section 4** Measurement and Safety in Physical Science . . 24

Chapter Highlights/Review 28

Feature Articles
- **Careers:** Electronics Engineer 32
- **Science Fiction:** "Inspiration" 33

LabBook
- Safety First! 622
- Exploring the Unseen 626
- Off to the Races! 627
- Measuring Liquid Volume 628
- Coin Operated 629

CHAPTER 2

Chapter Organizer 33A
Chapter Resources & Worksheets 33C
Chapter Background 33E

The Properties of Matter 34

- **Section 1** What Is Matter? 36
- **Section 2** Describing Matter 43

Chapter Highlights/Review 52

Feature Articles
- **Across the Sciences:** In the Dark About Dark Matter . . . 56
- **Health Watch:** Building a Better Body 57

LabBook
- Volumania! 630
- Determining Density 632
- Layering Liquids 633
- White Before Your Eyes 634

CHAPTER 3

Chapter Organizer 57A
Chapter Resources & Worksheets 57C
Chapter Background 57E

States of Matter 58

Section 1 Four States of Matter 60
Section 2 Changes of State 68

Chapter Highlights/Review 74

Feature Articles
Science, Technology, and Society: Guiding Lightning . . 78
Eureka!: Full Steam Ahead! 79

LabBook

- Full of Hot Air! 636
- Can Crusher 637
- A Hot and Cool Lab 638

CHAPTER 4

Chapter Organizer 79A
Chapter Resources & Worksheets 79C
Chapter Background 79E

Elements, Compounds, and Mixtures 80

Section 1 Elements 82
Section 2 Compounds 86
Section 3 Mixtures 90

Chapter Highlights/Review 98

Feature Articles
Science, Technology, and Society:
  Perfume: Fragrant Solutions 102
Science Fiction:
  "The Strange Case of Dr. Jekyll and Mr. Hyde" 103

LabBook

- Flame Tests 640
- A Sugar Cube Race! 642
- Making Butter 643
- Unpolluting Water 644

Contents

Unit 2 — Motion and Forces

Timeline 104

CHAPTER 5

Chapter Organizer 105A
Chapter Resources & Worksheets 105C
Chapter Background 105E

Matter in Motion 106

- **Section 1** Measuring Motion 108
- **Section 2** What Is a Force? 115
- **Section 3** Friction: A Force That Opposes Motion ... 119
- **Section 4** Gravity: A Force of Attraction 125

Chapter Highlights/Review 130

Feature Articles
- **Science, Technology, and Society:**
   Is It Real . . . or Is It Virtual? 134
- **Across the Sciences:** The Golden Gate Bridge 135

LabBook

- Built for Speed 646
- Detecting Acceleration 647
- Science Friction 650
- Relating Mass and Weight 651

CHAPTER 6

Chapter Organizer 135A
Chapter Resources & Worksheets 135C
Chapter Background 135E

Forces in Motion 136

- **Section 1** Gravity and Motion 138
- **Section 2** Newton's Laws of Motion 145

Chapter Highlights/Review 154

Feature Articles
- **Eureka!:** A Bat with Dimples 158
- **Careers:** Roller Coaster Designer 159

LabBook

- A Marshmallow Catapult 652
- Blast Off! 653
- Inertia-Rama! 654
- Quite a Reaction 656

viii Contents

CHAPTER 7

Chapter Organizer **159A**
Chapter Resources & Worksheets **159C**
Chapter Background **159E**

Forces in Fluids 160

Section 1 Fluids and Pressure 162
Section 2 Buoyant Force 168
Section 3 Bernoulli's Principle 173

Chapter Highlights/Review 178

Feature Articles
Eureka!: Stayin' Aloft—The Story of the Frisbee® 182
Science Fiction: "Wet Behind the Ears" 183

LabBook

■ Fluids, Force, and Floating 658   ■ Density Diver 660
■ Taking Flight 661

Unit 3 · · · Work, Machines, and Energy

⋮ **Timeline** 184

CHAPTER 8

Chapter Organizer **185A**
Chapter Resources & Worksheets **185C**
Chapter Background **185E**

Work and Machines 186

Section 1 Work and Power 188
Section 2 What Is a Machine? 192
Section 3 Types of Machines 198

Chapter Highlights/Review 206

Feature Articles
Science, Technology, and Society: Micromachines 210
Eureka!: Wheelchair Innovators 211

LabBook

■ A Powerful Workout 662   ■ Inclined to Move 664
■ Building Machines 665   ■ Wheeling and Dealing 666

Contents   **ix**

Contents

CHAPTER 9

Chapter Organizer 211A
Chapter Resources & Worksheets 211C
Chapter Background 211E

Energy and Energy Resources 212

- **Section 1** What Is Energy? 214
- **Section 2** Energy Conversions 222
- **Section 3** Conservation of Energy 229
- **Section 4** Energy Resources 232

Chapter Highlights/Review 238

Feature Articles

Across the Sciences: Green Buildings 242
Careers: Power-Plant Manager 243

LabBook

■ Finding Energy 668   ■ Energy of a Pendulum 670
■ Eggstremely Fragile 671

CHAPTER 10

Chapter Organizer 243A
Chapter Resources & Worksheets 243C
Chapter Background 243E

Heat and Heat Technology 244

- **Section 1** Temperature 246
- **Section 2** What Is Heat? 251
- **Section 3** Matter and Heat 260
- **Section 4** Heat Technology 263

Chapter Highlights/Review 270

Feature Articles

Science, Technology, and Society:
  The Deep Freeze 274
Across the Sciences:
  DiAPLEX®: The Intelligent Fabric 275

LabBook

■ Feel the Heat 672
■ Save the Cube! 674
■ Counting Calories 675

x   Contents

Unit 4 · · · The Atom

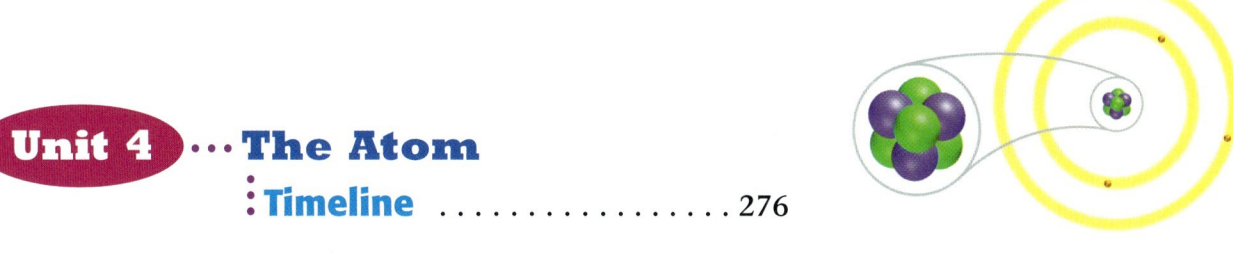

Timeline 276

CHAPTER 11

Chapter Organizer 277A
Chapter Resources & Worksheets 277C
Chapter Background 277E

Introduction to Atoms 278

Section 1 Development of the Atomic Theory 280
Section 2 The Atom 287

Chapter Highlights/Review 294

Feature Articles
Across the Sciences: Water on the Moon? 298
Careers: Experimental Physicist 299

LabBook
■ Made to Order 676

CHAPTER 12

Chapter Organizer 299A
Chapter Resources & Worksheets 299C
Chapter Background 299E

The Periodic Table 300

Section 1 Arranging the Elements 302
Section 2 Grouping the Elements 310

Chapter Highlights/Review 318

Feature Articles
Science, Technology, and Society:
   The Science of Fireworks 322
Weird Science: Buckyballs 323

LabBook
■ Create a Periodic Table 678

Contents **xi**

Unit 5 ··· Interactions of Matter

Timeline 324

CHAPTER 13

Chapter Organizer 325A
Chapter Resources & Worksheets 325C
Chapter Background 325E

Chemical Bonding 326

Section 1 Electrons and Chemical Bonding 328
Section 2 Types of Chemical Bonds 332

Chapter Highlights/Review 342

Feature Articles

Across the Sciences: Left-Handed Molecules 346
Eureka!: Here's Looking at Ya'! 347

LabBook

■ Covalent Marshmallows 680

CHAPTER 14

Chapter Organizer 347A
Chapter Resources & Worksheets 347C
Chapter Background 347E

Chemical Reactions 348

Section 1 Forming New Substances 350
Section 2 Types of Chemical Reactions 358
Section 3 Energy and Rates of Chemical Reactions .. 361

Chapter Highlights/Review 366

Feature Articles

Eye on the Environment: Slime That Fire! 370
Careers: Arson Investigator 371

LabBook

■ Finding a Balance 682
■ Cata-what? Catalyst! 683
■ Putting Elements Together 684
■ Speed Control 686

CHAPTER 15

Chapter Organizer 371A
Chapter Resources & Worksheets 371C
Chapter Background 371E

Chemical Compounds 372

Section 1 Ionic and Covalent Compounds 374
Section 2 Acids, Bases, and Salts 377
Section 3 Organic Compounds 383

Chapter Highlights/Review 390

Feature Articles
Across the Sciences: Unique Compounds 394
Weird Science: The Secrets of Spider Silk 395

- Cabbage Patch Indicators 688
- Making Salt 690

CHAPTER 16

Chapter Organizer 395A
Chapter Resources & Worksheets 395C
Chapter Background 395E

Atomic Energy 396

Section 1 Radioactivity 398
Section 2 Energy from the Nucleus 406

Chapter Highlights/Review 412

Feature Articles
Scientific Debate: Wasting Yucca Mountain? 416
Careers: Materials Scientist 417

- Domino Chain Reactions 692

Contents xiii

Contents

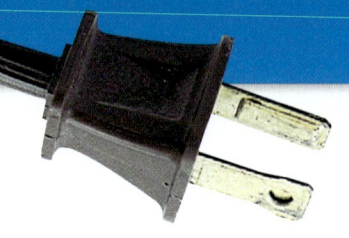

Unit 6 · Electricity

Timeline 418

CHAPTER 17

Chapter Organizer 419A
Chapter Resources & Worksheets 419C
Chapter Background 419E

Introduction to Electricity 420

Section 1 Electric Charge and Static Electricity 422
Section 2 Electrical Energy 430
Section 3 Electric Current 433
Section 4 Electric Circuits 440

Chapter Highlights/Review 446

Feature Articles

Science, Technology, and Society:
  Riding the Electric Rails 450
Across the Sciences: Sprites and Elves 451

LabBook

■ Stop the Static Electricity! 694 ■ Potato Power 695
■ Circuitry 101 696

CHAPTER 18

Chapter Organizer 451A
Chapter Resources & Worksheets 451C
Chapter Background 451E

Electromagnetism 452

Section 1 Magnets and Magnetism 454
Section 2 Magnetism from Electricity 462
Section 3 Electricity from Magnetism 468

Chapter Highlights/Review 474

Feature Articles

Across the Sciences: Geomagnetic Storms 478
Health Watch: Magnets in Medicine 479

LabBook

■ Magnetic Mystery 698 ■ Build a DC Motor 700
■ Electricity from Magnetism 699

xiv Contents

CHAPTER 19
Chapter Organizer 479A
Chapter Resources & Worksheets 479C
Chapter Background 479E

Electronic Technology 480

Section 1 Electronic Components 482
Section 2 Communication Technology 488
Section 3 Computers 494

Chapter Highlights/Review 500

Feature Articles
Health Watch: Listening Lower 504
Science Fiction: "There Will Come Soft Rains" 505

■ Tune In! 702

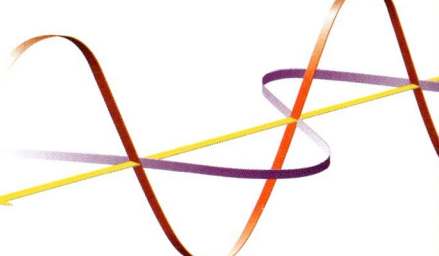

Unit 7 ··· **Waves, Sound, and Light**
⋮ **Timeline** 506

CHAPTER 20
Chapter Organizer 507A
Chapter Resources & Worksheets 507C
Chapter Background 507E

The Energy of Waves 508

Section 1 The Nature of Waves 510
Section 2 Properties of Waves 516
Section 3 Wave Interactions 520

Chapter Highlights/Review 526

Feature Articles
Science, Technology, and Society:
   The Ultimate Telescope 530
Across the Sciences: Sounds of Silence 531

■ Wave Energy and Speed 706
■ Wave Speed, Frequency, and Wavelength 708

Contents xv

Contents

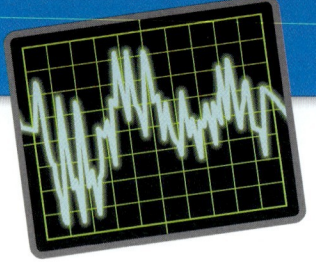

CHAPTER 21

Chapter Organizer 531A
Chapter Resources & Worksheets 531C
Chapter Background 531E

The Nature of Sound 532

Section 1 What Is Sound? 534
Section 2 Properties of Sound 539
Section 3 Interactions of Sound Waves ... 545
Section 4 Sound Quality 552

Chapter Highlights/Review 556

Feature Articles
Science, Technology, and Society: Jurassic Bark 560
Science Fiction: "Ear" 561

LabBook
- Easy Listening 710
- The Speed of Sound 712
- Tuneful Tube 713
- The Energy of Sound 714

CHAPTER 22

Chapter Organizer 561A
Chapter Resources & Worksheets 561C
Chapter Background 561E

The Nature of Light 562

Section 1 What Is Light? 564
Section 2 The Electromagnetic Spectrum ... 567
Section 3 Interactions of Light Waves ... 575
Section 4 Light and Color 581

Chapter Highlights/Review 586

Feature Articles
Science, Technology, and Society:
  Fireflies Light the Way 590
Eureka!: It's a Heat Wave! 591

LabBook
- What Color of Light Is Best for Green Plants? 716
- Which Color Is Hottest? 717
- Mixing Colors 718

CHAPTER 23

Chapter Organizer 591A
Chapter Resources & Worksheets 591C
Chapter Background 591E

Light and Our World 592

Section 1 Light Sources 594
Section 2 Mirrors and Lenses 598
Section 3 Light and Sight 605
Section 4 Light Technology 608

Chapter Highlights/Review 614

Feature Articles

Science, Technology, and Society: Traffic Lights 618
Eye on the Environment: Light Pollution 619

- Mirror Images 720
- Images from Convex Lenses 722

LabBook 620

Self-Check Answers 724

Appendix 727

Concept Mapping 728
SI Measurement 729
Temperature Scales 730
Measuring Skills 731
Scientific Method 732
Making Charts and Graphs 735
Math Refresher 738
Physical Science Refresher 742
Periodic Table of the Elements 744
Physical Science Laws and Principles 746

Glossary 750

Index 761

Answers to Concept Mapping Questions 779

Contents

The more labs, the better!
Take a minute to browse the **LabBook** located at the end of this textbook. You'll find a wide variety of exciting labs that will help you experience science firsthand. But please don't forget to be safe. Read the "Safety First!" section before starting any of the labs.

Safety First! 622

CHAPTER 1
The World of Physical Science
Exploring the Unseen 626
Off to the Races! 627
Measuring Liquid Volume 628
Coin Operated 629

CHAPTER 2
The Properties of Matter
Volumania! 630
Determining Density 632
Layering Liquids 633
White Before Your Eyes 634

CHAPTER 3
States of Matter
Full of Hot Air! 636
Can Crusher 637
A Hot and Cool Lab 638

CHAPTER 4
Elements, Compounds, and Mixtures
Flame Tests 640
A Sugar Cube Race! 642
Making Butter 643
Unpolluting Water 644

CHAPTER 5
Matter in Motion
Built for Speed 646
Detecting Acceleration 647
Science Friction 650
Relating Mass and Weight 651

CHAPTER 6
Forces in Motion
A Marshmallow Catapult 652
Blast Off! 653
Inertia-Rama! 654
Quite a Reaction 656

CHAPTER 7
Forces in Fluids
Fluids, Force, and Floating 658
Density Diver 660
Taking Flight 661

CHAPTER 8
Work and Machines
A Powerful Workout 662
Inclined to Move 664
Building Machines 665
Wheeling and Dealing 666

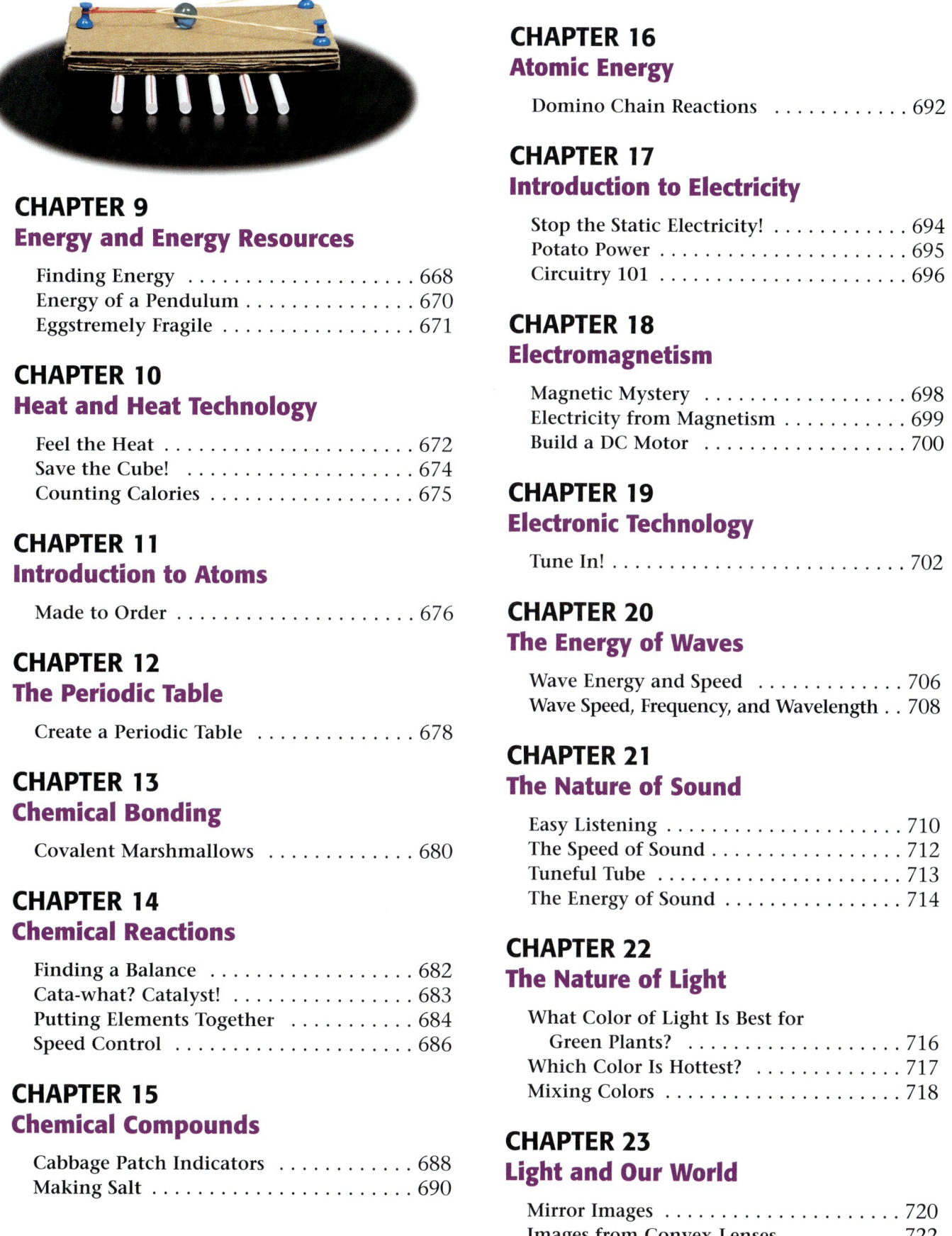

CHAPTER 9
Energy and Energy Resources
Finding Energy 668
Energy of a Pendulum 670
Eggstremely Fragile 671

CHAPTER 10
Heat and Heat Technology
Feel the Heat 672
Save the Cube! 674
Counting Calories 675

CHAPTER 11
Introduction to Atoms
Made to Order 676

CHAPTER 12
The Periodic Table
Create a Periodic Table 678

CHAPTER 13
Chemical Bonding
Covalent Marshmallows 680

CHAPTER 14
Chemical Reactions
Finding a Balance 682
Cata-what? Catalyst! 683
Putting Elements Together 684
Speed Control 686

CHAPTER 15
Chemical Compounds
Cabbage Patch Indicators 688
Making Salt 690

CHAPTER 16
Atomic Energy
Domino Chain Reactions 692

CHAPTER 17
Introduction to Electricity
Stop the Static Electricity! 694
Potato Power 695
Circuitry 101 696

CHAPTER 18
Electromagnetism
Magnetic Mystery 698
Electricity from Magnetism 699
Build a DC Motor 700

CHAPTER 19
Electronic Technology
Tune In! 702

CHAPTER 20
The Energy of Waves
Wave Energy and Speed 706
Wave Speed, Frequency, and Wavelength . . 708

CHAPTER 21
The Nature of Sound
Easy Listening 710
The Speed of Sound 712
Tuneful Tube 713
The Energy of Sound 714

CHAPTER 22
The Nature of Light
What Color of Light Is Best for
  Green Plants? 716
Which Color Is Hottest? 717
Mixing Colors 718

CHAPTER 23
Light and Our World
Mirror Images 720
Images from Convex Lenses 722

Contents

Now is the time to Investigate!
Science is a process in which investigation leads to information and understanding. The **Investigate!** at the beginning of each chapter helps you gain scientific understanding of the topic through hands-on experience.

Mission Impossible?	5
Sack Secrets	35
Vanishing Act	59
Mystery Mixture	81
The Domino Derby	107
Falling Water	137
Out the Spouts	161
C'mon, Lever a Little!	187
Blast-off to Energy	213
Some Like It Hot	245
Where Is It?	279
Placement Pattern	301
From Glue to Goop	327
Reaction Ready	349
Ionic Versus Covalent	373
Watch Your Headsium!	397
Charge over Matter	421
Magnetic Attraction	453
Talking Long Distance	481
Making Waves	509
A Homemade Guitar	533
Colors of Light	563
Mirror, Mirror	593

QuickLab

Not all laboratory investigations have to be long and involved.
The **QuickLabs** found throughout the chapters of this textbook require only a small amount of time and limited equipment. But just because they are quick, don't skimp on the safety.

That's Swingin'!	15
Space Case	36
Changing Change	49
Boiling Water Is Cool	71
Compound Confusion	87
The Friction 500	120
Penny Projectile Motion	144
First-Law Magic	147
Blown Away	166
Ship-Shape	171
Breathing Bernoulli-Style	173
More Power to You	191
Hear That Energy!	220
Hot or Cold?	247
Heat Exchange	253
Conduction Connection	307
Bending with Bonds	340
Mass Conservation	357
Which Is Quicker?	364
I'm Crushed!	365
pHast Relief!	380
Gone Fission	407
A Series of Circuits	442
A Parallel Lab	443
Electromagnets	464
Energetic Waves	510
Springy Waves	518
Good Vibrations	534
Sounding Board	543
Scattering Milk	577
Rose-Colored Glasses?	584
Now You See, Now You Don't	613

MATH BREAK

Science and math go hand in hand.
The **MathBreaks** in the margins of the chapters show you many ways that math applies directly to science and vice versa.

Using Area to Find Volume 26	
Calculating Volume 38	
Density 45	
Gas Law Graphs 66	Calculating Energy Transfer 257
Calculating Concentration 94	Atomic Mass 292
Calculating Average Speed 109	Charge! 334
Calculating Acceleration 113	Counting Atoms 352
Velocity of Falling Objects 139	Balancing Act 356
Second-Law Problems 149	How Old Is It? 404
Pressure, Force, and Area 162	Using Ohm's Law 437
How to Calculate Density 170	Computer Memory 497
Working It Out 190	Perpendicular Lines 513
Finding the Advantage 196	Wave Calculations 519
Calculating Energy 217	Speed of Sound 540
Converting Temperatures 249	Just How Fast Is Light? 566

APPLY

Science can be very useful in the real world.
It is interesting to learn how scientific information is being used in the real world. You can see for yourself in the **Apply** features. You will also be asked to apply your own knowledge. This is a good way to learn!

Models for Weather Forecasting 21	
Mass, Weight, and Bathroom Scales 42	
Density and Grease Separators 46	
Charles's Law and Bicycle Tires 67	
Shake Well Before Use 96	
Friction and Tires 124	
Stopping Motion 146	
Lift and Spoilers 176	
Oil Improves Efficiency 197	
Camping with Energy 224	
Keepin' It Cool 254	
Isotopes and Light Bulbs 291	
One Set of Symbols 308	
Metallic Bonding in Staples 341	
Fresh Hydrogen Peroxide 363	
Storage Site Selection 409	
How to Save Energy 439	
Compasses Near Magnets 463	Insightful Technology 547
Sound Waves in Movie Theaters 523	Blocking the Sun 573
	Convex Mirrors Help Drivers 602

Contents xxi

Science Connections

Biology CONNECTION

All About Penguins	14
Calcium Strengthens Bones	40
Blood: Part Suspension, Part Solution	96
Seeds Can "Sense" Gravity	125
Energy Conversions in the Body	231
Energy in Food	262
Covalent Bonds in Proteins	339
Photosynthesis, Cellular Respiration, and Energy	362
pH of Blood	381
Essential Amino Acids	386
"Jump Start" a Heart	435
Your Body's Wired	441
Do Birds Use Magnets to Navigate?	460
Vocal Cords and Speech	535
Waves of Therapy	541
Photosynthesis	572
Color Deficiency and Chromosomes	607

Environment CONNECTION

Chemical Changes and Acid Precipitation	51
Newton's Second Law and Air Pollution	148
Heat Island Effect	269
Recycling Aluminum	314
Radon in the Home	402
Noise Pollution and Butterflies	555

Geology CONNECTION

Density Differences Affect the Earth's Crust	172
From Alpha to Helium	399
Seismograms Are Analog Signals	489
Using Minerals in Paint	585

One science leads to another.

You may not realize it at first, but different areas of science are related to each other in many ways. Each **Connection** explores a topic from the viewpoint of another science discipline. In this way, areas of science merge to improve your understanding of the world around you.

Astronomy CONNECTION

The Gravitational Force of Black Holes	127
Hydrogen: The Most Abundant Element	290
Star Fuel	410
Light from the Stars	512
Communication Break	536
Speed of Electromagnetic Waves	567
What Makes the Moon Shine?	594

Physics CONNECTION

Breaking Down Compounds Using Electrolysis	88

Meteorology CONNECTION

Condensation and Fog Formation	71
Coastal Climates	256

Oceanography CONNECTION

Energy from the Ocean	266

Feature Articles

Feature articles for any appetite!
Science and technology affect us all in many ways. The following articles will give you an idea of just how interesting, strange, helpful, and action-packed science and technology are. At the end of each chapter, you will find two feature articles. Read them and you will be surprised at what you learn.

CAREERS

Electronics Engineer	32
Roller Coaster Designer	159
Power-Plant Manager	243
Experimental Physicist	299
Arson Investigator	371
Materials Scientist	417

ACROSS THE SCIENCES

In the Dark About Dark Matter	56
The Golden Gate Bridge	135
Green Buildings	242
DiAPLEX®: The Intelligent Fabric	275
Water on the Moon?	298
Left-Handed Molecules	346
Unique Compounds	394
Sprites and Elves	451
Geomagnetic Storms	478
Sounds of Silence	531

Science, Technology, and Society

Guiding Lightning	78
Perfume: Fragrant Solutions	102
Is It Real . . . or Is It Virtual?	134
Micromachines	210
The Deep Freeze	274
The Science of Fireworks	322
Riding the Electric Rails	450
The Ultimate Telescope	530
Jurassic Bark	560
Fireflies Light the Way	590
Traffic Lights	618

EYE ON THE ENVIRONMENT

Slime That Fire!	370
Light Pollution	619

Eureka!

Full Steam Ahead!	79
A Bat with Dimples	158
Stayin' Aloft—The Story of the Frisbee®	182
Wheelchair Innovators	211
Here's Looking at Ya'!	347
It's a Heat Wave!	591

Health WATCH

Building a Better Body	57
Magnets in Medicine	479
Listening Lower	504

SCIENTIFIC DEBATE

Wasting Yucca Mountain?	416

Science Fiction

"Inspiration"	33
"The Strange Case of Dr. Jekyll and Mr. Hyde"	103
"Wet Behind the Ears"	183
"There Will Come Soft Rains"	505
"Ear"	561

WEIRD SCIENCE

Buckyballs	323
The Secrets of Spider Silk	395

Master Materials List

The following chart provides a comprehensive list of all the materials you would need in order to teach all of the labs and investigations in *Holt Science and Technology, Physical Science*.

For added convenience, Science Kit® provides materials-ordering software on CD-ROM designed specifically for *Holt Science and Technology*. This software allows you to create an electronic materials list, complete with item numbers. Using this software, you can order complete kits or individual items, quickly and efficiently.

For more information about this software, contact your HRW representative, call Science Kit® directly at 1-800-828-7777, or visit the Web site: www.sciencekit.com.

As you can see from the listings, *Holt Science and Technology* is designed around readily available materials and equipment, with an emphasis on economy. More specific materials lists and information can be found with the lab or investigation in this *Annotated Teacher's Edition*.

MATERIALS AND EQUIPMENT CONSUMABLE	AMOUNT*	QuickLab PAGE NO.	Investigate! PAGE NO.	LabBook PAGE NO.
Aluminum foil, approx. 20 × 30 cm	1			702
Aluminum, approx. 5 × 1 cm	6			686
Antacid tablet	1	380		
Bag, paper lunch	1		35	678
Bag, sealable plastic	1	357	349	674
Baking powder	1 tsp			634
Baking soda	1 tsp	87, 357	349	634
Baking soda	1 tbsp		213	
Balloon, long, 12 in.	1			653
Balloon, round	1			636
Battery, 4.5 V or 6 V	1	442, 443		696, 700
Battery, D-cell	1	464		
Borax	approx. 2 tbsp		327	
Cabbage, red	1 leaf			688
Calcium chloride	2 tsp		349	
Calcium chloride solution	approx. 10 mL			640
Can, aluminum	2			637
Candle	1			720, 722
Cardboard, 10 × 15 cm	3			656
Cardboard, approx. 20 × 30 cm	1			702
Cardboard, approx. 60 × 30 cm	1	120	279	
Cardboard tube	1–2		563	699, 700, 702
Carton, egg, plastic-foam	1			634
Carton, empty milk	1		161	
Carton, empty milk, 1/2 pint	1			671, 674
Chalk	1 stick	340		
Charcoal, activated	4 oz			644
Clay, modeling	1 stick	171	593	647, 720, 722
Clothes hanger, wire	1			627
Colored paper, black, blue, red, and white, 2 × 2 cm	1 each			717
Copper powder	10 g			684
Corn syrup, dark	20 mL			633
Cornstarch	1 tsp			634

*Amount is for one group of students.

MATERIALS AND EQUIPMENT		QuickLab	Investigate!	LabBook
CONSUMABLE (continued)	AMOUNT*	PAGE NO.	PAGE NO.	PAGE NO.
Craft stick	1			640
Cream, heavy	4–6 fl oz			643
Cup, paper	1		137	653
Cup, paper, small	2		327	
Cup, plastic-foam	1	307	373	675, 700
Cup, plastic-foam	2			644, 672
Cup, plastic-foam with lid, small	1			675
Effervescent tablet	1	364, 365		
Egg, hard-boiled	1			654
Egg, raw	1			654, 671
Envelope, business-sized	2			682
Filter paper	2			644
Filter, coffee	1		81, 213	
Flashlight bulb with bulb holder	3	442, 443		696
Flashlight bulb with bulb holder (burned out)	1	442, 443		
Food coloring, dark red	1 bottle		137	633
Gloves, protective	1 pair			628, 634, 640, 683, 684, 686, 688, 690
Glue, white	1 bottle		327	627, 656
Graphite for mechanical pencil	1	307		
Hydrochloric acid 0.1 M (0.1 N)	10 mL			686
Hydrochloric acid 0.1 M (0.1 N)	15 mL			640
Hydrochloric acid 0.1 M (0.1 N)	30 mL			690
Hydrochloric acid 1.0 M (1.0 N)	40 mL			686
Hydrogen peroxide	15 mL			683
Iodine solution	5 drops			634
Litmus paper, blue and red	5 each	380		688
Liver, approx. 1 cm^3	2			683
Marker, permanent, black	1			628, 670, 700, 716
Marker, water-soluble, black	1		81	
Marshmallow, miniature	2			652
Marshmallow, any color	2			680
Marshmallow, any other color	1			680
Matches	1 box			720, 722
Milk	1 mL	577		
Oil, vegetable	10 mL			633
Paper, construction, black, approx. 8 × 8 cm	1		563	
Paper, graphing	1 sheet		397, 593	632, 651, 664, 710, 713, 717
Paper, graphing	2 sheets			638, 678
Paper, tissue 2 × 2 cm	6–8		421	
Paraffin wax	approx. 5 g		373	
Peanut, foam	1			694
Phenolphthalein	5 mL			690
Potassium chloride solution	approx. 10 mL			640
Potato	1			695
Rock salt	1 lb			638
Rubber band	1–2	220	533	644, 656, 672, 714
Rubbing alcohol	25 mL		59	
Salt	approx. 5 g		373	
Sand, fine	7 oz			644

* Amount is for one group of students.

Master Materials List

Master Materials List

MATERIALS AND EQUIPMENT CONSUMABLE (continued)	AMOUNT*	QuickLab PAGE NO.	Investigate! PAGE NO.	LabBook PAGE NO.
Sandpaper, medium, 9 × 11 in.	1 sheet	120		699, 700
Shoe box	1	397, 533		626, 698
Sodium chloride solution	approx. 10 mL			640
Sodium hydroxide 0.1 M	approx. 30 mL			690
Spoon, plastic	1		327, 349	652
Straw, jumbo	1–6			653, 656
String, 15 cm	2			653
String, approx. 10 cm	1			656
String, approx. 30–50 cm	1			647, 666, 672, 714
String, approx. 1–2 m	1	15, 191, 510	187, 481	650, 651, 654, 664, 670
Sugar cube	2			642
Sugar, granulated	1 tsp			634
Sugar, powdered	4 g	87		
Swab, cotton	1		59	
Tape, duct, 20–30 cm	1			652
Tape, electrical, 20–30 cm	1	464		700
Tape, masking, 20–30 cm	1		161, 563	628, 640, 646, 668, 683, 688, 698, 716, 718
Tape, transparent, 20–30 cm	1		81, 593	653, 694, 702, 717
Thread	1 spool			654
Toothpicks	20			676, 680
Twist tie	1		213	653
Vinegar	5 mL	357		634
Vinegar	10 mL	87		
Vinegar	50 mL	49, 380		
Vinegar	200 mL		213	
Water, distilled	approx. 20 mL			690
Water, distilled	100 mL			688
Watercolor paint	1 set			718
Wax paper	1 sheet	220		
Weighing paper	1			684

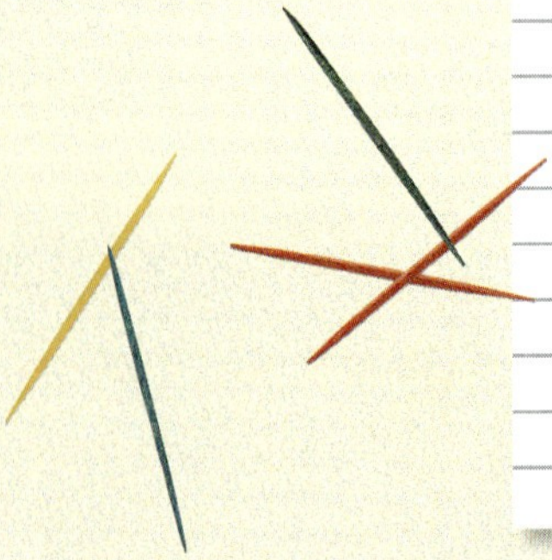

MATERIALS AND EQUIPMENT NONCONSUMABLE	AMOUNT*	QuickLab PAGE NO.	Investigate! PAGE NO.	LabBook PAGE NO.
Acetate, clear	1 sheet			698
Ammeter	1			696
Balance	1	357		629, 632, 651, 658, 668, 672, 674, 678, 684
Ball, styrene, 2–3 cm diam.	10			676
Beaker, large (or bucket)	1	36		
Beaker, 100 mL	1	71		633, 690
Beaker, 100 mL	3			628
Beaker, 250 mL	1	253		628, 636, 638, 688, 706
Beaker, 250 mL	2			640, 642
Beaker, 250 mL	4			644
Beaker, 600 mL	1			683
Beaker, 1 L	1			637
Block, wood, 3.5 × 3.5 × 1 cm	1			652
Block, wood, approx. 10 × 5 × 5 cm	10			664

* Amount is for one group of students.

MATERIALS AND EQUIPMENT		QuickLab	Investigate!	LabBook
NONCONSUMABLE (continued)	AMOUNT*	PAGE NO.	PAGE NO.	PAGE NO.
Board, wood, 1 m × 30 cm	1			627, 664, 668
Bottle, 2 L soda	1	166	213	630, 660
Bottle, plastic, 1 L	1	577		647
Bucket, rectangular (or fish tank)	1			658
Bunsen burner, adjustable	1			640, 684
Can, coffee	1	220		638
Can, coffee	2		481	
Car, toy	1	120		646
Card, index, 3 × 5 in.	1		5	654, 720, 722
Cardboard, 10 × 10 cm	1		245	
Clamp, C	2			666
Cloth, silk	1		421	694
Cloth, woolen	1			694
Colored filter, blue, green, red, and yellow	1 each	584		718
Colored glass, approx. 20 × 20 cm	1		593	
Comb, plastic	1		421	
Cork	1		213, 509	647
Cup, clear plastic	1–2	36, 87, 147, 364, 365, 380, 534	59, 81	654, 674, 714, 717, 718
Diffraction grating	1		563	
Diode	1			702
Domino	15			692
Domino	25		107	
Dowel, wood, 10 cm, 15 cm, 20 cm, and 25 cm	1 each			666
Dowel, wood, 30 cm	3–4			650
Dropper bottle	1			690
Dropper, medicine	1			660
Dropper, plastic	1–3			634, 688, 690
Earphone	1			702
Eraser, pink rubber	1	534	187	627, 710, 713, 714
Evaporating dish	1			684, 690
Film canister	1	253, 357	349	
Fishing line, 3 m	1			653
Flashlight	1	577		
Flashlight	3			718
Fluorescent light	1		563	
Friction rod, rubber	1			694
Funnel	1–3			628, 630, 633, 683, 686
Galvanometer	1			699
Gauze, wire, ceramic center	1			684
Gloves, heat-resistant	1 pair			636, 637, 638
Graduated cylinder, 10 mL	1		373	628, 683
Graduated cylinder, 10 mL	2			686
Graduated cylinder, 10 mL	3			633
Graduated cylinder, 100 mL	1			629, 630, 632, 638, 642, 644, 672, 675, 690, 713
Graduated cylinder, 100 mL	2		213	
Hot plate	1			636, 637, 638, 675, 688
Igniter	1			640, 684
Iron filings	approx. 10 g	459		698

* Amount is for one group of students.

Master Materials List

Master Materials List

MATERIALS AND EQUIPMENT NONCONSUMABLE (continued)	AMOUNT*	QuickLab PAGE NO.	Investigate! PAGE NO.	LabBook PAGE NO.
Iron nail	1	464	453	
Jar, clear plastic	1			643
Lamp, goose-neck	1		563	717
Lens, convex	1			722
Lid, jar	1			720, 722
Magnet, bar	1	459	453	698, 699
Magnet, disk	4			700
Magnet, horseshoe	1			698
Magnifying lens	1			690
Marble	1		279	626, 643, 656
Marble	8–10			632
Mass set	1			658
Mass, 1 kg	1			654, 666
Mass, hooked, 100 g	1			670
Metal strip, aluminum, copper, iron, and zinc, 0.5 × 2 cm	1 each			695
Meterstick	1			646, 652, 653, 654, 656, 664, 666, 668, 670, 708, 710, 722
Mirror, concave and convex	1 each			720
Mirror, plane	1		593	
Mortar and pestle	1			683
Nail, approx. 2 in.	12			672
Nail, small	1			644
Paintbrush	1			718
Pan or bucket, approx. 45 × 60 cm	1	171	137, 161	
Pan, aluminum pie	1			630
Pan, aluminum, 2.5 in. deep	2			636
Pan, rectangular baking	1			658
Pan, shallow, 20 × 30 cm	1		509	706
Pan or bucket, plastic	3	247		
Paper clip	1–6	340, 464	453	700, 702
Pencil, colored	1 box			717
Penny	1–3	49, 144		675
Penny	100		397	653
Penny, post-1982	5			629
Penny, pre-1982	5			629
Petri dish with cover	3			716
Pie plate, small	1	49		
Plastic tube, approx. 40 cm	1			713
Polarizing lens	2	613		
Protractor	1			652
Pushpin	1–3			647, 656
Quarter	1			654
Ring stand with ring clamp	1	15		684
Rod, glass	1			694
Rod, metal	1		421	
Rolling cart	1			668
Ruler, metric	1	120, 144, 191, 543	107, 187	627, 636, 644, 658, 662, 678, 694, 713, 718

* Amount is for one group of students.

MATERIALS AND EQUIPMENT NONCONSUMABLE (continued)	AMOUNT*	QuickLab PAGE NO.	Investigate! PAGE NO.	LabBook PAGE NO.
Scissors	1		5, 81, 563	644, 647, 650, 651, 654, 656, 686, 702
Screwdriver	1	442, 443		
Spatula	4			634
Spoon, plastic	2			644
Spring scale	1	191		650, 651, 664, 666
Spring toy, coiled	1	518		708
Stirring rod	1		373	634, 690
Stopwatch	1	15, 191	107	627, 638, 642, 643, 646, 662, 668, 675, 692, 706, 708
Switch, electric, knife	1			696
Syringe, small	1	71		
Test tube	2–6		373	628, 640, 683, 686, 688
Test-tube rack	1			628, 640, 686, 688
Thermometer	1			638, 672, 675, 717
Thermometer	2	253		
Thermometer, LCD strip	1		245	
Thread, 30 cm	1			694
Tongs, beaker with plain jaws	1			637, 688
Tongs, crucible	1			675, 684
Tuning fork	1	534		714
Tuning fork, different frequencies	4			710, 713
Tuning fork, same frequency	2			714
Tweezers	1			683
Voltmeter	1			695, 696
Washer, large	4	15		
Wire cutters	1			627
Wire, bare copper, 25 cm	1	307		638
Wire, bare Nichrome®, 30 cm	1			640
Wire, insulated copper, approx. 10 cm	6	442, 443		
Wire, insulated copper, approx. 15 cm	10			696
Wire, insulated copper, approx. 30 cm	7			702
Wire, insulated, with alligator clips, approx. 30 cm	2			699, 700
Wire, insulated, 1 m	1	464		
Wire, insulated, 2 m	1			702
Wire, magnet, 100–150 cm	1			699, 700

* Amount is for one group of students.

Master Materials List

Science & Math Skills Worksheets

The *Holt Science and Technology* program helps you meet the needs of a wide variety of students, regardless of their skill level. The following pages provide examples of the worksheets available to improve your students' science and math skills whether they already have a strong science and math background or are weak in these areas. Samples of assessment checklists and rubrics are also provided.

In addition to the skills worksheets represented here, *Holt Science and Technology* provides a variety of worksheets that are correlated directly with each chapter of the program. Representations of these worksheets are found at the beginning of each chapter in this Annotated Teacher's Edition.

Many worksheets are also available on the HRW Web site. The address is **go.hrw.com.**

Science Skills Worksheets: Thinking Skills

BEING FLEXIBLE
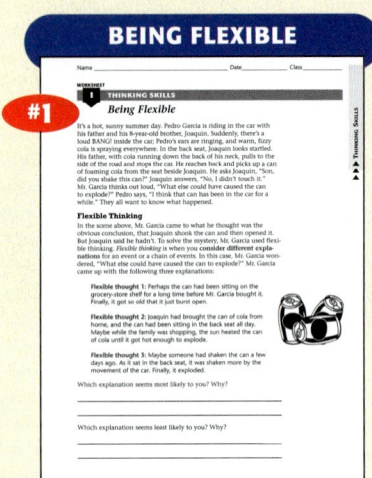

USING YOUR SENSES
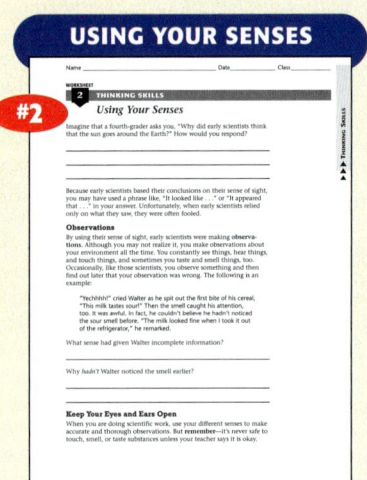

THINKING OBJECTIVELY
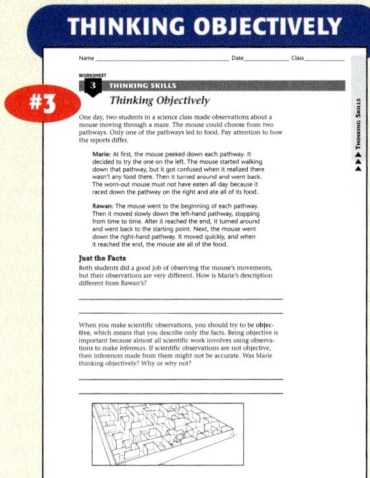

UNDERSTANDING BIAS
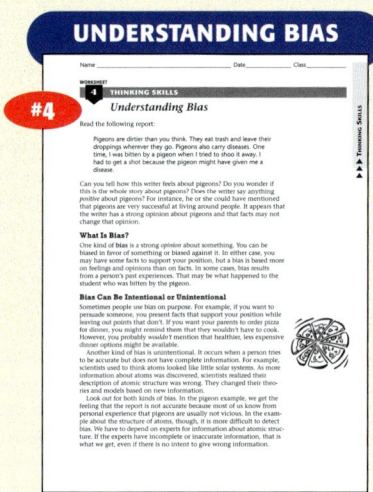

USING LOGIC

BOOSTING YOUR MEMORY
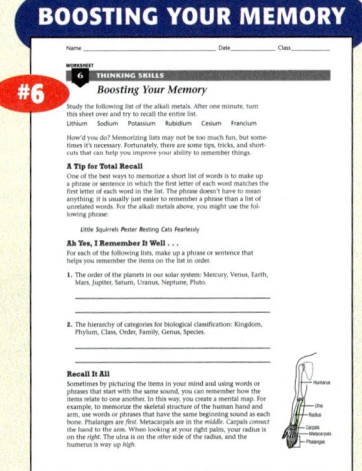

IMPROVING YOUR STUDY HABITS
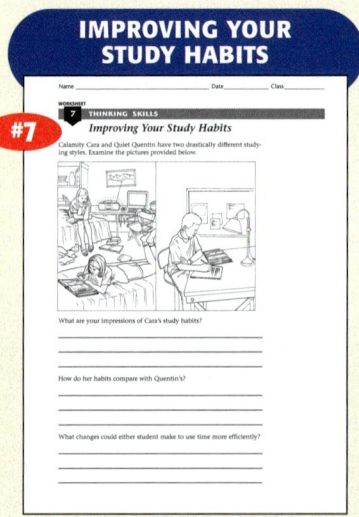

READING A SCIENCE TEXTBOOK
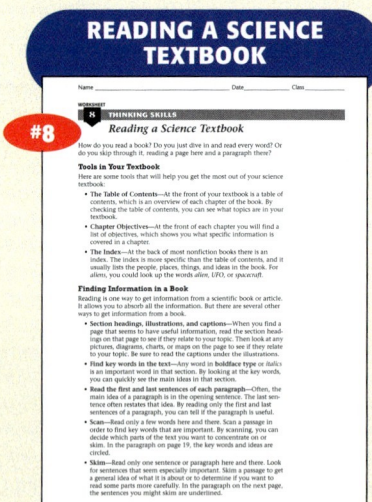

xxx Science & Math Skills Worksheets

Science Skills Worksheets: Experimenting Skills

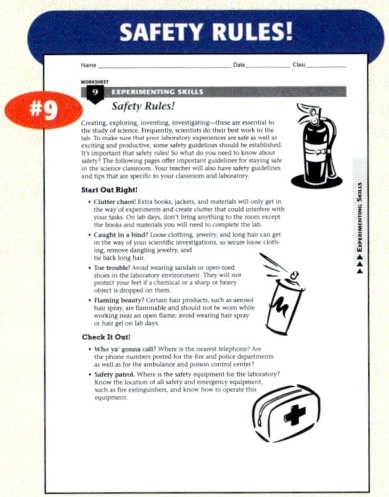
#9 SAFETY RULES!

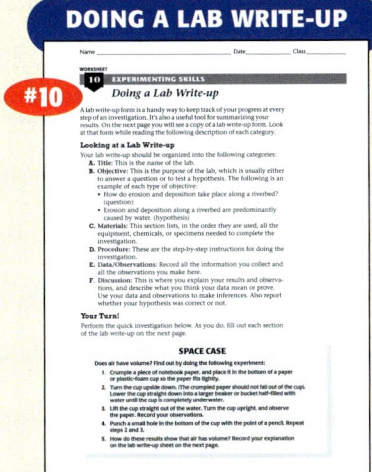
#10 DOING A LAB WRITE-UP

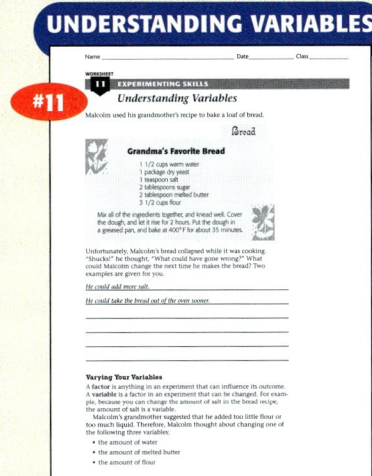
#11 UNDERSTANDING VARIABLES

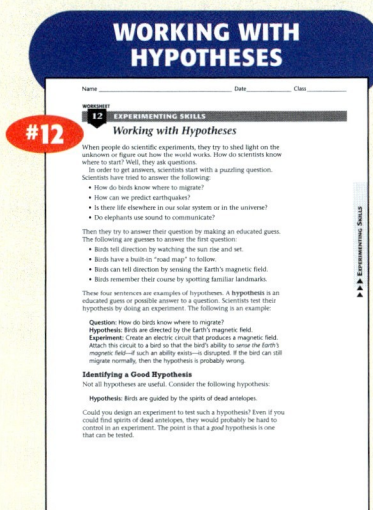
#12 WORKING WITH HYPOTHESES

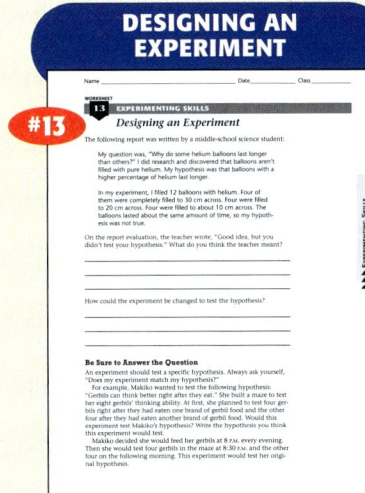
#13 DESIGNING AN EXPERIMENT

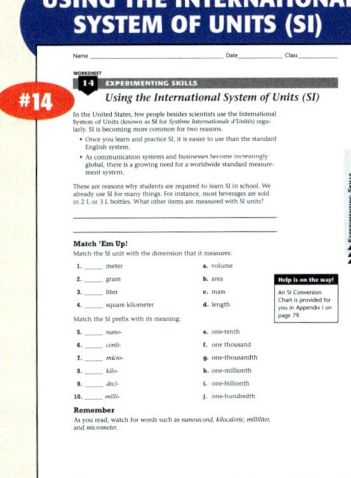
#14 USING THE INTERNATIONAL SYSTEM OF UNITS (SI)

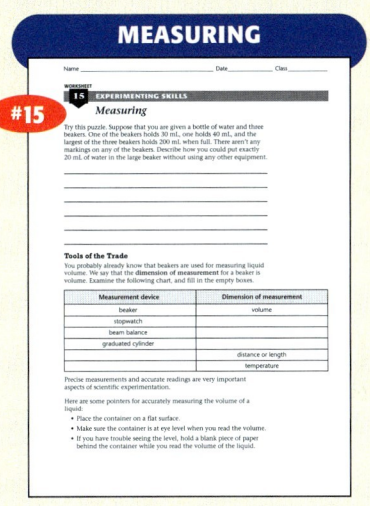
#15 MEASURING

Science Skills Worksheets: Researching Skills

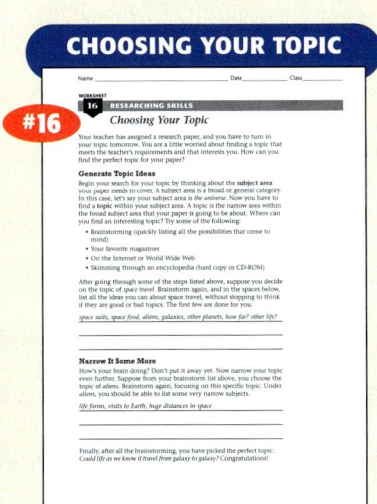
#16 CHOOSING YOUR TOPIC

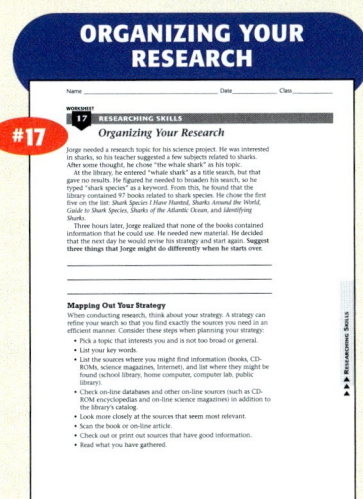
#17 ORGANIZING YOUR RESEARCH

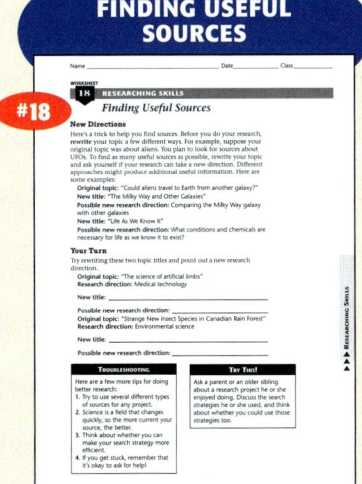
#18 FINDING USEFUL SOURCES

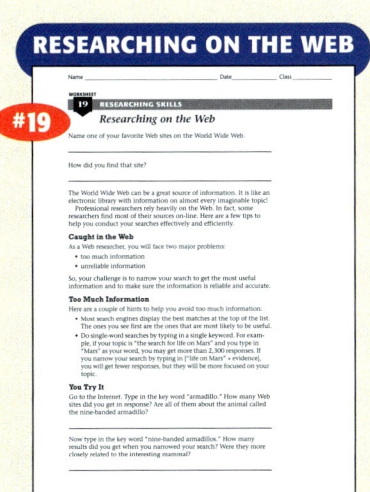
#19 RESEARCHING ON THE WEB

Science & Math Skills Worksheets   xxxi

Science & Math Skills Worksheets (continued)

Science Skills Worksheets: Researching Skills (continued)

IDENTIFYING BIAS
#20
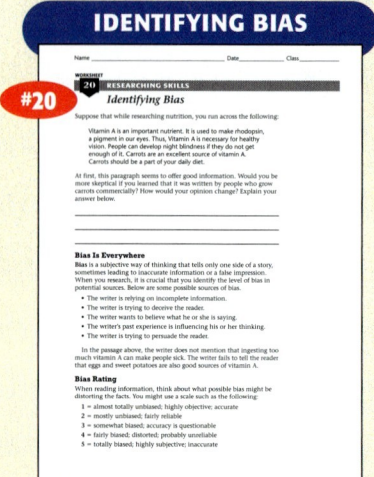

TAKING NOTES
#21

SCIENCE WRITING
#22
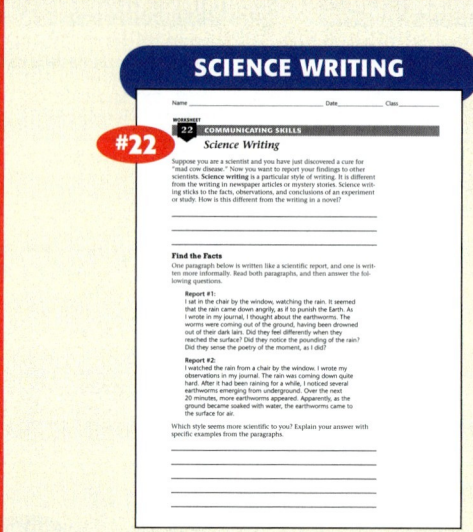

Science Skills Worksheets: Communicating Skills

SCIENCE DRAWING
#23
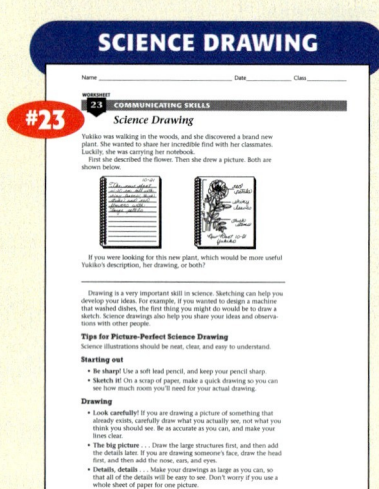

USING MODELS TO COMMUNICATE
#24
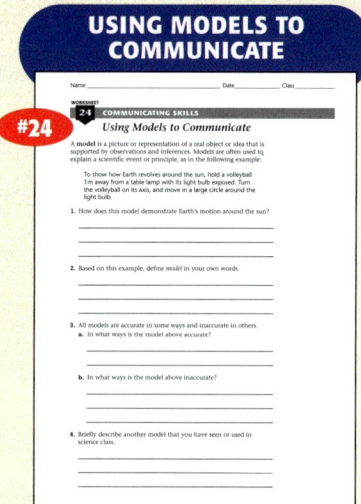

INTRODUCTION TO GRAPHS
#25
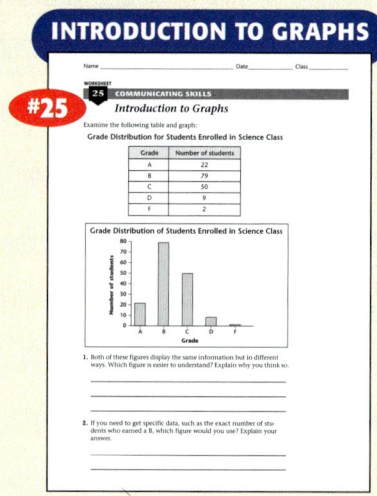

GRASPING GRAPHING
#26
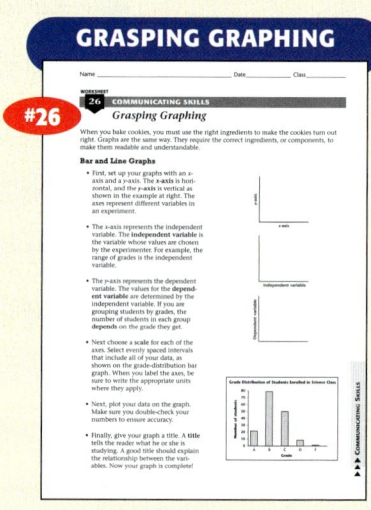

INTERPRETING YOUR DATA
#27

RECOGNIZING BIAS IN GRAPHS
#28
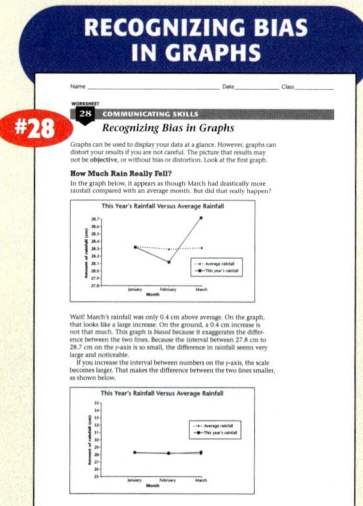

MAKING DATA MEANINGFUL
#29
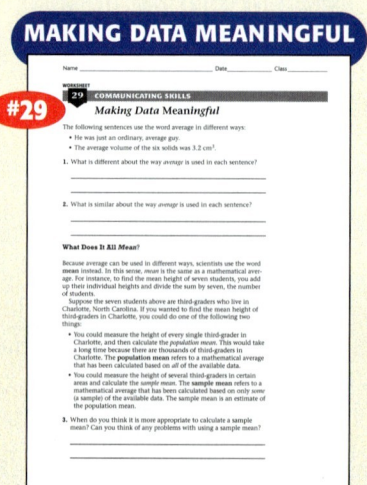

HINTS FOR ORAL PRESENTATIONS
#30
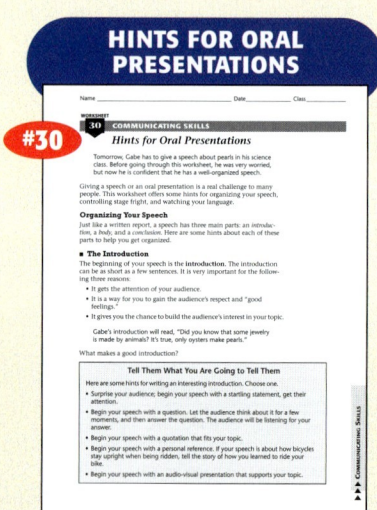

Math Skills for Science

ADDITION AND SUBTRACTION
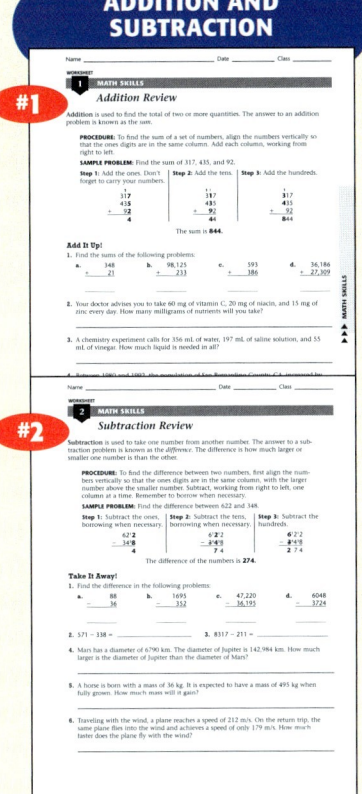

MULTIPLICATION
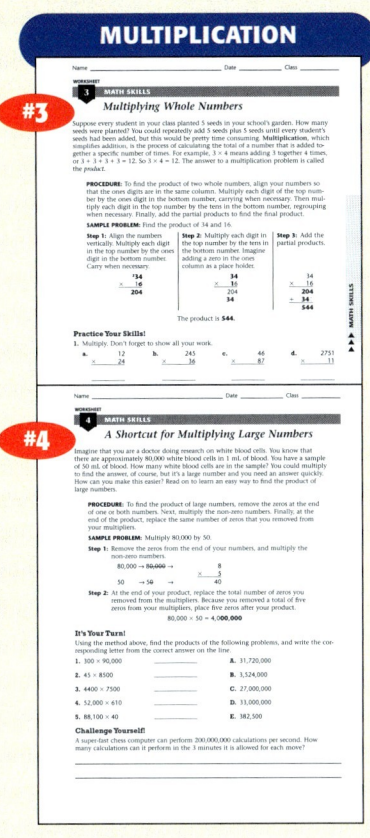

DIVISION
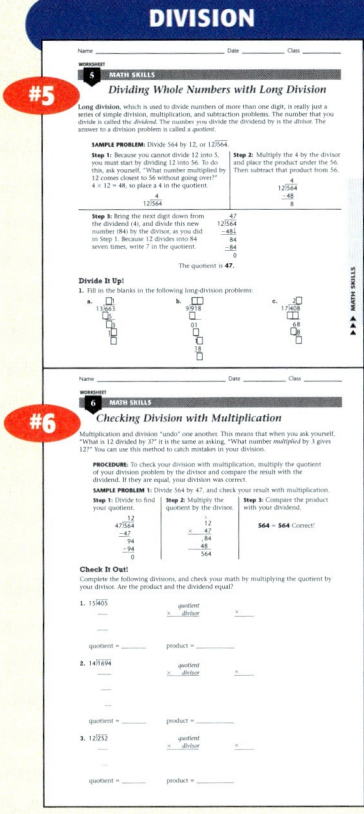

AVERAGES
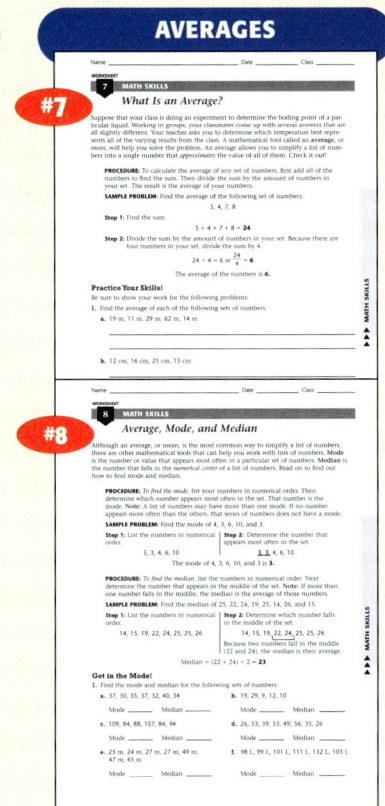

POSITIVE AND NEGATIVE NUMBERS
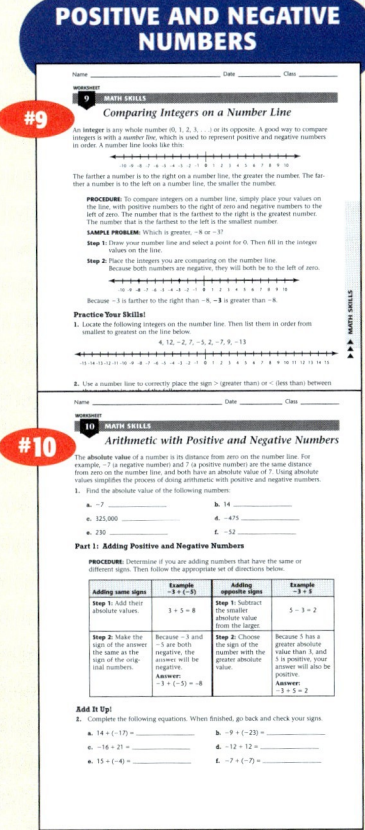

FRACTIONS
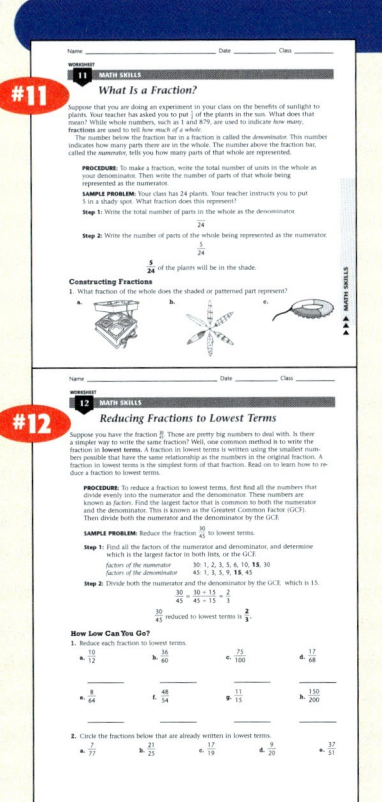
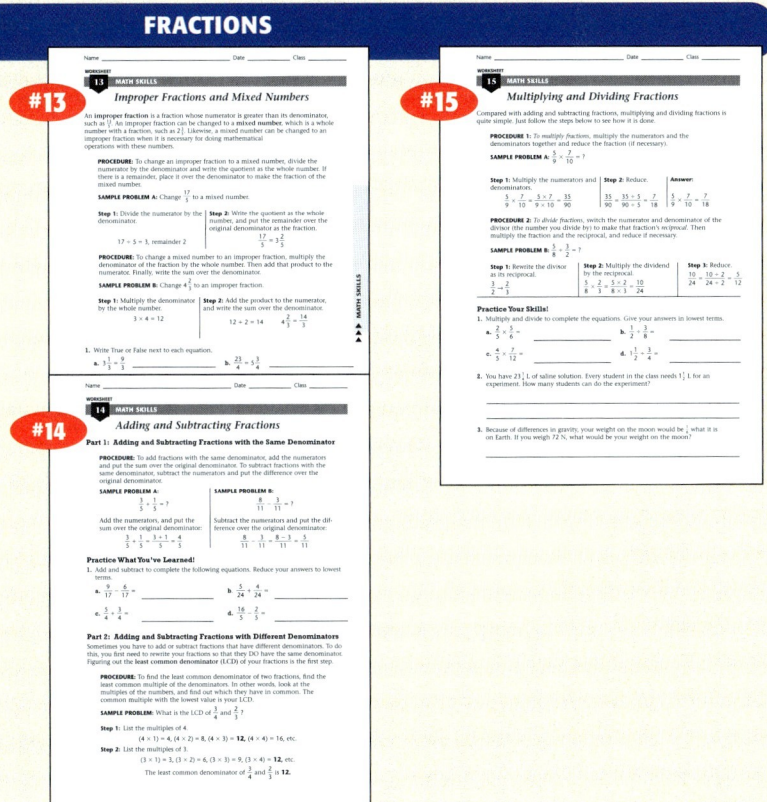

Science & Math Skills Worksheets

Science & Math Skills Worksheets (continued)

Math Skills for Science (continued)

RATIOS AND PROPORTIONS

DECIMALS

PERCENTAGES

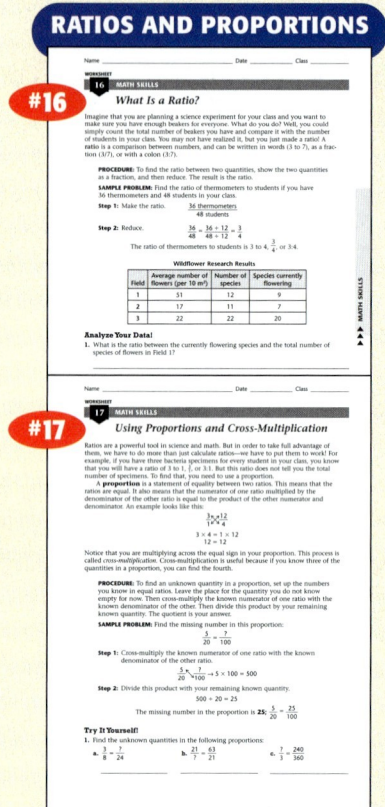
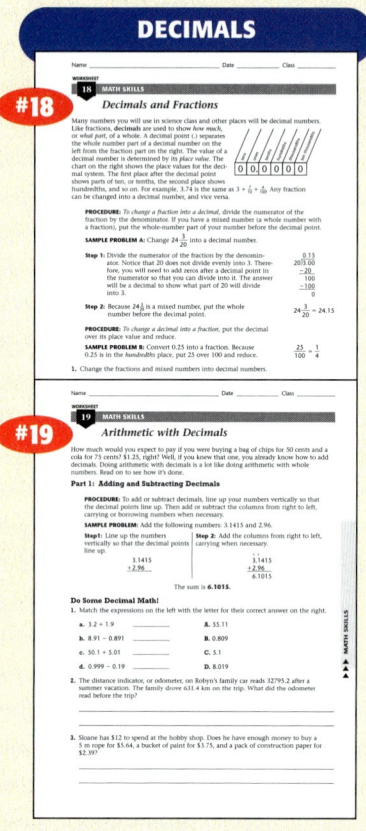
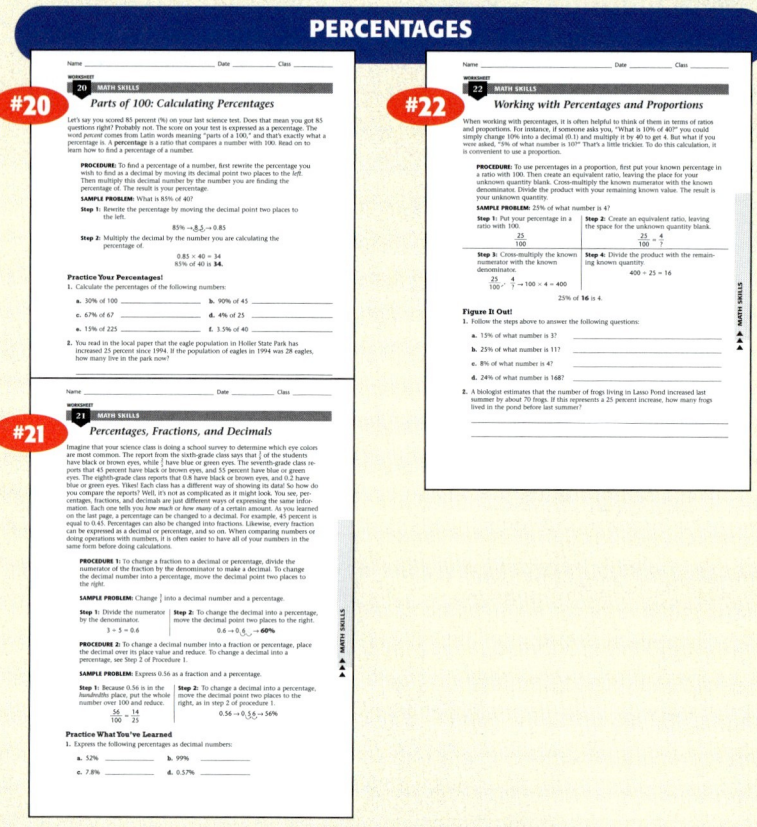

POWERS OF 10

SCIENTIFIC NOTATION

SI MEASUREMENT AND CONVERSION

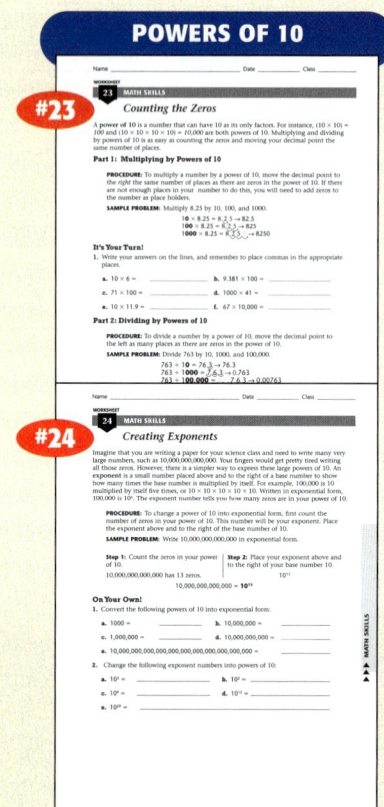
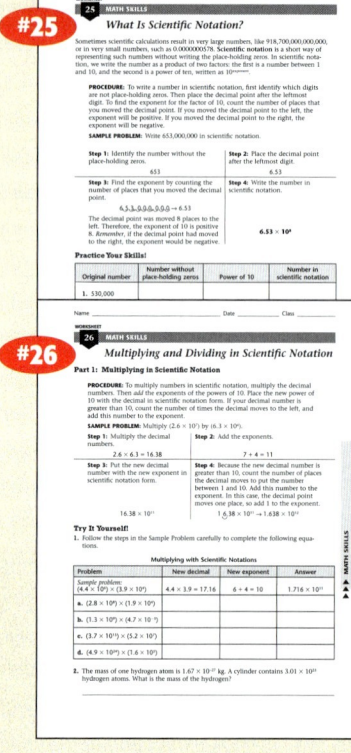
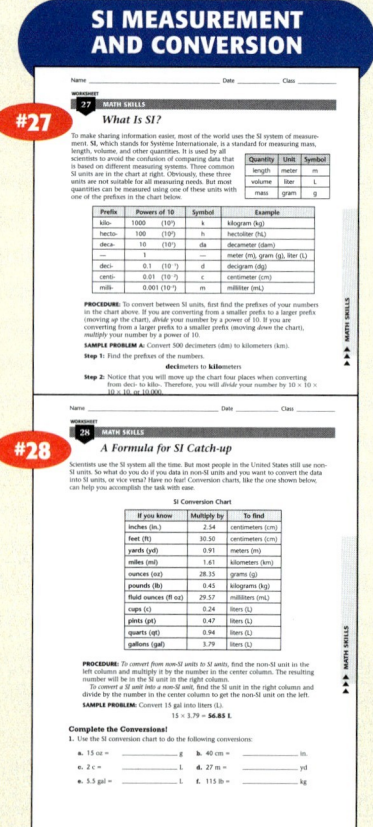

Math Skills for Science (continued)

GEOMETRY

#29 Finding Perimeter and Area

#30 Finding Volume

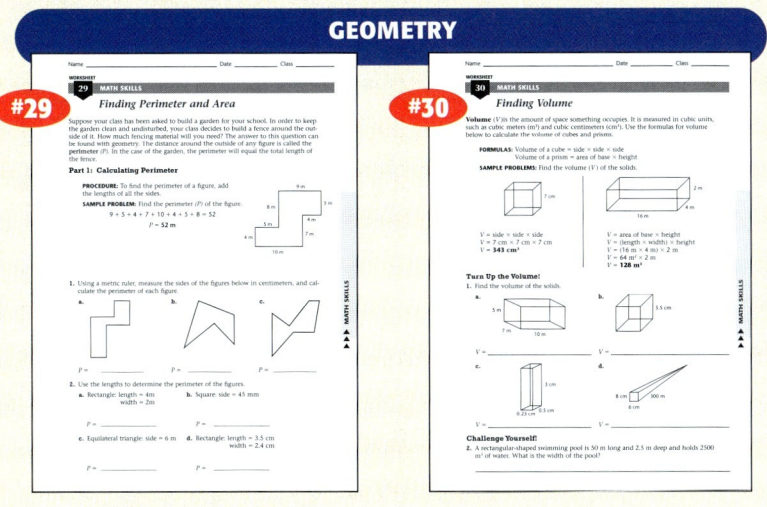

THE UNIT FACTOR AND DIMENSIONAL ANALYSIS

#31 The Unit Factor and Dimensional Analysis

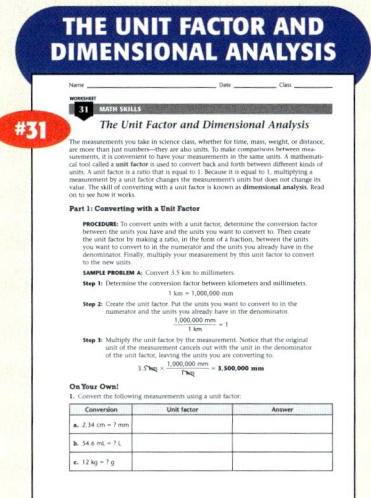

MATH IN SCIENCE: INTEGRATED SCIENCE

#32 Density

#33 The Pressure Is On!

#34 Sound Reasoning

#35 Using Temperature Scales

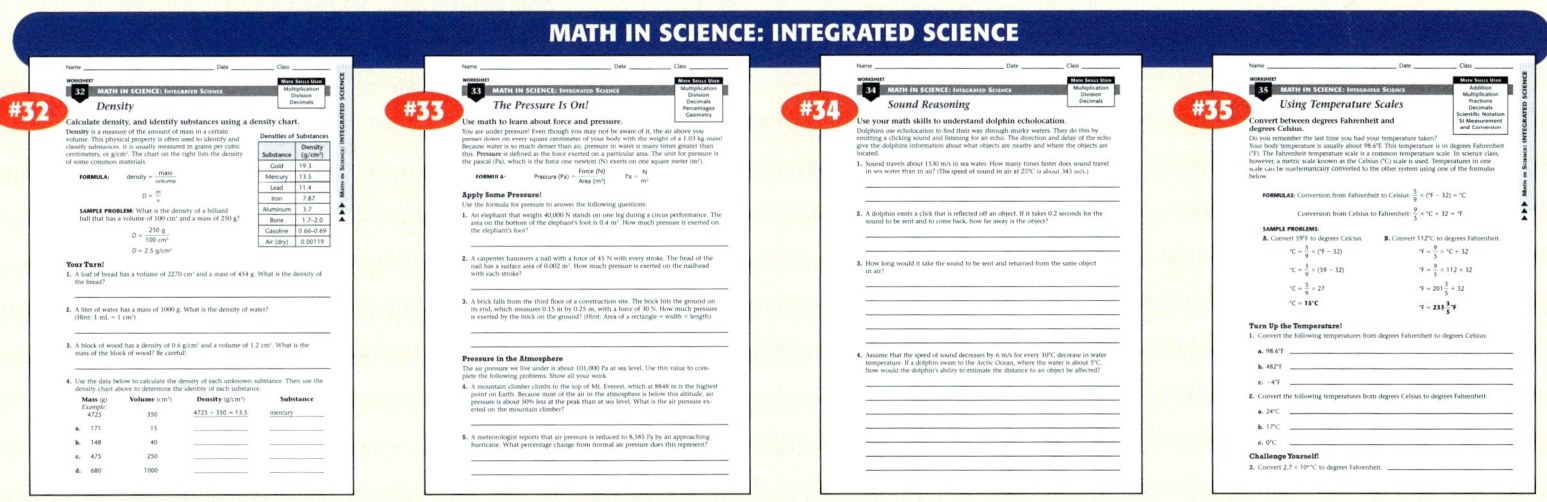

#36 Radioactive Decay and the Half-life

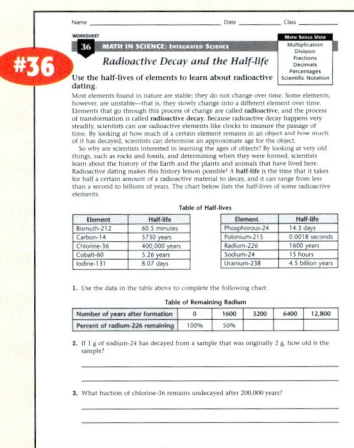

#37 Rain-Forest Math

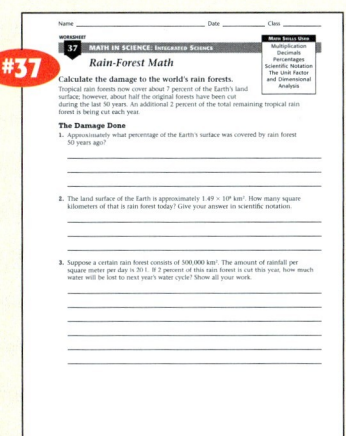

Science & Math Skills Worksheets

Science & Math Skills Worksheets (continued)

Math Skills for Science (continued)

MATH IN SCIENCE: LIFE SCIENCE

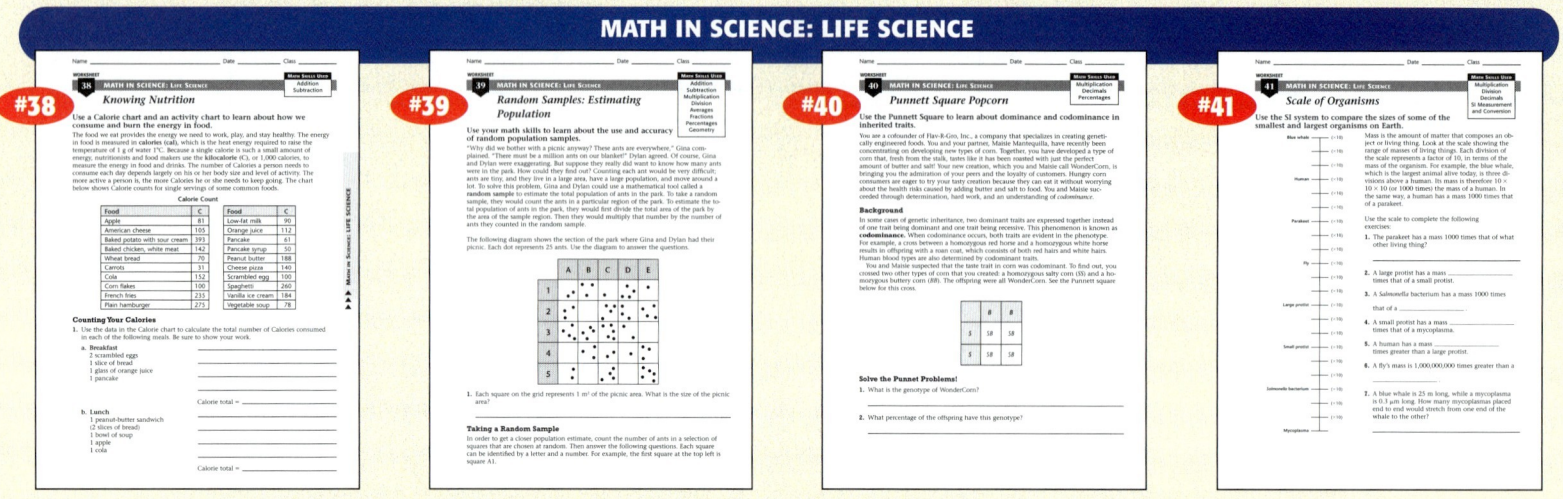

MATH IN SCIENCE: EARTH SCIENCE

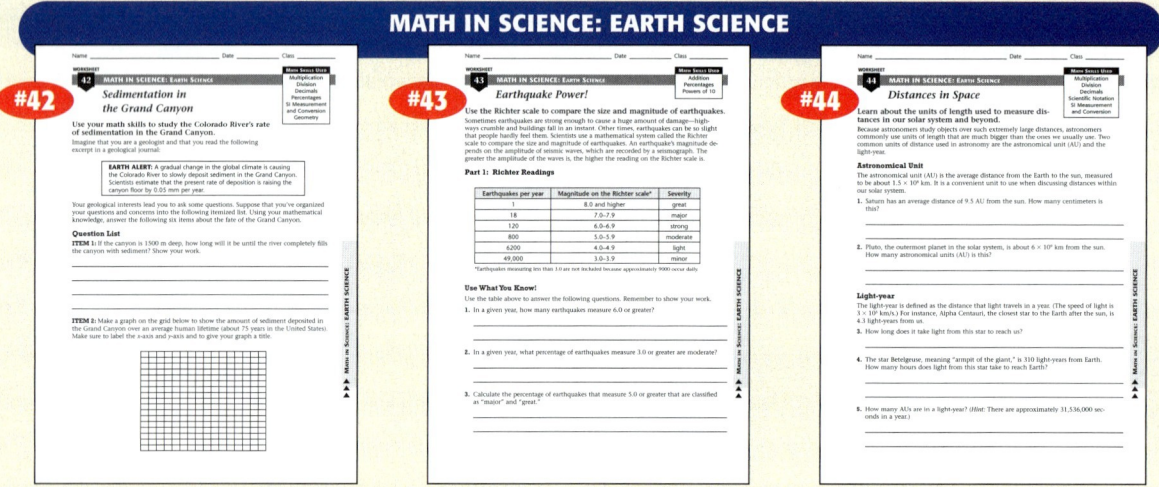

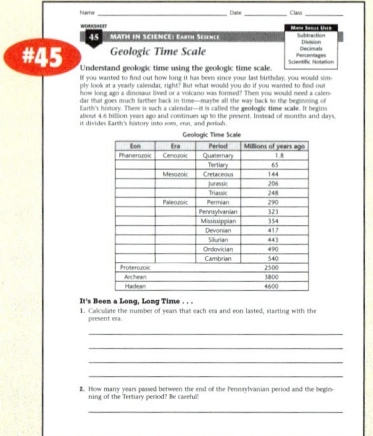
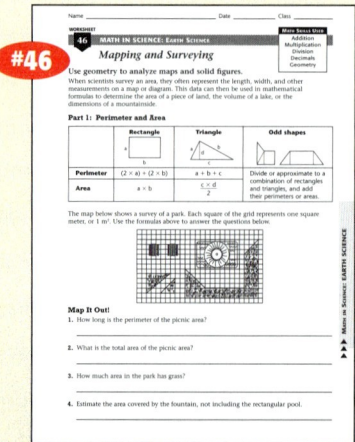

Math Skills for Science (continued)

MATH IN SCIENCE: PHYSICAL SCIENCE

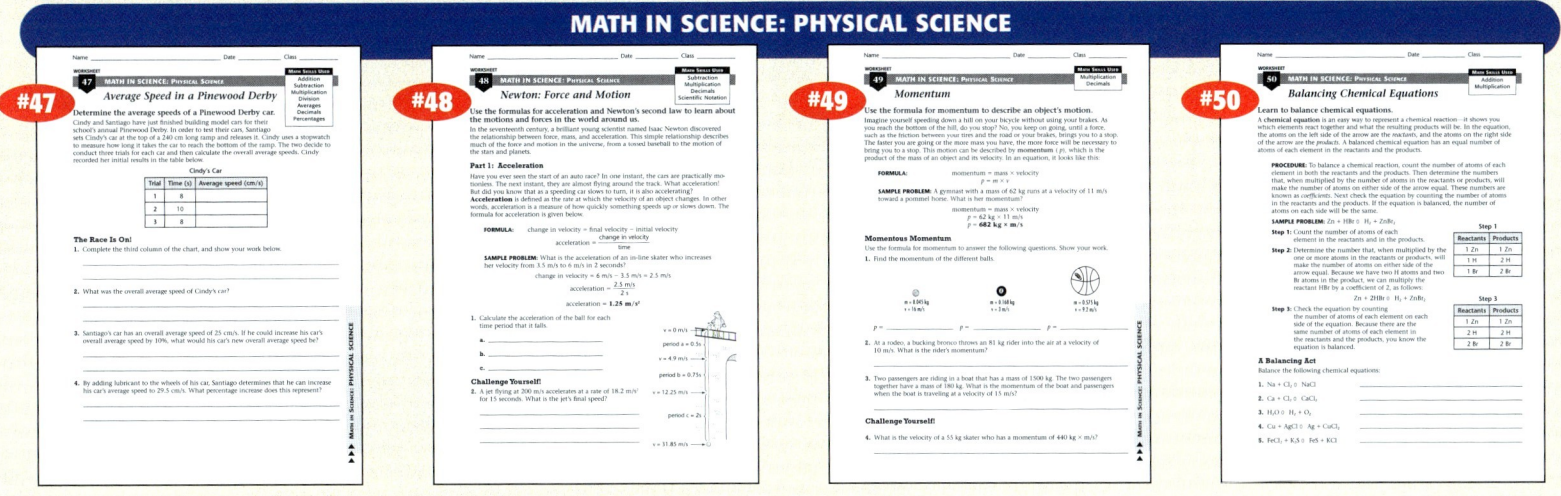

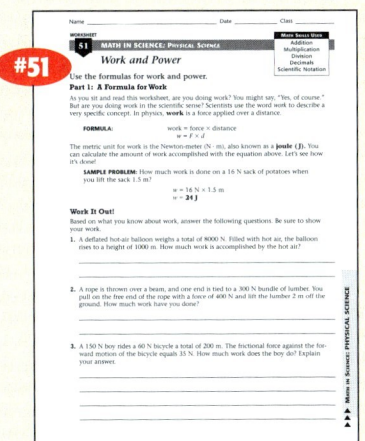
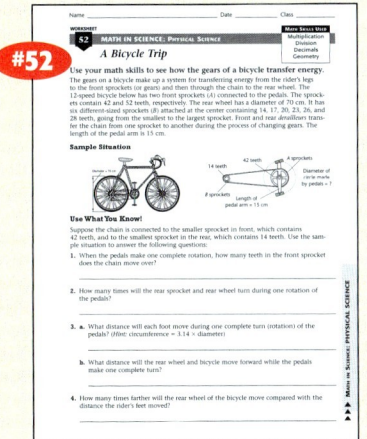
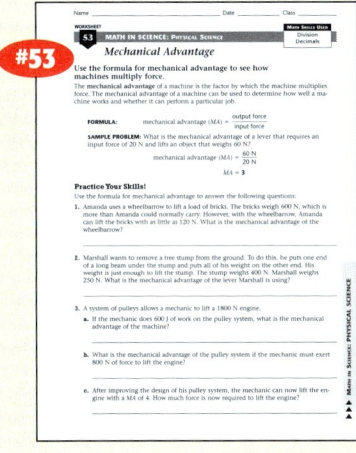
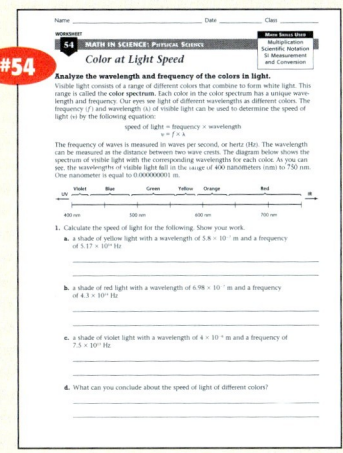

Assessment Checklist & Rubrics

The following is just a sample of over 50 checklists and rubrics contained in this booklet.

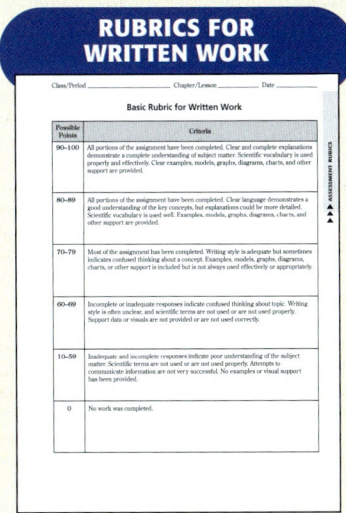
RUBRICS FOR WRITTEN WORK

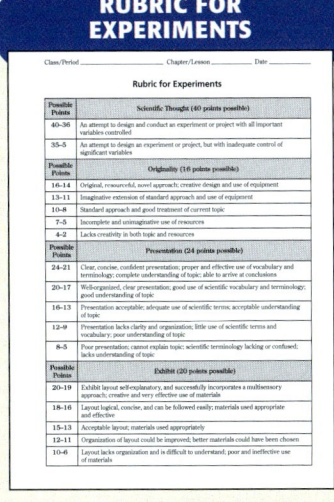
RUBRIC FOR EXPERIMENTS

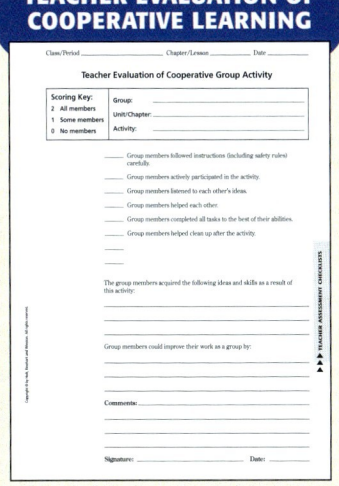
TEACHER EVALUATION OF COOPERATIVE LEARNING

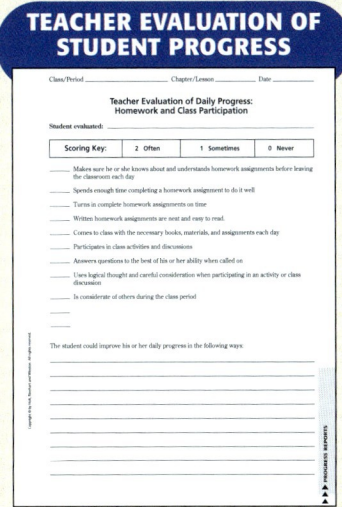
TEACHER EVALUATION OF STUDENT PROGRESS

UNIT 1

TIMELINE
Introduction to Matter

In this unit, you will explore a basic question that people have been pondering for centuries: What is the nature of matter? You will learn how to define the word *matter* and how to describe matter and the changes it goes through. You will also learn about the different states of matter and how to classify different arrangements of matter as elements, compounds, or mixtures. This timeline shows some of the events and discoveries that have occurred throughout history as scientists have sought to understand the nature of matter.

1661
Robert Boyle, a chemist in England, determines that elements are substances that cannot be broken down into anything simpler by chemical processes.

1712
Thomas Newcomen invents the first practical steam engine.

1949
Silly Putty® is sold in a toy store for the first time. The soft, gooey substance quickly becomes popular because of its strange properties, including the ability to "pick up" the print from a newspaper page.

1957
The space age begins when the Soviet Union launches *Sputnik I,* the first artificial satellite to circle the Earth.

1971
The first "pocket" calculator is introduced. It has a mass of more than 1 kg and a price of about $150—hardly the kind of pocket calculator that exists today.

1766
English chemist Henry Cavendish discovers and describes the properties of a highly flammable substance now known as hydrogen gas.

1800
Current from an electric battery is used to separate water into the elements hydrogen and oxygen for the first time.

1920
American women win the right to vote with the ratification of the 19th Amendment to the Constitution.

1937
The *Hindenburg* explodes while docking in Lakehurst, New Jersey. The airship was filled with flammable hydrogen gas to make it lighter than air.

1928
Sir Alexander Fleming discovers that the mold *Penicillium notatum,* shown here growing on an orange, is capable of killing some types of bacteria. The antibiotic penicillin is derived from this mold.

1989
An oil tanker strikes a reef in Prince William Sound, Alaska, spilling nearly 11 million gallons of oil. The floating oil injures or kills thousands of marine mammals and seabirds and damages the Alaskan coastline.

2000
The World's Fair, an international exhibition featuring exhibits and participants from around the world, is held in Hanover, Germany. The theme is "Humankind, Nature, and Technology."

Introduction to Matter

Chapter Organizer

CHAPTER ORGANIZATION	TIME MINUTES	OBJECTIVES	LABS, INVESTIGATIONS, AND DEMONSTRATIONS
Chapter Opener pp. 4–5	45	National Standards: SAI 1, HNS 1	**Investigate!** Mission Impossible? p. 5
Section 1 Exploring Physical Science	90	▶ Describe physical science as the study of energy and matter. ▶ Explain the role of physical science in the world around you. ▶ Name some careers that rely on physical science. SAI 2, SPSP 5, HNS 1, PS 3a, 3f	
Section 2 Using the Scientific Method	90	▶ Identify the steps used in the scientific method. ▶ Give examples of technology. ▶ Explain how the scientific method is used to answer questions and solve problems. ▶ Describe how our knowledge of science changes over time. UCP 2, SAI 1, 2, ST 2; LabBook SAI 1	**Demonstration,** p. 12 in ATE **Discovery Lab,** Exploring the Unseen, p. 626 **Datasheets for LabBook,** Exploring the Unseen, Datasheet 1 **QuickLab,** That's Swingin'! p. 15 **Whiz-Bang Demonstrations,** The Dollar-Bill Bridge, Demo 37
Section 3 Using Models in Physical Science	90	▶ Explain how models represent real objects or systems. ▶ Give examples of different ways models are used in science. UCP 2; LabBook UCP 2, 5, SAI 1, ST 1	**Making Models,** Off to the Races! p. 627 **Datasheets for LabBook,** Off to the Races! Datasheet 2
Section 4 Measurement and Safety in Physical Science	90	▶ Explain the importance of the International System of Units. ▶ Determine the appropriate units to use for particular measurements. ▶ Describe how area and density are derived quantities. UCP 3, SAI 1, 2, HNS 1; LabBook UCP 3	**Skill Builder,** Measuring Liquid Volume, p. 628 **Datasheets for LabBook,** Measuring Liquid Volume, Datasheet 3 **Skill Builder,** Coin Operated, p. 629 **Datasheets for LabBook,** Coin Operated, Datasheet 4 **Long-Term Projects & Research Ideas,** Project 51

See page T20 for a complete correlation of this book with the **NATIONAL SCIENCE EDUCATION STANDARDS.**

TECHNOLOGY RESOURCES

 Guided Reading Audio CD
English or Spanish, Chapter 1

 Science Discovery Videodiscs
Image and Activity Bank with Lesson Plans: Science and the Constitution, Models and Predictions
Science Sleuths: The Traffic Accident

 CNN. Scientists in Action, Remembering Richard Feynman, Segment 3
Multicultural Connection, Hopi Science, Segment 1

 One-Stop Planner CD-ROM with Test Generator

Chapter 1 • The World of Physical Science

CLASSROOM WORKSHEETS, TRANSPARENCIES, AND RESOURCES	SCIENCE INTEGRATION AND CONNECTIONS	REVIEW AND ASSESSMENT
Science Puzzlers, Twisters & Teasers, Worksheet 1 **Directed Reading Worksheet 1** **Science Skills Worksheet 8,** Reading a Science Textbook		
Directed Reading Worksheet 1, Section 1 **Science Skills Worksheet 30,** Hints for Oral Presentations	**Connect to Life Science,** p. 7 in ATE **Multicultural Connection,** p. 7 in ATE **Cross-Disciplinary Focus,** p. 8 in ATE **Careers:** Electronics Engineer– Julie Williams-Byrd, p. 32	**Review,** p. 10 **Quiz,** p. 10 in ATE **Alternative Assessment,** p. 10 in ATE
Directed Reading Worksheet 1, Section 2 **Math Skills for Science Worksheet 16,** What Is a Ratio? **Transparency 201,** The Scientific Method **Reinforcement Worksheet 1,** The Plane Truth	**Math and More,** p. 13 in ATE **Cross-Disciplinary Focus,** p. 13 in ATE **Biology Connection,** p. 14 **Real-World Connection,** p. 17 in ATE **Multicultural Connection,** p. 18 in ATE **Holt Anthology of Science Fiction,** *Inspiration*	**Review,** p. 14 **Homework,** p. 15 in ATE **Self-Check,** p. 16 **Review,** p. 19 **Quiz,** p. 19 in ATE **Alternative Assessment,** p. 19 in ATE
Directed Reading Worksheet 1, Section 3	**Apply,** p. 21 **Real-World Connection,** p. 21 in ATE **Cross-Disciplinary Focus,** p. 21 in ATE **Connect to Earth Science,** p. 22 in ATE	**Homework,** pp. 20, 22 in ATE **Review,** p. 23 **Quiz,** p. 23 in ATE **Alternative Assessment,** p. 23 in ATE
Transparency 202, Common SI Units **Math Skills for Science Worksheet 27,** What Is SI? **Math Skills for Science Worksheet 30,** Finding Volume **Transparency 4,** Scale of Sizes **Directed Reading Worksheet 1,** Section 4 **Math Skills for Science Worksheet 29,** Finding Perimeter and Area **Critical Thinking Worksheet 1,** A Solar Solution **Science Skills Worksheet 9,** Safety Rules!	**Math and More,** p. 25 in ATE **Connect to Life Science,** p. 25 in ATE **MathBreak,** Using Area to Find Volume, p. 26	**Homework,** p. 26 in ATE **Review,** p. 27 **Quiz,** p. 27 in ATE **Alternative Assessment,** p. 27 in ATE

END-OF-CHAPTER REVIEW AND ASSESSMENT

Chapter Review in Study Guide
Vocabulary and Notes in Study Guide
Chapter Tests with Performance-Based Assessment, Chapter 1 Test
Chapter Tests with Performance-Based Assessment, Performance-Based Assessment 1
Concept Mapping Transparency 1

internetconnect

Holt, Rinehart and Winston On-line Resources
go.hrw.com

For worksheets and other teaching aids related to this chapter, visit the HRW Web site and type in the keyword: **HSTWPS**

National Science Teachers Association
www.scilinks.org

Encourage students to use the *sci*LINKS numbers listed in the internet connect boxes to access information and resources on the **NSTA** Web site.

Chapter 1 • Chapter Organizer **3B**

Chapter Resources & Worksheets

Visual Resources

TEACHING TRANSPARENCIES

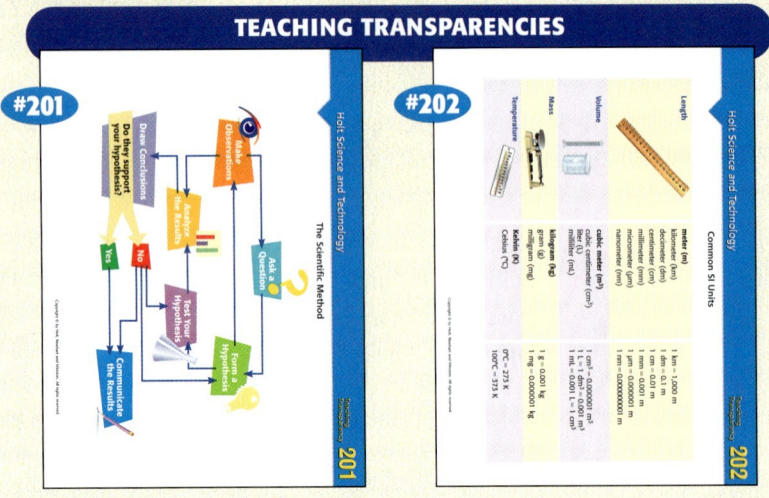

TEACHING TRANSPARENCIES

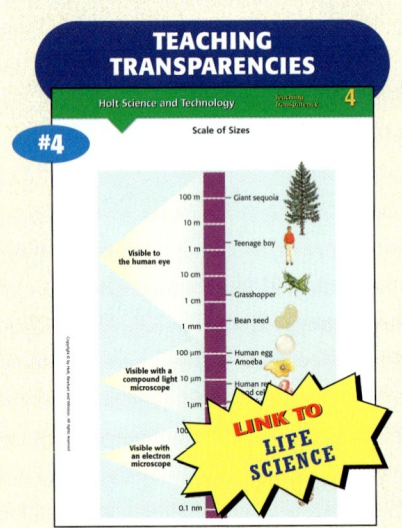

CONCEPT MAPPING TRANSPARENCY

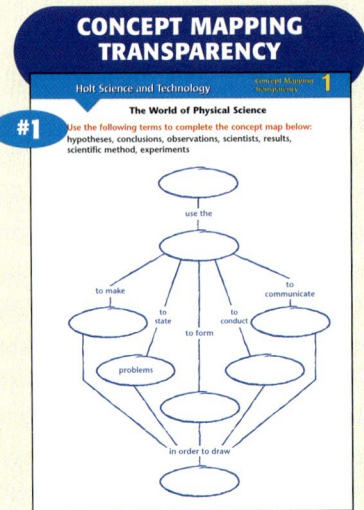

Meeting Individual Needs

DIRECTED READING

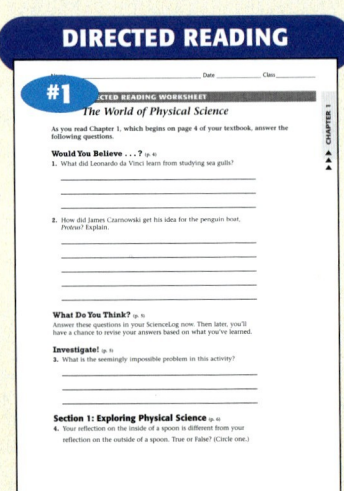

REINFORCEMENT & VOCABULARY REVIEW

SCIENCE PUZZLERS, TWISTERS & TEASERS

Chapter 1 • The World of Physical Science

Chapter 1 • The World of Physical Science

Review & Assessment

STUDY GUIDE
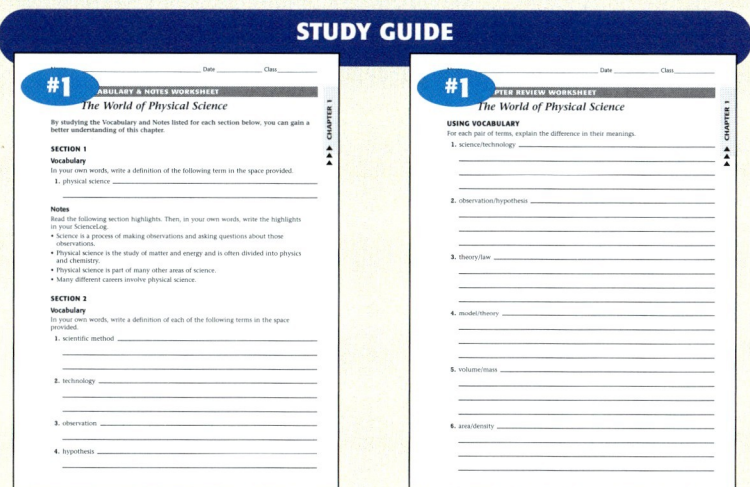

CHAPTER TESTS WITH PERFORMANCE-BASED ASSESSMENT
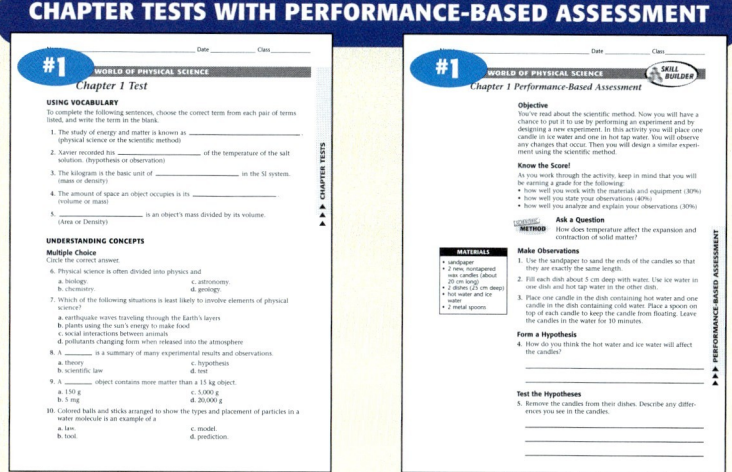

Lab Worksheets

WHIZ-BANG DEMONSTRATIONS
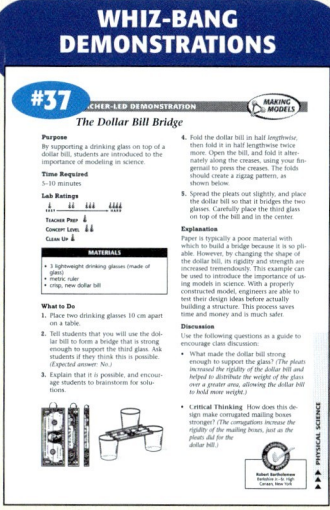

LONG-TERM PROJECTS & RESEARCH IDEAS
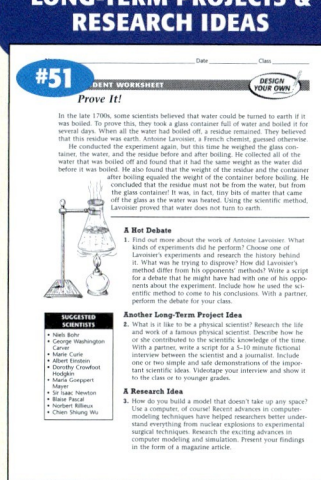

DATASHEETS FOR LABBOOK

Applications & Extensions

CRITICAL THINKING & PROBLEM SOLVING
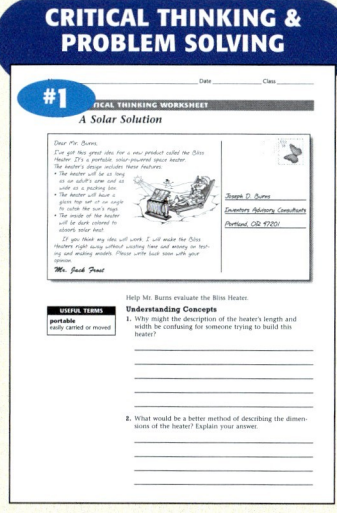

MULTICULTURAL CONNECTIONS
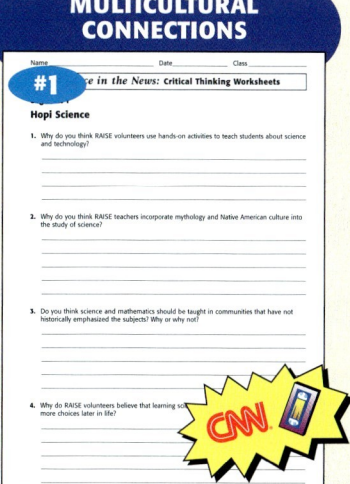

SCIENTISTS IN ACTION
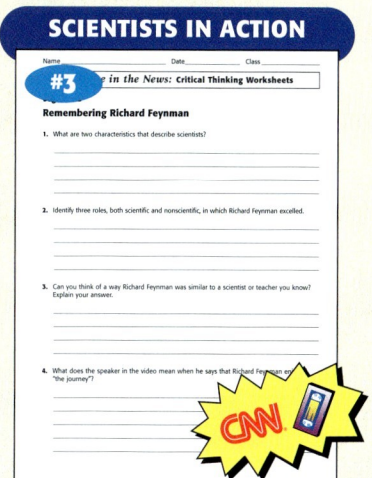

Chapter 1 • Chapter Resources & Worksheets

Chapter Background

SECTION 1
Exploring Physical Science

▶ **World of Physical Science**
Physical science covers a wide variety of scientific topics, including matter, energy, particles, chemistry, lasers, motion, forces, fluids, heat, light, sound, electricity, magnetism, and gravity. Almost every area of science involves some aspect of physical science.

- Physicists study the behavior of matter to learn how interactions between matter and energy work. For instance, research in plasma physics led to the invention of the laser, a device that produces a narrow, intense beam of light.

▶ **Archimedes**
Archimedes (287–212 B.C.) was a famous mathematician and inventor in ancient Greece. He is known for demonstrating the principle that the buoyant force on an object in a fluid is an upward force equal to the weight of the volume of fluid that the object replaces. He also calculated the relationship between the surface and the volume of a sphere, and he is known for building war machines. The Archimedes screw was a machine used for raising water for irrigation or removing water and sand from the hold of a ship.

▶ **Leonardo da Vinci**
Leonardo da Vinci (1452–1519) was born in Florence, Italy. He was an Italian sculptor, architect, engineer, draftsman, and painter (the "Last Supper" and "Mona Lisa"). He is known for carrying a notebook of scientific inquiry throughout his travels in Italy and France.

SECTION 2
Using the Scientific Method

▶ **Galileo**
Galileo Galilei (1564–1642) is known for his many achievements in science and math. Often called the founder of the experimental method, he clashed with the Catholic church about which was the center of the solar system, Earth or the sun. For some 1,500 years, most people believed Earth was the center. Galileo believed the Earth and other planets revolved around the sun, and he thought he could prove it.

IS THAT A FACT!

▪ The *Nei Ching*, a medical text attributed to the Chinese emperor Huang-ti from 2595 B.C., lists the four steps of medical diagnosis: observing the patient, listening to sounds from the organs, asking questions, and touching. Even 4,500 years ago, medical science investigations were conducted in an organized manner.

▶ **Printing**
With the development of the printing industry, scientific investigations and theories could be recorded and shared widely. The greatest impact was in the fifteenth century when Johannes Gutenburg, a German printer, developed movable metal type and improved the printing press.

▶ **Science for Everyone**
More recently, communication of scientific discoveries was enhanced by the development of radio. As technology has brought us television and computers, it has become easier and easier to communicate scientific discoveries (such as Einstein's theories) to more and more people.

Chapter 1 • The World of Physical Science

SECTION 3

Using Models in Physical Science

▶ **Da Vinci's Models**
Leonardo da Vinci's scientific models are well known from his notebooks. From his unpublished book of drawings, he is known to have studied and analyzed anatomy from cadavers. He also drew plans for what appears to be a helicopter as well as plans for draining swamps, and he designed a horizontal waterwheel. The combination of his artistry and his observation skills shows his works to be a practical use of models.

▶ **Models of Molecules**
Chemists often use models to represent molecules. One such model, called a ball-and-stick model, uses different colors and sizes of balls to represent atoms in a molecule. Sticks used to connect the balls represent bonds between the atoms.

- Today, powerful computer programs create three-dimensional virtual molecules on a computer screen. Scientists using computer models can make a change in some part of the molecule, and the computer will display the effects of that change on the shape and configuration of the molecule.

IS THAT A FACT!

◆ Around 50 years ago, there were only about 10 computers in the United States. Today, there are millions of computers in our homes, offices, toys, cars, televisions, stereos, traffic lights, gas pumps, and ATM machines. And someday "smart" computer software may drive your car, cook your food, and clean your house according to your instructions.

SECTION 4

Measurement and Safety in Physical Science

▶ **Ancient Sumeria**
Beginning around 2500 B.C., Sumerians began to develop a system of standard weights and measures that included a length roughly the same as the unit we call the foot.

▶ **Reaching Absolute Zero**
Absolute zero is −273.15°C, or 0 K. No one has ever achieved that temperature in the laboratory. But in a physics laboratory at Helsinki University of Technology, in Finland, physicists achieved the lowest temperature ever by bringing copper and silver to eight-tenths of a billionth of a kelvin above absolute zero. The temperature in space, by comparison, is about 2.7 K.

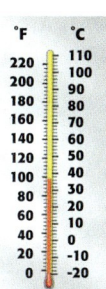

▶ **Global Positioning System**
If you have ever flown in an airplane, your safety was at least partly due to research in electronics and radio signals and to the development of the atomic clock. The Global Positioning System (GPS), which was completed in 1994, consists of 24 satellites that broadcast the location of objects to receivers on Earth.

- GPS is used to monitor earthquakes, find people stranded on mountaintops and in caves, guide drivers on unfamiliar roads, and even locate fishing holes and golf carts. Radar and global positioning devices used in aircraft help airplane pilots navigate in all kinds of weather and, therefore, make air travel safer.

*For background information about teaching strategies and issues, refer to the **Professional Reference for Teachers**.*

CHAPTER 1
The World of Physical Science

Chapter Preview

Section 1
Exploring Physical Science
- That's Science!
- Matter + Energy → Physical Science
- Physical Science Is All Around You
- Physical Science in Action

Section 2
Using the Scientific Method
- What Is the Scientific Method?
- Ask a Question
- Form a Hypothesis
- Test the Hypothesis
- Analyze the Results
- Draw Conclusions
- Communicate Results
- Breaking the Mold of the Scientific Method
- Building Scientific Knowledge

Section 3
Using Models in Physical Science
- What Is a Model?
- Models Help You Visualize Information
- Models Are Just the Right Size
- Models Build Scientific Knowledge
- Models Can Save Time and Money

Section 4
Measurement and Safety in Physical Science
- The International System of Units
- Derived Quantities
- Safety Rules!

CHAPTER 1
The World of Physical Science

Would You Believe . . . ?

Scientists are often inspired by nature. Just ask James Czarnowski (zahr NOW SKEE) and Michael Triantafyllou (tree AHN ti FEE loo), two scientists from the Massachusetts Institute of Technology (MIT), in Cambridge.

In 1997, Czarnowski and Triantafyllou were looking for an example from nature that could inspire a new way to power boats. On a trip to the New England Aquarium, in Boston, Czarnowski was watching penguins swim through the water when he realized that the penguins could be nature's answer. So he and Triantafyllou set out to create a boat that would imitate the way a penguin swims. After much thought, many questions, and a lot of research, *Proteus* (PROH tee uhs)— the penguin boat—was born.

Less than 4 meters long, *Proteus* is powered by two car batteries. Two broad paddles, similar to a penguin's flippers, flap together as often as 200 times per minute. At its top speed, this experimental boat can "swim" through the water at 2 meters per second. If a full-sized version of *Proteus* were developed, it could cruise easily at about 45 kilometers per hour. That's faster than most cargo carriers, which make up the majority of boats on the ocean. Also, full-sized penguin boats would use less fuel, which means that they would save money and produce less pollution.

Proteus is a creative solution to a scientific problem. In this chapter, you'll learn how Czarnowski and Triantafyllou used a series of steps called the *scientific method* to develop this amazing boat.

Proteus (shown above on the Charles River) is named after the son of Poseidon, the Greek god of the sea.

 Directed Reading Worksheet 1

 Science Puzzlers, Twisters & Teasers Worksheet 1

 Guided Reading Audio CD
English or Spanish, Chapter 1

Would You Believe . . . ?

Penguins are fast, efficient swimmers, but they are not the only animals whose swimming skills scientists have studied and tried to copy. Dolphins, sharks, tuna, and seals and sea lions have also served as models for scientists trying to improve the efficiency of boats and ships.

What Do You Think?

In your ScienceLog, try to answer the following questions based on what you already know:

1. What is physical science?
2. What are some steps scientists take to answer questions?
3. What purpose do models serve?

Mission Impossible?

In this activity, you will do some creative thinking to figure out a solution to what might seem like an impossible problem.

Procedure

1. Examine an **index card.** Take note of its size and shape. Your mission is to fit yourself through the card, as shown at right.

2. Brainstorm with a partner about possible ways to complete your mission, keeping the following guidelines in mind: You can use **scissors,** and you can fold the card, but you cannot use staples, paper clips, tape, glue, or any other form of adhesive.

3. When you and your partner have planned your strategy, write your procedure in your ScienceLog.

4. Test your strategy. Did it work? If necessary, get another index card and try again, recording your new strategy and results in your ScienceLog.

5. Share your strategies and results with other groups in your class.

Analysis

6. Why was it helpful to plan your strategy in advance?
7. How did testing your strategy help you complete your mission?
8. How did sharing your ideas with your classmates help you complete your mission? What did they do differently?

Answers to Investigate!

6. Responses should indicate that planning made students more efficient and prevented their making mistakes.
7. Responses should indicate a cursory understanding of testing a hypothesis.
8. Responses will vary but should indicate that sharing ideas leads to greater understanding of a problem.

Science Skills Worksheet 8 "Reading a Science Textbook"

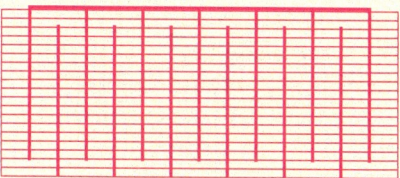

Smithsonian Institution®
Visit www.si.edu/hrw for additional on-line resources.

What Do You Think?

Accept all reasonable responses.

Students will have a chance to revise their answers in the Chapter Review under NOW What Do You Think?

Investigate!

Safety Caution: Remind students to review all safety cautions and icons before beginning this activity.

- This activity can be done using a regular 3 × 5 index card, but larger index cards may also be used.
- Students may need a hint in order to get started with their plan. Suggest that they consider how a combination of folds and cuts may help them accomplish their task.

The solution: Students should fold the card in half lengthwise. Using scissors, they can carefully cut a slit along the fold that doesn't quite reach either end of the card. Then they should fold the card along the slit. Next, students should make cuts into the card that alternate going from the center fold toward the outer edge (but not all the way!) and going from the outer edges toward the center fold (again not all the way!).

Finally, students should carefully open the index card by stretching the two ends apart. Now they can pull the index card over their head.

Chapter 1 • The World of Physical Science

Section 1

Focus

Exploring Physical Science

Physical science is the study of matter and energy. Students learn how physical science relates to the world around them and about a variety of careers that involve physical science.

🔔 Bellringer

Present the following scenario to students:

One day, you and a friend decide to have some popcorn while you do your homework. You put the bag of popcorn in the microwave oven, punch the buttons, and wait. The microwave sounds like it is working, but after a couple of minutes, it is clear the popcorn didn't pop.

In your ScienceLog, list some reasons why not. What steps could you take to help locate the problem?

1 Motivate

DISCUSSION

It is important for students to understand that science is a process, not just a set of facts. Information about the world around us is always changing. Discuss with students the idea that science always starts with a question. Ask them what they do when they have questions. Discuss their responses, and discuss the concept that every time they search for an answer to a question about the world, they are doing science.

Section 1

Terms to Learn

physical science

What You'll Do

- Describe physical science as the study of energy and matter.
- Explain the role of physical science in the world around you.
- Name some careers that rely on physical science.

Exploring Physical Science

It's Monday morning. You're eating breakfast and trying to pull yourself out of an early morning daze. As you eat a spoonful of Crunch Blasters, your favorite cereal, you look down and notice your reflection in your spoon. Something's funny about it—it's upside down! "Why is my reflection upside down even though I'm holding the spoon right side up?" you wonder. Is your spoon playing tricks on you? Next you look at the back of the spoon. "A-ha!" you think, "Now my reflection is right side up!" However, when you look back at the inside of the spoon, your reflection is upside down again. What is it about the spoon that makes your reflection look right side up on one side and upside down on the other?

That's Science!

You may not realize it, but you were just doing science. Science is all about being curious, making observations, and asking questions about those observations. For example, you noticed your reflection in your spoon and became curious about it. You observed that it was upside down, but that when you looked at the back of the spoon, your reflection was right side up. Then you asked what the two sides of the spoon had to do with your reflection. So you were definitely doing science!

Everyday Science Science is all around you, even if you're not thinking about it. Everyday actions such as putting on your sunglasses when you're outside, timing your microwave popcorn just right, and using the brakes on your bicycle all use your knowledge of science. But how do you know how to do these things? From experience—you've gained an understanding of your world by observing and discovering all your life.

Because science is all around, you might not be surprised to learn that there are different branches of science. This book is all about physical science. So just what is physical science?

6   Chapter 1 • The World of Physical Science

Matter + Energy → Physical Science

Physical science is the study of matter and energy. Matter is the "stuff" that everything is made of—even stuff that is so small you can't see it. Your shoes, your pencil, and even the air you breathe are made of matter. And all of that matter has energy. Energy is easier to describe than to explain. For example, energy is partly responsible for rainbows in the sky, but it isn't the rainbow itself. When you throw a ball, you give the ball energy. Moving objects have energy, as you can see in **Figure 1**. Food also has energy. When you eat food, the energy in the food is transferred to you, and you can use that energy to carry out your daily activities. But energy isn't always associated with motion or food. All matter has energy, even matter that isn't moving, like that shown in **Figure 2**.

Figure 1 *The cheetah, the fastest land mammal, has a lot of energy when running full speed. The cheetah also uses a lot of energy to run so fast. But a successful hunt will supply the energy the cheetah needs to live.*

As you explore physical science, you'll learn more about the relationship between matter and energy by answering questions such as the following: Why does paper burn but gold does not? Why is it harder to throw a bowling ball than a baseball? How can water turn into steam and back to water? All of the answers have to do with matter and energy. And although it is difficult to talk about matter without talking about energy, sometimes it is useful to focus on one or the other. That's why physical science is often divided into two categories—chemistry and physics.

Figure 2 *All matter has energy—even this monumental stone head that is over 1.5 m tall!*

2) Teach

CONNECT TO
LIFE SCIENCE

In preparing for space travel, scientists had to find the best way to process and store foods. As a result of their investigations, we enjoy better-preserved foods and better ways to preserve foods.

Have students research other benefits and new products derived from the science of space exploration. Student presentations can include samples, photos, and posters to depict products and benefits.
Sheltered English

DISCUSSION

Ask students to give examples of matter and energy. List their examples in two columns on the board. Discuss with students what all matter has in common and what all energy has in common. Help students articulate the difference between matter and energy.

Multicultural CONNECTION

The monumental stone head shown in **Figure 2** is from the Olmeca culture, one of the mother civilizations in Mesoamerica. Olmecan society flourished from about 1300 B.C. to about 600 B.C. in the area around the Mexican states of Tabasco and Veracruz.

Directed Reading Worksheet 1 Section 1

IS THAT A FACT!

Cheetahs once lived from southern Asia to Africa. Today, they are found exclusively in Africa. Cheetahs have been known to run at speeds of up to 110 km/h for short bursts while chasing prey. The world population of cheetahs is estimated to be between 10,000 and 15,000 animals.

2 Teach, continued

USING THE TABLE
Ask students to suggest other things they could learn from studying chemistry and from studying physics.

CROSS-DISCIPLINARY FOCUS

History Before modern chemistry there was an ancient art called *alchemy*. Alchemists tried to change common metals into gold or to find substances that would prolong life.

Alchemy is thought to have started in ancient China and India. It spread to ancient Egypt, then to Arabia, and then, in the twelfth and thirteenth centuries, through Spain into Europe. Alchemists discovered mineral acids and some compounds, and they developed some of the tools, techniques, and equipment that scientists use today.

Chemistry Studying all forms of matter and how they interact is what chemistry is all about. You'll learn about the properties and structure of matter and how different substances behave under certain conditions, such as high temperature and high pressure. You'll also discover how and why matter can go through changes, such as the one shown in **Figure 3.** Check out the chart below to find out what you can learn by studying chemistry.

Figure 3 When you wash your clothes, the detergent and the stains interact. The result? Clean clothes!

By studying chemistry, you can find out . . .
■ why yeast makes bread dough rise.
■ how the elements chlorine and sodium combine to form table salt, a compound.
■ why water boils at 100°C.
■ why sugar dissolves faster in hot tea than in iced tea.
■ how pollution affects our atmosphere.

Physics Like chemistry, physics deals with matter. But unlike chemistry, physics is mostly concerned with energy and how it affects matter. Studying different forms of energy is what physics is all about. When you study physics, you'll discover how energy can make matter do some interesting things, as shown in **Figure 4.** You'll also begin to understand aspects of your world such as motion, force, gravity, electricity, light, and heat. Check out the chart below to find out what you can learn by studying physics.

Figure 4 When you study physics you'll learn how energy causes the motion that makes a roller coaster ride so exciting.

By studying physics, you can find out . . .
■ why you move to the right when the car you're in turns left.
■ why you would weigh less on the moon than you do on Earth.
■ why you see a rainbow after a rainstorm.
■ how a compass works.
■ how your bicycle's gears help you pedal faster or slower.

 **SCIENCE**

Physical scientists are developing a "nose-on-a-chip" that is able to "smell" natural gas leaks to provide protection against explosions. One day the miniature nose may turn up in appliances such as stoves, clothes dryers, and heaters.

8 Chapter 1 • The World of Physical Science

Physical Science Is All Around You

Believe it or not, the things that you'll learn about matter and energy by studying physical science are important for what you'll learn in other science classes, too. Take a look below to see the role of physical science in areas that you might have thought only involved Earth science or life science.

Astronomy uses physical science to explain the composition of planets, the light given off by stars, and the motion of different galaxies in the universe.

Meteorology applies physical science in its study of the movement of air masses, weather patterns, and the composition of the atmosphere.

Botany, the study of plants, uses physical science to explain how plants use carbon dioxide and water to make food.

Geology uses physical science to explain earthquake waves and rock composition.

Oceanography uses physical science to explain waves, currents, and the chemistry of ocean water.

Ecology uses physical science to explain the nitrogen cycle and the transfer of energy between organisms in a food chain.

Biology uses physical science to explain how the heart pumps blood, how the eyes and ears work, and how the brain sends electrical impulses throughout the body.

Q: If the study of plants is called botany, what do you call the study of one-celled organisms?

A: monotany

TOPIC: Matter and Energy
GO TO: www.scilinks.org
*sci*LINKS NUMBER: HSTP005

3 Extend

GOING FURTHER

Give students a few moments to look at the images on this page and then discuss the images with them. Have students write in their ScienceLogs a question that they would like to find an answer for and how physical science might be used to find the answer.

MEETING INDIVIDUAL NEEDS

Learners Having Difficulty
Have students list each of the sciences shown on this page. Ask them to think of at least one example of each science in their daily lives. Have them put a star next to the examples they think are physical science. List student responses on the board, and discuss them with students.
`Sheltered English`

RESEARCH

After discussing the images on this page and talking about the careers using physical science (page 10), have students interview an adult whose life or career involves the physical sciences in some manner. (You might invite a retired person from the community or someone from a local college or university.) Ask students to present their findings to the class. Encourage them to be creative in their presentations.

 **Science Skills Worksheet 30** "Hints for Oral Presentations"

4 Close

Quiz
Ask students to fill in the blanks.
1. Physical science includes the study of ____ and ____. (matter; energy)
2. The study of interactions of various types of matter is called ____. (chemistry)
3. The science concerning the study of energy and how it affects matter is called ____. (physics)
4. Name three careers involving physical science. (Sample answer: astronomer, meteorologist, industrial chemist)

ALTERNATIVE ASSESSMENT

Concept Mapping
Ask students to create a concept map showing how physical science is linked to a number of other sciences and to some careers.
Sheltered English

Physical Science in Action

Now that you know physical science is all around you, you may not be surprised to learn that a lot of careers rely on physical science. What's more, you don't have to be a scientist to use physical science in your job! On this page, you can see some career opportunities that involve physical science.

Gene Webb is an auto mechanic. He understands how the parts of a car engine move and how to keep cars working efficiently.

Shirley Ann Jackson has done research in the semiconductor and optical physics industries. She became president of Rensselaer Polytechnic Institute in 1999.

Roberto Santibanez is a chef. He knows how ingredients interact and how energy can cause the chemical changes that produce his delicious meals.

Julie Fields is a chemist who studies chemical substances found in living organisms. She investigates how these substances can be made into products such as medicines.

internet connect

TOPIC: Matter and Energy
GO TO: www.scilinks.org
sciLINKS NUMBER: HSTP005

Other Careers Involving Physical Science
■ Architect
■ Pharmacist
■ Firefighter
■ Engineer
■ Construction worker
■ Optician
■ Pilot
■ Electrician
■ Computer technician

REVIEW
1. What is physical science all about?
2. List three things you do every day that use your experience with physical science.
3. **Applying Concepts** Choose one of the careers listed in the chart at left. How do you think physical science is involved in that career?

Answers to Review
1. Physical science is the study of matter and energy.
2. Acceptable answers include turning on a light, making popcorn in a microwave, getting a shock from touching a doorknob, washing dishes, sharpening a pencil, and listening to a CD.
3. Answers will vary, depending on the career chosen, but should show students' understanding of how concepts in physical science apply to the career. Sample answer: Architects use chemistry to decide what materials are best to use for the building. A knowledge of physics helps an architect determine the structural design of the building.

Section 2

Using the Scientific Method

Terms to Learn

scientific method
technology
observation
hypothesis
data
theory
law

What You'll Do

- Identify the steps used in the scientific method.
- Give examples of technology.
- Explain how the scientific method is used to answer questions and solve problems.
- Describe how our knowledge of science changes over time.

When you hear or read about advancements in science, do you wonder how they were made? How did the scientists make their discoveries? Were they just lucky? Maybe, but chances are that it was much more than luck. The scientific method probably had a lot to do with it!

What Is the Scientific Method?

The **scientific method** is a series of steps that scientists use to answer questions and solve problems. The chart below shows the steps that are commonly used in the scientific method. Although the scientific method has several distinct steps, it is not a rigid procedure whose steps must be followed in a certain order. Scientists may use the steps in a different order, skip steps, or repeat steps. It all depends on what works best to answer the question.

The Scientific Method

- Ask a question.
- Form a hypothesis.
- Test the hypothesis.
- Analyze the results.
- Draw conclusions.
- Communicate results.

Do you remember James Czarnowski and Michael Triantafyllou, the two scientists discussed at the beginning of this chapter? What scientific problem were they trying to solve? In the next few pages, you'll learn how they used the scientific method to develop new technology—*Proteus,* the penguin boat.

Spotlight on Technology

Technology is the application of knowledge, tools, and materials to solve problems and accomplish tasks. Technology can also refer to the objects used to accomplish tasks. For example, computers, headphones, and the Internet are all examples of technology. But even things like toothbrushes, light bulbs, and pencils are examples of technology.

Science and technology are not the same thing. The goal of science is to gain knowledge about the natural world. The goal of technology is to apply scientific understanding to solve problems. Technology is sometimes called *applied science.*

IS THAT A FACT!

Sir Isaac Newton was once asked how he happened to make so many important scientific discoveries. He replied, "By thinking night and day."

MISCONCEPTION ALERT

Emphasize that there is no single scientific method. Scientists approach problems from a variety of viewpoints. They conduct their research using available tools, data, time, and people. Research often leads to new problems and new hypotheses, which require further research and testing.

SECTION 2

Focus

Using the Scientific Method

This section presents the steps of the scientific method and the relationship between basic science and applied research or technology. Students learn that scientific knowledge changes over time, that new scientific knowledge often leads to new technology, and that new technology can lead to new scientific discoveries.

Bellringer

Ask students to answer the following question:

How can you prove that the world is not flat?

1) Motivate

GROUP ACTIVITY

Have groups of students work together to make lists of 10 observations about technology in the classroom. Have them explain how each example of technology is used to improve the classroom for teaching science.

Directed Reading Worksheet 1 Section 2

2) Teach

DEMONSTRATION

Before class, pour a small amount of 70 percent isopropyl alcohol in a beaker and the same amount of water in another beaker.

In class, tell students you have a question for them. Review and discuss with them the steps of the scientific method. Then show students the two beakers. Ask them if they can tell what the two liquids are. Your hypothesis: Although the two liquids look the same, you believe they are different.

Encourage students to think of practical ways to test your hypothesis. Then dim the lights in the classroom. Place the beakers on a safe surface, and put on safety goggles. Using a stick lighter or a long match, try to set the water on fire. Students will see that the liquid is not flammable. Then carefully set the alcohol on fire. Students will see that it burns with a blue flame. Ask students what conclusions they can draw from your demonstration.

MEETING INDIVIDUAL NEEDS

Learners Having Difficulty Students can create an outline of the scientific method to use and fill in as they read this chapter. They can start by writing down the steps listed on page 11. As they read about the different steps, have students fill in the outline with details. When they are finished, students will have a useful tool. `Sheltered English`

Figure 5 *Stopwatches and rulers are some of the many tools used to make observations.*

Ask a Question

Asking a question helps you focus your investigation and identify what you want to find out. Usually, scientists ask a question after they've made a lot of observations. An **observation** is any use of the senses to gather information. Measurements are observations that are made with instruments, such as those shown in **Figure 5**. The chart below gives you some examples of observations. Keep in mind that you can make observations at any point while using the scientific method.

Examples of Observations	
■ The sky is blue.	■ He is 125 centimeters tall.
■ The ice began to melt 30 seconds after it was taken out of the freezer.	■ Adding food coloring turned the water red. Adding bleach made the water clear again.
■ This soda bottle has a volume of 1 liter.	■ This brick feels heavier than this sponge.
■ Cotton balls feel soft.	■ Sandpaper is rough.

A Real-World Question So what question did the scientists who made *Proteus* ask? Czarnowski and Triantafyllou, shown in **Figure 6**, are engineers, scientists who put scientific knowledge to practical human use. Engineers create technology. While a graduate student at the Massachusetts Institute of Technology, Czarnowski worked with Triantafyllou, his professor, to observe boat propulsion systems and investigate how to make them work better. A propulsion (proh PUHL shuhn) system is what makes a boat move; most boats are driven by propellers.

One thing that Czarnowski and Triantafyllou were studying is the efficiency of boat propulsion systems. *Efficiency* (e FISH uhn see) compares energy output (the energy used to move the boat forward) with energy input (the energy supplied by the boat's engine). Czarnowski and Triantafyllou learned from their observations that boat propellers, shown in **Figure 7** on the next page, are not very efficient.

Figure 6 *James Czarnowski (left) and Michael Triantafyllou (right) made observations about how boats work in order to develop* Proteus.

IS THAT A FACT!

In 1864 and 1865, James Clerk Maxwell made observations about electricity and certain observations about magnetism and showed how the two phenomena are related. As a result of his investigations, he developed his theory of electromagnetism, one of the most important scientific advances of the nineteenth century.

Figure 7 Observations About the Efficiency of Boat Propellers

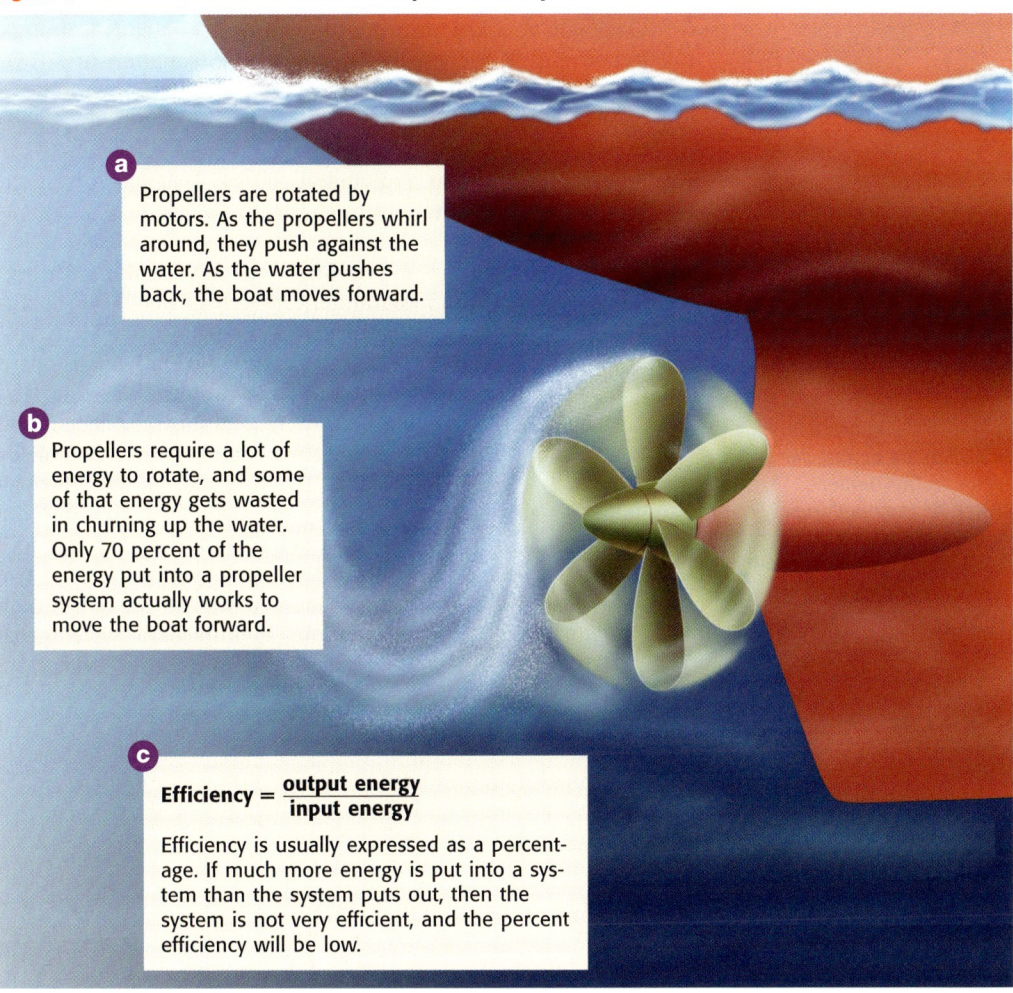

a Propellers are rotated by motors. As the propellers whirl around, they push against the water. As the water pushes back, the boat moves forward.

b Propellers require a lot of energy to rotate, and some of that energy gets wasted in churning up the water. Only 70 percent of the energy put into a propeller system actually works to move the boat forward.

c Efficiency = $\dfrac{\text{output energy}}{\text{input energy}}$

Efficiency is usually expressed as a percentage. If much more energy is put into a system than the system puts out, then the system is not very efficient, and the percent efficiency will be low.

Why is boat efficiency important? Most boats are only about 70 percent efficient. Making only a small fraction of the United States' boats and ships just 10 percent more efficient would save millions of liters of fuel per year. Saving fuel means saving money, but it also means using less of the Earth's supply of fossil fuels. Based on their observations and all of this information, Czarnowski and Triantafyllou knew what they wanted to find out.

Ask some questions of your own on page 626 in the LabBook.

The Question:
How can boat propulsion systems be made more efficient?

Q: Why is a science lesson like a worm in a cornfield?

A: They both go in one ear and out the other.

Exploring the Unseen

MATH and MORE

Point out that efficiency is a ratio of energy output to energy input. When expressed as a ratio or as a percentage, efficiency has no units. Remind students that to express efficiency as a percentage, they must divide the energy output (numerator) by the energy input (denominator) and multiply the result by 100.

Math Skills Worksheet 16 "What Is a Ratio?"

CROSS-DISCIPLINARY FOCUS

History Many early steamships were propelled by paddle wheels that hung over the sides of the ships. The most notable early steamship with a screw propeller was the British ship *Great Britain*. Her keel was laid in 1839, and she was launched in July 1844. The *Great Britain* had a single screw connected to a large steam engine. The ship was 98 m long and could carry over 3,500 metric tons of cargo. It could travel the open sea at a speed of about 28 km/h.

USING THE FIGURE

The motion described in **Figure 7,** label (a), is an example of a result of Newton's third law, which states that whenever one object exerts a force on a second object, the second object exerts an equal and opposite force on the first. The same force exerted by the propellers on the water is exerted by the water on the propellers.

Section 2 • Using the Scientific Method

Form a Hypothesis

Once you've asked your question, your next step is forming a hypothesis. A **hypothesis** is a possible explanation or answer to a question. You can use what you already know and any observations that you have made to form a hypothesis. A good hypothesis is testable. If no observations or information can be gathered or if no experiment can be designed to test the hypothesis, it is untestable.

Nature Provides a Possible Answer

Czarnowski and Triantafyllou were also looking for an example from nature on which to base their hypothesis. Czarnowski had made observations of penguins swimming at the New England Aquarium. **Figure 8** shows how penguins propel themselves. He observed how quickly and easily the penguins moved through the water. He also observed that penguins have a rigid body, similar to a boat. These observations led the two scientists to a possible answer to their question: a propulsion system that works the way a penguin swims!

Figure 8 Penguins use their flippers almost like wings to "fly" underwater. As they pull their flippers toward their body, they push against the water, which propels them forward.

Hypothesis:
A propulsion system that mimics the way a penguin swims will be more efficient than propulsion systems that use propellers.

Penguins, although flightless, are better adapted to water and extreme cold than any other bird. Most of the world's 18 penguin species live and breed on islands in the subantarctic waters. Penguins can swim as fast as 40 km/h, and some can leap more than 2 m above the water.

Before scientists test a hypothesis, they often make predictions that state what they think will happen during the actual test of the hypothesis. Scientists usually state predictions in an "If . . . then . . ." format. The engineers at MIT might have made the following prediction: *If* two flippers are attached to a boat, *then* the boat will be more efficient than a boat powered by propellers.

REVIEW

1. How do scientists and engineers use the scientific method?
2. Give three examples of technology from your everyday life.
3. **Analyzing Methods** Explain how the accuracy of your observations might affect how you develop a hypothesis.

Test the Hypothesis

After you form a hypothesis, you must test it to determine whether it is a reasonable answer to your question. In other words, testing helps you find out if your hypothesis is pointing you in the right direction or if it is way off the mark. Often a scientist will test a hypothesis by testing a prediction.

One way to test a hypothesis is to conduct a controlled experiment. In a controlled experiment, there is a control group and an experimental group. Both groups are the same except for one factor in the experimental group, called a *variable*. The experiment will then determine the effect of the variable.

Sometimes a controlled experiment is not possible. Stars, for example, are too far away to be used in an experiment. In such cases, you can test your hypothesis by making additional observations or by conducting research. If your investigation involves creating technology to solve a problem, you can make or build what you want to test and see if it does what you expected it to do. That's just what Czarnowski and Triantafyllou did—they built *Proteus*, the penguin boat, shown in **Figure 9.**

That's Swingin'!

1. Make a pendulum by tying a **piece of string** to a **ring stand** and hanging a **small mass,** such as a washer, from the end of the string.
2. Form a hypothesis about which factors (such as length of string, mass, etc.) affect the rate at which the pendulum swings.
3. In your ScienceLog, record what factors you will control and what factor will be your variable.
4. Test your hypothesis by conducting several trials, recording the number of swings made in a given time, such as 10 seconds, for each trial.
5. Was your hypothesis supported? In your ScienceLog, analyze your results.

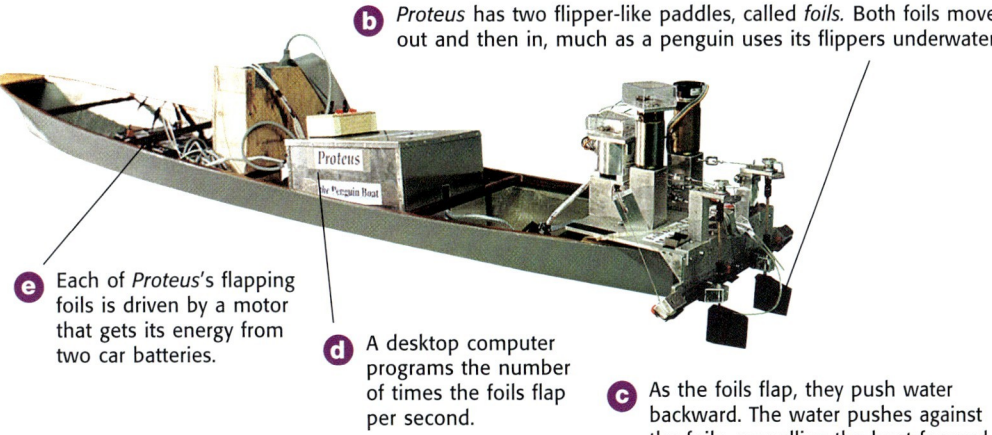

Figure 9 Testing Penguin Propulsion

a *Proteus* is only 3.4 m long and 50 cm wide, too narrow for even a single passenger.

b *Proteus* has two flipper-like paddles, called *foils*. Both foils move out and then in, much as a penguin uses its flippers underwater.

e Each of *Proteus*'s flapping foils is driven by a motor that gets its energy from two car batteries.

d A desktop computer programs the number of times the foils flap per second.

c As the foils flap, they push water backward. The water pushes against the foils, propelling the boat forward.

Homework

Give students the following quote from Thomas H. Huxley, in his *Collected Essays:*

"Science is nothing but trained and organized common sense."

Ask students to explain in their own words how this quote relates to observations, hypotheses, variables, and the scientific method.

2 Teach, continued

Answer to Self-Check

flapping rate

INDEPENDENT PRACTICE

Have students write an experiment to test the following hypothesis:

> Adding salt to water will change the temperature at which the water boils.

They should identify the controlled factors as well as the variable in the experiment. Ask them to make a chart or table they would use to record data.

USING THE GRAPH

Have students look at the line graph in **Figure 10**. Ask when *Proteus* was least efficient. Then ask students if the bar graph in **Figure 10** supports or refutes Czarnowski and Triantafyllou's original hypothesis.

Have students analyze the slope of the line graph. Point out that when the slope is positive, efficiency is increasing. When the slope is negative, efficiency is decreasing. Point out also that the relationship between the flapping rate and efficiency is not linear. If it were, the slope of the line would be constant.

> ### ✓ Self-Check
> What variable were Czarnowski and Triantafyllou testing? (See page 724 to check your answer.)

Testing Proteus Czarnowski and Triantafyllou took *Proteus* out into the open water of the Charles River when they were ready to collect data. **Data** are any pieces of information acquired through experimentation. The engineers did several tests, each time changing only the flapping rate. For each test, data such as the flapping rate, energy the motors used, and the speed achieved by the boat were carefully recorded. The input energy was determined by how much energy was used. The output energy was determined from the speed *Proteus* achieved.

Analyze the Results

After you collect and record your data, you must analyze them to determine whether the results of your test support the hypothesis. Sometimes doing calculations can help you learn more about your results. Organizing numerical data into tables and graphs makes relationships between information easier to see.

Analyzing Proteus Czarnowski and Triantafyllou used the data for input energy and output energy to calculate *Proteus*'s efficiency for different flapping rates. These data are graphed in **Figure 10**. The scientists compared *Proteus*'s highest level of efficiency with the average efficiency of a propeller-driven boat. Look at the bar graph in Figure 10 to see if their data support their hypothesis—that penguin propulsion would be more efficient than propeller propulsion.

Figure 10 Graphs of the Test Results

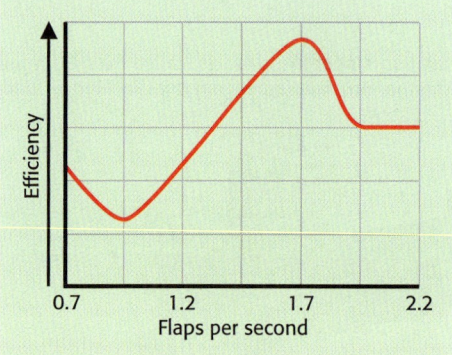

This line graph shows that *Proteus* was most efficient when its foils were flapping about 1.7 times per second.

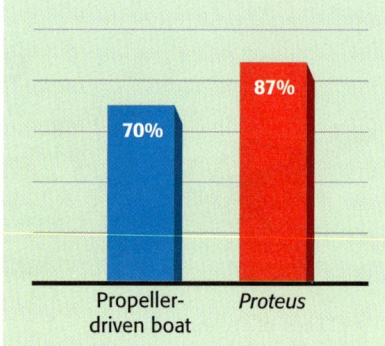

This bar graph shows that *Proteus* is 17 percent more efficient than a propeller-driven boat.

Science Bloopers

Experiments don't always turn out as expected. In 1856, William Henry Perkin was experimenting to synthesize the antimalarial drug quinine from coal tar. He didn't succeed, but he accidentally made aniline purple (mauve), the first synthetic dye. Mauve dye was used to color cotton, wool, and silk. Further experiments led to the development of many other dyes from coal tar.

16 Chapter 1 • The World of Physical Science

Draw Conclusions

At the end of an investigation, you must draw a conclusion. You could conclude that your results supported your hypothesis, that your results did *not* support your hypothesis, or that you need more information. If you conclude that your results support your hypothesis, you can ask further questions. If you conclude that your results do not support your hypothesis, you should check your results or calculations for errors. You may have to modify your hypothesis or form a new one and conduct another investigation. If you find that your results neither support nor disprove your hypothesis, you may need to gather more information, test your hypothesis again, or redesign the procedure.

The *Proteus* Conclusion After Czarnowski and Triantafyllou analyzed the results of their test, they conducted many more trials. Still they found that the penguin propulsion system was more efficient than a propeller propulsion system. So they concluded that their hypothesis was supported, which led to more questions, as you can see in **Figure 11**.

Figure 11 Could a penguin propulsion system be used on large ships, such as an oil tanker? The research continues!

Communicate Results

One of the most important steps in any investigation is to communicate your results. You can write a scientific paper, make a presentation, or create a Web site. Telling others what you learned is how science keeps going. Other scientists can conduct their own tests, modify your tests to learn something more specific, or study a new problem based on your results.

Communicating About *Proteus* Czarnowski and Triantafyllou published their results in academic papers, but they also displayed their project and its results on the Internet. In addition, science magazines and newspapers have reported the work of these engineers. These reports allow you to conduct some research of your own about *Proteus*.

REAL-WORLD CONNECTION

In 1933, Richard Hollingshead invented the first drive-in movie theater. It allowed people to watch movies in the privacy of their own vehicle. At first, the sound came from speakers built into the ground, and it was supposed to filter up through the floorboards of the car. Next, large speakers were placed on the edges of the 9.1 × 12.2 m screen. Unfortunately, everyone in the neighborhood could hear the movie! Neither idea worked. Finally, speakers were developed to hang on each car window.

MEETING INDIVIDUAL NEEDS

Advanced Learners Ask students to explain the following quote by Enrico Fermi in relation to the scientific method and the forming of a hypothesis. "There are two possible outcomes: If the result confirms the hypothesis, then you've made a measurement. If the result is contrary to the hypothesis, then you've made a discovery."

MISCONCEPTION ALERT

An investigation can be successful even when the hypothesis is not confirmed. The purpose of an investigation is to determine whether the hypothesis is valid—not to prove that it is true.

Two meteorologists decided to answer the old question: Do you stay drier by running in a rainstorm or by walking in it? Dressed in identical clothes, they covered the same course. One walked while the other ran. The results? The walker's clothes were drenched with almost twice as much water as the runner's. Their advice on a rainy day: Take an umbrella!

3) Extend

GOING FURTHER

Using **Figure 12,** have students select and analyze a problem from their everyday lives—something at school, at home, or in the community. Remind them that they can begin their analysis at any step but that they must include all the steps. The activity can be done for homework or in groups as a long-term assignment.

RESEARCH

Encourage students to research Sir Isaac Newton's famous quote, "If I have seen further it is by standing on the shoulders of Giants." Have them write a report explaining how Newton built his theories and laws on the work of scientists who had preceded him.

Teaching Transparency 201
"The Scientific Method"

internetconnect

SC/**LINKS**
NSTA

TOPIC: The Scientific Method
GO TO: www.scilinks.org
sciLINKS NUMBER: HSTP010

Breaking the Mold of the Scientific Method

Not all scientists use the same scientific method, nor do they always follow the same steps in the same order. Why not? Sometimes you may have a clear idea about the question you want to answer. Other times, you may have to revise your hypothesis and test it again. While you should always take accurate measurements and record data correctly, you don't always have to follow the scientific method in a certain order. **Figure 12** shows you some other paths through the scientific method.

Figure 12 *Scientific investigations do not always proceed from one step of the scientific method to the next. Sometimes steps are skipped, and sometimes they are repeated.*

Building Scientific Knowledge

Using the scientific method is a way to find answers to questions and solutions to problems. But you should understand that answers are very rarely *final* answers. As our understanding of science grows, our understanding of the world around us changes. New ideas and new experiments teach us new things. Sometimes, however, an idea is supported again and again by many experiments and tests. When this happens, the idea can become a theory or even a law. As you will read on the next page, theories and laws help to build new scientific knowledge.

Turn to page 33 to discover a tale of young Einstein's encounter with some other science heavyweights.

Multicultural CONNECTION

The Chinese book *Mo Ching,* from 250 B.C., contains evidence of a statement of the first law of motion, that an object at rest shall remain at rest. Sir Isaac Newton developed this law further in 1687.

Scientific Theories You've probably heard a detective on a TV show say, "I've got a theory about who committed the crime." Does the detective have a scientific theory? Probably not; it might be just a guess. A scientific theory is more complex than a simple guess.

In science, a **theory** is a unifying explanation for a broad range of hypotheses and observations that have been supported by testing. A theory not only can explain an observation you've made but also can predict an observation you might make in the future. Keep in mind that theories, like the one shown in **Figure 13,** can be changed or replaced as new observations are made or as new hypotheses are tested.

Scientific Laws What do you think of when you hear the word *law*? Traffic laws? Federal laws? Well, scientific laws are not like these laws. Scientific laws are determined by nature, and you can't break a scientific law!

In science, a **law** is a summary of many experimental results and observations. A law tells you how things work. Laws are not the same as theories because laws only tell you *what* happens, not *why* it happens, as shown in **Figure 14.** Although a law does not explain why something happens, the law tells you that you can expect the same thing to happen every time.

Figure 13 *According to the big-bang theory, the universe was once a small, hot, and dense volume of matter. About 10 to 20 billion years ago, an event called the big bang sent matter in all directions, forming the galaxies and planets.*

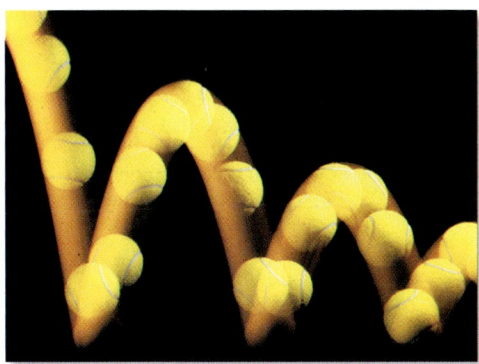

Figure 14 *Dropping a ball illustrates the law of conservation of energy. Although the ball doesn't bounce back to its original height, energy is not lost—it is transferred to the ground.*

REVIEW

1. Name the steps that can be used in the scientific method.
2. How is a theory different from a hypothesis?
3. **Analyzing Ideas** Describe how our knowledge of science changes over time.

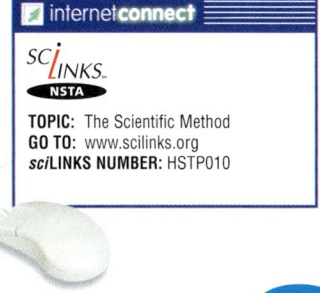

TOPIC: The Scientific Method
GO TO: www.scilinks.org
*sci*LINKS NUMBER: HSTP010

SECTION 3

Focus

Using Models in Physical Science

This section explains what scientific models are and why they are useful to scientists. Students also learn about different examples of models.

🔔 Bellringer

Pose the following to students:

To teach cardiopulmonary resuscitation (CPR), instructors most often use a mannequin to model a human upper torso and head. Why do you think CPR is taught with a model instead of a real human? Would the class be as effective if a model was not used? Explain your answer.

1) Motivate

ACTIVITY

Place students in groups. Give each group a globe or large ball, a flashlight, and a tennis ball. Explain to students that you want them to use only these materials to demonstrate both a solar and lunar eclipse. (You may have to refresh students' memories about what happens in an eclipse.) Have one group demonstrate a solar eclipse and another group demonstrate a lunar eclipse. Discuss whether using a model makes it easier to understand eclipses.

Directed Reading Worksheet 1 Section 3

Section 3

Using Models in Physical Science

Terms to Learn
model

What You'll Do
- Explain how models represent real objects or systems.
- Give examples of different ways models are used in science.

Think again about *Proteus*. How much like a penguin was it? Well, *Proteus* didn't have feathers and wasn't a living thing, but its "flippers" were designed to create the same kind of motion as a penguin's flippers. The MIT engineers built *Proteus* to mimic the way a penguin swims so that they could gain a greater understanding about boat propulsion. In other words, they created a *model*.

What Is a Model?

A **model** is a representation of an object or system. Models are used in science to describe or explain certain characteristics of things. Models can also be used for making predictions and explaining observations. A model is never exactly like the real object or system—if it were, it would no longer be a model. Models are particularly useful in physical science because many characteristics of matter and energy can be either hard to see or difficult to understand. You can see some examples of scientific models below.

Examples of Models

A model rocket is much smaller than a real rocket, but launching one in your backyard can help you understand how real rockets blast off into space.

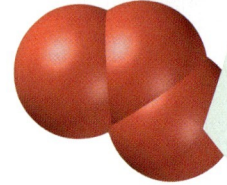

You can't see the tiny parts that make up matter, but you can make a model that shows how the parts fit together.

A cell diagram is a model that lets you look at all the parts of a cell up close—without using a microscope.

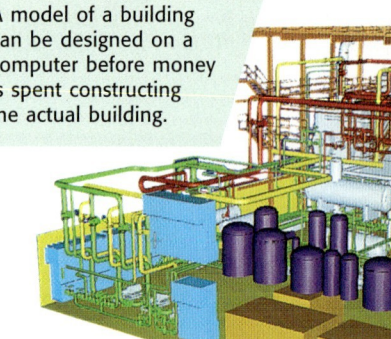

A model of a building can be designed on a computer before money is spent constructing the actual building.

Homework

Have students draw or diagram a model of something large or complex. Ask them to explain its purpose and its relationship to the original size and explain the advantages of using this particular model.

Models Help You Visualize Information

When you're trying to learn about something that you can't see or observe directly, a model can help you visualize it, or picture it in your mind. Familiar objects or ideas can help you understand something a little less familiar.

Objects as Models When you use an object as a model for something you cannot see, the object must have characteristics similar to those of the real thing. For example, a coiled spring toy is often used as a model of sound waves. You've probably used this kind of spring toy before, so it's a familiar object. Sound waves are probably a little less familiar—after all, you can't see them. But the spring toy behaves a lot like sound waves do. So using the spring toy as a model, as shown in **Figure 15,** can make the behavior of sound waves easier to understand.

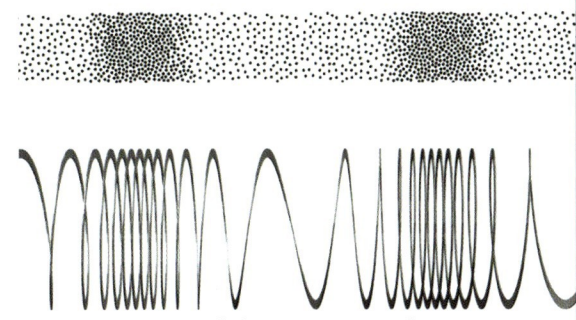

Figure 15 *A coiled spring toy can show you how air particles crowd together in parts of a sound wave.*

Ideas as Models When you're trying to understand something but don't have an object to use as a model, you can create a model from an idea. For example, when sugar dissolves in iced tea, it seems to disappear. To try to understand where the sugar goes, imagine a single drop of tea magnified until it is almost as big as you are, with tiny spaces between the particles of water in the tea. Using this model, as shown in **Figure 16,** you can understand that the sugar seems to disappear because the sugar particles fit into spaces between the water particles in the tea.

Figure 16 *Just by imagining a big drop of tea, you are creating a model!*

Models for Weather Forecasting

You've probably seen a weather report on television. Think about the models that a weather reporter uses to tell you about the weather: satellite pictures, color-coded maps, and live radar images. How are these models used to represent the weather? Why do you think that sometimes weather forecasts are wrong?

2) Teach

REAL-WORLD CONNECTION

Scientists are constantly trying to create better models to explain their theories. The model of the atom, for example, has changed many times. Atoms were once imagined as tiny balls that bounced against each other. Later, the atom was imagined to be something like a tiny chocolate-chip cookie with negative charges stuck in a positive substance. Still later, the atom was thought to be similar to a tiny solar system with a positive nucleus circled by orbiting negative charges. When you study atomic structure, you will learn that even this model is out of date.

CROSS-DISCIPLINARY FOCUS

Math Scientists and engineers make extensive use of mathematical models. Often these models are equations that represent the behavior of objects. Scientists compare the predictions of these equations with observations and then adjust the mathematical model if necessary. Mathematical models often determine the appearance or the use of other models, such as computer illustrations.

Answer to APPLY

Because the atmosphere is too big to see, models such as satellite pictures provide a glimpse of cloud cover and movement over a particular area. Storm maps represent weather patterns, and radar images show what kinds of weather a particular area is experiencing. Colors used on radar maps can represent the level of storm activity. When used together, these models help a forecaster predict upcoming weather. Forecasts can be wrong because they are a best guess about what will happen in the future based on what is happening now, and conditions may change.

3) Extend

RESEARCH
Have students find a newspaper or magazine article about a current science event in which models are being used. These models can be visual or they can be ideas new to technology. They might be weather patterns, a new sound system, or a model of the latest idea of what quarks look like.

CONNECT TO EARTH SCIENCE

You can approximate a model of the solar system by stepping off the distances between the sun and the planets. Each two steps (approximately 1 m) represent almost 50 million kilometers. In this model, Mercury would be one step from the sun. Earth would be three steps from the sun. Pluto would be 206 steps from the sun. The moon would be only one finger's width from Earth. Alpha Centauri, the closest star to our sun, would be many steps—about 320 km, or 640,000 steps—away!

Off to the Races!

TOPIC: Using Models in Physical Science
GO TO: www.scilinks.org
sciLINKS NUMBER: HSTP015

Models Are Just the Right Size

How can you observe how the phases of the moon occur? That's a tough problem, because you're on Earth and you can't easily get off of the Earth to observe the moon going around it. But you can observe a model of the moon, Earth, and sun, as shown in **Figure 17.** As you can see, models can represent things that are too large to easily observe.

Figure 17 *Using this model, you can see how the Earth's rotation, in addition to the moon's revolution around the Earth as the Earth revolves around the sun, results in the different phases of the moon.*

Figure 18 *The particles of matter in a grain of salt connect in a continuous pattern that forms a cube. That's why a grain of salt has a cubic shape.*

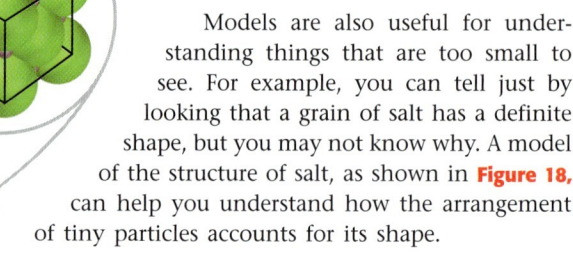

Models are also useful for understanding things that are too small to see. For example, you can tell just by looking that a grain of salt has a definite shape, but you may not know why. A model of the structure of salt, as shown in **Figure 18,** can help you understand how the arrangement of tiny particles accounts for its shape.

Models Build Scientific Knowledge

Models not only can represent scientific ideas and objects but also can be tools that you can use to conduct investigations and illustrate theories.

Testing Hypotheses The MIT engineers were trying to test their hypothesis that a boat that mimics the way a penguin swims would be more efficient than a boat powered by propellers. How did they test this hypothesis? By building a model, *Proteus*. When using the scientific method to develop new technology, testing a hypothesis often requires building a model. By conducting tests with *Proteus*, the MIT engineers tested their hypothesis and found out what factors affected the model's efficiency. Using the data they collected, they could consider building a full-sized penguin boat.

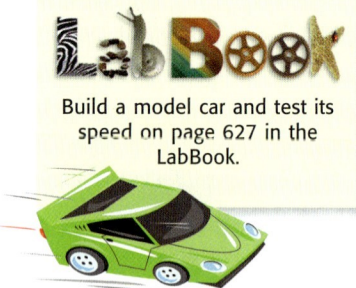
Build a model car and test its speed on page 627 in the LabBook.

Homework
Have students create a model of their bedroom to test different ways of rearranging the furniture. The models may be two-dimensional or three-dimensional, and they must include cutout pieces to represent the furniture. Have students use the model to demonstrate the current furniture layout and then manipulate the model to show a different furniture layout.

Illustrating Theories Recall that a theory explains why things happen the way they do. Sometimes, however, a theory is hard to picture. That's where models come in handy. A model is different from a theory, but a model can present a picture of what the theory explains when you cannot actually observe it. You can see an example of this in **Figure 19.**

Models Can Save Time and Money

When creating technology, scientists often create a model first so that they can test its characteristics and improve its design before building the real thing. You may recall that *Proteus* wasn't big enough to carry even a single passenger. Why didn't the MIT engineers begin by building a full-sized boat? Imagine if they had gone to all that trouble and found out that their design didn't work. What a waste! Models allow you to test ideas without having to spend the time and money necessary to make the real thing. In **Figure 20,** you can see another example of how models save time and money.

Figure 19 This model illustrates the atomic theory, which states that all matter is made of tiny particles called atoms.

Figure 20 Car engineers can conduct cyber-crashes, in which computer-simulated cars crash in various ways. Engineers use the results to determine which safety features to install on the car—all without damaging a single automobile.

REVIEW

1. What is the purpose of a model?
2. Give three examples of models that you see every day.
3. **Interpreting Models** Both a globe and a flat world map model certain features of the Earth. Give an example of when you would use a globe and an example of when you would use a flat map.

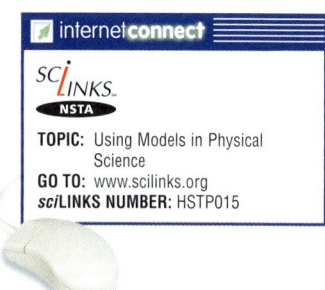

internetconnect

SC**L**INKS
NSTA

TOPIC: Using Models in Physical Science
GO TO: www.scilinks.org
sciLINKS NUMBER: HSTP015

4) Close

Quiz

1. What is meant by a scientific model? (a representation of an object or system)
2. Name five reasons for using models. (to visualize information, to represent objects that are very large or very small, to conduct investigations, to illustrate theories, and to save time and money)
3. Give an example of a model used in science that is larger than the real object and an example of a model that is smaller than the real object. (larger than real object: atoms, molecules; smaller than real object: rocket, weather map)

ALTERNATIVE ASSESSMENT

Concept Mapping Have students create a concept map to show how and why scientists use models. Each part of the map should contain an example of a model used in the real world.

Answers to Review

1. The purpose of a model is to represent concepts or characteristics of objects that are difficult to see or hard to explain. Models can also be tools used to conduct investigations and illustrate theories.
2. Acceptable answers include bus maps, an attendance record, a stuffed animal, assembly instructions for a bicycle, and sheet music.
3. Sample answer: A globe would be better if you wanted to compare the sizes of different countries; a flat map would be better if you wanted to carry a world map in your backpack.

SECTION 4

Focus

Measurement and Safety in Physical Science

This section explains SI, the International System of Units. (It is called SI and not IS because the official name of the system is French: Le Système International d'Unités.) Students learn about volume and mass. They also learn about derived units, such as area and density. Finally, students consider safety rules and safety icons.

 **Bellringer**

Pose the following question:

> How does a standard system of weights and measures, agreed to and used around the world, make life easier? Give examples.

1 Motivate

ACTIVITY

MATERIALS

FOR EACH STUDENT:
- string
- scissors

Safety Caution: Caution students to be careful when using scissors.

Many traditional units of measurement, such as the foot or the inch, were based on common objects. Have each student cut a piece of string one cubit long (the distance from elbow to fingertips). Have students compare their cubit strings with one another. Discuss why measurements made with their strings would vary. How could these variations pose problems for scientists? **Sheltered English**

Section 4

Terms to Learn

meter
volume
mass
temperature
area
density

What You'll Do

- Explain the importance of the International System of Units.
- Determine the appropriate units to use for particular measurements.
- Describe how area and density are derived quantities.

Figure 21 *Prefixes are used with SI units to convert them to larger or smaller units. For example* kilo *means 1,000 times, and* milli *indicates 1/1,000 times. The prefix used depends on the size of the object being measured.*

Measurement and Safety in Physical Science

Hundreds of years ago, different countries used different systems of measurement. In England, the standard for an inch used to be three grains of barley placed end to end. Other standardized units of the modern English system, which is used in the United States, used to be based on parts of the body, such as the foot. Such units were not very accurate because they were based on objects that varied in size.

Eventually people recognized that there was a need for a single measurement system that was simple and accurate. In the late 1700s, the French Academy of Sciences began to develop a global measurement system, now known as the International System of Units, or SI.

The International System of Units

Today most scientists in almost all countries use the International System of Units. One advantage of using SI measurements is that it helps scientists share and compare their observations and results. Another advantage of SI is that all units are based on the number 10, which makes conversions from one unit to another easy to do. The table in **Figure 21** contains the commonly used SI units for length, volume, mass, and temperature.

Common SI Units

Length	meter (m)	
	kilometer (km)	1 km = 1,000 m
	decimeter (dm)	1 dm = 0.1 m
	centimeter (cm)	1 cm = 0.01 m
	millimeter (mm)	1 mm = 0.001 m
	micrometer (μm)	1 μm = 0.000 001 m
	nanometer (nm)	1 nm = 0.000 000 001 m
Volume	cubic meter (m³)	
	cubic centimeter (cm³)	1 cm³ = 0.000 001 m³
	liter (L)	1 L = 1 dm³ = 0.001 m³
	milliliter (mL)	1 mL = 0.001 L = 1 cm³
Mass	kilogram (kg)	
	gram (g)	1 g = 0.001 kg
	milligram (mg)	1 mg = 0.000 001 kg
Temperature	Kelvin (K)	0°C = 273 K
	Celsius (°C)	100°C = 373 K

Teaching Transparency 202
"Common SI Units"

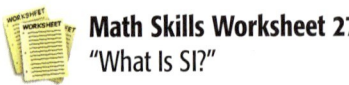

Math Skills Worksheet 27
"What Is SI?"

IS THAT A FACT!

In 1858, August Ferdinand Möbius invented the Möbius strip, a ribbon of paper with only one edge and one side. This invention was the beginning of the science of topology, a branch of geometry.

Length How long is an Olympic-sized swimming pool? To describe its length, a physical scientist would use **meters (m)**, the basic SI unit of length. Other SI units of length are larger or smaller than the meter by multiples of 10. For example, 1 kilometer (km) equals 1,000 meters. If you divide 1 m into 1,000 parts, each part equals 1 mm. This means that 1 mm is one-thousandth of a meter. Although that seems pretty small, some objects are so tiny that even smaller units must be used. To describe the length of a grain of salt, micrometers (μm) or nanometers (nm) are used.

Volume Imagine that you need to move some lenses to a laser laboratory. How many lenses will fit into a crate? That depends on the volume of the crate and the volume of each lens. **Volume** is the amount of space that something occupies.

Volumes of liquids are expressed in liters (L). Liters are based on the meter. A cubic meter (1 m^3) is equal to 1,000 L. So 1,000 L will fit into a box 1 m on each side. A milliliter (mL) will fit into a box 1 cm on each side. So 1 mL = 1 cm^3. Graduated cylinders are used to measure the volume of liquids.

Volumes of solid objects are expressed in cubic meters (m^3). Volumes of smaller objects can be expressed with cubic centimeters (cm^3) or cubic millimeters (mm^3). To find the volume of a crate, or any other rectangular shape, multiply the length by the width by the height. To find the volume of an irregularly shaped object, measure how much liquid that object displaces. You can see how this works in **Figure 22**.

Activity

Pick an object to use as a unit of measure. It could be a pencil, your hand, or anything else. Find how many units wide your desk is, and compare your measurement with those of your classmates. What were some of the units that your classmates used?

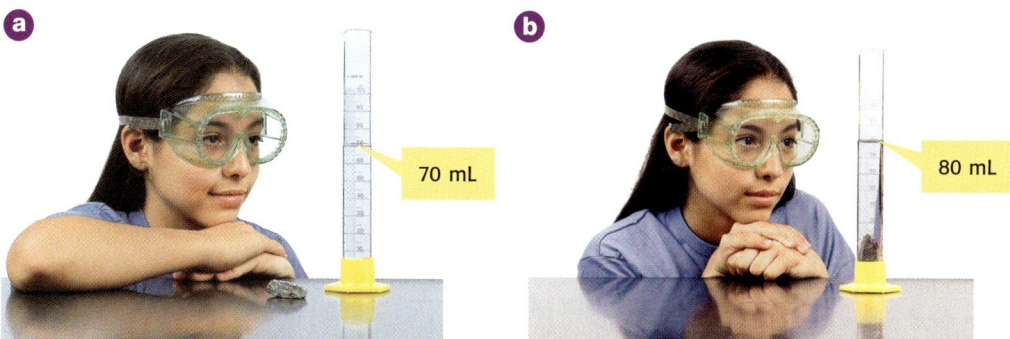

Figure 22 When the rock is added, the water level rises from 70 mL to 80 mL. Because the rock displaces 10 mL of water, and because 1 mL = 1 cm^3, the volume of the rock is 10 cm^3.

Answer to Activity
Measurements will vary, depending on the standard of measurement chosen. Some units might include hand width, hand length, finger width, or pencil length. (By comparing their units and measurements with others, students should recognize that a standard of measurement is important in order to communicate data and be understood.)

Measuring Liquid Volume PG 628

Directed Reading Worksheet 1 Section 4

2 Teach

MEETING INDIVIDUAL NEEDS
Students Having Difficulty
Have pairs of students make flash cards of the vocabulary words with the definitions and an example of each unit on the back. Have partners quiz one another using the cards.
Sheltered English

MATH and MORE
Have students calculate the following problems.
1. What is the volume of a box that is 1 m long, 0.5 m wide, and 2 m tall? (1.0 m^3)
2. What is the volume of a bar of soap that is 9 cm long, 5 cm wide, and 2 cm high? (90 cm^3)
3. A glass contains about 250 mL of milk. After adding a cookie to the milk, the level is 261 mL. What is the volume of the cookie? (11 cm^3)

Math Skills Worksheet 30 "Finding Volume"

CONNECT TO LIFE SCIENCE

Use Teaching Transparency 4, "Scale of Sizes," to help students understand how SI uses meters and multiples of 10 to measure length.

Teaching Transparency 4 "Scale of Sizes"

3) Extend

ACTIVITY

MATERIALS

FOR EACH GROUP:
- wooden blocks
- metric rulers
- balances

Have students work in small groups to measure the dimensions of a wooden block and the mass of the block. From their data, have groups calculate the areas of each surface of the block, the volume of the block, and the density of the block. **Sheltered English**

 **PG 629**

Coin Operated

Homework

Ask students to examine items from the grocery store they have at home. Ask them to determine whether each item is sold by volume or by mass. Have them make a list for each category.

Answers to MATHBREAK

1. 45 cm³
2. 3 m
3. 400 cm²

 Math Skills Worksheet 29 "Finding Perimeter and Area"

 Critical Thinking Worksheet 1 "A Solar Solution"

Figure 23 Measuring Temperature

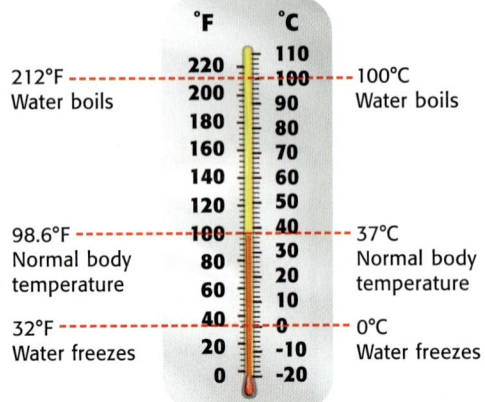

MATH BREAK

Using Area to Find Volume

Area can be used to find the volume of an object according to the following equation:

Volume = Area × height

1. What is the volume of a box 5 cm tall whose lid has an area of 9 cm²?
2. A crate has a volume of 48 m³. The area of its bottom side is 16 m². What is the height of the crate?
3. A cube with a volume of 8,000 cm³ has a height of 20 cm. What is the area of one of its sides?

TOPIC: SI Units
GO TO: www.scilinks.org
sciLINKS NUMBER: HSTP020

Mass How many cars can a bridge support? That depends on the strength of the bridge and the mass of the cars. **Mass** is the amount of matter that something is made of. The kilogram (kg) is the basic SI unit for mass and would be used to express the mass of a car. Grams (one-thousandth of a kilogram) are used to express the mass of small objects. A medium-sized apple has a mass of about 100 g. Masses of very large objects are expressed in metric tons. A metric ton equals 1,000 kg.

Temperature How hot is melted iron? To answer this question, a physical scientist would measure the temperature of the liquid metal. **Temperature** is a measure of how hot (or cold) something is. You are probably used to expressing temperature with degrees Fahrenheit (°F). Scientists often use degrees Celsius (°C), but the kelvin (K) is the SI unit for temperature. The thermometer in **Figure 23** compares °F with °C, the unit you will most often see in this book.

Derived Quantities

Some quantities are formed from combinations of other measurements. Such quantities are called *derived quantities*. Both area and density are derived quantities.

Area How much carpet would cover the floor of your classroom? It depends on the area of the floor. **Area** is a measure of how much surface an object has. To calculate the area of a rectangular surface, measure the length and width, then use this equation:

Area = length × width

The units for area are called square units, such as m², cm², and km². The area of the rectangle in **Figure 24** is 20 cm².

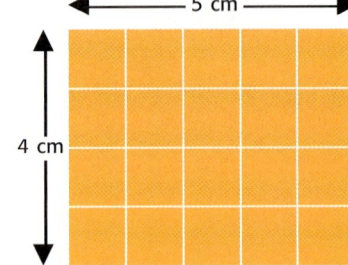

Figure 24 If you count the smaller squares within the rectangle, you'll count 20 squares that each measure 1 cm².

IS THAT A FACT!

The original standards for the kilogram and meter are kept in the International Bureau of Weights and Measures in Sèvres, France. They are made of 90 percent platinum and 10 percent iridium.

Density Another derived quantity is density. **Density** is mass per unit volume. So an object's density is the amount of matter it has in a given space. To find density (*D*), first measure mass (*m*) and volume (*V*). Then use the following equation:

$$D = \frac{m}{V}$$

For example, suppose you want to know the density of the gear shown at right. Its mass is 75 g and its volume is 20 cm³. You can calculate the gear's density like this:

$$D = \frac{m}{V} = \frac{75 \text{ g}}{20 \text{ cm}^3} = 3.75 \text{ g/cm}^3$$

Safety Rules!

Physical science is exciting and fun, but it can also be dangerous. So don't take any chances! Always follow your teacher's instructions, and don't take shortcuts—even when you think there is little or no danger.

Before starting an experiment, get your teacher's permission and read the lab procedures carefully. Pay particular attention to safety information and caution statements. The chart below shows the safety symbols used in this book. Get to know these symbols and what they mean by reading the safety information on page 622. **This is important!** If you are still unsure about what a safety symbol means, ask your teacher.

Stay on the safe side by reading the safety information on page 622. **You must do this before doing any experiment!**

Safety Symbols

Eye protection	Clothing protection	Hand safety
Heating safety	Electric safety	Sharp object
Chemical safety	Animal safety	Plant safety

REVIEW

1. Why is SI important?
2. Which SI unit would you use to express the height of your desk? Which SI unit would you use to express the volume of this textbook?
3. **Comparing Concepts** How is area different from volume?

TOPIC: SI Units
GO TO: www.scilinks.org
sciLINKS NUMBER: HSTP020

4) Close

Quiz

1. What does SI stand for? (International System of Units)
2. What is the SI unit of length? volume? mass? temperature? (Meter, cubic meter, kilogram, kelvin)
3. Name two safety rules of science. (Follow directions, and don't take shortcuts.)

Safety First!

Alternative Assessment

Have students explain why it is necessary to protect themselves when conducting scientific experiments. Ask them to list the safety symbols on this page and to think of at least one situation when the safety rule for each icon should be followed.

Synthesis

Have a "Guess the Size" contest. Place signs on several objects of different sizes and masses in your classroom. Ask students to guess the length, area, volume, or mass of each object. Then have students measure each object. Provide a "Best Guesser" certificate for the student who makes the closest estimates.

Answers to Review

1. SI, which is based on the number 10 (making conversion from one unit to another easy), allows scientists to communicate quantitative information more accurately than with older systems, which were based on objects that varied in size.
2. Answers will vary, but centimeters would probably be an appropriate unit. The volume of this textbook would best be expressed in cm³.
3. Area, the measure of an object's surface, is calculated by multiplying two dimensions, such as length and width. Volume, the measure of how much space an object takes up, is calculated by multiplying three dimensions, such as length, width, and height.

Science Skills Worksheet 9
"Safety Rules!"

Chapter Highlights

VOCABULARY DEFINITIONS

SECTION 1

physical science the study of matter and energy

SECTION 2

scientific method a series of steps that scientists use to answer questions and solve problems

technology the application of knowledge, tools, and materials to solve problems and accomplish tasks; can also refer to the objects used to accomplish tasks

observation any use of the senses to gather information

hypothesis a possible explanation or answer to a question

data any pieces of information acquired through experimentation

theory a unifying explanation for a broad range of hypotheses and observations that have been supported by testing

law a summary of many experimental results and observations; tells how things work

 Science Skills Worksheet 7 "Improving Your Study Habits"

Chapter Highlights

SECTION 1

Vocabulary
- physical science (p. 7)

Section Notes
- Science is a process of making observations and asking questions about those observations.
- Physical science is the study of matter and energy and is often divided into physics and chemistry.
- Physical science is part of many other areas of science.
- Many different careers involve physical science.

SECTION 2

Vocabulary
- scientific method (p. 11)
- technology (p. 11)
- observation (p. 12)
- hypothesis (p. 14)
- data (p. 16)
- theory (p. 19)
- law (p. 19)

Section Notes
- The scientific method is a series of steps that scientists use to answer questions and solve problems.
- Any information you gather through your senses is an observation. Observations often lead to questions or problems.
- A hypothesis is a possible explanation or answer to a question. A good hypothesis is testable.
- After you test a hypothesis, you should analyze your results and draw conclusions about whether your hypothesis was supported.
- Communicating your findings allows others to verify your results or continue to investigate your problem.
- A scientific theory is the result of many investigations and many hypotheses. Theories can be changed or modified by new evidence.
- A scientific law is a summary of many experimental results and hypotheses that have been supported over time.

Labs
Exploring the Unseen (p. 626)

✓ Skills Check

Math Concepts

AREA To calculate the area of a rectangular surface, first measure its length and width, then multiply those values. The area of a piece of notebook paper with a length of 28 cm and a width of 21.6 cm can be calculated as follows:

$$\text{Area} = \text{length} \times \text{width}$$
$$= 28 \text{ cm} \times 21.6 \text{ cm}$$
$$= 604.8 \text{ cm}^2$$

Visual Understanding

SCIENTIFIC METHOD To answer a question in science, you can use the scientific method. Review the flowchart on page 18 to see that the scientific method does not have to follow a specific order.

MODELS A model is a representation of an object or system. Look back at the examples on page 20 to learn more about different models.

Lab and Activity Highlights

Exploring the Unseen PG 626

Off to the Races! PG 627

Measuring Liquid Volume PG 628

Coin Operated PG 629

 Datasheets for LabBook (blackline masters for these labs)

SECTION 3

Vocabulary
model *(p. 20)*

Section Notes
- Scientific models are representations of objects or systems. Models make difficult concepts easier to understand.
- Models can represent things too small to see or too large to observe directly.
- Models can be used to test hypotheses and illustrate theories.

Labs
Off to the Races! *(p. 627)*

SECTION 4

Vocabulary
meter *(p. 25)*
volume *(p. 25)*
mass *(p. 26)*
temperature *(p. 26)*
area *(p. 26)*
density *(p. 27)*

Section Notes
- The International System of Units is the standard system of measurement used by scientists around the world.
- Length, volume, mass, and temperature are quantities of measurement. Each quantity of measurement is expressed with a particular SI unit.
- Area is a measure of how much surface an object has. Density is a measure of mass per unit volume.
- Safety rules are important and must be followed at all times during scientific investigations.

Labs
Measuring Liquid Volume *(p. 628)*
Coin Operated *(p. 629)*

VOCABULARY DEFINITIONS, continued

SECTION 3

model a representation of an object or system

SECTION 4

meter the basic unit of length in the SI system

volume the amount of space that something occupies or the amount of space that something contains

mass the amount of matter that something is made of; does not change with the object's location

temperature a measure of how hot (or cold) something is

area the amount of surface an object has

density the amount of matter in a given space; mass per unit volume

 Vocabulary Review Worksheet 1

 Blackline masters of these Chapter Highlights can be found in the **Study Guide.**

---

internet connect

 **GO TO:** go.hrw.com

Visit the **HRW** Web site for a variety of learning tools related to this chapter. Just type in the keyword:

KEYWORD: HSTWPS

 **GO TO:** www.scilinks.org

Visit the **National Science Teachers Association** on-line Web site for Internet resources related to this chapter. Just type in the *sci*LINKS number for more information about the topic:

TOPIC: Matter and Energy   *sci*LINKS NUMBER: HSTP005
TOPIC: The Scientific Method   *sci*LINKS NUMBER: HSTP010
TOPIC: Using Models in Physical Science   *sci*LINKS NUMBER: HSTP015
TOPIC: SI Units   *sci*LINKS NUMBER: HSTP020

Lab and Activity Highlights

LabBank

 Whiz-Bang Demonstrations, The Dollar-Bill Bridge, Demo 37

Long-Term Projects & Research Ideas, Prove It! Project 51

Chapter Review

USING VOCABULARY

For each pair of terms, explain the difference in their meanings.

1. science/technology
2. observation/hypothesis
3. theory/law
4. model/theory
5. volume/mass
6. area/density

UNDERSTANDING CONCEPTS

Multiple Choice

7. Physical science is the study of
   a. matter and motion.
   b. matter and energy.
   c. energy and motion.
   d. matter and composition.

8. 10 m is equal to
   a. 100 cm.   c. 10,000 mm.
   b. 1,000 cm.   d. Both (b) and (c)

9. For a hypothesis to be valid, it must be
   a. testable.
   b. supported by evidence.
   c. made into a law.
   d. Both (a) and (b)

10. The statement "Sheila has a stain on her shirt" is an example of a(n)
    a. law.
    b. hypothesis.
    c. observation.
    d. prediction.

11. A hypothesis is often developed out of
    a. observations.   c. laws.
    b. experiments.   d. Both (a) and (b)

12. How many milliliters are in 3.5 kL?
    a. 3,500   c. 3,500,000
    b. 0.0035   d. 35,000

13. A map of Seattle is an example of a
    a. law.   c. model.
    b. quantity.   d. unit.

14. Which of the following is an example of technology?
    a. mass
    b. physical science
    c. screwdriver
    d. none of the above

Short Answer

15. Name two areas of science other than chemistry and physics, and describe how physical science has a role in those areas of science.

16. Explain why the results of one experiment are never really final results.

17. Explain why area and density are called derived quantities.

18. If a hypothesis is not testable, does that mean that it is wrong? Explain.

Concept Mapping

19. Use the following terms to create a concept map: science, scientific method, hypothesis, problems, questions, experiments, observations.

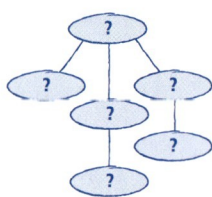

30

18. Sample answer: A hypothesis that is not testable is not necessarily wrong, but it cannot necessarily be supported either. Unless a hypothesis can be tested, there is no way to prove that it is wrong.

Concept Mapping

19. An answer to this exercise can be found at the end of this book.

Concept Mapping Transparency 1

Chapter Review Answers

USING VOCABULARY

1. Science is a process of observing and asking questions about the natural world. Technology is applying science knowledge and using tools to solve everyday practical problems.

2. An observation is any use of the senses to gather information. A hypothesis is a possible answer to a question. Hypotheses can be tested. Observations can be used to develop and test hypotheses.

3. A theory explains why something happens; a law only states what happens.

4. A theory is an explanation for how something happens. A model can represent an explanation or some aspect of the theory.

5. Volume is the amount of space taken up by an object, and mass is the amount of matter an object contains.

6. Area is the amount of surface an object has; density is the amount of matter in a given volume.

UNDERSTANDING CONCEPTS

Multiple Choice

7. b   10. c   13. c
8. d   11. d   14. c
9. d   12. c

Short Answer

15. Answers will vary, depending on the areas of science chosen, but they should reflect an understanding that physical science is all around.

16. Sample answer: The results of one experiment may provide evidence for future investigators. Sometimes new information shows that a hypothesis is not supported and may have to be revised or rejected.

17. Area and density are derived quantities because they are calculated from two or more measurements.

CRITICAL THINKING AND PROBLEM SOLVING

20. A tailor is someone who makes or alters items of clothing. Why might a standard system of measurement be helpful to a tailor?

21. Two classmates are having a debate about whether a spatula is an example of technology. Using what you know about science, technology, and spatulas, write a couple of sentences that will help your classmates settle their debate.

22. Imagine that you are conducting an experiment in which you are testing the effects of the height of a ramp on the speed at which a toy car goes down the ramp. What is the variable in this experiment? What factors must be controlled?

23. Suppose a classmate says, "I don't need to study physical science because I'm not going to be a scientist, and scientists are the only people who use physical science." How would you respond? (Hint: In your answer, give several examples of careers that use physical science.)

MATH IN SCIENCE

24. The cereal box at right has a mass of 340 g. Its dimensions are 27 cm × 19 cm × 6 cm.
    a. What is the volume of the box?
    b. What is its density?
    c. What is the area of the front side of the box?

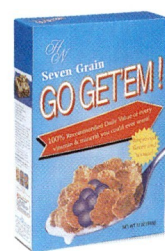

INTERPRETING GRAPHICS

Examine the picture below, and answer the questions that follow:

25. How similar to the real object is this model?
26. What characteristics of the real object does this model not show?
27. Why might this model be useful?

NOW What Do You Think?

Take a minute to review your answers to the ScienceLog questions on page 5. Have your answers changed? If necessary, revise your answers based on what you have learned since you began this chapter.

31

NOW WHAT DO YOU THINK?

Sample revised answers:
1. Physical science is the study of matter and energy.
2. Scientists use steps such as those in the scientific method to answer questions and solve problems. They ask questions, form hypotheses, test hypotheses, draw conclusions, and communicate their results.
3. Models serve the purpose of representing or explaining objects or concepts that are difficult to see or understand. Models can also be used to form hypotheses and make predictions.

CRITICAL THINKING AND PROBLEM SOLVING

20. Sample answer: A standard system of measurement allows a tailor to make clothing fit a customer exactly.
21. Sample answer: Technology is the application of science to accomplish tasks. A spatula used to lift or turn food is an example of technology.
22. The variable is the height of the ramp. Controlled factors include the type of car, the material the ramp is made of, and the point from which the car is released.
23. Sample answer: Scientists are not the only people who use physical science. Chefs have to understand how food ingredients will interact, and they have to measure quantities properly.

MATH IN SCIENCE

24. a. Volume = 27 cm × 19 cm × 6 cm = 3,078 cm^3
    b. Density = $\frac{340 \text{ g}}{3,078 \text{ cm}^3}$ = 0.110 g/cm^3
    c. Area of the front side = 27 cm × 19 cm = 513 cm^2

INTERPRETING GRAPHICS

25. Sample answer: The model is similar to the real object in terms of structure and the relative sizes of different parts of the building. It also shows the location of the windows and doors that will be built.
26. Sample answer: The model does not show the interior features, such as plumbing, furniture, or carpeting. It also has no electrical capabilities.
27. Sample answer: This model shows what features a building will have without having to build it full-size.

 Blackline masters of this Chapter Review can be found in the **Study Guide**.

CAREERS

Electronics Engineer– Julie Williams-Byrd

Background

Examining the real processes that make a laser work involves a discussion of atomic energy levels. An atom is in its ground state when all of its electrons occupy the lowest available energy levels. When energy is added to an atom, the electrons then move to higher energy levels and the atom is in an excited state. When a photon of energy passes near an atom in the excited state, it induces an electron in an upper energy level to drop into a lower energy level. As it drops, the electron gives off a photon of energy. This is the stimulated emission that is central to the process of lasing.

Remote sensing is a technique for measuring, observing, or monitoring a process or item from a distance (not physically touching the item under investigation). In this case, Julie Williams-Byrd uses lasers flown on the space shuttle or on airplanes to monitor activity in the atmosphere.

CAREERS

ELECTRONICS ENGINEER

Julie Williams-Byrd uses her knowledge of physics to develop better lasers. She started working with lasers as a graduate student at Hampton University, in Virginia. Today Williams-Byrd works as an electronics engineer in the Laser Systems Branch (LSB) of NASA. She designs and builds lasers that are used to monitor phenomena in the atmosphere, such as wind and ozone.

The white light we see every day is actually composed of all the colors of the spectrum. A laser emits a very small portion of this spectrum. That is why there are blue lasers, red lasers, and so on. High-voltage sources called laser "pumps" cause laser materials to emit certain wavelengths of light, depending on the material used. A laser material, such as helium neon gas, emits radiation (light) as a result of changes in the electron energy levels of its atoms. This process gives lasers their name: **L**ight **A**mplification of the **S**timulated **E**mission of **R**adiation.

Using Scientific Models

Julie Williams-Byrd uses scientific models to predict the nature of different aspects of laser design. Different laser materials emit radiation at different wavelengths, and specific pump sources must be used to induce "lasing." "Researchers at LSB use laser models to predict output energy, wavelength, efficiency, and a host of other properties of the laser system," Williams-Byrd says.

New Technologies

Her most challenging project has been building a laser-transmitter that will be used to measure winds in the atmosphere. This system, called *Lidar*, is very much like radar except that it uses light waves instead of sound waves to bounce off objects. To measure winds, a laser beam is transmitted into the atmosphere, where it illuminates particles. A receiver looks at these particles over a period of time and determines the changes in position of the particles. Wind velocity is then determined from this information. This new technology is expected to be used in a space shuttle mission called Sparcle.

Lasers All Around Us

Although Williams-Byrd works with high-tech lasers, she points out that lasers are a part of daily life for many people. For example, lasers are used in scanners at many retail stores. Ophthalmologists use lasers to correct nearsightedness. Some metal workers use them to cut metal. And lasers are even used to create spectacular light shows!

Going Further

▶ Can you think of any new uses for lasers? Make a list in your ScienceLog, and then do some research to find out if any of your ideas already exist.

▼ *Julie Williams-Byrd uses laser generators like this one in her work at NASA.*

Answer to Going Further

Students' answers will vary, but may include one or more of the following: to remove graffiti, to clean teeth, for security systems, and for shooting practice.

Science Fiction

"Inspiration"
by Ben Bova

No matter where you are on the face of the Earth, you can pinpoint your location. Most of the time, you use map coordinates, or latitude and longitude readings. And you can give your distance above sea level. With modern technology, you can give an accurate, three-dimensional description of where you are. But what about a fourth dimension? Consider for a moment traveling in *time.* Not just getting through today and into tomorrow but actually being able to leap back and forth through time.

Novelist H. G. Wells imagined such a possibility in his novelette *The Time Machine.* When the story was published in 1895, most physicists said that the notion of traveling in time was nonsense and against all the laws of physics that govern the universe. The idea that *time* was similar to *length, width,* or *height* was foolishness. Or so they thought.

It was up to Albert Einstein, in 1905, to propose a different view of the universe. However, when Wells's story was first published, Einstein was just 16 and not a very good student. What if Einstein had been discouraged and had not pursued his interest in physics? But Einstein did look at the universe and maybe, just maybe, he had an inspiration.

Ben Bova's story "Inspiration" describes just such a possibility. Young Einstein meets Wells and the great physicist of the time, Lord Kelvin. But was the meeting just a lucky coincidence or something else entirely? Escape to the *Holt Anthology of Science Fiction,* and read "Inspiration" to find out.

SCIENCE FICTION
"Inspiration"
by Ben Bova

Who inspires you? The great heroes of our time had their sources of inspiration too. But what if they hadn't? How different would our world be?

Teaching Strategy
Reading Level This is a relatively short story that may be of moderate difficulty for the average student to read and comprehend.

Background
About the Author Ben Bova has written many science fiction novels and collections of short stories. He has also written non-fiction books about science and about writing science fiction. Check your library for a complete listing.

Further Reading If you enjoyed "Inspiration," look for other stories by Ben Bova at your library. Some of Bova's recent collections of short stories include the following:

Challenges, Tor Books, 1993

Future Crime, Tor Books, 1990

Battle Station, Tor Books, 1987

Chapter Organizer

CHAPTER ORGANIZATION	TIME MINUTES	OBJECTIVES	LABS, INVESTIGATIONS, AND DEMONSTRATIONS
Chapter Opener pp. 34–35	45	National Standards: SAI 2, PS 1a	**Investigate!** Sack Secrets, p. 35
Section 1 What Is Matter?	90	▶ Name the two properties of all matter. ▶ Describe how volume and mass are measured. ▶ Compare mass and weight. ▶ Explain the relationship between mass and inertia. ST 1, 2, SPSP 1, 5, PS 1a, 1c; LabBook PS 1a	**QuickLab,** Space Case, p. 36 **Demonstration,** p. 36 in ATE **Demonstration,** p. 38 in ATE **Skill Builder,** Volumania! p. 630 **Datasheets for LabBook,** Volumania! Datasheet 5
Section 2 Describing Matter	90	▶ Give examples of matter's different properties. ▶ Describe how density is used to identify different substances. ▶ Compare physical and chemical properties. ▶ Explain what happens to matter during physical and chemical changes. PS 1a, 1b; LabBook PS 1a, 1b	**Demonstration,** p. 43 in ATE **QuickLab,** Changing Change, p. 49 **Skill Builder,** Determining Density, p. 632 **Datasheets for LabBook,** Determining Density, Datasheet 6 **Discovery Lab,** Layering Liquids, p. 633 **Datasheets for LabBook,** Layering Liquids, Datasheet 7 **Skill Builder,** White Before Your Eyes, p. 634 **Datasheets for LabBook,** White Before Your Eyes, Datasheet 8 **Inquiry Labs,** Whatever Floats Your Boat, Lab 17 **Whiz-Bang Demonstrations,** Curious Cubes, Demo 38 **Whiz-Bang Demonstrations,** The Dancing Toothpicks, Demo 39 **Whiz-Bang Demonstrations,** Does 2 + 2 = 4? Demo 40 **Long-Term Projects & Research Ideas,** Project 52

See page **T20** *for a complete correlation of this book with the*

NATIONAL SCIENCE EDUCATION STANDARDS.

TECHNOLOGY RESOURCES

 Guided Reading Audio CD
English or Spanish, Chapter 2

 Science Discovery Videodiscs
Image and Activity Bank with Lesson Plans:
In Search of Chemical Change,
Material Science

 CNN. Scientists in Action, Neutrino Breakthrough, Segment 4

 One-Stop Planner CD-ROM with Test Generator

Chapter 2 • The Properties of Matter

CLASSROOM WORKSHEETS, TRANSPARENCIES, AND RESOURCES	SCIENCE INTEGRATION AND CONNECTIONS	REVIEW AND ASSESSMENT
Directed Reading Worksheet 2 **Science Puzzlers, Twisters & Teasers,** Worksheet 2		
Directed Reading Worksheet 2, Section 1 **Math Skills for Science Worksheet 31,** The Unit Factor and Dimensional Analysis **Transparency 95,** Growth Chart **Transparency 203,** How Mass and Distance Affect Gravity Between Objects **Transparency 204,** Differences Between Mass and Weight **Science Skills Worksheet 15,** Measuring	**Cross-Disciplinary Focus,** p. 37 in ATE **MathBreak,** Calculating Volume, p. 38 **Math and More,** p. 38 in ATE **Biology Connection,** p. 40 **Connect to Life Science,** p. 40 in ATE **Multicultural Connection,** p. 41 in ATE **Apply,** p. 42 **Across the Sciences:** In the Dark About Dark Matter, p. 56	**Self-Check,** p. 41 **Review,** p. 42 **Quiz,** p. 42 in ATE **Alternative Assessment,** p. 42 in ATE
Directed Reading Worksheet 2, Section 2 **Math Skills for Science Worksheet 32,** Density **Transparency 205,** Examples of Chemical Changes **Reinforcement Worksheet 2,** A Matter of Density **Critical Thinking Worksheet 2,** As a Matter of Fact!	**Real-World Connection,** p. 44 in ATE **MathBreak,** Density, p. 45 **Math and More,** p. 45 in ATE **Apply,** p. 46 **Real-World Connection,** p. 47 in ATE **Environment Connection,** p. 51 **Health Watch:** Building a Better Body, p. 57	**Homework,** p. 44 in ATE **Review,** p. 46 **Review,** p. 51 **Quiz,** p. 51 in ATE **Alternative Assessment,** p. 51 in ATE

END-OF-CHAPTER REVIEW AND ASSESSMENT

Chapter Review in Study Guide
Vocabulary and Notes in Study Guide
Chapter Tests with Performance-Based Assessment, Chapter 2 Test
Chapter Tests with Performance-Based Assessment, Performance-Based Assessment 2
Concept Mapping Transparency 2

---

internet connect

 Holt, Rinehart and Winston On-line Resources
go.hrw.com

For worksheets and other teaching aids related to this chapter, visit the HRW Web site and type in the keyword: **HSTMAT**

 **National Science Teachers Association**
www.scilinks.org

Encourage students to use the *sci*LINKS numbers listed in the internet connect boxes to access information and resources on the **NSTA** Web site.

Chapter Resources & Worksheets

Visual Resources

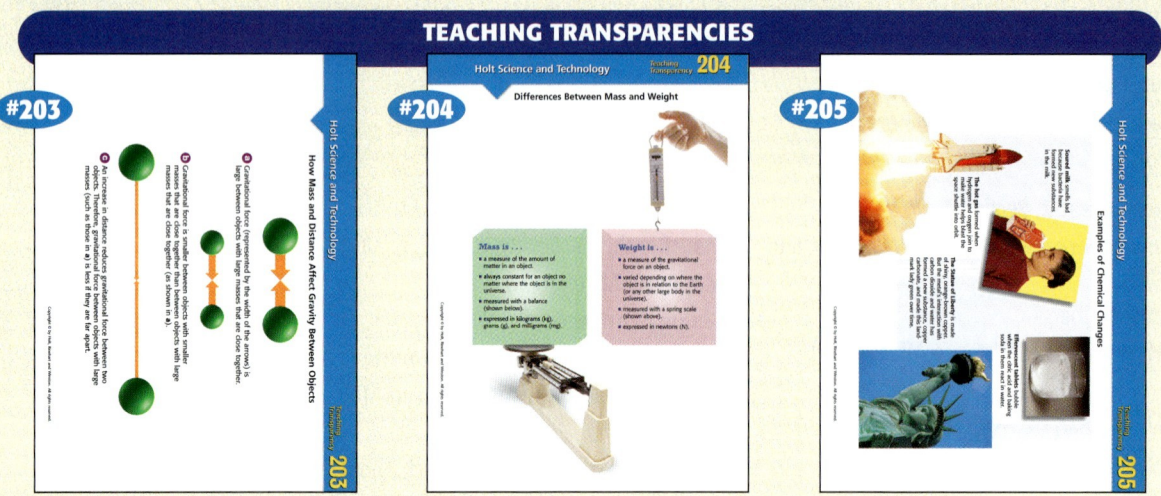

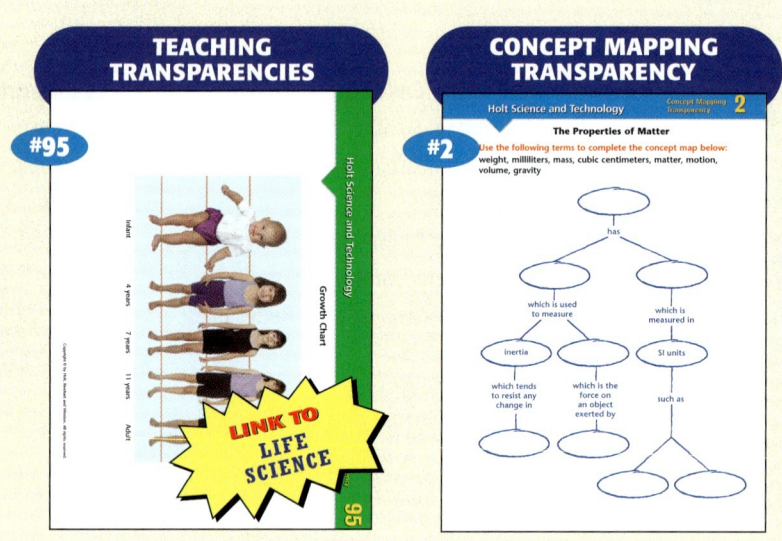

Meeting Individual Needs

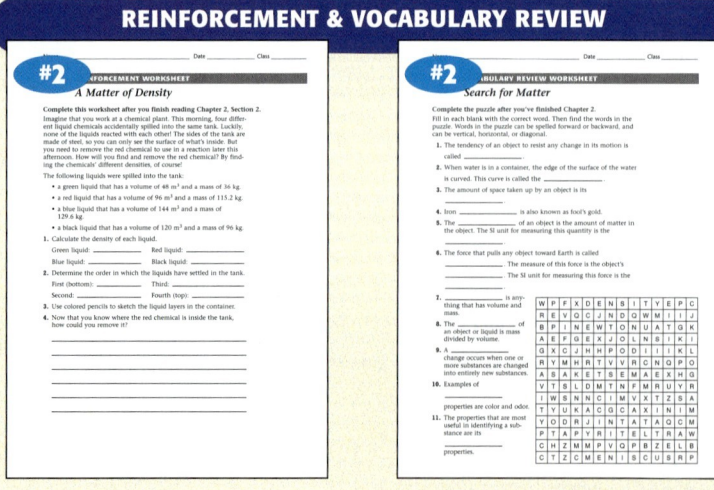

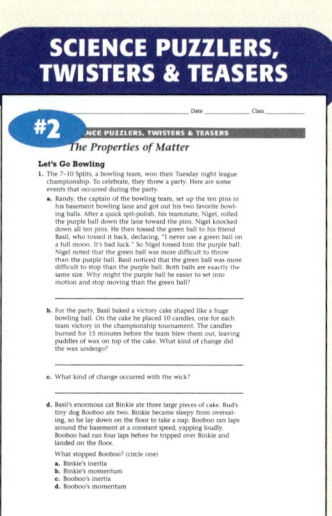

Chapter 2 • The Properties of Matter

Review & Assessment

STUDY GUIDE

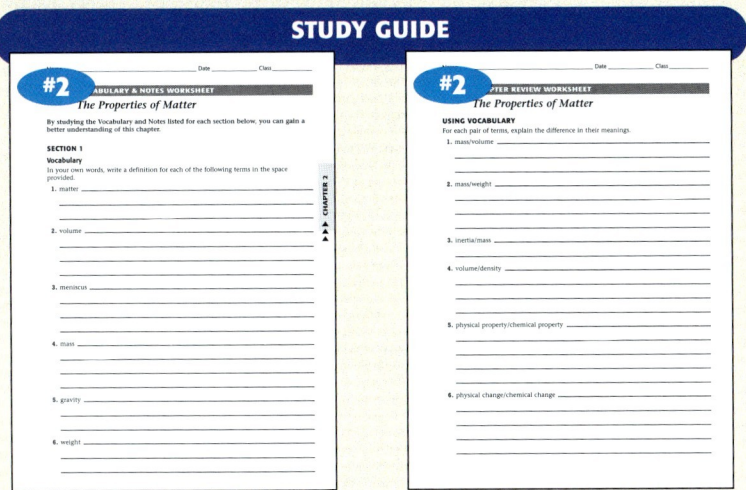

CHAPTER TESTS WITH PERFORMANCE-BASED ASSESSMENT

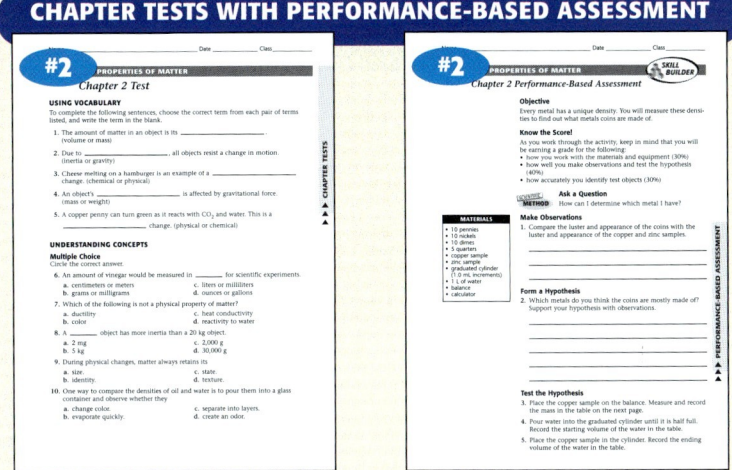

Lab Worksheets

INQUIRY LABS

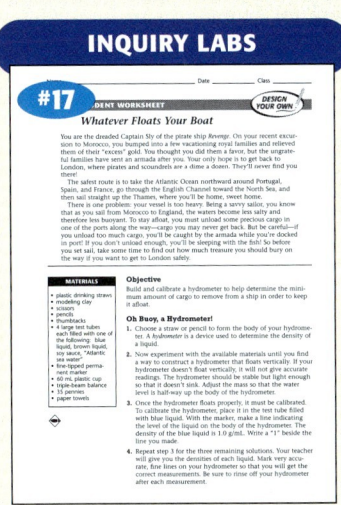

WHIZ-BANG DEMONSTRATIONS

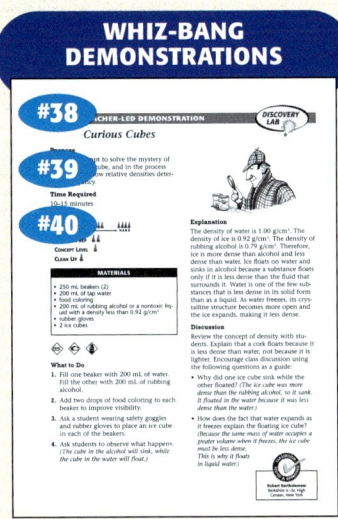

LONG-TERM PROJECTS & RESEARCH IDEAS

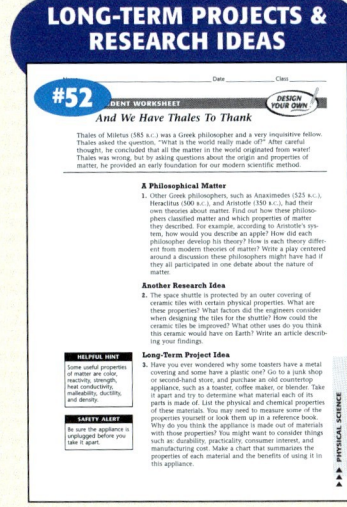

DATASHEETS FOR LABBOOK

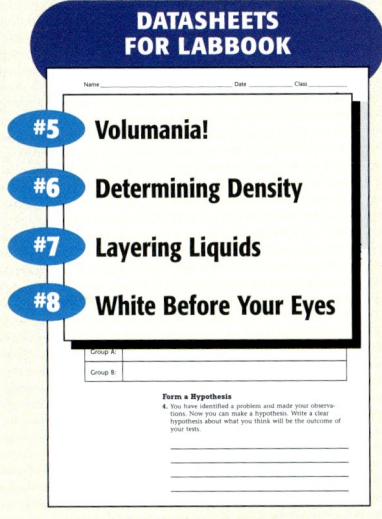

- #5 Volumania!
- #6 Determining Density
- #7 Layering Liquids
- #8 White Before Your Eyes

Applications & Extensions

CRITICAL THINKING & PROBLEM SOLVING

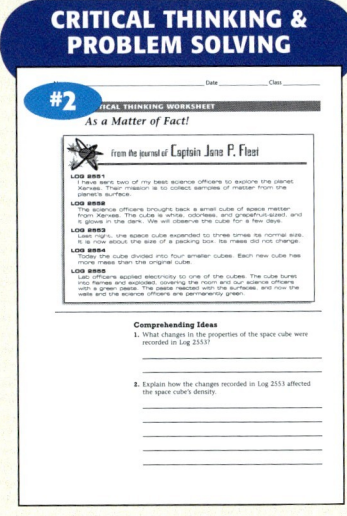

SCIENTISTS IN ACTION

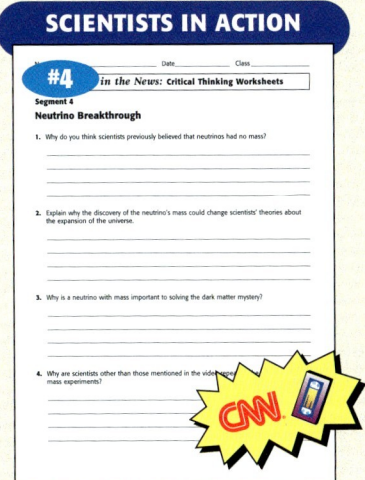

Chapter Background

SECTION 1
What Is Matter?

▶ **Measuring Volume**
Body measurements probably provided the basis for many early measurements. The Babylonian liquid measure, the *ka,* was the volume of a cube with sides of one handbreadth (between 99 and 102 mm). Three hundred *ka* equaled 3,000 *gin* or 1 *gur.* The *gur* was equal to a volume of approximately 50 L. The basic Roman unit of volume was the *sextarius*. It had several subdivisions and multiples. The largest multiple, the *amphora,* was equal to 48 *sextarii*. The *amphora* was equal to 25.5 L.

▶ **Weight on Other Planets**
The weight of a person on any given planet depends on the attraction between the person and the planet. The more massive the planet, the greater the gravitational force on the person, and the greater the person's weight. A person who weighs 445 N on Earth would have different weights on other planets. On Mercury, the person would weigh about 164.6 N, on Venus 400.3 N, on Mars 169 N, on Jupiter 1,169.8 N, on Saturn 502.6 N, on Uranus 351.4 N, on Neptune 498.2 N, and on Pluto about 22.2 N.

IS THAT A FACT!
◆ A balance is a freely suspended beam that is balanced by known and unknown masses. Balances have been used for almost 3,000 years.

▶ **Knife-Edge Balances**
The modern knife-edge balance was developed during the sixteenth and seventeenth centuries. At the end of the seventeenth century, balances were developed in which the mass and goods plates were positioned above the balance beam, allowing the goods or masses to be placed anywhere on the plates without affecting accuracy.

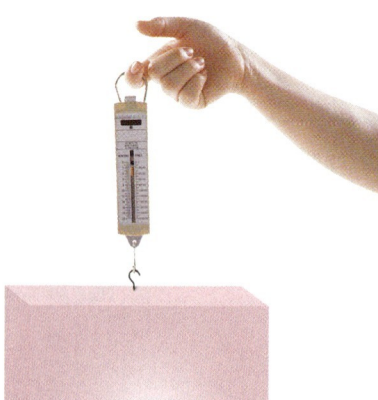

▶ **Spring Scales**
Another type of device used to measure weight is the spring scale. It uses the relationship between a spring's deflection and the weight of the object on the scale. Spring scales are not as accurate as balances, which compare a pair of masses.

Chapter 2 • The Properties of Matter

SECTION 2

Describing Matter

▶ **Physical and Chemical Properties**
The color and the density of a substance are physical properties. So are the temperatures at which a substance changes state. For example, chlorine is a greenish yellow gas with a density of 0.00321 g/cm³. It can be changed to a liquid by cooling it to −34.6°C.

- The ability of chlorine to react explosively with sodium to form sodium chloride (table salt) is a chemical property. When chlorine reacts with sodium, an entirely different substance is formed.

IS THAT A FACT!

◆ By comparing the density of King Hieron II's crown with that of a bar of pure gold, the Greek inventor and mathematician Archimedes was able to prove that the crown was not made of pure gold and that a goldsmith had cheated the king.

▶ **Dealing with Density**
Density is often a difficult concept for some middle school students to grasp. Discuss with students the principles that the world we know is made up of a variety of matter and that all matter has mass and volume.

- Not all matter is the same. Ask students which they would rather carry around all day, a backpack full of feathers or a backpack full of sand. Ask them to explain why. Lead them to the idea that even though the backpack is fixed in size (volume), there is more mass in it when it is full of sand because sand is more dense than feathers.

For background information about teaching strategies and issues, refer to the *Professional Reference for Teachers*.

CHAPTER 2
The Properties of Matter

Chapter Preview

Section 1
What Is Matter?
- Everything Is Made of Matter
- Matter Has Volume
- Matter Has Mass
- The Difference Between Mass and Weight
- Measuring Mass and Weight
- Mass Is a Measure of Inertia

Section 2
Describing Matter
- Physical Properties
- Chemical Properties
- Physical Vs. Chemical Properties
- Physical Changes Don't Form New Substances
- Chemical Changes Form New Substances

Directed Reading Worksheet 2

Science Puzzlers, Twisters & Teasers Worksheet 2

Guided Reading Audio CD
English or Spanish, Chapter 2

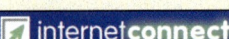

Smithsonian Institution®
Visit www.si.edu/hrw for additional on-line resources.

CHAPTER 2
The Properties of Matter

Imagine . . .

The year is 1849. You are one of thousands of people who have come to California to prospect for gold. But so far, no luck. In fact, you've decided that if you don't find gold today, you're going to head back home.

You swing your pickax into the granite bedrock, and a bright flash catches your eye. A shiny yellow chunk is sticking out of the rock. Such a sight used to make you catch your breath. Now you just sigh. More fool's gold, you think.

Fool's gold is the nickname for iron pyrite (PIE RIET), a mineral that looks like gold. But iron pyrite differs from gold in several ways. When hit with a hammer, iron pyrite shatters, and sparks fly everywhere. Gold just bends when it is hit, and no sparks are produced. Iron pyrite also produces foul-smelling smoke when it is heated. Gold does not.

Can You Tell the Difference?
One of these rocks contains valuable gold. The other rock contains iron pyrite that is worth . . . well, nothing.

You decide to test your shiny find. When you hit it with a hammer, it bends but does not shatter, and no sparks are produced. When you heat it, there is no smoke or odor. You'll have to perform a few more tests, but this time you're almost certain that you've struck gold. Congratulations! Your knowledge of the different properties of fool's gold and real gold may finally pay off.

In this chapter you'll learn more about the many different properties that objects can have and why they are important.

Imagine . . .

Gold is an element. It was one of the first metals used because it is found in nature in an uncombined state as gold nuggets. Iron pyrite, FeS_2, is a compound of sulfur, S, and the metal iron, Fe. Every type of matter has the physical and chemical properties discussed in this chapter.

When iron pyrite is heated, FeS_2 combines with O_2 in the air and produces a foul-smelling gas. Every substance has a unique set of characteristics that allows us to recognize it and distinguish it from other substances.

What Do You Think?

In your ScienceLog, try to answer the following questions based on what you already know:

1. What is matter?
2. What is the difference between a physical property and a chemical property?
3. What is the difference between a physical change and a chemical change?

Analysis

3. At the end of 5 minutes, take a couple of minutes to discuss your findings with your partners.
4. With your partners, list the object's properties, and make a conclusion about the object's identity. Write your conclusion in your ScienceLog.
5. Share your observations, list of properties, and conclusion with the class. Now you are ready to open the sack.
6. Did you properly identify the object? If so, how? If not, why not? Write your answers in your ScienceLog, and share them with the class.

Sack Secrets

In this activity, you will test your skills in determining the identity of an object based on its properties.

Procedure

1. You and two or three of your classmates will receive a **sealed paper sack** with a number on it. Write the number in your ScienceLog. Inside the sack is a **mystery object**. Do not open the sack!
2. For 5 minutes, make as many observations as you can about the object. You may shake the sack, touch the object through the sack, listen to the object in the sack, smell the object through the sack, and so on. Be sure to write down your observations.

What Do You Think?

Accept all reasonable responses.

Students will have a chance to revise their answers in the Chapter Review under NOW What Do You Think?

Investigate!

MATERIALS

FOR EACH GROUP:
Anything that fits in the sack can be used for the object. Objects with interesting shapes, odors, and textures are preferable. Some objects to consider are a rubber ball, a jack, a pink school eraser, a piece of chalk, an orange, and a potato. Almost anything that is not sharp, corrosive, or prone to spoilage will work. Giving each group a different object will add to the mystery.

Answer to Investigate!

6. Students may or may not be able to identify the object, but their observations should demonstrate an attempt to identify various properties of the object, such as mass, shape, sound when shaken, and so on.

IS THAT A FACT!

The average human nose can recognize about 10,000 different smells.

SECTION 1

Focus

What Is Matter?

This section explains that matter is anything that has volume and mass. Students explore how the volume of solids, liquids, and gases are measured. Students learn the difference between mass and weight and learn how both are measured. Finally, students learn about inertia.

Ask students to list in their ScienceLog what they think some of the components might be for the following items:

loaf of bread, textbook, bicycle

Discuss the variety of answers students come up with.

1 Motivate

DEMONSTRATION

Display the following objects for students to view:

a rock, a paper clip, a book, a pencil, and a large cardboard box

Point out that the objects are alike because they all take up space. Discuss with students which objects are largest and smallest, and what those terms mean. Then discuss the connection between "taking up space" and volume. This is what makes the game of musical chairs so much fun. Point out that the amount of space something takes up is its volume.

Sheltered English

Section 1

Terms to Learn

matter   gravity
volume   weight
meniscus newton
mass   inertia

What You'll Do

◆ Name the two properties of all matter.
◆ Describe how volume and mass are measured.
◆ Compare mass and weight.
◆ Explain the relationship between mass and inertia.

QuickLab

Space Case

1. Crumple a **piece of paper**, and fit it tightly in the bottom of a **cup** so that it won't fall out.
2. Turn the cup upside down. Lower the cup straight down into a **large beaker or bucket** half-filled with **water** until the cup is all the way underwater.
3. Lift the cup straight out of the water. Turn the cup upright and observe the paper. Record your observations in your ScienceLog.
4. Now punch a small hole in the bottom of the cup with the point of a **pencil.** Repeat steps 2 and 3.
5. How do these results show that air has volume? Record your explanation in your ScienceLog.

QuickLab

MATERIALS

FOR EACH STUDENT:
• piece of paper
• cup

FOR EACH GROUP:
• large beaker or bucket
• water
• pencil

What Is Matter?

Here's a strange question: What do you have in common with a toaster?

Give up? Okay, here's another question: What do you have in common with a steaming bowl of soup or a bright neon sign?

You are probably thinking these are trick questions. After all, it is hard to imagine that a human—you—has anything in common with a kitchen appliance, some hot soup, or a glowing neon sign.

Everything Is Made of Matter

From a scientific point of view you have at least one characteristic in common with these things. You, the toaster, the bowl, the soup, the steam, the glass tubing, and the glowing gas are all made of matter. But what is matter exactly? If so many different kinds of things are made of matter, you might expect the definition of the word *matter* to be complicated. But it is really quite simple. **Matter** is anything that has volume and mass.

Matter Has Volume

All matter takes up space. The amount of space taken up, or occupied, by an object is known as the object's **volume.** The sun, shown in **Figure 1,** has volume because it takes up space at the center of our solar system. Your fingernails, the Statue of Liberty, the continent of Africa, and a cloud all have volume. And because these things have volume, they cannot share the same space at the same time. Even the tiniest speck of dust takes up space, and there's no way another speck of dust can fit into that space without somehow bumping the first speck out of the way. Try the QuickLab on this page to see for yourself that matter takes up space.

Figure 1 *The volume of the sun is about 1,000,000 (1 million) times larger than the volume of the Earth.*

4. **Teacher Notes:** Students can feel the air being "moved out of the way" by the water if they hold a finger above the hole while they submerge the cup.

Answer to QuickLab

5. The water could not enter the cup because air occupied the space. Once the hole was punched, the water could force the air out of the cup and occupy the space in the cup.

36 Chapter 2 • The Properties of Matter

Liquid Volume Lake Erie, the smallest of the Great Lakes, has a volume of approximately 483,000,000,000,000 (483 trillion) liters of water. Can you imagine that much liquid? Well, think of a 2 liter bottle of soda. The water in Lake Erie could fill more than 241 trillion of those bottles. That's a lot of water! On a smaller scale, a can of soda has a volume of only 355 milliliters, which is approximately one-third of a liter. You can read the volume printed on the soda can. Or you can check the volume by pouring the soda into a large measuring cup from your kitchen, as shown in **Figure 2**.

Figure 2 *If the measurement is accurate, the volume measured should be the same as the volume printed on the can.*

Measuring the Volume of Liquids In your science class, you'll probably use a graduated cylinder to measure the volume of liquids. Keep in mind that the surface of a liquid in a graduated cylinder is not flat. The curve that you see at the liquid's surface has a special name—the **meniscus** (muh NIS kuhs). When you measure the volume of a liquid, you must look at the bottom of the meniscus, as shown in **Figure 3**. (A liquid in any container, including a measuring cup or a large beaker, has a meniscus. The meniscus is just too flat to see in a wider container.)

Liters (L) and milliliters (mL) are the units used most often to express the volume of liquids. The volume of any amount of liquid, from one raindrop to a can of soda to an entire ocean, can be expressed in these units.

Figure 3 *To measure volume correctly, read the scale at the lowest part of the meniscus (as indicated) at eye level.*

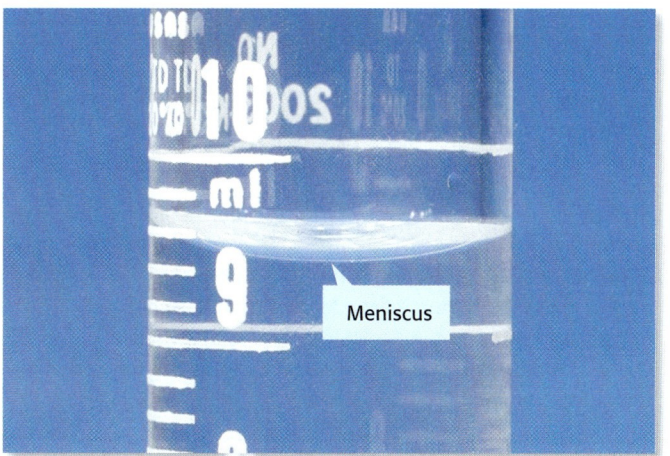

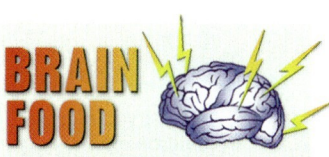

BRAIN FOOD

The volume of a typical raindrop is approximately 0.09 mL, which means that it would take almost 4,000 raindrops to fill a soda can.

2 Teach

READING STRATEGY

Prediction Guide Before students read the next four pages, ask them whether these statements are true or false.

- The volume of a gas can be measured with a graduated cylinder. (false)
- If you know the volume of the container a gas is in, you know the volume of the gas. (true)
- Volumes of solids can be expressed in liters or milliliters. (false)
- Weight and mass are the same thing. (false)

GROUP ACTIVITY

Provide small groups with a variety of jars, bottles, cans, and cartons. Allow students to use a measuring cup or a graduated cylinder to determine the volume of each container. A volume reading is always made at the flattest part of the meniscus—the bottom of the curve for water and the top for mercury.

DISCUSSION

Discuss with students the fact that we are surrounded by matter. Have students give examples of matter around them. Ask them to list some characteristics of matter. Discuss with them the notion that they are actually pushing air aside as they walk "through" it.

CROSS-DISCIPLINARY FOCUS

Music Provide each small group with several identical glass containers. Tell students to add a different amount of water to each container, then lightly strike each container with a pen to hear the pitch of the sound it makes. Ask students to arrange the containers in order from the lowest pitch to highest pitch. Finally, have students measure the volume of water in each container, and ask them to determine the relationship between pitch and the volume of water. **Sheltered English**

② Teach, continued

MATH and MORE

In 1997 Americans consumed an average of 204 L of soft drinks per person. How many cans of soft drinks would that be? Assume that a can holds 355 mL and remember that 1 L = 1,000 mL. **(more than 574 cans)**

The total volume of soft drinks consumed by Americans in 1997 was approximately 53 billion liters. How many cans of soft drinks would that be? **(more than 149 billion cans)**

Math Skills Worksheet 31 "The Unit Factor and Dimensional Analysis"

Answers to MATHBREAK

1. 1,800 cm^3
2. 95,000 cm^3, or 0.095 m^3
3. Answers will vary with the objects chosen. Students should show the units in each measurement and in the final answer.

Volumania! PG 630

DEMONSTRATION

Display a variety of classroom objects, such as pencils, books, and notebook paper. Ask students which objects contain the largest amount of matter and thus have the greatest mass. Then ask which contain the smallest amount of matter and thus have the smallest mass. Ask them if the objects with the greatest volume always have the most mass. **Sheltered English**

MATH BREAK

Calculating Volume

A typical compact disc (CD) case has a length of 14.2 cm, a width of 12.4 cm, and a height of 1.0 cm. The volume of the case is the length multiplied by the width multiplied by the height:

14.2 cm × 12.4 cm × 1.0 cm = 176.1 cm^3

Now It's Your Turn

1. A book has a length of 25 cm, a width of 18 cm, and a height of 4 cm. What is its volume?
2. What is the volume of a suitcase with a length of 95 cm, a width of 50 cm, and a height of 20 cm?
3. For additional practice, find the volume of other objects that have square or rectangular sides. Compare your results with those of your classmates.

How would you measure the volume of this strangely shaped object? To find out, turn to page 630 in the LabBook.

MISCONCEPTION ALERT

Students may not understand that a gas not only will expand to fill its container but also can be compressed, or squeezed, to fill a smaller container. Scuba divers' tanks contain compressed air. A 2.24 m^3 scuba tank holds enough air for an average adult to breathe underwater for 30 to 45 minutes.

Solid Volume The volume of any solid object is expressed in cubic units. *Cubic* means "having three dimensions." One cubic unit, a cubic meter, is shown in **Figure 4**. In science, cubic meters (m^3) and cubic centimeters (cm^3) are the units most often used to express the volume of solid items. The 3 in these unit abbreviations shows that three quantities were multiplied to get the final result. For a rectangular object, these three quantities are length, width, and height. Try this for yourself in the MathBreak at left.

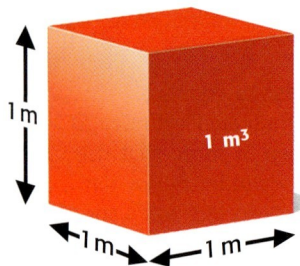
Figure 4 A cubic meter has a height of 1 m, a length of 1 m, and a width of 1 m, so its volume is 1 m × 1 m × 1 m = 1 m^3.

Comparing Solid and Liquid Volumes Suppose you want to determine whether the volume of an ice cube is equal to the volume of water that is left when the ice cube melts. Because 1 mL is equal to 1 cm^3, you can express the volume of the water in cubic centimeters and compare it with the volume of the ice cube. The volume of any liquid can be expressed in cubic units in this way. (However, in SI, volumes of solids are never expressed in liters or milliliters.)

Measuring the Volume of Gases How do you measure the volume of a gas? You can't hold a ruler up to a gas, and you can't pour a gas into a graduated cylinder. So it's impossible, right? Wrong! A gas expands to fill its container, so if you know the volume of the container the gas is in, then you know the volume of the gas.

Matter Has Mass

Another characteristic of all matter is mass. **Mass** is the amount of matter that something is made of. For example, the Earth is made of a very large amount of matter and therefore has a large mass. A peanut is made of a much smaller amount of matter and thus has a smaller mass. Remember, even something as small as a speck of dust is made of matter and therefore has mass.

WEIRD SCIENCE

Mauna Loa, in Hawaii, is the world's most active volcano. The volume of lava that has flowed from the volcano is enough to pave a four-lane highway that reaches around the world 30 times.

Is a Puppy Like a Bowling Ball? An object's mass can be changed only by changing the amount of matter in the object. Consider the bowling ball shown in **Figure 5.** Its mass is constant because the amount of matter in the bowling ball never changes (unless you use a sledgehammer to remove a chunk of it!). Now consider the puppy. Does its mass remain constant? No, because the puppy is growing. If you measured the puppy's mass next year or even next week, you'd find that it had increased. That's because more matter—more puppy—would be present.

Figure 5 The mass of the bowling ball does not change. The mass of the puppy increases as more matter is added—that is, as the puppy grows.

The Difference Between Mass and Weight

Weight is different from mass. To understand this difference, you must first understand gravity. **Gravity** is a force of attraction between objects that is due to their masses. This attraction causes objects to exert a pull on other objects. Because all matter has mass, all matter experiences gravity. The amount of attraction between objects depends on two things—the masses of the objects and the distance between them, as shown in **Figure 6.**

Figure 6 How Mass and Distance Affect Gravity Between Objects

a Gravitational force (represented by the width of the arrows) is large between objects with large masses that are close together.

b Gravitational force is smaller between objects with smaller masses that are close together than between objects with large masses that are close together (as shown in **a**).

c An increase in distance reduces gravitational force between two objects. Therefore, gravitational force between objects with large masses (such as those in **a**) is less if they are far apart.

Activity

Imagine the following items resting side by side on a table: an elephant, a tennis ball, a peanut, a bowling ball, and a housefly. In your ScienceLog, list these items in order of their attraction to the Earth due to gravity, from least to greatest amount of attraction. Follow your list with an explanation of why you arranged the items in the order that you did.

TRY at HOME

Science Bloopers

In July 1983, an Air Canada Boeing 767 airliner with 69 people on board ran out of fuel in mid-flight. Before leaving their previous stop, the crew had calculated that they had enough fuel to make it to their final destination. However, the plane's crew miscalculated the mass of the fuel because they had used the wrong units; they used pounds instead of kilograms! Fortunately, the plane was able to make a safe landing at an abandoned air force base in Manitoba, Canada.

2) Teach, continued

CONNECT TO LIFE SCIENCE

Although calcium makes up about 70 percent of the mass of the human skeleton, it is not the most abundant substance in the human body. The majority of the human body—between 70 and 80 percent—is composed of water.

RETEACHING

The gravitational force exerted on an astronaut on the moon is one-sixth that exerted on the astronaut by the Earth. Ask students to compare the mass and weight of an astronaut on Earth with the mass and weight of the astronaut on the moon. **(The astronaut's mass would not change at all. The astronaut's weight would be only one-sixth his or her weight on Earth.)**

GUIDED PRACTICE

Writing Ask students to write a paragraph or make a poster explaining how the weight of an object can change even though its mass does not change.

Teacher Notes: An object at sea level may weigh more than it would high above sea level, but the difference would be very small. For all practical purposes, mass and weight remain constant everywhere on Earth.

Biology CONNECTION

The mineral calcium is stored in bones, and it accounts for about 70 percent of the mass of the human skeleton. Calcium strengthens bones, helping the skeleton to remain upright against the strong force of gravity pulling it toward the Earth.

Figure 7 *This brick and sponge may be the same size, but their masses, and therefore their weights, are quite different.*

May the Force Be with You Gravitational force is experienced by all objects in the universe all the time. But the ordinary objects you see every day have masses so small (relative to, say, planets) that their attraction toward each other is hard to detect. Therefore, the gravitational force experienced by objects with small masses is very slight. However, the Earth's mass is so large that the gravitational force between objects, such as our atmosphere or the space shuttle, and the Earth is great. Gravitational force is what keeps you and everything else on Earth from floating into space.

So What About Weight? A measure of the gravitational force exerted on an object is called **weight**. Consider the brick in **Figure 7**. The brick has mass. The Earth also has mass. Therefore, the brick and the Earth are attracted to each other. A force is exerted on the brick because of its attraction to the Earth. The weight of the brick is a measure of this gravitational force.

Now look at the sponge in Figure 7. The sponge is the same size as the brick, but its mass is much less. Therefore, the sponge's attraction toward the Earth is not as great, and the gravitational force on the sponge is not as great. Thus, the *weight* of the sponge is less than the *weight* of the brick.

At a Distance The attraction between objects decreases as the distance between them increases. As a result, the gravitational force exerted on objects also decreases as the distance increases. For this reason, a brick floating in space would weigh less than it does resting on Earth's surface. However, the brick's mass would stay the same.

Massive Confusion Back on Earth, the gravitational force exerted on an object is about the same everywhere, so an object's weight is also about the same everywhere. Because mass and weight remain constant everywhere on Earth, the terms *mass* and *weight* are often used as though they mean the same thing. But using the terms interchangeably can lead to confusion. So remember, weight depends on mass, but weight is not the same thing as mass.

WEIRD SCIENCE

In 1993, while on its way to Jupiter, the *Galileo* spacecraft passed close enough to asteroid 243 to photograph it. This asteroid, named Ida, is approximately 52 × 24 × 21 km. When scientists analyzed the photo from *Galileo*, they noticed that Ida had a small moon circling it. The moon, which is approximately 1.5 km in diameter, is held in orbit by Ida's gravitational force.

Measuring Mass and Weight

The SI unit of mass is the kilogram (kg), but mass is often expressed in grams (g) and milligrams (mg) as well. These units can be used to express the mass of any object, from a single cell in your body to the entire solar system. Weight is a measure of gravitational force and must be expressed in units of force. The SI unit of force is the **newton (N).** So weight is expressed in newtons.

A newton is approximately equal to the weight of a 100 g mass on Earth. So if you know the mass of an object, you can calculate its weight on Earth. Conversely, if you know the weight of an object on Earth, you can determine its mass. **Figure 8** summarizes the differences between mass and weight.

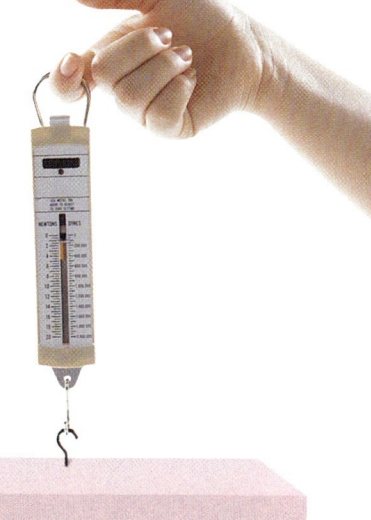

Figure 8 Differences Between Mass and Weight

Mass is . . .
- a measure of the amount of matter in an object.
- always constant for an object no matter where the object is in the universe.
- measured with a balance (shown below).
- expressed in kilograms (kg), grams (g), and milligrams (mg).

Weight is . . .
- a measure of the gravitational force on an object.
- varied depending on where the object is in relation to the Earth (or any other large body in the universe).
- measured with a spring scale (shown above).
- expressed in newtons (N).

Self-Check

If all of your school books combined have a mass of 3 kg, what is their total weight in newtons? Remember that 1 kg = 1,000 g. (See page 724 to check your answer.)

Scientists at Odds

The official standard kilogram is a cylinder made of platinum-iridium alloy. The mass of the cylinder is supposed to equal the mass of 1 dL^3 of pure water at 4°C. Some scientists believe that this cylinder is imprecise and needs to be changed. In fact, the kilogram is the only SI unit based on a single physical standard that can be destroyed or altered. Some scientists now suggest redefining the kilogram as the mass of an exact number of atoms of a particular element.

---

3) Extend

Multicultural CONNECTION

Cultures throughout history have developed different units to express mass, volume, and weight. Have students make a poster that shows or describes the units of measurement used by a particular culture.

Research

 Have students research the different kinds of instruments used to measure mass and weight. Have students draw or diagram an instrument and explain how it works. Sheltered English

Meeting Individual Needs

Students Having Difficulty
Rather than having students explain how volume, weight, and mass are measured, have them demonstrate the concepts. Provide them with instruments such as graduated cylinders and triple-beam balances. Have them explain step-by-step how to measure the volume and the mass of a given substance. Provide students with spring scales, and help them observe the difference between mass and weight.

Answer to Self-Check
approximately 30 N

 **Teaching Transparency 204**
"Differences Between Mass and Weight"

 Science Skills Worksheet 15
"Measuring"

Section 1 • What Is Matter?

4) Close

Answer to APPLY
A spring scale is used to measure weight, and the pound is a unit of weight. The kilogram, however, is a unit of mass. Having both units on the scale leads people to use them interchangeably.

Quiz
Allow students to use a balance and a spring scale to compare the masses and the weights of a variety of small objects, such as a stone, a marble, a washer, and a nail.

ALTERNATIVE ASSESSMENT
Writing Have students write a short science-fiction story in which matter does not behave in the ways described in this section. Ask them to consider what life would be like in this kind of universe. Some examples: a universe where gravity does not exist; a universe where objects repulse rather than attract one another; a universe where inertia becomes greater as mass decreases. Ask volunteers to share their stories with the class.

INDEPENDENT PRACTICE
Concept Mapping Have each student make a concept map comparing a golf ball with a table-tennis ball. Tell students they must use the terms *matter*, *mass*, *volume*, *weight*, and *inertia* in their map.

TOPIC: What Is Matter?
GO TO: www.scilinks.org
*sci*LINKS NUMBER: HSTP030

Mass, Weight, and Bathroom Scales
Ordinary bathroom scales are spring scales. Many scales available today show a reading in both pounds (a common, though not SI, unit of weight) and kilograms. How does such a reading contribute to the confusion between mass and weight?

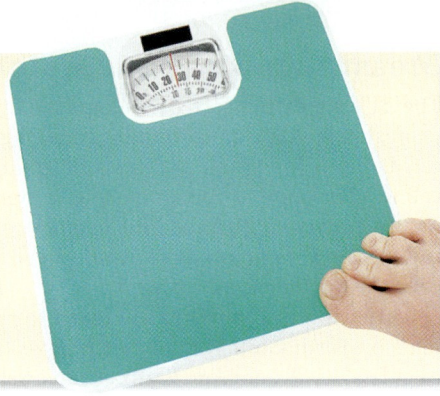

Mass Is a Measure of Inertia

Imagine trying to kick a soccer ball that has the mass of a bowling ball. It would be painful! The reason has to do with inertia (in UHR shuh). **Inertia** is the tendency of all objects to resist any change in motion. Because of inertia, an object at rest will remain at rest until something causes it to move. Likewise, a moving object continues to move at the same speed and in the same direction unless something acts on it to change its speed or direction.

Mass is a measure of inertia because an object with a large mass is harder to start in motion and harder to stop than an object with a smaller mass. This is because the object with the large mass has greater inertia. For example, imagine that you are going to push a grocery cart that has only one potato in it. No problem, right? But suppose the grocery cart is filled with potatoes, as in **Figure 9.** Now the total mass—and the inertia—of the cart full of potatoes is much greater. It will be harder to get the cart moving and harder to stop it once it is moving.

Figure 9 *Why is a cartload of potatoes harder to get moving than a single potato? Because of inertia, that's why!*

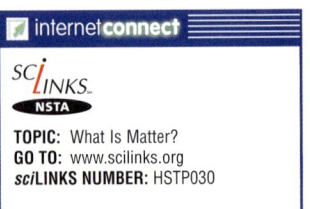
TOPIC: What Is Matter?
GO TO: www.scilinks.org
*sci*LINKS NUMBER: HSTP030

REVIEW
1. What are the two properties of all matter?
2. How is volume measured? How is mass measured?
3. **Analyzing Relationships** Do objects with large masses always have large weights? Explain your reasoning.

Answers to Review
1. All matter has mass and volume.
2. Volumes of liquids are measured with graduated cylinders and are expressed in liters and milliliters. Volumes of rectangular solids are calculated by multiplying length, width, and height measurements and are expressed in cubic units, such as m^3 or cm^3. Mass is measured with a balance and is expressed in kilograms, grams, and milligrams.
3. Not all objects with large masses have large weights because the weight of an object can change depending on where it is located in the universe. Mass remains the same everywhere in the universe. So a massive object in space may not have a large weight.

Section 2

Describing Matter

Terms to Learn

physical property physical change
density chemical change
chemical property

What You'll Do

◆ Give examples of matter's different properties.
◆ Describe how density is used to identify different substances.
◆ Compare physical and chemical properties.
◆ Explain what happens to matter during physical and chemical changes.

Have you ever heard of the game called "20 Questions"? In this game, your goal is to determine the identity of an object that another person is thinking of by asking questions about the object. The other person can respond with only a "yes" or a "no." If you can identify the object after asking 20 or fewer questions, you win! If you still can't figure out the object's identity after asking 20 questions, you may not be asking the right kinds of questions.

What kinds of questions should you ask? You might find it helpful to ask questions about the properties of the object. Knowing the properties of an object can help you determine the object's identity, as shown below.

Activity

With a partner, play a game of 20 Questions. One person will think of an object, and the other person will ask yes/no questions about it. Write the questions in your ScienceLog as you go along. Put a check mark next to the questions asked about physical properties. When the object is identified or when the 20 questions are up, switch roles. Good luck!

Physical Properties

Some of the questions shown above help the asker gather information about *color* (Is it orange?), *odor* (Does it have an odor?), and *mass* and *volume* (Could I hold it in my hand?). Each of these properties is a physical property of matter. A **physical property** of matter can be observed or measured without changing the identity of the matter. For example, you don't have to change what the apple is made of to see that it is red or to hold it in your hand.

IS THAT A FACT!

The element bromine gets its name from the Greek word *bromos*, which means "stench" or "bad smell."

SECTION 2

Focus

Describing Matter

This section introduces students to the properties of matter and compares physical properties and chemical properties of substances. It also explains how density is used to identify different substances. The section concludes with an explanation of what happens to matter during physical and chemical changes.

🔔 Bellringer

Ask your students the following question:

If you were asked to describe an orange to someone who had never seen an orange, what would you tell the person?

Write your description in your ScienceLog.

1) Motivate

DEMONSTRATION

Display several objects that have differences in color, odor, texture, size, shape, and state. Allow students to examine the objects. Then ask them to describe each object in terms of its color, odor, texture, size, shape, and state. Ask students why it is important to describe objects using a variety of properties.

Directed Reading Worksheet 2 Section 2

Section 2 • Describing Matter 43

2) Teach

DISCUSSION

Draw students' attention to the chart of physical properties. After reading through the definition and example of each property, ask volunteers to give another example of the same property.

REAL-WORLD CONNECTION

Electronic coin testers in vending machines can instantly identify the properties of real coins and reject fake coins. First, an electric current passes through the coin to measure its metal content and size. Only proper coins conduct the right amount of electricity. Next a magnet and light sensors are used to detect the coin's value. Incorrect coins are rejected.

Homework

Writing Have students write a description of the properties of a favorite object from home, such as a bicycle, a pet, a type of food, or an article of clothing. Let students read their description aloud, and have other class members try to guess the object being described. Sheltered English

LabBook PG 632
Determining Density

Physical Properties Identify Matter You rely on physical properties all the time. For example, physical properties help you determine whether your socks are clean (odor), whether you can fit all your books into your backpack (volume), or whether your shirt matches your pants (color). The table below lists some more physical properties that are useful in describing or identifying matter.

More Physical Properties		
Physical property	**Definition**	**Example**
Thermal conductivity	the ability to transfer thermal energy from one area to another	Plastic foam is a poor conductor, so hot chocolate in a plastic-foam cup will not burn your hand.
State	the physical form in which a substance exists, such as a solid, liquid, or gas	Ice is water in its solid state.
Malleability (MAL ee uh BIL uh tee)	the ability to be pounded into thin sheets	Aluminum can be rolled or pounded into sheets to make foil.
Ductility (duhk TIL uh tee)	the ability to be drawn or pulled into a wire	Copper is often used to make wiring.
Solubility (SAHL yoo BIL uh tee)	the ability to dissolve in another substance	Sugar dissolves in water.
Density	mass per unit volume	Lead is used to make sinkers for fishing line because lead is more dense than water.

Figure 10 *A golf ball is more dense than a table-tennis ball because the golf ball contains more matter in a similar volume.*

Spotlight on Density Density is a very helpful property when you need to distinguish different substances. Look at the definition of density in the table above—mass per unit volume. If you think back to what you learned in Section 1, you can define density in other terms: **density** is the amount of matter in a given space, or volume, as shown in **Figure 10.**

Two fish swim by a fisherman's baited hook. One fish says to the other, "You know, I never could figure out why those worms always go swimming with lead weights tied around their necks."

The other fish replies, "Yeah, they must be pretty dense."

44 Chapter 2 • The Properties of Matter

To find an object's density (D), first measure its mass (m) and volume (V). Then use the following equation:

$$D = \frac{m}{V}$$

Units for density are expressed using a mass unit divided by a volume unit, such as g/cm^3, g/mL, kg/m^3, and kg/L.

Using Density to Identify Substances Density is a useful property for identifying substances for two reasons. First, the density of a particular substance is always the same at a given pressure and temperature. For example, the helium in a huge airship has a density of $0.0001663\ g/cm^3$ at 20°C and normal atmospheric pressure. You can calculate the density of any other sample of helium at that same temperature and pressure—even the helium in a small balloon—and you will get $0.0001663\ g/cm^3$. Second, the density of one substance is usually different from that of another substance. Check out the table below to see how density varies among substances.

Densities of Common Substances*

Substance	Density (g/cm^3)	Substance	Density (g/cm^3)
Helium (gas)	0.0001663	Copper (solid)	8.96
Oxygen (gas)	0.001331	Silver (solid)	10.50
Water (liquid)	1.00	Lead (solid)	11.35
Iron pyrite (solid)	5.02	Mercury (liquid)	13.55
Zinc (solid)	7.13	Gold (solid)	19.32

* at 20°C and normal atmospheric pressure

Mass = 96.6 g
Volume = 5.0 cm³

Do you remember your imaginary attempt at gold prospecting? To make sure you hadn't found more fool's gold (iron pyrite), you could compare the density of a nugget from your sample, shown in **Figure 11**, with the known densities for gold and iron pyrite at the same temperature and pressure. By comparing densities, you'd know whether you'd actually struck gold or been fooled again.

Figure 11 Did you find gold or fool's gold?

MATH BREAK

Density

You can rearrange the equation for density to find mass and volume as shown below:

$$D = \frac{m}{V}$$
$$m = D \times V \qquad V = \frac{m}{D}$$

1. Find the density of a substance with a mass of 5 kg and a volume of 43 m³.
2. Suppose you have a lead ball with a mass of 454 g. What is its volume? (Hint: Use the table at left.)
3. What is the mass of a 15 mL sample of mercury? (Hint: Use the table at left.)

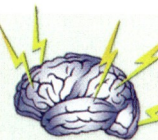

Pennies minted before 1982 are made mostly of copper and have a density of $8.85\ g/cm^3$. In 1982, a penny's worth of copper began to cost more than one cent, so the U.S. Department of the Treasury began producing pennies using mostly zinc with a copper coating. Pennies minted after 1982 have a density of $7.14\ g/cm^3$. Check it out for yourself!

IS THAT A FACT!

The density of a fresh egg is about 1.2 g/mL, while the density of a spoiled egg is about 0.9 g/mL. So don't eat an egg that floats. It's spoiled!

WEIRD SCIENCE

At one time, a person who was suspected of being a witch was tossed into a lake. It was believed that a witch would float, while a person who was not a witch would sink.

MATH and MORE

Ask students to use the equation for density to solve the following problems.

1. A block of pine wood has a mass of 120 g and a volume of 300 cm³. What is the density of the wood? (0.4 g/cm³)

   Extension Ask students to predict whether this block of pine would float in a pool of water. Why? (Yes; it is less dense than water.)

2. A sample of metal has a mass of 4,059 g and a volume of 453 cm³. What metal is it? (copper)

 Math Skills Worksheet 32 "Density"

Answers to MATHBREAK

1. $D = \frac{m}{V}$, so $D = \frac{5\ kg}{43\ m^3} = 0.12\ kg/m^3$

2. $V = \frac{m}{D}$, so $V = \frac{454 g}{11.35 g/cm^3} = 40\ cm^3$ (Students must use the density of lead from the table on this page.)

3. $m = D \times V$, so $m = 13.55\ g/mL \times 15\ mL = 203\ g$ (Students must use the density of mercury from the table on this page.)

MISCONCEPTION ALERT

The density of a substance changes as temperature and pressure change. This is especially true at the point at which a substance changes state. Remind students that densities such as those listed in the table on this page are valid only at the given temperature and pressure.

Section 2 • Describing Matter

Figure 12 *The yellow liquid is the least dense, and the green liquid is the densest.*

Liquid Layers What do you think causes the liquid in **Figure 12** to look the way it does? Is it magic? Is it trick photography? No, it's differences in density! There are actually four different liquids in the jar. Each liquid has a different density. Because of these differences in density, the liquids do not mix together but instead separate into layers, with the densest layer on the bottom and the least dense layer on top. The order in which the layers separate helps you determine how the densities of the liquids compare with one another.

The Density Challenge Imagine that you could put a lid on the jar in the picture and shake up the liquids. Would the different liquids mix together so that the four colors would blend into one interesting color? Maybe for a minute or two. But if the liquids are not soluble in one another, they would start to separate, and eventually you'd end up with the same four layers.

The same thing happens when you mix oil and vinegar to make salad dressing. When the layers separate, the oil is on top. But what do you think would happen if you added more oil? What if you added so much oil that there was several times as much oil as there was vinegar? Surely the oil would get so heavy that it would sink below the vinegar, right? Wrong! No matter how much oil you have, it will always be less dense than the vinegar, so it will always rise to the top. The same is true of the four liquids shown in Figure 12. Even if you add more yellow liquid than all of the other liquids combined, all of the yellow liquid will rise to the top. That's because density does not depend on how much of a substance you have.

APPLY

Density and Grease Separators

The grease separator shown here is a kitchen device that cooks use to collect the best meat juices for making gravies. Based on what you know about density, describe how a grease separator works. Be sure to explain why the spout is at the bottom.

REVIEW

1. List three physical properties of water.
2. Why does a golf ball feel heavier than a table-tennis ball?
3. Describe how you can determine the relative densities of liquids.
4. **Applying Concepts** How could you determine that a coin is not pure silver?

Chemical Properties

Physical properties are not the only properties that describe matter. **Chemical properties** describe a substance based on its ability to change into a new substance with different properties. For example, a piece of wood can be burned to create new substances (ash and smoke) with properties different from the original piece of wood. Wood has the chemical property of *flammability*—the ability to burn. A substance that does not burn, such as gold, has the chemical property of nonflammability. Other common chemical properties include reactivity with oxygen, reactivity with acid, and reactivity with water. (The word *reactivity* just means that when two substances get together, something can happen.)

Observing Chemical Properties Chemical properties can be observed with your senses. However, chemical properties aren't as easy to observe as physical properties. For example, you can observe the flammability of wood only while the wood is burning. Likewise, you can observe the nonflammability of gold only when you try to burn it and it won't burn. But a substance always has its chemical properties. A piece of wood is flammable even when it's not burning.

Some Chemical Properties of Car Maintenance Look at the old car shown in **Figure 13.** Its owner calls it Rust Bucket. Why has this car rusted so badly while some other cars the same age remain in great shape? Knowing about chemical properties can help answer this question.

Most car bodies are made from steel, which is mostly iron. Iron has many desirable physical properties, including strength, malleability, and a high melting point. Iron also has many desirable chemical properties, including nonreactivity with oil and gasoline. All in all, steel is a good material to use for car bodies. It's not perfect, however, as you can probably tell from the car shown here.

Paint doesn't react with oxygen, so it provides a barrier between oxygen and the iron in the steel.

This hole started as a small chip in the paint. The chip exposed the iron in the car's body to oxygen. The iron rusted and eventually crumbled away.

This bumper is rust free because it is coated with a barrier of chromium, which is nonreactive with oxygen.

Figure 13 **Rust Bucket**
One unfavorable chemical property of iron is its reactivity with oxygen. When iron is exposed to oxygen, it rusts.

READING STRATEGY

Prediction Guide Before students read this page, ask them:

What is one unfavorable chemical property of iron?
- **a.** its high melting point
- **b.** its nonreactivity with oil and gasoline
- **c.** its reactivity with oxygen
- **d.** its nonflammability

(c)

GUIDED PRACTICE

Show students a sheet of paper, and ask them to write a list of the physical and chemical properties of paper. (physical properties: white color, smooth texture, no odor; chemical properties: flammability)

DISCUSSION

After students have studied the picture of the car, have them describe where they have seen other examples of rusting.
Sheltered English

REAL-WORLD CONNECTION

Rustproofing is one way to help protect cars from rust. The process involves treating the car's underside and panels—such as the doors, the trunk, and the hood—with sealants. The sealants penetrate all the seams, cracks, and holes to keep out air and moisture, which can increase the rate at which rust forms.

Science Bloopers

In 1870, John and Isaiah Hyatt patented a plastic they called celluloid. It was to be used as a substitute for the ivory used in billiard balls. Unfortunately, one of the chemicals in celluloid was explosive, and billiard balls made from the Hyatt brothers' celluloid often blew up when struck with a pool cue.

IS THAT A FACT!

Galvanized steel is steel that is coated with zinc to prevent rusting. It is used in buckets and nails. And steel plated with tin was used in food cans and containers. Today, aluminum cans have replaced most steel cans.

Figure 14 Substances have different physical and chemical properties.

Physical Vs. Chemical Properties

You can describe matter by both physical and chemical properties. The properties that are most useful in identifying a substance, such as density, solubility, and reactivity with acids, are its characteristic properties. The *characteristic properties* of a substance are always the same whether the sample you're observing is large or small. Scientists rely on characteristic properties to identify and classify substances. **Figure 14** describes some physical and chemical properties.

It is important to remember the differences between physical and chemical properties. For example, you can observe physical properties without changing the identity of the substance. You can observe chemical properties only in situations in which the identity of the substance could change.

a Helium is used in airships because it is less dense than air and is nonflammable.

b If you add bleach to water that is mixed with red food coloring, the red color will disappear.

Comparing Physical and Chemical Properties		
Substance	Physical property	Chemical property
Helium	less dense than air	nonflammable
Wood	grainy texture	flammable
Baking soda	white powder	reacts with vinegar to produce bubbles
Powdered sugar	white powder	does not react with vinegar
Rubbing alcohol	clear liquid	flammable
Red food coloring	red color	reacts with bleach and loses color
Iron	malleable	reacts with oxygen

Physical Changes Don't Form New Substances

A **physical change** is a change that affects one or more physical properties of a substance. For example, if you break a piece of chalk in two, you change its physical properties of size and shape. But no matter how many times you break it, chalk is still chalk. The chemical properties of the chalk remain unchanged. Each piece of chalk would still produce bubbles if you placed it in vinegar.

Science Bloopers

The German zeppelin *Hindenburg*, which was filled with hydrogen, caught fire upon landing in 1937. The entire airship was engulfed in an orange fireball and burned in less than 32 seconds. For decades, most people believed the fire started when a spark ignited the flammable hydrogen. But hydrogen burns with a near-colorless flame, not an orange one. Scientists now think that the spark actually ignited the airship's highly flammable outer covering.

Examples of Physical Changes Melting is a good example of a physical change, as you can see in **Figure 15.** Still another physical change occurs when a substance dissolves into another substance. If you dissolve sugar in water, the sugar seems to disappear into the water. But the identity of the sugar does not change. If you taste the water, you will also still taste the sugar. The sugar has undergone a physical change. See the chart below for more examples of physical changes.

Figure 15 A physical change turned a stick of butter into the liquid butter that makes popcorn so tasty, but the identity of the butter did not change.

More Examples of Physical Changes	
▪ Freezing water for ice cubes	▪ Crushing an aluminum can
▪ Sanding a piece of wood	▪ Bending a paper clip
▪ Cutting your hair	▪ Mixing oil and vinegar

Can Physical Changes Be Undone? Because physical changes do not change the identity of substances, they are often easy to undo. If you leave butter out on a warm counter, it will undergo a physical change—it will melt. Putting it back in the refrigerator will reverse this change. Likewise, if you create a figure from a lump of clay, you change the clay's shape, causing a physical change. But because the identity of the clay does not change, you can crush your creation and form the clay back into its previous shape.

Chemical Changes Form New Substances

A **chemical change** occurs when one or more substances are changed into entirely new substances with different properties. Chemical changes will or will not occur as described by the chemical properties of substances. But chemical changes and chemical properties are not the same thing. A chemical property describes a substance's ability to go through a chemical change; a chemical change is the actual process in which that substance changes into another substance. You can observe chemical properties only when a chemical change might occur.

Changing Change

1. Place a folded **paper towel** in a **small pie plate.**
2. Pour **vinegar** into the pie plate until the entire paper towel is damp.
3. Place **two or three shiny pennies** on top of the paper towel.
4. Put the pie plate in a place where it won't be bothered, and wait 24 hours.
5. Describe the chemical change that took place.
6. Write your observations in your ScienceLog.

DISCUSSION

Encourage students to think of ways to cause physical changes in the following objects:
- a pencil (break, sharpen, grind, or sand it)
- hair (comb, cut, curl, or wash it)
- salt (crush it or dissolve it in water)

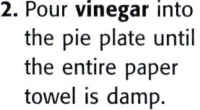

MATERIALS

FOR EACH STUDENT:
- paper towel
- pie plate
- vinegar
- 2 or 3 shiny pennies

Answers to QuickLab

5. The shiny copper surface became coated with a dull, green substance. The color change and change in the appearance of the coin indicated that a chemical change took place.

ACTIVITY

MATERIALS

FOR EACH STUDENT:
- spoon
- baking soda
- 2 plastic cups
- vinegar
- water

Safety Caution: Students should wear safety goggles, gloves, and an apron.

Have students place a teaspoon of baking soda in each of two plastic cups. Tell them to pour a small amount of water into one cup and a small amount of vinegar into the other. Ask students to describe what happens and to determine in which cup a chemical change occurred. (The chemical change occurred in the cup containing vinegar; gas bubbles were produced in this cup.)

The metal gallium has a melting point of 29.5°C, lower than human body temperature, which is 37°C. A piece of solid gallium will turn to a puddle of liquid metal if placed in a person's hand.

 **PG 634**
White Before Your Eyes

Section 2 • Describing Matter

3 Extend

GOING FURTHER

MATERIALS

FOR EACH STUDENT:
- self-sealing plastic bag
- small plastic pill bottle
- hydrogen peroxide (3% solution)
- clean steel wool

Safety Caution: Caution students to wear safety goggles, gloves, and an apron when doing this activity. Also caution them to handle the hydrogen peroxide with care.

Instruct students to fill the pill bottle halfway with hydrogen peroxide. Then have them place a small piece of steel wool and the pill bottle into the plastic bag, being careful not to spill the hydrogen peroxide. Tell them to force the air out of the bag and seal it tightly. Then instruct them to tip the bottle over so that the hydrogen peroxide comes in contact with the steel wool. Tell them to feel the bag and to observe what happens. Ask them how they know a chemical change has occurred. (A gas was formed that inflated the bag, and the bag heated up.)

MEETING INDIVIDUAL NEEDS

Advanced Learners Have students explore why desalination is so expensive. Then have them try to determine under what conditions it makes sense to use desalination on a large scale. (in places where it is less expensive than piping or shipping fresh water from distant sources)

Figure 16 Each of these ingredients has different physical and chemical properties.

A fun (and delicious) way to see what happens during chemical changes is to bake a cake. When you bake a cake, you combine eggs, flour, sugar, butter, and other ingredients as shown in **Figure 16.** Each ingredient has its own set of properties. But if you mix them together and bake the batter in the oven, you get something completely different. The heat of the oven and the interaction of the ingredients cause a chemical change. As shown in **Figure 17,** you get a cake that has properties completely different to any of the ingredients. Some more examples of chemical changes are shown below.

Figure 17 Chemical changes produce new substances with different properties.

Examples of Chemical Changes

Soured milk smells bad because bacteria have formed new substances in the milk.

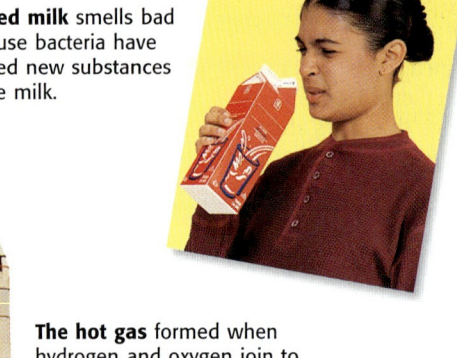

Effervescent tablets bubble when the citric acid and baking soda in them react with water.

The hot gas formed when hydrogen and oxygen join to make water helps blast the space shuttle into orbit.

The Statue of Liberty is made of shiny, orange-brown copper. But the metal's interaction with carbon dioxide and water has formed a new substance, copper carbonate, and made this landmark lady green over time.

TOPIC: Describing Matter
GO TO: www.scilinks.org
sciLINKS NUMBER: HSTP035

Chapter 2 • The Properties of Matter

Clues to Chemical Changes Look back at the bottom of the previous page. In each picture, there is at least one clue that signals a chemical change. Can you find the clues? Here's a hint: chemical changes often cause color changes, fizzing or foaming, heat, or the production of sound, light, or odor.

In the cake example, you would probably smell the sweet aroma of the cake as it baked. If you looked into the oven, you would see the batter rise and turn brown. When you cut the finished cake, you would see the spongy texture created by gas bubbles that formed in the batter (if you baked it right, that is!). All of these yummy clues are signals of chemical changes. But are the clues and the chemical changes the same thing? No, the clues just result from the chemical changes.

Can Chemical Changes Be Undone? Because new substances are formed, you cannot reverse chemical changes using physical means. In other words, you can't uncrumple or iron out a chemical change. Imagine trying to un-bake the cake shown in **Figure 18** by pulling out each ingredient. No way! Most of the chemical changes you see in your daily life, such as a cake baking or milk turning sour, would be difficult to reverse. However, some chemical changes can be reversed under the right conditions by other chemical changes. For example, the water formed in the space shuttle's rockets could be split back into hydrogen and oxygen using an electric current.

Environment CONNECTION

When fossil fuels are burned, a chemical change takes place involving sulfur (a substance in fossil fuels) and oxygen (from the air). This chemical change produces sulfur dioxide, a gas. When sulfur dioxide enters the atmosphere, it undergoes another chemical change by interacting with water and oxygen. This chemical change produces sulfuric acid, a contributor to acid precipitation. Acid precipitation can kill trees and make ponds and lakes unable to support life.

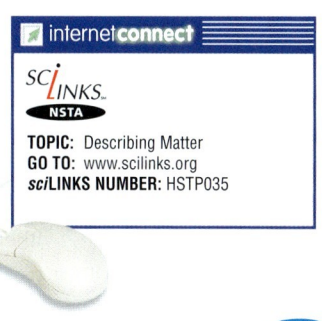

Figure 18 Looking for the original ingredients? You won't find them—their identities have changed.

REVIEW

1. Classify each of the following properties as either physical or chemical: reacts with water, dissolves in acetone, is blue, does not react with hydrogen.
2. List three clues that indicate a chemical change might be taking place.
3. **Comparing Concepts** Describe the difference between physical changes and chemical changes in terms of what happens to the matter involved in each kind of change.

internetconnect

SC*i*LINKS NSTA

TOPIC: Describing Matter
GO TO: www.scilinks.org
*sci*LINKS NUMBER: HSTP035

4) Close

Quiz

1. You have two objects, both about the size of an orange. Object A has a mass of 1,487 g, and object B has a mass of 878 g. Which object do you think has the greater density? Explain your answer. (Both objects have the same volume, so the object with more mass in the same volume has the greater density. Object A has the greater density.)

2. Give an example of a chemical change that occurs during the preparation of a meal. (Possible answers: burning of gas in an oven or a stove burner; cooking an egg; baking a pie or cake)

ALTERNATIVE ASSESSMENT

Concept Mapping Ask students what they could do to a sugar cube to cause it to undergo a physical change. (crush it, grind it, dissolve it in water)

Then ask what they could do that would cause the sugar cube to undergo a chemical change. (burn it, eat it, cause it to react with another chemical)

Have students make a concept map that shows physical changes and chemical changes to sugar.

Answers to Review

1. reacts with water: chemical; dissolves in acetone: physical; is blue: physical; does not react with hydrogen: chemical
2. Acceptable answers include color change; bubbling; fizzing or foaming; heat; and the production of light, sound, or odor.
3. In a physical change, the material does not change its identity. It is still the same matter it was before the change and has most of the same properties. In a chemical change, the initial matter changes its identity and becomes a new form of matter with a different identity and different properties.

 Reinforcement Worksheet 2 "A Matter of Density"

 Critical Thinking Worksheet 2 "As a Matter of Fact!"

Section 2 • Describing Matter

Chapter Highlights

Vocabulary Definitions

Section 1

matter anything that has volume and mass

volume the amount of space that something occupies or the amount of space that something contains

meniscus the curve at a liquid's surface by which you measure the volume of the liquid

mass the amount of matter that something is made of; its value does not change with the object's location in the universe

gravity a force of attraction between objects that is due to their masses

weight a measure of the gravitational force exerted on an object, usually by Earth

newton (N) the SI unit of force

inertia the tendency of all objects to resist any change in motion

Chapter Highlights

SECTION 1

Vocabulary
- matter (p. 36)
- volume (p. 36)
- meniscus (p. 37)
- mass (p. 38)
- gravity (p. 39)
- weight (p. 40)
- newton (p. 41)
- inertia (p. 42)

Section Notes
- Matter is anything that has volume and mass.
- Volume is the amount of space taken up by an object.
- The volume of liquids is expressed in liters and milliliters.
- The volume of solid objects is expressed in cubic units, such as cubic meters.
- Mass is the amount of matter that something is made of.
- Mass and weight are not the same thing. Weight is a measure of the gravitational force exerted on an object, usually in relation to the Earth.
- Mass is usually expressed in milligrams, grams, and kilograms.
- The newton is the SI unit of force, so weight is expressed in newtons.
- Inertia is the tendency of all objects to resist any change in motion. Mass is a measure of inertia. The more massive an object is, the greater its inertia.

Labs
Volumania! (p. 630)

✓ Skills Check

Math Concepts

DENSITY To calculate an object's density, divide the mass of the object by its volume. For example, the density of an object with a mass of 45 g and a volume of 5.5 cm³ is calculated as follows:

$$D = \frac{m}{V}$$
$$D = \frac{45 \text{ g}}{5.5 \text{ cm}^3}$$
$$D = 8.2 \text{ g/cm}^3$$

Visual Understanding

MASS AND WEIGHT Mass and weight are related, but they're not the same thing. Look back at Figure 8 on page 41 to learn about the differences between mass and weight.

PHYSICAL AND CHEMICAL PROPERTIES All substances have physical and chemical properties. You can compare some of those properties by reviewing the table on page 48.

Lab and Activity Highlights

Volumania! PG 630

Determining Density PG 632

Layering Liquids PG 633

White Before Your Eyes PG 634

 Datasheets for LabBook
(blackline masters for these labs)

SECTION 2

Vocabulary
- **physical property** *(p. 43)*
- **density** *(p. 44)*
- **chemical property** *(p. 47)*
- **physical change** *(p. 48)*
- **chemical change** *(p. 49)*

Section Notes
- Physical properties of matter can be observed without changing the identity of the matter.
- Density is the amount of matter in a given space, or the mass per unit volume.
- The density of a substance is always the same at a given pressure and temperature regardless of the size of the sample of the substance.
- Chemical properties describe a substance based on its ability to change into a new substance with different properties.
- Chemical properties can be observed only when one substance might become a new substance.
- The characteristic properties of a substance are always the same whether the sample observed is large or small.
- When a substance undergoes a physical change, its identity remains the same.
- A chemical change occurs when one or more substances are changed into new substances with different properties.

Labs
- **Determining Density** *(p. 632)*
- **Layering Liquids** *(p. 633)*
- **White Before Your Eyes** *(p. 634)*

VOCABULARY DEFINITIONS, continued

SECTION 2

physical property a property of matter that can be observed or measured without changing the identity of the matter

density the amount of matter in a given space; mass per unit volume

chemical property a property of matter that describes a substance based on its ability to change into a new substance with different properties

physical change a change that affects one or more physical properties of a substance; most physical changes are easy to undo

chemical change a change that occurs when one or more substances are changed into entirely new substances with different properties; cannot be reversed using physical means

---

internetconnect

GO TO: go.hrw.com

Visit the **HRW** Web site for a variety of learning tools related to this chapter. Just type in the keyword:

KEYWORD: HSTMAT

GO TO: www.scilinks.org

Visit the **National Science Teachers Association** on-line Web site for Internet resources related to this chapter. Just type in the *sci*LINKS number for more information about the topic:

TOPIC: What Is Matter?	*sci*LINKS NUMBER: HSTP030
TOPIC: Describing Matter	*sci*LINKS NUMBER: HSTP035
TOPIC: Dark Matter	*sci*LINKS NUMBER: HSTP040
TOPIC: Building a Better Body	*sci*LINKS NUMBER: HSTP045

 Vocabulary Review Worksheet 2

 Blackline masters of these Chapter Highlights can be found in the **Study Guide.**

Lab and Activity Highlights

LabBank

 Inquiry Labs, Whatever Floats Your Boat, Lab 17

Whiz-Bang Demonstrations
- Curious Cubes, Demo 38
- The Dancing Toothpicks, Demo 39
- Does 2 + 2 = 4? Demo 40

 Long-Term Projects & Research Ideas, And We Have Thales to Thank, Project 52

Chapter Review Answers

USING VOCABULARY

1. Mass is the amount of matter in an object; volume is the amount of space the object occupies.
2. Mass is the amount of matter in an object and is always constant. Weight is a measure of the gravitational force, and it will change, depending on the object's distance from the Earth or other bodies.
3. Mass is a measure of inertia. The more massive an object is, the more inertia it has.
4. Volume is the amount of space occupied by an object, and density is the amount of mass in a given volume.
5. physical property: can be observed without changing the identity of the matter; chemical property: can be observed only when a chemical change might occur that would change the matter into something new
6. When matter undergoes a physical change, its shape or form changes, but its identity remains the same. When matter undergoes a chemical change, its identity and properties change.

UNDERSTANDING CONCEPTS

Multiple Choice

7. c 11. a
8. d 12. a
9. b 13. c
10. d 14. c

Short Answer

15. Sample answer: Measure the volume of a liquid by pouring it into a graduated cylinder and reading the scale at the bottom of the meniscus. The volume of a rectangular solid is determined by multiplying the object's length, width, and height.
16. Sample answer: Mass is a measure of the inertia of an object. The more an object resists a change in motion, the greater its mass.

Chapter Review

USING VOCABULARY

For each pair of terms, explain the difference in their meanings.

1. mass/volume
2. mass/weight
3. inertia/mass
4. volume/density
5. physical property/chemical property
6. physical change/chemical change

UNDERSTANDING CONCEPTS

Multiple Choice

7. Which of these is *not* matter?
   a. a cloud   c. sunshine
   b. your hair   d. the sun

8. The mass of an elephant on the moon would be
   a. less than its mass on Mars.
   b. more than its mass on Mars.
   c. the same as its weight on the moon.
   d. None of the above

9. Which of the following is *not* a chemical property?
   a. reactivity with oxygen
   b. malleability
   c. flammability
   d. reactivity with acid

10. Your weight could be expressed in which of the following units?
    a. pounds
    b. newtons
    c. kilograms
    d. both (a) and (b)

11. You accidentally break your pencil in half. This is an example of
    a. a physical change.
    b. a chemical change.
    c. density.
    d. volume.

12. Which of the following statements about density is true?
    a. Density depends on mass and volume.
    b. Density is weight per unit volume.
    c. Density is measured in milliliters.
    d. Density is a chemical property.

13. Which of the following pairs of objects would have the greatest attraction toward each other due to gravity?
    a. a 10 kg object and a 10 kg object, 4 m apart
    b. a 5 kg object and a 5 kg object, 4 m apart
    c. a 10 kg object and a 10 kg object, 2 m apart
    d. a 5 kg object and a 5 kg object, 2 m apart

14. Inertia increases as __?__ increases.
    a. time   c. mass
    b. length d. volume

Short Answer

15. In one or two sentences, explain the different processes in measuring the volume of a liquid and measuring the volume of a solid.
16. In one or two sentences, explain the relationship between mass and inertia.
17. What is the formula for calculating density?
18. List three characteristic properties of matter.

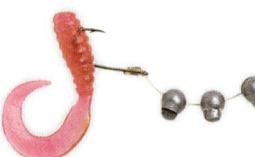

17. density = $\frac{mass}{volume}$
18. Characteristic properties include density, solubility, reactivity with acids, melting point, and boiling point.

Concept Mapping

19. 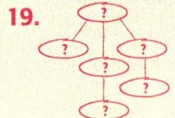 An answer to this exercise can be found at the end of this book.

CRITICAL THINKING AND PROBLEM SOLVING

20. Sample answer: Cooking eggs involves a chemical change. I cannot change the cooked eggs back to raw eggs in order to poach them.
21. Sample answer: If my neighbor has trouble lifting a small box, I would conclude that the box's inertia is large. The box resists my neighbor's attempt to move it. A large inertia means that the item(s) in the box has a large mass.

Concept Mapping

19. Use the following terms to create a concept map: matter, mass, inertia, volume, milliliters, cubic centimeters, weight, gravity.

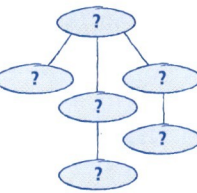

CRITICAL THINKING AND PROBLEM SOLVING

20. You are making breakfast for your picky friend, Filbert. You make him scrambled eggs. He asks, "Would you please take these eggs back to the kitchen and poach them?" What scientific reason do you give Filbert for not changing his eggs?

Poach these, please!

21. You look out your bedroom window and see your new neighbors moving in. Your neighbor bends over to pick up a small cardboard box, but he cannot lift it. What can you conclude about the item(s) in the box? Use the terms *mass* and *inertia* to explain how you came to this conclusion.

22. You may sometimes hear on the radio or on television that astronauts are "weightless" in space. Explain why this is not true.

23. People commonly use the term *volume* to describe the capacity of a container. How does this definition of volume differ from the scientific definition?

MATH IN SCIENCE

24. What is the volume of a book with the following dimensions: a width of 10 cm, a length that is two times the width, and a height that is half the width? Remember to express your answer in cubic units.

25. A jar contains 30 mL of glycerin (mass = 37.8 g) and 60 mL of corn syrup (mass = 82.8 g). Which liquid is on top? Show your work, and explain your answer.

INTERPRETING GRAPHICS

Examine the photograph below, and answer the following questions:

26. List three physical properties of this can.

27. Did a chemical change or a physical change cause the change in this can's appearance?

28. How does the density of the metal in the can compare before and after the change?

29. Can you tell what the chemical properties of the can are just by looking at the picture? Explain.

NOW What Do You Think?

Take a minute to review your answers to the ScienceLog questions on page 35. Have your answers changed? If necessary, revise your answers based on what you have learned since you began this chapter.

NOW WHAT DO YOU THINK?

1. Matter is anything that has volume and mass.
2. A physical property of matter can be observed without changing the identity of the matter. A chemical property of matter can be observed only when a chemical change might occur that would change the identity of the matter.
3. A physical change changes the shape or form of the matter without changing its identity. It is still the same matter as before the change and has most of the same properties. In a chemical change, the matter changes its identity and becomes a new form of matter with a different identity and different properties.

22. Sample answer: An astronaut weighs less in orbit than on Earth because of the astronaut's increased distance from the Earth. However, an astronaut is not weightless because there are still gravitational forces between the astronaut and all other objects in the universe.

23. Sample answer: The scientific definition of *volume* is the amount of space that matter, such as a container, occupies. The *capacity* of a container describes the maximum amount of space that matter inside the container can occupy.

MATH IN SCIENCE

24. volume = length × width × height = 20 cm × 10 cm × 5 cm = 1,000 cm³

25. Density of glycerin = $\frac{37.8 \text{ g}}{30 \text{ mL}}$ = 1.26 g/mL. Density of corn syrup = $\frac{82.8 \text{ g}}{60 \text{ mL}}$ = 1.38 g/mL. The glycerin will be on top because it is less dense than corn syrup.

INTERPRETING GRAPHICS

26. sample answer: crushed shape, somewhat shiny, metallic
27. a physical change
28. The density before and after the change is the same because density is a characteristic property of matter.
29. No; chemical properties cannot be determined simply by looking at a substance. Chemical properties can only be observed when a chemical change might occur.

Concept Mapping Transparency 2

Blackline masters of this Chapter Review can be found in the **Study Guide**.

ACROSS THE SCIENCES
In the Dark About Dark Matter

Background

Keep an eye out for new information about MACHOs and WIMPs. Bring relevant articles from newspapers or magazines to class to discuss with your students. Astronomy magazines, general-science magazines such as *Discover* and *Scientific American,* and science Web sites are a good source of up-to-date information. Web searches using the keywords "MACHO" and "WIMP" will produce results.

You may wish to review with students the types of astronomical bodies that are now known. You may also want to discuss the life cycle of a star.

Astronomers have proposed several candidates for MACHOs. These include brown dwarfs (stars that do not have enough mass to undergo combustion), neutron stars, and black holes.

In 1997, 1998, and 1999, scientists found evidence of MACHOs. They are still looking for convincing evidence of WIMPs.

TOPIC: Dark Matter
GO TO: www.scilinks.org
sciLINKS NUMBER: HSTP040

ACROSS THE SCIENCES

PHYSICAL SCIENCE • ASTRONOMY

In the Dark About Dark Matter

What is the universe made of? Believe it or not, when astronomers try to answer this question, they still find themselves in the dark. Surprisingly, there is more to the universe than meets the eye.

A Matter of Gravity

Astronomers noticed something odd when studying the motions of galaxies in space. They expected to find a lot of mass in the galaxies. Instead, they discovered that the mass of the galaxies was not great enough to explain the large gravitational force causing the galaxies' rapid rotation. So what was causing the additional gravitational force? Some scientists think the universe contains matter that we cannot see with our eyes or our telescopes. Astronomers call this invisible matter *dark matter.*

Dark matter doesn't reveal itself by giving off any kind of electromagnetic radiation, such as visible light, radio waves, or gamma radiation. According to scientific calculations, dark matter could account for between 90 and 99 percent of the total mass of the universe! What is dark matter? Would you believe MACHOs and WIMPs?

MACHOs

Scientists recently proved the existence of *MAssive Compact Halo Objects* (MACHOs) in our Milky Way galaxy by measuring their gravitational effects. Even though scientists know MACHOs exist, they aren't sure what MACHOs are made of. Scientists suggest that MACHOs may be brown dwarfs, old white dwarfs, neutron stars, or black holes. Others suggest they are some type of strange, new object whose properties still remain unknown. Even though the number of MACHOs is apparently very great, they still do not represent enough missing mass. So scientists offer another candidate for dark matter—WIMPs.

▲ *The Large Magellanic Cloud, located 180,000 light-years from Earth*

WIMPs

Theories predict that *Weakly Interacting Massive Particles* (WIMPs) exist, but scientists have never detected them. WIMPs are thought to be massive elementary particles that do not interact strongly with normal matter (which is why scientists have not found them).

More Answers Needed

So far, evidence supports the existence of MACHOs, but there is little or no solid evidence of WIMPs or any other form of dark matter. Scientists who support the idea of WIMPs are conducting studies of the particles that make up matter to see if they can detect WIMPs. Other theories are that gravity acts differently around galaxies or that the universe is filled with things called "cosmic strings." Scientists admit they have a lot of work to do before they will be able to describe the universe—and all the matter in it.

On Your Own

▶ What is microlensing, and what does it have to do with MACHOs? How might the neutrino provide valuable information to scientists who are interested in proving the existence of WIMPs? Find out on your own!

Answer to On Your Own

Students will find that microlensing is the occasional amplification of light from distant stars outside the Milky Way by the gravitational force of certain massive objects in the Milky Way. Neutrinos are important because some scientists think certain neutrinos are good candidates for WIMPs.

Health Watch

Building a Better Body

Have you ever broken an arm or a leg? If so, you probably wore a cast while the bone healed. But what happens when a bone is too badly damaged to heal? In some cases, a false bone made from a metal called titanium can take the original bone's place. Could using titanium bone implants be the first step in creating bionic body parts? Think about it as you read about some of titanium's amazing properties.

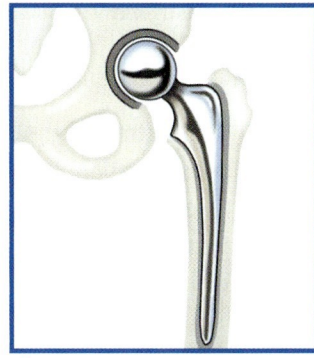

▲ *Titanium bones—even better than the real thing?*

Imitating the Original

Why would a metal like titanium be used to imitate natural bone? Well, it turns out that a titanium implant passes some key tests for bone replacement. First of all, real bones are incredibly lightweight and sturdy, and healthy bones last for many years. Therefore, a bone-replacement material has to be lightweight but also very durable. Titanium passes this test because it is well known for its strength, and it is also lightweight.

Second, the human body's immune system is always on the lookout for foreign substances. If a doctor puts a false bone in place and the patient's immune system attacks it, an infection can result. Somehow, the false bone must be able to chemically trick the body into thinking that the bone is real. Does titanium pass this test? Keep reading!

Accepting Imitation

By studying the human body's immune system, scientists found that the body accepts certain metals. The body almost always accepts one metal in particular. Yep, you guessed it—titanium! This turned out to be quite a discovery.

Doctors could implant pieces of titanium into a person's body without triggering an immune reaction. A bond can even form between titanium and existing bone tissue, fusing the bone to the metal!

Titanium is shaping up to be a great bone-replacement material. It is lightweight and strong, is accepted by the body, can attach to existing bone, and resists chemical changes, such as corrosion. But scientists have encountered a slight problem. Friction can wear away titanium bones, especially those used near the hips and elbows.

Real Success

An unexpected surprise, not from the field of medicine but from the field of nuclear physics, may have solved the problem. Researchers have learned that by implanting a special form of nitrogen on the surface of a piece of metal, they can create a surface layer on the metal that is especially durable and wear-resistant. When this form of nitrogen is implanted in titanium bones, the bones retain all the properties of pure titanium bones but also become very wear-resistant. The new bones should last through decades of heavy use without needing to be replaced.

Think About It

▶ What will the future hold? As time goes by, doctors become more successful at implanting titanium bones. What do you think would happen if the titanium bones were to eventually become better than real bones?

Chapter Organizer

CHAPTER ORGANIZATION	TIME MINUTES	OBJECTIVES	LABS, INVESTIGATIONS, AND DEMONSTRATIONS
Chapter Opener pp. 58–59	45	National Standards: UCP 2, 3, SAI 1, PS 1a, 3a	**Investigate!** Vanishing Act, p. 59
Section 1 Four States of Matter	60	▶ Describe the properties shared by particles of all matter. ▶ Describe the four states of matter discussed here. ▶ Describe the differences between the states of matter. ▶ Predict how a change in pressure or temperature will affect the volume of a gas. UCP 1, 2, PS 1a; LabBook UCP 2, 3, SAI 1, 2, PS 1a	**Demonstration,** p. 60 in ATE **Demonstration,** p. 64 in ATE **Discovery Lab,** Full of Hot Air! p. 636 **Datasheets for LabBook,** Full of Hot Air! Datasheet 9 **Whiz-Bang Demonstrations,** Demonstration with a CRUNCH! Demo 41
Section 2 Changes of State	90	▶ Describe how substances change from state to state. ▶ Explain the difference between an exothermic change and an endothermic change. ▶ Compare the changes of state. UCP 1, 3, SAI 1, 2, ST 1, SPSP 3, 5, HNS 3, PS 1a, 3a; LabBook UCP 2, 3, SAI 1, 2, PS 1a, 3a	**Demonstration,** p. 68 in ATE **QuickLab,** Boiling Water Is Cool, p. 71 **Skill Builder,** Can Crusher, p. 637 **Datasheets for LabBook,** Can Crusher, Datasheet 10 **Discovery Lab,** A Hot and Cool Lab, p. 638 **Datasheets for LabBook,** A Hot and Cool Lab, Datasheet 11 **Labs You Can Eat,** How Cold Is Ice-Cream Cold? Lab 18 **Long-Term Projects & Research Ideas,** Project 53

*See page **T20** for a complete correlation of this book with the*

NATIONAL SCIENCE EDUCATION STANDARDS.

TECHNOLOGY RESOURCES

 Guided Reading Audio CD
English or Spanish, Chapter 3

 Science Discovery Videodiscs
Image and Activity Bank with Lesson Plans: States of Change

 CNN Scientists in Action, In Search of Absolute Zero, Segment 5

 One-Stop Planner CD-ROM with Test Generator

Chapter 3 • States of Matter

CLASSROOM WORKSHEETS, TRANSPARENCIES, AND RESOURCES	SCIENCE INTEGRATION AND CONNECTIONS	REVIEW AND ASSESSMENT
Directed Reading Worksheet 3 **Science Puzzlers, Twisters & Teasers,** Worksheet 3		
Directed Reading Worksheet 3, Section 1 **Transparency 206,** Models of a Solid, a Liquid, and a Gas **Transparency 207,** Boyle's Law **Transparency 207,** Charles's Law **Reinforcement Worksheet 3,** Make a State-ment	**Connect to Life Science,** p. 63 in ATE **Math and More,** p. 65 in ATE **MathBreak,** Gas Law Graphs, p. 66 **Apply,** p. 67	**Self-Check,** p. 64 **Review,** p. 64 **Homework,** p. 66 in ATE **Review,** p. 67 **Quiz,** p. 67 in ATE **Alternative Assessment,** p. 67 in ATE
Directed Reading Worksheet 3, Section 2 **Math Skills for Science Worksheet 6,** Checking Division with Multiplication **Transparency 208,** Summarizing the Changes of State **Critical Thinking Worksheet 3,** What a State! **Transparency 141,** The Water Cycle **Transparency 209,** Changing the State of Water	**Multicultural Connection,** p. 69 in ATE **Meteorology Connection,** p. 71 **Math and More,** p. 71 in ATE **Science, Technology, and Society:** Guiding Lightning, p. 78 **Eureka!** Full Steam Ahead! p. 79	**Self-Check,** p. 70 **Homework,** p. 70 in ATE **Review,** p. 73 **Quiz,** p. 73 in ATE **Alternative Assessment,** p. 73 in ATE

internet connect

  Holt, Rinehart and Winston On-line Resources
go.hrw.com

For worksheets and other teaching aids related to this chapter, visit the HRW Web site and type in the keyword: **HSTSTA**

 **National Science Teachers Association**
www.scilinks.org

Encourage students to use the *sci*LINKS numbers listed in the internet connect boxes to access information and resources on the **NSTA** Web site.

END-OF-CHAPTER REVIEW AND ASSESSMENT

Chapter Review in Study Guide
Vocabulary and Notes in Study Guide
Chapter Tests with Performance-Based Assessment, Chapter 3 Test
Chapter Tests with Performance-Based Assessment, Performance-Based Assessment 3
Concept Mapping Transparency 3

Chapter Resources & Worksheets

Visual Resources

TEACHING TRANSPARENCIES

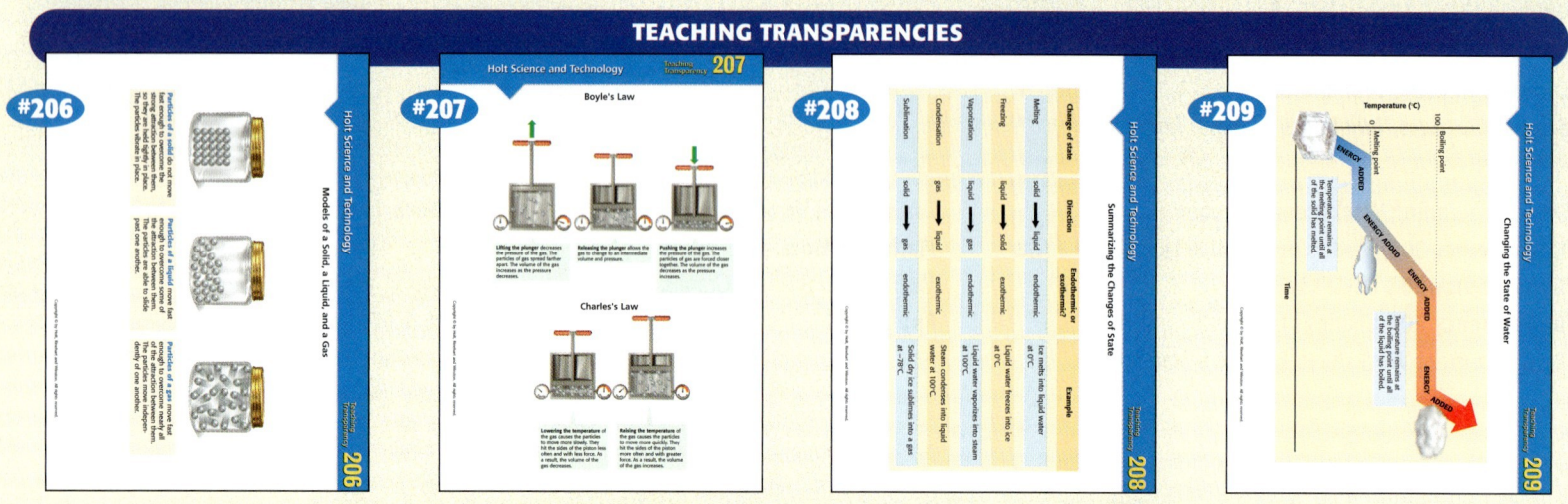

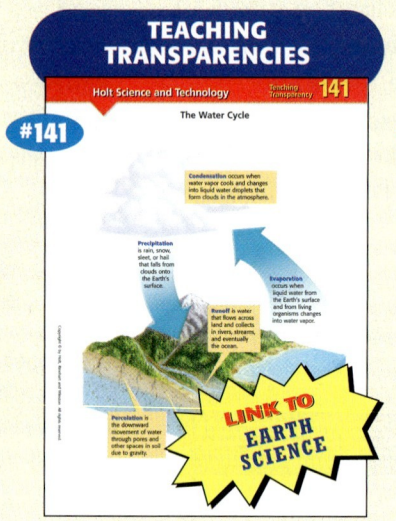

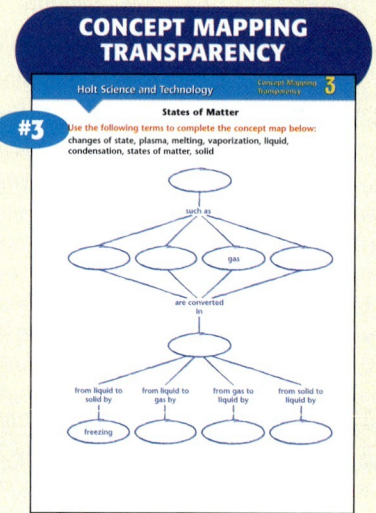

Meeting Individual Needs

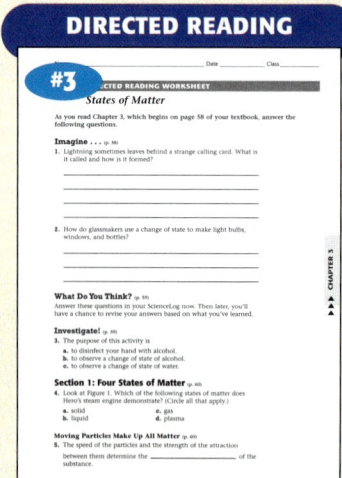

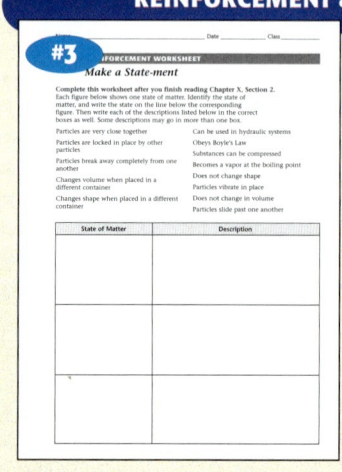

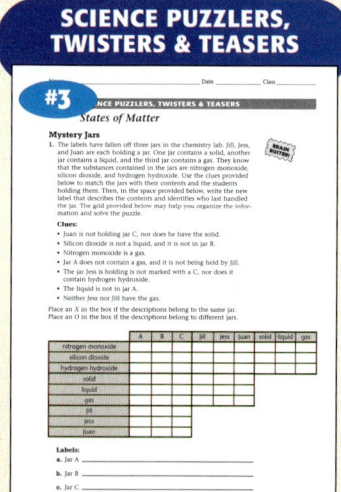

57C   Chapter 3 • States of Matter

Chapter 3 • States of Matter

Review & Assessment

STUDY GUIDE

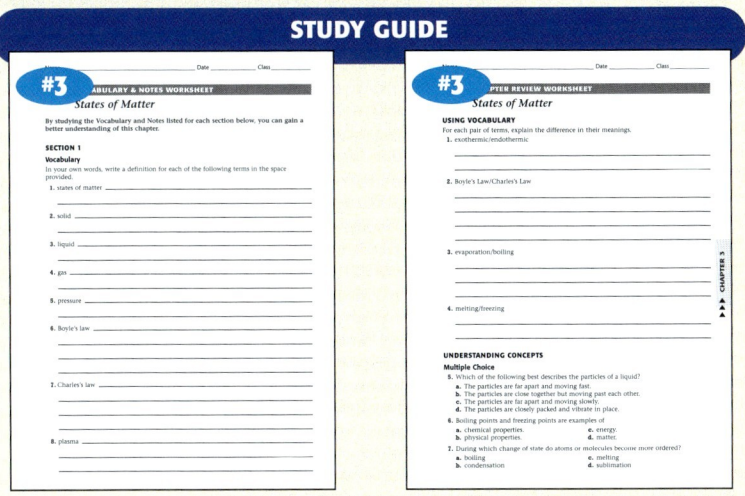

CHAPTER TESTS WITH PERFORMANCE-BASED ASSESSMENT

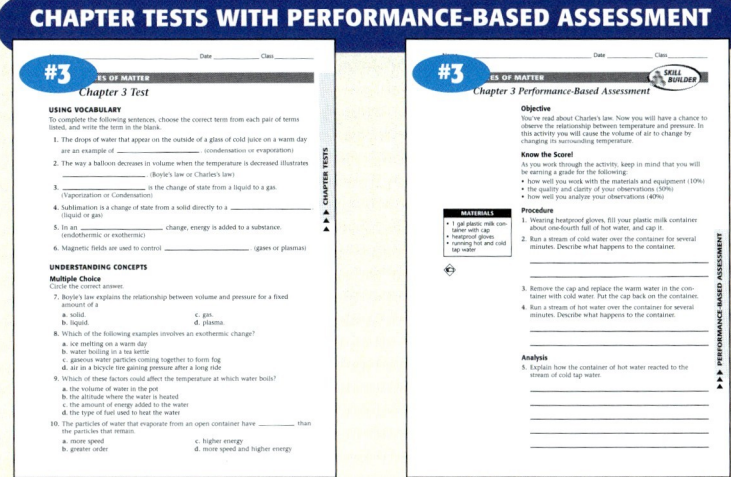

Lab Worksheets

LABS YOU CAN EAT

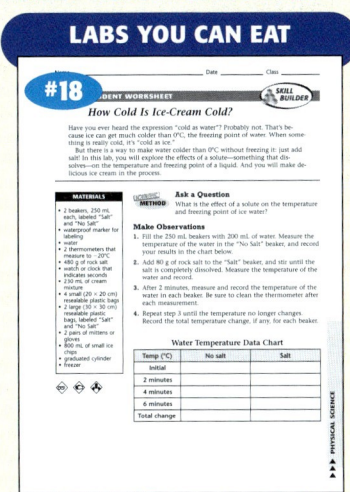

WHIZ-BANG DEMONSTRATIONS

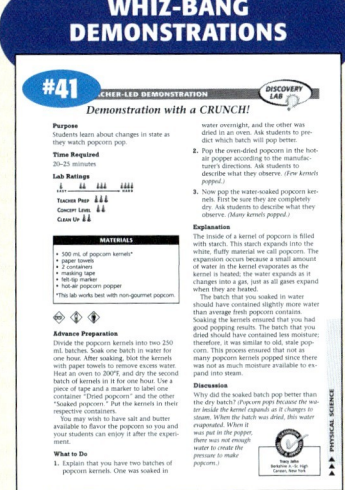

LONG-TERM PROJECTS & RESEARCH IDEAS

DATASHEETS FOR LABBOOK

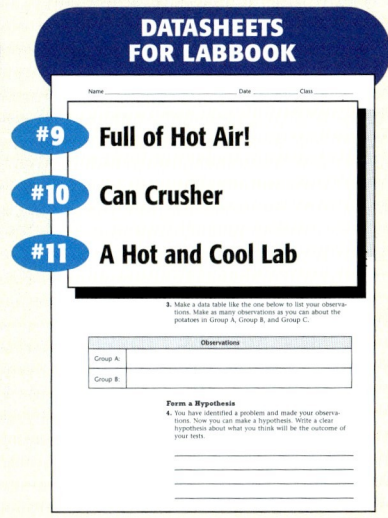

Applications & Extensions

CRITICAL THINKING & PROBLEM SOLVING

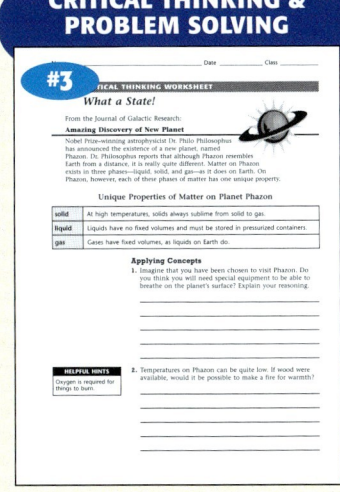

SCIENTISTS IN ACTION

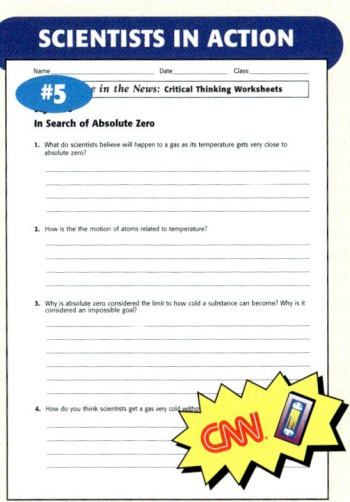

Chapter 3 • Chapter Resources & Worksheets

57D

Chapter Background

SECTION 1

Four States of Matter

▶ **Solids**
In solids, particles vibrate about fixed points. If the particles are arranged in a regular, repeating pattern, the solid is defined as a crystalline solid. If a crystalline solid is melted and cooled down quickly, it usually forms an amorphous solid. Amorphous solid particles are not arranged in regular, repeating patterns.

▶ **Liquids**
The properties of liquids are caused by *cohesion*, the attraction between atoms and molecules of the liquid, and *adhesion*, the attraction between atoms and molecules of the liquid and other atoms and molecules. Because the surface of a liquid has no liquid particles above it, the particles at the surface cohere to the liquid below, and the surface exhibits surface tension.

▶ **Gases**
The defining property of gases is the ability to expand indefinitely. Gases are extremely compressible. Gases are also miscible with other gases in all proportions.

▶ **Plasma**
Plasma is ionized gas. Matter changes into the plasma state when gaseous particles collide with such intensity that electrons are torn away from the atoms, producing an ionized gas that conducts electric current and is affected by magnetic fields. Slightly ionized plasmas, like those found in plasma balls and fluorescent lights, can also conduct an electric current. Fluorescent lights and plasma balls are cool to the touch because electrical energy, instead of thermal energy, is used to break apart the particles.

- A great deal of scientific research is being done to find useful applications for plasmas. For example, plasmas are being used to destroy chemical weapons. Plasmas are also necessary in fusion research.

- In 1920, American chemist Irving Langmuir coined the name *plasma*. Langmuir and other scientists discovered that many substances reach a unique state at temperatures above 3,000°C in which their particles have properties like a gas (no definite shape or volume) but are electrically charged.

▶ **Robert Boyle and Boyle's Law**
Robert Boyle (1627–1691) was born in Ireland and educated at Eton, Geneva, and Oxford. In 1662, Boyle was experimenting with mercury in a closed J-shaped tube. He discovered the inverse relationship between the volume of a confined gas and its pressure. Through experimentation, Boyle discovered that if the volume of a gas at a constant temperature is doubled, the pressure is reduced by half. And for any decrease in volume, there is a proportional increase in pressure.

▶ **Jacques Charles and Charles's Law**
Jacques Alexander Charles (1746–1823) was a professor of physics at the University of Paris and a friend of Benjamin Franklin. Charles was an avid balloonist. From his work with balloons and gases, he realized that hydrogen would be ideal for balloon flight. He built a balloon and used hydrogen to fill it. He made several flights with his hydrogen balloon and once flew to a height of over 1.7 km.

- Charles's law states that if an ideal gas is held at a constant pressure, its volume will increase as temperature increases and decrease as temperature decreases. Charles's research with gases was used by Lord Kelvin to formulate the absolute, or Kelvin, temperature scale.

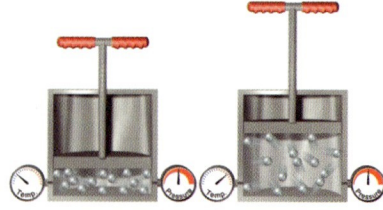

IS THAT A FACT!

▶ Many purists argue that amorphous materials are not true solids. When defining amorphous substances, these scientists prefer to call such substances supercooled liquids.

▶ Crystalline solids can be classified into seven crystal systems: cubic, tetragonal, hexagonal, rhombohedral,

Chapter 3 • States of Matter

orthorhombic, monoclinic, and triclinic. A few examples of common substances with their corresponding crystal system are: table salt—cubic system; most metals—cubic or hexagonal system; diamond—cubic system (but graphite, which, like diamond, is a form of carbon, has a layered hexagonal system).

- All stars, fluorescent lights, fire, and lightning are examples of matter in the plasma state.

SECTION 2
Changes of State

▶ Change of State
For a solid substance to melt, it must gain sufficient energy to overcome intermolecular attraction. As a substance such as ice absorbs energy, the individual molecules of the ice vibrate faster and faster, breaking the bonds that hold the molecules together. This allows the molecules to begin sliding past one another. If sufficient energy is added, the liquid begins to boil.

▶ Temperature
Temperature is a measure of the average speed of a substance's particles. Temperature differences indicate in which direction thermal energy will move.

▶ Fahrenheit Scale
Gabriel Daniel Fahrenheit (1686–1736), a German physicist, developed the Fahrenheit temperature scale.

Fahrenheit's zero point was the freezing temperature of icy brine water. He chose icy brine water because in the late 1600s, it was the lowest known temperature. Pure water froze at 32° on Fahrenheit's scale. The scale has 180 divisions between the freezing point and boiling point of pure water.

▶ Celsius Scale
Swedish astronomer Anders Celsius (1704–1744) developed his thermometer so scientists could have a common scale and standard by which to compare experiments. The Celsius scale, also known as the centigrade scale, has 100 divisions between the freezing and boiling points of pure water at 1 atm. Celsius assigned the freezing point of water as 100° and the boiling point as 0°. This was later changed to the scale we use today.

▶ William Thomson, Lord Kelvin
William Thomson, Lord Kelvin, (1824–1907) was born in Ireland. Thomson was considered a child prodigy—he began his studies at the University of Glasgow when he was only 11 years old. Thomson had many interests (for instance, he investigated the age of Earth), but he is probably best known for his work with absolute temperature.

▶ Kelvin Scale
The Kelvin scale's divisions are based on the centigrade scale, but the scale does not have any negative numbers. Pure water boils at 373 K and freezes at 273 K.

IS THAT A FACT!

- There is no apparent limit to how hot a substance can become, but there is a limit to how cold something can become. Lord Kelvin stated that temperature is related to volume and energy, and at absolute zero a substance's volume and energy would achieve their lowest values.

For background information about teaching strategies and issues, refer to the *Professional Reference for Teachers*.

CHAPTER 3
States of Matter

Chapter Preview

Section 1
Four States of Matter
- Moving Particles Make Up All Matter
- Solids Have Definite Shape and Volume
- Liquids Change Shape but Not Volume
- Gases Change Both Shape and Volume
- Gas Under Pressure
- Laws Describe Gas Behavior
- Plasmas

Section 2
Changes of State
- Energy and Changes of State
- Melting: Solids to Liquids
- Freezing: Liquids to Solids
- Vaporization: Liquids to Gases
- Condensation: Gases to Liquids
- Sublimation: Solids Directly to Gases
- Comparing Changes of State
- Temperature Change Versus Change of State

Guided Reading Audio CD
English or Spanish, Chapter 3

TOPIC: Forms and Uses of Glass
GO TO: www.scilinks.org
sciLINKS NUMBER: HSTP055

CHAPTER 3
States of Matter

Imagine...

You arrive at the beach as the last of a thunderstorm heads out to sea. Suddenly lightning strikes a short distance down the beach.

After the storm passes, you hurry to the spot where the lightning bolt hit. There you notice an odd mark in the sand. You dig down and find a glassy object like the one shown below. What is it?

You have found a rare type of natural glass called *fulgurite* (FUHL gyoo RIET) that sometimes forms when lightning strikes sand. In the instant that the lightning bolt strikes, the sand may reach a temperature of 33,000°C (about the same as the sun's surface). The solid sand melts into a liquid, then quickly cools and hardens into glass. A *change of state*, from solid to liquid and back again, has taken place—right on the beach!

The same basic process is used to make the light bulbs, windows, and bottles you use every day. Instead of lightning, however, glassmakers use hot ovens to melt solid silica (the main mineral in sand) and other ingredients into liquid glass. Then, before the glass cools and solidifies, the glassmaker forms it into the desired shape. Read on to discover more about states of matter.

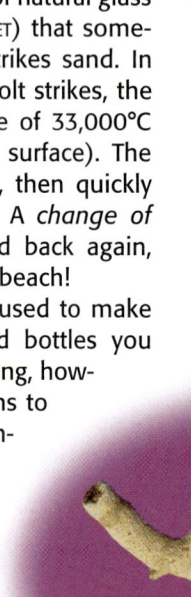

Imagine...

Imagine being an astronaut and finding amorphous moon rocks. The moon doesn't have lightning strikes or volcanoes. What caused the amorphous rocks to form? Scientists theorize that they may have formed when meteorites hit the moon, causing some of the moon's surface to melt. This melted material cooled very rapidly, forming rocks with no crystal structure.

What Do You Think?

In your ScienceLog, try to answer the following questions based on what you already know:

1. What are the four most familiar states of matter?
2. Compare the motion of the particles in a solid, a liquid, and a gas.
3. Name three ways matter changes from one state to another.

Vanishing Act

In this activity, you will use rubbing alcohol to investigate a change of state.

Procedure

1. Pour **rubbing alcohol** into a small **plastic cup** until the alcohol just covers the bottom of the cup.
2. Moisten the tip of a **cotton swab** by dipping it into the alcohol in the cup.
3. Rub the cotton swab on the palm of your hand.
4. Record your observations in your ScienceLog.
5. Wash your hands thoroughly.

Analysis

6. Explain what happened to the alcohol.
7. Did you feel a sensation of hot or cold? If so, how do you explain what you observed?
8. Record your answers in your ScienceLog.

What Do You Think?

Accept all reasonable responses.

Students will have a chance to revise their answers in the Chapter Review under NOW What Do You Think?

Investigate!

MATERIALS

For Each Group:
- rubbing alcohol
- small plastic cup
- cotton swab

Safety Caution: Remind students to review all safety cautions and icons before beginning this activity. Students should wear safety goggles and aprons during this activity.

Only a small amount of alcohol is needed for this activity. Demonstrate how little alcohol is needed by pouring an amount sufficient for this activity into your cup.

Answers to Analysis

6. The alcohol disappeared by evaporating.
7. Students should feel a cooling sensation. As the alcohol evaporates, it absorbs energy from the student's hand.

 Directed Reading Worksheet 3

 Science Puzzlers, Twisters & Teasers Worksheet 3

MISCONCEPTION ALERT

Glass in windows of old buildings is frequently used as evidence that glass flows over time. However, the process that was used to manufacture windowpane glass caused one end of the pane to be thicker than the other. The thicker end was usually installed at the bottom to provide stability.

Smithsonian Institution®
Visit **www.si.edu/hrw** for additional on-line resources.

Chapter 3 • States of Matter   **59**

SECTION 1

Focus

Four States of Matter

This section introduces four states of matter, and students explore the similarities and differences among these four states. Students also examine the effect of temperature and pressure on gases.

The terms *phase* and *state* are sometimes used interchangeably, but they are not the same. *State* refers to states of matter (solid, liquid, gas, plasma). *Phase* refers to a region of material with distinct boundaries and uniform properties for that region. For example, both corn oil and water are in the liquid state. A mixture of corn oil and water has two phases, the corn oil phase and the water phase.

🔔 Bellringer

Pose the following question to your students:

In the kitchen, you might find three different forms of water. What are these three forms of water, and where exactly in the kitchen would you find them?

1 Motivate

DEMONSTRATION

From one corner of the room, or from the very front, spray room deodorizer into the air. Ask students to raise their hand when they smell the deodorizer. Discuss a possible model that would explain why different students smelled the deodorizer at different times. Sheltered English

---

Section 1

Four States of Matter

Terms to Learn

states of matter
solid
liquid
gas
pressure
Boyle's law
Charles's law
plasma

What You'll Do

- Describe the properties shared by particles of all matter.
- Describe the four states of matter discussed here.
- Describe the differences between the states of matter.
- Predict how a change in pressure or temperature will affect the volume of a gas.

Figure 1 shows a model of the earliest known steam engine, invented about A.D. 60 by Hero, a scientist who lived in Alexandria, Egypt. This model also demonstrates the four most familiar states of matter: solid, liquid, gas, and plasma. The **states of matter** are the physical forms in which a substance can exist. For example, water commonly exists in three different states of matter: solid (ice), liquid (water), and gas (steam).

Figure 1 This model of Hero's steam engine spins as steam escapes through the nozzles.

Moving Particles Make Up All Matter

Matter consists of tiny particles called atoms and molecules (MAHL i KYOOLZ) that are too small to see without an amazingly powerful microscope. These atoms and molecules are always in motion and are constantly bumping into one another. The state of matter of a substance is determined by how fast the particles move and how strongly the particles are attracted to one another. **Figure 2** illustrates three of the states of matter—solid, liquid, and gas—in terms of the speed and attraction of the particles.

Figure 2 Models of a Solid, a Liquid, and a Gas

Particles of a solid do not move fast enough to overcome the strong attraction between them, so they are held tightly in place. The particles vibrate in place.

Particles of a liquid move fast enough to overcome some of the attraction between them. The particles are able to slide past one another.

Particles of a gas move fast enough to overcome nearly all of the attraction between them. The particles move independently of one another.

 Teaching Transparency 206 "Models of a Solid, a Liquid, and a Gas"

 Directed Reading Worksheet 3 Section 1

60 Chapter 3 • States of Matter

Solids Have Definite Shape and Volume

Look at the ship in **Figure 3.** Even in a bottle, it keeps its original shape and volume. If you moved the ship to a larger bottle, the ship's shape and volume would not change. Scientifically, the state in which matter has a definite shape and volume is **solid.** The particles of a substance in a solid are very close together. The attraction between them is stronger than the attraction between the particles of the same substance in the liquid or gaseous state. The atoms or molecules in a solid move, but not fast enough to overcome the attraction between them. Each particle vibrates in place because it is locked in position by the particles around it.

Figure 3 *Because this ship is a solid, it does not take the shape of the bottle.*

Two Types of Solids Solids are often divided into two categories—*crystalline* and *amorphous* (uh MOHR fuhs). Crystalline solids have a very orderly, three-dimensional arrangement of atoms or molecules. That is, the particles are arranged in a repeating pattern of rows. Examples of crystalline solids include iron, diamond, and ice. Amorphous solids are composed of atoms or molecules that are in no particular order. That is, each particle is in a particular spot, but the particles are in no organized pattern. Examples of amorphous solids include rubber and wax. **Figure 4** illustrates the differences in the arrangement of particles in these two solids.

Activity

Imagine that you are a particle in a solid. Your position in the solid is your chair. In your ScienceLog, describe the different types of motion that are possible even though you cannot leave your chair.

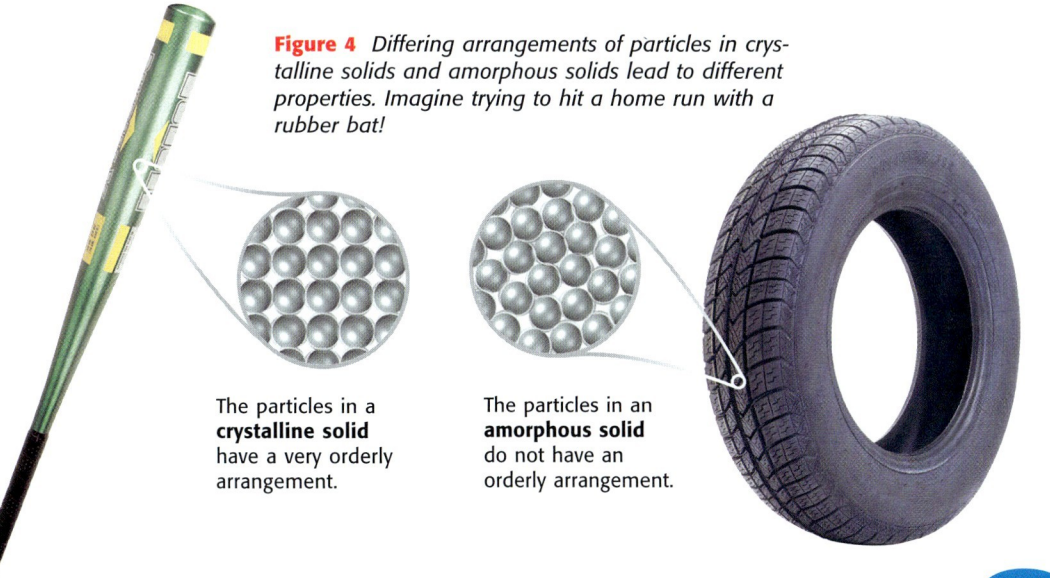

Figure 4 *Differing arrangements of particles in crystalline solids and amorphous solids lead to different properties. Imagine trying to hit a home run with a rubber bat!*

The particles in a **crystalline solid** have a very orderly arrangement.

The particles in an **amorphous solid** do not have an orderly arrangement.

WEIRD SCIENCE

Even the atoms or molecules that make up a solid are constantly in motion. However, as matter is cooled to extremely cold temperatures, its particles move more slowly. Theoretically, matter can be cooled enough for all particle motion to stop. This temperature is known as absolute zero, or 0 K (–273°C). A temperature of absolute zero has never been achieved by scientists in a laboratory.

2) Teach, continued

MEETING INDIVIDUAL NEEDS

Learners Having Difficulty
Provide students with a hand lens and samples of salt, flour, sugar, margarine or butter, and a rubber band. Give them time to look at and compare all the samples. Encourage them to investigate and describe the visual differences between an amorphous solid and a crystalline solid.

DISCUSSION

Lead a discussion about the differences between solids and liquids. Ask students to explain the differences in terms of molecular attraction, motion, and distances. Ask students to explain the behavior of salt, sugar, dust, and so on. These substances pour easily but are considered solids. Explaining this pouring behavior of small solid particles can lead to a discussion of how a liquid's molecules slide past one another while still remaining in contact with one another.

MISCONCEPTION ALERT

Students often believe erroneously that the distances between liquid molecules are much greater than distances between molecules of a solid. Point out that while most materials are more dense in the solid state than in the liquid, the densities of solids and liquids are very similar. In fact, water molecules are closer in the liquid state than they are in the solid state.

Liquids Change Shape but Not Volume

A liquid will take the shape of whatever container it is put in. You are reminded of this every time you pour yourself a glass of juice. The state in which matter takes the shape of its container and has a definite volume is **liquid**. The atoms or molecules in liquids move fast enough to overcome some of the attractions between them. The particles slide past each other until the liquid takes the shape of its container. **Figure 5** shows how the particles in juice might look if they were large enough to see.

Even though liquids change shape, they do not readily change volume. You know that a can of soda contains a certain volume of liquid regardless of whether you pour it into a large container or a small one. **Figure 6** illustrates this point using a beaker and a graduated cylinder.

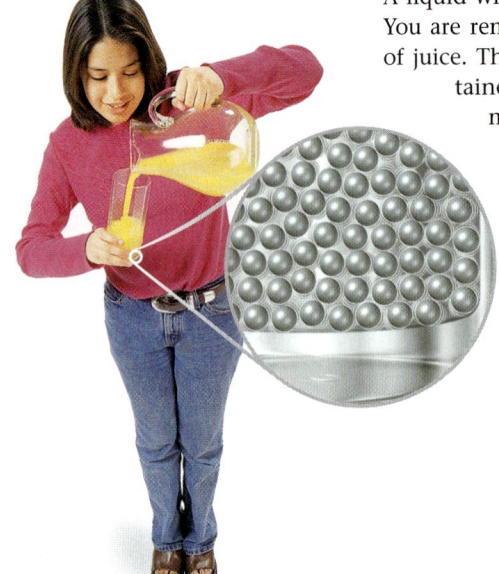

Figure 5 Particles in a liquid slide past one another until the liquid conforms to the shape of its container.

Figure 6 Even when liquids change shape, they don't change volume.

The Squeeze Is On Because the particles in liquids are close to one another, it is difficult to push them closer together. This makes liquids ideal for use in hydraulic (hie DRAW lik) systems. For example, brake fluid is the liquid used in the brake systems of cars. Stepping on the brake pedal applies a force to the liquid. The particles in the liquid move away rather than squeezing closer together. As a result, the fluid pushes the brake pads outward against the wheels, which slows the car.

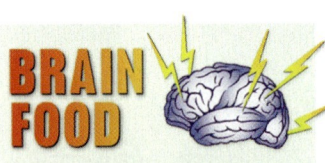

The Boeing 767 Freighter, a type of commercial airliner, has 187 km (116 mi) of hydraulic tubing.

IS THAT A FACT!

A gel is a liquid that has tiny particles of a solid suspended in it. Gels are best known for their elasticity or ability to bounce. In a gel, the solid particles remain suspended, unaffected by gravity. These suspended solids give gels their limited firmness. Examples of gels are flavored gelatin and some kinds of toothpaste.

A Drop in the Bucket Two other important properties of liquids are *surface tension* and *viscosity* (vis KAHS uh tee). Surface tension is the force acting on the particles at the surface of a liquid that causes the liquid to form spherical drops, as shown in **Figure 7.** Different liquids have different surface tensions. For example, rubbing alcohol has a lower surface tension than water, but mercury has a higher surface tension than water.

Viscosity is a liquid's resistance to flow. In general, the stronger the attractions between a liquid's particles are, the more viscous the liquid is. Think of the difference between pouring honey and pouring water. Honey flows more slowly than water because it has a higher viscosity than water.

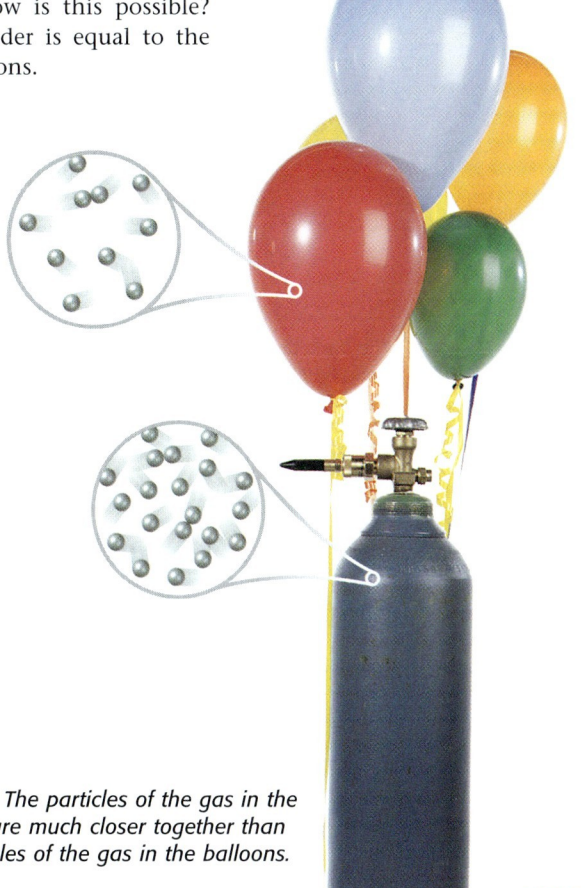

Figure 7 *Liquids form spherical drops as a result of surface tension.*

Gases Change Both Shape and Volume

How many balloons can be filled from a single metal cylinder of helium? The number may surprise you. One cylinder can fill approximately 700 balloons. How is this possible? After all, the volume of the metal cylinder is equal to the volume of only about five inflated balloons.

It's a Gas! Helium is a gas. **Gas** is the state in which matter changes in both shape and volume. The atoms or molecules in a gas move fast enough to break away completely from one another. Therefore, the particles of a substance in the gaseous state have less attraction between them than particles of the same substance in the solid or liquid state. In a gas, there is empty space between particles.

The amount of empty space in a gas can change. For example, the helium in the metal cylinder consists of atoms that have been forced very close together, as shown in **Figure 8.** As the helium fills the balloon, the atoms spread out, and the amount of empty space in the gas increases. As you continue reading, you will learn how this empty space is related to pressure.

Figure 8 *The particles of the gas in the cylinder are much closer together than the particles of the gas in the balloons.*

CONNECT TO LIFE SCIENCE

The tallest living organism is a tree known as the giant sequoia. These trees, which grow primarily in California, can grow 100 m tall. Surface tension, at least in part, helps water reach the top of these giant trees. As water evaporates from the leaves, a thin column of water molecules travels up through the tissues of the trunk and limbs. The surface tension of the water molecules, a result of cohesion, causes the molecules to stick together and, along with adhesion, allows them to be pulled all the way to the top of the tree.

ACTIVITY

Safety Caution: Caution students to wear safety goggles and an apron when performing this activity.

Provide groups with flour, paper plates, food coloring (with eyedropper), one toothpick or pin dipped in liquid dish soap, and one clean toothpick or pin. Have students drop one or two drops of food coloring onto the flour. Ask what happened. (Surface tension causes beading of the water.)

Have students insert the toothpick with soap gently into one of the spheres and note any changes. (Spheres will disappear and leave a wet spot on the powder.)

Have students insert the clean toothpick in a different sphere. Discuss any differences. (The clean toothpick should produce no changes in the sphere.)
Sheltered English

TOPIC: Solids, Liquids, and Gases
GO TO: www.scilinks.org
sciLINKS NUMBER: HSTP060

Some liquids lose all viscosity, or resistance to flow, when cooled to extremely cold temperatures. This phenomenon is called superfluidity. Helium, which is normally a gas, liquefies at about –268°C. At about –271°C, helium becomes superfluid. It will flow through extremely small holes that it normally could not flow through. It also forms a thin film on the walls of its container. This film is made up of helium atoms that are actually flowing up and out of the container!

Section 1 • Four States of Matter

Gas Under Pressure

Pressure is the amount of force exerted on a given area. You can think of this as the number of collisions of particles against the inside of the container. Compare the basketball with the beach ball in **Figure 9**. The balls have the same volume and contain particles of gas (air) that constantly collide with one another and with the inside surface of the balls. Notice, however, that there are more particles in the basketball than in the beach ball. As a result, more particles collide with the inside surface of the basketball than with the inside surface of the beach ball. When the number of collisions increases, the force on the inside surface of the ball increases. This increased force leads to increased pressure.

Self-Check

How would an increase in the speed of the particles affect the pressure of gas in a metal cylinder? (See page 724 to check your answer.)

Figure 9 Both balls shown here are full of air, but the pressure in the basketball is higher than the pressure in the beach ball.

The basketball has a higher pressure than the beach ball because the greater number of particles of gas are closer together. Therefore, they collide with the inside of the ball at a faster rate.

The beach ball has a lower pressure than the basketball because the lesser number of particles of gas are farther apart. Therefore, they collide with the inside of the ball at a slower rate.

internetconnect

*sci*LINKS
NSTA

TOPIC: Solids, Liquids, and Gases
GO TO: www.scilinks.org
*sci*LINKS NUMBER: HSTP060

REVIEW

1. List two properties that all particles of matter have in common.
2. Describe solids, liquids, and gases in terms of shape and volume.
3. Why can the volume of a gas change?
4. **Applying Concepts** Explain what happens inside the ball when you pump up a flat basketball.

Laws Describe Gas Behavior

Earlier in this chapter, you learned about the atoms and molecules in both solids and liquids. You learned that compared with gas particles, the particles of solids and liquids are closely packed together. As a result, solids and liquids do not change volume very much. Gases, on the other hand, behave differently; their volume can change by a large amount.

It is easy to measure the volume of a solid or liquid, but how do you measure the volume of a gas? Isn't the volume of a gas the same as the volume of its container? The answer is yes, but there are other factors, such as pressure, to consider.

Boyle's Law Imagine a diver at a depth of 10 m blowing a bubble of air. As the bubble rises, its volume increases. By the time the bubble reaches the surface, its original volume will have doubled due to the decrease in pressure. The relationship between the volume and pressure of a gas is known as Boyle's law because it was first described by Robert Boyle, a seventeenth-century Irish chemist. **Boyle's law** states that for a fixed amount of gas at a constant temperature, the volume of a gas increases as its pressure decreases. Likewise, the volume of a gas decreases as its pressure increases. Boyle's law is illustrated by the model in **Figure 10**.

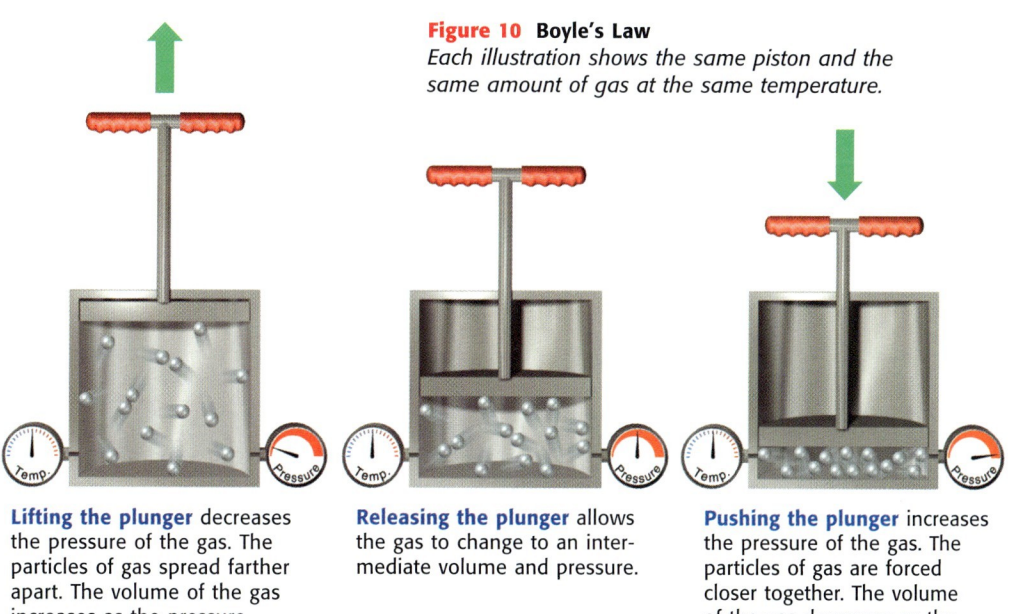

Figure 10 Boyle's Law
Each illustration shows the same piston and the same amount of gas at the same temperature.

Lifting the plunger decreases the pressure of the gas. The particles of gas spread farther apart. The volume of the gas increases as the pressure decreases.

Releasing the plunger allows the gas to change to an intermediate volume and pressure.

Pushing the plunger increases the pressure of the gas. The particles of gas are forced closer together. The volume of the gas decreases as the pressure increases.

SCIENTISTS AT ODDS

Many early scientists believed that all matter was made of four elements: earth, air, fire, and water. In 1661, Robert Boyle wrote a book called the *Sceptical Chymist* in which he disagreed with this belief. Boyle proposed that matter was made of primitive and simple bodies called corpuscles. He believed that corpuscles had different shapes and sizes that mixed together to give elements their unique properties.

Teaching Transparency 207
"Boyle's Law"

3) Extend

USING THE FIGURE

The temperature and volume of a gas are proportional, and they are directly proportional when the temperature is measured in kelvins. When the Kelvin temperature is doubled, the volume of the gas is also doubled. In **Figure 11,** what happens to the gas in the piston when the temperature is changed? Have students predict what might happen to solids or liquids in a container when the temperature is changed.

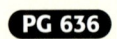

Full of Hot Air! PG 636

Answers to MATHBREAK

1. In Graph A, the missing variable increases as the volume increases. In Graph B, the missing variable decreases as the volume increases.
2. Graph A represents Charles's law. Graph B represents Boyle's law.
3. In Graph A, the *x*-axis should be labeled "Temperature." In Graph B, the label for the *x*-axis should be "Pressure."
4. Graph A is linear and shows that both variables increase together. Graph B is nonlinear and shows that as one variable increases, the other variable decreases.

Teaching Transparency 207
"Charles's Law"

internetconnect
SC_{LINKS} **TOPIC:** Natural and Artificial Plasma
NSTA **GO TO:** www.scilinks.org
sciLINKS NUMBER: HSTP065

See Charles's law in action for yourself using a balloon on page 636 of the LabBook.

MATH BREAK

Gas Law Graphs

Each graph below illustrates a gas law. However, the variable on one axis of each graph is not labeled. Answer the following questions for each graph:

1. As the volume increases, what happens to the missing variable?
2. Which gas law is shown?
3. What label belongs on the axis?
4. Is the graph linear or nonlinear? What does this tell you?

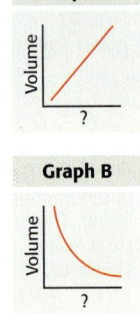

Weather balloons demonstrate a practical use of Boyle's law. A weather balloon carries equipment into the atmosphere to collect information used to predict the weather. This balloon is filled with only a small amount of gas because the pressure of the gas decreases and the volume increases as the balloon rises. If the balloon were filled with too much gas, it would pop as the volume of the gas increased.

Charles's Law An inflated balloon will also pop when it gets too hot, demonstrating another gas law—Charles's law. **Charles's law** states that for a fixed amount of gas at a constant pressure, the volume of the gas increases as its temperature increases. Likewise, the volume of the gas decreases as its temperature decreases. Charles's law is illustrated by the model in **Figure 11.** You can see Charles's law in action by putting an inflated balloon in the freezer. Wait about 10 minutes, and see what happens!

Figure 11 Charles's Law
Each illustration shows the same piston and the same amount of gas at the same pressure.

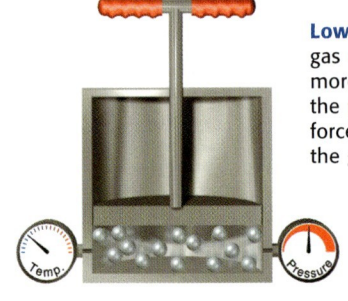

Lowering the temperature of the gas causes the particles to move more slowly. They hit the sides of the piston less often and with less force. As a result, the volume of the gas decreases.

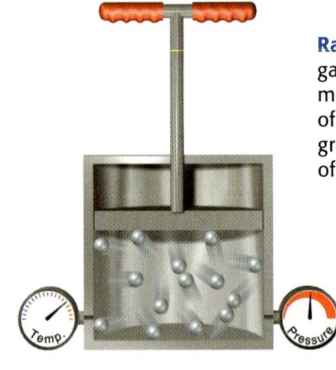

Raising the temperature of the gas causes the particles to move more quickly. They hit the sides of the piston more often and with greater force. As a result, the volume of the gas increases.

Homework

Plasmas (page 67) may be the key to an almost unlimited energy resource—nuclear fusion. Have students research nuclear fusion and plasma containment. Have them make a poster showing the powerful magnets and the tokamak reactor. Remind them to explain the possible benefits of controlling nuclear fusion on Earth.

IS THAT A FACT!

Scuba is an acronym for *s*elf-*c*ontained *u*nderwater *b*reathing *a*pparatus. Credit for the invention of scuba in 1943 is usually given to Jacques-Yves Cousteau and Emile Gagnan.

Charles's Law and Bicycle Tires

One of your friends overinflated the tires on her bicycle. Use Charles's law to explain why she should let out some of the air before going for a ride on a hot day.

Plasmas

Scientists estimate that more than 99 percent of the known matter in the universe, including the sun and other stars, is made of a state of matter called plasma. **Plasma** is the state of matter that does not have a definite shape or volume and whose particles have broken apart.

Plasmas have some properties that are quite different from the properties of gases. Plasmas conduct electric current, while gases do not. Electric and magnetic fields affect plasmas but do not affect gases. In fact, strong magnetic fields are used to contain very hot plasmas that would destroy any other container.

Natural plasmas are found in lightning, fire, and the incredible light show in **Figure 12,** called the aurora borealis (ah ROHR uh BOHR ee AL is). Artificial plasmas, found in fluorescent lights and plasma balls, are created by passing electric charges through gases.

Figure 12 Auroras, like the aurora borealis seen here, form when high-energy plasma collides with gas particles in the upper atmosphere.

REVIEW

1. When scientists record the volume of a gas, why do they also record the temperature and the pressure?
2. List two differences between gases and plasmas.
3. **Applying Concepts** What happens to the volume of a balloon left on a sunny windowsill? Explain.

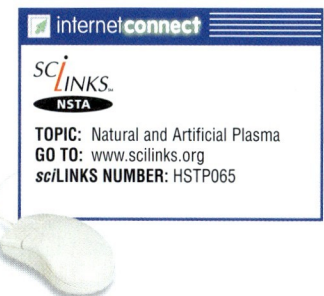

TOPIC: Natural and Artificial Plasma
GO TO: www.scilinks.org
sciLINKS NUMBER: HSTP065

SECTION 2

Focus

Changes of State

This section examines how matter changes from state to state. Changes in state are explained in terms of matter gaining or losing energy. Certain physical properties are explained in terms of molecular motion and molecular attraction.

Bellringer

Have students describe what must be done to liquid water to change it to ice or to change it to steam. Then have students use these explanations to predict what must happen, in general, to cause matter to change state. Have them write their explanations and predictions in their ScienceLog.

1 Motivate

DEMONSTRATION

Ask four student volunteers to stand close together to form a square. Wrap masking tape around the students several times. Tell the class that the four students represent the particles in a solid. Have the students demonstrate that they can still move a bit without breaking the tape, just as particles in a solid move a bit but generally stay close together. Then have the four students move around more and more until they break the tape. Discuss with the class that when particles in a solid move faster, they move apart, and the solid changes to the liquid state.

Section 2

Terms to Learn

change of state · boiling
melting · evaporation
freezing · condensation
vaporization · sublimation

What You'll Do

◆ Describe how substances change from state to state.
◆ Explain the difference between an exothermic change and an endothermic change.
◆ Compare the changes of state.

Want to learn how to get power from changes of state? Steam ahead to page 79.

Changes of State

A **change of state** is the conversion of a substance from one physical form to another. All changes of state are physical changes. In a physical change, the identity of a substance does not change. In **Figure 13,** the ice, liquid water, and steam are all the same substance—water. In this section, you will learn about the four changes of state illustrated in Figure 13 as well as a fifth change of state called *sublimation* (SUHB li MAY shuhn).

Figure 13 *The terms in the arrows are changes of state. Water commonly goes through the changes of state shown here.*

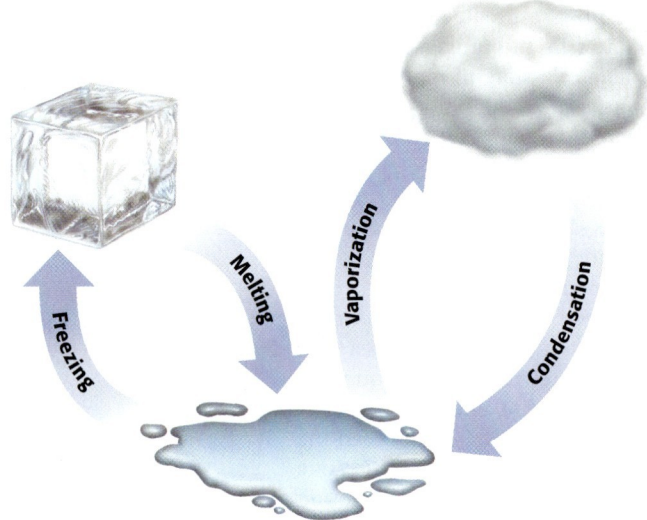

Energy and Changes of State

During a change of state, the energy of a substance changes. The *energy* of a substance is related to the motion of its particles. The molecules in the liquid water in Figure 13 move faster than the molecules in the ice. Therefore, the liquid water has more energy than the ice.

If energy is added to a substance, its particles move faster. If energy is removed, its particles move slower. The *temperature* of a substance is a measure of the speed of its particles and therefore is a measure of its energy. For example, steam has a higher temperature than liquid water, so particles in steam have more energy than particles in liquid water. A transfer of energy, known as *heat,* causes the temperature of a substance to change, which can lead to a change of state.

IS THAT A FACT!

Water is the only substance that can be found as a solid, a liquid, and a gas at normal surface temperatures on Earth.

---

68   Chapter 3 • States of Matter

Melting: Solids to Liquids

Melting is the change of state from a solid to a liquid. This is what happens when an ice cube melts. **Figure 14** shows a metal called gallium melting. What is unusual about this metal is that it melts at around 30°C. Because your normal body temperature is about 37°C, gallium will melt right in your hand!

The *melting point* of a substance is the temperature at which the substance changes from a solid to a liquid. Melting points of substances vary widely. The melting point of gallium is 30°C. Common table salt, however, has a melting point of 801°C.

Most substances have a unique melting point that can be used with other data to identify them. Because the melting point does not change with different amounts of the substance, melting point is a *characteristic property* of a substance.

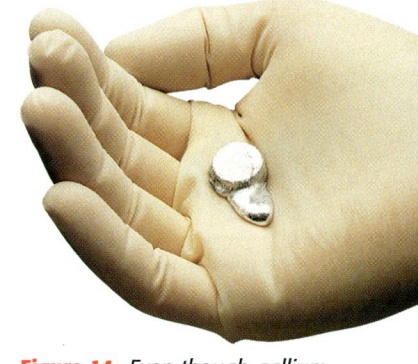

Figure 14 Even though gallium is a metal, it would not be very useful as jewelry!

Absorbing Energy For a solid to melt, particles must overcome some of their attractions to each other. When a solid is at its melting point, any energy it absorbs increases the motion of its atoms or molecules until they overcome the attractions that hold them in place. Melting is an *endothermic* change because energy is absorbed by the substance as it changes state.

Freezing: Liquids to Solids

Freezing is the change of state from a liquid to a solid. The temperature at which a liquid changes into a solid is its *freezing point*. Freezing is the reverse process of melting, so freezing and melting occur at the same temperature, as shown in **Figure 15**.

Removing Energy For a liquid to freeze, the motion of its atoms or molecules must slow to the point where attractions between them overcome their motion. If a liquid is at its freezing point, removing more energy causes the particles to begin locking into place. Freezing is an *exothermic* change because energy is removed from, or taken out of, the substance as it changes state.

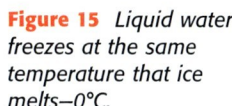

Figure 15 Liquid water freezes at the same temperature that ice melts—0°C.

If energy is added at 0°C, the ice will melt.

If energy is removed at 0°C, the liquid water will freeze.

WEIRD SCIENCE

To change the freezing point of water, just add salt. People rely on this phenomenon when making homemade ice cream. To achieve temperatures cold enough to help freeze the ice cream, rock salt is added to the ice, thus lowering the freezing point of the ice-salt mixture.

2) Teach

USING THE FIGURE

Have students look at **Figure 13**. During which changes are the substances gaining energy? (melting and vaporization)

How can students tell? Help them make a concept map to describe and compare the particle motion before and after the change in state.

MISCONCEPTION ALERT

Most students associate the term *freezing* with cold temperatures. However, be sure to point out that the term applies to any change of state from liquid to solid, regardless of temperature. Freezing can occur at high or low temperatures. For example, ammonia freezes at −77.7°C, while magnesium freezes at 650°C.

Multicultural CONNECTION

Frederick McKinley Jones (1892–1961) was an African-American inventor with more than 60 patents to his name. Perhaps his most important invention was his compact, shockproof, automatic-refrigeration unit for trucks hauling meat or produce to market. This invention, which was later adapted for trains, is still in use around the world today.

Have students find out more about Jones's inventions, especially the one that gave us "talking movies."

Directed Reading Worksheet 3 Section 2

Section 2 • Changes of State

② Teach, continued

READING 📖 STRATEGY

Prediction Guide Before students read this page, ask them if they agree with the following three statements.

- Evaporation can occur at any temperature. (true)
- Boiling occurs only at the surface of a liquid. (false)
- Vaporization is simply a liquid changing to a gas. (true)

Homework

Traditional clothing varies from culture to culture. People who live in warm climates wear lightweight and loose-fitting clothes that allow air to circulate near the body. This causes perspiration to evaporate, which cools the body. Examples of cultures that wear such lightweight clothing are those of the Middle East and Northern Africa. Ask students to research other examples of how people dress to fit the climate where they live. Have them make posters showing the examples they found.

Answer to Self-Check
endothermic

Vaporization: Liquids to Gases

One way to experience vaporization (VAY puhr i ZAY shuhn) is to iron a shirt—carefully!—using a steam iron. You will notice steam coming up from the iron as the wrinkles are eliminated. This steam results from the vaporization of liquid water by the iron. **Vaporization** is simply the change of state from a liquid to a gas.

Boiling is vaporization that occurs throughout a liquid. The temperature at which a liquid boils is called its *boiling point*. Like the melting point, the boiling point is a characteristic property of a substance. The boiling point of water is 100°C, whereas the boiling point of liquid mercury is 357°C. **Figure 16** illustrates the process of boiling and a second form of vaporization—evaporation (ee VAP uh RAY shuhn).

Evaporation is vaporization that occurs at the surface of a liquid below its boiling point, as shown in Figure 16. When you perspire, your body is cooled through the process of evaporation. Perspiration is mostly water. Water absorbs energy from your skin as it evaporates. You feel cooler because your body transfers energy to the water. Evaporation also explains why water in a glass on a table disappears after several days.

> ✓ **Self-Check**
> Is vaporization an endothermic or exothermic change? *(See page 724 to check your answer.)*

Figure 16 *Both boiling and evaporation change a liquid to a gas.*

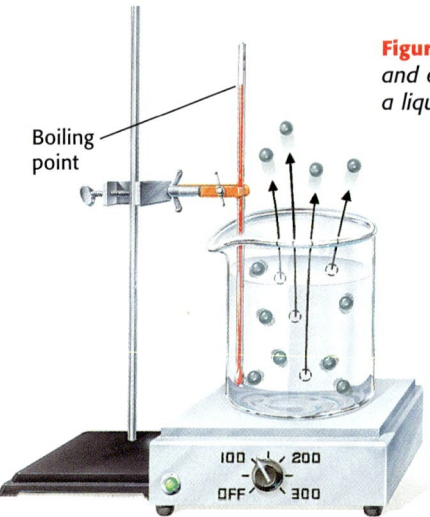

Boiling occurs in a liquid at its boiling point. As energy is added to the liquid, particles throughout the liquid move fast enough to break away from the particles around them and become a gas.

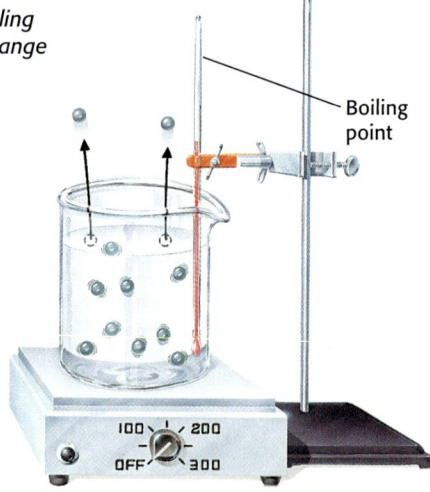

Evaporation occurs in a liquid below its boiling point. Some particles at the surface of the liquid move fast enough to break away from the particles around them and become a gas.

Science Bloopers

Most people do not want to get too sweaty, so they wear an antiperspirant. In addition to covering unpleasant odors, antiperspirants contain compounds that clog pores in the skin. This prevents sweat from being excreted by the body. However, sweat is the body's natural air conditioner. When sweat evaporates, it cools the skin. By wearing antiperspirant, people cause their bodies to cool less efficiently.

Pressure Affects Boiling Point Earlier you learned that water boils at 100°C. In fact, water only boils at 100°C at sea level because of atmospheric pressure. Atmospheric pressure is caused by the weight of the gases that make up the atmosphere. Atmospheric pressure varies depending on where you are in relation to sea level. Atmospheric pressure is lower at higher elevations. The higher you go above sea level, the less air there is above you, and the lower the atmospheric pressure is. If you were to boil water at the top of a mountain, the boiling point would be lower than 100°C. For example, Denver, Colorado, is 1.6 km (1 mi) above sea level and water boils there at about 95°C. You can make water boil at an even lower temperature by doing the QuickLab at right.

Condensation: Gases to Liquids

Look at the cool glass of lemonade in **Figure 17**. Notice the beads of water on the outside of the glass. These form as a result of condensation. **Condensation** is the change of state from a gas to a liquid. The *condensation point* of a substance is the temperature at which the gas becomes a liquid and is the same temperature as the boiling point at a given pressure. Thus, at sea level, steam condenses to form water at 100°C—the same temperature at which water boils.

For a gas to become a liquid, large numbers of atoms or molecules must clump together. Particles clump together when the attraction between them overcomes their motion. For this to occur, energy must be removed from the gas to slow the particles down. Therefore, condensation is an exothermic change.

Figure 17 *Gaseous water in the air will become liquid when it contacts a cool surface.*

QuickLab

Boiling Water Is Cool

1. Remove the cap from a **syringe**.
2. Place the tip of the syringe in the **warm water** provided by your teacher. Pull the plunger out until you have 10 mL of water in the syringe.
3. Tightly cap the syringe.
4. Hold the syringe, and slowly pull the plunger out.
5. Observe any changes you see in the water. Record your observations in your ScienceLog.
6. Why are you not burned by the boiling water in the syringe?

Meteorology CONNECTION

The amount of gaseous water that air can hold decreases as the temperature of the air decreases. As the air cools, some of the gaseous water condenses to form small drops of liquid water. These drops form clouds in the sky and fog near the ground.

IS THAT A FACT!

If all of the water vapor in Earth's atmosphere were to suddenly condense, the falling water would cover the United States to a depth of 8 m.

Can Crusher PG 637

QuickLab

MATERIALS

FOR EACH STUDENT:
- syringe
- warm water

Safety Caution: Remind all students to review all safety cautions and icons before beginning this activity. Students should wear safety goggles and aprons during this activity.

Answers to QuickLab

Since the temperature of the water required depends on the size of the syringes used, it would be best to determine the necessary temperature for the syringes your students will be using.

5. Bubbles form in the water as the plunger is pulled out.
6. The boiling water is not 100°C. The lower pressure causes the water to boil at a much lower temperature.

MATH and MORE

The average atmospheric pressure on top of Mount Everest, at an elevation of 8,850 m, is only about 33,000 Pa. The average atmospheric pressure at sea level is 101,000 Pa. Assuming that the boiling point of water is approximately 1°C lower for every decrease of 2,230 Pa, what would be the approximate boiling point of water on the top of Mount Everest? *(The pressure drops approximately 68,000 Pa, so the boiling point drops approximately 30° to 70°C.)*

Math Skills Worksheet 6 "Checking Division with Multiplication"

Sublimation: Solids Directly to Gases

Look at the solids shown in **Figure 18**. The solid on the left is ice. Notice the drops of liquid collecting as it melts. On the right, you see carbon dioxide in the solid state, also called dry ice. It is called dry ice because instead of melting into a liquid, it goes through a change of state called sublimation. **Sublimation** is the change of state from a solid directly into a gas. Dry ice is colder than ice, and it doesn't melt into a puddle of liquid. It is often used to keep food, medicine, and other materials cold without getting them wet.

For a solid to change directly into a gas, the atoms or molecules must move from being very tightly packed to being very spread apart. The attractions between the particles must be completely overcome. Because this requires the addition of energy, sublimation is an endothermic change.

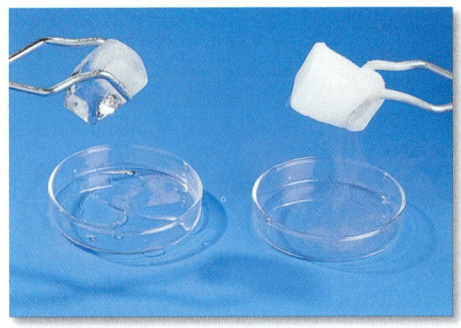

Figure 18 *Ice melts, but dry ice, on the right, turns directly into a gas.*

Comparing Changes of State

As you learned in Section 1 of this chapter, the state of a substance depends on how fast its atoms or molecules move and how strongly they are attracted to each other. A substance may undergo a physical change from one state to another by an endothermic change (if energy is added) or an exothermic change (if energy is removed). The table below shows the differences between the changes of state discussed in this section.

Summarizing the Changes of State

Change of state	Direction	Endothermic or exothermic?	Example
Melting	solid → liquid	endothermic	Ice melts into liquid water at 0°C.
Freezing	liquid → solid	exothermic	Liquid water freezes into ice at 0°C.
Vaporization	liquid → gas	endothermic	Liquid water vaporizes into steam at 100°C.
Condensation	gas → liquid	exothermic	Steam condenses into liquid water at 100°C.
Sublimation	solid → gas	endothermic	Solid dry ice sublimes into a gas at −78°C.

IS THAT A FACT!

Helium, an unreactive gas, has one of the lowest boiling points. Helium boils at 4.2 K, a little above absolute zero.

WEIRD SCIENCE

Ice and snow sometimes sublime directly to water vapor. If the air is dry after a snowstorm, a thin layer of ice on a driveway or street may simply disappear in a matter of hours, even though the temperature never rises above freezing.

Temperature Change Versus Change of State

When most substances lose or absorb energy, one of two things happens to the substance: its temperature changes or its state changes. Earlier in the chapter, you learned that the temperature of a substance is a measure of the speed of the particles. This means that when the temperature of a substance changes, the speed of the particles also changes. But while a substance changes state, its temperature does not change until the change of state is complete, as shown in **Figure 19.**

Figure 19 Changing the State of Water

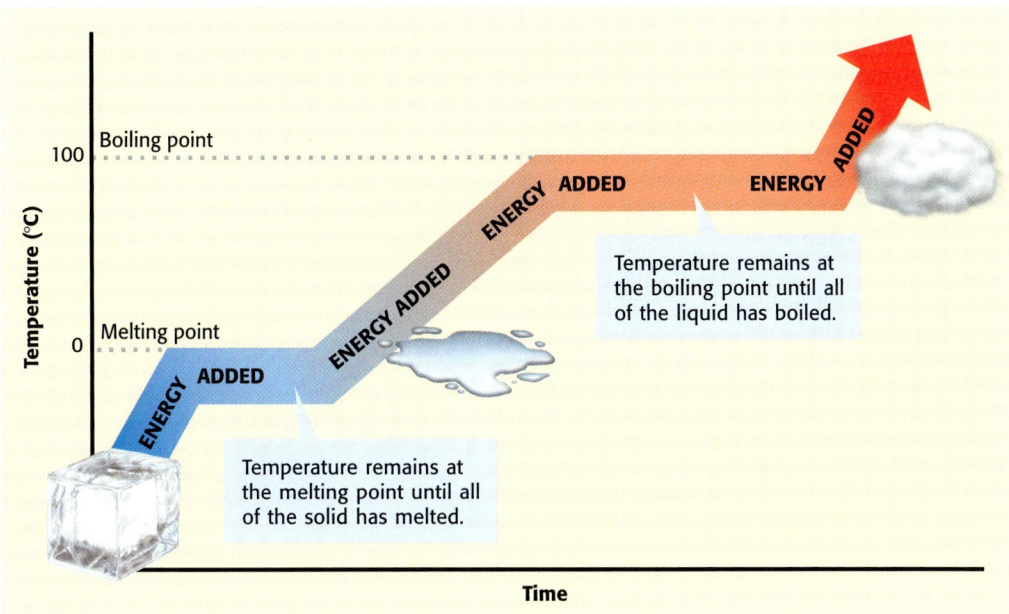

Temperature remains at the boiling point until all of the liquid has boiled.

Temperature remains at the melting point until all of the solid has melted.

REVIEW

1. Compare endothermic and exothermic changes.
2. Classify each change of state (melting, freezing, vaporization, condensation, and sublimation) as endothermic or exothermic.
3. Describe how the motion and arrangement of particles change as a substance freezes.
4. **Comparing Concepts** How are evaporation and boiling different? How are they similar?

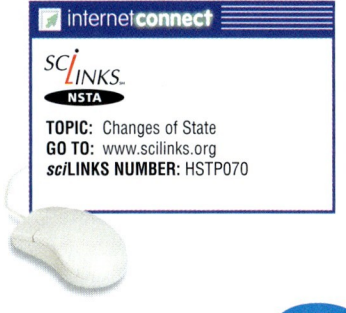

TOPIC: Changes of State
GO TO: www.scilinks.org
*sci*LINKS NUMBER: HSTP070

4) Close

Quiz

Pose the following situation to students:

A scientist and her assistant have an unmarked thermometer on which they want to mark the temperatures of 0°C and 100°C. They heat a beaker of water and take several cubes of ice out of the freezer. Just as they are about to mark the thermometer, the phone rings. The scientist spends 15 minutes on the phone. When she is finished, she again places the thermometer on the ice to mark 0°C. The scientist's assistant stops her and says that after 15 minutes the ice has begun to melt and must be warmer than 0°C. Also, since the water has been boiling for 15 minutes, it must be hotter than 100°C. Explain why the assistant's assumptions are not correct.

ALTERNATIVE ASSESSMENT

Use "The Water Cycle" teaching transparency to help students understand the changes of state that water undergoes as it cycles through the environment. Have students explain in their own words how changing the state of water **(Figure 19)** relates to the water cycle.

Teaching Transparency 141
"The Water Cycle"

Teaching Transparency 209
"Changing the State of Water"

▼ Answers to Review

1. During endothermic changes, energy is absorbed. During exothermic changes, energy is released.
2. exothermic: freezing, condensation; endothermic: melting, vaporization, sublimation
3. As a substance freezes, its particles lose some of their freedom of motion and become more orderly.
4. Evaporation occurs only at the surface of a liquid while boiling occurs throughout a liquid. Both evaporation and boiling are endothermic processes that change a liquid to a gas.

Section 2 • Changes of State

Chapter Highlights

VOCABULARY DEFINITIONS

SECTION 1

states of matter the physical forms in which a substance can exist; states include solid, liquid, gas, and plasma

solid the state in which matter has a definite shape and volume

liquid the state in which matter takes the shape of its container and has a definite volume

gas the state in which matter changes in both shape and volume

pressure the amount of force exerted on a given area

Boyle's law the law that states that for a fixed amount of gas at a constant temperature, the volume of a gas increases as its pressure decreases

Charles's law the law that states that for a fixed amount of gas at a constant pressure, the volume of a gas increases as its temperature increases

plasma the state of matter that does not have a definite shape or volume and whose particles have broken apart

Chapter Highlights

SECTION 1

Vocabulary
- **states of matter** (p. 60)
- **solid** (p. 61)
- **liquid** (p. 62)
- **gas** (p. 63)
- **pressure** (p. 64)
- **Boyle's law** (p. 65)
- **Charles's law** (p. 66)
- **plasma** (p. 67)

Section Notes
- The states of matter are the physical forms in which a substance can exist. The four most familiar states are solid, liquid, gas, and plasma.
- All matter is made of tiny particles called atoms and molecules that attract each other and move constantly.
- A solid has a definite shape and volume.
- A liquid has a definite volume but not a definite shape.
- A gas does not have a definite shape or volume. A gas takes the shape and volume of its container.
- Pressure is a force per unit area. Gas pressure increases as the number of collisions of gas particles increases.
- Boyle's law states that the volume of a gas increases as the pressure decreases if the temperature does not change.
- Charles's law states that the volume of a gas increases as the temperature increases if the pressure does not change.
- Plasmas are composed of particles that have broken apart. Plasmas do not have a definite shape or volume.

Labs
Full of Hot Air! (p. 636)

✓ Skills Check

Math Concepts

GRAPHING DATA The relationship between measured values can be seen by plotting the data on a graph. The top graph shows the linear relationship described by Charles's law—as the temperature of a gas increases, its volume increases. The bottom graph shows the nonlinear relationship described by Boyle's law—as the pressure of a gas increases, its volume decreases.

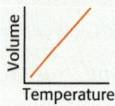
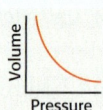

Visual Understanding

PARTICLE ARRANGEMENT Many of the properties of solids, liquids, and gases are due to the arrangement of the atoms or molecules of the substance. Review the models in Figure 2 on page 60 to study the differences in particle arrangement between the solid, liquid, and gaseous states.

SUMMARY OF THE CHANGES OF STATE Review the table on page 72 to study the direction of each change of state and whether energy is absorbed or removed during each change.

Lab and Activity Highlights

Full of Hot Air! PG 636

Can Crusher PG 637

A Hot and Cool Lab PG 638

 Datasheets for LabBook (blackline masters for these labs)

SECTION 2

Vocabulary
- change of state *(p. 68)*
- melting *(p. 69)*
- freezing *(p. 69)*
- vaporization *(p. 70)*
- boiling *(p. 70)*
- evaporation *(p. 70)*
- condensation *(p. 71)*
- sublimation *(p. 72)*

Section Notes
- A change of state is the conversion of a substance from one physical form to another. All changes of state are physical changes.
- Exothermic changes release energy. Endothermic changes absorb energy.
- Melting changes a solid to a liquid. Freezing changes a liquid to a solid. The freezing point and melting point of a substance are the same temperature.
- Vaporization changes a liquid to a gas. There are two kinds of vaporization: boiling and evaporation.
- Boiling occurs throughout a liquid at the boiling point.
- Evaporation occurs at the surface of a liquid, at a temperature below the boiling point.
- Condensation changes a gas to a liquid.
- Sublimation changes a solid directly to a gas.
- Temperature does not change during a change of state.

Labs
- Can Crusher *(p. 637)*
- A Hot and Cool Lab *(p. 638)*

VOCABULARY DEFINITIONS, continued

SECTION 2

change of state the conversion of a substance from one physical form to another

melting the change of state from a solid to a liquid

freezing the change of state from a liquid to a solid

vaporization the change of state from a liquid to a gas; includes boiling and evaporation

boiling vaporization that occurs throughout a liquid

evaporation vaporization that occurs at the surface of a liquid below its boiling point

condensation the change of state from a gas to a liquid

sublimation the change of state from a solid directly into a gas

 Vocabulary Review Worksheet 3

 Blackline masters of these Chapter Highlights can be found in the **Study Guide**.

---

internet connect

 **GO TO:** go.hrw.com

Visit the **HRW** Web site for a variety of learning tools related to this chapter. Just type in the keyword:

KEYWORD: HSTSTA

 **GO TO:** www.scilinks.org

Visit the **National Science Teachers Association** on-line Web site for Internet resources related to this chapter. Just type in the *sciLINKS* number for more information about the topic:

TOPIC: Forms and Uses of Glass	*sci*LINKS NUMBER: HSTP055
TOPIC: Solids, Liquids, and Gases	*sci*LINKS NUMBER: HSTP060
TOPIC: Natural and Artificial Plasma	*sci*LINKS NUMBER: HSTP065
TOPIC: Changes of State	*sci*LINKS NUMBER: HSTP070
TOPIC: The Steam Engine	*sci*LINKS NUMBER: HSTP075

75

Lab and Activity Highlights

LabBank

 Whiz-Bang Demonstrations, Demonstration with a CRUNCH! Demo 41

Labs You Can Eat, How Cold Is Ice-Cream Cold? Lab 18

 Long-Term Projects & Research Ideas, Episode IV: Sam and His Elephants Get That Sinking Feeling, Project 53

Chapter 3 • Chapter Highlights **75**

Chapter Review Answers

USING VOCABULARY

1. Solid is the state of matter in which the substance has a definite shape and volume; liquid is the state in which the substance takes the shape of its container but has a definite volume.
2. Boyle's law states that when the pressure of a gas increases, its volume decreases. Charles's law states that when the temperature of a gas increases, its volume increases.
3. Evaporation is the change of a liquid to a gas at the surface of a liquid. Boiling is the change of a liquid to a gas throughout a liquid.
4. Melting changes a solid to a liquid. Freezing changes a liquid to a solid.

UNDERSTANDING CONCEPTS

Multiple Choice

5. b
6. b
7. b
8. b
9. a
10. c
11. a
12. d
13. c

Short Answer

14. The particles of liquid water can move past one another and take the shape of a container. Particles in an ice cube are locked in place and cannot move past one another. An ice cube holds its shape no matter what container you put it in.
15. gases, liquids, solids
16. Iron in the solid state is more dense than iron in the liquid or gaseous state. The density of gaseous iron is lower than the density of solid or liquid iron.

Chapter Review

USING VOCABULARY

For each pair of terms, explain the difference in meaning.

1. solid/liquid
2. Boyle's law/Charles's law
3. evaporation/boiling
4. melting/freezing

UNDERSTANDING CONCEPTS

Multiple Choice

5. Which of the following best describes the particles of a liquid?
   a. The particles are far apart and moving fast.
   b. The particles are close together but moving past each other.
   c. The particles are far apart and moving slowly.
   d. The particles are closely packed and vibrate in place.

6. Boiling points and freezing points are examples of
   a. chemical properties.   c. energy.
   b. physical properties.   d. matter.

7. During which change of state do atoms or molecules become more ordered?
   a. boiling   c. melting
   b. condensation   d. sublimation

8. Which of the following describes what happens as the temperature of a gas in a balloon increases?
   a. The speed of the particles decreases.
   b. The volume of the gas increases and the speed of the particles increases.
   c. The volume decreases.
   d. The pressure decreases.

9. Dew collects on a spider web in the early morning. This is an example of
   a. condensation.   c. sublimation.
   b. evaporation.   d. melting.

10. Which of the following changes of state is exothermic?
    a. evaporation   c. freezing
    b. sublimation   d. melting

11. What happens to the volume of a gas inside a piston if the temperature does not change but the pressure is reduced?
    a. increases
    b. stays the same
    c. decreases
    d. not enough information

12. The atoms and molecules in matter
    a. are attracted to one another.
    b. are constantly moving.
    c. move faster at higher temperatures.
    d. All of the above

13. Which of the following contains plasma?
    a. dry ice   c. a fire
    b. steam   d. a hot iron

Short Answer

14. Explain why liquid water takes the shape of its container but an ice cube does not.

15. Rank solids, liquids, and gases in order of decreasing particle speed.

16. Compare the density of iron in the solid, liquid, and gaseous states.

Concept Mapping

17. 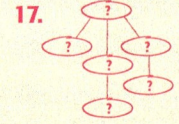 An answer to this exercise can be found at the end of this book.

Concept Mapping Transparency 3

Chapter 3 • States of Matter

Concept Mapping

17. Use the following terms to create a concept map: states of matter, solid, liquid, gas, plasma, changes of state, freezing, vaporization, condensation, melting.

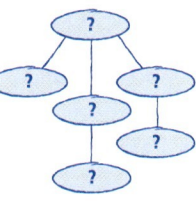

CRITICAL THINKING AND PROBLEM SOLVING

18. After taking a shower, you notice that small droplets of water cover the mirror. Explain how this happens. Be sure to describe where the water comes from and the changes it goes through.

19. In the photo below, water is being split to form two new substances, hydrogen and oxygen. Is this a change of state? Explain your answer.

20. To protect their crops during freezing temperatures, orange growers spray water onto the trees and allow it to freeze. In terms of energy lost and energy gained, explain why this practice protects the oranges from damage.

21. At sea level, water boils at 100°C, while methane boils at −161°C. Which of these substances has a stronger force of attraction between its particles? Explain your reasoning.

MATH IN SCIENCE

22. Kate placed 100 mL of water in five different pans, placed the pans on a windowsill for a week, and measured how much water evaporated. Draw a graph of her data, shown below, with surface area on the *x*-axis. Is the graph linear or nonlinear? What does this tell you?

Pan number	1	2	3	4	5
Surface area (cm²)	44	82	20	30	65
Volume evaporated (mL)	42	79	19	29	62

23. Examine the graph below, and answer the following questions:
    a. What is the boiling point of the substance? What is the melting point?
    b. Which state is present at 30°C?
    c. How will the substance change if energy is added to the liquid at 20°C?

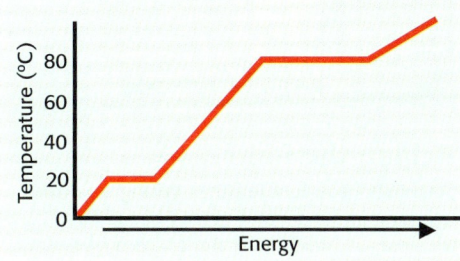

NOW What Do You Think?

Take a minute to review your answers to the ScienceLog questions on page 59. Have your answers changed? If necessary, revise your answers based on what you have learned since you began this chapter.

CRITICAL THINKING AND PROBLEM SOLVING

18. As you take a shower, some of the liquid water evaporates and becomes a gas. When the gaseous water touches the mirror, the water releases energy to the mirror and condenses into drops of liquid water.

19. The splitting of water into hydrogen and oxygen is not a change of state because the substance (water) does not keep its identity during the change. The water is changed into two new substances, hydrogen and oxygen.

20. Freezing is an exothermic change. As the water freezes, it releases energy. The oranges absorb some of this energy and warm up. (The ice also helps to insulate the oranges from the cold air.)

21. Water has a stronger force of attraction between its particles. A higher temperature, and therefore more energy, is required to separate the water particles from one another than is needed to separate the methane particles from one another.

MATH IN SCIENCE

22.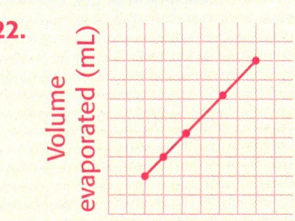

The graph is linear, which tells you that both variables (surface area and volume evaporated) increase together.

23. a. 80°C; 20°C
    b. liquid
    c. The temperature of the liquid will rise.

NOW WHAT DO YOU THINK?

1. solid, liquid, gas, and plasma
2. Particles in a solid have limited motion. They mainly vibrate around fixed points. Particles in a liquid can move past one another but are still very close together. Particles in a gas have the greatest freedom of motion. They are able to move apart to fill a container.
3. melting, freezing, vaporization, condensation, and sublimation

 Blackline masters of this Chapter Review can be found in the **Study Guide.**

SCIENCE, TECHNOLOGY, AND SOCIETY

Guiding Lightning

Teaching Strategy
In order to help students connect this feature with the topic of the unit, review the term *plasma* with students.

Research Activity You may wish to have a group of students do research on different types of lightning that exist planetwide. Examples include ribbon lightning, sheet lightning, and bead lightning. Ribbon lightning looks like a broad stream of fire; sheet lightning causes a cloud to glow; and bead lightning breaks up, creating a beadlike chain across the sky.

Students may also find information about "sprites" (red and blue balls of lightning generated in some thunderstorms). This type of lightning is not well understood and may be related to particulate matter in the atmosphere. There was a great increase in the number of sprites following the forest fires in Mexico in 1998.

Science, Technology, and Society

Guiding Lightning

By the time you finish reading this sentence, lightning will have flashed more than 500 times around the world. This common phenomenon can have devastating results. Each year in the United States alone, lightning kills almost a hundred people and causes several hundred million dollars in damage. While controlling this awesome outburst of Mother Nature may seem impossible, scientists around the world are searching for ways to reduce the destruction caused by lightning.

Behind the Bolts
Scientists have learned that during a normal lightning strike several events occur. First, electric charges build up at the bottom of a cloud. The cloud then emits a line of negatively charged air particles that zigzags toward the Earth. The attraction between these negatively charged air particles and positively charged particles from objects on the ground forms a *plasma channel.* This channel is the pathway for a lightning bolt. As soon as the plasma channel is complete, BLAM!—between 3 and 20 lightning bolts separated by thousandths of a second travel along it.

A Stroke of Genius
Armed with this information, scientists have begun thinking of ways to redirect these naturally occurring plasma channels. One idea is to use laser beams. In theory, a laser beam directed into a thundercloud can charge the air particles in its path, causing a plasma channel to develop and forcing lightning to strike.

By creating the plasma channels themselves, scientists can, in a way, catch a bolt of lightning before it strikes and direct it to a safe area of the ground. So scientists simply use lasers to direct naturally occurring lightning to strike where they want it to.

A Bright Future?
Laser technology is not without its problems, however. The machines that generate laser beams are large and expensive, and they can themselves be struck by misguided lightning bolts. Also, it is not clear whether creating these plasma channels will be enough to prevent the devastating effects of lightning.

▲ *Sometime in the future, a laser like this might be used to guide lightning away from sensitive areas.*

Find Out for Yourself
▶ Use the Internet or an electronic database to find out how rockets have been used in lightning research. Share your findings with the class.

78

Sample Answer to Find Out for Yourself

Researchers from NASA have sent up test rockets with trailing wires to try to determine the atmospheric conditions necessary for aircraft and rockets to trigger lightning strikes. Scientists have found that a rocket is more likely to trigger lightning when a thunderstorm is relatively inactive.

The Electric Power Research Institute uses small rockets to provoke and direct lightning strikes in order to study the impact of lightning on electric utility equipment, such as power lines and transformers.

Eureka!

Full Steam Ahead!

It was huge. It was 40 m long, about 5 m high, and it weighed 245 metric tons. It could pull a 3.28 million kilogram train at 100 km/h. It was a 4-8-8-4 locomotive, called a Big Boy, delivered in 1941 to the Union Pacific Railroad in Omaha, Nebraska. It was also one of the final steps in a 2,000-year search to harness steam power.

A Simple Observation

For thousands of years, people used wind, water, gravity, dogs, horses, and cattle to replace manual labor. But until about 300 years ago, they had limited success. Then in 1690, Denis Papin, a French mathematician and physicist, observed that steam expanding in a cylinder pushed a piston up. As the steam then cooled and contracted, the piston fell. Watching the motion of the piston, Papin had an idea: attach a water-pump handle to the piston. As the pump handle rose and fell with the piston, water was pumped.

More Uplifting Ideas

Eight years later, an English naval captain named Thomas Savery made Papin's device more efficient by using water to cool and condense the steam. Savery's improved pump was used in British coal mines. As good as Savery's pump was, the development of steam power didn't stop there!

In 1712, an English blacksmith named Thomas Newcomen improved Savery's device by adding a second piston and a horizontal beam that acted like a seesaw. One end of the beam was attached to the piston in the steam cylinder. The other end of the beam was attached to the pump piston. As the steam piston moved up and down, it created a vacuum in the pump cylinder and sucked water up from the mine. Newcomen's engine was the most widely used steam engine for more than 50 years.

Watt a Great Idea!

In 1764, James Watt, a Scottish technician, was repairing a Newcomen engine. He realized that heating the cylinder, letting it cool, then heating it again wasted an enormous amount of energy. Watt added a separate chamber where the steam could cool and condense. The two chambers were connected by a valve that let the steam escape from the boiler. This improved the engine's efficiency—the boiler could stay hot all the time!

A few years later, Watt turned the whole apparatus on its side so that the piston was moving horizontally. He added a slide valve that admitted steam first to one end of the chamber (pushing the piston in one direction) and then to the other end (pushing the piston back). This changed the steam pump into a true steam engine that could drive a locomotive the size of Big Boy!

Explore Other Inventions

▶ Watt's engine helped trigger the Industrial Revolution as many new uses for steam power were found. Find out more about the many other inventors, from tinkerers to engineers, who harnessed the power of steam.

Eureka!
Full Steam Ahead!

Background

In A.D. 60, an Egyptian writer named Hero wrote about a machine made of a metal sphere supported by two hollow pipes over a kettle of water. When a fire was lit under the kettle, the water turned into steam, which traveled through the pipes into the sphere. Two L-shaped nozzles in the sphere allowed the steam to escape, causing the sphere to rotate. This interesting device was invented just for fun, but it is an early example of how steam can be used to set objects in motion.

James Watt is also well known for his patented design of the double-acting piston. In this engine, the steam entered the cylinder on one side of the piston, pushing the piston to one end of the cylinder, and then on the other side of the piston, pushing the piston back to the other end of the cylinder. This allowed the steam engine to operate continuously. The addition of a flywheel made rotary motion possible.

TOPIC: The Steam Engine
GO TO: www.scilinks.org
sciLINKS NUMBER: HSTP075

Sample Answer to Explore Other Inventions

In the early nineteenth century, Oliver Evans, an American inventor, built a stationary high-pressure steam engine. His engine was originally used to drive a rotary crusher to produce pulverized limestone for agricultural use. Later, he designed a high-pressure steam engine that was used in driving sawmills, sowing grain, and powering a dredge to clear the Philadelphia waterfront. Evans's steam engines were also used to process paper, cotton, and tobacco.

Richard Trevithick, an English mechanical engineer and inventor, used the high-pressure steam engine to construct the world's first steam railway locomotive in 1803. By 1805, Trevithick had adapted his high-pressure steam engine to propel a barge using paddle wheels and to drive an iron-rolling mill. Trevithick's engines also powered one of the first steam dredges in 1806 and drove a threshing machine on a farm in 1812.

Chapter Organizer

CHAPTER ORGANIZATION	TIME MINUTES	OBJECTIVES	LABS, INVESTIGATIONS, AND DEMONSTRATIONS
Chapter Opener pp. 80–81	45	National Standards: UCP 1, 2, 3, SAI 1, 2, ST 1, SPSP 3, 4, 5, HNS 1, PS 1a, 1b	**Investigate!** Mystery Mixture, p. 81
Section 1 Elements	90	▶ Describe pure substances. ▶ Describe the characteristics of elements, and give examples. ▶ Explain how elements can be identified. ▶ Classify elements according to their properties. UCP 1, 2, SAI 1, PS 1a, 1b, 1c	**Demonstration,** p. 82 in ATE **Interactive Explorations CD-ROM,** What's the Matter? A **Worksheet** is also available in the **Interactive Explorations Teacher's Edition.** **Labs You Can Eat,** An Iron-ic Cereal Experience, Lab 19
Section 2 Compounds	90	▶ Describe the properties of compounds. ▶ Identify the differences between an element and a compound. ▶ Give examples of common compounds. UCP 1, 2, SAI 2, SPSP 5, PS 1b, 1c; LabBook UCP 1, 2, SPSP 5	**Demonstration,** p. 86 in ATE **QuickLab,** Compound Confusion, p. 87 **Discovery Lab,** Flame Tests, p. 640 **Datasheets for LabBook,** Flame Tests, Datasheet 12
Section 3 Mixtures	90	▶ Describe the properties of mixtures. ▶ Describe methods of separating the components of a mixture. ▶ Analyze a solution in terms of its solute, solvent, and concentration. ▶ Compare the properties of solutions, suspensions, and colloids. UCP 1, 2, ST 2, SPSP 1, 3, PS 1a; LabBook UCP 1, 2, SAI 1, 2, ST 2, SPSP 5	**Demonstration,** Separation, p. 91 in ATE **Discovery Lab,** A Sugar Cube Race! p. 642 **Datasheets for LabBook,** A Sugar Cube Race! Datasheet 13 **Skill Builder,** Making Butter, p. 643 **Datasheets for LabBook,** Making Butter, Datasheet 14 **Making Models,** Unpolluting Water, p. 644 **Datasheets for LabBook,** Unpolluting Water, Datasheet 15 **Inquiry Labs,** Separation Anxiety, Lab 16 **Whiz-Bang Demonstrations,** Dense Suspense, Demo 42 **EcoLabs & Field Activities,** Ozone News Zone, EcoLab 17 **Long-Term Projects & Research Ideas,** Project 54

See page T20 for a complete correlation of this book with the

NATIONAL SCIENCE EDUCATION STANDARDS.

TECHNOLOGY RESOURCES

 Guided Reading Audio CD
English or Spanish, Chapter 4

 Science Discovery Videodiscs
Image and Activity Bank with Lesson Plans: It Takes Concentration
Science Sleuths: Fortune or Fraud?

 CNN Eye on the Environment, Treating Toxic Waste, Segment 24

  Interactive Explorations CD-ROM
CD 1, Exploration 4, What's the Matter?

 One-Stop Planner CD-ROM with Test Generator

Chapter 4 • Elements, Compounds, and Mixtures

CLASSROOM WORKSHEETS, TRANSPARENCIES, AND RESOURCES	SCIENCE INTEGRATION AND CONNECTIONS	REVIEW AND ASSESSMENT
Directed Reading Worksheet 4 **Science Puzzlers, Twisters & Teasers,** Worksheet 4		
Directed Reading Worksheet 4, Section 1 **Math Skills for Science Worksheet 21,** Percentages, Fractions, and Decimals **Science Skills Worksheet 25,** Introduction to Graphs **Transparency 210,** The Three Major Categories of Elements **Problem Solving Worksheet 4,** Jet Smart	**Math and More,** p. 83 in ATE **Multicultural Connection,** p. 83 in ATE **Real-World Connection,** p. 85 in ATE	**Review,** p. 85 **Quiz,** p. 85 in ATE **Alternative Assessment,** p. 85 in ATE
Directed Reading Worksheet 4, Section 2	**Physics Connection,** p. 88 **Holt Anthology of Science Fiction,** *The Strange Case of Dr. Jekyll and Mr. Hyde*	**Self-Check,** p. 87 **Review,** p. 89 **Quiz,** p. 89 in ATE **Alternative Assessment,** p. 89 in ATE
Transparency 211, Separation of a Mixture **Directed Reading Worksheet 4,** Section 3 **Math Skills for Science Worksheet 20,** Parts of 100: Calculating Percentages **Math Skills for Science Worksheet 17,** Using Proportions and Cross-Multiplication **Transparency 212,** Solubility Graph **Transparency 134,** Three Types of Volcanoes **Reinforcement Worksheet 4,** It's All Mixed Up	**Cross-Disciplinary Focus,** p. 92 in ATE **Math and More,** p. 93 in ATE **Cross-Disciplinary Focus,** p. 93 in ATE **MathBreak,** Calculating Concentration, p. 94 **Math and More,** p. 94 in ATE **Connect to Earth Science,** p. 94 in ATE **Connect to Life Science,** p. 95 in ATE **Biology Connection,** p. 96 **Apply,** p. 96 **Connect to Earth Science,** p. 96 in ATE **Science, Technology, and Society:** Perfume, p. 102	**Review,** p. 92 **Homework,** pp. 92, 95 in ATE **Self-Check,** p. 93 **Review,** p. 97 **Quiz,** p. 97 in ATE **Alternative Assessment,** p. 97 in ATE

END-OF-CHAPTER REVIEW AND ASSESSMENT

Chapter Review in Study Guide
Vocabulary and Notes in Study Guide
Chapter Tests with Performance-Based Assessment, Chapter 4 Test
Chapter Tests with Performance-Based Assessment, Performance-Based Assessment 4
Concept Mapping Transparency 4

 Holt, Rinehart and Winston On-line Resources
go.hrw.com

For worksheets and other teaching aids related to this chapter, visit the HRW Web site and type in the keyword: **HSTMIX**

 **National Science Teachers Association**
www.scilinks.org

Encourage students to use the *sci*LINKS numbers listed in the internet connect boxes to access information and resources on the **NSTA** Web site.

Chapter 4 • Chapter Organizer

Chapter Resources & Worksheets

Visual Resources

TEACHING TRANSPARENCIES

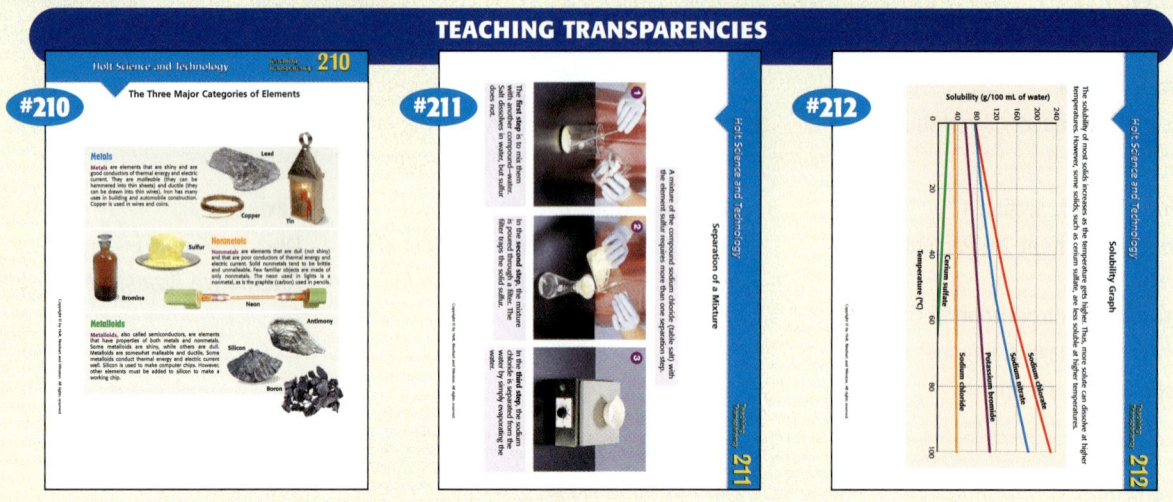

#210 The Three Major Categories of Elements
#211 Separation of a Mixture
#212 Solubility Graph

TEACHING TRANSPARENCIES

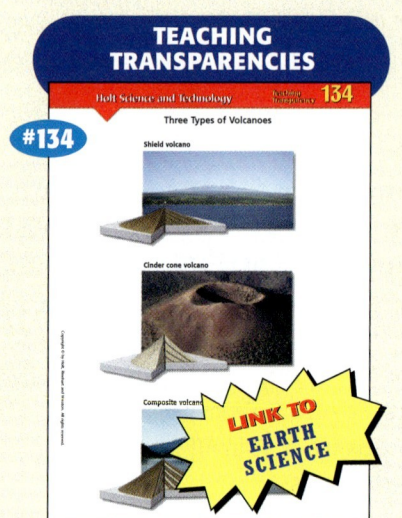

#134 Three Types of Volcanoes — LINK TO EARTH SCIENCE

CONCEPT MAPPING TRANSPARENCY

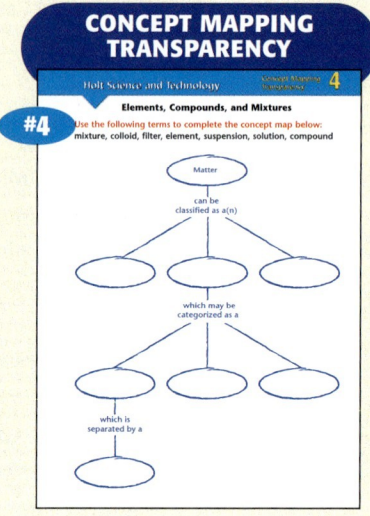

#4 Elements, Compounds, and Mixtures

Meeting Individual Needs

DIRECTED READING

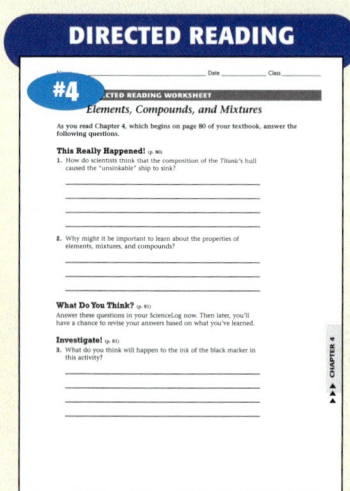

#4 Elements, Compounds, and Mixtures

REINFORCEMENT & VOCABULARY REVIEW

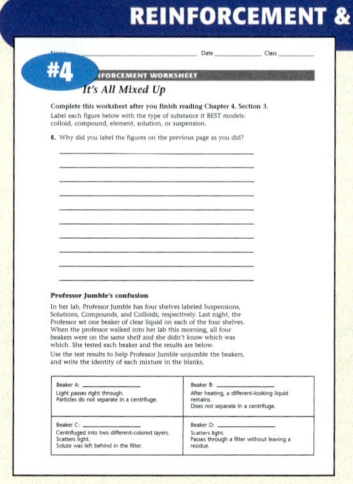

#4 It's All Mixed Up

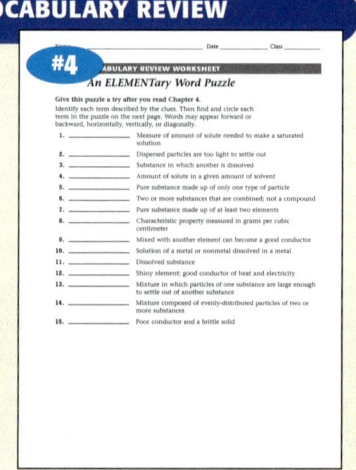

#4 An ELEMENTary Word Puzzle

SCIENCE PUZZLERS, TWISTERS & TEASERS

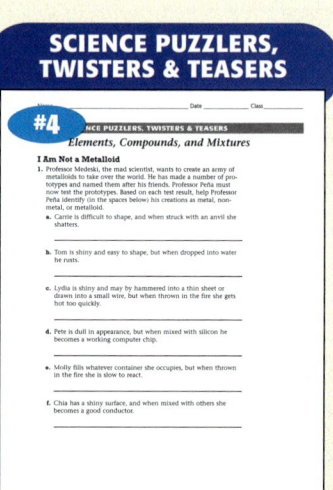

#4 Elements, Compounds, and Mixtures — I Am Not a Metalloid

79C Chapter 4 • Elements, Compounds, and Mixtures

Chapter 4 • Elements, Compounds, and Mixtures

Review & Assessment

STUDY GUIDE

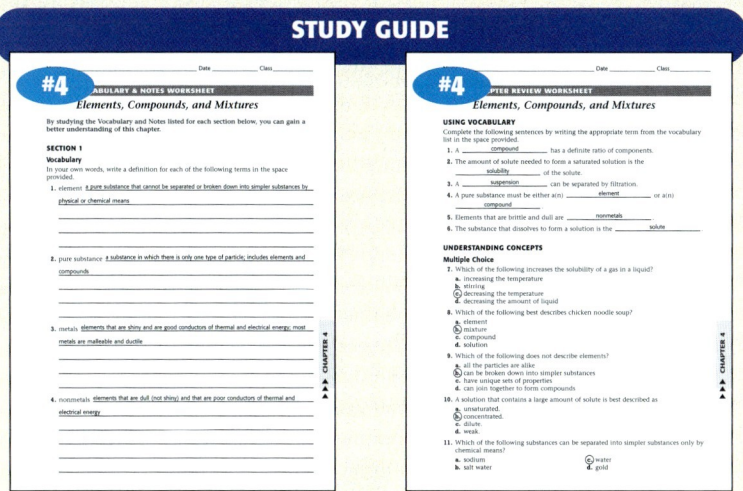

CHAPTER TESTS WITH PERFORMANCE-BASED ASSESSMENT

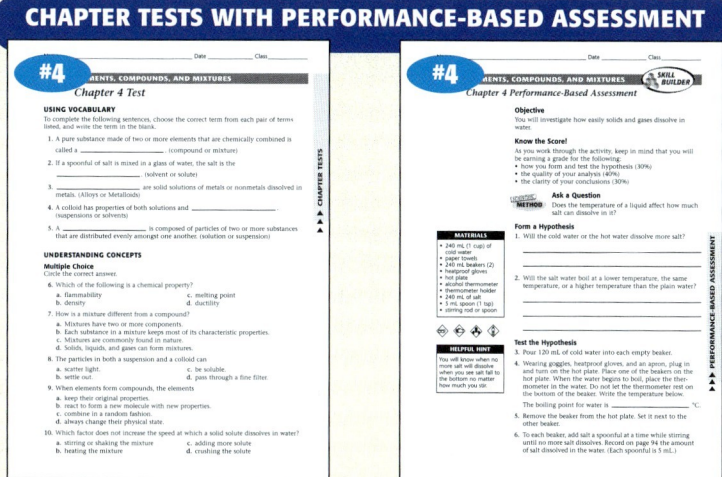

Lab Worksheets

INQUIRY LABS

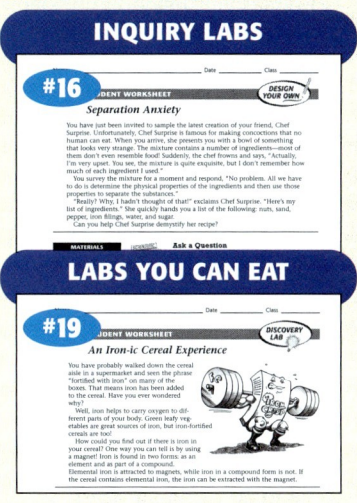

LABS YOU CAN EAT

WHIZ-BANG DEMONSTRATIONS

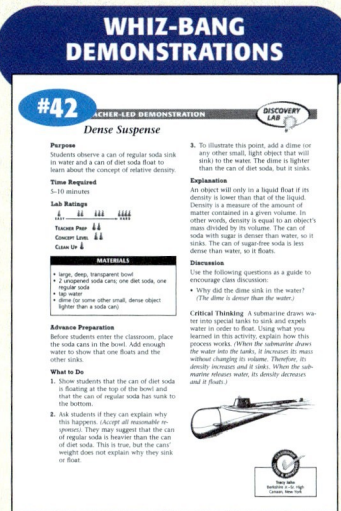

ECOLABS & FIELD ACTIVITIES

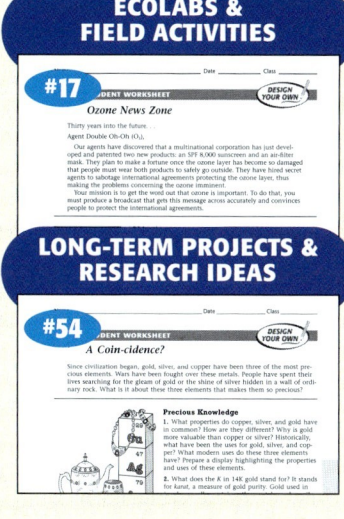

LONG-TERM PROJECTS & RESEARCH IDEAS

DATASHEETS FOR LABBOOK

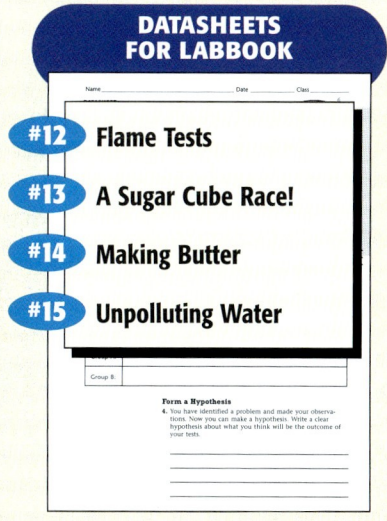

- #12 Flame Tests
- #13 A Sugar Cube Race!
- #14 Making Butter
- #15 Unpolluting Water

Applications & Extensions

CRITICAL THINKING & PROBLEM SOLVING

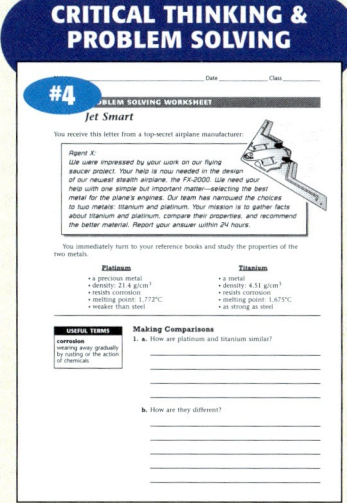

EYE ON THE ENVIRONMENT

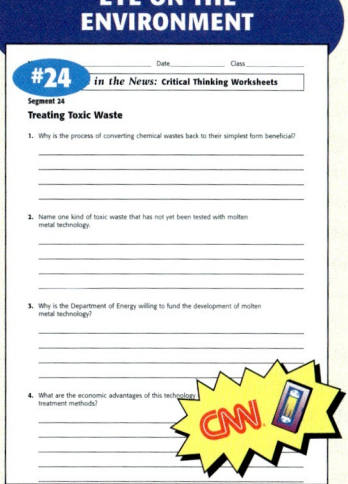

INTERACTIVE EXPLORATIONS

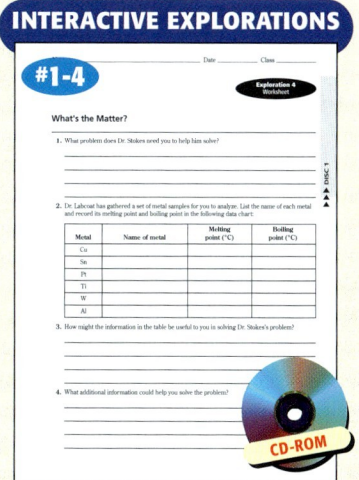

Chapter 4 • Chapter Resources & Worksheets **79D**

Chapter Background

SECTION 1
Elements

▶ **Electrolysis**
Sir Humphry Davy (1778–1829) was a professor at England's Royal Institution. After the creation of the voltaic pile in 1800, Davy built a battery made of voltaic cells and applied the electric current to potash and to soda. The compounds decomposed to form two previously unknown elements—potassium and sodium. He later used electrolysis to isolate the elements magnesium, calcium, strontium, barium, boron, and silicon.

▶ **Gold—a Metal**
Gold is often found in its elemental state because it is not a chemically reactive element. The ancient Egyptians hammered gold into a sheet so thin that it took 367,000 leaves to make a pile 2.5 cm high. Gold is often used with other metals in jewelry because it can be reshaped easily.

▶ **Sulfur—a Nonmetal**
Sulfur is found both uncombined and combined in nature. Sulfur is found in deposits on the slopes of volcanoes and in crystals at the mouth of volcanic vents. A series of chemical reactions causes uncombined sulfur to form and fall onto the volcanoes' slopes.

IS THAT A FACT!

- Jupiter's moon Io appears yellow due to large deposits of sulfur from volcanic activity.

▶ **Elements in the Body**
Sodium and potassium compounds are vital to the human body in blood, muscle tissue, and nerve tissue. These are only two of many elements present in compounds that keep the human body functioning properly.

SECTION 2
Compounds

▶ **Sodium Compounds**
Sodium compounds are very important commercially. For example, several million tons of sodium hydroxide are used each year to make paper, other chemicals, and petroleum products. Sodium sulfate is used in the manufacture of paper, glass, and detergents, and sodium silicate is used in the manufacture of soaps and detergents.

▶ **Silicon Compounds**
In nature, most silicon is combined with oxygen to form silicon dioxide. Silicon dioxide makes up sand, flint, quartz, and opal. Silicon is also found combined with iron, aluminum, magnesium, and other metals. One reason for the large number of silicon compounds is that silicon forms long chains of atoms, often in the form of silicates (compounds of silicon, a metal, and oxygen).

- When silicon dioxide contains small amounts of manganese or iron, it forms a type of quartz called amethyst, which is purple in color and is used as a gemstone. Many silicates, such as emerald, jade, aquamarine, garnet, opal, onyx, and moonstone, are valued as gemstones.

IS THAT A FACT!

- The greenish color of the Statue of Liberty is caused by the compound copper(II) carbonate, which formed when the copper in the statue reacted with carbon dioxide and water.

▶ **Carbon Compounds**
The science of carbon compounds, organic chemistry, has produced plastics, fuels, medicines, fibers, and armor. Carbon compounds are everywhere, and our

Chapter 4 • Elements, Compounds, and Mixtures

Chapter 4 • Elements, Compounds, and Mixtures

lives would be vastly different without plastic containers, gasoline, penicillin, nylon, and Teflon®, all of which are made from carbon compounds.

- In 1945, Dorothy Hodgkin used X-ray diffraction to determine the structure of penicillin. Once its structure was known, penicillin could be synthesized and mass produced. Hodgkin went on to determine the structures of insulin and vitamin B_{12}.

SECTION 3

Mixtures

▶ Describing Solutions
Students are shown three methods of describing how much solute is dissolved in a solvent. The most general method uses the terms *concentrated* and *dilute*. Describing a solution in terms of its *saturation* is a little more specific because it relates the amount of solute to a specific number value. Calculating the *concentration* is the most specific method because it gives a number value for the solution.

▶ Supersaturated Solutions
A solution that contains more dissolved solute than is normally possible is *supersaturated*. Supersaturated solutions will become saturated solutions when solute comes out of solution. This can occur if more solute is added or if the solution is shaken. To make a supersaturated solution, make a saturated solution at a higher temperature; then allow it to cool undisturbed. Several varieties of reusable hand warmers make use of supersaturated solutions.

▶ Colloids

Colloids resist separation for several reasons. The small particle size makes gravitational force less effective in causing their separation. Another factor is the constant, random motion of the colloid particles, called Brownian motion. Third, most colloid particles are electrically charged. In any colloid, all the particles have the same charge and should repel each other. This keeps them from clumping together and from settling out.

▶ Colloids You Know
Gels are colloids in which solid particles are spread out in a liquid. Aerosols are colloids made with solid or liquid particles that are suspended in a gas. Emulsions are colloids made of two liquids. Smog is a colloid of dust and other solid particles in the air.

For background information about teaching strategies and issues, refer to the *Professional Reference for Teachers*.

CHAPTER 4
Elements, Compounds, and Mixtures

Chapter Preview

Section 1
Elements
- An Element Has Only One Type of Particle
- Every Element Has a Unique Set of Properties
- Elements Are Classified by Their Properties

Section 2
Compounds
- Elements Combine in a Definite Ratio to Form a Compound
- Every Compound Has a Unique Set of Properties
- Compounds Can Be Broken Down into Simpler Substances
- Compounds in Your World

Section 3
Mixtures
- Properties of Mixtures
- Solutions
- Suspensions
- Colloids

Directed Reading Worksheet 4

Science Puzzlers, Twisters & Teasers Worksheet 4

Guided Reading Audio CD
English or Spanish, Chapter 4

CHAPTER 4
Elements, Compounds, and Mixtures

This Really Happened!

In the early morning hours of April 15, 1912, the *Titanic*, the largest ship ever to set sail, sank on its first voyage. The *Titanic* was considered to be unsinkable, yet more than 1,500 of its passengers and crew were killed after it hit an iceberg and sank.

How could an iceberg, which is made of ice, destroy the 2.5 cm thick steel plates that made up the *Titanic*'s hull? Analysis of a recovered piece of the *Titanic*'s hull showed that the steel contained large amounts of the element sulfur, which is a normal component of steel. However, in this case, the steel contained much more sulfur than is the standard for steel made today. The excess sulfur may have caused the steel to be brittle, much like glass. Scientists suspect that this brittle steel may have cracked on impact with the iceberg, allowing water to enter the hull.

Could something as simple as using less sulfur in the *Titanic*'s steel have prevented the ship from sinking? We may never know. What is known, however, is that the composition of compounds and mixtures is very important in preventing future disasters. In this chapter, you will learn about elements and how they are assembled into compounds and mixtures with some very different properties.

This piece of steel hull from the Titanic (at left) was recovered from the wreck.

This Really Happened!

Another theory of why the RMS (Royal Mail Ship) *Titanic* sank so quickly was that the wrought iron rivets that held the hull plates together failed. This caused the weak rivets to pop, "unzipping" the seams of the hull plates and allowing sea water to enter the ship. This theory has been discounted as later evidence showed that the *Titanic*'s hull suffered a series of several thin cracks that allowed water into the ship.

internetconnect

TOPIC: The Titanic
GO TO: www.scilinks.org
sciLINKS NUMBER: HSTP080

Smithsonian Institution®
Visit **www.si.edu/hrw** for additional on-line resources.

What Do You Think?

In your ScienceLog, try to answer the following questions based on what you already know:

1. What is an element?
2. What is a compound? How are compounds and mixtures different?
3. What are the components of a solution called?

Mystery Mixture

Steel is just one of the many mixtures that you encounter every day. In fact, you might be using a mixture to write notes for this activity! Some inks used in pens and markers are a mixture of several dyes. In this lab, you will separate the parts of an ink mixture.

Procedure

1. Cut a **3 × 15 cm strip of paper** from a **coffee filter**. Wrap one end around a **pencil** so that the other end will just touch the bottom of a **clear plastic cup** (as shown in the photo above). Secure the strip of paper to the pencil with a **piece of tape**.
2. Take the paper out of the cup. Using a **water-soluble black marker**, make a small dot in the center of the strip about 2 cm from the bottom end of the paper.
3. Pour **water** in the cup to a depth of 1 cm.
4. Carefully lower the paper into the cup so that the end is in the water but the dot you made is not under water.
5. Watch the filter paper. Remove the paper when the water is 1 cm from the top of the paper. Record your observations in your ScienceLog.

Analysis

6. What happened as the filter paper soaked up the water? What colors were mixed to make black ink?
7. Compare your results with those of your classmates. How did the mixture in your marker compare with the mixtures in their markers?
8. Do you think the process used to create the ink involved a physical or chemical change? Explain.

Going Further

The procedure you used to separate the components of ink is a scientific technique called chromatography. Find out more about chromatography and its uses by looking in a chemistry or reference book.

What Do You Think?

Accept all reasonable answers.

Students will have a chance to revise their answers in the Chapter Review under NOW What Do You Think?

Investigate!

MATERIALS

FOR EACH GROUP:
- 3 × 15 cm strip of paper cut from a coffee filter or filter paper
- pencil
- clear plastic cup or beaker
- piece of tape
- water-soluble, black felt-tip marker or pen (not permanent marker)
- water

Safety Caution: Caution students to be careful when handling sharp objects. Remind students to wear an apron when doing this activity.

This activity works best if students are given a variety of brands of markers. Brands that are known to work include Mr. Sketch®, Vis-à-vis®, Crayola Washable®, and Flair®. Test the markers for suitability. Demonstrate how to use chromatography to identify a sample: students can determine the type of marker you used by comparing the pattern of colors on your paper with the pattern on theirs.

Answers to Analysis

6. The ink in the dot separated into several colors and moved up the paper. (The colors will vary with the brand of marker used.)
7. Answers will vary. If several varieties of markers are used, differences in the order and colors of ink can be seen.
8. The process involved a physical change. The colors of ink are separated without changing their chemical makeup.

SECTION 1

Focus

Elements

This section explains the characteristics of elements and gives examples of these characteristics. It also explains how to identify and classify elements as metals, nonmetals, and metalloids based on their properties.

 **Bellringer**

Pose the following questions to your students:

What do gold, iron, and aluminum have in common? What do oxygen, neon, and sulfur have in common? How is silicon different from aluminum or oxygen?

1) Motivate

DEMONSTRATION

Hold up a large piece of heavy-duty aluminum foil, and ask students to identify it. Fold the foil into a strip. Demonstrate that it will conduct electric current by touching both electrodes of a conductivity apparatus to the strip. (Do not touch the metal strip while it is attached to the apparatus.)

Next bunch the foil into a ball, then flatten it by pounding it with a hammer. Ask students to list as many properties of aluminum as they can.

 **Directed Reading Worksheet 4** Section 1

SECTION 1

Terms to Learn

element   nonmetals
pure substance   metalloids
metals

What You'll Do

- Describe pure substances.
- Describe the characteristics of elements, and give examples.
- Explain how elements can be identified.
- Classify elements according to their properties.

Elements

Imagine you are working as a lab technician for the Break-It-Down Corporation. Your job is to break down materials into the simplest substances you can obtain. One day a material seems particularly difficult to break down. You crush and grind it. You notice that the resulting pieces are smaller, but they are still the same material. You try other physical changes, including melting, boiling, and filtering it, but the material does not change into anything simpler.

Next you try some chemical changes. You pass an electric current through the material but it still does not become any simpler. After recording your observations, you analyze the results of your tests. You then draw a conclusion: the substance must be an element. An **element** is a pure substance that cannot be separated into simpler substances by physical or chemical means, as shown in **Figure 1**.

Figure 1 No matter what kind of physical or chemical change you attempt, an element cannot be changed into a simpler substance!

Figure 2 The atoms of the element iron are alike whether they are in a meteorite or in a common iron skillet.

An Element Has Only One Type of Particle

A **pure substance** is a substance in which there is only one type of particle. Because elements are pure substances, each element contains only one type of particle. For example, every particle (atom) in a 5 g nugget of the element gold is like every other particle of gold. The particles of a pure substance are alike no matter where that substance is found, as shown in **Figure 2**. Although a meteorite might travel more than 400 million kilometers (about 248 million miles) to reach Earth, the particles of iron in a meteorite are identical to the particles of iron in objects around your home!

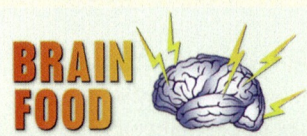

Three types of particles are used when discussing pure substances. The term *atom* is used for most elements. The term *molecule* is used for diatomic elements. Molecule is also used for covalent compounds. The term *formula unit* is used for ionic compounds, although the term *molecule* is also widely used and accepted.

82 Chapter 4 • Elements, Compounds, and Mixtures

Every Element Has a Unique Set of Properties

Each element has a unique set of properties that allows you to identify it. For example, each element has its own *characteristic properties*. These properties do not depend on the amount of material present in a sample of the element. Characteristic properties include some physical properties, such as boiling point, melting point, and density, as well as chemical properties, such as reactivity with acid. The elements helium and krypton are unreactive gases. However, the density (mass per unit volume) of helium is less than the density of air. Therefore, a helium-filled balloon will float up if it is released. Krypton is more dense than air, so a krypton-filled balloon will sink to the ground if it is released.

Identifying Elements by Their Properties Look at the elements cobalt, iron, and nickel, shown in **Figure 3.** Even though these three elements have some similar properties, each can be identified by its unique set of properties.

Notice that the physical properties for the elements in Figure 3 include melting point and density. Other physical properties, such as color, hardness, and texture, could be added to the list. Also, depending on the elements being identified, other chemical properties might be useful. For example, some elements, such as hydrogen and carbon, are flammable. Other elements, such as sodium, react immediately with oxygen. Still other elements, such as zinc, are reactive with acid.

Cobalt

Melting point is 1,495°C.
Density is 8.9 g/cm^3.
Conducts electric current and thermal energy.
Unreactive with oxygen in the air.

Iron

Melting point is 1,535°C.
Density is 7.9 g/cm^3.
Conducts electric current and thermal energy.
Combines slowly with oxygen in the air to form rust.

Nickel

Melting point is 1,455°C.
Density is 8.9 g/cm^3.
Conducts electric current and thermal energy.
Unreactive with oxygen in the air.

Figure 3 *Like all other elements, cobalt, iron, and nickel can be identified by their unique combination of properties.*

IS THAT A FACT!

People in ancient times are thought to have used iron from meteorites before they learned to mine and process ore. A dagger found in the tomb of the Egyptian pharaoh Tutankhamen is thought to have been made from an iron meteorite.

Multicultural CONNECTION

People have long enjoyed the special characteristics and beauty of gold. Gold has also been vital to commerce. Have students research the importance and use of gold in different cultures, such as the ancient Egyptians and Minoans. Students can present their findings on a poster or in a story.

---

2) Teach

USING THE FIGURE

Have students look at the elements shown in **Figure 3.** Ask them if they could use density to tell the three elements apart. (Students could identify iron but could not tell nickel and cobalt apart because these two elements have the same density.)

Ask students if they could use conductivity or reactivity with oxygen to tell them apart. (No; all three conduct thermal energy and electric current, and only iron reacts with oxygen.)

Ask if melting point could be used to identify the elements. (Yes; each has a different melting point.)

Emphasize that it is the *set* of properties of an element, and not any one single property, that identifies an element.

MATH and MORE

The percentages by mass of the elements composing the compounds that make up the human body are:

oxygen, 64.6 percent; carbon, 18.0 percent; hydrogen, 10.0 percent; nitrogen, 3.1 percent; calcium, 1.9 percent; phosphorus, 1.1 percent; other elements, 1.3 percent.

Have students prepare a pie chart or bar graph to illustrate this information.

Math Skills Worksheet 21
"Percentages, Fractions, and Decimals"

Science Skills Worksheet 25
"Introduction to Graphs"

Section 1 • Elements

2) Teach, continued

MEETING INDIVIDUAL NEEDS

Learners Having Difficulty
Allow students to observe samples of elements, such as aluminum, iron, sulfur, iodine, and silicon, in closed plastic containers. Ask students to describe the properties of the elements that they can see. Then ask them to classify the elements as metals, nonmetals, or metalloids.

MISCONCEPTION ALERT

It is useful to group objects with similar properties into categories based on those properties. However, students should realize that exceptions exist in many categories. For example, all metals except mercury are solids at room temperature. Students should be prepared for exceptions and "gray areas."

3) Extend

GOING FURTHER

Have students find out which elements are nutrients needed by the human body for proper functioning and which foods are good sources of these elements. Have them make a poster or a concept map that shows the major and minor elements and their food sources.

RESEARCH

Ask each student to choose an element to gather information about. Students should research the properties of the element, the history of its discovery, and how it is used. Have them create a poster or a booklet showing their results. **Sheltered English**

Elements Are Classified by Their Properties

Consider how many different breeds of dogs there are. Consider also how you tell one breed from another. Most often you can tell just by their appearance, or what might be called physical properties. **Figure 4** shows several breeds of dogs, which all happen to be terriers. Many terriers are fairly small in size and have short hair. Although not all terriers are exactly alike, they share enough common properties to be classified in the same group.

Figure 4 Even though these dogs are different breeds, they have enough in common to be classified as terriers.

Elements Are Grouped into Categories

Elements are classified into groups according to their shared properties. Recall the elements iron, nickel, and cobalt. All three are shiny, and all three conduct thermal energy and electric current. Using these shared properties, scientists have grouped these three elements, along with other similar elements, into one large group called metals. Metals are not all exactly alike, but they do have some properties in common.

If You Know the Category, You Know the Properties If you have ever browsed at a music store, you know that the CDs are categorized by type of music. If you like rock-and-roll, you would go to the rock-and-roll section. You might not recognize a particular CD, but you know that it must have the characteristics of rock-and-roll for it to be in this section.

Likewise, you can predict some of the properties of an unfamiliar element by knowing the category to which it belongs. As shown in the concept map in **Figure 5,** elements are classified into three categories—metals, nonmetals, and metalloids. Cobalt, iron, and nickel are classified as metals. If you know that a particular element is a metal, you know that it shares certain properties with iron, nickel, and cobalt. The chart on the next page shows examples of each category and describes the properties that identify elements in each category.

Figure 5 Elements are divided into three categories: metals, nonmetals, and metalloids.

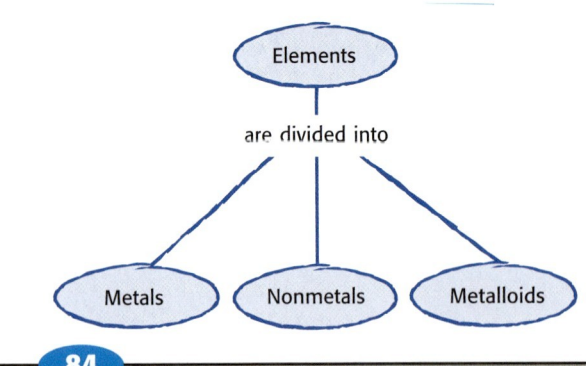

TOPIC: Elements
GO TO: www.scilinks.org
sciLINKS NUMBER: HSTP085

WEIRD SCIENCE

Nitrogen forms about four-fifths of Earth's atmosphere but is so unreactive with other elements that it makes up only a tiny percentage of Earth's crust.

84 Chapter 4 • Elements, Compounds, and Mixtures

The Three Major Categories of Elements

Metals

Metals are elements that are shiny and are good conductors of thermal energy and electric current. They are *malleable* (they can be hammered into thin sheets) and *ductile* (they can be drawn into thin wires). Iron has many uses in building and automobile construction. Copper is used in wires and coins.

Nonmetals

Nonmetals are elements that are dull (not shiny) and that are poor conductors of thermal energy and electric current. Solid nonmetals tend to be brittle and unmalleable. Few familiar objects are made of only nonmetals. The neon used in lights is a nonmetal, as is the graphite (carbon) used in pencils.

Metalloids

Metalloids, also called semiconductors, are elements that have properties of both metals and nonmetals. Some metalloids are shiny, while others are dull. Metalloids are somewhat malleable and ductile. Some metalloids conduct thermal energy and electric current well. Silicon is used to make computer chips. However, other elements must be added to silicon to make a working chip.

REVIEW

1. What is a pure substance?
2. List three properties that can be used to classify elements.
3. **Applying Concepts** Which category of element would be the least appropriate choice for making a container that can be dropped without shattering? Explain your reasoning.

internet connect

SCILINKS
NSTA

TOPIC: Elements
GO TO: www.scilinks.org
sciLINKS NUMBER: HSTP085

85

4) Close

Quiz

Ask students to identify the group or groups of elements that have each of the following properties:

1. good conductors of electric current (metals, some metalloids)
2. brittle and nonmalleable (nonmetals)
3. shiny (metals, some metalloids)
4. poor conductors of thermal energy (nonmetals, some metalloids)

ALTERNATIVE ASSESSMENT

Concept Mapping Have students make a concept map that compares the properties of metals, nonmetals, and metalloids.
Sheltered English

REAL-WORLD CONNECTION

For hundreds of years, lead and lead compounds have been used in and around homes. But lead, although common, is toxic to humans (especially to children). It disrupts enzymes that are important to the function of brain cells.

Teaching Transparency 210 "Three Major Categories of Elements"

Problem Solving Worksheet 4 "Jet Smart"

Interactive Explorations CD-ROM "What's the Matter?"

▼ Answers to Review

1. A pure substance is a substance in which there is only one type of particle.
2. Accept all reasonable responses. Answers may include melting point, boiling point, density, reactivity with acid, color, hardness, texture, and flammability.
3. Sample answer: The least appropriate choice for this container would be a nonmetal. Nonmetals tend to be brittle and would most likely crack when dropped.

Section 1 • Elements   **85**

SECTION 2

Focus

Compounds

This section describes the properties of compounds and explains the differences between compounds and elements. Students also learn about the properties and importance of common compounds.

Bellringer

Point out to students that the word *compound* refers to something that consists of two or more parts. Ask students to write in their ScienceLog how they might make a compound using elements. Have them list any compounds they know about.

1) Motivate

DEMONSTRATION

Safety Caution: Follow and model proper safety procedures.

The reaction between magnesium and oxygen is easily demonstrated for your students. The light produced in the chemical change is VERY bright. Looking directly at the flame may cause damage to the retina. Inform students of this, and remind them to look away as the magnesium begins to burn. In a darkened classroom, this demonstration is even more dramatic. This reaction was used in old flashbulbs.

Directed Reading Worksheet 4 Section 2

Section 2

Compounds

Terms to Learn
compound

What You'll Do
- Describe the properties of compounds.
- Identify the differences between an element and a compound.
- Give examples of common compounds.

Familiar Compounds

- **table salt—** sodium and chlorine
- **water—** hydrogen and oxygen
- **sugar—** carbon, hydrogen, and oxygen
- **carbon dioxide—** carbon and oxygen
- **baking soda—** sodium, hydrogen, carbon, and oxygen

Most elements take part in chemical changes fairly easily, so few elements are found alone in nature. Instead, most elements are found combined with other elements as compounds.

A **compound** is a pure substance composed of two or more elements that are chemically combined. In a compound, a particle is formed when atoms of two or more elements join together. In order for elements to combine, they must *react*, or undergo a chemical change, with one another. In **Figure 6,** you see magnesium reacting with oxygen to form a compound called magnesium oxide. The compound is a new pure substance that is different from the elements that reacted to form it. Most substances you encounter every day are compounds. The table at left lists some familiar examples.

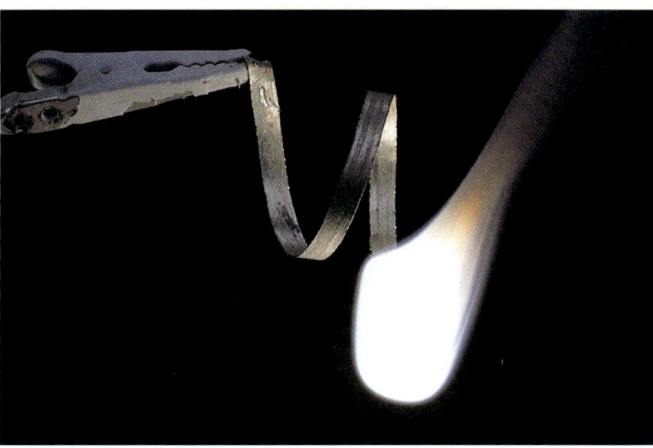

Figure 6 As magnesium burns, it reacts with oxygen and forms the compound magnesium oxide.

Elements Combine in a Definite Ratio to Form a Compound

Compounds are not random combinations of elements. When a compound forms, the elements join in a specific ratio according to their masses. For example, the ratio of the mass of hydrogen to the mass of oxygen in water is always the same—1 g of hydrogen to 8 g of oxygen. This mass ratio can be written as 1:8 or as the fraction 1/8. Every sample of water has this 1:8 mass ratio of hydrogen to oxygen. If a sample of a compound has a different mass ratio of hydrogen to oxygen, the compound cannot be water.

IS THAT A FACT!

Rubber is a compound of hydrogen and carbon, with the basic formula of $(C_5H_8)n$, where n is about 3,000. The basic unit in the molecule is isoprene. The composition of rubber was proved in 1860 when rubber was heated and broken down into isoprene; its composition was confirmed in 1884 when rubber was produced by the accidental polymerization of isoprene that had been left in a bottle.

Every Compound Has a Unique Set of Properties

Each compound has a unique set of properties that allows you to distinguish it from other compounds. Like elements, each compound has its own physical properties, such as boiling point, melting point, density, and color. Compounds can also be identified by their different chemical properties. Some compounds, such as the calcium carbonate found in chalk, react with acid. Others, such as hydrogen peroxide, react when exposed to light. You can see how chemical properties can be used to identify compounds in the QuickLab at right.

A compound has different properties from the elements that form it. Did you know that ordinary table salt is a compound made from two very dangerous elements? Table salt—sodium chloride—consists of sodium (which reacts violently with water) and chlorine (which is poisonous). Together, however, these elements form a harmless compound with unique properties. Take a look at **Figure 7.** Because a compound has different properties from the elements that react to form it, sodium chloride is safe to eat and dissolves (without exploding!) in water.

QuickLab

Compound Confusion

1. Measure 4 g (1 tsp) of **compound A,** and place it in a **clear plastic cup.**
2. Measure 4 g (1 tsp) of **compound B,** and place it in a **second clear plastic cup.**
3. Observe the color and texture of each compound. Record your observations.
4. Add 5 mL (1 tsp) of **vinegar** to each cup. Record your observations.
5. Baking soda reacts with vinegar, while powdered sugar does not. Which of these compounds is compound A, and which is compound B?

Figure 7 Table salt is formed when the elements sodium and chlorine join. The properties of salt are different from the properties of sodium and chlorine.

Sodium is a soft, silvery white metal that reacts violently with water.

Chlorine is a poisonous, greenish yellow gas.

Sodium chloride, or table salt, is a white solid that dissolves easily in water and is safe to eat.

Self-Check

Do the properties of pure water from a glacier and from a desert oasis differ? *(See page 724 to check your answer.)*

BRAIN FOOD

In ancient times, salt was a precious commodity. It was even traded for an equal weight of gold. Soldiers in ancient Rome, as part of their pay, often received a *salarium,* a special ration of salt. (The Latin word for salt is *sal.*) This term eventually evolved into the English word *salary,* a payment for work. Have students research how salt is produced, and have them present their results to the class in some sort of demonstration, a report, or a poster.

Compounds Can Be Broken Down into Simpler Substances

Some compounds can be broken down into elements through chemical changes. Look at **Figure 8.** When the compound mercury(II) oxide is heated, it breaks down into the elements mercury and oxygen. Likewise, if an electric current is passed through melted table salt, the elements sodium and chlorine are produced.

Other compounds undergo chemical changes to form simpler compounds. These compounds can be broken down into elements through additional chemical changes. For example, carbonic acid is a compound that helps to give carbonated beverages their "fizz," as shown in **Figure 9.** The carbon dioxide and water that are formed can be further broken down into the elements carbon, oxygen, and hydrogen through additional chemical changes.

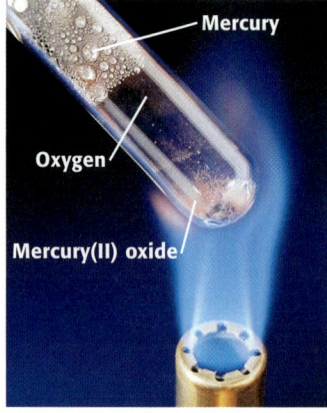

Figure 8 Heating mercury(II) oxide causes a chemical change that separates it into the elements mercury and oxygen.

Figure 9 Opening a carbonated drink can be messy as carbonic acid breaks down into two simpler compounds—carbon dioxide and water.

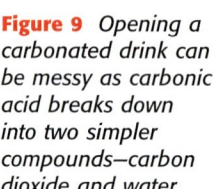

Physics CONNECTION

The process of using electric current to break compounds into simpler compounds and elements is known as electrolysis. Electrolysis can be used to separate water into hydrogen and oxygen. The elements aluminum and copper and the compound hydrogen peroxide are important industrial products obtained through electrolysis.

Compounds Cannot Be Broken Down by Physical Changes

The only way to break down a compound is through a chemical change. If you pour water through a filter, the water will pass through the filter unchanged. Filtration is a physical change, so it cannot be used to break down a compound. Likewise, a compound cannot be broken down by being ground into a powder or by any other physical process.

IS THAT A FACT!

Some metals can have more than one charge when they form compounds. To identify the charge used in a particular compound, a Roman numeral is used in the name. Thus, the mercury in mercury(II) oxide has a 2+ charge.

WEIRD SCIENCE

In 1772, Joseph Priestly discovered nitrous oxide. This gas was nontoxic, but it produced unusual effects when inhaled. People would often sing, fight, or laugh. This led to the popular name for nitrous oxide—"laughing gas." The gas is still used in dental surgery.

Compounds in Your World

You are always surrounded by compounds. Compounds make up the food you eat, the school supplies you use, the clothes you wear—even you!

Compounds in Nature Proteins are compounds found in all living things. The element nitrogen is needed to make proteins. **Figure 10** shows how some plants get the nitrogen they need. Other plants use nitrogen compounds that are in the soil. Animals get the nitrogen they need by eating plants or by eating animals that have eaten plants. As an animal digests food, the proteins in the food are broken down into smaller compounds that the animal's cells can use.

Another compound that plays an important role in life is carbon dioxide. You exhale carbon dioxide that was made in your body. Plants take in carbon dioxide and use it to make other compounds, including sugar.

Figure 10 The bumps on the roots of this pea plant are home to bacteria that form compounds from atmospheric nitrogen. The pea plant makes proteins from these compounds.

Compounds in Industry The element nitrogen is combined with the element hydrogen to form a compound called ammonia. Ammonia is manufactured for use in fertilizers. Plants can use ammonia as a source of nitrogen for their proteins. Other manufactured compounds are used in medicines, food preservatives, and synthetic fabrics.

The compounds found in nature are usually not the raw materials needed by industry. Often, these compounds must be broken down to provide elements used as raw material. For example, the element aluminum, used in cans, airplanes, and building materials, is not found alone in nature. It is produced by breaking down the compound aluminum oxide.

REVIEW

1. What is a compound?
2. What type of change is needed to break down a compound?
3. **Analyzing Ideas** A jar contains samples of the elements carbon and oxygen. Does the jar contain a compound? Explain.

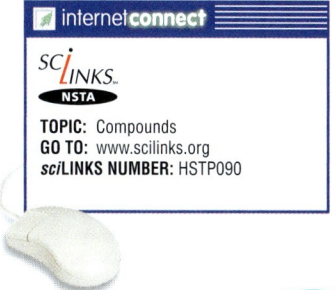

internetconnect

SC*I*NKS
NSTA

TOPIC: Compounds
GO TO: www.scilinks.org
*sci*LINKS NUMBER: HSTP090

SECTION 3

Focus

Mixtures

This section explains the properties of mixtures. Students learn how mixtures can be separated. The concepts of solutes, concentration, and solvents are covered. Finally, students compare solutions, suspensions, and colloids.

 **Bellringer**

Have students respond to the following situation:

When you add sugar to coffee, tea, iced tea, or lemonade, the sugar disappears. What do you think happens to the sugar? Write your answer in your ScienceLog.

1) Motivate

ACTIVITY

MATERIALS

FOR EACH GROUP:
- two beakers with water
- tablespoon of ground coffee (not instant)
- two sugar cubes or sugar packets
- funnel
- coffee filters or filter paper
- paper towels
- stirring rod

Divide students into groups of three or four. Have students put the coffee into a beaker of water and stir it vigorously. Their task is to recover as much of the coffee as possible. Give them time. Have them record their steps, observations, and results in their ScienceLog.

Repeat the activity using the sugar. Have students record everything in their ScienceLog. Discuss the results.

Section 3

Terms to Learn

mixture concentration
solution solubility
solute suspension
solvent colloid

What You'll Do

- Describe the properties of mixtures.
- Describe methods of separating the components of a mixture.
- Analyze a solution in terms of its solute, solvent, and concentration.
- Compare the properties of solutions, suspensions, and colloids.

Mixtures

Have you ever made your own pizza? You roll out the dough, add a layer of tomato sauce, then add toppings like green peppers, mushrooms, and olives—maybe even some pepperoni! Sprinkle cheese on top, and you're ready to bake. You have just created not only a pizza but also a mixture—and a delicious one at that!

Properties of Mixtures

All mixtures—even pizza—share certain properties. A **mixture** is a combination of two or more substances that are not chemically combined. Two or more materials together form a mixture if they do not react to form a compound. For example, cheese and tomato sauce do not react when they are used to make a pizza.

Figure 11 *Colorless quartz, pink feldspar, and black mica make up the mixture granite.*

Substances in a Mixture Retain Their Identity Because no chemical change occurs, each substance in a mixture has the same chemical makeup it had before the mixture formed. That is, each substance in a mixture keeps its identity. In some mixtures, such as the pizza above or the piece of granite shown in **Figure 11,** you can even see the individual components. In other mixtures, such as salt water, you cannot see all the components.

Mixtures Can Be Physically Separated If you don't like mushrooms on your pizza, you can pick them off. This is a physical change of the mixture. The identities of the substances did not change. In contrast, compounds can be broken down only through chemical changes.

Not all mixtures are as easy to separate as a pizza. You cannot simply pick salt out of a saltwater mixture, but you can separate the salt from the water by heating the mixture. When the water changes from a liquid to a gas, the salt remains behind. Several common techniques for separating mixtures are shown on the following page.

IS THAT A FACT!

The Liberty Bell is a mixture of 70 percent copper, 25 percent tin, and small amounts of lead, zinc, arsenic, gold, and silver.

Common Techniques for Separating Mixtures

Distillation is a process that separates a mixture based on the boiling points of the components. Here you see pure water being distilled from a saltwater mixture. In addition to water purification, distillation is used to separate crude oil into its components, such as gasoline and kerosene.

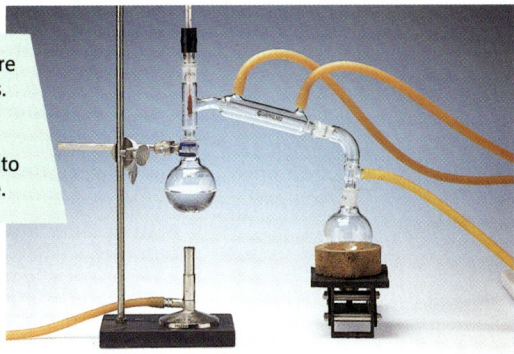

A **magnet** can be used to separate a mixture of the elements iron and aluminum. Iron is attracted to the magnet, but aluminum is not.

The components that make up blood are separated using a machine called a **centrifuge.** This machine separates mixtures according to the densities of the components.

A mixture of the compound sodium chloride (table salt) with the element sulfur requires more than one separation step.

 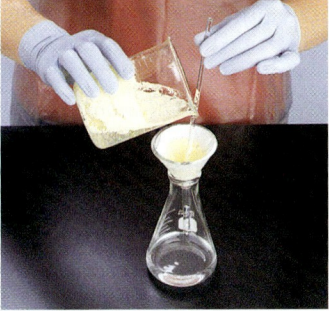 

❶ The **first step** is to mix them with another compound—water. Salt dissolves in water, but sulfur does not.

❷ In the **second step,** the mixture is poured through a filter. The filter traps the solid sulfur.

❸ In the **third step,** the sodium chloride is separated from the water by simply evaporating the water.

91

BRAIN FOOD

The property of density is used to separate a mixture of ripe and unripe cranberries. Ripe cranberries float in water, but unripe cranberries sink. During harvesting, cranberry bogs are flooded, and the floating cranberries are skimmed from the water.

2) Teach

DISCUSSION
Discuss with students the idea that pizza is a mixture. Ask students to write a recipe for their favorite pizza. Have volunteers write their pizza recipes on the board. Have the class compare recipes and discuss how they vary.

MEETING INDIVIDUAL NEEDS
Advanced Learners Have students prepare posters that illustrate how the components of crude oil are separated by distillation. Encourage students to be creative as they share their work with the class. Sheltered English

DEMONSTRATION
Separation Demonstrate the separation of salt (sodium chloride) and sand (silicon dioxide) using the method shown in the text. Ask students which compound dissolves in water and which does not.

GROUP ACTIVITY
Have students work in small groups to figure out a way to separate a mixture of sand, sawdust, and gravel into its components. Let each group come up with a method and present the results to the class.

Teaching Transparency 211
"Separation of a Mixture"

Directed Reading Worksheet 4 Section 3

Section 3 • Mixtures **91**

2 Teach, continued

RETEACHING
Show students a bottle of an oil-and-vinegar salad dressing. Read aloud the ingredients label. Allow the bottle to sit undisturbed so that the ingredients separate. Discuss how the ingredients in the dressing retain their identity and how they could be mixed in any proportions.

CROSS-DISCIPLINARY FOCUS

Art Give students samples of red, blue, and yellow paint. Allow students to discover how many different colors they can make by mixing various amounts of two or three of the colors. Let students make paintings using their mixtures.

Homework
Remind students that many garments are mixtures of fibers. Ask students to examine clothing labels and to list the mixtures and percentages of each material in the mixture. What fabrics are most common? Which ones are not used very often?

Mixtures vs. Compounds	
Mixtures	**Compounds**
Components are elements, compounds, or both	Components are elements
Components keep their original properties	Components lose their original properties
Separated by physical means	Separated by chemical means
Formed using any ratio of components	Formed using a set mass ratio of components

The Components of a Mixture Do Not Have a Definite Ratio Recall that a compound has a specific mass ratio of the elements that form it. Unlike compounds, the components of a mixture do not need to be combined in a definite ratio. For example, granite that has a greater amount of feldspar than mica or quartz appears to have a pink color. Granite that has a greater amount of mica than feldspar or quartz appears black. Regardless of which ratio is present, this combination of materials is always a mixture—and it is always called granite.

Air is a mixture composed mostly of nitrogen and oxygen, with smaller amounts of other gases, such as carbon dioxide and water vapor. Some days the air has more water vapor, or is more humid, than on other days. But regardless of the ratio of the components, air is still a mixture. The chart at left summarizes the differences between mixtures and compounds.

REVIEW

1. What is a mixture?
2. Is a mixture separated by physical or chemical changes?
3. **Applying Concepts** Suggest a procedure to separate iron filings from sawdust. Explain why this procedure works.

Solutions

A **solution** is a mixture that appears to be a single substance but is composed of particles of two or more substances that are distributed evenly amongst each other. Solutions are often described as *homogeneous mixtures* because they have the same appearance and properties throughout the mixture.

The process in which particles of substances separate and spread evenly throughout a mixture is known as *dissolving*. In solutions, the **solute** is the substance that is dissolved, and the **solvent** is the substance in which the solute is dissolved. A solute is *soluble*, or able to dissolve, in the solvent. A substance that is *insoluble*, or unable to dissolve, forms a mixture that is not homogeneous and therefore is not a solution.

Salt water is a solution. Salt is soluble in water, meaning that salt dissolves in water. Therefore, salt is the solute and water is the solvent. When two liquids or two gases form a solution, the substance with the greater volume is the solvent.

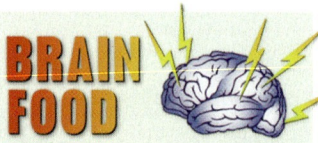

BRAIN FOOD
Many substances are soluble in water, including salt, sugar, alcohol, and oxygen. Water does not dissolve everything, but it dissolves so many different solutes that it is often called the universal solvent.

Answers to Review

1. A mixture is a combination of two or more substances that are not chemically combined.
2. physical
3. Sample answer: Use a magnet to attract the iron filings away from the sawdust. Iron is attracted to a magnet, while sawdust is not.

Chapter 4 • Elements, Compounds, and Mixtures

You may think of solutions as being liquids. And, in fact, tap water, soft drinks, gasoline, and many cleaning supplies are liquid solutions. However, solutions may also be gases, such as air, and solids, such as steel. *Alloys* are solid solutions of metals or nonmetals dissolved in metals. Brass is an alloy of the metal zinc dissolved in copper. Steel, including that used to build the *Titanic,* is an alloy made of the nonmetal carbon and other elements dissolved in iron. Look at the chart below for examples of the different states of matter used as solutes and solvents in solutions.

Examples of Different States in Solutions

Gas in gas	Dry air (oxygen in nitrogen)
Gas in liquid	Soft drinks (carbon dioxide in water)
Liquid in liquid	Antifreeze (alcohol in water)
Solid in liquid	Salt water (salt in water)
Solid in solid	Brass (zinc in copper)

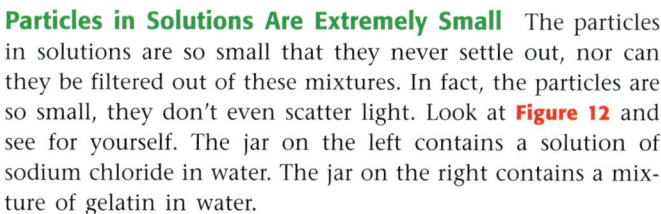

Particles in Solutions Are Extremely Small The particles in solutions are so small that they never settle out, nor can they be filtered out of these mixtures. In fact, the particles are so small, they don't even scatter light. Look at **Figure 12** and see for yourself. The jar on the left contains a solution of sodium chloride in water. The jar on the right contains a mixture of gelatin in water.

Figure 12 Both of these jars contain mixtures. The mixture in the jar on the left, however, is a solution. The particles in solutions are so small they don't scatter light. Therefore, you can't see the path of light through it.

✓ Self-Check

Yellow gold is an alloy made from equal parts copper and silver combined with a greater amount of gold. Identify each component of yellow gold as a solute or solvent. (See page 724 to check your answer.)

SCIENCE HUMOR

Q: What did the compound say to the solution?

A: You're all mixed up!

CROSS-DISCIPLINARY FOCUS

Music The most commonly used brass instruments in a symphony orchestra are the trumpet, the French horn, the trombone, and the tuba. Brass instruments are based on ancient valveless horns that were used for signaling or hunting.

READING STRATEGY

Prediction Guide Before students read this page, ask them:

Which of these are solutions:

air, soft drinks, ocean water, antifreeze, and brass (all)

Discuss students' answers.

USING THE CHART

Discuss with students that although they may be most familiar with solutions of solids dissolved in liquids, there are many other kinds of solutions. Use the chart **Examples of Different States in Solutions** to start a discussion of the different kinds of solutions.

Answer to Self-Check

Copper and silver are solutes. Gold is the solvent.

MATH and MORE

Pure gold is said to be 24 karat. A 12-karat gold item is 50 percent gold. The common alloy used in jewelry is 14 karat. Have students calculate the percentage of gold in 14-karat gold. (58 percent) Tell them that gold coins are 22 karat. Ask what percentage of gold that is. (92 percent)

Math Skills Worksheet 20 "Parts of 100: Calculating Percentages"

internetconnect

TOPIC: Mixtures
GO TO: www.scilinks.org
sciLINKS NUMBER: HSTP095

Section 3 • Mixtures

2) Teach, continued

ACTIVITY

MATERIALS

FOR EACH PAIR:
- food coloring
- water
- clear plastic cups

Safety Caution: Caution students to wear an apron while doing this activity.

Students work in pairs. One member of each pair makes a concentrated solution of food coloring and water. The other partner makes a dilute solution of the same.

Place all the cups containing concentrated solutions in front of a white sheet of paper so that students can compare the solutions' colors. Do the same thing with all the dilute solutions. Mention that not all of the concentrated solutions have the same color, nor do all the dilute solutions. This will reinforce that the terms *concentrated* and *dilute* are relative and do not specify amounts.

MATH and MORE

Extend the MathBreak: Suppose you have 45 g of sodium chloride (salt) dissolved in 150 mL of water, and you need 250 mL more of the same solution. How much sodium chloride do you need to make the additional solution? (75 g)

What is the concentration of the solution? (0.3 g/mL)

 Math Skills Worksheet 17 "Using Proportions and Cross-Multiplication"

MATH BREAK

Calculating Concentration

Many solutions are colorless. Therefore, you cannot always compare the concentrations of solutions by looking at the color—you have to compare the actual calculated concentrations. One way to calculate the concentration of a liquid solution is to divide the grams of solute by the milliliters of solvent. For example, the concentration of a solution in which 35 g of salt is dissolved in 175 mL of water is

$$\frac{35 \text{ g salt}}{175 \text{ mL water}} = 0.2 \text{ g/mL}$$

Now It's Your Turn

Calculate the concentrations of each solution below. Solution A has 55 g of sugar dissolved in 500 mL of water. Solution B has 36 g of sugar dissolved in 144 mL of water. Which solution is the more dilute one? Which is the more concentrated?

Smelly solutions? Follow your nose and learn more on page 102.

Answers to MATHBREAK

Solution A: 55 g/500 mL = 0.11 g/mL

Solution B: 36 g/144 mL = 0.25 g/mL

Solution A is more dilute.

Solution B is more concentrated.

Concentration: How Much Solute Is Dissolved? A measure of the amount of solute dissolved in a solvent is **concentration**. Concentration can be expressed in grams of solute per milliliter of solvent. Knowing the exact concentration of a solution is very important in chemistry and medicine because using the wrong concentration can be dangerous.

Solutions can be described as being *concentrated* or *dilute*. Look at **Figure 13.** Both solutions have the same amount of solvent, but the solution on the left contains less solute than the solution on the right. The solution on the left is dilute while the solution on the right is concentrated. Keep in mind that the terms *concentrated* and *dilute* do not specify the amount of solute that is actually dissolved. Try your hand at calculating concentration and describing solutions as concentrated or dilute in the MathBreak at left.

Figure 13 *The dilute solution on the left contains less solute than the concentrated solution on the right.*

A solution that contains all the solute it can hold at a given temperature is said to be *saturated*. An *unsaturated* solution contains less solute than it can hold at a given temperature. More solute can dissolve in an unsaturated solution.

Solubility: How Much Solute Can Dissolve? If you add too much sugar to a glass of lemonade, not all of the sugar can dissolve. Some of the sugar collects on the bottom of the glass. To determine the maximum amount of sugar that can dissolve, you would need to know the solubility of sugar. The **solubility** of a solute is the amount of solute needed to make a saturated solution using a given amount of solvent at a certain temperature. Solubility is usually expressed in grams of solute per 100 mL of solvent. **Figure 14** on the next page shows the solubility of several different substances in water at different temperatures.

CONNECT TO EARTH SCIENCE

Many caves, such as Carlsbad Caverns in New Mexico and Mammoth Cave in Kentucky, were formed by calcium carbonate alternately dissolving in water and being deposited when water evaporated. Have students find out how these caves formed and make a model or a poster or write a report. **Sheltered English**

Chapter 4 • Elements, Compounds, and Mixtures

Figure 14 Solubility of Different Substances

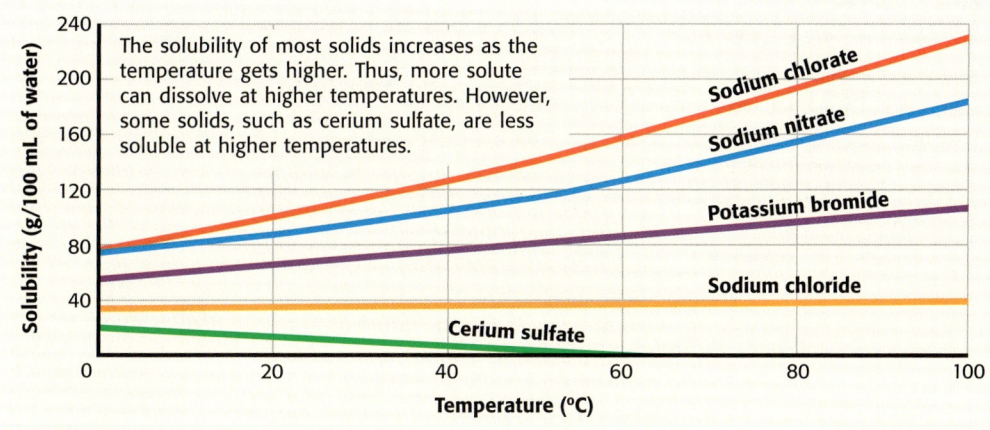

The solubility of most solids increases as the temperature gets higher. Thus, more solute can dissolve at higher temperatures. However, some solids, such as cerium sulfate, are less soluble at higher temperatures.

Unlike the solubility of most solids in liquids, the solubility of gases in liquids decreases as the temperature is raised. Bubbles of gas appear in hot water long before the water begins to boil. The gases that are dissolved in the water cannot remain dissolved as the temperature increases because the solubility of the gases is lower at higher temperatures.

What Affects How Quickly Solids Dissolve in Liquids?

Many familiar solutions are formed when a solid solute is dissolved in water. Several factors affect how fast the solid will dissolve. Look at **Figure 15** to see three methods used to make a solute dissolve faster. You can see why you will enjoy a glass of lemonade sooner if you stir granulated sugar into the lemonade before adding ice!

Figure 15 Mixing, heating, and crushing iron(III) chloride increase the speed at which it will dissolve.

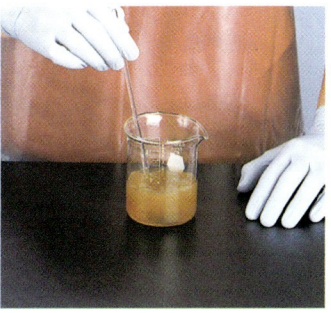

Mixing by stirring or shaking causes the solute particles to separate from one another and spread out more quickly among the solvent particles.

Heating causes particles to move more quickly. The solvent particles can separate the solute particles and spread them out more quickly.

Crushing the solute increases the amount of contact between the solute and the solvent. The particles of solute mix with the solvent more quickly.

CONNECT TO LIFE SCIENCE

Because less gas dissolves in a liquid if the temperature is raised, fish can suffocate when aquarium water becomes too warm—there may not be enough oxygen dissolved in the water.

LabBook PG 642
A Sugar Cube Race!

USING THE GRAPH

Using the graph in **Figure 14**, ask students to compare the solubility of the different solids at different temperatures. Which solid's solubility decreases as temperature increases? (cerium sulfate)

Point out to students that some elements and compounds, such as iodine and calcium carbonate, are not soluble (or are only slightly soluble) in water. Iodine is, however, soluble in alcohol, forming a solution called tincture of iodine.

DISCUSSION

Ask students how the solubility of gases varies with temperature. (Solubility decreases as temperature increases.)

Ask students how that explains why a glass of soda goes "flat" when it sits in a warm room. (The CO_2 gas that gives the soda its "fizz" comes out of the solution as the soda warms up.)

Homework

Concept Mapping
Have students describe three ways to increase the speed at which a solid will dissolve in a liquid. (mixing or stirring, heating the solvent, or crushing the solute)

Then ask them to name some home appliances that are used to speed the solution process. (mixers, food processors, heating elements or burners on a stove, microwaves)

Have students create a concept map to display their answers.
<mark>Sheltered English</mark>

Teaching Transparency 212
"Solubility Graph"

Section 3 • Mixtures

3 Extend

GOING FURTHER

Darken the room, and turn on the light from a projector. Clap two chalkboard erasers together in the beam of light. Ask students if they can explain what they are observing. (chalk particles suspended in the air scatter the light)

The mixture of chalk dust in air is a suspension. Eventually, the particles of chalk settle out of the air.

Answer to APPLY

The bottle must be shaken to remix the suspension. If the medicine is not mixed, the amount of the medicine taken may not contain the correct dosage of each component and therefore may not be effective.

LabBook PG 644
Unpolluting Water

CONNECT TO EARTH SCIENCE

Research Have students research what happens when a major volcanic eruption sends particulate matter into the atmosphere. They could start with the 1991 eruption of Mount Pinatubo, in the Philippines. Use Teaching Transparency 134, "Three Types of Volcanoes," to help students begin their project.

 **Teaching Transparency 134** "Three Types of Volcanoes"

Blood is a suspension. The suspended particles, mainly red blood cells, white blood cells, and platelets, are actually suspended in a solution called plasma. Plasma is 90 percent water and 10 percent dissolved solutes, including sugar, vitamins, and proteins.

Figure 16 Dirty air is a suspension that could damage a car's engine. The air filter in a car separates dust from air to keep the dust from getting into the engine.

Suspensions

When you shake up a snow globe, you are mixing the solid snow particles with the clear liquid. When you stop shaking the globe, the snow particles settle to the bottom of the globe. This mixture is called a suspension. A **suspension** is a mixture in which particles of a material are dispersed throughout a liquid or gas but are large enough that they settle out. The particles are insoluble, so they do not dissolve in the liquid or gas. Suspensions are often described as *heterogeneous mixtures* because the different components are easily seen. Other examples of suspensions include muddy water and Italian salad dressing.

The particles in a suspension are fairly large, and they scatter or block light. This often makes a suspension difficult to see through. But the particles are too heavy to remain mixed without being stirred or shaken. If a suspension is allowed to sit undisturbed, the particles will settle out, as in a snow globe.

A suspension can be separated by passing it through a filter. The liquid or gas passes through, but the solid particles are large enough to be trapped by the filter, as shown in **Figure 16**.

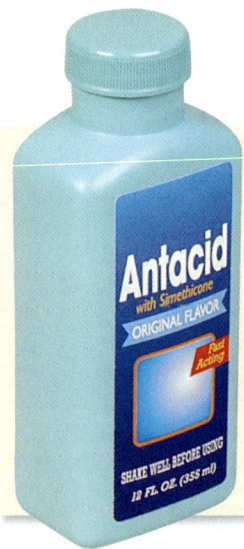

APPLY

Shake Well Before Use

Many medicines, such as remedies for upset stomach, are suspensions. The directions on the label instruct you to shake the bottle well before use. Why must you shake the bottle? What problem could arise if you don't?

 **SCIENCE HUMOR**

Q: What did the chemist say to the suspension?

A: "Settle down!"

IS THAT A FACT!

Blood is a suspension, but cells contain colloids of solid particles suspended in water.

---

96   Chapter 4 • Elements, Compounds, and Mixtures

Colloids

Some mixtures have properties of both solutions and suspensions. These mixtures are known as colloids (KAWL OYDZ). A **colloid** is a mixture in which the particles are dispersed throughout but are not heavy enough to settle out. The particles in a colloid are relatively small and are fairly well mixed. Solids, liquids, and gases can be used to make colloids. You might be surprised at the number of colloids you encounter each day. Milk, mayonnaise, stick deodorant—even the gelatin and whipped cream in **Figure 17**—are colloids. The materials that compose these products do not separate between uses because their particles do not settle out.

Figure 17 This dessert includes two delicious examples of colloids—fruity gelatin and whipped cream.

Although the particles in a colloid are much smaller than the particles in a suspension, they are still large enough to scatter a beam of light shined through the colloid, as shown in **Figure 18**. Finally, unlike a suspension, a colloid cannot be separated by filtration. The particles are small enough to pass through a filter.

Figure 18 The particles in the colloid fog scatter light, making it difficult for drivers to see the road ahead.

Make a colloid found in your kitchen on page 643 of the LabBook.

REVIEW

1. List two methods of making a solute dissolve faster.
2. Identify the solute and solvent in a solution made from 15 mL of oxygen and 5 mL of helium.
3. **Comparing Concepts** What are three differences between solutions and suspensions?

TOPIC: Mixtures
GO TO: www.scilinks.org
sciLINKS NUMBER: HSTP095

Answers to Review

1. Answers may include mixing, heating, or crushing the solute.
2. Helium is the solute, and oxygen is the solvent.
3. Sample answer: Unlike particles in a solution, particles in a suspension are large enough to settle out, block light, and be trapped by a filter. Particles in a solution do none of those.

4) Close

Quiz

1. Which of the following is not a solution: air in a scuba tank, muddy water, a soft drink, or salt water? **(muddy water)**
2. When solid iodine is dissolved in alcohol, which is the solute? the solvent? **(iodine—solute, alcohol—solvent)**
3. Why might a lake in a tropical area contain more dissolved minerals than a lake in Maine? **(The temperature of the tropical lake is probably higher, and many minerals are more soluble in warmer water than in colder water.)**

Making Butter PG 643

ALTERNATIVE ASSESSMENT

MATERIALS

FOR EACH SMALL GROUP:
- paper cups and straws
- container of warm water
- small amounts of vinegar, vegetable oil, ground coffee, instant coffee, and sand

Safety Caution: Caution students to wear safety goggles, gloves, and an apron.

Ask students to determine how many solutions and suspensions they can make by mixing these materials. Have them make two lists: solutions and suspensions. (Possible answers: Solutions—water and sugar, water and instant coffee; Suspensions—water and oil; sand and water)

Reinforcement Worksheet 4
"It's All Mixed Up"

Section 3 • Mixtures

Chapter Highlights

VOCABULARY DEFINITIONS

SECTION 1

element a pure substance that cannot be separated or broken down into simpler substances by physical or chemical means

pure substance a substance in which there is only one type of particle; includes elements and compounds

metals elements that are shiny and are good conductors of thermal and electrical energy; most metals are malleable and ductile

nonmetals elements that are dull (not shiny) and that are poor conductors of thermal and electrical energy

metalloids elements that have properties of both metals and nonmetals; sometimes referred to as semiconductors

SECTION 2

compound a pure substance composed of two or more elements that are chemically combined

Chapter Highlights

SECTION 1

Vocabulary
- element (p. 82)
- pure substance (p. 82)
- metals (p. 85)
- nonmetals (p. 85)
- metalloids (p. 85)

Section Notes
- A substance in which all the particles are alike is a pure substance.
- An element is a pure substance that cannot be broken down into anything simpler by physical or chemical means.
- Each element has a unique set of physical and chemical properties.
- Elements are classified as metals, nonmetals, or metalloids, based on their properties.

SECTION 2

Vocabulary
- compound (p. 86)

Section Notes
- A compound is a pure substance composed of two or more elements chemically combined.
- Each compound has a unique set of physical and chemical properties that are different from the properties of the elements that compose it.
- The elements that form a compound always combine in a specific ratio according to their masses.
- Compounds can be broken down into simpler substances by chemical changes.

Labs
Flame Tests (p. 640)

✓ Skills Check

Math Concepts
CONCENTRATION The concentration of a solution is a measure of the amount of solute dissolved in a solvent. For example, a solution is formed by dissolving 85 g of sodium nitrate in 170 mL of water. The concentration of the solution is calculated as follows:

$$\frac{85 \text{ g sodium nitrate}}{170 \text{ mL water}} = 0.5 \text{ g/mL}$$

Visual Understanding
THREE CATEGORIES OF ELEMENTS Elements are classified as metals, nonmetals, or metalloids, based on their properties. The chart on page 85 provides a summary of the properties that distinguish each category.

SEPARATING MIXTURES Mixtures can be separated through physical changes based on differences in the physical properties of their components. Review the illustrations on page 91 for some techniques for separating mixtures.

Lab and Activity Highlights

Flame Tests PG 640

A Sugar Cube Race! PG 642

Making Butter PG 643

Unpolluting Water PG 644

Datasheets for LabBook
(blackline masters for these labs)

98 Chapter 4 • Elements, Compounds, and Mixtures

SECTION 3

Vocabulary
- mixture *(p. 90)*
- solution *(p. 92)*
- solute *(p. 92)*
- solvent *(p. 92)*
- concentration *(p. 94)*
- solubility *(p. 94)*
- suspension *(p. 96)*
- colloid *(p. 97)*

Section Notes
- A mixture is a combination of two or more substances, each of which keeps its own characteristics.
- Mixtures can be separated by physical means, such as filtration and evaporation.
- The components of a mixture can be mixed in any proportion.
- A solution is a mixture that appears to be a single substance but is composed of a solute dissolved in a solvent. Solutions do not settle, cannot be filtered, and do not scatter light.
- Concentration is a measure of the amount of solute dissolved in a solvent.
- The solubility of a solute is the amount of solute needed to make a saturated solution using a given amount of solvent at a certain temperature.
- Suspensions are heterogeneous mixtures that contain particles large enough to settle out, be filtered, and block or scatter light.
- Colloids are mixtures that contain particles too small to settle out or be filtered but large enough to scatter light.

Labs
- **A Sugar Cube Race!** *(p. 642)*
- **Making Butter** *(p. 643)*
- **Unpolluting Water** *(p. 644)*

VOCABULARY DEFINITIONS, continued

SECTION 3

mixture a combination of two or more substances that are not chemically combined

solution a mixture that appears to be a single substance but is composed of particles of two or more substances that are distributed evenly amongst each other

solute the substance that is dissolved to form a solution

solvent the substance in which a solute is dissolved to form a solution

concentration a measure of the amount of solute dissolved in a solvent

solubility the ability to dissolve in another substance; more specifically, the amount of solute needed to make a saturated solution using a given amount of solvent at a certain temperature

suspension a mixture in which particles of a material are dispersed throughout a liquid or gas but are large enough that they settle out

colloid a mixture in which the particles are dispersed throughout but are not heavy enough to settle out

---

internet connect

GO TO: go.hrw.com

Visit the **HRW** Web site for a variety of learning tools related to this chapter. Just type in the keyword:

KEYWORD: HSTMIX

GO TO: www.scilinks.org

Visit the **National Science Teachers Association** on-line Web site for Internet resources related to this chapter. Just type in the *sci*LINKS number for more information about the topic:

TOPIC:	*sci*LINKS NUMBER:
The *Titanic*	HSTP080
Elements	HSTP085
Compounds	HSTP090
Mixtures	HSTP095

Vocabulary Review Worksheet 4

Blackline masters of these Chapter Highlights can be found in the **Study Guide.**

99

Lab and Activity Highlights

LabBank

Labs You Can Eat, An Iron-ic Cereal Experience, Lab 19

EcoLabs & Field Activities, Ozone News Zone, EcoLab 17

Whiz-Bang Demonstrations, Dense Suspense, Demo 42

Inquiry Labs, Separation Anxiety, Lab 16

Long-Term Projects & Research Ideas, A Coin-cidence, Project 54

Interactive Explorations CD-ROM

CD 1, Exploration 4, "What's the Matter?"

Chapter 4 • Chapter Highlights **99**

Chapter Review Answers

USING VOCABULARY

1. compound
2. solubility
3. suspension
4. element; compound
5. nonmetals
6. solute

UNDERSTANDING CONCEPTS

Multiple Choice

7. c   11. c
8. b   12. a
9. b   13. a
10. b   14. c

Short Answer

15. Elements cannot be separated into simpler substances, but compounds can be separated by chemical means.
16. Nail polish is the solute. Acetone is the solvent.

Concept Mapping

17. 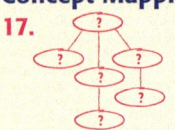 An answer to this exercise can be found at the end of this book.

CRITICAL THINKING AND PROBLEM SOLVING

18. Sample answer: Pass the mixture through a screen that allows the salt and pepper to pass through but traps the pebbles. Mix the salt and pepper with water to dissolve the salt. Filter the mixture to trap the pepper. Evaporate the water to recover the salt.
19. The powder is a compound. The change in color and the formation of a gas imply that a chemical change took place. Compounds can be broken down by chemical changes.

Concept Mapping Transparency 4

Chapter Review

USING VOCABULARY

Complete the following sentences by choosing the appropriate term from the vocabulary list to fill in each blank:

1. A __?__ has a definite ratio of components.
2. The amount of solute needed to form a saturated solution is the __?__ of the solute.
3. A __?__ can be separated by filtration.
4. A pure substance must be either a(n) __?__ or a(n) __?__.
5. Elements that are brittle and dull are __?__.
6. The substance that dissolves to form a solution is the __?__.

UNDERSTANDING CONCEPTS

Multiple Choice

7. Which of the following increases the solubility of a gas in a liquid?
   a. increasing the temperature
   b. stirring
   c. decreasing the temperature
   d. decreasing the amount of liquid

8. Which of the following best describes chicken noodle soup?
   a. element   c. compound
   b. mixture   d. solution

9. Which of the following does not describe elements?
   a. all the particles are alike
   b. can be broken down into simpler substances
   c. have unique sets of properties
   d. can join together to form compounds

10. A solution that contains a large amount of solute is best described as
    a. unsaturated.   c. dilute.
    b. concentrated.   d. weak.

11. Which of the following substances can be separated into simpler substances only by chemical means?
    a. sodium   c. water
    b. salt water   d. gold

12. Which of the following would not increase the rate at which a solid dissolves?
    a. decreasing the temperature
    b. crushing the solid
    c. stirring
    d. increasing the temperature

13. An element that conducts thermal energy well and is easily shaped is a
    a. metal.
    b. metalloid.
    c. nonmetal.
    d. None of the above

14. In which classification of matter are the components chemically combined?
    a. alloy   c. compound
    b. colloid   d. suspension

Short Answer

15. What is the difference between an element and a compound?

16. When nail polish is dissolved in acetone, which substance is the solute and which is the solvent?

---

20. The exact concentration tells you exactly how much solute is dissolved in the solvent. *Concentrated* and *dilute* are descriptive terms that do not tell you the amount of solute.
21. Each piece of fruit in a fruit salad keeps the appearance and flavor of that fruit, demonstrating that components of a mixture keep their original properties. You can separate each type of fruit using a fork, which is a physical process, demonstrating that a mixture can be separated by physical means. The amount of each fruit used in a salad can be changed, demonstrating that a mixture can be formed from any ratio of components.

Concept Mapping

17. Use the following terms to create a concept map: matter, element, compound, mixture, solution, suspension, colloid.

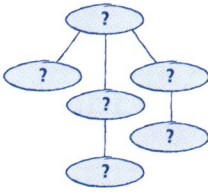

CRITICAL THINKING AND PROBLEM SOLVING

18. Describe a procedure to separate a mixture of salt, finely ground pepper, and pebbles.

19. A light green powder is heated in a test tube. A gas is given off, while the solid becomes black. In which classification of matter does the green powder belong? Explain your reasoning.

20. Why is it desirable to know the exact concentration of solutions rather than whether they are concentrated or dilute?

21. Explain the three properties of mixtures using a fruit salad as an example.

22. To keep the "fizz" in carbonated beverages after they have been opened, should you store them in a refrigerator or in a cabinet? Explain.

MATH IN SCIENCE

23. What is the concentration of a solution prepared by mixing 50 g of salt with 200 mL of water?

24. How many grams of sugar must be dissolved in 150 mL of water to make a solution with a concentration of 0.6 g/mL?

INTERPRETING GRAPHICS

25. Use Figure 14 on page 95 to answer the following questions:
    a. Can 50 g of sodium chloride dissolve in 100 mL of water at 60°C?
    b. How much cerium sulfate is needed to make a saturated solution in 100 mL of water at 30°C?
    c. Is sodium chloride or sodium nitrate more soluble in water at 20°C?

26. Dr. Sol Vent tested the solubility of a compound. The data below was collected using 100 mL of water. Graph Dr. Vent's results. To increase the solubility, would you increase or decrease the temperature? Explain.

Temperature (°C)	10	25	40	60	95
Dissolved solute (g)	150	70	34	25	15

27. What type of mixture is shown in the photo below? Explain.

NOW What Do You Think?

Take a minute to review your answers to the ScienceLog questions on page 81. Have your answers changed? If necessary, revise your answers based on what you have learned since you began this chapter.

SCIENCE, TECHNOLOGY, AND SOCIETY

Perfume: Fragrant Solutions

Background
A perfume is any substance used as a pleasant fragrance. Many cosmetics contain perfumes. Low-priced perfumes called *oderants* are added to many products, including paper, plastics, and rubber products, to hide unpleasant odors or to make the products more attractive to consumers.

Discussion
Perfume scents are often grouped according to their dominant odor. The major groups are floral, spicy, woody, and herbal. Using some of the scents listed below, have a class "smelling test" in which the students smell each scent and guess which category the scent belongs in. Discuss the results. Common scents you can use include the following:
- floral: jasmine, lily of the valley, rose, gardenia
- spicy: clove, cinnamon, nutmeg
- woody: sandalwood, cedar
- herbal: clover, rosemary
- other: vanilla, balsam, patchouli

Note: After students smell two or three scents, their olfactory functions may become desensitized. To restore their ability, allow students to sniff coffee beans after each scent.

Science, Technology, and Society
Perfume: Fragrant Solutions

Making perfume is an ancient art. It was practiced, for example, by the ancient Egyptians, who rubbed their bodies with a substance made by soaking fragrant woods and resins in water and oil. From certain references and formulas in the Bible, we know that the ancient Israelites also practiced the art of perfume making. Other sources indicate that this art was also known to the early Chinese, Arabs, Greeks, and Romans.

▲ *Perfumes have been found in the tombs of Egyptians who lived more than 3,000 years ago.*

Only the E-scent-ials
Over time, perfume making has developed into a complicated art. A fine perfume may contain more than 100 different ingredients. The most familiar ingredients come from fragrant plants or flowers, such as sandalwood or roses. These plants get their pleasant odor from their essential oils, which are stored in tiny, baglike parts called sacs. The parts of plants that are used for perfumes include the flowers, roots, and leaves. Other perfume ingredients come from animals and from man-made chemicals.

Making Scents
Perfume makers first remove essential oils from the plants using distillation or reactions with solvents. Then the essential oils are blended with other ingredients to create perfumes. Fixatives, which usually come from animals, make the other odors in the perfume last longer. Oddly enough, most natural fixatives smell awful! For example, civet musk is a foul-smelling liquid that the civet cat sprays on its enemies.

Taking Notes
When you take a whiff from a bottle of perfume, the first odor you detect is called the top note. It is a very fragrant odor that evaporates rather quickly. The middle note, or modifier, adds a different character to the odor of the top note. The base note, or end note, is the odor that lasts the longest.

▲ *Not all perfume ingredients smell good. The foul-smelling oil from the African civet cat is used as a fixative in some perfumes.*

Smell for Yourself
▶ Test a number of different perfumes and colognes to see if you can identify three different notes in each.

Answer to Smell for Yourself
You may wish to use the same scents mentioned above for this activity. Alternatively, you might bring in some popular colognes for students to test. These scents will most likely be more complex because they may include as many as 100 different ingredients.

Did You Know . . .
- Other fixatives include castor from the beaver, musk from the male musk deer, and ambergris from the sperm whale.
- The word *perfume* comes from the Latin phrase *per fumum,* which means "through smoke."

Science Fiction

"The Strange Case of Dr. Jekyll and Mr. Hyde"

by Robert Louis Stevenson

A vicious, detestable man murders an old gentleman. A wealthy and respectable scientist commits suicide. Are these two tragedies connected in some way?

Dr. Henry Jekyll is an admirable member of society. He is a doctor and a scientist. Although wild as a young man, Jekyll has become cold and analytical as he has aged and has pursued his scientific theories. Now he wants to understand the nature of human identity. He wants to explore the different parts of the human personality that usually fit together smoothly to make a complete person. His theory is that if he can separate his personality into "good" and "evil" parts, he can get rid of his evil side and lead a happy, useful life. So Jekyll develops a chemical mixture that will allow him to test his theory. The results are startling!

Who is the mysterious Mr. Hyde? He is not a scientist. He is a man of action and anger, who sparks fear in the hearts of those he comes in contact with. Where did he come from? What does he do? How can local residents be protected from his wrath?

Robert Louis Stevenson's story of the decent doctor Henry Jekyll and the violent Edward Hyde is a classic science-fiction story. When Jekyll mixes his "salts" and drinks his chemical mixture, he changes his life—and Edward Hyde's—completely. To find out more, read Stevenson's "The Strange Case of Dr. Jekyll and Mr. Hyde" in the *Holt Anthology of Science Fiction*.

SCIENCE FICTION

"The Strange Case of Dr. Jekyll and Mr. Hyde"
by Robert Louis Stevenson

When Dr. Jekyll mixes his "salts" and drinks his chemical mixture, he changes his life—and Edward Hyde's—completely.

Teaching Strategy

Reading Level This novelette is challenging for middle school readers. It may be helpful for you to review the story in advance and review some of the unfamiliar words and phrases with students ahead of time.

Background

The science connection in this story is that Dr. Jekyll is a "man of science" who conducts experiments with chemical compounds to explore his own personality. He wants to separate out the purely good part of himself from the brutish and evil. Jekyll experiments until he finds a mixture of "salts" that creates the split. But once he has released Mr. Hyde, it becomes increasingly difficult for Jekyll to control him!

About the Author Stevenson was a sickly child and was plagued by health problems all his life. Some critics argue that Hyde represents the anger and frustration that Stevenson felt as a result of his ill health. Other critics compare the story to Mary Shelley's *Frankenstein* because both deal with the idea that humans can be perfected. Still others see a reflection of the conflict between good and evil, which people have talked about and written about for more than 4,000 years. All three of these themes are in the story, and any one of them would be a good starting point for a class discussion.

UNIT 2

TIMELINE
Motion and Forces

It's hard to imagine a world where nothing ever moves. Without motion or forces to cause motion, life would be very dull! The relationship between force and motion is the subject of this unit. You will learn how to describe the motion of objects, how forces affect motion, and how fluids exert force. This timeline shows some events and discoveries that have occurred as scientists have worked to understand the motion of objects here on Earth and in space.

Around 250 B.C.
Archimedes, a Greek mathematician, develops the principle that bears his name. The principle relates the buoyant force on an object in a fluid to the amount of fluid the object displaces.

Around 240 B.C.
Chinese astronomers are the first to record a sighting of Halley's Comet.

1905
While employed as a patent clerk, German physicist Albert Einstein publishes his special theory of relativity. The theory states that the speed of light is constant, no matter what the reference point is.

1921
Bessie Coleman becomes the first African-American woman licensed to fly an airplane.

1947
While flying a Bell X-1 rocket-powered airplane, American pilot Chuck Yeager becomes the first human to travel faster than the speed of sound.

1519
Portuguese explorer Ferdinand Magellan begins the first voyage around the world.

1687
Sir Isaac Newton, a British mathematician and scientist, publishes *Principia,* a book describing his laws of motion and the law of universal gravitation.

1764
In London, Wolfgang Amadeus Mozart composes his first symphony—at the age of 9.

1846
After determining that the orbit of Uranus is different from what is predicted from the law of universal gravitation, scientists discover Neptune, shown here, whose gravitational force is causing Uranus's unusual orbit.

1971
American astronaut Alan Shepard takes a break from gathering lunar data to play golf on the moon during the *Apollo 14* mission.

1990
The *Magellan* spacecraft begins orbiting Venus for a four-year mission to map the planet. The spacecraft uses the sun's gravitational force to propel it to Venus without burning much fuel.

1999
NASA launches the Mars *Polar Lander* spacecraft, one of a series sent to explore Mars.

Motion and Forces **105**

Chapter Organizer

CHAPTER ORGANIZATION	TIME MINUTES	OBJECTIVES	LABS, INVESTIGATIONS, AND DEMONSTRATIONS
Chapter Opener pp. 106–107	45	National Standards: UCP 3, SAI 1, PS 2a	**Investigate!** The Domino Derby, p. 107
Section 1 Measuring Motion	120	▶ Identify the relationship between motion and a reference point. ▶ Identify the two factors that speed depends on. ▶ Determine the difference between speed and velocity. ▶ Analyze the relationship of velocity to acceleration. ▶ Interpret a graph showing acceleration. UCP 1, UCP 3, PS 2a; LabBook UCP 3, SAI 1–2, PS 2a	**Demonstration,** Models, p. 108 in ATE **Interactive Explorations CD-ROM,** Force in the Forest A **Worksheet** is also available in the **Interactive Explorations Teacher's Edition.** **Design Your Own,** Built for Speed, p. 646 **Datasheets for LabBook,** Built for Speed, Datasheet 16 **Skill Builder,** Detecting Acceleration, p. 647 **Datasheets for LabBook,** Detecting Acceleration, Datasheet 17
Section 2 What Is a Force?	120	▶ Give examples of different kinds of forces. ▶ Determine the net force on an object. ▶ Compare balanced and unbalanced forces. UCP 1, UCP 4, SPSP 5, PS 2b, PS 2c	**Demonstration,** p. 117 in ATE
Section 3 Friction: A Force That Opposes Motion	120	▶ Explain why friction occurs. ▶ List the types of friction, and give examples of each. ▶ Explain how friction can be both harmful and helpful. UCP 3, SAI 1, PS 2c; LabBook SAI 1–2	**Demonstration,** p. 119 in ATE **QuickLab,** The Friction 500, p. 120 **Interactive Explorations CD-ROM,** Stranger Than Friction **Discovery Lab,** Science Friction, p. 650 **Datasheets for LabBook,** Science Friction, Datasheet 18
Section 4 Gravity: A Force of Attraction	120	▶ Define *gravity*. ▶ State the law of universal gravitation. ▶ Describe the difference between mass and weight. UCP 1, UCP 3, ST 2, SPSP 5, HNS 1, HNS 3, PS 2c; LabBook UCP 3, SAI 1	**Demonstration,** p. 125 in ATE **Skill Builder,** Relating Mass and Weight, p. 651 **Datasheets for LabBook,** Relating Mass and Weight, Datasheet 19 **Long-Term Projects & Research Ideas,** Project 55

See page T20 for a complete correlation of this book with the

NATIONAL SCIENCE EDUCATION STANDARDS.

TECHNOLOGY RESOURCES

 Guided Reading Audio CD
English or Spanish, Chapter 5

 **Interactive Explorations CD-ROM**
CD 2, Exploration 4, Force in the Forest
CD 3, Exploration 3, Stranger Than Friction

 One-Stop Planner CD-ROM
with Test Generator

 CNN Science, Technology & Society,
The Science of Bowling, Segment 7
Scientists in Action, Segments 16 and 25

 Science Discovery Videodiscs
Image and Activity Bank with Lesson Plans:
Friction Finder, Name That Structure
Science Sleuths: The Collapsing Bleachers

Chapter 5 • Matter in Motion

Chapter 5 • Matter in Motion

CLASSROOM WORKSHEETS, TRANSPARENCIES, AND RESOURCES	SCIENCE INTEGRATION AND CONNECTIONS	REVIEW AND ASSESSMENT
Directed Reading Worksheet 5 **Science Puzzlers, Twisters & Teasers,** Worksheet 5		
Directed Reading Worksheet 5, Section 1 **Math Skills for Science Worksheet 47,** Average Speed in a Pinewood Derby **Transparency 213,** A Graph Showing Speed **Math Skills for Science Worksheet 31,** The Unit Factor and Dimensional Analysis **Science Skills Worksheet 17,** Organizing Your Research **Transparency 214,** Determining Resultant Velocity **Transparency 215,** Calculating Acceleration **Transparency 216,** A Graph Showing Acceleration **Reinforcement Worksheet 5,** Bug Race	**MathBreak,** Calculating Average Speed, p. 109 **Math and More,** p. 109 in ATE **MathBreak,** Calculating Acceleration, p. 113 **Math and More,** p. 113 in ATE **Holt Anthology of Science Fiction,** *Direction of the Road*	**Homework,** pp. 109, 112 in ATE **Self-Check,** p. 110 **Review,** p. 111 **Review,** p. 114 **Quiz,** p. 114 in ATE **Alternative Assessment,** p. 114 in ATE
Directed Reading Worksheet 5, Section 2 **Transparency 217,** Forces in the Same Direction **Transparency 217,** Forces in Different Directions	**Science, Technology, and Society:** Is It Real . . . or Is It Virtual? p. 134 **Across the Sciences:** The Golden Gate Bridge, p. 135	**Self-Check,** p. 117 **Review,** p. 118 **Quiz,** p. 118 in ATE **Alternative Assessment,** p. 118 in ATE
Directed Reading Worksheet 5, Section 3 **Transparency 218,** Force and Friction **Transparency 219,** Static Friction **Reinforcement Worksheet 5,** Friction Action	**Connect to Life Science,** p. 119 in ATE **Real-World Connection,** p. 121 in ATE **Cross-Disciplinary Focus,** p. 121 in ATE **Apply,** p. 124	**Self-Check,** p. 122 **Homework,** pp. 122, 123 in ATE **Review,** p. 124 **Quiz,** p. 124 in ATE **Alternative Assessment,** p. 124 in ATE
Directed Reading Worksheet 5, Section 4 **Transparency 161,** Tidal Variations **Transparency 220,** The Law of Universal Gravitation **Reinforcement Worksheet 5,** A Weighty Problem **Critical Thinking Worksheet 5,** A Mission in Motion **Transparency 221,** Weight and Mass Are Different	**Biology Connection,** p. 125 **Connect to Earth Science,** p. 126 in ATE **Astronomy Connection,** p. 127 **Connect to Earth Science,** p. 127 in ATE **Real-World Connection,** p. 127 in ATE	**Self-Check,** p. 126 **Homework,** p. 127 in ATE **Review,** p. 129 **Quiz,** p. 129 in ATE **Alternative Assessment,** p. 129 in ATE

END-OF-CHAPTER REVIEW AND ASSESSMENT

Chapter Review in Study Guide
Vocabulary and Notes in Study Guide
Chapter Tests with Performance-Based Assessment, Chapter 5 Test
Chapter Tests with Performance-Based Assessment, Performance-Based Assessment 5
Concept Mapping Transparency 5

 Holt, Rinehart and Winston On-line Resources
go.hrw.com
For worksheets and other teaching aids related to this chapter, visit the HRW Web site and type in the keyword: **HSTMOT**

 **National Science Teachers Association**
www.scilinks.org
Encourage students to use the *sci*LINKS numbers listed in the internet connect boxes to access information and resources on the **NSTA** Web site.

Chapter 5 • Chapter Organizer **105B**

Chapter Resources & Worksheets

Visual Resources

TEACHING TRANSPARENCIES

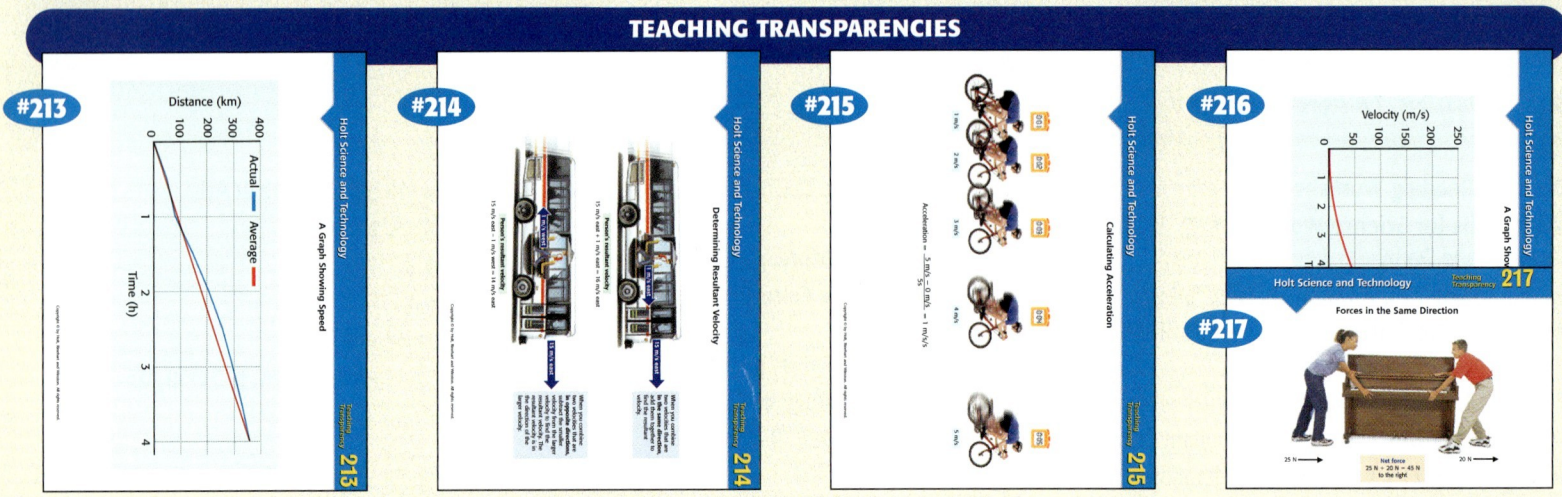

TEACHING TRANSPARENCIES

CONCEPT MAPPING TRANSPARENCY

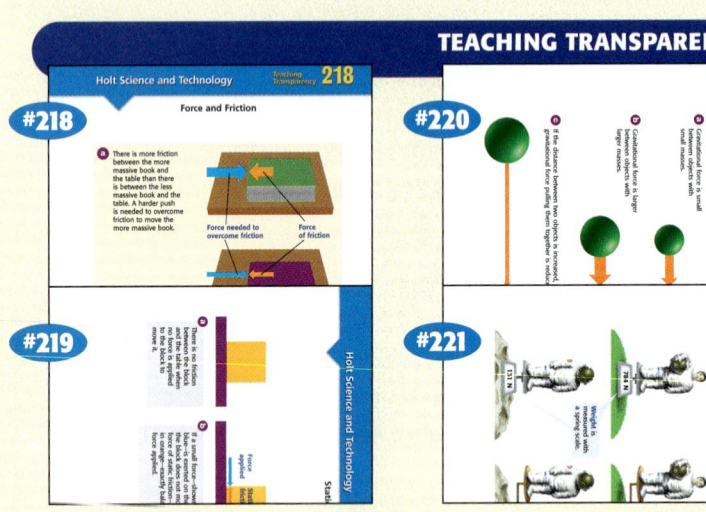
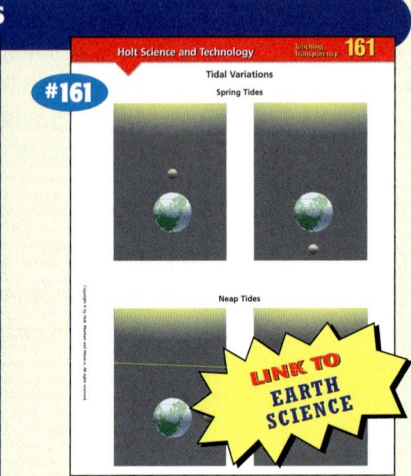
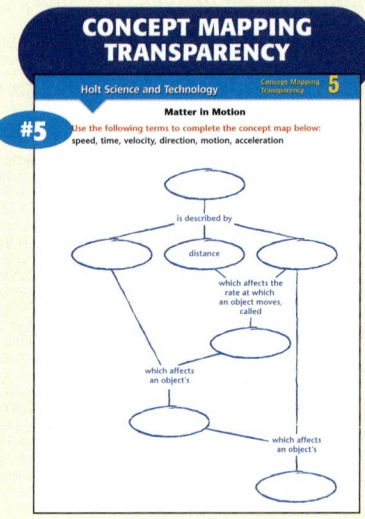

Meeting Individual Needs

DIRECTED READING

REINFORCEMENT & VOCABULARY REVIEW

SCIENCE PUZZLERS, TWISTERS & TEASERS

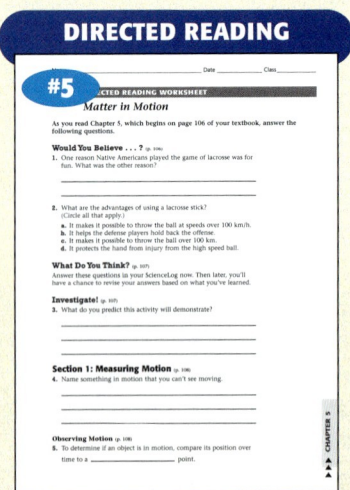
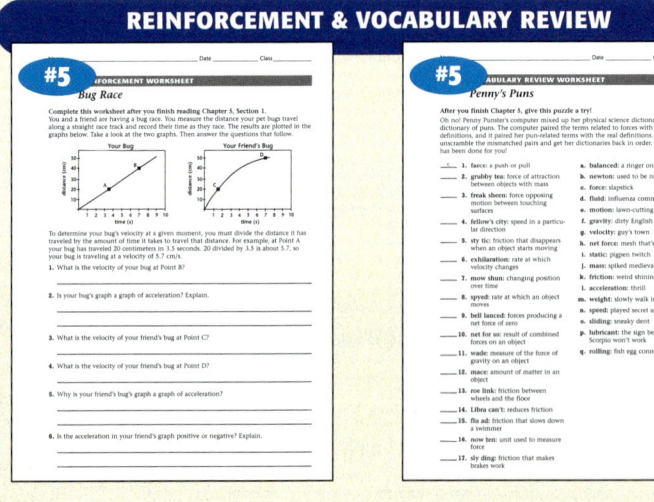
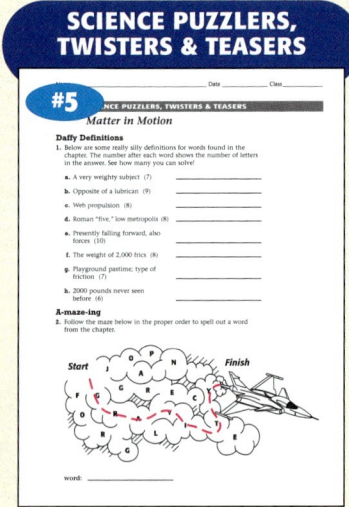

Chapter 5 • Matter in Motion

Chapter 5 • Matter in Motion

Review & Assessment

STUDY GUIDE

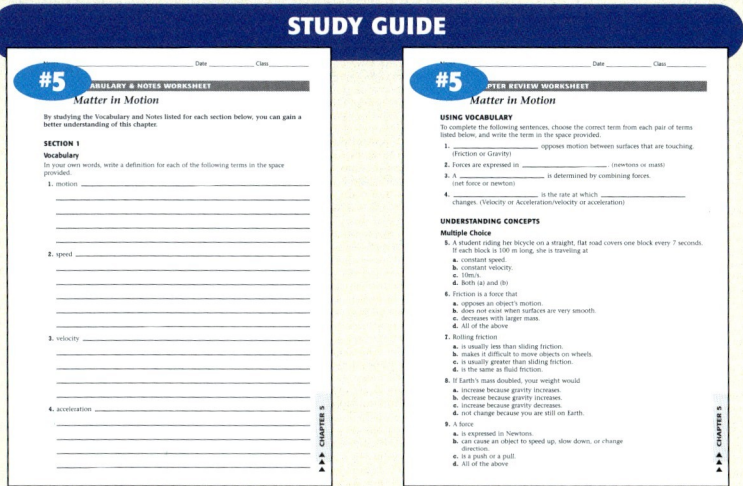

CHAPTER TESTS WITH PERFORMANCE-BASED ASSESSMENT

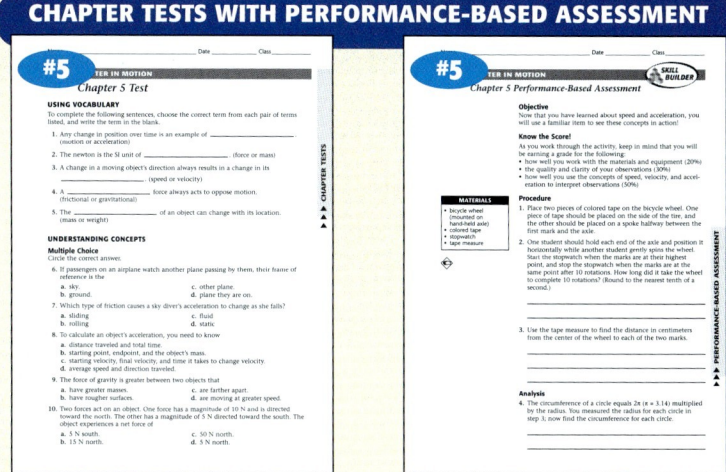

Lab Worksheets

LONG-TERM PROJECTS & RESEARCH IDEAS

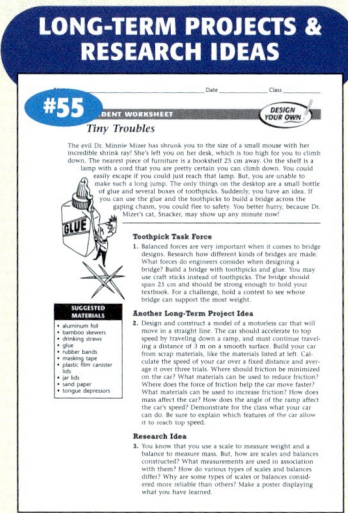

DATASHEETS FOR LABBOOK

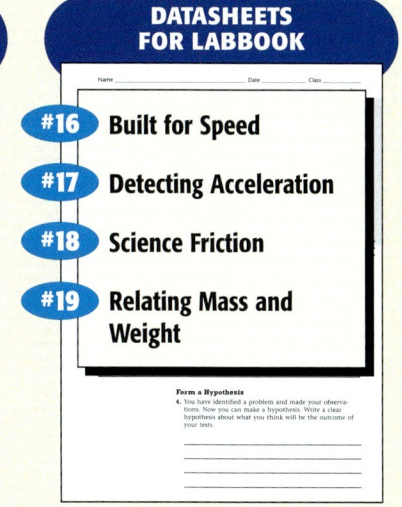

Applications & Extensions

CRITICAL THINKING & PROBLEM SOLVING

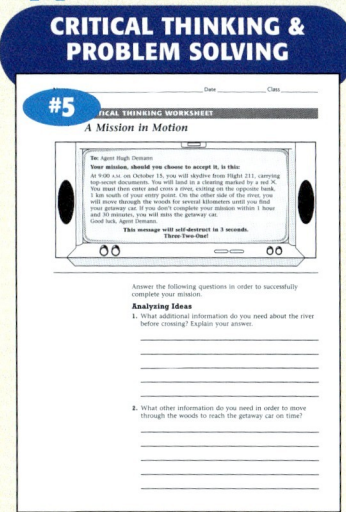

SCIENCE TECHNOLOGY

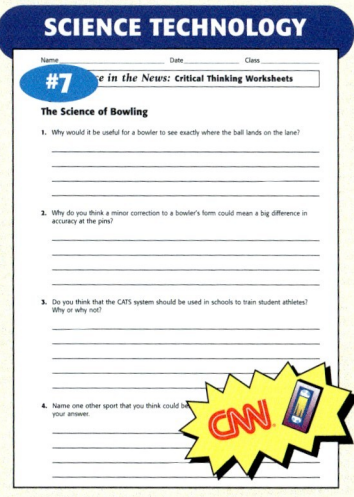

SCIENTISTS IN ACTION

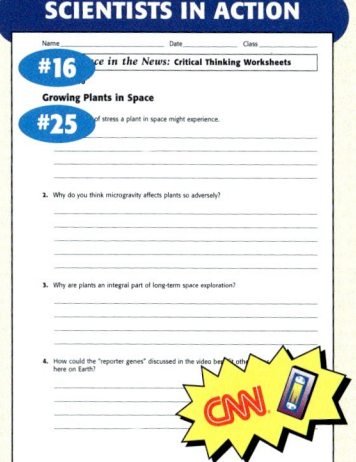

INTERACTIVE EXPLORATIONS

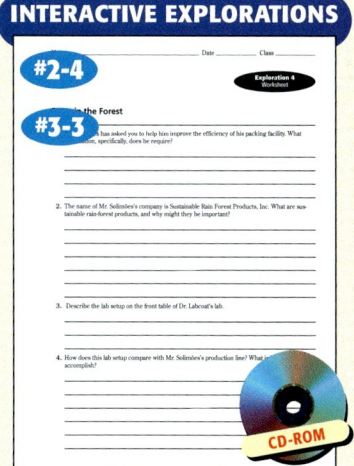

Chapter 5 • Chapter Resources & Worksheets 105D

Chapter Background

SECTION 1

Measuring Motion

▶ **The Scientific Revolution**
The movement now called the Scientific Revolution took place between the sixteenth and eighteenth centuries. Mainstream science of the time still taught the classical Aristotelian view of the universe. With the translation of Greek, Roman, and Arabic texts and the improvement of the printing press, ideas that are now the basis of modern science first became available to a large number of people.

- In astronomy, the theory that the sun is the center of the solar system was established by Copernicus. Galileo laid the foundations of the principles of mechanics and first turned a telescope toward the sky. Philosophers such as Descartes began to develop the idea of nature as a complicated system of particles in motion.

▶ **Sir Isaac Newton (1642–1727)**
Sir Isaac Newton was a central figure in the Scientific Revolution during the seventeenth century. He was born in 1642, the year Galileo died.

▶ **Acceleration**
Remember that acceleration, just like velocity, always includes direction. However, the relationship between acceleration and motion is different from the relationship between velocity and motion. An object's motion is always in the same direction as its velocity. An object's motion is not always in the same direction as its acceleration.

▶ **Lacrosse and Physics**
The sport lacrosse takes advantage of the physics of circular motion, and skilled lacrosse players can use a lacrosse stick to send the ball flying at speeds approaching 42 m/s, or about as fast as a typical fastball in Major League Baseball.

- Think of a line of students in a marching band making a turn. One student serves as the pivot point around which the others turn (similar to the bottom of the handle of the lacrosse stick). The far end of the line (or the web end of the stick) is moving very fast compared with the pivot. In lacrosse, some of that speed is imparted to the ball.

IS THAT A FACT!

- A fast runner can reach a speed of 32 km/h. The highest speed a person can attain when swimming, however, is only about 8 km/h.

SECTION 2

What Is a Force?

▶ **Basic Forces of Nature**
Scientists believe that the interactions of only four basic forces can describe all the physical properties and relationships in nature. These forces are:

- the gravitational force, which acts on all matter that has mass and on light, which has no mass

- the electromagnetic force, which is responsible for the attraction and repulsion of certain kinds of matter (including the electrical and magnetic forces)

- the strong nuclear force, which binds the protons and neutrons of atoms together in the nucleus

- the weak nuclear force, which describes some interactions between subatomic particles

- The electromagnetic, strong nuclear, and weak nuclear forces are covered briefly in Chapter 11, "Introduction to Atoms."

Chapter 5 • Matter in Motion

IS THAT A FACT!

- Gravitational force and electromagnetic force were discovered long before nuclear forces because we can observe their effects on ordinary matter. The strong and weak nuclear forces were not discovered until the twentieth century, when we were able to probe the structure of atoms.

▶ Tug-of-War and Force
In a tug-of-war contest, the losing team always moves in the direction of the net force.

SECTION 3

Friction: A Force That Opposes Motion

▶ Sports and Friction
Many sports participants want to reduce friction as much as possible. Downhill skiers wax their skis to reduce friction between the skis and the snow. Surfers wax their boards to reduce friction between the boards and the water. However, in some sports, increased friction is what the athlete wants. A runner in the 100 m dash wants maximum friction between his or her shoes and the running track.

▶ Wheels
A wheel makes movement easier by reducing friction. Yet without friction between the wheel and the ground, the wheel would just spin around and the object to which the wheel is attached would go nowhere. Rolling friction usually dissipates much less energy than sliding friction.

IS THAT A FACT!

- Because friction can increase the temperature of objects, the space shuttle glows bright pink as it reenters the thick atmosphere of Earth. One astronaut reported that reentry is like riding in a neon tube.

- Athletic shoes come in so many varieties because they are designed to provide the proper amount of friction for maximum performance in each sport.

SECTION 4

Gravity: A Force of Attraction

▶ Gravity
Every object in the universe is constantly subject to the pull of gravity. The gravitational force acting on the object may be extremely small, but it is always present.

▶ Newton's Universal Law of Gravitation
The gravitational force exists between two objects anywhere in the universe. It exists regardless of the mass of the objects, the medium they are in, their composition, or the distance between them.

Newton's universal law of gravitation is $F_g = G \frac{m_1 m_2}{d^2}$, which means that the gravitational force
(F_g) = constant of universal gravitation $\times \left(\frac{\text{mass}_1 \times \text{mass}_2}{(\text{distance between the centers of mass})^2} \right)$.

The size of the gravitational force is related to the masses of the objects and the distance between them.

IS THAT A FACT!

- When the gravitational force of the moon and sun pull together on the same side of Earth or pull on opposite sides of Earth, ocean tides are highest.

- If a person could hover at a distance of 6,400 km above Earth, twice Earth's radius, he or she would weigh only one-fourth his or her weight on Earth.

For background information about teaching strategies and issues, refer to the *Professional Reference for Teachers*.

Chapter 5 • Chapter Background   **105F**

CHAPTER 5
Matter in Motion

Chapter Preview

Section 1
Measuring Motion
- Observing Motion
- Speed Depends on Distance and Time
- Velocity: Direction Matters
- Acceleration: The Rate at Which Velocity Changes

Section 2
What Is a Force?
- Forces Act on Objects
- Forces in Combination
- Unbalanced and Balanced Forces

Section 3
Friction: A Force That Opposes Motion
- The Source of Friction
- Types of Friction
- Friction Can Be Harmful or Helpful

Section 4
Gravity: A Force of Attraction
- All Matter Is Affected by Gravity
- The Law of Universal Gravitation
- Weight Is a Measure of Gravitational Force

Science Puzzlers, Twisters & Teasers Worksheet 5

Guided Reading Audio CD
English or Spanish, Chapter 5

CHAPTER 5
Matter in Motion

Would You Believe...?

There was once a game that could be played by as few as 5 or as many as 1,000 players. The game could be played on a small field for a few hours or on a huge tract of land for several days. The game was not just for fun—in fact, it was often used as a substitute for war. One of the few rules was that the players couldn't touch the ball with their hands—they had to use a special stick with webbing on one end. Would you believe that this game is the same as the game of lacrosse played today?

Lacrosse is a game that was originally played by Native Americans, as shown above. They called the game *baggataway* (bag AT uh way), which means "little brother of war." Although lacrosse has changed and is now played all over the world, it still requires special webbed sticks.

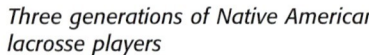
Detail of Ball Play of the Choctaw by George Catlin, National Museum of American Art, Smithsonian Institution, Washington D.C./Art Resouce, N.Y.

Using a lacrosse stick, a player can throw the ball at speeds well over 100 km/h. In order to move the ball this fast, a large force (push or pull) has to be supplied. Likewise, in order to stop the ball, another large force is needed. Imagine using your bare hand, instead of the stick, to supply this force—Ouch!

Even though you may have never played lacrosse, you have experienced motion and the forces that cause it or prevent it. As you read this chapter, you'll have no trouble thinking of your own examples.

Three generations of Native American lacrosse players

Would You Believe...?

Many games and sports rely on an understanding of motion. Variations of a game called *chunkee* were played by Native Americans throughout much of North America. *Chunkee* involved one person rolling a stone disk along a path while other players attempted to hit the disk with their spears.

106 Chapter 5 • Matter in Motion

What Do You Think?

In your ScienceLog, try to answer the following questions based on what you already know:

1. How is motion measured?
2. What is a force?
3. How does friction affect motion?
4. How does gravity affect objects?

The Domino Derby

You are probably familiar with the term *speed*. Speed is the rate at which an object moves. In this activity, you will determine the factors that affect the speed of falling dominoes.

Procedure

1. Set up **25 dominoes** in a straight line. Try to keep equal spacing between the dominoes.
2. Using a **metric ruler,** measure the total length of your row of dominoes, and record it in your ScienceLog.
3. Using a **stopwatch,** time how long it takes for the entire row of dominoes to fall. Record the time in your ScienceLog.
4. Predict what would happen to that amount of time if you changed the distance between the dominoes. Write your predictions in your ScienceLog.
5. Repeat steps 2 and 3 several times, using distances between the dominoes that are smaller and larger than in your original setup.

Analysis

6. Calculate the average speed for each trial by dividing the total distance (the length of the domino row) by the time taken to fall.
7. How did the spacing between dominoes affect the average speed? Did your results confirm your predictions? If not, explain.

Going Further

Make a graph of your results. Explain why your graph has the shape that it does.

internet connect

Smithsonian Institution®
Visit **www.si.edu/hrw** for additional on-line resources.

Answer to Going Further

The curve of the graph shows that speed decreases as the spacing gets too small or too large. The speed is fastest at the highest point of the curve.

What Do You Think?

Accept all reasonable responses.

Students will have a chance to revise their answers in the Chapter Review under NOW What Do You Think?

Investigate!

MATERIALS

FOR EACH GROUP:
- 25 dominoes
- metric ruler
- stopwatch

You might want to allow students to line up their dominoes along the side edge of a meterstick to assure that the dominoes are in a straight line.

Answers to Investigate!

4. Accept all reasonable predictions.
6. Answers will vary.
7. Students should determine that putting dominoes very close together and putting them very far apart *both* lead to slower average speed. The average speed is fastest when the dominoes are set about half a domino's length apart. Accept all reasonable answers regarding predictions. Students will likely find that the results do *not* confirm their predictions. It would seem most predictable that setting the dominoes very close together would reduce the time taken for all the dominoes to fall, thus increasing the average speed.

Directed Reading Worksheet 5

Chapter 5 • Matter in Motion **107**

SECTION 1

Focus

Measuring Motion

This section introduces students to the concept of motion. It introduces the idea of a *reference point* as a necessary starting point to observe motion. Students learn about average speed, velocity, and acceleration, and learn to calculate all three.

Bellringer

Have students describe their position in the classroom using a reference point and a set of reference directions. For example, a student might say, "I sit three desks behind Ahmed's desk," or "I sit 2 m east of the vent hood and 10 m north of the emergency shower."

1) Motivate

DEMONSTRATION

Models Place two identical wind-up toys on a table, one wound, the other not wound, so that one toy moves across the table while the other one remains motionless. Ask students to explain the difference between the toys. Help students understand that the difference is movement. Ask students to define motion in their own terms. Explain that in this section they will learn how to identify and measure different quantities related to motion.

Directed Reading Worksheet 5 Section 1

Section 1

Terms to Learn
motion velocity
speed acceleration

What You'll Do
- Identify the relationship between motion and a reference point.
- Identify the two factors that speed depends on.
- Determine the difference between speed and velocity.
- Analyze the relationship of velocity to acceleration.
- Interpret a graph showing acceleration.

Measuring Motion

Look around you—you're likely to see something in motion. Your teacher may be walking across the room, or perhaps a bird is flying outside a window. Even if you don't see anything moving, motion is still occurring all around you. Tiny air particles are whizzing around, the moon is circling the Earth, and blood is traveling through your veins and arteries!

Observing Motion

You might think that the motion of an object is easy to detect—you just observe the object. But you actually must observe the object in relation to another object that appears to stay in place. The object that appears to stay in place is a *reference point*. When an object changes position over time when compared with a reference point, the object is in **motion**. When an object is in motion, you can describe the direction of its motion with a reference direction, such as north, south, east, west, or up and down.

Common Reference Points The Earth's surface is a common reference point for determining position and motion. Nonmoving objects on Earth's surface, such as buildings, trees, and mountains, are also useful reference points, as shown in **Figure 1**.

A moving object can also be used as a reference point. For example, if you were on the hot-air balloon shown below, you could watch a bird fly by and see that it was changing position in relation to your moving balloon. Furthermore, Earth itself is a moving reference point—it is moving around the sun.

Figure 1 During the time it took for these pictures to be taken, the hot-air balloon changed position compared with a reference point—the mountain.

MISCONCEPTION ALERT

The text defines *motion* as an object's change in position over time when compared with a reference point. Remind students that an object's *position* can be described in terms of a reference point and a set of reference directions. Common reference directions are compass directions (such as south and west) and relative directions (such as left of, just beyond, and in front of).

Speed Depends on Distance and Time

The rate at which an object moves is its **speed.** Speed depends on the distance traveled and the time taken to travel that distance. Look back at Figure 1. Suppose the time interval between the pictures was 10 seconds and the balloon traveled 50 m in that time. The speed (distance divided by time) of the balloon is 50 m/10 s, or 5 m/s.

The SI unit for speed is meters per second (m/s). Kilometers per hour, feet per second, and miles per hour are other units commonly used to express speed.

Determining Average Speed Most of the time, objects do not travel at a constant speed. For example, you probably do not walk at a constant speed from one class to the next. Therefore, it is very useful to calculate *average speed* using the following equation:

$$\text{Average speed} = \frac{\text{total distance}}{\text{total time}}$$

Recognizing Speed on a Graph Suppose a person drives from one city to another. The blue line in the graph below shows the distance traveled every hour. Notice that the distance traveled every hour is different. This is because the speed (distance/time) is not constant—the driver changes speed often because of weather, traffic, or varying speed limits. The average speed can be calculated by adding up the total distance and dividing it by the total time:

$$\text{Average speed} = \frac{360 \text{ km}}{4 \text{ h}} = 90 \text{ km/h}$$

The red line shows the average distance traveled each hour. The slope of this line is the average speed.

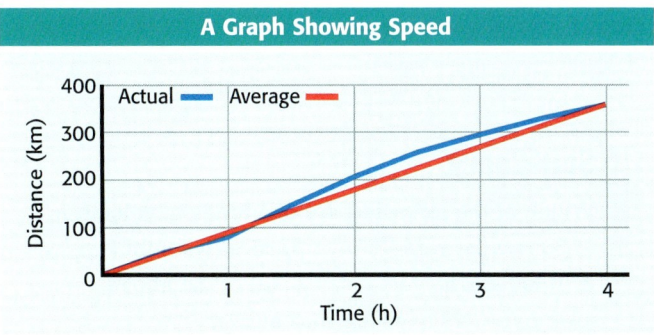

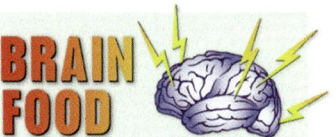

The list below shows a comparison of some interesting speeds:

Cockroach . . . . . . 1.25 m/s
Kangaroo . . . . 15 m/s
Cheetah (the fastest land animal) . . . . 27 m/s
Sound (in air) . . . . . 343 m/s
Space shuttle . . . 10,000 m/s
Light . . . . . 300,000,000 m/s

MATH BREAK

Calculating Average Speed

Practice calculating average speed in the problems listed below:

1. If you walk for 1.5 hours and travel 7.5 km, what is your average speed?
2. A bird flies at a speed of 15 m/s for 10 s, 20 m/s for 10 s, and 25 m/s for 5 s. What is the bird's average speed?

2) Teach

USING THE FIGURE

In the figure **A Graph Showing Speed,** the linear curve (straight line) on the graph shows that the average speed is constant for the entire trip, while the nonlinear curve (crooked line) indicates that the speed of the car changed several times during the trip.

Answers to MATHBREAK

1. 5 km/h
2. 19 m/s

Item 2 requires dimensional analysis.

LabBook PG 646
Built for Speed

MATH and MORE

Give students the following problems to solve:

- What is your average speed if you take 0.5 hour to walk 4,000 m? (8,000 m/h)
- If the average speed of a car is 110 km/h, how long will it take the car to travel 715 km? (6.5 hours)

 Math Skills Worksheet 47 "Average Speed in a Pinewood Derby"

Teaching Transparency 213 "A Graph Showing Speed"

 Math Skills Worksheet 31 "The Unit Factor and Dimensional Analysis"

Homework

Obtain bus, train, or airplane schedules that list departure and arrival times. Help students plan a trip with at least four segments.

Using a map of the route, have students estimate the distance between points on the route as accurately as possible. Have them calculate the average speed of the vehicle between checkpoints and compare the average speed for each segment. Does the average speed remain constant or does it change? What might account for any differences?

Section 1 • Measuring Motion

Velocity: Direction Matters

Here's a riddle for you: Two birds leave the same tree at the same time. They both fly at 10 km/h for 1 hour, 15 km/h for 30 minutes, and 5 km/h for 1 hour. Why don't they end up at the same destination?

Have you figured it out? The birds traveled at the same speeds for the same amounts of time, but they did not end up at the same place because they went in different directions. In other words, they had different velocities. The speed of an object in a particular direction is the object's **velocity** (vuh LAHS uh tee).

Be careful not to confuse the terms *speed* and *velocity;* they do not mean the same thing. Because velocity must include direction, it would not be correct to say that an airplane's velocity is 600 km/h. However, you could say the plane's velocity is 600 km/h south. Velocity always includes a reference direction. **Figure 2** further illustrates the difference between speed and velocity.

Figure 2 The speeds of these cars may be similar, but their velocities are different because they are going in different directions.

Velocity Changes as Speed or Direction Changes You can think of velocity as the rate of change of an object's position. An object's velocity is constant only if its speed and direction don't change. Therefore, constant velocity is always along a straight line. An object's velocity will change if either its speed or direction changes. For example, if a bus traveling at 15 m/s south speeds up to 20 m/s, a change in velocity has occurred. But a change in velocity also occurs if the bus continues to travel at the same speed but changes direction to travel east.

Self-Check

Which of the following are examples of velocity?
1. 25 m/s forward
2. 1,500 km/h
3. 55 m/h south
4. all of the above

(See page 724 to check your answer.)

IS THAT A FACT!

A 14-year-old land-speed record was broken in 1997 when the jet-powered *ThrustSSC* traveled faster than the speed of sound. The vehicle reached a speed of 1,230 km/h. The speed of sound in air at 0°C is about 1,192 km/h.

Combining Velocities If you're riding in a bus traveling east at 15 m/s, you and all the other passengers are also traveling at a velocity of 15 m/s east. But suppose you stand up and walk down the bus's aisle while it is moving. Are you still moving at the same velocity as the bus? No! **Figure 3** shows how you can combine velocities to determine the *resultant velocity*.

Figure 3 Determining Resultant Velocity

Person's resultant velocity
15 m/s east + 1 m/s east = 16 m/s east

When you combine two velocities that are **in the same direction,** add them together to find the resultant velocity.

Person's resultant velocity
15 m/s east − 1 m/s west = 14 m/s east

When you combine two velocities that are **in opposite directions,** subtract the smaller velocity from the larger velocity to find the resultant velocity. The resultant velocity is in the direction of the larger velocity.

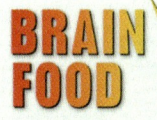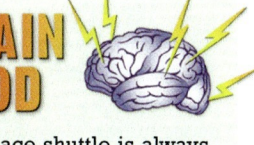

The space shuttle is always launched in the same direction that the Earth rotates, thus taking advantage of the Earth's rotational velocity (over 1,500 km/h east). This allows the shuttle to use less fuel to reach space than if it had to achieve such a great velocity on its own.

REVIEW

1. What is a reference point?
2. What two things must you know to determine speed?
3. What is the difference between speed and velocity?
4. **Applying Concepts** Explain why it is important to know a tornado's velocity and not just its speed.

RETEACHING

Have students use graph paper or make a number line to practice adding and subtracting velocities. Have them draw a number line on the graph paper. Starting with the problems listed in **Figure 3,** have students draw arrows representing the velocities of the bus and of the walker. Show them that by placing the arrows in sequence, they can add the velocities. By superimposing the arrows, they can subtract the velocities. (This is a form of vector addition and subtraction.)

INDEPENDENT PRACTICE

Have students develop three of their own problems involving the addition and subtraction of velocities. The problems should come from events in their own experience. For example, they might develop a problem based on kicking a soccer ball down the field or from watching actors running along the top of a train in an adventure movie. Students should provide answers to their problems.

MISCONCEPTION ALERT

When a plane is in the air, the Earth rotates beneath it. Remind students that the Earth's atmosphere rotates with the Earth. If it didn't, a plane flying from Los Angeles to New York would never reach its destination. It would be as if the plane were flying into a 1,600 km/h headwind.

 Teaching Transparency 214 "Determining Resultant Velocity"

Answers to Review

1. A reference point is an object that appears to stay in place in relation to an object being observed and is used to determine if the object is in motion.
2. the distance traveled and the time taken to travel that distance
3. Speed does not include direction; velocity does.
4. It would be important to know the velocity because velocity includes direction. Knowing only the speed of a tornado would not tell the direction that the tornado is traveling. Knowing a tornado's direction of travel would allow people to avoid or escape its path.

2) Teach, continued

READING STRATEGY

Prediction Guide Before reading about acceleration, ask students to predict whether the following sentences are true or false:

- If you slow down on your bicycle, you accelerate. (true)
- If you ride your bicycle at a constant speed, you cannot accelerate. (false)
- Changing the speed and changing the direction of your bicycle are both examples of acceleration. (true)

MEETING INDIVIDUAL NEEDS

Learners Having Difficulty Read aloud each of the following situations. Diagram them on the board or overhead projector. Then discuss with students whether or not acceleration occurred and why.

- You are riding your bike at 9 km/h. Ten minutes later, your speed is 6 km/h. (Acceleration occurred because speed decreased.)
- You ride your bike around the block at a constant speed of 11 km/h. (Acceleration occurred because direction changed.)
- You ride your bike in a straight line at a constant speed of 10 km/h. (No acceleration occurred because neither speed nor direction changed.) **Sheltered English**

Detecting Acceleration PG 647

Acceleration: The Rate at Which Velocity Changes

Imagine that you are in-line skating and you see a large rock in your path. You slow down and swerve to avoid the rock. A neighbor sees you and exclaims, "That was great acceleration! I'm amazed that you could slow down and turn so quickly!" You're puzzled. Doesn't *accelerate* mean to speed up? But you didn't speed up—you slowed down and turned. So how could you have accelerated?

Defining Acceleration Although the word *accelerate* is commonly used to mean "speed up," there's more to its meaning scientifically. **Acceleration** (ak SEL uhr AY shuhn) is the rate at which velocity changes. To *accelerate* means to change velocity. You just learned that velocity changes if speed changes, direction changes, or both. So your neighbor was right! Your speed and direction changed, so you accelerated.

Keep in mind that acceleration is not just how much velocity changes. It is also *how fast* velocity changes. The faster velocity changes, the greater the acceleration is.

Calculating Acceleration You can calculate acceleration by using the following equation:

$$\text{Acceleration} = \frac{\text{final velocity} - \text{starting velocity}}{\text{time it takes to change velocity}}$$

Velocity is expressed in meters per second (m/s), and time is expressed in seconds (s). Therefore, acceleration is expressed in meters per second per second (m/s/s).

Suppose you get on your bicycle and accelerate southward at a rate of 1 m/s/s. (Like velocity, acceleration has size and direction.) This means that every second, your southward velocity increases by 1 m/s, as shown in **Figure 4** on the next page.

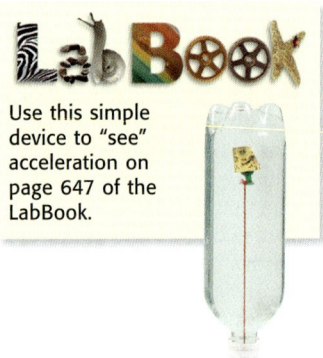
Use this simple device to "see" acceleration on page 647 of the LabBook.

Homework

Have students record examples of acceleration that they observe around their homes. Ask them to make a chart like the one at the bottom of page 113 to include each example of acceleration and to show how velocity changed in each example.

MISCONCEPTION ALERT

The unit for acceleration is often written m/s², not m/s/s. This section uses m/s/s because many students lack experience with exponents. You may wish to use m/s² in this section if your students are familiar with exponents.

112 Chapter 5 • Matter in Motion

Figure 4 Acceleration at 1 m/s/s South

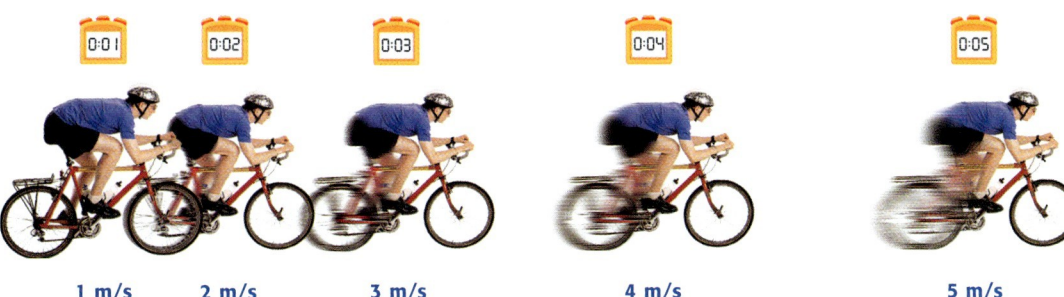

After 1 second, you have a velocity of 1 m/s south, as shown in Figure 4. After 2 seconds, you have a velocity of 2 m/s south. After 3 seconds, you have a velocity of 3 m/s south, and so on. If your final velocity after 5 seconds is 5 m/s south, your acceleration can be calculated as follows:

$$\text{Acceleration} = \frac{5 \text{ m/s} - 0 \text{ m/s}}{5 \text{ s}} = 1 \text{ m/s/s south}$$

You can practice calculating acceleration by doing the MathBreak shown here.

Examples of Acceleration In the example above, your velocity was originally zero and then it increased. Because your velocity changed, you accelerated. Acceleration in which velocity increases is sometimes called *positive acceleration*.

Acceleration also occurs when velocity decreases. In the skating example, you accelerated because you slowed down. Acceleration in which velocity decreases is sometimes called *negative acceleration* or *deceleration*.

Remember that velocity has direction, so velocity will change if your direction changes. Therefore, a change in direction is acceleration, even if there is no change in speed. Some more examples of acceleration are shown in the chart below.

Example of Acceleration	How Velocity Changes
A plane taking off	Increase in speed
A car stopping at a stop sign	Decrease in speed
Jogging on a winding trail	Change in direction
Driving around a corner	Change in direction
Standing at Earth's equator	Change in direction

MATH BREAK

Calculating Acceleration

Use the equation shown on the previous page to do the following problems. Be sure to express your answers in m/s/s and include direction.

1. A plane passes over Point A with a velocity of 8,000 m/s north. Forty seconds later it passes over Point B at a velocity of 10,000 m/s north. What is the plane's acceleration from A to B?

2. A coconut falls from the top of a tree and reaches a velocity of 19.6 m/s when it hits the ground. It takes 2 seconds to reach the ground. What is the coconut's acceleration?

Answers to MATHBREAK

1. 50 m/s/s north
2. 9.8 m/s/s downward (Note: Some students may recognize this answer as the acceleration due to gravity. Take this opportunity to set the tone for Section 4, "Gravity: A Force of Attraction," and for the next chapter, "Forces in Motion.")

 Teaching Transparency 215 "Calculating Acceleration"

 Interactive Explorations CD-ROM "Force in the Forest"

3) Extend

RESEARCH

Have small groups of students apply the idea of acceleration to the design of roller coasters. Have them research a particular roller coaster and create a drawing or diagram of its features. Have them describe the motion of the roller coaster in terms of velocity and acceleration.

MATH and MORE

Practice calculating acceleration with the following problems:

1. At point A, a runner is jogging at 3 m/s. Forty seconds later, at point B —on a hill—the jogger's velocity is only 1 m/s. What is the jogger's acceleration from point A to point B? (−0.05 m/s/s up)

2. In a summer storm, the wind is blowing with a velocity of 8 m/s north. Suddenly, in 3 seconds, the wind's velocity is 23 m/s north. What is the acceleration in the wind? (5 m/s/s north)

USING SCIENCE FICTION

Have students read the story "Direction of the Road" by Ursula K. LeGuin in the *Holt Anthology of Science Fiction*. As you discuss the story, ask students to describe the importance of identifying reference points.

4 Close

Quiz

1. What distinguishes the measurement of speed from that of velocity and acceleration? (Speed does not involve direction, as both velocity and acceleration do.)
2. What is centripetal acceleration? (acceleration that occurs in circular motion)
3. How do you calculate speed? velocity? acceleration? (divide the distance traveled by the time; divide the distance and direction traveled by the time; subtract the starting velocity from the final velocity, and divide by the time it takes to change velocity)

ALTERNATIVE ASSESSMENT

Ask students to draw two pictures of rolling balls as they would appear at 1 second intervals that would illustrate the difference between a ball rolling at a constant speed and a ball that is accelerating.

Teaching Transparency 216 "A Graph Showing Acceleration"

Reinforcement Worksheet 5 "Bug Race"

TOPIC: Measuring Motion
GO TO: www.scilinks.org
sciLINKS NUMBER: HSTP105

Figure 5 The blades of this windmill are constantly changing direction as they travel in a circle. Thus, centripetal acceleration is occurring.

TOPIC: Measuring Motion
GO TO: www.scilinks.org
sciLINKS NUMBER: HSTP105

Circular Motion: Continuous Acceleration Does it surprise you to find out that standing at Earth's equator is an example of acceleration? After all, you're not changing speed, and you're not changing direction . . . or are you? In fact, you are traveling in a circle as the Earth rotates. An object traveling in a circular motion is always changing its direction. Therefore, its velocity is always changing, so acceleration is occurring. The acceleration that occurs in circular motion is known as *centripetal* (sen TRIP uht uhl) *acceleration*. Another example of centripetal acceleration is shown in **Figure 5**.

Recognizing Acceleration on a Graph Suppose that you have just gotten on a roller coaster. The roller coaster moves slowly up the first hill until it stops at the top. Then you're off, racing down the hill! The graph below shows your acceleration for the 10 seconds coming down the hill. You can tell from this graph that your acceleration is positive because your velocity increases as time passes. Because the graph is not a straight line, you can also tell that your acceleration is not constant for each second.

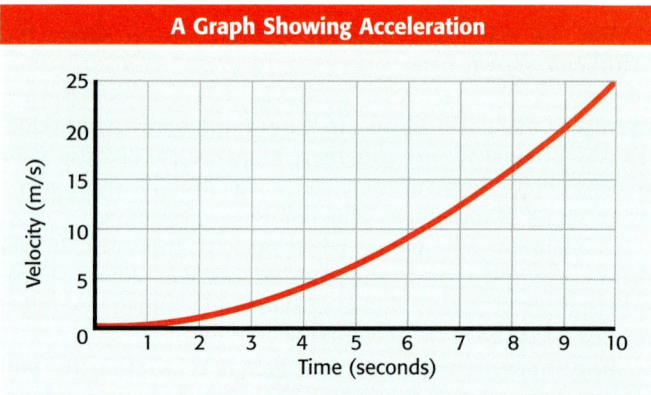

REVIEW

1. What is acceleration?
2. Does a change in direction affect acceleration? Explain your answer.
3. **Interpreting Graphics** How do you think a graph of deceleration would differ from the graph shown above? Explain your reasoning.

Answers to Review

1. Acceleration is the rate at which velocity changes.
2. Yes, a change in direction does affect acceleration. Acceleration is a measure of velocity change. Velocity is speed in a given direction, and velocity changes if direction changes.
3. The graph showing acceleration has a positive slope. A graph showing deceleration would have a negative slope. The graph would take this shape because velocity would be decreasing as time passes.

Section 2

What Is a Force?

Terms to Learn

force   net force
newton

What You'll Do

- Give examples of different kinds of forces.
- Determine the net force on an object.
- Compare balanced and unbalanced forces.

You often hear the word *force* in everyday conversation:

"That storm had a lot of force!"
"Our basketball team is a force to be reckoned with."
"A flat tire forced me to stop riding my bicycle."
"The inning ended with a force-out at second base."

But what exactly is a force? In science, a **force** is simply a push or a pull. All forces have both size and direction.

Forces are everywhere. In fact, any time you see something moving, you can be sure that its motion was created by a force. Scientists express force using a unit called the **newton (N).** The more newtons, the greater the force.

Forces Act on Objects

All forces are exerted by one object on another object. For any push to occur, something has to receive the push. You can't push nothing! The same is true for any pull. When doing schoolwork, you use your fingers to pull open books or to push the buttons on a computer keyboard. In these examples, your fingers are exerting forces on the books and the keys. However, just because a force is being exerted by one object on another doesn't mean that motion will occur. For example, you are probably sitting on a chair as you read this. But the force you are exerting on the chair does not cause the chair to move. That's because the Earth is also exerting a force on the chair. In most cases, it is easy to determine where the push or pull is coming from, as shown in **Figure 6.**

Figure 6 It is obvious that the bulldozer is exerting a force on the pile of soil. But did you know that the pile of soil also exerts a force, even when it is just sitting on the ground?

TOPIC: Forces
GO TO: www.scilinks.org
*sci*LINKS NUMBER: HSTP107

2 Teach

READING STRATEGY

Prediction Guide Before reading about forces in combination, have students look at **Figures 8** and **9**. While they are looking at these pictures, ask students to predict what happens when forces are exerted in the same direction and when forces are exerted in opposite directions.

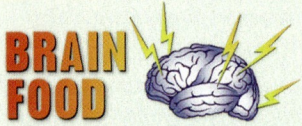

Some people confuse *force* and *pressure* because they are related to each other.

Magicians depend on this difference when they lie down on a bed of nails. The **force**—the magician's weight—is fairly large, but because there are hundreds or even thousands of nails, the **pressure** (the amount of force exerted on a given area) from each nail is not enough to break the magician's skin.

Ask students for other examples of spreading force over a wide area to reduce pressure.

 Teaching Transparency 217 "Forces in the Same Direction"

Figure 7 Something unseen exerts a force that makes your socks cling together when they come out of the dryer. You have to exert a force to separate the socks.

It is not always so easy to tell what is exerting a force or what is receiving a force, as shown in **Figure 7.** You cannot see what exerts the force that pulls magnets to refrigerators, and the air you breathe is an unseen receiver of a force called *gravity*. You will learn more about gravity later in this chapter.

Forces in Combination

Often more than one force is exerted on an object at the same time. The **net force** is the force that results from combining all the forces exerted on an object. So how do you determine the net force? The examples below can help you answer this question.

Forces in the Same Direction Suppose you and a friend are asked to move a piano for the music teacher. To do this, you pull on one end of the piano, and your friend pushes on the other end. Together, your forces add up to enough force to move the piano. This is because your forces are in the same direction. **Figure 8** shows this situation. Because the forces are in the same direction, they can be added together to determine the net force. In this case, the net force is 45 N, which is plenty to move a piano—if it is on wheels, that is!

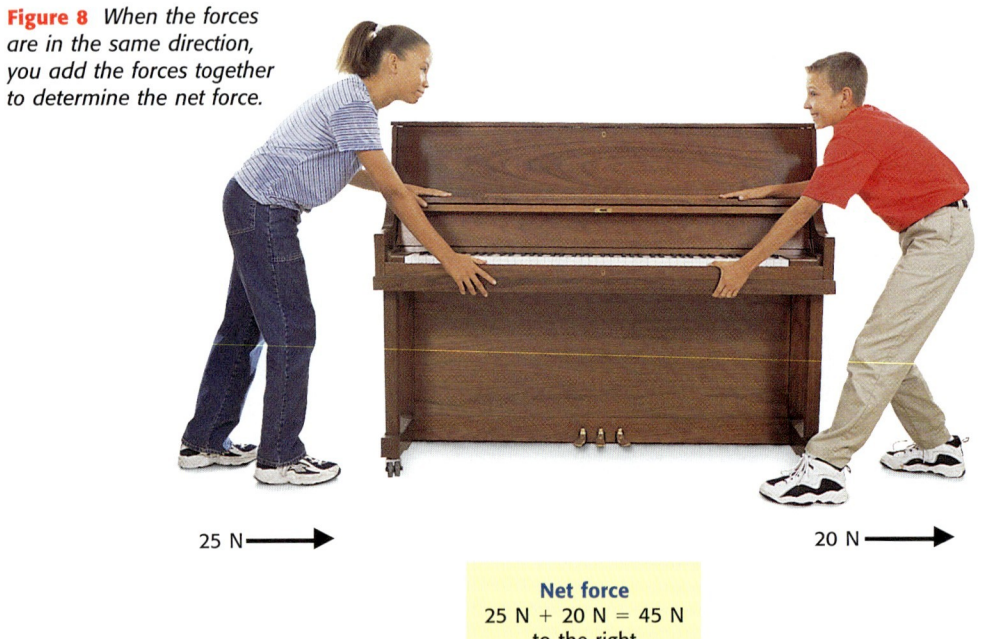

Figure 8 When the forces are in the same direction, you add the forces together to determine the net force.

25 N ⟶   20 N ⟶

Net force
25 N + 20 N = 45 N
to the right

IS THAT A FACT!

Some trains are too massive to be moved by one locomotive. To compensate for the larger mass, extra locomotives are added until the net force of all the locomotives is large enough to move the train.

116   Chapter 5 • Matter in Motion

Forces in Different Directions Consider two dogs playing tug of war with a short piece of rope. Each is exerting a force, but in opposite directions. **Figure 9** shows this scene. Notice that the dog on the left is pulling with a force of 10 N and the dog on the right is pulling with a force of 12 N. Which dog do you think will win the tug of war?

Because the forces are in opposite directions, the net force is determined by subtracting the smaller force from the larger one. In this case, the net force is 2 N in the direction of the dog on the right. Give that dog a dog biscuit!

Science CONNECTION

Every moment, forces in several directions are exerted on the Golden Gate Bridge. For example, Earth exerts a powerful downward force on the bridge while elastic forces pull and push portions of the bridge up and down. To learn how the bridge stands up to these forces, turn to page 135.

← 10 N   12 N →

Net force
12 N − 10 N = 2 N
to the right

Figure 9 When the forces are in different directions, you subtract the smaller force from the larger force to determine the net force.

Unbalanced and Balanced Forces

If you know the net force on an object, you can determine the effect the force will have on the object's motion. Why? The net force tells you whether the forces on the object are balanced or unbalanced.

Unbalanced Forces Produce a Change in Motion In the examples shown in Figures 8 and 9, the net force on the object is greater than zero. When the net force on an object is not zero, the forces on the object are *unbalanced*. Unbalanced forces produce a change in motion (acceleration). In the two previous examples, the receivers of the forces—the piano and the rope—move. Unbalanced forces are necessary to cause a nonmoving object to start moving.

✓ Self-Check

What is the net force when you combine a force of 7 N north with a force of 5 N south? (See page 724 to check your answer.)

Teaching Transparency 217
"Forces in Different Directions"

3 Extend

ACTIVITY

MATERIALS

FOR EACH STUDENT:
- toothpicks
- string and glue
- gumdrops
- cardboard

Making Models Students work in small groups to research, design, and build a bridge that spans a 60 cm gap and that is wide enough to accommodate a model car. The goal is to construct the strongest bridge that meets these requirements. Bridges will be rated according to the mass they can support without collapsing. Students should identify the forces acting on their bridge. A good place to start is the feature about the Golden Gate Bridge on page 135.

4 Close

Quiz

1. What is a net force? (the sum of all the forces acting on an object)
2. Are the forces on a kicked soccer ball balanced or unbalanced? How do you know? (Unbalanced; because the ball changes speed and/or direction.)

ALTERNATIVE ASSESSMENT

Poster Project Have students make a poster that shows an example of balanced forces (such as an elevator at rest or a gymnast motionless on a balance beam). The poster should show all forces acting on the object and should show what happens to the object if the forces become unbalanced.

Unbalanced forces are also necessary to change the motion of moving objects. For example, consider a soccer game. The soccer ball is already moving when it is passed from one player to another. When the ball reaches the second player, the player exerts an unbalanced force—a kick—on the ball. After the kick, the ball moves in a new direction and with a new speed.

Keep in mind that an object can continue to move even when the unbalanced forces are removed. A soccer ball, for example, receives an unbalanced force when it is kicked. However, the ball continues to roll along the ground long after the force of the kick has ended.

Balanced Forces Produce No Change in Motion When the forces applied to an object produce a net force of zero, the forces are *balanced*. Balanced forces do not cause a nonmoving object to start moving. Furthermore, balanced forces will not cause a change in the motion of a moving object.

Many objects around you have only balanced forces acting on them. For example, a light hanging from the ceiling does not move because the force of gravity pulling down on the light is balanced by an elastic force due to tension that pulls the light up. A bird's nest in a tree and a hat resting on your head are also examples of objects with only balanced forces acting on them. **Figure 10** shows another case where the forces on an object are balanced. Because all the forces are balanced, the house of cards does not move.

Figure 10 *The forces on this house of cards are balanced. An unbalanced force on one of the cards would cause motion— and probably a mess!*

REVIEW

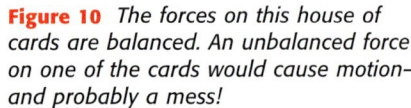

1. Give four examples of a force being exerted.
2. Explain the difference between balanced and unbalanced forces and how each affects the motion of an object.
3. **Interpreting Graphics** In the picture at left, two bighorn sheep push on each other's horns. The arrow shows the direction the two sheep are moving. Describe the forces the sheep are exerting and how the forces combine to produce the sheep's motion.

▼ **Answers to Review**

1. Accept all reasonable answers. Examples include: kicking a ball, writing with a pencil, pulling a rope, and pushing a stalled car.
2. Unbalanced forces occur when the net force on an object is not zero; balanced forces occur when the net force equals zero. Unbalanced forces cause a change in an object's motion; balanced forces cause no change.
3. Because the sheep are moving (as indicated by the arrow), the forces they are exerting on each other are unbalanced. The sheep on the left is exerting a larger force, so the total net force is in the direction it is pushing.

Section 3

Friction: A Force That Opposes Motion

Terms to Learn
friction

What You'll Do
- Explain why friction occurs.
- List the types of friction, and give examples of each.
- Explain how friction can be both harmful and helpful.

Picture a warm summer day. You are enjoying the day by wearing shorts and tossing a ball with your friends. By accident, one of your friends tosses the ball just out of your reach. You have to make a split-second decision to dive for it or not. You look down and notice that if you dove for it, you would most likely slide across pavement rather than the surrounding grass. What would you decide?

Unless you enjoy scraped knees, you probably would not want to slide on the pavement. The painful difference between sliding on grass and sliding on pavement has to do with friction. **Friction** is a force that opposes motion between two surfaces that are touching.

The Source of Friction

Friction occurs because the surface of any object is rough. Even surfaces that look or feel very smooth are actually covered with microscopic hills and valleys. When two surfaces are in contact, the hills and valleys of one surface stick to the hills and valleys of the other surface, as shown in **Figure 11.** This contact causes friction even when the surfaces appear smooth.

The amount of friction between two surfaces depends on many factors, including the roughness of the surfaces and the force pushing the surfaces together.

Figure 11 When the hills and valleys of one surface stick to the hills and valleys of another surface, friction is created.

CONNECT TO LIFE SCIENCE

Humans have tiny ridges in the skin of their hands and feet. These ridges increase friction between the skin and objects the hands or feet touch. This friction helps humans grasp objects with their hands and avoid slipping with their feet.

 Directed Reading Worksheet 5 Section 3

2) Teach

MISCONCEPTION ALERT

The roughness of an object is not the only contributor to friction. Frictional forces are also influenced by the electrical attraction between the molecules of substances. The attraction makes it more difficult to slide the surfaces past one another.

MATERIALS

FOR EACH GROUP:
- cardboard (corrugated is best)
- 2 books
- toy car
- meterstick
- sandpaper or cloth (sandpaper should be very coarse; cloth should be fuzzy or nappy)

Teacher Notes: You can substitute pieces of plywood or several metersticks for the corrugated cardboard.

If your classroom is carpeted, you can move the ramp to the floor for one of the trials.

Answers to QuickLab

5. The covered surface had the most friction because it is the roughest. A heavier car would result in even more friction between the car and the surface because the force pushing the surfaces together would be increased.

Teaching Transparency 218
"Force and Friction"

The Friction 500

1. Make a short ramp out of a **piece of cardboard** and **one or two books** on a table.

2. Put a **toy car** at the top of the ramp and let go. If necessary, adjust the ramp height so that your car does not roll off the table.

3. Put the car at the top of the ramp again and let go. Record the distance the car travels after leaving the ramp. Do this three times, and calculate the average for your results.

4. Change the surface of the table by covering it with **sandpaper** or **cloth**. Repeat step 3. Change the surface one more time, and repeat step 3 again.

5. Which surface had the most friction? Why? What do you predict would happen if the car were heavier? Record your results and answers in your ScienceLog.

TRY at HOME

Rougher Surfaces Create More Friction Rougher surfaces have more microscopic hills and valleys. Thus, the rougher the surface, the greater the friction. Think back to the example on the previous page. Pavement is much rougher than grass. Therefore, more friction is produced when you slide on the pavement than when you slide on grass. This increased friction is more effective at stopping your sliding, but it is also more painful! On the other hand, if the surfaces are smooth, there is less friction. If you were to slide on ice instead of on grass, your landing would be even more comfortable—but also much colder!

Greater Force Creates More Friction The amount of friction also depends on the force pushing the surfaces together. If this force is increased, the hills and valleys of the surfaces can come into closer contact. This causes the friction between the surfaces to increase. Less massive objects exert less force on surfaces than more massive objects do, as illustrated in **Figure 12**. However, changing the amounts of the surfaces that touch does not change the amount of friction.

Figure 12 Force and Friction

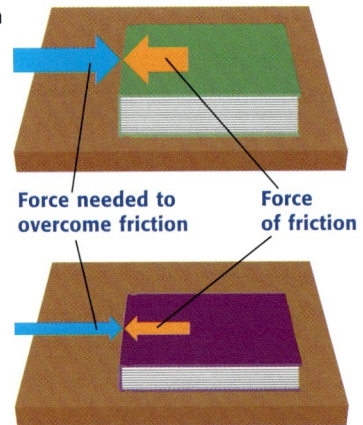

a There is more friction between the more massive book and the table than there is between the less massive book and the table. A harder push is needed to overcome friction to move the more massive book.

Force needed to overcome friction

Force of friction

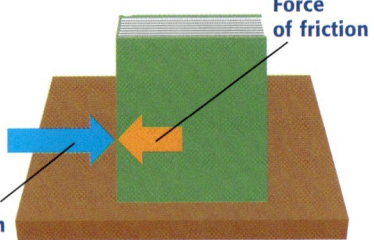

b Turning the more massive book on its edge does not change the amount of friction between the table and the book.

Force of friction

Force needed to overcome friction

120

Tom: This match won't light.

Jerry: What's the matter with it?

Tom: I don't know; it worked a minute ago.

WEIRD SCIENCE

Air hockey is challenging because the puck floats on a very thin layer of air. Tiny holes in the table surface allow pressurized air to escape from underneath. The puck moves with very little friction.

Types of Friction

The friction you observe when sliding books across a tabletop is called sliding friction. Other types of friction include rolling friction, fluid friction, and static friction. As you will learn, the name of each type of friction is a big clue as to the conditions where it can be found.

Sliding Friction If you push an eraser across your desk, the eraser will move for a short distance and then stop. This is an example of *sliding friction*. Sliding friction is very effective at opposing the movement of objects and is the force that causes the eraser to stop moving. You can feel the effect of sliding friction when you try to move a heavy dresser by pushing it along the floor. You must exert a lot of force to overcome the sliding friction, as shown in **Figure 13.**

You use sliding friction when you go sledding, when you apply the brakes on a bicycle or a car, or when you write with a piece of chalk.

Rolling Friction If the same heavy dresser were on wheels, you would have an easier time moving it. The friction between the wheels and the floor is an example of *rolling friction*. The force of rolling friction is usually less than the force of sliding friction. Therefore, it is generally easier to move objects on wheels than it is to slide them along the floor, as shown at right.

Rolling friction is an important part of almost all means of transportation. Anything with wheels—bicycles, in-line skates, cars, trains, and planes—uses rolling friction between the wheels and the ground to move forward.

Figure 13 Comparing Sliding Friction and Rolling Friction

Moving a heavy piece of furniture in your room can be hard work because **the force of sliding friction is large.**

It is easier to move a heavy piece of furniture if you put it on wheels. **The force of rolling friction is smaller** and easier to overcome.

Synthesis

When two very smooth surfaces move past each other, friction is mostly caused by "stickiness"—chemical bonding between the moving surfaces. When you picture friction between very smooth surfaces, don't think about hills and valleys sticking together. A better image is that of trying to drag very sticky tape along a surface. When there is a lot of friction, you may see pieces of one surface sticking onto the other surface.

MISCONCEPTION ALERT

Rolling friction is usually smaller than sliding friction, but it really depends on the situation. If both surfaces are hard, rolling friction is smaller. But if one of the surfaces is soft, such as deep snow, the sliding friction of skis or a sled might be a lot smaller than the rolling friction of a loaded wagon. Friction depends on several characteristics of both surfaces.

REAL-WORLD CONNECTION

Vehicle tires are designed to use friction to increase grip. Have students find information on as many different kinds of tires, tire compounds, and tread designs as they can. Have them do a poster or other project showing some of the types of tires and treads they have learned about. Sheltered English

TOPIC: Force and Friction
GO TO: www.scilinks.org
*sci*LINKS NUMBER: HSTP110

Cross-Disciplinary Focus

History Scientists believe that the first wheeled vehicles were used in ancient Mesopotamia sometime between 3500 and 3000 B.C. Before wheels, people used a plank or a sled dragged along the ground to carry loads. With the invention of wheels, sleds were replaced with carts. The invention of the wheel is considered a major step in the advancement of human civilization. Ask students to write a short story about a day in their lives if wheels did not exist.

Section 3 • Friction: A Force That Opposes Motion

2 Teach, continued

SYNTHESIS

Some competitive swimmers try to imitate the swimming style of marine mammals. Many swimmers shave off all of their body hair before a competition. Ask students to hypothesize how this relates to friction and to predict whether shaving might be helpful to a competitive swimmer. Ask students what other things might help a swimmer reduce friction and increase speed. (Studies seem to show that body shaving has no effect on swimmers' performance. It does seem to give swimmers a psychological boost, but it is hard to tell if that reduces a swimmer's time.)

Homework

Ask students to experiment with friction at home. Show them how to make a ramp using a piece of cardboard that has been covered tightly with plastic wrap. Have students select three or four different common objects they think might have different amounts of friction. Students can experiment by placing objects on the ramp while it is flat then lifting one end until each object slides down. Have them use a ruler to measure how high the ramp must be lifted before each object slides down. Ask them to record their observations in a chart or table and then write an explanation for their findings.
Sheltered English

Answer to Self-Check
sliding friction

Figure 14 *Swimming provides a good workout because you must exert force to overcome fluid friction.*

Fluid Friction Why is it harder to walk on a freshly mopped floor than on a dry floor? The reason is that on the wet floor the sliding friction between your feet and the floor is replaced by *fluid friction* between your feet and the water. In this case, fluid friction is less than sliding friction, so the floor is slippery. The term *fluid* includes liquids, such as water and milk, and gases, such as air and helium.

Fluid friction opposes the motion of objects traveling through a fluid, as illustrated in **Figure 14.** For example, fluid friction between air and a fast moving car is the largest force opposing the motion of the car. You can observe this friction by holding your hand out the window of a moving car.

Static Friction When a force is applied to an object but does not cause the object to move, *static friction* occurs. The object does not move because the force of static friction balances the force applied. Static friction disappears as soon as an object starts moving, and then another type of friction immediately occurs. Look at **Figure 15** to understand when static friction affects an object.

Figure 15 Static Friction

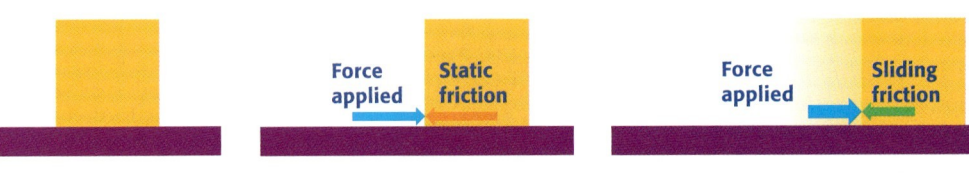

a There is no friction between the block and the table when no force is applied to the block to move it.

b If a small force—shown in blue—is exerted on the block, the block does not move. The force of static friction—shown in orange—exactly balances the force applied.

c When the force exerted on the block is greater than the force of static friction, the block starts moving. Once the block starts moving, all static friction is gone, and the force applied opposes sliding friction—shown in green.

Self-Check

What type of friction was involved in the imaginary situation at the beginning of this section? *(See page 724 to check your answer.)*

Teaching Transparency 219 "Static Friction"

Interactive Explorations CD-ROM "Stranger Than Friction"

An impatient young girl named Lenore
Tried to run on a freshly waxed floor.
Since the friction was less,
She made quite a mess
As she slid right under the door.

Friction Can Be Harmful or Helpful

Think about how friction affects a car. Without friction, the tires could not push against the ground to move the car forward and the brakes could not stop the car. Without friction, a car is useless. However, friction can cause problems in a car too. Friction between moving engine parts increases their temperature and causes the parts to wear down. A liquid coolant is added to the engine to keep it from overheating, and engine parts need to be changed as they wear out.

Friction is both harmful and helpful to you and the world around you. Friction can cause holes in your socks and in the knees of your jeans. Friction by wind and water can cause erosion of the topsoil that nourishes plants. On the other hand, friction between your pencil and your paper is necessary for the pencil to leave a mark. Without friction, you would just slip and fall when you tried to walk. Because friction can be both harmful and helpful, it is sometimes necessary to reduce or increase friction.

Some Ways to Reduce Friction One way to reduce friction is to use lubricants. *Lubricants* (LOO bri kuhnts) are substances that are applied to surfaces to reduce the friction between them. Some examples of common lubricants are motor oil, wax, and grease. **Figure 16** shows why lubricants are important to maintaining car parts.

Friction can also be reduced by switching from sliding friction to rolling friction. Ball bearings are placed between the wheels and axles of in-line skates and bicycles to make it easier for the wheels to turn by reducing friction.

Have some fun with friction! Investigate three types of friction on page 650 of the LabBook.

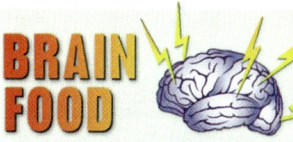
Lubricants are usually liquids, but they can be solids or gases too. Graphite is a shiny black solid that is used in pencils. Graphite dust is very slippery and is often used as a lubricant for ball bearings in bicycle and skate wheels. An example of a gas lubricant is the air that comes out of the tiny holes of an air-hockey table.

Figure 16 *Motor oil is used as a lubricant in car engines. Without oil, engine parts would wear down quickly, as the connecting rod on the bottom has.*

3) Extend

MISCONCEPTION ALERT

Because friction hinders motion, people may assume that friction is a negative force that must be overcome. Have students **imagine** the following activities to reinforce the fact that friction helps as much as it hinders:

- Apply dishwashing soap to your hands. Then try to open a tightly sealed jar.
- Apply petroleum jelly to a doorknob and try to turn it.
- Try picking up a bowling ball that has been coated with oil.

RESEARCH

Have students do research on types of lubricants. Have them describe the different products on the market, their different uses, and the improvements that have been made to them over the years. What are the qualities that make one lubricant different from another?

GOING FURTHER

 Polytetrafluoroethylene (PTFE), also known as Teflon®, is one of the slipperiest substances known to humans. It was discovered by accident in 1938. Most students know Teflon as a nonstick coating for frying pans. Have them research the many uses of Teflon and make posters or other presentations to the class.

Q: Why did the teacher insist that her students wear rain slickers to class?

A: She wanted to reduce the friction between them.

Homework

Writing — Have students write a short poem, song, or rap that explains ways that friction can be helpful and ways it can be harmful. Encourage students to be creative by using humor. Put finished poems up for display on a classroom bulletin board. **Sheltered English**

Science Friction

Section 3 • Friction: A Force That Opposes Motion

4) Close

Quiz

1. Which of the following would NOT help you move a heavy object across a concrete floor?

    water, ball bearings, oil, soapsuds, steel rods, foam rubber **(foam rubber)**

2. Name three common items you might use to increase friction. **(Possible answers: sticky tape, sand, work gloves)**

3. Name three common items you might use to reduce friction. **(Possible answers: oil, water, wax, grease)**

ALTERNATIVE ASSESSMENT

Ask students to imagine that they have been asked to design a bowling alley. Have them describe the areas where they would try to reduce friction and the areas where they would try to increase friction. Have them describe what materials they would use and why.

Answers to APPLY

Friction caused the treads (the raised surfaces that grip the road) to wear away, making the tire very smooth. Rolling friction is mainly responsible for the tire's appearance. Car owners should change their tires after several thousand kilometers because the tire surfaces are worn smooth by rolling friction. This decreases the friction between the tires and the road, which could cause the car to slide or skid when the brakes are applied.

Reinforcement Worksheet 5 "Friction Action"

Figure 17 *No one enjoys cleaning pans with baked-on food! To make this chore pass quickly, press down with the scrubber to increase friction.*

Another way to reduce friction is to make surfaces that rub against each other smoother. For example, rough wood on a park bench is painful to slide across because there is a large amount of friction between your leg and the bench. Rubbing the bench with sandpaper makes it smoother and more comfortable to sit on because the friction between your leg and the bench is reduced.

Some Ways to Increase Friction One way to increase friction is to make surfaces rougher. For example, sand scattered on icy roads keeps cars from skidding. Baseball players sometimes wear textured batting gloves to increase the friction between their hands and the bat so that the bat does not fly out of their hands.

Another way to increase friction is to increase the force pushing the surfaces together. For example, you can ensure that your magazine will not blow away at the park by putting a heavy rock on it. The added mass of the rock increases the friction between the magazine and the ground. Or if you are sanding a piece of wood, you can sand the wood faster by pressing harder on the sandpaper. **Figure 17** shows another situation where friction is increased by pushing on an object.

Friction and Tires
The tire shown here was used for more than 80,000 km. What effect did friction have on the rubber? What kind of friction is mainly responsible for the tire's appearance? Why are car owners warned to change their car tires after using them for several thousand kilometers?

internetconnect

sciLINKS NSTA

TOPIC: Force and Friction
GO TO: www.scilinks.org
sciLINKS NUMBER: HSTP110

REVIEW

1. Explain why friction occurs.
2. Name two ways in which friction can be increased.
3. Give an example of each of the following types of friction: sliding, rolling, and fluid.
4. **Applying Concepts** Name two ways that friction is harmful and two ways that friction is helpful to you when riding a bicycle.

Answers to Review

1. Friction occurs because the microscopic hills and valleys of two touching surfaces "stick" to each other.
2. Friction can be increased by making surfaces rougher and by increasing the force pushing the surfaces together.
3. Answers will vary; accept all reasonable answers. Examples: sliding—skiing and writing with a pencil; rolling—riding a bicycle and pushing a handcart; fluid—swimming and throwing a softball.
4. Accept all reasonable answers. Sample answer: harmful—it causes tire tread to wear down and the wind can slow you down; helpful—the wheels grip the road, and your feet and hands stay on the pedals and handlebars.

Section 4

Terms to Learn

gravity   mass
weight

What You'll Do

- Define gravity.
- State the law of universal gravitation.
- Describe the difference between mass and weight.

Gravity: A Force of Attraction

If you watch videotape of astronauts on the moon, you will notice that when the astronauts tried to walk on the lunar surface, they bounced around like beach balls instead.

Why did the astronauts—who were wearing heavy spacesuits—bounce so easily on the moon (as shown in **Figure 18**), while you must exert effort to jump a few centimeters off Earth's surface? The answer has to do with gravity. **Gravity** is a force of attraction between objects that is due to their masses. In this section, you will learn about gravity and the effects it has on objects.

Figure 18 *Because gravity is less on the moon than on Earth, walking on the moon's surface was a very bouncy experience for the Apollo astronauts.*

Biology CONNECTION

Scientists think seeds can "sense" gravity. The ability to sense gravity is what causes seeds to always send roots down and the green shoot up. But scientists do not understand just *how* seeds do this. Astronauts have grown seedlings during space shuttle missions to see how seeds respond to changes in gravity. So far, there are no definite answers from the results of these experiments.

All Matter Is Affected by Gravity

All matter has mass. Gravity is a result of mass. Therefore, all matter experiences gravity. That is, all objects experience an attraction toward all other objects. This gravitational force "pulls" objects toward each other. Right now, because of gravity, you are being pulled toward this book, your pencil, and every other object around you.

These objects are also being pulled toward you and toward each other because of gravity. So why don't you see the effects of this attraction? In other words, why don't you notice objects moving toward each other? The reason is that the mass of most objects is too small to cause an attraction large enough to move objects toward each other. However, you are familiar with one object that is massive enough to cause a noticeable attraction—the Earth.

Directed Reading Worksheet 5 Section 4

2 Teach

READING STRATEGY

Prediction Guide Before students read this section, ask them to predict whether the following statements are true or false:

- Objects of any size exert a gravitational force. (true)
- The planets are held in their orbits by unbalanced forces. (true)
- If you traveled to Jupiter and you neither gained nor lost mass, your weight on Jupiter would be much greater than your weight on Earth. (true)

Answer to Self-Check

Gravity is a force of attraction between objects that is due to the masses of the objects.

MISCONCEPTION ALERT

Although the gravitational attraction of an object toward Earth does decrease with altitude, this difference is very small. For all practical purposes, Earth's gravitational force on any object remains essentially the same anywhere in the atmosphere.

CONNECT TO EARTH SCIENCE

Use Teaching Transparency 161 to help students understand the effects the moon's gravitational force has on Earth's tides.

Teaching Transparency 161 "Tidal Variations" LINK TO EARTH SCIENCE

Self-Check

What is gravity? (See page 724 to check your answer.)

Figure 19
Newton Makes the Connection

Earth's Gravitational Force Is Large Compared with all the objects around you, Earth has an enormous mass. Therefore, Earth's gravitational force is very large. You must apply forces to overcome Earth's gravitational force any time you lift objects or even parts of your body.

Earth's gravitational force pulls everything toward the center of Earth. Because of this, the books, tables, and chairs in the room stay in place, and dropped objects fall to Earth rather than moving together or toward you.

The Law of Universal Gravitation

For thousands of years, two very puzzling questions were "Why do objects fall toward Earth?" and "What keeps the planets in motion in the sky?" The two questions were treated as separate topics until a British scientist named Sir Isaac Newton (1642–1727) realized that they were two parts of the same question.

The Core of an Idea Legend has it that Newton made the connection when he observed a falling apple during a summer night, as shown in **Figure 19**. He knew that unbalanced forces are necessary to move or change the motion of objects. He concluded that there had to be an unbalanced force on the apple to make it fall, just as there had to be an unbalanced force on the moon to keep it moving around Earth. He realized that these two forces are actually the same force—a force of attraction called gravity.

A Law Is Born Newton generalized his observations on gravity in a law now known as the *law of universal gravitation.* This law describes the relationships between gravitational force, mass, and distance. It is called universal because it applies to all objects in the universe.

IS THAT A FACT!

In the reduced gravity of space, astronauts lose bone and muscle mass, even after a very short period of time. Sleep patterns may be affected and so may cardiovascular strength and the immune response. These same effects happen more gradually as people age on Earth. Scientists are interested in studying the effects of microgravity so they can find ways to counteract them in space and here on Earth.

The law of universal gravitation states the following: All objects in the universe attract each other through gravitational force. The size of the force depends on the masses of the objects and the distance between them. The examples in **Figure 20** show the effects of the law of universal gravitation. It is easier to understand the law if you consider it in two parts.

a Gravitational force is small between objects with small masses.

Figure 20 *The arrows indicate the gravitational force between the objects. The width of the arrows indicates the strength of the force.*

b Gravitational force is larger between objects with larger masses.

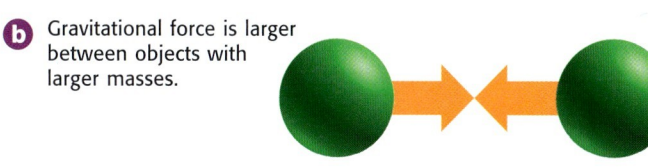

c If the distance between two objects is increased, the gravitational force pulling them together is reduced.

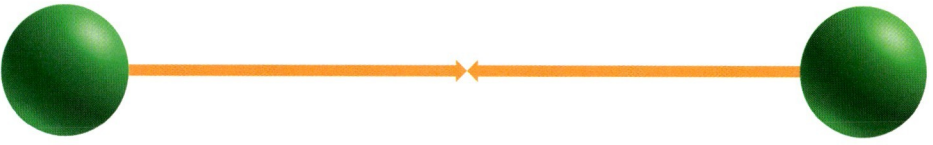

Part 1: Gravitational Force Increases as Mass Increases

Imagine an elephant and a cat. Because an elephant has a larger mass than a cat, the amount of gravity between an elephant and Earth is greater than the amount of gravity between a cat and Earth. That is why a cat is much easier to pick up than an elephant! There is gravity between the cat and the elephant, but it is very small because the cat's mass and the elephant's mass are so much smaller than Earth's mass.

The moon has less mass than Earth. Therefore, the moon's gravitational force is less than Earth's. Remember the astronauts on the moon? They bounced around as they walked because they were not being pulled down with as much force as they would have been on Earth.

Astronomy CONNECTION

Black holes are formed when massive stars collapse. Black holes are 10 times to 1 billion times more massive than our sun. Thus, their gravitational force is incredibly large. The gravity of a black hole is so large that an object that enters a black hole can never get out. Even light cannot escape from a black hole. Because black holes do not emit light, they cannot be seen—hence their name.

 **SCIENCE**

Black holes are much more massive than the sun, but they are extremely small relative to other celestial objects. A black hole 10 times more massive than our sun may have a radius of only 30 km. The gravitational force exerted by a black hole is so powerful that it crushes any matter that falls into it down to a point of zero volume and infinite density. This phenomenon is called a singularity.

2) Teach, continued

MEETING INDIVIDUAL NEEDS

Advanced Learners Have students read H. G. Wells's 1901 story "The First Men in the Moon." Take one class to discuss the story and Wells's use of "Cavorite." Discuss how well the story fits with current scientific knowledge of the moon and gravity. How might the story be different if it were written today?

Answer to Activity

Accept all reasonable answers. Generally, students should demonstrate an understanding that increasing gravitational force would make things weigh more on Earth and make them harder to pick up; decreasing gravitational force would have the opposite effect.

3) Extend

DEBATE

Some scientists argue that the planet Pluto should not be called a planet. Other scientists believe that Pluto is a perfectly good planet. Help students research the issue and conduct a class debate about what is a planet and what isn't.

PG 651
Relating Mass and Weight

Reinforcement Worksheet 5
"A Weighty Problem"

Critical Thinking Worksheet 5
"A Mission in Motion"

128 Chapter 5 • Matter in Motion

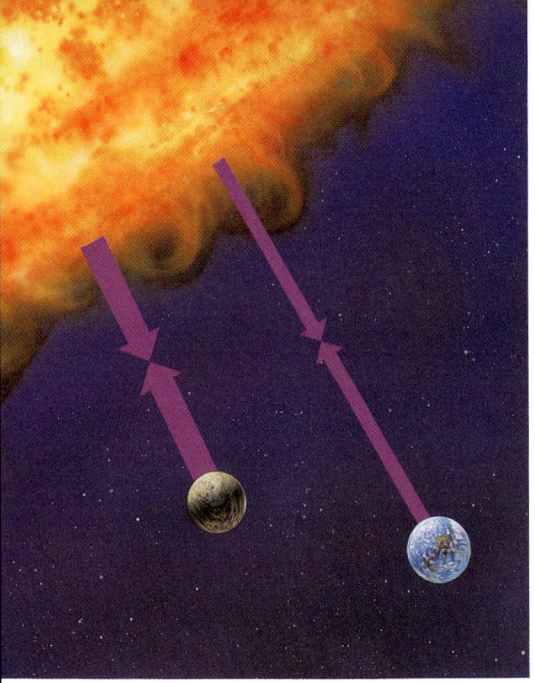

Figure 21 Venus and Earth have approximately the same mass. However, Venus is closer to the sun. Thus, the gravity between Venus and the sun is greater than the gravity between Earth and the sun.

Activity

Suppose you had a device that could increase or decrease the gravitational force of objects around you (including small sections of Earth). In your ScienceLog, describe what you might do with the device, what you would expect to see, and what effect the device would have on the weight of objects.

TRY at HOME

Part 2: Gravitational Force Decreases as Distance Increases The gravity between you and Earth is large. Whenever you jump up, you are pulled back down by Earth's gravitational force. On the other hand, the sun is more than 300,000 times more massive than Earth. So why doesn't the sun's gravitational force affect you more than Earth's does? The reason is that the sun is so far away.

You are approximately 150 million kilometers away from the sun. At this distance, the gravity between you and the sun is very small. If there were some way you could stand on the sun (and not burn up), you would find it impossible to jump or even walk. The gravitational force acting on you would be so great that your muscles could not lift any part of your body!

Although the sun's gravitational force does not have much of an effect on your body here, it does have a big effect on Earth itself and the other planets, as shown in **Figure 21**. The gravity between the sun and the planets is large because the objects have large masses. If the sun's gravitational force did not have such an effect on the planets, the planets would not stay in orbit around the sun.

Weight Is a Measure of Gravitational Force

You have learned that gravity is a force of attraction between objects that is due to their masses. **Weight** is a measure of the gravitational force exerted on an object. When you see or hear the word *weight*, it usually refers to Earth's gravitational force on an object. But weight can also be a measure of the gravitational force exerted on objects by the moon or other planets.

You have learned that the unit of force is a newton. Because gravity is a force and weight is a measure of gravity, weight is also expressed in newtons (N). On Earth, a 100 g object, such as a medium-sized apple, weighs approximately 1 N.

Science Bloopers

The moon used to be blamed for some strange behaviors in humans and animals (the word *lunatic* comes from the Latin word *luna*, meaning "moon"). Scientists once thought the moon affected the human body's fluids the same way it affects ocean tides. Women's menstrual cycles reinforced this belief. Today, scientists know that there is no evidence to support these beliefs.

Weight and Mass Are Different Weight is related to mass, but the two are not the same. Weight changes when gravitational force changes. **Mass** is the amount of matter in an object, and its value does not change. If an object is moved to a place with a greater gravitational force—like Jupiter—its weight will increase, but its mass will remain the same. **Figure 22** shows the weight and mass of an object on Earth and a place with about one-sixth the gravitational force—the moon.

Gravitational force is about the same everywhere on Earth, so the weight of any object is about the same everywhere. Because mass and weight are constant on Earth, the terms are often used to mean the same thing. This can lead to confusion. Be sure you understand the difference!

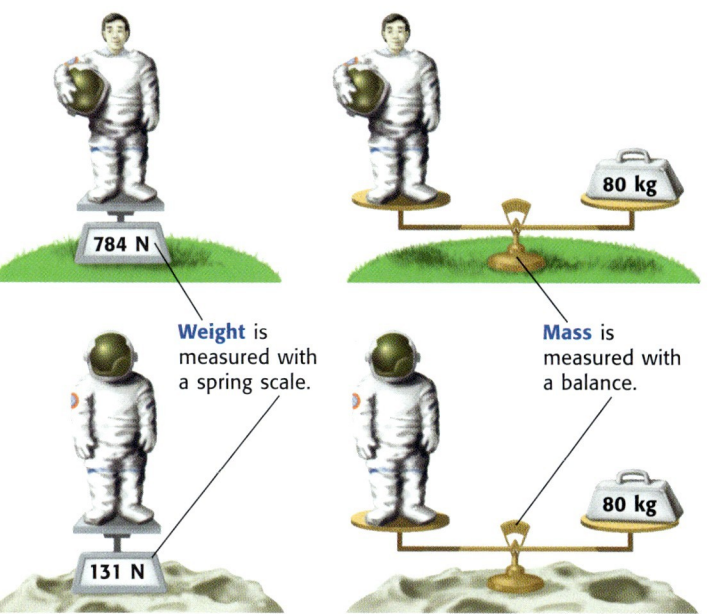

Figure 22 The astronaut's weight on the moon is about one-sixth of his weight on Earth, but his mass remains constant.

Weight is measured with a spring scale.

Mass is measured with a balance.

REVIEW

1. How does the mass of an object relate to the gravitational force the object exerts on other objects?
2. How does the distance between objects affect the gravity between them?
3. **Comparing Concepts** Explain why your weight would change if you orbited Earth in the space shuttle but your mass would not.

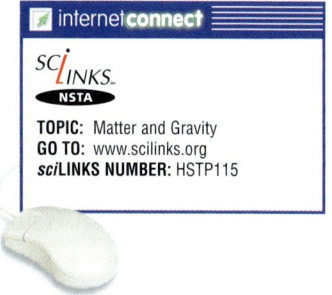

internet connect

TOPIC: Matter and Gravity
GO TO: www.scilinks.org
sciLINKS NUMBER: HSTP115

Chapter Highlights

Vocabulary Definitions

SECTION 1

motion an object's change in position over time when compared with a reference point

speed the rate at which an object moves; speed depends on the distance traveled and the time taken to travel that distance

velocity the speed of an object in a particular direction

acceleration the rate at which velocity changes; an object accelerates if its speed changes, if its direction changes, or if both its speed and its direction change

SECTION 2

force a push or a pull; all forces have both size and direction

newton the SI unit of force

net force the force that results from combining all the forces exerted on an object

Chapter Highlights

SECTION 1

Vocabulary
- motion (p. 108)
- speed (p. 109)
- velocity (p. 110)
- acceleration (p. 112)

Section Notes
- An object is in motion if it changes position over time when compared with a reference point.
- The speed of a moving object depends on the distance traveled by the object and the time taken to travel that distance.
- Speed and velocity are not the same thing. Velocity is speed in a given direction.
- Acceleration is the rate at which velocity changes.
- An object can accelerate by changing speed, changing direction, or both.
- Acceleration is calculated by subtracting starting velocity from final velocity, then dividing by the time required to change velocity.

Labs
Built for Speed (p. 646)
Detecting Acceleration (p. 647)

SECTION 2

Vocabulary
- force (p. 115)
- newton (p. 115)
- net force (p. 116)

Section Notes
- A force is a push or a pull.
- Forces are expressed in newtons.
- Force is always exerted by one object on another object.
- Net force is determined by combining forces.
- Unbalanced forces produce a change in motion. Balanced forces produce no change in motion.

✓ Skills Check

Math Concepts

ACCELERATION An object's acceleration can be determined using the following equation:

$$\text{Acceleration} = \frac{\text{final velocity} - \text{starting velocity}}{\text{time it takes to change velocity}}$$

For example, suppose a cheetah running at a velocity of 27 m/s east slows down. After 15 seconds, the cheetah has stopped.

$$\frac{0 \text{ m/s} - 27 \text{ m/s}}{15 \text{ s}} = -1.8 \text{ m/s/s east}$$

Visual Understanding

THE SOURCE OF FRICTION Even surfaces that look or feel very smooth are actually rough at the microscopic level. To understand how this roughness causes friction, review Figure 11 on page 119.

THE LAW OF UNIVERSAL GRAVITATION This law explains that the gravity between objects depends on their masses and the distance between them. Review the effects of this law by looking at Figure 20 on page 127.

Lab and Activity Highlights

Built for Speed PG 646

Detecting Acceleration PG 647

Science Friction PG 650

Relating Mass and Weight PG 651

 Datasheets for LabBook (blackline masters for these labs)

SECTION 3

Vocabulary

friction *(p. 119)*

Section Notes

- Friction is a force that opposes motion.
- Friction is caused by "hills and valleys" touching on the surfaces of two objects.
- The amount of friction depends on factors such as the roughness of the surfaces and the force pushing the surfaces together.
- Four kinds of friction that affect your life are sliding friction, rolling friction, fluid friction, and static friction.
- Friction can be harmful or helpful.

Labs

Science Friction *(p. 650)*

SECTION 4

Vocabulary

gravity *(p. 125)*
weight *(p. 128)*
mass *(p. 129)*

Section Notes

- Gravity is a force of attraction between objects that is due to their masses.
- The law of universal gravitation states that all objects in the universe attract each other through gravitational force. The size of the force depends on the masses of the objects and the distance between them.
- Weight and mass are not the same. Mass is the amount of matter in an object; weight is a measure of the gravitational force on an object.

Labs

Relating Mass and Weight *(p. 651)*

VOCABULARY DEFINITIONS, continued

SECTION 3

friction a force that opposes motion between two surfaces that are touching

SECTION 4

gravity a force of attraction between objects that is due to their masses

weight a measure of the gravitational force exerted on an object, usually by the Earth

mass the amount of matter that something is made of; its value does not change with the object's location

Vocabulary Review Worksheet 5

Blackline masters of these Chapter Highlights can be found in the **Study Guide**.

---

internetconnect

GO TO: go.hrw.com

Visit the **HRW** Web site for a variety of learning tools related to this chapter. Just type in the keyword:

KEYWORD: HSTMOT

GO TO: www.scilinks.org

Visit the **National Science Teachers Association** on-line Web site for Internet resources related to this chapter. Just type in the *sci*LINKS number for more information about the topic:

TOPIC: Measuring Motion	*sci*LINKS NUMBER: HSTP105
TOPIC: Forces	*sci*LINKS NUMBER: HSTP107
TOPIC: Force and Friction	*sci*LINKS NUMBER: HSTP110
TOPIC: Matter and Gravity	*sci*LINKS NUMBER: HSTP115
TOPIC: The Science of Bridges	*sci*LINKS NUMBER: HSTP125

131

Lab and Activity Highlights

LabBank

Long-Term Projects & Research Ideas,
Tiny Troubles, Project 55

Interactive Explorations CD-ROM

CD 2, Exploration 4, "Force in the Forest"

CD 3, Exploration 3, "Stranger Than Friction"

Chapter Review Answers

USING VOCABULARY

1. Friction
2. newtons
3. net force
4. Acceleration, velocity

UNDERSTANDING CONCEPTS

Multiple Choice

5. d
6. a
7. a
8. a
9. d
10. c

Short Answer

11. Motion occurs when an object changes position over time when compared with a reference point (an object that appears to stay in place).

12. Acceleration can occur simply by a change in direction. Thus, no change in speed is necessary for acceleration.

13. Mass is the amount of matter in an object, and its value does not change with the object's location. Weight measures the gravitational force on an object, so it can change as the amount of gravitational force changes.

Chapter Review

USING VOCABULARY

To complete the following sentences, choose the correct term from each pair of terms listed below:

1. ___?___ opposes motion between surfaces that are touching. (*Friction* or *Gravity*)

2. Forces are expressed in ___?___. (*newtons* or *mass*)

3. A ___?___ is determined by combining forces. (*net force* or *newton*)

4. ___?___ is the rate at which ___?___ changes. (*Velocity* or *Acceleration*/*velocity* or *acceleration*)

UNDERSTANDING CONCEPTS

Multiple Choice

5. A student riding her bicycle on a straight, flat road covers one block every 7 seconds. If each block is 100 m long, she is traveling at
   a. constant speed.
   b. constant velocity.
   c. 10 m/s.
   d. Both (a) and (b)

6. Friction is a force that
   a. opposes an object's motion.
   b. does not exist when surfaces are very smooth.
   c. decreases with larger mass.
   d. All of the above

7. Rolling friction
   a. is usually less than sliding friction.
   b. makes it difficult to move objects on wheels.
   c. is usually greater than sliding friction.
   d. is the same as fluid friction.

8. If Earth's mass doubled, your weight would
   a. increase because gravity increases.
   b. decrease because gravity increases.
   c. increase because gravity decreases.
   d. not change because you are still on Earth.

9. A force
   a. is expressed in newtons.
   b. can cause an object to speed up, slow down, or change direction.
   c. is a push or a pull.
   d. All of the above

10. The amount of gravity between 1 kg of lead and Earth is _____ the amount of gravity between 1 kg of marshmallows and Earth.
    a. greater than   c. the same as
    b. less than   d. none of the above

Short Answer

11. Describe the relationship between motion and a reference point.

12. How is it possible to be accelerating and traveling at a constant speed?

13. Explain the difference between mass and weight.

132 Chapter 5 • Matter in Motion

Concept Mapping

14. Use the following terms to create a concept map: speed, velocity, acceleration, force, direction, motion.

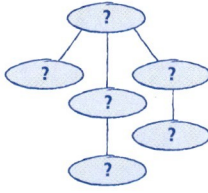

CRITICAL THINKING AND PROBLEM SOLVING

15. Your family is moving, and you are asked to help move some boxes. One box is so heavy that you must push it across the room rather than lift it. What are some ways you could reduce friction to make moving the box easier?

16. Explain how using the term *accelerator* when talking about a car's gas pedal can lead to confusion, considering the scientific meaning of the word *acceleration*.

17. Explain why it is important for airplane pilots to know wind velocity, not just wind speed, during a flight.

MATH IN SCIENCE

18. A kangaroo hops 60 m to the east in 5 seconds.
    a. What is the kangaroo's speed?
    b. What is the kangaroo's velocity?
    c. The kangaroo stops at a lake for a drink of water, then starts hopping again to the south. Every second, the kangaroo's velocity increases 2.5 m/s. What is the kangaroo's acceleration after 5 seconds?

INTERPRETING GRAPHICS

19. Is this a graph of positive or negative acceleration? How can you tell?

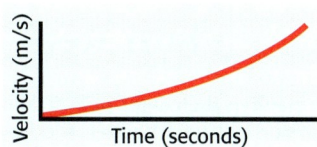

20. You know how to combine two forces that act in one or two directions. The same method you learned can be used to combine several forces acting in several directions. Examine the diagrams below, and predict with how much force and in what direction the object will move.

a)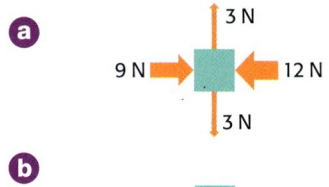

b)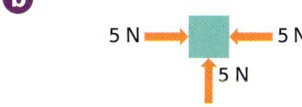

c)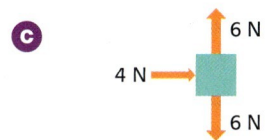

NOW What Do You Think?

Take a minute to review your answers to the ScienceLog questions on page 107. Have your answers changed? If necessary, revise your answers based on what you have learned since you began this chapter.

Concept Mapping

14. An answer to this exercise can be found at the end of this book.

CRITICAL THINKING AND PROBLEM SOLVING

15. Accept all reasonable answers. Examples include using a handcart or dolly to take advantage of rolling friction and polishing the floor to reduce sliding friction.

16. The car's gas pedal is pressed by the driver to increase the car's velocity. Since the scientific meaning of the term *acceleration* can include slowing down and even changing direction, accelerator is not an accurate term for this device.

17. It is helpful for pilots to know wind velocity because velocity includes direction. Pilots need to know the wind's speed and direction so that they will know whether the wind is blowing in the same direction as the plane (which could increase the plane's resultant velocity and lead to an earlier arrival time) or in a different direction than the plane (which might lead to a later arrival).

MATH IN SCIENCE

18. a. 12 m/s
    b. 12 m/s east
    c. 2.5 m/s/s south

INTERPRETING GRAPHICS

19. Positive, because velocity increases as time passes.
20. a. 3 N to the left
    b. 5 N up
    c. 4 N to the right

NOW WHAT DO YOU THINK?

1. Motion is measured with speed (distance divided by time), velocity (speed in a given direction), and acceleration (the rate of change of velocity).
2. A force is a push or pull.
3. Friction opposes motion.
4. Gravity, a force of attraction, causes objects to be pulled toward each other.

Concept Mapping Transparency 5

 Blackline masters of this Chapter Review can be found in the **Study Guide**.

SCIENCE, TECHNOLOGY, AND SOCIETY

Is It Real . . . or Is It Virtual?

Background

- Flight simulators have been popular computer applications for many years, but now powerful computers have brought motion simulation to a far more common experience—driving.

- VR machines can imitate the experience of driving many makes and models of cars for potential buyers to sample.

- Engineers might use driving simulators to test different features of a car or to test the design of intersections and roads before they are built.

- Golfers can practice in VR. They hit a real ball with a real club. The ball hits a vinyl screen, and sensors determine how the ball would fare on the course shown on the screen.

- Surgeons at the Virtual Reality in Medicine Laboratory at the University of Illinois at Chicago have created a virtual tour of the human ear, and they use the display (on a 6 m screen!) to learn their way around the inner ear.

- Scientists are working on a semi-transparent helmet for surgeons performing delicate operations, such as brain surgery. With this see-through helmet, a computer-generated three-dimensional image of a brain tumor, for example, is added to the surgeon's own view of the operation.

Science, Technology, and Society

Is It Real . . . or Is It Virtual?

You stand in the center of a darkened room and put on a helmet. The helmet covers your head and face, making it impossible for you to see or hear anything from outside. Wires run from the helmet to a series of computers, carrying information about how your head is positioned and where you are looking. Other wires carry back to you the sights and sounds the computer wants you to "see" and "hear." All of a sudden you find yourself driving a race car around a tricky course at 300 km/h. Then in another instant, you are in the middle of a rain forest staring at a live snake!

It's All an Illusion

Such simulated-reality experiences were once thought the stuff of science fiction alone. But today devices called motion simulators can stimulate the senses of sight and sound to create illusions of movement.

Virtual-reality devices, as these motion simulators are called, were first used during World War II to train pilots. Mock-ups of fighter-plane cockpits, films of simulated terrain, and a joystick that manipulated large hydraulic arms simulated the plane in "virtual flight." Today's jet pilots train with similar equipment, except the simulators use extremely sophisticated computer graphics instead of films.

Fooled You!

Virtual-reality hoods and gloves take people into a variety of "realities." Inside the hood, two small television cameras or computer-graphic images fool the wearer's sense of vision. The brain perceives the image as three-dimensional because one image is placed in front of each eye. As the images change, the computer adjusts the scene's perspective so that it appears to the viewer as though he or she is moving through the scene. When the position of the head changes, the computer adjusts the scene to account for the movement. All the while, sounds coming through the headphones trick the wearer's ears into thinking he or she is moving too.

In addition to hoods, gloves, and images, virtual-reality devices may have other types of sensors. Driving simulators, for instance, often have a steering wheel, a gas pedal, and a brake so that the participant has the sensation of driving. So whether you want spine-tingling excitement or on-the-job training, virtual reality could very well take *you* places!

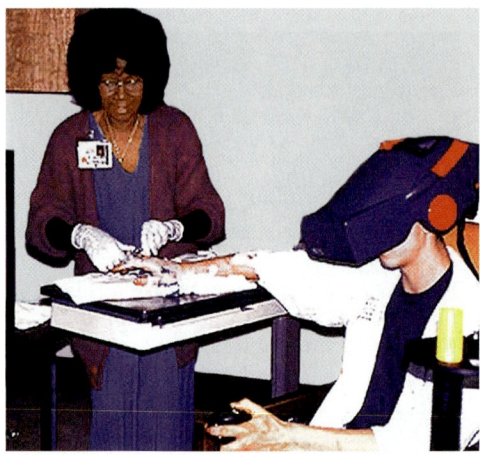

▲ Wearing a virtual-reality helmet helps to lessen the pain this burn patient feels while his dressings are changed.

Explore New Realities

▶ What other activities or skills could be learned or practiced with virtual reality? What are some problems with relying on this technology? Record your ideas in your ScienceLog.

Suggestions for Explore New Realities
Other activities in which virtual reality might be useful are hitting a baseball, operating complicated machinery, shopping, learning to dance, and practicing self-defense. Some problems with VR are its expense, the fact that what you learn through VR practice may not easily transfer to the real world, and that VR equipment may cause disorientation and discomfort in some users.

ACROSS THE SCIENCES

PHYSICAL SCIENCE • EARTH SCIENCE

The Golden Gate Bridge

Have you ever relaxed in a hammock? If so, you may have noticed how tense the strings got when the hammock supported your weight. Now imagine a hammock 1,965 m long supporting a 20-ton roadway with more than 100,000 cars traveling along its length each day. That describes the Golden Gate Bridge! Because of the way the bridge is built, it is very much like a giant hammock.

Tug of War

The bridge's roadway is suspended from main cables 2.33 km long that sweep from one end of the bridge to the other and that are anchored at each end. Smaller cables called *hangers* connect the main cables to the roadway. Tension, the force of being pulled apart, is created as the cables are pulled down by the weight of the roadway while being pulled up by their attachment to the top of each tower.

▲ *The Golden Gate Bridge spans the San Francisco Bay.*

Towering Above

Towers 227 m tall support the cables over the long distance across San Francisco Bay, making the Golden Gate the tallest bridge in the world. The towers receive a force that is the exact opposite of tension—compression. Compression is the force of being pushed together. The main cables holding the weight of the roadway push down on the top of the towers while Earth pushes up on the bottom.

Stretching the Limits

Tension and compression are elastic forces, which means they are dependent on elasticity, the ability of an object to return to its original shape after being stretched or compressed. If an object is not very elastic, it breaks easily or becomes permanently deformed when subjected to an elastic force. The cables and towers of the Golden Gate Bridge are made of steel, a material with great elastic strength. A single steel wire 2.54 mm thick can support over half a ton without breaking!

On the Road

The roadway of the Golden Gate Bridge is subjected to multiple forces at the same time, including friction, gravity, and elastic forces. Rolling friction is caused by the wheels of each vehicle moving across the roadway's surface. Gravity pulls down on the roadway but is counteracted by the support of the towers and cables. This causes each roadway span to bend slightly and experience both tension and compression. The bottom of each span is under tension because the cables and towers pull up along the road's sides, while gravity pulls down at its center. These same forces cause compression of the top of each span. Did you ever imagine that so many forces were at work on a bridge?

Bridge the Gap

▶ Find out more about another type of bridge, such as an arch, a beam, or a cable-stayed bridge. How do forces such as friction, gravity, tension, and compression affect these types of bridges?

Teaching Strategies

Build a people bridge. Students lean toward each other with palms touching. Have them move their feet back until they can't back up without falling. Where do they feel tension and compression? How about friction and gravity? Repeat the exercise with students facing each other and standing with their feet close to their partner's. Have them then hold hands and lean back.

internet connect

TOPIC: The Science of Bridges
GO TO: www.scilinks.org
*sci*LINKS NUMBER: HSTP125

ACROSS THE SCIENCES
The Golden Gate Bridge

Background

- The Golden Gate Bridge took 4 years to build and was completed in 1937. It was the longest suspension bridge (1,280 m) in the world for 27 years.
- 128,720 km of wire was used to create each main cable. Each cable contains 27,572 wires bundled into 61 strands and will support a mass of 90,718,000 kg.
- The longest suspension bridge, the Akashi Kaikyo Bridge, opened in Japan in 1998 with a center span of 1,990 m.

Answers to Bridge the Gap

All of the bridge types are affected by gravity. All the bridges are exposed to rolling friction from vehicles traveling across them.

- **Arch:** The weight of an arch bridge is carried out along the arch to the abutments at each end. When supporting its own weight and the weight of traffic, the entire arch is under compression.
- **Beam:** A beam bridge is a horizontal beam supported by piers at each end. The beam's weight pushes straight down, placing the bottom of the beam under tension and the top under compression. The strength of a beam bridge decreases with length.
- **Cable-stayed:** A cable-stayed bridge hangs the roadway from cables that extend from single towers to the deck. No cable anchorage is used, so the towers in compression bear the entire load from the cables, which are in tension.

Chapter Organizer

CHAPTER ORGANIZATION	TIME MINUTES	OBJECTIVES	LABS, INVESTIGATIONS, AND DEMONSTRATIONS
Chapter Opener pp. 136–137	45	National Standards: SAI 1, SPSP 5	**Investigate!** Falling Water, p. 137
Section 1 Gravity and Motion	90	▶ Explain how gravity and air resistance affect the acceleration of falling objects. ▶ Explain why objects in orbit appear to be weightless. ▶ Describe how an orbit is formed. ▶ Describe projectile motion. UCP 3, ST 1, HNS 1; LabBook: SAI 1	**QuickLab**, Penny Projectile Motion, p. 144 **Interactive Explorations CD-ROM,** Extreme Skiing A **Worksheet** is also available in the **Interactive Explorations Teacher's Edition.** **Discovery Lab**, A Marshmallow Catapult, p. 652 **Datasheets for LabBook,** A Marshmallow Catapult, Datasheet 20 **Inquiry Labs**, On the Fast Track, Lab 18
Section 2 Newton's Laws of Motion	135	▶ State and apply Newton's laws of motion. ▶ Compare the momentum of different objects. ▶ State and apply the law of conservation of momentum. UCP 3, 4, SAI 1, 2, PS 2b, 2c; LabBook: SAI 1, PS 2b, 2c	**Demonstration,** Egg in a Buggy, p. 145 in ATE **QuickLab,** First-Law Magic, p. 147 **Making Models,** Blast Off! p. 653 **Datasheets for LabBook,** Blast Off! Datasheet 21 **Skill Builder,** Inertia-Rama! p. 654 **Datasheets for LabBook,** Inertia-Rama! Datasheet 22 **Skill Builder,** Quite a Reaction, p. 656 **Datasheets for LabBook,** Quite a Reaction, Datasheet 23 **Whiz-Bang Demonstrations,** Newton's Eggciting Experiment, Demo 43 **Whiz-Bang Demonstrations,** Inertia Can Hurt Ya, Demo 44 **Whiz-Bang Demonstrations,** Fountain of Knowledge, Demo 45 **Long-Term Projects & Research Ideas,** Project 56

See page T20 for a complete correlation of this book with the

NATIONAL SCIENCE EDUCATION STANDARDS.

TECHNOLOGY RESOURCES

 Guided Reading Audio CD
English or Spanish, Chapter 6

 Science Discovery Videodiscs
Science Sleuths: A Day at the Races

 CNN Scientists in Action, Force in the Circus, Segment 8

 Interactive Explorations CD-ROM
CD 2, Exploration 5, Extreme Skiing

 One-Stop Planner CD-ROM with Test Generator

Chapter 6 • Forces in Motion

Chapter 6 • Forces in Motion

CLASSROOM WORKSHEETS, TRANSPARENCIES, AND RESOURCES	SCIENCE INTEGRATION AND CONNECTIONS	REVIEW AND ASSESSMENT
Directed Reading Worksheet 6 **Science Puzzlers, Twisters, & Teasers,** Worksheet 6		
Directed Reading Worksheet 6, Section 1 **Math Skills for Science Worksheet 19,** Arithmetic with Decimals **Transparency 222,** Falling Objects Accelerate at a Constant Rate **Transparency 162,** Profile of the Earth's Atmosphere **Transparency 223,** Two Motions Combine to Form Projectile Motion **Reinforcement Worksheet 6,** Falling Fast	**MathBreak,** Velocity of Falling Objects, p. 139 **Math and More,** p. 139 in ATE **Cross-Disciplinary Focus,** p. 140 in ATE **Connect to Earth Science,** p. 140 in ATE **Multicultural Connection,** p. 142 in ATE **Connect to Life Science,** p. 143 in ATE **Eureka!** A Bat with Dimples, p. 158 **Careers:** Roller Coaster Designer–Steve Okamoto, p. 159	**Self-Check,** p. 140 **Quiz,** p. 143 in ATE **Review,** p. 144 **Alternative Assessment,** p. 144 in ATE
Directed Reading Worksheet 6, Section 2 **Math Skills for Science Worksheet 48,** Newton: Force and Motion **Transparency 224,** Newton's Second Law and Acceleration Due to Gravity **Critical Thinking Worksheet 6,** Forces to Reckon With **Math Skills for Science Worksheet 49,** Momentum	**Cross-Disciplinary Focus,** p. 145 in ATE **Apply,** p. 146 **Real-World Connection,** p. 146 in ATE **Environment Connection,** p. 148 **MathBreak,** Second-Law Problems, p. 149 **Math and More,** p. 149 in ATE **Connect to Life Science,** p. 150 in ATE **Real-World Connection,** p. 151 in ATE **Multicultural Connection,** p. 151 in ATE	**Self-Check,** p. 147 **Review,** p. 149 **Homework,** pp. 151, 152 in ATE **Review,** p. 153 **Quiz,** p. 153 in ATE **Alternative Assessment,** p. 153 in ATE

END-OF-CHAPTER REVIEW AND ASSESSMENT

Chapter Review in Study Guide
Vocabulary and Notes in Study Guide
Chapter Tests with Performance-Based Assessment, Chapter 6 Test
Chapter Tests with Performance-Based Assessment, Performance-Based Assessment 6
Concept Mapping Transparency 6

internet connect

Holt, Rinehart and Winston On-line Resources
go.hrw.com

For worksheets and other teaching aids related to this chapter, visit the HRW Web site and type in the keyword: **HSTFOR**

National Science Teachers Association
www.scilinks.org

Encourage students to use the *sci*LINKS numbers listed in the internet connect boxes to access information and resources on the **NSTA** Web site.

Chapter 6 • Chapter Organizer   **135B**

Chapter Resources & Worksheets

Visual Resources

TEACHING TRANSPARENCIES

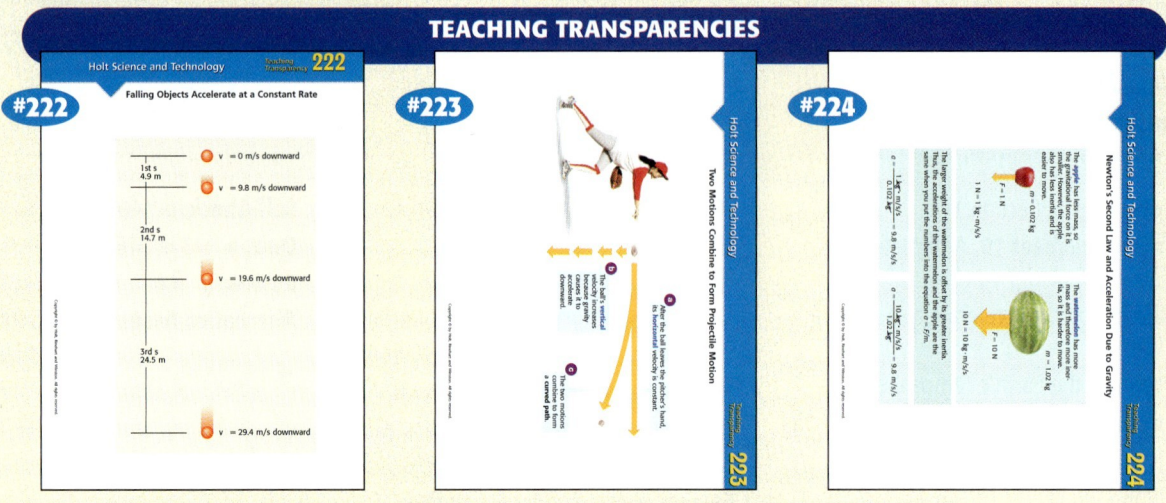

TEACHING TRANSPARENCIES

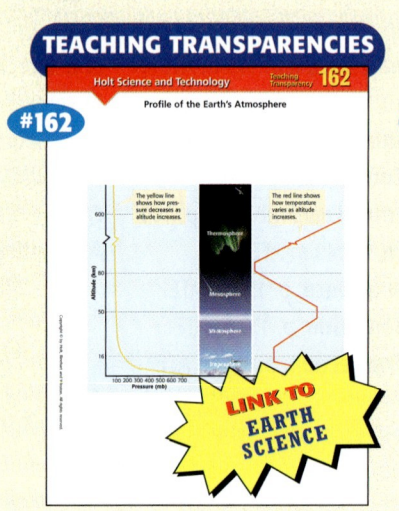

CONCEPT MAPPING TRANSPARENCY

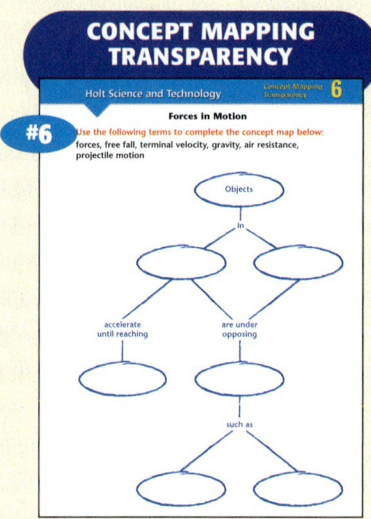

Meeting Individual Needs

DIRECTED READING

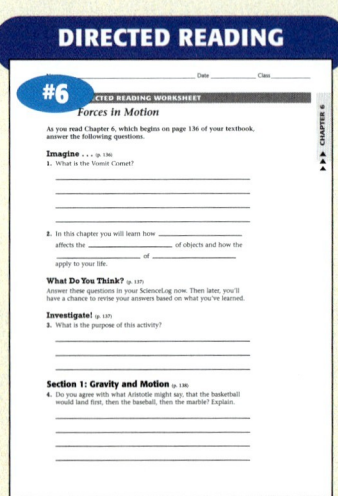

REINFORCEMENT & VOCABULARY REVIEW

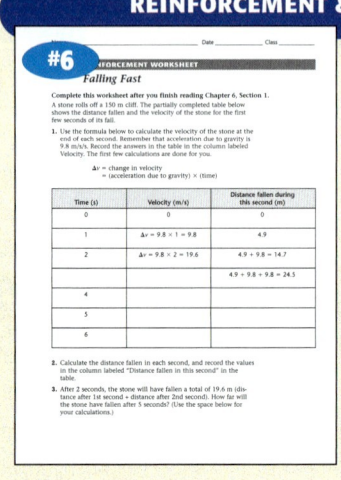

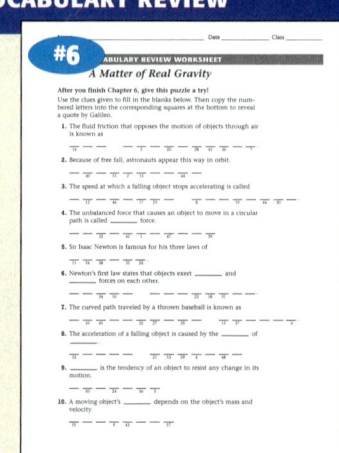

SCIENCE PUZZLERS, TWISTERS & TEASERS

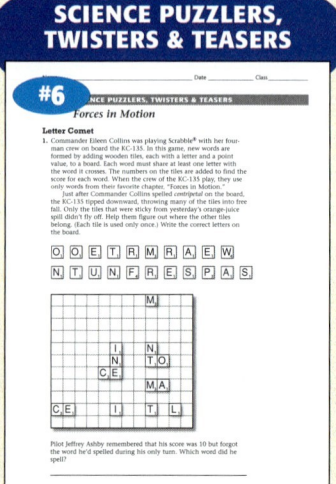

Chapter 6 • Forces in Motion

Chapter 6 • Forces in Motion

Review & Assessment

STUDY GUIDE

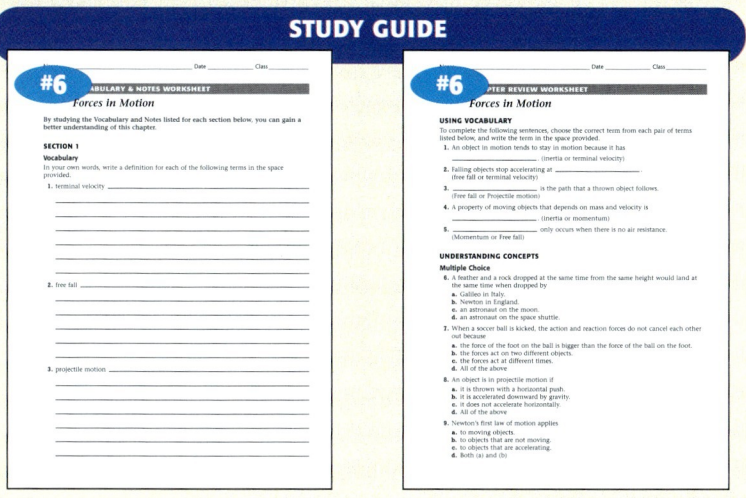

CHAPTER TESTS WITH PERFORMANCE-BASED ASSESSMENT

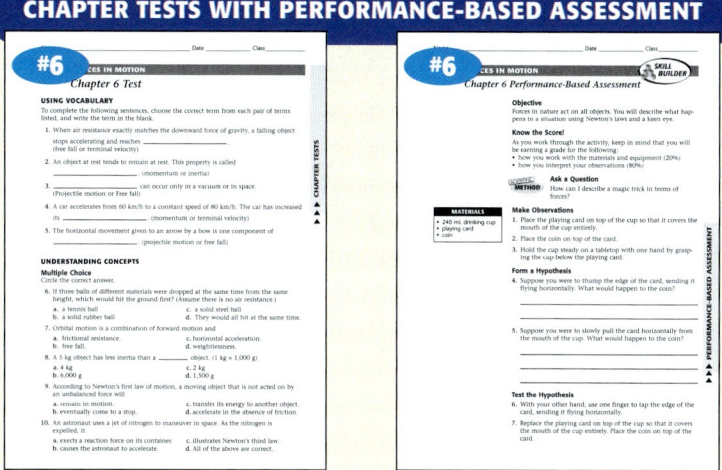

Lab Worksheets

INQUIRY LABS

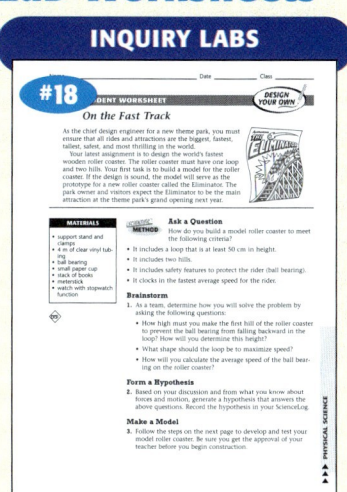

WHIZ-BANG DEMONSTRATIONS

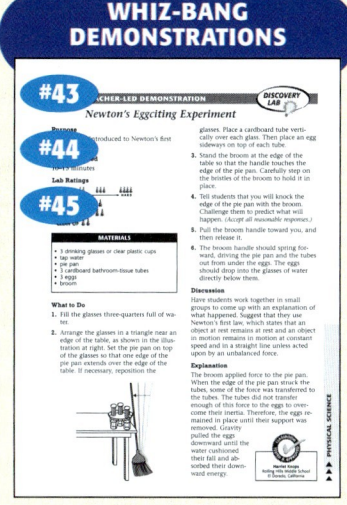

LONG-TERM PROJECTS & RESEARCH IDEAS

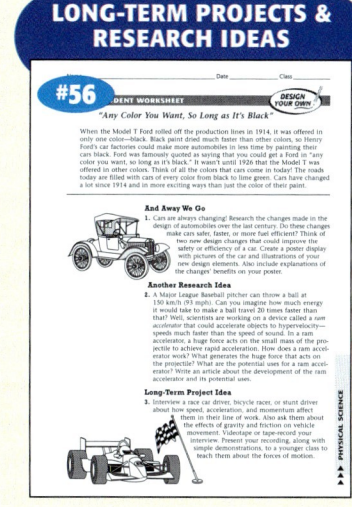

DATASHEETS FOR LABBOOK

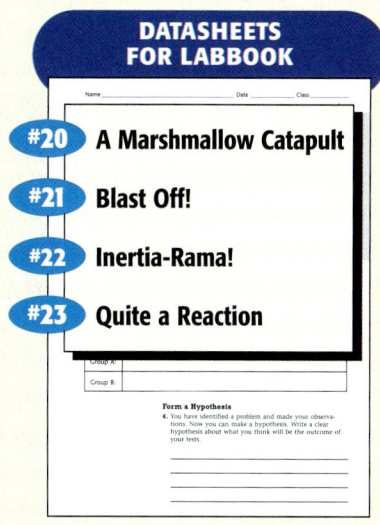

#20 A Marshmallow Catapult

#21 Blast Off!

#22 Inertia-Rama!

#23 Quite a Reaction

Applications & Extensions

CRITICAL THINKING & PROBLEM SOLVING

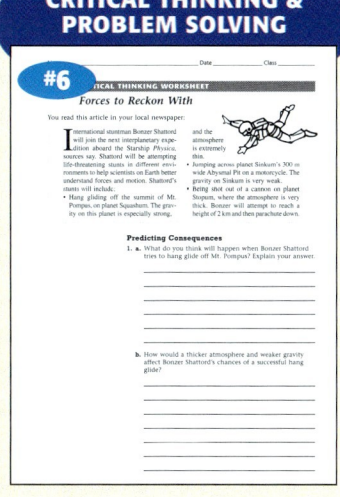

SCIENTISTS IN ACTION

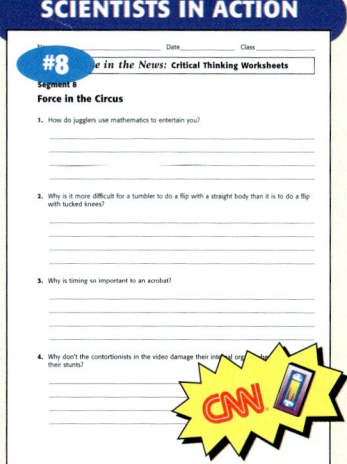

INTERACTIVE EXPLORATIONS

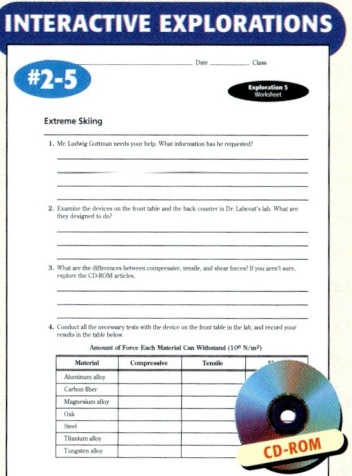

Chapter 6 • Chapter Resources & Worksheets   135D

Chapter Background

SECTION 1
Gravity and Motion

▶ **Space Shuttles and Sky Divers**
What does the space shuttle have in common with a sky diver? What does a jumping frog have in common with a 42 m/s fastball? They are all affected by gravity, and their flights are governed by certain laws of motion. Although some observers in ancient China theorized about objects in motion and objects at rest, Sir Isaac Newton is usually given credit for stating and testing the three basic laws that describe and predict motion.

▶ **The Apple and the Moon**
Galileo's theory that all objects fall with the same acceleration in a vacuum has been verified on Earth many times. It wasn't the same old proof, though, on July 30, 1971, when astronaut David Randolph Scott stood on the surface of the moon and dropped a feather and a hammer simultaneously. Just as Galileo had predicted, in the absence of air resistance, the feather hit the ground at the same time as the hammer.

- Sir Isaac Newton is said to have realized the importance of gravitational force in 1666, when he watched an apple fall from a tree in his garden. One of Newton's contemporaries said, "It came into his thought that the power of gravity (which brought the apple from the tree to the ground) was not limited to a certain distance from the Earth, but that this power must extend much further than is usually thought. Why not as high as the moon, he said to himself, and if so that must influence her motion. Whereupon he fell a-calculating what would be the effect."

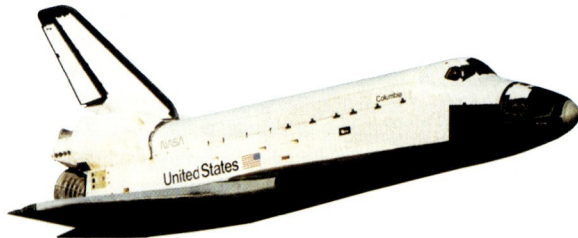

- Newton calculated the acceleration of the moon in a circular orbit around Earth and compared this with an apple's downward acceleration. He found that the accelerations were the same. He concluded that the orbital motion of the moon and the fall of the apple were the results of the same force.

▶ **Parachutes**
Older parachutes without holes trapped air in the canopy as they fell. These parachutes were difficult to control. As the air escaped, the parachute rocked back and forth, and many parachutists would get airsick. Modern parachutes are shaped like a wing and have holes or slits that the jumper can open and close. Today, a parachutist can steer a parachute to within a few meters of a desired spot and, by controlling the rate of descent, can land as gently as walking down stairs.

IS THAT A FACT!

▶ Galileo timed the motion of balls rolling down an inclined plane to prove that all objects fall at the same rate.

Chapter 6 • Forces in Motion

SECTION 2
Newton's Laws of Motion

▶ **Sir Isaac Newton (1642–1727)**
In 1661, Isaac Newton went to study at Cambridge University. But Newton made many of his most important discoveries while spending time at the family home, Woolsthorpe Manor, near Grantham, in Lincolnshire, England, in 1665 and 1666.

▶ ***Principia***
Newton's *Principia,* published in 1687, explains the three basic laws that govern the way objects move and Newton's theory of gravity. Newton explained how the force of gravity keeps the planets moving around the sun. Interestingly, Newton used his laws to predict that Earth must be a slightly flattened sphere and that comets orbit the sun in elongated elliptical paths. These predictions were later shown to be true.

▶ **Friction**
You may want to refer students back to Chapter 5 for a review of friction.

- How is simple friction different from air resistance? Simple friction depends only on the nature of the surfaces that are interacting with each other. Air resistance depends on both that kind of friction and on the amount of air that must be moved out of the way each second.

- How do parachutes work to increase air resistance? The parachute provides a larger surface area to pull through the air. This in turn requires that a much larger amount of air be moved out of the way each second as the parachute falls toward the Earth.

IS THAT A FACT!

- When a heavy steel wrecking ball is swung on a cable, it has a very large momentum. When the ball collides with a brick wall, the momentum of the ball is transferred to the wall. The wall starts to move and the cement between the bricks is torn apart. Because the individual bricks have relatively small masses, they are knocked away.

▶ **Terminal Velocity**
Air resistance, a type of friction, limits the velocity of an object as it falls to the Earth. As long as a falling object is somewhat streamlined and has not accelerated to high velocity, its acceleration due to gravity is a constant 9.8 m/s^2 until it reaches the Earth.

- But as the falling object speeds up, fluid friction increases as a result of turbulent flow. More and more air must be pushed out of the way each second. Eventually, the force of the air pushing upward on the falling object is equal to Earth's gravitational force pulling downward on the falling object.

- When the upward and downward forces are equal, the net force on the falling object is zero. With a zero net force, the object falls at constant velocity.

For background information about teaching strategies and issues, refer to the *Professional Reference for Teachers.*

CHAPTER 6
Forces in Motion

Chapter Preview

Section 1
Gravity and Motion
- All Objects Fall with the Same Acceleration
- Air Resistance Slows Down Acceleration
- Orbiting Objects Are in Free Fall
- Projectile Motion and Gravity

Section 2
Newton's Laws of Motion
- Newton's First Law of Motion
- Newton's Second Law of Motion
- Newton's Third Law of Motion
- Momentum Is a Property of Moving Objects

MISCONCEPTION ALERT

Every bit of matter in the universe exerts a gravitational force. Because humans are made of matter, each person exerts his or her own gravitational force. However, that force is very weak compared with that of Earth, with its much larger mass.

Directed Reading Worksheet 6

Science Puzzlers, Twisters & Teasers Worksheet 6

Guided Reading Audio CD
English or Spanish, Chapter 6

CHAPTER 6
Forces in Motion

Imagine...

You have been selected to travel on the space shuttle as NASA's first student astronaut. Like all astronauts, you must go through a year of training to prepare for space travel. When you are in the space shuttle, many different forces will be acting on your body that might make you dizzy or disoriented. You must get used to these forces quickly before you go into space.

There are many parts to your training. For instance, there is a machine that spins you around in all directions. There is also underwater training that lets you experience what reduced gravity feels like. But the most exciting part of your training is riding on the KC-135 airplane.

The KC-135 is a modified airplane that simulates what it feels like to orbit Earth in the space shuttle. The KC-135 flies upward at a steep angle, then flies downward at a 45° angle. When the airplane flies downward, the effect of reduced gravity is produced inside. As the plane "falls" out from under the passengers, the astronaut trainees inside the plane can "float," as shown above. Because the floating often makes passengers queasy, the KC-135 has earned a nickname—the Vomit Comet.

NASA scientists used their knowledge of forces, gravity, and the laws of motion to develop these training procedures. In this chapter, you will learn how gravity affects the motion of objects and how the laws of motion apply to your life.

Imagine...

Sir Isaac Newton first formalized the laws that determine the motion of spacecraft. His laws led to, among other fields, *astronautics*, the area of engineering and technology concerned with spaceflight. Astronautics includes *astrodynamics*, which is the study of spacecraft motion.

Spacecraft can follow four different types of flight paths in space. These are elliptical orbit, circular orbit, parabolic trajectory, and hyperbolic trajectory. All orbits of Earth's satellites are either circular or elliptical orbits.

 **What Do You Think?**

In your ScienceLog, try to answer the following questions based on what you already know:

1. How does the force of gravity affect falling objects?
2. What is projectile motion?
3. What are Newton's laws of motion?
4. What is momentum?

What Do You Think?
Accept all reasonable responses.
Students will have a chance to revise their answers in the Chapter Review under NOW What Do You Think?

Investigate!

MATERIALS

FOR EACH GROUP:
- wide plastic tub
- paper cup
- water colored with food coloring
- paper towels

Making solutions of colored water before class will save time and food coloring. The colors do not have to be very intense, just enough to make the water easier to see.

To reduce the mess, have students fill the cups only half full. Spread plenty of newspapers on the floor.

Falling Water

Gravity is one of the most important forces you encounter in your daily life. Without it, objects that are thrown or dropped would never land on the ground—they would just float in space. In this activity, you will observe the effect of gravity on a falling object.

Procedure

1. Place a **wide plastic tub** on the floor. Punch a small hole in the side of a **paper cup,** near the bottom.
2. Hold your finger over the hole, and fill the cup with **water colored with food coloring.** Keeping your finger over the hole, hold the cup about waist high above the tub.
3. Uncover the hole. Describe your observations in your ScienceLog.
4. Cover the hole with your finger again, and refill the cup.
5. Predict what will happen to the water if you drop the cup at the same time you uncover the hole. Write your predictions in your ScienceLog.
6. Uncover the hole, and drop the cup at the same time. Record your observations.
7. Clean up any spilled water with **paper towels.**

Analysis

8. What differences did you observe in the behavior of the water during the two trials?
9. In the second trial, how fast did the cup fall compared with the water?
10. How is the water in the cup similar to passengers in the KC-135 jet?

Answers to Investigate!

8. In the first trial, students should see the water coming out of the hole and falling to the ground. In the second trial, they should see no water coming out of the hole as the cup falls.
9. The cup and the water fall at the same rate. Students may not know that both are accelerating and may say that both fell at the same velocity or speed. This is acceptable at this point.
10. The water in the cup falls at the same rate as the cup, just as the people in the KC-135 fall at the same rate as the jet.

IS THAT A FACT!

Although it is primarily used for training and research, the Vomit Comet is occasionally used for filming scenes about space travel. The film director Ron Howard spent more than 6 months renting the Vomit Comet for the movie *Apollo 13*.

internetconnect

 Smithsonian Institution®
Visit **www.si.edu/hrw** for additional on-line resources.

Chapter 6 • Forces in Motion   **137**

SECTION 1

Focus

Gravity and Motion

In this section students explore how gravity and air resistance affect falling objects. Students learn how an orbit is formed and why objects in orbit appear to be weightless. Finally, they explore the relationship between gravity and projectile motion.

🔔 Bellringer

Warner Brothers cartoon character Wile E. Coyote often finds himself falling off a cliff. Then a giant boulder lands on top of him after he hits the ground. Before students read the first section, have them answer the following question:

If Wile E. Coyote and a boulder fall off a cliff at the same time, which do you think will hit the ground first?

Write your predictions in your ScienceLog.

1 Motivate

ACTIVITY

You will need a 12 in. softball, a women's size shot, a sturdy table to stand on, and a board or pad to protect the floor. First, show students the softball and the shot. Discuss their similar size but different masses. Then stand on top of the table. Tell students that you will drop both objects from the same height. As you hold both objects at arm's length, have them predict which will hit first. Discuss and question their predictions. Now drop both objects *at the same time*. Ask students for their observations; repeat as necessary.

Section 1

Terms to Learn
terminal velocity
free fall
projectile motion

What You'll Do
- Explain how gravity and air resistance affect the acceleration of falling objects.
- Explain why objects in orbit appear to be weightless.
- Describe how an orbit is formed.
- Describe projectile motion.

Gravity and Motion

Suppose you drop a baseball and a marble at the same time from the same height. Which do you think would land first? In ancient Greece around 400 B.C., an important philosopher named Aristotle (ER is TAWT uhl) believed that the rate at which an object falls depends on the object's mass. Imagine that you could ask Aristotle which object would land first. He would predict that the baseball would land first.

All Objects Fall with the Same Acceleration

In the late 1500s, a young Italian scientist named Galileo questioned Aristotle's idea about falling objects. Galileo proved that the mass of an object does not affect the rate at which it falls. According to one story, Galileo did this by dropping two cannonballs of different masses from the top of the Leaning Tower of Pisa. The crowd watching from the ground was amazed to see the two cannonballs land at the same time. Whether or not this story is true, Galileo's idea changed people's understanding of gravity and falling objects.

Acceleration Due to Gravity Objects fall to the ground at the same rate because the acceleration due to gravity is the same for all objects. Does that seem odd? The force of gravity is greater between Earth and an object with a large mass than between Earth and a less massive object, so you may think that the acceleration due to gravity should be greater too. But a greater force must be applied to a large mass than to a small mass to produce the same acceleration. Thus, the difference in force is canceled by the difference in mass. **Figure 1** shows objects with different masses falling with the same acceleration.

Figure 1 *A table tennis ball and a golf ball fall with the same acceleration even though they have different masses.*

SCIENTISTS AT ODDS

When Galileo attended the University of Pisa in the 1500s, scholars generally accepted Aristotle's theory that bodies fall to Earth at different velocities depending on their mass. Galileo questioned Aristotle's teachings after observing different-sized hailstones hitting the ground at the same time.

 **WEIRD SCIENCE**

If a penny fell from the top of the Empire State Building (about 385 m), it would be traveling with enough velocity to dent almost anything it struck at ground level.

Chapter 6 • Forces in Motion

Accelerating at a Constant Rate All objects accelerate toward Earth at a rate of 9.8 meters per second per second, which is expressed as 9.8 m/s/s. This means that for every second that an object falls, the object's downward velocity increases by 9.8 m/s, as shown in **Figure 2.** Remember, this acceleration is the same for all objects regardless of their mass. Do the MathBreak at right to learn how to calculate the velocity of a falling object.

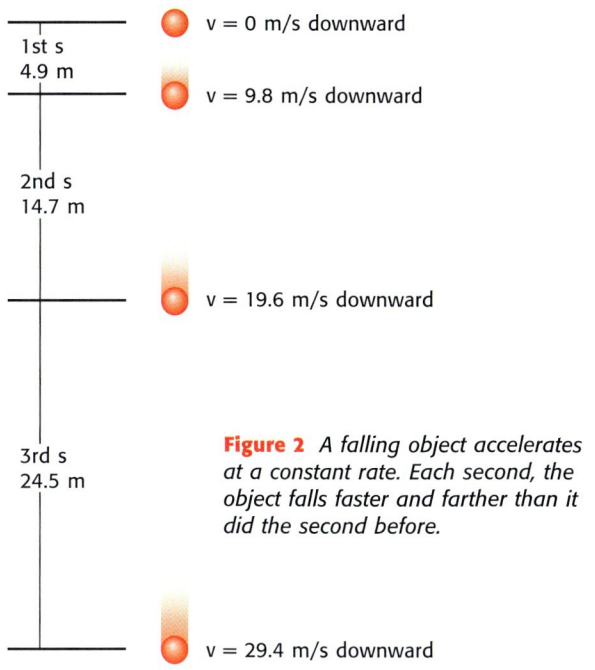

Figure 2 A falling object accelerates at a constant rate. Each second, the object falls faster and farther than it did the second before.

MATH BREAK

Velocity of Falling Objects

To find the change in velocity (Δv) of a falling object, multiply the acceleration due to gravity (g) by the time it takes for the object to fall in seconds (t):

$$\Delta v = g \times t$$

For example, a stone at rest is dropped from a cliff, and it takes 3 seconds to hit the ground. Its downward velocity when it hits the ground is as follows:

$$\Delta v = 9.8 \, \frac{m/s}{s} \times 3 \, s$$
$$= 29.4 \, m/s$$

Now It's Your Turn

A penny at rest is dropped from the top of a tall stairwell.

1. What is the penny's velocity after it has fallen for 2 seconds?
2. The penny hits the ground in 4.5 seconds. What is its final velocity?

Gravity helps make roller coasters thrilling to ride. Read about a roller coaster designer on page 159.

Air Resistance Slows Down Acceleration

Try this simple experiment. Drop two sheets of paper—one crumpled in a tight ball and the other kept flat. Did your results contradict what you just learned about falling objects? The flat paper fell more slowly because of fluid friction that opposes the motion of objects through air. This fluid friction is also known as *air resistance*. Air resistance occurs between the surface of the falling object and the air that surrounds it.

IS THAT A FACT!

Air resistance is a result of the fluid friction between the falling object and the air and also the inertia of the particles of the air. The air particles have to "move out of the way" of the falling object. Because the particles have mass, they also have inertia that resists movement.

 Teaching Transparency 222
"Falling Objects Accelerate at a Constant Rate"

 Directed Reading Worksheet 6 Section 1

2) Teach

USING THE FIGURE

Draw students' attention to **Figures 1** and **2**. Be sure students understand that objects falling vertically do not fall at a constant speed but constantly accelerate. Have students note how the distance between the position of each ball increases with time as the ball falls. Point out that although the strobe images were photographed at equal intervals, each of the balls moves faster and travels a greater distance during each interval.

Answers to MATHBREAK

1. $9.8 \, \frac{m/s}{s} \times 2 \, s = 19.6 \, m/s$ downward
2. $9.8 \, \frac{m/s}{s} \times 4.5 \, s = 44.1 \, m/s$ downward

MATH and MORE

Have students do the following problems for additional practice:

1. A boy standing on a high cliff dives into the ocean below and strikes the water after 3 seconds. What is the boy's velocity when he hits the water? **(29.4 m/s downward)**

2. A rocks falls from a high cliff and hits the ground in 6.5 seconds. What is its final velocity? **(63.7 m/s downward)**

3. A brick falls from the top of a building and strikes the ground with a velocity of 19.6 m/s downward. How long does the brick fall? **(2 seconds)**

 Math Skills Worksheet 19 "Arithmetic with Decimals"

Section 1 • Gravity and Motion **139**

2 Teach, continued

READING STRATEGY

Prediction Guide Before students read pages 140 and 141, ask them to explain whether a school bus or a racing car would be affected less by air resistance. (a racing car, because a racing car is built low to the ground, with smooth lines to reduce air resistance)

Answer to Self-Check
A leaf is more affected by air resistance.

CROSS-DISCIPLINARY FOCUS

History The first recorded parachute jump was completed by André-Jacques Garnerin near Paris, France, in 1797. Garnerin, a hot-air balloon pilot, was demonstrating his balloon as part of a traveling show. The balloon rose to about 700 m when it burst. As the gondola fell, many of the people in the crowd turned their heads so they would not see Garnerin fall to his death. Much to their surprise, Garnerin did not fall because he was in the balloon gondola, which floated safely to the ground under his makeshift parachute.

CONNECT TO EARTH SCIENCE

Use the Teaching Transparency "Profile of the Earth's Atmosphere" to discuss how air resistance changes as one goes higher in the atmosphere.

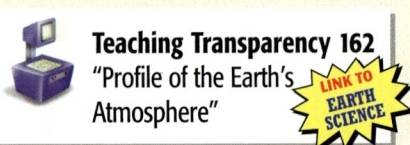
Teaching Transparency 162 "Profile of the Earth's Atmosphere"

Self-Check

Which is more affected by air resistance—a leaf or an acorn? *(See page 724 to check your answer.)*

Figure 3 *The force of gravity pulls the object downward as the force of air resistance pushes it upward.*

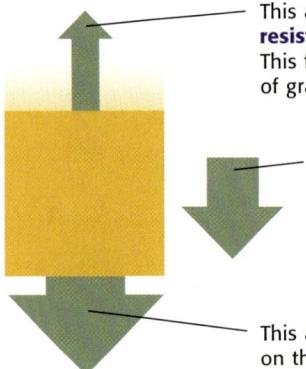

This arrow represents **the force of air resistance** pushing up on the object. This force is subtracted from the force of gravity to produce the net force.

This arrow represents **the net force** on the object. Because the net force is not zero, the object still accelerates downward, but not as fast as it would without air resistance.

This arrow represents **the force of gravity** on the object. If this were the only force acting on the object, it would accelerate at a rate of 9.8 m/s/s.

Figure 4
The parachute increases the air resistance of this sky diver, slowing him to a safe terminal velocity.

Air Resistance Affects Some Objects More than Others

The amount of air resistance acting on an object depends on the size and shape of the object. Air resistance affects the flat sheet of paper more than the crumpled one, causing the flat sheet to fall more slowly than the crumpled one. Because air is all around you, any falling object you see is affected by air resistance. **Figure 3** shows the effect of air resistance on the downward acceleration of a falling object.

Acceleration Stops at the Terminal Velocity

As long as the net force on a falling object is not zero, the object accelerates downward. But the amount of air resistance on an object increases as the speed of the object increases. As an object falls, the upward force of air resistance continues to increase until it exactly matches the downward force of gravity. When this happens, the net force is zero, and the object stops accelerating. The object then falls at a constant velocity, which is called the **terminal velocity.**

Sometimes the fact that falling objects have a terminal velocity is a good thing. The terminal velocity of hailstones is between 5 and 40 m/s, depending on the size of the stones. Every year cars, buildings, and vegetation are all severely damaged in hail storms. Imagine how much more destructive hail would be if there were no air resistance—hailstones would hit the Earth at velocities near 350 m/s! **Figure 4** shows another situation in which terminal velocity is helpful.

SCIENCE HUMOR

When asked why he wasn't interested in being a paratrooper, an Army pilot said, "I will never understand why anyone would want to jump out of a perfectly good airplane." Ask students if they share the pilot's opinion or if they might enjoy sky diving.

140   Chapter 6 • Forces in Motion

Free Fall Occurs When There Is No Air Resistance Sky divers are often described as being in free fall before they open their parachutes. However, that is an incorrect description, because air resistance is always acting on the sky diver.

An object is in **free fall** only if gravity is pulling it down and no other forces are acting on it. Because air resistance is a force (fluid friction), free fall can occur only where there is no air—in a vacuum (a place in which there is no matter) or in space. **Figure 5** shows objects falling in a vacuum. Because there is no air resistance, the two objects are in free fall.

Figure 5 *Air resistance normally causes a feather to fall more slowly than an apple. But in a vacuum, the feather and the apple fall with the same acceleration because both are in free fall.*

Orbiting Objects Are in Free Fall

Look at the astronaut in **Figure 6.** Why is the astronaut floating inside the space shuttle? It might be tempting to say it is because she is "weightless" in space. In fact, you may have read or heard that objects are weightless in space. However, it is impossible to be weightless anywhere in the universe.

Weight is a measure of gravitational force. The size of the force depends on the masses of objects and the distances between them. If you traveled in space far away from all the stars and planets, the gravitational force acting on you would be almost undetectable because the distance between you and other objects would be great. But you would still have mass, and so would all the other objects in the universe. Therefore, gravity would still attract you to other objects—even if just slightly—so you would still have weight.

Astronauts "float" in orbiting spaceships because of free fall. To understand this better, you need to understand what *orbiting* means and then consider the astronauts inside the ship.

Figure 6 *Astronauts appear to be weightless while floating inside the space shuttle—but they're not!*

MISCONCEPTION ALERT

Free fall can be either ascending or descending. If you could toss a ball upward with no forces other than gravity acting on it (i.e., no air resistance), its entire path (up and down) would be in free fall.

TOPIC: The Force of Gravity
GO TO: www.scilinks.org
*sci*LINKS NUMBER: HSTP130

DISCUSSION

Concept Mapping Ask students what problems they might encounter if they tried to sky dive on the moon. (The absence of an atmosphere would mean no air resistance to slow a parachute. But they would still fall because the moon does have gravity.)

Have students create a concept map showing the difference between sky diving on Earth and sky diving on the moon.

USING THE FIGURE

The strobe photo in **Figure 5** shows a feather and an apple falling in a vacuum. Students may notice that the feather appears to be falling slower. In the top image, the feather is lined up with the bottom of the apple. In the bottom image, the feather is lined up with the top of the apple. Explain that it is very difficult to create a total vacuum—especially one that is large enough to allow a feather and apple to fall side by side. Although the feather and the apple are not in a total vacuum, the photo shows that their accelerations in a partial vacuum are nearly equal. **Sheltered English**

MEETING INDIVIDUAL NEEDS

Learners Having Difficulty Review with students what a vacuum is (a space with no matter). Point out that the partial vacuum in which the feather and apple were placed has almost no air left in it. Therefore, the feather cannot be affected very much by air resistance and will fall with almost the same acceleration as the apple. **Sheltered English**

Section 1 • Gravity and Motion

2 Teach, continued

MISCONCEPTION ALERT

The shuttle in **Figure 7** is shown in orbit facing forward and oriented right side up (called "airplane mode"). In orbit, the shuttle spends most of the time upside down and backward. It also orbits upside down and sideways (wing first), but it rarely orbits in airplane mode. It is only in airplane mode for landings.

USING THE FIGURE

Draw students' attention to **Figure 7**. Ask students why the shuttle does not fall to Earth if gravity is pulling downward on it. (The forward motion of the shuttle occurs together with free fall to produce a path that follows the curve of Earth's surface.)

Ask what would happen if the shuttle started moving much faster or much slower. (If the shuttle moved fast enough, it would escape Earth's gravitational force and move forward, off into space. If the shuttle moved more slowly, it would begin to fall toward Earth. This is exactly what it does on reentry.)

Multicultural CONNECTION

On September 12, 1992, Dr. Mae Jemison became the first African-American woman to orbit Earth on the space shuttle *Endeavor*. Dr. Jemison, who has degrees in chemical engineering and medicine, was in charge of many of the experiments conducted during the mission.

Two Motions Combine to Cause Orbiting An object is said to be orbiting when it is traveling in a circular or nearly circular path around another object. When a spaceship orbits Earth, it is moving forward, but it is also in free fall toward Earth. **Figure 7** shows how these two motions occur together to cause orbiting.

Figure 7 How an Orbit Is Formed

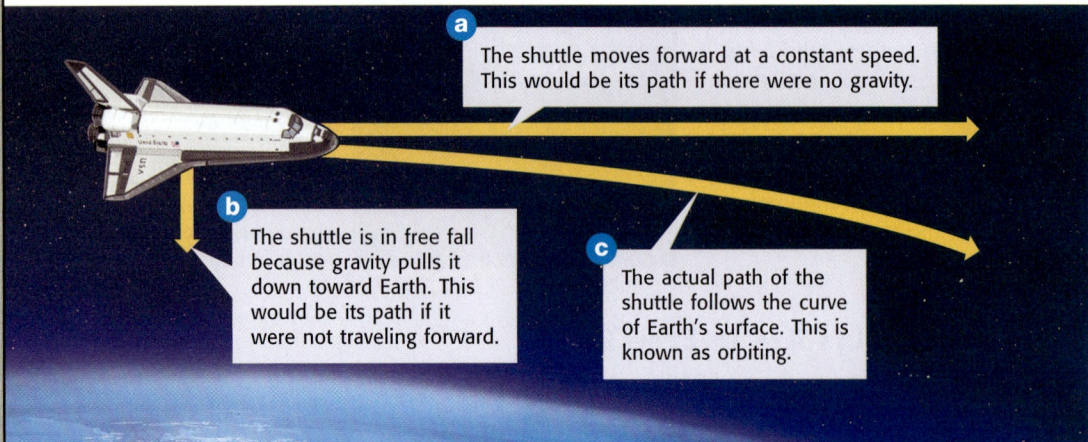

a. The shuttle moves forward at a constant speed. This would be its path if there were no gravity.

b. The shuttle is in free fall because gravity pulls it down toward Earth. This would be its path if it were not traveling forward.

c. The actual path of the shuttle follows the curve of Earth's surface. This is known as orbiting.

As you can see in the illustration above, the space shuttle is always falling while it is in orbit. So why don't astronauts hit their heads on the ceiling of the falling shuttle? Because they are also in free fall—they are always falling, too. Because the astronaut in Figure 6 is in free fall, she appears to be floating.

The Role of Gravity in Orbiting Besides spaceships and satellites, many other objects in the universe are in orbit. The moon orbits the Earth, Earth and the other planets orbit the sun, and many stars orbit large masses in the center of galaxies. All of these objects are traveling in a circular or nearly circular path. Remember, any object in circular motion is constantly changing direction. Because an unbalanced force is necessary to change the motion of any object, there must be an unbalanced force working on any object in circular motion.

The unbalanced force that causes objects to move in a circular path is called a *centripetal force*. Gravity provides the centripetal force that keeps objects in orbit. The word *centripetal* means "toward the center." As you can see in **Figure 8**, the centripetal force on the moon points toward the center of the circle traced by the moon's orbit.

Figure 8 The moon stays in orbit around the Earth because Earth's gravitational force provides a centripetal force on the moon.

TOPIC: Gravity and Orbiting Objects
GO TO: www.scilinks.org
sciLINKS NUMBER: HSTP135

IS THAT A FACT!

In the text, the definition of an orbit is somewhat simplified. All orbits are ellipses. However, some orbits are ellipses that are *not* nearly circular. The orbits of comets around the sun are very eccentric (very oblong), but they are still elliptical.

142 Chapter 6 • Forces in Motion

Projectile Motion and Gravity

The orbit of the space shuttle around the Earth is an example of projectile (proh JEK tuhl) motion. **Projectile motion** is the curved path an object follows when thrown or propelled near the surface of the Earth. The motions of leaping dancers, thrown balls, hopping grasshoppers, and arrows shot from a bow are all examples of projectile motion. Projectile motion has two components—horizontal and vertical. The two components are independent; that is, they have no effect on each other. When the two motions are combined, they form a curved path, as shown in **Figure 9**.

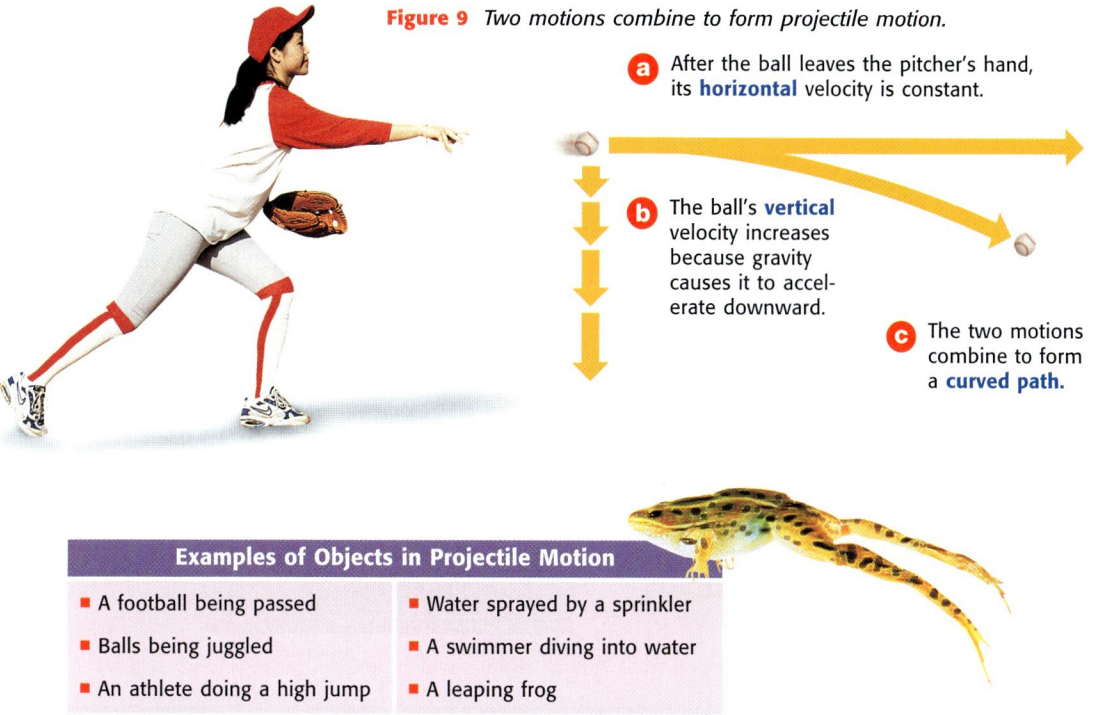

Figure 9 Two motions combine to form projectile motion.

a After the ball leaves the pitcher's hand, its **horizontal** velocity is constant.

b The ball's **vertical** velocity increases because gravity causes it to accelerate downward.

c The two motions combine to form a **curved path**.

Examples of Objects in Projectile Motion

- A football being passed
- Balls being juggled
- An athlete doing a high jump
- Water sprayed by a sprinkler
- A swimmer diving into water
- A leaping frog

Horizontal Motion When you throw a ball, your hand exerts a force on the ball that makes the ball move forward. This force gives the ball its horizontal motion. Horizontal motion is motion that is parallel to the ground.

After you let go of the ball, there are no horizontal forces acting on the ball (if you ignore air resistance). Therefore, there are no forces to change the ball's horizontal motion. Thus, the horizontal velocity of the ball is constant after the ball leaves your hand, as shown in Figure 9.

CONNECT TO LIFE SCIENCE

To launch itself into projectile motion, a bullfrog *(Rana catesbeiana)* uses its very large hind legs. Those hind legs can be up to 25 cm long, which is longer than the frog's body! Some people consider those hind legs quite tasty! The bullfrog is the largest frog in the United States.

internet connect

TOPIC: Projectile Motion
GO TO: www.scilinks.org
***sci*LINKS NUMBER:** HSTP140

3) Extend

RESEARCH

Have students research the effects that prolonged time in microgravity has on the bodies of astronauts and what doctors recommend the astronauts do to counteract these effects. Ask students to make a poster showing the results of their research.

4) Close

Quiz

1. Explain why a ball moves in a straight line as it rolls across a table but follows a curved path once it rolls off the edge of the table. (A ball rolling across the table has only horizontal motion; once the ball rolls off the edge, gravity pulls it downward, giving it both vertical and horizontal motion, which causes a curved path.)

2. Explain why results differ on the moon and on Earth when a hammer and a feather are dropped from the same height at exactly the same time. (On the moon, both will hit the ground at the same time because there is no atmosphere and no air resistance; on Earth, the hammer will hit the ground first because the feather will be slowed much more by air resistance.)

Teaching Transparency 223 "Two Motions Combine to Form Projectile Motion"

Section 1 • Gravity and Motion   143

4) Close, continued

ALTERNATIVE ASSESSMENT

Making Models Give each group some small, thin plastic trash bags; some string; tape; metal washers; a pair of scissors; and a stopwatch. Have each group design one or more parachutes. Have students use the parachutes to lower a washer slowly from a high point in the room. Challenge the groups to make the parachute that descends the slowest. How does the size and design of a parachute affect its rate of fall?

QuickLab

Make sure students have plenty of room. The penny in projectile motion may travel 1–2 m from its starting point. If the QuickLab is done in a room without a carpet, students can listen for the sound of the pennies hitting the floor.

Answer to QuickLab

3. The penny that was knocked off the table with the ruler was in projectile motion. The pennies should land at the same time because gravity gives both pennies the same acceleration downward. The horizontal motion does not affect the vertical motion.

A Marshmallow Catapult PG 652

Reinforcement Worksheet 6 "Falling Fast"

Interactive Explorations CD-ROM "Extreme Skiing"

QuickLab

Penny Projectile Motion

1. Position a **flat ruler** and **two pennies** on a desk or table as shown below.

2. Hold the ruler by the end that is on the desk. Move the ruler quickly in the direction shown so that the ruler knocks the penny off the table and so that the other penny also drops. Repeat several times.

3. Which penny travels with projectile motion? In what order do the pennies hit the ground? Record and explain your answers in your ScienceLog.

---

internetconnect

SC*i*LINKS
NSTA

TOPIC: The Force of Gravity, Projectile Motion
GO TO: www.scilinks.org
*sci*LINKS NUMBER: HSTP130, HSTP140

Vertical Motion After you throw a ball, gravity pulls it downward, giving the ball vertical motion. Vertical motion is motion that is perpendicular to the ground. Because objects in projectile motion accelerate downward, you always have to aim above a target if you want to hit it with a thrown or propelled object. That's why when you aim an arrow directly at a bull's-eye, your arrow strikes the bottom of the target rather than the middle.

Gravity pulls objects in projectile motion down with an acceleration of 9.8 m/s/s (if air resistance is ignored), just as it does all falling objects. **Figure 10** shows that the downward acceleration of a thrown object and a falling object are the same.

Figure 10 Projectile Motion and Acceleration Due to Gravity

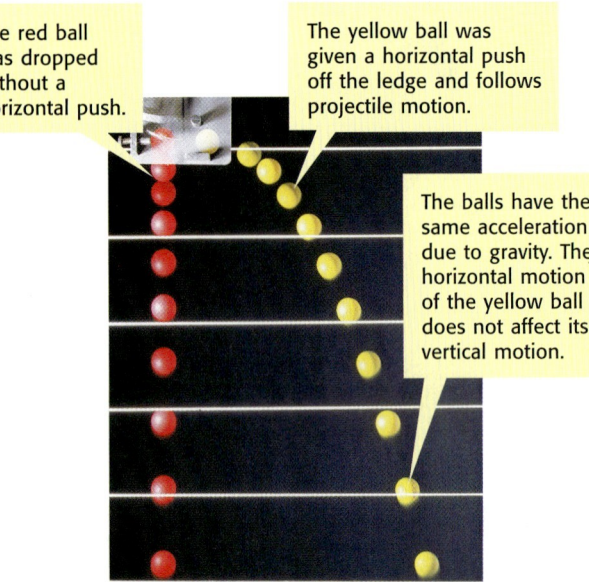

The red ball was dropped without a horizontal push.

The yellow ball was given a horizontal push off the ledge and follows projectile motion.

The balls have the same acceleration due to gravity. The horizontal motion of the yellow ball does not affect its vertical motion.

REVIEW

1. How does air resistance affect the acceleration of falling objects?
2. Explain why an astronaut in an orbiting spaceship floats.
3. How is an orbit formed?
4. **Applying Concepts** Think about a sport you play that involves a ball. Identify at least four different instances in which an object is in projectile motion.

Answers to Review

1. Air resistance slows or stops acceleration of falling objects.

2. An astronaut on an orbiting spaceship floats because both the astronaut and the spaceship are in free fall. Since both fall at the same rate, the astronaut floats inside. The astronaut has no sensation of falling.

3. An orbit is formed by combining two motions: a forward motion and free fall toward Earth. The path that results is a curve that matches the curve of Earth's surface.

4. Accept all reasonable answers. A basketball example: a player jumping to dunk the ball; a ball passed from one player to another; a ball shot toward the basket; a ball bounced on the floor.

Chapter 6 • Forces in Motion

Newton's Laws of Motion

Section 2

Terms to Learn

inertia   momentum

What You'll Do

- State and apply Newton's laws of motion.
- Compare the momentum of different objects.
- State and apply the law of conservation of momentum.

In 1686, Sir Isaac Newton published his book *Principia*. In it, he described three laws that relate forces to the motion of objects. Although he did not discover all three of the laws, he explained them in a way that helped many people understand them. Thus, the three laws are commonly known as Newton's laws of motion. In this section, you will learn about these laws and how they influence the motion of objects.

Newton's First Law of Motion

An object at rest remains at rest and an object in motion remains in motion at constant speed and in a straight line unless acted on by an unbalanced force.

Newton's first law of motion describes the motion of an object that has a net force of zero acting on it. This law may seem complicated when you first read it, but it's easy to understand when you consider its two parts separately.

Part 1: Objects at Rest What does it mean for an object to be at rest? Objects don't get tired! An object that is not moving is said to be at rest. Objects are at rest all around you. A plane parked on a runway, a chair on the floor, and a golf ball balanced on a tee are all examples of objects at rest.

Newton's first law says that objects at rest will remain at rest unless they are acted on by an unbalanced force. That means that objects will not start moving until a push or a pull is exerted on them. A plane won't soar in the air unless it is pushed by the exhaust from its jet engines, a chair won't slide across the room unless you push it, and a golf ball won't move off the tee unless struck by a golf club, as shown in **Figure 11**.

Figure 11 A golf ball will remain at rest on a tee until it is acted on by the unbalanced force of a moving club.

CROSS-DISCIPLINARY FOCUS

History Long before Newton, others had observed relationships between forces and motion, rest, and acceleration. When Newton extended their work with his three laws of motion, he said, "If I have seen further, it is by standing on the shoulders of Giants." Newton's genius was that he combined previous discoveries plus his own observations into a unified picture of how the universe worked.

2 Teach

REAL-WORLD CONNECTION

A tractor trailer will often jackknife on an icy road when the driver suddenly applies the brakes. The brakes are applied to the tractor wheels and the front part of the rig (the tractor) stops. However, the back half (the trailer) skids and continues moving in accordance with Newton's first law, causing the rig to jackknife. Ask students to speculate on how jackknife accidents might be prevented.

GUIDED PRACTICE

Have students prepare one list of situations in which people would want to avoid friction and another list of situations in which friction is helpful. (List 1: opening windows, attaining high speeds, and so on; List 2: walking, braking a car or bicycle, and so on)

Answer to APPLY

Students should notice that the dummy's head hit the steering wheel even when it was wearing a seat belt. Newton's first law says that an object in motion tends to stay in motion unless it is acted on by an unbalanced force. Thus, when the car is stopped in the collision, the dummy's body continues in motion until it is stopped by the seat belt. But the dummy's head *still* stays in motion because there is no unbalanced force—such as that from an air bag—to stop its motion.

a An unbalanced force from another car acts on your car, changing its motion.

b The collision changes your car's motion, but not yours. Your motion continues with the same velocity.

c Another unbalanced force, from your seat belt, changes your motion.

Figure 12 Bumper cars let you have fun with Newton's first law.

Part 2: Objects in Motion

Think about riding in a bumper car at an amusement park. Your ride is pleasant as long as you are driving in an open space. But the name of the game is bumper cars, so sooner or later you are likely to run into another car, as shown in **Figure 12**.

The second part of Newton's first law explains that an object moving at a certain velocity will continue to move *forever* at the same speed and in the same direction unless some unbalanced force acts on it. Thus, your bumper car stops, but you continue to move forward until your seat belt stops you.

Friction and Newton's First Law Because an object in motion will stay in motion forever unless it is acted on by an unbalanced force, you should be able to give your desk a small push and send it sailing across the floor. If you try it, you will find that the desk quickly comes to a stop. What does this tell you?

There must be an unbalanced force that acts on the desk to stop its motion. That unbalanced force is friction. The friction between the desk and the floor works against the motion of the desk. Because of friction, it is often difficult to observe the effects of Newton's first law on the motion of everyday objects. For example, friction will cause a ball rolling on grass to slow down and stop. Friction will also make a car decelerate on a flat surface if the driver lets up on the gas pedal. Because of friction, the motion of these objects changes.

Stopping Motion

The dummy in this crash test is wearing a seat belt, but the car does not have an air bag. Explain why Newton's first law of motion could lead to serious injuries in accidents involving cars without air bags.

Blast Off! PG 653

IS THAT A FACT!

Antilock braking systems (ABS) controlled by a computer prevent skidding by sensing when the wheels are about to lock. They release and reapply the brakes up to 25 times a second. Instead of skidding out of control, the car slows down and stops safely.

146 Chapter 6 • Forces in Motion

Inertia Is Related to Mass Newton's first law of motion is sometimes called the law of inertia. **Inertia** (in UHR shuh) is the tendency of all objects to resist any change in motion. Due to inertia, an object at rest will remain at rest until something makes it move. Likewise, inertia is why a moving object stays in motion with the same velocity unless a force acts on it to change its speed or direction. Inertia causes you to slide toward the side of a car when the driver makes a sharp turn. Inertia is also why it is impossible for a plane, car, or bicycle to stop instantaneously.

Mass Is a Measure of Inertia An object with a small mass has less inertia than an object with a large mass. Therefore, it is easier to start and to change the motion of an object with a small mass. For example, a softball has less mass and therefore less inertia than a bowling ball. Because the softball has a small amount of inertia, it is easy to pitch a softball and to change its motion by hitting it with a bat. Imagine how difficult it would be to play softball with a bowling ball! **Figure 13** further illustrates the relationship between mass and inertia. Try the QuickLab at right to test the relationship yourself.

Figure 13 *Inertia makes it harder to push a car than to push a bicycle. Inertia also makes it easier to stop a moving bicycle than a car moving at the same speed.*

QuickLab

First-Law Magic

1. On a table or desk, place a **large, empty plastic cup** on top of a **paper towel**.
2. Without touching the cup or tipping it over, remove the paper towel from under the cup. What did you do to accomplish this?
3. Repeat the first two steps a few times until you are comfortable with the procedure.
4. Fill the cup half full with **water,** and place the cup on the paper towel.
5. Once again, remove the paper towel from under the cup. Was it easier or harder to do this? Explain your answer in terms of mass and inertia.

Self-Check

When you stand while riding a bus, why do you tend to fall backward when the bus starts moving?
(See page 724 to check your answer.)

Inertia-Rama!

2 Teach, continued

READING STRATEGY

Prediction Guide Before students read pages 148 and 149, have them read Newton's second law of motion. Without reading further in the section, have them try to explain the second law in their own words. They might suggest activities or draw diagrams to demonstrate how the second law works. Accept all responses. After reading the section, discuss with the class some of their activities and diagrams.

RETEACHING

When you introduce the equation for Newton's second law, point out to students that acceleration and force are directly proportional (i.e., as force increases, acceleration increases) and that acceleration and mass are inversely proportional (i.e., as mass increases, acceleration decreases). These relationships are explained qualitatively, but students may not see the connection on their own.

- 1 newton = 1 kilogram-meter per second per second
   OR
   1 N = 1 kg•m/s/s

This is important for helping students through the unit cancellation in the MathBreak and in **Figure 16**. Sheltered English

TOPIC: Newton's Laws of Motion
GO TO: www.scilinks.org
sciLINKS NUMBER: HSTP145

Environment CONNECTION

Modern cars pollute the air less than older cars. One reason for this is that modern cars are less massive than older models and have considerably smaller engines. According to Newton's second law, a less massive object requires less force to achieve the same acceleration as a more massive object. This is why a smaller car can have a smaller engine and still have acceptable acceleration. And because smaller engines use less fuel, they pollute less.

Newton's Second Law of Motion

The acceleration of an object depends on the mass of the object and the amount of force applied.

Newton's second law describes the motion of an object when an unbalanced force is acting on it. As with Newton's first law, it is easier to consider the parts of this law separately.

Part 1: Acceleration Depends on Mass Suppose you are pushing a shopping cart at the grocery store. At the beginning of your shopping trip, you have to exert only a small force on the cart to accelerate it. But when the cart is full, the same amount of force will not accelerate the cart as much as before, as shown in **Figure 14**. This example illustrates that for the same force, an object's acceleration *decreases* as its mass *increases* and its acceleration *increases* as its mass *decreases*.

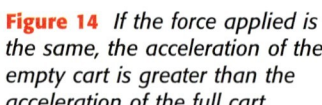

Figure 14 *If the force applied is the same, the acceleration of the empty cart is greater than the acceleration of the full cart.*

Part 2: Acceleration Depends on Force Now suppose you give the shopping cart a hard push, as shown in **Figure 15**. The cart will start moving faster than if you only gave it a soft push. This illustrates that an object's acceleration *increases* as the force on it *increases*. Conversely, an object's acceleration *decreases* as the force on it *decreases*.

The acceleration of an object is always in the same direction as the force applied. The shopping cart moved forward because the push was in the forward direction. To change the direction of an object, you must exert a force in the direction you want the object to go.

Figure 15 *Acceleration will increase when a larger force is exerted.*

There once was a trucker from Nome,
Whose rig was loaded with foam.
Its very small mass
Made him able to pass
The other trucks all the way home.

148 Chapter 6 • Forces in Motion

Expressing Newton's Second Law Mathematically The relationship of acceleration (*a*) to mass (*m*) and force (*F*) can be expressed mathematically with the following equation:

$$a = \frac{F}{m}$$

This equation is often rearranged to the following form:

$$F = m \times a$$

Both forms of the equation can be used to solve problems. Try the MathBreak at right to practice using the equations. Newton's second law explains why objects fall to Earth with the same acceleration. In **Figure 16,** you can see how the larger weight of the watermelon is offset by its greater inertia. Thus, the accelerations of the watermelon and the apple are the same when you put the numbers into the equation for acceleration.

Figure 16 Newton's Second Law and Acceleration Due to Gravity

The **apple** has less mass, so the gravitational force on it is smaller. However, the apple also has less inertia and is easier to move.

The **watermelon** has more mass and therefore more inertia, so it is harder to move.

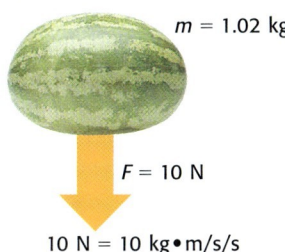

$m = 0.102$ kg

$F = 1$ N

1 N $= 1$ kg•m/s/s

$$a = \frac{1 \text{ kg•m/s/s}}{0.102 \text{ kg}} = 9.8 \text{ m/s/s}$$

$m = 1.02$ kg

$F = 10$ N

10 N $= 10$ kg•m/s/s

$$a = \frac{10 \text{ kg•m/s/s}}{1.02 \text{ kg}} = 9.8 \text{ m/s/s}$$

MATH BREAK

Second-Law Problems

You can rearrange the equation $F = m \times a$ to find acceleration and mass as shown below.

$$a = \frac{F}{m} \qquad m = \frac{F}{a}$$

1. What is the acceleration of a 7 kg mass if a force of 68.6 N is used to move it toward Earth? (Hint: 1 N is equal to 1 kg•m/s/s.)
2. What force is necessary to accelerate a 1,250 kg car at a rate of 40 m/s/s?
3. What is the mass of an object if a force of 34 N produces an acceleration of 4 m/s/s?

REVIEW

1. How is inertia related to Newton's first law of motion?
2. Name two ways to increase the acceleration of an object.
3. **Making Predictions** If the acceleration due to gravity were somehow doubled to 19.6 m/s/s, what would happen to your weight?

internetconnect

TOPIC: Newton's Laws of Motion
GO TO: www.scilinks.org
***sci*LINKS NUMBER:** HSTP145

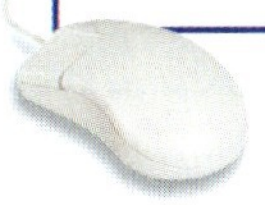

Newton's Third Law of Motion

Whenever one object exerts a force on a second object, the second object exerts an equal and opposite force on the first.

Newton's third law can be simply stated as follows: All forces act in pairs. If a force is exerted, another force occurs that is equal in size and opposite in direction. The law itself addresses only forces. But the way that force pairs interact affects the motion of objects.

What is meant by "forces act in pairs"? Study **Figure 17** to learn how one force pair helps propel a swimmer through water.

Figure 17 The action force and reaction force are a pair. The two forces are equal in size but opposite in direction.

The **action force** is the swimmer's hands and feet pushing on the water.

The **reaction force** is the water pushing on the hands and feet. The reaction force moves the swimmer forward.

Action and reaction force pairs occur even when there is no motion. For example, you exert a force on a chair when you sit on it. Your weight pushing down on the chair is the action force. The reaction force is the force exerted by the chair that pushes up on your body and is equal to your weight.

Force Pairs Do Not Act on the Same Object You know that a force is always exerted by one object on another object. This is true for all forces, including action and reaction forces. However, it is important to remember that action and reaction forces in a pair do not act on the same object. If they did, the net force would always be zero and nothing would ever move! To understand this better, look back at Figure 17. In this example, the action force was exerted on the water by the swimmer's hands and feet. But the reaction force was exerted on the swimmer's hands and feet by the water. The forces did not act on the same object.

Activity

Choose a sport that you enjoy playing or watching. In your ScienceLog, list five ways that Newton's laws of motion are involved in the game you selected. **TRY at HOME**

The Effect of a Reaction Can Be Difficult to See Another example of a force pair is shown in **Figure 18.** Remember, gravity is a force of attraction between objects that is due to their masses. If you drop a ball off a ledge, the force of gravity pulls the ball toward Earth. This is the action force exerted by Earth on the ball. But the force of gravity also pulls Earth toward the ball. That is the reaction force exerted by the ball on Earth.

It's easy to see the effect of the action force—the ball falls to Earth. Why don't you notice the effect of the reaction force—Earth being pulled upward? To find the answer to this question, think back to Newton's second law. It states that the acceleration of an object depends on the force applied to it and on the mass of the object. The force on Earth is equal to the force on the ball, but the mass of Earth is much *larger* than the mass of the ball. Therefore, the acceleration of Earth is much *smaller* than the acceleration of the ball. The acceleration is so small that you can't even see it or feel it. Thus, it is difficult to observe the effect of Newton's third law on falling objects.

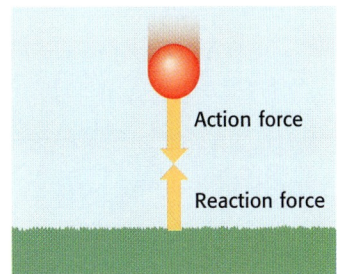

Figure 18 *The force of gravity between Earth and a falling object is a force pair.*

More Examples of Action and Reaction Force Pairs The examples below illustrate a variety of action and reaction force pairs. In each example, notice which object exerts the action force and which object exerts the reaction force.

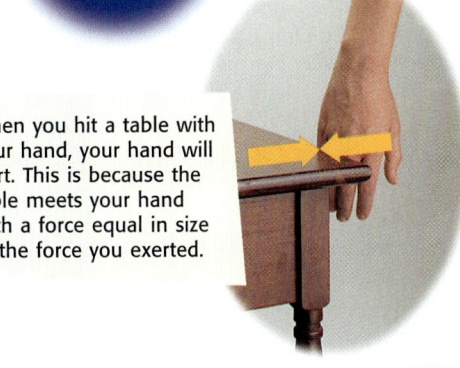

The rabbit's legs exert a force on Earth. Earth exerts an equal force on the rabbit's legs, causing the rabbit to accelerate upward.

The bat exerts a force on the ball, sending the ball into the outfield. The ball exerts an equal force on the bat, but the bat does not fly toward the catcher because the batter is exerting another force on the bat.

The shuttle's thrusters push the exhaust gases downward as the gases push the shuttle upward with an equal force.

When you hit a table with your hand, your hand will hurt. This is because the table meets your hand with a force equal in size to the force you exerted.

Homework

 **Poster Project** Ask students to find several magazine pictures of sporting events. Have students identify the action-reaction force pairs in each picture. Sheltered English

USING THE FIGURE

Study **Figures 17** and **18** with students. Be sure they understand that in any force pair, the distinction between the action and reaction force is totally arbitrary. It doesn't matter which force we call the *action* and which force we call the *reaction*.

REAL-WORLD CONNECTION

Heavy artillery has been used in warfare for hundreds of years. Newton's third law explains that when a shell is fired from a large artillery piece, the force opposite to that which propels the shell forward causes the gun to recoil, or move backward. Because the mass of the gun is so much greater than the mass of the shell, the shell moves forward with a far greater velocity than the gun moves backward. This same law applies to the human cannonball at the circus!

Multicultural CONNECTION

The Chinese invented gunpowder in the tenth century and used it in rockets for fireworks used for celebrations. These rockets were later adapted to warfare. In the thirteenth century Chinese armies launched rockets over enemy troops. In the twentieth century, rockets took humans into space and robots to other planets.

Section 2 • Newton's Laws of Motion

3) Extend

GOING FURTHER

The momentum (*p*) of an object can be found by multiplying its mass (*m*) times its velocity (*v*), as in the following equation:

$$p = m \times v$$

The units of momentum are kilogram meters per second. Have students find the momentum of an 80 kg basketball player driving to the basket with a constant velocity of 8 m/s. **(640 kg•m/s to the basket)**

Ask students to predict what will happen if the player collides with another player whose mass is 100 kg but whose velocity is 0 m/s.

USING THE FIGURE

Teacher Notes: The momentum arrows, or vectors, in **Figures 19** and **20** do not represent forces. Momentum, like force, is a vector quantity and can therefore be shown with arrows.

Critical Thinking Worksheet 6
"Forces to Reckon With"

Math Skills Worksheet 49
"Momentum"

152   Chapter 6 • Forces in Motion

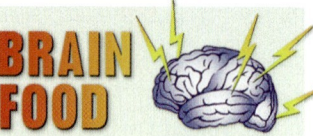

Jumping beans appear to leap into the air with no forces acting on them. However, inside each bean is a small insect larva. When the larva moves suddenly, it applies a force to the shell of the bean. The momentum of the larva is transferred to the bean, and the bean "jumps."

Figure 19 *The momentum before a collision is equal to the momentum after the collision.*

Homework

Concept Mapping Ask students to create a concept map using Newton's three laws and momentum to explain how seat belts and air bags protect passengers.

Momentum Is a Property of Moving Objects

If a compact car and a large truck are traveling with the same velocity, it takes longer for the truck to stop than it does for the car if the same braking force is applied. Likewise, it takes longer for a fast moving car to stop than it does for a slow moving car with the same mass. The truck and the fast moving car have more momentum than the compact car and the slow moving car.

Momentum is a property of a moving object that depends on the object's mass and velocity. The more momentum an object has, the harder it is to stop the object or change its direction. Although the compact car and the truck are traveling with the same velocity, the truck has more mass and therefore more momentum, so it is harder to stop than the car. Similarly, the fast moving car has a greater velocity and thus more momentum than the slow moving car.

Momentum Is Conserved When a moving object hits another object, some or all of the momentum of the first object is transferred to the other object. If only some of the momentum is transferred, the rest of the momentum stays with the first object.

Imagine you hit a billiard ball with a cue ball so that the billiard ball starts moving and the cue ball stops, as shown in **Figure 19**. The cue ball had a certain amount of momentum before the collision. During the collision, all of the cue ball's momentum was transferred to the billiard ball. After the collision, the billiard ball moved away with the same amount of momentum the cue ball had. This example illustrates the *law of conservation of momentum*. Any time two or more objects interact, they may exchange momentum, but the total amount of momentum stays the same.

IS THAT A FACT!

Edmond Halley used Newton's ideas to predict that a comet seen in 1531, 1607, and 1682, would return in 1758. When the comet returned as predicted, it became known as Halley's comet. It last appeared in 1986. When will the comet appear again? **(2061)**

Bowling is another example of how conservation of momentum is used in a game. The bowling ball rolls down the lane with a certain amount of momentum. When the ball hits the pins, some of the ball's momentum is transferred to the pins and the pins move off in different directions. Furthermore, some of the pins that were hit by the ball go on to hit other pins, transferring the momentum again.

Conservation of Momentum and Newton's Third Law

Conservation of momentum can be explained by Newton's third law. In the example with the billiard ball, the cue ball hit the billiard ball with a certain amount of force. This was the action force. The reaction force was the equal but opposite force exerted by the billiard ball on the cue ball. The action force made the billiard ball start moving, and the reaction force made the cue ball stop moving, as shown in **Figure 20.** Because the action and reaction forces are equal and opposite, momentum is conserved.

Figure 20 *The action force makes the billiard ball begin moving, and the reaction force stops the cue ball's motion.*

REVIEW

1. Name three action and reaction force pairs involved in doing your homework. Name what object is exerting and what object is receiving the forces.

2. Which has more momentum, a mouse running at 1 m/s north or an elephant walking at 3 m/s east? Explain your answer.

3. **Applying Concepts** When a truck pulls a trailer, the trailer and truck accelerate forward even though the action and reaction forces are the same size but in opposite directions. Why don't these forces balance each other out?

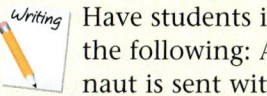

Catapult forward! Or is it backward? Find out on page 656 of the LabBook.

Chapter Highlights

VOCABULARY DEFINITIONS

SECTION 1

terminal velocity the constant velocity of a falling object when the size of the upward force of air resistance matches the size of the downward force of gravity

free fall the condition an object is in when gravity is the only force acting on it

projectile motion the curved path an object follows when thrown or propelled near the surface of Earth

Chapter Highlights

SECTION 1

Vocabulary
- terminal velocity (p. 140)
- free fall (p. 141)
- projectile motion (p. 143)

Section Notes
- All objects accelerate toward Earth at 9.8 m/s/s.
- Air resistance slows the acceleration of falling objects.
- An object is in free fall if gravity is the only force acting on it.
- An orbit is formed by combining forward motion and free fall.
- Objects in orbit appear to be weightless because they are in free fall.
- A centripetal force is needed to keep objects in circular motion. Gravity acts as a centripetal force to keep objects in orbit.
- Projectile motion is the curved path an object follows when thrown or propelled near the surface of Earth.
- Projectile motion has two components—horizontal and vertical. Gravity affects only the vertical motion of projectile motion.

Labs
A Marshmallow Catapult (p. 652)

✓ Skills Check

Math Concepts

NEWTON'S SECOND LAW The equation $a = F/m$ on page 149 summarizes Newton's second law of motion. The equation shows the relationship between the acceleration of an object, the force causing the acceleration, and the object's mass. For example, if you apply a force of 18 N to a 6 kg object, the object's acceleration is

$$a = \frac{F}{m} = \frac{18 \text{ N}}{6 \text{ kg}} = \frac{18 \text{ kg} \cdot \text{m/s/s}}{6 \text{ kg}} = 3 \text{ m/s/s}$$

Visual Understanding

HOW AN ORBIT IS FORMED An orbit is a combination of two motions—forward motion and free fall. Figure 7 on page 142 shows how the two motions combine to form an orbit.

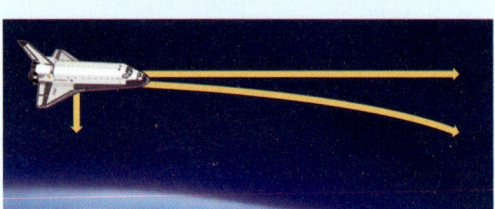

Lab and Activity Highlights

A Marshmallow Catapult **PG 652**

Blast Off! **PG 653**

Inertia-Rama! **PG 654**

Quite a Reaction **PG 656**

 Datasheets for LabBook (blackline masters for these labs)

SECTION 2

Vocabulary
- inertia *(p. 147)*
- momentum *(p. 152)*

Section Notes
- Newton's first law of motion states that the motion of an object will not change if no unbalanced forces act on it.
- Inertia is the tendency of matter to resist a change in motion. Mass is a measure of inertia.
- Newton's second law of motion states that the acceleration of an object depends on its mass and on the force exerted on it.
- Newton's third law of motion states that whenever one object exerts a force on a second object, the second object exerts an equal and opposite force on the first.
- Momentum is the property of a moving object that depends on its mass and velocity.
- When two or more objects interact, momentum may be exchanged, but the total amount of momentum does not change. This is the law of conservation of momentum.

Labs
- Blast Off! *(p. 653)*
- Inertia-Rama! *(p. 654)*
- Quite a Reaction *(p. 656)*

VOCABULARY DEFINITIONS, continued

SECTION 2

inertia the tendency of all objects to resist any change in motion

momentum a property of a moving object that depends on the object's mass and velocity

 Vocabulary Review Worksheet 6

 Blackline masters of these Chapter Highlights can be found in the **Study Guide.**

---

internet connect

GO TO: go.hrw.com

Visit the **HRW** Web site for a variety of learning tools related to this chapter. Just type in the keyword:

KEYWORD: HSTFOR

GO TO: www.scilinks.org

Visit the **National Science Teachers Association** on-line Web site for Internet resources related to this chapter. Just type in the *sci*LINKS number for more information about the topic:

TOPIC:	The Force of Gravity	*sci*LINKS NUMBER:	HSTP130
TOPIC:	Gravity and Orbiting Objects	*sci*LINKS NUMBER:	HSTP135
TOPIC:	Projectile Motion	*sci*LINKS NUMBER:	HSTP140
TOPIC:	Newton's Laws of Motion	*sci*LINKS NUMBER:	HSTP145

Lab and Activity Highlights

LabBank

 Inquiry Labs, On the Fast Track, Lab 18

Whiz-Bang Demonstrations,
- Newton's Eggciting Experiment, Demo 43
- Inertia Can Hurt Ya, Demo 44
- Fountain of Knowledge, Demo 45

 Long-Term Projects & Research Ideas, "Any Color You Want, so Long as It's Black", Project 56

Interactive Explorations CD-ROM

 CD 2, Exploration 5, "Extreme Skiing"

Chapter Review

USING VOCABULARY

To complete the following sentences, choose the correct term from each pair of terms listed below:

1. An object in motion tends to stay in motion because it has ___?___. (*inertia* or *terminal velocity*)

2. Falling objects stop accelerating at ___?___. (*free fall* or *terminal velocity*)

3. ___?___ is the path that a thrown object follows. (*Free fall* or *Projectile motion*)

4. A property of moving objects that depends on mass and velocity is ___?___. (*inertia* or *momentum*)

5. ___?___ only occurs when there is no air resistance. (*Momentum* or *Free fall*)

UNDERSTANDING CONCEPTS

Multiple Choice

6. A feather and a rock dropped at the same time from the same height would land at the same time when dropped by
   a. Galileo in Italy.
   b. Newton in England.
   c. an astronaut on the moon.
   d. an astronaut on the space shuttle.

7. When a soccer ball is kicked, the action and reaction forces do not cancel each other out because
   a. the force of the foot on the ball is bigger than the force of the ball on the foot.
   b. the forces act on two different objects.
   c. the forces act at different times.
   d. All of the above

8. An object is in projectile motion if
   a. it is thrown with a horizontal push.
   b. it is accelerated downward by gravity.
   c. it does not accelerate horizontally.
   d. All of the above

9. Newton's first law of motion applies
   a. to moving objects.
   b. to objects that are not moving.
   c. to objects that are accelerating.
   d. Both (a) and (b)

10. Acceleration of an object
    a. decreases as the mass of the object increases.
    b. increases as the force on the object increases.
    c. is in the same direction as the force on the object.
    d. All of the above

11. A golf ball and a bowling ball are moving at the same velocity. Which has more momentum?
    a. the golf ball, because it has less mass
    b. the bowling ball, because it has more mass
    c. They both have the same momentum because they have the same velocity.
    d. There is no way to know without additional information.

Short Answer

12. Explain how an orbit is formed.

13. Describe how gravity and air resistance combine when an object reaches terminal velocity.

14. Explain why friction can make observing Newton's first law of motion difficult.

156   Chapter 6 • Forces in Motion

Concept Mapping

15. Use the following terms to create a concept map: gravity, free fall, terminal velocity, projectile motion, air resistance.

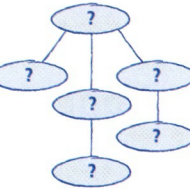

CRITICAL THINKING AND PROBLEM SOLVING

16. During a shuttle launch, about 830,000 kg of fuel is burned in 8 minutes. The fuel provides the shuttle with a constant thrust, or push off the ground. How does Newton's second law of motion explain why the shuttle's acceleration increases during takeoff?

17. When using a hammer to drive a nail into wood, you have to swing the hammer through the air with a certain velocity. Because the hammer has both mass and velocity, it has momentum. Describe what happens to the hammer's momentum after the hammer hits the nail.

18. Suppose you are standing on a skateboard or on in-line skates and you toss a backpack full of heavy books toward your friend. What do you think will happen to you and why? Explain your answer in terms of Newton's third law of motion.

MATH IN SCIENCE

19. A 12 kg rock falls from rest off a cliff and hits the ground in 1.5 seconds.
    a. Ignoring air resistance, what is the rock's velocity just before it hits the ground?
    b. What is the rock's weight after it hits the ground? (Hint: Weight is a measure of the gravitational force on an object.)

INTERPRETING GRAPHICS

20. The picture below shows a common desk toy. If you pull one ball up and release it, it hits the balls at the bottom and comes to a stop. In the same instant, the ball on the other side swings up and repeats the cycle. How does conservation of momentum explain how this toy works?

NOW What Do You Think?

Take a minute to review your answers to the ScienceLog questions on page 137. Have your answers changed? If necessary, revise your answers based on what you have learned since you began this chapter.

CRITICAL THINKING AND PROBLEM SOLVING

16. Newton's second law: $a = F/m$. During takeoff, the shuttle burns fuel and therefore loses mass. However, the upward force on the shuttle remains the same. So the shuttle's acceleration increases because its mass constantly gets smaller during takeoff.

17. When the hammer hits the nail, the hammer stops. Its momentum is transferred to the nail, driving it into the wood. Momentum is also transferred from the nail to the wood and to the work bench or table top.

18. You will move away from your friend (in the direction opposite from where you throw the backpack). The action force is you pushing the backpack toward your friend. The reaction force is the backpack pushing you away from your friend.

MATH IN SCIENCE

19. a. $\Delta v = g \times t = 9.8$ m/s/s $\times$ 1.5 s = 14.7 m/s
    b. $F = m \times a$ = 12 kg $\times$ 9.8 m/s/s = 117.6 N

20. The law of conservation of momentum: when two or more objects interact, the total amount of momentum must stay the same. The ball moving in the air has a certain amount of momentum, and the balls at rest have no momentum. When the moving ball hits the balls at rest, all of its momentum is transferred to them, and it comes to a stop. The momentum is transferred from ball to ball until it reaches the ball on the other end. The ball on the other end keeps all the momentum, and it moves away from the other balls.

NOW WHAT DO YOU THINK?

1. The force of gravity causes all objects to fall toward the ground with the same acceleration, 9.8 m/s/s.
2. Projectile motion is the curved path an object follows when it is thrown or propelled near the surface of the Earth. Good examples are a leaping frog or a pass in a football game.
3. Newton's three laws of motion are physical laws that explain the relationship of forces to the motion of objects. For complete statements of Newton's laws, refer to the explanations on pages 145, 148, and 150.
4. Momentum is a property of a moving object that is related to the object's mass and velocity. The more momentum an object has, the harder it is to stop the object or change its direction.

 Blackline masters of this Chapter Review can be found in the **Study Guide**.

Eureka!

A Bat with Dimples

Wouldn't it be nice to hit a home run every time? Jeff DiTullio, a teacher at MIT, in Cambridge, Massachusetts, has found a way for you to get more bang from your bat. Would you believe *dimples*?

Building a Better Bat

If you look closely at the surface of a golf ball, you'll see dozens of tiny craterlike dimples. When air flows past these dimples, it gets stirred up. By keeping air moving near the surface of the ball, the dimples help the golf ball move faster and farther through the air.

DiTullio decided to apply this same idea to a baseball bat. His hypothesis was that dimples would allow a bat to move more easily through the air. This would help batters swing the bat faster and hit the ball harder. To test his hypothesis, DiTullio pressed hundreds of little dimples about 1 mm deep and 2 mm across into the surface of a bat.

When DiTullio tested his dimpled bat in a wind tunnel, he found that it could be swung 3 to 5 percent faster. That may not sound like much, but it could add about 5 m to a fly ball!

Safe . . . or Out?

As you might imagine, many baseball players would love to have a bat that could turn a long fly ball into a home run. But are dimpled baseball bats legal?

The size and shape of every piece of equipment used in Major League Baseball games are regulated. A baseball bat, for instance, must be no more than 107 cm long and no more than 7 cm across at its widest point. When DiTullio designed his dimpled bat, there was no rule stating that bats had to be smooth. But when Major League Baseball found out about the new bat, they changed the rules! Today official rules require that all bats be smooth, and they prohibit any type of "experimental" bat. Someday the rules may be revised to allow DiTullio's dimpled bat. When that happens, fans of the dimpled baseball bat will all shout, "Play ball!"

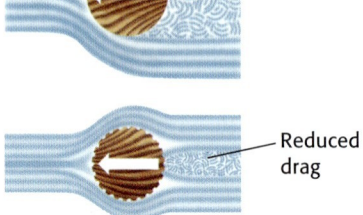

▲ *By reducing the amount of drag behind the bat, dimples help the bat move faster through the air.*

Dimple Madness

▶ Now that you know how dimples can improve baseball bats, think of other uses for dimples. How might dimples improve the way other objects move through the air? Draw a sketch of a dimpled object, and describe how the dimples improve the design.

▶ *Jeff DiTullio, pictured with his dimpled baseball bat, is an aeronautical engineer—someone who studies both the way air moves and the way things move through air.*

CAREERS

CAREERS
Roller Coaster Designer—Steve Okamoto

ROLLER COASTER DESIGNER

Roller coasters have fascinated **Steve Okamoto** ever since his first ride on one. "I remember going to Disneyland as a kid. My mother was always upset with me because I kept looking over the sides of the rides, trying to figure out how they worked," he laughs. To satisfy his curiosity, Okamoto became a mechanical engineer. Today he uses his scientific knowledge to design and build machines, systems, and buildings. But his specialty is roller coasters.

His West Coaster, which sits on the Santa Monica pier in Santa Monica, California, towers five stories above the Pacific Ocean. The cars on the Steel Force, at Dorney Park, in Pennsylvania, reach speeds of over 120 km/h and drop more than 60 m to disappear into a 37 m long tunnel. The Mamba, at Worlds of Fun, in Missouri, sends cars flying along as high and as fast as the Steel Force does, but it also has two giant back-to-back hills, a fast spiral, and five "camelback" humps. The camelbacks are designed to pull riders' seats out from under them, giving the riders "air time."

Coaster Motion
Roller-coaster cars really do coast along the track. A motor pulls the cars up a high hill to start the ride. After that, the cars are powered by gravity alone. As the cars roll downhill, they pick up enough speed to whiz through the rest of the curves, loops, twists, and bumps in the track.

Designing a successful coaster is no simple task. Steve Okamoto has to calculate the cars' speed and acceleration on each part of the track. "The coaster has to go fast enough to make it up the next hill," he explains. Okamoto uses his knowledge of geometry and physics to create safe but scary curves, loops, humps, and dips. Okamoto must also keep in mind that the ride's towers and structures need to be strong enough to support both the track and the speeding cars full of people. The cars themselves need special wheels to keep them locked onto the track and seat belts or bars to keep passengers safely inside. "It's like putting together a puzzle, except the pieces haven't been cut out yet," says Okamoto.

Take the Challenge
▶ Step outside for a moment. Gather some rope and a medium-sized plastic bucket half-full of water. Can you get the bucket over your head and upside down without any water escaping? How does this relate to roller coasters?

▲ *The Wild Thing, in Shakopee, Minnesota, was designed by Steve Okamoto.*

Background
Steve Okamoto has a degree in product design. He studied not only mechanical engineering but also studio art. Product designers consider an object's form as well as its function and take into account the interests and abilities of the product's consumer.

Two of Okamoto's first coasters were the Ninjas at Six Flags Over Mid-America, in St. Louis, Missouri, and Six Flags Magic Mountain, in Los Angeles, California.

When designing a ride, Okamoto studies site maps of the location, then goes to the amusement park to look at the actual site. Since most rides he designs are for older parks, fitting a coaster around, above, and between existing rides and buildings is one of his biggest challenges. Most rides and parks also have some kind of theme, so marketing goals and concerns figure into his designs as well. (As an example, the *Mamba* is named for one of the fastest snakes in Africa and is designed around this theme.)

Sample Answer to Take the Challenge
The water is falling down to Earth due to gravity. But if the bucket (and thus the water in it) is moving fast enough, the water's forward motion will combine with its downward motion to produce a path similar to an orbit. By the time the water falls down far enough to hit the ground, the bucket is already underneath it. The loop-the-loop in a roller coaster relies on a similar principle.

Chapter Organizer

CHAPTER ORGANIZATION	TIME MINUTES	OBJECTIVES	LABS, INVESTIGATIONS, AND DEMONSTRATIONS
Chapter Opener pp. 160–161	45	National Standards: SAI 1, 2, ST 2	**Investigate!** Out the Spouts, p. 161
Section 1 Fluids and Pressure	90	▶ Describe how fluids exert pressure. ▶ Analyze how fluid depth affects pressure. ▶ Give examples of fluids flowing from high to low pressure. ▶ State and apply Pascal's principle. SAI 1, 2, ST 2	**Demonstration,** p. 163 in ATE **QuickLab,** Blown Away, p. 166 **Whiz-Bang Demonstrations,** The Rise and Fall of Raisins, Demo 46 **Whiz-Bang Demonstrations,** Going Against the Flow, Demo 47
Section 2 Buoyant Force	90	▶ Explain the relationship between fluid pressure and buoyant force. ▶ Predict whether an object will float or sink in a fluid. ▶ Analyze the role of density in an object's ability to float. UCP 4, ST 2; LabBook SAI 1	**Demonstration,** p. 168 in ATE **QuickLab,** Ship-Shape, p. 171 **Interactive Explorations CD-ROM,** Sea the Light A **Worksheet** is also available in the **Interactive Explorations Teacher's Edition.** **Skill Builder,** Fluids, Force, and Floating, p. 658 **Datasheets for LabBook,** Fluids, Force, and Floating, Datasheet 24 **Discovery Lab,** Density Diver, p. 660 **Datasheets for LabBook,** Density Diver, Datasheet 25
Section 3 Bernoulli's Principle	135	▶ Describe the relationship between pressure and fluid speed. ▶ Analyze the roles of lift, thrust, and drag in flight. ▶ Give examples of Bernoulli's principle in real-life situations. UCP 2, 5, SAI 1, ST 2; LabBook UCP 5, SAI 1	**QuickLab,** Breathing Bernoulli-Style, p. 173 **Demonstration,** p. 173 in ATE **Demonstration,** p. 174 in ATE **Making Models,** Taking Flight, p. 661 **Datasheets for LabBook,** Taking Flight, Datasheet 26 **EcoLabs & Field Activities,** What's the Flap All About? Field Activity 18 **Long-Term Projects & Research Ideas,** Project 57

*See page **T20** for a complete correlation of this book with the* **NATIONAL SCIENCE EDUCATION STANDARDS.**

TECHNOLOGY RESOURCES

 Guided Reading Audio CD
English or Spanish, Chapter 7

 Interactive Explorations CD-ROM
CD 3, Exploration 2, Sea the Light

 One-Stop Planner CD-ROM with Test Generator

 Science, Technology & Society,
Pressure Paint, Segment 11
High-Tech Hang Gliders, Segment 12
Scientists in Action, Deep Flight, Segment 17

Chapter 7 • Forces in Fluids

CLASSROOM WORKSHEETS, TRANSPARENCIES, AND RESOURCES	SCIENCE INTEGRATION AND CONNECTIONS	REVIEW AND ASSESSMENT
Directed Reading Worksheet 7 **Science Puzzlers, Twisters & Teasers,** Worksheet 7		
Directed Reading Worksheet 7, Section 1 **Math Skills for Science Worksheet 33,** The Pressure Is On! **Transparency 8,** Surface-to-Volume Ratio **Math Skills for Science Worksheet 32,** Density **Transparency 225,** Air Pressure and Breathing	**MathBreak,** Pressure, Force, and Area, p. 162 **Connect to Life Science,** p. 163 in ATE **Cross-Disciplinary Focus,** p. 163 in ATE **Connect to Earth Science,** p. 164 in ATE **Real-World Connection,** p. 165 in ATE **Multicultural Connection,** p. 165 in ATE **Real-World Connection,** p. 166 in ATE	**Review,** p. 164 **Review,** p. 167 **Quiz,** p. 167 in ATE **Alternative Assessment,** p. 167 in ATE
Directed Reading Worksheet 7, Section 2 **Transparency 226,** Why Does a Steel Ship Float?	**Math and More,** p. 169 in ATE **MathBreak,** How to Calculate Density, p. 170 **Connect to Life Science,** p. 171 in ATE **Geology Connection,** p. 172	**Homework,** pp. 169, 170 in ATE **Review,** p. 172 **Quiz,** p. 172 in ATE **Alternative Assessment,** p. 172 in ATE
Directed Reading Worksheet 7, Section 3 **Transparency 227,** Wing Shape Creates Differences in Air Speed **Critical Thinking Worksheet 7,** Build a Better Submarine **Transparency 228,** Pitching a Curve Ball **Reinforcement Worksheet 7,** Building Up Pressure	**Multicultural Connection,** p. 175 in ATE **Apply,** p. 176 **Cross-Disciplinary Focus,** p. 176 in ATE **Connect to Earth Science,** p. 177 in ATE **Eureka!** Stayin' Aloft—The Story of the Frisbee®, p. 182 **Holt Anthology of Science Fiction,** Wet Behind the Ears	**Self-Check,** p. 175 **Review,** p. 177 **Quiz,** p. 177 in ATE **Alternative Assessment,** p. 177 in ATE

END-OF-CHAPTER REVIEW AND ASSESSMENT

Chapter Review in Study Guide
Vocabulary and Notes in Study Guide
Chapter Tests with Performance-Based Assessment, Chapter 7 Test
Chapter Tests with Performance-Based Assessment, Performance-Based Assessment 7
Concept Mapping Transparency 7

internetconnect

 Holt, Rinehart and Winston On-line Resources
go.hrw.com

For worksheets and other teaching aids related to this chapter, visit the HRW Web site and type in the keyword: **HSTFLU**

 **National Science Teachers Association**
www.scilinks.org

Encourage students to use the *sci*LINKS numbers listed in the internet connect boxes to access information and resources on the **NSTA** Web site.

Chapter 7 • Chapter Organizer **159B**

Chapter Resources & Worksheets

Visual Resources

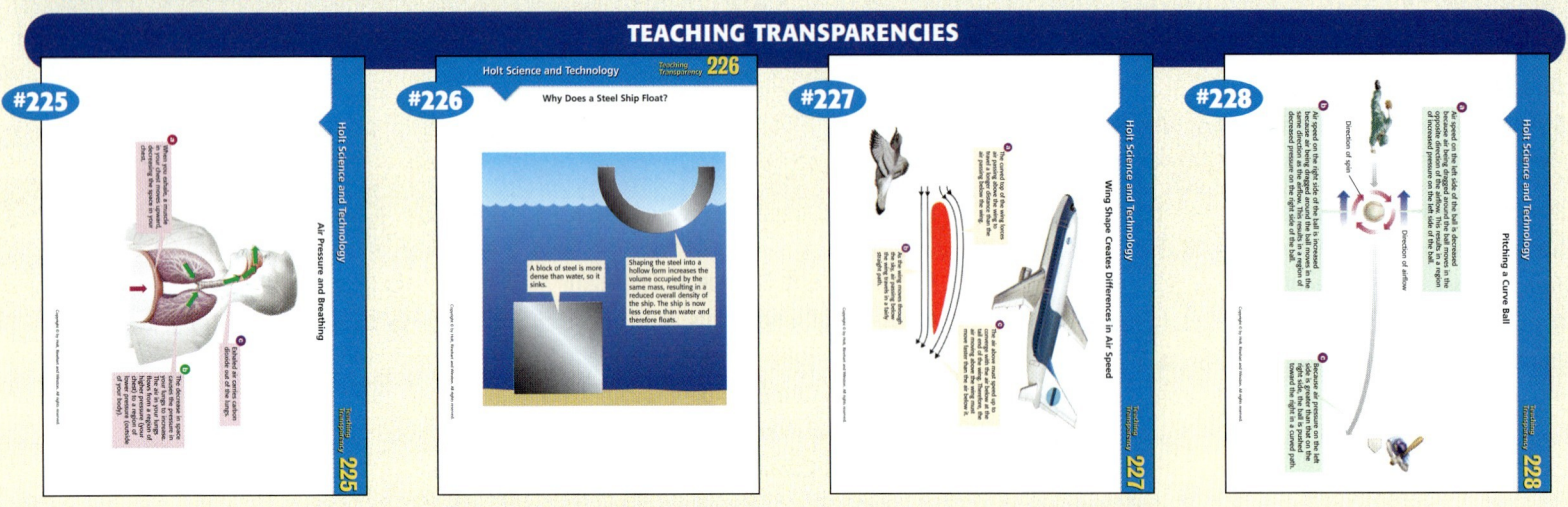

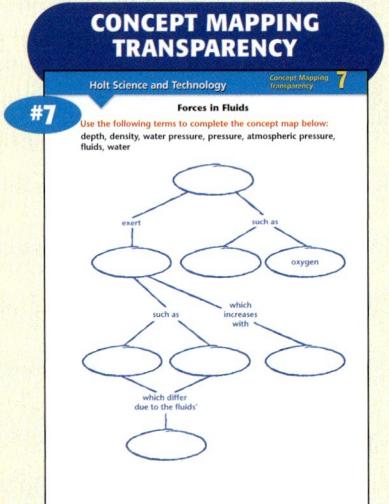

Meeting Individual Needs

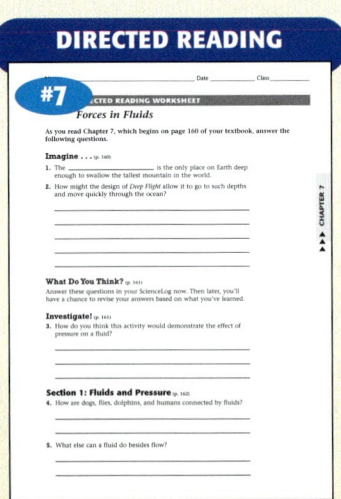

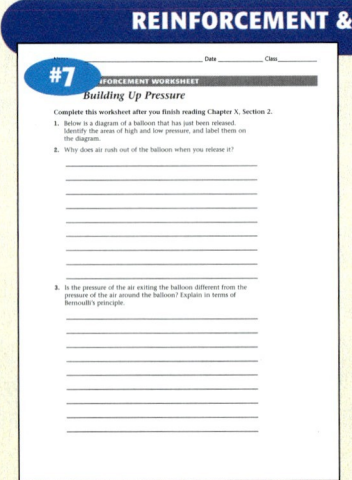

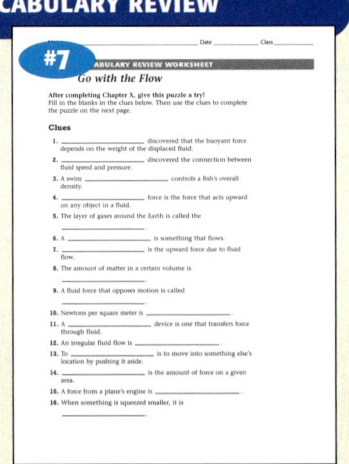

Chapter 7 • Forces in Fluids

Review & Assessment

STUDY GUIDE

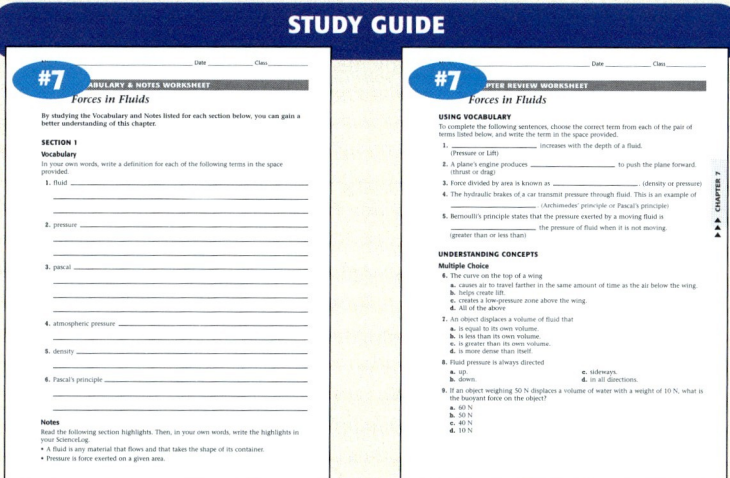

CHAPTER TESTS WITH PERFORMANCE-BASED ASSESSMENT

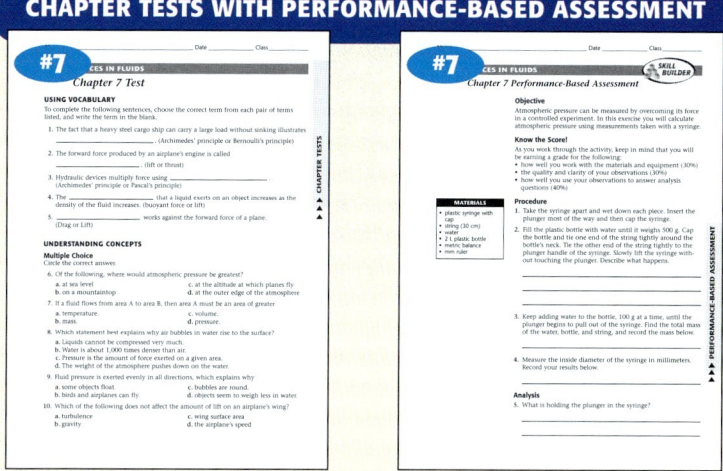

Lab Worksheets

ECOLABS & FIELD ACTIVITIES

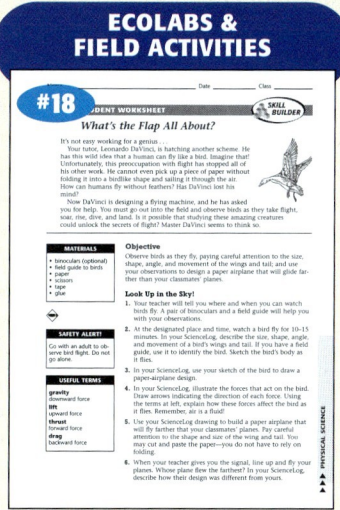

WHIZ-BANG DEMONSTRATIONS

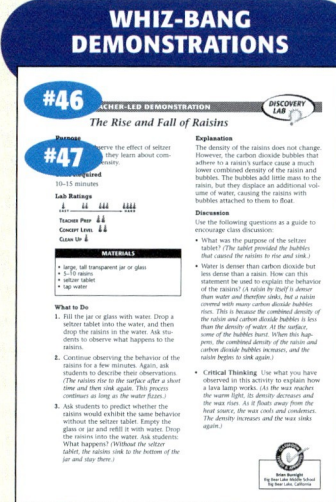

LONG-TERM PROJECTS & RESEARCH IDEAS

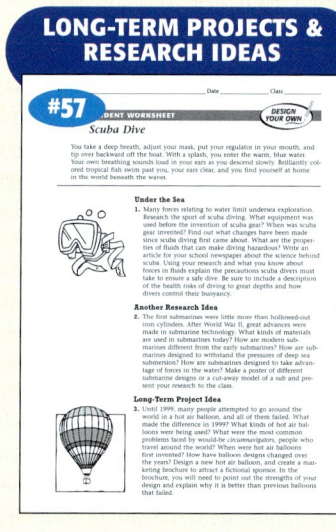

DATASHEETS FOR LABBOOK

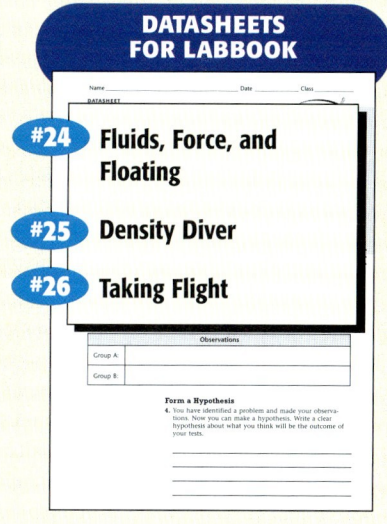

Applications & Extensions

CRITICAL THINKING & PROBLEM SOLVING

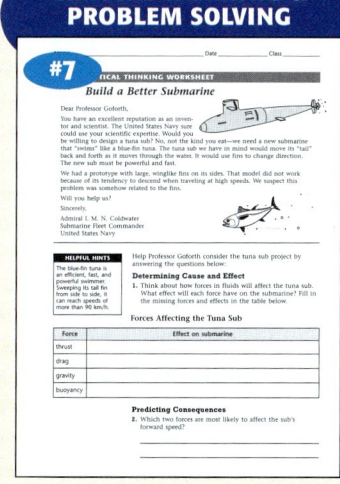

SCIENCE, TECHNOLOGY & SOCIETY

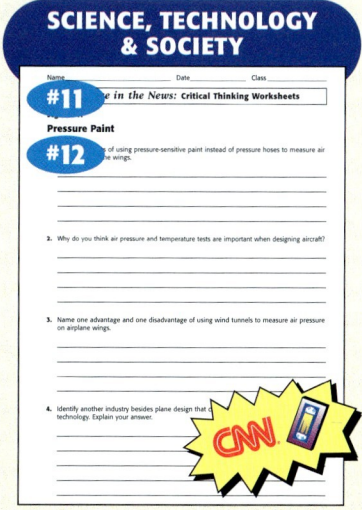

SCIENTISTS IN ACTION

INTERACTIVE EXPLORATIONS

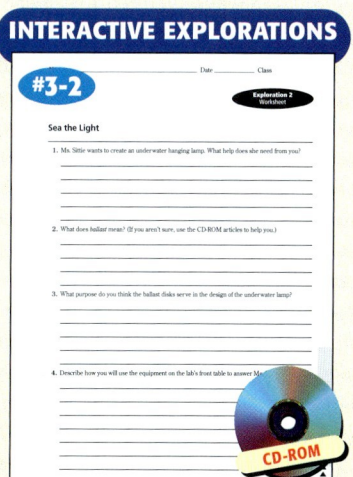

Chapter 7 • Chapter Resources & Worksheets   159D

Chapter Background

SECTION 1

Fluids and Pressure

▶ **Blaise Pascal**
Blaise Pascal (1623–1662) was a famous French scientist, mathematician, philosopher, and writer of prose. He had no formal schooling but pursued his interests under his father's guidance. Pascal's father forbade him to study mathematics until he was 15 years old, but Pascal's curiosity led him to begin studying geometry in secret at the age of 12. By the time he was 14, Pascal was regularly attending sessions with the leading geometricians of his time. Pascal presented his first mathematics paper at the age of 16.

▶ **Refresher on Gas Laws**
Nearly all materials expand when they are heated and contract when they are cooled. Gases are not an exception. A gas expands as it gets hotter because the kinetic energy of its particles increases. When the kinetic energy increases, the particles move faster and bounce against each other harder. This causes them to move farther apart, and the gas expands. If the pressure does not change, the volume of the gas will increase as the temperature increases. This is known as Charles's law.

- The air pressure inside the tires of an automobile can be much greater than the pressure outside the tires. This is because air, like all gases, is compressible. If the temperature does not change, the pressure of a gas will increase as the volume decreases. This is known as Boyle's law.

IS THAT A FACT!

▶ The water pressure at the bottom of a small, deep pond is greater than the pressure at the bottom of a large, shallow lake because water pressure is determined by the depth of the water, not the volume of the water.

SECTION 2

Buoyant Force

▶ **Archimedes (287–212 B.C.)**
Archimedes, a Greek mathematician, inventor, and physicist, lived in the ancient city of Syracuse from 287 B.C. to 212 B.C. He is famous for his work in geometry, physics, mechanics, and water and water pressure.

▶ **Diving and Water Pressure**
Scuba diving relies in part on the principles of buoyancy and fluid pressure. Some of the effects of water pressure can even be felt in a swimming pool. Just a few meters under water, your ears begin to hurt from the pressure of the water on your eardrums.

- As a diver descends deeper into the water with scuba gear, the diver's lungs hold more air because the air is compressed by the water pressure. As a diver rises to the surface, the air expands again. Under certain circumstances, the air in a diver's lungs could expand enough to rupture the air sacs in the diver's lungs.

▶ **Neutral Buoyancy**
Scuba divers use weights to compensate for the buoyancy of their body and diving gear. When a diver weighs exactly the same as an equal volume of the surrounding water, the diver can swim to any depth and remain there effortlessly. This state is called neutral buoyancy.

▶ **Buoyancy and Microgravity**
NASA uses large neutral-buoyancy tanks to simulate microgravity. The weight of an astronaut in a space suit can be adjusted so that the astronaut is neutrally buoyant. Astronauts practice maneuvering and working with instruments in this environment to prepare for the almost "weightless" environment of Earth orbit.

Chapter 7 • Forces in Fluids

IS THAT A FACT!

- *Deep Flight* (p. 160) may be futuristic, but humans have built underwater vessels for hundreds of years. In 1620, the Dutch inventor Cornelis van Drebbel built what is thought to be the first submarine. His vessel was not much more than a rowboat covered with greased leather. It traveled at a depth of 4 to 5 m under water in the Thames River, in London, England. King James I of England is said to have taken a short ride in this vessel.

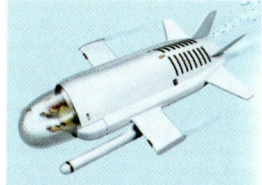

SECTION 3

Bernoulli's Principle

▶ Daniel Bernoulli (1700–1782)

Daniel Bernoulli was born in the Netherlands in 1700. For most of his life, he lived in Basel, Switzerland.

- Bernoulli was born into a family distinguished for accomplishments in science and mathematics. His father, Johann, was famous for his work in calculus, trigonometry, and the study of geodesics. Bernoulli's uncle Jacob was integral in the development of the calculus. Bernoulli's brothers, Nicolaus and Johann II, were also noted mathematicians and physicists.

- Bernoulli's greatest work was *Hydrodynamica*, which was published in 1738. It included the concept now known as Bernoulli's principle. He also made important contributions to probability theory and studied astronomy, botany, physiology, gravity, and magnetism.

▶ Looking for Bernoulli's Principle?

Even on a calm night, air moves across the top of a chimney. This causes the pressure at the top of the chimney to be lower than the pressure in the house. According to Bernoulli's principle, the smoke in the fireplace is pushed up the chimney by the greater air pressure in the house.

- Animals that burrow must have air circulating in their burrows, or they will suffocate. The burrows always have two entrances. Usually, one is higher than the other. Wind speed usually varies with height, so the air flows at different speeds across the holes. This causes a pressure difference that forces air to circulate.

- Bernoulli's principle also explains why a soft convertible top on a car bulges when the car travels at high speeds. The air moving over the top causes an area of low pressure, and the higher pressure inside the car pushes the soft top up.

▶ The Venturi Effect

A Venturi meter is a device that uses Bernoulli's principle to determine the velocity of a fluid by measuring differences in pressure. Venturi meters are found in carburetors, flow meters, and aircraft-speed indicators. In carburetors, a Venturi meter is used to mix fuel with air.

IS THAT A FACT!

- Water flowing in a stream speeds up when it flows through a narrow part of the stream bed. According to Bernoulli's principle, the water pressure decreases as the speed increases.

For background information about teaching strategies and issues, refer to the *Professional Reference for Teachers*.

Chapter 7 • Chapter Background 159F

CHAPTER 7
Forces in Fluids

Chapter Preview

Section 1
Fluids and Pressure
- All Fluids Exert Pressure
- Atmospheric Pressure
- Water Pressure
- Fluids Flow from High Pressure to Low Pressure
- Pascal's Principle

Section 2
Buoyant Force
- Buoyant Force Is Caused by Differences in Fluid Pressure
- Weight Vs. Buoyant Force
- An Object Will Float or Sink Based on Its Density
- The Mystery of Floating Steel

Section 3
Bernoulli's Principle
- Fluid Pressure Decreases as Speed Increases
- It's a Bird! It's a Plane! It's Bernoulli's Principle!
- Thrust and Wing Size Determine Lift
- Drag Opposes Motion in Fluids
- Wings Are Not Always Required

Directed Reading Worksheet 7

Science Puzzlers, Twisters & Teasers Worksheet 7

Guided Reading Audio CD
English or Spanish, Chapter 7

CHAPTER 7
Forces in Fluids

Imagine....

You're the pilot of a revolutionary new undersea vessel, *Deep Flight*, and today is the day of your first undersea voyage. Your destination: the Mariana Trench, which is the deepest spot in the ocean. The Mariana Trench is about 11 km deep—that's deep enough to swallow Mount Everest, the tallest mountain in the world. Fewer than a dozen undersea vessels have ever ventured this far down. The reason? Water exerts tremendous pressure at this depth. Luckily, *Deep Flight*'s hull is made of an extremely strong ceramic material that can withstand the pressure.

What makes *Deep Flight* so revolutionary? *Deep Flight* actually "flies" through the water. In fact, *Deep Flight* looks a lot like an airplane with stubby wings. Controls allow you to adjust the curvature of the wings to move faster through the water.

With its battery-powered motor and your ability to change the curvature of the wings, *Deep Flight* can reach speeds of up to 25 km/h! By adjusting *Deep Flight*'s wing flaps and tail fins, you can do dives, spins, and turns. Ready to race a whale?

As futuristic as this story sounds, *Deep Flight* is a real undersea vessel that is currently being tested. Although *Deep Flight* has not yet made it to the bottom of the Mariana Trench, some scientists believe this type of undersea vessel will one day be used routinely to explore the ocean floor.

In this chapter you will explore fluids. You'll learn how pressure is exerted by water and other fluids. You'll also learn why some things sink and others float and how the curvature of a wing affects speed. Dive in!

Imagine ...

"With respect to the ocean, it's easy to be the first for a lot of things. Less than one percent of the deep sea has been seen at all, let alone explored." So says Sylvia Earle, oceanographer, marine biologist, author, and former chief scientist of the National Oceanic and Atmospheric Administration. Earle's life is dedicated to protecting the oceans. Earle says, "If the sea is sick, we'll feel it. If it dies, we die. Our future and the state of the oceans are one...."

What Do You Think?

In your ScienceLog, try to answer the following questions based on what you already know:

1. What is a fluid?
2. How is fluid pressure exerted?
3. Do moving fluids exert different forces than nonmoving fluids?

Investigate!

Out the Spouts

The undersea vessel *Deep Flight* was built to withstand the pressure exerted by water. In this activity you'll witness one of the effects of this pressure firsthand.

Procedure

1. With a sharp **pencil,** punch a small hole in the center of one side of an empty **cardboard milk container.**
2. Make another hole 4 cm above the center hole. Then make another hole 8 cm above the center hole.
3. With a single piece of **masking tape,** carefully cover the holes. Leave a little tape free at the bottom for easy removal.
4. Fill the container with **water,** and place it in a **large plastic tray or sink.**
5. Quickly pull the tape off the container.
6. Record your observations in your ScienceLog.

Analysis

7. Did the same thing happen at each hole after you removed the tape? If not, what do you think caused the different results? Record your answers in your ScienceLog.

What Do You Think?

Accept all reasonable responses. Students will have a chance to revise their answers in the Chapter Review under NOW What Do You Think?

Investigate!

MATERIALS

For Each Group:
- pencil
- empty cardboard milk container
- metric ruler
- masking tape
- water
- large plastic tray or sink

Safety Caution: Make sure students wear safety goggles and an apron when doing this activity.

Answers to Investigate!

7. The same thing does not happen at each hole after the tape is removed. Water spurts out farther from the middle hole than from the top hole, and even farther out of the bottom hole than out of the top two holes. The difference in how far each stream of water travels is due to the difference in water pressure. Water pressure increases with depth. More pressure is pushing on the bottom of the column, so the water is pushed out with greater force and travels farther.

IS THAT A FACT!

Robotic submersibles are smaller and less expensive than manned diving vessels. They do not need life-support systems, and they can work under water far longer than humans. The Autonomous Benthic Explorer (ABE) works as deep as 5,500 m. Computer programs guide ABE's movement, video cameras, sensors, and scanning sonar. Instead of returning to the surface when a job is done, ABE can "sleep" on the bottom until it gets more instructions.

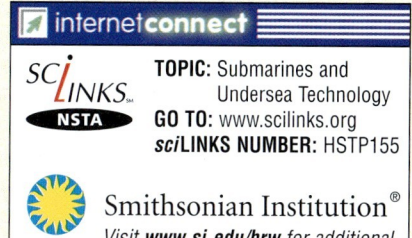

TOPIC: Submarines and Undersea Technology
GO TO: www.scilinks.org
sciLINKS NUMBER: HSTP155

Smithsonian Institution®
Visit www.si.edu/hrw for additional on-line resources.

Chapter 7 • Forces in Fluids

SECTION 1

Focus

Fluids and Pressure

In this section students learn about the physical properties of fluids. They also learn how pressure is related to depth and density, and how fluids flow from areas of high pressure to areas of low pressure. Students learn the practical applications of Pascal's principle.

 **Bellringer**

Pose the following situation to your students:

One afternoon, you go outside to find your younger sister standing by her bike with a nail in her hand. The bike has a flat tire. She wants to know why the air came out of the tire when she pulled the nail out.

Have students write a few sentences to explain why air rushes out of a hole in a tire.

Answers to MATHBREAK

1. 1,500 Pa
2. 2,500 N

 Directed Reading Worksheet 7 Section 1

 Math Skills Worksheet 33 "The Pressure Is On!"

Section 1

Terms to Learn
fluid
pressure
pascal
atmospheric pressure
density
Pascal's principle

What You'll Do
- Describe how fluids exert pressure.
- Analyze how fluid depth affects pressure.
- Give examples of fluids flowing from high to low pressure.
- State and apply Pascal's principle.

MATH BREAK

Pressure, Force, and Area

The equation on this page can be used to find pressure or rearranged to find force or area.

Force = Pressure × Area

Area = $\dfrac{\text{Force}}{\text{Pressure}}$

1. Find the pressure exerted by a 3,000 N crate with an area of 2 m².
2. Find the weight of a rock with an area of 10 m² that exerts a pressure of 250 Pa.
(Be sure to express your answers in the correct SI unit.)

Fluids and Pressure

What does a dolphin have in common with a sea gull? What does a dog have in common with a fly? What do you have in common with all these living things? The answer is that you and all these other living things spend a lifetime moving through and even breathing fluids. A **fluid** is any material that can flow and that takes the shape of its container. Fluids include liquids (such as water and oil) and gases (such as oxygen and carbon dioxide). Fluids are able to flow because the particles in fluids, unlike the particles in solids, can move easily past each other. As you will find out, the remarkable properties of fluids allow huge ships to float, divers to explore the ocean depths, and jumbo jets to soar across the skies.

All Fluids Exert Pressure

You probably have heard the terms *air pressure, water pressure,* and *blood pressure*. Air, water, and blood are all fluids, and all fluids exert pressure. So what's pressure? Well, think about this example. When you pump up a bicycle tire, you push air into the tire. And like all matter, air is made of tiny particles that are constantly moving. Inside the tire, the air particles push against each other and against the walls of the tire, as shown in **Figure 1.** The more air you pump into the tire, the more the air particles push against the inside of your tire. Together, these pushes create a force against the tire. The amount of force exerted on a given area is **pressure.** Pressure can be calculated by dividing the force that a fluid exerts by the area over which the force is exerted:

$$\text{Pressure} = \dfrac{\text{Force}}{\text{Area}}$$

The SI unit for pressure is the **pascal.** One pascal (1 Pa) is the force of one newton exerted over an area of one square meter (1 N/m²). Try the MathBreak at left to practice calculating pressure.

Figure 1 *The force of the air particles hitting the inner surface of the tire creates pressure, which keeps the tire inflated.*

MISCONCEPTION ALERT

Students might assume that pressure calculations will always involve the force of a fluid. Explain that because weight is a measure of gravitational force, anything that has weight exerts pressure. Thus, a crate on a floor exerts pressure on the floor.

162 Chapter 7 • Forces in Fluids

Why Are Bubbles Round? When you blow a soap bubble, you blow in only one direction. So why doesn't the bubble get longer and longer as you blow instead of rounder and rounder? The shape of the bubble is due in part to an important property of fluids: Fluids exert pressure evenly in all directions. The air you blow into the bubble exerts pressure evenly in every direction, so the bubble expands in every direction, helping to create a sphere, as shown in **Figure 2**. This property also explains why tires inflate evenly (unless there is a weak spot in the tire).

Atmospheric Pressure

The *atmosphere* is the layer of nitrogen, oxygen, and other gases that surrounds the Earth. The atmosphere stretches about 150 km above us. If you could stack 500 Eiffel Towers on top of each other, they would come close to reaching the top of the atmosphere. However, approximately 80 percent of the gases in the atmosphere are found within 10 km of the Earth's surface. Earth's atmosphere is held in place by gravity, which pulls the gases toward Earth. The pressure caused by the weight of the atmosphere is called **atmospheric pressure.**

Atmospheric pressure is exerted on everything on Earth, including you. The atmosphere exerts a pressure of approximately 101,300 N on every square meter, or 101,300 Pa. This means that there is a weight of about 10 N (roughly the weight of a pineapple) on every square centimeter (roughly the area of the tip of your little finger) of your body. Ouch!

Why don't you feel this crushing pressure? The fluids inside your body also exert pressure, just like the air inside a balloon exerts pressure. **Figure 3** can help you understand.

Figure 2 *You can't blow a square bubble, because fluids exert pressure equally in every direction.*

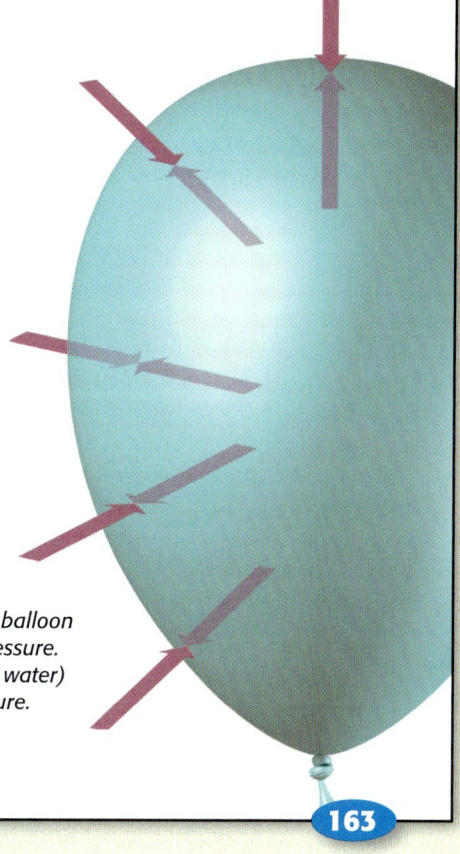

Figure 3 *The pressure exerted by the air inside a balloon keeps the balloon inflated against atmospheric pressure. Similarly, the pressure exerted by the fluid (mostly water) inside your body works against atmospheric pressure.*

163

IS THAT A FACT!
The air in a large room in your house weighs about as much as an average adult male! (about 736 N)

CROSS-DISCIPLINARY FOCUS
Language Arts Have students compose a short poem describing something about flowing fluids (examples: water, mixing liquids, air, steam, clouds, fog, or food).

1) Motivate

DEMONSTRATION
Safety Caution: Remind students to wear protective goggles.

Place two soda bottles half-filled with water in front of the classroom. Add some fizzing powder or crushed fizzing tablets. Immediately place a cork snugly in one of the bottles. Place the mouth of a balloon over the other bottle, sealing the opening. Have the class observe what happens. Ask them to explain what happened in each bottle. Have students predict what would happen to the bottles in different environments, such as at the bottom of the ocean, in the refrigerator, in a hot room, or in outer space.

2) Teach

MEETING INDIVIDUAL NEEDS
Learners Having Difficulty Have students think of all the ways they can use the word *pressure*. Have them collect pictures from magazines, then write short captions using the word *pressure*. Encourage students to be creative and even humorous with their captions.

CONNECT TO LIFE SCIENCE

Use Teaching Transparency 8 to help students understand how objects, including human bodies, can withstand atmospheric pressure.

 **Teaching Transparency 8** "Surface-to-Volume Ratio"

Section 1 • Fluids and Pressure **163**

2 Teach, continued

CONNECT TO EARTH SCIENCE

Have students research the effects of atmospheric pressure on weather. Have them make a poster or concept map to display their results.

BRAIN FOOD
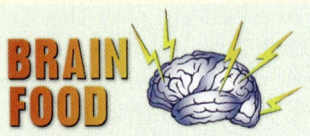

The extremely high altitude of Mount Everest makes even base camps on the mountain hazardous to visitors' health. Most of these base camps are more than 4,000 m above sea level. Altitude sickness affects most people who reach that elevation. Most climbers must use oxygen masks above 5,500 m because there is not enough oxygen to sustain normal body functions.

RETEACHING

Writing Have students write an essay describing how they are affected by fluid pressure on a typical day. Students should include examples such as weather, transportation, plumbing, breathing, bathing, playing outside, and so on. Encourage them to be creative.

Figure 4 Differences in Atmospheric Pressure

At 150,000 m above sea level, atmospheric pressure is almost zero. Humans cannot travel this high without protection. The space shuttle travels past this point on its way into orbit.

The atmospheric pressure at 12,000 m is about 20 kPa. Airplane cabins must be pressurized for passenger safety.

At the top of Mount Everest (8,847 m above sea level), atmospheric pressure is about a third that at sea level.

Atmospheric pressure at La Paz, Bolivia (the world's highest capital city at 4,000 m) is about 51 kPa.

At sea level (0 m), the full pressure of the atmosphere— 101 kPa—is exerted on you.

Atmospheric Pressure Varies At the top of the atmosphere, pressure is almost nonexistent because there is no atmosphere pressing down. At the top of Mount Everest in south-central Asia (which is the highest point on Earth), atmospheric pressure is about 33,000 Pa, or 33 kilopascals (kPa). At sea level, atmospheric pressure is about 101 kPa.

Pressure Depends on Depth As shown in **Figure 4,** pressure increases as you descend through the atmosphere. In other words, the pressure increases as the atmosphere gets "deeper." This is an important point about fluids: Pressure depends on the depth of the fluid. At lower levels of the atmosphere, there is more fluid above you being pulled by Earth's gravitational force, so there is more pressure.

If you travel to higher or lower points in the atmosphere, the fluids in your body have to adjust to maintain equal pressure. You may have experienced this if your ears have "popped" when you were in a plane taking off or a car traveling down a steep mountain road. Small pockets of air behind your eardrums contract or expand as atmospheric pressure increases or decreases. The "pop" occurs when air is released due to these pressure changes.

REVIEW

1. How do particles in a fluid exert pressure on a container?
2. Why are you not crushed by atmospheric pressure?
3. **Applying Concepts** Explain why dams on deep lakes should be thicker at the bottom than near the top.

Answers to Review

1. The moving particles in a fluid collide against each other and against the walls of the container. This creates pressure.
2. The pressure exerted by the fluids in your body works against atmospheric pressure.
3. Water pressure increases with depth. Therefore, more pressure is exerted at the bottom of the dam than at the top. The dam must be thicker at the bottom to withstand this added pressure.

Water Pressure

Water is a fluid; therefore, it exerts pressure, just like the atmosphere does. Water pressure also increases with depth because of gravity. Take a look at **Figure 5.** The deeper a diver goes in the water, the greater the pressure becomes because more water above the diver is being pulled by Earth's gravitational force. In addition, the atmosphere presses down on the water, so the total pressure on the diver includes water pressure as well as atmospheric pressure.

But pressure does not depend on the total amount of fluid present, only on the depth of the fluid. A swimmer would feel the same pressure swimming at 5 m below the surface of a small pond as at 5 m below the surface of an ocean, even though there is more water in the ocean.

Density Makes a Difference Water is about 1,000 times more dense than air. (Remember, **density** is the amount of matter in a certain volume, or mass per unit volume.) Because water is more dense than air, a certain volume of water has more mass—and therefore weighs more—than the same volume of air. Therefore, water exerts greater pressure than air.

For example, if you climb a 10 m tree, the decrease in atmospheric pressure is too small to notice. But if you dive 10 m underwater, the pressure on you increases to 201 kPa, which is almost twice the atmospheric pressure at the surface!

Figure 5 Differences in Water Pressure

Pressure exerted on a diver 10 m below the water's surface is twice the pressure at the surface.

At 500 m below the surface, pressure is about 5,000 kPa. Divers at or below this level must wear special suits to survive the pressure.

The wreck of the *Titanic* rests 3,660 m below sea level. The water pressure at this depth is 36,600 kPa.

The viper fish lives 8,000 m below the ocean's surface. No fish are found below this level. The water pressure at this depth is 80,000 kPa.

In 1960, the *Trieste* descended to the deepest part of the ocean (11,000 m), where the pressure is 110,000 kPa.

REAL-WORLD CONNECTION

The pressure on a diver's body increases as the diver goes deeper underwater. The increased pressure on the diver's chest makes breathing more difficult. Scuba divers use a pressure regulator to solve this problem. As they go deeper, the regulator increases the pressure of the air released from the diver's air tanks. The pressure of the released air equals the pressure of the water on the diver, making breathing easier.

Multicultural CONNECTION

Have students do research on Japanese pearl divers. They should investigate the techniques these deep divers use to cope with the water pressure and the effects of pressure on the divers.

Math Skills Worksheet 32 "Density"

SCIENCE HUMOR

Q: What do you call a pod of whales on a deep dive?

A: grays under pressure

Section 1 • Fluids and Pressure

2 Teach, continued

REAL-WORLD CONNECTION

Have students make a poster showing the airflow in their homes. Have them write a short description of the circulation of the air using the concept of fluid pressure. Students should include one or more ways they have used to track air movement accurately.

ACTIVITY

MATERIALS

FOR EACH STUDENT:
- clean plastic cups
- water
- straws
- pins

Safety Caution: Remind students to handle pins carefully and that everyone should wear safety goggles.

Tell students to sip some water through the straw. Then have them make a small hole in the straw about 5 cm from the top. Have students explain what happens when they try to drink water through the straw again. (Some liquid will rise up the straw, but air flowing through the hole will tend to push the liquid down.)

Teaching Transparency 225
"Air Pressure and Breathing"

TOPIC: Fluids and Pressure
GO TO: www.scilinks.org
sciLINKS NUMBER: HSTP160

Fluids Flow from High Pressure to Low Pressure

Look at **Figure 6.** When you drink through a straw, you remove some of the air in the straw. Because there is less air, the pressure in the straw is reduced. But the atmospheric pressure on the surface of the liquid remains the same. This creates a difference between the pressure inside the straw and the pressure outside the straw. The outside pressure forces the liquid up into the straw and into your mouth. So just by sipping your drink through a straw, you can observe another important property of fluids: Fluids flow from regions of high pressure to regions of low pressure.

Figure 6 Atmospheric pressure helps you sip through a straw!

Go with the Flow Take a deep breath—that's fluid flowing from high to low pressure! When you inhale, a muscle increases the space in your chest, giving your lungs room to expand. This expansion lowers the pressure in your lungs so that it becomes lower than the outside air pressure. Air then flows into your lungs—from higher to lower pressure. This air carries oxygen that you need to live. **Figure 7** shows how exhaling also causes fluids to flow from higher to lower pressure. You can see this same exchange when you open a carbonated beverage or squeeze toothpaste onto your toothbrush.

QuickLab

Blown Away

1. Lay an **empty plastic soda bottle** on its side.
2. Wad **a small piece of paper** (about 4 × 4 cm) into a ball.
3. Place the paper ball just inside the bottle's opening.
4. Blow straight into the opening.
5. Record your observations in your ScienceLog.
6. Explain your results in terms of high and low fluid pressures.

TRY at HOME

Figure 7 Just as when you inhale, fluids flow from high to low pressure when you exhale.

a When you exhale, a muscle in your chest moves upward, decreasing the space in your chest.

b The decrease in space causes the pressure in your lungs to increase. The air in your lungs flows from a region of higher pressure (your chest) to a region of lower pressure (outside of your body).

c Exhaled air carries carbon dioxide out of the lungs.

QuickLab

MATERIALS

FOR EACH STUDENT:
- empty plastic soda bottle
- 4 × 4 cm paper

Answers to QuickLab

5. Students should observe that the paper wad flies out of the bottle.
6. By blowing into the bottle, the air pressure inside the bottle is increased. Fluids flow from high pressure to low pressure, so the air inside flows out of the bottle, carrying the paper wad with it.

Chapter 7 • Forces in Fluids

Pascal's Principle

Imagine that the water-pumping station in your town can now increase the water pressure by 20 Pa. Will the water pressure be increased more at a supermarket two blocks away or at a home 2 km away?

Believe it or not, the increase in water pressure will be transmitted through all of the water and will be the same—20 Pa—at both locations. This is explained by Pascal's principle, named for Blaise Pascal, the seventeenth-century French scientist who discovered it. **Pascal's principle** states that a change in pressure at any point in an enclosed fluid will be transmitted equally to all parts of that fluid.

Putting Pascal's Principle to Work

Devices that use liquids to transmit pressure from one point to another are called *hydraulic* (hie DRAW lik) devices. Hydraulic devices use liquids because they cannot be compressed, or squeezed, into a smaller space very much. This property allows liquids to transmit pressure more efficiently than gases, which can be compressed a great deal.

Hydraulic devices can multiply forces. The brakes of a typical car are a good example. In **Figure 8,** a driver's foot exerts pressure on a cylinder of liquid. Pascal's principle tells you that this pressure is transmitted equally to all parts of the liquid-filled brake system. This liquid presses a brake pad against each wheel, and friction brings the car to a stop. The force is multiplied because the pistons that push the brake pads on each wheel are much larger than the piston that is pushed by the brake pedal.

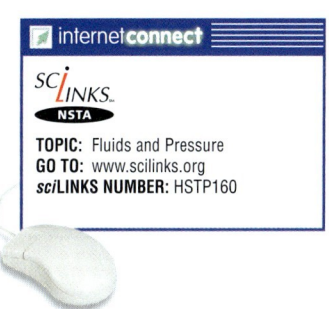

Figure 8 *Thanks to Pascal's principle, the touch of a foot can stop tons of moving metal.*

REVIEW

1. Explain how atmospheric pressure helps you drink through a straw.
2. What does Pascal's principle state?
3. **Making Predictions** When you squeeze a balloon, where is the pressure inside the balloon increased the most? Explain your answer in terms of Pascal's principle.

internet connect

SC_/**LINKS**
NSTA

TOPIC: Fluids and Pressure
GO TO: www.scilinks.org
*sci*LINKS NUMBER: HSTP160

SECTION 2

Focus

Buoyant Force

This section describes how differences in fluid pressure create buoyant force. Students are introduced to Archimedes' principle and learn how to calculate the buoyant force exerted on an object. Finally, students learn the factors that determine whether an object floats or sinks in a fluid.

Bellringer

Pose the following question to your students:

Which of the following objects will float in water?

    a rock, an orange, a screw, a quarter, a candle, a plastic-foam "peanut," a chalkboard eraser

Ask them to write a hypothesis about why an aircraft carrier, which has a mass of thousands of tons, does not sink.

1 Motivate

DEMONSTRATION

Add 20 mL each of molasses, cooking oil, and water to a 100 mL graduated cylinder. Either before students enter the classroom or while they observe, insert several different objects that will float on different layers. You might also try adding droplets of alcohol. Use the results of the demonstration to launch a discussion about buoyant force.

Directed Reading Worksheet 7 Section 2

SECTION 2

Terms to Learn

buoyant force
Archimedes' principle

What You'll Do

- Explain the relationship between fluid pressure and buoyant force.
- Predict whether an object will float or sink in a fluid.
- Analyze the role of density in an object's ability to float.

Buoyant Force

Why does a rubber duck float on water? Why doesn't it sink to the bottom of your bathtub? Even if you pushed the rubber duck to the bottom, it would pop back to the surface when you released it. Some force pushes the rubber duck to the top of the water. That force is **buoyant force**, the upward force that fluids exert on all matter.

Air is a fluid, so it exerts a buoyant force. But why don't you ever see rubber ducks floating in air? Read on to find out!

Buoyant Force Is Caused by Differences in Fluid Pressure

Look at **Figure 9**. Water exerts fluid pressure on all sides of an object. The pressure exerted horizontally on one side of the object is equal to the pressure exerted horizontally on the opposite side. These equal pressures cancel one another. Thus, the only fluid pressures affecting the object are at the top and at the bottom. Because pressure increases with depth, the pressure on the bottom of the object is greater than the pressure at the top, as shown by the width of the arrows. Therefore, the water exerts a net upward force on the object. This upward force is buoyant force.

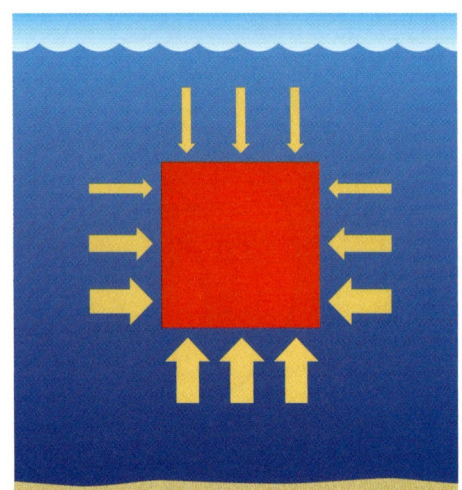

Figure 9 There is more fluid pressure on the bottom of an object because pressure increases with depth. This results in an upward force on the object—buoyant force.

Determining Buoyant Force Archimedes (ahr kuh MEE deez), a Greek mathematician who lived in the third century B.C., discovered how to determine buoyant force. **Archimedes' principle** states that the buoyant force on an object in a fluid is an upward force equal to the weight of the volume of fluid that the object displaces. (*Displace* means "to take the place of.") For example, suppose the object in Figure 9 displaces 250 mL of water. The weight of that volume of displaced water is about 2.5 N. Therefore, the buoyant force on the object is 2.5 N. Notice that the weight of the object has nothing to do with the buoyant force. Only the weight of the displaced fluid determines the buoyant force on an object.

Q: Why did the banker jump into the swimming pool?

A: He needed to float a loan.

168   Chapter 7 • Forces in Fluids

Weight Vs. Buoyant Force

An object in a fluid will sink if it has a weight greater than the weight of the fluid that is displaced. In other words, an object will sink if its weight is greater than the buoyant force acting on it. An object floats only when it displaces a volume of fluid that has a weight equal to the object's weight—that is, if the buoyant force on the object is equal to the object's weight.

Sinking The lake scene in **Figure 10** looks quite peaceful, but there are forces being exerted! The rock weighs 75 N. It displaces 5 L of water. According to Archimedes' principle, the buoyant force is equal to the weight of the displaced water—about 50 N. Because the rock's weight is greater than the buoyant force, the rock sinks.

Floating The fish weighs 12 N. It displaces a volume of water that has a weight of 12 N. Because the fish's weight is equal to the buoyant force, the fish floats in the water. Now look at the duck. The duck weighs 9 N. The duck does not sink. What does that tell you? The buoyant force on the duck must be equal to the duck's weight. But the duck isn't even all the way underwater! Only the duck's feet, legs, and stomach have to be underwater in order to displace enough water to equal 9 N. Thus, the duck floats.

Buoying Up If the duck dove underwater, it would then displace more water, and the buoyant force would therefore be greater. When the buoyant force on an object is greater than the object's weight, the object is *buoyed up* (pushed up) out of the water until what's left underwater displaces an amount of water that equals the object's entire weight. That's why a rubber duck pops to the surface when it is pushed to the bottom of a filled bathtub.

Activity

Find five things that float in water and five things that sink in water. What do the floating objects have in common? What do the sinking objects have in common?

TRY at HOME

Figure 10 Will an object sink or float? It depends on whether the buoyant force is less than or equal to the object's weight.

Weight = 12 N
Buoyant force = 12 N
Fish floats in the water

Weight = 9 N
Buoyant force = 9 N
Duck floats on the surface

Weight = 75 N
Buoyant force = 50 N
Rock sinks

169

Homework

Concept Mapping Have students create a buoyant force concept map and discuss objects that float on the surface, objects that float between the surface and the bottom, and objects that sink to the bottom.

Answer to Activity

Accept all reasonable answers. Students may answer that floating objects are light and sinking objects are heavy. Drop a penny in a glass of water, and ask students if the penny weighs more than an aircraft carrier. Review and discuss the concept of density. If necessary, reread with them the "Weight Vs. Buoyant Force" section to help clarify this difficult concept.

2) Teach

READING STRATEGY

Prediction Guide Before students read the next three pages, ask them whether the following statements are true or false:

1. The shape of an object helps determine whether it will float. (true)
2. Something made of steel cannot float in water. (false)
3. The force of gravity is less in water than on dry land. (false)

Have students evaluate their answers after they read the next three pages.

MATH and MORE

Ask students to solve the following problem:

A force of 15 N is required to lift an object that is underwater. The object displaces 2 L of water (1 L of water weighs 10 N). What is the weight of the object out of water? (force required to lift object in water = weight of object out of water − buoyant force

15 N = weight of object out of water − 20 N

weight of object out of water = 20 N + 15 N = 35 N)

Fluids, Force, and Floating

Section 2 • Buoyant Force 169

2 Teach, continued

Answers to MATHBREAK
1. 1.25 g/cm³
2. 1.3 g/cm³

BRAIN FOOD

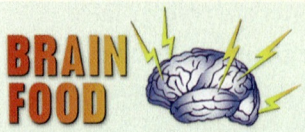

Can a helium balloon keep rising forever? Helium is less dense than air, so a balloon filled with helium weighs less than the same volume of air. Air exerts a buoyant force on the balloon and pushes it up. The balloon will continue to rise as long as the weight of the displaced air is greater than the weight of the balloon. Eventually, the weight of the balloon will equal the weight of the displaced air, and the balloon will stop rising.

ACTIVITY

Making Models Students will make a model of a hot-air balloon. Before they begin, discuss how heating the air inside the balloon changes the balloon's overall density and therefore changes its buoyancy. Provide students with tissue paper, tape, glue, string, and other materials to make a model balloon. Hold each completed model in place and fill it with hot air from a hair dryer. Release the model to see if it flies. Have students evaluate their balloon's performance.

Density Diver PG 660

MATH BREAK

How to Calculate Density
The volume of any sample of matter, no matter what state or shape, can be calculated using this equation:

$$\text{Density} = \frac{\text{Mass}}{\text{Volume}}$$

1. What is the density of a 20 cm³ sample of liquid with a mass of 25 g?
2. A 546 g fish displaces 420 cm³ of water. What is the density of the fish?

An Object Will Float or Sink Based on Its Density

Think again about the rock at the bottom of the lake. The rock displaces 5 L of water, which means that the volume of the rock is 5,000 cm³. (Remember that liters are used only for fluid volumes.) But 5,000 cm³ of rock weighs more than an equal volume of water. This is why the rock sinks. Because mass is proportional to weight on Earth, you can say that the rock has more mass per volume than water. Remember, mass per unit volume is *density*. The rock sinks because it is more dense than water. The duck floats because it is less dense than water. In Figure 10, the density of the fish is exactly equal to the density of the water.

More Dense Than Air Think back to the question about the rubber duck: "Why does it float on water but not in air?" The rubber duck floats because it is less dense than water. However, most substances are *more* dense than air. Therefore, there are few substances that float in air. The plastic that makes up the rubber duck is more dense than air, so the rubber duck doesn't float in air.

Less Dense Than Air One substance that is less dense than air is helium, a gas. In fact, helium is over 70 times less dense than air. A volume of helium displaces a volume of air that is much heavier than itself, so helium floats. That's why helium is used in airships and parade balloons, like the one shown in **Figure 11.**

Figure 11 *Helium in a balloon floats in air for the same reason a duck floats in water—it is less dense than the surrounding fluid.*

Homework

Concept Mapping Have students create a concept map showing how an airship is similar to an aircraft carrier or a cruise ship.

IS THAT A FACT!

Before plastics can be recycled, they must first be separated by type. Most containers display a number that identifies the type of plastic used. Containers that do not display number codes can be separated by density by floating them in liquids of different densities.

The Mystery of Floating Steel

Steel is almost eight times more dense than water. And yet huge steel ships cruise the oceans with ease, even while carrying enormous loads. But hold on! Didn't you just learn that substances that are more dense than water will sink in water? You bet! So how does a steel ship float?

The secret is in the shape of the ship. What if a ship were just a big block of steel, as shown in **Figure 12**? If you put that steel block into water, the block would sink because it is more dense than water. For this reason, ships are built with a hollow shape, as shown below. The amount of steel in the ship is the same as in the block, but the hollow shape increases the volume of the ship. Because density is mass per volume, an increase in the ship's volume leads to a decrease in its density. Therefore, ships made of steel float because their *overall density* is less than the density of water. This is true of boats of any size, made of any material. Most ships are actually built to displace even more water than is necessary for the ship to float so that the ship won't sink when people and cargo are loaded onboard.

The *Seawise Giant* is the largest ship in the world. It is so large that crew members often use bicycles to travel around the ship.

Figure 12 A Ship's Shape Makes the Difference

A block of steel is more dense than water, so it sinks.

Shaping the steel into a hollow form increases the volume occupied by the same mass, resulting in a reduced overall density of the ship. The ship is now less dense than water and therefore floats.

Ship-Shape

1. Roll a **piece of clay** into a ball the size of a golf ball, and drop it into a **container of water**. Record your observations in your ScienceLog.

2. With your hands, flatten the ball of clay until it is a bit thinner than your little finger, and press it into the shape of a bowl or canoe.

3. Place the clay boat gently in the water. How does the change of shape affect the buoyant force on the clay? How is that change related to the average density of the clay boat? Record your answers in your ScienceLog.

GROUP ACTIVITY

Invite a scuba diver to talk to the class about diving, and ask the diver to touch on some of the principles of buoyant force. Have the diver bring a regulator and a tank to demonstrate their use. Encourage students to ask questions.

CONNECT TO LIFE SCIENCE

Have students investigate the physical adaptations that enable sea organisms to utilize buoyant force. Have them select an organism that interests them and write a report or create a poster or other presentation describing it.

3) Extend

ACTIVITY

Fill a tall, transparent glass or jar about one-third full with water. Mark the level of the water. Add a golf ball to the glass, and ask students to describe what happens. (The ball sinks.)

Mark the water level again. Next add salt to the water until the golf ball floats. Finally, slowly add fresh water that has been colored with food coloring. Ask students to describe the process they have just seen in terms of buoyant force, weight, and density.

QuickLab

MATERIALS

FOR EACH STUDENT:
- clay
- medium-sized bowl or pail for every two or three students
- water

Safety Caution: Caution students to wear an apron when doing this lab.

Answer to QuickLab

3. Forming the clay into a boat shape causes it to displace more water, which increases the buoyant force. The change in shape causes the average density of the clay boat to decrease so that the clay boat is less dense than the water. Therefore, the clay boat floats.

Teaching Transparency 226 "Why Does a Steel Ship Float?"

TOPIC: The Buoyant Force
GO TO: www.scilinks.org
*sci*LINKS NUMBER: HSTP165

Section 2 • Buoyant Force

Geology CONNECTION

The rock that makes up the Earth's continents is about 15 percent less dense than the molten (melted) mantle rock below it. Because of this difference in densities, the continents are "floating" on the mantle.

Density on the Move A submarine is a special kind of ship that can travel on the surface of the water and underwater. Submarines have special tanks that can be opened to allow sea water to flow in. This water adds mass, thus increasing the submarine's overall density so it can descend into the ocean. Crew members can control the amount of water taken in, thereby controlling the submarine's change in density and thus its depth in the ocean. Compressed air is used to blow the water out of the tanks so the submarine can rise through the water. Most submarines are built of high-strength metals that withstand water pressure. Still, most submarines can go no deeper than 400 m below the surface of the ocean.

How Is a Fish Like a Submarine? No, this is not a trick question! Like a submarine, some fish adjust their overall density in order to stay at a certain depth in the water. Most bony fish have an organ called a *swim bladder*, shown in **Figure 13**. This swim bladder is filled with gases produced in the fish's blood. The inflated swim bladder increases the fish's volume, thereby decreasing the fish's overall density and keeping it from sinking in the water. The fish's nervous system controls the amount of gas in the bladder according to the fish's depth in the water. Some fish, such as sharks, do not have a swim bladder. These fish must swim constantly to keep from sinking to the bottom of the water.

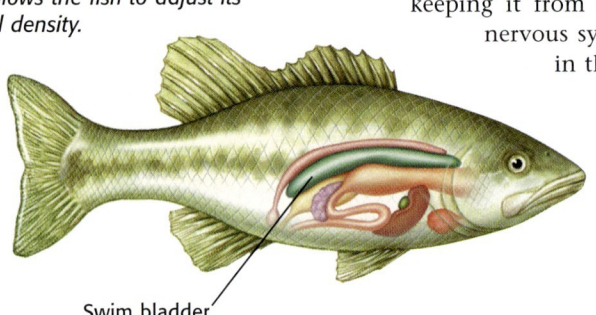

Figure 13 *Most bony fish have an organ called a swim bladder that allows the fish to adjust its overall density.*

Swim bladder

REVIEW

internetconnect

*sci*LINKS NSTA

TOPIC: The Buoyant Force
GO TO: www.scilinks.org
*sci*LINKS NUMBER: HSTP165

1. Explain how differences in fluid pressure create buoyant force on an object.

2. An object weighs 20 N. It displaces a volume of water that weighs 15 N.
   a. What is the buoyant force on the object?
   b. Will this object float or sink? Explain your answer.

3. Iron has a density of 7.9 g/cm^3. Mercury has a density of 13.6 g/cm^3. Will iron float or sink in mercury? Explain your answer.

4. **Applying Concepts** Why is it inaccurate to say that all heavy objects will sink in water?

Section 3

Terms to Learn

Bernoulli's principle
lift
thrust
drag

What You'll Do

- Describe the relationship between pressure and fluid speed.
- Analyze the roles of lift, thrust, and drag in flight.
- Give examples of Bernoulli's principle in real-life situations.

Bernoulli's Principle

Has this ever happened to you? You've just turned on the shower. Upon stepping into the water stream, you decide that the water pressure is not strong enough. You turn the faucet to provide more water, and all of a sudden the bottom edge of the shower curtain starts swirling around your legs. What's going on? It might surprise you that the explanation for this unusual occurrence also explains how wings help birds and planes fly and how pitchers throw curve balls.

Fluid Pressure Decreases as Speed Increases

The strange reaction of the shower curtain is caused by a property of moving fluids that was first described in the eighteenth century by Daniel Bernoulli (buhr NOO lee), a Swiss mathematician. **Bernoulli's principle** states that as the speed of a moving fluid increases, its pressure decreases. In the case of the shower curtain, the faster the water moves, the less pressure it exerts. This creates an imbalance between the pressure inside the shower curtain and the pressure outside it. Because the pressure outside is now greater than the pressure inside, the shower curtain is pushed toward the water stream.

Science in a Sink You can see Bernoulli's principle at work in **Figure 14**. A table-tennis ball is attached to a string and swung gently into a moving stream of water. Instead of being pushed back out, the ball is actually held in the moving water when the string is given a tug. Why does the ball do that? The water is moving, so it has a lower pressure than the surrounding air. The higher air pressure then pushes the ball into the area of lower pressure—the water stream. Try this at home to see for yourself!

Figure 14 This ball is pushed by the higher pressure of the air into an area of reduced pressure—the water stream.

QuickLab

Breathing Bernoulli-Style

1. Hold **two pieces of paper** by their top edges, one in each hand, so that they hang next to one another about 5 cm apart.
2. Blow a steady stream of air between the two sheets of paper.
3. Record your observations in your ScienceLog. Explain the results according to Bernoulli's principle.

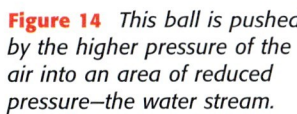

QuickLab

MATERIALS

For Each Student:
- two pieces of paper

Answer to QuickLab

3. Blowing a steady stream of air between the pieces of paper causes them to move toward each other—an example of Bernoulli's principle. The fast-moving air between the pieces of paper has a lower pressure than the air outside the pieces of paper. The higher pressure outside pushes the pieces of paper together.

SECTION 3

Focus

Bernoulli's Principle

In this section students learn about Bernoulli's principle. They then explore how heavier-than-air objects can achieve flight. Students learn about thrust, drag, and lift, three other basic aspects of flight.

Bellringer

Pose the following problem to your students:

You have been asked to design two kites. One kite will be flown in areas where there is almost always a good breeze. The other kite will be flown in areas with very little wind.

What differences in design and materials are there between your two kites? Write your answer in your ScienceLog.

1) Motivate

DEMONSTRATION

Place a straw upright in a glass of water. Hold a second straw at a right angle at the top of the first so that the straws are just touching. Blow very hard through the horizontal straw. Water will rise up in the vertical straw and form a spray. Tell students they will learn why this occurs in this section.

Directed Reading Worksheet 7 Section 3

Section 3 • Bernoulli's Principle   **173**

2 Teach

MEETING INDIVIDUAL NEEDS

Learners Having Difficulty Before you discuss Bernoulli's principle, it may help some students to imagine the pressure of a fluid as the combined pressure of many particles striking a surface. Have students imagine a swarm of bees trapped in a short section of a long piece of pipe. As the bees fly around inside the pipe, they bounce off each other and off the walls of the pipe, creating pressure. Now imagine the bees are suddenly able to fly the entire length of the pipe. Because they now have more room, they bounce against the walls of the pipe much less frequently, creating less pressure inside the pipe.

MEETING INDIVIDUAL NEEDS

Advanced Learners Ask students to examine the wing shapes shown in **Figure 15.** Have students use their knowledge of Bernoulli's principle to hypothesize about what type of wings might work in flight. Does the wing have to be curved? How does each of Newton's laws apply to both curved and flat wings? Is flight possible without wings?

DEMONSTRATION

Point the airflow of a portable hair dryer straight up, and suspend a table-tennis ball in the airstream. Change the direction of the airflow slightly to maneuver the ball. Have students speculate on the forces that are at work in this demonstration.

BRAIN FOOD

The first successful flight of an engine-driven heavier-than-air machine occurred in Kitty Hawk, North Carolina, in 1903. Orville Wright was the pilot. The plane flew only 37 m (about the length of a 737 jet) before landing, and the entire flight lasted only 12 seconds.

It's a Bird! It's a Plane! It's Bernoulli's Principle!

The most common commercial airplane in the skies today is the Boeing 737 jet. A 737 jet is almost 37 m long and has a wingspan of 30 m. Even without passengers, the plane weighs 350,000 N. That's more than 35 times heavier than an average car! How can something so big and heavy get off the ground, much less fly 10,000 m into the sky? Wing shape plays a role in helping these big planes—as well as smaller planes and even birds—achieve flight, as shown in **Figure 15.**

According to Bernoulli's principle, the faster-moving air above the wing exerts less pressure than the slower-moving air below the wing. The increased pressure that results below the wing exerts an upward force. This upward force, known as **lift,** pushes the wings (and the rest of the airplane or bird) upward against the downward pull of gravity.

Figure 15 Wing Shape Creates Differences in Air Speed

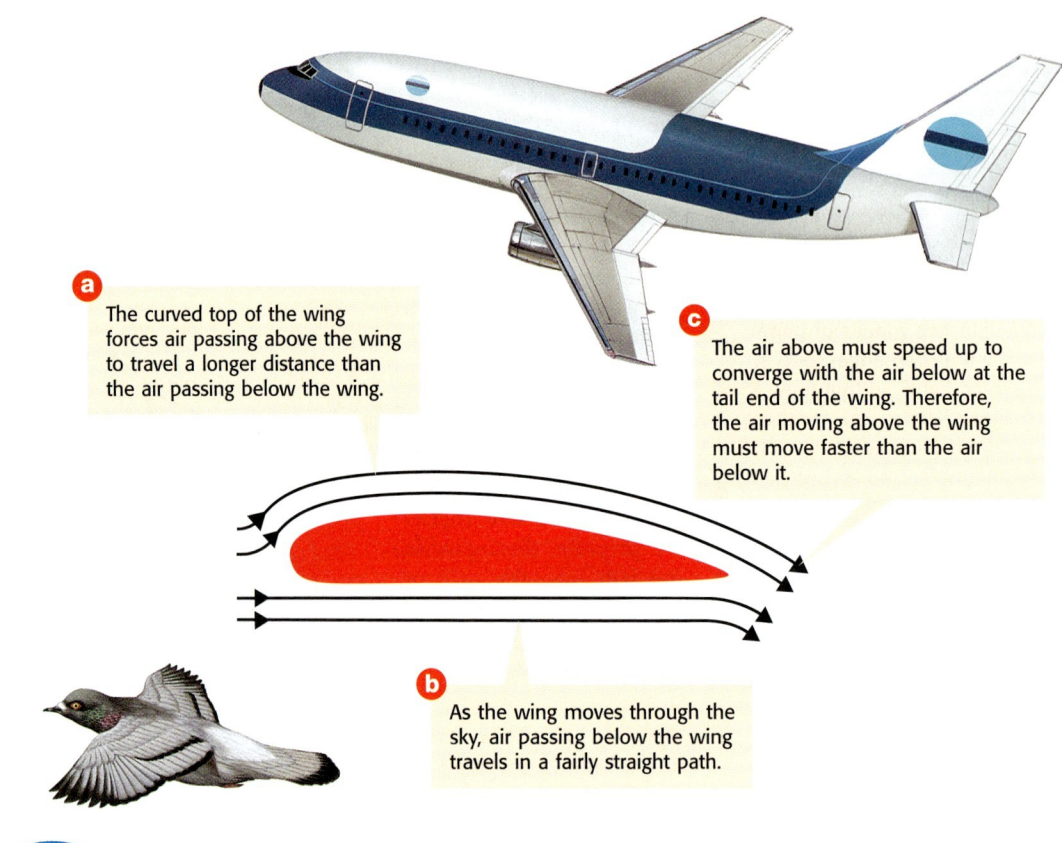

a The curved top of the wing forces air passing above the wing to travel a longer distance than the air passing below the wing.

c The air above must speed up to converge with the air below at the tail end of the wing. Therefore, the air moving above the wing must move faster than the air below it.

b As the wing moves through the sky, air passing below the wing travels in a fairly straight path.

MISCONCEPTION ALERT

In teaching about airplane flight, emphasize that there is more to understanding lift than can be explained by Bernoulli's principle alone. Newton's third law also plays a part—a tilted wing deflects horizontal airflow downward (the action force exerted by the wing on the air). In reaction, the air exerts an upward force on the wing. This effect also contributes to lift.

174 Chapter 7 • Forces in Fluids

Thrust and Wing Size Determine Lift

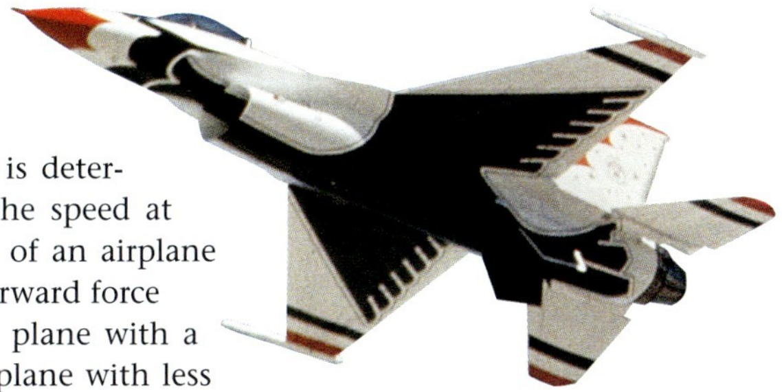

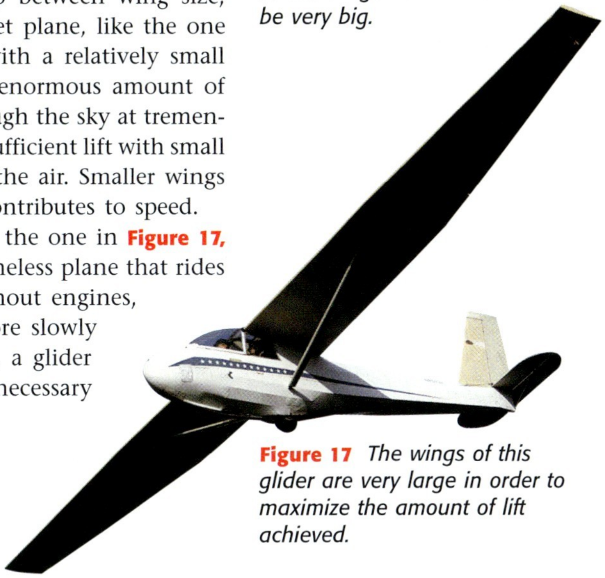

Figure 16 *The engine of this jet creates a great deal of thrust, so the wings don't have to be very big.*

The amount of lift created by a plane's wing is determined in part by the size of the wing and the speed at which air travels around the wing. The speed of an airplane is in large part determined by its **thrust**—the forward force produced by the plane's engine. In general, a plane with a greater amount of thrust moves faster than a plane with less thrust. This faster speed means air travels around the wing at a greater speed, which increases lift.

You can understand the relationship between wing size, thrust, and speed by thinking about a jet plane, like the one in **Figure 16.** This plane is able to fly with a relatively small wing size because its engine creates an enormous amount of thrust. This thrust pushes the plane through the sky at tremendous speeds. Therefore, the jet generates sufficient lift with small wings by moving very quickly through the air. Smaller wings keep a plane's weight low, which also contributes to speed.

Compared with the jet, a glider, like the one in **Figure 17,** has a large wing area. A glider is an engineless plane that rides rising air currents to stay in flight. Without engines, gliders produce no thrust and move more slowly than many other kinds of planes. Thus, a glider must have large wings to create the lift necessary to keep it in the air.

Figure 17 *The wings of this glider are very large in order to maximize the amount of lift achieved.*

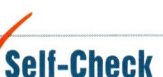

Self-Check

Does air travel faster or slower over the top of a wing? *(See page 724 to check your answer.)*

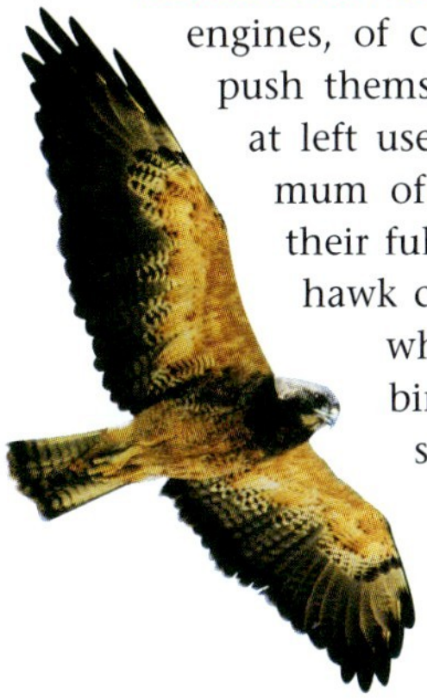

Bernoulli's Principle Is for the Birds Birds don't have engines, of course, so they must flap their wings to push themselves through the air. The hawk shown at left uses its large wing size to fly with a minimum of effort. By extending its large wings to their full length and gliding on wind currents, a hawk can achieve enough lift to stay in the air while flapping only occasionally. Smaller birds must flap their wings more often to stay in the air.

LabBook

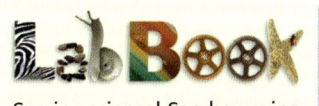

Soaring science! See how wing shape affects the flight of your own airplane on page 661 of the LabBook.

Group Activity

Safety Caution: Caution students to wear goggles, gloves, and aprons while doing this activity.

Prepare a solution consisting of 250 mL of dishwashing liquid, 50–60 drops of glycerin, and 4.5 L of water. Give small groups of students containers of the solution and straws or other bubble-blowing tools. You may also want to provide them with index cards or fans to help create a breeze.

Ask the groups to devise ways to keep the bubbles from hitting the floor. Have them describe methods that increase the pressure under the bubble or decrease the pressure over it.

LabBook PG 661
Taking Flight

Meeting Individual Needs

Advanced Learners Have students research how engineers use wind tunnels to test the design of airplane wings. Then have students use what they have learned to build their own wings and wind tunnel, and show the class how to test the wing designs.

Answer to Self-Check

Air travels faster over the top of a wing.

Multicultural Connection

More than 8,000 years ago, Australian aborigines discovered the aerodynamic qualities of a type of hunting stick called a boomerang. Have students research boomerangs and compare a boomerang's flight to airplane flight.

Teaching Transparency 227
"Wing Shape Creates Differences in Air Speed"

Critical Thinking Worksheet 7
"Build a Better Submarine"

internetconnect
SciLINKS NSTA
TOPIC: Bernoulli's Principle
GO TO: www.scilinks.org
***sci*LINKS NUMBER:** HSTP170

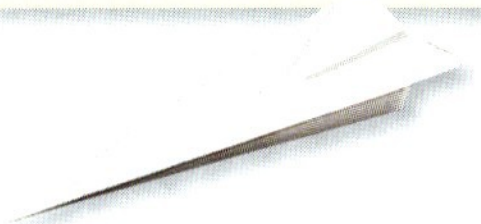

2 Teach, continued

Answer to APPLY

The upside-down wing shape causes air to travel faster under the spoiler, reducing the air pressure. The higher air pressure above the spoiler "pushes" the car down, reducing the chances that the rear wheels will lose contact with the ground.

CROSS-DISCIPLINARY FOCUS

Language Arts Have students imagine being a hawk or an albatross. (They may need to do a little research.) Have students write a report or make a poster or concept map describing how the principles of flight apply to them as they travel through the sky.

3 Extend

GOING FURTHER

Have students work together in groups to research and select a design for a paper airplane they think would have the longest flight time. When all groups have made their plane, take the class outside to fly the planes. Each group should select a member to throw their plane gently from the same location. Have students record the results for five flights, then average the times and write the data on the board. Discuss the differences in the planes that may account for the observed results.

Teaching Transparency 228
"Pitching a Curve Ball"

Lift and Spoilers

At high speeds, air moving around the body of this race car could lift the car just as it lifts a plane's wing. This could cause the wheels to lose contact with the ground, sending the car out of control. To prevent this situation, an upside-down wing, or spoiler, is mounted on the rear of the car. How do spoilers help reduce the danger of accidents?

Drag Opposes Motion in Fluids

Have you ever walked into a strong wind and noticed that the wind seemed to slow you down? Fluids exert a force that opposes motion. The force that opposes or restricts motion in a fluid is called **drag.** In a strong wind, air "drags" on your clothes and body, making it difficult for you to move forward. Drag forces in flight work against the forward motion of a plane or bird and are usually caused by an irregular flow of air around the wings. An irregular or unpredictable flow of fluids is known as *turbulence*.

Lift is often reduced when turbulence causes drag. At faster speeds, drag can become a serious problem, so airplanes are equipped with ways to reduce turbulence as much as possible when in flight. For example, flaps like those shown in **Figure 18** can be used to change the shape or area of a wing, thereby reducing drag and increasing lift. Similarly, birds can adjust their wing feathers in response to turbulence to achieve greater lift.

Figure 18 During flight, the pilot of this airplane can adjust these flaps to help increase lift.

SCIENTISTS AT ODDS

In the 1940s, pilots of high-speed airplanes reported that as they approached the speed of sound (343 m/s at 20°C), their planes began to shake and the controls did not function properly. At these speeds, shock waves formed a cone of turbulence around the plane, interrupting the airflow over the wings. Some scientists believed that an airplane could not go faster than the speed of sound because the turbulence from shock waves would tear the wings apart. Others believed that with better designs, planes could pass this speed. Jet planes with swept-back wings and stronger frames eventually surpassed the speed of sound.

176 Chapter 7 • Forces in Fluids

Wings Are Not Always Required

You don't have to look up at a bird or a plane flying through the sky to see Bernoulli's principle in your world. In fact, you've already learned how Bernoulli's principle can affect such things as shower curtains and race cars. Any time fluids are moving, Bernoulli's principle is at work. In **Figure 19,** you can see how Bernoulli's principle can mean the difference between a home run and a strike during a baseball game.

Bernoulli's principle at play—read how Frisbees® were invented on page 182.

Figure 19 *A pitcher can take advantage of Bernoulli's principle to produce a confusing curveball that is difficult for the batter to hit.*

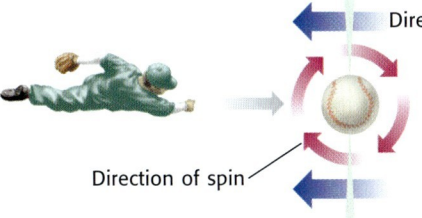

a Air speed on the left side of the ball is decreased because air being dragged around the ball moves in the opposite direction of the airflow. This results in a region of increased pressure on the left side of the ball.

b Air speed on the right side of the ball is increased because air being dragged around the ball moves in the same direction as the airflow. This results in a region of decreased pressure on the right side of the ball.

c Because air pressure on the left side is greater than that on the right side, the ball is pushed toward the right in a curved path.

REVIEW

1. Does fluid pressure increase or decrease as fluid speed increases?
2. Explain how wing shape can contribute to lift during flight.
3. What force opposes motion through a fluid?
4. **Interpreting Graphics** When the space through which a fluid flows becomes narrow, fluid speed increases. Explain how this could lead to a collision for the two boats shown at right.

CONNECT TO
EARTH SCIENCE

A hurricane is a large, circular storm system that usually occurs in late summer or early fall. In a powerful hurricane, winds can reach speeds of 150 km/h. This fast-moving wind may reduce outside air pressure so much that the higher air pressure inside a house causes windows to break and the roof to fly off.

4) Close

Quiz

1. What forces act on an aircraft? (lift, thrust, drag, and gravity)
2. When an airplane is flying, how does the air pressure above a wing compare with that below the wing? (Air pressure above the wing is lower.)
3. Why do shower curtains often have weights or magnets at the bottom? (to prevent them from being pushed toward the water stream)

ALTERNATIVE ASSESSMENT

Display two or three photographs or models of different types of aircraft, such as a glider, a jet, a biplane, or even an airship. Ask students to select two of the aircraft to compare and contrast them in terms of lift, drag, thrust, and gravity. What are the characteristics of each aircraft that allow it to fly?

Reinforcement Worksheet 7 "Building Up Pressure"

Answers to Review

1. Fluid pressure decreases.
2. Many wings are shaped so that air passing over the wing travels a longer distance than air traveling under the wing. The air above the wing must speed up to converge with the air below. This faster-moving air reduces the pressure above the wing, and higher pressure below the wing results in lift (upward force on the wing).
3. drag
4. As the fluid speed between the boats increases, the fluid pressure decreases. The pressure on the outer sides of the boats then becomes greater than the pressure between them. This increased pressure from the outside can push the boats together, causing them to collide.

Chapter Highlights

VOCABULARY DEFINITIONS

SECTION 1

fluid any material that can flow and that takes the shape of its container

pressure the amount of force exerted on a given area

pascal the SI unit for pressure; equal to the force of one newton exerted over an area of one square meter

atmospheric pressure the pressure caused by the weight of the atmosphere

density the amount of matter in a given space; mass per unit volume

Pascal's principle the principle that states that a change in pressure at any point in an enclosed fluid is transmitted equally to all parts of that fluid

SECTION 2

buoyant force the upward force that fluids exert on all matter; buoyant force opposes gravitational force

Archimedes' principle the principle that states that the buoyant force on an object in a fluid is an upward force equal to the weight of the volume of fluid that the object displaces

Chapter Highlights

SECTION 1

Vocabulary
fluid (p. 162)
pressure (p. 162)
pascal (p. 162)
atmospheric pressure (p. 163)
density (p. 165)
Pascal's principle (p. 167)

Section Notes

- A fluid is any material that flows and that takes the shape of its container.
- Pressure is force exerted on a given area.
- Moving particles of matter create pressure by colliding with one another and with the walls of their container.
- Fluids exert pressure equally in all directions.
- The pressure caused by the weight of Earth's atmosphere is called atmospheric pressure.
- Fluid pressure increases as depth increases.
- Fluids flow from areas of high pressure to areas of low pressure.
- Pascal's principle states that a change in pressure at any point in an enclosed fluid will be transmitted equally to all parts of the fluid.
- Hydraulic devices transmit changes of pressure through liquids.

SECTION 2

Vocabulary
buoyant force (p. 168)
Archimedes' principle (p. 168)

Section Notes

- All fluids exert an upward force called buoyant force.
- Buoyant force is caused by differences in fluid pressure.
- Archimedes' principle states that the buoyant force on an object is equal to the weight of the fluid displaced by the object.

✓ Skills Check

Math Concepts

PRESSURE If an object exerts a force of 10 N over an area of 2 m², the pressure exerted can be calculated as follows:

$$\text{Pressure} = \frac{\text{Force}}{\text{Area}}$$
$$= \frac{10 \text{ N}}{2 \text{ m}^2}$$
$$= \frac{5 \text{ N}}{1 \text{ m}^2}, \text{ or } 5 \text{ Pa}$$

Visual Understanding

ATMOSPHERIC PRESSURE Why aren't you crushed by atmospheric pressure? Figure 3 on page 163 can help you understand.

BUOYANT FORCE To understand how differences in fluid pressure cause buoyant force, review Figure 9 on page 168.

BERNOULLI'S PRINCIPLE AND WING SHAPE Turn to page 174 to review how a wing is often shaped to take advantage of Bernoulli's principle in creating lift.

Lab and Activity Highlights

Fluids, Force, and Floating   PG 658

Density Diver   PG 660

Taking Flight   PG 661

Datasheets for LabBook
(blackline masters for these labs)

178   Chapter 7 • Forces in Fluids

SECTION 2

- Any object that is more dense than the surrounding fluid will sink; any object that is less dense than the surrounding fluid will float.

Labs

Fluids, Force, and Floating (p. 658)

Density Diver (p. 660)

SECTION 3

Vocabulary
Bernoulli's principle (p. 173)
lift (p. 174)
thrust (p. 175)
drag (p. 176)

Section Notes

- Bernoulli's principle states that fluid pressure decreases as the speed of a moving fluid increases.

- Wings are often shaped to allow airplanes to take advantage of decreased pressure in moving air in order to achieve flight.

- Lift is an upward force that acts against gravity.

- Lift on an airplane is determined by wing size and thrust (the forward force produced by the engine).

- Drag opposes motion through fluids.

Labs

Taking Flight (p. 661)

VOCABULARY DEFINITIONS, continued

SECTION 3

Bernoulli's principle the principle that states that as the speed of a moving fluid increases, its pressure decreases

lift an upward force on an object (such as a wing) caused by differences in pressure above and below the object; lift opposes the downward pull of gravity

thrust the forward force produced by an airplane's engines; thrust opposes drag

drag the force that opposes or restricts motion in a fluid; drag opposes thrust

 Vocabulary Review Worksheet 7

 Blackline masters of these Chapter Highlights can be found in the **Study Guide.**

internet connect

 **GO TO:** go.hrw.com

Visit the **HRW** Web site for a variety of learning tools related to this chapter. Just type in the keyword:

KEYWORD: HSTFLU

 **GO TO:** www.scilinks.org

Visit the **National Science Teachers Association** on-line Web site for Internet resources related to this chapter. Just type in the *sci*LINKS number for more information about the topic:

TOPIC: Submarines and Undersea Technology   *sci*LINKS NUMBER: HSTP155
TOPIC: Fluids and Pressure   *sci*LINKS NUMBER: HSTP160
TOPIC: The Buoyant Force   *sci*LINKS NUMBER: HSTP165
TOPIC: Bernoulli's Principle   *sci*LINKS NUMBER: HSTP170

Lab and Activity Highlights

LabBank

 Whiz-Bang Demonstrations
- The Rise and Fall of Raisins, Demo 46
- Going Against the Flow, Demo 47

EcoLabs & Field Activities, What's the Flap All About? Field Activity 18

 Long-Term Projects & Research Ideas, Scuba Dive, Project 57

Interactive Explorations CD-ROM

 CD 3, Exploration 2, "Sea the Light"

Chapter 7 • Chapter Highlights   **179**

Chapter Review

USING VOCABULARY

To complete the following sentences, choose the correct term from each of the pair of terms listed below:

1. __?__ increases with the depth of a fluid. (*Pressure* or *Lift*)

2. A plane's engine produces __?__ to push the plane forward. (*thrust* or *drag*)

3. Force divided by area is known as __?__. (*density* or *pressure*)

4. The hydraulic brakes of a car transmit pressure through fluid. This is an example of __?__. (*Archimedes' principle* or *Pascal's principle*)

5. Bernoulli's principle states that the pressure exerted by a moving fluid is __?__ (*greater than* or *less than*) the pressure of the fluid when it is not moving.

UNDERSTANDING CONCEPTS

Multiple Choice

6. The curve on the top of a wing
   a. causes air to travel farther in the same amount of time as the air below the wing.
   b. helps create lift.
   c. creates a low-pressure zone above the wing.
   d. All of the above

7. An object displaces a volume of fluid that
   a. is equal to its own volume.
   b. is less than its own volume.
   c. is greater than its own volume.
   d. is more dense than itself.

8. Fluid pressure is always directed
   a. up.
   b. down.
   c. sideways.
   d. in all directions.

9. If an object weighing 50 N displaces a volume of water with a weight of 10 N, what is the buoyant force on the object?
   a. 60 N
   b. 50 N
   c. 40 N
   d. 10 N

10. A helium-filled balloon will float in air because
    a. there is more air than helium.
    b. helium is less dense than air.
    c. helium is as dense as air.
    d. helium is more dense than air.

11. Materials that can flow to fit their containers include
    a. gases.
    b. liquids.
    c. both gases and liquids.
    d. neither gases nor liquids.

Short Answer

12. What two factors determine the amount of lift achieved by an airplane?

13. Where is water pressure greater, at a depth of 1 m in a large lake or at a depth of 2 m in a small pond? Explain.

14. Is there buoyant force on an object at the bottom of an ocean? Explain your reasoning.

15. Why are liquids used in hydraulic brakes instead of gases?

Concept Mapping

16. Use the following terms to create a concept map: fluid, pressure, depth, buoyant force, density.

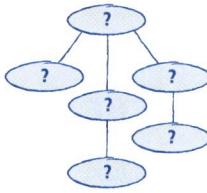

CRITICAL THINKING AND PROBLEM SOLVING

17. Compared with an empty ship, will a ship loaded with plastic-foam balls float higher or lower in the water? Explain your reasoning.

18. Inside all vacuum cleaners is a high-speed fan. Explain how this fan causes dirt to be picked up by the vacuum cleaner.

19. A 600 N clown on stilts says to two 600 N clowns sitting on the ground, "I am exerting twice as much pressure as the two of you together!" Could this statement be true? Explain your reasoning.

MATH IN SCIENCE

20. Calculate the area of a 1,500 N object that exerts a pressure of 500 Pa (N/m^2). Then calculate the pressure exerted by the same object over twice that area. Be sure to express your answers in the correct SI unit.

INTERPRETING GRAPHICS

Examine the illustration of an iceberg below, and answer the questions that follow.

21. At what point (*a*, *b*, or *c*) is water pressure greatest on the iceberg?

22. How much of the iceberg has a weight equal to the buoyant force?
    a. all of it
    b. the section from *a* to *b*
    c. the section from *b* to *c*

23. How does the density of ice compare with the density of water?

24. Why do you think icebergs are so dangerous to passing ships?

NOW What Do You Think?

Take a minute to review your answers to the ScienceLog questions on page 161. Have your answers changed? If necessary, revise your answers based on what you have learned since you began this chapter.

CRITICAL THINKING AND PROBLEM SOLVING

17. The ship will float lower in the water because the plastic-foam balls will add to the total mass of the ship but will not increase the volume. Therefore, the overall density of the ship will increase, causing the ship to sink a little.

18. The fan causes the air inside the vacuum cleaner to move faster, which decreases pressure. The higher air pressure outside of the vacuum then pushes dirt into the vacuum cleaner.

19. Yes, the statement could be true. Pressure is equal to force over area, that is, an amount of force applied over a certain area. The clown on stilts is exerting force over a much smaller area than the two clowns on the ground are. Therefore, it is possible that the clown on stilts is exerting twice as much pressure as the other two clowns are.

MATH IN SCIENCE

20. 3 m^2; 250 Pa

INTERPRETING GRAPHICS

21. c
22. a
23. Ice is less dense than water.
24. Only a small portion of an iceberg floats above water, as shown in the image. A ship may actually be closer to running into a massive block of ice underwater than it would appear on the surface. If the ship is not turned or stopped in time, it could collide with or scrape the iceberg.

NOW WHAT DO YOU THINK?

1. A fluid is any material that can flow and that takes the shape of its container.
2. Fluid pressure is exerted by fluid particles colliding with each other and with the walls of their container.
3. Moving fluids travel at faster speeds than nonmoving fluids and therefore exert less pressure (less force per unit area).

 Blackline masters of this Chapter Review can be found in the **Study Guide**.

Eureka!
Stayin' Aloft—The Story of the Frisbee®

Whoa! Nice catch! Your friend 30 m away just sent a disk spinning toward you. As you reached for it, a gust of wind floated it up over your head. With a quick jump, you snagged it. A snap of your wrist sends the disk soaring back. You are "Frisbee-ing," a game more than 100 years old. But back then, there were no plastic disks, only pie plates.

From Pie Plate...

In the late 1800s, ready-made pies baked in tin plates began to appear in stores and restaurants. A bakery near Yale University, in New Haven, Connecticut, embossed its name, Frisbie's Pies, on its pie plates. When a few fun-loving college students tossed empty pie plates, they found that the metal plates had a marvelous ability to stay in the air. Soon the students began alerting their companions of an incoming pie plate by shouting "Frisbie!" So tossing pie plates became known as Frisbie-ing. By the late 1940s, the game was played across the country.

...to Plastic

In 1947, California businessmen Fred Morrison and Warren Franscioni needed to make a little extra money. They were familiar with pie-plate tossing, and they knew the plates often cracked when they landed and developed sharp edges that caused injuries. At the time, plastic was becoming widely available. Plastic is more durable and flexible than metal, and it isn't as likely to injure fingers. Why not make a "pie plate" out of plastic, thought Morrison and Franscioni? They did, and their idea was a huge success.

Years later, a toy company bought the rights to make the toy. One day the president of the company heard someone yelling "Frisbie!" while tossing a disk and decided to use that name, changing the spelling to "Frisbee."

Saucer Science

It looks simple, but Frisbee flight is quite complicated. It involves *thrust*, the force you give the disk to move it through the air; *angle of attack*, the slight upward tilt you give the disk when you throw it; and *lift*, the upward forces (explained by Bernoulli's principle) acting on the Frisbee to counteract gravity. But perhaps the most important aspect of Frisbee physics is *spin*, which gives the Frisbee stability as it flies. The faster a Frisbee spins, the more stable it is and the farther it can fly.

What Do You Think?

▶ From what you've learned in class, why do you think the Frisbee has a curved lip? Would a completely flat Frisbee fly as well? Why or why not? Find out more about the interesting aerodynamics of Frisbee flight. Fly a Frisbee for the class, and explain what you've learned.

Science Fiction

"Wet Behind the Ears"

by Jack C. Haldeman II

Willie Joe Thomas is a college student who lied to get into college and cheated to get a swimming scholarship. Now he is faced with a major swim meet, and his coach has told him that he has to swim or be kicked off the team. Willie Joe could lose his scholarship. What's worse, he would have to get a *job*.

"Wet Behind the Ears" is Willie Joe's story. It's the story of someone who has always taken the easy way (even if it takes more work), of someone who lies and cheats as easily as he breathes. Willie Joe could probably do things the right way, but it never even occurred to him to try it!

So when Willie Joe's roommate, Frank Emerson, announces that he has made an amazing discovery in the chemistry lab, Willie Joe doesn't much care. Frank works too hard. Frank follows the rules. Willie Joe isn't impressed.

But when he is running late for the all-important swim meet, Willie Joe remembers what Frank's new compound does. Frank said it was a "sliding compound." Willie Joe may not know chemistry, but "slippery" he understands. And Frank also said something about selling the stuff to the Navy to make its ships go faster. Hey, if it works for ships . . .

See what happens when Willie Joe tries to save his scholarship. Go to the *Holt Anthology of Science Fiction,* and read "Wet Behind the Ears," by Jack C. Haldeman II.

Further Reading Try some of Haldeman's other sports-related science fiction stories, such as the following:

"Louisville Slugger," *Isaac Asimov's Science Fiction Magazine,* Summer 1977.

"Thrill of Victory," *Isaac Asimov's Science Fiction Magazine,* Summer 1978.

"Dirt Track Demon," *Aladdin: Master of the Lamp,* Resnick & Greenberg, eds. New York: D.A.W. Books, 1992.

"South of Eden, Somewhere Near Salinas," *By Any Other Fame,* Mike Resnick, ed. New York: D.A.W. Books, 1994.

SCIENCE FICTION

"Wet Behind the Ears"
by Jack C. Haldeman II

Genuine effort can be less work than cheating, but Willie Joe just isn't the kind of person who exerts himself—even in a sink-or-swim situation.

Teaching Strategy

Reading Level This is a relatively short story that should not be difficult for the average student to read and comprehend.

Background

About the Author Sports and science fiction may seem like an unlikely combination, but Jack C. Haldeman enjoys both. He has written science fiction stories, sports stories, and stories such as "Wet Behind the Ears," which is a bit of both! Before becoming a writer, Haldeman received a college degree in life science and worked as a research assistant, a medical technician, a statistician, a photographer, and an apprentice in a print shop.

Many of Haldeman's stories are funny. For instance, "What Weighs 8,000 Pounds and Wears Red Sneakers?" describes a family that discovers their front yard is an elephant graveyard. Haldeman has also written several science fiction novels that explore issues in biology and in weapons development.

UNIT 3

TIMELINE
Work, Machines, and Energy

Can you imagine living in a world with no machines? In this unit, you will explore the scientific meaning of *work* and learn how machines make work easier. You will find out how energy allows you to do work and how different forms of energy can be converted into other forms of energy. You will also learn about heat and how heating and cooling systems work. This timeline shows some of the inventions and discoveries made throughout history as people have advanced their understanding of work, machines, and energy.

Around 3000 B.C.
The sail is used in Egypt. Sails use the wind rather than human power to move boats through the water.

Around 200 B.C.
Under the Han dynasty, the Chinese become one of the first civilizations to use coal as fuel.

1926
American scientist Robert Goddard launches the first rocket powered by liquid fuel. It reaches a height of 56 m and a speed of 97 km/h.

1948
Maria Telkes, a Hungarian-born physicist, designs the heating system for the first solar-heated house.

1972
The first American self-service gas station opens.

1656
Dutch scientist Christiaan Huygens invents the pendulum clock.

1776
The American colonies declare their independence from Great Britain.

1818
The first two-wheeled, rider-propelled machine is invented by German Baron Karl von Drais de Sauerbrun. Made of wood, this early machine paves the way for the invention of the bicycle.

1893
The zipper is patented.

1908
The automobile age begins with the mass production of the Ford Model T.

1988
The world's most powerful wind-powered generator begins generating electrical energy in Scotland's Orkney Islands.

2000
The 2000 Olympic Summer Games are held in Sydney, Australia.

Work, Machines, and Energy **185**

Chapter Organizer

CHAPTER ORGANIZATION	TIME MINUTES	OBJECTIVES	LABS, INVESTIGATIONS, AND DEMONSTRATIONS
Chapter Opener pp. 186–187	45	National Standards: SAI 1, ST 2, HNS 3	**Investigate!** C'mon, Lever a Little! p. 187
Section 1 Work and Power	90	▶ Determine when work is being done on an object. ▶ Calculate the amount of work done on an object. ▶ Explain the difference between work and power. UCP 3, SAI 1; LabBook SAI 1	**QuickLab,** More Power to You, p. 191 **Discovery Lab,** A Powerful Workout, p. 662 **Datasheets for LabBook,** A Powerful Workout, Datasheet 27 **Inquiry Labs,** Get an Arm and an Egg Up, Lab 19
Section 2 What Is a Machine?	90	▶ Explain how a machine makes work easier. ▶ Describe and give examples of the force-distance trade-off that occurs when a machine is used. ▶ Calculate mechanical advantage. ▶ Explain why machines are not 100 percent efficient. UCP 3, ST 2, SPSP 5, HNS 1	**Whiz-Bang Demonstrations,** Pull-Ease, Please! Demo 48 **Whiz-Bang Demonstrations,** A Clever Lever, Demo 49
Section 3 Types of Machines	90	▶ Identify and give examples of the six types of simple machines. ▶ Analyze the mechanical advantage provided by each simple machine. ▶ Identify the simple machines that make up a compound machine. UCP 5, ST 2, SPSP 5; LabBook UCP 3, SAI 1, ST 1	**Skill Builder,** Inclined to Move, p. 664 **Datasheets for LabBook,** Inclined to Move, Datasheet 28 **Skill Builder,** Wheeling and Dealing, p. 666 **Datasheets for LabBook,** Wheeling and Dealing, Datasheet 30 **Design Your Own,** Building Machines, p. 665 **Datasheets for LabBook,** Building Machines, Datasheet 29 **Long-Term Projects & Research Ideas,** Project 58

*See page **T20** for a complete correlation of this book with the*

NATIONAL SCIENCE EDUCATION STANDARDS.

TECHNOLOGY RESOURCES

 Guided Reading Audio CD
English or Spanish, Chapter 8

 Science Discovery Videodiscs
Image and Activity Bank with Lesson Plans: Mechancial Advantage
Science Sleuths: The Moving Monument

 CNN Multicultural Connections, Who Built the Egyptian Pyramids? Segment 7
Science, Technology & Society, Snake Robots, Segment 13

 One-Stop Planner CD-ROM with Test Generator

185A Chapter 8 • Work and Machines

Chapter 8 • Work and Machines

CLASSROOM WORKSHEETS, TRANSPARENCIES, AND RESOURCES	SCIENCE INTEGRATION AND CONNECTIONS	REVIEW AND ASSESSMENT
Directed Reading Worksheet 8 **Science Puzzlers, Twisters & Teasers,** Worksheet 8		
Transparency 229, Work or Not Work? **Directed Reading Worksheet 8,** Section 1 **Transparency 230,** Work Depends on Force and Distance **Math Skills for Science Worksheet 51,** Work and Power	**MathBreak,** Working It Out, p. 190 **Math and More,** p. 190 in ATE	**Self-Check,** p. 189 **Review,** p. 191 **Quiz,** p. 191 in ATE **Alternative Assessment,** p. 191 in ATE
Directed Reading Worksheet 8, Section 2 **Transparency 230,** Input Force and Distance **Transparency 231,** Machines Change the Size or Direction (or Both) of a Force **Math Skills for Science Worksheet 53,** Mechanical Advantage	**Cross-Disciplinary Focus,** p. 192 in ATE **Holt Anthology of Science Fiction,** *Clean Up Your Room* **Cross-Disciplinary Focus,** p. 194 in ATE **Connect to Life Science,** p. 195 in ATE **MathBreak,** Finding the Advantage, p. 196 **Math and More,** p. 196 in ATE **Apply,** p. 197 **Eureka!** Wheelchair Innovators, p. 211	**Homework,** pp. 194, 195 in ATE **Review,** p. 197 **Quiz,** p. 197 in ATE **Alternative Assessment,** p. 197 in ATE
Directed Reading Worksheet 8, Section 3 **Critical Thinking Worksheet 8,** Building Works of Art **Reinforcement Worksheet 8,** Finding Machines in Everyday Life **Reinforcement Worksheet 8,** Mechanical Advantage and Efficiency	**Math and More,** p. 202 in ATE **Real-World Connection,** p. 203 in ATE **Science, Technology, and Society:** Micromachines, p. 210	**Review,** p. 202 **Review,** p. 205 **Quiz,** p. 205 in ATE **Alternative Assessment,** p. 205 in ATE

END-OF-CHAPTER REVIEW AND ASSESSMENT

Chapter Review in Study Guide
Vocabulary and Notes in Study Guide
Chapter Tests with Performance-Based Assessment, Chapter 8 Test
Chapter Tests with Performance-Based Assessment, Performance-Based Assessment 8
Concept Mapping Transparency 8

---

internetconnect

 Holt, Rinehart and Winston On-line Resources
go.hrw.com

For worksheets and other teaching aids related to this chapter, visit the HRW Web site and type in the keyword: **HSTWRK**

 **National Science Teachers Association**
www.scilinks.org

Encourage students to use the *sci*LINKS numbers listed in the internet connect boxes to access information and resources on the **NSTA** Web site.

Chapter Resources & Worksheets

Visual Resources

TEACHING TRANSPARENCIES

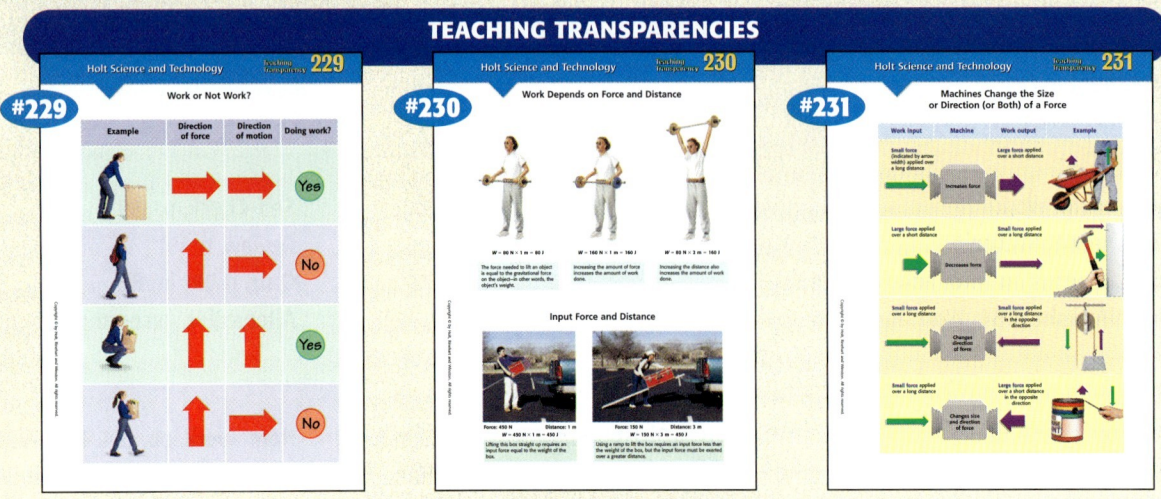

#229 Work or Not Work?
#230 Work Depends on Force and Distance
#231 Machines Change the Size or Direction (or Both) of a Force

CONCEPT MAPPING TRANSPARENCY

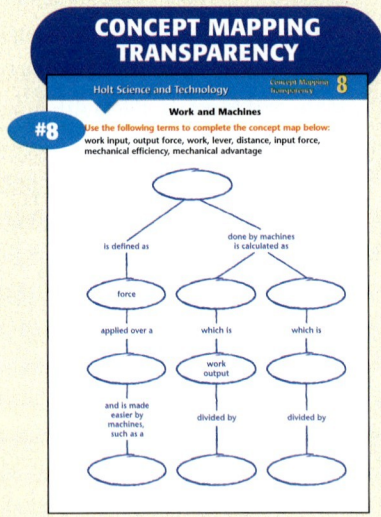

#8 Work and Machines

Meeting Individual Needs

DIRECTED READING

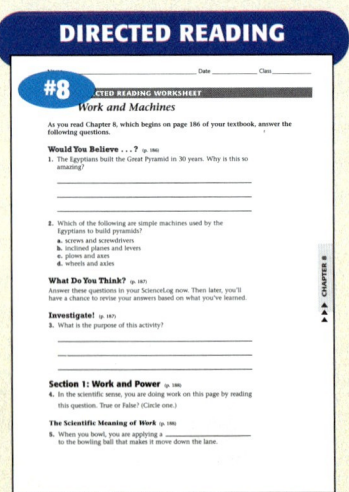

#8 Work and Machines

REINFORCEMENT & VOCABULARY REVIEW

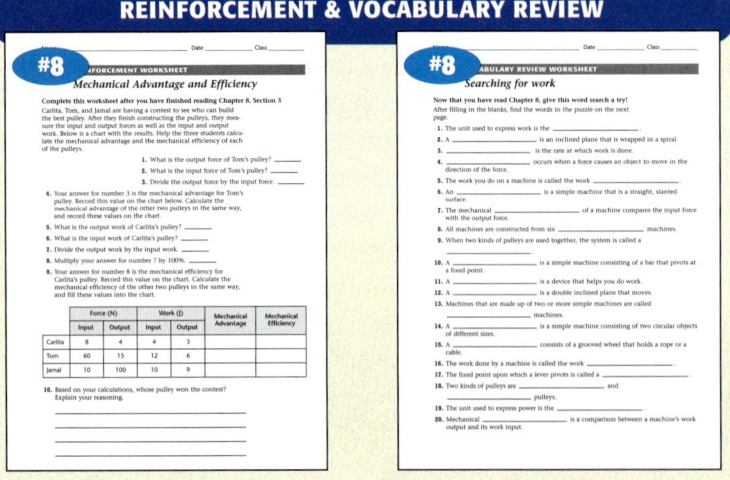

#8 Mechanical Advantage and Efficiency
#8 Searching for work

SCIENCE PUZZLERS, TWISTERS & TEASERS

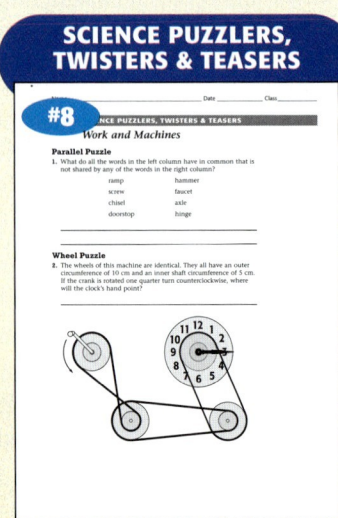

#8 Work and Machines

Chapter 8 • Work and Machines

Chapter 8 • Work and Machines

Review & Assessment

STUDY GUIDE

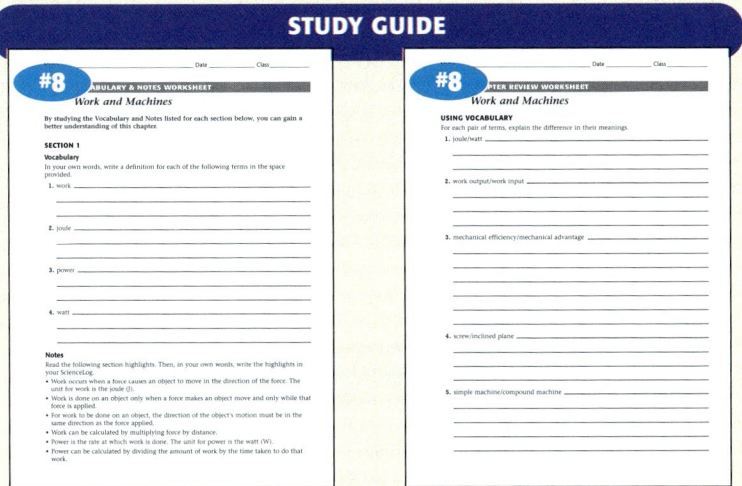

CHAPTER TESTS WITH PERFORMANCE-BASED ASSESSMENT

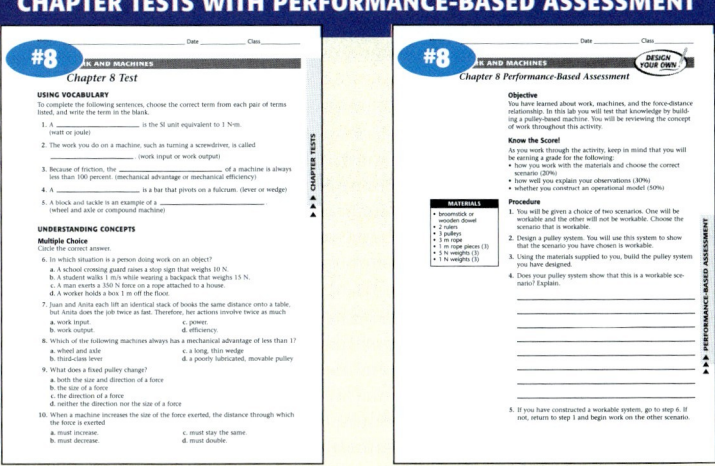

Lab Worksheets

INQUIRY LABS

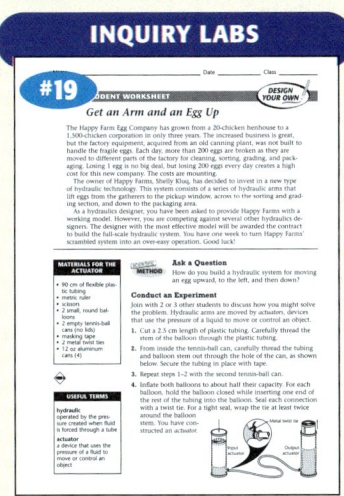

WHIZ-BANG DEMONSTRATIONS

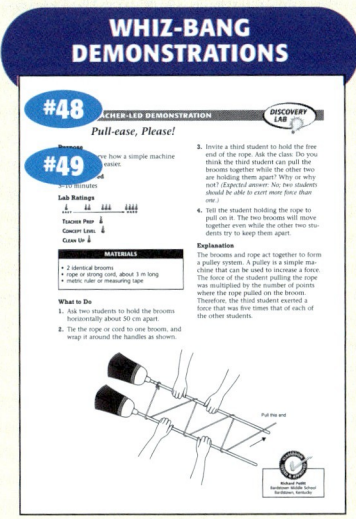

LONG-TERM PROJECTS & RESEARCH IDEAS

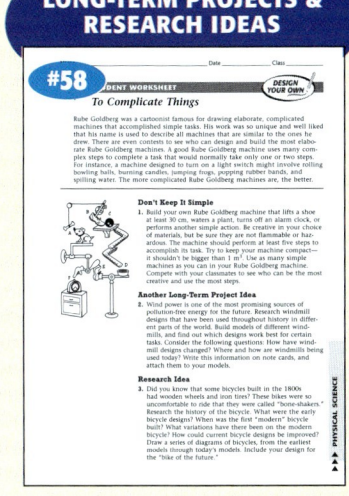

DATASHEETS FOR LABBOOK

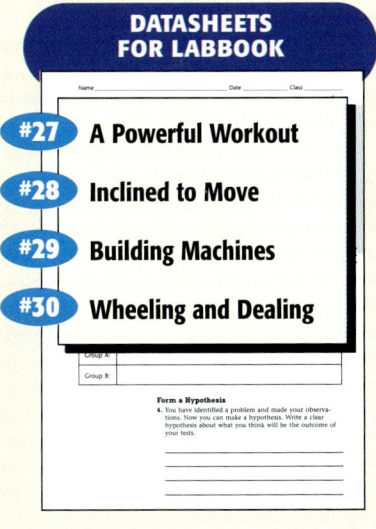

Applications & Extensions

CRITICAL THINKING & PROBLEM SOLVING

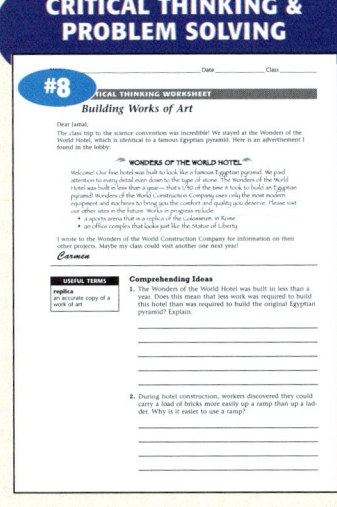

MULTICULTURAL CONNECTIONS

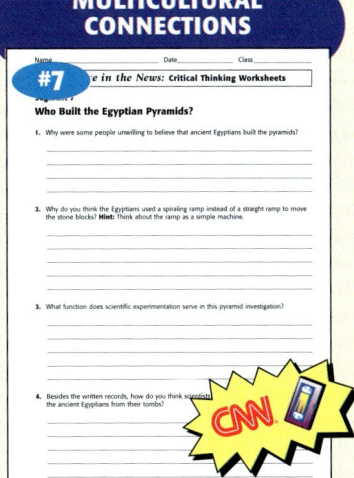

SCIENCE TECHNOLOGY

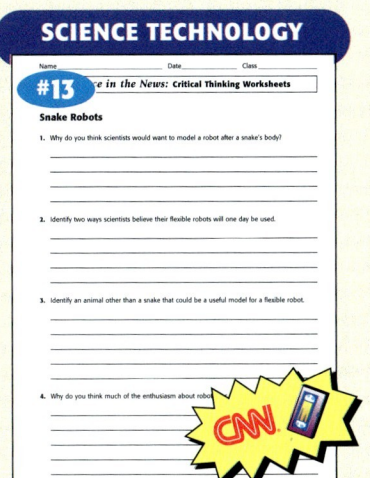

Chapter 8 • Chapter Resources & Worksheets

Chapter Background

SECTION 1

Work and Power

▶ **James Prescott Joule (1818–1889)**
James Joule was an English physicist who established that mechanical energy, electrical energy, and thermal energy are basically the same and that one type of energy can be converted into another. This principle is the basis of the first law of thermodynamics, the conservation of energy. It states that the total energy in any closed system remains the same, even when the energy is converted from one type to another.

- Joule developed mathematical equations that described the thermal energy of current in electrical wire and the amount of work needed to produce a unit of thermal energy. The standard unit of work is called the *joule,* named in his honor.

▶ **Converting Energy**
In physics, energy is the ability to do work. Energy can exist in different forms, such as thermal, electrical, nuclear, potential, kinetic, and chemical. All forms of energy have to do with motion or position. Energy can be converted from one form to another. The electrical energy used to drive all sorts of devices is generated by engines that create thermal energy, batteries, or fuel cells. Energy and energy resources are covered in Chapter 9.

IS THAT A FACT!

▶ The term *horsepower* was coined in the late eighteenth century by Scottish engineer James Watt, who used horses as a measure of power in his experiments. In the English system, one horsepower is 33,000 ft-lb of work per minute, or the force necessary to lift 33,000 lb 1 ft in 1 minute. This unit was based on the dray horse, a horse adapted for drawing heavy loads.

SECTION 2

What Is a Machine?

▶ **Leonardo da Vinci (1452–1519)**
Leonardo da Vinci was an Italian painter, sculptor, and inventor. The motivating interest behind all of his work was the appearance of everyday things and how they operated. He studied the flight of birds, the movement of water, the growth of plants, and the anatomy of the human body.

- One of da Vinci's interests was the mechanical advantage that could be obtained with gears. Da Vinci made drawings of complex machines that were centuries ahead of their time. Among his drawings were plans for tanks, a helicopter, and other aircraft. He was especially concerned with the problems of friction and resistance. He described and drew screws, gears, hydraulic jacks, transmission gears, and swiveling devices.

- Da Vinci felt that the basic laws of mechanics operated the same way in all aspects of the world and were the keys to understanding the world and reproducing it through art.

Chapter 8 • Work and Machines

IS THAT A FACT!

▶ Many industrial towns in early America were located where water flow could be assured all year. Water and wind were the primary sources of mechanical energy until the end of the eighteenth century, when steam power was developed. Steam-powered mechanical devices launched the Industrial Revolution.

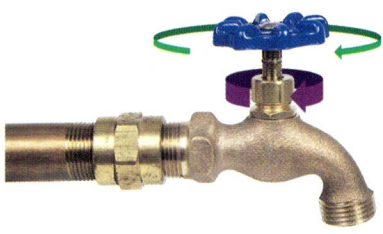

▶ Perpetual Motion
Inventors for centuries have tried to build a perpetual-motion machine—a device that would run forever once it is set in motion. Unfortunately, no such machines can ever work because they would violate the laws of thermodynamics.

- A perpetual-motion machine would work by delivering as much or more energy than is put into it. The first law of thermodynamics states that the total energy of a closed system is constant. The second law states that some energy is always lost as thermal energy from a closed system when energy is used to do work. The practical effect of these two laws is that the output energy from any machine will never be as great as the energy put into it.

- Friction—in which kinetic energy is converted to waste thermal energy—can be reduced but never eliminated. While some machines can be made to run very efficiently, they will always need a source of energy to operate, and they will never be able to produce more energy than is put into them.

SECTION 3
Types of Machines

▶ The Invention of Machines
The first machines were tools used by prehistoric people to help them hunt and gather food. A wedge shaped out of stone made an excellent cutting tool. Early axes were wedges made of stone. Levers were used in hoes, oars, and slings. Because simple machines multiply force or distance, they provided our early ancestors with a tremendous survival advantage.

▶ The Plow
The plow was one of the first agricultural machines to be invented, and it is still one of the most important. Evidence shows that plows first appeared more than 6,000 years ago. The first plow was not much more than a digging stick drawn by a person or an animal. As primitive as it was, the plow allowed people to dig deeper to turn over and loosen the soil. Plants could put down deeper, stronger roots in plowed soil, increasing crop yields. This simple machine magnified the effort of a single person enough to produce food for many people. The plow freed some people from having to grow food so they could begin to build, sew, or trade.

IS THAT A FACT!

▶ Tiny machines are being built with gears and levers so small they can only be seen under a powerful microscope. Scientists are learning how to make even tinier machines out of molecules. Tiny gears have been shaped out of strands of DNA molecules, and hydrogen molecules may one day control microscopic computers. For more information, see "Micromachines," on page 210.

For background information about teaching strategies and issues, refer to the *Professional Reference for Teachers*.

Chapter 8 • Chapter Background   **185F**

CHAPTER 8
Work and Machines

Chapter Preview

Section 1
Work and Power
- The Scientific Meaning of *Work*
- Calculating Work
- Power—How Fast Work Is Done

Section 2
What Is a Machine?
- Machines—Making Work Easier
- Mechanical Advantage
- Mechanical Efficiency

Section 3
Types of Machines
- Levers
- Inclined Planes
- Wedges
- Screws
- Wheel and Axle
- Pulleys
- Compound Machines

Directed Reading Worksheet 8

Science Puzzlers, Twisters & Teasers Worksheet 8

Guided Reading Audio CD
English or Spanish, Chapter 8

CHAPTER 8 Work and Machines

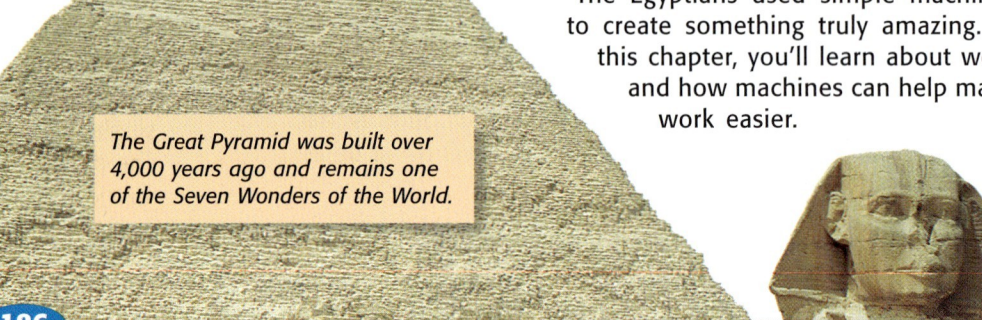

Would You Believe . . . ?

The Great Pyramid, located in Giza (GEE zuh), Egypt, could be called the largest tombstone ever created. A monument and tomb for the pharaoh King Khufu (KOO foo), it covers an area the size of seven city blocks and rises about 40 stories high. The Great Pyramid is the largest of the three pyramids of Giza. It was built around 2600 B.C. and took less than 30 years to complete—a relatively short period of time considering that construction equipment didn't exist 4,000 years ago. So how did the Egyptians do it?

To build the Great Pyramid, the Egyptians cut and moved more than 2 million stone blocks, most averaging 2,000 kg (probably over 40 times your own mass). The blocks were cut from a stone quarry, moved near the pyramid, and then lifted into place. To finish in less than 30 years, the Egyptians would have had to cut, move, and lift about 200 blocks per day! The Egyptians did not have cranes, bulldozers, or any other heavy-duty machines. What they had were two simple machines—the inclined plane and the lever.

Archaeologists have found the remains of inclined planes, or ramps, made from mud, stone, and wood. The Egyptians pushed or pulled the blocks along these ramps to raise them to the proper height. Using ramps required less force than lifting the blocks straight up. In addition, notches in many blocks indicate that huge levers were used like giant crowbars to lift and move the heavy blocks. The workers pushed down on the lever, and the lever pushed up on a stone block, lifting it into place.

The Egyptians used simple machines to create something truly amazing. In this chapter, you'll learn about work and how machines can help make work easier.

The Great Pyramid was built over 4,000 years ago and remains one of the Seven Wonders of the World.

Would You Believe . . . ?

Although the ancient Egyptians used only levers and inclined planes to move the huge stone blocks, they did have other tools that were used to quarry and shape the blocks of stone. Among these tools were copper chisels and copper mallets that were used by masons to quarry limestone blocks. Once the blocks were quarried, they were dragged on wooden sledges (strong, heavy sleds) to the Nile River and carried by barges to the pyramid site. Ancient Egyptians also had hard stone pounders, which were used as chisels in conjunction with wooden mallets for shaping blocks of stone.

186 Chapter 8 • Work and Machines

What Do You Think?

In your ScienceLog, try to answer the following questions based on what you already know:

1. What does it mean to do work?
2. How are machines helpful when doing work?
3. What are some examples of simple machines?

What Do You Think?

Accept all reasonable responses. Students will have a chance to revise their answers in the Chapter Review under NOW What Do You Think?

Investigate!

MATERIALS

FOR EACH GROUP:
- a couple of books
- string
- wooden ruler
- large pencil eraser

Safety Caution: The rulers should be fairly stiff and sturdy. Use lightweight books if necessary. If the books are not too heavy and the activity is done carefully, the rulers should not get broken. Caution students to wear safety goggles during this activity.

Teacher Notes: The word *lever* comes from the Latin word *levare*, "to lift." The lever was one of the first simple machines to be developed. It is thought that tree limbs may have been used by early humans as pry bars to move heavy rocks.

Answers to Investigate

5. Students should find that lifting the books with the ruler was easier because it took less effort (force).
6. The direction of the force applied by students' fingers on the books was up, and the direction of the force applied on the ruler was down. The ruler changed the direction of the force.
7. Sample answer: A lever, such as a ruler, is useful because it makes doing work easier by changing the direction of the force and by requiring less force to be applied.

Investigate!

C'mon, Lever a Little!

In this activity, you will use a simple machine, a lever, to make your task a little easier.

Procedure

1. Gather a couple of **books**, such as dictionaries, encyclopedias, or textbooks, and stack them on a table one on top of the other. If necessary, tie some **string** around them to keep them from slipping.

2. Slide your index finger underneath the edge of the bottom book. Using the force of your finger only, try to lift one side of the books 2 or 3 cm off the table. Is it difficult? Write your observations in your ScienceLog.

3. Slide the end of a **wooden ruler** underneath the edge of the bottom book. Then slip a **large pencil eraser** under the ruler.

4. Again using the force of your index finger only, push down on the ruler and try to lift the books as shown at right.
   Caution: Push down slowly to keep the ruler and eraser from flipping.

Analysis

5. Which was easier, lifting the books with your finger or with the ruler? Explain.
6. What was different about the direction of the force your finger applied on the books compared with the force you applied on the ruler?
7. Based on your results, how would you explain the usefulness of a lever, such as a ruler?

IS THAT A FACT!

The "jaws of life" used by fire departments and rescue squads to extricate people trapped in vehicles is a form of lever.

 internetconnect

Smithsonian Institution®
Visit **www.si.edu/hrw** for additional on-line resources.

Chapter 8 • Work and Machines **187**

SECTION 1

Focus

Work and Power

This section introduces the scientific definitions of work and power. Students learn how to calculate work and power.

Bellringer

On the board, give students the following task:

Select the activities below that require the least amount of work. Write your answers in your ScienceLog.

- carrying heavy books home
- reading a 300-page novel
- skiing for 1 hour
- lifting a 45 kg mass
- holding a steel beam in place for 3 hours
- jacking up a car

Remind students to explain what work is being done in each of their selections.

1) Motivate

DISCUSSION

After reading the section on work and power, discuss with students the use of the words *work* and *power* in everyday language. Identify usages that do not match the scientific definition of work, and discuss why they are different. Remind them that in this section work is discussed in terms of physically moving objects rather than in terms of energy expenditure.

Section 1

Terms to Learn

work   power
joule   watt

What You'll Do

- Determine when work is being done on an object.
- Calculate the amount of work done on an object.
- Explain the difference between work and power.

Work and Power

Suppose your science teacher has just given you a homework assignment. You have to read an entire chapter by tomorrow! Wow, that's a lot of work, isn't it? Actually, in the scientific sense, you won't be doing any work at all! How can that be?

The Scientific Meaning of *Work*

In science, **work** occurs when a force causes an object to move in the direction of the force. In the example above, you may put a lot of mental effort into doing your homework, but you won't be using a force to move an object. Therefore, in the scientific sense, you will not be doing work.

Now think about the example shown in **Figure 1.** This student is having a lot of fun, isn't she? But she is doing work, even though she is having fun. That's because she's applying a force to the bowling ball to make it move through a distance. However, it's important to understand that she is doing work on the ball only as long as she is touching it. The ball will continue to move away from her after she releases it, but she will no longer be doing work on the ball because she will no longer be applying a force to it.

Figure 1 *You might be surprised to find out that bowling is doing work!*

Working Hard or Hardly Working? You should understand that applying a force doesn't always result in work being done. Suppose your neighbor asks you to help push his stalled car. You push and push, but the car doesn't budge. Even though you may be exhausted and sweaty, you haven't done any work on the car. Why? Because the car hasn't moved. Remember, work is done on an object only when a force makes that object move. In this case, your pushing doesn't make the car move. You only do work on the car if it starts to move.

188

MISCONCEPTION ALERT

In the second paragraph, the text states that the girl does work on the bowling ball only when she is touching it. The ball continues to move when she lets go of it, but she's no longer applying a force to it. Review the Forces in Motion chapter and Newton's first law. It takes a little force to get the ball moving because the resistance of mass to changes in motion must be overcome. Disregarding friction, once the ball is moving, no additional force is needed to keep it moving at constant speed because no other force impedes its horizontal motion.

188   Chapter 8 • Work and Machines

Force and Motion in the Same Direction Suppose you're in the airport and you're late for a flight. You have to run through the airport carrying a heavy suitcase. Because you're making the suitcase move, you're doing work on it, right? Wrong! For work to be done, the object must move in the same direction as the force. In this case, the motion is in a different direction than the force, as shown in **Figure 2.** So no work is done on the suitcase. However, work *is* done on the suitcase when you lift it off the ground.

You'll know that work is done on an object if two things occur: (1) the object moves as a force is applied and (2) the direction of the object's motion is the same as the direction of the force applied. The pictures and the arrows in the chart below will help you understand how to determine when work is being done on an object.

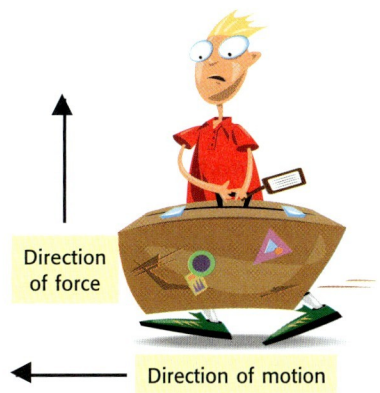

Direction of force

Direction of motion

Figure 2 *You exert an upward force on the suitcase. But the motion of the suitcase is forward. Therefore, you are not doing work on the suitcase.*

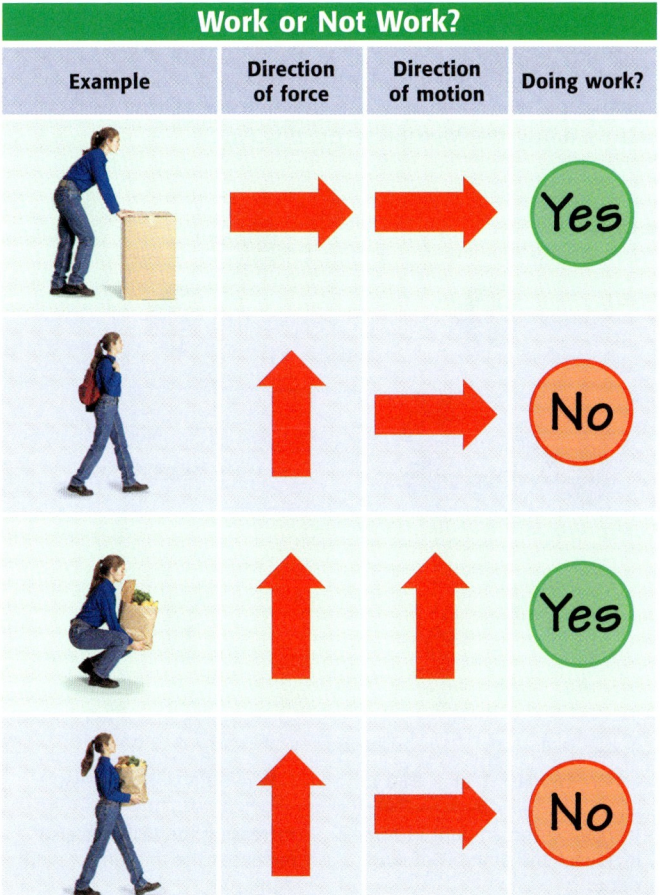

Self-Check

If you pulled a wheeled suitcase instead of carrying it, would you be doing work on the suitcase? Why or why not? *(See page 724 to check your answer.)*

IS THAT A FACT!

The word *energy* is derived from the Latin *en,* meaning "in," and *ergon,* meaning "work."

Q: Did you hear about the criminals who never had to do any work?

A: They were joule thieves.

3 Extend

Answers to MATHBREAK
1. 50,000 J
2. lifting the 75 N ball a distance of 2 m (150 J)

MATH and MORE

Have students, in groups of three or four, select a sport, and discuss the different ways work is done in that sport. Have them estimate how much work is done in an average game.

ACTIVITY

MATERIALS

FOR EACH PAIR:
- meterstick and string
- spring scale
- objects to lift

Have each pair attach each object in turn to the spring scale and slowly lift or pull it, then record how much force was used. Next have them measure the distance the object moved and record it in meters. Have them calculate how much work was done.

Teaching Transparency 230 "Work Depends on Force and Distance"

MATH BREAK

Working It Out
Use the equation for work shown on this page to solve the following problems:
1. A man applies a force of 500 N to push a truck 100 m down the street. How much work does he do?
2. In which situation do you do more work?
   a. You lift a 75 N bowling ball 2 m off the floor.
   b. You lift two 50 N bowling balls 1 m off the floor.

Calculating Work

Do you do more work when you lift an 80 N barbell or a 160 N barbell? It would be tempting to say that you do more work when you lift the 160 N barbell because it weighs more. But actually, you can't answer this question with the information given. You also need to know how high each barbell is being lifted. Remember, work is a force applied through a distance. The greater the distance through which you exert a given force, the more work you do. Similarly, the greater the force you exert through a given distance, the more work you do.

The amount of work (W) done in moving an object can be calculated by multiplying the force (F) applied to the object by the distance (d) through which the force is applied, as shown in the following equation:

$$W = F \times d$$

Recall that force is expressed in newtons, and the meter is the basic SI unit for length or distance. Therefore, the unit used to express work is the newton-meter (N•m), which is more simply called the **joule (J)**. Look at **Figure 3** to learn more about calculating work. You can also practice calculating work yourself by doing the MathBreak on this page.

Figure 3 Work Depends on Force and Distance

$W = 80 \text{ N} \times 1 \text{ m} = 80 \text{ J}$

The force needed to lift an object is equal to the gravitational force on the object—in other words, the object's weight.

$W = 160 \text{ N} \times 1 \text{ m} = 160 \text{ J}$

Increasing the amount of force increases the amount of work done.

$W = 80 \text{ N} \times 2 \text{ m} = 160 \text{ J}$

Increasing the distance also increases the amount of work done.

internetconnect
TOPIC: Work and Power
GO TO: www.scilinks.org
sciLINKS NUMBER: HSTP180

SCIENCE HUMOR

Q: What is the unit of power?
A: Watt.
Q: I said, What is the unit of power?
A: Watt!
Q: I SAID...

190 Chapter 8 • Work and Machines

Power—How Fast Work Is Done

Like *work,* the term *power* is used a lot in everyday language but has a very specific meaning in science. **Power** is the rate at which work is done. To calculate power (*P*), you divide the amount of work done (*W*) by the time (*t*) it takes to do that work, as shown in the following equation:

$$P = \frac{W}{t}$$

You just learned that the unit for work is the joule, and the basic unit for time is the second. Therefore, the unit used to express power is joules per second (J/s), which is more simply called the **watt (W).** So if you do 50 J of work in 5 seconds, your power is 10 J/s, or 10 W. You can calculate your own power in the QuickLab at right.

Increasing Power Power is how fast work happens. Power is increased when more work is done in a given amount of time. Power is also increased when the time it takes to do a certain amount of work is decreased, as shown in **Figure 4.**

Figure 4 *No matter how fast you can sand with sandpaper, an electric sander can do the same amount of work faster. Therefore, the electric sander has more power.*

QuickLab

More Power to You

1. Use a loop of **string** to attach a **spring scale** to a **book.**
2. Slowly pull the book across a table by the spring scale. Use a **stopwatch** to determine the time this takes. In your ScienceLog, record the amount of time it took and the force used as the book reached the edge of the table.
3. With a **metric ruler,** measure the distance you pulled the book.
4. Now quickly pull the book across the same distance. Again record the time and force.
5. Calculate work and power for both trials.
6. How were the amounts of work and power affected by your pulling the book faster? Record your answers in your ScienceLog.

REVIEW

1. Work is done on a ball when a pitcher throws it. Is the pitcher still doing work on the ball as it flies through the air? Explain.
2. Explain the difference between work and power.
3. **Doing Calculations** You lift a chair that weighs 50 N to a height of 0.5 m and carry it 10 m across the room. How much work do you do on the chair?

TOPIC: Work and Power
GO TO: www.scilinks.org
sciLINKS NUMBER: HSTP180

SECTION 2

Focus

What Is a Machine?
This section explains how machines make work easier. Students learn to calculate and compare the mechanical advantage of machines and their mechanical efficiency.

 **Bellringer**

Pose the following question to your students, and have them write a one-paragraph answer in their ScienceLog:

Why do we use machines?

1) Motivate

DISCUSSION

Show students a selection of pictures of familiar objects that represent simple machines either alone or in combination. Discuss with students how each of the objects can be used to make work easier. Save the pictures for Section 3 of this chapter, when you can use them to have students identify the simple machines in each picture.

 **Directed Reading Worksheet 8** Section 2

Section 2

Terms to Learn
machine
work input
work output
mechanical advantage
mechanical efficiency

What You'll Do
- Explain how a machine makes work easier.
- Describe and give examples of the force-distance trade-off that occurs when a machine is used.
- Calculate mechanical advantage.
- Explain why machines are not 100 percent efficient.

What Is a Machine?

Imagine you're in the car with your mom on the way to a party when suddenly— *KABLOOM hisssss*—a tire blows out. "Now I'm going to be late!" you think as your mom pulls over to the side of the road. You watch as she opens the trunk and gets out a jack and a tire iron. Using the tire iron, she pries the hubcap off and begins to unscrew the lug nuts from the wheel. She then puts the jack under the car and turns the handle several times until the flat tire no longer touches the ground. After exchanging the flat tire with the spare, she lowers the jack and puts the lug nuts and hubcap back on the wheel. "Wow!" you think, "That wasn't as hard as I thought it would be." As your mom drops you off at the party, you think how lucky it was that she had the right equipment to change the tire.

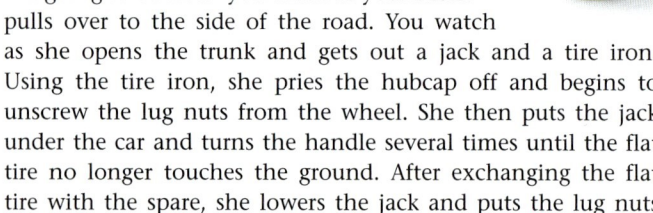

Machines—Making Work Easier
Now imagine changing a tire without the jack and the tire iron. Would it have been so easy? No, you would have needed several people just to hold up the car! Sometimes you need a little help to do work. That's where machines come in. A **machine** is a device that helps make work easier by changing the size or direction of a force.

When you think of machines, you might think of things like cars, big construction equipment, or even computers. But not all machines are complicated or even have moving parts. In fact, the tire iron, jack, and lug nut shown above are all machines. Even the items shown in **Figure 5** are machines.

Figure 5 *You might be surprised to find out that all of these common objects are machines.*

192

CROSS-DISCIPLINARY FOCUS

Home Economics Show students some common kitchen utensils, such as knives, forks, can and bottle openers, nutcrackers, and manual egg beaters. Allow students to examine the utensils and discuss their uses. Then have students speculate about how each machine makes work easier.

192 Chapter 8 • Work and Machines

Work In, Work Out Suppose you need to get the lid off a can of paint. What do you do? Well, one way to pry the lid off is to use the flat end of a common machine known as a screwdriver, as shown in **Figure 6.** You place the tip of the screwdriver under the edge of the lid and then push down on the handle. The other end of the screwdriver lifts the lid as you push down. In other words, you do work on the screwdriver, and the screwdriver does work on the lid. This example illustrates that two kinds of work are always involved when a machine is used—the work done on the machine and the work the machine does on another object.

Figure 6 *When you use a machine, you do work on the machine, and the machine does work on something else.*

The width of the arrows representing **input force** and **output force** indicates the relative size of the forces. The length of the arrows indicates the distance through which they are exerted.

Remember that work is a force applied through a distance. Look again at Figure 6. The work you do on a machine is called **work input.** You apply a force, called the *input force,* to the machine and move it through a distance. The work done by the machine is called **work output.** The machine applies a force, called the *output force,* through a distance. The output force opposes the forces you and the machine are working against—in this case, the weight of the lid and the friction between the can and the lid.

How Machines Help You might think that machines help you because they increase the amount of work done. But that's not true. If you multiplied the forces by the distances through which they are applied in Figure 6 (remember, $W = F \times d$), you would find that the screwdriver does *not* do more work on the lid than you do on the screwdriver. Work output can *never* be greater than work input.

Science Bloopers

Even though it is a physical law that the work output of a machine is always less than the work input, people have always tried to invent machines that will run forever. Known as perpetual-motion machines, these devices promise unlimited operation but can never deliver because they violate the laws of physics.

2 Teach, continued

MEETING INDIVIDUAL NEEDS

Advanced Learners Have students think of a problem that has no apparent solution. The problem may also be something that students think may become a problem in the future. Challenge them to invent a machine that solves that problem. Have them describe it as carefully as possible and illustrate it with their own artwork.

CROSS-DISCIPLINARY FOCUS

History Have students research prehistoric uses of machines, especially the earliest occurrences of machines that change the size or direction of force in the same ways as the examples in the chart on page 195.

ACTIVITY

Graphing A certain task takes 480 J of work. Remind students that many combinations of $F \times d$ result in 480 J of work (480 N × 1 m; or 64 N × 7.5 m). Help students find combinations of forces and distances whose products are 480 J. Have them use these number pairs to plot and connect points on a graph (with F on the x-axis and d on the y-axis). Discuss the graphs and what they show about the relationship between force and distance. (*F and d are inversely related.*) (Students can start with any two of the quantities, calculate the third, then do the graph.)

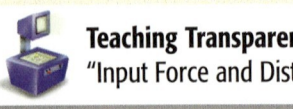
Teaching Transparency 230 "Input Force and Distance"

Machines Do Not Save Work Machines make work easier because they change the size or direction of the input force. And using a screwdriver to open a paint can changes *both* the size and direction of the input force. Just remember that using a machine does not mean that you do less work. As you can see in **Figure 7**, the same amount of work is involved with or without the ramp. The ramp decreases the amount of input force necessary to do the work of lifting the box. But the distance over which the force is exerted increases. In other words, the machine allows a smaller force to be applied over a longer distance.

Figure 7 *A simple plank of wood acts as a machine when it is used to help raise a load.*

Force: 450 N   Distance: 1 m

$W = 450 \text{ N} \times 1 \text{ m} = 450 \text{ J}$

Lifting this box straight up requires an input force equal to the weight of the box.

Force: 150 N   Distance: 3 m

$W = 150 \text{ N} \times 3 \text{ m} = 450 \text{ J}$

Using a ramp to lift the box requires an input force less than the weight of the box, but the input force must be exerted over a greater distance.

The Force-Distance Trade-off When a machine changes the size of the force, the distance through which the force is exerted must also change. Force or distance can increase, but not together. When one increases, the other must decrease. This is because the work output is never greater than the work input.

The diagram on the next page will help you better understand this force-distance trade-off. It also shows that some machines affect only the direction of the force, not the size of the force or the distance through which it is exerted.

Homework

Have students keep a "machine diary" for a week. Each day, they should describe the machines they used or came in contact with over the course of the day. Have them expand their ideas of what a machine is by examining ordinary actions like writing or playing and deciding whether a machine is involved.

Machines Change the Size or Direction (or Both) of a Force

Work input	Machine	Work output	Example
Small force (indicated by arrow width) applied over a long distance	Increases force	**Large force** applied over a short distance	 wheelbarrow
Large force applied over a short distance	Decreases force	**Small force** applied over a long distance	 hammer pulling nail
Small force applied over a long distance	Changes direction of force	**Small force** applied over a long distance in the opposite direction	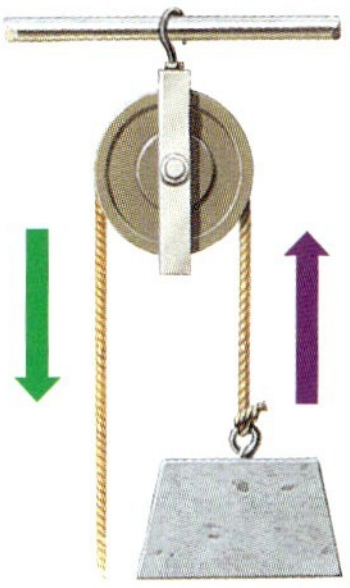 pulley
Small force applied over a long distance	Changes size and direction of force	**Large force** applied over a short distance in the opposite direction	 opening paint can

---

CONNECT TO LIFE SCIENCE

Humans aren't the only animals that use tools. Chimpanzees fashion specialized twigs to snare termites from inside their mounds, and some otters use carefully selected rocks to crack open shellfish. There are examples of other species using tools—a distinct evolutionary advantage. Have students find information about such tool use and make some creative presentations to the class.

GUIDED PRACTICE

Concept Mapping Give students examples of several different types of machines, such as those used in construction or industry. Have them analyze whether each machine changes the size or direction (or both) of a force. When they have finished their analysis, have students make a concept map showing their results.
Sheltered English

RETEACHING

For each of the examples of machines on page 195, have students design a different machine that would accomplish the same job. The machine can be as simple or as elaborate as desired. Does the new machine change force in the same way as the original?

Homework

Writing Have students go through their homes and select five machines that they find there. Encourage them to find unusual examples, things they might not use everyday. Have them write one-paragraph descriptions of these machines in terms of the mechanical advantage they offer.

 Teaching Transparency 231 "Machines Change the Size or Direction (or Both) of a Force"

Section 2 • What Is a Machine? **195**

3) Extend

Answers to MATHBREAK

1. $MA = \frac{2000 \text{ N}}{200 \text{ N}} = 10$
2. 1; it could be useful for tasks in which it is necessary to change the direction of a force.
3. Both a and b make work easier than doing work without a machine. A task would be easier with b because it has a larger mechanical advantage.

MATH and MORE

Teacher Notes: When the output force is greater than the input force, the mechanical advantage is greater than 1. When the output force is less than the input force, the mechanical advantage is less than 1.

Have students determine which of the following machines has a greater mechanical advantage:

- a machine to which you apply a force of 50 N and the machine applies a force of 150 N *(MA = 3)*
- a machine to which you apply a force of 60 N and the machine applies a force of 200 N *(MA = 3.3)*

 Math Skills Worksheet 53 "Mechanical Advantage"

GOING FURTHER

Show students one of Rube Goldberg's cartoons. Ask them to decipher what is happening in the cartoon. Focus students' attention on the action in each step and the results of the action. Challenge students to design and draw their own machine that uses multiple steps to perform a simple task.

196 Chapter 8 • Work and Machines

MATH BREAK

Finding the Advantage

1. You apply 200 N to a machine, and the machine applies 2,000 N to an object. What is the mechanical advantage?
2. You apply 10 N to a machine, and the machine applies 10 N to another object. What is the mechanical advantage? Can such a machine be useful? Why or why not?
3. Which of the following makes work easier to do?
   a. a machine with a mechanical advantage of 15
   b. a machine to which you apply 15 N and that exerts 255 N

Figure 8 A machine that has a large mechanical advantage can make lifting a heavy load a whole lot easier.

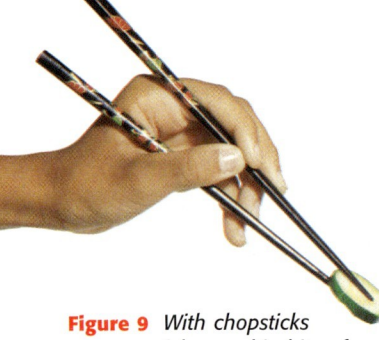

Figure 9 With chopsticks you can pick up a big bite of food with just a little wiggle of your fingers.

TOPIC: Mechanical Efficiency
GO TO: www.scilinks.org
sciLINKS NUMBER: HSTP185

Mechanical Advantage

Do some machines make work easier than others? Yes, because some machines can increase force more than others. A machine's **mechanical advantage** tells you how many times the machine multiplies force. In other words, it compares the input force with the output force. You can find mechanical advantage by using the following equation:

$$\text{Mechanical advantage } (MA) = \frac{\text{output force}}{\text{input force}}$$

Take a look at **Figure 8.** In this example, the output force is greater than the input force. Using the equation above, you can find the mechanical advantage of the handcart:

$$MA = \frac{500 \text{ N}}{50 \text{ N}} = 10$$

Input force = 50 N
Output force = 500 N

Because the mechanical advantage of the handcart is 10, the output force is 10 times bigger than the input force. The larger the mechanical advantage, the easier a machine makes your work. But as mechanical advantage increases, the distance that the output force moves the object decreases.

Remember that some machines only change the direction of the force. In such cases, the output force is equal to the input force, and the mechanical advantage is 1. Other machines have a mechanical advantage that is less than 1. That means that the input force is greater than the output force. Although such a machine actually decreases your force, it does allow you to exert the force over a longer distance, as shown in **Figure 9.**

Mechanical Efficiency

As mentioned earlier, the work output of a machine can never be greater than the work input. In fact, the work output of a machine is always *less* than the work input. Why? Because some of the work done by the machine is used to overcome the friction created by the use of the machine. But keep in mind that no work is *lost*. The work output plus the work done to overcome friction equals the work input.

The less work a machine has to do to overcome friction, the more *efficient* it is. **Mechanical efficiency** (e FISH uhn see) is a comparison of a machine's work output with the work input. A machine's mechanical efficiency is calculated using the following equation:

$$\text{Mechanical efficiency} = \frac{\text{work output}}{\text{work input}} \times 100$$

The 100 in this equation means that mechanical efficiency is expressed as a percentage. Mechanical efficiency tells you what percentage of the work input gets converted into work output. No machine is 100 percent efficient, but reducing the amount of friction in a machine is a way to increase its mechanical efficiency. Inventors have tried for many years to create a machine that has no friction to overcome, but so far they have been unsuccessful. If a machine could be made that had 100 percent mechanical efficiency, it would be called an *ideal machine*.

Oil Improves Efficiency

Car manufacturers recommend regular oil changes. That's because over time, motor oil in a car's engine starts to get dark and thick and doesn't flow as well as fresh motor oil. Why do you think a car engine needs motor oil? How does getting regular oil changes improve the mechanical efficiency of a car's engine?

REVIEW

1. Explain how using a ramp makes work easier.
2. Why can't a machine be 100 percent efficient?
3. Suppose you exert 15 N on a machine, and the machine exerts 300 N on another object. What is the machine's mechanical advantage?
4. **Comparing Concepts** For the machine described in question 3, how does the distance through which the output force is exerted differ from the distance through which the input force is exerted?

internetconnect

SC*i*LINKS.
NSTA

TOPIC: Mechanical Efficiency
GO TO: www.scilinks.org
sciLINKS NUMBER: HSTP185

SECTION 3

Focus

Types of Machines

This section describes the six simple machines and explains how to determine the mechanical advantage of each. Students learn about compound machines (combinations of simple machines) they commonly encounter, and they learn how combining simple machines affects efficiency.

Pose the following question:

What type of machine can be found on at least half the students in this room right now? (zipper)

1) Motivate

ACTIVITY

MATERIALS

FOR EACH GROUP:
- string
- meterstick
- ring stand with ring
- scissors
- 5 large metal washers tied together

Divide the class into small groups. Tell each group to use the string to hang the meterstick from the ring so the meterstick is balanced (hangs level). Then tell them to tie the washers to the meterstick at the 2-cm mark. Challenge them to find a way to again balance the meterstick without adding any weights to the opposite end. Discuss the students' solutions to the problem.

Section 3

Terms to Learn

lever
inclined plane
wedge
screw
wheel and axle
pulley
compound machine

What You'll Do

- Identify and give examples of the six types of simple machines.
- Analyze the mechanical advantage provided by each simple machine.
- Identify the simple machines that make up a compound machine.

Figure 10 A First Class Lever

Input force — Output force
Load
Fulcrum

Types of Machines

All machines are constructed from these six simple machines: *lever, inclined plane, wedge, screw, wheel and axle,* and *pulley.* You've seen a couple of these machines already—a screwdriver can be used as a lever, and a ramp is an inclined plane. In the next few pages, each of the six simple machines will be discussed separately. Then you'll learn how compound machines are formed from combining simple machines.

Levers

Have you ever used the claw end of a hammer to remove a nail from a piece of wood? If so, you were using the hammer as a lever. A **lever** is a simple machine consisting of a bar that pivots at a fixed point, called a *fulcrum.* Levers are used to apply a force to a load. There are three classes of levers, based on the locations of the fulcrum, the load, and the input force.

First Class Levers With a first class lever, the fulcrum is between the input force and the load, as shown in **Figure 10**. First class levers always change the direction of the input force. And depending on the location of the fulcrum, first class levers can be used to increase force or to increase distance. Some examples of first class levers are shown below.

Examples of First Class Levers

When the fulcrum is closer to the load than to the input force, a **mechanical advantage of greater than 1 results.** The output force is increased because it is exerted over a shorter distance.

When the fulcrum is exactly in the middle, a **mechanical advantage of 1 results.** The output force is not increased because the input force's distance is not increased.

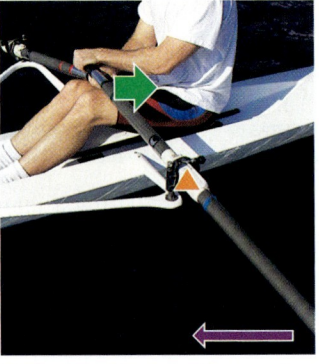
When the fulcrum is closer to the input force than to the load, a **mechanical advantage of less than 1 results.** Although the output force is less than the input force, a gain in distance occurs.

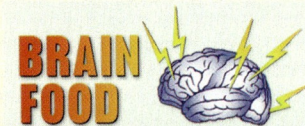

Besides their obvious uses in bottle openers and nail pullers, levers are also used in devices such as fishing rods, cranes, typewriters, pianos, parking meters, and scales.

Second Class Levers With a second class lever, the load is between the fulcrum and the input force, as shown in **Figure 11.** Second class levers do not change the direction of the input force, but they allow you to apply less force than the force exerted by the load. Because the output force is greater than the input force, you must exert the input force over a greater distance. Some examples of second class levers are shown at right.

Figure 11 A Second Class Lever

Examples of Second Class Levers

Using a second class lever results in a **mechanical advantage of greater than 1.** The closer the load is to the fulcrum, the more the force is increased and the greater the mechanical advantage.

Third Class Levers With a third class lever, the input force is between the fulcrum and the load, as shown in **Figure 12.** Third class levers do not change the direction of the input force. In addition, they do *not* increase the input force. Therefore, the output force is always less than the input force. Some examples of third class levers are shown at right.

Figure 12 A Third Class Lever

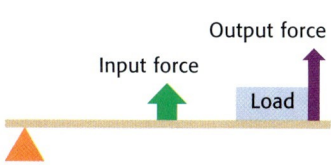

Examples of Third Class Levers

Using a third class lever results in a **mechanical advantage of less than 1** because force is decreased. But third class levers are helpful because they increase the distance through which the output force is exerted.

2) Teach

MAKING MODELS
Provide students with triangular blocks and long pieces of wood so they can make small seesaws. Have students experiment with the position and size of the weights and the placement of the fulcrum. Have them write their observations and descriptions in their ScienceLog.
Sheltered English

ACTIVITY
Classifying Tools Gather a selection of tools, such as brooms, shovels, crowbars, fishing poles, ice or sugar-cube tongs, pliers, scissors, baseball bats, tennis rackets, hockey sticks, golf clubs, canoe paddles, boat oars, wheelbarrows, nutcrackers, tweezers, and bottle openers. Divide the class into groups, and assign each group several tools. Have each group work together to locate the fulcrum, load, location of input force, and location of output force in each tool. Then have each group share its information with other groups.
Sheltered English

Directed Reading Worksheet 8 Section 3

IS THAT A FACT!
The human body uses simple machines. Muscles and bones form first class and third class levers. When you look up, the skull pivots on the neck vertebrae, forming a first class lever. When you kick a soccer ball, the contracting muscle pulls your leg upward, acting like a third class lever.

Section 3 • Types of Machines

2 Teach, continued

ACTIVITY

MATERIALS

FOR EACH GROUP:
• paper fastener
• rubber band
• ruler
• thick cardboard (16 × 5 cm)
• string
• model car or truck

Have students form groups of 2–3. Have each group use a paper fastener to attach a rubber band near one end of a piece of thick cardboard. Have them tie a piece of string to the other end of the rubber band and tie it to a model car or truck. Have them use a ruler to make a scale on the cardboard to measure the length of the rubber band as it stretches.

Ask students to make charts recording the changes in forces on inclined planes of varying heights.

USING THE FIGURE

Use **Figure 13** and the diagram below it to explain how you can determine mechanical advantage of an inclined plane using distances. Explain it as follows:

Work input = work output
F (input) × d (input) =
F (output) × d (output)

This equation can be rearranged into ratios to show

$$\frac{F \text{ (input)}}{F \text{ (output)}} = \frac{d \text{ (output)}}{d \text{ (input)}}$$

The force ratio can be used to determine mechanical advantage. But because the distance ratio is equivalent to the force ratio, it can also be used to determine mechanical advantage.

BRAIN FOOD

When Napoleon Bonaparte's army invaded Egypt in 1798, one of his engineers reportedly calculated that the three pyramids of Giza contained enough stone to build a wall about 2.5 m tall and 0.3 m thick around the entire country of France.

Compare work done with and without an inclined plane on page 664 of the LabBook.

 **PG 664**
Inclined to Move

Inclined Planes

Do you remember the story about how the Egyptians built the Great Pyramid? One of the machines they used was the *inclined plane*. An **inclined plane** is a simple machine that is a straight, slanted surface. A ramp is an example of an inclined plane.

Inclined planes can make work easier. Look at **Figure 13**. Using an inclined plane to load an upright piano into the back of a truck is easier than just lifting it into the truck. Rolling the piano into the truck along an inclined plane requires a smaller input force than is required to lift the piano into the truck. But remember that machines do not save work—therefore, the input force must be exerted over a longer distance.

Figure 13 *The work you do on the piano to roll it up the ramp is the same as the work you would do to lift it straight up. An inclined plane simply allows you to apply a smaller force over a greater distance.*

Mechanical Advantage of Inclined Planes The longer the inclined plane is compared with its height, the greater the mechanical advantage. The mechanical advantage (MA) of an inclined plane can be calculated by dividing the *length* of the inclined plane by the *height* to which the load is lifted, as shown below:

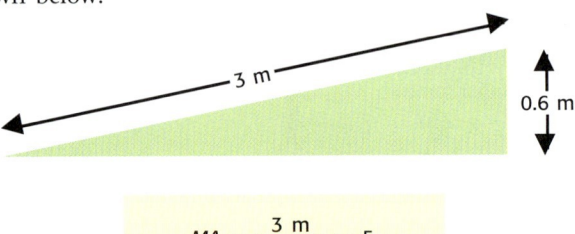

$$MA = \frac{3 \text{ m}}{0.6 \text{ m}} = 5$$

Q: Why didn't the ramp help out when the piano was being loaded onto the truck?

A: It didn't have the inclination.

Chapter 8 • Work and Machines

Wedges

Imagine trying to cut a watermelon in half with a spoon. It wouldn't be easy, would it? A knife is a much more useful utensil for cutting because it's a *wedge*. A **wedge** is a double inclined plane that moves. When you move a wedge through a distance, it applies a force on an object. A wedge applies an output force that is greater than your input force, but you apply the input force over a greater distance. The greater the distance you move the wedge, the greater the force it applies on the object. For example, the deeper you move a knife into a watermelon, as shown in **Figure 14,** the more force the knife applies to the two halves. Eventually, it pushes them apart. Other useful wedges include doorstops, plows, axe heads, and chisels.

Figure 14 Wedges, which are often used to cut materials, allow you to exert your force over an increased distance.

Mechanical Advantage of Wedges The longer and thinner the wedge is, the greater the mechanical advantage. That's why axes and knives cut better when you sharpen them—you are making the wedge thinner. Therefore, less input force is required. The mechanical advantage of a wedge can be determined by dividing the *length* of the wedge by its greatest *thickness*, as shown below.

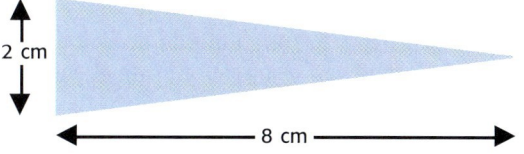

$$MA = \frac{8 \text{ cm}}{2 \text{ cm}} = 4$$

Screws

A **screw** is an inclined plane that is wrapped in a spiral. When a screw is rotated, a small force is applied over the long distance along the inclined plane of the screw. Meanwhile, the screw applies a large force through the short distance it is pushed. In other words, you apply a small input force over a large distance, while the screw exerts a large output force over a small distance. Screws are used most commonly as fasteners. Some examples of screws are shown in **Figure 15.**

Figure 15 When you turn a screw, you exert a small input force over a large turning distance, but the screw itself doesn't move very far.

IS THAT A FACT!
Both a jar lid and the top of a jar are screws. The ridges on the jar and on the lid act as screws, holding the jar and the lid together.

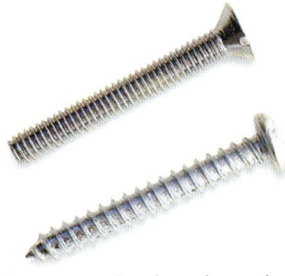

Figure 16 The threads on the top screw are closer together and wrap more times around, so that screw has a greater mechanical advantage than the one below it.

Mechanical Advantage of Screws If you could "unwind" the inclined plane of a screw, you would see that it is very long and has a gentle slope. Recall that the longer an inclined plane is compared with its height, the greater its mechanical advantage. Similarly, the longer the spiral on a screw is and the closer together the threads, the greater the screw's mechanical advantage, as shown in **Figure 16.**

REVIEW

1. Give an example of each of the following simple machines: first class lever, second class lever, third class lever, inclined plane, wedge, and screw.
2. A third class lever has a mechanical advantage of less than 1. Explain why it is useful for some tasks.
3. **Interpreting Graphics** Look back at Figures 6, 7, and 8 in Section 2. Identify the type of simple machine shown in each case. (If a lever is shown, identify its class.)

Wheel and Axle

Did you know that when you turn a doorknob you are using a machine? A doorknob is an example of a **wheel and axle,** a simple machine consisting of two circular objects of different sizes. A wheel can be a crank, such as the handle on a fishing reel, or it can be a knob, such as a volume knob on a radio. The axle is the smaller of the two circular objects. Doorknobs, wrenches, ferris wheels, screwdrivers, and steering wheels all use a wheel and axle. **Figure 17** shows how a wheel and axle works.

Figure 17
How a Wheel and Axle Works

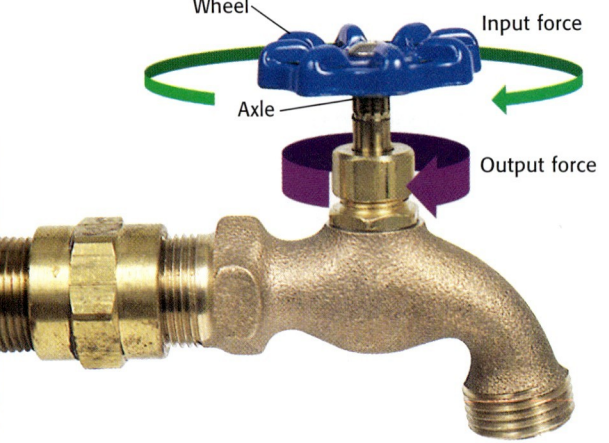

a When a small input force is applied to the wheel, it rotates through a circular distance.

b As the wheel turns, so does the axle. But because the axle is smaller than the wheel, it rotates through a smaller distance, which makes the output force larger than the input force.

202 Chapter 8 • Work and Machines

Mechanical Advantage of a Wheel and Axle The mechanical advantage of a wheel and axle can be determined by dividing the *radius* (the distance from the center to the edge) of the wheel by the radius of the axle, as shown at right. Turning the wheel results in a mechanical advantage of greater than 1 because the radius of the wheel is larger than the radius of the axle.

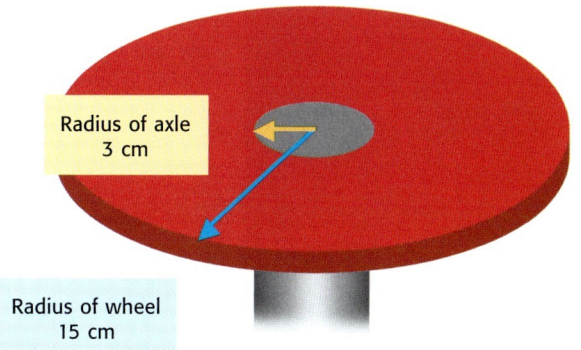

$$MA = \frac{15 \text{ cm}}{3 \text{ cm}} = 5$$

Pulleys

When you open window blinds by pulling on a cord, you're using a pulley. A **pulley** is a simple machine consisting of a grooved wheel that holds a rope or a cable. A load is attached to one end of the rope, and an input force is applied to the other end. There are two kinds of pulleys—*fixed* and *movable*. Fixed and movable pulleys can be combined to form a *block and tackle*.

Fixed Pulleys Some pulleys only change the direction of a force. This kind of pulley is called a fixed pulley. Fixed pulleys do not increase force. A fixed pulley is attached to something that does not move. By using a fixed pulley, you can pull down on the rope in order to lift the load up. This is usually easier than trying to lift the load straight up. Elevators make use of fixed pulleys.

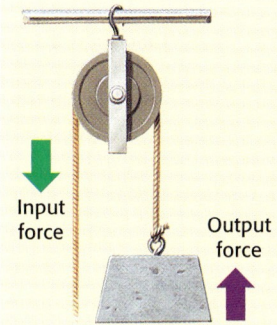

A **fixed pulley** only spins. So the distance through which the input force and the output force are exerted—and thus the forces themselves—are the same. Therefore, a fixed pulley provides a mechanical advantage of 1.

Movable Pulleys Unlike fixed pulleys, movable pulleys are attached to the object being moved. A movable pulley does not change a force's direction. Movable pulleys do increase force, but you must exert the input force over a greater distance than the load is moved. This is because you must make *both* sides of the rope move in order to lift the load.

A **movable pulley** moves up with the load as it is lifted. Force is multiplied because the combined input force is exerted over twice the distance of the output force. The mechanical advantage of a movable pulley is the number of rope segments that support the load. In this example, the mechanical advantage is 2.

TOPIC: Simple Machines
GO TO: www.scilinks.org
*sci*LINKS NUMBER: HSTP190

3) Extend

GOING FURTHER

Obtain discarded machines, such as turntables, door locks and keys, table fans, mechanical clocks, or other compound machines. Make several of them available in areas where students can disassemble them. Over a period of a few days, have each student make a chart comparing pieces of the devices with the set of simple machines. Which devices are the most complex?

GROUP ACTIVITY

Divide the classroom into groups. Assign a simple machine to each group. Each group will be responsible for developing a tabletop display that describes its simple machine. The display should make use of models, objects, photographs and drawings, text labels, and other ways of presenting information on the topic. Encourage students to have fun and to be creative in their presentations.

Building Machines

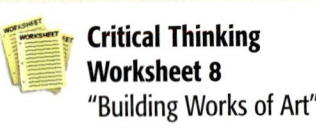
Critical Thinking Worksheet 8 "Building Works of Art"

Reinforcement Worksheet 8 "Finding Machines in Everyday Life"

TOPIC: Compound Machines
GO TO: www.scilinks.org
sciLINKS NUMBER: HSTP195

Figure 18 The combination of pulleys used by this crane allows it to lift heavy pieces of scrap metal.

Block and Tackles When a fixed pulley and a movable pulley are used together, the pulley system is called a *block and tackle*. A block and tackle can have a large mechanical advantage if several pulleys are used. A block and tackle used within a larger pulley system is shown in **Figure 18**.

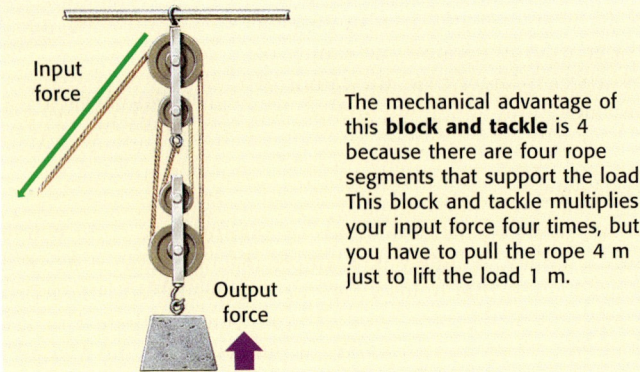

The mechanical advantage of this **block and tackle** is 4 because there are four rope segments that support the load. This block and tackle multiplies your input force four times, but you have to pull the rope 4 m just to lift the load 1 m.

Compound Machines

You are surrounded by machines. As you saw earlier, you even have machines in your body! But most of the machines in your world are **compound machines,** machines that are made of two or more simple machines. You've already seen one example of a compound machine: a block and tackle. A block and tackle consists of two or more pulleys. On this page and the next, you'll see some other examples of compound machines.

Activity

List five machines that you have encountered today and indicate what type of machine each is. Try to include at least one compound machine and one machine that is part of your body.

TRY at HOME

Can Opener

The axle has gear teeth on it that grip the can and act as tiny levers to push the can along when the axle turns.

- Wheel and axle
- Wedge
- Second class lever

204 Chapter 8 • Work and Machines

Answer to Activity

Student responses will vary. Some machines students might name include: a doorknob (wheel and axle), a wheelchair ramp (inclined plane), a cap on a shampoo bottle (screw), a garage door (by pulling down on a rope that runs through a pulley), and a fingernail (when used as a wedge to turn pages in a book).

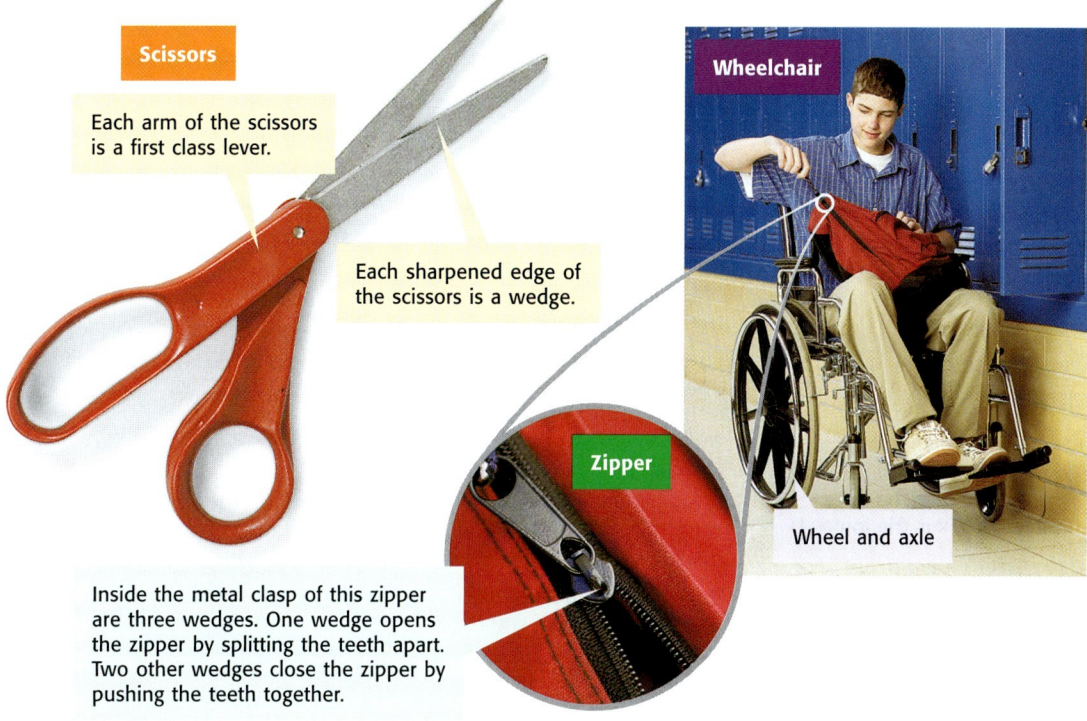

Scissors

Each arm of the scissors is a first class lever.

Each sharpened edge of the scissors is a wedge.

Wheelchair

Zipper

Wheel and axle

Inside the metal clasp of this zipper are three wedges. One wedge opens the zipper by splitting the teeth apart. Two other wedges close the zipper by pushing the teeth together.

Mechanical Efficiency of Compound Machines In general, the more moving parts a machine has, the lower its mechanical efficiency. Thus the mechanical efficiency of compound machines is often quite low. For compound machines that involve many simple machines, such as automobiles and airplanes, it is very important that friction be reduced as much as possible through the use of lubrication and other techniques. Too much friction could cause heating and damage the simple machines involved, which could create safety problems and could be expensive to repair.

REVIEW

1. Give an example of a wheel and axle.
2. Identify the simple machines that make up tweezers and nail clippers.
3. **Doing Calculations** The radius of the wheel of a wheel and axle is four times greater than the radius of the axle. What is the mechanical advantage of this machine?

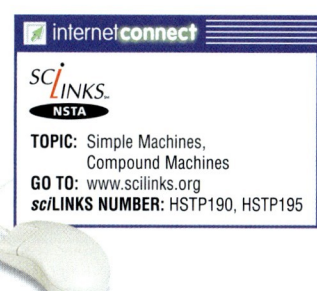

internet connect

SC_iLINKS NSTA

TOPIC: Simple Machines, Compound Machines
GO TO: www.scilinks.org
*sci*LINKS NUMBER: HSTP190, HSTP195

4) Close

Quiz

1. Why are simple machines so useful? (They make work easier.)
2. Identify types of simple machines you might find on a playground. Describe how each of them modifies work. (seesaw: lever changes direction of input force; merry-go-round: wheel and axle makes the input force on the axle cause the wheel to move in a circle)
3. How does reducing friction increase the mechanical efficiency of a compound machine? (Less work input is used to overcome friction, so work output is higher and mechanical efficiency is higher.)

ALTERNATIVE ASSESSMENT

Have each student write a story that incorporates six simple or compound machines. The machines must operate in some way appropriate to the story line. Suggest that students illustrate their stories.

Examples of Compound Machines:

- tweezers
- bicycle
- automobile
- jack
- airplane
- nail clippers
- typewriter
- pencil sharpener
- tire iron

Reinforcement Worksheet 8 "Mechanical Advantage and Efficiency"

Answers to Review

1. Examples include the crank on a can opener, the reel on a fishing rod, a screwdriver, a doorknob, the crank on an ice cream maker, and the film-advance mechanism on an old camera.
2. Each side of the tweezers is a third class lever. The sharpened edges of nail clippers are wedges, and the arm that activates the clipper is a second class lever.
3. The mechanical advantage of a wheel and axle is determined by the ratio of the wheel radius to the axle radius. So this machine would have a mechanical advantage of 4.

Section 3 • Types of Machines

Chapter Highlights

Vocabulary Definitions

Section 1

work the action that results when a force causes an object to move in the direction of the force; $W = F \times d$

joule the unit used to express work and energy; equivalent to the newton-meter (N•m)

power the rate at which work is done; $P = W/t$

watt the unit used to express power; equivalent to joules per second (J/s)

Section 2

machine a device that helps make work easier by changing the size or direction (or both) of a force

work input the work done on a machine; the product of the input force and the distance through which it is exerted

work output the work done by a machine; the product of the output force and the distance through which it is exerted

mechanical advantage a number that tells how many times a machine multiplies force; can be calculated by dividing the output force by the input force

mechanical efficiency a comparison expressed as a percentage of a machine's work output with the work input; can be calculated by dividing work output by work input and then multiplying by 100

Chapter Highlights

SECTION 1

Vocabulary
- work (p. 188)
- joule (p. 190)
- power (p. 191)
- watt (p. 191)

Section Notes
- Work occurs when a force causes an object to move in the direction of the force. The unit for work is the joule (J).
- Work is done on an object only when a force makes an object move and only while that force is applied.
- For work to be done on an object, the direction of the object's motion must be in the same direction as the force applied.
- Work can be calculated by multiplying force by distance.
- Power is the rate at which work is done. The unit for power is the watt (W).
- Power can be calculated by dividing the amount of work by the time taken to do that work.

Labs
- A Powerful Workout (p. 662)

SECTION 2

Vocabulary
- machine (p. 192)
- work input (p. 193)
- work output (p. 193)
- mechanical advantage (p. 196)
- mechanical efficiency (p. 197)

Section Notes
- A machine makes work easier by changing the size or direction (or both) of a force.
- When a machine changes the size of a force, the distance through which the force is exerted must also change. Force or distance can increase, but not together.

✓ Skills Check

Math Concepts

WORK AND POWER Suppose a woman raises a 65 N object 1.6 m in 4 s. The work done and her power can be calculated as follows:

$$W = F \times d \qquad P = \frac{W}{t}$$
$$= 65 \text{ N} \times 1.6 \text{ m} \qquad = \frac{104 \text{ J}}{4 \text{ s}}$$
$$= 104 \text{ J} \qquad = 26 \text{ W}$$

Visual Understanding

MACHINES MAKE WORK EASIER A machine can change the size or direction (or both) of a force. Review the table on page 195 to learn more about how machines make work easier.

COMPOUND MACHINES A compound machine is made of two or more simple machines. Review the examples on pages 204 and 205.

Lab and Activity Highlights

A Powerful Workout **PG 662**

Inclined to Move **PG 664**

Building Machines **PG 665**

Wheeling and Dealing **PG 666**

 Datasheets for LabBook
(blackline masters for these labs)

206 Chapter 8 • Work and Machines

SECTION 2

- Mechanical advantage tells how many times a machine multiplies force. It can be calculated by dividing the output force by the input force.

- Mechanical efficiency is a comparison of a machine's work output with work input. Mechanical efficiency is calculated by dividing work output by work input and is expressed as a percentage.

- Machines are not 100 percent efficient because some of the work done by a machine is used to overcome friction. So work output is always less than work input.

SECTION 3

Vocabulary
lever (p. 198)
inclined plane (p. 200)
wedge (p. 201)
screw (p. 201)
wheel and axle (p. 202)
pulley (p. 203)
compound machine (p. 204)

Section Notes

- All machines are constructed from these six simple machines: lever, inclined plane, wedge, screw, wheel and axle, and pulley.

- Compound machines consist of two or more simple machines.

- Compound machines have low mechanical efficiencies because they have more moving parts and thus more friction to overcome.

Labs
Inclined to Move (p. 664)
Building Machines (p. 665)
Wheeling and Dealing (p. 666)

VOCABULARY DEFINITIONS, continued

SECTION 3

lever a simple machine consisting of a bar that pivots at a fixed point, called a fulcrum; there are three classes of levers, based on where the input force, output force, and fulcrum are placed in relation to the load: first class levers, second class levers, and third class levers

inclined plane a simple machine that is a straight, slanted surface; a ramp

wedge a simple machine that is a double inclined plane that moves; a wedge is often used for cutting

screw a simple machine that is an inclined plane wrapped in a spiral

wheel and axle a simple machine consisting of two circular objects of different sizes; the wheel is the larger of the two circular objects

pulley a simple machine consisting of a grooved wheel that holds a rope or a cable; there are two kinds of pulleys—fixed and movable

compound machine machine that is made of two or more simple machines

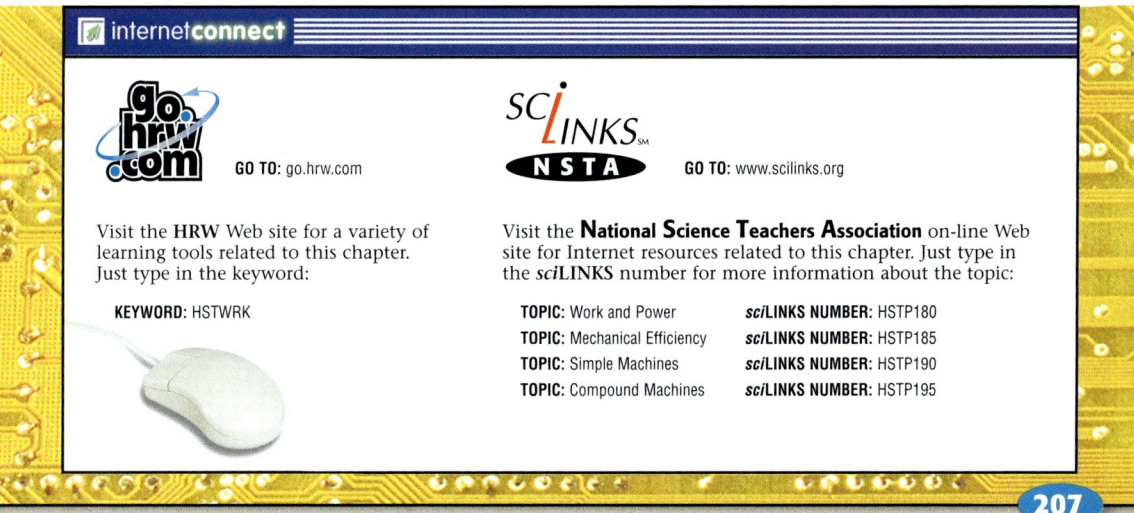

internetconnect

GO TO: go.hrw.com

Visit the **HRW** Web site for a variety of learning tools related to this chapter. Just type in the keyword:

KEYWORD: HSTWRK

GO TO: www.scilinks.org

Visit the **National Science Teachers Association** on-line Web site for Internet resources related to this chapter. Just type in the *sci*LINKS number for more information about the topic:

TOPIC: Work and Power — *sci*LINKS NUMBER: HSTP180
TOPIC: Mechanical Efficiency — *sci*LINKS NUMBER: HSTP185
TOPIC: Simple Machines — *sci*LINKS NUMBER: HSTP190
TOPIC: Compound Machines — *sci*LINKS NUMBER: HSTP195

Vocabulary Review Worksheet 8

Blackline masters of these Chapter Highlights can be found in the **Study Guide.**

207

Lab and Activity Highlights

LabBank

Inquiry Labs, Get an Arm and an Egg Up, Lab 19

Long-Term Projects & Research Ideas, To Complicate Things, Project 58

Whiz-Bang Demonstrations
- Pull-Ease, Please! Demo 48
- A Clever Lever, Demo 49

Chapter Review

USING VOCABULARY

For each pair of terms, explain the difference in their meanings.

1. joule/watt
2. work output/work input
3. mechanical efficiency/mechanical advantage
4. screw/inclined plane
5. simple machine/compound machine

UNDERSTANDING CONCEPTS

Multiple Choice

6. Work is being done when
   a. you apply a force to an object.
   b. an object is moving after you apply a force to it.
   c. you exert a force that moves an object in the direction of the force.
   d. you do something that is difficult.

7. The work output for a machine is always less than the work input because
   a. all machines have a mechanical advantage.
   b. some of the work done is used to overcome friction.
   c. some of the work done is used to overcome distance.
   d. power is the rate at which work is done.

8. The unit for work is the
   a. joule.   c. newton.
   b. joule per second.   d. watt.

9. Which of the following is not a simple machine?
   a. a faucet handle
   b. a jar lid
   c. a can opener
   d. a seesaw

10. Power is
    a. how strong someone or something is.
    b. how much force is being used.
    c. how much work is being done.
    d. how fast work is being done.

11. The unit for power is the
    a. newton.   c. watt.
    b. kilogram.   d. joule.

12. A machine can increase
    a. distance at the expense of force.
    b. force at the expense of distance.
    c. neither distance nor force.
    d. Both (a) and (b)

Short Answer

13. Identify the simple machines that make up a pair of scissors.

14. In two or three sentences, explain the force-distance trade-off that occurs when a machine is used to make work easier.

15. Explain why you do work on a bag of groceries when you pick it up but not when you are carrying it.

a little distance to move the ends of the chopsticks a larger distance.

Concept Mapping

16. 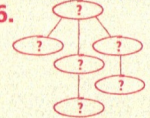 An answer to this exercise can be found at the end of this book.

Concept Mapping

16. Create a concept map using the following terms: work, force, distance, machine, mechanical advantage.

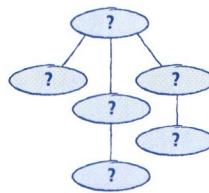

CRITICAL THINKING AND PROBLEM SOLVING

17. Why do you think levers usually have a greater mechanical efficiency than other simple machines do?

18. The winding road shown below is actually a series of inclined planes. Describe how a winding road makes it easier for vehicles to travel up a hill.

19. Why do you think you would not want to reduce the friction involved in using a winding road?

MATH IN SCIENCE

20. You and a friend together apply a force of 1,000 N to a 3,000 N automobile to make it roll 10 m in 1 minute and 40 seconds.
    a. How much work did you and your friend do together?
    b. What was your combined power?

INTERPRETING GRAPHICS

For each of the images below, identify the class of lever used and calculate the mechanical advantage.

21.

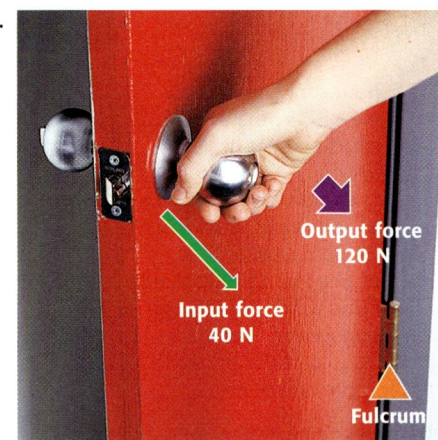

22.

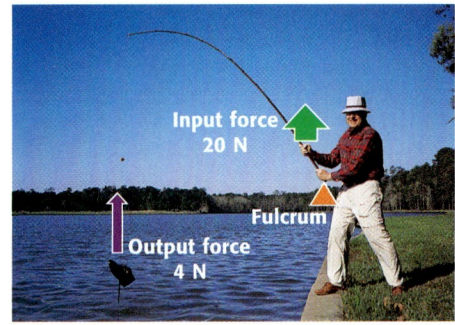

NOW What Do You Think?

Take a minute to review your answers to the ScienceLog questions on page 187. Have your answers changed? If necessary, revise your answers based on what you have learned since you began this chapter.

CRITICAL THINKING AND PROBLEM SOLVING

17. Sample answer: Because some work input is used to overcome friction, work output is always less than work input. Levers do not have a lot of moving parts, so they don't generate as much friction as other machines. Less work input is used to overcome friction. As a result, the mechanical efficiency of a lever is usually greater than that of other simple machines.

18. Sample answer: A winding road makes climbing a hill easier because the length of the winding road is longer than the length of a road straight up the hill. Because the mechanical advantage of an inclined plane is determined by dividing the length of the inclined plane by its height, the more the road winds, the easier it is for a car to get up the hill.

19. Sample answer: Friction between the road and car tires is necessary for a car to travel along a road. Although friction reduces mechanical efficiency, reducing the friction between tires and the roadway would prevent cars from traveling safely along a winding road.

MATH IN SCIENCE

20. a. Work = 1,000 N × 10 m = 10,000 J
    b. Power = $\frac{10,000 \text{ J}}{100 \text{ s}}$ = 100 W

INTERPRETING GRAPHICS

21. second class lever, $MA = \frac{120 \text{ N}}{40 \text{ N}} = 3$

22. third class lever, $MA = \frac{4 \text{ N}}{20 \text{ N}} = 0.20$

NOW WHAT DO YOU THINK?

Sample answers:

1. Doing work means making an object move in the direction of the force applied to it.
2. Machines make doing work easier by changing the size or direction (or both) of a force. Machines increase force at the expense of distance or increase distance at the expense of force.
3. Simple machines include levers (a hammer pulling a nail), inclined planes (a ramp), wedges (a knife), screws (a jar lid), wheel and axle (a doorknob), and pulleys (the cord mechanism on horizontal blinds).

Concept Mapping Transparency 8

Blackline masters of this Chapter Review can be found in the **Study Guide**.

SCIENCE, TECHNOLOGY, AND SOCIETY

Micromachines

Background
Advances in microtechnology have allowed scientists to achieve impressive results in many fields. For example, medical researchers are working on special pills equipped with sensors, tiny pumps, and drug reservoirs.

Other technological advances include microscopic filters and air turbines for controlling the temperature of microchip arrays. One team of scientists has created a molecular "on-off switch" that could be used to store information in computers.

A scanning tunneling microscope (STM) can be used to study the surfaces of materials that can carry electric current. As the probe of the STM approaches a material, a current called a tunneling current is created between the material and the probe. The strength of the current at different locations allows the STM to create an image of the material's surface. The inventors of the STM won the Nobel Prize in physics in 1986.

Science, Technology, and Society

Micromachines

The technology of making things smaller and smaller keeps growing and growing. Powerful computers can now be held in the palm of your hand. But what about motors smaller than a grain of pepper? Or gnat-sized robots that can swim through the bloodstream? These are just a couple of the possibilities for micromachines.

Microscopic Motors
Researchers have already built gears, motors, and other devices so small that you could accidentally inhale one! For example, one engineer devised a motor so small that five of the motors would fit on the period at the end of this sentence. This micromotor is powered by static electricity instead of electric current, and the motor spins at 15,000 revolutions per minute. This is about twice as fast as most automobile engines running at top speed.

Small Sensors
So far micromachines have been most useful as sensing devices. Micromechanical sensors can be used in places too small for ordinary instruments. For example, blood-pressure sensors can fit inside blood vessels and can detect minute changes in a person's blood pressure. Each sensor has a patch so thin that it bends when the pressure changes.

Cell-Sized Robots
Some scientists are investigating the possibility of creating cell-sized machines called nanobots. These tiny robots may have many uses in medicine. For instance, if nanobots could be injected into a person's bloodstream, they might be used to destroy disease-causing organisms such as viruses and bacteria. Nanobots might also be used to count blood cells or to deliver medicine.

The ultimate in micromachines would be machines created from individual atoms and molecules. Although these machines do not currently exist, scientists are already able to manipulate single atoms and molecules. For example, the "molecular man" shown below is made of individual molecules. These molecules are moved by using a scanning tunneling microscope.

▲ *The earliest working micromachine had a turning central rotor.*

A Nanobot's "Life"
▶ Imagine that you are a nanobot traveling through a person's body. What types of things do you think you would see? What type of work could you do? Write a story that describes what your experiences as a nanobot might be like.

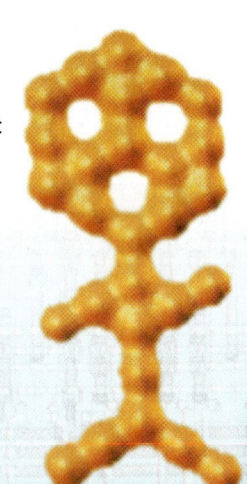

▶ *"Molecular man" is composed of 28 carbon monoxide molecules.*

Answer to A Nanobot's "Life"
Encourage creativity and scientific accuracy by providing students with a body atlas or similar reference work. Tell them that they are all specialized nanobots who can travel through only certain systems of the body (such as the circulatory, endocrine, or nervous system) and certain organs or types of tissue. Ask them to describe their environment. What common problems might occur in their environment, and what could they do to help? (For example, a nanobot inside a lung would see bronchial tubes, alveoli, and capillaries. It could break down contaminants in the air sacs, help fight off infections, or remove fluids in patients who have pneumonia.)

Eureka!
Wheelchair Innovators

Two recent inventions have dramatically improved the technology of wheelchairs. With these new inventions, some wheelchair riders can now control their chairs with voice commands and others can take a cruise over a sandy beach.

Voice-Command Wheelchair

At age 27, Martine Kemph invented a voice-recognition system that enables people without arms or legs to use spoken commands to operate their motorized wheelchairs. Here's how it works: The voice-recognition computer translates spoken words into digital commands, which are then directed to electric motors. These commands completely control the operating speed and direction of the motors, giving the operator total control over the chair's movement.

Kemph's system can execute spoken commands almost instantly. In addition, the system is easy to program, so each user can tailor the computer's list of commands to his or her needs.

Kemph named the computer Katalvox, using the root words *katal*, which is Greek for "to understand," and *vox*, which is Latin for "voice."

The Surf Chair

Mike Hensler was a lifeguard at Daytona Beach, Florida, when he realized that it was next to impossible for someone in a wheelchair to come onto the beach. Although he had never invented a machine before, Hensler decided to build a wheelchair that could be maneuvered across sand without getting stuck. He began spending many evenings in his driveway with a pile of lawn-chair parts, designing the chair by trial and error.

The result of Hensler's efforts looks very different from a conventional wheelchair. With huge rubber wheels and a thick frame of white PVC pipe, the Surf Chair not only moves easily over sandy terrain but also is weather resistant and easy to clean. The newest models of the Surf Chair come with optional attachments, such as a variety of umbrellas, detachable armrests and footrests, and even places to attach fishing rods.

▲ *Mike Hensler tries out his Surf Chair.*

Design One Yourself

▶ Can you think of any other ways to improve wheelchairs? Think about it, and put your ideas down on paper. To inspire creative thinking, consider how a wheelchair could be made lighter, faster, safer, or easier to maneuver.

Answer to Design One Yourself
Accept all reasonable designs. Make sure students have properly considered safety features and usefulness in their designs.

Eureka!
Wheelchair Innovators

Background

Martine Kemph's Katalvox-driven wheelchair is already being used in medical institutions in Moscow and Paris, at Stanford University Hospital, and at the Mayo Clinic. Also, NASA is testing Katalvox for its ability to control cameras mounted on robotic arms. As an inventor intent on helping people, Kemph has had a very good role model: her father is a polio survivor who invented a car that could be driven without the use of legs.

In designing the Surf Chair, Hensler purposefully avoided materials that would make the chair look cumbersome or clinical. Since the beach is a place to relax and have fun, Hensler designed his chair to blend easily into such an environment. This fun and practical wheelchair is now available at many public beaches. Daytona Beach, for example, provides free use of the Surf Chair for people who need wheelchairs.

Teaching Strategies

Have students design a device to help mobility-impaired people in the home. You might want to give them a specific goal, such as designing a device to retrieve something from the refrigerator.

Chapter Organizer

CHAPTER ORGANIZATION	TIME MINUTES	OBJECTIVES	LABS, INVESTIGATIONS, AND DEMONSTRATIONS
Chapter Opener pp. 212–213	45	National Standards: SAI 1, PS 3a	**Investigate!** Blast-off to Energy, p. 213
Section 1 What Is Energy?	90	▶ Explain the relationship between energy and work. ▶ Compare kinetic and potential energy. ▶ Summarize the different forms of energy. UCP 3, PS 3a, 3d–3f	**Demonstration,** p. 214 in ATE **Demonstration,** All Wound Up! p. 215 in ATE **QuickLab,** Hear That Energy! p. 220 **Whiz-Bang Demonstrations,** Wrong-Way Roller? Demo 51
Section 2 Energy Conversions	90	▶ Describe an energy conversion. ▶ Give examples of energy conversions among the different forms of energy. ▶ Explain the role of machines in energy conversions. ▶ Explain how energy conversions make energy useful. ST 2, SPSP 5, PS 3a, 3f; LabBook SAI 1, PS 3a	**Discovery Lab,** Finding Energy, p. 668 **Datasheets for LabBook,** Finding Energy, Datasheet 31 **Skill Builder,** Energy of a Pendulum, p. 670 **Datasheets for LabBook,** Energy of a Pendulum, Datasheet 32 **Whiz-Bang Demonstrations,** Pendulum Peril, Demo 50
Section 3 Conservation of Energy	90	▶ Explain how energy is conserved within a closed system. ▶ Explain the law of conservation of energy. ▶ Give examples of how thermal energy is always a result of energy conversion. ▶ Explain why perpetual motion is impossible. UCP 1, 3, ST 2; LabBook ST 1	**Demonstration,** p. 229 in ATE **Design Your Own,** Eggstremely Fragile, p. 671 **Datasheets for LabBook,** Eggstremely Fragile, Datasheet 33 **Labs You Can Eat,** Power-Packed Peanuts, Lab 20
Section 4 Energy Resources	90	▶ Name several energy resources. ▶ Explain how the sun is the source of most energy on Earth. ▶ Evaluate the advantages and disadvantages of using various energy resources. ST 2, SPSP 4, HNS 1, PS 3e, 3f	**Interactive Explorations CD-ROM,** The Generation Gap A **Worksheet** is also available in the **Interactive Explorations Teacher's Edition.** **Labs You Can Eat,** Now You're Cooking! Lab 21 **Long-Term Projects & Research Ideas,** Project 59

*See page **T20** for a complete correlation of this book with the*

NATIONAL SCIENCE EDUCATION STANDARDS.

TECHNOLOGY RESOURCES

 Guided Reading Audio CD English or Spanish, Chapter 9

 Interactive Explorations CD-ROM CD 1, Exploration 6, The Generation Gap

 One-Stop Planner CD-ROM with Test Generator

  Science, Technology & Society, Segments 6 and 14

Multicultural Connections, Segment 8

Scientists in Action, Segment 7

Chapter 9 • Energy and Energy Resources

Chapter 9 • Energy and Energy Resources

CLASSROOM WORKSHEETS, TRANSPARENCIES, AND RESOURCES	SCIENCE INTEGRATION AND CONNECTIONS	REVIEW AND ASSESSMENT
Directed Reading Worksheet 9 **Science Puzzlers, Twisters & Teasers,** Worksheet 9		
Transparency 232, Energy and Work **Directed Reading Worksheet 9,** Section 1 **Transparency 233,** Thermal Energy	**Multicultural Connection,** p. 216 in ATE **MathBreak,** Calculating Energy, p. 217 **Math and More,** p. 217 in ATE **Cross-Disciplinary Focus,** p. 219, 220 in ATE **Real-World Connection,** p. 220 in ATE	**Review,** p. 217 **Review,** p. 221 **Quiz,** p. 221 in ATE **Alternative Assessment,** p. 221 in ATE
Transparency 234, Energy Conversion on a Trampoline **Directed Reading Worksheet 9,** Section 2 **Transparency 235,** Photosynthesis **Transparency 236,** Energy Transfer in a Bicycle **Transparency 237,** Energy Conversions in a Car Engine **Math Skills for Science Worksheet 52,** A Bicycle Trip **Reinforcement Worksheet 9,** See What I Saw, Energetic Cooking	**Apply,** p. 224 **Connect to Environmental Science,** p. 224 in ATE **Multicultural Connection,** p. 225 in ATE **Real-World Connection,** p. 228 in ATE **Across the Sciences:** Green Buildings, p. 242	**Self-Check,** p. 223 **Review,** p. 225 **Homework,** p. 227 in ATE **Review,** p. 228 **Quiz,** p. 228 in ATE **Alternative Assessment,** p. 228 in ATE
Directed Reading Worksheet 9, Section 3	**Real-World Connection,** p. 230 in ATE **Biology Connection,** p. 231	**Review,** p. 231 **Quiz,** p. 231 in ATE **Alternative Assessment,** p. 231 in ATE
Directed Reading Worksheet 9, Section 4 **Science Skills Worksheet 26,** Grasping Graphing **Transparency 116,** Formation of Coal **Critical Thinking Worksheet 9,** The Armchair Enviro-Challenge	**Cross-Disciplinary Focus,** p. 233 in ATE **Connect to Earth Science,** p. 233 in ATE **Multicultural Connection,** p. 236 in ATE **Connect to Environmental Science,** p. 237 in ATE **Careers:** Power-Plant Manager—Cheryl Mele, p. 243	**Homework,** p. 234 in ATE **Review,** p. 237 **Quiz,** p. 237 in ATE **Alternative Assessment,** p. 237 in ATE

 Holt, Rinehart and Winston On-line Resources
go.hrw.com

For worksheets and other teaching aids related to this chapter, visit the HRW Web site and type in the keyword: **HSTENG**

 **National Science Teachers Association**
www.scilinks.org

Encourage students to use the *sci*LINKS numbers listed in the internet connect boxes to access information and resources on the **NSTA** Web site.

END-OF-CHAPTER REVIEW AND ASSESSMENT

Chapter Review in Study Guide
Vocabulary and Notes in Study Guide
Chapter Tests with Performance-Based Assessment, Chapter 9 Test, Performance-Based Assessment 9
Concept Mapping Transparency 9

Chapter Resources & Worksheets

Visual Resources

TEACHING TRANSPARENCIES

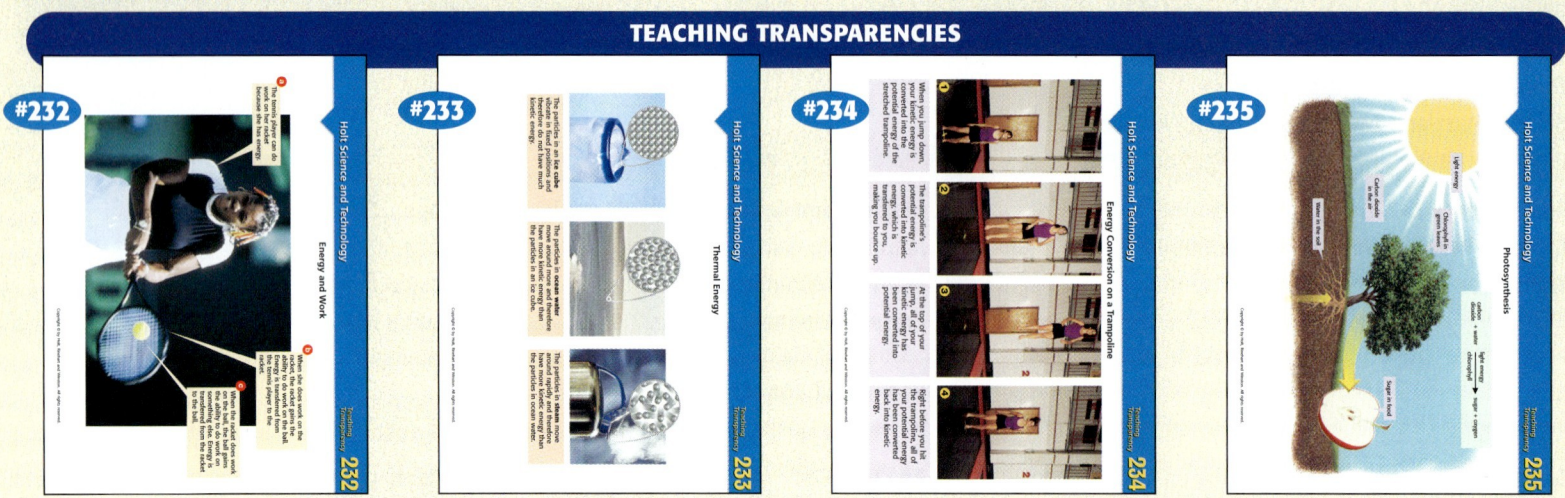

TEACHING TRANSPARENCIES

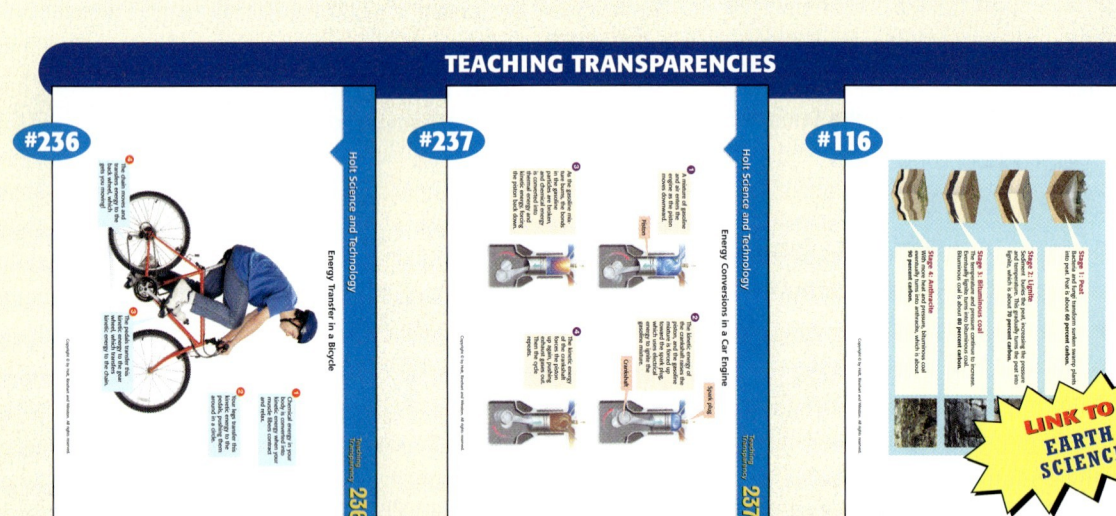

CONCEPT MAPPING TRANSPARENCY

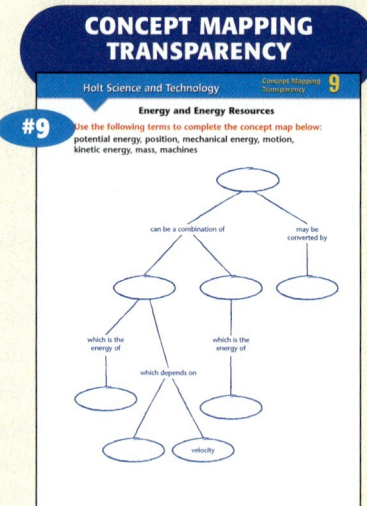

Meeting Individual Needs

DIRECTED READING

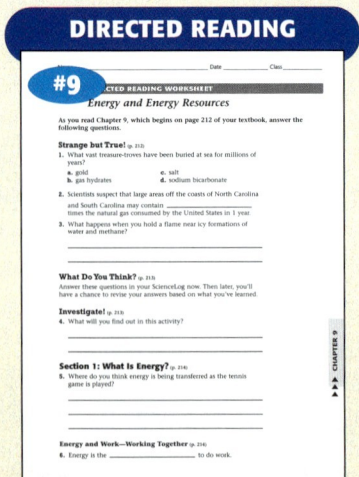

REINFORCEMENT & VOCABULARY REVIEW

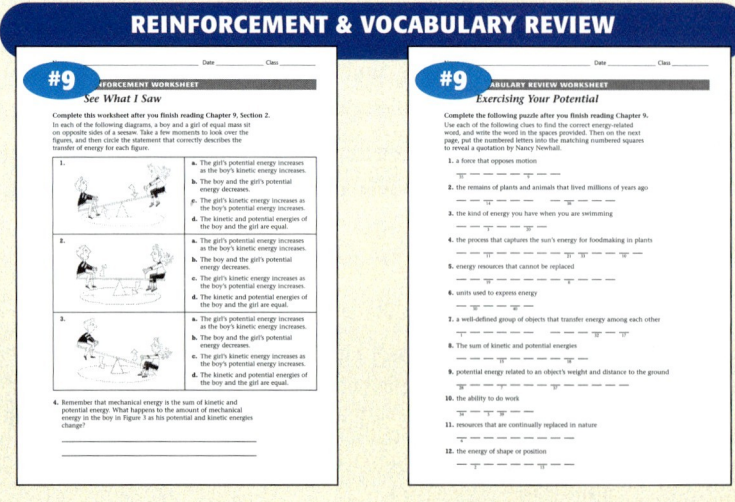

SCIENCE PUZZLERS, TWISTERS & TEASERS

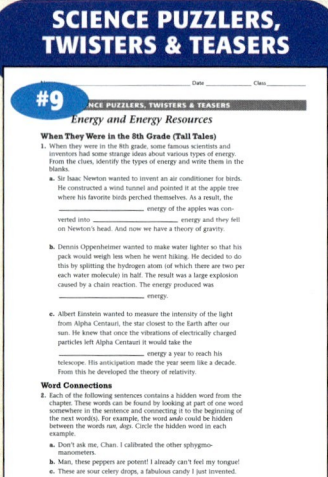

Chapter 9 • Energy and Energy Resources

Chapter 9 • Energy and Energy Resources

Review & Assessment

STUDY GUIDE

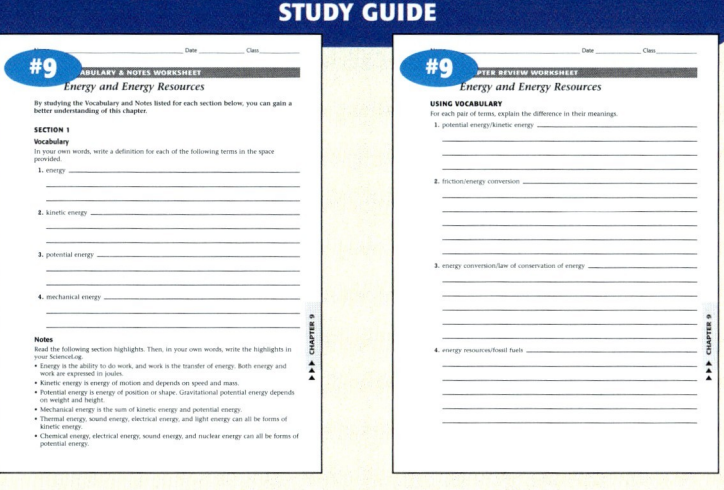

CHAPTER TESTS WITH PERFORMANCE-BASED ASSESSMENT

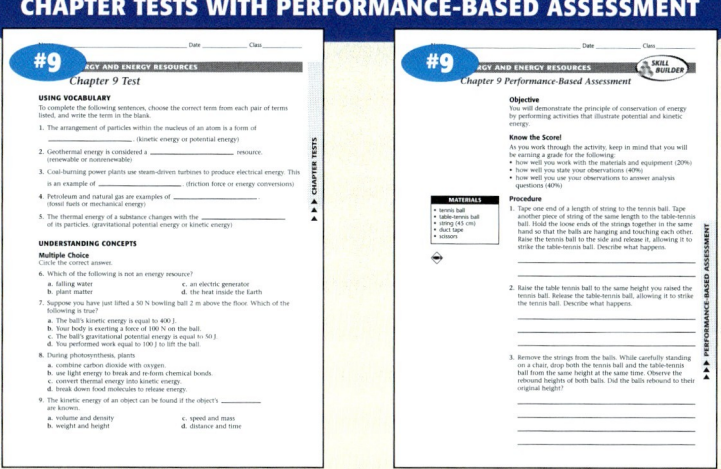

Lab Worksheets

LABS YOU CAN EAT

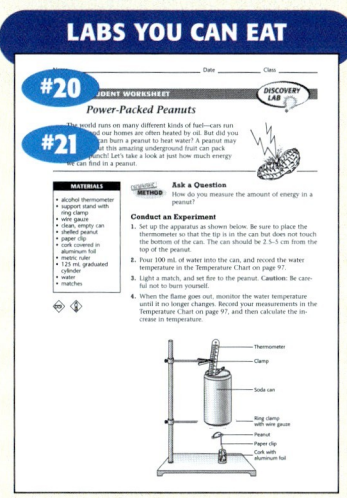

WHIZ-BANG DEMONSTRATIONS

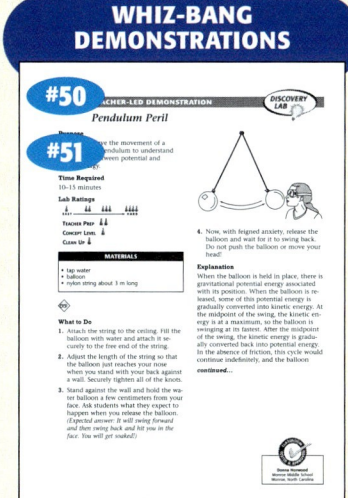

LONG-TERM PROJECTS & RESEARCH IDEAS

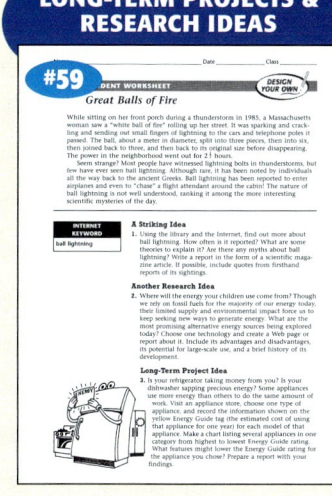

DATASHEETS FOR LABBOOK

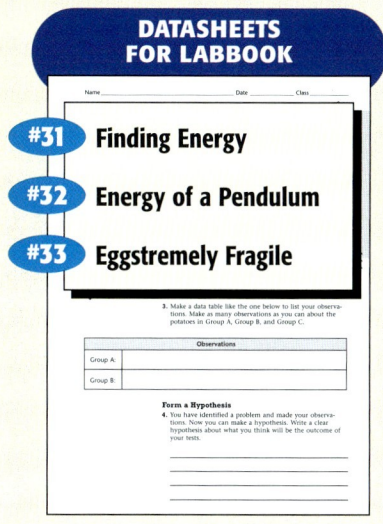

Applications & Extensions

CRITICAL THINKING & PROBLEM SOLVING

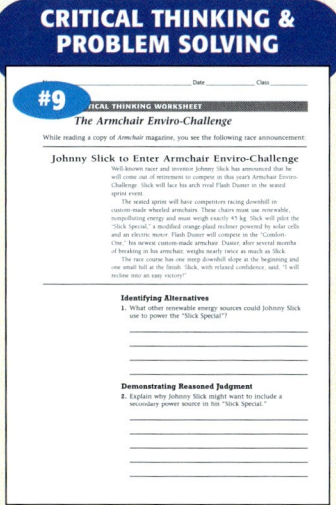

MULTICULTURAL CONNECTIONS / SCIENCE TECHNOLOGY

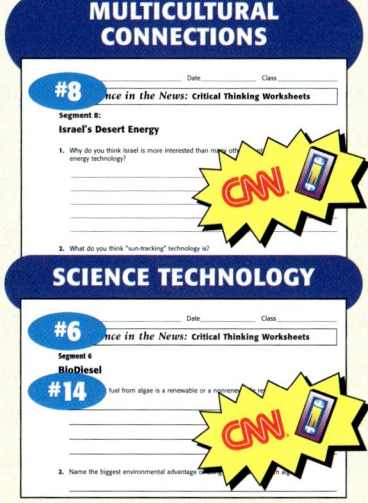

SCIENTISTS IN ACTION

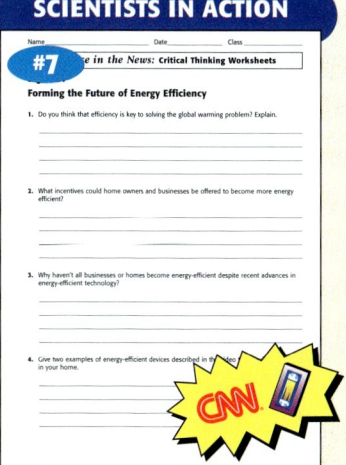

INTERACTIVE EXPLORATIONS

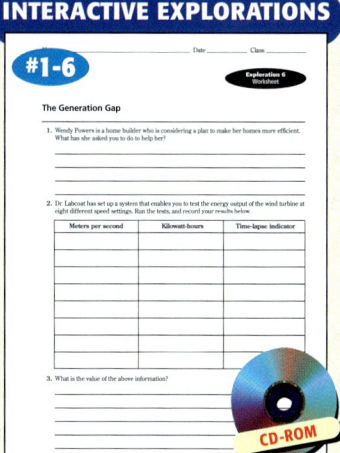

Chapter 9 • Chapter Resources & Worksheets   211D

Chapter Background

SECTION 1

What Is Energy?

▶ **Energy**
Energy is the ability to do work. *Work* occurs when a force causes an object to move in the direction of the force. Both energy and work are expressed in units called *joules* (J), named for James Prescott Joule. One joule is the amount of work done when a force of 1 N acts through a distance of 1 m (1 J = 1 N × 1 m).

▶ **James Prescott Joule**
The English scientist James Prescott Joule (1818–1889) was the son of a wealthy brewery owner. Joule used his financial resources to conduct research in a variety of areas.

- Joule worked to improve the efficiency of electric motors so they could be used to replace steam engines. His research was some of the first to show the connection between thermal energy and other forms of energy.

IS THAT A FACT!

- The countries of North America consume about 30 percent of the total world energy output. The countries of the former Soviet Union consume about 11 to 15 percent.

SECTION 2

Energy Conversions

▶ **Kinetic and Potential Energy**
The conversion of potential energy to kinetic energy and vice versa is classically demonstrated by lifting and dropping an object.

- A moving object has kinetic energy. The amount of kinetic energy depends on the mass of the object and the speed at which it is moving.

▶ **Gravitational Potential Energy**
An object that has been lifted from its position on the Earth has gravitational potential energy. If you drop the object and nothing is in its way, the gravitational potential energy will immediately begin to change into kinetic energy as the object accelerates toward the Earth.

▶ **Conversion of Light Energy to Chemical Energy**
Plants use photosynthesis to make molecules with high chemical energy, such as sugars, from water and carbon dioxide, which have low chemical energy. To increase the amount of chemical energy, light energy is converted to chemical energy, and ATP is formed. In a separate series of reactions, plants convert sugars to starches.

- When you eat plants, your digestive system transforms the high-energy sugars and starches into smaller, lower-energy molecules. The chemical energy in the sugars and starches fuels all your body functions and movements and provides the thermal energy that keeps your body temperature constant.

Chapter 9 • Energy and Energy Resources

▶ **Conversion of Chemical Energy to Electrical Energy**
Batteries consist of cells. A cell converts chemical energy into electrical energy. Any cell has two electrodes and an electrolyte. Between the electrodes are positive and negative ions. Positively charged ions have fewer electrons than protons, and negatively charged ions have more electrons than protons. When a circuit is completed, the electrodes react with the electrolyte, causing electrons to leave one of the electrodes and build up on the other. Work is done in separating the charges, and that work is stored in the battery as electrical potential energy.

- Whenever the electrodes of the battery are connected with a wire, work is done on the electrons in the wire as electrical energy flows from the negative electrode of the battery to the positive electrode.

SECTION 3

Conservation of Energy

▶ **The Law of Conservation of Energy**
In the presence of friction, mechanical energy *(KE + PE)* is *not* conserved. But mechanical energy does not take into account the other objects and conversions within a closed system. Total energy is always conserved, even if mechanical energy is not.

IS THAT A FACT!

- The British Patent Office does not accept applications for perpetual motion machines. Such a machine would violate the laws of physics and is therefore considered impossible.

- The United States Patent Office receives (and accepts) about 100 applications yearly for perpetual motion machines.

SECTION 4

Energy Resources

▶ **Fossil Fuels**
Fossil fuels require hundreds of thousands, or even millions, of years to form.

- Coal is formed from plant material that is compressed in swamps.

- Petroleum and natural gas both form from decayed organisms.

▶ **Energy Alternatives**
Nature can supply energy in a variety of ways. Wind energy, tidal energy, hydroelectric energy, and solar energy are all alternatives to the nonrenewable fossil fuels used today.

- Although the sun is technically a limited energy source, it still has approximately 5 billion years left in its life span. For the time being, it is considered a limitless source of energy.

For background information about teaching strategies and issues, refer to the *Professional Reference for Teachers*.

Chapter 9 • Chapter Background   **211F**

CHAPTER 9
Energy and Energy Resources

Chapter Preview

Section 1
What Is Energy?
- Energy and Work—Working Together
- Kinetic Energy Is Energy of Motion
- Potential Energy Is Energy of Position
- Mechanical Energy Sums It All Up
- Forms of Energy

Section 2
Energy Conversions
- From Kinetic to Potential and Back
- Conversions Involving Chemical Energy
- Conversions Involving Electrical Energy
- Energy and Machines
- Why Energy Conversions Are Important

Section 3
Conservation of Energy
- Where Does the Energy Go?
- Energy Is Conserved Within a Closed System
- No Conversion Without Thermal Energy

Section 4
Energy Resources
- Nonrenewable Resources
- Renewable Resources
- The Two Sides to Energy Resources

Strange but True!

Vast treasures are buried at sea. No, they're not gold doubloons—they're gas hydrates (HIE DRAYTS), energy resources that may become more important in the future.

Gas hydrates are icy formations of water and methane, the main component of natural gas. The methane in hydrates is produced by bacteria that help decompose organic material in the ocean. Hydrates form at depths of 300–800 m.

Gas-hydrate deposits are found under the Arctic permafrost and in marine sediments. Off the coasts of North Carolina and South Carolina, scientists have found two deposits that may contain 37 trillion cubic meters of methane gas. That's 70 times the amount of natural gas consumed by the United States in 1 year!

When brought to temperatures of around 15°C, the snowball-like hydrates fizz like effervescent tablets. And holding a flame near a hydrate ignites the evaporating methane, making the gas hydrate look like a burning ice cube. In both instances, the energy released could be used to drive machinery or generate electrical energy.

Unfortunately, mining gas hydrates is expensive. But as more research is done, gas hydrates may play a bigger role in the way energy is used every day. In this chapter, you'll learn about energy, energy conversions, and energy resources.

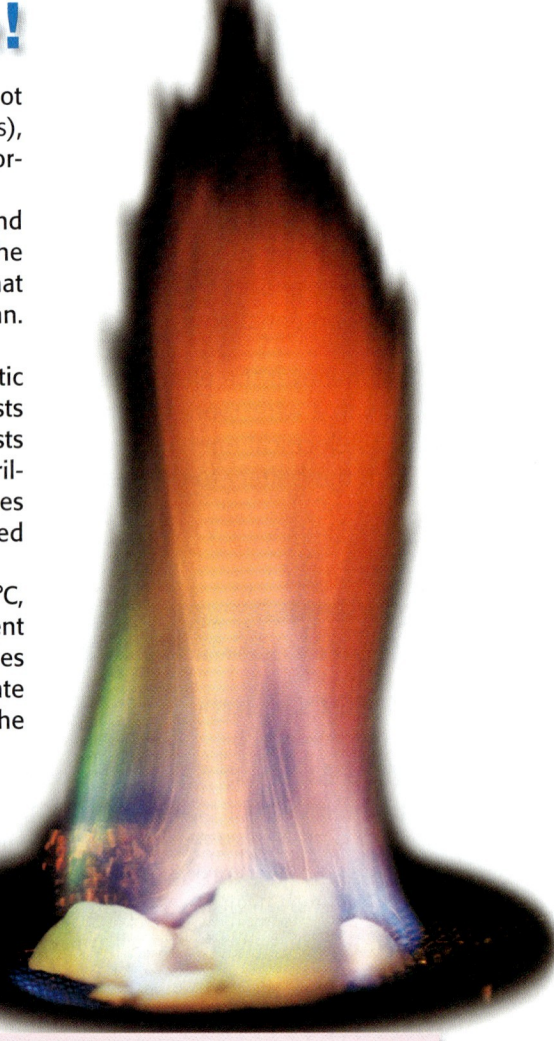

Because of the methane locked inside these icy formations, gas hydrates may become a very valuable energy resource.

Strange but True!

Gas hydrates may be one of the largest sources of energy ever discovered. For the United States, developing hydrates as an energy source would cost more than producing natural gas from conventional sources. For other countries, though, it may be worth the expense to develop gas hydrates as a source of energy.

For instance, Japan imports nearly 95 percent of its natural gas, and the Japanese pay very high prices for it. In 1995, the Japanese government announced plans to try to tap its offshore gas hydrate deposits. India and Russia are doing similar research.

What Do You Think?

In your ScienceLog, try to answer the following questions based on what you already know:

1. What is energy?
2. How is energy converted from one form to another?
3. What is an energy resource?

Blast-off to Energy

In this activity, you will find out what happens when energy stored in matter is released.

Procedure

1. Use a **measuring spoon** to put a tablespoon of **baking soda** into the center of a **coffee filter**. Twist the ends of the filter tightly shut. (You can use a **twist tie** if necessary.)

2. Use a **graduated cylinder** to pour 200 mL of **water** into an empty **2 L soda bottle**. Use **another graduated cylinder** to pour 200 mL of **vinegar** into the same soda bottle. Place the bottle upright on several pieces of **newspaper** on a table or on the floor.

3. Drop the coffee filter into the soda bottle, and quickly place a **cork** in the mouth of the bottle. Take several steps back from the bottle. **Caution:** Do not lean over the bottle.

4. Observe what happens inside the bottle and what happens to the cork. Record your observations in your ScienceLog.

Analysis

5. Do you think the water, vinegar, or baking soda has energy? Explain your answer.

6. How does what happened to the cork show that the cork had energy? Where do you think the cork's energy came from?

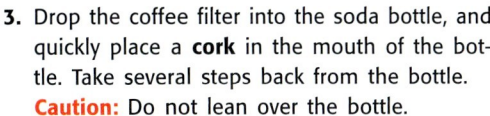

What Do You Think?

Accept all reasonable responses. Students will have a chance to revise their answers in the Chapter Review under NOW What Do You Think?

Investigate!

MATERIALS

FOR EACH GROUP:
- measuring spoon
- 1 tablespoon of baking soda
- coffee filter
- twist tie (optional)
- 2 graduated cylinders
- 2 L soda bottle
- cork
- 200 mL water
- 200 mL vinegar
- newspaper

Safety Caution: Goggles, safety gloves, and aprons must be worn for this activity. Emphasize to students that they should stand away from their bottle to observe the results. The pressure built up behind the cork could produce a significant force.

Answers to Investigate!

4. Students should observe bubbles being formed inside their bottle and should note that the cork was launched out of the bottle.

5. Answers will vary, but students should infer that the water, vinegar, and baking soda have energy because they produced a reaction that popped the cork.

6. Answers will vary, but students should mention that the movement of the cork indicates that it has energy. Students can infer that the energy came from the reaction in the bottle.

 internetconnect

Smithsonian Institution®
Visit *www.si.edu/hrw* for additional on-line resources.

 Directed Reading Worksheet 9

 Science Puzzlers, Twisters & Teasers Worksheet 9

 Guided Reading Audio CD
English or Spanish, Chapter 9

Chapter 9 • Energy and Energy Resources

Section 1

Focus

What Is Energy?
This section introduces the concept of energy. Students will learn about the relationship between energy and work. They will also learn about the difference between kinetic and potential energy and how they relate to mechanical energy. This section also discusses and compares different forms of energy.

Bellringer
Write the following on the board:

"Energy is the ability to ____."

Ask students to think about this phrase and to write in their ScienceLog how they think it should be completed. Lead a brief discussion to introduce the concept that energy is the ability to do work.

1 Motivate

DEMONSTRATION
At the beginning of class, do the following:

Strike a match and let it burn for a few moments. Wind up a windup toy and let it run. Turn off the lights in the classroom and turn on a flashlight. Finally, knock a tennis ball off a table so that it bounces onto the floor.

After these demonstrations, ask students to explain how energy was involved in each event. Lead students to conclude that there are many different forms of energy.

Section 1

Terms to Learn
energy
kinetic energy
potential energy
mechanical energy

What You'll Do
- Explain the relationship between energy and work.
- Compare kinetic and potential energy.
- Summarize the different forms of energy.

What Is Energy?
It's match point. The crowd is dead silent. The tennis player steps up to serve. With a look of determination, she bounces the tennis ball several times. Next, in one fluid movement, she tosses the ball into the air and then slams it with her racket. The ball flies toward her opponent, who steps up and swings her racket at the ball. Suddenly, THWOOSH!! The ball goes into the net, and the net wiggles from the impact. Game, set, and match!!

Energy and Work—Working Together
Energy is around you all the time. So what is it exactly? In science, you can think of **energy** as the ability to do work. Work occurs when a force causes an object to move in the direction of the force. How are energy and work involved in playing tennis? In this example, the tennis player does work on her racket, the racket does work on the ball, and the ball does work on the net. Each time work is done, something is given by one object to another that allows it to do work. That "something" is energy. As you can see in **Figure 1,** work is a transfer of energy.

Because work and energy are so closely related, they are expressed in the same units—joules (J). When a given amount of work is done, the same amount of energy is involved.

Figure 1 When one object does work on another, energy is transferred.

a The tennis player can do work on her racket because she has energy.

b When she does work on the racket, the racket gains the ability to do work on the ball. Energy is transferred from the tennis player to the racket.

c When the racket does work on the ball, the ball gains the ability to do work on something else. Energy is transferred from the racket to the ball.

Teaching Transparency 232
"Energy and Work"

Directed Reading Worksheet 9 Section 1

IS THAT A FACT!
One joule is approximately the amount of energy it takes to lift an apple 1 m. In sports, some activities take a bit more energy. The average serve of a tennis ball takes 75 J of kinetic energy, a single fastball pitch takes 120 J, and a forward pass in football takes 150 J.

214   Chapter 9 • Energy and Energy Resources

Kinetic Energy Is Energy of Motion

From the tennis example on the previous page, you learned that energy is transferred from the racket to the ball. As the ball flies over the net, it has **kinetic** (ki NET ik) **energy,** the energy of motion. All moving objects have kinetic energy. Does the tennis player have kinetic energy? Definitely! She has kinetic energy when she steps up to serve and when she swings the racket. When she's standing still, she doesn't have any kinetic energy. However, the parts of her body that are moving—her eyes, her heart, and her lungs—do have some kinetic energy.

Objects with kinetic energy can do work. If you've ever gone bowling, you've done work using kinetic energy. When you throw the ball down the lane, you do work on it, transferring your kinetic energy to the ball. As a result, the bowling ball can do work on the pins. Another example of doing work with kinetic energy is shown in **Figure 2.**

Figure 2 When you swing a hammer, you give it kinetic energy, which it uses to do work on the nail.

Kinetic Energy Depends on Speed and Mass An object's kinetic energy can be determined with the following equation:

$$\text{Kinetic energy} = \frac{mv^2}{2}$$

In this equation, m stands for an object's mass, and v stands for an object's speed. The faster something is moving, the more kinetic energy it has. In addition, the more massive a moving object is, the more kinetic energy it has. But which do you think has more of an effect on an object's kinetic energy, its mass or its speed? As you can see from the equation, speed is squared, so speed has a greater effect on kinetic energy than does mass. You can see an example of how kinetic energy depends on speed and mass in **Figure 3.**

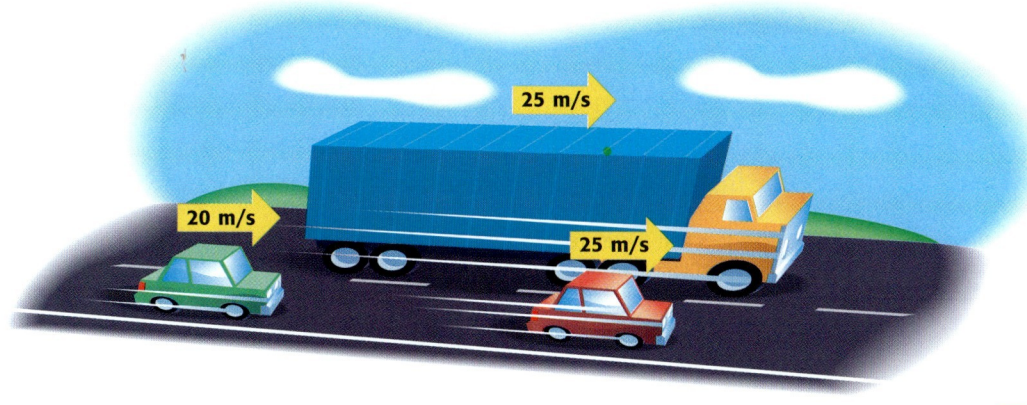

Figure 3 The red car has more kinetic energy than the green car because the red car is moving faster. But the truck has more kinetic energy than the red car because the truck is more massive.

 **SCIENCE**

The kinetic energy of a snail with a mass of 5 g traveling at 0.014 m/s is 0.00000048 J. By comparison, the kinetic energy of an 18-wheel truck traveling at 26.69 m/s is 2,200,000 J.

2) Teach, continued

MEETING INDIVIDUAL NEEDS

Students Having Difficulty
Use a pendulum to show the difference between potential energy and kinetic energy. As you pull the pendulum to the side, explain that you are giving it energy. Hold the pendulum to the side. Write the term *potential energy* on the board. Draw a picture of the pendulum's position next to the term. Allow the pendulum to swing down, and write the term *kinetic energy* on the board. Draw a picture of the pendulum moving away from its potential-energy position. Discuss with students the difference between kinetic energy and potential energy.
Sheltered English

Bungee jumping began as a ritual ceremony, called land diving, of the people of Pentecost Island, in the Pacific archipelago of Vanuatu. Every year, the men of the community build a tower about 25 m tall. They then dive from platforms on the tower with vines attached to their ankles. After seeing a film of the land divers, the members of the Dangerous Sport Club, at Oxford University, in England, held the first bungee jump off of a bridge in 1979. (You may want to inform students that the potential energy of a stretched bow or a stretched rubber band is called *elastic potential energy*.)

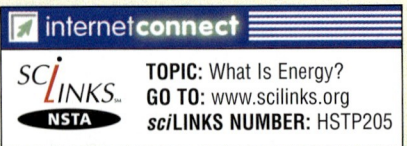
TOPIC: What Is Energy?
GO TO: www.scilinks.org
*sci*LINKS NUMBER: HSTP205

Figure 4 *The stored potential energy of the bow and string allows them to do work on the arrow when the string is released.*

Potential Energy Is Energy of Position

Not all energy involves motion. **Potential energy** is the energy an object has because of its position or shape. For example, the stretched bow shown in **Figure 4** has potential energy. The bow is not moving, but it has energy because work has been done to change its shape. A similar example of potential energy is in a stretched rubber band.

Gravitational Potential Energy Depends on Weight and Height When you lift an object, you do work on it by using a force that opposes gravitational force. As a result, you give that object *gravitational potential energy*. Books on a bookshelf have gravitational potential energy, as does your backpack after you lift it onto your back. As you can see in **Figure 5,** the amount of gravitational potential energy an object has depends on its weight and its distance above Earth's surface.

Figure 5 Weight and Height Affect Gravitational Potential Energy

a The diver on the left weighs less and therefore has less gravitational potential energy than the diver on the right. The diver on the left did less work to climb up the platform.

b The diver on the higher platform has more gravitational potential energy than the diver on the lower platform. The diver on the higher platform did more work to climb up to the platform.

Calculating Gravitational Potential Energy You can calculate gravitational potential energy by using the following equation:

Gravitational potential energy = weight × height

Because weight is expressed in newtons and height is expressed in meters, gravitational potential energy is expressed in newton-meters (N•m), or joules (J). So a 25 N object at a height of 3 m has 25 N × 3 m = 75 J of gravitational potential energy.

Recall that work = force × distance. Weight is the amount of force you must exert on an object in order to lift it, and height is a distance. So calculating an object's gravitational potential energy is done by calculating the amount of work done on the object to lift it to a given height. You can practice calculating gravitational potential energy as well as kinetic energy in the MathBreak at right.

MATH BREAK

Calculating Energy

1. What is the kinetic energy of a 4,000 kg elephant running at 3 m/s? at 4 m/s?
2. If you lift a 50 N watermelon to the top of a 2 m refrigerator, how much gravitational potential energy do you give the watermelon?

Mechanical Energy Sums It All Up

How would you describe the energy of the juggler's pins in **Figure 6**? Well, to describe their total energy, you would describe their mechanical energy. **Mechanical energy** is the total energy of motion and position of an object. Mechanical energy can be all potential energy, all kinetic energy, or some of both. The following equation defines mechanical energy as the sum of kinetic and potential energy:

Mechanical energy = potential energy + kinetic energy

When potential energy increases (or decreases), kinetic energy has to decrease (or increase) in order for mechanical energy to remain constant. So the amount of an object's kinetic or potential energy may change, but its mechanical energy remains the same. You'll learn more about these changes in the next section.

Figure 6 As a pin is juggled, its mechanical energy is the sum of its potential energy and its kinetic energy at any point.

REVIEW

1. How are energy and work related?
2. What is the difference between kinetic and potential energy?
3. **Applying Concepts** Explain why a high-speed collision might cause more damage to vehicles than a low-speed collision.

Section 1 • What Is Energy?   **217**

2) Teach, continued

MISCONCEPTION ALERT

Students may confuse heat with thermal energy. In this textbook, heat is a transfer of energy from a higher temperature object to a lower temperature object. The energy that is transferred is thermal energy.

MEETING INDIVIDUAL NEEDS

Advanced Learners The thermal energy of Earth's oceans has a profound effect on climate and weather. An example of this is the phenomenon known as El Niño, and its counterpart, La Niña. Have students research these two phenomena and in a report or on a poster, describe how thermal energy is responsible for them.

USING THE FIGURE

Use **Figure 7** to help students understand that the thermal energy of a substance is related to the substance's temperature as well as its state. Point out the difference in the appearance of the particles of ocean water and the particles of steam. Explain that equal masses of liquid water and steam at the same temperature (100°C) have different amounts of thermal energy. The reason is that work must be done to force particles of liquid water apart when water changes to steam. The energy used to do this work is stored by the particles of steam as potential energy. The particles of liquid water and the particles of steam may have the same average kinetic energy, but the particles of steam have more potential energy. As a result, the steam has more thermal energy than the liquid water. Students will learn more about this process in the chapter titled "Heat and Heat Technology."

218   Chapter 9 • Energy and Energy Resources

Forms of Energy

All energy involves either motion or position. But energy takes different forms. These forms of energy include thermal, chemical, electrical, sound, light, and nuclear energy. In the next few pages, you will learn how the different forms of energy relate to kinetic and potential energy.

Thermal Energy All matter is made of particles that are constantly in motion. Because the particles are in motion, they have kinetic energy. The particles also have energy because of how they are arranged. *Thermal energy* is the total energy of the particles that make up an object. At higher temperatures, particles move faster. The faster the particles move, the more kinetic energy they have and the greater the object's thermal energy is. In addition, particles of a substance that are farther apart have more energy than particles of the same substance that are closer together. Look at **Figure 7**. Thermal energy also depends on the number of particles in a substance.

Figure 7 *The particles in steam have more energy than the particles in ice or ocean water. But the ocean has the most thermal energy because it has the most particles.*

The particles in an **ice cube** vibrate in fixed positions and therefore do not have a lot of energy.

The particles in **ocean water** are not in fixed positions and can move around. They have more energy than the particles in an ice cube.

The particles in **steam** are far apart. They move rapidly, so they have more energy than the particles in ocean water.

Chemical Energy What is the source of the energy in food? Food consists of chemical compounds. When compounds, such as the sugar in some foods, are formed, work is done to join, or bond, the different atoms together to form molecules. *Chemical energy* is the energy of a compound that changes as its atoms are rearranged to form new compounds. Chemical energy is a form of potential energy. Some molecules that have many atoms bonded together, such as gasoline, have a lot of chemical energy. In **Figure 8** on the next page, you can see an example of chemical energy.

 Teaching Transparency 233 "Thermal Energy"

IS THAT A FACT!

The chemical energy of glucose (sugar) is released slowly by the cells in your body. You cannot perceive this reaction taking place. Energy is released more rapidly when wood burns. You feel this energy as thermal energy. A very rapid release of energy is called an explosion.

Figure 8 Examples of Chemical Energy

When wood is burned, the chemical energy stored in the wood is used to toast your marshmallows.

When you eat a marshmallow, chemical energy stored in the sugar becomes available for you to use.

Chemical energy is stored in the marshmallow's sugar molecules.

Electrical Energy The electrical outlets in your home allow you to use electrical energy. *Electrical energy* is the energy of moving electrons. Electrons are the negatively charged particles of atoms. An atom is the smallest particle into which an element can be divided.

Suppose you plug an electrical device, such as the portable stereo shown in **Figure 9,** into an outlet and turn it on. The electrons in the wires will move back and forth, changing directions 120 times per second. As they do, energy is transferred to different parts within the stereo. The electrical energy created by moving electrons is used to do work. The work of a stereo is to produce sound.

The electrical energy available to your home is produced at power plants. Huge generators rotate magnets within coils of wire to produce electrical energy. Because the electrical energy results from the changing position of the magnet, electrical energy can be considered a form of potential energy. As soon as a device is plugged into an outlet and turned on, electrons move back and forth within the wires of the cord and within parts of the device. So electrical energy can also be considered a form of kinetic energy.

Figure 9 The movement of electrons produces the electrical energy that a stereo uses to produce sound.

CROSS-DISCIPLINARY FOCUS

History Today we take electrical energy for granted. It is always there at the flick of a switch. However, as late as 1930, only one out of 10 rural homes in the United States had electric service. Running lines many miles out to homes in the countryside was costly, and many power companies did not spend the money to do so. In 1935 and 1936, the Rural Electrification Administration (REA) was established to provide electrical energy to rural homes and farms. The REA made loans to nonprofit cooperatives to build electric systems in rural areas. Because of the REA, more than 99 percent of rural homes and farms in the United States now have electric service.

MEETING INDIVIDUAL NEEDS

Advanced Learners Have students find out how dry cells and batteries work. How do dry cells and batteries supply electrical energy? Why do they "run out"? How does a rechargeable battery work? Why are there so many different kinds of dry cells and batteries? Students can present their results on a poster or in a short report.

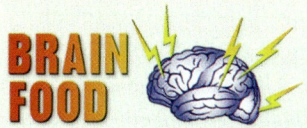

The plant with the ability to generate the most electric power from solar energy is the Harper Lake Site, in the Mojave Desert, California. It has the capability to produce about 160 MW. The largest wind-powered generator is on Oahu, Hawaii, which can produce about 7,300 kW when the wind reaches 32 mph.

Section 1 • What Is Energy?

3 Extend

QuickLab

MATERIALS

FOR EACH STUDENT:
- empty coffee can
- wax paper
- rubber band
- pencil with an eraser

Answers to QuickLab

2. Sample answer: a sound something like a drum.

3. Sample answer: The sound was louder when I tapped harder. The paper has a larger vibration when it is hit harder, so it causes the air particles near it to vibrate harder. More energy is transmitted by the air particles, so the sound is louder.

4. Sample answer: The paper was not able to vibrate as much when it was held still, so the sound was more muffled. Sound energy is a form of mechanical energy because vibration involves a change of position (potential energy) and changes in back-and-forth motion (kinetic energy).

REAL-WORLD CONNECTION

Lasers are a special kind of light energy. Lasers are used to read discs in CD and DVD players. Most supermarkets and retail stores have price scanners that use lasers to read bar codes on packages, and many stores use a portable laser to take inventory. Lasers are also used in several types of surgery, especially in skin and eye surgery. A variety of industries use lasers to measure, weld, cut, and drill metal objects.

Figure 10 As the guitar strings vibrate, they cause particles in the air to vibrate. These vibrations transmit energy.

Hear That Energy!

1. Make a simple drum by covering the open end of an **empty coffee can** with **wax paper.** Secure the wax paper with a **rubber band.**

2. Using the eraser end of a **pencil,** tap lightly on the wax paper. In your ScienceLog, describe how the paper responds. What do you hear?

3. Repeat step 2, but tap the paper a bit harder. In your ScienceLog, compare your results with those of step 2.

4. Cover half of the wax paper with one hand. Now tap the paper. What happened? How can you describe sound energy as a form of mechanical energy?

TRY at HOME

TOPIC: Forms of Energy
GO TO: www.scilinks.org
sciLINKS NUMBER: HSTP210

Sound Energy You probably know that your vocal cords determine the sound of your voice. When you speak, air passes through your vocal cords, making them vibrate, or move back and forth. *Sound energy* is caused by an object's vibrations. **Figure 10** describes how a vibrating object transmits energy through the air around it.

Sound energy is a form of potential and kinetic energy. To make an object vibrate, work must be done to change its position. For example, when you pluck a guitar string, you stretch it and release it. The stretching changes the string's position. As a result, the string stores potential energy. In the release, the string uses its potential energy to move back to its original position. The moving guitar string has kinetic energy, which the string uses to do work on the air particles around it. The air particles vibrate and transmit this kinetic energy from particle to particle. When the vibrating air particles cause your eardrum to vibrate, you hear the sound of the guitar.

Light Energy Light allows us to see, but did you know that not all light can be seen? **Figure 11** shows a type of light that we use but can't see. *Light energy* is produced by the vibrations of electrically charged particles. Like sound vibrations, light vibrations cause energy to be transmitted. But unlike sound, the vibrations that transmit light energy don't cause other particles to vibrate. In fact, light energy can be transmitted through a vacuum (the absence of matter).

Figure 11 The energy used to cook food in a microwave is a form of light energy.

CROSS-DISCIPLINARY FOCUS

Music Look at different musical instruments to illustrate the many ways sound energy is produced. Discuss the sources of the work that produces musical sounds; for example, a harpist's fingers pluck the strings of a harp, whereas a trombone player's lips vibrate a column of air.

Nuclear Energy What form of energy can come from a tiny amount of matter, can be used to generate electrical energy, and gives the sun its energy? It's *nuclear* (NOO klee uhr) *energy,* the energy associated with changes in the nucleus (NOO klee uhs) of an atom. Nuclear energy is produced in two ways—when two or more nuclei (NOO klee IE) join together or when the nucleus of an atom splits apart.

In the sun, shown in **Figure 12,** hydrogen nuclei join together to make a larger helium nucleus. This reaction releases a huge amount of energy, which allows the sun to light and heat the Earth.

The nuclei of some atoms, such as uranium, store a lot of potential energy. When work is done to split these nuclei apart, that energy is released. This type of nuclear energy is used to generate electrical energy at nuclear power plants, such as the one shown in **Figure 13.**

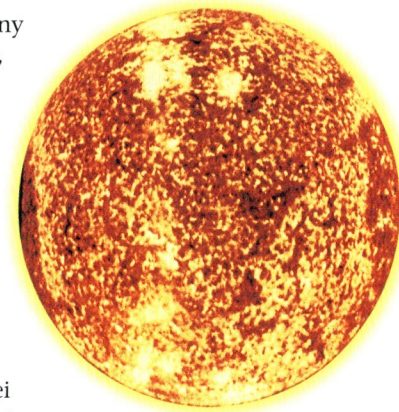

Figure 12 *Without the nuclear energy from the sun, life on Earth would not be possible.*

Figure 13 *In a nuclear power plant, small amounts of matter can produce large amounts of nuclear energy.*

REVIEW

1. What determines an object's thermal energy?
2. Describe why chemical energy is a form of potential energy.
3. Explain how sound energy is produced when you beat a drum.
4. **Analyzing Relationships** When you hit a nail into a board using a hammer, the head of the nail gets warm. In terms of kinetic and thermal energy, describe why you think this happens.

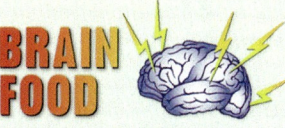

TOPIC: What Is Energy?, Forms of Energy
GO TO: www.scilinks.org
*sci*LINKS NUMBER: HSTP205, HSTP210

SECTION 2

Focus

Energy Conversions

This lesson discusses energy conversions. Students will be given examples of ways that energy is converted from one form to another. This section also explains the role of machines in energy conversions.

Bellringer

Display a plant, a Bunsen burner or small propane camping stove, and a pendulum. Ask students what they think these objects have in common. (They are all capable of converting energy from one form to another.)

1 Motivate

DISCUSSION

Have a windup alarm clock set up for students to see. Display a label next to the clock that reads "Potential Energy." The clock should be wound and set to go off when students are seated and attentive. When the clock alarm sounds, turn the label around so that it reads "Kinetic Energy." Ask students to try to define *kinetic energy* and *potential energy* based on the demonstration. Guide the discussion so that it addresses energy conversions. Encourage students to explain how the clock converted energy.

Finding Energy

Section 2

Terms to Learn
energy conversion

What You'll Do
- Describe an energy conversion.
- Give examples of energy conversions among the different forms of energy.
- Explain the role of machines in energy conversions.
- Explain how energy conversions make energy useful.

Energy Conversions

When you use a hammer to pound a nail into a board, you transfer your kinetic energy to the hammer, and the hammer transfers that kinetic energy to the nail. But energy is involved in other ways too. For example, sound energy is produced when you hit the nail. An energy transfer often leads to an **energy conversion,** a change from one form of energy into another. Any form of energy can be converted into any other form of energy, and often one form of energy is converted into more than one other form. In this section, you'll learn how energy conversions make your daily activities possible.

From Kinetic to Potential and Back

Take a look at **Figure 14.** Have you ever jumped on a trampoline? What types of energy are involved in this bouncing activity? Because you're moving when you jump, you have kinetic energy. And each time you jump into the air, you change your position with respect to the ground, so you also have gravitational potential energy. Another kind of potential energy is involved too—that of the trampoline stretching when you jump on it.

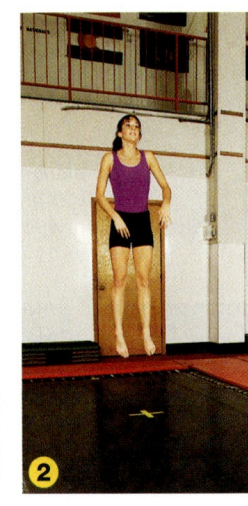  

Figure 14 *Kinetic and potential energy are converted back and forth as you jump up and down on a trampoline.*

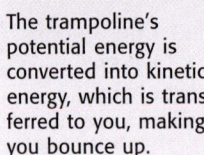

① When you jump down, your kinetic energy is converted into the potential energy of the stretched trampoline.

② The trampoline's potential energy is converted into kinetic energy, which is transferred to you, making you bounce up.

③ At the top of your jump, all of your kinetic energy has been converted into potential energy.

④ Right before you hit the trampoline, all of your potential energy has been converted back into kinetic energy.

Teaching Transparency 234
"Energy Conversion on a Trampoline"

Directed Reading Worksheet 9 Section 2

Another example of the energy conversions between kinetic and potential energy is the motion of a pendulum (PEN dyoo luhm). Shown in **Figure 15,** a pendulum is a mass hung from a fixed point so that it can swing freely. When you lift the pendulum to one side, you do work on it, and the energy used to do that work is stored by the pendulum as potential energy. As soon as you let the pendulum go, it swings because the Earth exerts a force on it. The work the Earth does converts the pendulum's potential energy into kinetic energy.

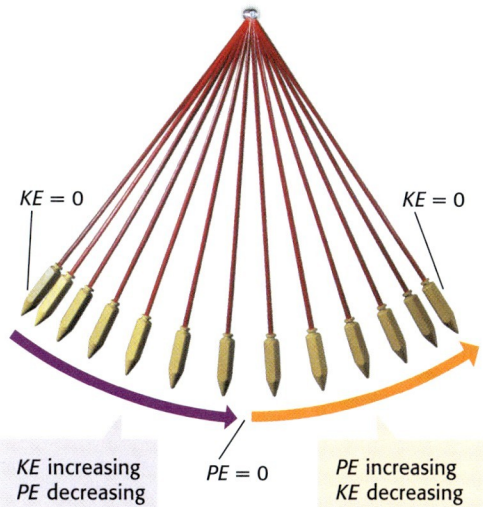

Figure 15 A pendulum's mechanical energy is all kinetic (KE) at the bottom of its swing and all potential (PE) at the top of its swing.

Self-Check

At what point does a roller coaster have the greatest potential energy? the greatest kinetic energy? *(See page 724 to check your answer.)*

Conversions Involving Chemical Energy

You've probably heard the expression "Breakfast is the most important meal of the day." What does this statement mean? Why does eating breakfast help you start the day? As your body digests food, chemical energy is released and is available to you, as discussed in **Figure 16.**

Figure 16 Your body performs energy conversions.

Chemical energy of food is converted into . . .

. . . kinetic energy when you are active and thermal energy to maintain body temperature.

Energy of a Pendulum

WEIRD SCIENCE

If sound waves could be converted into electrical energy, 100 quadrillion mosquito buzzes could power a reading lamp.

IS THAT A FACT!

One appliance that uses a great deal of electrical energy is the water heater (4,200–4,800 kWh/year). At the other extreme, an electric toothbrush uses only about 5 kWh/year.

2 Teach, continued

MISCONCEPTION ALERT

Students may assume that they only get energy from the sun when they eat plants or plant products. However, when a person eats meat, that person is still getting energy from the sun. For example, a cow gets energy from the sun by eating plants. The cow stores some of this energy in its cells. When a person eats beef, that person's body uses the energy that was stored in the cow's cells. This energy originally came from the sun.

CONNECT TO ENVIRONMENTAL SCIENCE

Divide the class into two groups. Have one group research the rate of growth and the rate of photosynthesis in tropical rain forests. Have the second group research the rate of rain-forest destruction. Ask both groups to present their information to the class. Encourage a discussion of the usefulness of photosynthesis versus the usefulness of clearing the land occupied by rain forests. Use Teaching Transparency 235, "Photosynthesis," to help students understand why photosynthesis is so important.

Answers to APPLY

Sample answer: Chemical energy in the stove fuel is converted to thermal energy when the stove is lit. Chemical energy in the food you eat is converted to the kinetic energy of your body's movement as you hike. Chemical energy in the food is converted to thermal energy that maintains your body temperature.

Would you believe that the chemical energy in the food you eat is a result of the sun's energy? It's true! When you eat fruits, vegetables, grains, or meat from animals that ate fruits, vegetables, or grains, you are taking in chemical energy that resulted from a chemical change involving the sun's energy. As shown in **Figure 17,** photosynthesis (FOHT oh SIN thuh sis) uses light energy to produce new substances with chemical energy. In this way light energy is converted into chemical energy.

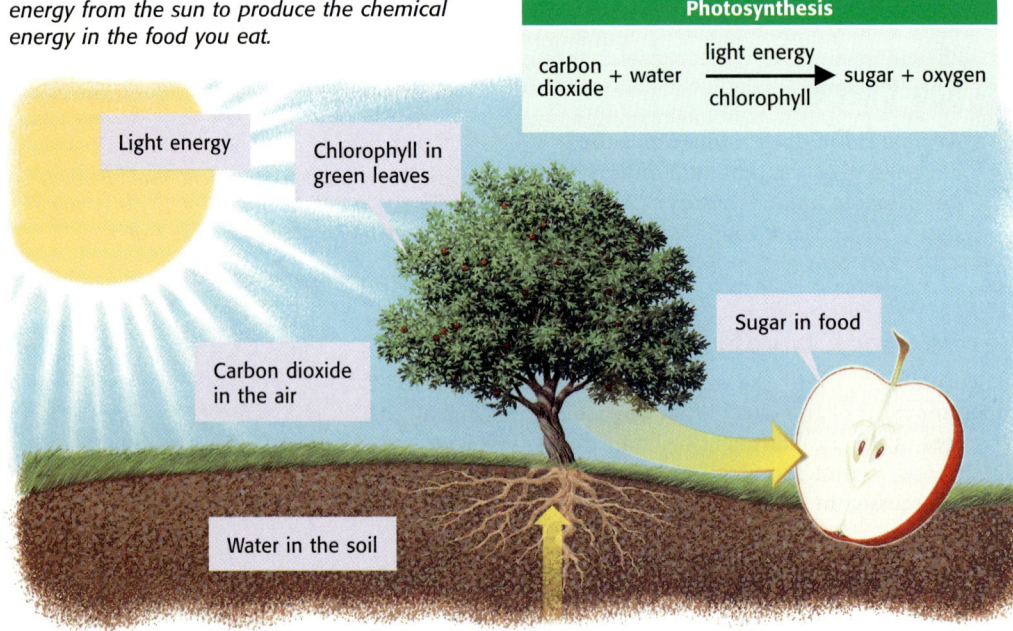

Figure 17 Green plants use chlorophyll and light energy from the sun to produce the chemical energy in the food you eat.

Teaching Transparency 235
"Photosynthesis"

APPLY

Camping with Energy
If you go camping, you probably use a stove, such as the one shown here, to prepare meals. Describe some of the energy conversions that take place when lighting the stove, cooking the food, eating the prepared meal, and then setting out on a long hike.

IS THAT A FACT!

Using the process of photosynthesis, plants and phytoplankton are able to convert carbon dioxide and water into 500 billion metric tons of carbohydrate per year. Of that 500 billion tons, 80 percent is produced in the sea.

224 Chapter 9 • Energy and Energy Resources

Conversions Involving Electrical Energy

You use electrical energy all the time—when you listen to the radio, when you make toast, and when you take a picture with a camera. Electrical energy can be easily converted into other forms of energy. **Figure 18** shows how electrical energy is converted in a hair dryer.

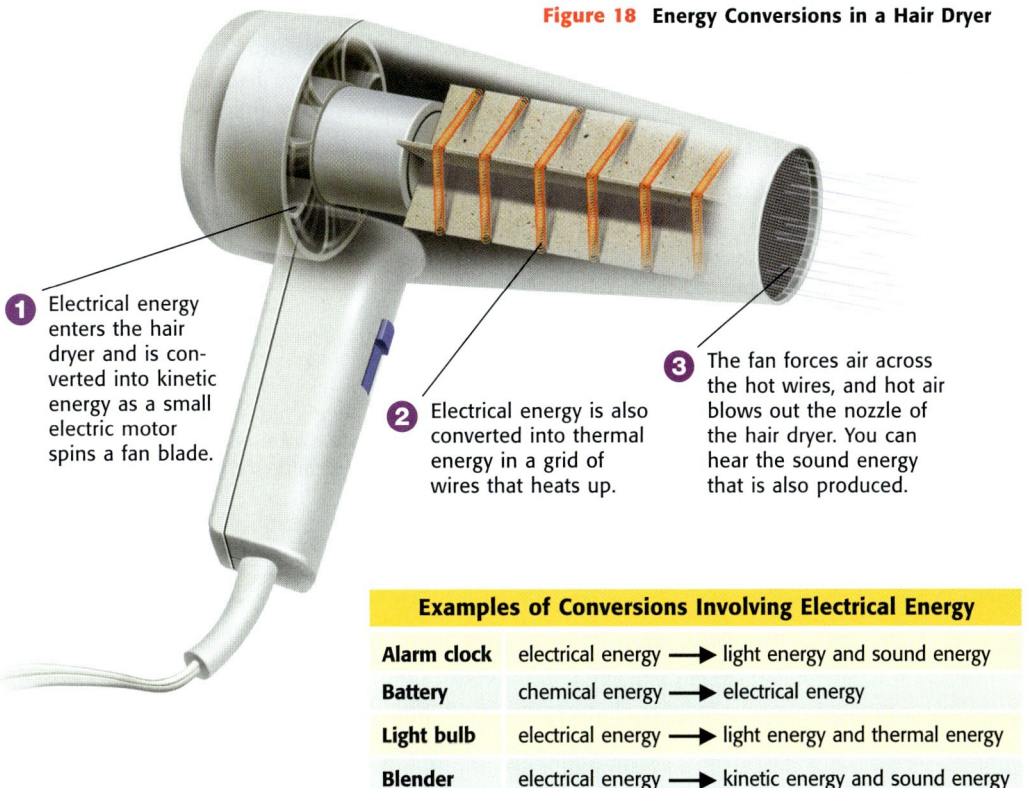

Figure 18 Energy Conversions in a Hair Dryer

1. Electrical energy enters the hair dryer and is converted into kinetic energy as a small electric motor spins a fan blade.

2. Electrical energy is also converted into thermal energy in a grid of wires that heats up.

3. The fan forces air across the hot wires, and hot air blows out the nozzle of the hair dryer. You can hear the sound energy that is also produced.

Examples of Conversions Involving Electrical Energy

Alarm clock	electrical energy → light energy and sound energy
Battery	chemical energy → electrical energy
Light bulb	electrical energy → light energy and thermal energy
Blender	electrical energy → kinetic energy and sound energy

REVIEW

1. What is an energy conversion?
2. Describe an example in which electrical energy is converted into thermal energy.
3. Describe an energy conversion involving chemical energy.
4. **Applying Concepts** Describe the kinetic-potential energy conversions that occur when you bounce a basketball.

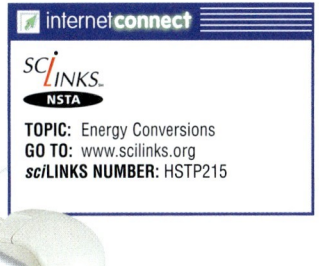

TOPIC: Energy Conversions
GO TO: www.scilinks.org
sciLINKS NUMBER: HSTP215

2) Teach, continued

MEETING INDIVIDUAL NEEDS

Advanced Learners Ball bearings are round, smooth objects that reduce friction between two objects. The more perfectly rounded the ball bearing is, the more friction is reduced. Ball bearings produced on Earth cannot be perfectly round and smooth because of the effect of gravity on the manufacturing process. Bearings produced in space would eliminate almost all of gravity's effects and produce a perfectly smooth ball bearing. Have interested students report on the process of making ball bearings on Earth and in space.

 Teaching Transparency 236 "Energy Transfer in a Bicycle"

 Teaching Transparency 237 "Energy Conversions in a Car Engine"

 Math Skills Worksheet 52 "A Bicycle Trip"

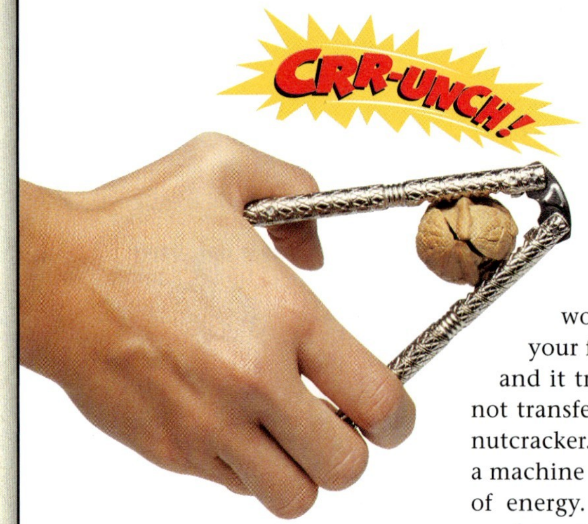

Figure 19 Some of the kinetic energy you transfer to a nutcracker is converted into sound energy as the nutcracker transfers energy to the nut.

Energy and Machines

You've been learning about energy, its different forms, and how it can undergo conversions. Another way to learn about energy is to look at how machines use energy. A machine can make work easier by changing the size or direction (or both) of the force required to do the work. Suppose you want to crack open a walnut. Using a nutcracker, like the one shown in **Figure 19**, would be much easier (and less painful) than using your fingers. You transfer your energy to the nutcracker, and it transfers energy to the nut. But the nutcracker will not transfer more energy to the nut than you transfer to the nutcracker. In addition, some of the energy you transfer to a machine can be converted by the machine into other forms of energy. Another example of how energy is used by a machine is shown in **Figure 20**.

Figure 20 To start and keep your bike moving, energy must be converted and transferred.

① Chemical energy in your body is converted into kinetic energy when your muscle fibers contract and relax.

② Your legs transfer this kinetic energy to the pedals, pushing them around in a circle.

③ The pedals transfer this kinetic energy to the gear wheel, which transfers kinetic energy to the chain.

④ The chain moves and transfers energy to the back wheel, which gets you moving!

IS THAT A FACT!

The pedicar, introduced in 1973, was a pedal-powered, one-passenger, all-weather vehicle. It was conceived as an alternative to the gas-powered automobile and cost about $550 at the time of its introduction. The pedicar was capable of reaching speeds of 8–15 mph.

Machines Are Energy Converters As you saw in the examples on the previous page, when machines transfer energy, energy conversions can often result. For example, you can hear the sounds that your bike makes when you pedal it, change gears, or brake swiftly. That means that some of the kinetic energy being transferred gets converted into sound energy as the bike moves. Some machines are especially useful because they are energy converters. **Figure 21** shows an example of a machine specifically designed to convert energy from one form to another. In addition, the chart at right lists other machines that perform useful energy conversions.

Some Machines that Convert Energy	
■ electric motor	■ microphone
■ windmill	■ toaster
■ doorbell	■ dishwasher
■ gas heater	■ lawn mower
■ telephone	■ clock

Figure 21 *The continuous conversion of chemical energy into thermal energy and kinetic energy in a car's engine is necessary to make a car move.*

① A mixture of gasoline and air enters the engine as the piston moves downward.

Piston

② The kinetic energy of the crankshaft raises the piston, and the gasoline mixture is forced up toward the spark plug, which uses electrical energy to ignite the gasoline mixture.

Spark plug

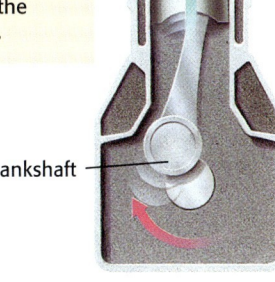

Crankshaft

③ As the gasoline mixture burns, chemical energy is converted into thermal energy and kinetic energy, forcing the piston back down.

④ The kinetic energy of the crankshaft forces the piston up again, pushing exhaust gases out. Then the cycle repeats.

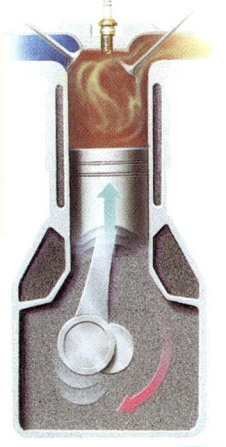

3 Extend

Homework
Have students list machines in their home that convert energy. Students can use the examples given on this page as a reference. Instruct students to list the machine and the kind of energy conversion that occurs.

ACTIVITY
Arrange a field trip to the machine shop at a local high school or college. Ask the instructor or mechanic to explain to the students how the piston and the crankshaft work to convert chemical energy into kinetic energy. If a field trip is not possible, invite a knowledgeable mechanic or machine-shop instructor to visit the classroom with examples of a piston and crankshaft.

GOING FURTHER
To investigate the principle of wind power more closely, have students construct a windmill. Instruct students to work in pairs or in small groups to create a windmill out of any materials they choose. The only requirement for the assignment is that the windmill must do some type of work when the blades turn. Finished windmills can be demonstrated to the rest of the class.

Science Bloopers
The design for a nuclear-powered automobile was proposed by Ford automotive designers in the 1950s. The name of the car was to be the Ford Nucleon, and it was to be propelled by a small atomic reactor located in the rear of the car. The car was never built for several reasons.

IS THAT A FACT!
Only about 20 percent of the energy released by burning gasoline in a car engine is converted to kinetic energy to move the car forward. Most of the rest is converted to thermal energy, which is wasted.

 Reinforcement Worksheet 9 "See What I Saw"

 Reinforcement Worksheet 9 "Energetic Cooking"

Section 2 • Energy Conversions

4) Close

Quiz

1. Give an example of an energy conversion that produces a useful result. (Answers will vary, but students might mention the conversion of chemical energy in their food into the kinetic energy of their movements.)
2. Demonstrate the conversion of potential to kinetic energy using a pendulum model. (As the pendulum is lifted upward, it gains potential energy. When the pendulum is released and swings downward, that potential energy is converted to kinetic energy.)

ALTERNATIVE ASSESSMENT

Ask students to categorize their daily activities according to the forms of energy they use. Categories could include electrical energy, chemical energy, and mechanical energy. Instruct students to try to list five activities for each category.
Sheltered English

REAL-WORLD CONNECTION

Windmills were first used in about the fifth century A.D. to pump water or to turn grindstones. Today, wind power offers a viable alternative to the energy crisis. Especially promising is the melding of computer technology with the wind turbine. In the past, windmills turned at a single speed. In the 1990s, windmills were designed to move at whatever rate the wind moves them. A computer-controlled electronic circuit allows turbines to generate current with a constant frequency, regardless of wind speed.

Figure 22 In a wind turbine, the kinetic energy of the wind can be collected and converted into electrical energy.

Turn to page 242 to find out about buildings that are energy efficient as well as environmentally friendly.

Why Energy Conversions Are Important

Everything we do is related to energy conversions. Heating our homes, obtaining energy from a meal, growing plants, and many other activities all require energy conversions.

Making Energy Useful You can think of energy conversions as a way of getting energy in the form that you need. Machines help harness existing energy and make that energy work for you. Did you know that the wind could help you cook a meal? A wind turbine, shown in **Figure 22,** can perform an energy conversion that would allow you to use an electric stove to do just that.

Making Conversions Efficient You may have heard that a car may be considered energy efficient if it gets good gas mileage, and your home may be energy efficient if it is well insulated. In terms of energy conversions, *energy efficiency* (e FISH uhn see) is a comparison of the amount of energy before a conversion with the amount of useful energy after a conversion. For example, the energy efficiency of a light bulb would be a comparison of the electrical energy going into it with the light energy coming out of it. The less electrical energy that is converted into thermal energy instead of into light energy, the more efficient the bulb.

Not all of the energy in a conversion becomes useful energy. Just as work input is always greater than work output, energy input is also always greater than energy output. But the closer the energy output is to the energy input, the more efficient the conversion is. Making energy conversions more efficient is important because greater efficiency means less waste.

REVIEW

1. What is the role of machines in energy conversions?
2. Give an example of a machine that is an energy converter, and explain how the machine converts one form of energy to another.
3. **Applying Concepts** A car that brakes suddenly comes to a screeching halt. Is the sound energy produced in this conversion a useful form of energy? Explain your answer.

Answers to Review

1. Machines can transfer energy from one object to another as they make work easier. For example, when you use a crowbar to remove a hubcap, you transfer energy to the crowbar, and the crowbar transfers energy to the hubcap. The way the energy is transferred determines how much easier the work is to do.
2. Accept all reasonable answers. Sample answer: A wind turbine converts the kinetic energy of wind into electrical energy.
3. The sound energy of the screeching is not a useful form of energy because it cannot be used to do work.

Section 3

Conservation of Energy

Terms to Learn
friction
law of conservation of energy

What You'll Do
- Explain how energy is conserved within a closed system.
- Explain the law of conservation of energy.
- Give examples of how thermal energy is always a result of energy conversion.
- Explain why perpetual motion is impossible.

Many roller coasters have a mechanism that pulls the cars up to the top of the first hill, but the cars are on their own the rest of the ride. As the cars go up and down the hills on the track, their potential energy is converted into kinetic energy and back again. But the cars never return to the same height they started from. Does that mean that energy gets *lost* somewhere along the way? Nope—it just gets converted into other forms of energy.

Where Does the Energy Go?

In order to find out where a roller coaster's original potential energy goes, you have to consider more than just the hills of the roller coaster. You have to consider friction too. **Friction** is a force that opposes motion between two surfaces that are touching. For the roller coaster to move, work must be done to overcome the friction between the cars' wheels and the coaster track and between the cars and the surrounding air. The energy used to do this work comes from the original amount of potential energy that the cars have on the top of the first hill. The need to overcome friction affects the design of a roller coaster track. In **Figure 23,** you can see that the second hill will always be shorter than the first.

When energy is used to overcome friction, some of the energy is converted into thermal energy. Some of the cars' potential energy is converted into thermal energy on the way down the first hill, and then some of their kinetic energy is converted into thermal energy on the way up the second hill. So energy isn't lost at all—it just undergoes a conversion.

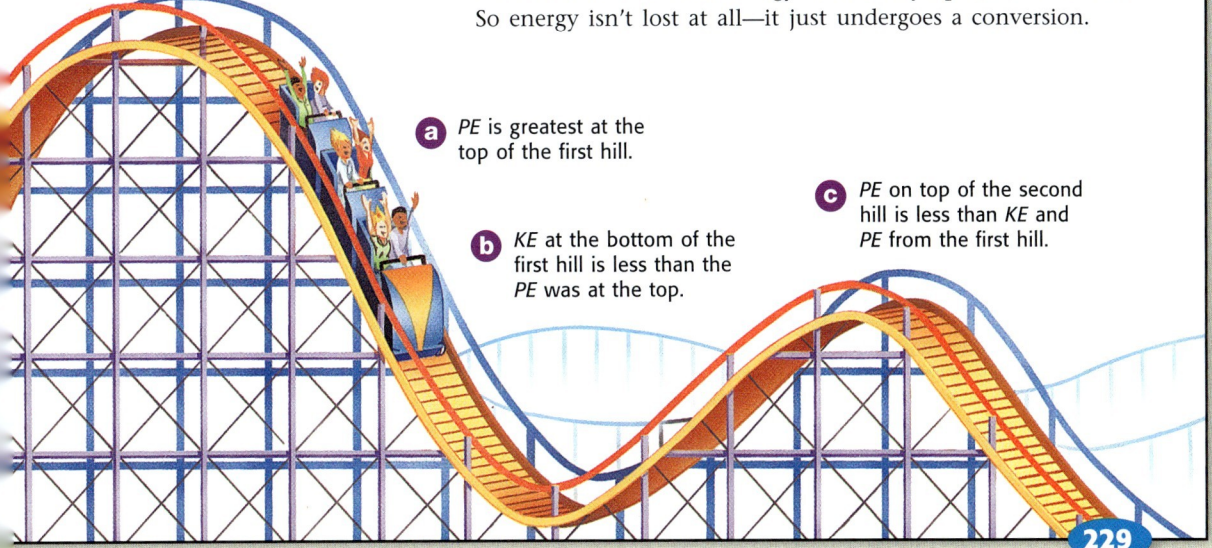

Figure 23 *Due to friction, not all of the cars' potential energy (PE) is converted into kinetic energy (KE) as the cars go down the first hill. In addition, not all of the cars' kinetic energy is converted into potential energy as the cars go up the second hill.*

a PE is greatest at the top of the first hill.

b KE at the bottom of the first hill is less than the PE was at the top.

c PE on top of the second hill is less than KE and PE from the first hill.

Students may assume that all processes involving work and energy are 100 percent efficient. Remind students that all motion and all processes involving work are opposed by friction. It is because of friction that so much kinetic energy is converted to thermal energy. Let students create their own thermal energy by rapidly rubbing their palms together for 30 seconds. They will feel the thermal energy produced by the friction between their hands.

SECTION 3

Focus

Conservation of Energy
This section introduces the law of conservation of energy. Students will learn how all energy is continuously being converted into other forms, and they will discover why the law of conservation of energy makes the concept of perpetual motion impossible.

🔔 Bellringer
Pose the following questions to students:

How does a roller coaster work? Where does the energy come from to make the car go along the track? Where does all the energy go? Explain the meaning of the sentence, "All of the energy put into a process still exists somewhere at the end of that process."

1 Motivate

DEMONSTRATION
Show students a simple, high-density rubber ball. Explain to students that this ball was designed to bounce for a long time, but that it must eventually stop according to the law of conservation of energy. Allow the ball to begin bouncing. As it bounces, ask students to observe both the height and the number of bounces. Ask them to theorize why the ball eventually stops. What happens to the kinetic energy of the ball's movement?

Directed Reading
Worksheet 9 Section 3

2) Teach

READING STRATEGY

Prediction Guide Ask students to interpret the sentence, "Energy can be neither created nor destroyed." Write the predictions on the board, and discuss them before students read pages 230 and 231.

Eggstremely Fragile

REAL-WORLD CONNECTION

Resistance to the flow of electrical energy is a major concern to electric utility companies that transmit electrical energy through miles of wire. To reduce the amount of energy lost to resistance, power companies use very high voltages in the transmission lines that carry electrical energy from generating stations to cities. Voltage in these lines ranges from 138,000 to 765,000 V. These higher voltages minimize the amount of energy lost to resistance. Transformers reduce the voltage for distribution in cities and neighborhoods. Finally, neighborhood transformers reduce the voltage to 120 to 240 V for use in the home.

TOPIC: Law of Conservation of Energy
GO TO: www.scilinks.org
sciLINKS NUMBER: HSTP217

Energy Is Conserved Within a Closed System

A *closed system* is a well-defined group of objects that transfer energy between one another. For example, a closed system that involves a roller coaster consists of the track, the cars, and the surrounding air. On a roller coaster, some mechanical energy (the sum of kinetic and potential energy) is always converted into thermal energy because of friction. Sound energy is also a result of the energy conversions in a roller coaster. You can understand that energy is not lost on a roller coaster only when you consider all of the factors involved in a closed system. If you add together the cars' kinetic energy at the bottom of the first hill, the thermal energy due to overcoming friction, and the sound energy produced, you end up with the same total amount of energy as the original amount of potential energy. In other words, energy is conserved.

Try to keep an egg from breaking while learning more about the law of conservation of energy on page 671 in the LabBook.

Law of Conservation of Energy No situation has been found where energy is not conserved. Because this phenomenon is always observed during energy conversions, it is described as a law. According to the **law of conservation of energy**, energy can be neither created nor destroyed. The total amount of energy in a closed system is always the same. Energy can be changed from one form to another, but all the different forms of energy in a system always add up to the same total amount of energy, no matter how many energy conversions occur.

Consider the energy conversions in a light bulb, shown in **Figure 24**. You can define the closed system to include the outlet, the wires, and the parts of the bulb. While not all of the original electrical energy is converted into light energy, no energy is lost. At any point during its use, the total amount of electrical energy entering the light bulb is equal to the total amount of light and thermal energy that leaves the bulb. Energy is conserved.

Figure 24 Energy Conservation in a Light Bulb

Some energy is converted to thermal energy, which makes the bulb feel warm.

Some electrical energy is converted into light energy.

Some electrical energy is converted into thermal energy because of friction in the wire.

IS THAT A FACT!

At extremely low temperatures, some materials become *superconductors,* materials that have almost no resistance to the flow of electrical energy. These materials are used to create giant electromagnets that generate strong magnetic fields with very little thermal-energy loss.

Q: What happened when the sandpaper and the wood got together to settle their differences?

A: The discussion got heated! There was just too much friction between them.

230 Chapter 9 • Energy and Energy Resources

No Conversion Without Thermal Energy

Any time one form of energy is converted into another form, some of the original energy always gets converted into thermal energy. The thermal energy due to friction that results from energy conversions is not useful energy. That is, this thermal energy is not used to do work. Think about a car. You put gas into a car, but not all of the gasoline's chemical energy makes the car move. Some waste thermal energy will always result from the energy conversions. Much of this waste thermal energy exits a car engine through the radiator and the exhaust pipe.

Perpetual Motion? No Way! People have dreamed of constructing a machine that runs forever without any additional energy—a *perpetual* (puhr PECH oo uhl) *motion machine*. Such a machine would put out exactly as much energy as it takes in. But because some waste thermal energy always results from energy conversions, perpetual motion is impossible. The only way a machine can keep moving is to have a continuous supply of energy. For example, the "drinking bird" shown in **Figure 25** continually uses thermal energy from the air to evaporate the water from its head. So it is *not* a perpetual motion machine.

Biology CONNECTION

Whenever you do work, you use chemical energy stored in your body that comes from food you've eaten. As you do work, some of that chemical energy is always converted into thermal energy. That's why your body heats up after performing a task, such as raking leaves, for several minutes.

Figure 25 The "Drinking Bird"

a When the bird "drinks," the felt covering its head gets wet.

b When the bird is upright, water evaporates from the felt, decreasing the temperature and pressure in the head. Fluid is drawn up from the tail, where pressure is higher, and the bird tips.

c After the bird "drinks," fluid returns to the tail, the bird flips upright, and the cycle repeats.

REVIEW

1. Describe the energy conversions that take place in a pendulum, and explain how energy is conserved.
2. Why is perpetual motion impossible?
3. **Analyzing Viewpoints** Imagine that you drop a ball. It bounces a few times, but then it stops. Your friend says that the ball has lost all of its energy. Using what you know about the law of conservation of energy, respond to your friend's statement.

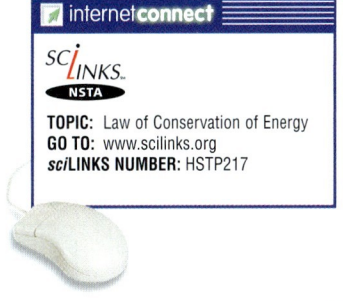

TOPIC: Law of Conservation of Energy
GO TO: www.scilinks.org
sciLINKS NUMBER: HSTP217

SECTION 4

Focus

Energy Resources

Students learn about renewable and nonrenewable energy resources and about advantages and disadvantages of energy resources.

Write the names of several different energy resources on the board (sunlight, coal, wind). Ask students to predict which ones are nonrenewable (a finite supply) and renewable (an endless supply) resources.

1) Motivate

ACTIVITY

Give each student a large piece of paper and colored pencils. Tell them to pick an activity they do every day. Ask them to trace the energy involved in their activity back to its source. For example, if their activity is playing computer games, they would trace the light and sound energy from the computer. The light and sound were made possible by the electrical energy from the outlet in their home, so they would trace the production of the electrical energy back to its source. The power plant produced electrical energy from some fuel, such as coal or natural gas. If they can, have students trace the fuel back to its source as well.

Directed Reading Worksheet 9 Section 4

Section 4

Terms to Learn

energy resource
nonrenewable resources
fossil fuels
renewable resources

What You'll Do

- Name several energy resources.
- Explain how the sun is the source of most energy on Earth.
- Evaluate the advantages and disadvantages of using various energy resources.

This piece of coal containing a fern fossil shows that coal formed from plants that lived millions of years ago.

BRAIN FOOD

It takes about 454 kg of lead-acid batteries (like the one in most cars) to store the same amount of energy that about 4 L of gasoline contains.

Energy Resources

Energy is used to light and warm our homes; to produce food, clothing, and other products; and to transport people and products from place to place. Where does all this energy come from? An **energy resource** is a natural resource that can be converted by humans into other forms of energy in order to do useful work. In this section, you will learn about several energy resources, including the resource responsible for most other energy resources—the sun.

Nonrenewable Resources

Some energy resources, called **nonrenewable resources,** cannot be replaced after they are used or can be replaced only over thousands or millions of years. Fossil fuels are the most important nonrenewable resources.

Fossil Fuels Coal, petroleum, and natural gas, shown in **Figure 26,** are the most common fossil fuels. **Fossil fuels** are energy resources that formed from the buried remains of plants and animals that lived millions of years ago. These plants stored energy from the sun by photosynthesis. Animals used and stored this energy by eating the plants or by eating animals that ate plants. So fossil fuels are concentrated forms of the sun's energy.

Figure 26 Formation of Fossil Fuels

Petroleum, or oil, was formed from organisms that lived in prehistoric lakes and seas. Crushed by layers of sediment and heated by the Earth, the remains were slowly changed into petroleum.

Natural gas was formed much in the same way that petroleum was formed, and it is often found along with petroleum deposits.

IS THAT A FACT!

Recycling just one aluminum can saves enough energy to run a television set for 4 hours.

232 Chapter 9 • Energy and Energy Resources

Now, millions of years later, energy from the sun is released when fossil fuels are burned. Any fossil fuel contains stored energy from the sun that can be converted into other types of energy. The information below shows how important fossil fuels are to our society.

Coal

Most coal used in the United States is burned to produce steam to run electric generators.

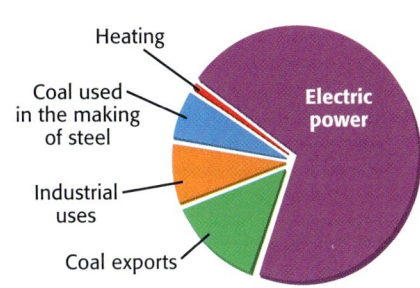

Coal Use (U.S.)
- Heating
- Coal used in the making of steel
- Electric power
- Industrial uses
- Coal exports

Petroleum

Petroleum supplies us with gasoline, kerosene, and wax as well as petrochemicals, which are used to make synthetic fibers, such as rayon.

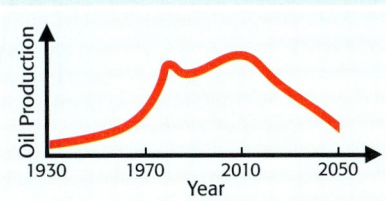

Annual Oil Production—Past & Predicted

Finding alternative energy resources will become more important in years to come.

Natural Gas

Natural gas is used in heating systems, in stoves and ovens, and in vehicles as an alternative to gasoline.

Natural gas is the cleanest burning fossil fuel.

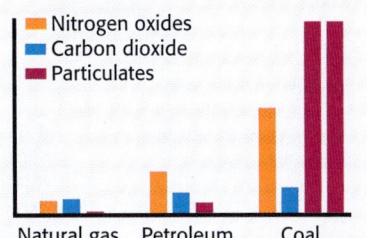

Comparing Fossil Fuel Emissions
- Nitrogen oxides
- Carbon dioxide
- Particulates

Natural gas · Petroleum · Coal

2) Teach, continued

USING THE FIGURE
Have students study **Figure 27** on this page. Make sure students understand each step for converting fossil fuels into electrical energy by discussing each one. Ask students to create a concept map explaining each of the steps. Sheltered English

Homework
Instruct students to find out what type of power their home uses. Many homes use a combination of energy sources. Have students find out the names of the companies that supply power to their home.

REAL-WORLD CONNECTION
Here are two ways to get more kilometers to the gallon. First, decrease driving speed from 113 km/h (70 mph) to 88 km/h (55 mph); this will increase fuel economy by 21 percent. Second, keep tires properly inflated. Under-inflated tires decrease fuel economy by 5 percent.

BRAIN FOOD
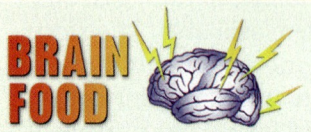
In 1882, Thomas Edison built the first electrical generating station designed to provide electrical energy to homes and businesses in Manhattan.

Turn to page 243 to read about a day in the life of a power-plant manager.

Electrical Energy from Fossil Fuels One way to generate electrical energy is to burn fossil fuels. In fact, fossil fuels are the primary source of electrical energy generated in the United States. Earlier in this chapter, you learned that electrical energy can result from energy conversions. Kinetic energy is converted into electrical energy by an *electric generator*. This energy conversion is part of a larger process, shown in **Figure 27**, of converting the chemical energy in fossil fuels into the electrical energy you use every day.

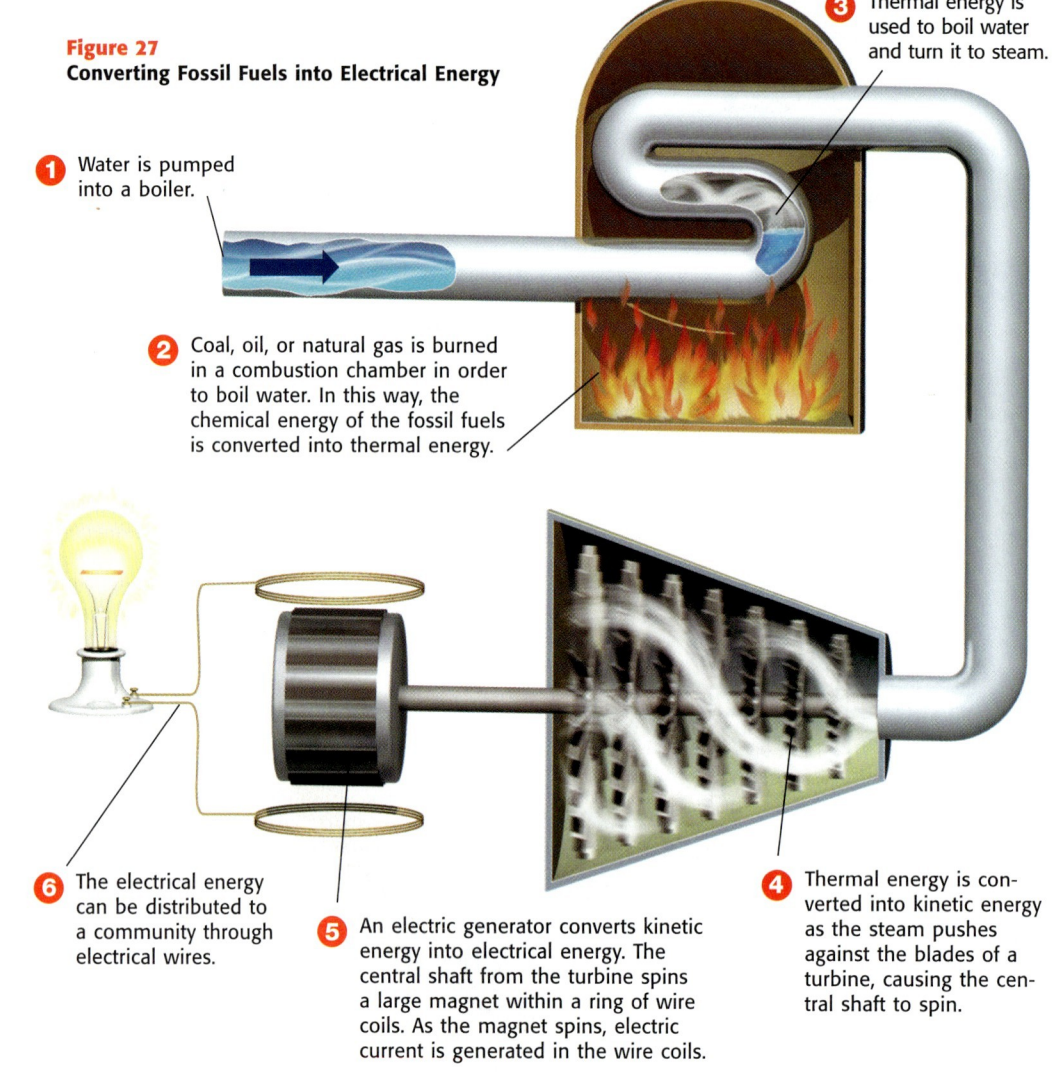

Figure 27
Converting Fossil Fuels into Electrical Energy

① Water is pumped into a boiler.

② Coal, oil, or natural gas is burned in a combustion chamber in order to boil water. In this way, the chemical energy of the fossil fuels is converted into thermal energy.

③ Thermal energy is used to boil water and turn it to steam.

④ Thermal energy is converted into kinetic energy as the steam pushes against the blades of a turbine, causing the central shaft to spin.

⑤ An electric generator converts kinetic energy into electrical energy. The central shaft from the turbine spins a large magnet within a ring of wire coils. As the magnet spins, electric current is generated in the wire coils.

⑥ The electrical energy can be distributed to a community through electrical wires.

IS THAT A FACT!
Of all the energy used by a standard incandescent light bulb, only one-tenth is converted to light energy. The rest is thermal energy. That's why light bulbs are so hot after they have been on for a while!

Nuclear Energy Another way to generate electrical energy is to use nuclear energy. Like fossil-fuel power plants, a nuclear power plant generates thermal energy that boils water to produce steam. The steam then turns a turbine, which rotates a generator that converts kinetic energy into electrical energy. However, the fuels used in nuclear power plants are different from fossil fuels. Nuclear energy is generated from radioactive elements, such as uranium, shown in **Figure 28.** In a process called *nuclear fission* (FISH uhn), the nucleus of a uranium atom is split into two smaller nuclei, releasing nuclear energy. Because the supply of these elements is limited, nuclear energy can be thought of as a nonrenewable resource.

Renewable Resources

Some energy resources, called **renewable resources,** can be used and replaced in nature over a relatively short period of time. Some renewable resources, such as solar energy and wind energy, are considered practically limitless.

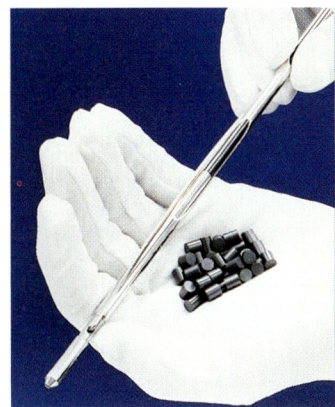

Figure 28 *A single uranium fuel pellet contains the energy equivalent of about 1 metric ton of coal.*

Solar Energy

Sunlight can be converted into electrical energy through solar cells, which can be used in devices such as calculators or installed in a home to provide electrical energy.

Some houses allow sunlight into the house through large windows. The sunlight is converted into thermal energy that heats the house naturally.

Energy from Water

The sun causes water to evaporate and fall again as rain that flows through rivers. The potential energy of water in a reservoir is converted into kinetic energy as the water flows downhill through a dam.

Falling water turns a turbine in a dam, which is connected to a generator that converts kinetic energy into electrical energy. Electrical energy produced from falling water is called *hydroelectricity*.

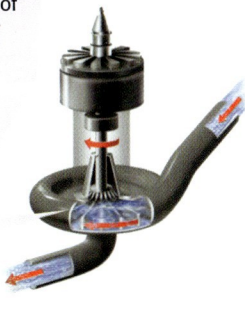

MEETING INDIVIDUAL NEEDS

Advanced Learners Have students research and prepare a presentation about the importance of the ozone layer of the atmosphere and the effects of its depletion on the environment and on solar energy. How might the amount of thermal energy received from the sun be affected? How do "holes" in the ozone layer affect the efficiency of solar energy as an energy resource? Encourage students to be creative in their presentations.

DEBATE

It is estimated that Earth has reserves of shale oil and tar sands that are about 500 times larger than the known crude-oil reserves. Shale oil and tar sands could provide the world with petroleum products long after crude oil reserves have been exhausted. However, producing petroleum from shale oil and tar sands is quite a bit more expensive than producing crude oil. Have students debate whether resources should be spent to produce petroleum from shale oil and tar sands or to develop renewable energy resources.

TOPIC: Energy Resources
GO TO: www.scilinks.org
***sci*LINKS NUMBER:** HSTP225

3 Extend

MAKING MODELS

Ask students to choose one of the alternative energy sources described in this section. Have students create either a poster or a model of their choice. Models or posters should show how the resource is harnessed as well as how it produces electrical energy. Arrange for students to present their projects to other classes.
Sheltered English

DEBATE

Energy Alternatives Ask groups of students to represent different alternative energy resources. Using this section and the table on page 237 as a reference, each group should research its energy resource. Have the class debate which energy resources should be developed and which ones shouldn't. Be sure students offer full explanations for their positions. At the end of the debate, ask students to vote for the most effective alternative energy resource. This debate can also be part of the debate described on page 235.

GOING FURTHER

Invite an expert in the field of alternative energy sources to visit the classroom. If this is not possible, have students find information about such experts. Then have students prepare a short report on their findings.

Interactive Explorations CD-ROM, "The Generation Gap"

Wind Energy

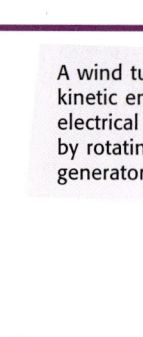
Wind is caused by the sun's uneven heating of the Earth's surface, which creates currents of air. The kinetic energy of wind can turn the blades of a windmill. Windmills are often used to pump water from the ground.

A wind turbine converts kinetic energy into electrical energy by rotating a generator.

Geothermal Energy

Thermal energy resulting from the heating of Earth's crust is called *geothermal energy*. Ground water that seeps into hot spots near the surface of the Earth can form geysers.

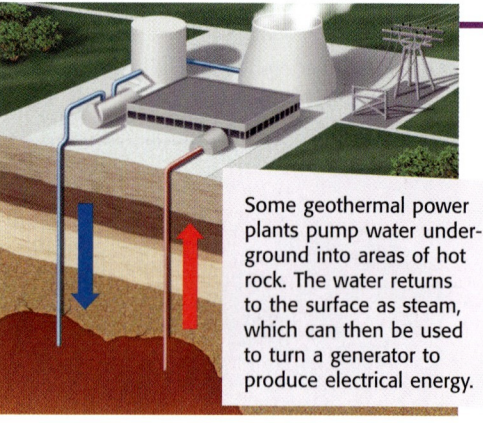
Some geothermal power plants pump water underground into areas of hot rock. The water returns to the surface as steam, which can then be used to turn a generator to produce electrical energy.

Biomass

Plants capture and store energy from the sun. Organic matter, such as plants, wood, and waste, that can be burned to release energy is called *biomass*. Nonindustrialized countries rely heavily on biomass for energy.

Certain plants can also be converted into liquid fuel. For example, corn can be used to make ethanol, which is often mixed with gasoline to make a cleaner-burning fuel for cars.

Multicultural CONNECTION

The island nation of Japan utilizes the surrounding ocean to produce energy. Tidal energy is an alternative energy source that uses the rise and fall of the ocean tides to run turbines that produce electrical energy. Ask students to think of other countries that might use tidal energy to produce electrical energy.

The Two Sides to Energy Resources

The table below compares several energy resources. Depending on where you live, what you need energy for, and how much you need, sometimes one energy resource is a better choice than another.

Energy resource	Advantages	Disadvantages
Fossil fuels	- provide a large amount of thermal energy per unit of mass - easy to get and easy to transport - can be used to generate electrical energy and make products, such as plastic	- nonrenewable - burning produces smog - burning coal releases substances that can cause acid precipitation - risk of oil spills
Nuclear	- very concentrated form of energy - power plants do not produce smog	- produces radioactive waste - radioactive elements are nonrenewable
Solar	- almost limitless source of energy - does not produce pollution	- expensive to use for large-scale energy production - only practical in sunny areas
Water	- renewable - does not produce air pollution	- dams disrupt a river's ecosystem - available only in areas that have rivers
Wind	- renewable - relatively inexpensive to generate - does not produce air pollution	- only practical in windy areas
Geothermal	- almost limitless source of energy - power plants require little land	- only practical in locations near hot spots - waste water can damage soil
Biomass	- renewable	- requires large areas of farmland - produces smoke

REVIEW

1. Compare fossil fuels and biomass.
2. Why is nuclear energy a nonrenewable resource?
3. Trace electrical energy back to the sun.
4. **Interpreting Graphics** Use the pie chart at right to explain why renewable resources will become more important in years to come.

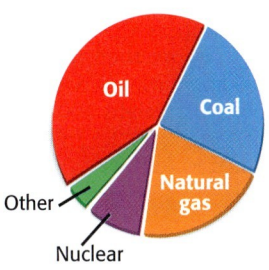

U.S. Energy Sources (Oil, Coal, Natural gas, Nuclear, Other)

4) Close

Quiz

1. Explain the process of fossil fuel formation. (Organisms that lived millions of years ago died and were covered by layers of sediment. The pressure and the temperatures produced by the overlying layers caused chemical reactions that changed the organic matter into fossil fuel.)

2. Name the five types of energy that are considered renewable resources. (solar energy, energy from water, wind energy, geothermal energy, and biomass)

ALTERNATIVE ASSESSMENT

Ask students to think about how life will change when fossil fuels run out. How will the environment, jobs, travel, sports, and industry be affected? Ask them to write or illustrate a short story that describes a day in such a time.

CONNECT TO ENVIRONMENTAL SCIENCE

One disadvantage of mining coal is the impact on the environment. Strip mining destroys large areas of land. Reclamation efforts can restore the strip-mined land to its original condition, but the process is very expensive.

Critical Thinking Worksheet 9 "The Armchair Enviro-Challenge"

Answers to Review

1. Answers will vary but should include the fact that both result from living things and both can be burned to release energy. Fossil fuels are millions of years old, while biomass is organic matter obtained from living things today.
2. because the elements from which it is generated are in limited supply
3. Sample answer: The steam turning the turbine that generates electrical energy comes from water heated by the burning of a fossil fuel, such as coal. The coal is a result of organisms that lived millions of years ago that used light energy from the sun.
4. When the nonrenewable resources we rely on are used up, we will have to use renewable resources.

Chapter Highlights

VOCABULARY DEFINITIONS

SECTION 1

energy the ability to do work

kinetic energy the energy of motion; kinetic energy depends on speed and mass

potential energy the energy of position or shape

mechanical energy the total energy of motion and position of an object

SECTION 2

energy conversion a change from one form of energy into another; any form of energy can be converted into any other form of energy

Chapter Highlights

SECTION 1

Vocabulary
energy (p. 214)
kinetic energy (p. 215)
potential energy (p. 216)
mechanical energy (p. 217)

Section Notes

- Energy is the ability to do work, and work is the transfer of energy. Both energy and work are expressed in joules.
- Kinetic energy is energy of motion and depends on speed and mass.
- Potential energy is energy of position or shape. Gravitational potential energy depends on weight and height.
- Mechanical energy is the sum of kinetic energy and potential energy.
- Thermal energy, sound energy, electrical energy, and light energy can all be forms of kinetic energy.
- Chemical energy, electrical energy, sound energy, and nuclear energy can all be forms of potential energy.

SECTION 2

Vocabulary
energy conversion (p. 222)

Section Notes

- An energy conversion is a change from one form of energy to another. Any form of energy can be converted into any other form of energy.
- Machines can transfer energy and convert energy into a more useful form.
- Energy conversions help to make energy useful by changing energy into the form you need.

Labs
Finding Energy (p. 668)
Energy of a Pendulum (p. 670)

✓ Skills Check

Math Concepts

GRAVITATIONAL POTENTIAL ENERGY To calculate an object's gravitational potential energy, multiply the weight of the object by its height above the Earth's surface. For example, the gravitational potential energy (GPE) of a box that weighs 100 N and that is sitting in a moving truck 1.5 m above the ground is calculated as follows:

$$GPE = \text{weight} \times \text{height}$$
$$GPE = 100 \text{ N} \times 1.5 \text{ m} = 150 \text{ J}$$

Visual Understanding

POTENTIAL-KINETIC ENERGY CONVERSIONS When you jump up and down on a trampoline, potential and kinetic energy are converted back and forth. Review the picture of the pendulum on page 223 for another example of potential-kinetic energy conversions.

ENERGY RESOURCES Look back at the diagram on page 234. Converting fossil fuels into electrical energy requires several energy conversions.

Lab and Activity Highlights

Finding Energy PG 668

Energy of a Pendulum PG 670

Eggstremely Fragile PG 671

Datasheets for LabBook
(blackline masters for these labs)

238   Chapter 9 • Energy and Energy Resources

SECTION 3

Vocabulary

friction (p. 229)
law of conservation of energy (p. 230)

Section Notes

- Because of friction, some energy is always converted into thermal energy during an energy conversion.
- Energy is conserved within a closed system. According to the law of conservation of energy, energy can be neither created nor destroyed.
- Perpetual motion is impossible because some of the energy put into a machine will be converted into thermal energy due to friction.

Labs

Eggstremely Fragile (p. 671)

SECTION 4

Vocabulary

energy resource (p. 232)
nonrenewable resources (p. 232)
fossil fuels (p. 232)
renewable resources (p. 235)

Section Notes

- An energy resource is a natural resource that can be converted into other forms of energy in order to do useful work.
- Nonrenewable resources cannot be replaced after they are used or can only be replaced after long periods of time. They include fossil fuels and nuclear energy.
- Fossil fuels are nonrenewable resources formed from the remains of ancient organisms. Coal, petroleum, and natural gas are fossil fuels.
- Renewable resources can be used and replaced in nature over a relatively short period of time. They include solar energy, wind energy, energy from water, geothermal energy, and biomass.
- The sun is the source of most energy on Earth.
- Depending on where you live and what you need energy for, one energy resource can be a better choice than another.

VOCABULARY DEFINITIONS, continued

SECTION 3

friction a force that opposes motion between two surfaces that are touching

law of conservation of energy the law that states that energy is neither created nor destroyed

SECTION 4

energy resource a natural resource that can be converted by humans into other forms of energy in order to do useful work

nonrenewable resources natural resources that cannot be replaced or that can be replaced only over thousands or millions of years

fossil fuels nonrenewable energy resources that form in the Earth's crust over millions of years from the buried remains of once-living organisms

renewable resources natural resources that can be used and replaced over a relatively short time

---

internet connect

GO TO: go.hrw.com

Visit the **HRW** Web site for a variety of learning tools related to this chapter. Just type in the keyword:

KEYWORD: HSTENG

GO TO: www.scilinks.org

Visit the **National Science Teachers Association** on-line Web site for Internet resources related to this chapter. Just type in the *sci*LINKS number for more information about the topic:

TOPIC:	What Is Energy?	*sci*LINKS NUMBER:	HSTP205
TOPIC:	Forms of Energy	*sci*LINKS NUMBER:	HSTP210
TOPIC:	Energy Conversions	*sci*LINKS NUMBER:	HSTP215
TOPIC:	Law of Conservation of Energy	*sci*LINKS NUMBER:	HSTP217
TOPIC:	Energy Resources	*sci*LINKS NUMBER:	HSTP225

 Vocabulary Review Worksheet 9

 Blackline masters of these Chapter Highlights can be found in the **Study Guide.**

Lab and Activity Highlights

LabBank

 Whiz-Bang Demonstrations
- Wrong-Way Roller? Demo 51
- Pendulum Peril, Demo 50

Labs You Can Eat
- Power-Packed Peanuts, Lab 20
- Now You're Cooking! Lab 21

 Long-Term Projects & Research Ideas, Great Balls of Fire, Project 59

Interactive Explorations CD-ROM

 CD 1, Exploration 6, "The Generation Gap"

Chapter Review

Chapter Review Answers

USING VOCABULARY

1. Potential energy is energy of position or shape. Kinetic energy is energy of motion.
2. Friction is a force that opposes motion between two surfaces that are touching. In an energy conversion, friction always causes some form of energy to be converted into thermal energy.
3. During an energy conversion, one form of energy is changed into another form of energy. The law of conservation of energy states that energy is neither created nor destroyed during any energy conversion.
4. Energy resources are natural resources that can be converted by humans into other forms of energy in order to do useful work. Fossil fuels are an energy resource that formed from the remains of organisms that lived millions of years ago.
5. Renewable resources are natural resources that can be used and replaced over a relatively short time. Nonrenewable resources are natural resources that cannot be replaced or that can be replaced only over thousands or millions of years.

UNDERSTANDING CONCEPTS

Multiple Choice

6. d	10. d
7. b	11. c
8. b	12. c
9. d	13. c

Short Answer

14. Sample answer: Thermal energy depends partly on the kinetic energy of the particles that make up an object. The more kinetic energy the particles have, the more thermal energy the object has. Chemical energy is a kind of potential energy because when a substance forms, work is done to bond particles of matter together. The energy required to do this work is stored in the new compound as potential energy that can be released when the compound is broken down.
15. Sample answers: When a person jumps off a diving board, his or her potential energy is converted into kinetic energy. When steam turns the blades of a turbine, the thermal energy of the steam is converted into the kinetic energy of the moving turbine. When a hair dryer is turned on, electrical energy is converted into kinetic energy of the turning fan and thermal energy of the hot coils inside the hair dryer.
16. A closed system is a well-defined group of objects that transfer energy among one another. Within a closed system, energy is neither created or destroyed; it just gets converted into other forms of energy.

Chapter Review

USING VOCABULARY

For each pair of terms, explain the difference in their meanings.

1. potential energy/kinetic energy
2. friction/energy conversion
3. energy conversion/law of conservation of energy
4. energy resources/fossil fuels
5. renewable resources/nonrenewable resources

UNDERSTANDING CONCEPTS

Multiple Choice

6. Kinetic energy depends on
   a. mass and volume.
   b. speed and weight.
   c. weight and height.
   d. speed and mass.

7. Gravitational potential energy depends on
   a. mass and speed.
   b. weight and height.
   c. mass and weight.
   d. height and distance.

8. Which of the following is not a renewable resource?
   a. wind energy
   b. nuclear energy
   c. solar energy
   d. geothermal energy

9. Which of the following is a conversion from chemical energy to thermal energy?
   a. Food is digested and used to regulate body temperature.
   b. Charcoal is burned in a barbecue pit.
   c. Coal is burned to boil water.
   d. all of the above

10. Machines can
    a. increase energy.
    b. transfer energy.
    c. convert energy.
    d. Both (b) and (c)

11. In every energy conversion, some energy is always converted into
    a. kinetic energy.
    b. potential energy.
    c. thermal energy.
    d. mechanical energy.

12. An object that has kinetic energy must be
    a. at rest.
    b. lifted above the Earth's surface.
    c. in motion.
    d. None of the above

13. Which of the following is *not* a fossil fuel?
    a. gasoline   c. firewood
    b. coal   d. natural gas

Short Answer

14. Name two forms of energy, and relate them to kinetic or potential energy.
15. Give three specific examples of energy conversions.
16. Explain how energy is conserved within a closed system.
17. How are fossil fuels formed?

Concept Mapping

18. Use the following terms to create a concept map: energy, machines, energy conversions, thermal energy, friction.

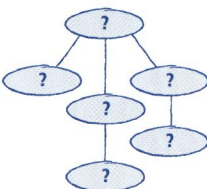

CRITICAL THINKING AND PROBLEM SOLVING

19. What happens when you blow up a balloon and release it? Describe what you would see in terms of energy.

20. After you coast down a hill on your bike, you eventually come to a complete stop unless you keep pedaling. Relate this to the reason why perpetual motion is impossible.

21. Look at the photo of the pole-vaulter below. Trace the energy conversions involved in this event, beginning with the pole-vaulter's breakfast of an orange-banana smoothie.

22. If the sun were exhausted of its nuclear energy, what would happen to our energy resources on Earth?

MATH IN SCIENCE

23. A box has 400 J of gravitational potential energy.
    a. How much work had to be done to give the box that energy?
    b. If the box weighs 100 N, how far was it lifted?

INTERPRETING GRAPHICS

24. Look at the illustration below, and answer the questions that follow.

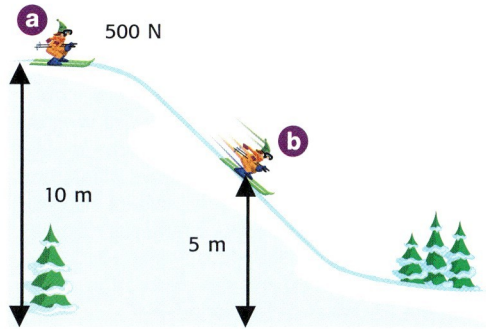

a. What is the skier's gravitational potential energy at point A?
b. What is the skier's gravitational potential energy at point B?
c. What is the skier's kinetic energy at point B? (Hint: mechanical energy = potential energy + kinetic energy.)

NOW What Do You Think?

Take a minute to review your answers to the ScienceLog questions on page 213. Have your answers changed? If necessary, revise your answers based on what you have learned since you began this chapter.

NOW WHAT DO YOU THINK?

1. Energy is the ability to do work.
2. Energy is converted from one form to another when you do work.
3. An energy resource is a natural resource, such as coal or oil, that can be converted into useful forms of energy.

Concept Mapping Transparency 9

Blackline masters of this Chapter Review can be found in the **Study Guide**.

---

17. Fossil fuels are the remains of plants and animals that lived millions of years ago. Plants converted energy from the sun by photosynthesis. Animals got this energy by eating plants or other animals. Over millions of years, the remains of these organisms became coal, petroleum, and natural gas.

Concept Mapping

18. 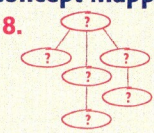 An answer to this exercise can be found at the end of this book.

CRITICAL THINKING AND PROBLEM SOLVING

19. Sample answer: When you blow up a balloon, you stretch it. Because you change the balloon's shape, you give it potential energy. When you release the balloon, it zooms around because the potential energy is converted into kinetic energy.

20. Sample answer: Your bike can't keep moving because kinetic energy is converted into thermal energy due to friction between the tires and the road.

21. Sample answer: The pole-vaulter's breakfast provided chemical energy that was converted into kinetic energy as he started his vault. As his pole bends, it stores potential energy. This is then converted into the kinetic energy that lifts him into the air. As he rises, his kinetic energy is converted into gravitational potential energy. This is converted to kinetic energy as he falls.

22. Sample answer: Without the sun as the source of most energy, we would eventually run out of energy resources.

MATH IN SCIENCE

23. a. 400 J
    b. 4 m

INTERPRETING GRAPHICS

24. a. 5,000 J
    b. 2,500 J
    c. 2,500 J

ACROSS THE SCIENCES
Green Buildings

Background

According to the Environmental Protection Agency, more than 240 million tires are discarded every year. However, because many landfills do not accept tires, these tires are often simply stockpiled aboveground, where they sit indefinitely. They are not only an eyesore and a fire hazard but also can be a health hazard: water-filled tires are ideal breeding grounds for insects such as mosquitoes and flies.

Old tires can be recycled for use in "green" buildings. Sturdy walls can be made by stacking old tires like bricks. The tires are filled with dirt and covered with cement or clay. This technique recycles materials and is energy efficient. Tire walls absorb thermal energy when the weather is hot and release thermal energy when the weather is cool; they act as temperature regulators without setting a single thermostat control.

Discussion

Conduct a discussion about ways students could make the classroom into a "green" room. (Examples might include installing low-wattage lights and putting insulating sheets of plastic over the windows in winter.)

ACROSS THE SCIENCES

PHYSICAL SCIENCE • LIFE SCIENCE

Green Buildings

How do you make a building green without painting it? You make sure it does as little damage to the environment as possible. *Green,* in this case, does not refer to the color of pine trees or grass. Instead, *green* means "environmentally safe." And the "green movement" is growing quickly.

Green Methods and Materials

One strategy that architects employ to turn a building green is to minimize its energy consumption. They also reduce water use wherever possible. One way to do this would be to create landscapes that use only native plants that require little watering. Green builders also use recycled building materials whenever possible. For example, crushed light bulbs can be recycled into floor tiles, and recycled cotton can replace fiberglass as insulation.

Seeing Green

Although green buildings cost more than conventional buildings to construct, they save a lot of money in the long run. For example, the Audubon Building, in Manhattan, saves $100,000 in maintenance costs every year—that is $60,000 in electricity bills alone! The building uses more than 60 percent less energy and electricity than a conventional building does. Inside, the workers enjoy natural lighting, cleaner air, and an environment that is free of unnecessary chemicals.

Some designers want to create buildings that are even more environmentally friendly than the Audubon Building. Walls can be made of straw bales or packed dirt, and landscapes can be maintained with rainwater collected from rooftops. By conserving, recycling, and reducing waste, green builders are doing a great deal to help the environment.

Design It Yourself!

▶ Design a building, a home, or even a doghouse that is made of only recycled materials. Be inventive! When you think you have the perfect design, create a scale model. Describe how your green structure saves resources.

◀ *The walls of this building are being made out of worn-out tires packed with soil. The walls will later be covered with stucco.*

Answers to Design It Yourself!
In their design, students may wish to incorporate some of the materials discussed in the text. Encourage them to be innovative by thinking about what materials are available and what use these materials might serve. For example, they could use cardboard for walls, soda straws for thatched roofs, or old clothes for curtains or tablecloths.

CAREERS

POWER-PLANT MANAGER

As a power-plant manager, **Cheryl Mele** is responsible for almost a billion watts of electric power generation at the Decker Power Plant in Austin, Texas. More than 700 MW are produced using a steam-driven turbine system with natural gas fuel and oil as a backup fuel. Another 200 MW are generated by gas turbines. The steam-driven turbine system and gas turbines together provide enough electrical energy for many homes and businesses.

According to Cheryl Mele, her job as plant manager includes "anything that needs doing." Her training as a mechanical engineer allows her to conduct routine testing and to diagnose problems successfully. A firm believer in protecting our environment, Mele operates the plant responsibly. Mele states, "It is very important to keep the plant running properly and burning as efficiently as possible." Her previous job helping to design more-efficient gas turbines helped make her a top candidate for the job of plant manager.

The Team Approach

Mele uses the team approach to maintain the power plant. She says, "We think better as a team. We all have areas of expertise and interest, and we maximize our effectiveness." Mele observes that working together makes everyone's job easier.

Advice to Young People

Mele believes that mechanical engineering and managing a power plant are interesting careers because you get to work with many exciting new technologies. These professions are excellent choices for both men and women. In these careers you interact with creative people as you try to improve mechanical equipment to make it more efficient and reduce harm to the environment. Her advice for young people is to pursue what interests you. "Be sure to connect the math you learn to the science you are doing," she says. "This will help you to understand both."

A Challenge

▶ With the help of an adult, find out how much electrical energy your home uses each month. How many homes like yours could Mele's billion-watt power plant supply energy to each month?

▶ *Cheryl Mele manages the Decker Power Plant in Austin, Texas.*

CAREERS

Power-Plant Manager— Cheryl Mele

Background

Cheryl Mele earned a bachelor of science degree in mechanical engineering. She worked as a programmer for General Electric, became interested in power-plant design, and joined a General Electric design group. Mele worked as a mechanical engineer for Austin Energy, where her diverse experiences made her the top choice for plant manager.

Students should be familiar with the general principles of the generation of electrical energy, including the use of different fuel sources to power a turbine (steam from coal, natural gas, or nuclear energy).

Teaching Strategy

As an extension of the investigation, students can find ways to use less electrical energy in order to minimize their impact on the environment.

Answers to A Challenge

Answers will vary depending on a variety of factors, such as the size of the student's home, the number of people in the family, and what the structure is made of. Answers to the second part of the challenge will vary, but a billion-watt power plant could provide enough electrical energy for hundreds of thousands, or even millions, of ordinary homes.

Chapter Organizer

CHAPTER ORGANIZATION	TIME MINUTES	OBJECTIVES	LABS, INVESTIGATIONS, AND DEMONSTRATIONS
Chapter Opener pp. 244–245	45	National Standards: UCP 2, 5, SAI 2, ST 1, SPSP 2, 5, HNS 1, PS 3a, 3b, 3f	**Investigate!** Some Like It Hot, p. 245
Section 1 Temperature	90	▶ Describe how temperature relates to kinetic energy. ▶ Give examples of thermal expansion. ▶ Compare temperatures on different temperature scales. UCP 1, 2, 3, SAI 2, SPSP 5, PS 3a, 3b	**Demonstration,** p. 246 in ATE **QuickLab,** Hot or Cold? p. 247 **Whiz-Bang Demonstrations,** Cool It, Demo 52
Section 2 What Is Heat?	90	▶ Define *heat* as the transfer of energy between objects at different temperatures. ▶ Compare conduction, convection, and radiation. ▶ Use specific heat capacity to calculate heat. ▶ Explain the differences between temperature, thermal energy, and heat. UCP 2, 3, SPSP 2, 5, PS 3a, 3b, 3f; LabBook UCP 2, 3, SAI 1, ST 1, PS 3a, 3b	**Demonstration,** p. 252 in ATE **QuickLab,** Heat Exchange, p. 253 **Demonstration,** Convection Currents, p. 254 in ATE **Discovery Lab,** Feel the Heat, p. 672 **Datasheets for LabBook,** Feel the Heat, Datasheet 34 **Design Your Own,** Save the Cube! p. 674 **Datasheets for LabBook,** Save the Cube! Datasheet 35 **Making Models,** Counting Calories, p. 675 **Datasheets for LabBook,** Counting Calories, Datasheet 36
Section 3 Matter and Heat	90	▶ Identify three states of matter. ▶ Explain how heat affects matter during a change of state. ▶ Describe how heat affects matter during a chemical change. UCP 2, 3, SPSP 5, PS 1a, 1b	**Demonstration,** p. 260 in ATE **Labs You Can Eat,** Baked Alaska, Lab 22
Section 4 Heat Technology	90	▶ Analyze several kinds of heating systems. ▶ Describe how a heat engine works. ▶ Explain how a refrigerator keeps food cold. ▶ Give examples of some effects of heat technology on the environment. SPSP 2, 5, PS 3a, 3b	**EcoLabs & Field Activities,** Energy-Efficient Home, EcoLab 19 **Long-Term Projects & Research Ideas,** Project 60

*See page **T20** for a complete correlation of this book with the*

NATIONAL SCIENCE EDUCATION STANDARDS.

TECHNOLOGY RESOURCES

 Guided Reading Audio CD English or Spanish, Chapter 10

One-Stop Planner CD-ROM with Test Generator

 CNN. Eye on the Environment, Geothermal Energy, Segment 22

Chapter 10 • Heat and Heat Technology

Chapter 10 • Heat and Heat Technology

CLASSROOM WORKSHEETS, TRANSPARENCIES, AND RESOURCES	SCIENCE INTEGRATION AND CONNECTIONS	REVIEW AND ASSESSMENT
Science Puzzlers, Twisters & Teasers, Worksheet 10 **Directed Reading Worksheet 10**		
Directed Reading Worksheet 10, Section 1 **Transparency 238,** Three Temperature Scales **Math Skills for Science Worksheet 35,** Using Temperature Scales	**MathBreak,** Converting Temperatures, p. 249 **Math and More,** p. 249 in ATE **Science, Technology, and Society:** The Deep Freeze, p. 274	**Review,** p. 250 **Quiz,** p. 250 in ATE **Alternative Assessment,** p. 250 in ATE **Homework,** p. 250 in ATE
Directed Reading Worksheet 10, Section 2 **Transparency 239,** Reaching Thermal Equilibrium **Transparency 240,** Conduction **Transparency 165,** The Greenhouse Effect **Transparency 240,** Convection **Critical Thinking Worksheet 10,** Try and Try Again **Math Skills for Science Worksheet 38,** Knowing Nutrition **Reinforcement Worksheet 10,** Feel the Heat	**Apply,** p. 254 **Connect to Earth Science,** p. 254 in ATE **Connect to Astronomy,** p. 255 in ATE **Meteorology Connection,** p. 256 **Cross-Disciplinary Focus,** p. 256 in ATE **MathBreak,** Calculating Energy Transfer, p. 257 **Math and More,** p. 257 in ATE **Cross-Disciplinary Focus,** p. 257 in ATE **Cross-Disciplinary Focus,** p. 258 in ATE	**Homework,** pp. 252, 257 in ATE **Review,** p. 255 **Self-Check,** p. 259 **Review,** p. 259 **Quiz,** p. 259 in ATE **Alternative Assessment,** p. 259 in ATE
Directed Reading Worksheet 10, Section 3 **Transparency 241,** Models of a Solid, a Liquid, and a Gas **Transparency 242,** Changes of State for Water	**Connect to Life Science,** p. 260 in ATE **Biology Connection,** p. 262 **Across the Sciences:** Diaplex, p. 275	**Self-Check,** p. 261 **Review,** p. 262 **Quiz,** p. 262 in ATE **Alternative Assessment,** p. 262 in ATE
Directed Reading Worksheet 10, Section 4 **Transparency 243,** Solar Heating Systems **Transparency 237,** Energy Conversions in a Car Engine	**Cross-Disciplinary Focus,** pp. 263, 266, 268 in ATE **Oceanography Connection,** p. 266 **Real-World Connection,** p. 267 in ATE **Environment Connection,** p. 269	**Homework,** p. 264 in ATE **Review,** p. 269 **Quiz,** p. 269 in ATE **Alternative Assessment,** p. 269 in ATE

 Holt, Rinehart and Winston On-line Resources
go.hrw.com
For worksheets and other teaching aids related to this chapter, visit the HRW Web site and type in the keyword: **HSTHOT**

 **National Science Teachers Association**
www.scilinks.org
Encourage students to use the sciLINKS numbers listed in the internet connect boxes to access information and resources on the **NSTA** Web site.

END-OF-CHAPTER REVIEW AND ASSESSMENT

Chapter Review in Study Guide
Vocabulary and Notes in Study Guide
Chapter Tests with Performance-Based Assessment, Chapter 10 Test, Performance-Based Assessment 10
Concept Mapping Transparency 10

Chapter Resources & Worksheets

Visual Resources

TEACHING TRANSPARENCIES

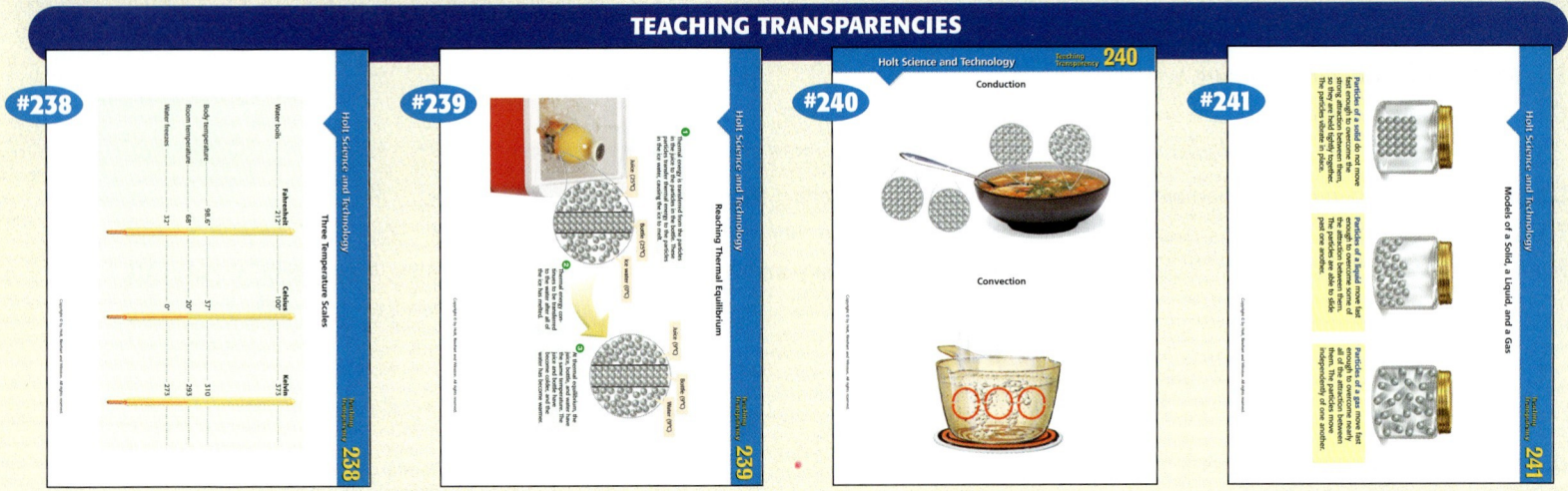

TEACHING TRANSPARENCIES

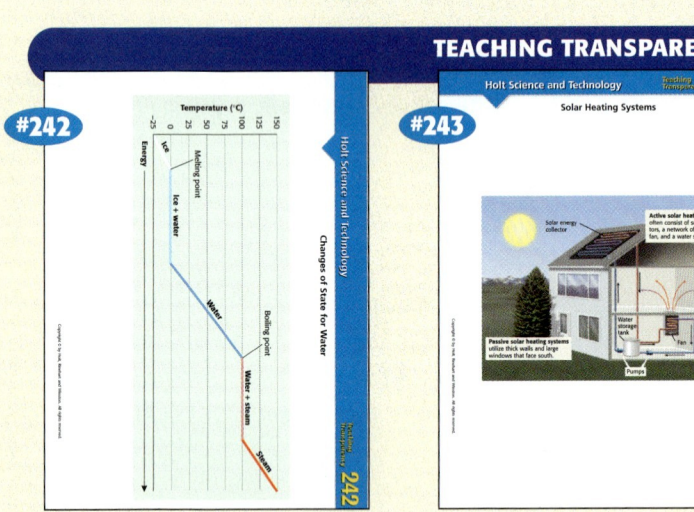
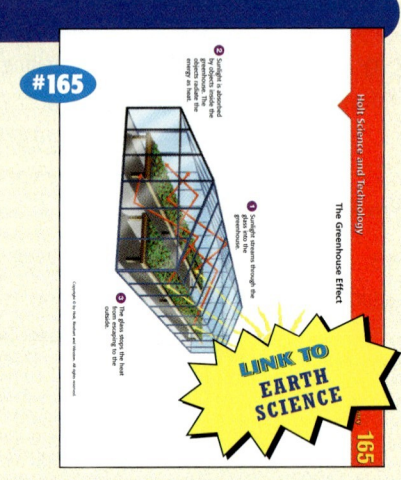

CONCEPT MAPPING TRANSPARENCY

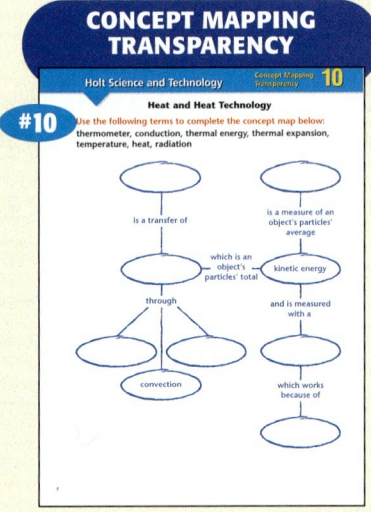

Meeting Individual Needs

DIRECTED READING

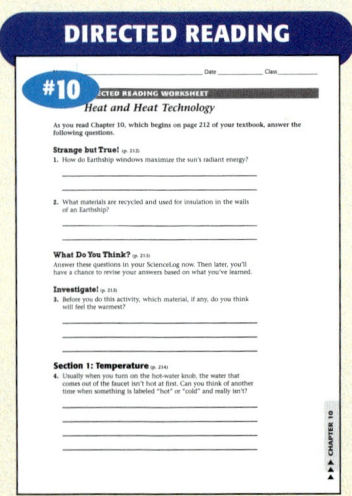

REINFORCEMENT & VOCABULARY REVIEW

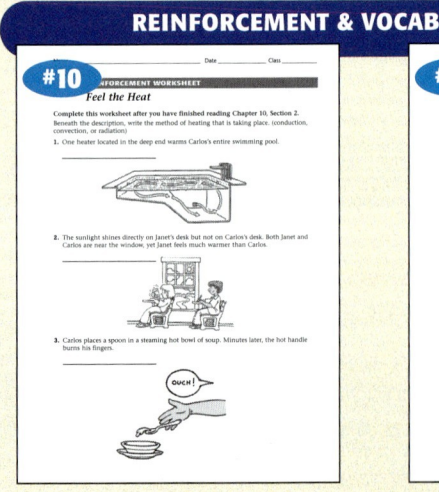
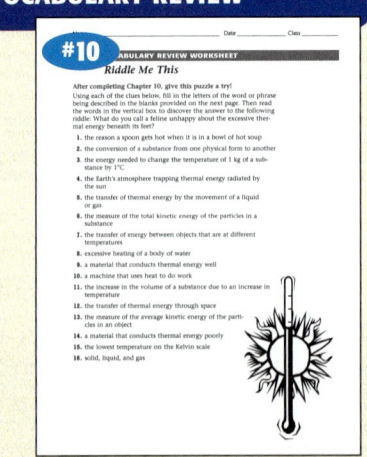

SCIENCE PUZZLERS, TWISTERS & TEASERS

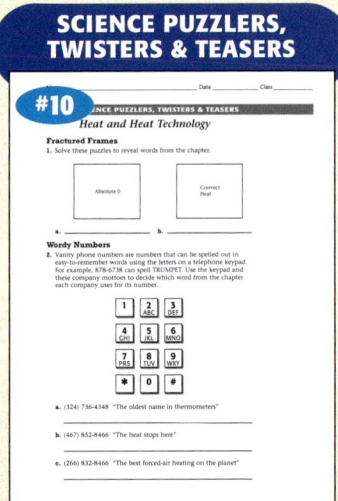

Chapter 10 • Heat and Heat Technology

Review & Assessment

STUDY GUIDE

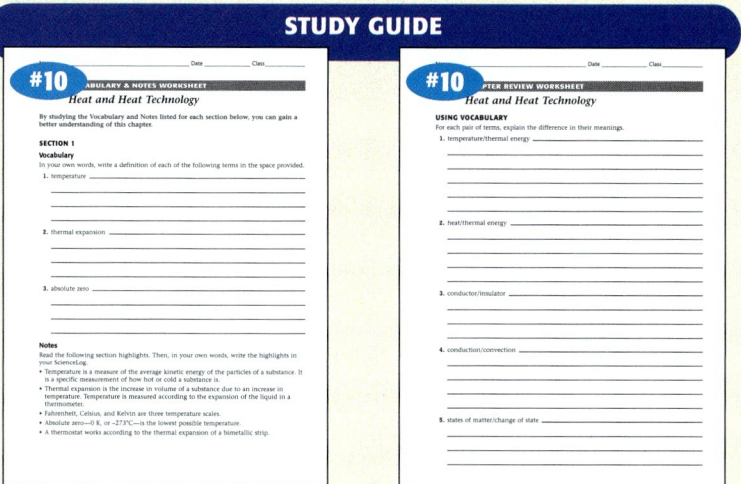

CHAPTER TESTS WITH PERFORMANCE-BASED ASSESSMENT

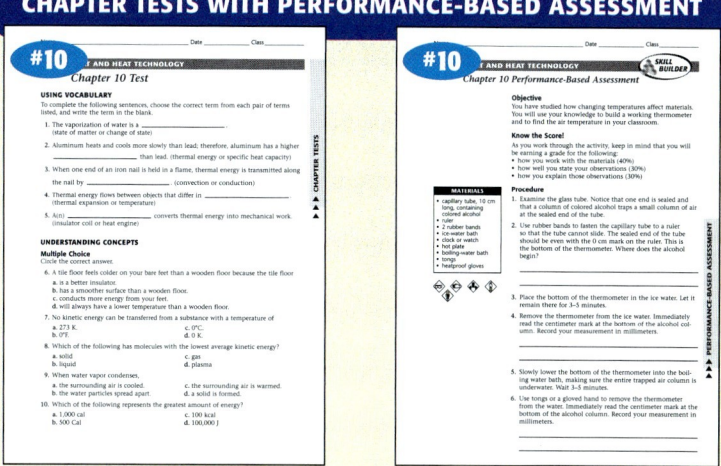

Lab Worksheets

LABS YOU CAN EAT

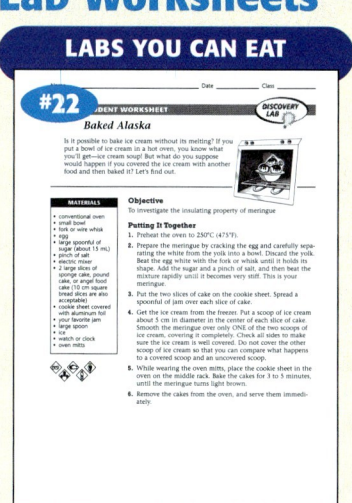

ECOLABS & FIELD ACTIVITIES

LONG-TERM PROJECTS & RESEARCH IDEAS

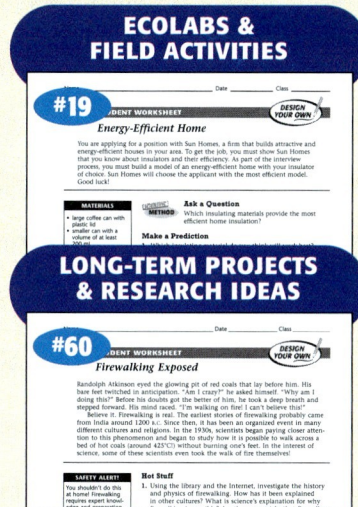

WHIZ-BANG DEMONSTRATIONS

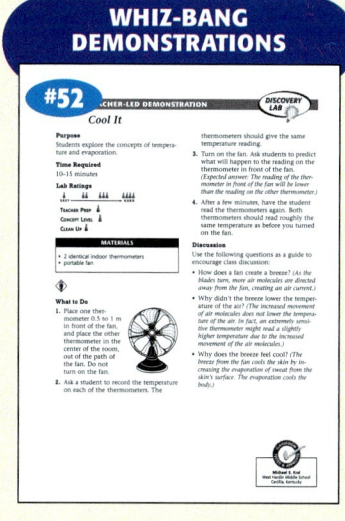

DATASHEETS FOR LABBOOK

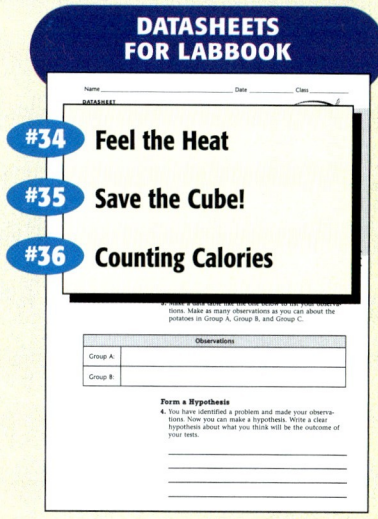

Applications & Extensions

CRITICAL THINKING & PROBLEM SOLVING

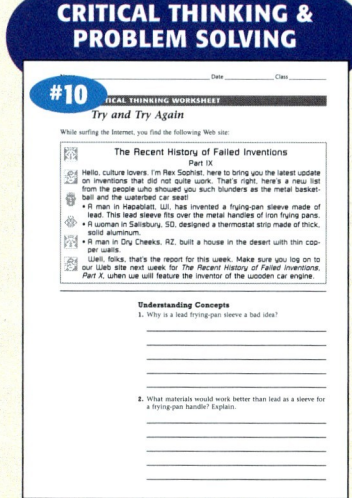

EYE ON THE ENVIRONMENT

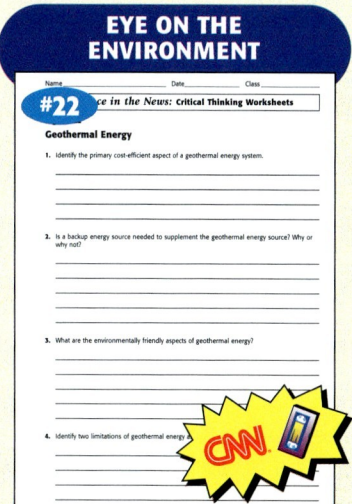

Chapter 10 • Chapter Resources & Worksheets   **243D**

Chapter Background

SECTION 1

Temperature

▶ **Temperature Scales**
Daniel Gabriel Fahrenheit (1686–1736) developed the first mercury thermometer in 1714. His scale used the temperature of a brine solution of ice and salt as 0°. He chose 30° for the freezing temperature of water and 90° for the temperature of the human body. These were later adjusted to 32° and 98.6°.

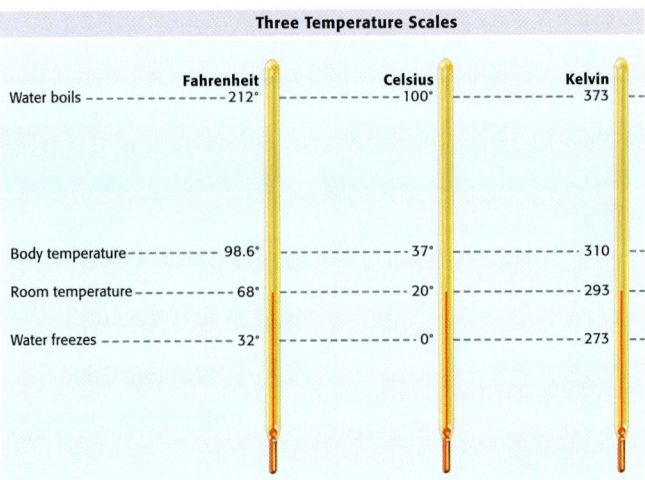

- Anders Celsius (1701–1744) developed the centigrade temperature scale using two physical properties of pure water as his standards. The modern Celsius scale assigns 0° to the freezing point of pure water and 100° to the boiling point of pure water. The Celsius scale has been adopted for use by the scientific community.

- In 1848, British physicist and mathematician William Thomson (1824–1907), later Lord Kelvin, developed the absolute temperature scale. Using J.A.C. Charles's (1746–1823) work with gases, Kelvin realized that a gas decreased by $\frac{1}{273}$ of its volume for each Celsius-degree decrease in temperature. Kelvin theorized that a substance would lose all energy at a temperature of −273°C, so he assigned that point a value of zero on his scale.

IS THAT A FACT!

▰ How much energy does the human body radiate in 1 second? It uses as much as a 60 W light bulb.

SECTION 2

What Is Heat?

▶ **Benjamin Thompson (1753–1814)**
In the eighteenth century, most scientists defined heat as an invisible and weightless fluid that soaked into an object as it was heated and left an object as it cooled.

- Benjamin Thompson, also known as Count von Rumford, an American-born British physicist, noticed that metal became very hot during the process of boring cannons. He set up an experiment to find out why.

- In his experiment, Thompson encased the cannon form in a wooden barrel filled with water. After hours of drilling, the water began to boil. When the drilling stopped, the water stopped boiling. When the drilling began again, the water once again boiled. The water continued to boil for as long as the drill was turned. If heat had been a material substance, it would have run out eventually and the cannon would have become cold—no matter how much drilling was done.

- Because there was no source of heat, Thompson decided that heat was actually a form of energy supplied by the work of the horses turning the drill. Thompson reasoned that the drilling caused the molecules in the cannon to vibrate faster and that the cannon's molecules caused the water molecules to vibrate faster. When the drilling stopped, the source of energy also stopped.

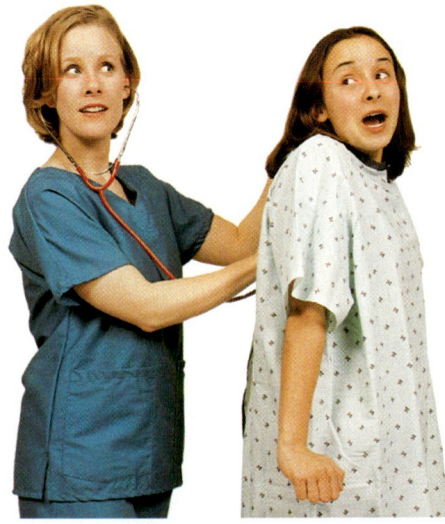

Chapter 10 • Heat and Heat Technology

Chapter 10 • Heat and Heat Technology

SECTION 3

Matter and Heat

▶ **Water and Heat**

When thermal energy is added to substances, they usually expand. When thermal energy is subtracted, they usually contract. Water behaves this way until it reaches the temperature range between 4°C and 0°C. In this range, water expands as it cools and freezes, making its solid form (ice) less dense than its liquid form.

▶ **Latent Heat**

The amount of thermal energy that is lost or gained during a phase change is called latent heat. During a phase change, there is no change in temperature. The energy that is absorbed or released is used to break or to recreate physical bonds.

IS THAT A FACT!

◆ More than 2 million joules of thermal energy are lost from a mammal's body as 1 L of perspiration is evaporated.

SECTION 4

Heat Technology

▶ **Central Heating**

Central-heating systems that used hot water were developed in the 1800s. The first successful central-heating system, used in 1835, relied on warm air. In 1850, steam heating was developed.

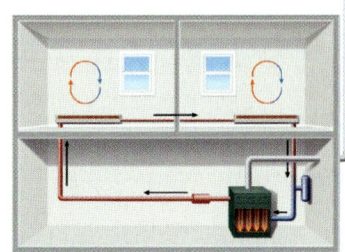

• Radiant heating refers to systems in which floors, walls, and ceilings are used as radiant-heating units. When floors and walls are used, steam or hot-water pipes are placed in the floors or the walls during the construction of the building.

• Radiant heating can be provided by electrical resistance. If electrical resistance is used, the panels containing coils are placed in the baseboard or the ceiling.

▶ **Steam Engines**

Hero of Alexandria (first century A.D.) invented a type of steam engine, but the French physicist Denis Papin (c. 1647–1712) developed the first piston steam engine in 1690. Thomas Savery (c. 1650–1715) and Thomas Newcomen (1663–1729) made improvements on Papin's design, but it was James Watt (1736–1819) who produced the modern steam engine.

▶ **Internal Combustion Engines**

Jean Joseph Etienne Lenoir (1822–1900) is given credit for inventing the first practical internal combustion engine. Nikolaus August Otto (1832–1891) and Rudolf Diesel (1858–1913) also did extensive work with

internal combustion engines. Gottlieb Daimler (1834–1900) assisted Otto with this engine. Daimler, who developed both two- and four-cycle engines, patented his own engine in 1887.

• Karl Benz (1844–1929), a German engineer, developed a two-cycle internal combustion engine and a light four-cycle engine. In 1886, Benz patented a vehicle that had his engine.

• Benz and Daimler, who worked independently of each other and who never met, were each credited with building the first automobile.

IS THAT A FACT!

◆ Heating, cooling, and breathing produce hazardous waste gases and vapors. An adequate ventilation system provides about 280 to 850 L of outside air per minute for each person in a room.

For background information about teaching strategies and issues, refer to the *Professional Reference for Teachers*.

Chapter 10 • Chapter Background **243F**

CHAPTER 10
Heat and Heat Technology

Chapter Preview

Section 1
Temperature
- What Is Temperature?
- Measuring Temperature
- More About Thermal Expansion

Section 2
What Is Heat?
- Heat Is a Transfer of Energy
- Conduction, Convection, and Radiation
- Heat and Temperature Change
- The Differences Between Temperature, Thermal Energy, and Heat

Section 3
Matter and Heat
- States of Matter
- Changes of State
- Heat and Chemical Changes

Section 4
Heat Technology
- Heating Systems
- Heat Engines
- Cooling Systems
- Heat Technology and Thermal Pollution

Science Puzzlers, Twisters & Teasers Worksheet 10

Guided Reading Audio CD
English or Spanish, Chapter 10

CHAPTER 10 Heat and Heat Technology

Strange but True!

Would you want to live in a house without a heating system? You could if you lived in an Earthship! Earthships are the brainchild of Michael Reynolds, an architect in Taos, New Mexico. These houses are designed to make the most of our planet's most abundant source of energy, the sun.

Each Earthship takes full advantage of passive solar heating. For example, large windows face south in order to maximize the amount of energy the house receives from the sun. Each home is partially buried in the ground, with the excavated soil piled almost to the roof. The energy-absorbing soil helps keep the energy that comes in through the windows inside the house.

To absorb the sun's energy, the outer walls of Earthships are massive and thick. The walls may be made with crushed aluminum cans or stacks of old automobile tires filled with dirt. These materials absorb the sun's energy during daylight hours and naturally heat the house from the walls inward. Because an Earthship maintains a temperature around 15°C (about 60°F), it can keep its occupants comfortable through all but the coldest winter nights.

Technology that keeps you warm or cool is very important. In this chapter, you'll learn about temperature and heat, the transfer of energy by different materials, and the use of heat technology in everyday life.

Strange but True!

One of the main purposes of housing is to provide shelter from the elements. The inside climate must be kept comfortable when the outside climate is not. Traditional houses accomplish this at high energy costs. The thermal mass of an Earthship's walls is used to store thermal energy and to regulate temperature for the living area. Air pockets between the packed cans and the dirt filling the tires provide extra insulation. As a result, a lot of energy is prevented from leaving the house, even as the sun goes down and the outside air grows cold.

What Do You Think?

In your ScienceLog, try to answer the following questions based on what you already know:

1. How do you measure how hot or cold an object is?
2. What makes an object hot or cold?
3. How can heat be used in your home?

TRY at HOME

Some Like It Hot

Sometimes you can tell the relative temperature of something by touching it with your hand. But how well does your hand work as a thermometer? In this activity, you will find out!

Procedure

1. Gather small pieces of the following materials from your teacher: **metal, wood, plastic foam, rock, plastic,** and **cardboard.**
2. Allow the materials to sit untouched on a table for several minutes.
3. Put your hands palms down on each of the various materials. Compare how warm or cool the materials feel.
4. In your ScienceLog, list the materials in order from coolest to warmest. Compare your results with those of your classmates.
5. Based on your discussion, arrange the materials in order from coolest to warmest.
6. Place a **thermometer strip** on the surface of each material. In your ScienceLog, record the temperature of each material.

Analysis

7. Which material felt the warmest?
8. Which material had the highest temperature?
9. Why do you think some materials felt warmer than others?
10. Was your hand a good thermometer? Why or why not?

What Do You Think?

Accept all reasonable responses.

Students will have a chance to revise their answers in the Chapter Review under NOW What Do You Think?

Investigate!

MATERIALS

FOR EACH GROUP:
- small pieces of metal, wood, plastic foam, rock, plastic, cardboard
- thermometer strip (You can use bulb thermometers, but liquid crystal thermometer strips or cards, available from a science store or supply house, may measure temperature on the materials more accurately.)

Answers to Investigate!

7. Answers will vary, but students may say that the plastic foam felt the warmest.
8. Students should find that the materials were all about the same temperature.
9. Answers will vary, but students may conclude that the material of which something is made determines how warm or cold it feels.
10. Students will probably conclude that their hands were not a good thermometer because some materials felt warmer than others, even though they were all about the same temperature.

 Directed Reading Worksheet 10

 internetconnect

Smithsonian Institution®
Visit **www.si.edu/hrw** for additional on-line resources.

IS THAT A FACT!

In the mid-1800s, in some warm parts of the United States, people built houses that had a "dog run" to help cool the house. The simplest of these homes consisted of two rooms separated by a hallway (the dog run) that ran from the front of the house all the way through to the back. A wide porch stretched across the front. Later designs included more rooms and a second story. The dog run was an efficient way of cooling the house because it allowed the breeze to blow between the two parts of the building and create air flow.

Chapter 10 • **HEAT AND HEAT TECHNOLOGY**

SECTION 1

Focus

Temperature

This section explains temperature and how it is measured. Students learn how temperature relates to kinetic energy. They will explore thermal expansion and learn how to convert between the three temperature scales.

 **Bellringer**

Write the following on the board:

The temperature of boiling water is 100° on the Celsius scale and 212° on the Fahrenheit scale.

Look at each of the following temperatures carefully, and decide whether you think that it is hot or cold:

60°F, 60°C, 37°F, 37°C, 0°C, 100°F, 70°F

Write your responses in your ScienceLog.

1 Motivate

DEMONSTRATION

Using a metal ball-and-ring set, demonstrate how the ball easily slips through the ring. Be sure to use tongs or protective gloves. Heat the ball for a minute or two, then try to pass the ball through the ring. Ask students to theorize why the ball no longer passes through the ring. Next heat the ring and pass the ball through it. Ask students to theorize why the ball again passed through the ring. **(The ball expanded when it was heated, so it would not fit through the ring. When the ring was heated, the ring expanded enough to allow the ball to pass through.)**

246 Chapter 10 • Heat and Heat Technology

Section 1

Terms to Learn

temperature
thermal expansion
absolute zero

What You'll Do

◆ Describe how temperature relates to kinetic energy.
◆ Give examples of thermal expansion.
◆ Compare temperatures on different temperature scales.

Temperature

You probably put on a sweater or a jacket when it's cold outside. Likewise, you probably wear shorts in the summer when it gets hot. But how hot is hot, and how cold is cold? Think about how the knobs on a water faucet are labeled "H" for hot and "C" for cold. But does only hot water come out when the hot water knob is on? You may have noticed that when you first turn on the water, it is warm or even cool. Are you being misled by the label on the knob? The terms *hot* and *cold* are not very scientific terms. If you really want to specify how hot or cold something is, you must use temperature.

What Is Temperature?

You probably think of temperature as a measure of how hot or cold something is. But scientifically, **temperature** is a measure of the average kinetic energy of the particles in an object. Using *temperature* instead of words like *hot* or *cold* reduces confusion. The scenario below emphasizes the importance of communicating about temperature. You can learn more about hot and cold comparisons by doing the QuickLab on the next page.

246

Directed Reading Worksheet 10 Section 1

internetconnect

SC**LINKS**
NSTA

TOPIC: What Is Temperature?
GO TO: www.scilinks.org
KEYWORD: HSTP230

Students often think that heat and temperature are the same. Stress that temperature is the measure of the average kinetic energy of the molecules in a substance. Heat is the transfer of thermal energy between objects that are at different temperatures. These concepts are covered in Section 2 of this chapter.

Temperature Depends on the Kinetic Energy of Particles

All matter is made of particles—atoms or molecules—that are in constant motion. Because the particles are in motion, they have kinetic energy. The faster the particles are moving, the more kinetic energy they have. What does temperature have to do with kinetic energy? Well, as described in **Figure 1**, the more kinetic energy the particles of an object have, the higher the temperature of the object.

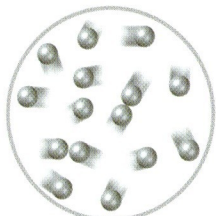 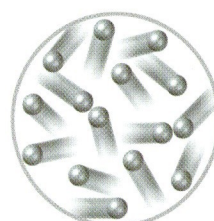

Figure 1 *The gas particles on the right have more kinetic energy than those on the left. So, the gas on the right is at a higher temperature.*

Temperature Is an Average Measure
Particles of matter are constantly moving, but they don't all move at the same speed and in the same direction all the time. Look back at Figure 1. As you can see, the motion of the particles is random. The particles of matter in an object move in different directions, and some particles move faster than others. As a result, some particles have more kinetic energy than others. So what determines an object's temperature? An object's temperature is the best approximation of the kinetic energy of the particles. When you measure an object's temperature, you measure the average kinetic energy of the particles in the object.

The temperature of a substance is not determined by how much of the substance you have. As shown in **Figure 2,** different amounts of the same substance can have the same temperature. However, the total kinetic energy of the particles in each amount is different. You will learn more about total kinetic energy in the next section.

Figure 2 *Even though there is more tea in the teapot than in the mug, the temperature of the tea in the mug is the same as the temperature of the tea in the teapot.*

Hot or Cold?
1. Put both your hands into a **bucket of warm water,** and note how it feels.
2. Now put one hand into a **bucket of cold water** and the other into a **bucket of hot water.**
3. After a minute, take your hands out of the hot and cold water and put them back in the warm water.
4. Can you rely on your hands to determine temperature? In your ScienceLog, explain your observations.

Science Bloopers
When Anders Celsius invented his temperature scale, he set the freezing point of water as 100° and the boiling point of water at 0°. Apparently, the person who made thermometers for Celsius got the two numbers reversed, and ever since, 0° has been the freezing point of water and 100° has been the boiling point of water.

IS THAT A FACT!
There are five temperature scales used today: Fahrenheit, Celsius, Kelvin, the international thermodynamic temperature scale, and Rankine. Scientists use the Celsius and Kelvin scales almost exclusively.

2 Teach, continued

USING THE FIGURE

Ask students to use the figure of the **Three Temperature Scales** on this page to determine human body temperature on the Kelvin scale (310 K), the Celsius scale (37°C), and the Fahrenheit scale (98.6°F).

At what temperature does water boil on the Celsius scale? (100°C) on the Kelvin scale? (373 K)

DISCUSSION

The Fahrenheit scale defines the freezing point of water as 32°F. By the time 0°F is reached, the temperature is well below the freezing point of water. Human body temperature is 98.6°F. Discuss with the class what would happen if normal human body temperature suddenly shot up to 98.6°C. Would air temperatures of 70–75°C feel comfortable? Why do doctors worry more about a fever of a couple of degrees Celsius than a fever of a couple of degrees Fahrenheit?

Teaching Transparency 238 "Three Temperature Scales"

Measuring Temperature

How would you measure the temperature of a steaming cup of hot chocolate? Would you take a sip of it or stick your finger into it? Probably not—you would use a thermometer.

Using a Thermometer Many thermometers are a thin glass tube filled with a liquid. Mercury and alcohol are often used in thermometers because they remain liquids over a large temperature range. Thermometers can measure temperature because of thermal expansion. **Thermal expansion** is the increase in volume of a substance due to an increase in temperature. As a substance gets hotter, its particles move faster. The particles themselves do not expand; they just spread out so that the entire substance expands. Different substances expand by different amounts for a given temperature change. When you insert a thermometer into a hot substance, the liquid inside the thermometer expands and rises. You measure the temperature of a substance by measuring the expansion of the liquid in the thermometer.

Temperature Scales Temperature can be expressed according to different scales. Notice how the same temperatures have different readings on the three temperature scales shown below.

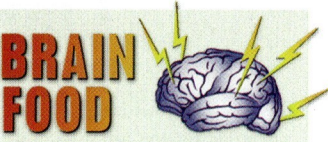

BRAIN FOOD

The coldest temperature on record occurred in Vostok Station, Antarctica. In 1983, the temperature dropped to −89°C (about −192°F). The hottest temperature on record occurred in 1922 in a Libyan desert. A scorching temperature of 58°C (about 136°F) was recorded—in the shade!

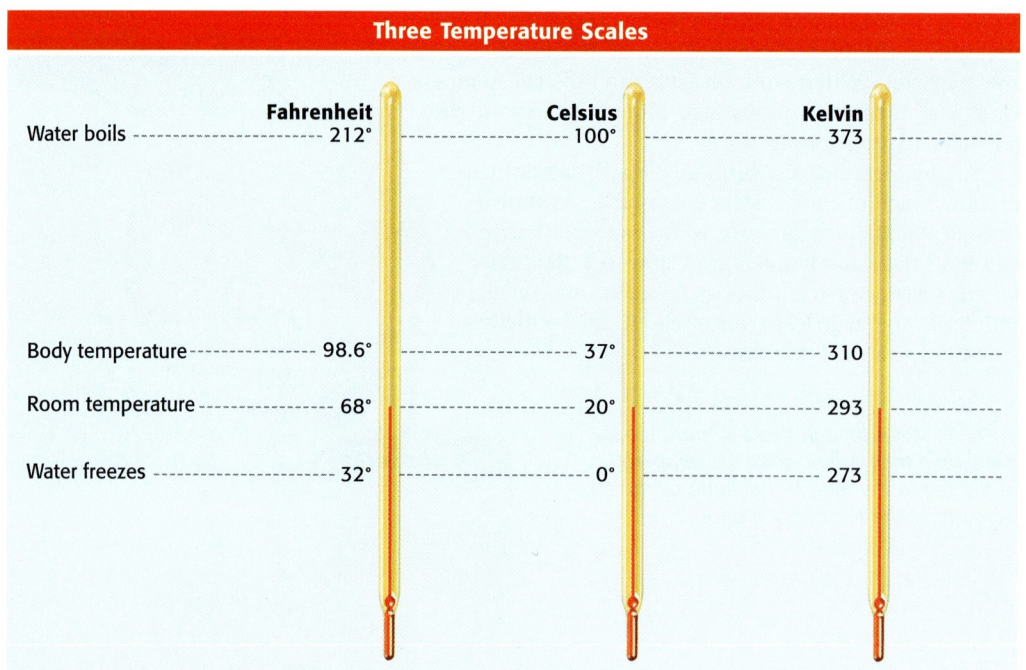

Three Temperature Scales

	Fahrenheit	Celsius	Kelvin
Water boils	212°	100°	373
Body temperature	98.6°	37°	310
Room temperature	68°	20°	293
Water freezes	32°	0°	273

Chapter 10 • Heat and Heat Technology

When you hear a weather report that gives the current temperature as 65°, chances are that you are given the temperature in degrees Fahrenheit (°F). In science, the Celsius scale is used more often than the Fahrenheit scale. The Celsius scale is divided into 100 equal parts, called degrees Celsius (°C), between the freezing point and boiling point of water. A third scale, called the Kelvin (or absolute) scale, is the official SI temperature scale. The Kelvin scale is divided into units called kelvins (K)—not degrees kelvin. The lowest temperature on the Kelvin scale is 0 K, which is called **absolute zero.** It is not possible to reach a temperature lower than absolute zero. In fact, temperatures within a few billionths of a kelvin above absolute zero have been achieved in laboratories, but absolute zero itself has never been reached.

What can you do at temperatures near absolute zero? Turn to page 274 to find out!

Temperature Conversion As shown by the thermometers illustrated on the previous page, a given temperature is represented by different numbers on the three temperature scales. For example, the freezing point of water is 32°F, 0°C, or 273 K. As you can see, 0°C is actually a much higher temperature than 0 K, but a change of 1 K is equal to a change of one Celsius degree. In addition, 0°C is a higher temperature than 0°F, but a change of one Fahrenheit degree is *not* equal to a change of one Celsius degree. You can convert from one scale to another using the simple equations shown below. After reading the examples given, try the MathBreak on this page.

To convert	Use this equation:	Example
Celsius to Fahrenheit °C → °F	$°F = \left(\frac{9}{5} \times °C\right) + 32$	Convert 45°C to °F. $°F = \left(\frac{9}{5} \times 45°C\right) + 32 = 113°F$
Fahrenheit to Celsius °F → °C	$°C = \frac{5}{9} \times (°F - 32)$	Convert 68°F to °C. $°C = \frac{5}{9} \times (68°F - 32) = 20°C$
Celsius to Kelvin °C → K	$K = °C + 273$	Convert 45°C to K. $K = 45°C + 273 = 318 K$
Kelvin to Celsius K → °C	$°C = K - 273$	Convert 32 K to °C. $°C = 32 K - 273 = -241°C$

MATH BREAK

Converting Temperatures

Use the equations at left to answer the following questions:

1. What temperature on the Celsius scale is equivalent to 373 K?
2. Absolute zero is 0 K. What is the equivalent temperature on the Celsius scale? on the Fahrenheit scale?
3. Which temperature is colder, 0°F or 200 K?

Answers to MATHBREAK
1. 100°C
2. −273°C; −459.4°F
3. 200 K is colder

---

3) Extend

RESEARCH

Writing — Encourage students to research the lives and work of Anders Celsius, Gabriel Fahrenheit, William Rankine, and William Thomson (Lord Kelvin). Students can present their findings on posters, by writing a story or skit, or in a report.

MATH and MORE

When solving equations, it is important to follow the order of operations. Remind students to do what is inside the parentheses first, then multiply or divide from left to right, and finally add or subtract from left to right.

Have students do the following conversion problems:

- Normal body temperature is 98.6°F. Marie has a temperature of 38.5°C. Does Marie have a fever? (yes; 38.5°C = 101.3°F)
- The temperature tonight is supposed to be 265 K. Will water left in a bucket outside freeze? (yes; 265 K = −8°C, which is below water's freezing point, 0°C)

 Math Skills Worksheet 35 "Using Temperature Scales"

4) Close

Quiz

1. Most substances _____ when they are cooled. (contract)
2. The common temperature scale used by most Americans is the _____ scale. (Fahrenheit)
3. Scientists use either the _____ scale or the _____ scale. (Celsius, Kelvin)
4. Temperature _____ as average kinetic energy decreases. (decreases)

ALTERNATIVE ASSESSMENT

Ask students to theorize why large buildings and sidewalks are constructed with expansion joints. (to allow for thermal expansion)

Ask them to explain what would happen in hot or cold weather if there were no expansion joints.

Homework

Writing Have students explain how they could measure temperature if they were given a thermometer without marks on it. Remind students that water would help them with their measurements.

Figure 3 *The concrete segments of a bridge can expand on hot days. When the temperature drops, the segments contract.*

More About Thermal Expansion

Have you ever gone across a highway bridge in a car? You probably heard and felt a *"thuh-thunk"* every couple of seconds as you went over the bridge. That sound occurs when the car goes over small gaps called expansion joints, shown in **Figure 3**. These joints keep the bridge from buckling as a result of thermal expansion. Recall that thermal expansion is the increase in volume of a substance due to an increase in temperature.

Thermal expansion also occurs in a thermostat, the device that controls the heater in your home. Inside a thermostat is a bimetallic strip. A *bimetallic strip* is made of two different metals stacked in a thin strip. Because different materials expand at different rates, one of the metals expands more than the other when the strip gets hot. This makes the strip coil and uncoil in response to changes in temperature. This coiling and uncoiling closes and opens an electric circuit that turns the heater on and off in your home, as shown in **Figure 4**.

Figure 4 How a Thermostat Works

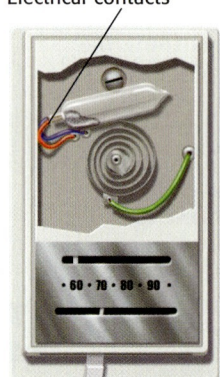

a As the room temperature drops below the desired level, the bimetallic strip coils up and the glass tube tilts. A drop of mercury closes an electric circuit that turns the heater on.

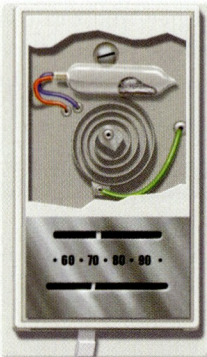

b As the room temperature rises above the desired level, the bimetallic strip uncoils. The drop of mercury rolls back in the tube, opening the electric circuit, and the heater turns off.

internetconnect
SCILINKS
NSTA
TOPIC: What Is Temperature?
GO TO: www.scilinks.org
*sci*LINKS NUMBER: HSTP230

REVIEW

1. What is temperature?
2. What is the coldest temperature possible?
3. Convert 35°C to degrees Fahrenheit.
4. **Inferring Conclusions** Why do you think heating a full pot of soup on the stove could cause the soup to overflow?

250

▼ Answers to Review

1. Temperature is a measure of how hot or cold an object is. Specifically, temperature is a direct measure of the average kinetic energy of the particles in an object.

2. The coldest possible temperature is absolute zero (0 K or −273°C).

3. °F = ($\frac{9}{5}$ × °C) + 32
   °F = $\frac{9}{5}$ × 35°C + 32
   °F = 95, or 95°F

4. The soup could overflow its pot as it cooks on the stove because of thermal expansion. The soup will expand in volume as its temperature increases. If the cold soup is too close to the top of a pot, it will likely overflow as it expands.

Section 2

What Is Heat?

Terms to Learn

heat
thermal energy
conduction
conductor
insulator
convection
radiation
specific heat capacity

What You'll Do

- Define *heat* as the transfer of energy between objects at different temperatures.
- Compare conduction, convection, and radiation.
- Use specific heat capacity to calculate heat.
- Explain the differences between temperature, thermal energy, and heat.

It's time for your annual physical. The doctor comes in and begins her exam by looking down your throat using a wooden tongue depressor. Next she listens to your heart and lungs. But when she places a metal stethoscope on your back, as shown in **Figure 5,** you jump a little and say, "Whoa! That's cold!" The doctor apologizes and continues with your checkup.

Why did the metal stethoscope feel cold? After all, it was at the same temperature as the tongue depressor, which didn't make you jump. What is it about the stethoscope that made it feel cold? The answer has to do with how energy is transferred between the metal and your skin. In this section, you'll learn about this kind of energy transfer.

Heat Is a Transfer of Energy

You might think of the word *heat* as having to do with things that feel hot. But heat also has to do with things that feel cold—like the stethoscope. In fact, heat is what causes objects to feel hot or cold or to get hot or cold under the right conditions. You probably use the word *heat* every day to mean different things. However, in this chapter, you will learn a specific meaning for it. **Heat** is the transfer of energy between objects that are at different temperatures.

Why do some things feel hot, while others feel cold? When two objects at different temperatures come in contact, energy is always transferred from the object with the higher temperature to the object with the lower temperature. When the doctor's stethoscope touches your back, energy is transferred from your back to the stethoscope because your back has a higher temperature (37°C) than the stethoscope (probably room temperature, 20°C). So to you, the stethoscope is cold, but compared to the stethoscope, you are hot! You'll learn why the tongue depressor didn't feel cold to you a little later in this section.

Figure 5 The reason the metal stethoscope feels cold is actually because of heat!

1 Motivate

DEMONSTRATION

Place three small objects with similar masses, such as a rock, a block of brass, and a block of steel, in boiling water. After 2 minutes, remove each object and place it on a block of wax. When the objects have cooled, remove them from the wax. Measure the depth of the indentation made by each object on the wax. Ask the students to explain the differences. (Each object had a different amount of thermal energy.)

MISCONCEPTION ALERT

The thermal energy of a substance is related to the substance's temperature as well as its state. For example, equal masses of liquid water and steam at the same temperature (100°C) have different amounts of thermal energy. Because the steam stores the energy used to separate the particles of liquid water to change it to steam, the steam has more thermal energy than the liquid water.

2 Teach

READING STRATEGY

Prediction Guide Before students read the section about heat and thermal energy, ask them whether the following statements are true or false.

- Thermal energy depends partly on the temperature of a substance. (true)
- A cup of water at 283 K and a pot of water at 283 K have the same thermal energy. (false)

Heat and Thermal Energy If heat is a transfer of energy, what form of energy is being transferred? The answer is thermal energy. **Thermal energy** is the total energy of the particles that make up a substance. Thermal energy, which is expressed in joules (J), depends partly on temperature. An object at a high temperature has more thermal energy than it would at a lower temperature. Thermal energy also depends on how much of a substance you have. As described in **Figure 6,** the more moving particles there are in a substance at a given temperature, the greater the thermal energy of the substance.

When you hold an ice cube, thermal energy is transferred from your hand to the ice cube. The ice cube's thermal energy increases, and it starts to melt. But your hand's thermal energy decreases. The particles in the surface of your skin move more slowly, and the surface temperature of your skin drops slightly. So your hand feels cold!

Figure 6 Although both soups are at the same temperature, the soup in the pan has more thermal energy than the soup in the bowl.

Reaching the Same Temperature Take a look at **Figure 7.** When objects at different temperatures come in contact, energy will always be transferred from the higher-temperature object to the lower-temperature object until both objects reach the same temperature. This point is called *thermal equilibrium* (EE kwi LIB ree uhm). When objects are at thermal equilibrium, no net change in either object's thermal energy occurs. Although one object may have more thermal energy, both objects have the same temperature.

Figure 7
Reaching Thermal Equilibrium

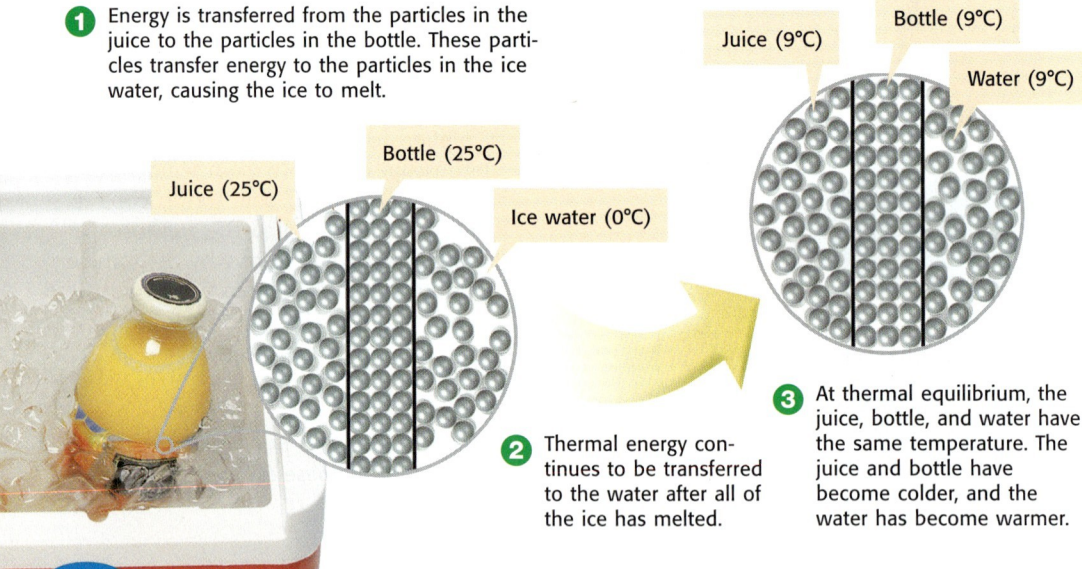

1. Energy is transferred from the particles in the juice to the particles in the bottle. These particles transfer energy to the particles in the ice water, causing the ice to melt.

2. Thermal energy continues to be transferred to the water after all of the ice has melted.

3. At thermal equilibrium, the juice, bottle, and water have the same temperature. The juice and bottle have become colder, and the water has become warmer.

Homework

Ask students this question:
When energy has been transferred by heat, what happens to it? Explain your answer. (Energy transferred by heat moves from a higher-temperature object to a lower-temperature object. The thermal energy of the lower-temperature object increases, as does its temperature. The thermal energy of the higher-temperature object decreases, as does its temperature.)

Conduction, Convection, and Radiation

So far you've read about several examples of energy transfer: stoves transfer energy to substances in pots and pans; you can adjust the temperature of your bath water by adding cold or hot water to the tub; and the sun warms your skin. In the next couple of pages you'll learn about three processes involving this type of energy transfer: *conduction, convection,* and *radiation.*

Conduction Imagine that you put a cold metal spoon in a bowl of hot soup, as shown in **Figure 8.** Soon the handle of the spoon warms up—even though it is not in the soup! The entire spoon gets warm because of conduction. **Conduction** is the transfer of thermal energy from one substance to another through direct contact. Conduction can also occur within a substance, such as the spoon in Figure 8.

How does conduction work? As substances come in contact, particles collide and thermal energy is transferred from the higher-temperature substance to the lower-temperature substance. Remember that particles of substances at different temperatures have different average kinetic energy. So when particles collide, higher-kinetic-energy particles transfer kinetic energy to lower-kinetic-energy particles. This makes some particles slow down and other particles speed up until all particles have the same average kinetic energy. As a result, the substances have the same temperature.

Heat Exchange

1. Fill a **film canister** with **hot water.** Insert the **thermometer apparatus** prepared by your teacher. Record the temperature.
2. Fill a **250 mL beaker** two-thirds full with **cool water.** Insert **another thermometer** in the cool water, and record its temperature.
3. Place the canister in the cool water. Record the temperature measured by each thermometer every 30 seconds.
4. When the thermometers read nearly the same temperature, stop and graph your data. Plot temperature (*y*-axis) versus time (*x*-axis).
5. In your ScienceLog, describe what happens to the rate of energy transfer as the two temperatures get closer.

Figure 8 The end of this spoon will warm up because conduction, the transfer of energy through direct contact, occurs all the way up the handle.

Q: Why did the music teacher bring a metal pole to orchestra rehearsal?

A: He wanted the orchestra to have a good conductor.

IS THAT A FACT!

Special ceramic tiles were created for use on the underside of the space shuttle. These tiles transfer so little energy that one side can be exposed to a welder's torch while the other side remains cool to the touch.

2 Teach, continued

Answer to APPLY

The drink holder is an insulator because it does not conduct thermal energy very well. It protects the can, which is a conductor, from energy that transfers from the warmer air to the cooler can.

DEMONSTRATION

Convection Currents Fill a 250 mL beaker about two-thirds full of water. Place the beaker on a hot plate turned on low or medium. Roll some very small pieces of aluminum foil into small, tightly packed balls. Drop the foil balls into the water, and direct students to observe what happens to the balls as the water warms up. Ask students what the movement of the foil balls suggests about the movement of water within the beaker. (The circulation of the foil balls suggests that the water in the beaker is circulating too.)

Then ask what method of heating is shown in this demonstration. (convection)

CONNECT TO EARTH SCIENCE

Convection currents caused by the uneven heating of Earth's surface are responsible for Earth's winds, weather patterns, and ocean currents. Without these currents, Earth's climates might be very different and life on Earth might also be greatly changed.

Teaching Transparency 240 "Convection"

Conductors	Insulators
Curling iron	Flannel shirt
Iron skillet	Oven mitt
Cookie sheet	Plastic spatula
Copper pipes	Fiberglass insulation
Stove coils	Ceramic bowl

Conductors and Insulators Substances that conduct thermal energy very well are called **conductors**. For example, the metal in a doctor's stethoscope is a conductor. Energy is transferred rapidly from your higher-temperature skin to the room-temperature stethoscope. That's why the stethoscope feels cold. Substances that do not conduct thermal energy very well are called **insulators**. For example, the doctor's wooden tongue depressor is an insulator. It has the same temperature as the stethoscope, but the tongue depressor doesn't feel cold. That's because thermal energy is transferred very slowly from your tongue to the wood. Compare some typical conductors and insulators in the chart at left.

Keepin' It Cool

The drink holder shown here is made from a foamlike material that helps keep your can of soda cold. How is this drink holder an insulator?

Figure 9 *The repeated rising and sinking of water during boiling is due to convection.*

Convection When you boil a pot of water, like the one shown in **Figure 9**, the water moves in roughly circular patterns because of convection. **Convection** is the transfer of thermal energy by the movement of a liquid or a gas. The water at the bottom of a pot on a stove burner gets hot because of contact with the pot itself (conduction). As a result, the hot water becomes less dense because its higher-energy particles have spread apart. The warmer water rises through the denser, cooler water above it. At the surface, the warm water begins to cool, and the lower-energy particles move closer together, making the water denser. The denser, cooler water sinks back to the bottom, where it will be heated again. This circular motion of liquids or gases due to density differences that result from temperature differences is called a *convection current*.

Science Bloopers

The use of glass fibers goes back to the ancient Egyptians, but making useful fiberglass was hard to do. Then, in 1932, as a researcher was trying to weld glass blocks together, a burst of compressed air accidentally hit some molten glass. The burst blew the molten glass into very fine glass fibers. This accident led to one of today's most common insulating materials, fiberglass.

254 Chapter 10 • Heat and Heat Technology

Radiation Unlike conduction and convection, radiation can involve either an energy transfer between particles of matter or an energy transfer across empty space. **Radiation** is the transfer of energy through matter or space as electromagnetic waves, such as visible light and infrared waves.

All objects, including the heater in **Figure 10,** radiate electromagnetic waves. The sun emits mostly visible light, which you can see and your body can absorb, making you feel warmer. The Earth emits mostly infrared waves, which you cannot see but can still make you feel warmer.

Figure 10 *The coils of this portable heater warm a room by radiating visible light and infrared waves.*

Radiation and the Greenhouse Effect Earth's atmosphere, like the windows of a greenhouse, allows the sun's visible light to pass through it. But like the windows of a greenhouse keep energy inside the greenhouse, the atmosphere traps some reradiated energy. This process, called the *greenhouse effect,* is illustrated in **Figure 11.** Some scientists are concerned that high levels of greenhouse gases (water vapor, carbon dioxide, and methane) in the atmosphere may trap too much energy and make Earth too warm. However, if not for the greenhouse effect, the Earth would be a cold, lifeless planet.

Figure 11 The Greenhouse Effect

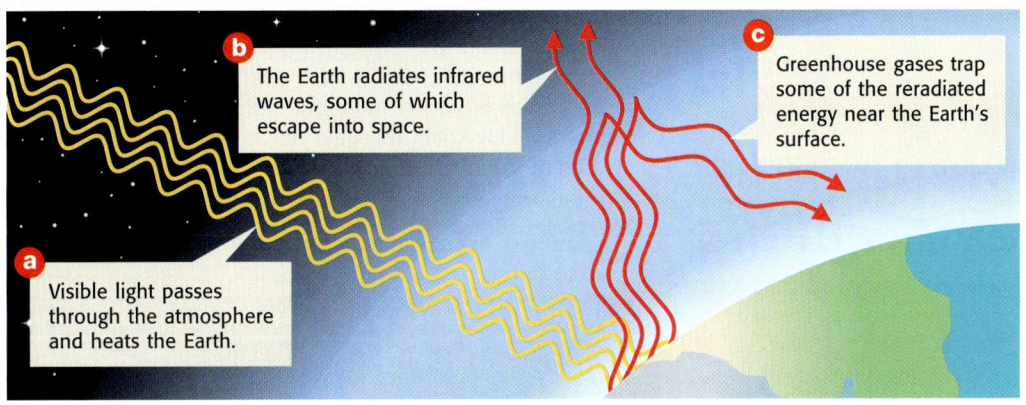

a. Visible light passes through the atmosphere and heats the Earth.

b. The Earth radiates infrared waves, some of which escape into space.

c. Greenhouse gases trap some of the reradiated energy near the Earth's surface.

REVIEW

1. What is heat?
2. Explain how radiation is different from conduction and convection.
3. **Applying Concepts** Why do many metal cooking utensils have wooden handles?

TOPIC: What Is Heat?; Conduction, Convection, and Radiation
GO TO: www.scilinks.org
*sci*LINKS NUMBER: HSTP240, HSTP245

CONNECT TO
ASTRONOMY

The very dense atmosphere of Venus is composed mostly of carbon dioxide. The high amount of carbon dioxide results in a greenhouse effect that traps most of the thermal energy from sunlight. The surface temperature of Venus is therefore the hottest of any planet in the solar system. It remains at about 460°C—hot enough to melt zinc metal.

USING THE FIGURE

Draw students' attention to **Figure 11.** Ask students why they think clouds would keep an area of Earth from heating up as much as it would on a clear day. (Clouds prevent some radiation from reaching Earth.)

Then ask what would happen if greenhouse gases kept most of the thermal energy that reaches Earth from escaping into space. (Earth would gradually warm up.) Sheltered English

Use Teaching Transparency 165, "The Greenhouse Effect," to help students understand how the atmospheres of Venus and Earth can act as a greenhouse.

Teaching Transparency 165 "The Greenhouse Effect"

Save the Cube! PG 674

TOPIC: Conduction, Convection, and Radiation
GO TO: www.scilinks.org
KEYWORD: HSTP245

Answers to Review

1. Heat is the transfer of energy between objects that are at different temperatures. Energy is always transferred from an object with a higher temperature to an object with a lower temperature.
2. Radiation is different from conduction and convection in that it does not require an energy transfer among particles of matter. Radiation is the transfer of energy through matter or space as electromagnetic waves, such as visible light or infrared waves.
3. Sample answer: Many metal cooking utensils have wooden handles because wood is an insulator. When you are preparing hot food, a wooden handle will prevent the thermal energy of the food from being conducted to your hand.

2 Teach, continued

USING THE TABLE

Have students study the table of **Specific Heat Capacities of Some Common Substances** found on this page. Then ask the following questions:

- If you have equal masses of each of the following pairs of substances, which will become hotter faster: some silver coins or water (silver coins); a copper pan on a hot stove or its wooden handle (pan); a car's aluminum door handle sitting in the hot summer sun or the windshield (the windshield).

- Explain why water is used as a coolant. (Water has a very high specific heat capacity.)

CROSS-DISCIPLINARY FOCUS

Home Economics When an apple pie is taken from the oven, the crust cools faster than the filling. Ask students to compare the specific heat capacity of the crust with that of the filling.

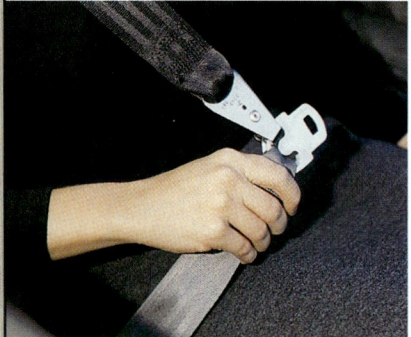

Figure 12 On a hot summer day, the metal part of a seat belt feels hotter than the cloth part.

Water has a higher specific heat capacity than land. This difference affects the climate of different areas on Earth. Climates in coastal areas are moderated by the ocean. Because of water's high specific heat capacity, the ocean retains a lot of thermal energy. So even in the winter, when inland temperatures drop, coastal areas stay moderately warm. Because water does not heat up as easily as land does, oceans can help to keep coastal areas cool during the summer when inland temperatures soar.

Heat and Temperature Change

On a hot summer day, have you ever fastened your seat belt in a car, as shown in **Figure 12**? If so, you may have noticed that the metal buckle felt hotter than the cloth belt. Why? Keep reading to learn more.

Thermal Conductivity Different substances have different thermal conductivities. *Thermal conductivity* is the rate at which a substance conducts thermal energy. Conductors, such as the metal buckle, have higher thermal conductivities than do insulators, such as the cloth belt. Because of the metal's higher thermal conductivity, it transfers energy more rapidly to your hand when you touch it than the cloth does. So even when the cloth and metal are the same temperature, the metal feels hotter.

Specific Heat Capacity Another difference between the metal and the cloth is how easily they change temperature when they absorb or lose energy. When equal amounts of energy are transferred to or from equal masses of different substances, the change in temperature for each substance will differ. **Specific heat capacity** is the amount of energy needed to change the temperature of 1 kg of a substance by 1°C.

Look at the table below. Notice that the specific heat capacity of the cloth of a seat belt is more than twice that of the metal seat belt buckle. This means that for equal masses of metal and cloth, less energy is required to change the temperature of the metal. So the metal buckle gets hot (and cools off) more quickly than an equal mass of the cloth belt.

Different substances have different specific heat capacities. Check out the specific heat capacities for various substances in the table below.

Specific Heat Capacities of Some Common Substances

Substance	Specific heat capacity (J/kg•°C)	Substance	Specific heat capacity (J/kg•°C)
Lead	128	Glass	837
Gold	129	Aluminum	899
Mercury	138	Cloth of seat belt	1,340
Silver	234	Wood	1,760
Copper	387	Steam	2,010
Iron	448	Ice	2,090
Metal of seat belt	500	Water	4,184

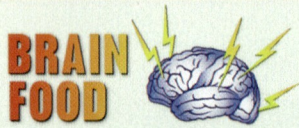

Challenge students to explain whether water would be a good insulator for a home with passive solar heating, such as the Earthship that students read about in the chapter opener.

Chapter 10 • Heat and Heat Technology

Heat—The Amount of Energy Transferred

Unlike temperature, energy transferred between objects cannot be measured directly—it must be calculated. When calculating energy transferred between objects, it is helpful to define *heat* as the amount of energy that is transferred between two objects that are at different temperatures. Heat can then be expressed in joules (J).

How much energy is required to heat a cup of water to make tea? To answer this question, you have to consider the water's mass, its change in temperature, and its specific heat capacity. In general, if you know an object's mass, its change in temperature, and its specific heat capacity, you can use the equation below to calculate heat (the amount of energy transferred).

Heat (J) = specific heat capacity (J/kg•°C) × mass (kg) × change in temperature (°C)

Figure 13 *Information used to calculate heat, the amount of energy transferred to the water, is shown above.*

Mass of water = 0.2 kg
Temperature (before) = 25°C
Temperature (after) = 80°C
Specific heat capacity of water = 4,184 J/kg•°C

Calculating Heat Using the equation above and the data in **Figure 13**, you can follow the steps below to calculate the heat added to the water. Because the water's temperature increases, the value of heat is positive. You can also use this equation to calculate the heat removed from an object when it cools down. The value for heat would then be negative because the temperature decreases.

① Write down what you know.
Specific heat capacity of water = 4,184 J/kg•°C
Mass of water = 0.2 kg
Change in temperature = 80°C − 25°C = 55°C

② Substitute the values into the equation.
Heat = specific heat capacity × mass × change in temperature
= 4,184 J/kg•°C × 0.2 kg × 55°C

③ Solve and cancel units.
Heat = 4,184 J/kg•°C × 0.2 kg × 55°C
= 4,184 J × 0.2 × 55
= 46,024 J

MATH BREAK

Calculating Energy Transfer
Use the equation at left to solve the following problems:

1. Imagine that you heat 2 L of water to make pasta. The temperature of the water before is 40°C, and the temperature after is 100°C. What is the heat involved? (Hint: 1 L of water = 1 kg of water)

2. Suppose you put a glass filled with 180 mL of water into the refrigerator. The temperature of the water before is 25°C, and the temperature after is 10°C. How much energy was transferred away from the water as it became colder?

3) Extend

Research

Have students find out how insulating materials are rated. Ask them to research what the R-values are based on and what R-values are recommended for homes in your geographic area. Students can present their results on a poster or with a model.

Going Further

A typical use of calorimetry is to figure out how much energy is transferred in a chemical reaction. When acids and bases react with each other, there is less chemical potential energy in the products than in the reacting acid and base molecules. Because energy is conserved, energy will be transferred to the reaction's environment.

Water is used in calorimeters because its specific heat capacity is well known. Have students propose a way to use water to calculate the change in chemical potential energy. (Perform the reaction in water. Measure the mass of the water and the temperature increase to calculate the amount of energy transferred to the water.)

Counting Calories

Critical Thinking Worksheet 10
"Try and Try Again"

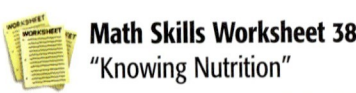
Math Skills Worksheet 38
"Knowing Nutrition"

Build your own calorimeter! Try the lab on page 675 of the LabBook.

Calorimeters When one object transfers thermal energy to another object, the energy lost by one object is gained by the other object. This is the key to how a *calorimeter* (KAL uh RIM uh ter) works. Inside a calorimeter, shown in **Figure 14,** thermal energy is transferred from a known mass of a test substance to a known mass of another substance, usually water.

Using a Calorimeter If a hot test substance is placed inside the calorimeter's inner container of water, the substance transfers energy to the water until thermal equilibrium is reached. By measuring the temperature change of the water and using water's specific heat capacity, you can determine the exact amount of energy transferred by the test substance to the water. You can then use this amount of energy (heat), the change in the test substance's temperature, and the mass of the test substance to calculate that substance's specific heat capacity.

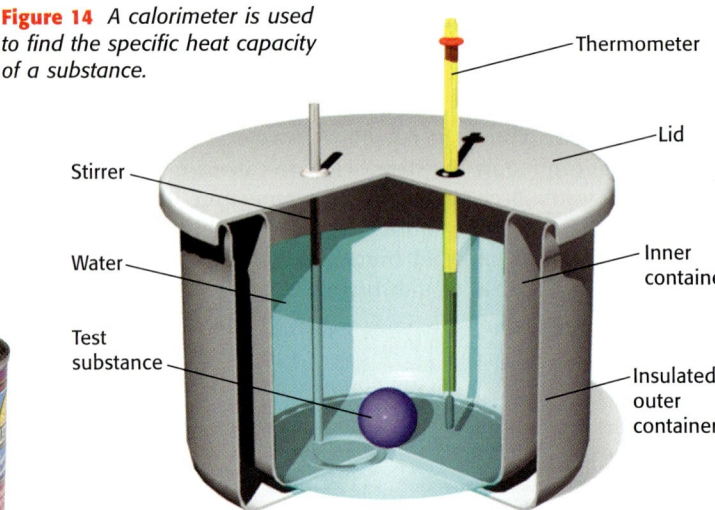
Figure 14 A calorimeter is used to find the specific heat capacity of a substance.

Figure 15 A serving of this fruit contains 120 Cal (502,080 J) of energy that becomes available when it is eaten and digested.

Calories and Kilocalories Heat can also be expressed in units called calories. A *calorie (cal)* is the amount of energy needed to change the temperature of 0.001 kg of water by 1°C. Therefore, 1,000 calories are required to change the temperature of 1 kg of water by 1°C. One calorie is equivalent to 4.184 J. Another unit used to express heat is the *kilocalorie (kcal)*, which is equivalent to 1,000 calories. The kilocalorie is also known as a *Calorie* (with a capital C). These are the Calories listed on food labels, such as the label shown in **Figure 15.**

Cross-Disciplinary Focus

Health Have students examine the nutrition information labels from several packages of prepared foods or snacks to determine the number of kilocalories (Calories, with a capital C) contained in one serving. One Calorie is 1,000 calories. One calorie (lowercase c) can also be defined as the amount of energy needed to change the temperature of 1 g of water by 1°C. Then have students calculate the joules of energy that would be transferred to their body by eating one serving of each of the foods.

The Differences Between Temperature, Thermal Energy, and Heat

So far in this chapter, you have been learning about some concepts that are closely related: temperature, heat, and thermal energy. But the differences between these concepts are very important.

Temperature Versus Thermal Energy Temperature is a measure of the average kinetic energy of an object's particles, and thermal energy is the total energy of an object's particles. While thermal energy varies with the mass of an object, temperature does not. A drop of boiling water has the same temperature as a pot of boiling water, but the pot has more thermal energy because there are more particles.

Thermal Energy Versus Heat Heat and thermal energy are not the same thing; heat is a transfer of thermal energy. In addition, heat can refer to the amount of energy transferred from one object to another. Objects contain thermal energy, but they do not contain heat. The table below summarizes the differences between temperature, thermal energy, and heat.

Self-Check

How can two substances have the same temperature but different amounts of thermal energy? *(See page 724 to check your answer.)*

Temperature	Thermal energy	Heat
A measure of the average kinetic energy of the particles in a substance	The total energy of the particles in a substance	The transfer of energy between objects that are at different temperatures
Expressed in degrees Fahrenheit, degrees Celsius, or kelvins	Expressed in joules	Amount of energy transferred expressed in joules or calories
Does not vary with the mass of a substance	Varies with the mass and temperature of a substance	Varies with the mass, specific heat capacity, and temperature change of a substance

REVIEW

1. Some objects get hot more quickly than others. Why?
2. How are temperature and heat different?
3. **Applying Concepts** Examine the photo at right. How do you think the specific heat capacities for water and air influence the temperature of a swimming pool and the area around it?

SECTION 3

Focus

Matter and Heat

In this section, students learn how substances change from state to state and how heat affects matter during changes of state. They also learn how heat affects matter during chemical changes.

🔔 Bellringer

Ask students to predict what changes would occur if they added an equal number of ice cubes to a glass of cold water and a glass of warm water. Ask them to explain their answer.

1 Motivate

DEMONSTRATION

On an overhead projector, place a beaker half-full of very hot water. Place a second beaker half-full of very cold water next to the first. Before turning on the projector, ask students to watch the screen. As you drop food coloring into each beaker, have students describe what they see happening in the beaker. Ask them these questions:

From your observations, which beaker contained the hotter water? How did you come to this conclusion? Predict what will happen to the molecules of a liquid if more thermal energy is added.

Teaching Transparency 241
"Models of a Solid, a Liquid, and a Gas"

Teaching Transparency 242
"Changes of State for Water"

260 Chapter 10 • Heat and Heat Technology

SECTION 3

Terms to Learn
states of matter
change of state

What You'll Do
- Identify three states of matter.
- Explain how heat affects matter during a change of state.
- Describe how heat affects matter during a chemical change.

Matter and Heat

Have you ever eaten a frozen juice bar outside on a hot summer day? It's pretty hard to finish the entire thing before it starts to drip and make a big mess! The juice bar melts because the sun radiates energy to the air, which transfers energy to the frozen juice bar. The energy absorbed by the juice bar increases the kinetic energy of the molecules in the juice bar, which starts to turn to a liquid. In this section, you'll learn more about how heat affects matter.

States of Matter

The matter that makes up a frozen juice bar has the same identity whether the juice bar is frozen or has melted. The matter is just in a different form, or state. The **states of matter** are the physical forms in which a substance can exist. Recall that matter consists of particles—atoms or molecules—that can move around at different speeds. The state a substance is in depends on the speed of its particles and the attraction between them. Three familiar states of matter are solid, liquid, and gas, represented in **Figure 16.** You may recall that thermal energy is the total energy of the particles that make up a substance. Suppose you have equal masses of a substance in its three states, each at a different temperature. The substance will have the most thermal energy as a gas and the least thermal energy as a solid. That's because the particles move around fastest in a gas.

Figure 16 Models of a Solid, a Liquid, and a Gas

Particles of a solid do not move fast enough to overcome the strong attraction between them, so they are held tightly together. The particles vibrate in place.

Particles of a liquid move fast enough to overcome some of the attraction between them. The particles are able to slide past one another.

Particles of a gas move fast enough to overcome nearly all of the attraction between them. The particles move independently of one another.

260

 Directed Reading Worksheet 10 Section 3

CONNECT TO
LIFE SCIENCE

Life on Earth would end if there were no water. Water occurs in three states—solid, liquid, and gas—and all three are critical to survival. Even though water vapor (a gas) is invisible, it is just as important as the water we can see.

Changes of State

When you melt cheese to make a cheese dip, like that shown in **Figure 17,** the cheese changes from a solid to a thick, gooey liquid. A **change of state** is the conversion of a substance from one physical form to another. A change of state is a *physical change* that affects one or more physical properties of a substance without changing the substance's identity. Changes of state include *freezing* (liquid to solid), *melting* (solid to liquid), *boiling* (liquid to gas), and *condensing* (gas to liquid).

Graphing Changes of State Suppose you put an ice cube in a pan and set the pan on a stove burner. Soon the ice will turn to water and then to steam. If you made a graph of the energy involved versus the temperature of the ice during this process, it would look something like the graph below.

As the ice is heated, its temperature increases from −25°C to 0°C. At 0°C, the ice begins to melt. Notice that the temperature of the ice remains 0°C even as more energy is added. This added energy changes the arrangement of the particles, or molecules, in the ice. The temperature of the ice remains constant until all of the ice has become liquid water. At that point, the water's temperature will start to increase from 0°C to 100°C. At 100°C, the water will begin to turn into steam. Even as more energy is added, the water's temperature stays at 100°C. The energy added at the boiling point changes the arrangement of the particles until the water has entirely changed to a gaseous state. When all of the water has become steam, the temperature again increases.

Figure 17 When you melt cheese, you change the state of the cheese but not its identity.

Self-Check

Why do you think you can get a more severe burn from steam than from boiling water? *(See page 724 to check your answer.)*

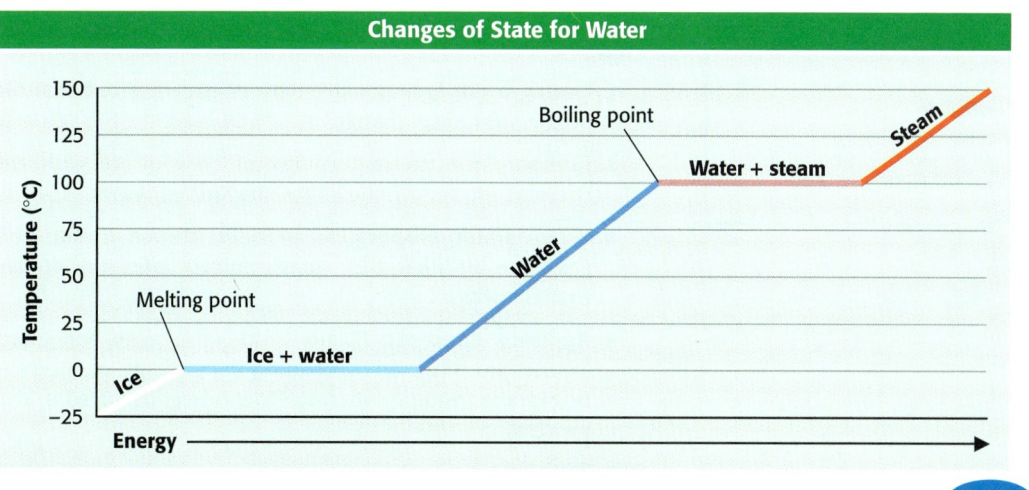

Changes of State for Water

MISCONCEPTION ALERT

The graph at the bottom of the page is not drawn to scale. The slope of the portions where temperature is increasing represents specific heat capacity. If the graph were drawn to scale, the slopes where ice and steam are increasing in temperature would be twice as steep as the slope where water is increasing in temperature. That's because water's specific heat capacity is roughly twice that of ice or steam. In addition, more energy is required for water to vaporize than for ice to melt. If the graph were drawn to scale, the length of the horizontal segment representing ice melting would be shorter than that for water vaporizing.

3) Extend

RESEARCH

 Writing Ask students to find out about French chemist Pierre E. M. Berthelot (1827–1907). Have them find out what contributions he made to the study of chemical changes. **(He synthesized many organic compounds, including alcohols, methane, benzene, and acetylene.)**

Students can display their results in a concept map, on a poster, or by writing a poem or skit.

4) Close

Quiz

Ask students whether these statements are true or false.

1. When ice changes to a liquid, it absorbs energy. **(true)**
2. When a liquid evaporates, it absorbs energy. **(true)**
3. When a vapor condenses to a liquid, energy is given off. **(true)**
4. When a liquid boils, energy is absorbed. **(true)**

ALTERNATIVE ASSESSMENT

Concept Mapping Have students make a concept map showing how heat affects matter during a change of state and during a chemical change.

TOPIC: Changes of State
GO TO: www.scilinks.org
KEYWORD: HSTP250

The substances your body needs to survive and grow come from food. Carbohydrates, proteins, and fats are major sources of energy for the body. The energy content of food can be found by burning a dry food sample in a special calorimeter. Both carbohydrates and proteins provide 4 Cal of energy per gram, while fats provide 9 Cal of energy per gram.

Figure 18 *In a natural-gas fireplace, the methane in natural gas and the oxygen in air change into carbon dioxide and water. As a result of the change, energy is given off, making a room feel warmer.*

TOPIC: Changes of State
GO TO: www.scilinks.org
sciLINKS NUMBER: HSTP250

Heat and Chemical Changes

Heat is involved not only in changes of state, which are physical changes, but also in *chemical changes*—changes that occur when one or more substances are changed into entirely new substances with different properties. During a chemical change, new substances are formed. For a new substance to form, old bonds between particles must be broken and new bonds must be created. The breaking and creating of bonds between particles involves energy. Sometimes a chemical change requires that thermal energy be absorbed. For example, photosynthesis is a chemical change in which carbon dioxide and water combine to form sugar and oxygen. In order for this change to occur, energy must be absorbed. That energy is radiated by the sun. Other times, a chemical change, such as the one shown in **Figure 18,** will result in energy being released.

REVIEW

1. During a change of state, why doesn't the temperature of the substance change?
2. Compare the thermal energy of 10 g of ice with the thermal energy of the same amount of water.
3. When water evaporates (changes from a liquid to a gas), the air near the water's surface becomes cooler. Explain why.
4. **Applying Concepts** Many cold packs used for sports injuries are activated by bending the package, causing the substances inside to interact. How is heat involved in this process?

▼ Answers to Review

1. Energy added to or removed from a substance during a change of state rearranges the particles of the substance rather than raising or lowering the temperature.
2. Particles of water in the liquid state have more kinetic energy than particles of water in the solid state, so 10 mL of water has more thermal energy than 10 g of ice (if the water and ice are not at the same temperature).
3. Sample answer: For water to evaporate, it must absorb energy. The air near the water's surface transfers energy to the water to make it evaporate. Because the air loses energy, it becomes cooler.
4. Sample answer: When you bend the ice pack, the substances inside interact. That interaction absorbs so much energy that the pack feels colder.

Section 4

Terms to Learn
insulation
heat engine
thermal pollution

What You'll Do
- Analyze several kinds of heating systems.
- Describe how a heat engine works.
- Explain how a refrigerator keeps food cold.
- Give examples of some effects of heat technology on the environment.

Heat Technology

You probably wouldn't be surprised to learn that the heater in your home is an example of heat technology. But did you know that automobiles, refrigerators, and air conditioners are also examples of heat technology? It's true! You can travel long distances, you can keep your food cold, and you can feel comfortable indoors during the summer—all because of heat technology.

Heating Systems

Many homes and buildings have a central heating system that controls the temperature in every room. On the next few pages, you will see some different central heating systems.

Hot-Water Heating The high specific heat capacity of water makes it useful for heating systems. In a hot-water heating system, shown in **Figure 19,** water is heated by burning fuel (usually natural gas or fuel oil) in a hot-water heater. The hot water is pumped through pipes that lead to radiators in each room. The hot water heats the radiators, and the radiators then heat the colder air surrounding them. The water returns to the hot-water heater to be heated again. A *steam-heating system* is similar, except that steam is used in place of water.

Figure 19
A Hot-Water Heating System

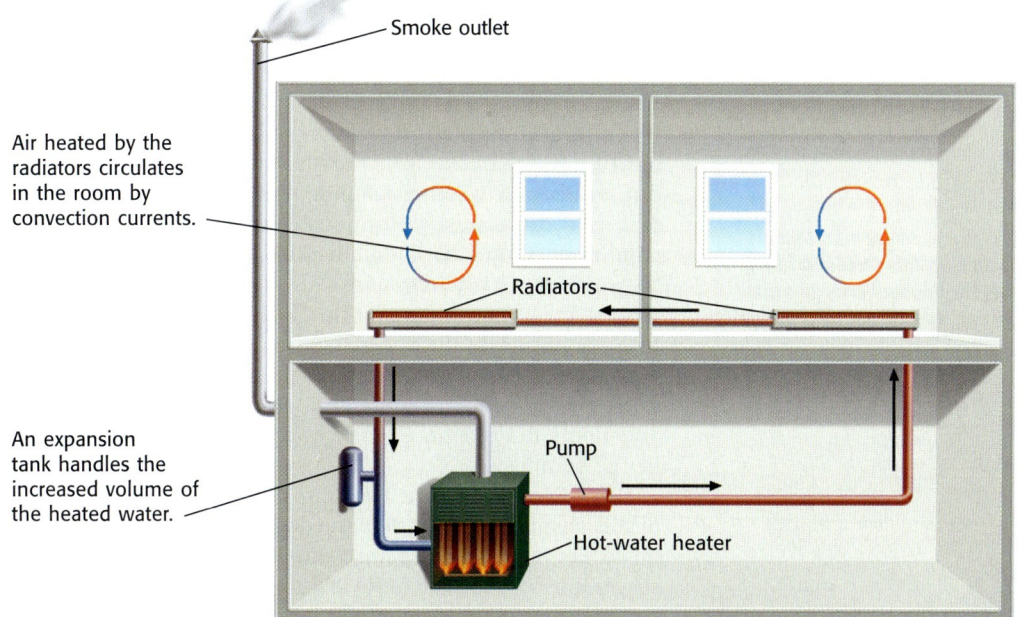

- Smoke outlet
- Air heated by the radiators circulates in the room by convection currents.
- Radiators
- An expansion tank handles the increased volume of the heated water.
- Pump
- Hot-water heater

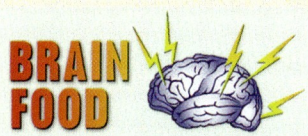

An advantage to using steam instead of water is that steam has a higher temperature than hot water. However, it is more difficult to regulate room temperature with a steam-heating system than with a hot-water heating system.

CROSS-DISCIPLINARY FOCUS

History The first heating systems developed by people were probably open fires in caves. When people found a way to make a hole in the side or top of the cave to let the smoke out, a type of fireplace was created. Fireplaces with a chimney tall enough to provide adequate draft for fires were first built in the twelfth century.

SECTION 4

Focus
Heat Technology
In this section, students learn about different kinds of heating systems, heat engines, and cooling systems. They also learn about some effects of heat on the environment.

Bellringer
Write the following on the board:

Predict whether leaving the refrigerator door open on a hot summer day will help to cool the kitchen. Explain your answer.

Have students write their responses in their ScienceLog. Review these predictions after students have read pages 267 and 268.

1) Motivate

DISCUSSION
Have students work together to hypothesize about how a refrigerator or an air conditioner works and how heat is involved in an appliance that cools. Have the groups share their hypotheses with the class. Discuss with students some ways people may have cooled their homes before air conditioners were invented, and have them imagine what their lives would be like today without heating or air conditioning.

Directed Reading Worksheet 10 Section 4

Section 4 • Heat Technology

2) Teach

READING STRATEGY

Prediction Before students read this section, have them predict the answers to the following questions about heating and cooling systems:

- Where should a heat register or heating vent be placed for maximum effect? (on the floor)
- Where should the cold-air return be placed? (on the floor)
- If you were cooling a house with central air conditioning, where would you place the cold-air register? (on the ceiling) the warm-air return? (on the ceiling)

Students often believe that blankets provide thermal energy. Explain that blankets insulate the body; the air pockets in the blanket material slow the escape of thermal energy from the body into the air, and the feeling of warmth results. Electric blankets are an exception.

Homework

Have students investigate the type of heating and cooling systems used in their home. Ask them to draw a diagram of their home showing the placement of the equipment (fireplaces, registers, cold-air intakes, hot-water pipes, radiators, and so on) used to keep their home warm or cool.

Warm-Air Heating Although air has a lower specific heat capacity than water, warm-air heating systems are used in many homes and offices in the United States. In a warm-air heating system, shown in **Figure 20,** air is heated in a separate chamber by burning fuel (usually natural gas) in a furnace. The warm air travels through ducts to different rooms, which it enters through vents. The warm air heats air in the rooms. Cooler air sinks below the warm air and enters a vent near the floor. Then a fan forces the cooler air into the furnace, where the air will be heated and returned to the ducts. An air filter cleans the air as it circulates through the system.

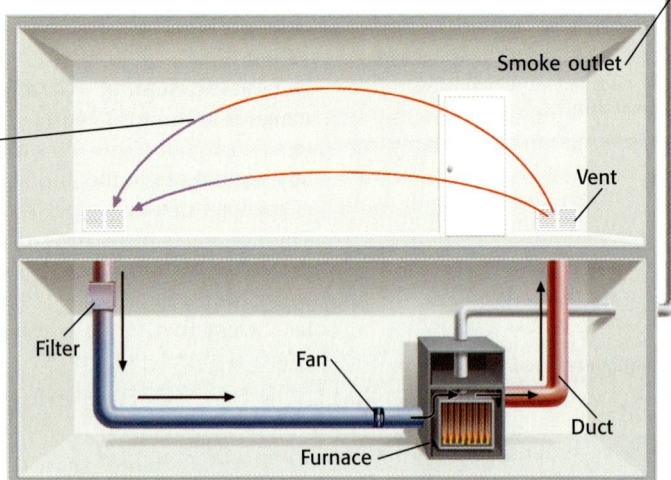

Figure 20
A Warm-Air Heating System

Heating and Insulation Thermal energy may be transferred out of a house during cold weather and into a house during hot weather. To keep the house comfortable, a heating system must run almost continuously during the winter, and air conditioners often do the same during the summer. This can be wasteful. That's where insulation comes in. **Insulation** is a substance that reduces the transfer of thermal energy. Insulation, such as the fiberglass insulation shown in **Figure 21,** is made of insulators—materials that do not conduct thermal energy very well. Insulation that is used in walls, ceilings, and floors helps a house stay warm in the winter and cool in the summer.

Do you remember the Earthships described at the beginning of this chapter? The tightly packed aluminum cans in the walls of an Earthship have spaces between them. Air filling these spaces insulates the Earthship. These homes also rely on a solar heating system, which you will learn about on the next page.

Figure 21 Millions of tiny air pockets in this insulation help prevent thermal energy from flowing into or out of a building.

Solar Heating The sun radiates an enormous amount of energy. Solar heating systems use this energy to heat houses and buildings. *Passive solar heating* systems do not have moving parts. They rely on a building's structural design and materials to use energy from the sun as a means of heating. *Active solar heating* systems do have moving parts. They use pumps and fans to distribute the sun's energy throughout a building.

Look at the house in **Figure 22.** The large windows on the south side of the house are part of the passive solar heating system. These windows receive maximum sunlight, and energy is radiated through the windows into the rooms. Thick, well-insulated concrete walls absorb energy and heat the house at night or when it is cloudy. In the active solar heating system, water is pumped to the solar collector, where it is heated. The hot water is pumped through pipes and transfers its energy to them. A fan blowing over the pipes helps the pipes transfer their thermal energy to the air. Warm air is then sent into rooms through vents. Cooler water returns to the water storage tank to be pumped back through the solar collector.

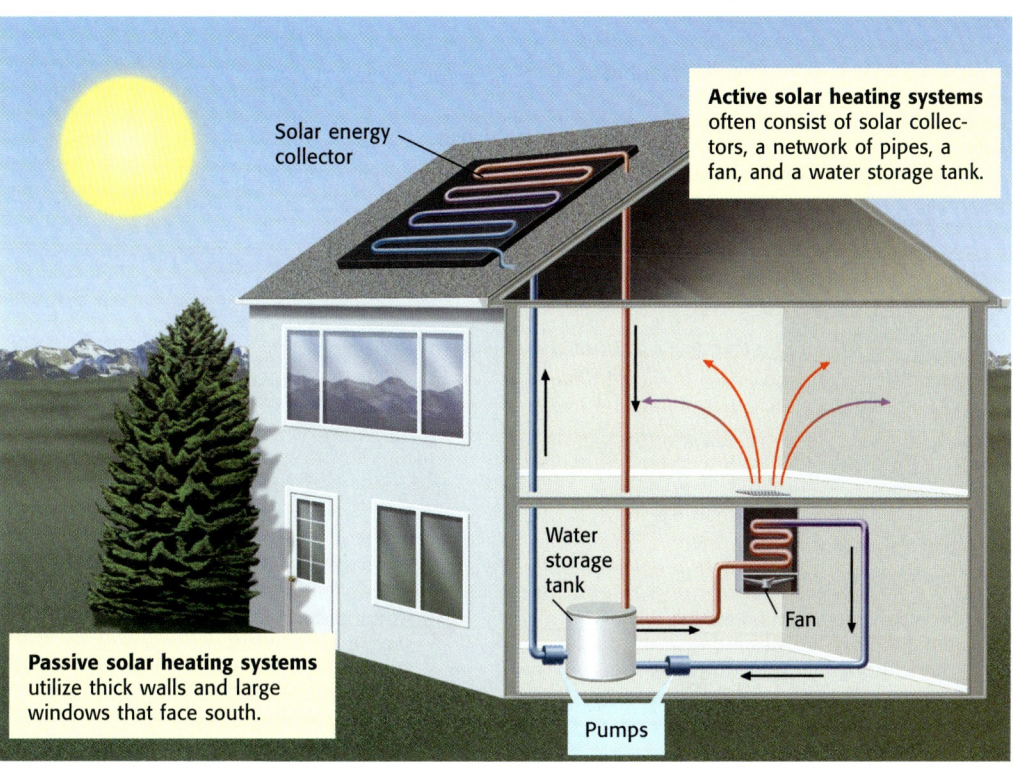

Figure 22 *Passive and active solar heating systems work together to use the sun's energy to heat an entire house.*

USING THE FIGURE
Draw students' attention to **Figure 22.** Ask which parts of the house are part of the passive solar heating system and which are part of the active solar heating system. (passive: large, south-facing windows and thick walls; active: solar collectors, network of pipes, fan, and water-storage tank)

GROUP ACTIVITY
Provide groups with shoe boxes painted flat black inside and out, jars or cans painted white and black, water, thermometers, and tubing. Challenge students to construct a model of a solar heating system.

MEETING INDIVIDUAL NEEDS
Learners Having Difficulty
Help students draw diagrams of the heating systems shown in **Figures 19, 20,** and **22.** Have them use red arrows to indicate the flow of hot air and blue arrows to indicate the flow of cold air. Sheltered English

Teaching Transparency 243
"Solar Heating Systems"

IS THAT A FACT!
Earth receives enough energy from the sun in 1 minute to meet the planet's energy demands for an entire year. If humans could find better ways to capture and use solar energy, dependence on fossil fuels for energy sources could be reduced.

2) Teach, continued

CROSS-DISCIPLINARY FOCUS

History In 1769, Nicolas-Joseph Cugnot (1725–1804), a French Army engineer, built a three-wheeled, steam-powered tractor. It traveled very slowly (3.6 km/h) and had to stop every 20 minutes to build up a fresh head of steam. Cugnot's tractor was hard to drive and not very practical, but his ideas led others to create better self-propelled vehicles.

USING THE FIGURE

Concept Mapping Ask students to study **Figures 23** and **24.** Have them create a concept map that shows the similarities and differences between an external combustion engine and an internal combustion engine. The concept map should show the source of the energy, what the energy does, where the combustion takes place, and any other features of the two types of engines.

Ask students which type of engine is more efficient and why.

Oceanography CONNECTION

Ocean engineers are developing a new technology known as Ocean Thermal Energy Conversion, or OTEC. OTEC uses temperature differences between surface water and deep water in the ocean to do work like a heat engine does. Warm surface water vaporizes a fluid, such as ammonia, causing it to expand. Then cool water from ocean depths causes the fluid to condense and contract. The continuous cycle of vaporizing and condensing converts thermal energy into kinetic energy that can be used to generate electrical energy.

Heat Engines

Did you know that automobiles work because of heat? A car has a **heat engine,** a machine that uses heat to do work. In a heat engine, fuel combines with oxygen in a chemical change that produces thermal energy. This process, called *combustion,* is how engines burn fuel. Heat engines that burn fuel outside the engine are called *external combustion engines.* Heat engines that burn fuel inside the engine are called *internal combustion engines.* In both types of engines, fuel is burned to produce thermal energy that can be used to do work.

External Combustion Engine A simple steam engine, shown in **Figure 23,** is an example of an external combustion engine. Coal is burned to heat water in a boiler and change the water to steam. When water changes to steam, it expands. The expanding steam is used to drive a piston, which can be attached to other mechanisms that do work, such as a flywheel. Modern steam engines, such as those used to generate electrical energy at a power plant, drive turbines instead of pistons.

Figure 23 An External Combustion Engine

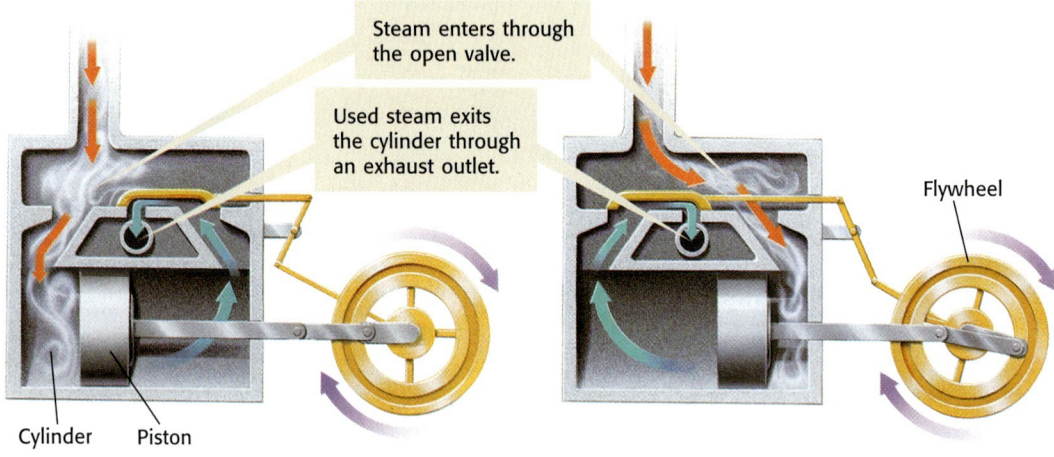

a The expanding steam enters the cylinder from one side. The steam does work on the piston, forcing the piston to move.

b As the piston moves to the other side, a second valve opens and steam enters. The steam does work on the piston and moves it back. The motion of the piston turns a flywheel.

Science Bloopers

When automobiles were first built, they shared the roads with horses. Horses were often quite frightened by the cars. Uriah Smith, founder of a "horseless carriage" company in Michigan, came up with a solution to this problem: He made an automobile with a wooden, life-size horse head on the front. Unfortunately, this did nothing to quiet the noise of the engine, and horses were still frightened by cars.

Internal Combustion Engine In the six-cylinder car engine shown in **Figure 24,** fuel is burned inside the engine. During the intake stroke, a mixture of gasoline and air enters each cylinder as the piston moves down. Next the crankshaft turns and pushes the piston up, compressing the fuel mixture. This is called the compression stroke. Next comes the power stroke, in which the spark plug uses electrical energy to ignite the compressed fuel mixture, causing the mixture to expand and force the piston down. Finally, during the exhaust stroke, the crankshaft turns and the piston is forced back up, pushing exhaust gases out of the cylinder.

Figure 24 *The continuous cycling of the four strokes in the cylinders converts thermal energy into the kinetic energy required to make a car move.*

Cooling Systems

When it gets hot in the summer, an air-conditioned room can feel very refreshing. Cooling systems are used to transfer thermal energy out of a particular area so that it feels cooler. An air conditioner, shown in **Figure 25,** is a cooling system that transfers thermal energy from a warm area inside a building or car to an area outside, where it is often even warmer. But wait a minute—doesn't that go against the natural direction of heat—from higher temperatures to lower temperatures? Well, yes. A cooling system moves thermal energy from cooler temperatures to warmer temperatures. But in order to do that, the cooling system must do work.

Figure 25 *This air conditioning unit keeps a building cool by moving thermal energy from inside the building to the outside.*

IS THAT A FACT!

A heat pump is a "refrigerator" that can be run in two directions. When a heat pump is used for cooling, energy is extracted from the air in the house and is pumped outside. When a heat pump is used for heating, energy is taken from the air outside and is pumped inside.

MEETING INDIVIDUAL NEEDS

Advanced Learners Encourage interested students to research different types of heat engines, such as external and internal heat engines, the Carnot engine, and Hero's engine. Encourage them to include information on the laws of thermodynamics, perpetual motion machines, and entropy and chaos.

REAL-WORLD CONNECTION

Swamp coolers, or evaporative cooling systems, are used in areas of hot, dry weather, such as the southwestern United States. Swamp coolers work in a manner similar to the way evaporating sweat cools the body. A swamp cooler consists of a simple fan that draws in hot, dry outside air and passes it through wet filters. The evaporation process lowers the temperature of the indoor air, which the fan then distributes throughout the building.

USING THE FIGURE

Have students draw a series of cylinders similar to the ones in **Figure 24,** showing the four-stroke process. The strokes should be labeled to indicate the intake stroke, compression stroke, power stroke, and exhaust stroke. Ask students to then write a brief description of the processes that are occurring during each stroke. Use Teaching Transparency 237 to help students understand how each of the four strokes helps convert thermal energy into kinetic energy.

Teaching Transparency 237
"Energy Conversions in a Car Engine"

Section 4 • Heat Technology   **267**

3) Extend

USING THE FIGURE

After students have studied **Figure 26,** discuss with them how refrigeration has affected food storage and the kinds of foods we eat. What did refrigeration allow that had never been possible before?

GOING FURTHER

Have interested students investigate the controversy about the effect of Freon™ on the environment. Students should also research the alternatives to Freon. Explain that Freon used to be a commonly used refrigerant in the United States.

CROSS-DISCIPLINARY FOCUS

History The air conditioning systems we use today evolved from commercial refrigeration systems. In 1902, a young engineer named Willis Carrier helped a printing company that was having a problem with its color printing. Humidity caused the paper to expand or shrink. The colored inks would not align correctly, which caused fuzzy pictures. Carrier intended to control humidity with his device. To his surprise, the air was not only drier but also cooler. Carrier patented his machine in 1906 and made his first international sale to a silk mill in Japan in 1907. In this country, textile mills in the southern states were among the first to use Carrier's machines. The Carrier Corporation still manufactures air conditioners for homes and businesses today.

BRAIN FOOD

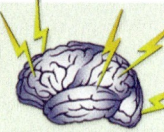

If you had a refrigerator in Antarctica, you would have to heat it to keep it running. Otherwise, the refrigerator would transfer energy to its surroundings until it reached the same temperature as its surroundings. It would freeze!

Cooling Takes Energy Most cooling systems require electrical energy to do the work of cooling. The electrical energy is used by a device called a compressor. The compressor does the work of compressing the refrigerant, a gas that has a boiling point below room temperature. This property of the refrigerant allows it to condense easily.

To keep many foods fresh, you store them in a refrigerator. A refrigerator is another example of a cooling system. **Figure 26** shows how a refrigerator continuously transfers thermal energy from inside the refrigerator to the condenser coils on the outside of the refrigerator. That's why the area near the back of a refrigerator feels warm.

Figure 26 How a Refrigerator Works

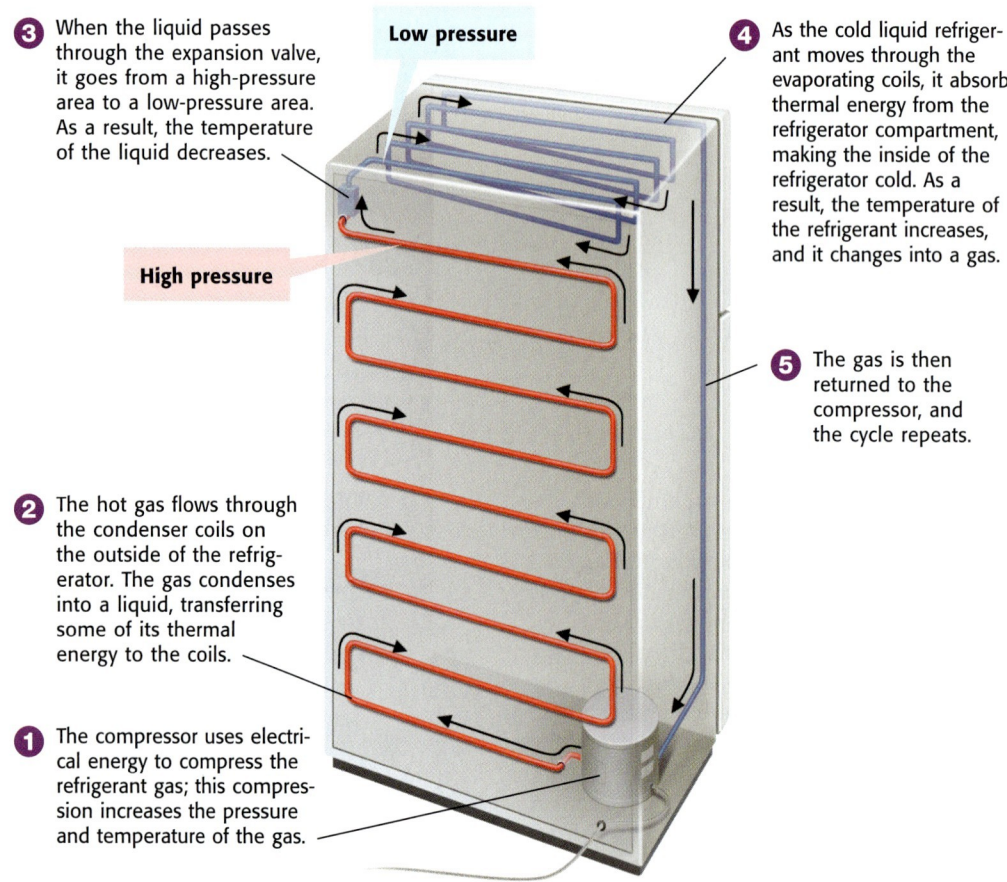

① The compressor uses electrical energy to compress the refrigerant gas; this compression increases the pressure and temperature of the gas.

② The hot gas flows through the condenser coils on the outside of the refrigerator. The gas condenses into a liquid, transferring some of its thermal energy to the coils.

③ When the liquid passes through the expansion valve, it goes from a high-pressure area to a low-pressure area. As a result, the temperature of the liquid decreases.

④ As the cold liquid refrigerant moves through the evaporating coils, it absorbs thermal energy from the refrigerator compartment, making the inside of the refrigerator cold. As a result, the temperature of the refrigerant increases, and it changes into a gas.

⑤ The gas is then returned to the compressor, and the cycle repeats.

IS THAT A FACT!

A German scientist named Karl von Linde (1842–1934) made the first practical refrigerator, which used ammonia as the refrigerant.

Heat Technology and Thermal Pollution

Heating systems, car engines, and cooling systems all transfer thermal energy to the environment. Unfortunately, too much thermal energy can have a negative effect on the environment.

One of the negative effects of excess thermal energy is **thermal pollution,** the excessive heating of a body of water. Thermal pollution can occur near large power plants, which are often located near a body of water. Electric power plants burn fuel to produce thermal energy that is used to generate electrical energy. Unfortunately, it is not possible for all of that thermal energy to do work, so some waste thermal energy results. **Figure 27** shows how a cooling tower helps remove this waste thermal energy in order to keep the power plants operating smoothly. In extreme cases, the increase in temperature downstream from a power plant can adversely affect the ecosystem of the river or lake. Some power plants reduce thermal pollution by reducing the temperature of the water before it is returned to the river.

Environment CONNECTION

Large cities can exhibit something called a heat island effect when excessive amounts of waste thermal energy are added to the urban environment. This thermal energy comes from automobiles, factories, home heating and cooling, lighting, and even just the number of people living in a relatively small area. The heat island effect can make the temperature of the air in a city higher than that of the air in the surrounding countryside.

Figure 27 Cool water is circulated through a power plant to absorb waste thermal energy.

Cool water   Warm water

REVIEW

1. Compare a hot-water heating system with a warm-air heating system.
2. What is the difference between an external combustion engine and an internal combustion engine?
3. **Analyzing Relationships** How are changes of state an important part of the way a refrigerator works?

TOPIC: Heating Systems
GO TO: www.scilinks.org
*sci*LINKS NUMBER: HSTP252

Chapter Highlights

Vocabulary Definitions

Section 1

temperature a measure of how hot (or cold) something is; specifically, a measure of the average kinetic energy of the particles in an object

thermal expansion the increase in volume of a substance due to an increase in temperature

absolute zero the lowest possible temperature (0 K, –273°C)

Section 2

heat the transfer of energy between objects that are at different temperatures; the amount of energy that is transferred between objects that are at different temperatures; energy is always transferred from higher-temperature objects to lower-temperature objects until thermal equilibrium is reached

thermal energy the total energy of the particles that make up an object

conduction the transfer of thermal energy from one substance to another through direct contact; conduction can also occur within a substance

conductor a substance that conducts thermal energy very well

insulator a substance that does not conduct thermal energy very well

convection the transfer of thermal energy by the movement of a liquid or a gas

radiation the transfer of energy through matter or space as electromagnetic waves, such as visible light and infrared waves

specific heat capacity the amount of energy needed to change the temperature of 1 kg of a substance by 1°C; specific heat capacity is a characteristic property of a substance

Chapter Highlights

SECTION 1

Vocabulary
- temperature (p. 246)
- thermal expansion (p. 248)
- absolute zero (p. 249)

Section Notes
- Temperature is a measure of the average kinetic energy of the particles of a substance. It is a specific measurement of how hot or cold a substance is.
- Thermal expansion is the increase in volume of a substance due to an increase in temperature. Temperature is measured according to the expansion of the liquid in a thermometer.
- Fahrenheit, Celsius, and Kelvin are three temperature scales.
- Absolute zero—0 K, or –273°C— is the lowest possible temperature.
- A thermostat works according to the thermal expansion of a bimetallic strip.

SECTION 2

Vocabulary
- heat (p. 251)
- thermal energy (p. 252)
- conduction (p. 253)
- conductor (p. 254)
- insulator (p. 254)
- convection (p. 254)
- radiation (p. 255)
- specific heat capacity (p. 256)

Section Notes
- Heat is the transfer of energy between objects that are at different temperatures.
- Thermal energy is the total energy of the particles that make up a substance.
- Energy transfer will always occur from higher temperatures to lower temperatures until thermal equilibrium is reached.

✓ Skills Check

Math Concepts

TEMPERATURE CONVERSION To convert between different temperature scales, you can use the equations found on page 249. The example below shows you how to convert a Fahrenheit temperature to a Celsius temperature.

Convert 41°F to °C.

$$°C = \frac{5}{9} \times (°F - 32)$$
$$°C = \frac{5}{9} \times (41°F - 32)$$
$$°C = \frac{5}{9} \times 9 = 5°C$$

Visual Understanding

HEAT—A TRANSFER OF ENERGY Remember that thermal energy is transferred between objects at different temperatures until both objects reach the same temperature. Look back at Figure 7, on page 252, to review what you've learned about heat.

Lab and Activity Highlights

Feel the Heat PG 672

Save the Cube! PG 674

Counting Calories PG 675

 Datasheets for LabBook (blackline masters for these labs)

Chapter 10 • Heat and Heat Technology

VOCABULARY DEFINITIONS, continued

SECTION 3

states of matter the physical forms in which a substance can exist

change of state the conversion of a substance from one physical form to another

SECTION 4

insulation a substance that reduces the transfer of thermal energy

heat engine a machine that uses heat to do work

thermal pollution the excessive heating of a body of water

Vocabulary Review Worksheet 10

Blackline masters of these Chapter Highlights can be found in the **Study Guide**.

SECTION 2

- Conduction, convection, and radiation are three methods of energy transfer.
- Specific heat capacity is the amount of energy needed to change the temperature of 1 kg of a substance by 1°C. Different substances have different specific heat capacities.
- Energy transferred by heat cannot be measured directly. It must be calculated using specific heat capacity, mass, and change in temperature.
- A calorimeter is used to determine the specific heat capacity of a substance.

Labs
Feel the Heat *(p. 672)*
Save the Cube! *(p. 674)*
Counting Calories *(p. 675)*

SECTION 3

Vocabulary
states of matter *(p. 260)*
change of state *(p. 261)*

Section Notes
- A substance's state is determined by the speed of its particles and the attraction between them.
- Thermal energy transferred during a change of state does not change a substance's temperature. Rather, it causes a substance's particles to be rearranged.
- Chemical changes can cause thermal energy to be absorbed or released.

SECTION 4

Vocabulary
insulation *(p. 264)*
heat engine *(p. 266)*
thermal pollution *(p. 269)*

Section Notes
- Central heating systems include hot-water heating systems and warm-air heating systems.
- Solar heating systems can be passive or active.
- Heat engines use heat to do work. External combustion engines burn fuel outside the engine. Internal combustion engines burn fuel inside the engine.
- A cooling system transfers thermal energy from cooler temperatures to warmer temperatures by doing work.
- Transferring excess thermal energy to lakes and rivers can result in thermal pollution.

---

internetconnect

GO TO: go.hrw.com

Visit the **HRW** Web site for a variety of learning tools related to this chapter. Just type in the keyword:

KEYWORD: HSTHOT

GO TO: www.scilinks.org

Visit the **National Science Teachers Association** on-line Web site for Internet resources related to this chapter. Just type in the *sci*LINKS number for more information about the topic:

TOPIC: What Is Temperature?	*sci*LINKS NUMBER: HSTP230
TOPIC: What Is Heat?	*sci*LINKS NUMBER: HSTP240
TOPIC: Conduction, Convection, and Radiation	*sci*LINKS NUMBER: HSTP245
TOPIC: Changes of State	*sci*LINKS NUMBER: HSTP250
TOPIC: Heating Systems	*sci*LINKS NUMBER: HSTP252

271

Lab and Activity Highlights

LabBank

Whiz-Bang Demonstrations, Cool It, Demo 52

Labs You Can Eat, Baked Alaska, Lab 22

EcoLabs & Field Activities, Energy-Efficient Home, EcoLab 19

Long-Term Projects & Research Ideas, Firewalking Exposed, Project 60

Chapter 10 • Chapter Highlights   **271**

Chapter Review Answers

USING VOCABULARY

1. Temperature is a direct measure of the average kinetic energy of the particles of a substance; thermal energy is the total kinetic energy of the particles of the substance.
2. Heat is the transfer of energy between objects at different temperatures. Thermal energy is energy transferred by heat.
3. A conductor is a material that conducts energy easily. An insulator is a material that does not conduct energy easily.
4. Conduction is the transfer of energy from one substance to another through direct contact. Convection is the transfer of energy by the movement of a gas or a liquid.
5. The states of matter are the physical forms in which a substance can exist. A change of state occurs when a substance changes from one state to another.

UNDERSTANDING CONCEPTS

Multiple Choice

6. c   10. d
7. b   11. a
8. b   12. b
9. c

Short Answer

13. Temperature is a direct measure of the average kinetic energy of the particles in a substance. The more kinetic energy the particles have, the higher the temperature of the substance.
14. Specific heat capacity is the amount of energy needed to change the temperature of 1 kg of a substance by 1°C. Specific heat capacity determines the rate at which a substance changes temperature. Every substance has a unique specific heat capacity.

Chapter Review

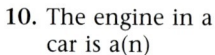

USING VOCABULARY

For each pair of terms, explain the difference in their meanings.

1. temperature/thermal energy
2. heat/thermal energy
3. conductor/insulator
4. conduction/convection
5. states of matter/change of state

UNDERSTANDING CONCEPTS

Multiple Choice

6. Which of the following temperatures is the lowest?
   a. 100°C   c. 100 K
   b. 100°F   d. They are the same.

7. Compared with the Pacific Ocean, a cup of hot chocolate has
   a. more thermal energy and a higher temperature.
   b. less thermal energy and a higher temperature.
   c. more thermal energy and a lower temperature.
   d. less thermal energy and a lower temperature.

8. The energy units on a food label are
   a. degrees.   c. calories.
   b. Calories.   d. joules.

9. Which of the following materials would not be a good insulator?
   a. wood   c. metal
   b. cloth   d. rubber

10. The engine in a car is a(n)
    a. heat engine.
    b. external combustion engine.
    c. internal combustion engine.
    d. Both (a) and (c)

11. Materials that warm up or cool down very quickly have a
    a. low specific heat capacity.
    b. high specific heat capacity.
    c. low temperature.
    d. high temperature.

12. In an air conditioner, thermal energy is
    a. transferred from higher to lower temperatures.
    b. transferred from lower to higher temperatures.
    c. used to do work.
    d. taken from air outside a building and transferred to air inside the building.

Short Answer

13. How does temperature relate to kinetic energy?
14. What is specific heat capacity?
15. Explain how heat affects matter during a change of state.
16. Describe how a bimetallic strip works in a thermostat.

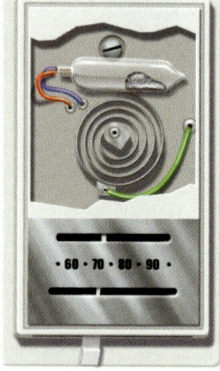

15. During a change of state, the thermal energy transferred to or from the matter is used to rearrange the particles of the matter. This rearranging involves overcoming the attraction between particles (as when a solid changes to a liquid) or increasing the attraction between particles (as when a liquid changes to a solid).

16. A bimetallic strip is made of two metals that expand and contract at different rates with changes in temperature. If the temperature drops below the thermostat setting, the strip coils up. This causes a glass tube to tilt, and a drop of mercury rolls down the tube to close an electric circuit that turns on the heater. When the temperature rises, the process is reversed.

272   Chapter 10 • Heat and Heat Technology

Concept Mapping

17. Use the following terms to create a concept map: thermal energy, temperature, radiation, heat, conduction, convection.

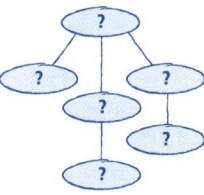

CRITICAL THINKING AND PROBLEM SOLVING

18. Why does placing a jar under warm running water help loosen the lid on the jar?

19. Why do you think a down-filled jacket keeps you so warm? (Hint: Think about what insulation does.)

20. Would opening the refrigerator cool a room in a house? Why or why not?

21. In a hot-air balloon, air is heated by a flame. Explain how this enables the balloon to float in the air.

MATH IN SCIENCE

22. The weather forecast calls for a temperature of 86°F. What is the corresponding temperature in degrees Celsius? in kelvins?

23. Suppose 1,300 mL of water are heated from 20°C to 100°C. How much energy was transferred to the water? (Hint: Water's specific heat capacity is 4,184 J/kg•°C.)

INTERPRETING GRAPHICS

Examine the graph below, and then answer the questions that follow.

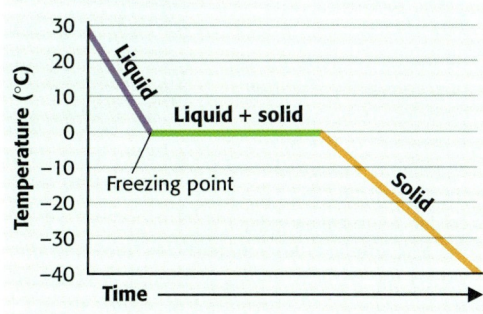

24. What physical change does this graph illustrate?

25. What is the freezing point of this liquid?

26. What is happening at the point where the line is horizontal?

NOW What Do You Think?

Take a minute to review your answers to the ScienceLog questions on page 245. Have your answers changed? If necessary, revise your answers based on what you have learned since you began this chapter.

Concept Mapping

17.  An answer to this exercise can be found at the end of this book.

CRITICAL THINKING AND PROBLEM SOLVING

18. The water warms the lid, causing it to expand so that it can be removed more easily.

19. Inside a down-filled jacket are thousands of air pockets between the feathers. You stay warm because these air pockets slow the transfer of energy from your body to the cooler air outside the jacket.

20. No; a refrigerator transfers thermal energy from its interior into the room. If you open the refrigerator door, its interior warms up, and it has to transfer even more thermal energy away from its interior.

21. Heating the air increases the kinetic energy of the air particles, causing them to move faster and spread apart. As a result, the warmer air rises and the balloon floats.

MATH IN SCIENCE

22. 30°C; 303 K
23. Energy transferred = 4,184 J/kg•°C × 1.3 kg × 80°C = 435,136 J

INTERPRETING GRAPHICS

24. freezing; a change of state from liquid to a solid
25. 0°C
26. a change of state; Energy is being transferred away from the substance and the attraction between particles is increasing.

NOW What Do You Think?

1. Use a thermometer to measure how hot or cold objects are.
2. An object is hot or cold relative to another object. For example, if an object's temperature is higher than your body temperature, energy transfers from the object to your body and the object feels hot. If an object's temperature is lower than your body temperature, energy transfers from your body to the object and the object feels cold.
3. Central heating systems, such as hot-water or warm-air heating systems, use a combination of conduction and convection to heat the air in the house.

Concept Mapping Transparency 10

Blackline masters of this Chapter Review can be found in the **Study Guide**.

SCIENCE, TECHNOLOGY, AND SOCIETY
The Deep Freeze

Background

Scientists know that as gases approach absolute zero, they condense into a state of matter called a Bose-Einstein condensate. This state is named for physicists Satyendra Nath Bose and Albert Einstein. At these very low temperatures, almost all particle motion ceases and the particles overlap one another. In 1999, scientists used a thick Bose-Einstein condensate of sodium atoms to slow the speed of a beam of light to 61 km/h.

Discussion

Why is cryogenics useful to biological researchers? (Scientists can preserve tissues and test the effects of extremely low temperatures on living tissue.)

Science, Technology, and Society
The Deep Freeze

In the dark reaches of outer space, temperatures can drop below −270°C. Perhaps the only place colder is a laboratory here on Earth!

The Quest for Zero

All matter is made up of tiny, constantly vibrating particles. Temperature is a measure of the average kinetic energy of these particles. The colder a substance gets, the less kinetic energy its particles have and the slower the particles move. In theory, at absolute zero (−273°C), all movement of matter should stop. Scientists are working in laboratories to slow down matter so much that the temperature approaches absolute zero.

How Low Can They Go?

Using lasers, along with magnets, mirrors, and supercold chemicals, scientists have cooled matter to within a few billionths of a degree of absolute zero. In one method, scientists aim lasers at tiny gas particles inside a special chamber. The lasers hold the particles so still that their temperature approaches −272.999998°C.

To get an idea of what takes place, imagine turning on several garden hoses as high as they can go. Then direct the streams of water at a soccer ball so that each stream pushes the ball from a different angle. If the hoses are aimed properly, the ball won't roll in any direction. That's similar to what happens to the particles in the scientists' experiment.

▲ *This laser device is used to cool matter to nearly absolute zero.*

Cryogenics—Cold Temperature Technology

Supercold temperatures have led to some super-cool technology. Cryosurgery, which is surgery that uses extremely low temperatures, allows doctors to seal off tiny blood vessels during an operation or to freeze diseased cells and destroy them.

Cooling materials to near absolute zero has also led to the discovery of superconductors. Superconductors are materials that lose all of their electrical resistance when they are cooled to a low enough temperature. Imagine the possibilities for materials that could conduct electricity indefinitely without any energy loss. Unfortunately, it takes a great deal of energy to cool such materials. Right now, applications for superconductors are still just the stuff of dreams.

Freezing Fun on Your Own

▶ You can try your hand at cryoinvestigation. Place 50 mL of tap water, 50 mL of salt water (50 mL of water plus 15 g of salt), and 50 mL of rubbing alcohol (isopropanol) in three separate plastic containers. Then put all three containers in your freezer at the same time. Check the containers every 5 minutes for 40 minutes. Which liquid freezes first? How can you explain any differences?

Answers to Freezing Fun on Your Own

The tap water should freeze first. The salt water should freeze second. The alcohol should not freeze at all because alcohol's freezing point (−117.3°C) is below the temperature of the freezer. Different liquids freeze at different temperatures. (Remind students not to ingest these substances.)

EARTH SCIENCE • PHYSICAL SCIENCE

DiAPLEX®: The Intelligent Fabric

Wouldn't it be great if you had a winter coat that could automatically adjust to keep you cozy regardless of the outside temperature? Well, scientists have developed a new fabric, called DiAPLEX, that can be used to make such a coat!

With Pores or Without?

Winter adventurers usually wear nylon fabrics to keep warm. These nylon fabrics are laminated with a thin coating that contains thousands of tiny pores, or openings. The pores allow moisture, such as sweat from your body, and excess thermal energy to escape. You might think the pores would let moisture and cold air into the fabric, but that's not the case. Because the pores are so small, the nylon fabric is windproof and waterproof.

DiAPLEX is also made from laminated nylon, but the coating is different. DiAPLEX doesn't have pores; it is a solid film. This film makes DiAPLEX even more waterproof and breathable than other laminated nylon fabrics. So how does it work?

Moving Particles

DiAPLEX keeps you warm by taking advantage of how particles move. When the air outside is cold, the particles of DiAPLEX arrange themselves into a solid sheet, forming an insulator and preventing the transfer of thermal energy from your body to colder surroundings. As your body gets warm, such as after exercising, the fabric's particles respond to your body's increased thermal energy. Their kinetic energy increases, and they rearrange to create millions of tiny openings that allow excess thermal energy and moisture to escape.

Donning DiAPLEX

DiAPLEX has a number of important advantages over traditional nylon fabrics. Salts in perspiration and ice can clog the pores of traditional nylon fabrics, decreasing their ability to keep you warm and dry. But DiAPLEX does not have this problem because it contains no pores. Because DiAPLEX is unaffected by UV light and is machine washable, it is also a durable fabric that is easy to care for.

Anatomy Connection

▶ Do some research to find out how your skin lets thermal energy and moisture escape.

▶ When your body is cold, the DiAPLEX garment adjusts to prevent the transfer of thermal energy from your body to its surroundings, and you feel warmer.

▶ When your body gets too warm, the DiAPLEX garment adjusts to allow your body to transfer excess thermal energy and moisture to your surroundings, and you feel cooler.

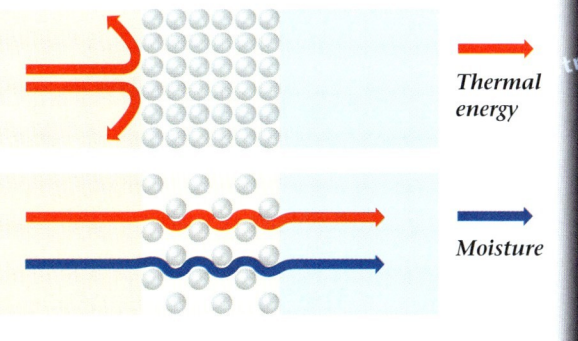

Thermal energy

Moisture

Across the Sciences
DiAPLEX®: The Intelligent Fabric

Background

DiAPLEX™ fabric allows moisture to escape twice as fast as regular microporous fabrics do, and it maintains a constant internal temperature of 0°C. This may sound cold, but at temperatures above 0°C, skiers begin to leave their microporous jackets on the slopes. The jackets don't allow enough body heat to escape, and the skiers start to sweat. People who wear DiAPLEX garments, however, remove layers of clothing far less frequently.

DiAPLEX works on the principles of micro-Brownian motion, the random, zigzag motion of particles in solution. This phenomenon was first observed by the British botanist Robert Brown in 1827.

Students may find DiAPLEX intriguing because the molecules of this solid fabric are capable of moving and reconfiguring, properties usually believed to occur only in liquids and gases. As the temperature rises, the molecules of DiAPLEX become more excited and move more rapidly. Although DiAPLEX is a solid fabric, the temperature range over which its molecules are active is conveniently the temperature range where we change our clothes most often.

Answer to Anatomy Connection

Sweat is one way our bodies remove excess thermal energy. Our skin contains about 100 sweat glands per square centimeter. The evaporation of sweat from the skin's surface removes thermal energy from the body much more efficiently than simply radiating thermal energy from the blood into the air. Without sweat, we would have great difficulty cooling our bodies on a hot day or after exercising. Most sweat is about 99 percent water, mixed with small amounts of salts, acids, and waste products.

UNIT 4

TIMELINE: The Atom

Thousands of years ago, people began asking the question, "What is matter made of?" This unit follows the discoveries and ideas that have led to our current theories about what makes up matter. You will learn about the atom—the building block of all matter—and its structure. You will also learn how the periodic table is used to classify and organize elements according to patterns in atomic structure and other properties. This timeline illustrates some of the events that have brought us to our current understanding of atoms and of the periodic table in which they are organized.

Around 400 B.C.
The Greek philosopher Democritus proposes that small particles called atoms make up all matter.

1911
Ernest Rutherford, a physicist from New Zealand, discovers the positively charged nucleus of the atom.

1932
The neutron, one of the particles in the nucleus of an atom, is discovered by British physicist James Chadwick.

1945
The United Nations is formed. Its purpose is to maintain world peace and develop friendly relations between countries.

1964
Scientists propose the idea that smaller particles make up protons and neutrons. The particles are named quarks after a word used by James Joyce in his book *Finnegans Wake*.

1803
British scientist and school teacher John Dalton reintroduces the concept of atoms with evidence to support his ideas.

1848
James Marshall finds gold while building Sutter's Mill, starting the California gold rush.

1898
British scientists Sir William Ramsay and Morris W. Travers discover three elements—krypton, neon, and xenon—in three months. The periodic table developed by Mendeleev helps guide their research.

1897
British scientist J. J. Thomson identifies electrons as particles that are present in every atom.

1869
Russian chemist Dmitri Mendeleev develops a periodic table that organizes the elements known at the time.

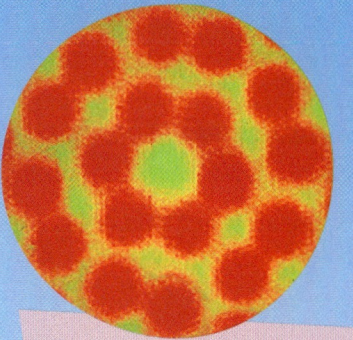

1981
Scientists in Switzerland develop a scanning tunneling microscope, which is used to see atoms for the first time.

1989
Germans celebrate when the Berlin Wall ceases to function as a barrier between East and West Germany.

1996
Another element is added to the periodic table after a team of German scientists synthesize an atom containing 112 protons in its nucleus.

The Atom

Chapter Organizer

CHAPTER ORGANIZATION	TIME MINUTES	OBJECTIVES	LABS, INVESTIGATIONS, AND DEMONSTRATIONS
Chapter Opener pp. 278–279	45	National Standards: UCP 2, SAI 1, HNS 2	**Investigate!** Where Is It? p. 279
Section 1 Development of the Atomic Theory	135	▶ Describe some of the experiments that led to the current atomic theory. ▶ Compare the different models of the atom. ▶ Explain how the atomic theory has changed as scientists have discovered new information about the atom. UCP 1, 2, SAI 2, ST 2, SPSP 5, HNS 1–3	**Whiz-Bang Demonstrations,** As a Matter of Space, Demo 54
Section 2 The Atom	135	▶ Compare the charge, location, and relative mass of protons, neutrons, and electrons. ▶ Calculate the number of particles in an atom using the atomic number, mass number, and overall charge. ▶ Calculate the atomic mass of elements. UCP 1–3, HNS 2; LabBook UCP 1, 2	**Making Models,** Made to Order, p. 676 **Datasheets for LabBook,** Made to Order, Datasheet 37 **Whiz-Bang Demonstrations,** Candy Lights, Demo 53 **Long-Term Projects & Research Ideas,** Project 61

*See page **T20** for a complete correlation of this book with the*

NATIONAL SCIENCE EDUCATION STANDARDS.

TECHNOLOGY RESOURCES

 **Guided Reading Audio CD** English or Spanish, Chapter 11

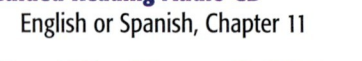 **One-Stop Planner CD-ROM with Test Generator**

 Scientists in Action, Nobel Prize Physicists, Segment 14

Chapter 11 • Introduction to Atoms

Chapter 11 • Introduction to Atoms

CLASSROOM WORKSHEETS, TRANSPARENCIES, AND RESOURCES	SCIENCE INTEGRATION AND CONNECTIONS	REVIEW AND ASSESSMENT
Directed Reading Worksheet 11 **Science Puzzlers, Twisters & Teasers,** Worksheet 11		
Directed Reading Worksheet 11, Section 1 **Transparency 244,** Thomson's Cathode-Ray Tube Experiment **Transparency 107,** Gold Crystal Structure **Transparency 245,** Rutherford's Gold Foil Experiment **Math Skills for Science Worksheet 17,** Using Proportions and Cross-Multiplication	**Cross-Disciplinary Focus,** p. 283 in ATE **Math and More,** p. 284 in ATE **Connect to Earth Science,** p. 284 in ATE **Math and More,** p. 285 in ATE **Real-World Connection,** p. 285 in ATE **Careers:** Experimental Physicist—Melissa Franklin, p. 299	**Review,** p. 283 **Self-Check,** p. 285 **Homework,** p. 285 in ATE **Review,** p. 286 **Quiz,** p. 286 in ATE **Alternative Assessment,** p. 286 in ATE
Directed Reading Worksheet 11, Section 2 **Transparency 246,** Parts of an Atom **Math Skills for Science Worksheet 19,** Arithmetic with Decimals **Transparency 247,** Forces in the Atom **Reinforcement Worksheet 11,** Atomic Timeline **Critical Thinking Worksheet 11,** Incredible Shrinking Scientist!	**Real-World Connection,** p. 288 in ATE **Astronomy Connection,** p. 290 **Connect to Paleontology,** p. 290 in ATE **Apply,** p. 291 **Real-World Connection,** p. 291 in ATE **MathBreak,** Atomic Mass, p. 292 **Math and More,** p. 292 in ATE **Across the Sciences:** Water on the Moon? p. 298	**Review,** p. 289 **Review,** p. 293 **Quiz,** p. 293 in ATE **Alternative Assessment,** p. 293 in ATE

 Holt, Rinehart and Winston On-line Resources
go.hrw.com
For worksheets and other teaching aids related to this chapter, visit the HRW Web site and type in the keyword: **HSTATS**

 **National Science Teachers Association**
www.scilinks.org
Encourage students to use the *sci*LINKS numbers listed in the internet connect boxes to access information and resources on the **NSTA** Web site.

END-OF-CHAPTER REVIEW AND ASSESSMENT

Chapter Review in Study Guide
Vocabulary and Notes in Study Guide
Chapter Tests with Performance-Based Assessment, Chapter 11 Test
Chapter Tests with Performance-Based Assessment, Performance-Based Assessment 11
Concept Mapping Transparency 11

Chapter Resources & Worksheets

Visual Resources

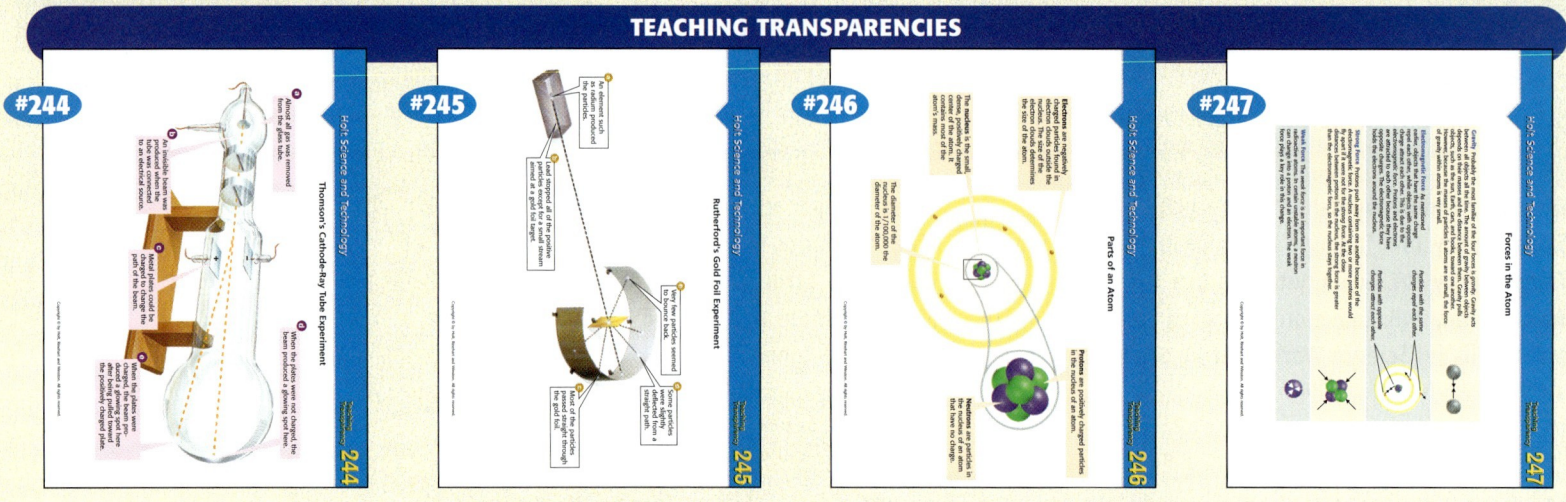

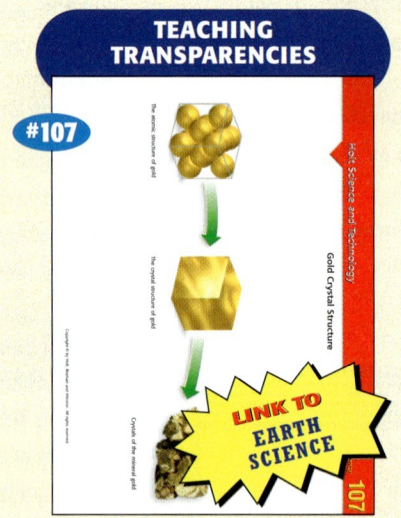

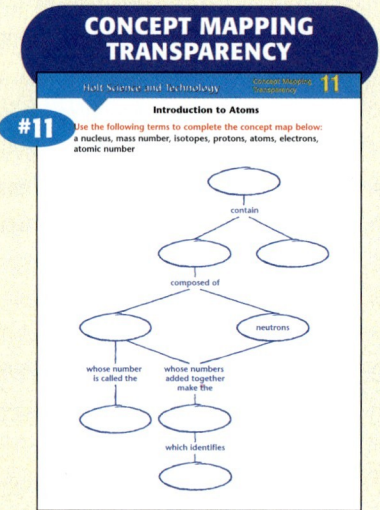

Meeting Individual Needs

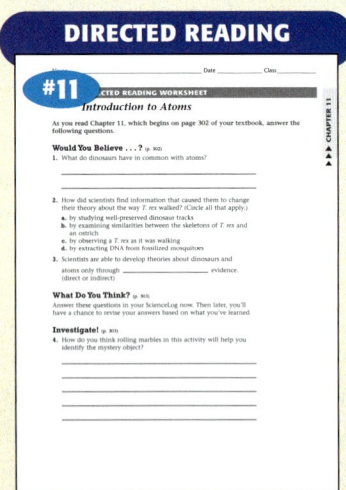

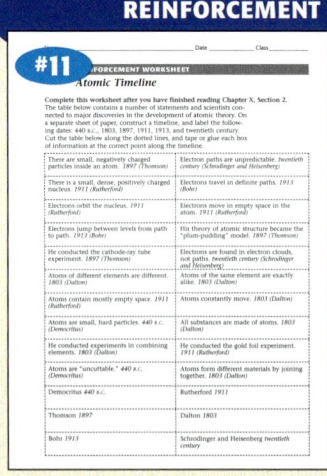

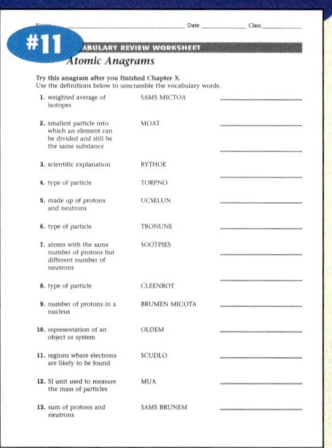

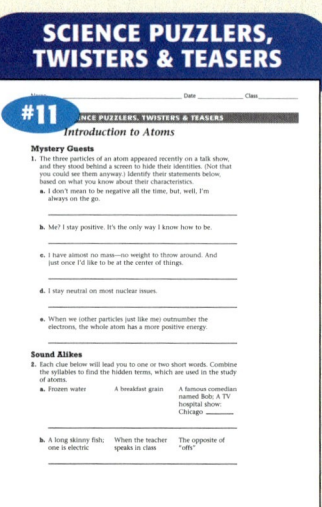

Chapter 11 • Introduction to Atoms

Review & Assessment

STUDY GUIDE

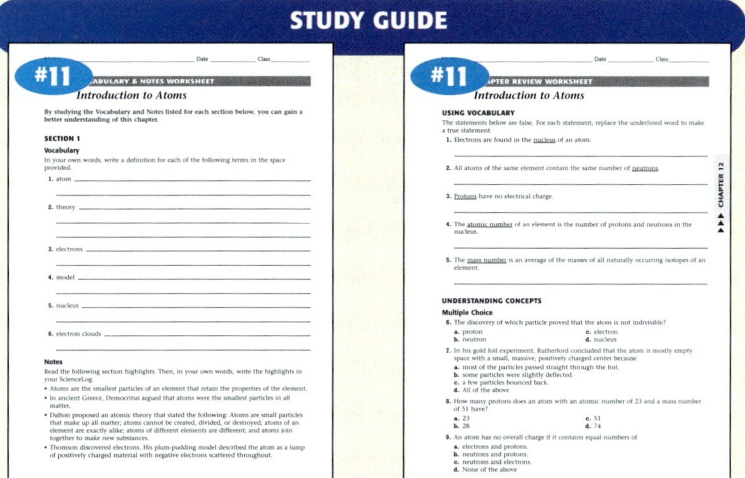

CHAPTER TESTS WITH PERFORMANCE-BASED ASSESSMENT

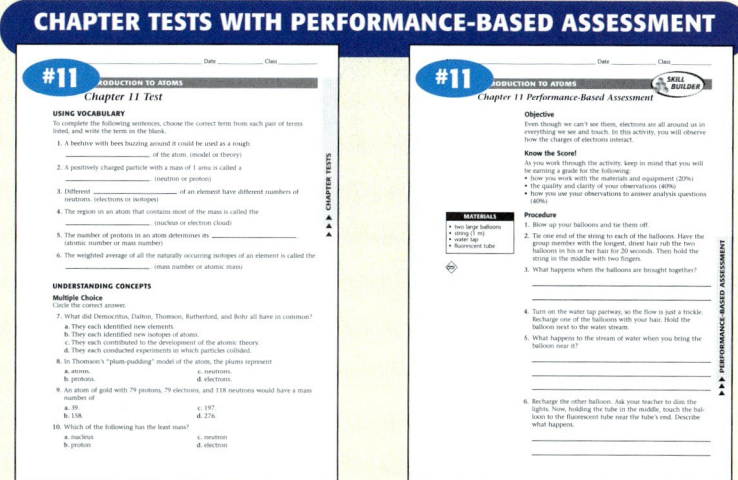

Lab Worksheets

WHIZ-BANG DEMONSTRATIONS

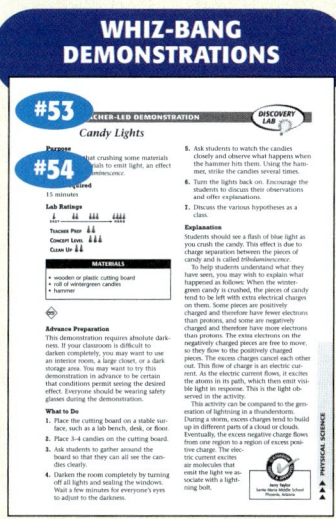

LONG-TERM PROJECTS & RESEARCH IDEAS

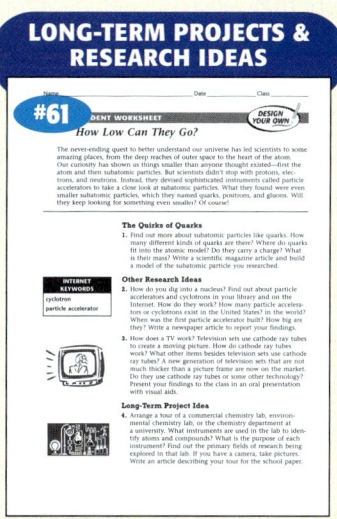

DATASHEETS FOR LABBOOK

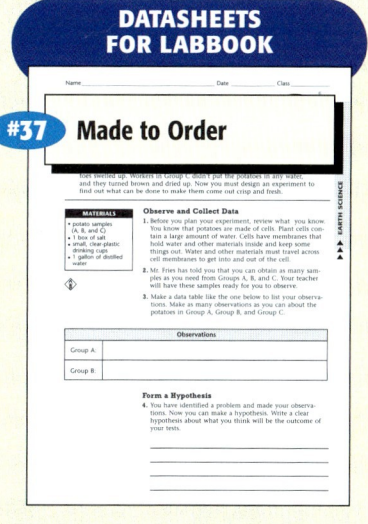

Applications & Extensions

CRITICAL THINKING & PROBLEM SOLVING

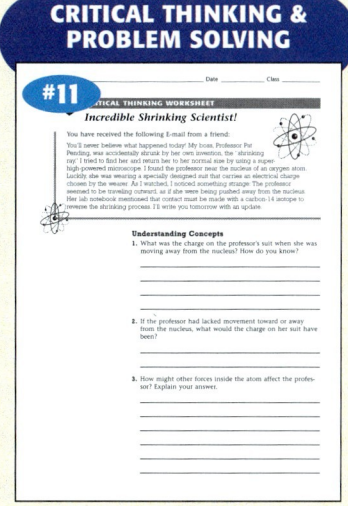

SCIENTISTS IN ACTION

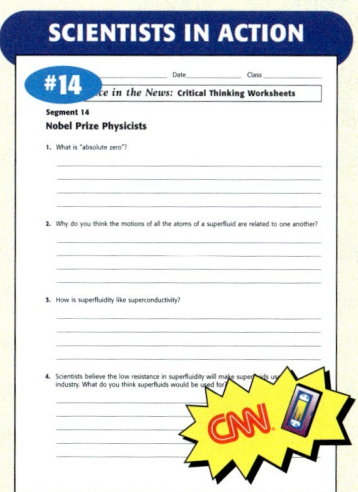

Chapter 11 • Chapter Resources & Worksheets **277D**

Chapter Background

SECTION 1

Development of the Atomic Theory

▶ **Democritus**

Democritus (c. 460–c. 370 B.C.) was a Greek philosopher and leading advocate of the theory that all phenomena in nature could be understood in terms of the movements of particles called atoms (from the Greek word *atomos*, meaning "indivisible").

- The views of Democritus sharply contrasted those of Aristotle and others, who held to the theory that all matter could be reduced to a combination of four elements: earth, water, air, and fire.

IS THAT A FACT!

▶ Democritus's ideas were not widely accepted because Aristotle, who was better known and respected, did not accept the idea of atoms. Only fragments of Democritus's writings survive, and most of our knowledge of his ideas comes from negative remarks about his theories in other people's writings.

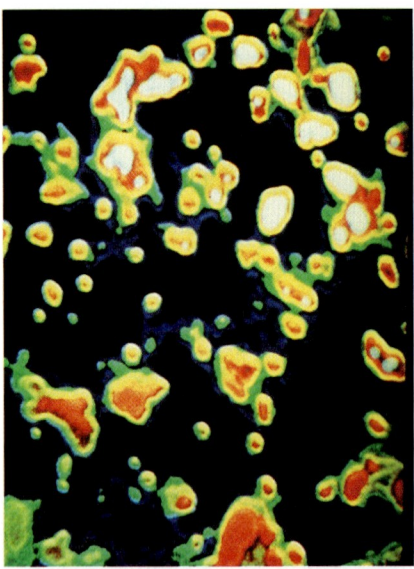

▶ **From Greek to Modern Atomic Theory**

Democritus and other Greek philosophers laid the groundwork for the modern atomic theory, but it was not until the sixteenth and seventeenth centuries that interest in atoms and atomic structure was renewed. During that time, the work of Sir Isaac Newton, Robert Boyle, and Pierre Gassendi helped to further the development of the atomic theory.

- In the nineteenth century, experiments by John Dalton, Amedeo Avogadro, James Clerk Maxwell, and Rudolf Clausius began to reveal the nature and structure of atoms.

- Sir Joseph John Thomson's discovery of electrons in 1897 and his later research on protons and gases indicated that atoms were not the smallest indivisible units of matter, as previously thought. He showed that subatomic particles with either a negative or positive charge form at least part of the structure of an atom. Thomson won the Nobel Prize in Physics in 1906.

- While Thomson was director of the Cavendish Laboratory, at Cambridge University, in Cambridge, England, one of his graduate students was Ernest Rutherford. Rutherford went on to win the Nobel Prize in Chemistry in 1908 for his work on radioactivity.

Chapter 11 • Introduction to Atoms

Section 2

The Atom

▶ **How Small Are They?**
Determining the diameter of an atom is difficult because atoms are not small, hard spheres. Measurement often varies, depending on the method used. On average, the diameter of an atom ranges from about 7×10^{-9} cm to 5×10^{-8} cm.

▶ **Quarks and Gluons: the Smallest ... So Far**
Protons and neutrons are composed of smaller particles called *quarks*. The existence of quarks was suggested in 1963 by two physicists, Murray Gell-Mann and George Zweig.

- Hadrons are all particles that feel the strong force. They include baryons, quark triplets; antibaryons; and mesons, quark-antiquark pairs. Baryons include protons and neutrons.

- A gluon is believed to be a subatomic particle that "glues" quarks together with the strong nuclear force.

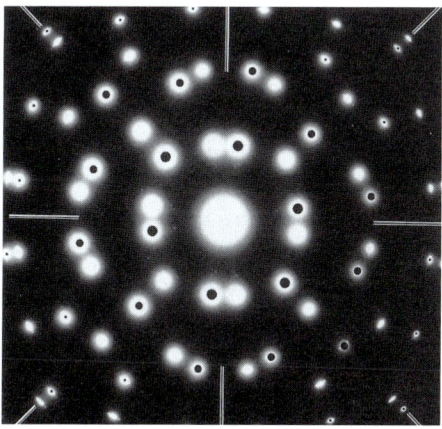

IS THAT A FACT!

- When gluons bind to each other, they are referred to as "glueballs."

- The term *quark* originated from a line in James Joyce's novel *Finnegans Wake*: "Three quarks for Muster Mark."

▶ **Isotopes**
Two major types of isotopes exist: stable and unstable. Stable isotopes persist in nature, whereas unstable isotopes undergo radioactive decay toward a more stable state.

- There are approximately 280 stable isotopes of the natural elements. A natural element is usually predominantly one stable isotope with smaller amounts of other stable and unstable isotopes.

- Radioactive isotopes can be natural or artificial. The naturally occurring radioisotopes have existed since Earth's formation.

- The first artificial radioisotopes were produced in 1934 by Frederic and Irene Joliot-Curie. Since then, more than 1,800 artificial radioisotopes have been produced using a variety of nuclear bombardment techniques.

For background information about teaching strategies and issues, refer to the *Professional Reference for Teachers.*

CHAPTER 11
Introduction to Atoms

Chapter Preview

Section 1
Development of the Atomic Theory
- Democritus Proposes the Atom
- Dalton Creates an Atomic Theory Based on Experiments
- Thomson Finds Electrons in the Atom
- Rutherford Opens an Atomic "Shooting Gallery"
- Bohr States That Electrons Can Jump Between Levels
- The Modern Theory: Electron Clouds Surround the Nucleus

Section 2
The Atom
- How Small Is an Atom?
- What's Inside an Atom?
- How Do Atoms of Different Elements Differ?
- Are All Atoms of an Element the Same?
- Calculating the Mass of an Element
- What Forces Are at Work in Atoms?

Science Puzzlers, Twisters & Teasers Worksheet 11

Guided Reading Audio CD
English or Spanish, Chapter 11

Would You Believe . . . ?

Tiny atoms have something in common with huge dinosaurs. In both cases, scientists have had to try to understand something they could not observe firsthand!

No one has ever seen a living dinosaur, but scientists have determined the appearance of *Tyrannosaurus rex* by studying fossilized skeletons. Scientists theorize that these now-extinct creatures had big hind legs, small front legs, a long, whip-like tail, and a mouth full of dagger-shaped teeth.

However, theories of how *T. rex* walked have been harder to develop. For many years, most scientists thought that *T. rex* plodded slowly like a big, lazy lizard.

However, after studying well-preserved dinosaur tracks, like those shown below, and noticing skeletal similarities between certain dinosaur fossils and living creatures such as the ostrich, many scientists now theorize that *T. rex* could turn on the speed. Some scientists estimate that *T. rex* had bursts of speed of 32 km/h (20 mi/h)!

Theories about *T. rex* and other dinosaurs have changed gradually based on indirect evidence, such as dinosaur tracks. Likewise, our theory of the atom has changed as scientists have uncovered more evidence about the atom, even though they were unable to see an atom directly. In this chapter, you'll learn about the development of the atomic theory and our current understanding of atomic structure.

Would You Believe . . . ?

One hundred years ago, scientists were just beginning to explore the structure of atoms. Today's technology applies what we know about atoms in many different areas—medicine, health, environmental science, and food science, to name just a few. Try to imagine 100 years from now. What new information might scientists have uncovered about atoms? What new technology might have been developed?

What Do You Think?

In your ScienceLog, try to answer the following questions based on what you already know:

1. What are some ways that scientists have described the atom?
2. What are the parts of the atom, and how are they arranged?
3. How are atoms of all elements alike?

Where Is It?

Theories about the internal structure of atoms were developed by aiming moving particles at atoms. In this activity you will develop an idea about the location and size of a hidden object by rolling marbles at the object.

Procedure

1. Place a rectangular piece of **cardboard** on **four books or blocks** so that each corner of the cardboard rests on a book or block.
2. Ask your teacher to place the **unknown object** under the cardboard. Be sure that you do not see it.
3. Place a **large piece of paper** on top of the cardboard.
4. Gently roll a **marble** under the cardboard, and record on the paper the position where the marble enters and exits and the direction it travels.
5. Continue rolling the marble from different directions to determine the shape and location of the object.
6. Write down all your observations in your ScienceLog.

Analysis

7. Form a conclusion about the object's shape, size, and location. Record your conclusion in your ScienceLog.

What Do You Think?

Accept all reasonable responses.

Students will have a chance to revise their answers in the Chapter Review under NOW What Do You Think?

Investigate!

MATERIALS

FOR EACH SMALL GROUP:
- rectangular piece of cardboard
- unknown object
- piece of plain paper
- books or blocks
- marble
- pencil

Teacher Notes: The size of the cardboard should be large enough to prevent students from seeing the hidden object after you place it under the cardboard. Students will need to cover the cardboard completely with paper in order to mark the information they need to gather. Small pieces of wood cut into simple geometric shapes would work well as the objects used by each group.

Remind students to roll the marble gently as they try to establish where and what the object is.

Answer to Investigate!

7. Accept all reasonable answers.

 Directed Reading Worksheet 11

 Smithsonian Institution®
Visit **www.si.edu/hrw** for additional on-line resources.

SCIENTISTS AT ODDS

For years, many scientists assumed that *Tyrannosaurus rex* was a predator because fossil evidence suggested that it had very strong jaws and sharp teeth and was a carnivore. But some scientists think it is more likely that *T. rex* was a scavenger that fed on already dead animals. These scientists argue that *T. rex*'s eyes and front legs were too small to belong to a predator. Other scientists believe that *T. rex*, like lions and hyenas today, was both a predator and a scavenger, eating fresh meat when it could catch prey and eating carrion when it was available.

Chapter 11 • Introduction to Atoms   **279**

SECTION 1

Focus

Development of the Atomic Theory

Students learn the early history of the atomic theory. Students also trace changes in atomic theory as scientists have discovered more about atomic structure.

Bellringer

Display the following quote by Democritus (c. 460–c. 370 B.C.). Have students write in their ScienceLog what they think the statement means. Do not divulge the source.

"Color exists by convention, sweet by convention, bitter by convention; in reality nothing exists but atoms and the void."

Discuss Democritus and his statement with students.

1) Motivate

ACTIVITY

Give students a newspaper and magnifying lens. Have them use the magnifier to examine photographs in the newspaper. Have them describe what they see. Students should notice that the pictures are made up of thousands of tiny dots of ink. Explain that many objects that appear to be whole are actually made up of many smaller parts. It was this idea that led the first philosophers and scientists to theorize that all matter is made up of tiny, indivisible parts. These tiny bits of matter became known as atoms. Sheltered English

Section 1

Terms to Learn
atom   model
theory   nucleus
electrons   electron clouds

What You'll Do
- Describe some of the experiments that led to the current atomic theory.
- Compare the different models of the atom.
- Explain how the atomic theory has changed as scientists have discovered new information about the atom.

Development of the Atomic Theory

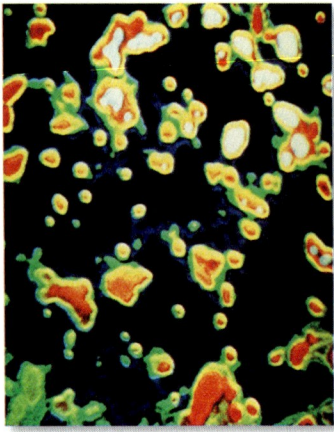

The photo at right shows uranium atoms magnified 3.5 million times by a scanning tunneling microscope. An **atom** is the smallest particle into which an element can be divided and still be the same substance. Atoms make up elements; elements combine to form compounds. Because all matter is made of elements or compounds, atoms are often called the building blocks of matter.

Before the scanning tunneling microscope was invented, in 1981, no one had ever seen an atom. But the existence of atoms is not a new idea. In fact, atomic theory has been around for more than 2,000 years. A **theory** is a unifying explanation for a broad range of hypotheses and observations that have been supported by testing. In this section, you will travel through history to see how our understanding of atoms has developed. Your first stop—ancient Greece.

Democritus Proposes the Atom

Imagine that you cut the silver coin shown in **Figure 1** in half, then cut those halves in half, and so on. Could you keep cutting the pieces in half forever? Around 440 B.C., a Greek philosopher named Democritus (di MAHK ruh tuhs) proposed that you would eventually end up with an "uncuttable" particle. He called this particle an *atom* (from the Greek word *atomos,* meaning "indivisible"). Democritus proposed that all atoms are small, hard particles made of a single material formed into different shapes and sizes. He also claimed that atoms are always moving and that they form different materials by joining together.

Figure 1 This coin was in use during Democritus's time. Democritus thought the smallest particle in an object like this silver coin was an atom.

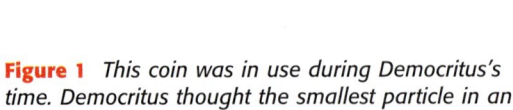

MISCONCEPTION ALERT

The photo at the top of this page does not show individual uranium atoms but rather clumps of uranium atoms. The colors were added to the photograph to make the clumps easier to see.

IS THAT A FACT!

It would take 1.05×10^{17} gold atoms to cover the entire surface of a dollar bill. That's 105 quadrillion gold atoms!

Aristotle Disagrees Aristotle (ER is TAHT uhl), a Greek philosopher who lived from 384 to 322 B.C., disagreed with Democritus's ideas. He believed that you would never end up with an indivisible particle. Although Aristotle's ideas were eventually proved incorrect, he had such a strong influence on popular belief that Democritus's ideas were largely ignored for centuries.

Dalton Creates an Atomic Theory Based on Experiments

By the late 1700s, scientists had learned that elements combine in specific proportions based on mass to form compounds. For example, hydrogen and oxygen always combine in the same proportion to form water. John Dalton, a British chemist and school teacher, wanted to know why. He performed experiments with different substances. His results demonstrated that elements combine in specific proportions because they are made of individual atoms. Dalton, shown in **Figure 2,** published his own atomic theory in 1803. His theory stated the following:

In 342 or 343 B.C., King Phillip II of Macedon appointed Aristotle to be a tutor for his son, Alexander. Alexander later conquered Greece and the Persian Empire (in what is now Iran) and became known as Alexander the Great.

- All substances are made of atoms. Atoms are small particles that cannot be created, divided, or destroyed.
- Atoms of the same element are exactly alike, and atoms of different elements are different.
- Atoms join with other atoms to make new substances.

Figure 2 *John Dalton developed his atomic theory from observations gathered from many experiments.*

Not Quite Correct Toward the end of the nineteenth century scientists agreed that Dalton's theory explained many of their observations. However, as new information was discovered that could not be explained by Dalton's ideas, the atomic theory was revised to more correctly describe the atom. As you read on, you will learn how Dalton's theory has changed, step by step, into the current atomic theory.

IS THAT A FACT!

Along with contributing to the atomic theory, John Dalton was also the first to describe colorblindness. Dalton himself was colorblind. The paper that contains his article describing the condition was published in 1794.

2) Teach

READING STRATEGY

Making a Prediction Before students read this section, ask them to predict whether Democritus's theory about the atom is correct or even partly correct. Then ask them which parts of his theory might have been changed in the 2,500 years since it was first proposed. Have students write their predictions in their ScienceLog.

ACTIVITY

Dalton Discussion Discuss how Dalton's atomic theory explains his observations. Use diagrams of different compounds (water, carbon dioxide, table salt) to show how elements combine in proportions and how the same elements always combine in the same proportions to make the same compounds. Talk about the meaning of the terms *indestructible* and *indivisible* and how such properties affect chemical changes.

MEETING INDIVIDUAL NEEDS

Learners Having Difficulty Some students may benefit from making and using flashcards that connect the scientists profiled in this section with their accomplishments. Have students make their own sets of flashcards. One side of the card should feature the name of the scientist, and the other side should include a small illustration representing the model or experiment associated with the scientist.
Sheltered English

Directed Reading Worksheet 11 Section 1

Section 1 • Development of the Atomic Theory

2 Teach, continued

MISCONCEPTION ALERT

The terms *positive* and *negative* are arbitrary. Particles do not have little plus and minus signs on them. The terms were first used by Benjamin Franklin to describe phenomena he observed. They were quickly adopted by other eighteenth-century scientists. Today, the terms are the standard terms applied to a variety of particles and interactions.

ACTIVITY

Students should study **Figure 3**, then read the section on electric charge. Have them work in pairs to do this activity on static electricity.

MATERIALS

FOR EACH PAIR:
- round balloon 23 cm in diameter
- 3 small saucerlike dishes
- 15 g (1 tbsp) each of salt, sugar, and confetti paper

1. Inflate the balloon, and tie a knot at the end.
2. Stroke the balloon on clean, oil-free hair.
3. Hold the balloon over the dish of salt. Observe the result.
4. Clean off the balloon if necessary, repeat step 2, and hold the balloon over the sugar.
5. Repeat the same procedure for the confetti.

The balloon that was rubbed on the hair gained electrons. Ask students to explain their results.

Thomson Finds Electrons in the Atom

In 1897, a British scientist named J. J. Thomson made a discovery that identified an error in Dalton's theory. Using simple equipment (compared with modern equipment), Thomson discovered that there are small particles *inside* the atom. Therefore, atoms *can* be divided into even smaller parts.

Thomson experimented with a cathode-ray tube, as shown in **Figure 3.** He discovered that a positively charged plate (marked with a positive sign in the illustration) attracts the beam. Thomson concluded that the beam was made of particles with a negative electric charge.

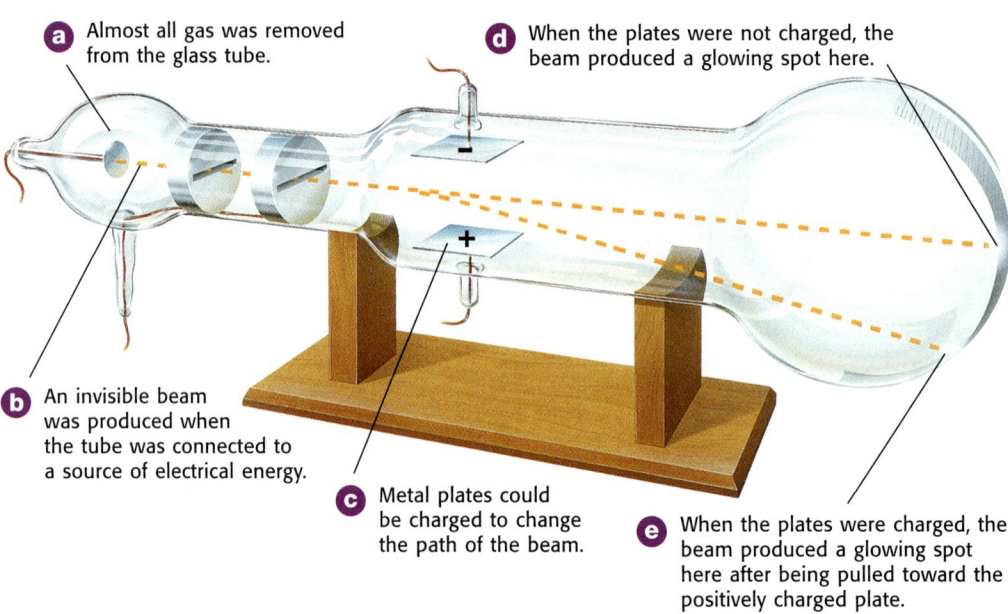

Figure 3 Thomson's Cathode-Ray Tube Experiment

a Almost all gas was removed from the glass tube.

b An invisible beam was produced when the tube was connected to a source of electrical energy.

c Metal plates could be charged to change the path of the beam.

d When the plates were not charged, the beam produced a glowing spot here.

e When the plates were charged, the beam produced a glowing spot here after being pulled toward the positively charged plate.

Just What Is Electric Charge?

Have you ever rubbed a balloon on your hair? The properties of your hair and the balloon seem to change, making them attract one another. To describe these observations, scientists say that the balloon and your hair become "charged." There are two types of electric charges—positive and negative. Objects with opposite charges attract each other, while objects with the same charge push each other away.

 Teaching Transparency 244 "Thomson's Cathode-Ray Tube Experiment"

IS THAT A FACT!

Thales of Miletus, the earliest known Greek philosopher and scientist, is said to have been the first to observe static electricity. He rubbed a piece of amber with a wool cloth and observed that lightweight objects were attracted to it.

282 Chapter 11 • Introduction to Atoms

Negative Corpuscles Thomson repeated his experiment several times and found that the particle beam behaved in exactly the same way each time. He called the particles in the beam corpuscles (KOR puhs uhls). His results led him to conclude that corpuscles are present in every type of atom and that all corpuscles are identical. The negatively charged particles found in all atoms are now called **electrons.**

Like Plums in a Pudding Thomson revised the atomic theory to account for the presence of electrons. Because Thomson knew that atoms have no overall charge, he realized that positive charges must be present to balance the negative charges of the electrons. But Thomson didn't know the location of the electrons or of the positive charges. So he proposed a model to describe a possible structure of the atom. A **model** is a representation of an object or system. A model is different from a theory in that a model presents a picture of what the theory explains.

Thomson's model, illustrated in **Figure 4,** came to be known as the plum-pudding model, named for an English dessert that was popular at the time. Today you might call Thomson's model the chocolate-chip-ice-cream model; electrons in the atom could be compared to the chocolate chips found throughout the ice cream!

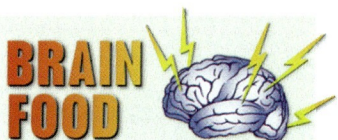

The word *electron* comes from a Greek word meaning "amber." A piece of amber (the solidified sap from ancient trees) attracts small bits of paper after being rubbed with cloth.

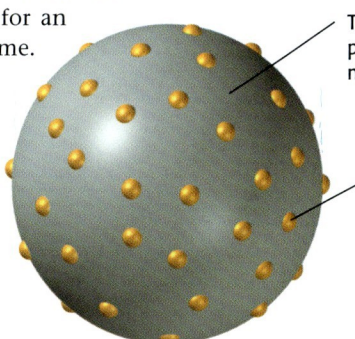

The atom is mostly positively charged material.

Electrons are small, negatively charged particles located throughout the positive material.

Figure 4 Thomson's plum-pudding model of the atom is shown above. A modern version of Thomson's model might be chocolate-chip ice cream.

REVIEW

1. What discovery demonstrated that atoms are not the smallest particles?
2. What did Dalton do in developing his theory that Democritus did not do?
3. **Analyzing Methods** Why was it important for Thomson to repeat his experiment?

TOPIC: Development of the Atomic Theory
GO TO: www.scilinks.org
sciLINKS NUMBER: HSTP255

2 Teach, continued

MEETING INDIVIDUAL NEEDS

 Advanced Learners Rutherford was influenced by the ideas of Japanese physicist Hantaro Nagaoka, who in 1904 suggested that electrons circled in orbits within the atom. Have advanced learners research Japanese scientists such as Nagaoka, Hideki Yukawa, and Kenjiro Takayanagi and share with the class the contributions these scientists made to modern science.

MATH and MORE

The length of a dollar bill is 15.70 cm. The width is 6.65 cm. If it takes 500 million gold atoms laid end to end to measure the length of a dollar bill, how many gold atoms would it take to measure the width? (almost 212 million gold atoms)

CONNECT TO EARTH SCIENCE

Use Teaching Transparency 107, "Gold Crystal Structure," to show students the arrangement of gold atoms in a sample of gold and to help them understand how Rutherford's experiment worked. The positively charged alpha particles in Rutherford's experiment **(Figures 5 and 6)** did not actually collide with the nuclei of the gold atoms in the foil. Because alpha particles and gold nuclei both have positive charges, their like charges repelled each other before a collision between the particles could take place. (The Investigate! activity at the beginning of this chapter is modeled after Rutherford's gold foil experiment.)

Rutherford Opens an Atomic "Shooting Gallery"

 Find out about Melissa Franklin, a modern atom explorer, on page 299.

In 1909, a former student of Thomson's named Ernest Rutherford decided to test Thomson's theory. He designed an experiment to investigate the structure of the atom. He aimed a beam of small, positively charged particles at a thin sheet of gold foil. These particles were larger than *protons*, even smaller positive particles identified in 1902. **Figure 5** shows a diagram of Rutherford's experiment. To find out where the particles went after being "shot" at the gold foil, Rutherford surrounded the foil with a screen coated with zinc sulfide, a substance that glowed when struck by the particles.

Figure 5 Rutherford's Gold Foil Experiment

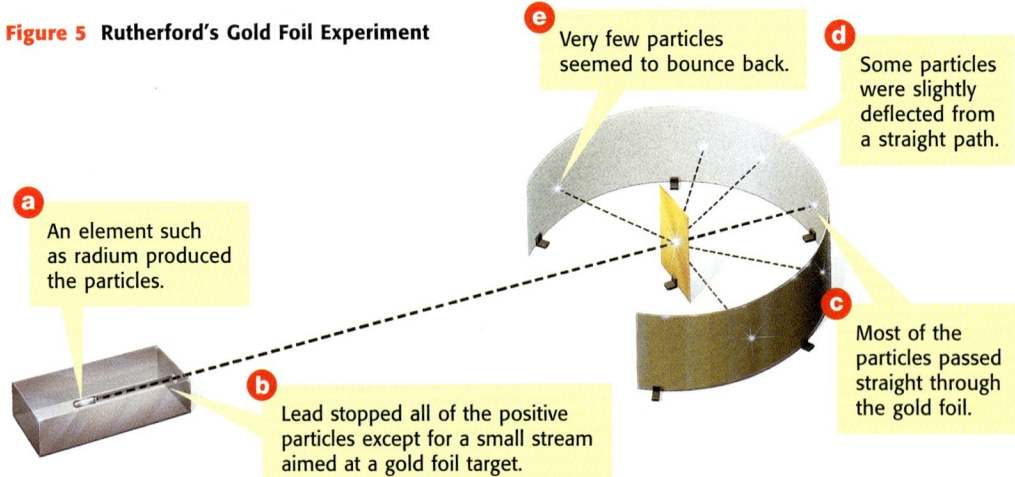

a An element such as radium produced the particles.

b Lead stopped all of the positive particles except for a small stream aimed at a gold foil target.

c Most of the particles passed straight through the gold foil.

d Some particles were slightly deflected from a straight path.

e Very few particles seemed to bounce back.

Rutherford Gets Surprising Results Rutherford thought that if atoms were soft "blobs" of material, as suggested by Thomson, then the particles would pass through the gold and continue in a straight line. Most of the particles did just that. But to Rutherford's great surprise, some of the particles were deflected (turned to one side) a little, some were deflected a great deal, and some particles seemed to bounce back. Rutherford reportedly said,

"It was quite the most incredible event that has ever happened to me in my life. It was almost as if you fired a fifteen-inch shell into a piece of tissue paper and it came back and hit you."

 **Teaching Transparency 107** "Gold Crystal Structure"

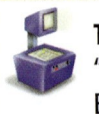 LINK TO EARTH SCIENCE

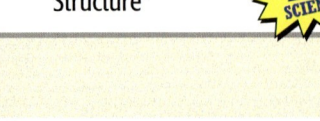 **Teaching Transparency 245** "Rutherford's Gold Foil Experiment"

IS THAT A FACT!

The gold foil experiments were actually performed by Ernest Marsden and Hans Geiger (who later invented the Geiger counter), two research assistants working in Rutherford's lab.

Rutherford Presents a New Atomic Model Rutherford realized that the plum-pudding model of the atom did not explain his results. In 1911, he revised the atomic theory and developed a new model of the atom, as shown in **Figure 6.** To explain the deflection of the particles, Rutherford proposed that in the center of the atom is a tiny, extremely dense, positively charged region called the **nucleus** (NOO klee uhs). Most of the atom's mass is concentrated here. Rutherford reasoned that positively charged particles that passed close by the nucleus were pushed away by the positive charges in the nucleus. A particle that headed straight for a nucleus would be pushed almost straight back in the direction from which it came. From his results, Rutherford calculated that the diameter of the nucleus was 100,000 times smaller than the diameter of the gold atom. To imagine how small this is, look at **Figure 7.**

Figure 6
Rutherford's Model of the Atom

The atom has a small, dense, positively charged **nucleus.**

The atom is mostly **empty space** through which electrons travel.

Electrons travel around the nucleus like planets around the sun, but their exact arrangement could not be described.

Figure 7 *The diameter of this pinhead is 100,000 times smaller than the diameter of the stadium.*

✓ Self-Check

Why did Thomson think the atom contains positive charges? *(See page 724 to check your answer.)*

Answer to Self-Check
The particles Thomson discovered had negative charges. Because an atom has no charge, it must contain positively charged particles to cancel the negative charges.

TOPIC: Development of the Atomic Theory
GO TO: www.scilinks.org
***sci*LINKS NUMBER:** HSTP255

MATH and MORE

Have students measure the diameter of a penny in millimeters and imagine that this penny represents the nucleus of an atom. Ask them to calculate the diameter of the whole atom to which this nucleus belongs. Have students report their answers in millimeters and meters. (A penny has a diameter of 19 mm. Thus, the diameter of the atom with a nucleus the size of a penny would be 19 mm × 100,000 = 1,900,000 mm, or 1,900 m.)

 Math Skills Worksheet 17 "Using Proportions and Cross-Multiplication"

REAL-WORLD CONNECTION

By the mid 1900s, many nations shared a deep concern about the misuse of nuclear energy. In response to this concern, the Atomic Energy Commission was formed in 1946 to oversee civilian uses of nuclear power. The first international conference on nuclear energy was held in Geneva, Switzerland, in 1955.

Homework

Writing Thomson's model of the atom was the first of many models created to explain the atom's structure. Each model is revised or replaced as scientists learn more. Current models may be changed when scientists discover something new. Have students write a paragraph explaining why making and using models of scientific discoveries is important. They should give at least two reasons.

3) Extend

GOING FURTHER

Electrons can move from level to level only by absorbing or losing a fixed amount of energy called a *quantum*. If the electron absorbs a quantum of energy, it moves to a higher level (farther away from the nucleus). If it releases energy, it moves to a lower level. Have students research the quantum phenomenon and present their results to the class on a poster or in a skit.

Teacher's Note: The Bohr model **(Figure 8)** is used in this chapter and Chapter 13, Chemical Bonding, because it is easier to use and allows students to understand the number of electrons in each energy level.

4) Close

Quiz

Prepare large index cards with the names of the scientists discussed in this section—Democritus, Dalton, Thomson, Rutherford, and Bohr. On separate cards, write the major discovery or accomplishment associated with each scientist. Students should be able to match correctly the scientists with their discovery or accomplishment.

ALTERNATIVE ASSESSMENT

Concept Mapping Have students make a concept map comparing the different models of the atom.

TOPIC: Modern Atomic Theory
GO TO: www.scilinks.org
sciLINKS NUMBER: HSTP260

286 Chapter 11 • Introduction to Atoms

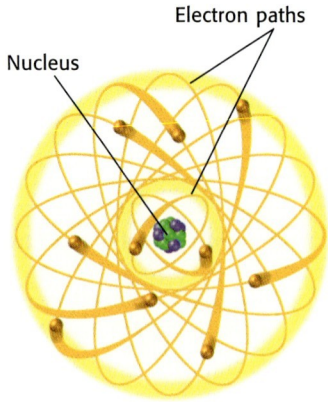

Figure 8 Bohr's Model of the Atom

Electron paths
Nucleus

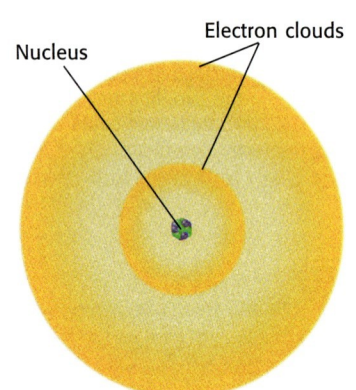

Figure 9 The Current Model of the Atom

Electron clouds
Nucleus

TOPIC: Modern Atomic Theory
GO TO: www.scilinks.org
sciLINKS NUMBER: HSTP260

Bohr States That Electrons Can Jump Between Levels

In 1913, Niels Bohr, a Danish scientist who worked with Rutherford, suggested that electrons travel around the nucleus in definite paths. These paths are located in levels at certain distances from the nucleus, as illustrated in **Figure 8**. Bohr proposed that no paths are located between the levels, but electrons can jump from a path in one level to a path in another level. Think of the levels as rungs on a ladder. You can stand *on* the rungs of a ladder but not *between* the rungs. Bohr's model was a valuable tool in predicting some atomic behavior, but the atomic theory still had room for improvement.

The Modern Theory: Electron Clouds Surround the Nucleus

Many twentieth-century scientists have contributed to our current understanding of the atom. An Austrian physicist named Erwin Schrödinger and a German physicist named Werner Heisenberg made particularly important contributions. Their work further explained the nature of electrons in the atom. For example, electrons do not travel in definite paths as Bohr suggested. In fact, the exact path of a moving electron cannot be predicted. According to the current theory, there are regions inside the atom where electrons are *likely* to be found—these regions are called **electron clouds.** Electron clouds are related to the paths described in Bohr's model. The electron-cloud model of the atom is illustrated in **Figure 9**.

REVIEW

1. In what part of an atom is most of its mass located?
2. What are two differences between the atomic theory described by Thomson and that described by Rutherford?
3. **Comparing Concepts** Identify the difference in how Bohr's theory and the modern theory describe the location of electrons.

Answers to Review

1. the nucleus
2. Two differences in the theories are that Thomson's model had the negatively charged particles in the positive material but Rutherford's model had them moving around the positive material. Thomson's model does not have a nucleus in the atom, but Rutherford's model does.
3. Sample answer: Bohr's theory was that electrons move in definite paths around the nucleus. The modern theory states that the path of an electron cannot be known. Only the areas of the atom where electrons are likely to be found can be described.

Section 2

The Atom

Terms to Learn

protons
atomic mass unit
neutrons
atomic number
isotopes
mass number
atomic mass

What You'll Do

- Compare the charge, location, and relative mass of protons, neutrons, and electrons.
- Calculate the number of particles in an atom using the atomic number, mass number, and overall charge.
- Calculate the atomic mass of elements.

In the last section, you learned how the atomic theory developed through centuries of observation and experimentation. Now it's time to learn about the atom itself. In this section, you'll learn about the particles inside the atom, and you'll learn about the forces that act on those particles. But first you'll find out just how small an atom really is.

How Small Is an Atom?

The photograph below shows the pattern that forms when a beam of electrons is directed at a sample of aluminum. By analyzing this pattern, scientists can determine the size of an atom. Analysis of similar patterns for many elements has shown that aluminum atoms, which are average-sized atoms, have a diameter of about 0.00000003 cm. That's three hundred-millionths of a centimeter. That is so small that it would take a stack of 50,000 aluminum atoms to equal the thickness of a sheet of aluminum foil from your kitchen!

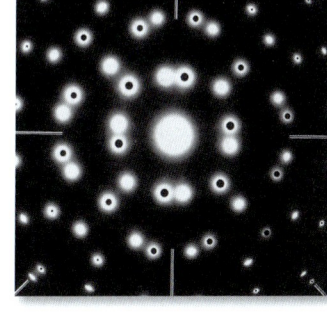

As another example, consider an ordinary penny. Believe it or not, a penny contains about 2×10^{22} atoms, which can be written as 20,000,000,000,000,000,000,000 atoms, of copper and zinc. That's twenty thousand billion billion atoms—over 3,000,000,000,000 times more atoms than there are people on Earth! So if there are that many atoms in a penny, each atom must be very small. You can get a better idea of just how small an atom is in **Figure 10.**

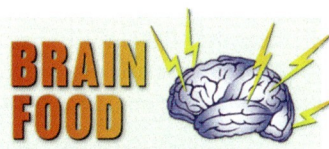

The size of atoms varies widely. Helium atoms have the smallest diameter, and francium atoms have the largest diameter. In fact, about 600 atoms of helium would fit in the space occupied by a single francium atom!

Figure 10 *If you could enlarge a penny until it was as wide as the continental United States, each of its atoms would be only about 3 cm in diameter—about the size of this table-tennis ball.*

IS THAT A FACT!

One molecule of water is composed of three atoms—two of hydrogen and one of oxygen. One molecule of natural rubber is composed of approximately 295,000 atoms—175,000 carbon atoms and about 120,000 hydrogen atoms.

WEIRD SCIENCE

What do you get if you take particles of silica and oxygen and link them together in long strands? The lightest solid material known! Some of these silica aerogels have a density of only 0.003 g/cm³ and are used, among other things, for collecting cosmic dust in space.

2) Teach

READING STRATEGY

Activity As students learn about the particles inside an atom, have them create and label diagrams of several different atoms in their ScienceLog. Students can use **Figures 11–15** as guidelines. The diagrams should show the different particles, where they are located, and other information, such as mass and charge.
Sheltered English

MISCONCEPTION ALERT

When students think of the smallest particle possible, they may picture a dust particle. As they read through this section, help them understand how small atomic size really is. Even one dust particle is made of millions of atoms!

REAL-WORLD CONNECTION

Attempting to comprehend the size of atoms and their components interests people other than chemists and physicists. Charles and Ray Eames were architects and designers who were also fascinated with size and numbers. This interest led them to make the award-winning film *Powers of Ten* (1977). The film is available on video and is a fascinating exploration into the "small" of atoms and the "large" of the universe.

Teaching Transparency 246
"Parts of an Atom"

What's Inside an Atom?

As tiny as an atom is, it consists of even smaller particles—protons, neutrons, and electrons—as shown in the model in **Figure 11.** (The particles represented in the figures are not shown in their correct proportions because the electrons would be too small to see.)

Figure 11 Parts of an Atom

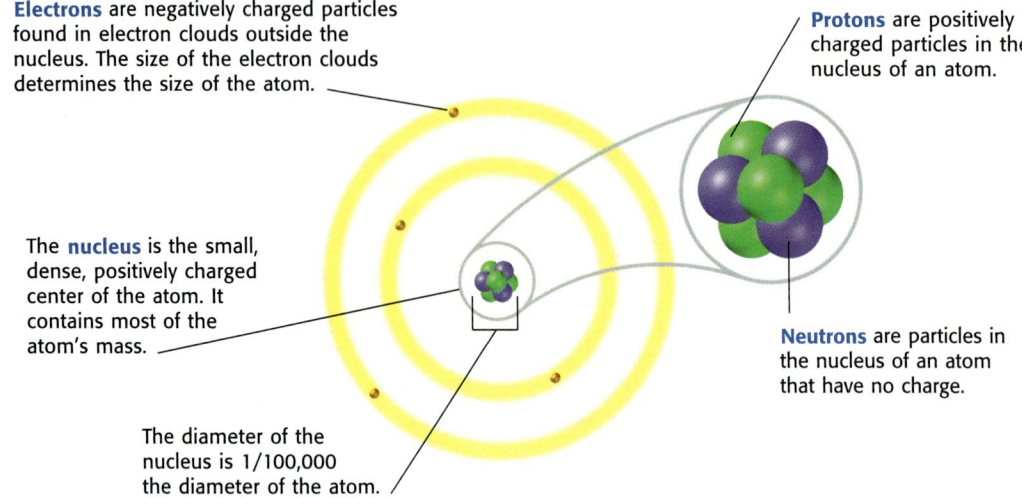

Electrons are negatively charged particles found in electron clouds outside the nucleus. The size of the electron clouds determines the size of the atom.

The **nucleus** is the small, dense, positively charged center of the atom. It contains most of the atom's mass.

The diameter of the nucleus is 1/100,000 the diameter of the atom.

Protons are positively charged particles in the nucleus of an atom.

Neutrons are particles in the nucleus of an atom that have no charge.

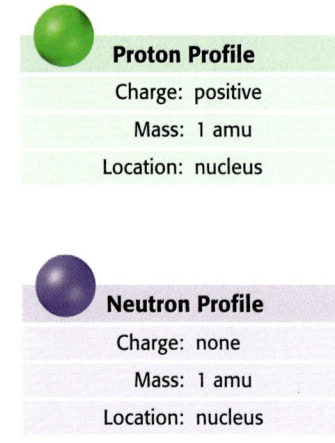

Proton Profile
Charge: positive
Mass: 1 amu
Location: nucleus

Neutron Profile
Charge: none
Mass: 1 amu
Location: nucleus

The Nucleus Protons are the positively charged particles of the nucleus. It was these particles that repelled Rutherford's "bullets." All protons are identical. The mass of a proton is approximately 1.7×10^{-24} g, which can also be written as 0.00000000000000000000000017 g. Because the masses of particles in atoms are so small, scientists developed a new unit for them. The SI unit used to express the masses of particles in atoms is the **atomic mass unit (amu).** Scientists assign each proton a mass of 1 amu.

Neutrons are the particles of the nucleus that have no charge. All neutrons are identical. Neutrons are slightly more massive than protons, but the difference in mass is so small that neutrons are also given a mass of 1 amu.

Protons and neutrons are the most massive particles in an atom, yet the nucleus has a very small volume. So the nucleus is very dense. If it were possible to have a nucleus the volume of an average grape, that nucleus would have a mass greater than 9 million metric tons!

IS THAT A FACT!

Carbon-12 is used by scientists to determine an atomic mass unit (amu). The amu is exactly one-twelfth the mass of a carbon-12 atom. Because carbon-12 has 6 protons and 6 neutrons in its nucleus, the mass of a proton and a neutron are each considered to be 1 amu.

SCIENCE HUMOR

A neutron walks into a diner and orders a glass of orange juice at the lunch counter. When the waiter brings the juice, the neutron asks, "How much do I owe you?"

The waiter replies, "For you, no charge."

Chapter 11 • Introduction to Atoms

Outside of the Nucleus *Electrons* are the negatively charged particles in atoms. Electrons are likely to be found around the nucleus within electron clouds. The charges of protons and electrons are opposite but equal in size. An atom is neutral (has no overall charge) because there are equal numbers of protons and electrons, so their charges cancel out. If the numbers of electrons and protons are not equal, the atom becomes a charged particle called an *ion* (IE ahn). Ions are positively charged if the protons outnumber the electrons, and they are negatively charged if the electrons outnumber the protons.

Electrons are very small in mass compared with protons and neutrons. It takes more than 1,800 electrons to equal the mass of 1 proton. In fact, the mass of an electron is so small that it is usually considered to be zero.

Electron Profile
Charge: negative
Mass: almost zero
Location: electron clouds

REVIEW

1. What particles form the nucleus?
2. Explain why atoms are neutral.
3. **Summarizing Data** Why do scientists say that most of the mass of an atom is located in the nucleus?

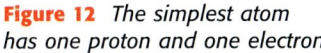

Help wanted! Elements-4-U needs qualified nucleus builders. Report to page 676 of the LabBook.

How Do Atoms of Different Elements Differ?

There are over 110 different elements, each of which is made of different atoms. What makes atoms different from each other? To find out, imagine that it's possible to "build" an atom by putting together protons, neutrons, and electrons.

Starting Simply It's easiest to start with the simplest atom. Protons and electrons are found in all atoms, and the simplest atom consists of just one of each. It's so simple it doesn't even have a neutron. Put just one proton in the center of the atom for the nucleus. Then put one electron in the electron cloud, as shown in the model in **Figure 12.** Congratulations! You have just made the simplest atom—a hydrogen atom.

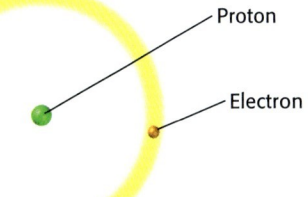

Figure 12 *The simplest atom has one proton and one electron.*

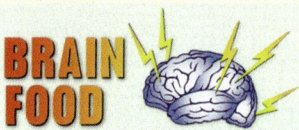

Scientists have learned that protons and neutrons are composed of even smaller particles called quarks. There are six kinds of quarks; scientists have labeled them "up," "down," "charm," "strange," "top," and "bottom." The labels are used to tell one type of quark from another; they don't really describe the quarks. Have students research these particles and make a concept map using the following terms: element, atom, nucleus, electron, proton, neutron, quark.

Made to Order

MISCONCEPTION ALERT

Scientists often ignore the mass of electrons, but they cannot ignore the space that electrons occupy; in fact, the electron clouds—the regions of space where you are most likely to find electrons—determine the size of the atom. The relative masses of the particles are:

electron	0.0005486 amu
proton	1.007276 amu
neutron	1.008665 amu

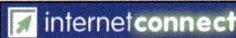

TOPIC: Inside the Atom
GO TO: www.scilinks.org
*sci*LINKS NUMBER: HSTP265

▼ **Answers to Review**

1. protons and neutrons
2. Atoms are neutral because the number of protons and the number of electrons are the same. Thus, the positive charges and negative charges cancel out.
3. Sample answer: Protons and neutrons are located in the nucleus, and electrons are outside the nucleus. Because an electron has almost zero mass and a proton and a neutron have a mass of 1 amu each, most of the mass of an atom is in the nucleus.

2) Teach, continued

GUIDED PRACTICE

Display a large version of the periodic table, and distribute a copy of the periodic table to each student. Explain to students that this is a table of all the known elements. Help students find the atomic number of different elements using the periodic table (the atomic number is the number above the chemical symbol). Remind students that the atomic number is the number of protons in the nucleus of each atom of a particular element. **Sheltered English**

CONNECT TO PALEONTOLOGY

The isotope carbon-14 is used in radiocarbon-dating of animal and plant fossils. Uranium-238, uranium-235, and thorium-232 are isotopes that scientists use to tell the age of rocks and meteorites.

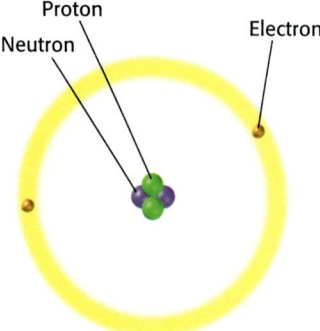

Figure 13 *A helium nucleus must have neutrons in it to keep the protons from moving apart.*

Astronomy CONNECTION

Hydrogen is the most abundant element in the universe. It is the fuel for the sun and other stars. It is currently believed that there are roughly 2,000 times more hydrogen atoms than oxygen atoms and 10,000 times more hydrogen atoms than carbon atoms.

Now for Some Neutrons Now build an atom containing two protons. Both of the protons are positively charged, so they repel one another. You cannot form a nucleus with them unless you add some neutrons. For this atom, two neutrons will do. Your new atom will also need two electrons outside the nucleus, as shown in the model in **Figure 13.** This is an atom of the element helium.

Building Bigger Atoms You could build a carbon atom using 6 protons, 6 neutrons, and 6 electrons; or you could build an oxygen atom using 8 protons, 9 neutrons, and 8 electrons. You could even build a gold atom with 79 protons, 118 neutrons, and 79 electrons! As you can see, an atom does not have to have equal numbers of protons and neutrons.

The Number of Protons Determines the Element How can you tell which elements these atoms represent? The key is the number of protons. The number of protons in the nucleus of an atom is the **atomic number** of that atom. All atoms of an element have the same atomic number. Every hydrogen atom has only one proton in its nucleus, so hydrogen has an atomic number of 1. Every carbon atom has six protons in its nucleus, so carbon has an atomic number of 6.

Are All Atoms of an Element the Same?

Back in the atom-building workshop, you make an atom that has one proton, one electron, and one neutron, as shown in **Figure 14.** The atomic number of this new atom is 1, so the atom is hydrogen. However, this hydrogen atom's nucleus has two particles; therefore, this atom has a greater mass than the first hydrogen atom you made. What you have is another isotope (IE suh TOHP) of hydrogen. **Isotopes** are atoms that have the same number of protons but have different numbers of neutrons. Atoms that are isotopes of each other are always the same element because the number of protons in each atom is the same.

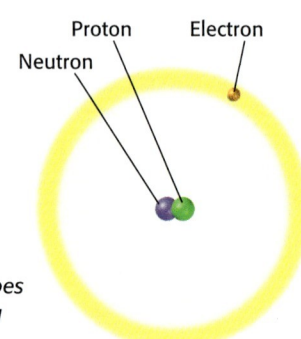

Figure 14 *The atom in this model and the one in Figure 12 are isotopes because each has one proton but a different number of neutrons.*

290

Have you heard the one about the chemist who was reading a book about helium? He couldn't put it down.

Science Bloopers

In 1811, Bernard Courtois was washing seaweed ashes in sulfuric acid. A black precipitate appeared unexpectedly. The precipitate was an unknown element and was later named iodine (from the Greek word for "violet-like") because of the purple vapor it produces when heated.

290 Chapter 11 • Introduction to Atoms

Properties of Isotopes Each element has a limited number of isotopes that occur naturally. Some isotopes of an element have unique properties because they are unstable. An unstable atom is an atom whose nucleus can change its composition. This type of isotope is *radioactive*. However, isotopes of an element share most of the same chemical and physical properties. For example, the most common oxygen isotope has 8 neutrons in the nucleus, but other isotopes have 9 or 10 neutrons. All three isotopes are colorless, odorless gases at room temperature. Each isotope has the chemical property of combining with a substance as it burns and even behaves the same in chemical changes in your body.

Isotopes and Light Bulbs

Oxygen reacts, or undergoes a chemical change, with the hot filament in a light bulb, quickly burning out the bulb. Argon does not react with the filament, so a light bulb filled with argon burns out more slowly than one filled with oxygen. Do all three naturally-occurring isotopes of argon have the same effect in light bulbs? Explain your reasoning.

How Can You Tell One Isotope from Another?

You can identify each isotope of an element by its mass number. The **mass number** is the sum of the protons and neutrons in an atom. Electrons are not included in an atom's mass number because their mass is so small that they have very little effect on the atom's total mass. Look at the boron isotope models shown in **Figure 15** to see how to calculate an atom's mass number.

Figure 15 *Each of these boron isotopes has five protons. But because each has a different number of neutrons, each has a different mass number.*

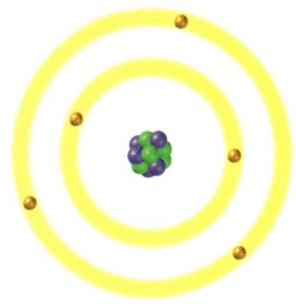

Protons: 5
Neutrons: 5
Electrons: 5
Mass number = protons + neutrons = 10

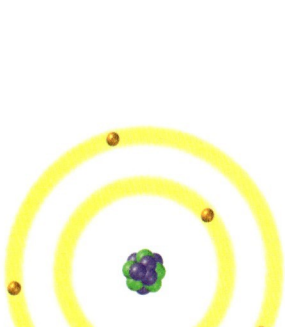

Protons: 5
Neutrons: 6
Electrons: 5
Mass number = protons + neutrons = 11

2) Teach, continued

Answer to Activity

hydrogen-2: 1 proton and 1 neutron in the nucleus; 1 electron in the electron cloud

helium-3: 2 protons and 1 neutron in the nucleus; 2 electrons in the electron cloud

carbon-14: 6 protons and 8 neutrons in the nucleus; 6 electrons in the electron cloud

MATH and MORE

Do an example of calculating atomic mass with students. Use the information given for copper-63 and copper-65 on this page. Let students fill in some missing numbers. Label each of the values.

(63 × 0.69) = 43.47 amu
(65 × 0.31) = 20.15 amu
(43.47) + (20.15) = 63.62 amu

Now have students calculate the atomic mass of titanium. Its five isotopes are:

titanium-46 (8.0 percent)
titanium-47 (7.3 percent)
titanium-48 (73.8 percent)
titanium-49 (5.5 percent)
titanium-50 (5.4 percent)

47.9 amu

 Math Skills Worksheet 19 "Arithmetic with Decimals"

Answer to MATHBREAK

(11 × 0.80) = 8.8 amu
(10 × 0.20) = +2.0 amu
10.8 amu

 **Reinforcement Worksheet 11** "Atomic Timeline"

Activity

Draw diagrams of hydrogen-2, helium-3, and carbon-14. Show the correct number and location of each type of particle. For the electrons, simply write the total number of electrons in the electron cloud. Use colored pencils or markers to represent the protons, neutrons, and electrons.

TRY at HOME

MATH BREAK

Atomic Mass

To calculate the atomic mass of an element, multiply the mass number of each isotope by its percentage abundance in decimal form. Then add these amounts together to find the atomic mass. For example, chlorine-35 makes up 76 percent (its percentage abundance) of all the chlorine in nature, and chlorine-37 makes up the other 24 percent. The atomic mass of chlorine is calculated as follows:

(35 × 0.76) = 26.6
(37 × 0.24) = +8.9
35.5 amu

Now It's Your Turn

Calculate the atomic mass of boron, which occurs naturally as 20 percent boron-10 and 80 percent boron-11.

MISCONCEPTION ALERT

The atomic mass of copper shown on this page differs from that shown on the periodic table. The atomic mass of an element is calculated from the relative atomic masses of each isotope, not from the mass numbers. Relative atomic masses account for the fact that protons and neutrons are not exactly 1 amu and that electrons do have some mass.

Naming Isotopes To identify a specific isotope of an element, write the name of the element followed by a hyphen and the mass number of the isotope. A hydrogen atom with one proton and no neutrons has a mass number of 1. Its name is hydrogen-1. Hydrogen-2 has one proton and one neutron. The carbon isotope with a mass number of 12 is called carbon-12. If you know that the atomic number for carbon is 6, you can calculate the number of neutrons in carbon-12 by subtracting the atomic number from the mass number. For carbon-12, the number of neutrons is 12 − 6, or 6.

12	Mass number
−6	Number of protons (atomic number)
6	Number of neutrons

Calculating the Mass of an Element

Most elements found in nature contain a mixture of two or more stable (nonradioactive) isotopes. For example, all copper is composed of copper-63 atoms and copper-65 atoms. The term *atomic mass* describes the mass of a mixture of isotopes. **Atomic mass** is the weighted average of the masses of all the naturally occurring isotopes of an element. A weighted average accounts for the percentages of each isotope that are present. Copper, including the copper in the Statue of Liberty (shown in **Figure 16**), is 69 percent copper-63 and 31 percent copper-65. The atomic mass of copper is 63.6 amu. You can try your hand at calculating atomic mass by doing the MathBreak at left.

Figure 16 The copper used to make the Statue of Liberty includes both copper-63 and copper-65. Copper's atomic mass is 63.6 amu.

What Forces Are at Work in Atoms?

You have seen how atoms are composed of protons, neutrons, and electrons. But what are the *forces* (the pushes or pulls between two objects) acting between these particles? Four basic forces are at work everywhere, including within the atom—gravity, the electromagnetic force, the strong force, and the weak force. These forces are discussed below.

Forces in the Atom

Gravity Probably the most familiar of the four forces is *gravity*. Gravity acts between all objects all the time. The amount of gravity between objects depends on their masses and the distance between them. Gravity pulls objects, such as the sun, Earth, cars, and books, toward one another. However, because the masses of particles in atoms are so small, the force of gravity within atoms is very small.

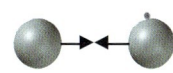

Electromagnetic Force As mentioned earlier, objects that have the same charge repel each other, while objects with opposite charge attract each other. This is due to the *electromagnetic force*. Protons and electrons are attracted to each other because they have opposite charges. The electromagnetic force holds the electrons around the nucleus.

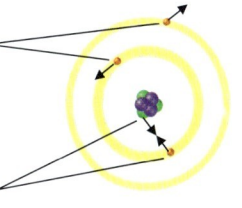

Particles with the same charges repel each other.

Particles with opposite charges attract each other.

Strong Force Protons push away from one another because of the electromagnetic force. A nucleus containing two or more protons would fly apart if it were not for the *strong force*. At the close distances between protons in the nucleus, the strong force is greater than the electromagnetic force, so the nucleus stays together.

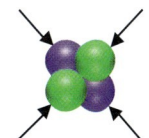

Weak Force The *weak force* is an important force in radioactive atoms. In certain unstable atoms, a neutron can change into a proton and an electron. The weak force plays a key role in this change.

REVIEW

1. List the charge, location, and mass of a proton, a neutron, and an electron.
2. Determine the number of protons, neutrons, and electrons in an atom of aluminum-27.
3. **Doing Calculations** The metal thallium occurs naturally as 30 percent thallium-203 and 70 percent thallium-205. Calculate the atomic mass of thallium.

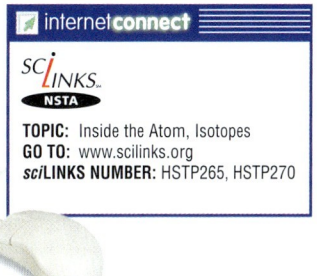

internetconnect

TOPIC: Inside the Atom, Isotopes
GO TO: www.scilinks.org
sciLINKS NUMBER: HSTP265, HSTP270

Chapter Highlights

VOCABULARY DEFINITIONS

SECTION 1

atom the smallest particle into which an element can be divided and still be the same substance

theory a unifying explanation for a broad range of hypotheses and observations that have been supported by testing

electrons the negatively charged particles found in all atoms

model a representation of an object or system

nucleus the tiny, extremely dense, positively charged region in the center of an atom

electron clouds the regions inside an atom where electrons are likely to be found

Chapter Highlights

SECTION 1

Vocabulary
- **atom** (p. 280)
- **theory** (p. 280)
- **electrons** (p. 283)
- **model** (p. 283)
- **nucleus** (p. 285)
- **electron clouds** (p. 286)

Section Notes
- Atoms are the smallest particles of an element that retain the properties of the element.
- In ancient Greece, Democritus argued that atoms were the smallest particles in all matter.
- Dalton proposed an atomic theory that stated the following: Atoms are small particles that make up all matter; atoms cannot be created, divided, or destroyed; atoms of an element are exactly alike; atoms of different elements are different; and atoms join together to make new substances.
- Thomson discovered electrons. His plum-pudding model described the atom as a lump of positively charged material with negative electrons scattered throughout.
- Rutherford discovered that atoms contain a small, dense, positively charged center called the nucleus.
- Bohr suggested that electrons move around the nucleus at only certain distances.
- According to the current atomic theory, electron clouds are where electrons are most likely to be in the space around the nucleus.

✓ Skills Check

Math Concepts

ATOMIC MASS The atomic mass of an element takes into account the mass of each isotope and the percentage of the element that exists as that isotope. For example, magnesium occurs naturally as 79 percent magnesium-24, 10 percent magnesium-25, and 11 percent magnesium-26. The atomic mass is calculated as follows:

$$(24 \times 0.79) = 19.0$$
$$(25 \times 0.10) = 2.5$$
$$(26 \times 0.11) = \underline{+\,\,2.8}$$
$$24.3 \text{ amu}$$

Visual Understanding

ATOMIC MODELS The atomic theory has changed over the past several hundred years. To understand the different models of the atom, look over Figures 2, 4, 6, 8, and 9.

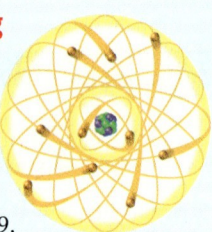

PARTS OF THE ATOM Atoms are composed of protons, neutrons, and electrons. To review the particles and their placement in the atom, study Figure 11 on page 288.

Lab and Activity Highlights

Made to Order PG 676

 Datasheets for LabBook (blackline masters for this lab)

SECTION 2

Vocabulary
- protons (p. 288)
- atomic mass unit (p. 288)
- neutrons (p. 288)
- atomic number (p. 290)
- isotopes (p. 290)
- mass number (p. 291)
- atomic mass (p. 292)

Section Notes
- A proton is a positively charged particle with a mass of 1 amu.
- A neutron is a particle with no charge that has a mass of 1 amu.
- An electron is a negatively charged particle with an extremely small mass.
- Protons and neutrons make up the nucleus. Electrons are found in electron clouds outside the nucleus.
- The number of protons in the nucleus of an atom is the atomic number. The atomic number identifies the atoms of a particular element.
- Isotopes of an atom have the same number of protons but have different numbers of neutrons. Isotopes share most of the same chemical and physical properties.
- The mass number of an atom is the sum of the atom's neutrons and protons.
- The atomic mass is an average of the masses of all naturally occurring isotopes of an element.
- The four forces at work in an atom are gravity, the electromagnetic force, the strong force, and the weak force.

Labs
Made to Order (p. 676)

VOCABULARY DEFINITIONS, continued

SECTION 2

protons the positively charged particles of the nucleus

atomic mass unit the SI unit used to express the masses of particles in atoms

neutrons the particles of the nucleus that have no charge

atomic number the number of protons in the nucleus of an atom

isotopes atoms that have the same number of protons but have different numbers of neutrons

mass number the sum of the protons and neutrons in an atom

atomic mass the weighted average of the masses of all the naturally occurring isotopes of an element

 Vocabulary Review Worksheet 11

 Blackline masters of these Chapter Highlights can be found in the **Study Guide.**

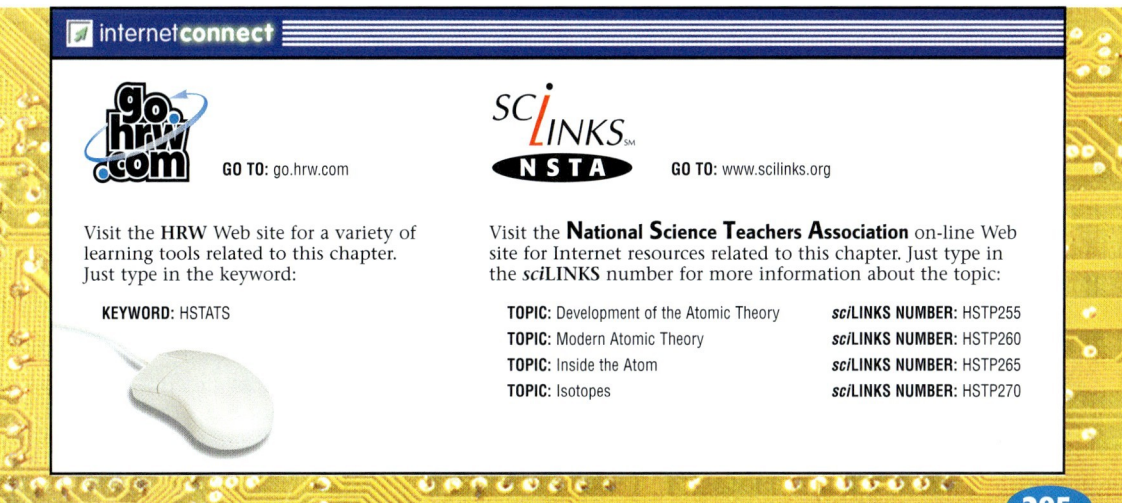

internet connect

GO TO: go.hrw.com

Visit the **HRW** Web site for a variety of learning tools related to this chapter. Just type in the keyword:

KEYWORD: HSTATS

GO TO: www.scilinks.org

Visit the **National Science Teachers Association** on-line Web site for Internet resources related to this chapter. Just type in the *sci*LINKS number for more information about the topic:

TOPIC	sciLINKS NUMBER
Development of the Atomic Theory	HSTP255
Modern Atomic Theory	HSTP260
Inside the Atom	HSTP265
Isotopes	HSTP270

Lab and Activity Highlights

LabBank

 Whiz-Bang Demonstrations,
- As a Matter of Space, Demo 54
- Candy Lights, Demo 53

Long-Term Projects & Research Ideas,
How Low Can They Go? Project 61

Chapter Review Answers

USING VOCABULARY

1. electron clouds
2. protons
3. Neutrons
4. mass number
5. atomic mass

UNDERSTANDING CONCEPTS

Multiple Choice

6. c
7. d
8. a
9. a
10. c
11. a
12. a
13. b

Short Answer

14. Sample answers: New information is discovered that proves a previous theory to be incorrect; a new theory explains existing information better.
15. electromagnetic force
16. Sample answer: The plum-pudding model describes the atom as a lump of positively charged material with negatively charged particles throughout. The positively charged material is like the dough, and the negative particles are like the plums in a plum pudding.

Chapter Review

USING VOCABULARY

The statements below are false. For each statement, replace the underlined word to make a true statement.

1. Electrons are found in the <u>nucleus</u> of an atom.
2. All atoms of the same element contain the same number of <u>neutrons</u>.
3. <u>Protons</u> have no electric charge.
4. The <u>atomic number</u> of an element is the number of protons and neutrons in the nucleus.
5. The <u>mass number</u> is an average of the masses of all naturally occurring isotopes of an element.

UNDERSTANDING CONCEPTS

Multiple Choice

6. The discovery of which particle proved that the atom is not indivisible?
    a. proton
    b. neutron
    c. electron
    d. nucleus

7. In his gold foil experiment, Rutherford concluded that the atom is mostly empty space with a small, massive, positively charged center because
    a. most of the particles passed straight through the foil.
    b. some particles were slightly deflected.
    c. a few particles bounced back.
    d. All of the above

8. How many protons does an atom with an atomic number of 23 and a mass number of 51 have?
    a. 23
    b. 28
    c. 51
    d. 74

9. An atom has no overall charge if it contains equal numbers of
    a. electrons and protons.
    b. neutrons and protons.
    c. neutrons and electrons.
    d. None of the above

10. Which statement about protons is true?
    a. Protons have a mass of 1/1,840 amu.
    b. Protons have no charge.
    c. Protons are part of the nucleus of an atom.
    d. Protons circle the nucleus of an atom.

11. Which statement about neutrons is true?
    a. Neutrons have a mass of 1 amu.
    b. Neutrons circle the nucleus of an atom.
    c. Neutrons are the only particles that make up the nucleus.
    d. Neutrons have a negative charge.

12. Which of the following determines the identity of an element?
    a. atomic number
    b. mass number
    c. atomic mass
    d. overall charge

13. Isotopes exist because atoms of the same element can have different numbers of
    a. protons.
    b. neutrons.
    c. electrons.
    d. None of the above

Short Answer

14. Why do scientific theories change?
15. What force holds electrons in atoms?
16. In two or three sentences, describe the plum-pudding model of the atom.

Concept Mapping

17. Use the following terms to create a concept map: atom, nucleus, protons, neutrons, electrons, isotopes, atomic number, mass number.

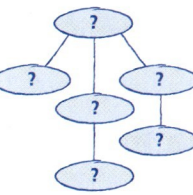

CRITICAL THINKING AND PROBLEM SOLVING

18. Particle accelerators, like the one shown below, are devices that speed up charged particles in order to smash them together. Sometimes the result of the collision is a new nucleus. How can scientists determine whether the nucleus formed is that of a new element or that of a new isotope of a known element?

19. John Dalton made a number of statements about atoms that are now known to be incorrect. Why do you think his atomic theory is still found in science textbooks?

MATH IN SCIENCE

20. Calculate the atomic mass of gallium consisting of 60 percent gallium-69 and 40 percent gallium-71.

21. Calculate the number of protons, neutrons, and electrons in an atom of zirconium-90, which has an atomic number of 40.

INTERPRETING GRAPHICS

22. Study the models below, and answer the questions that follow:

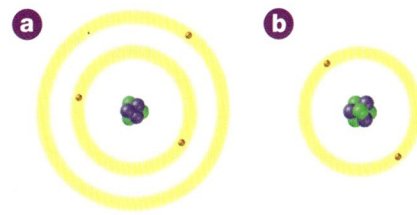

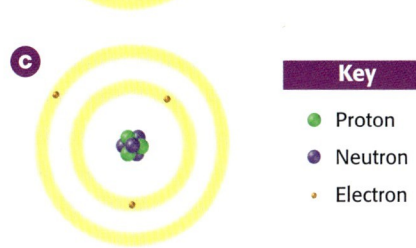

Key
- Proton
- Neutron
- Electron

a. Which models represent isotopes of the same element?
b. What is the atomic number for (a)?
c. What is the mass number for (b)?

23. Predict how the direction of the moving particle in the figure below will change, and explain what causes the change to occur.

NOW What Do You Think?

Take a minute to review your answers to the ScienceLog questions on page 279. Have your answers changed? If necessary, revise your answers based on what you have learned since you began this chapter.

297

Concept Mapping

17. An answer to this exercise can be found at the end of this book.

CRITICAL THINKING AND PROBLEM SOLVING

18. Scientists must determine the atomic number, or the number of protons, in the newly formed nucleus. The nucleus is that of a new element only if the number of protons is different from all known elements.

19. Sample answer: Dalton's atomic theory was the first one based on experimental evidence. It helps show how a theory develops as new information is discovered.

MATH IN SCIENCE

20. $(69 \times 0.60) + (71 \times 0.40) =$ 69.8 amu
21. 40 protons, 50 neutrons, and 40 electrons

INTERPRETING GRAPHICS

22. a. a and c
    b. 3
    c. 7
23. The particle will move downward, away from the group of particles. The moving particle has a positive charge, and the group of particles is composed of positively charged and neutral particles. The electromagnetic force causes like charges to repel, so the moving particle will be pushed away from the group of particles.

Concept Mapping Transparency 11

Blackline masters of this Chapter Review can be found in the **Study Guide**.

NOW WHAT DO YOU THINK?

1. Scientists have described atoms in several ways: as a solid sphere; as a plum pudding; and as a dense, central nucleus with electrons moving around it. The later models have electrons moving in paths at certain distances around the nucleus or have electron clouds around the nucleus, where electrons are most likely found.

2. Atoms are composed of protons and neutrons, which make up the nucleus in the center of the atom, and electrons, which are most likely found in regions around the nucleus called electron clouds.

3. All atoms have a small, dense, positively charged nucleus with electrons in electron clouds around the nucleus. Atoms are neutral because the number of protons equals the number of electrons.

ACROSS THE SCIENCES
Water on the Moon?

Background
- Not only are the elements hydrogen and oxygen essential for human life, they are also necessary for space travel and exploration. Solar energy striking the moon could be used to break down the water into hydrogen and oxygen.
- These two elements are a valuable rocket fuel. Lack of a refueling station has been a limiting factor in space travel thus far. The amount of water on the moon may be vast and could make space travel far more feasible.
- The sun and other stars are always giving off protons, electrons, and neutrons. The solar wind from our sun bombards the moon with neutrons and other particles.
- Many of these particles bounce straight back into space when they collide with something, but some remain and bounce around on the surface. As a result, the moon is abuzz with neutrons whirring around. Fast neutrons usually fly right back into space.
- When an epithermal neutron bounces into something that is nearly the same size and weight as itself, it slows into a thermal neutron.

ACROSS THE SCIENCES

PHYSICAL SCIENCE • ASTRONOMY

Water on the Moon?

When the astronauts of the Apollo space mission explored the surface of the moon in 1969, all they found was rock powder. None of the many samples of moon rocks they carried back to Earth contained any hint of water. Because the astronauts didn't see water on the moon and scientists didn't detect any in the lab, scientists believed there was no water on the moon.

Then in 1994, radio waves suggested another possibility. On a 4-month lunar jaunt, an American spacecraft called *Clementine* beamed radio waves toward various areas of the moon, including a few craters that never receive sunlight. Mostly, the radio waves were reflected by what appeared to be ground-up rock. However, in part of one huge, dark crater, the radio waves were reflected as if by . . . ice.

Hunting for Hydrogen Atoms
Scientists were intrigued by *Clementine's* evidence. Two years later, another spacecraft, *Lunar Prospector*, traveled to the moon. Instead of trying to detect water with radio waves, *Prospector* scanned the moon's surface with a device called a *neutron spectrometer* (NS). A neutron spectrometer counts the number of slow neutrons bouncing off a surface. When a neutron hits something about the same mass as itself, it slows down. As it turns out, the only thing close to the mass of a neutron is an *atom* of the lightest of all elements, hydrogen. So when the NS located high concentrations of slow-moving neutrons on the moon, it indicated to scientists that the neutrons were crashing into hydrogen atoms.

As you know, water consists of two atoms of hydrogen and one atom of oxygen. The presence of hydrogen atoms on the moon is more evidence that water may exist there.

▲ The Lunar Prospector *spacecraft may have found water on the moon.*

How Did It Get There?
Some scientists speculate that the water molecules came from comets (which are 90 percent water) that hit the moon more than 4 billion years ago. Water from comets may have landed in the frigid, shadowed craters of the moon, where it mixed with the soil and froze. The Aitken Basin, at the south pole of the moon, where much of the ice was detected, is more than 12 km deep in places. Sunlight never touches most of the crater. And it is very cold—temperatures there may fall to −229°C. The conditions seem right to lock water into place for a very long time.

Think About Lunar Life
▶ Do some research on conditions on the moon. What conditions would humans have to overcome before we could establish a colony there?

Answers for Think About Lunar Life
Among other things, travelers to the moon must overcome the great expense of taking all of their life-support materials with them, including fuel, water, oxygen, food, and protective clothing. Moon dwellers would also face temperature extremes and intense radiation. They would be in danger of being hit by meteorites. They would also have to find a safe way to get around on the moon.

Accept all reasonable answers for solving these problems.

CAREERS

EXPERIMENTAL PHYSICIST

In the course of a single day, you could find **Melissa Franklin** operating a huge drill, giving a tour of her lab to a 10-year-old, putting together a gigantic piece of electronic equipment, or even telling a joke. Then you'd see her really get down to business—studying the smallest particles of matter in the universe.

Melissa Franklin is an experimental physicist. "I am trying to understand the forces that describe how everything in the world moves—especially the smallest things," she explains. "I want to find the things that make up all matter in the universe and then try to understand the forces between them."

Other scientists rely on her to test some of the most important hypotheses in physics. For instance, Franklin and her team recently contributed to the discovery of a particle called the top quark. (Quarks are the tiny particles that make up protons and neutrons.)

Physicists had theorized that the top quark might exist but had no evidence. Franklin and more than 450 other scientists worked together to prove the existence of the top quark. Finding it required the use of a massive machine called a particle accelerator. Basically, a particle accelerator smashes particles together, and then scientists look for the remains of the collision. The physicists had to build some very complicated machines to detect the top quark, but the discovery was worth the effort. Franklin and the other researchers have earned the praise of scientists all over the world.

Getting Her Start

"I didn't always want to be a scientist, but what happens is that when you get hooked, you really get hooked. The next thing you know, you're driving forklifts and using overhead cranes while at the same time working on really tiny, incredibly complicated electronics. What I do is a combination of exciting things. It's better than watching TV."

It isn't just the best students who grow up to be scientists. "You can understand the ideas without having to be a math genius," Franklin says. Anyone can have good ideas, she says, absolutely anyone.

Don't Be Shy!

▶ Franklin also has some good advice for young people interested in physics. "Go and bug people at the local university. Just call up a physics person and say, 'Can I come visit you for a couple of hours?' Kids do that with me, and it's really fun." Why don't you give it a try? Prepare for the visit by making a list of questions you would like answered.

▲ *This particle accelerator was used in the discovery of the top quark.*

CAREERS

Experimental Physicist— Melissa Franklin

Background

An experimental physicist is different from a theoretical physicist. Theoretical physicists deal with formulas, calculations, and predictions. Experimental physicists, such as Franklin, test the theories developed by other scientists. Often, experimental physicists must build machines and develop new technologies to test their theories.

A person who wants to pursue a career in physics will find it important to study science and mathematics in high school. In college, physics students study chemistry and higher mathematics in addition to physics. Most people who have careers in physics have advanced degrees.

Teaching Strategy

Invite a physicist to speak to your class. Many colleges, universities, and community colleges have programs that make professors available for such visits. Prior to the visit, help your students develop questions to ask your speaker.

Discussion

Talk about the difference between a theoretical physicist and an experimental physicist. Have students discuss which they might like to be and why. Have them discuss which type of scientist is more important, if either, and why they think so.

Chapter Organizer

CHAPTER ORGANIZATION	TIME MINUTES	OBJECTIVES	LABS, INVESTIGATIONS, AND DEMONSTRATIONS
Chapter Opener pp. 300–301	45	National Standards: UCP 1, 2, SAI 1, ST 2, SPSP 5, HNS 1, 3, PS 1b	**Investigate!** Placement Pattern, p. 301
Section 1 Arranging the Elements	90	▶ Describe how elements are arranged in the periodic table. ▶ Compare metals, nonmetals, and metalloids based on their properties and on their location in the periodic table. ▶ Describe the difference between a period and a group. UCP 1, ST 2, SPSP 5, HNS 1–3, PS 1b; LabBook UCP 1, SAI 1	**Demonstration,** p. 302 in ATE **QuickLab,** Conduction Connection, p. 307 **Making Models,** Create a Periodic Table, p. 678 **Datasheets for LabBook,** Create a Periodic Table, Datasheet 38
Section 2 Grouping the Elements	90	▶ Explain why elements in a group often have similar properties. ▶ Describe the properties of the elements in the groups of the periodic table. UCP 2, 3, ST 2, SPSP 1, 5, HNS 3, PS 1b, 3e	**Interactive Explorations CD-ROM,** Element of Surprise A **Worksheet** is also available in the **Interactive Explorations Teacher's Edition.** **Inquiry Labs,** The Chemical Side of Light, Lab 20 **Whiz-Bang Demonstrations,** Waiter, There's Carbon in My Sugar Bowl! Demo 55 **Long-Term Projects & Research Ideas,** Project 62

*See page **T20** for a complete correlation of this book with the*

NATIONAL SCIENCE EDUCATION STANDARDS.

TECHNOLOGY RESOURCES

Guided Reading Audio CD
English or Spanish, Chapter 12

Interactive Explorations CD-ROM
CD 1, Exploration 5, Element of Surprise

 **Scientists in Action,** Tracking Mercury in the Everglades, Segment 15

One-Stop Planner CD-ROM with Test Generator

Chapter 12 • The Periodic Table

CLASSROOM WORKSHEETS, TRANSPARENCIES, AND RESOURCES	SCIENCE INTEGRATION AND CONNECTIONS	REVIEW AND ASSESSMENT
Directed Reading Worksheet 12 **Science Puzzlers, Twisters & Teasers,** Worksheet 12		
Directed Reading Worksheet 12, Section 1 **Transparency 248,** The Periodic Table of the Elements **Reinforcement Worksheet 12,** Placing All Your Elements on the Table	**Cross-Disciplinary Focus,** p. 305 in ATE **Real-World Connection,** p. 306 in ATE **Apply,** p. 308	**Review,** p. 309 **Quiz,** p. 309 in ATE **Alternative Assessment,** p. 309 in ATE
Directed Reading Worksheet 12, Section 2 **Transparency 79,** What's in a Bone? **Math Skills for Science Worksheet 6,** Checking Division with Multiplication **Science Skills Worksheet 18,** Finding Useful Sources **Critical Thinking Worksheet 12,** Believe It or Not	**Multicultural Connection,** p. 311 in ATE **Connect to Life Science,** p. 311 in ATE **Real-World Connection,** p. 312 in ATE **Math and More,** p. 313 in ATE **Environment Connection,** p. 314 **Cross-Disciplinary Focus,** p. 314 in ATE **Real-World Connection,** p. 314 in ATE **Multicultural Connection,** p. 315 in ATE **Connect to Astronomy,** p. 316 in ATE **Science, Technology, and Society:** The Science of Fireworks, p. 322 **Weird Science:** Buckyballs, p. 323	**Self-Check,** p. 312 **Review,** p. 313 **Review,** p. 317 **Quiz,** p. 317 in ATE **Alternative Assessment,** p. 317 in ATE

 Holt, Rinehart and Winston On-line Resources
go.hrw.com
For worksheets and other teaching aids related to this chapter, visit the HRW Web site and type in the keyword: **HSTPRT**

 **National Science Teachers Association**
www.scilinks.org
Encourage students to use the *sci*LINKS numbers listed in the internet connect boxes to access information and resources on the **NSTA** Web site.

END-OF-CHAPTER REVIEW AND ASSESSMENT

Chapter Review in Study Guide
Vocabulary and Notes in Study Guide
Chapter Tests with Performance-Based Assessment, Chapter 12 Test
Chapter Tests with Performance-Based Assessment, Performance-Based Assessment 12
Concept Mapping Transparency 12

Chapter Resources & Worksheets

Visual Resources

TEACHING TRANSPARENCIES

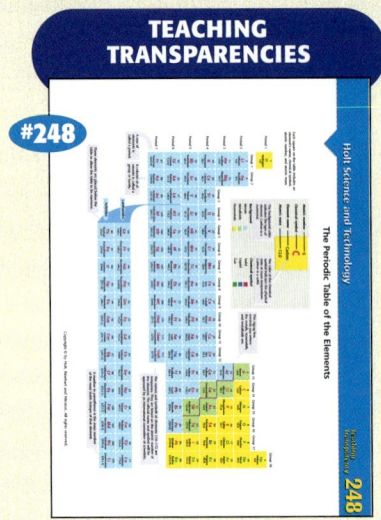

TEACHING TRANSPARENCIES   **CONCEPT MAPPING TRANSPARENCY**

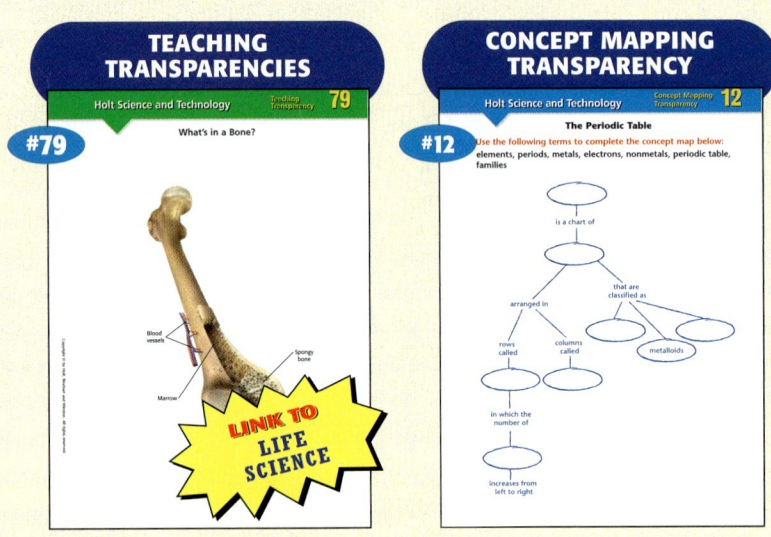

Meeting Individual Needs

DIRECTED READING   **REINFORCEMENT & VOCABULARY REVIEW**   **SCIENCE PUZZLERS, TWISTERS & TEASERS**

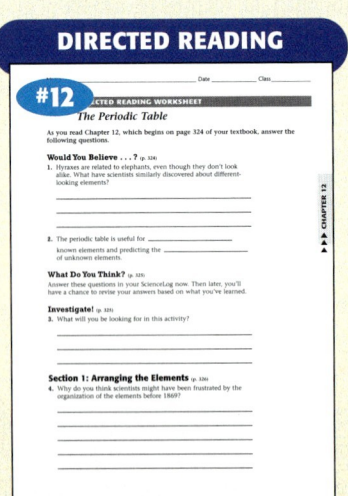 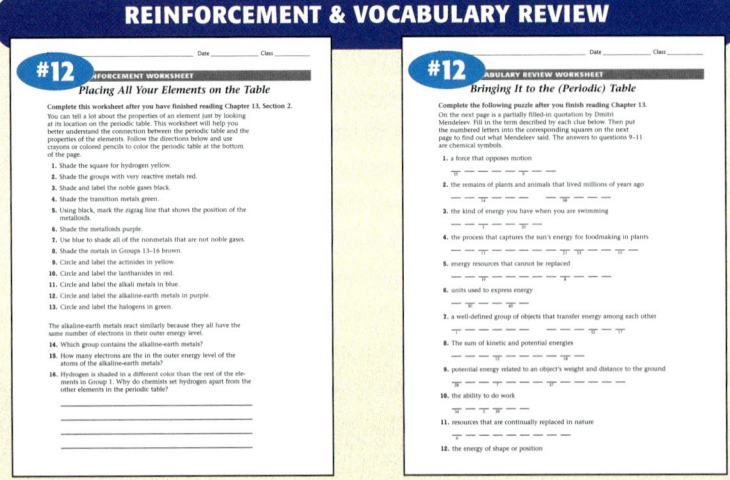 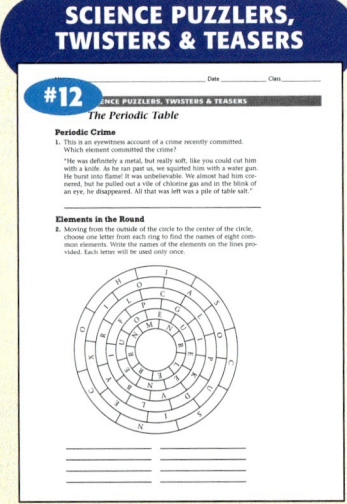

Chapter 12 • The Periodic Table

Chapter 12 • The Periodic Table

Review & Assessment

STUDY GUIDE

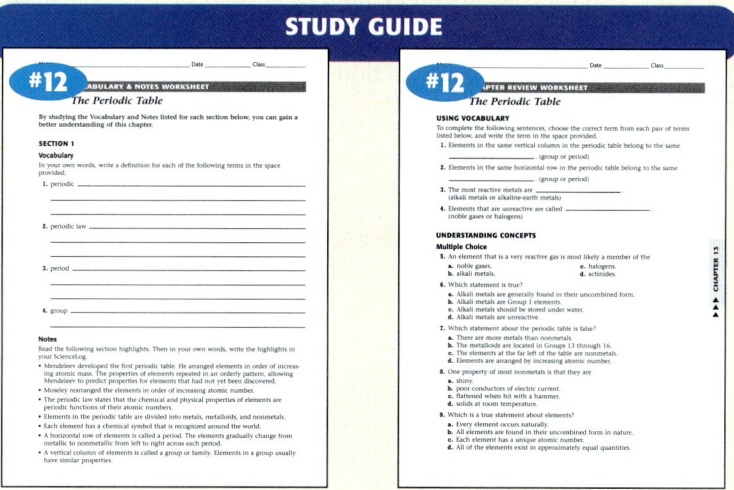

CHAPTER TESTS WITH PERFORMANCE-BASED ASSESSMENT

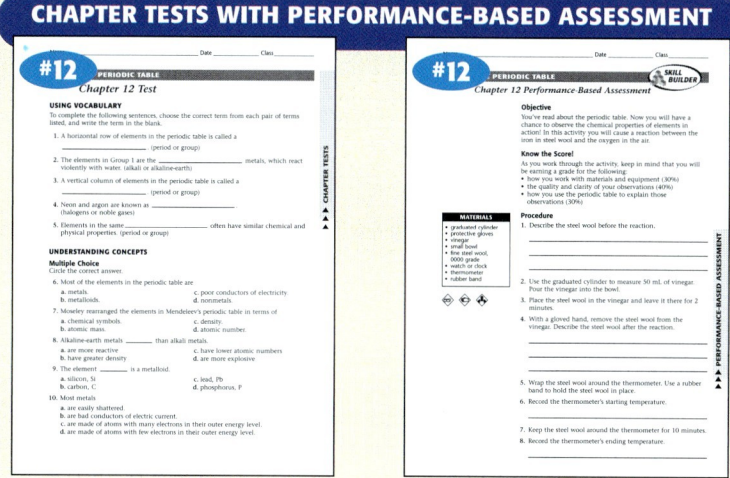

Lab Worksheets

INQUIRY LABS
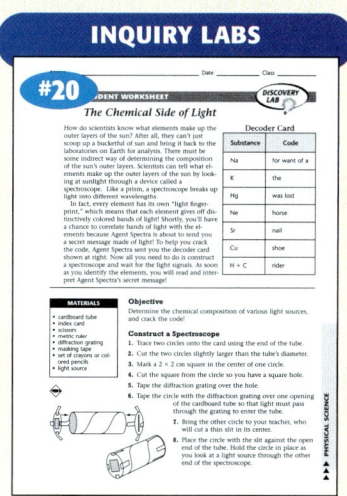

WHIZ-BANG DEMONSTRATIONS
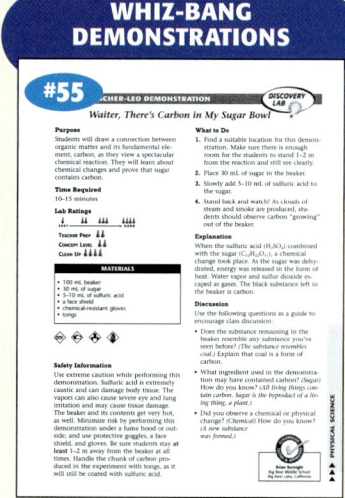

LONG-TERM PROJECTS & RESEARCH IDEAS
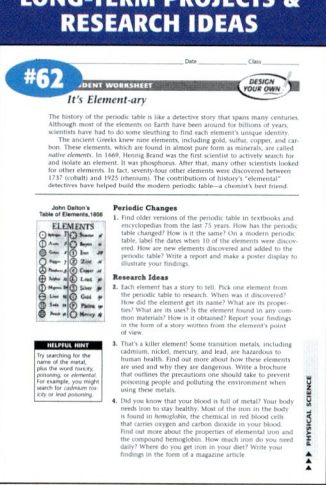

DATASHEETS FOR LABBOOK
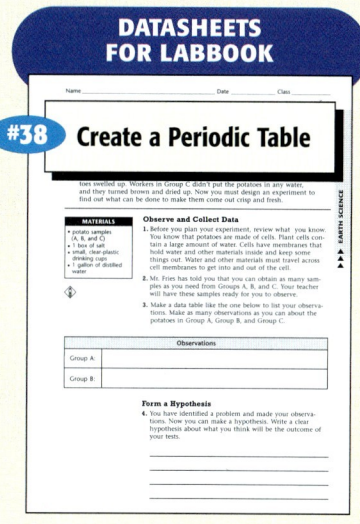

Applications & Extensions

CRITICAL THINKING & PROBLEM SOLVING
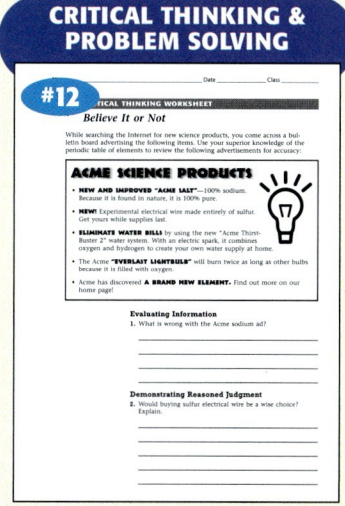

SCIENTISTS IN ACTION
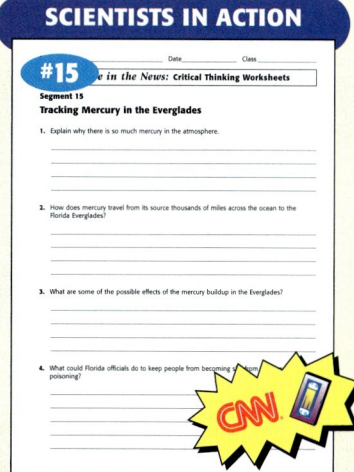

INTERACTIVE EXPLORATIONS
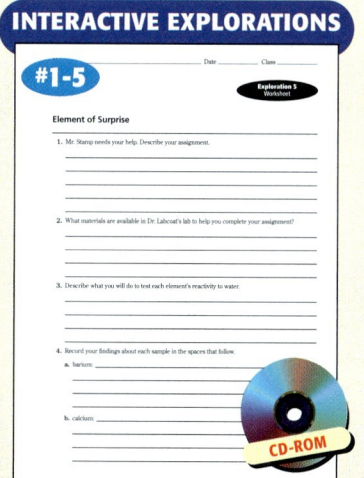

Chapter 12 • Chapter Resources & Worksheets 299D

Chapter Background

SECTION 1

Arranging the Elements

▶ **Before the Periodic Table**
Elements such as gold, silver, tin, copper, lead, and mercury have been known for thousands of years.

- The first modern discovery of an element was in 1669 when German alchemist Hennig Brand discovered phosphorus by precipitating it out of urine.

- Sixty-three elements had been discovered by 1869. As more and more elements were discovered, scientists recognized similarities and patterns in the properties of elements, and some scientists proposed classification schemes.

- In 1817, Johann Döbereiner (1780–1849) realized that the elements calcium, strontium, and barium had similar properties and that the atomic weight of strontium was about halfway between that of the other two elements.

▶ **The Law of Triads**
In 1829, Döbereiner made the first significant observation of chemical periodicity. After discovering two more triads—chlorine, bromine, and iodine (the halogen group) and lithium, sodium, and potassium (alkali metals)—Döbereiner proposed his law of triads: in nature there are triads of elements in which the middle element has properties that are an average of the other two when the elements are grouped by atomic weight.

- Between 1829 and 1858, several scientists worked on the idea of triads. They discovered that the chemical relationship extended beyond groups of three. Fluorine was added to the halogen group; oxygen, sulfur, selenium, and tellurium were grouped into another family; and nitrogen, phosphorus, arsenic, antimony, and bismuth were grouped into another family.

IS THAT A FACT!

- The first comprehensive arrangement of the elements showing the periodicity of chemical and physical properties was published in 1862 by French geologist A. E. Beguyer de Chancourtois. De Chancourtois positioned the elements on a cylinder in order of increasing atomic weight.

- When de Chancourtois arranged the elements so there were 16 on the cylinder per turn, he noted that closely related elements lined up vertically.

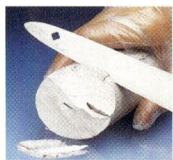

▶ **The Law of Octaves**
English chemist John Newlands (1837–1898) noticed that several pairs of similar elements were separated in atomic weight by some multiple of eight. In 1864, Newlands proposed his law of octaves: any element will exhibit properties similar to the eighth element following it in the table.

▶ **The Father of the Periodic Table?**
Two chemists, a German named Lothar Meyer (1830–1895) and a Russian named Dmitri Mendeleev (1834–1907), produced almost identical tables of the elements at almost the same time, completely independent of each other.

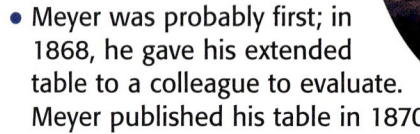

- Meyer was probably first; in 1868, he gave his extended table to a colleague to evaluate. Meyer published his table in 1870.

- Unfortunately for Meyer, Mendeleev published his table in 1869 and received credit for the first modern periodic table of the elements.

IS THAT A FACT!

- Mendeleev's (and Meyer's) table was a pioneering development because Mendeleev and other scientists used it to predict the existence of elements that had not yet been discovered.

- When Mendeleev first demonstrated his table, most scientists were skeptical. But then the element gallium was discovered in 1875 and was found to closely match Mendeleev's predicted properties!

Chapter 12 • The Periodic Table

SECTION 2

Grouping the Elements

▶ **What Goes Where?**
Mendeleev's table showed that the elements could be grouped in periods, but it didn't explain why. As the modern periodic table took shape, scientists realized that the underlying order was based on atomic structure, namely the number of protons in each atom.

- The known elements fall into three main categories, or classes, called metals, metalloids (semiconductors), and nonmetals.

▶ **The Noble Gases**
One of the most important additions to the periodic table was the discovery of the noble gases. English physicists John William Strutt, Lord Rayleigh (1842–1919), and William Ramsay (1852–1916) discovered argon in 1894.

- In 1895, Ramsay also discovered that helium exists on Earth. Then in 1898, Ramsay (and his assistant, Morris W. Travers) discovered three more noble gases—neon, krypton, and xenon.

- The final noble gas, radon, was discovered by German scientist Friedrich Ernst Dorn (1848–1916) in 1900.

IS THAT A FACT!

- Argon makes up about 1 percent of Earth's atmosphere, but it remained completely undetected until 1894 because it lacks chemical reactivity under normal conditions.

▶ **The Modern Periodic Table**
In the early 1940s, chemist Glenn Seaborg and his team worked on the Manhattan Project, America's secret effort to make the atomic bomb. Seaborg and his colleagues discovered the element plutonium in 1940.

- In the 1940s and 1950s, Seaborg's team synthesized and identified all the transuranic elements with atomic numbers 94 to 102.

- Seaborg also rearranged the periodic table by placing the actinide series below the lanthanide series. This was the last major change to the modern periodic table.

IS THAT A FACT!

- Some elements are highly reactive and combine explosively. When these reactive elements combine, the compounds they form are usually very stable. It takes a lot of energy to decompose the compound back into elements.

▶ **Transuranic Elements**
The chemical elements with atomic numbers greater than 92, known as transuranic elements, have been created in laboratories by bombarding heavy elements with neutrons or other subatomic particles. Plutonium (atomic number 94) occurs in small amounts in nature.

- All transuranic elements are radioactive, and some exist for only short amounts of time before they decay into other, lighter elements.

- Scientists continue to synthesize heavier transuranic elements, such as numbers 114, 116, and 118.

IS THAT A FACT!

- When elements after uranium were discovered, scientists first named them for the planets beyond Uranus: Neptune (neptunium) and Pluto (plutonium). This worked fine until an element was discovered after plutonium and there were no other planets!

- Early chemists, called alchemists, tried to change common metals, such as lead, into precious metals, such as gold. They weren't aware that this can be done only by removing protons from the lead atom.

For background information about teaching strategies and issues, refer to the *Professional Reference for Teachers*.

CHAPTER 12
The Periodic Table

Chapter Preview

Section 1
Arranging the Elements
- Discovering a Pattern
- Changing the Arrangement
- Finding Your Way Around the Periodic Table

Section 2
Grouping the Elements
- Groups 1 and 2: Very Reactive Metals
- Groups 3–12: Transition Metals
- Groups 13–16: Groups with Metalloids
- Groups 17 and 18: Nonmetals Only
- Hydrogen Stands Apart

 Directed Reading Worksheet 12

 Science Puzzlers, Twisters & Teasers Worksheet 12

 Guided Reading Audio CD English or Spanish, Chapter 12

 Smithsonian Institution® Visit www.si.edu/hrw for additional on-line resources.

CHAPTER 12
The Periodic Table

Would You Believe . . . ?

Suppose someone told you that the small animal shown above—a yellow-spotted rock hyrax—is genetically related to an elephant. Impossible, you say? But it's true! Even though this animal looks more like a rabbit or a rodent, scientists have determined through DNA studies that the closest relatives of the hyrax are aardvarks, sea cows, and elephants. Biologists have uncovered similar genetic links between other seemingly different species.

Scientists have also discovered that many different-looking elements, like those shown at right, actually have common properties. For almost 150 years, scientists have organized elements by observing the similarities (both obvious and not so obvious) between them. One scientist in particular—a Russian named Dmitri Mendeleev (MEN duh LAY uhf)—organized the known elements in such a way that a repeating pattern emerged. Mendeleev actually used this pattern to predict the properties of elements that had not even been discovered! His method of organization became known as the periodic table.

The modern periodic table is arranged somewhat differently than Mendeleev's, but it is still a useful tool for organizing the known elements and predicting the properties of elements still unknown. Read on to learn about the development of this remarkable table and the patterns it reveals.

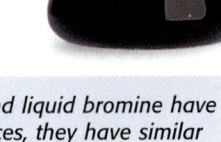

Although solid iodine and liquid bromine have very different appearances, they have similar chemical properties.

Would You Believe . . . ?

When Mendeleev organized the known elements in order of increasing atomic mass, he left gaps in his chart where the pattern seemed to require another element or elements that had not yet been discovered. But the noble gases had not been discovered, and no one predicted their existence, so Mendeleev's chart had no column for these elements.

What Do You Think?

In your ScienceLog, try to answer the following questions based on what you already know:

1. How are elements organized in the periodic table?
2. Why is the table of the elements called "periodic"?
3. What one property is shared by elements in a group?

Placement Pattern

You can find patterns—right in your classroom! By gathering and analyzing information about your classmates, you can determine the pattern behind a new seating chart your teacher has created.

Procedure

1. In your ScienceLog, draw a seating chart for the classroom arrangement designated by your teacher. Write the name of each of your classmates in the correct place on the chart.
2. Write information about yourself, such as your name, date of birth, hair color, and height, in the space that represents you on the chart.
3. Starting with the people around you, ask questions to gather information about them. Write the information about each person in the corresponding spaces on the seating chart.

Analysis

4. In your ScienceLog, identify a pattern within the information you gathered that could be used to explain the order of people in the seating chart. If you cannot find a pattern, collect more information and look again.
5. Test your pattern by gathering information from a person you did not talk to before.
6. If the new information does not support your pattern, reanalyze your data and collect more information to determine another pattern.

Going Further

The science of classifying organisms is called *taxonomy*. Find out more about the way the Swedish scientist Carolus Linnaeus classified organisms.

IS THAT A FACT!

The yellow spotted hyrax is an African animal whose range is from southern Egypt to Angola to northern South Africa. It ranges in size from 30 to 38 cm. Hyraxes usually live in rocky areas in colonies with hundreds of other hyraxes. Hyraxes eat a variety of vegetation and are eaten by predators such as pythons, leopards, and mongooses.

What Do You Think?

Accept all reasonable responses.

Students will have a chance to revise their answers in the Chapter Review under NOW What Do You Think?

Investigate!

Teacher Notes: To do this activity, you will need to make a seating chart before the class period. Possible organizational ideas for the arrangement include placing students by birth date, height, or alphabetically by their first names.

SECTION 1

Focus

Arranging the Elements

This section gives a short history of the periodic table. Students learn about the modern periodic table and are shown how to interpret it, and they learn how characteristics of elements led to their being grouped in a logical way.

Ask students to think of all the ways a deck of cards could be laid out so that the cards form some sort of identifiable pattern. Have them write as many different patterns as they can in their ScienceLog.

1) Motivate

DEMONSTRATION

Ask three volunteers to stand at the front of the class. Put two of them together, and ask the third to step off to the side for a moment. Ask the class what similar characteristics the two students share—in other words, why would these two be grouped together? List student responses on the board. Encourage students to look for as many similarities as possible.

Now separate the two; ask the third student to stand next to one of them. Repeat the exercise. Compare the two lists of characteristics. Discuss with the class the similarities and differences in the lists.

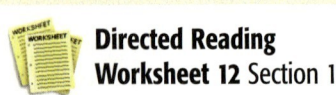

302 Chapter 12 • The Periodic Table

Section 1

Arranging the Elements

Terms to Learn
periodic   period
periodic law   group

What You'll Do
- Describe how elements are arranged in the periodic table.
- Compare metals, nonmetals, and metalloids based on their properties and on their location in the periodic table.
- Describe the difference between a period and a group.

Imagine you go to a new grocery store to buy a box of cereal. You are surprised by what you find. None of the aisles are labeled, and there is no pattern to the products on the shelves! You think it might take you days to find your cereal.

Some scientists probably felt a similar frustration before 1869. By that time, more than 60 elements had been discovered and described. However, it was not until 1869 that the elements were organized in any special way.

Discovering a Pattern

In the 1860s, a Russian chemist named Dmitri Mendeleev began looking for patterns among the properties of the elements. He wrote the names and properties of the elements on pieces of paper. He included density, appearance, atomic mass, melting point, and information about the compounds formed from the element. He then arranged and rearranged the pieces of paper, as shown in **Figure 1**. After much thought and work, he determined that there was a repeating pattern to the properties of the elements when the elements were arranged in order of increasing atomic mass.

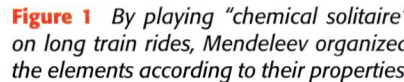

Figure 1 By playing "chemical solitaire" on long train rides, Mendeleev organized the elements according to their properties.

The Properties of Elements Are Periodic Mendeleev saw that the properties of the elements were **periodic**, meaning they had a regular, repeating pattern. Many things that are familiar to you are periodic. For example, the days of the week are periodic because they repeat in the same order every 7 days.

When the elements were arranged in order of increasing atomic mass, similar chemical and physical properties were observed in every eighth element. Mendeleev's arrangement of the elements came to be known as a periodic table because the properties of the elements change in a periodic way.

Predicting Properties of Missing Elements Look at the section of Mendeleev's periodic table shown in **Figure 2**. Notice the question marks. Mendeleev recognized that there were elements missing and boldly predicted that elements yet to be discovered would fill the gaps. He also predicted the properties of the missing elements by using the pattern of properties in the periodic table. When one of the missing elements, gallium, was discovered a few years later, its properties matched Mendeleev's predictions very well. Since that time, all of the missing elements on Mendeleev's periodic table have been discovered. In the chart below, you can see Mendeleev's predictions for another missing element—germanium—and the actual properties of that element.

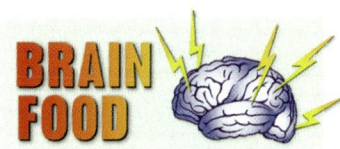

Figure 2 Mendeleev used question marks to indicate some elements that he believed would later be identified.

Properties of Germanium		
	Mendeleev's predictions	Actual properties
Atomic mass	72	72.6
Density	5.5 g/cm³	5.3 g/cm³
Appearance	dark gray metal	gray metal
Melting point	high melting point	937°C

Changing the Arrangement

Mendeleev noticed that a few elements in the table were not in the correct place according to their properties. He thought that the calculated atomic masses were incorrect and that more accurate atomic masses would eventually be determined. However, new measurements of the atomic masses showed that the masses were in fact correct.

The mystery was solved in 1914 by a British scientist named Henry Moseley (MOHZ lee). From the results of his experiments, Moseley was able to determine the number of protons—the atomic number—in an atom. When he rearranged the elements by atomic number, every element fell into its proper place in an improved periodic table.

Since 1914, more elements have been discovered. Each discovery has supported the periodic law, considered to be the basis of the periodic table. The **periodic law** states that the chemical and physical properties of elements are periodic functions of their atomic numbers. The modern version of the periodic table is shown on the following pages.

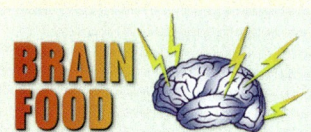

BRAIN FOOD

Moseley was 26 when he made his discovery. His work allowed him to predict that only three elements were yet to be found between aluminum and gold. The following year, as he fought for the British in World War I, he was killed in action at Gallipoli, Turkey. The British government no longer assigns scientists to combat duty.

2 Teach, continued

READING STRATEGY

Discussion Assist students in recognizing the layout pattern for the periodic table of the elements. Have them count across, group by group, to see that there are a total of 18 groups. Do the same for the seven periods. Discuss the triads that Döbereiner found (see Background material on page 299E), the expanded triads, and the noble gases. Emphasize that the lanthanides and actinides are parts of periods 6 and 7 and are not periods by themselves.

USING THE FIGURE

Look at the **Periodic Table of the Elements** on pages 304 and 305. The use of the colors on this periodic table will be continued throughout the book. Any time a square from the periodic table is shown, the color pattern for the type of element it is and its state will match what is shown here. This will help remind students which elements are in a group as they learn about each individual group.

The groups on this periodic table are numbered in the format most currently accepted by the International Union of Pure and Applied Chemistry (IUPAC). Be aware that older copies of the periodic table may have Roman numerals and letters to designate the various groups.

Periodic Table of the Elements

Each square on the table includes an element's name, chemical symbol, atomic number, and atomic mass.

Atomic number — 6
Chemical symbol — C
Element name — Carbon
Atomic mass — 12.0

The background color indicates the type of element. Carbon is a nonmetal.

The color of the chemical symbol indicates the physical state at room temperature. Carbon is a solid.

Background
- Metals
- Metalloids
- Nonmetals

Chemical symbol
- Solid
- Liquid
- Gas

A row of elements is called a period.

A column of elements is called a group or family.

Lanthanides
Actinides

These elements are placed below the table to allow the table to be narrower.

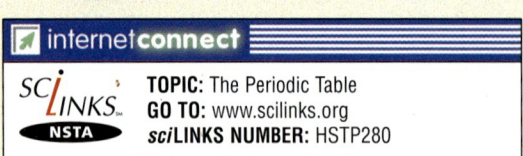

TOPIC: The Periodic Table
GO TO: www.scilinks.org
sciLINKS NUMBER: HSTP280

304 Chapter 12 • The Periodic Table

This zigzag line reminds you where the metals, nonmetals, and metalloids are.

			Group 13	Group 14	Group 15	Group 16	Group 17	Group 18
								2 **He** Helium 4.0
			5 **B** Boron 10.8	6 **C** Carbon 12.0	7 **N** Nitrogen 14.0	8 **O** Oxygen 16.0	9 **F** Fluorine 19.0	10 **Ne** Neon 20.2
Group 10	Group 11	Group 12	13 **Al** Aluminum 27.0	14 **Si** Silicon 28.1	15 **P** Phosphorus 31.0	16 **S** Sulfur 32.1	17 **Cl** Chlorine 35.5	18 **Ar** Argon 39.9
28 **Ni** Nickel 58.7	29 **Cu** Copper 63.5	30 **Zn** Zinc 65.4	31 **Ga** Gallium 69.7	32 **Ge** Germanium 72.6	33 **As** Arsenic 74.9	34 **Se** Selenium 79.0	35 **Br** Bromine 79.9	36 **Kr** Krypton 83.8
46 **Pd** Palladium 106.4	47 **Ag** Silver 107.9	48 **Cd** Cadmium 112.4	49 **In** Indium 114.8	50 **Sn** Tin 118.7	51 **Sb** Antimony 121.8	52 **Te** Tellurium 127.6	53 **I** Iodine 126.9	54 **Xe** Xenon 131.3
78 **Pt** Platinum 195.1	79 **Au** Gold 197.0	80 **Hg** Mercury 200.6	81 **Tl** Thallium 204.4	82 **Pb** Lead 207.2	83 **Bi** Bismuth 209.0	84 **Po** Polonium (209.0)	85 **At** Astatine (210.0)	86 **Rn** Radon (222.0)
110 **Uun** Ununnilium (271)	111 **Uuu** Unununium (272)	112 **Uub** Ununbium (277)						

The names and symbols of elements 110–112 are temporary. They are based on the atomic number of the element. The official name and symbol will be approved by an international committee of scientists.

63 **Eu** Europium 152.0	64 **Gd** Gadolinium 157.3	65 **Tb** Terbium 158.9	66 **Dy** Dysprosium 162.5	67 **Ho** Holmium 164.9	68 **Er** Erbium 167.3	69 **Tm** Thulium 168.9	70 **Yb** Ytterbium 173.0	71 **Lu** Lutetium 175.0
95 **Am** Americium (243.1)	96 **Cm** Curium (247.1)	97 **Bk** Berkelium (247.1)	98 **Cf** Californium (251.1)	99 **Es** Einsteinium (252.1)	100 **Fm** Fermium (257.1)	101 **Md** Mendelevium (258.1)	102 **No** Nobelium (259.1)	103 **Lr** Lawrencium (262.1)

A number in parentheses is the mass number of the most stable isotope of that element.

MEETING INDIVIDUAL NEEDS

Advanced Learners Have students consider the progression of atomic mass across the periodic table, where atoms differ in number by one proton. Ask them to consider how scientists can be sure that there are no undiscovered elements between hydrogen and uranium.

RESEARCH

Scientists are continually trying to synthesize new elements. Ask students to do some research to find out if any new elements have been synthesized since this book was published. Students may present their findings in a short report or poster.

CROSS-DISCIPLINARY FOCUS

History Before you can create a periodic table of the elements, there must be elements to arrange. Several elements, such as gold, silver, copper, tin, and a few others, were known to ancient people. But there weren't enough elements to show any patterns or relationships.

It wasn't until 1669, with the discovery of phosphorus, that steps toward creating the modern periodic table were taken. By 1869, a total of 63 elements (out of the 92 that occur in nature) had been discovered. As more elements were discovered, scientists began to see patterns of properties among them and began to create classification schemes.

Teaching Transparency 248
"The Periodic Table of the Elements"

Section 1 • Arranging the Elements

2 Teach, continued

MEETING INDIVIDUAL NEEDS

Learners Having Difficulty
Make a board game consisting of a dozen or so flip pages. Select 24–36 elements from the periodic table. Have students write short descriptions of these elements on the tops of one set of flip pages. Ask other students to find images or photographs of something made from those elements. Under the second flip page is the answer.

Students play the game by trying to guess the element from its description or its uses. The game works best if a wide variety of elements are available. Keeping score is up to you. **Sheltered English**

REAL-WORLD CONNECTION

Homes built between 1965 and 1973 may contain aluminum wiring, which can be very dangerous. This type of wiring has conductors made of aluminum that may corrode at any connection. Corrosion causes increased electrical resistance, and this may cause the wire to overheat and start a fire. By 1973, manufacturers had corrected this problem, making aluminum wiring used after 1973 much safer. To be safe, people who buy homes that were wired between 1965 and 1973 should check the wiring and replace it if necessary.

Finding Your Way Around the Periodic Table

At first glance, you might think studying the periodic table is like trying to explore a thick jungle without a guide—it would be easy to get lost! However, the table itself contains a lot of information that will help you along the way.

Classes of Elements Elements are classified as metals, nonmetals, and metalloids, according to their properties. The number of electrons in the outer energy level of an atom also helps determine which category an element belongs in. The zigzag line on the periodic table can help you recognize which elements are metals, which are nonmetals, and which are metalloids.

Metals

Most elements are metals. Metals are found to the left of the zigzag line on the periodic table. Atoms of most metals have few electrons in their outer energy level, as shown at right.

Most metals are solid at room temperature. Mercury, however, is a liquid. Some additional information on properties shared by most metals is shown below.

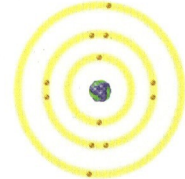
A model of a magnesium atom

Most metals are **good conductors** of thermal energy. This iron griddle conducts thermal energy from a stovetop to cook your favorite foods.

Most metals are **malleable,** meaning that they can be flattened with a hammer without shattering. Aluminum is flattened into sheets to make cans and foil.

Most metals are **ductile,** which means that they can be drawn into thin wires. All metals are good conductors of electric current. The wires in the electrical devices in your home are made from the metal copper.

Metals tend to be **shiny.** You can see a reflection in a mirror because light reflects off the shiny surface of a thin layer of silver behind the glass.

IS THAT A FACT!

Mercury is the only metal that is liquid at room temperature. It was not thought to be a metal until it was frozen in 1759. The metal cesium is almost a liquid metal. It has a melting point of 28.4°C, so on a hot day in Phoenix, Arizona, (or anywhere else) cesium metal would melt into a puddle.

Nonmetals

Nonmetals are found to the right of the zigzag line on the periodic table. Atoms of most nonmetals have an almost complete set of electrons in their outer level, as shown at right. (Atoms of one group of nonmetals, the noble gases, have a complete set of electrons, with most having eight electrons in their outer energy level.)

More than half of the nonmetals are gases at room temperature. The properties of nonmetals are the opposite of the properties of metals, as shown below.

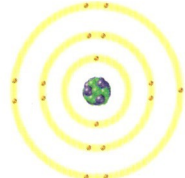

A model of a chlorine atom

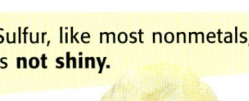

Sulfur, like most nonmetals, is **not shiny.**

Nonmetals are **not malleable or ductile.** In fact, solid nonmetals, like carbon (shown here in the graphite of the pencil lead), are brittle and will break or shatter when hit with a hammer.

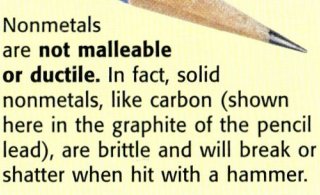

Nonmetals are **poor conductors** of thermal energy and electric current. If the gap in a spark plug is too wide, the nonmetals nitrogen and oxygen in the air will stop the spark, and a car's engine will not run.

QuickLab

Conduction Connection

1. Fill a **plastic-foam cup** with **hot water.**
2. Stand a piece of **copper wire** and a **graphite lead** from a mechanical pencil in the water.
3. After 1 minute, touch the top of each object. Record your observations.
4. Which material conducted thermal energy the best? Why?

Metalloids

Metalloids, also called semiconductors, are the elements that border the zigzag line on the periodic table. Atoms of metalloids have about a half-complete set of electrons in their outer energy level, as shown at right.

Metalloids have some properties of metals and some properties of nonmetals, as shown below.

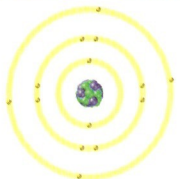

A model of a silicon atom

Tellurium is **shiny,** but it is also **brittle** and is easily smashed into a powder.

Boron is almost as **hard** as diamond, but it is also **very brittle.** At high temperatures, boron is a good conductor of electric current.

IS THAT A FACT!

Metalloids are also called semiconductors because they conduct electric current more easily than nonmetals but less easily than metals. The semiconductors silicon and germanium are extremely important in your everyday life. These elements are used to create microprocessor chips for computers.

QuickLab

MATERIALS

FOR EACH STUDENT:
• copper wire
• pencil lead
• plastic-foam cup
• hot water

Safety Caution: Remind students to review all safety cautions and icons before beginning this lab activity and the Reteaching activity below.

Teacher Notes: The wire should be approximately the same thickness as the pencil lead. Test the procedure; adjust the time if necessary.

Answer to QuickLab

4. The wire conducted thermal energy better than the pencil lead. The wire is made of the metal copper; pencil lead is made of graphite, a form of the nonmetal carbon. Metals conduct thermal energy better than nonmetals.

RETEACHING

Reinforce the meanings of the terms *malleable* and *brittle* as they apply to metals and nonmetals.

Safety Caution: Students should wear safety goggles when doing this activity.

Pass out to pairs or small groups of students small pieces of lead, such as fishing weights, and small hammers. Students can hammer and shape the lead to demonstrate malleability. Students may discover that malleability is not perfect, as the lead may break.

To demonstrate brittleness, wrap a charcoal briquette in an old towel and strike the wrapped briquette with a hammer. Select a piece of the briquette, and snap it to further demonstrate brittleness.

3) Extend

GOING FURTHER

Have students check the ingredients of foods and other products in their homes and write down the ingredients that have recognizable chemicals (such as sodium fluoride). In class, have students place self-adhesive notes containing product names on the corresponding elements on a wall-chart periodic table. Discuss with students the wide variety of elements in everyday use.

Answer to Activity

One column should include the following: H—hydrogen, B—boron, C—carbon, N—nitrogen, O—oxygen, F—fluorine. The chemical symbols for these elements are the first letter of the name of the element.

The second column should include the following: He—helium, Li—lithium, Be—beryllium, Ne—neon. The chemical symbols for these elements are the first two letters of the name of the element.

Create a Periodic Table PG 678

Answer to APPLY

The periodic table has the same shape, atomic numbers, and chemical symbols. The names of the elements are in a different language (Japanese). One reason it is important that the same chemical symbols are used around the world is so people can understand one another when discussing chemical substances.

Activity

Draw a line down a sheet of paper to divide it into two columns. Look at the elements with atomic numbers 1 through 10 on the periodic table. Write all the chemical symbols and names that follow one pattern in one column on your paper and all chemical symbols and names that follow a second pattern in the second column. Write a sentence describing each pattern you found.

TRY at HOME

You can create your own well-rounded periodic table using coins, washers, and buttons on page 678 of the LabBook.

308

Each Element Is Identified by a Chemical Symbol

Each square on the periodic table contains information about an element, including its atomic number, atomic mass, name, and chemical symbol. An international committee of scientists is responsible for approving the names and chemical symbols of the elements. The names of the elements come from many sources. For example, some elements are named after important scientists (mendelevium, einsteinium), and others are named for geographical regions (germanium, californium).

The chemical symbol for each element usually consists of one or two letters. The first letter in the symbol is always capitalized, and the second letter, if there is one, is always written in lowercase. The chart below lists the patterns that the chemical symbols follow, and the Activity will help you investigate two of those patterns further.

Writing the Chemical Symbols

Pattern of chemical symbols	Examples
first letter of the name	S—sulfur
first two letters of the name	Ca—calcium
first letter and third or later letter of the name	Mg—magnesium
letter(s) of a word other than the English name	Pb—lead (from the Latin *plumbum,* meaning "lead")
first letter of root words that stand for the atomic number (used for elements whose official names have not yet been chosen)	Uun—unnunilium (uhn uhn NIL ee uhm) (for atomic number 110)

APPLY

One Set of Symbols

Look at the periodic table shown here. How is it the same as the periodic table you saw earlier? How is it different? Explain why it is important for scientific communication that the chemical symbols used are the same around the world.

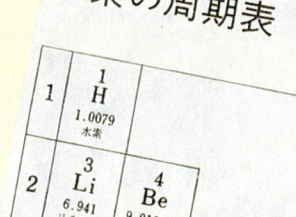

SCIENTISTS AT ODDS

When a new element is synthesized, the scientists who created the element submit a proposed name for it. Sometimes two or more scientists claim to have created the new element, and each claimant may submit a proposed name. Names are reviewed and suggested by a committee of the International Union of Pure and Applied Chemistry (IUPAC). But the committee for naming elements is made up of scientists who are competing with each other to create new elements, so the naming process is sometimes difficult. Eventually, the IUPAC designates one name as the official name, and most scientists use it from then on.

Rows Are Called Periods Each horizontal row of elements (from left to right) on the periodic table is called a **period.** For example, the row from lithium (Li) to neon (Ne) is Period 2. A row is called a period because the properties of elements in a row follow a repeating, or periodic, pattern as you move across each period. The physical and chemical properties of elements, such as conductivity and the number of electrons in the outer level of atoms, change gradually from those of a metal to those of a nonmetal in each period, as shown in **Figure 3.**

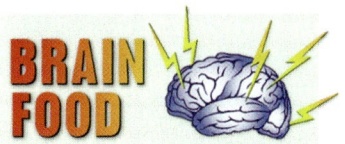

To remember that a period goes from left to right across the periodic table, just think of reading a sentence. You read from left to right across the page until you come to a period.

Figure 3 *The elements in a row become less metallic from left to right.*

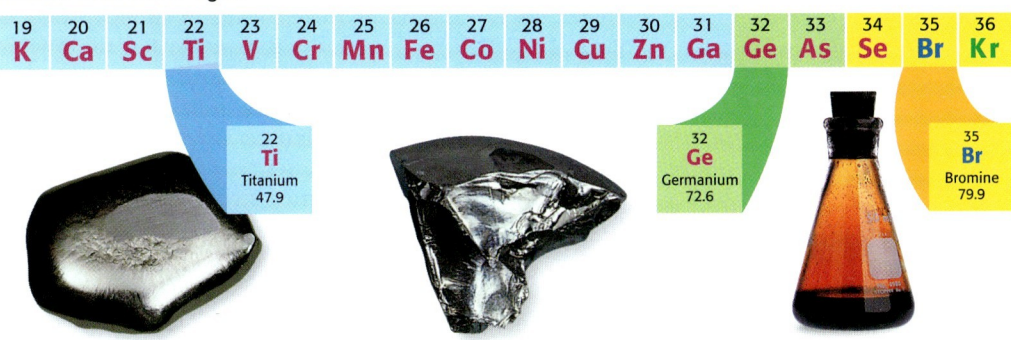

Elements at the left end of a period, such as titanium, are very metallic in their properties.

Elements farther to the right, like germanium, are less metallic in their properties.

Elements at the far right end of a period, such as bromine, are nonmetallic in their properties.

Columns Are Called Groups Each column of elements (from top to bottom) on the periodic table is called a **group.** Elements in the same group often have similar chemical and physical properties. For this reason, sometimes a group is also called a family. You will learn more about each group in the next section.

> **REVIEW**
>
> 1. Compare a period and a group on the periodic table.
> 2. How are the elements arranged in the modern periodic table?
> 3. **Comparing Concepts** Compare metals, nonmetals, and metalloids in terms of their electrical conductivity.

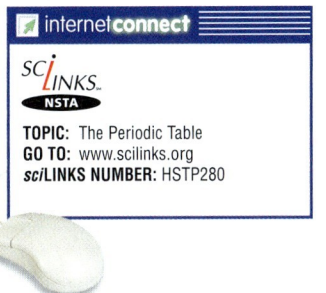

internetconnect

SC_i**LINKS**
NSTA

TOPIC: The Periodic Table
GO TO: www.scilinks.org
***sci*LINKS NUMBER:** HSTP280

309

▼ **Answers to Review**

1. A period in the periodic table is a horizontal row of elements. A group is a vertical column of elements.
2. Elements are arranged by increasing atomic number.
3. Metals have the highest conductivity. Metalloids are less conductive than metals but more conductive than nonmetals. Nonmetals are the least conductive elements.

4) Close

Quiz

1. What does the periodic law state? (The chemical and physical properties of elements are periodic functions of their atomic numbers.)

2. Which elements are in the same group as oxygen? You can use the periodic table to answer this. (sulfur, selenium, tellurium, and polonium)

3. List five elements that have symbols that don't seem to be derived from their English names; for example, Fe is iron. (Others include K—potassium, Na—sodium, W—tungsten, Cu—copper, Ag—silver, Au—gold, and Pb—lead.)

ALTERNATIVE ASSESSMENT

Photocopy the periodic table, and cut the elements apart. Fold each square in half, and put them into a jar or box.

Ask each student to select three squares and then write a short report for each element that includes:

- the full chemical name of each element
- whether each element is a metal, a metalloid, or a nonmetal
- the order of the three by increasing atomic mass
- identification of each element's group and period
- any interesting facts about or important uses of each element

Reinforcement Worksheet 12 "Placing All Your Elements on the Table"

Section 1 • Arranging the Elements

SECTION 2

Focus

Grouping the Elements

Students learn how properties of elements are used to group them in the periodic table. Students also study the relationship that elements have to each other and to the overall layout of elements within the table.

Bellringer

Ask students the following:

How do you know a bird is a bird? a kangaroo is a kangaroo? a shark is a shark? What characteristics of each animal help you to tell them apart? How does this apply to elements?

1 Motivate

DISCUSSION

Pass out several different kinds of cookies. Ask students to brainstorm about the various ingredients. (The goal is to create a long list of all the things from which you can make cookies.) Show students the list of ingredients for the entire universe—the periodic table of the elements. Discuss with students how these eight dozen or so elements combine to make everything we see around us.

Discuss with them the interesting idea that the basic ingredients of the atoms of the elements are simply the proton, neutron, and electron.

Don't forget to eat the cookies!

Section 2

Terms to Learn

alkali metals
alkaline-earth metals
halogens
noble gases

What You'll Do

- Explain why elements in a group often have similar properties.
- Describe the properties of the elements in the groups of the periodic table.

Grouping the Elements

You probably know a family with several members that look a lot alike. Or you may have a friend whose little brother or sister acts just like your friend. Members of a family often—but not always—have a similar appearance or behavior. Likewise, the elements in a family or group in the periodic table often—but not always—share similar properties. The properties are similar because the atoms of the elements have the same number of electrons in their outer energy level.

Groups 1 and 2: Very Reactive Metals

The most reactive metals are the elements in Groups 1 and 2. What makes an element reactive? The answer has to do with electrons in the outer energy level of atoms. Atoms will often take, give, or share electrons with other atoms in order to have a complete set of electrons in their outer energy level. Elements whose atoms undergo such processes are *reactive* and combine to form compounds. Elements whose atoms need to take, give, or share only one or two electrons to have a filled outer level tend to be very reactive.

The elements in Groups 1 and 2 are so reactive that they are only found combined with other elements in nature. To study the elements separately, the naturally occurring compounds must first be broken apart through chemical changes.

Group 1: Alkali Metals

Although the element hydrogen appears above the alkali metals on the periodic table, it is not considered a member of Group 1. It will be described separately at the end of this section.

Group contains: Metals
Electrons in the outer level: 1
Reactivity: Very reactive
Other shared properties: Soft; silver-colored; shiny; low density

Alkali (AL kuh LIE) **metals** are soft enough to be cut with a knife, as shown in **Figure 4**. The densities of the alkali metals are so low that lithium, sodium, and potassium are actually less dense than water.

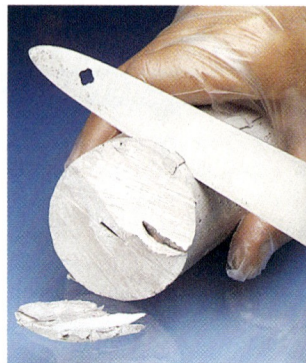

Figure 4 *Metals so soft that they can be cut with a knife? Welcome to the alkali metals.*

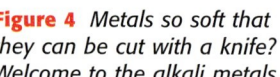
Directed Reading Worksheet 12 Section 2

Alkali metals are the most reactive of the metals. This is because their atoms can easily give away the single electron in their outer level. For example, alkali metals react violently with water, as shown in **Figure 5.** Alkali metals are usually stored in oil to prevent them from reacting with water and oxygen in the atmosphere.

The compounds formed from alkali metals have many uses. Sodium chloride (table salt) can be used to add flavor to your food. Sodium hydroxide can be used to unclog your drains. Potassium bromide is one of several potassium compounds used in photography.

Lithium

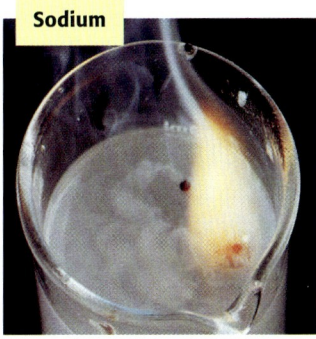
Sodium

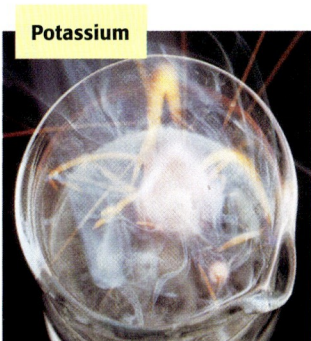
Potassium

Figure 5 *As alkali metals react with water, they form hydrogen gas.*

Group 2: Alkaline-earth Metals

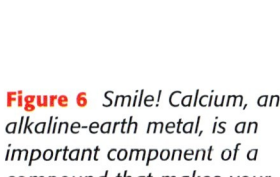

Group contains: Metals
Electrons in the outer level: 2
Reactivity: Very reactive, but less reactive than alkali metals
Other shared properties: Silver-colored; more dense than alkali metals

Alkaline-earth metals are not as reactive as alkali metals because it is more difficult for atoms to give away two electrons than to give away only one when joining with other atoms.

The alkaline-earth metal magnesium is often mixed with other metals to make low-density materials used in airplanes. Compounds of alkaline-earth metals also have many uses. For example, compounds of calcium are found in cement, plaster, chalk, and even you, as shown in **Figure 6.**

Figure 6 *Smile! Calcium, an alkaline-earth metal, is an important component of a compound that makes your bones and teeth healthy.*

2) Teach

Multicultural CONNECTION

The alkali metals in Group 1, which include potassium, got their group name from Arabic. Hundreds of years ago, to isolate potassium compounds from plant matter, plants were burned, the ashes were dissolved in water, and then the water was boiled off in large pots. The powdery residue left behind, potassium carbonate, was called potash. The Arabic word for potash is *al-qili*.

CONNECT TO LIFE SCIENCE

Calcium is an element that is very important to everyone's health. Calcium is used and stored by the body in the form of calcium compounds. Almost all of the calcium compounds in the body are found in bones. Only 1 percent of calcium in the body is found in compounds in the blood and other tissues. However, this 1 percent is essential for muscle contractions, blood clotting, and nerve functioning. Refer to Teaching Transparency 79, "What's in a Bone?" to help students understand how calcium and other substances make up bones.

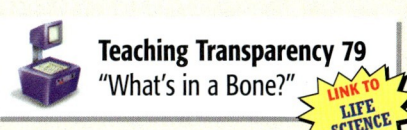
Teaching Transparency 79 "What's in a Bone?"

MISCONCEPTION ALERT

Textbooks often show photos of alkali metals reacting explosively with water and producing flames. Students should be aware that the metal itself is not burning. When the metal reacts with water, one of the products of the reaction is hydrogen gas. The energy released during the reaction often ignites the flammable hydrogen, producing flames. Not all alkali metals have the same reactivity with water. **Figure 5** illustrates that as you move down the group (lithium to sodium to potassium), the reactivity of the element with water increases.

Section 2 • Grouping the Elements

2 Teach, continued

REAL-WORLD CONNECTION

Mercury has been the liquid of choice for use in thermometers because it expands and contracts with temperature changes at a nearly constant rate. This means that for every one-degree change in temperature, the volume of mercury changes consistently.

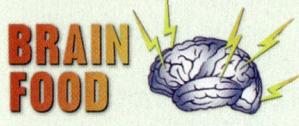

Titanium is a very light but very strong structural metal. Because of these properties, it is often used in airframes and jet engines. It is also highly resistant to corrosion or erosion, so it can be used in very corrosive places, such as in salt water or in the human body.

Answer to Self-Check

It is easier for atoms of alkali metals to lose one electron than for atoms of alkaline-earth metals to lose two electrons. Therefore, alkali metals are more reactive than alkaline-earth metals.

TOPIC: Metals
GO TO: www.scilinks.org
sciLINKS NUMBER: HSTP285

Groups 3–12: Transition Metals

Groups 3–12 do not have individual names. Instead, these groups are described together under the name *transition metals*.

Group contains: Metals
Electrons in the outer level: 1 or 2
Reactivity: Less reactive than alkaline-earth metals
Other shared properties: Shiny; good conductors of thermal energy and electric current; higher densities and melting points (except for mercury) than elements in Groups 1 and 2

21 Sc Scandium	22 Ti Titanium	23 V Vanadium	24 Cr Chromium	25 Mn Manganese	26 Fe Iron	27 Co Cobalt	28 Ni Nickel	29 Cu Copper	30 Zn Zinc
39 Y Yttrium	40 Zr Zirconium	41 Nb Niobium	42 Mo Molybdenum	43 Tc Technetium	44 Ru Ruthenium	45 Rh Rhodium	46 Pd Palladium	47 Ag Silver	48 Cd Cadmium
57 La Lanthanum	72 Hf Hafnium	73 Ta Tantalum	74 W Tungsten	75 Re Rhenium	76 Os Osmium	77 Ir Iridium	78 Pt Platinum	79 Au Gold	80 Hg Mercury
89 Ac Actinium	104 Rf Rutherfordium	105 Db Dubnium	106 Sg Seaborgium	107 Bh Bohrium	108 Hs Hassium	109 Mt Meitnerium	110 Uun Ununnilium	111 Uuu Unununium	112 Uub Ununbium

The atoms of transition metals do not give away their electrons as easily as atoms of the Group 1 and Group 2 metals do, making transition metals less reactive than the alkali metals and the alkaline-earth metals. The properties of the transition metals vary widely, as shown in **Figure 7**.

Figure 7 Transition metals have a wide range of physical and chemical properties.

Mercury is used in thermometers because, unlike the other transition metals, it is in the liquid state at room temperature.

Many transition metals are silver-colored—but not all! This **gold** ring proves it!

Some transition metals, including the **titanium** in the artificial hip at right, are not very reactive. But others, such as **iron**, are reactive. The iron in the steel trowel above has reacted with oxygen to form rust.

✓ Self-Check

Why are alkali metals more reactive than alkaline-earth metals? *(See page 724 to check your answer.)*

In a meeting of the transition metals, mercury wished to speak to the entire group. But the group didn't let mercury speak because they didn't like to listen to heavy metal.

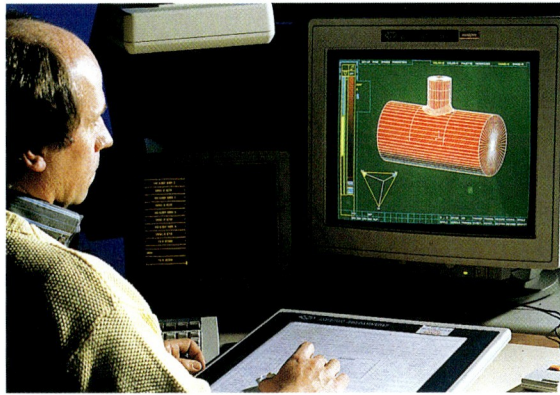

Lanthanides and Actinides Some transition metals from Periods 6 and 7 are placed at the bottom of the periodic table to keep the table from being too wide. The properties of the elements in each row tend to be very similar.

Elements in the first row are called *lanthanides* because they follow the transition metal lanthanum. The lanthanides are shiny, reactive metals. Some of these elements are used to make different types of steel. An important use of a compound of one lanthanide element is shown in **Figure 8.**

Elements in the second row are called *actinides* because they follow the transition metal actinium. All atoms of actinides are radioactive, which means they are unstable. The atoms of a radioactive element can change into atoms of a different element. Elements listed after plutonium, element 94, do not occur in nature but are instead produced in laboratories. You might have one of these elements in your home. Very small amounts of americium (AM uhr ISH ee uhm), element 95, are used in some smoke detectors.

Figure 8 Seeing red? The color red appears on a computer monitor because of a compound formed from europium that coats the back of the screen.

REVIEW

1. What are two properties of the alkali metals?
2. What causes the properties of elements in a group to be similar?
3. **Applying Concepts** Why are neither the alkali metals nor the alkaline-earth metals found uncombined in nature?

TOPIC: Metals
GO TO: www.scilinks.org
sciLINKS NUMBER: HSTP285

2) Teach, continued

CROSS-DISCIPLINARY FOCUS

History Food preservation through canning was invented in 1809 by Frenchman Nicolas-François Appert (c. 1750–1841). Tin-plated cans were first used for canning in 1810 by English inventor Peter Durand. Commercial canning was brought to the United States in 1821 when it was introduced by the William Underwood Company in Boston. In 1874, the canning process was greatly improved when cans were first heated by high-pressure steam. The high pressure in this process kept cans from bursting during heating.

REAL-WORLD CONNECTION

Aluminum alloys are often used in above-deck parts of cruise ships. They are strong, resistant to corrosion, and lightweight.

USING THE FIGURE

Many elements have several forms, called allotropes. For example, oxygen gas and ozone are allotropes of oxygen. Allotropes are usually stable at different temperatures and pressures. For example, diamond, graphite, and buckyballs are allotropes of carbon. Refer to **Figure 10** on page 315.

Groups 13–16: Groups with Metalloids

Moving from Group 13 across to Group 16, the elements shift from metals to nonmetals. Along the way, you find the metalloids. These elements have some properties of metals and some properties of nonmetals.

Group 13: Boron Group

Group contains: One metalloid and four metals
Electrons in the outer level: 3
Reactivity: Reactive
Other shared properties: Solid at room temperature

The most common element from Group 13 is aluminum. In fact, aluminum is the most abundant metal in Earth's crust. Until the 1880s, it was considered a precious metal because the process used to produce pure aluminum was very expensive. In fact, aluminum was even more valuable than gold, as shown in **Figure 9.**

Today, the process is not as difficult or expensive. Aluminum is now an important metal used in making lightweight automobile parts and aircraft, as well as foil, cans, and wires.

Figure 9 During the 1850s and 1860s, Emperor Napoleon III of France used aluminum dinnerware because aluminum was more valuable than gold!

Environment CONNECTION

Recycling aluminum uses less energy than obtaining aluminum in the first place. Aluminum must be separated from bauxite, a mixture containing naturally occurring compounds of aluminum. Twenty times more electrical energy is required to separate aluminum from bauxite than to recycle used aluminum.

Group 14: Carbon Group

Group contains: One nonmetal, two metalloids, and two metals
Electrons in the outer level: 4
Reactivity: Varies among the elements
Other shared properties: Solid at room temperature

The metalloids silicon and germanium are used to make computer chips. The metal tin is useful because it is not very reactive. A tin can is really made of steel coated with tin. The tin is less reactive than the steel, and it keeps the steel from rusting.

IS THAT A FACT!

Less than 50 years ago, most scientists believed that silicon had little commercial use. They didn't foresee the invention of the silicon transistor chip, which led the way for the development of computer chips. Now, industrial processes using silicon employ millions of people worldwide. The main silicon product, integrated circuits for computer and game chips, has changed the world.

314 Chapter 12 • The Periodic Table

The nonmetal carbon can be found uncombined in nature, as shown in **Figure 10.** Carbon forms a wide variety of compounds. Some of these compounds, including proteins, fats, and carbohydrates, are essential to life on Earth.

Figure 10 *Diamonds and soot have very different properties, yet both are natural forms of carbon.*

Diamond is the hardest material known. It is used as a jewel and on cutting tools such as saws, drills, and files.

Soot—formed from burning oil, coal, and wood—is used as a pigment in paints and crayons.

Group 15: Nitrogen Group

Group contains: Two nonmetals, two metalloids, and one metal
Electrons in the outer level: 5
Reactivity: Varies among the elements
Other shared properties: All but nitrogen are solid at room temperature.

Nitrogen, which is a gas at room temperature, makes up about 80 percent of the air you breathe. Nitrogen removed from air is reacted with hydrogen to make ammonia for fertilizers.

Although nitrogen is unreactive, phosphorus is extremely reactive, as shown in **Figure 11.** In fact, phosphorus is only found combined with other elements in nature.

Figure 11 *Simply striking a match on the side of this box causes chemicals on the match to react with phosphorus on the box and begin to burn.*

Group 16: Oxygen Group

Group contains: Three nonmetals, one metalloid, and one metal
Electrons in the outer level: 6
Reactivity: Reactive
Other shared properties: All but oxygen are solid at room temperature.

Oxygen makes up about 20 percent of air. Oxygen is necessary for substances to burn, such as the chemicals on the match in Figure 11. Sulfur, another common member of Group 16, can be found as a yellow solid in nature. The principal use of sulfur is to make sulfuric acid, the most widely used compound in the chemical industry.

Multicultural CONNECTION

About a century ago, Marie Sklodowska Curie (1867–1934) made many contributions to the study of radioactivity and radioactive elements. In 1903, Marie, her husband, Pierre Curie (1859–1906), and French physicist Henri Becquerel (1852–1908) were awarded the Nobel Prize in Physics for their contributions to understanding radioactivity. The Curies discovered the radioactive elements polonium and radium and isolated samples of these elements from tons of ore. For her discoveries of polonium and radium, Marie Curie was awarded the 1911 Nobel Prize in Chemistry.

3 Extend, continued

CONNECT TO ASTRONOMY

Astronomers have evidence that the universe began with nothing more than hydrogen and helium. Where did all of the other elements come from?

Stars seem to be the factories that created all of the naturally occurring elements throughout the universe. Students can find information about and photographs of areas in the universe where new stars are born and other areas where old stars have exploded. Have students research how elements may be created or changed in these violent reactions.

MEETING INDIVIDUAL NEEDS

Advanced Learners The word *halogen* comes from the Greek words meaning "salt former." Sodium chloride, table salt, is composed of the halogen chlorine and the alkali metal sodium. Have students research halogens and their uses and then prepare a chart or a poster that shows what they learned.

Interactive Explorations CD-ROM "Element of Surprise"

internetconnect
SCILINKS **TOPIC:** Nonmetals
GO TO: www.scilinks.org
NSTA **sciLINKS NUMBER:** HSTP295

Groups 17 and 18: Nonmetals Only

The elements in Groups 17 and 18 are nonmetals. The elements in Group 17 are the most reactive nonmetals, but the elements in Group 18 are the least reactive nonmetals. In fact, the elements in Group 18 normally won't react at all with other elements.

Group 17: Halogens

Chlorine is a yellowish green gas.

Bromine is a dark red liquid.

Iodine is a dark gray solid.

Figure 12 Physical properties of some halogens at room temperature are shown here.

| 9 F Fluorine |
| 17 Cl Chlorine |
| 35 Br Bromine |
| 53 I Iodine |
| 85 At Astatine |

Group contains: Nonmetals
Electrons in the outer level: 7
Reactivity: Very reactive
Other shared properties: Poor conductors of electric current; react violently with alkali metals to form salts; never found uncombined in nature

Halogens are very reactive nonmetals because their atoms need to gain only one electron to have a complete outer level. The atoms of halogens combine readily with other atoms, especially metals, to gain that missing electron.

Although the chemical properties of the halogens are similar, the physical properties are quite different, as shown in **Figure 12.**

Both chlorine and iodine are used as disinfectants. Chlorine is used to treat water, while iodine mixed with alcohol is used in hospitals.

Group 18: Noble Gases

| 2 He Helium |
| 10 Ne Neon |
| 18 Ar Argon |
| 36 Kr Krypton |
| 54 Xe Xenon |
| 86 Rn Radon |

Group contains: Nonmetals
Electrons in the outer level: 8 (2 for helium)
Reactivity: Unreactive
Other shared properties: Colorless, odorless gases at room temperature

Noble gases are unreactive nonmetals. Because the atoms of the elements in this group have a complete set of electrons in their outer level, they do not need to lose or gain any electrons. Therefore, they do not react with other elements under normal conditions.

All of the noble gases are found in Earth's atmosphere in small amounts. Argon, the most abundant noble gas in the atmosphere, makes up almost 1 percent of the atmosphere.

BRAIN FOOD

The term *noble gases* describes the nonreactivity of these elements. Just as nobles, such as kings and queens, did not often mix with common people, the noble gases do not normally react with other elements.

MISCONCEPTION ALERT

Noble gases were originally called *inert gases* because it was thought that they would not react with any elements. However, scientists are able to use high temperatures and pressures to cause some of the elements in Group 18 to react. Thus, the term *inert* is not correct, and the term *noble* is preferred.

The nonreactivity of the noble gases makes them useful. Ordinary light bulbs last longer when filled with argon than they would if filled with a reactive gas. Because argon is unreactive, it does not react with the metal filament in the light bulb even when the filament gets hot. The low density of helium causes blimps and weather balloons to float, and its nonreactivity makes helium safer to use than hydrogen. One popular use of noble gases that does *not* rely on their nonreactivity is shown in **Figure 13.**

Figure 13 Besides neon, other noble gases are often used in "neon" lights.

Hydrogen Stands Apart

Electrons in the outer level: 1
Reactivity: Reactive
Other properties: Colorless, odorless gas at room temperature; low density; reacts explosively with oxygen

The properties of hydrogen do not match the properties of any single group, so hydrogen is set apart from the other elements in the table.

Hydrogen is placed above Group 1 in the periodic table because atoms of the alkali metals also have only one electron in their outer level. Atoms of hydrogen, like atoms of alkali metals, can give away one electron when joining with other atoms. However, hydrogen's physical properties are more like the properties of nonmetals than of metals. As you can see, hydrogen really is in a group of its own.

Hydrogen is the most abundant element in the universe. Hydrogen's reactive nature makes it useful as a fuel in rockets, as shown in **Figure 14.**

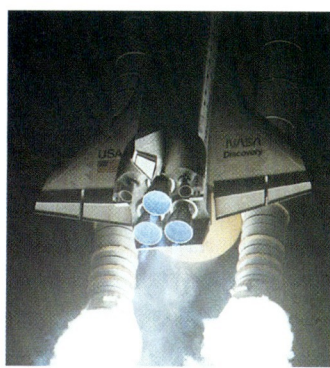

Figure 14 Hydrogen reacts violently with oxygen. The hot water vapor that forms as a result pushes the space shuttle into orbit.

REVIEW

1. In which group are the unreactive nonmetals found?
2. What are two properties of the halogens?
3. **Making Predictions** In the future, a new halogen may be synthesized. Predict its atomic number and properties.
4. **Comparing Concepts** Compare the element hydrogen with the alkali metal sodium.

Chapter Highlights

Vocabulary Definitions

Section 1

periodic having a regular, repeating pattern

periodic law the law that states that the chemical and physical properties of elements are periodic functions of their atomic numbers

period a horizontal row of elements on the periodic table

group a column of elements on the periodic table

Chapter Highlights

SECTION 1

Vocabulary
periodic (p. 302)
periodic law (p. 303)
period (p. 309)
group (p. 309)

Section Notes
- Mendeleev developed the first periodic table. He arranged elements in order of increasing atomic mass. The properties of elements repeated in an orderly pattern, allowing Mendeleev to predict properties for elements that had not yet been discovered.
- Moseley rearranged the elements in order of increasing atomic number.
- The periodic law states that the chemical and physical properties of elements are periodic functions of their atomic numbers.
- Elements in the periodic table are divided into metals, metalloids, and nonmetals.
- Each element has a chemical symbol that is recognized around the world.
- A horizontal row of elements is called a period. The elements gradually change from metallic to nonmetallic from left to right across each period.
- A vertical column of elements is called a group or family. Elements in a group usually have similar properties.

Labs
Create a Periodic Table (p. 678)

✓ Skills Check

Visual Understanding

PERIODIC TABLE OF THE ELEMENTS Scientists rely on the periodic table as a resource for a large amount of information. Review the periodic table on pages 304–305. Pay close attention to the labels and the key; they will help you understand the information presented in the table.

CLASSES OF ELEMENTS Identifying an element as a metal, nonmetal, or metalloid gives you a better idea of the properties of that element. Review the figures on pages 306–307 to understand how to use the zigzag line on the periodic table to identify the classes of elements and to review the properties of elements in each category.

Lab and Activity Highlights

Create a Periodic Table PG 678

 Datasheets for LabBook
(blackline masters for this lab)

318 Chapter 12 • The Periodic Table

SECTION 2

Vocabulary
- alkali metals (p. 310)
- alkaline-earth metals (p. 311)
- halogens (p. 316)
- noble gases (p. 316)

Section Notes
- The alkali metals (Group 1) are the most reactive metals. Atoms of the alkali metals have one electron in their outer level.
- The alkaline-earth metals (Group 2) are less reactive than the alkali metals. Atoms of the alkaline-earth metals have two electrons in their outer level.
- The transition metals (Groups 3–12) include most of the well-known metals as well as the lanthanides and actinides located below the periodic table.
- Groups 13–16 contain the metalloids along with some metals and nonmetals. The atoms of the elements in each of these groups have the same number of electrons in their outer level.
- The halogens (Group 17) are very reactive nonmetals. Atoms of the halogens have seven electrons in their outer level.
- The noble gases (Group 18) are unreactive nonmetals. Atoms of the noble gases have a complete set of electrons in their outer level.
- Hydrogen is set off by itself because its properties do not match the properties of any one group.

VOCABULARY DEFINITIONS, continued

SECTION 2

alkali metals the elements in Group 1 of the periodic table; they are the most reactive metals, and their atoms have one electron in their outer level

alkaline-earth metals the elements in Group 2 of the periodic table; they are reactive metals but less reactive than alkali metals; their atoms have two electrons in their outer level

halogens the elements in Group 17 of the periodic table; they are very reactive nonmetals, and their atoms have seven electrons in their outer level

noble gases the unreactive elements in Group 18 of the periodic table; their atoms have eight electrons in their outer level (except for helium, which has two electrons)

 Vocabulary Review Worksheet 12

 Blackline masters of these Chapter Highlights can be found in the **Study Guide**.

internet connect

 GO TO: go.hrw.com

Visit the **HRW** Web site for a variety of learning tools related to this chapter. Just type in the keyword:

KEYWORD: HSTPRT

 GO TO: www.scilinks.org

Visit the **National Science Teachers Association** on-line Web site for Internet resources related to this chapter. Just type in the *sci*LINKS number for more information about the topic:

TOPIC: The Periodic Table	*sci*LINKS NUMBER: HSTP280
TOPIC: Metals	*sci*LINKS NUMBER: HSTP285
TOPIC: Metalloids	*sci*LINKS NUMBER: HSTP290
TOPIC: Nonmetals	*sci*LINKS NUMBER: HSTP295
TOPIC: Buckminster Fuller and the Buckyball	*sci*LINKS NUMBER: HSTP300

Lab and Activity Highlights

LabBank

 Inquiry Labs, The Chemical Side of Light, Lab 20

Whiz-Bang Demonstrations, Waiter, There's Carbon in My Sugar Bowl! Demo 55

 Long-Term Projects & Research Ideas, It's Element-ary, Project 62

Interactive Explorations CD-ROM

 CD 1, Exploration 5, "Element of Surprise"

Chapter 12 • Chapter Highlights

Chapter Review Answers

USING VOCABULARY
1. group
2. period
3. alkali metals
4. noble gases

UNDERSTANDING CONCEPTS

Multiple Choice
5. c
6. b
7. c
8. b
9. c
10. c

Short Answer
11. Mendeleev's periodic table allowed scientists to predict properties of elements that had not yet been found.
12. Moseley arranged elements by increasing atomic number. Mendeleev arranged elements by increasing atomic mass.
13. Both are periodic. The periodic table has repeating properties of elements. The calendar has repeating days and months.
14. Metals are located to the left of the zigzag on the periodic table. Metalloids border the zigzag. Nonmetals are to the right of the zigzag.

Concept Mapping
15. 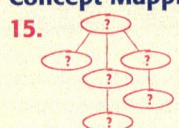 An answer to this exercise can be found at the end of this book.

Concept Mapping Transparency 12

Chapter Review

USING VOCABULARY

Complete the following sentences by choosing the appropriate term from each pair of terms listed below.

1. Elements in the same vertical column in the periodic table belong to the same __?__. (*group* or *period*)

2. Elements in the same horizontal row in the periodic table belong to the same __?__. (*group* or *period*)

3. The most reactive metals are __?__. (*alkali metals* or *alkaline-earth metals*)

4. Elements that are unreactive are called __?__. (*noble gases* or *halogens*)

UNDERSTANDING CONCEPTS

Multiple Choice

5. An element that is a very reactive gas is most likely a member of the
   a. noble gases.
   b. alkali metals.
   c. halogens.
   d. actinides.

6. Which statement is true?
   a. Alkali metals are generally found in their uncombined form.
   b. Alkali metals are Group 1 elements.
   c. Alkali metals should be stored under water.
   d. Alkali metals are unreactive.

7. Which statement about the periodic table is false?
   a. There are more metals than nonmetals.
   b. The metalloids are located in Groups 13 through 16.
   c. The elements at the far left of the table are nonmetals.
   d. Elements are arranged by increasing atomic number.

8. One property of most nonmetals is that they are
   a. shiny.
   b. poor conductors of electric current.
   c. flattened when hit with a hammer.
   d. solids at room temperature.

9. Which is a true statement about elements?
   a. Every element occurs naturally.
   b. All elements are found in their uncombined form in nature.
   c. Each element has a unique atomic number.
   d. All of the elements exist in approximately equal quantities.

10. Which is NOT found on the periodic table?
    a. the atomic number of each element
    b. the symbol of each element
    c. the density of each element
    d. the atomic mass of each element

Short Answer

11. Why was Mendeleev's periodic table useful?

12. How is Moseley's basis for arranging the elements different from Mendeleev's?

13. How is the periodic table like a calendar?

14. Describe the location of metals, metalloids, and nonmetals on the periodic table.

320 Chapter 12 • The Periodic Table

Concept Mapping

15. Use the following terms to create a concept map: periodic table, elements, groups, periods, metals, nonmetals, metalloids.

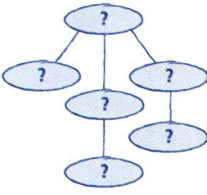

CRITICAL THINKING AND PROBLEM SOLVING

16. When an element with 115 protons in its nucleus is synthesized, will it be a metal, a nonmetal, or a metalloid? Explain.

17. Look at Mendeleev's periodic table in Figure 2. Why was Mendeleev not able to make any predictions about the noble gas elements?

18. Your classmate offers to give you a piece of sodium he found while hiking. What is your response? Explain.

19. Determine the identity of each element described below:
    a. This metal is very reactive, has properties similar to magnesium, and is in the same period as bromine.
    b. This nonmetal is in the same group as lead.
    c. This metal is the most reactive metal in its period and cannot be found uncombined in nature. Each atom of the element contains 19 protons.

MATH IN SCIENCE

20. The chart below shows the percentages of elements in the Earth's crust.

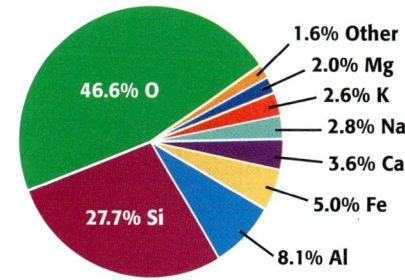

Excluding the "Other" category, what percentage of the Earth's crust is
a. alkali metals?
b. alkaline-earth metals?

INTERPRETING GRAPHICS

21. Study the diagram below to determine the pattern of the images. Predict the missing image, and draw it. Identify which properties are periodic and which properties are shared within a group.

  ?

NOW What Do You Think?

Take a minute to review your answers to the ScienceLog questions on page 301. Have your answers changed? If necessary, revise your answers based on what you have learned since you began this chapter.

CRITICAL THINKING AND PROBLEM SOLVING

16. Metal; it will be located below the metal bismuth to the left of the zigzag.
17. Mendeleev could only make predictions about elements where there were clear gaps in his table. Because no noble gases were known at the time, there were no obvious gaps in the table and no way he could have known a whole column was missing.
18. I would tell my classmate that he didn't find sodium. Sodium is very reactive and cannot be found uncombined in nature. It would react with oxygen and water in the air and form a compound.
19. a. calcium
    b. carbon
    c. potassium

MATH IN SCIENCE

20. a. 5.4 percent (sodium and potassium)
    b. 5.6 percent (magnesium and calcium)

INTERPRETING GRAPHICS

21.

Periodic properties are the order of the shapes and the number of lines inside the shape. The properties shared in a group are the shape and the color of the lines inside the shape.

NOW What Do You Think?

1. Elements are organized by their atomic number.
2. The properties of elements repeat in a pattern as you move across the table.
3. The elements in a group have the same number of electrons in their outer level.

Blackline masters of this Chapter Review can be found in the **Study Guide**.

SCIENCE, TECHNOLOGY, AND SOCIETY

The Science of Fireworks

Background

The colors in a fireworks display depend on the wavelengths of the light emitted by different chemicals as they burn. Light with the shortest wavelength appears violet in color. Light with the longest wavelength appears red. Refer to the chart at the bottom of the page for the colors produced by various elements.

When the fuse in the fireworks is lit, the gunpowder ignites and produces gases that propel the fireworks into the air. Charcoal gives the fireworks a sparkling, flaming tail.

Energy is necessary to start the reaction in a fireworks display. If the fireworks are not packed correctly, the thermal reaction fails, resulting in what is called a dud.

Teaching Strategy

Show students that each element produces a certain color. Obtain samples of calcium chloride, strontium chloride, and sodium chloride. To prepare 0.5 M solutions, dissolve the following quantities in separate containers with enough water to make 100 mL of each solution: 5.5 g of $CaCl_2$, 8.83 g of $SrCl_2 \cdot H_2O$, and 2.9 g of NaCl. Dip a different wooden splint in each solution, and use tongs to insert each splint into the flame of a portable burner to burn the chemical from the splint. Try not to ignite the splints. The splints can be dipped into the solutions again if necessary.

Science, Technology, and Society

The Science of Fireworks

What do the space shuttle and the Fourth of July have in common? The same scientific principles that help scientists launch a space shuttle also help pyrotechnicians create spectacular fireworks shows. The word *pyrotechnics* comes from the Greek words for "fire art." Explosive and dazzling, a fireworks display is both a science and an art.

An Ancient History

More than 1,000 years ago, Chinese civilizations made black powder, the original gunpowder used in pyrotechnics. They used the powder to set off firecrackers and primitive missiles. Black powder is still used today to launch fireworks into the air and to give fireworks an explosive charge. Even the ingredients—saltpeter (potassium nitrate), charcoal, and sulfur—haven't changed since ancient times.

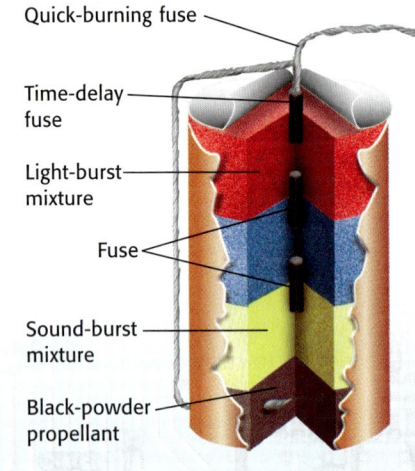

▲ *Cutaway view of a typical firework. Each shell creates a different type of display.*

Snap, Crackle, Pop!

The shells of fireworks contain the ingredients that create the explosions. Inside the shells, black powder and other chemicals are packed in layers. When ignited, one layer may cause a bright burst of light while a second layer produces a loud booming sound. The shell's shape affects the shape of the explosion. Cylindrical shells produce a trail of lights that looks like an umbrella. Round shells produce a star-burst pattern of lights.

The color and sound of fireworks depend on the chemicals used. To create colors, chemicals like strontium (for red), magnesium (for white), and copper (for blue) can be mixed with the gunpowder.

Explosion in the Sky

Fireworks are launched from metal, plastic, or cardboard tubes. Black powder at the bottom of the shell explodes and shoots the shell into the sky. A fuse begins to burn when the shell is launched. Seconds later, when the explosive chemicals are high in the air, the burning fuse lights another charge of black powder. This ignites the rest of the ingredients in the shell, causing an explosion that lights up the sky!

Bang for Your Buck

▶ The fireworks used during New Year's Eve and Fourth of July celebrations can cost anywhere from $200 to $2,000 apiece. Count the number of explosions at the next fireworks show you see. If each of the fireworks cost just $200 to produce, how much would the fireworks for the entire show cost?

Answer to Bang for Your Buck

Students should be aware that a fireworks display is costly. If a fireworks display consists of 50 explosions at $200 per explosion, the display would cost $10,000.

Element	Color
sodium	yellow
barium	green
nickel	green
copper	blue
strontium	crimson
lithium	bright red
calcium	dark red
magnesium	white

322 Chapter 12 • Science, Technology, and Society

WEIRD SCIENCE

BUCKYBALLS

Researchers are scrambling for the ball—the buckyball, that is. This special form of carbon has 60 carbon atoms linked together in a shape much like a soccer ball. Scientists are having a field day trying to find new uses for this unusual molecule.

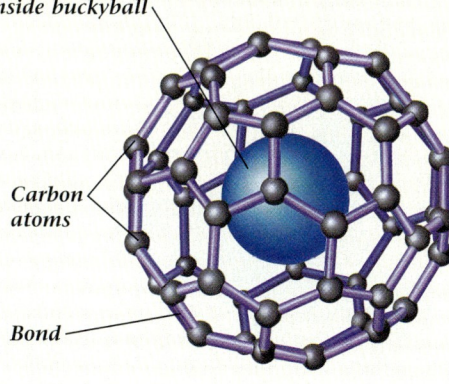

▲ The buckyball, short for buckminsterfullerene, was named after architect Buckminster Fuller.

The Starting Lineup

Named for architect Buckminster Fuller, buckyballs resemble the geodesic domes that are characteristic of the architect's work. Excitement over buckyballs began in 1985 when scientists projected light from a laser onto a piece of graphite. In the soot that remained, researchers found a completely new kind of molecule! Buckyballs are also found in the soot from a candle flame. Some scientists claim to have detected buckyballs in outer space. In fact, one hypothesis suggests that buckyballs might be at the center of the condensing clouds of gas, dust, and debris that form galaxies.

The Game Plan

Ever since buckyballs were discovered, chemists have been busy trying to identify the molecules' properties. One interesting property is that substances can be trapped inside a buckyball. A buckyball can act like a cage that surrounds smaller substances, such as individual atoms. Buckyballs also appear to be both slippery and strong. They can be opened to insert materials, and they can even link together in tubes.

How can buckyballs be used? They may have a variety of uses, from carrying messages through atom-sized wires in computer chips to delivering medicines right where the body needs them. Making tough plastics and cutting tools are uses that are also under investigation. With so many possibilities, scientists expect to get a kick out of buckyballs for some time!

The Kickoff

▶ A soccer ball is a great model for a buckyball. On the model, the places where three seams meet correspond to the carbon atoms on a buckyball. What represents the bonds between carbon atoms? Does your soccer-ball model have space for all 60 carbon atoms? You'll have to count and see for yourself.

UNIT 5

TIMELINE

Interactions of Matter

In this unit you will study the interactions through which matter can change its identity. You will learn how atoms bond with one another to form compounds and how atoms join in different combinations to form new substances through chemical reactions. You will also learn about the properties of several categories of compounds. Finally, you will learn how nuclear interactions can actually change the identity of an atom. This timeline includes some of the events leading to the current understanding of these interactions of matter.

1828
Urea, a compound found in urine, is produced in a laboratory. Until this time, chemists had believed that compounds created by living organisms could not be produced in the laboratory.

1858
German chemist Friedrich August Kekulé suggests that carbon forms four chemical bonds and can form long chains of carbon bonded to itself.

1964
Dr. Martin Luther King, Jr., American civil rights leader, is awarded the Nobel Peace Prize.

1969
The *Nimbus III* weather satellite is launched by the United States, representing the first civilian use of nuclear batteries.

1979
Public fear about nuclear power grows after an accident occurs at the Three Mile Island nuclear power station, in Pennsylvania.

1867
Swedish chemist Alfred Nobel develops dynamite. Dynamite's explosive power is a result of the decomposition reaction of nitroglycerin.

1898
The United States defeats Spain in the Spanish-American War.

1942
The first nuclear chain reaction is carried out in a squash court under the football stadium at the University of Chicago.

1903
Marie Curie, Pierre Curie, and Henri Becquerel are awarded the Nobel Prize in Physics for the discovery of radioactivity.

1996
Evidence of organic compounds in a meteorite leads scientists to speculate that life may have existed on Mars more than 3.6 billion years ago.

2001
The first total solar eclipse of the millenium occurs on June 21.

Interactions of Matter **325**

Chapter Organizer

CHAPTER ORGANIZATION	TIME MINUTES	OBJECTIVES	LABS, INVESTIGATIONS, AND DEMONSTRATIONS
Chapter Opener pp. 326–327	45	National Standards: SAI 1, ST 2, PS 1a	**Investigate!** From Glue to Goop, p. 327
Section 1 Electrons and Chemical Bonding	90	▶ Describe chemical bonding. ▶ Identify the number of valence electrons in an atom. ▶ Predict whether an atom is likely to form bonds. UCP 1, 2, SAI 2, ST 2, SPSP 5, HNS 1–3, PS 1b, 1c	**Demonstration,** p. 329 in ATE
Section 2 Types of Chemical Bonds	90	▶ Describe ionic, covalent, and metallic bonding. ▶ Describe the properties associated with substances containing each type of bond. UCP 1–3, PS 1b, 3e; LabBook UCP 2	**QuickLab,** Bending with Bonds, p. 340 **Making Models,** Covalent Marshmallows, p. 680 **Datasheets for LabBook,** Covalent Marshmallows, Datasheet 39 **Long-Term Projects & Research Ideas,** Project 63

*See page **T20** for a complete correlation of this book with the*

NATIONAL SCIENCE EDUCATION STANDARDS.

TECHNOLOGY RESOURCES

 **Guided Reading Audio CD** English or Spanish, Chapter 13

 **One-Stop Planner CD-ROM** with Test Generator

 CNN. Science, Technology & Society, Brittle Book Repair, Segment 18

325A Chapter 13 • Chemical Bonding

Chapter 13 • Chemical Bonding

CLASSROOM WORKSHEETS, TRANSPARENCIES, AND RESOURCES	SCIENCE INTEGRATION AND CONNECTIONS	REVIEW AND ASSESSMENT
Directed Reading Worksheet 13 **Science Puzzlers, Twisters & Teasers,** Worksheet 13		
Directed Reading Worksheet 13, Section 1 **Transparency 249,** Electron Arrangement in an Atom **Transparency 250,** Valence Electrons and the Periodic Table	**Across the Sciences:** Left-Handed Molecules, p. 346	**Homework,** p. 330 in ATE **Review,** p. 331 **Quiz,** p. 331 in ATE **Alternative Assessment,** p. 331 in ATE
Directed Reading Worksheet 13, Section 2 **Transparency 251,** Forming Positive and Negative Ions **Math Skills for Science Worksheet 9,** Comparing Integers on a Number Line **Math Skills for Science Worksheet 10,** Arithmetic with Positive and Negative Numbers **Transparency 252,** Covalent Bonds **Transparency 253,** Covalent Bonds in a Water Molecule **Transparency 21,** The Making of a Protein **Reinforcement Worksheet 13,** Is It an Ion? **Reinforcement Worksheet 13,** Interview with an Electron **Critical Thinking Worksheet 13,** The Road to Knowledge	**Connect to Life Science,** p. 333 in ATE **MathBreak,** Charge! p. 334 **Connect to Earth Science,** p. 334 in ATE **Real-World Connection,** p. 334 in ATE **Math and More,** p. 335 in ATE **Biology Connection,** p. 339 **Real-World Connection,** p. 339 in ATE **Cross-Disciplinary Focus,** p. 340 in ATE **Apply,** p. 341 **Eureka!** Here's Looking at Ya'! p. 347	**Self-Check,** p. 333 **Review,** p. 335 **Self-Check,** p. 337 **Homework,** pp. 338, 339 in ATE **Review,** p. 341 **Quiz,** p. 341 in ATE **Alternative Assessment,** p. 341 in ATE

 Holt, Rinehart and Winston On-line Resources
go.hrw.com

For worksheets and other teaching aids related to this chapter, visit the HRW Web site and type in the keyword: **HSTBND**

 **National Science Teachers Association**
www.scilinks.org

Encourage students to use the *sci*LINKS numbers listed in the internet connect boxes to access information and resources on the **NSTA** Web site.

END-OF-CHAPTER REVIEW AND ASSESSMENT

Chapter Review in Study Guide
Vocabulary and Notes in Study Guide
Chapter Tests with Performance-Based Assessment, Chapter 13 Test
Chapter Tests with Performance-Based Assessment, Performance-Based Assessment 13
Concept Mapping Transparency 13

Chapter Resources & Worksheets

Visual Resources

TEACHING TRANSPARENCIES

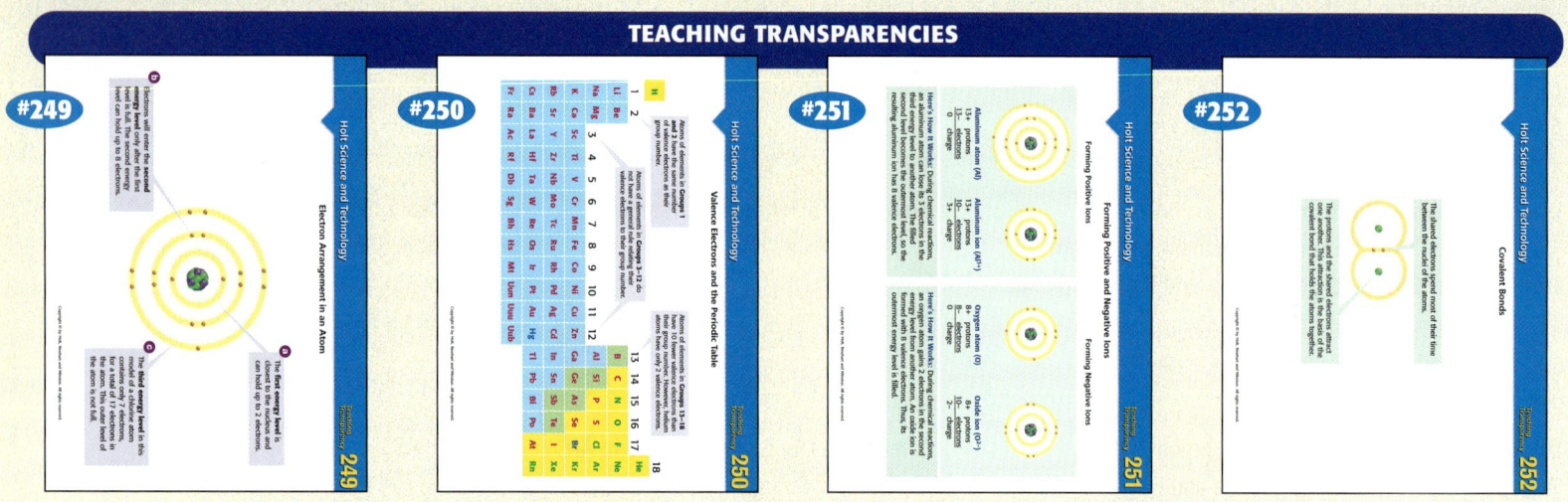

TEACHING TRANSPARENCIES

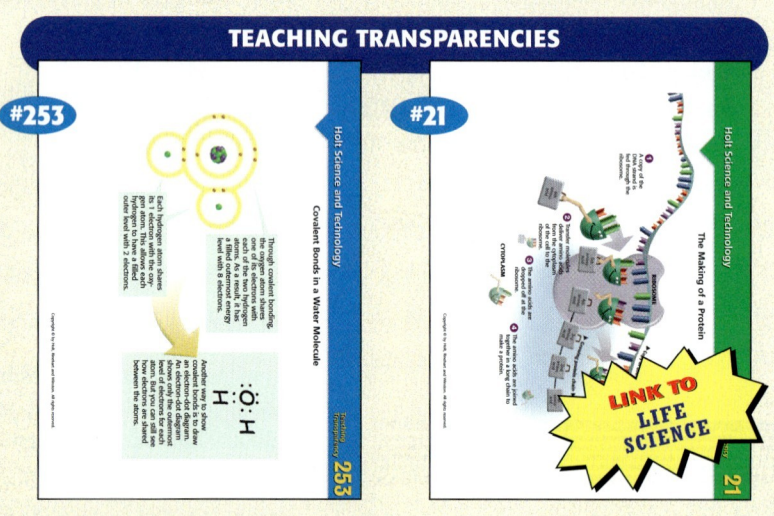

CONCEPT MAPPING TRANSPARENCY

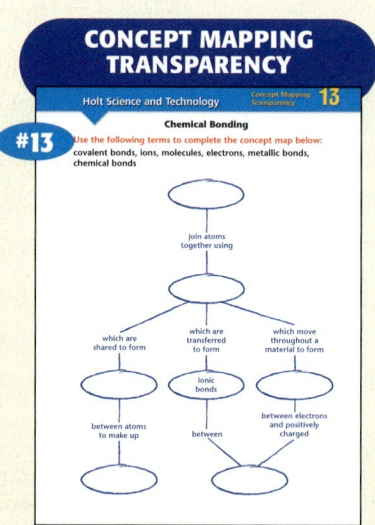

Meeting Individual Needs

DIRECTED READING
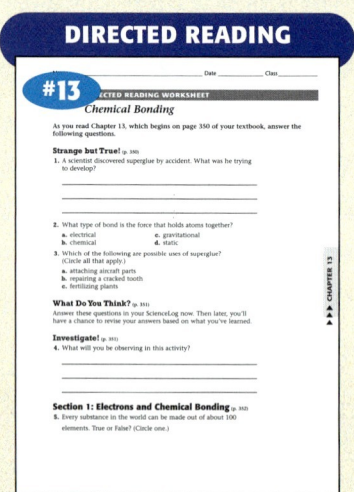

REINFORCEMENT & VOCABULARY REVIEW
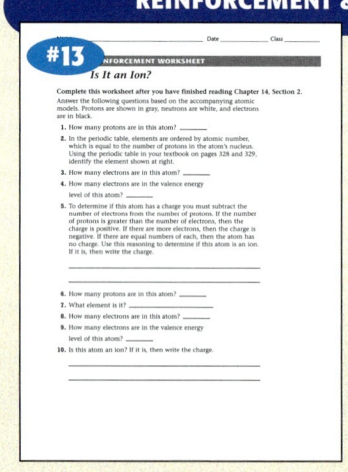
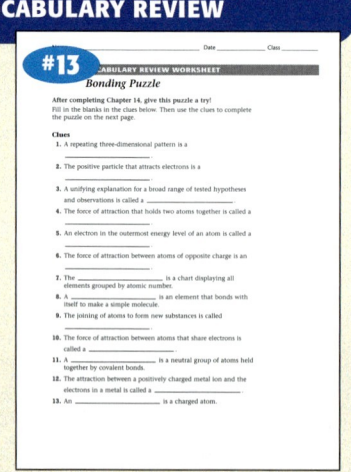

SCIENCE PUZZLERS, TWISTERS & TEASERS
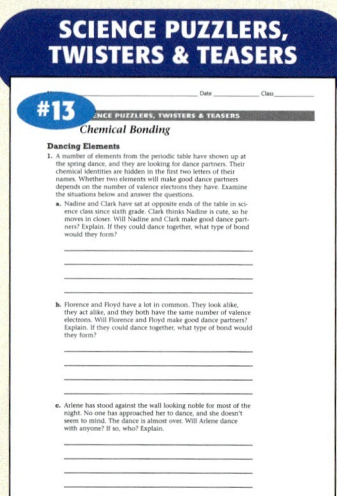

325C Chapter 13 • Chemical Bonding

Chapter 13 • Chemical Bonding

Review & Assessment

STUDY GUIDE

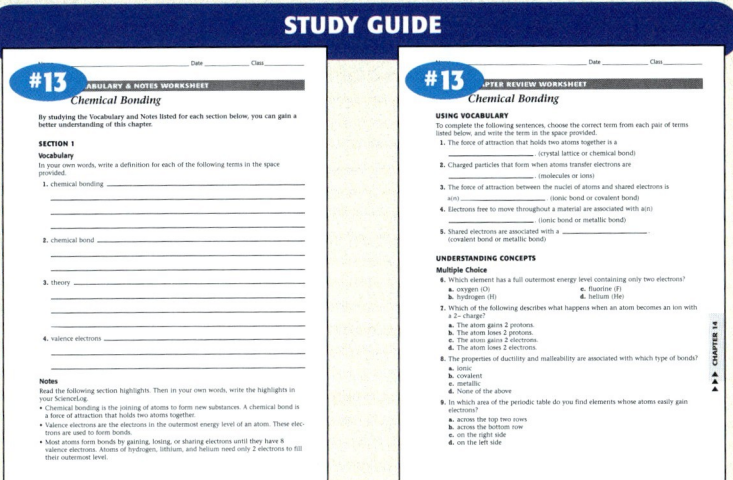

CHAPTER TESTS WITH PERFORMANCE-BASED ASSESSMENT

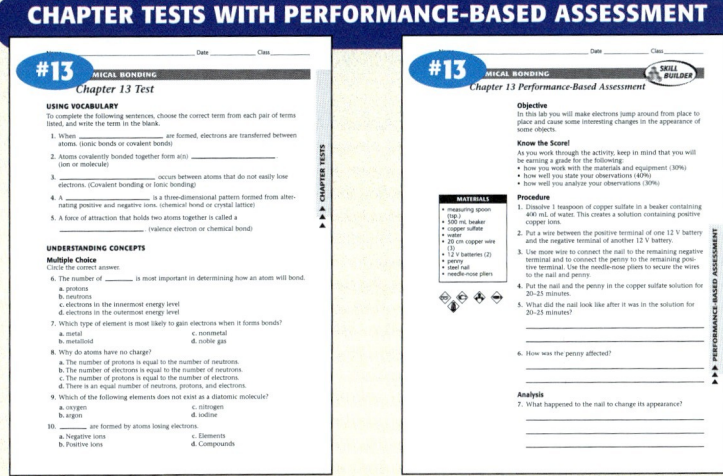

Lab Worksheets

LONG-TERM PROJECTS & RESEARCH IDEAS

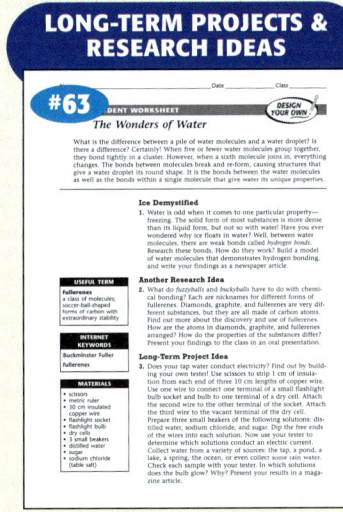

DATASHEETS FOR LABBOOK

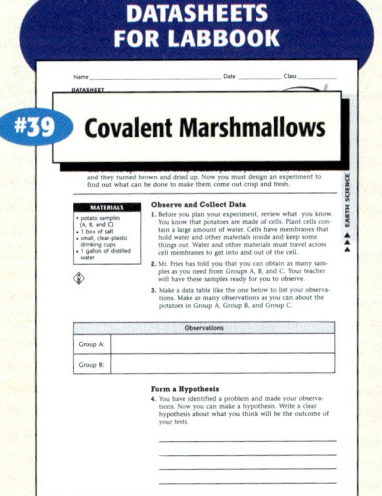

Applications & Extensions

CRITICAL THINKING & PROBLEM SOLVING

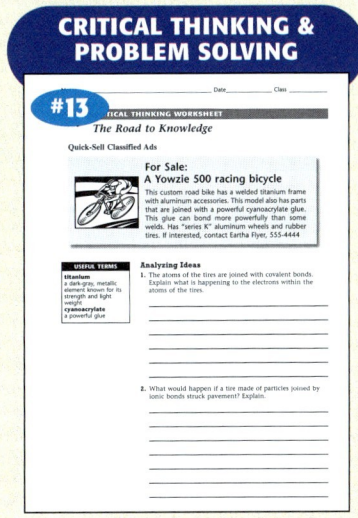

SCIENCE TECHNOLOGY

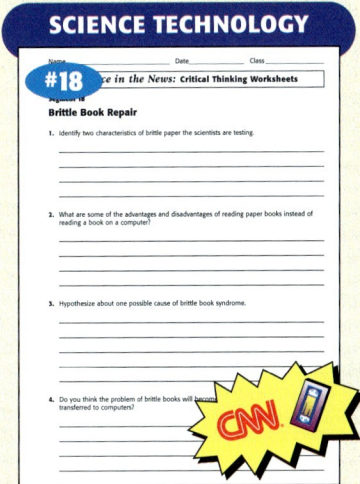

Chapter 13 • Chapter Resources & Worksheets **325D**

Chapter Background

SECTION 1

Electrons and Chemical Bonding

▶ Discovery of the Electron

Electrons are key to the way all atoms bond with other atoms. An English physicist named Joseph John Thomson (1856–1940) discovered the electron in 1897 as a result of his attempts to discover the nature of cathode rays, the invisible beam emitted from the negative electrode when electrical energy is passed through a vacuum tube.

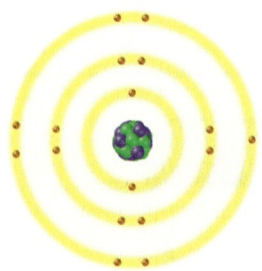

- Thomson believed that cathode rays were composed of particles of matter that he called corpuscles. He also theorized that the corpuscles—later renamed electrons—were negatively charged and were identical, no matter what type of gas or metal carried the electrical energy.

- For his discovery of the electron and his work shedding light on atomic structure, Thomson was awarded the Nobel Prize in Physics in 1906.

IS THAT A FACT!

▶ J. J. Thomson's model of the atom, which was eventually superseded by other models, was dubbed the plum-pudding model because some people visualized Thomson's model as a positively charged sphere of "pudding" interspersed with negatively charged "plums," or electrons.

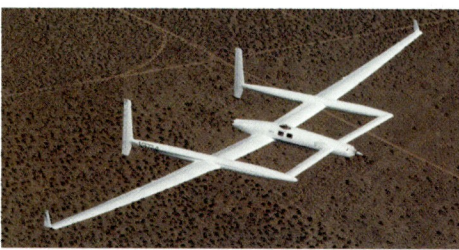

▶ Bohr's Theory of Atomic Structure

In 1913, the Danish physicist Niels Bohr (1885–1962) theorized that electrons occupy energy levels, which are at certain specified distances from an atom's nucleus. Known atoms have an unexcited electron configuration of up to seven energy levels, but only the heaviest and largest atoms have electrons in all seven energy levels.

- Energy is absorbed when an electron moves from a lower energy level to a higher energy level. Energy is released when an electron moves from a higher level to a lower one. Bohr's model of the atom has been compared to the structure of an onion, with the layers of onion corresponding to the energy levels occupied by electrons.

- Scientists now describe electrons as particles with properties similar to those of waves. These properties led scientists to describe regions in the atom where electrons are likely to be found because the exact path of an electron cannot be predicted. These regions are called electron clouds.

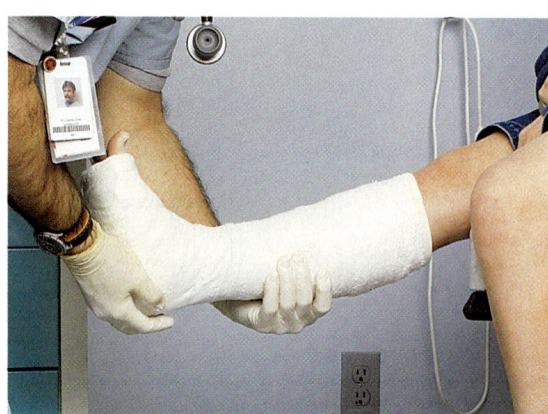

SECTION 2

Types of Chemical Bonds

▶ G. N. Lewis and the Theory of the Electron Pair

In the early 1900s, an American chemist named Gilbert Newton Lewis (1875–1946) noticed that elements with certain numbers of electrons seemed to be especially unreactive, while other elements were highly reactive.

Chapter 13 • Chemical Bonding

Helium, which has 2 electrons, is inert, but hydrogen, which has 1 electron, is reactive. Lewis also noticed that the next nonreactive element on the periodic table, neon, had 8 more electrons than helium.

- Lewis theorized that atoms have "layers" of electrons and that a specific number of electrons—8, for example—is required to fill the outer layer. From this observation came Lewis's "octet rule"—ions or atoms with a filled outer layer of 8 electrons are unreactive.

- Lewis envisioned atoms as cubes that need to have all their corners occupied by electrons. When all the corners filled, a new cube could be started. Lewis revised his model when he read a paper that suggested that a chemical bond could be formed by the sharing of 2 electrons between two atoms.

- Lewis published his theory in 1916. It was the first explanation of the covalent bond and went a long way toward explaining the mechanism of many chemical reactions.

- Electron-dot diagrams, often called Lewis structures, are the legacy of Lewis's cube model and have helped several generations of chemistry students visualize molecular structures and bonding.

▶ **The Unique Bonding Properties of Carbon**

Carbon and carbon compounds are the basis of all living things. Because carbon atoms have 4 valence electrons, they can combine with other carbon atoms indefinitely to form molecules with high molecular weight. These large molecules may take rather unusual forms, such as long chains or rings.

- Carbon rings can form when carbon atoms bond to other carbon atoms. The carbon compound benzene, C_6H_6, for example, is a hexagonal ring consisting of six carbon atoms bonded to each other with a hydrogen atom bonded to each carbon. The benzene ring is the parent compound of many familiar substances, including aromatics, such as vanilla, perfumes, and mothballs.

- Long carbon-based chains of repeating molecular units are known as polymers. The wide variety of plastics we use, with all their different physical properties, are examples of polymers. These different properties are the result of the type of repeating unit and the way in which these units are bonded together.

IS THAT A FACT!

▶ To some people, the word *polymer* is synonymous with *plastic*. However, many polymers exist in nature. Cellulose, a polymer chain containing repeating units of the molecule glucose, is the chief constituent of plant cells. Wood is about 50 percent cellulose, and cotton is 90 percent cellulose.

▶ The first plastic, celluloid, was synthesized from cotton fibers that had been dissolved in nitric acid and then further processed.

For background information about teaching strategies and issues, refer to the *Professional Reference for Teachers*.

Chapter 13 • Chapter Background   **325F**

CHAPTER 13
Chemical Bonding

Chapter Preview

Section 1
Electrons and Chemical Bonding
- Atoms Combine Through Chemical Bonding
- Electron Number and Organization
- To Bond or Not to Bond

Section 2
Types of Chemical Bonds
- Ionic Bonds
- Covalent Bonds
- Metallic Bonds

Directed Reading Worksheet 13

Science Puzzlers, Twisters & Teasers Worksheet 13

Guided Reading Audio CD
English or Spanish, Chapter 13

Smithsonian Institution®
Visit www.si.edu/hrw for additional on-line resources.

CHAPTER 13 Chemical Bonding

Strange but True!

In 1987, pilots Richard Rutan and Jeana Yeager flew the *Voyager* aircraft, shown above, around the world without refueling. The record-breaking trip lasted just over 9 days. In order to carry enough fuel for the trip, the plane had to be as lightweight as possible. Using fewer bolts than usual to attach parts would make the airplane lighter. But without the bolts, what would hold the parts together? The designers decided to use glue!

Not just any glue would do. They used superglue. When superglue is applied, it combines with water from the air to form chemical bonds. The result—the materials stick together as if they were one material. Superglue is so strong that the weight of a two-ton elephant cannot separate two metal plates glued together with just a few drops!

Along with household uses, superglue also has uses in industry and medicine. To make shoes stronger and lighter, manufacturers can replace some of the stitching with superglue. And dentists can use superglue to hold a cracked tooth together.

Chemical bonding is responsible for the properties of materials. In this chapter, you will learn about the different types of bonds that hold atoms together and how those bonds affect the properties of the materials.

Superglue was discovered in the early 1950s by a scientist who was trying to develop a new plastic for the cockpit bubble of a jet plane.

Strange but True!

As anyone whose fingers have been stuck together knows, superglue bonds readily with human skin! Recently, doctors have found a way to take advantage of this fact by using a type of superglue as an alternative to stitches. Using glue to close wounds has several advantages over stitches. Glue is less painful than stitches, so an anesthetic is not necessary. Patients don't have to return to have their stitches removed. And gluing wounds leaves less noticeable scars.

What Do You Think?

In your ScienceLog, try to answer the following questions based on what you already know:

1. What is a chemical bond?
2. How are ionic bonds different from covalent bonds?
3. How are the properties of metals related to the type of bonds in them?

From Glue to Goop

Particles of glue can bond to other particles and hold objects together. Different types of bonds create differences in the properties of substances. In this activity, you will see how the formation of bonds causes an interesting change in the properties of a very common material—white glue.

Procedure

1. Fill a **small paper cup** 1/4 full of **white glue**. Observe the properties of the glue, and record your observations in your ScienceLog.
2. Fill a second **small paper cup** 1/4 full of **borax solution**.
3. Pour the borax solution into the cup containing the white glue, and stir well using a **plastic spoon**.
4. When it becomes too thick to stir, remove the material from the cup and knead it with your fingers. Observe the properties of the material, and record your observations in your ScienceLog.

Analysis

5. Compare the properties of the glue with those of the new material.
6. The properties of the new material resulted from the bonds between the borax and the particles in the glue. If too little borax were used, in what way would the properties of the material have been different?

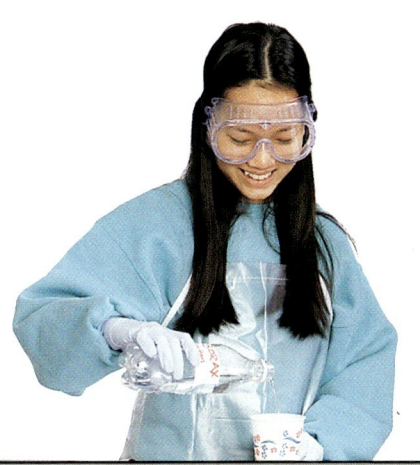

What Do You Think?

Accept all reasonable responses.

Students will have a chance to revise their answers in the Chapter Review under NOW What Do You Think?

Investigate!

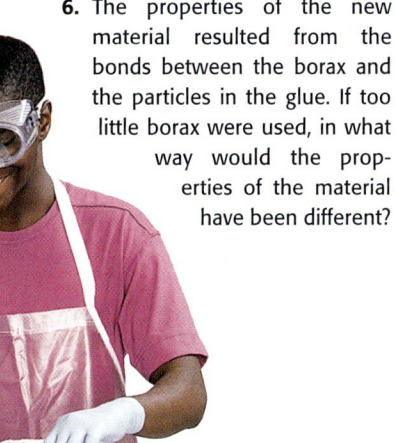

MATERIALS

FOR EACH STUDENT:
- 2 small paper cups
- diluted white glue ($\frac{1}{2}$ glue: $\frac{1}{2}$ water)
- borax solution (4 g borax: 100 mL water)
- plastic spoon

Safety Cautions:

- Remind students to review all safety cautions and icons before beginning this lab activity. Caution students to wear safety goggles, gloves, and aprons during this lab activity. Caution students to keep their hands away from their eyes and face during this lab activity.
- Ingestion of large amounts of borax can cause severe vomiting, diarrhea, and shock. Have the telephone number for your local poison control center available during this activity.
- Be sure eyewash equipment is available and is working.
- Caution students to wash their hands thoroughly when they are finished with this activity.
- Use only nontoxic white glue.

If time allows, have one group repeat the activity to find out what happens if less borax is used. Have students compare the result with their prediction in question 6.

Answers to Investigate!

5. The glue is a white liquid that flows easily. The new material is white and has properties that are more like those of a solid than like those of a liquid.
6. The properties of the material would be closer to the properties of the glue. The material would flow more easily and would not hold its shape as well.

Chapter 13 • Chemical Bonding

SECTION 1

Focus

Electrons and Chemical Bonding

This section defines chemical bonding and introduces the atomic components that are involved in the formation of chemical bonds.

Bellringer

Display the following chemical formulas but not their identities:

$C_6H_{12}O_6$ (glucose, a sugar)

C_2H_5OH (ethanol, an alcohol)

$C_6H_8O_6$ (vitamin C, found in citrus fruits)

$C_6H_8O_7$ (citric acid, found in lemons and other citrus fruits)

Ask students to identify the elements in these compounds and to predict whether the compounds are similar to each other and why. Identify and discuss the compounds and their similarities.

 Teaching Transparency 249 "Electron Arrangement in an Atom"

 **Directed Reading Worksheet 13** Section 1

TOPIC: The Electron
GO TO: www.scilinks.org
sciLINKS NUMBER: HSTP305

Section 1

Terms to Learn

chemical bonding
chemical bond
valence electrons

What You'll Do

- Describe chemical bonding.
- Identify the number of valence electrons in an atom.
- Predict whether an atom is likely to form bonds.

 **Science CONNECTION**

Why are the amino acids that are chemically bonded together to form your proteins all left-handed? Read about one cosmic explanation on page 346.

Electrons and Chemical Bonding

Have you ever stopped to consider that by using just the 26 letters of the alphabet, you make all of the words you use every day? Even though the number of letters is limited, their ability to be combined in different ways allows you to make an enormous number of words.

Now look around the room. Everything around you—desks, chalk, paper, even your friends—is made of atoms of elements. How can so many substances be formed from about 100 elements? In the same way that words can be formed by combining letters, different substances can be formed by combining atoms.

Atoms Combine Through Chemical Bonding

The atoms of just three elements—carbon, hydrogen, and oxygen—combine in different patterns to form the substances sugar, alcohol, and citric acid. **Chemical bonding** is the joining of atoms to form new substances. The properties of these new substances are different from those of the original elements. A force of attraction that holds two atoms together is called a **chemical bond.** As you will see, chemical bonds involve the electrons in the atoms.

Atoms and the chemical bonds that connect them cannot be observed with your eyes. During the past 150 years, scientists have performed many experiments that have led to the development of a theory of chemical bonding. Remember that a *theory* is a unifying explanation for a broad range of hypotheses and observations that have been supported by testing. The use of models helps people to discuss the theory of how and why atoms form chemical bonds.

IS THAT A FACT!

One of the earliest theories of chemical bonding was developed by the Swedish chemist Jöns Jacob Berzelius (1779–1848). Berzelius theorized that all elements had either a positive or a negative charge and that only positive and negative elements would bond with each other. His theory was widely accepted. In many ways, it is a fairly accurate explanation of ionic bonding. Berzelius's theory fell short, however, by implying that molecules containing more than one atom of the same element could not exist because those atoms would repel each other.

Electron Number and Organization

To understand how atoms form chemical bonds, you first need to know how many electrons are in a particular atom and how the electrons in an atom are organized. The number of electrons in an atom can be determined from the atomic number of the element. The atomic number is the number of protons in an atom. However, atoms have no charge, so the atomic number also represents the number of electrons in the atom.

The electrons in an atom are organized in energy levels. The levels farther from the nucleus contain electrons that have more energy than levels closer to the nucleus. The arrangement of electrons in a chlorine atom is shown in **Figure 1.**

Figure 1 Electron Arrangement in an Atom

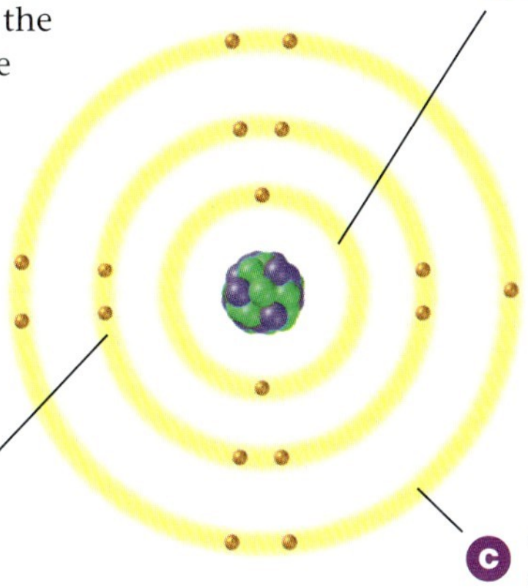

a The **first energy level** is closest to the nucleus and can hold up to 2 electrons.

b Electrons will enter the **second energy level** only after the first level is full. The second energy level can hold up to 8 electrons.

c The **third energy level** in this model of a chlorine atom contains only 7 electrons, for a total of 17 electrons in the atom. This outer level of the atom is not full.

Outer-Level Electrons Are the Key to Bonding As you just saw in Figure 1, a chlorine atom has a total of 17 electrons. When a chlorine atom bonds to another atom, not all of these electrons are used to create the bond. Most atoms form bonds using only the electrons in their outermost energy level. The electrons in the outermost energy level of an atom are called **valence** (VAY luhns) **electrons.** Thus, a chlorine atom has 7 valence electrons. You can see the valence electrons for atoms of some other elements in **Figure 2.**

Figure 2 *Valence electrons are the electrons in the outermost energy level of an atom.*

Oxygen

Electron total: 8
First level: 2 electrons
Second level: 6 electrons

The second energy level is the outermost level, so an oxygen atom has 6 valence electrons.

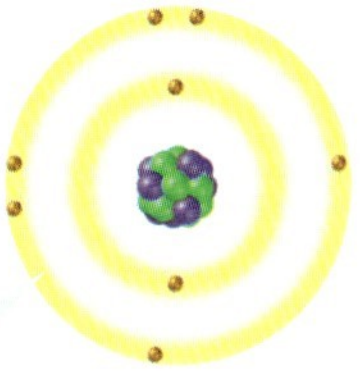

Sodium

Electron total: 11
First level: 2 electrons
Second level: 8 electrons
Third level: 1 electron

The third energy level is the outermost level, so a sodium atom has 1 valence electron.

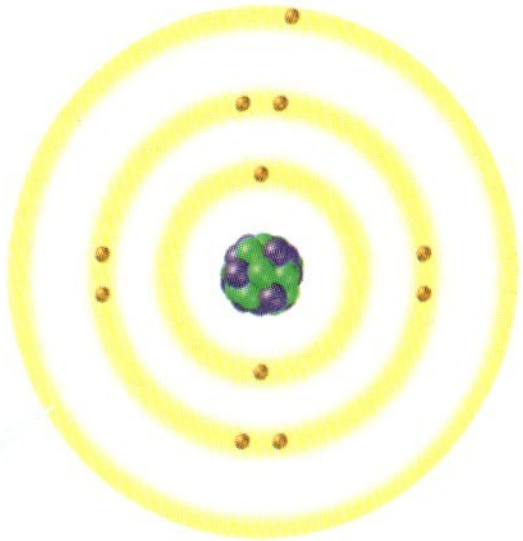

Scientists at Odds

Before 1962, most scientists believed that noble gases could not form compounds with other elements. After all, none were known to exist. In that year, though, chemists first created a compound of xenon and fluorine called xenon tetrafluoride, XeF_4. Much to their surprise, these chemists found that xenon and fluorine reacted quite easily to form the compound. Krypton and radon can also form compounds under the right conditions.

1 Motivate

Demonstration

Heat sugar over a Bunsen burner until only a black goo remains. Ask students to identify the black goo. (carbon)

Ask students to explain why the sugar turned into carbon. (Sugar is composed of carbon, hydrogen, and oxygen. The thermal energy drives off the hydrogen and oxygen in the form of water.)

Explain that the energy broke the chemical bonds that were holding the atoms of the three elements together.

2 Teach

MISCONCEPTION ALERT

Remind students that electrons are not arranged in precise circular levels around the nuclei of atoms. These diagrams are intended only to illustrate the concept of energy levels and to help students understand chemical bonding. The locations of electrons are best described as regions called *orbitals*. Orbitals have many shapes, and scientists cannot predict exactly where the electrons are within the orbitals.

Meeting Individual Needs

Learners Having Difficulty
After students read this page, have them draw the valence electrons of the elements magnesium, neon, aluminum, sulfur, and argon. Students should refer to a periodic table and write down the number of electrons in each of the five elements. Students can model their diagrams after **Figure 1** and **Figure 2.** Sheltered English

2 Teach, continued

USING THE FIGURE

Energy levels do not fill with electrons exactly in order. Levels are divided into sublevels that begin to overlap with the 19th electron in an atom. To avoid confusion, all examples using Bohr diagrams will have 18 or fewer electrons.

Have students refer to **Figure 3** and answer the following questions:

- How many valence electrons are there in an atom of radium? of lead? of iodine? of neon? of cesium? *(2, 4, 7, 8, 1)*
- Which of those elements would be the most likely to bond with other atoms? *(radium, lead, iodine, cesium)*
- Which element would be least likely to bond with other atoms? *(neon)*

Sheltered English

Answers to Activity

The valence electrons in each atom are as follows: lithium (1), beryllium (2), aluminum (3), carbon (4), nitrogen (5), sulfur (6), bromine (7), and krypton (8).

Homework

 *Writing* The atomic models shown in this section are known as Bohr models. Bohr models were developed by the Danish physicist Niels Bohr (1885–1962). Bohr was awarded the Nobel Prize in physics in 1922, largely for his work on atomic structure. Have students research Bohr's work and write a report.

Teaching Transparency 250 "Valence Electrons and the Periodic Table"

Valence Electrons and the Periodic Table You can determine the number of valence electrons in Figure 2 because you have a model to look at. But what if you didn't have a model? You have a tool that helps you determine the number of valence electrons for some elements—the periodic table!

Remember that elements in a group often have similar properties, including the number of electrons in the outermost energy level of their atoms. The number of valence electrons for many elements is related to the group number, as shown in **Figure 3**.

Figure 3 Determining the Number of Valence Electrons

Atoms of elements in **Groups 1 and 2** have the same number of valence electrons as their group number.

Atoms of elements in **Groups 13–18** have 10 fewer valence electrons than their group number. However, helium atoms have only 2 valence electrons.

Atoms of elements in **Groups 3–12** do not have a general rule relating their valence electrons to their group number.

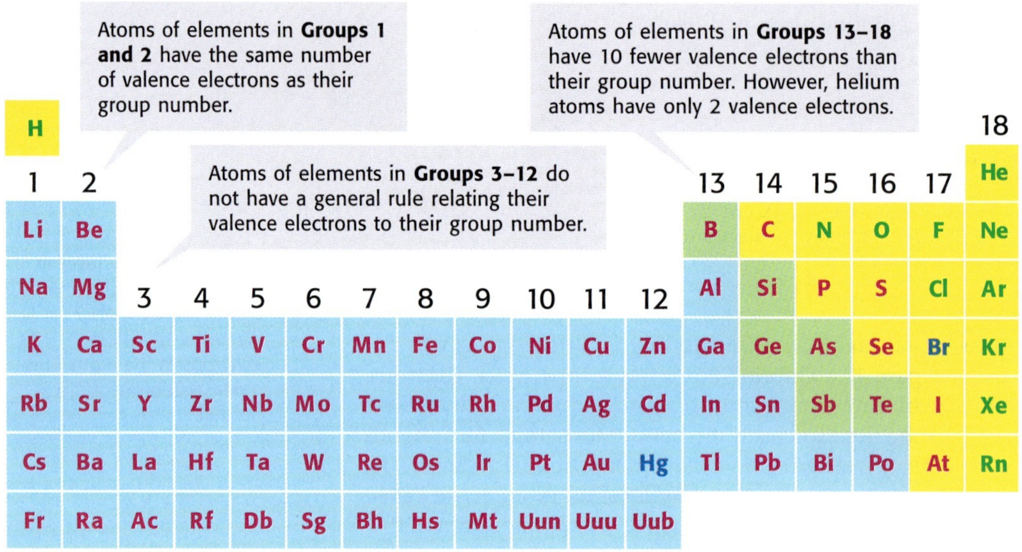

Activity

Determine the number of valence electrons in each of the following atoms: lithium (Li), beryllium (Be), aluminum (Al), carbon (C), nitrogen (N), sulfur (S), bromine (Br), and krypton (Kr).

TRY at HOME

To Bond or Not to Bond

Atoms do not all bond in the same manner. In fact, some atoms rarely bond at all! The number of electrons in the outermost energy level of an atom determines whether an atom will form bonds.

Atoms of the noble, or inert, gases (Group 18) do not normally form chemical bonds. As you just learned, atoms of Group 18 elements (except helium) have 8 valence electrons. Therefore, having 8 valence electrons must be a special condition. In fact, atoms that have 8 electrons in their outermost energy level do not normally form new bonds. The outermost energy level of an atom is considered to be full if it contains 8 electrons.

WEIRD SCIENCE

Vegetable oils are usually liquid. Margarine is 100 percent vegetable oil but is a solid. A process called *hydrogenation* uses a catalyst, such as nickel, to add hydrogen atoms to molecules of the oils. These hydrogen atoms bond with atoms in the oil molecules and change the substance to a solid. This solid has properties different from those of the original materials.

330   Chapter 13 • Chemical Bonding

Atoms Bond to Have a Filled Outermost Level An atom that has fewer than 8 valence electrons is more reactive, or more likely to form bonds, than an atom with 8 valence electrons. Atoms bond by gaining, losing, or sharing electrons in order to have a filled outermost energy level with 8 valence electrons. **Figure 4** describes the ways in which atoms can achieve a filled outermost energy level.

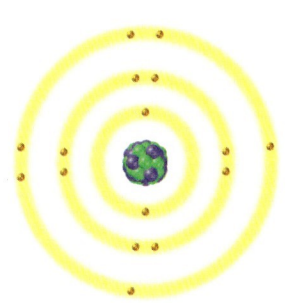
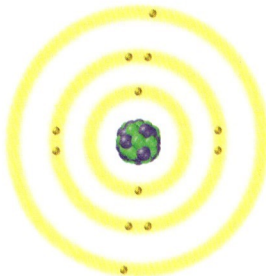

Figure 4 *These atoms achieve a full set of valence electrons in different ways.*

Sulfur
An atom of sulfur has 6 valence electrons. It can have 8 valence electrons by sharing 2 electrons with or gaining 2 electrons from other atoms to fill its outermost energy level.

Magnesium
An atom of magnesium has 2 valence electrons. It can have a full outer level by losing 2 electrons. The second energy level becomes the outermost energy level and contains a full set of 8 electrons.

A Full Set—with Two? Not all atoms need 8 valence electrons for a filled outermost energy level. Helium atoms need only 2 valence electrons. With only 2 electrons in the entire atom, the first energy level (which is also the outermost energy level) is full. Atoms of hydrogen and lithium form bonds with other atoms in order to have 2 electrons.

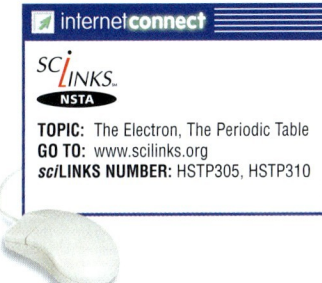

internetconnect
TOPIC: The Electron, The Periodic Table
GO TO: www.scilinks.org
sciLINKS NUMBER: HSTP305, HSTP310

REVIEW

1. What is a chemical bond?
2. What are valence electrons?
3. How many valence electrons does a silicon atom have?
4. Predict how atoms with 5 valence electrons will achieve a full set of valence electrons.
5. **Interpreting Graphics** At right is a diagram of a fluorine atom. Will fluorine form bonds? Explain.

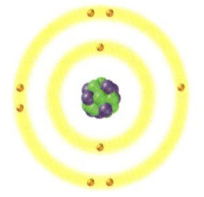

Fluorine

Section 1 • Electrons and Chemical Bonding 331

SECTION 2

Focus

Types of Chemical Bonds

In this section, students are introduced to ionic bonds and covalent bonds, and they learn how these bonds form different kinds of compounds. Students also learn about metallic bonds and how they relate to various properties of metals.

🔔 Bellringer

Give students the following scenario:

Suppose you decide to build a wooden birdhouse. You are not sure how to fasten the wooden pieces together. What are three ways you could fasten the wood together? Can you think of any other ways? Explain which you think would work best.

1 Motivate

DISCUSSION

Most convenience stores have a small container near the cash register with pennies in it. Discuss with students what purpose this container of pennies serves. (Many people leave a penny or two in it when they receive change. Others take a penny or two when they need to.) Discuss with students how this give-a-penny, take-a-penny strategy is similar to what atoms do when they form ionic bonds.

Directed Reading Worksheet 13 Section 2

SECTION 2

Types of Chemical Bonds

Terms to Learn
ionic bond covalent bond
ions molecule
crystal lattice metallic bond

What You'll Do
◆ Describe ionic, covalent, and metallic bonding.
◆ Describe the properties associated with substances containing each type of bond.

Atoms bond by gaining, losing, or sharing electrons to have a filled outermost energy level containing eight valence electrons. The way in which atoms interact through their valence electrons determines the type of bond that forms. The three types of bonds are ionic (ie AHN ik), covalent (кон VAY luhnt), and metallic.

Ionic Bonds

The materials shown in **Figure 5** have much in common. They are all hard, brittle solids at room temperature, they all have high melting points, and they all contain ionic bonds. An **ionic bond** is the force of attraction between oppositely charged ions. **Ions** are charged particles that form during chemical changes when one or more valence electrons transfer from one atom to another.

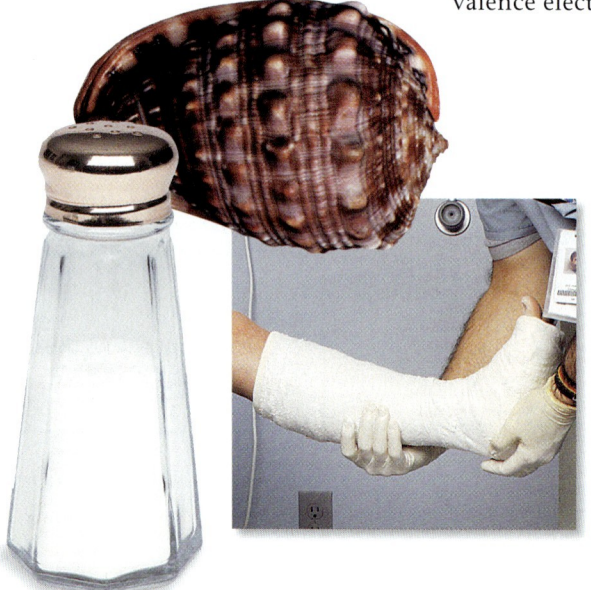

Figure 5 Calcium carbonate in seashells, sodium chloride in table salt, and calcium sulfate used to make plaster of Paris casts all contain ionic bonds.

A Transfer of Electrons An atom is neutral because the number of electrons equals the number of protons. So their charges cancel each other. A transfer of electrons between atoms changes the number of electrons in each atom, while the number of protons stays the same. The negative charges and positive charges no longer cancel out, and the atoms become ions. Although an atom cannot gain (or lose) electrons without another atom nearby to lose (or gain) electrons, it is easier to study the formation of ions one at a time.

Atoms That Lose Electrons Form Positive Ions Ionic bonds form during chemical changes when atoms pull electrons away from other atoms. The atoms that lose electrons form ions that have fewer electrons than protons. Because the positive charges outnumber the negative charges, these ions have an overall positive charge.

⚛ WEIRD SCIENCE

A compound with ionic bonds has properties completely different from those of the elements that form it. Table salt is a good example. Salt is sodium and chloride ions bonded together. However, elemental chlorine gas is extremely toxic to humans; it may cause severe respiratory damage and even death. Elemental sodium is highly reactive—when it is exposed to chlorine gas under certain conditions, it bursts into flame! But when these two elements join under the right conditions the resultant compound, sodium chloride, is nonreactive and harmless.

Chapter 13 • Chemical Bonding

Metal Atoms Lose Electrons Atoms of most metals have few electrons in their outer energy level. When metal atoms bond with other atoms, the metal atoms tend to lose these valence electrons and form positive ions. For example, look at the model in **Figure 6**. An atom of sodium has one valence electron. When a sodium atom loses this electron to another atom, it becomes a sodium ion. A sodium ion has a charge of 1+ because it contains 1 more proton than electrons. To show the difference between a sodium atom and a sodium ion, the chemical symbol for the ion is written as Na^+. Notice that the charge is written to the upper right of the chemical symbol. Figure 6 also shows a model for the formation of an aluminum ion.

Figure 6 Forming Positive Ions

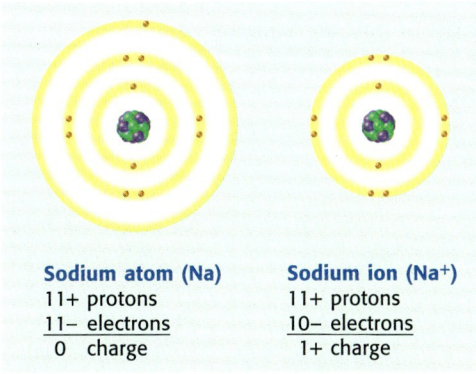

Sodium atom (Na)
11+ protons
11– electrons
0 charge

Sodium ion (Na$^+$)
11+ protons
10– electrons
1+ charge

Aluminum atom (Al)
13+ protons
13– electrons
0 charge

Aluminum ion (Al^{3+})
13+ protons
10– electrons
3+ charge

Here's How It Works: During chemical changes, a sodium atom can lose its 1 electron in the third energy level to another atom. The filled second level becomes the outermost level, so the resulting sodium ion has 8 valence electrons.

Here's How It Works: During chemical changes, an aluminum atom can lose its 3 electrons in the third energy level to another atom. The filled second level becomes the outermost level, so the resulting aluminum ion has 8 valence electrons.

The Energy of Losing Electrons When an atom loses electrons, energy is needed to overcome the attraction between the electrons and the protons in the atom's nucleus. Removing electrons from atoms of metals requires only a small amount of energy, so metal atoms lose electrons easily. In fact, the energy needed to remove electrons from atoms of elements in Groups 1 and 2 is so low that these elements react very easily and can be found only as ions in nature. On the other hand, removing electrons from atoms of nonmetals requires a large amount of energy. Rather than give up electrons, these atoms gain electrons when they form ionic bonds.

 **Self-Check**

Look at the periodic table, and determine which noble gas has the same electron arrangement as a sodium ion. (See page 724 to check your answer.)

 **SCIENCE HUMOR**

Q: What do you call a bond that is fond of sarcasm?

A: an ironic bond

IS THAT A FACT!

Negative ions are slightly larger than the neutral atoms they form from. As a result of *shielding effects*, the attractive force between protons in the nucleus and the added electrons is smaller than the force between the protons and the original electrons.

2) Teach, continued

CONNECT TO EARTH SCIENCE

Phenomena such as the *aurora borealis*, or northern lights, occur when charged particles from the sun enter Earth's magnetic field and travel toward the poles. When the particles strike atoms or molecules in Earth's atmosphere, they ionize them and move electrons to a higher energy state. These "excited" atoms and molecules quickly return to their ground state by releasing the extra energy as a small burst of light. The northern lights are usually greenish in color and may look like flickering curtains, arches, or streaks of light.

Sheltered English

Answer to MATHBREAK

$(16+) + (18-) = 2-$
S^{2-}; sulfide ion

REAL-WORLD CONNECTION

The World Health Organization estimates that about a quarter of the world's population does not have access to safe drinking water and that about 5 million people die every year from diseases linked to unsafe water. Since the late 1800s, chlorine has been added to drinking water to kill bacteria and other pathogens that cause diseases in humans. When chlorine gas dissolves in water, it forms ions that kill most pathogens.

 Math Skills Worksheet 9 "Comparing Integers on a Number Line"

MATH BREAK

Charge!

Calculating the charge of an ion is the same as adding integers (positive or negative whole numbers or zero) with opposite signs. You write the number of protons as a positive integer and the number of electrons as a negative integer and then add the integers. Calculate the charge of an ion that contains 16 protons and 18 electrons. Write the ion's symbol and name.

Atoms That Gain Electrons Form Negative Ions Atoms that gain electrons from other atoms during chemical changes form ions that have more electrons than protons. The negative charges outnumber the positive charges, giving each of these ions an overall negative charge.

The outermost energy level of nonmetal atoms is almost full. Only a few electrons are needed to fill the outer level, so atoms of nonmetals tend to gain electrons from other atoms. For example, look at the model in **Figure 7.** An atom of chlorine has 7 valence electrons. When a chlorine atom gains 1 electron to complete its outer level, it becomes an ion with a 1– charge called a chloride ion. The symbol for the chloride ion is Cl^-. Notice that the name of the negative ion formed from chlorine has the ending *-ide*. This ending is used for the names of the negative ions formed when atoms gain electrons. Figure 7 also shows a model of how an oxide ion is formed.

Figure 7 Forming Negative Ions

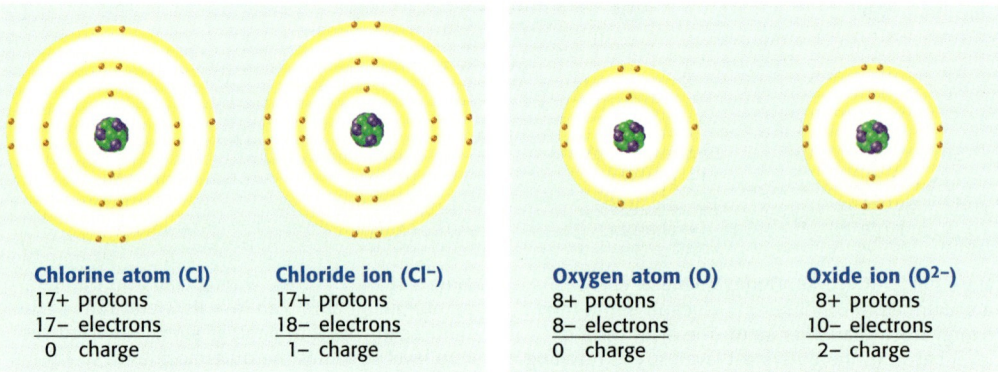

Chlorine atom (Cl)
17+ protons
17– electrons
0 charge

Chloride ion (Cl^-)
17+ protons
18– electrons
1– charge

Oxygen atom (O)
8+ protons
8– electrons
0 charge

Oxide ion (O^{2-})
8+ protons
10– electrons
2– charge

Here's How It Works: During chemical changes, a chlorine atom gains 1 electron in the third energy level from another atom. A chloride ion is formed with 8 valence electrons. Thus, its outermost energy level is filled.

Here's How It Works: During chemical changes, an oxygen atom gains 2 electrons in the second energy level from another atom. An oxide ion is formed with 8 valence electrons. Thus, its outermost energy level is filled.

The Energy of Gaining Electrons Atoms of most nonmetals fill their outermost energy level by gaining electrons. Energy is given off by most nonmetal atoms during this process. The more easily an atom gains an electron, the more energy an atom gives off. Atoms of the Group 17 elements (the halogens) give off the most energy when they gain an electron. The halogens, such as fluorine and chlorine, are extremely reactive nonmetals because they release a large amount of energy.

Science Bloopers

In 1774, a Swedish chemist named Carl Scheele (1742–1786) added hydrochloric acid to manganese dioxide and got an unpleasant yellowish green gas, chlorine. Scheele decided that the gas was a compound and named it marine acid. Nearly 40 years later, English chemist Sir Humphry Davy (1778–1829) demonstrated that the gas was an element, not a compound.

Charged Ions Form a Neutral Compound When a metal reacts with a nonmetal, the same number of electrons is lost by the metal atoms as is gained by the nonmetal atoms. Even though the ions that bond are charged, the compound formed is neutral because the charges of the ions cancel each other through ionic bonding. An ionic bond is an example of electrostatic attraction in which opposite electric charges stick together. Another example is static cling, illustrated in **Figure 8.**

Figure 8 *Like ionic bonds, static cling is the result of the attraction between opposite charges.*

Ions Bond to Form a Crystal Lattice The ions that make up an ionic compound are bonded in a repeating three-dimensional pattern called a **crystal lattice** (KRI stuhl LAT is). In ionic compounds, such as table salt, the ions in the crystal lattice are arranged as alternating positive and negative ions, forming a solid. The model in **Figure 9** shows a small part of a crystal lattice. The arrangement of bonded ions in a crystal lattice determines the shape of the crystals of an ionic compound.

The strong force of attraction between bonded ions in a crystal lattice gives ionic compounds certain properties, including a high melting point and boiling point. Ionic compounds tend to be brittle solids at room temperature and usually break apart when hit with a hammer.

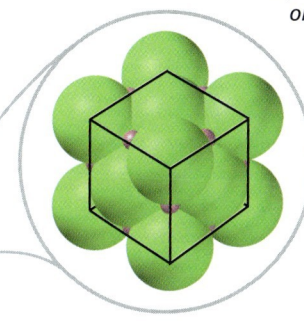

Figure 9 *This model of the crystal lattice of sodium chloride, or table salt, shows a three-dimensional view of the bonded ions.*

REVIEW

1. How does an atom become a negative ion?
2. What are two properties of ionic compounds?
3. **Applying Concepts** Which group of elements lose 2 valence electrons when their atoms form ionic bonds? What charge would the ions formed have?

2) Teach, continued

MEETING INDIVIDUAL NEEDS

Advanced Learners At room temperature, hydrogen, H_2, is a gas composed of molecules consisting of two hydrogen atoms held together by a covalent bond, as shown in **Figure 11.** Surprisingly, such a simple molecule is capable of releasing a great deal of energy. Have students research how hydrogen has been used as a fuel in the space program and why some scientists think it is one of the fuels of the future.

Covalent Marshmallows

In certain covalent compounds, atoms can end up sharing fewer or more than 8 electrons in their outer energy level. In boron trifluoride, BF_3, the boron atom ends up sharing only 6 electrons in its outer energy level. In sulfur hexafluoride, SF_6, sulfur ends up sharing 12 electrons in its outer energy level. For the purposes of this chapter, students can assume that sharing 8 electrons in the outer energy level is the rule.

Teaching Transparency 252
"Covalent Bonds"

Covalent Bonds

Most materials you encounter every day, such as water, sugar, and carbon dioxide, are held together by bonds that do not involve ions. These substances tend to have low melting and boiling points, and some of these substances are brittle in the solid state. The type of bonds found in these substances, including the substances shown in **Figure 10,** are covalent bonds.

A **covalent bond** is the force of attraction between the nuclei of atoms and the electrons shared by the atoms. When two atoms of nonmetals bond, a large amount of energy is required for either atom to lose an electron, so no ions are formed. Rather than transferring electrons to complete their outermost energy levels, two nonmetal atoms bond by sharing electrons with one another, as shown in the model in **Figure 11.**

Figure 10 Covalent bonds are found in this plastic ball, the paddle's rubber covering, the cotton fibers in clothes, and even many of the substances that make up the human body!

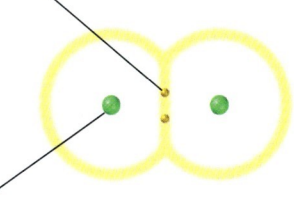

Figure 11 By sharing electrons in a covalent bond, each hydrogen atom (the smallest atom known) has a full outermost energy level containing two electrons.

The shared electrons spend most of their time between the nuclei of the atoms.

The protons and the shared electrons attract one another. This attraction is the basis of the covalent bond that holds the atoms together.

Make models of molecules out of marshmallows on page 680 of the LabBook.

Covalently Bonded Atoms Make Up Molecules The particles of substances containing covalent bonds differ from those containing ionic bonds. Ionic compounds consist of ions organized in a crystal. Covalent compounds consist of individual particles called molecules (MAHL i KYOOLZ). A **molecule** is a neutral group of atoms held together by covalent bonds. In Figure 11, you saw a model of a hydrogen molecule, which is composed of two hydrogen atoms covalently bonded. However, most molecules are composed of atoms of two or more elements. The models in **Figure 12** show two ways to represent the covalent bonds in a molecule.

IS THAT A FACT!

Even though a molecule of water is bigger than the hydrogen and oxygen atoms it comprises, it is still an extremely tiny particle. There are about 2 million quadrillion (2 followed by 21 zeros) molecules in a single drop of water!

Figure 12 Covalent Bonds in a Water Molecule

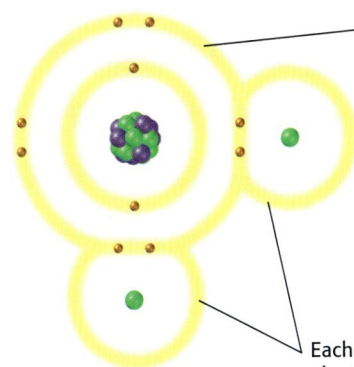

Through covalent bonding, the oxygen atom shares one of its electrons with each of the two hydrogen atoms. As a result, it has a filled outermost energy level with 8 electrons.

Each hydrogen atom shares its 1 electron with the oxygen atom. This allows each hydrogen to have a filled outer level with 2 electrons.

$$\ddot{\text{:O:H}}$$
$$\text{H}$$

Another way to show covalent bonds is to draw an electron-dot diagram. An electron-dot diagram shows only the outermost level of electrons for each atom. But you can still see how electrons are shared between the atoms.

Making Electron-Dot Diagrams

An electron-dot diagram is a model that shows only the valence electrons in an atom. Electron-dot diagrams are helpful when predicting how atoms might bond. You draw an electron-dot diagram by writing the symbol of the element and placing the correct number of dots around it. This type of model can help you to better understand bonding by showing the number of valence electrons and how atoms share electrons to fill their outermost energy levels, as shown below.

$\cdot\dot{\text{C}}\cdot$ $:\ddot{\text{O}}\cdot$ $:\ddot{\text{Kr}}:$ H:H

Carbon atoms have 4 valence electrons, so 4 dots are placed around the symbol. A carbon atom needs 4 more electrons for a filled outermost energy level.

Oxygen atoms have 6 valence electrons, so 6 dots are placed around the symbol. An oxygen atom needs only 2 more electrons for a filled outermost energy level.

The noble gas krypton has a full set of 8 valence electrons in its atoms. Thus, krypton is nonreactive because its atoms do not need any more electrons.

This electron-dot diagram represents hydrogen gas, the same substance shown in the model in Figure 11.

✓ Self-Check

1. How many dots does the electron-dot diagram of a sulfur atom have?
2. How is a covalent bond different from an ionic bond?

(See page 724 to check your answers.)

MEETING INDIVIDUAL NEEDS

Advanced Learners In addition to the covalent bonds that link hydrogen atoms to an oxygen atom in a molecule of water, another type of bond is important in water. This bond, which is actually an intermolecular force, is known as the hydrogen bond. It is the force that causes water molecules to attract one another and form drops. Have students investigate hydrogen bonds and the properties they impart to water and other substances.

MAKING MODELS

Discuss with students different ways of visualizing molecules. Why are electron-dot diagrams useful? What drawbacks do they have? Demonstrate how to make three-dimensional models of hydrogen sulfide molecules, H_2S, using gumdrops and toothpicks. One color of gumdrop represents the sulfur atom, and another color represents the two hydrogen atoms. Use toothpicks to "bond" the hydrogen gumdrops to the sulfur gumdrop. Give students gumdrops and toothpicks, and have them make their own models of ammonia, NH_3, and methane, CH_4. **Sheltered English**

Teaching Transparency 253 "Covalent Bonds in a Water Molecule"

SCIENCE HUMOR

Q: What is the one thing that atoms in molecules do not have to teach their children?

A: how to share with others

Answers to Self-Check

1. 6
2. In a covalent bond, electrons are shared between atoms. In an ionic bond, electrons are transferred from one atom to another.

Section 2 • Types of Chemical Bonds

② Teach, continued

GUIDED PRACTICE

Remind students that they can use the periodic table to find the number of valence electrons for atoms of elements in Groups 13–18. They have 10 fewer valence electrons than their group number. Display a periodic table, and have students determine the number of valence electrons for bromine (7) and iodine (7).

Invite volunteers to the board to draw electron-dot diagrams for diatomic molecules of these elements.

ACTIVITY

You may want to explain to students that molecules form when atoms share electrons in a way that achieves a full set of valence electrons, like the nearest noble gas on the periodic table. Follow these guidelines to construct electron-dot diagrams for chlorine and ammonia:

1. Add up the valence electrons for all of the atoms that make up the molecule.

2. Use one pair of electrons to indicate the bond(s) shared by atoms.

3. Arrange the remaining electrons to form a stable molecule. For example, each atom from second-row nonmetals (carbon, nitrogen, oxygen, and fluorine) needs 8 electrons to fill its outermost energy level; hydrogen needs to share 2 electrons. **Sheltered English**

TOPIC: Types of Chemical Bonds
GO TO: www.scilinks.org
sciLINKS NUMBER: HSTP315

Figure 13 The water in this fishbowl is made up of many tiny water molecules. Each molecule is the smallest particle that still has the chemical properties of water.

Activity

Try your hand at drawing electron-dot diagrams for a molecule of chlorine (a diatomic molecule) and a molecule of ammonia (one nitrogen atom bonded with three hydrogen atoms).
TRY at HOME

Homework

Concept Mapping Have students construct concept maps for ionic bonding, covalent bonding, and metallic bonding. Suggest they include terms such as the following:

electrons lost, electrons gained, positive ion, negative ion, compound, crystal, electrons shared, molecule

A Molecule Is the Smallest Particle of a Covalent Compound An atom is the smallest particle into which an element can be divided and still be the same substance. Likewise, a molecule is the smallest particle into which a covalently bonded compound can be divided and still be the same compound. **Figure 13** illustrates how a sample of water is made up of many individual molecules of water (shown as three-dimensional models). If you could divide water over and over, you would eventually end up with a single molecule of water. However, if you separated the hydrogen and oxygen atoms that make up a water molecule, you would no longer have water.

The Simplest Molecules All molecules are composed of at least two covalently bonded atoms. The simplest molecules, known as *diatomic molecules,* consist of two atoms bonded together. Some elements are called diatomic elements because they are found in nature as diatomic molecules composed of two atoms of the element. Hydrogen is a diatomic element, as you saw in Figure 11. Oxygen, nitrogen, and the halogens fluorine, chlorine, bromine, and iodine are also diatomic. By sharing electrons, both atoms of a diatomic molecule can fill their outer energy level, as shown in **Figure 14.**

Figure 14 Models of a Diatomic Fluorine Molecule

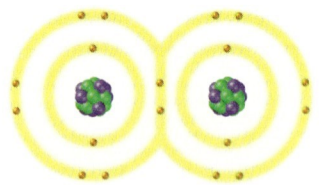 

Two covalently bonded fluorine atoms have filled outermost energy levels. The pair of electrons shared by the atoms are counted as valence electrons for each atom.

This is a three-dimensional model of a fluorine molecule.

MISCONCEPTION ALERT

For clarity, the model of liquid water in **Figure 13** shows only one layer of molecules with spaces between them. Make sure students understand that in reality the molecules are always in contact with and sliding past molecules above and below the layer shown.

338 Chapter 13 • Chemical Bonding

More-Complex Molecules Diatomic molecules are the simplest—and some of the most important—of all molecules. You could not live without diatomic oxygen molecules. But other important molecules are much more complex. Gasoline, plastic, and even proteins in the cells of your body are examples of complex molecules. Carbon atoms are the basis of many of these complex molecules. Each carbon atom needs to make 4 covalent bonds to have 8 valence electrons. These bonds can be with atoms of other elements or with other carbon atoms, as shown in the model in **Figure 15.**

Proteins perform many functions throughout your body, such as digesting your food, building components of your cells, and transporting nutrients to each cell. A single protein can have a chain of 7,000 atoms of carbon and nitrogen with atoms of other elements covalently bonded to it.

Figure 15 *A granola bar contains sucrose, or table sugar. A molecule of sucrose is composed of carbon atoms, hydrogen atoms, and oxygen atoms joined by covalent bonds.*

Metallic Bonds

Look at the unusual metal sculpture shown in **Figure 16.** Notice that some metal pieces have been flattened, while other metal pieces have been shaped into wires. How could the artist change the shape of the metal into all of these different forms without breaking the metal into pieces? A metal can be shaped because of the presence of a special type of bond called a metallic bond. A **metallic bond** is the force of attraction between a positively charged metal ion and the electrons in a metal. (Remember that metal atoms tend to lose electrons and form positively charged ions.)

Figure 16 *The different shapes of metal in this sculpture are possible because of the bonds that hold the metal together.*

WEIRD SCIENCE

In 1985, chemists Richard Smalley, Sir Harold W. Kroto, and Robert F. Curl, Jr., discovered an unusually large type of pure carbon molecule that looks like a soccer ball. The new molecule, C_{60}, was named Buckminsterfullerene because it resembles the geodesic domes designed by American architect R. Buckminster Fuller. "Buckyballs" are hollow, so atoms or molecules of other substances can be inserted into their center. Such "doped" molecules may someday be used as superconductors or delivery systems for some medications.

DISCUSSION

Review with students the properties of compounds having ionic bonds, covalent bonds, and metallic bonds. Then have students suppose that they have been asked to determine what kind of bond holds an unknown solid together. Work with them to develop ideas for tests that would serve as indicators of a certain type of bond. (Students may suggest tests to determine melting or boiling point, brittleness, or malleability.)

Homework

Materials made of covalently bonded molecules are all around you. Plastics are a prime example. Make a list of all of the plastic items you use during the day. How would your life be different without plastics?

REAL-WORLD CONNECTION

Very large molecules that are made of many smaller, repeating units are called polymers. Many polymers are found in nature; protein, cellulose, chitin, and rubber are examples. Use Teaching Transparency 21 to show how proteins are made. Synthetic polymers, such as plastics, are also very common. Many synthetic polymers are formed from long chains of carbon atoms. For this reason, petroleum products are the raw materials for almost all plastics.

Section 2 • Types of Chemical Bonds

3) Extend

GOING FURTHER

Explain to students that atoms can form double or triple covalent bonds if they need more than one electron to complete their outermost energy level. An atom of oxygen, for example, forms a double bond with another atom of oxygen. Demonstrate this by writing an electron-dot diagram on the chalkboard. Point out that each oxygen atom's outer energy level has 4 shared electrons (2 per bond) and 4 unshared electrons, so that the outermost energy level has a total of 8 electrons. Challenge students to make electron-dot diagrams for nitrogen, N_2, and carbon dioxide, CO_2, to determine the type of multiple bond needed.

MATERIALS
FOR EACH STUDENT: • wire paper clip • piece of chalk

Safety Caution: Remind students to review all safety cautions and icons before beginning this lab activity.

Answers to QuickLab

3. metallic bonds
4. The metallic bonds give the paper clip the ability to bend without breaking because the electrons move within the metal. The ionic bonds in the piece of chalk cause the chalk to be brittle.

Bending with Bonds

1. Straighten out a **wire paper clip**. Record the result in your ScienceLog.
2. Bend a **piece of chalk**. Record the result in your ScienceLog.
3. Chalk is composed of calcium carbonate, a compound containing ionic bonds. What type of bonds are present in the paper clip?
4. In your ScienceLog, explain why you could change the shape of the paper clip but could not bend the chalk without breaking it.

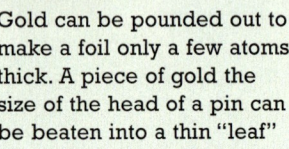

Gold can be pounded out to make a foil only a few atoms thick. A piece of gold the size of the head of a pin can be beaten into a thin "leaf" that would cover this page!

 Reinforcement Worksheet 13
"Is It an Ion?"

 Reinforcement Worksheet 13
"Interview with an Electron"

Electrons Move Throughout a Metal The scientific understanding of the bonding in metals is that the metal atoms get so close to one another that their outermost energy levels overlap. This allows their valence electrons to move throughout the metal from the energy level of one atom to the energy levels of the atoms nearby. The atoms form a crystal much like the ions associated with ionic bonding. However, the negative charges (electrons) in the metal are free to move about. You can think of a metal as being made up of positive metal ions with enough valence electrons "swimming" about to keep the ions together and to cancel the positive charge of the ions, as shown in **Figure 17**. The ions are held together because metallic bonds extend throughout the metal in all directions.

Figure 17 *The moving electrons are attracted to the metal ions, forming metallic bonds.*

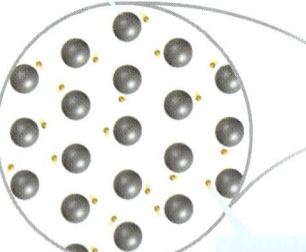

The positive metal ions are in fixed positions in the metal.

Negative electrons are free to move about.

Metals Conduct Electric Current Metallic bonding is the reason why metals have particular properties. One of these properties is electrical conductivity—the ability to conduct electric current. For example, when you turn on a lamp, electrons move within the copper wire that connects the lamp with the outlet. The electrons that move are the valence electrons in the copper atoms. These electrons are free to move because of metallic bonds—they are not connected to any one atom.

Metals Can Be Reshaped Metallic bonds allow atoms in metals to be rearranged. As a result, metals can be reshaped. The properties of *ductility* (the ability to be drawn into wires) and *malleability* (the ability to be hammered into sheets) describe a metal's ability to be reshaped. For example, copper is made into wires for use in electrical cords. Aluminum can be pounded into thin sheets and made into aluminum foil and cans.

CROSS-DISCIPLINARY FOCUS

Art Copper is so malleable that it is not necessary to heat the metal in order to shape it. Give students some 18-gauge copper wire, and allow them to investigate its malleability by challenging them to create a small sculpture or piece of jewelry.

How Metals Can Bend Without Breaking When a piece of metal is bent, some of the metal ions are forced closer together. You might expect the metal to break because the positive ions repel one another. However, even in their new positions, the positive ions are surrounded by and attracted to the electrons, as shown in **Figure 18.** (Ionic compounds do break when hit because neither the positive ions nor the negative ions are free to move.)

Figure 18 *The shape of a metal can be changed without breaking because metallic bonds occur in many directions.*

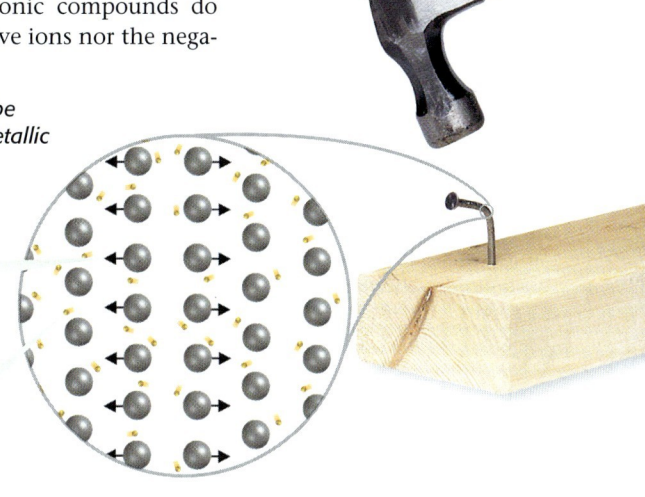

The repulsion between the positively charged metal ions increases as the ions are pushed closer to one another.

The moving electrons maintain the metallic bonds no matter how the shape of the metal changes.

Metallic Bonding in Staples

Although they are not very glamorous, metal staples are very useful in holding things such as sheets of paper together. Explain how the metallic bonds in a staple allow it to change shape so that it can function properly.

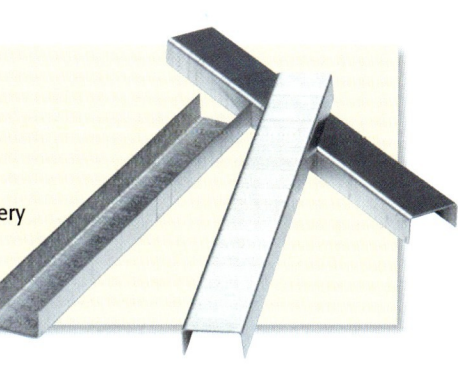

REVIEW

1. What happens to electrons in covalent bonding?
2. What type of element is most likely to form covalent bonds?
3. What is a metallic bond?
4. **Interpreting Graphics** This electron-dot diagram is not yet complete. Which atom needs to form another covalent bond? How do you know?

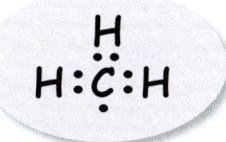

TOPIC: Types of Chemical Bonds, Properties of Metals
GO TO: www.scilinks.org
*sci*LINKS NUMBER: HSTP315, HSTP320

Answers to Review

1. Electrons are shared between atoms.
2. nonmetals
3. the force of attraction between a positively charged metal ion and the electrons in a metal
4. Carbon; the carbon in the diagram has only 7 dots around it, representing 7 valence electrons. It needs one more electron to have a filled outer energy level (8 valence electrons).

4) Close

Quiz

1. How does an atom develop a charge? (by gaining or losing electrons)
2. What properties are characteristic of ionic compounds? (They tend to have a high melting and boiling point. At room temperature, they are brittle solids and may break apart if hit with a hammer.)
3. What is the smallest particle of a covalently bonded compound? (a molecule)
4. What properties of metals are due to the fact that metal ions can be rearranged? (ductility and malleability)

ALTERNATIVE ASSESSMENT

Organize students in small groups. Have them develop a charade that depicts either ionic, covalent, or metallic bonding. Students may want to use a few props, such as signs that indicate positive or negative charge or the name of an atom. Have each group present its charade, and then have the remainder of the class determine the type of bond being portrayed.

Answer to APPLY

A staple must bend to hold papers together. The freely moving electrons in the metal allow the staple to bend without breaking. These flowing electrons maintain the metallic bonds holding the metal atoms together even after the metal is bent.

Critical Thinking Worksheet 13 "The Road to Knowledge"

Chapter Highlights

VOCABULARY DEFINITIONS

SECTION 1

chemical bonding the joining of atoms to form new substances

chemical bond a force of attraction that holds two atoms together

valence electrons the electrons in the outermost energy level of an atom

Chapter Highlights

SECTION 1

Vocabulary
- chemical bonding (p. 328)
- chemical bond (p. 328)
- valence electrons (p. 329)

Section Notes
- Chemical bonding is the joining of atoms to form new substances. A chemical bond is a force of attraction that holds two atoms together.
- Valence electrons are the electrons in the outermost energy level of an atom. These electrons are used to form bonds.
- Most atoms form bonds by gaining, losing, or sharing electrons until they have 8 valence electrons. Atoms of hydrogen, lithium, and helium need only 2 electrons to fill their outermost level.

SECTION 2

Vocabulary
- ionic bond (p. 332)
- ions (p. 332)
- crystal lattice (p. 335)
- covalent bond (p. 336)
- molecule (p. 336)
- metallic bond (p. 339)

Section Notes
- In ionic bonding, electrons are transferred between two atoms. The atom that loses electrons becomes a positive ion. The atom that gains electrons becomes a negative ion. The force of attraction between these oppositely charged ions is an ionic bond.
- Ionic bonding usually occurs between atoms of metals and atoms of nonmetals.

✓ Skills Check

Math Concepts

CALCULATING CHARGE To calculate the charge of an ion, you must add integers with opposite signs. The total positive charge of the ion (the number of protons) is written as a positive integer. The total negative charge of the ion (the number of electrons) is written as a negative integer. For example, the charge of an ion containing 11 protons and 10 electrons would be calculated as follows:

$$(11+) + (10-) = 1+$$

Visual Understanding

DETERMINING VALENCE ELECTRONS Knowing the number of valence electrons in an atom is important in predicting how it will bond with other atoms. Review Figure 3 on page 330 to learn how an element's location on the periodic table helps you determine the number of valence electrons in an atom.

FORMING IONS Turn back to Figures 6 and 7 on pages 333–334 to review how ions are formed when atoms lose or gain electrons.

Lab and Activity Highlights

Covalent Marshmallows   PG 680

 Datasheets for LabBook
(blackline masters for this lab)

SECTION 2

- Energy is needed to remove electrons from metal atoms to form positive ions. Energy is released when most nonmetal atoms gain electrons to form negative ions.

- In covalent bonding, electrons are shared by two atoms. The force of attraction between the nuclei of the atoms and the shared electrons is a covalent bond.

- Covalent bonding usually occurs between atoms of nonmetals.

- Electron-dot diagrams are a simple way to represent the valence electrons in an atom.

- Covalently bonded atoms form a particle called a molecule. A molecule is the smallest particle of a compound with the chemical properties of the compound.

- Diatomic elements are the only elements found in nature as diatomic molecules consisting of two atoms of the same element covalently bonded together.

- In metallic bonding, the outermost energy levels of metal atoms overlap, allowing the valence electrons to move throughout the metal. The force of attraction between a positive metal ion and the electrons in the metal is a metallic bond.

- Many properties of metals, such as conductivity, ductility, and malleability, result from the freely moving electrons in the metal.

Labs
Covalent Marshmallows (p. 680)

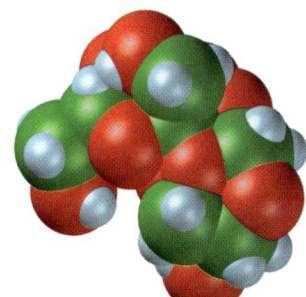

VOCABULARY DEFINITIONS, continued

SECTION 2

ionic bond the force of attraction between oppositely charged ions

ions charged particles that form during chemical changes when one or more valence electrons transfer from one atom to another

crystal lattice a repeating three-dimensional pattern of ions

covalent bond the force of attraction between the nuclei of atoms and the electrons shared by the atoms

molecule a neutral group of atoms held together by covalent bonds

metallic bond the force of attraction between a positively charged metal ion and the electrons in a metal

 Vocabulary Review Worksheet 13

 Blackline masters of these Chapter Highlights can be found in the **Study Guide**.

internetconnect

GO TO: go.hrw.com

Visit the **HRW** Web site for a variety of learning tools related to this chapter. Just type in the keyword:

KEYWORD: HSTBND

GO TO: www.scilinks.org

Visit the **National Science Teachers Association** on-line Web site for Internet resources related to this chapter. Just type in the sciLINKS number for more information about the topic:

TOPIC:	sciLINKS NUMBER:
The Electron	HSTP305
The Periodic Table	HSTP310
Types of Chemical Bonds	HSTP315
Properties of Metals	HSTP320

Lab and Activity Highlights

LabBank

 Long-Term Projects & Research Ideas,
The Wonders of Water, Project 63

Chapter 13 • Chapter Highlights **343**

Chapter Review

USING VOCABULARY

To complete the following sentences, choose the correct term from each pair of terms listed below.

1. The force of attraction that holds two atoms together is a ____. (*crystal lattice* or *chemical bond*)

2. Charged particles that form when atoms transfer electrons are ____. (*molecules* or *ions*)

3. The force of attraction between the nuclei of atoms and shared electrons is a(n) ____. (*ionic bond* or *covalent bond*)

4. Electrons free to move throughout a material are associated with a(n) ____. (*ionic bond* or *metallic bond*)

5. Shared electrons are associated with a ____. (*covalent bond* or *metallic bond*)

UNDERSTANDING CONCEPTS

Multiple Choice

6. Which element has a full outermost energy level containing only two electrons?
   a. oxygen (O)
   b. hydrogen (H)
   c. fluorine (F)
   d. helium (He)

7. Which of the following describes what happens when an atom becomes an ion with a 2– charge?
   a. The atom gains 2 protons.
   b. The atom loses 2 protons.
   c. The atom gains 2 electrons.
   d. The atom loses 2 electrons.

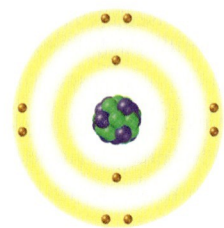

8. The properties of ductility and malleability are associated with which type of bonds?
   a. ionic
   b. covalent
   c. metallic
   d. none of the above

9. In which area of the periodic table do you find elements whose atoms easily gain electrons?
   a. across the top two rows
   b. across the bottom row
   c. on the right side
   d. on the left side

10. What type of element tends to lose electrons when it forms bonds?
    a. metal
    b. metalloid
    c. nonmetal
    d. noble gas

11. Which pair of atoms can form an ionic bond?
    a. sodium (Na) and potassium (K)
    b. potassium (K) and fluorine (F)
    c. fluorine (F) and chlorine (Cl)
    d. sodium (Na) and neon (Ne)

Short Answer

12. List two properties of covalent compounds.

13. Explain why an iron ion is attracted to a sulfide ion but not to a zinc ion.

14. Using your knowledge of valence electrons, explain the main reason so many different molecules are made from carbon atoms.

15. Compare the three types of bonds based on what happens to the valence electrons of the atoms.

Concept Mapping

16. Use the following terms to create a concept map: chemical bonds, ionic bonds, covalent bonds, metallic bonds, molecule, ions.

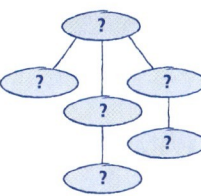

CRITICAL THINKING AND PROBLEM SOLVING

17. Predict the type of bond each of the following pairs of atoms would form:
    a. zinc (Zn) and zinc (Zn)
    b. oxygen (O) and nitrogen (N)
    c. phosphorus (P) and oxygen (O)
    d. magnesium (Mg) and chlorine (Cl)

18. Draw electron-dot diagrams for each of the following atoms, and state how many bonds it will have to make to fill its outer energy level.
    a. sulfur (S)
    b. nitrogen (N)
    c. neon (Ne)
    d. iodine (I)
    e. silicon (Si)

19. Does the substance being hit in the photo below contain ionic or metallic bonds? Explain.

MATH IN SCIENCE

20. For each atom below, write the number of electrons it must gain or lose to have 8 valence electrons. Then calculate the charge of the ion that would form.
    a. calcium (Ca)   c. bromine (Br)
    b. phosphorus (P)   d. sulfur (S)

INTERPRETING GRAPHICS

Look at the picture of the wooden pencil below, and answer the following questions.

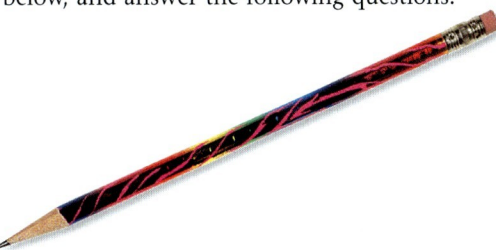

21. In which part of the pencil are metallic bonds found?

22. List three materials composed of molecules with covalent bonds.

23. Identify two differences between the properties of the metallically bonded material and one of the covalently bonded materials.

NOW What Do You Think?

Take a minute to review your answers to the ScienceLog questions on page 327. Have your answers changed? If necessary, revise your answers based on what you have learned since you began this chapter.

345

NOW WHAT DO YOU THINK?

1. A chemical bond is a force of attraction that holds two atoms together.
2. Electrons in ionic bonds are transferred between atoms, forming ions. Electrons in covalent bonds are shared between neutral atoms.
3. The properties of metals—such as malleability, ductility, and the ability to conduct electric current—are a result of the electrons in a metal moving freely within the metal. The metallic bonds occur between each metal ion and the electrons moving near it. The bonds can move as the shape of a piece of metal changes.

Concept Mapping

16. An answer to this exercise can be found at the end of this book.

CRITICAL THINKING AND PROBLEM SOLVING

17. a. metallic
    b. covalent
    c. covalent
    d. ionic
18. a. 6 dots; 2 bonds
    b. 5 dots; 3 bonds
    c. 8 dots; no bonds
    d. 7 dots; 1 bond
    e. 4 dots; 4 bonds
19. Ionic bonds; the substance is breaking into smaller pieces as the hammer hits it. The substance is brittle, so the bonds are more likely to be ionic.

MATH IN SCIENCE

20. a. lose 2 electrons; 2+
    b. gain 3 electrons; 3−
    c. gain 1 electron; 1−
    d. gain 2 electrons; 2−

INTERPRETING GRAPHICS

21. the metal band near the eraser
22. graphite, wood, eraser
23. Answers can include the following: The metallically bonded material is shiny, and the covalently bonded materials are not shiny. The metal is hard, but the eraser is soft. The metal can be bent without breaking, but the wood or graphite will break if bent.

Concept Mapping Transparency 13

Blackline masters of this Chapter Review can be found in the **Study Guide.**

Chapter 13 • Chapter Review   **345**

Across the Sciences

Left-Handed Molecules

PHYSICAL SCIENCE • EARTH SCIENCE

Some researchers think that light from a newly forming star 1,500 light-years away (1 light-year is equal to about 9.6 trillion kilometers) may hold the answer to an Earthly riddle that has been puzzling scientists for over 100 years!

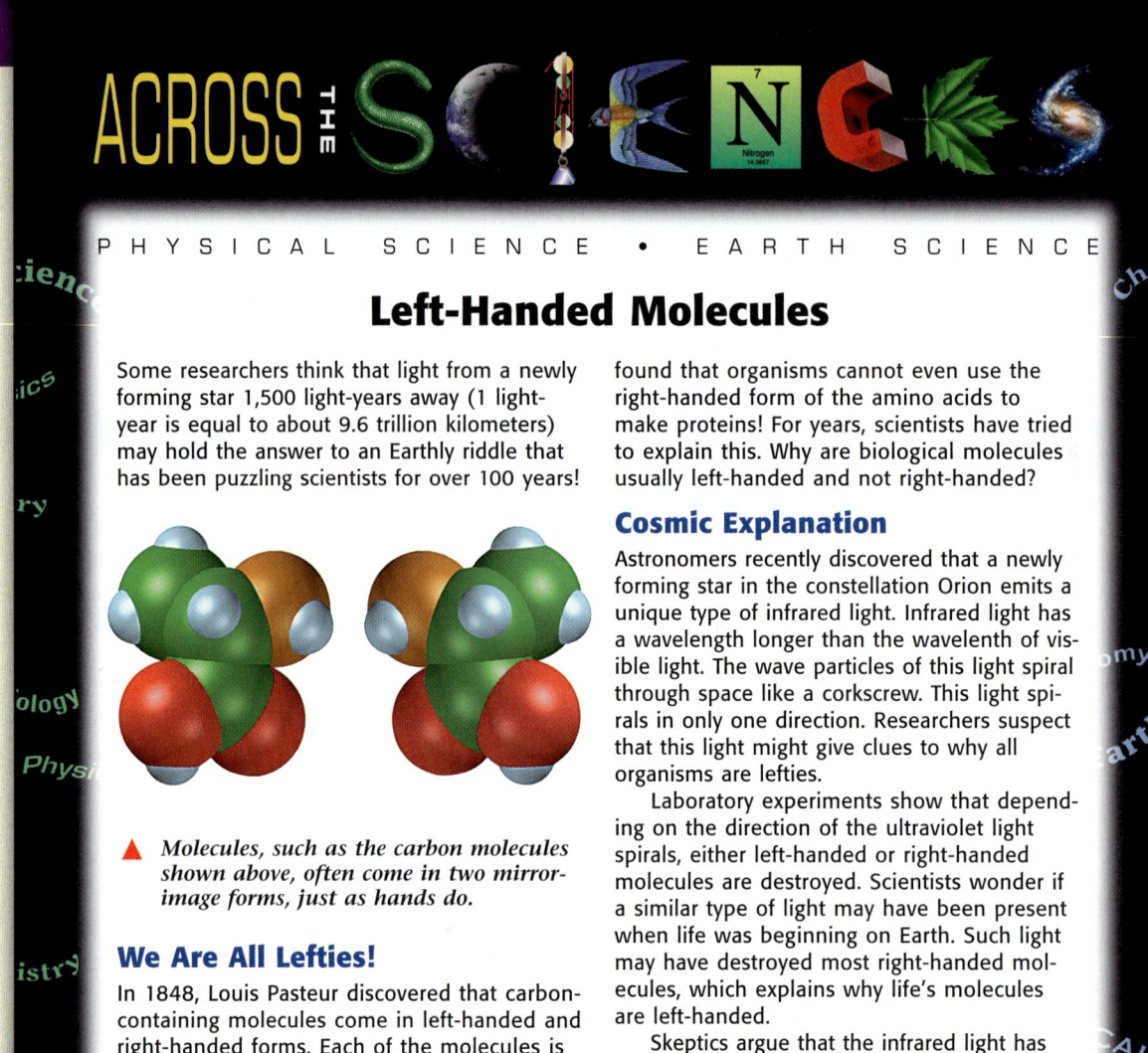

▲ Molecules, such as the carbon molecules shown above, often come in two mirror-image forms, just as hands do.

We Are All Lefties!

In 1848, Louis Pasteur discovered that carbon-containing molecules come in left-handed and right-handed forms. Each of the molecules is an exact mirror image of the other, just as each of your hands is a mirror image of the other. These molecules are made of the same elements, but they differ in the elements' arrangement in space.

Shortly after Pasteur's discovery, researchers stumbled across an interesting but unexplained phenomenon—all organisms, including humans, are made almost entirely of left-handed molecules! Chemists were puzzled by this observation because when they made amino acids in the laboratory, the amino acids came out in equal numbers of right- and left-handed forms. Scientists also found that organisms cannot even use the right-handed form of the amino acids to make proteins! For years, scientists have tried to explain this. Why are biological molecules usually left-handed and not right-handed?

Cosmic Explanation

Astronomers recently discovered that a newly forming star in the constellation Orion emits a unique type of infrared light. Infrared light has a wavelength longer than the wavelength of visible light. The wave particles of this light spiral through space like a corkscrew. This light spirals in only one direction. Researchers suspect that this light might give clues to why all organisms are lefties.

Laboratory experiments show that depending on the direction of the ultraviolet light spirals, either left-handed or right-handed molecules are destroyed. Scientists wonder if a similar type of light may have been present when life was beginning on Earth. Such light may have destroyed most right-handed molecules, which explains why life's molecules are left-handed.

Skeptics argue that the infrared light has less energy than the ultraviolet light used in the laboratory experiments and thus is not a valid comparison. Some researchers, however, hypothesize that both infrared and ultraviolet light may be emitted from the newly forming star that is 1,500 light-years away.

Find Out More

▶ The French chemist Pasteur discovered left-handed and right-handed molecules in tartaric acid. Do some research to find out more about Pasteur and his discovery. Share your findings with the class.

Eureka!
Here's Looking At Ya'!

To some people, just the thought of putting small pieces of plastic in their eyes is uncomfortable. But for millions of others, those little pieces of plastic, known as contact lenses, are a part of daily life. So what would you think about putting a piece of glass in your eye instead? Strangely enough, the humble beginning of the contact lens began with doing just that—inserting a glass lens right in the eye! Ouch!

Molded Glass

Early developers of contact lenses had only glass to use until plastics were discovered. In 1929, a Hungarian physician named Joseph Dallos came up with a way to make a mold of the human eye. This was a critical step in the development of contact lenses. He used these molds to make a glass lens that followed the shape of the eye rather than laying flat against it. In combination with the eye's natural lens, light was refocused to improve a person's eyesight. As you can probably guess, glass lenses weren't very comfortable.

Still Too Hard

Seven years later, an American optometrist, William Feinbloom, introduced contact lenses made of hard plastic. Plastic was a newly developed material made from long, stable chains of carbon, hydrogen, and oxygen molecules called polymers. But polymers required a lot of work to make. Chemists heated short chains, forcing them to chemically bond to form a longer, more-stable polymer. The whole process was also expensive. To make matters worse, the hard-plastic lenses made from polymers weren't much more comfortable than the glass lenses.

How About Spinning Plastic Gel?

In an effort to solve the comfort problem, Czech chemists Otto Wichterle and Drahoslav Lim invented a water-absorbing plastic gel. The lenses made from this gel were soft and pliable, and they allowed air to pass through the lens to the eye. These characteristics made the lenses much more comfortable to wear than the glass lenses.

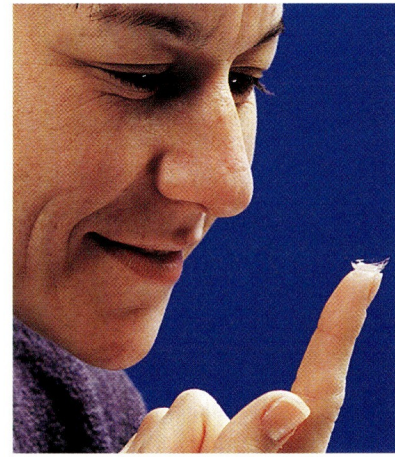
▲ *Does the thought of putting something in your eye make you squirm?*

Wichterle solved the cost problem by developing a simple and inexpensive process to make the plastic-gel lenses. In this process, called spin casting, liquid plastic is added to a spinning mold of an eye. When the plastic forms the correct shape, it is treated with ultraviolet and infrared light, which hardens the plastic. Both plastic gel and spin casting were patented in 1963, becoming the foundation for the contact lenses people wear today.

Look Toward the Future

▶ What do you think contact lenses might be like in 20 years? Let your imagination run wild. Sometimes the strangest ideas are the best seeds of new inventions!

Teaching Strategy

Students may want to know how contact lenses are made or shaped. The front surface of the lens is shaped by the curvature of the lens mold. The inner part of the lens is shaped by a combination of temperature, gravity, surface tension, the amount of liquid in the mold, and the rate of spin of the lens-making machine. Invite a technician or lens maker to visit the class and explain the material used in today's lenses and the process by which lenses are shaped and fitted.

Eureka!
Here's Looking at Ya'!

Background

The idea of contact lenses may go back to Leonardo da Vinci. In 1508, da Vinci sketched a lens that some people believe was meant to be a corrective lens worn on the eye—the first contact lens. Others believe da Vinci sketched how an image is transferred in the human eye from the cornea to the optic nerve. But everyone agrees that da Vinci's sketch describes the basic principles that are used in today's contact lenses.

More than a century later, in 1636, the French philosopher and scientist René Descartes described and illustrated a lens that would rest directly on the cornea, without touching the rest of the eye.

Between 1636 and 1887, there were a number of ideas for contact lenses. Most of the lenses were impractical, painful, or likely to lead to eye infections. Finally in 1887, a German glassblower named F. E. Muller shaped the first contact lens that not only corrected vision but also was tolerable to wear.

Answer to Look Toward the Future

Accept all reasonable responses.

Chapter Organizer

CHAPTER ORGANIZATION	TIME MINUTES	OBJECTIVES	LABS, INVESTIGATIONS, AND DEMONSTRATIONS
Chapter Opener pp. 348–349	45	National Standards: UCP 3, SAI 1, SPSP 5, PS 1b, 3a, 3d, 3e	**Investigate!** Reaction Ready, p. 349
Section 1 Forming New Substances	135	▶ Identify the clues that indicate a chemical reaction might be taking place. ▶ Interpret and write simple chemical formulas. ▶ Interpret and write simple balanced chemical equations. ▶ Explain how a balanced equation illustrates the law of conservation of mass. UCP 3, SAI 1, ST 2, SPSP 5, HNS 1, 3, PS 1b, 3a, 3e; LabBook PS 3e	**QuickLab,** Mass Conservation, p. 357 **Making Models,** Finding a Balance, p. 682 **Datasheets for LabBook,** Finding a Balance, Datasheet 40
Section 2 Types of Chemical Reactions	90	▶ Describe four types of chemical reactions. ▶ Classify a chemical equation as one of the four types of chemical reactions described here. UCP 3, PS 1b; LabBook UCP 3, SAI 1, 2, PS 1b, 3e	**Demonstration,** p. 359 in ATE **Skill Builder,** Putting Elements Together, p. 684 **Datasheets for LabBook,** Putting Elements Together, Datasheet 42 **Inquiry Labs,** Curses, Foiled Again! Lab 21 **Labs You Can Eat,** How to Fluff a Muffin, Lab 24
Section 3 Energy and Rates of Chemical Reactions	90	▶ Compare exothermic and endothermic reactions. ▶ Explain activation energy. ▶ Interpret an energy diagram. ▶ Describe the factors that affect the rate of a reaction. UCP 3, SAI 1, 2, ST 2, HNS 1, 2, SPSP 5, PS 1b, 3a, 3e, 3f; LabBook UCP 3, SAI 1, PS 3e	**QuickLab,** Which Is Quicker? p. 364 **QuickLab,** I'm Crushed! p. 365 **Discovery Lab,** Cata-what? Catalyst! p. 683 **Datasheets for LabBook,** Cata-what? Catalyst! Datasheet 41 **Discovery Lab,** Speed Control, p. 686 **Datasheets for LabBook,** Speed Control, Datasheet 43 **Whiz-Bang Demonstrations,** Fire and Ice, Demo 56 **Long-Term Projects & Research Ideas,** Project 64

*See page **T20** for a complete correlation of this book with the*

NATIONAL SCIENCE EDUCATION STANDARDS.

TECHNOLOGY RESOURCES

 Guided Reading Audio CD
English or Spanish, Chapter 14

Science Discovery Videodiscs
Science Sleuths: Exploding Lawnmowers

 CNN Science, Technology & Society, The Chemistry of Dry Cleaning, Segment 19

 One-Stop Planner CD-ROM with Test Generator

347A   Chapter 14 • Chemical Reactions

Chapter 14 • Chemical Reactions

CLASSROOM WORKSHEETS, TRANSPARENCIES, AND RESOURCES	SCIENCE INTEGRATION AND CONNECTIONS	REVIEW AND ASSESSMENT
Directed Reading Worksheet 14 **Science Puzzlers, Twisters & Teasers,** Worksheet 14		
Directed Reading Worksheet 14, Section 1 **Transparency 254,** Reaction of Hydrogen and Chlorine **Transparency 255,** Writing Chemical Formulas and Equations **Math Skills for Science Worksheet 50,** Balancing Chemical Equations **Transparency 256,** Balancing a Chemical Equation	**MathBreak,** Counting Atoms, p. 352 **Math and More,** p. 352 in ATE **Cross-Disciplinary Focus,** p. 353 in ATE **Cross-Disciplinary Focus,** p. 355 in ATE **MathBreak,** Balancing Act, p. 356 **Math and More,** p. 356 in ATE	**Homework,** pp. 351, 353 in ATE **Self-Check,** p. 353 **Self-Check,** p. 355 **Review,** p. 357 **Quiz,** p. 357 in ATE **Alternative Assessment,** p. 357 in ATE
Directed Reading Worksheet 14, Section 2 **Transparency 257,** Models of Reactions **Reinforcement Worksheet 14,** Fabulous Food Reactions	**Connect to Environmental Science,** p. 358 in ATE	**Review,** p. 360 **Quiz,** p. 360 in ATE **Alternative Assessment,** p. 360 in ATE
Directed Reading Worksheet 14, Section 3 **Transparency 51,** Photosynthesis **Reinforcement Worksheet 14,** Activation Energy **Transparency 258,** Energy Diagrams **Critical Thinking Worksheet 14,** Shedding Light on Landfills	**Biology Connection,** p. 362 **Connect to Life Science,** p. 362 in ATE **Apply,** p. 363 **Real-World Connection,** p. 363 in ATE **Cross-Disciplinary Focus,** p. 363 in ATE **Eye on the Environment:** Slime That Fire! p. 370 **Careers:** Arson Investigator—Lt. Larry McKee, p. 371	**Review,** p. 365 **Quiz,** p. 365 in ATE **Alternative Assessment,** p. 365 in ATE

END-OF-CHAPTER REVIEW AND ASSESSMENT

Chapter Review in Study Guide
Vocabulary and Notes in Study Guide
Chapter Tests with Performance-Based Assessment, Chapter 14 Test
Chapter Tests with Performance-Based Assessment, Performance-Based Assessment 14
Concept Mapping Transparency 14

 Holt, Rinehart and Winston On-line Resources
go.hrw.com
For worksheets and other teaching aids related to this chapter, visit the HRW Web site and type in the keyword: **HSTREA**

 **National Science Teachers Association**
www.scilinks.org
Encourage students to use the *sci*LINKS numbers listed in the internet connect boxes to access information and resources on the **NSTA** Web site.

Chapter Resources & Worksheets

Visual Resources

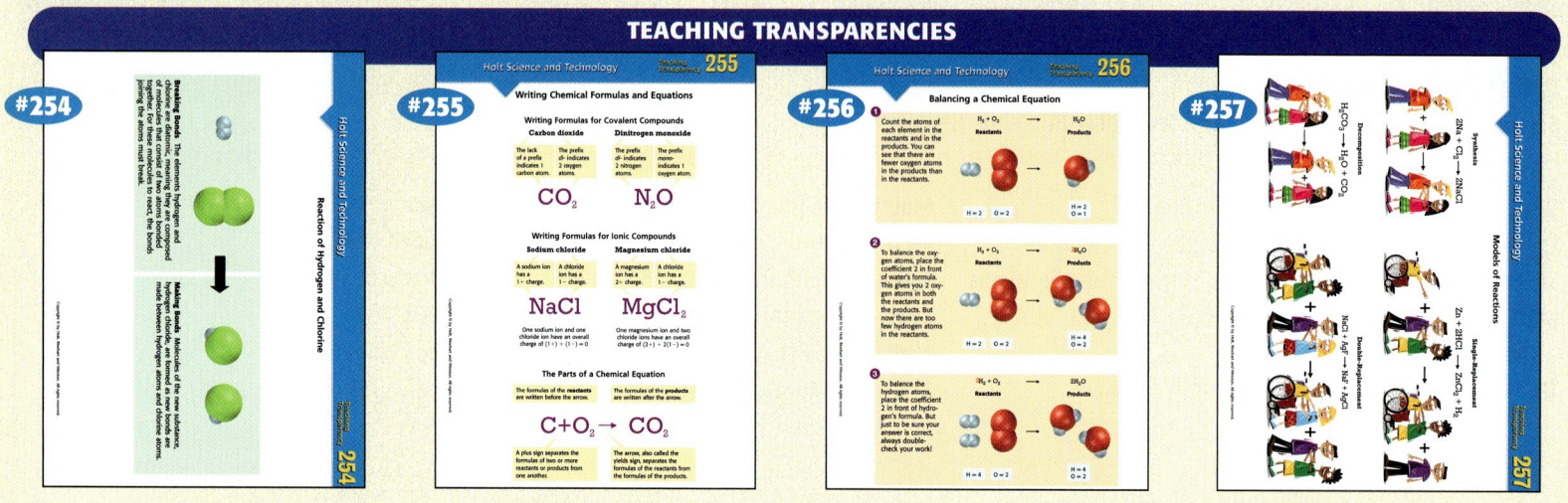

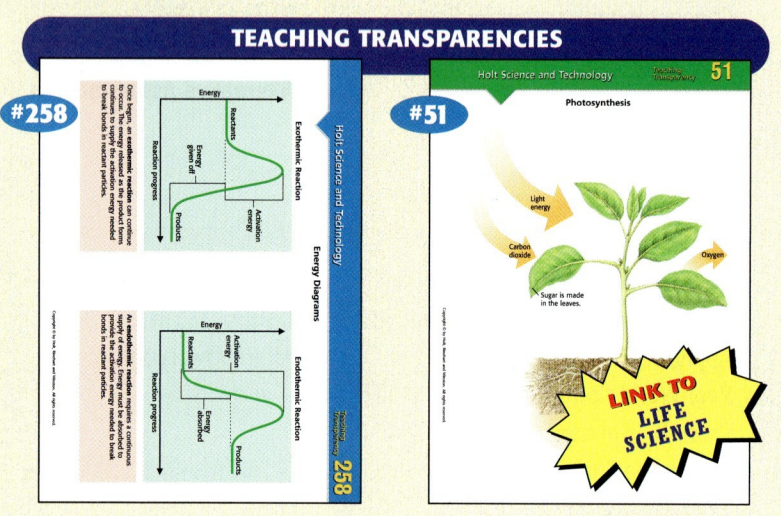

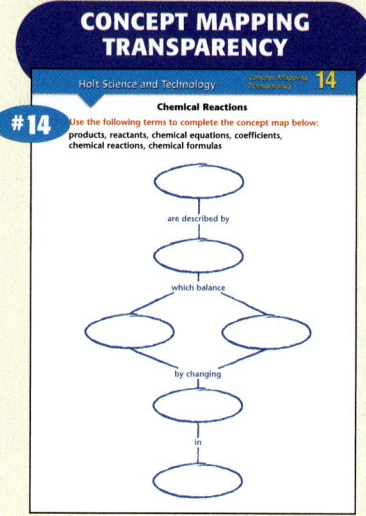

Meeting Individual Needs

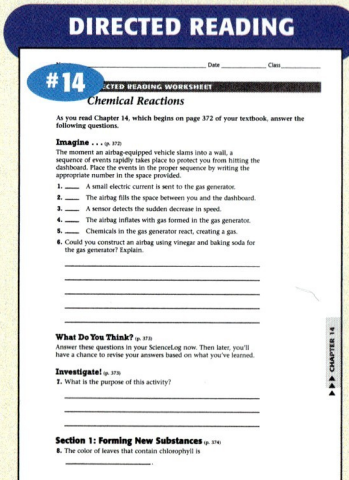

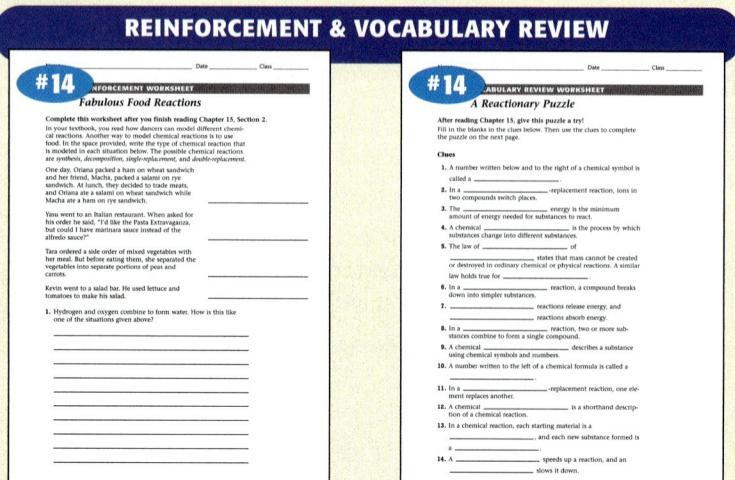

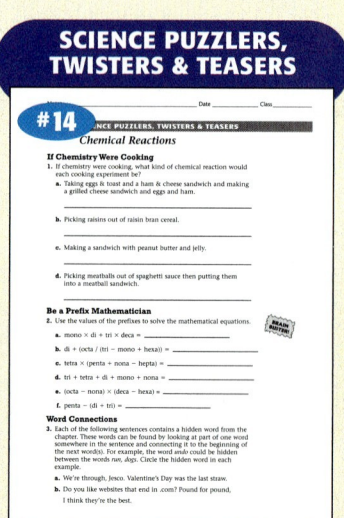

Chapter 14 • Chemical Reactions

Chapter 14 • Chemical Reactions

Review & Assessment

STUDY GUIDE

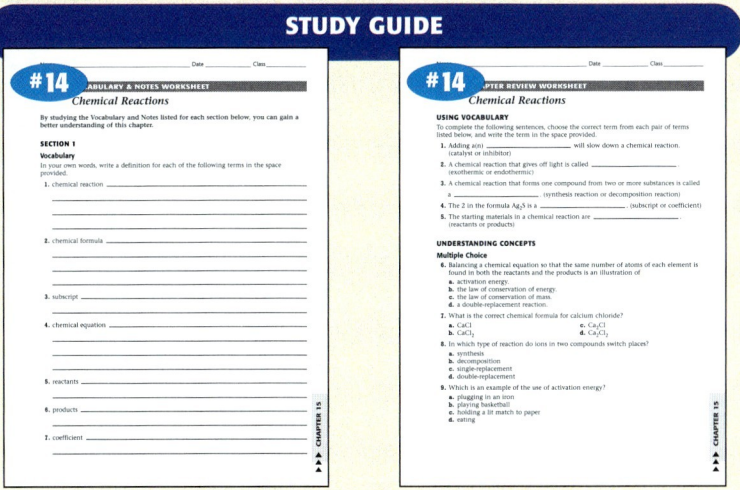

CHAPTER TESTS WITH PERFORMANCE-BASED ASSESSMENT

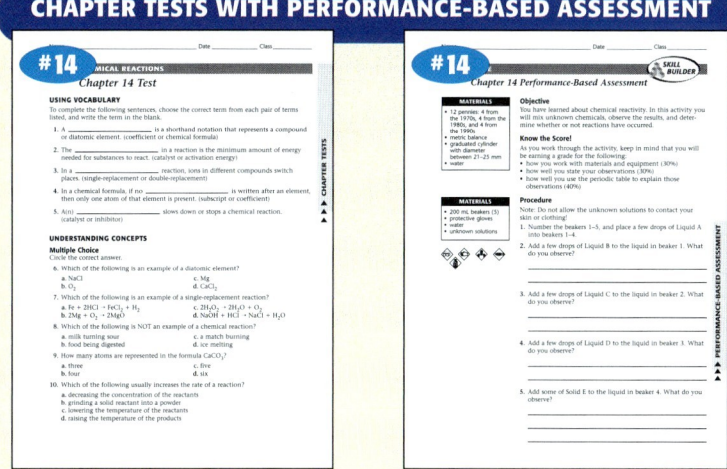

Lab Worksheets

INQUIRY LABS
LONG-TERM PROJECTS & RESEARCH IDEAS

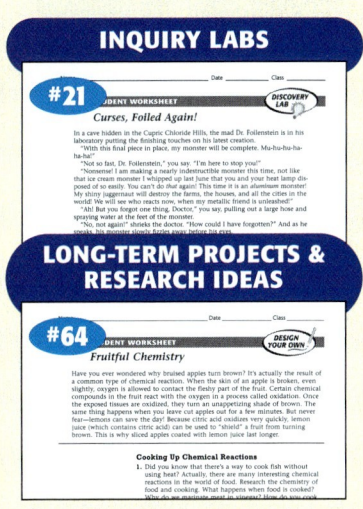

WHIZ-BANG DEMONSTRATIONS

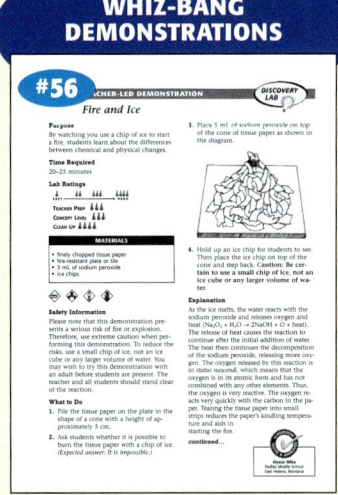

LABS YOU CAN EAT

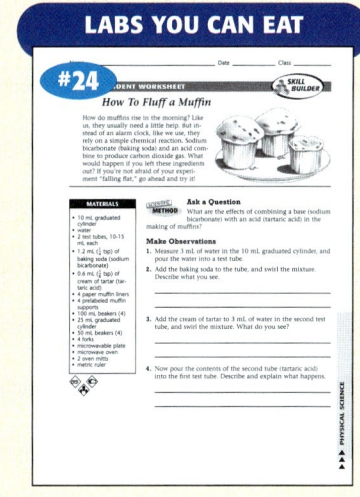

DATASHEETS FOR LABBOOK

- #40 Finding a Balance
- #41 Cata-what? Catalyst!
- #42 Putting Elements Together
- #43 Speed Control

Applications & Extensions

CRITICAL THINKING & PROBLEM SOLVING
SCIENCE TECHNOLOGY

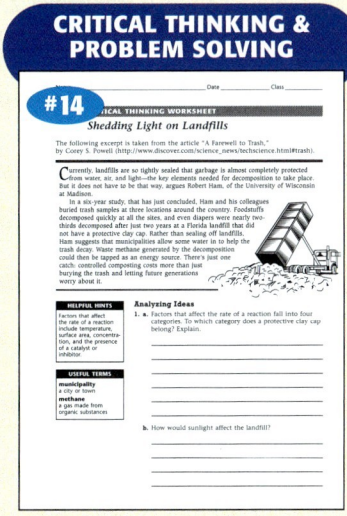

Chapter 14 • Chapter Resources & Worksheets

Chapter Background

SECTION 1

Forming New Substances

▶ **Chemical Symbols**
To be able to discuss the nature of chemical reactions, scientists identify elements with one- or two-letter symbols. In this way, the language of chemical reactions can be understood universally.

▶ **Conserved Quantities**
In any chemical or physical change, the total amount of mass and energy in the reaction is unchanged. Both the law of conservation of mass and the law of conservation of energy apply to the chemical reactions discussed in this chapter.

▶ **Chemical Formulas**
Chemical formulas describe compounds and diatomic elements. A chemical formula represents the composition of one formula unit of an ionic compound or one molecule of a covalent compound or diatomic element. For example, the chemical formula for the ionic compound calcium chloride is $CaCl_2$, because each formula unit consists of one calcium ion and two chloride ions. The chemical formula for the covalent compound water is H_2O, because each molecule of water consists of two hydrogen atoms and one oxygen atom.

▶ **Chemical Equations**
Chemical symbols and formulas are used together to form chemical equations that describe a chemical reaction. A chemical equation states which elements or compounds are used up and which are formed, and it shows the relative amounts of each.

IS THAT A FACT!

◆ The reaction between hydrogen gas and oxygen gas to form water can be started with a small flame. However, water cannot be changed back into hydrogen and oxygen merely by cooling. The reverse chemical reaction can be accomplished only if some type of energy, such as electrical energy, is used to break the bonds between the hydrogen and oxygen atoms in the water molecules.

SECTION 2

Types of Chemical Reactions

▶ **Synthesis Reactions**
The formation of one product from two or more reactants is a synthesis reaction. For example, the formation of magnesium oxide from magnesium and oxygen (in early flashbulbs) and the formation of ammonia from nitrogen and hydrogen are synthesis reactions.

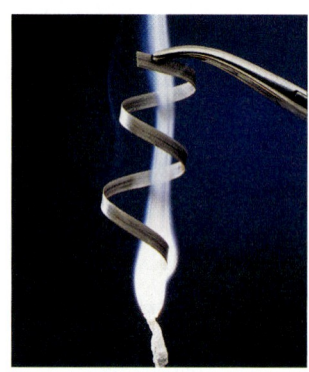

▶ **Decomposition Reactions**
A decomposition reaction is one in which a single compound produces two or more simpler substances. For example, the breakdown of water molecules into hydrogen and oxygen molecules is a decomposition reaction in which energy is used to break the bonds in the water molecules.

▶ **Single-Replacement Reactions**
Both metals and nonmetals undergo single-replacement reactions; for example, zinc, a metal, will react with hydrochloric acid to form zinc chloride and hydrogen gas. Chlorine, a nonmetal, will replace the bromine in sodium bromide to form sodium chloride and bromine.

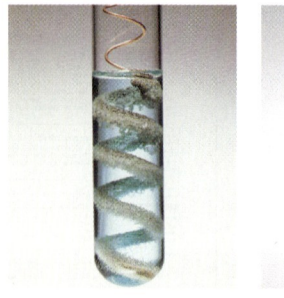 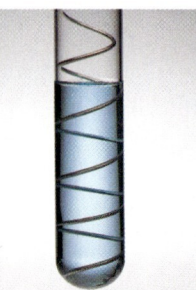

Chapter 14 • Chemical Reactions

▶ Double-Replacement Reactions
Double-replacement reactions usually "go to completion." This means that they continue until one or more of the reactants is entirely used up. When a person takes milk of magnesia (magnesium hydroxide) to neutralize stomach acid, a double-replacement reaction occurs. The two products formed are magnesium chloride and water.

IS THAT A FACT!
▶ The reaction between baking soda, $NaHCO_3$, and tartaric acid, $H_2C_4H_4O_6$, in baking powder is a double-replacement reaction, followed by a decomposition reaction that produces carbon dioxide. The bubbles of CO_2 make some doughs rise.

SECTION 3

Energy and Rates of Chemical Reactions

▶ Chemical Kinetics
For a chemical reaction to occur at all, reactant molecules must collide with enough energy and in the proper orientation to allow bonds to break and new bonds to form.

▶ Endothermic Reactions
Endothermic reactions are those that absorb energy. Photosynthesis in plants is an example of an endothermic reaction. Light energy from the sun drives the formation of glucose from carbon dioxide and water.

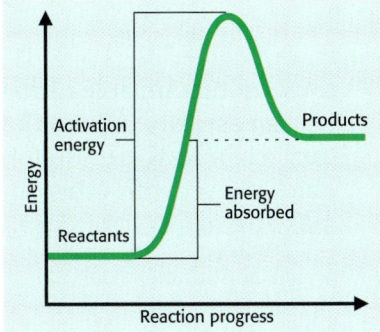

▶ Exothermic Reactions
Exothermic reactions are those in which energy is removed or given off. For example, when hydrogen and oxygen react to form water, light and thermal energy are given off.

- In the body, exothermic reactions take place when food molecules are broken down and absorbed by cells in a series of reactions.

▶ Catalysts
Catalysts are substances that significantly increase the rate of a chemical reaction. *Enzymes* are catalysts in living systems. These large protein molecules speed up many of the reactions in our body. For instance, the enzyme *amylase*, found in saliva, breaks down starch.

For background information about teaching strategies and issues, refer to the *Professional Reference for Teachers*.

CHAPTER 14
Chemical Reactions

Chapter Preview

Section 1
Forming New Substances
- Chemical Reactions
- Chemical Formulas
- Chemical Equations

Section 2
Types of Chemical Reactions
- Synthesis Reactions
- Decomposition Reactions
- Single-Replacement Reactions
- Double-Replacement Reactions

Section 3
Energy and Rates of Chemical Reactions
- Every Reaction Involves Energy
- Factors Affecting Rates of Reactions

Directed Reading Worksheet 14

Science Puzzlers, Twisters & Teasers Worksheet 14

Guided Reading Audio CD
English or Spanish, Chapter 14

internetconnect
Smithsonian Institution®
Visit www.si.edu/hrw for additional on-line resources.

CHAPTER 14 Chemical Reactions

Imagine . . .

A car slams into a wall at 97 km/h (60 mph). Although both occupants are wearing seat belts, one suffers a crushing blow to the head as he strikes the dashboard. The other occupant suffers only minor bruises thanks to the presence of an air bag. Fortunately, no one was really injured because this was just a crash test using dummies. The results of this test could lead to the design of better air bags.

The key to an air bag's success during a crash is the speed at which it inflates. Inside the bag is a gas generator that contains the compounds sodium azide, potassium nitrate, and silicon dioxide. At the moment of a crash, an electronic sensor in the vehicle detects the sudden decrease in speed. The sensor sends a small electric current to the gas generator. This provides the *activation energy*, or the energy needed for substances to react, for the chemicals in the gas generator.

The rate, or speed, at which the reaction occurs is very fast. In 1/25 of a second—less than the blink of an eye—the gas formed in the reaction inflates the bag. The air bag fills upward and outward. By filling the space between a person and the car's dashboard, the air bag protects him or her from injury.

Designers of air bags must understand a lot about chemical reactions. In this chapter, you will learn about different types of chemical reactions. You will learn the clues that will help you identify when a chemical reaction is taking place. You will also learn about the factors that affect the rate of a reaction.

The reaction between vinegar and baking soda produces a gas. However, the reaction is too slow for use in an air bag.

Imagine . . .

The force that triggers the inflation of an airbag is approximately the same as that of hitting a solid barrier head-on at 20 km/h. On impact, the chemicals sodium azide and potassium nitrate react to form nontoxic, nonflammable nitrogen gas, which is what actually inflates the bag. (Several toxic chemicals are also formed, but they quickly react with other substances to make them less hazardous.)

Reaction Ready

The reactions that occur in an air bag produce the gas that fills the bag. In fact, the production of a gas is often a sign that a chemical reaction is taking place. In this activity, you will observe a reaction and identify signs that indicate that a reaction is taking place.

Procedure

1. In a **large, sealable plastic bag,** place one plastic spoonful of **baking soda** and two spoonfuls of **calcium chloride.**
2. Fill a **plastic film canister** two-thirds full with **water.**
3. Carefully place the canister in the bag without spilling the water. Squeeze the air out of the bag, and seal it tightly.
4. Tip the canister over, and mix the contents of the bag.

Analysis

5. Observe the contents of the bag. Record your observations in your ScienceLog.
6. What evidence did you see that a chemical reaction was taking place?

What Do You Think?

In your ScienceLog, try to answer the following questions based on what you already know:

1. What clues can help you identify a chemical reaction?
2. What are some types of chemical reactions?
3. How can you change the rate of a chemical reaction?

What Do You Think?

Accept all reasonable responses. Students will have a chance to revise their answers in the Chapter Review under NOW What Do You Think?

Investigate!

MATERIALS

FOR EACH GROUP:
- large, strong, sealable plastic bag
- baking soda
- calcium chloride
- plastic spoons (one for each chemical)
- plastic film canister
- water

Safety Caution: Remind students to review all safety cautions and icons before beginning this activity. Caution students to wear goggles, gloves, and an apron when doing this activity.

Teacher Notes: Try this reaction ahead of time to be sure the gases will not pop the plastic bag.

Squeezing as much air as possible out of the bag before sealing it will produce the best results.

For an optimum reaction, check to make sure the baking soda has not expired.

Disposal Information: One at a time, slowly combine all the solutions while stirring. Adjust the pH of the final waste liquid with 1.0 M acid or base until the pH is between 5 and 9. Pour the neutralized liquid down the drain.

The rate at which the carbon dioxide gas is released determines the size of the bubbles in dough. Bakers use baking soda as a leavening agent in most cakes and quickbreads. Yeast, another leavening agent, produces a fine-grained bread with a denser texture.

Answers to Investigate!

5. Students should observe the formation of gas bubbles, the formation of a solid white substance that does not dissolve, and possibly a decrease in the temperature of the mixture.
6. formation of gas, formation of an insoluble solid, change in temperature

Chapter 14 • Chemical Reactions

SECTION 1

Focus

Forming New Substances

This section discusses chemical reactions. Students learn how to write chemical formulas and how to balance chemical equations. The section also explains how the law of conservation of mass is maintained in a balanced chemical equation.

Bellringer

Ask students the following question:

What do baking bread, launching the space shuttle, and digesting food have in common? **(They all involve chemical reactions.)**

Have them write their answer in their ScienceLog.

1 Motivate

DISCUSSION

Ask students to think about the chemical reactions that occur in school every day. Have them consider the reactions in the meals cooking in the school cafeteria and in the dry cells and batteries that provide energy to run equipment. List their responses on the board, and discuss the clues to look for in each chemical reaction.

Directed Reading Worksheet 14 Section 1

Section 1

Terms to Learn
chemical reaction
chemical formula
chemical equation
reactants
products
law of conservation of mass

What You'll Do
- Identify the clues that indicate a chemical reaction might be taking place.
- Interpret and write simple chemical formulas.
- Interpret and write simple balanced chemical equations.
- Explain how a balanced equation illustrates the law of conservation of mass.

Forming New Substances

Each fall, an amazing transformation takes place. Leaves change color, as shown in **Figure 1**. Vibrant reds, oranges, and yellows that had been hidden by green all year are seen as the temperatures get cooler and the hours of sunlight become fewer. What is happening to cause this change? Leaves have a green color as a result of a compound called chlorophyll (KLOR uh FIL). Each fall, the chlorophyll undergoes a chemical change and forms simpler substances that have no color. You can see the red, orange, and yellow colors in the leaves because the green color of the chlorophyll no longer hides them.

Figure 1 *The change of color in the fall is a result of chemical changes in the leaves.*

Chemical Reactions

The chemical change that occurs as chlorophyll breaks down into simpler substances is one example of a chemical reaction. A **chemical reaction** is the process by which one or more substances undergo change to produce one or more different substances. These new substances have different chemical and physical properties from the original substances. Many of the changes you are familiar with are chemical reactions, including the ones shown in **Figure 2**.

Figure 2 Examples of Chemical Reactions

The substances that make up baking powder undergo a chemical reaction when mixed with water. One new substance that forms is carbon dioxide gas, which causes the bubbles in this muffin.

Once ignited, gasoline reacts with oxygen gas in the air. The new substances that form, carbon dioxide and water, push against the pistons in the engine to keep the car moving.

IS THAT A FACT!

Carbon dioxide has a number of notable applications. When dissolved under pressure, it produces the effervescence in carbonated beverages. Because carbon dioxide gas does not combust and is denser than air, it is used in fire extinguishers to smother flames. Dry ice, or solid carbon dioxide, is valuable for its cooling effect, which is almost twice that of water ice. Carbon dioxide also changes directly from a solid to a gas, bypassing the liquid state.

Clues to Chemical Reactions How can you tell when a chemical reaction is taking place? There are several clues that indicate when a reaction might be occurring. The more of these clues you observe, the more likely it is that the change is a chemical reaction. Several of these clues are described below.

Some Clues to Chemical Reactions

Gas Formation
The formation of gas bubbles is a clue that a chemical reaction might be taking place. For example, bubbles of carbon dioxide are produced when hydrochloric acid is placed on a piece of limestone.

Solid Formation
A solid formed in a solution as a result of a chemical reaction is called a *precipitate* (pruh SIP uh TAYT). Here you see potassium chromate solution being added to a silver nitrate solution. The dark red solid is a precipitate of silver chromate.

Color Change
Chlorine bleach is great for removing the color from stains on white clothes. But don't spill it on your jeans. The bleach reacts with the blue dye on the fabric, causing the color of the material to change.

Energy Change
Energy is released during some chemical reactions. A fire heats a room and provides light. Electrical energy is released when chemicals in a battery react. During some other chemical reactions, energy is absorbed. Chemicals on photographic film react when they absorb energy from light shining on the film.

2) Teach, continued

GUIDED PRACTICE

Allow students to make and break bonds using toothpicks and plastic-foam balls of two different sizes. Use the examples given in **Figure 3** to guide students through the breaking of bonds between atoms of hydrogen (small balls) and chlorine (large balls) and the making of new bonds in hydrogen chloride.

MATH and MORE

Have students list the name and number of each type of atom in these well-known compounds:

1. DDT—$C_{14}H_9Cl_5$ (14 carbon, 9 hydrogen, 5 chlorine)
2. vitamin C (ascorbic acid)—$C_6H_8O_6$ (6 carbon, 8 hydrogen, 6 oxygen)
3. nitroglycerin—$C_3H_5N_3O_9$ (3 carbon, 5 hydrogen, 3 nitrogen, 9 oxygen)
4. rubbing alcohol—C_3H_8O (3 carbon, 8 hydrogen, 1 oxygen)
5. nicotine—$C_{10}H_{14}N_2$ (10 carbon, 14 hydrogen, 2 nitrogen)

If students have trouble identifying the elements in these compounds, refer them to the periodic table on pp. 304–305.

Answers to MATHBREAK

$Mg(OH)_2$: 1 magnesium atom, 2 oxygen atoms, 2 hydrogen atoms;
$Al_2(SO_4)_3$: 2 aluminum atoms, 3 sulfur atoms, 12 oxygen atoms

Teaching Transparency 254
"Reaction of Hydrogen and Chlorine"

Figure 3
Reaction of Hydrogen and Chlorine

Breaking Bonds The elements hydrogen and chlorine are diatomic, meaning they are composed of molecules that consist of two atoms bonded together. For these molecules to react, the bonds joining the atoms must break.

Making Bonds Molecules of the new substance, hydrogen chloride, are formed as new bonds are made between hydrogen atoms and chlorine atoms.

Breaking and Making Bonds New substances are formed in a chemical reaction because chemical bonds in the starting substances break, atoms rearrange, and new bonds form to make the new substances. Look at the model in **Figure 3** to understand how this process occurs.

Chemical Formulas

Remember that a chemical symbol is a shorthand method of identifying an element. A **chemical formula** is a shorthand notation for a compound or a diatomic element using chemical symbols and numbers. A chemical formula indicates the chemical makeup by showing how many of each kind of atom is present in a molecule.

The chemical formula for water, H_2O, tells you that a water molecule is composed of two atoms of hydrogen and one atom of oxygen. The small number 2 in the formula is a subscript. A *subscript* is a number written below and to the right of a chemical symbol in a formula. When no subscript is written after a symbol, as with the oxygen in water's formula, only one atom of that element is present. **Figure 4** shows two more chemical formulas and what they mean.

Figure 4 *A chemical formula shows the number of atoms of each element present.*

$$O_2$$

Oxygen is a diatomic element. Each molecule of oxygen gas is composed of two atoms of oxygen bonded together.

$$C_6H_{12}O_6$$

Every molecule of **glucose** (the sugar formed by plants during photosynthesis) is composed of six atoms of carbon, twelve atoms of hydrogen, and six atoms of oxygen.

MATH BREAK

Counting Atoms

Some chemical formulas contain two or more chemical symbols enclosed by parentheses. When counting atoms in these formulas, multiply everything inside the parentheses by the subscript as though they were part of a mathematical equation. For example, $Ca(NO_3)_2$ contains:

- 1 calcium atom
- 2 nitrogen atoms (2 × 1)
- 6 oxygen atoms (2 × 3)

Now It's Your Turn
Determine the number of atoms of each element in the formulas $Mg(OH)_2$ and $Al_2(SO_4)_3$.

Q: Name the compound $Ba(Na)_2$.

A: banana

IS THAT A FACT!

When hydrogen chloride gas is dissolved in water, it is known as hydrochloric acid. There is a small amount of concentrated hydrochloric acid in your stomach, where it is necessary for the digestion of food.

Writing Formulas for Covalent Compounds You can often write a chemical formula if you know the name of the substance. Remember that covalent compounds are usually composed of two nonmetals. The names of covalent compounds use prefixes to tell you how many atoms of each element are in the formula. A *prefix* is a syllable or syllables joined to the beginning of a word. Each prefix used in a chemical name represents a number, as shown in the table at right. **Figure 5** demonstrates how to write a chemical formula from the name of a covalent compound.

Prefixes Used in Chemical Names			
mono-	1	hexa-	6
di-	2	hepta-	7
tri-	3	octa-	8
tetra-	4	nona-	9
penta-	5	deca-	10

Carbon dioxide

$$CO_2$$

The *lack of a prefix* indicates 1 carbon atom.
The prefix *di-* indicates 2 oxygen atoms.

Dinitrogen monoxide

$$N_2O$$

The prefix *di-* indicates 2 nitrogen atoms.
The prefix *mono-* indicates 1 oxygen atom.

Figure 5 *The formulas of these covalent compounds can be written using the prefixes in their names.*

Self-Check

How many atoms of each element make up Na_2SO_4? (See page 724 to check your answer.)

Writing Formulas for Ionic Compounds If the name of a compound contains the name of a metal and a nonmetal, the compound is probably ionic. To write the formula for an ionic compound, you must make sure the compound's overall charge is zero. In other words, the formula must have subscripts that cause the charges of the ions to cancel out. (Remember that the charge of many ions can be determined by looking at the periodic table.) **Figure 6** demonstrates how to write a chemical formula from the name of an ionic compound.

Figure 6 *The formula of an ionic compound is written by using enough of each ion so the overall charge is zero.*

Sodium chloride

$$NaCl$$

A sodium ion has a 1+ **charge**.
A chloride ion has a 1− **charge**.

One sodium ion and one chloride ion have an overall **charge of** $(1+) + (1-) = 0$

Magnesium chloride

$$MgCl_2$$

A magnesium ion has a 2+ **charge**.
A chloride ion has a 1− **charge**.

One magnesium ion and two chloride ions have an overall **charge of** $(2+) + 2(1-) = 0$

CROSS-DISCIPLINARY FOCUS

Language Arts The prefixes in the names of covalent compounds have their origins in the Greek language. Each prefix is a Greek numeric representation.

Answer to Self-Check
2 sodium atoms, 1 sulfur atom, and 4 oxygen atoms

Homework
Write the chemical names given below on the board. Have students identify each compound as ionic or covalent, then use the table of prefixes on this page and a periodic table to write the formula for each compound.

sulfur trioxide (covalent; SO_3)

calcium fluoride (ionic; CaF_2)

phosphorus pentachloride (covalent; PCl_5)

dinitrogen trioxide (covalent; N_2O_3)

lithium oxide (ionic; Li_2O)

MEETING INDIVIDUAL NEEDS

Advanced Learners Have students write the names of compounds in the list of ingredients of substances found around their homes. Encourage students to identify substances as ionic or covalent and to attempt to write the chemical formulas for each of the compounds. Many of the compounds can be found in chemistry references.

Teaching Transparency 255 "Writing Chemical Formulas and Equations"

TOPIC: Chemical Formulas
GO TO: www.scilinks.org
sciLINKS NUMBER: HSTP335

Section 1 • Forming New Substances

2 Teach, continued

DISCUSSION
Have students discuss how the yields sign in a chemical equation is like an "equals" sign in a mathematical equation. Also discuss how the two signs are different.

ACTIVITY
Concept Mapping Have students create a concept map with "chemical equations" as the title concept. The concept map should include the different components of a chemical equation:

reactants, products, coefficients, yields sign

MEETING INDIVIDUAL NEEDS
Advanced Learners Have students research the chemical reactants and products for the reactions that produce acid precipitation and ozone in the atmosphere. Ask them to diagram the processes involved. Have them present their results on a poster to show to the class.

MISCONCEPTION ALERT
Some students may assume that triatomic molecules such as H_2O, CO_2, and N_2O consist of only two particles bonded together. For example, students may think that H_2O consists of a molecule of hydrogen, H_2, bonded to an atom of oxygen. Be sure to point out that in such molecules there are three particles bonded together. In the case of H_2O, there are two hydrogen atoms bonded to one oxygen atom.

Figure 7 The symbols on this music are understood around the world—just like chemical symbols!

Chemical Equations

A composer writing a piece of music, like the one in **Figure 7,** must communicate to the musician what notes to play, how long to play each note, and in what style each note should be played. The composer does not use words to describe what must happen. Instead, he or she uses musical symbols to communicate in a way that can be easily understood by anyone in the world who can read music.

Similarly, people who work with chemical reactions need to communicate information about reactions clearly to other people throughout the world. Describing reactions using long descriptive sentences would require translations into other languages. Chemists have developed a method of describing reactions that is short and easily understood by anyone in the world who understands chemical formulas. A **chemical equation** is a shorthand description of a chemical reaction using chemical formulas and symbols. Because each element's chemical symbol is understood around the world, a chemical equation needs no translation.

Reactants Yield Products Consider the example of carbon reacting with oxygen to yield carbon dioxide, as shown in **Figure 8.** The starting materials in a chemical reaction are **reactants** (ree AKT uhnts). The substances formed from a reaction are **products.** In this example, carbon and oxygen are reactants, and carbon dioxide is the product formed. The parts of the chemical equation for this reaction are described in **Figure 9.**

Figure 8 Charcoal is used to cook food on a barbecue. When carbon in charcoal reacts with oxygen in the air, the primary product is carbon dioxide.

Figure 9 The Parts of a Chemical Equation

The formulas of the **reactants** are written before the arrow.

The formulas of the **products** are written after the arrow.

A **plus sign** separates the formulas of two or more reactants or products from one another.

The **arrow,** also called the yields sign, separates the formulas of the reactants from the formulas of the products.

SCIENCE HUMOR

Q: What does a doctor do with an injured chemist?

A: helium

Q: And what does a doctor do with a sick chemist?

A: curium

Q: And if the doctor can't cure him?

A: barium

Accuracy Is Important The symbol or formula for each substance in the reaction must be written correctly. For a compound, determine if it is covalent or ionic, and write the appropriate formula. For an element, use the proper chemical symbol, and be sure to use a subscript of 2 for the diatomic elements. (The seven diatomic elements are hydrogen, nitrogen, oxygen, fluorine, chlorine, bromine, and iodine.) An equation with an incorrect chemical symbol or formula will not accurately describe the reaction. In fact, even a simple mistake can make a huge difference, as shown in **Figure 10**.

BRAIN FOOD

Hydrogen gas, H_2, is an important fuel that may help reduce air pollution. Because water is the only product formed as hydrogen burns, there is little air pollution from vehicles that use hydrogen as fuel.

Figure 10 *The symbols and formulas shown here are similar, but don't confuse them while writing an equation!*

The chemical formula for the compound carbon dioxide is **CO_2**. Carbon dioxide is a colorless, odorless gas that you exhale.

The chemical formula for the compound carbon monoxide is **CO**. Carbon monoxide is a colorless, odorless, poisonous gas.

The chemical symbol for the element cobalt is **Co**. Cobalt is a hard, bluish gray metal.

✓ Self-Check

When calcium bromide reacts with chlorine, bromine and calcium chloride are produced. Write an equation to describe this reaction. Identify each substance as either a reactant or a product. *(See page 724 to check your answers.)*

An Equation Must Be Balanced In a chemical reaction, every atom in the reactants becomes part of the products. Atoms are never lost or gained in a chemical reaction. When writing a chemical equation, you must show that the number of atoms of each element in the reactants equals the number of atoms of those elements in the products by writing a balanced equation.

RETEACHING

Remind students of the importance of writing chemical formulas correctly. As an example, write the formulas for water, H_2O, and hydrogen peroxide, H_2O_2, or for oxygen, O_2, and ozone, O_3, on the board. Discuss with students the properties of each substance and the dangers of mistaking one for the other. **Sheltered English**

Answer to Self-Check

$CaBr_2 + Cl_2 \rightarrow Br_2 + CaCl_2$

reactants: $CaBr_2$ and Cl_2

products: Br_2 and $CaCl_2$

CROSS-DISCIPLINARY FOCUS

History As long ago as the mid-1800s, hydrogen gas was used to inflate rigid, semirigid, and nonrigid dirigibles. These gas-filled aircraft were first used for military defense. Later the dirigible became a commercial airship. After the 1936 explosion of the German-built *Hindenburg*, in which 36 people were killed, the use of hydrogen-filled rigid airships was halted.

IS THAT A FACT!

Hydrogen peroxide is a compound that can be made by combining barium peroxide and phosphoric acid. In a 3-percent solution, hydrogen peroxide is an effective antiseptic and germicide. Undiluted, however, it is caustic and highly toxic.

3) Extend

USING THE FIGURE

It is important not to change a subscript. In step 1 of **Figure 11,** if the formula H_2O were changed to H_2O_2, although the equation would be balanced, it would no longer describe the formation of water. It would show the formation of hydrogen peroxide, a different substance.

Answers to MATHBREAK

$2HCl + Na_2S \rightarrow H_2S + 2NaCl$

$2Al + 3Cl_2 \rightarrow 2AlCl_3$

MATH and MORE

When students have balanced the equations in Now It's Your Turn in the MathBreak, ask them to write in their ScienceLog what the two equations are describing. Remind students to be specific and not to forget any of the symbols. *(Two molecules of hydrogen chloride—hydrochloric acid—combine with one molecule of sodium sulfide to form one molecule of hydrogen sulfide and two molecules of sodium chloride. Two atoms of aluminum combine with three molecules of diatomic chlorine to form two molecules of aluminum chloride.)*

Math Skills Worksheet 50 "Balancing Chemical Equations"

Finding a Balance

MATH BREAK

Balancing Act

When balancing a chemical equation, you must place coefficients in front of an entire chemical formula, never in the middle of a formula. Notice where the coefficients are in the balanced equation below:

$F_2 + 2KCl \rightarrow 2KF + Cl_2$

Now It's Your Turn

Write balanced equations for the following:

$HCl + Na_2S \rightarrow H_2S + NaCl$

$Al + Cl_2 \rightarrow AlCl_3$

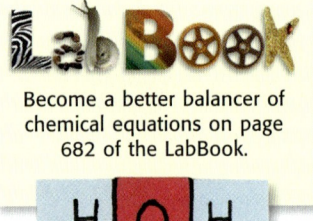
Become a better balancer of chemical equations on page 682 of the LabBook.

How to Balance an Equation Writing a balanced equation requires the use of coefficients (кон uh FISH uhnts). A *coefficient* is a number placed in front of a chemical symbol or formula. When counting atoms, you multiply a coefficient by the subscript of each of the elements in the formula that follows it. Thus, $2CO_2$ represents 2 carbon dioxide molecules. Together the two molecules contain a total of 2 carbon atoms and 4 oxygen atoms. Coefficients are used when balancing equations because the subscripts in the formulas cannot be changed. Changing a subscript changes the formula so that it no longer represents the correct substance. Study **Figure 11** to see how to use coefficients to balance an equation. Then you can practice balancing equations by doing the MathBreak at left.

Figure 11 Follow these steps to write a balanced equation for $H_2 + O_2 \rightarrow H_2O$.

1 **Count the atoms** of each element in the reactants and in the products. You can see that there are fewer oxygen atoms in the products than in the reactants.

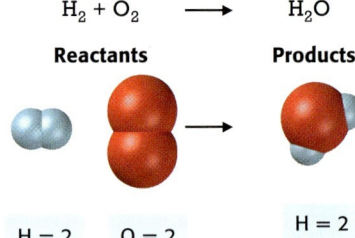

$H_2 + O_2 \rightarrow H_2O$

Reactants: H = 2, O = 2

Products: H = 2, O = 1

2 **To balance the oxygen atoms,** place the coefficient 2 in front of water's formula. This gives you 2 oxygen atoms in both the reactants and the products. But now there are too few hydrogen atoms in the reactants.

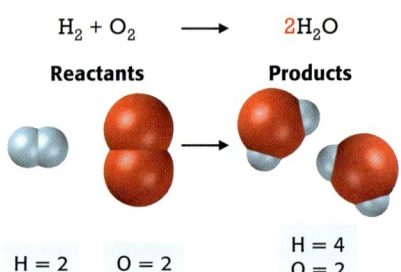

$H_2 + O_2 \rightarrow 2H_2O$

Reactants: H = 2, O = 2

Products: H = 4, O = 2

3 **To balance the hydrogen atoms,** place the coefficient 2 in front of hydrogen's formula. But just to be sure your answer is correct, always double-check your work!

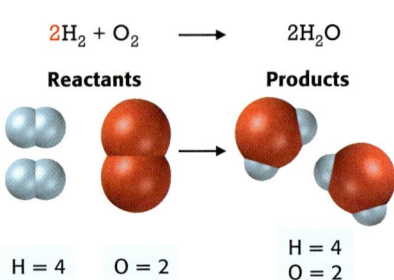

$2H_2 + O_2 \rightarrow 2H_2O$

Reactants: H = 4, O = 2

Products: H = 4, O = 2

Teaching Transparency 256 "Balancing a Chemical Equation"

internetconnect
SC LINKS **TOPIC:** Chemical Equations
GO TO: www.scilinks.org
NSTA **sciLINKS NUMBER:** HSTP340

Mass Is Conserved—It's a Law! The practice of balancing equations is a result of the work of a French chemist, Antoine Lavoisier (luh vwa ZYAY). In the 1700s, Lavoisier performed experiments in which he carefully measured and compared the masses of the substances involved in chemical reactions. He determined that the total mass of the reactants equaled the total mass of the products. Lavoisier's work led to the **law of conservation of mass,** which states that mass is neither created nor destroyed in ordinary chemical and physical changes. Thus, a chemical equation must show the same number and kind of atom on both sides of the arrow. The law of conservation of mass is demonstrated in **Figure 12.** You can explore this law for yourself in the QuickLab at right.

Figure 12 In this demonstration, magnesium in the flashbulb of a camera reacts with oxygen. Notice that the mass is the same before and after the reaction takes place.

QuickLab

Mass Conservation

1. Place 5 g (1 tsp) of **baking soda** into a **sealable plastic bag.**
2. Place 5 mL (1 tsp) of **vinegar** into a **plastic film canister.** Close the lid.
3. Use a **balance** to determine the masses of the bag with baking soda and the canister with vinegar, and record both values in your ScienceLog.
4. Place the canister into the bag. Squeeze the air out of the bag, and tightly seal it.
5. Open the canister in the bag. Mix the vinegar with the baking soda.
6. When the reaction has stopped, measure the total mass of the bag and its contents.
7. Compare the mass of the materials before and after the reaction.

REVIEW

1. List four clues that a chemical reaction is occurring.
2. How many atoms of each element make up $2Na_3PO_4$?
3. Write the chemical formulas for carbon tetrachloride and calcium bromide.
4. Explain how a balanced chemical equation illustrates that mass is never lost or gained in a chemical reaction.
5. **Applying Concepts** Write the balanced chemical equation for methane, CH_4, reacting with oxygen gas to produce water and carbon dioxide.

internet connect

SC_iLINKS NSTA
TOPIC: Chemical Formulas, Chemical Equations
GO TO: www.scilinks.org
sciLINKS NUMBER: HSTP335, HSTP340

▼ **Answers to Review**

1. gas formation, solid formation, color change, energy change
2. 6 sodium atoms, 2 phosphorus atoms, 8 oxygen atoms
3. CCl_4, $CaBr_2$
4. A balanced chemical equation shows the same number and kind of atom in both the reactants and the products. Therefore, the total mass of all the atoms in the reactants is the same as the total mass of the same atoms in the products.
5. $CH_4 + 2O_2 \rightarrow 2H_2O + CO_2$

SECTION 2

Focus

Types of Chemical Reactions

This section describes four different types of chemical reactions. Students will learn how to determine the type of reaction that is represented by a chemical equation.

 **Bellringer**

In the last section, you learned that chemical reactions have reactants and products. Do you think that the products of a reaction are always more complex than the reactants? Could products be simpler than the reactants? Explain your answer.

1 Motivate

DISCUSSION

Ask students to define the words *decompose* and *synthesize*. Challenge them to explain what happens during decomposition and synthesis reactions.

CONNECT TO ENVIRONMENTAL SCIENCE

Some synthesis reactions have two compounds, or an element and a compound, as reactants forming a larger compound. For example, the formation of sulfuric acid, a major component of acid precipitation, involves the following synthesis reactions:

$S + O_2 \rightarrow SO_2$

$2SO_2 + O_2 \rightarrow 2SO_3$

$SO_3 + H_2O \rightarrow H_2SO_4$

Section 2

Terms to Learn

synthesis reaction
decomposition reaction
single-replacement reaction
double-replacement reaction

What You'll Do

- Describe four types of chemical reactions.
- Classify a chemical equation as one of the four types of chemical reactions described here.

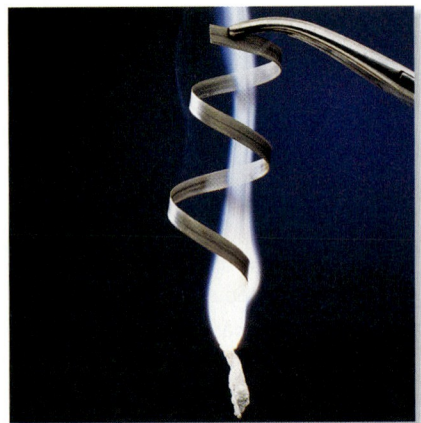

Figure 13 The synthesis reaction that occurs when magnesium reacts with oxygen in the air forms the compound magnesium oxide.

 Teaching Transparency 257 "Models of Reactions"

 Directed Reading Worksheet 14 Section 2

Types of Chemical Reactions

Imagine having to learn 50 chemical reactions. Sound tough? Well, there are thousands of known chemical reactions. It would be impossible to remember them all. But there is help! Remember that the elements are divided into categories based on their properties. In a similar way, reactions can be classified according to their similarities.

Many reactions can be grouped into one of four categories: synthesis (SIN thuh sis), decomposition, single replacement, and double replacement. By dividing reactions into these categories, you can better understand the patterns of how reactants become products. As you learn about each type of reaction, study the models provided to help you recognize each type of reaction.

Synthesis Reactions

A **synthesis reaction** is a reaction in which two or more substances combine to form a single compound. For example, the synthesis reaction in which the compound magnesium oxide is produced is seen in **Figure 13.** (This is the same reaction that occurs in the flashbulb in Figure 12.) One way to remember what happens in each type of reaction is to imagine people at a dance. A synthesis reaction would be modeled by two people joining to form a dancing couple, as shown in **Figure 14.**

Figure 14 A model for the synthesis reaction of sodium reacting with chlorine to form sodium chloride is shown below.

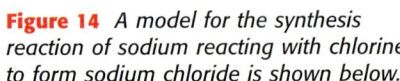

 **MISCONCEPTION ALERT**

The four types of reactions discussed in this section are not the only types of reactions that substances can undergo. For example, combustion (reaction with oxygen) is an important type of reaction not discussed here.

358 Chapter 14 • Chemical Reactions

Decomposition Reactions

A **decomposition reaction** is a reaction in which a single compound breaks down to form two or more simpler substances. The decomposition of water is shown in **Figure 15**. Decomposition is the reverse of synthesis. The dance model would represent a decomposition reaction as a dancing couple splitting up, as shown in **Figure 16**.

Figure 16 *A model for the decomposition reaction of carbonic acid to form water and carbon dioxide is shown below.*

$$H_2CO_3 \rightarrow H_2O + CO_2$$

Figure 15 *Water can be decomposed into the elements hydrogen and oxygen through electrolysis.*

Single-Replacement Reactions

A **single-replacement reaction** is a reaction in which an element takes the place of another element that is part of a compound. The products of single-replacement reactions are a new compound and a different element. The dance model for single-replacement reactions is a person who cuts in on a couple dancing. A new couple is formed and a different person is left alone, as shown in **Figure 17**.

Figure 17 *A model for a single-replacement reaction of zinc reacting with hydrochloric acid to form zinc chloride and hydrogen is shown below.*

$$Zn + 2HCl \rightarrow ZnCl_2 + H_2$$

Q: What happens to songwriters when they are buried?

A: They decompose.

MISCONCEPTION ALERT

The dancing models used in this section only represent general types of reactions. They do not show what happens in a particular reaction, nor do they show that reactants in a reaction undergo changes and form products that are different substances, with different properties, from those reactants.

2) Teach

DEMONSTRATION

Obtain silver nitrate from a high-school chemistry lab to demonstrate the single-replacement reaction shown on page 360.

1. Write the following equation on the board:

   $Cu + 2AgNO_3 \rightarrow 2Ag + Cu(NO_3)_2$

2. Guide students through this equation by identifying the reactants and products:

   copper + silver nitrate → silver + copper(II) nitrate

3. Explain to students that you will demonstrate this reaction by dropping a copper penny into water that contains silver nitrate.

4. Ask students to share their observations about the penny. (The penny becomes coated with silver.)

5. Ask students to refer to the equation to determine which metal is more reactive. (Copper replaced the silver so copper is more reactive than silver.)

3) Extend

GOING FURTHER

Discuss with students the reactions for photosynthesis, $6CO_2 + 6H_2O + energy \rightarrow C_6H_{12}O_6 + 6O_2$, and respiration, $C_6H_{12}O_6 + 6O_2 \rightarrow 6CO_2 + 6H_2O + energy$.

Ask them to discuss how the two reactions are complementary.

TOPIC: Reaction Types
GO TO: www.scilinks.org
sciLINKS NUMBER: HSTP343

Section 2 • Types of Chemical Reactions **359**

4) Close

Quiz

Write each of the following definitions on the board. Have students choose any two definitions to explain in their own words. Ask them to give examples of the reactions they select. Accept all reasonable examples, but make sure students balance the equations if necessary.

1. Two reactants exchange ions to form two new compounds.
2. One element takes the place of another element in a compound.
3. A compound breaks down into simpler compounds or elements.
4. Two or more reactants combine to form one product.

ALTERNATIVE ASSESSMENT

This section uses dance partners as an analogy to explain the different kinds of chemical reactions. Ask each student to come up with another analogy to describe chemical reactions. (For example, objects or food could be used.)

PG 684
Putting Elements Together

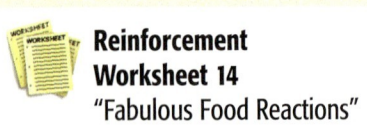
Reinforcement Worksheet 14
"Fabulous Food Reactions"

Some Elements Are More Reactive Than Others In a single-replacement reaction, a more-reactive element can replace a less-reactive one from a compound. However, the opposite reaction does not occur, as shown in **Figure 18**.

Figure 18 *More-reactive elements replace less-reactive elements in single-replacement reactions.*

$Cu + 2AgNO_3 \rightarrow 2Ag + Cu(NO_3)_2$
Copper is more reactive than silver.

$Ag + Cu(NO_3)_2 \rightarrow$ **No reaction**
Silver is less reactive than copper.

Double-Replacement Reactions

A **double-replacement reaction** is a reaction in which ions in two compounds switch places. One of the products of this reaction is often a gas or a precipitate. A double-replacement reaction in the dance model would be two couples dancing and switching partners, as shown in **Figure 19**.

Figure 19 *A model for the double-replacement reaction of sodium chloride reacting with silver fluoride to form sodium fluoride and the precipitate silver chloride is shown below.*

$NaCl + AgF \rightarrow NaF + AgCl$

internetconnect

SCLINKS
NSTA
TOPIC: Reaction Types
GO TO: www.scilinks.org
*sci*LINKS NUMBER: HSTP343

REVIEW

1. What type of reaction does each of the following equations represent?
   a. $FeS + 2HCl \rightarrow FeCl_2 + H_2S$
   b. $NH_4OH \rightarrow NH_3 + H_2O$
2. Which type of reaction always has an element and a compound as reactants?
3. **Comparing Concepts** Compare synthesis and decomposition reactions.

360 Chapter 14 • Chemical Reactions

▼ **Answers to Review**

1. a. double-replacement
   b. decomposition
2. single-replacement
3. Synthesis reactions combine two or more reactants to form a single product. Decomposition reactions take a single reactant and break it into two or more products.

Section 3
Energy and Rates of Chemical Reactions

Terms to Learn
exothermic
endothermic
law of conservation of energy
activation energy
catalyst
inhibitor

What You'll Do
- Compare exothermic and endothermic reactions.
- Explain activation energy.
- Interpret an energy diagram.
- Describe the factors that affect the rate of a reaction.

You just learned one method of classifying chemical reactions. In this section, you will learn how to classify reactions in terms of the energy associated with the reaction and learn how to change the rate at which the reaction occurs.

Every Reaction Involves Energy

All chemical reactions involve chemical energy. Remember that during a reaction, chemical bonds in the reactants break as they absorb energy. As new bonds form in the products, energy is released. Energy is released or absorbed in the overall reaction depending on how the chemical energy of the reactants compares with the chemical energy of the products.

Energy Is Released in Exothermic Reactions If the chemical energy of the reactants is greater than the chemical energy of the products, the difference in energy is released during the reaction. A chemical reaction in which energy is released or removed is called **exothermic**. *Exo* means "go out" or "exit," and *thermic* means "heat" or "energy." The energy can be released in several different forms, as shown in **Figure 20**. The energy released in an exothermic reaction is often written as a product in a chemical equation, as in this equation:

$$2Na + Cl_2 \longrightarrow 2NaCl + energy$$

Figure 20 Types of Energy Released in Reactions

Light energy is released in the exothermic reaction taking place in these light sticks.

Electrical energy is released in the exothermic reaction taking place in the dry cells in this flashlight.

Light and thermal energy are released in the exothermic reaction taking place in this campfire.

SCIENCE HUMOR

There once was a chemist named Rexo,
Who combined things in reactions quite "exo."
He took a swift fall,
And combusted it all,
From the tips of his toes to his necks-o!

2) Teach

MISCONCEPTION ALERT

Students may mistakenly think that endothermic reactions do not produce any energy. Explain that a certain amount of activation energy is required for any reaction to occur. However, in exothermic reactions, the energy produced during the formation of products is greater than the activation energy, and energy is given off. In endothermic reactions, the activation energy required is greater than the energy produced in the reaction, so overall, energy is absorbed.

CONNECT TO LIFE SCIENCE

One of the most important endothermic reactions is the one carried on continuously by plants and some protists—*photosynthesis*. The photosynthetic capability of terrestrial plants is well known. In the uppermost layer of the ocean (the top 100 m or so), tiny geometrically shaped organisms called phytoplankton also make food using photosynthesis. Many fish and other sea animals depend on phytoplankton as their food source. Use Teaching Transparency 51 to help students understand this important chemical reaction.

Teaching Transparency 51
"Photosynthesis"
LINK TO LIFE SCIENCE

Reinforcement Worksheet 14
"Activation Energy"

Biology CONNECTION

Photosynthesis is an endothermic process in which light energy from the sun is used to produce glucose, a simple sugar. The equation that describes photosynthesis is as follows:

$6CO_2 + 6H_2O + \text{energy} \longrightarrow C_6H_{12}O_6 + 6O_2$

The cells in your body use glucose to get the energy they need through cellular respiration, an exothermic process described by the reverse of the above reaction:

$C_6H_{12}O_6 + 6O_2 \longrightarrow 6CO_2 + 6H_2O + \text{energy}$

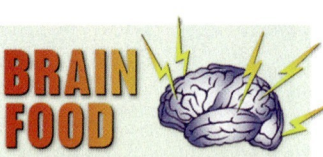
BRAIN FOOD

Matches rubbing together in a box could provide the activation energy to light a strike-anywhere match. Safety matches, which must be struck on a strike plate on the box, were developed to prevent such accidents.

IS THAT A FACT!

Endothermic changes can be very useful if you sprain your ankle. Many manufacturers make "instant cold packs" that can be used to treat the swelling of a sprain or bruise. The packs are plastic bags that contain water and another chemical (such as ammonium nitrate) separated by a plastic barrier. When the barrier is broken, the water dissolves the ammonium nitrate, which is an endothermic change. This causes the pack to get very cold without refrigeration.

Energy Is Absorbed in Endothermic Reactions If the chemical energy of the reactants is less than the chemical energy of the products, the difference in energy is absorbed during the reaction. A chemical reaction in which energy is absorbed is called **endothermic**. *Endo* means "go in," and *thermic* means "heat" or "energy." The energy absorbed in an endothermic reaction is often written as a reactant in a chemical equation, as in this equation:

$$2H_2O + \text{energy} \longrightarrow 2H_2 + O_2$$

Energy Is Conserved—It's a Law! You learned that mass is never created or destroyed in chemical reactions. The same holds true for energy. The **law of conservation of energy** states that energy can be neither created nor destroyed. The energy released in exothermic reactions was originally stored in the reactants. And the energy absorbed in endothermic reactions does not just vanish. It is stored in the products that form. If you could carefully measure all the energy in a reaction, you would find that the total amount of energy (of all types) is the same before and after the reaction.

Activation Energy Gets a Reaction Started A match can be used to light a campfire—but only if the match is lit! A strike-anywhere match, like the one shown in **Figure 21**, has all the reactants it needs to be able to burn. And though the chemicals on a match are intended to react and burn, they will not ignite by themselves. Energy is needed to start the reaction. The minimum amount of energy needed for substances to react is called **activation energy**.

Figure 21 *Rubbing the tip of this strike-anywhere match on a rough surface provides the energy needed to get the chemicals to react.*

The friction of striking a match heats the substances on the match, breaking bonds in the reactants and allowing the new bonds in the products to form. Chemical reactions require some energy to get started. An electric spark in a car's engine provides activation energy to begin the burning of gasoline. Light can also provide the activation energy for a reaction. You can better understand activation energy and the differences between exothermic reactions and endothermic reactions by studying the diagrams in **Figure 22**.

Figure 22 Energy Diagrams

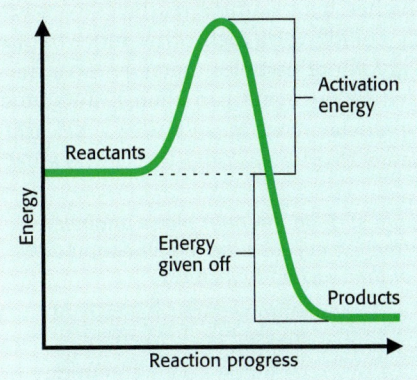

Exothermic Reaction Once begun, an exothermic reaction can continue to occur, as in a fire. The energy released as the product forms continues to supply the activation energy needed for the substances to react.

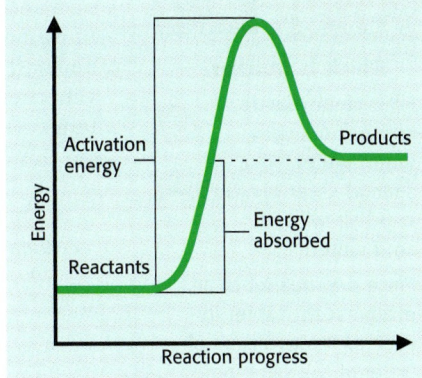

Endothermic Reaction An endothermic reaction requires a continuous supply of energy. Energy must be absorbed to provide the activation energy needed for the substances to react.

Fresh Hydrogen Peroxide

Hydrogen peroxide is used as a disinfectant for minor scrapes and cuts because it decomposes to produce oxygen gas and water, which help cleanse the wound. The decomposition of hydrogen peroxide is an exothermic reaction. Explain why hydrogen peroxide must be stored in a dark bottle to maintain its freshness. (HINT: What type of energy would be blocked by this type of container?

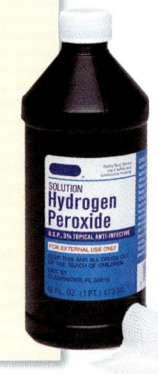

Factors Affecting Rates of Reactions

You can think of a reaction as occurring only if the particles of reactants collide when they have enough energy to break the appropriate bonds. The rate of a reaction is a measure of how rapidly the reaction takes place. Four factors that affect the rate of a reaction are temperature, concentration, surface area, and the presence of a catalyst or inhibitor.

Fighting fires with slime? Read more about it on page 370.

IS THAT A FACT!

Diesel engines have no spark plugs to provide activation energy to ignite the fuel in their cylinders. While this may seem like a flaw in the design of the engine, spark plugs are actually not necessary in diesel engines. Air in the cylinders of a diesel engine is compressed so much that its temperature is very high. When the fuel is squirted into the cylinder, it ignites instantly because of the high temperature of the compressed air.

REAL-WORLD CONNECTION

Some packaged meals used by the military, campers, hunters, and others are called Meals Ready to Eat, or MREs. MREs come in plastic containers and are fully cooked. The meals can be eaten cold but can also be heated by a flameless ration heater that uses an exothermic reaction. In about 12 minutes, the reaction in the ration heater releases enough energy to warm the MRE to 38°C.

CROSS-DISCIPLINARY FOCUS

History Humans have been using fire since before recorded history. However, until the early 1800s, no fire had ever been started with a match. Matches that light from friction were invented in the 1820s by a British chemist named John Walker. Walker's matches were coated with phosphorus at one end. They caught fire when the phosphorus ignited because of the thermal energy produced by the friction of rubbing the match on a rough surface. Many matches today are safety matches. They light only if rubbed against the striking surface of their package, because the red phosphorus necessary for the reaction is on that surface, not in the match itself.

Answer to APPLY

A dark bottle blocks light that could provide the activation energy needed to begin the decomposition of the hydrogen peroxide. If hydrogen peroxide decomposes, it is no longer useful as a disinfectant.

Teaching Transparency 258 "Energy Diagrams"

Section 3 • Energy and Rates of Chemical Reactions

3) Extend

QuickLab

MATERIALS

FOR EACH STUDENT:
- 2 clear plastic cups
- warm water
- cold water
- 2 quarters of an effervescent tablet

Safety Cautions: Remind students to review all safety cautions and icons before beginning this lab activity. Caution students to wear goggles and an apron when doing this activity. Students should not put the tablets in their mouth.

Teacher Notes: A rule of thumb is that the rate of a reaction doubles with each increase of 10°C. A difference in temperature of about 30°C should be sufficient to see a marked difference in the rate of gas production.

Answers to QuickLab

4. The reaction occurred at a faster rate in the warm water. The reaction produced gas bubbles at a faster rate in the warm water.

Speed Control

MEETING INDIVIDUAL NEEDS

Learners Having Difficulty
Have students make a concept map of the four factors that affect the rates of reactions. Their map should include an explanation of how each factor affects the rate. **Sheltered English**

 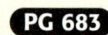
Cata-what? Catalyst!

364 Chapter 14 • Chemical Reactions

QuickLab

Which Is Quicker?

1. Fill a **clear plastic cup** half-full with **warm water.** Fill a **second clear plastic cup** half-full with **cold water.**
2. Place one-quarter of an **effervescent tablet** in each of the two cups of water at the same time.
3. Observe the reaction, and record your observations in your ScienceLog.
4. In which cup did the reaction occur at a greater rate? What evidence supports your answer?

LabBook

Do you feel as though you are not up to speed on controlling the rate of a reaction? Then hurry over to page 686 of the LabBook.

Temperature An increase in temperature increases the rate of a reaction. At higher temperatures, particles of reactants move faster, so they collide with each other more frequently and with more energy. More particles therefore have the activation energy needed to react and can change into products faster. Thus, more particles react in a shorter time. You can see this effect in **Figure 23** and by doing the QuickLab at left.

Figure 23 *The light stick on the right glows brighter than the one on the left because the higher temperature causes the rate of the reaction to increase.*

Concentration Generally, increasing the concentration of reactants increases the rate of a reaction, as shown in **Figure 24.** *Concentration* is a measure of the amount of one substance dissolved in another. Increasing the concentration increases the number of reactant particles present and decreases the distance between them. The reactant particles collide more often, so more particles react each second. Increasing the concentration is similar to having more people in a room. The more people that are in the room, the more frequently they will collide and interact.

Figure 24 *The reaction on the right produces bubbles of hydrogen gas at a faster rate because the concentration of hydrochloric acid used is higher.*

IS THAT A FACT!

Cold temperatures can make diesel engines difficult to start. When it is cold, there is not enough thermal energy to ignite the fuel and start the reaction. To solve this problem, combustion chambers in diesel engines have small heaters called glow plugs. Before the engine starts, an electric current causes the glow plugs to warm up the combustion chambers to a temperature that will ignite the fuel.

Surface Area Increasing the surface area, or the amount of exposed surface, of solid reactants increases the rate of a reaction. Grinding a solid into a powder exposes more particles of the reactant to other reactant particles. The number of collisions between reactant particles increases, increasing the rate of the reaction. You can see the effect of increasing the surface area in the QuickLab at right.

Catalysts and Inhibitors Some reactions would be too slow to be useful without a catalyst (KAT uh LIST). A **catalyst** is a substance that speeds up a reaction without being permanently changed. A catalyst lowers the activation energy of a reaction, which allows the reaction to occur more rapidly. Most reactions in your body are sped up using catalysts called enzymes. Catalysts are even found in cars, as seen in **Figure 25.**

An **inhibitor** is a substance that slows down or stops a chemical reaction. Preservatives added to foods are inhibitors that slow down reactions in the bacteria or fungus that can spoil food. Many poisons are also inhibitors.

I'm Crushed!

1. Fill **two clear plastic cups** half-full with **room-temperature water.**
2. Fold a **sheet of paper** around one-quarter of an **effervescent tablet.** Carefully crush the tablet.
3. Get another one-quarter of an effervescent tablet. Carefully pour the crushed tablet into one cup, and place the uncrushed tablet in the second cup.
4. Observe the reaction, and record your observations in your ScienceLog.
5. In which cup did the reaction occur at a greater rate? What evidence supports your answer?
6. Explain why the water in each cup must have the same temperature.

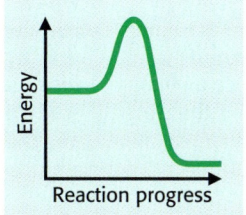

Figure 25 This catalytic converter contains platinum and palladium—two catalysts that increase the rate of reactions that make the car's exhaust less polluting.

REVIEW

1. What is activation energy?
2. List four ways to increase the rate of a reaction.
3. **Comparing Concepts** Compare exothermic and endothermic reactions.
4. **Interpreting Graphics** Does this energy diagram show an exothermic or an endothermic reaction? How can you tell?

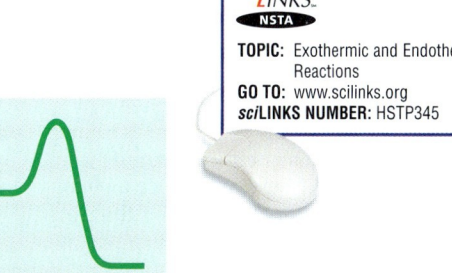

internetconnect

SC_{*i*}**LINKS**
NSTA

TOPIC: Exothermic and Endothermic Reactions
GO TO: www.scilinks.org
*sci*LINKS NUMBER: HSTP345

Chapter Highlights

VOCABULARY DEFINITIONS

SECTION 1

chemical reaction the process by which one or more substances undergo change to produce one or more different substances

chemical formula a shorthand notation for a compound or a diatomic element using chemical symbols and numbers

chemical equation a shorthand description of a chemical reaction using chemical formulas and symbols

reactants the starting materials in a chemical reaction

products the substances formed from a chemical reaction

law of conservation of mass the law that states that mass is neither created nor destroyed in ordinary chemical and physical changes

SECTION 2

synthesis reaction a reaction in which two or more substances combine to form a single compound

decomposition reaction a reaction in which a single compound breaks down to form two or more simpler substances

single-replacement reaction a reaction in which an element takes the place of another element in a compound

double-replacement reaction a reaction in which ions in two compounds switch places

Chapter Highlights

SECTION 1

Vocabulary
- chemical reaction (p. 350)
- chemical formula (p. 352)
- chemical equation (p. 354)
- reactants (p. 354)
- products (p. 354)
- law of conservation of mass (p. 357)

Section Notes
- Chemical reactions form new substances with different properties than the starting substances.
- Clues that a chemical reaction is taking place include formation of a gas or solid, a color change, and an energy change.
- A chemical formula tells the composition of a compound using chemical symbols and subscripts. Subscripts are small numbers written below and to the right of a symbol in a formula.
- Chemical formulas can sometimes be written from the names of covalent compounds and ionic compounds.
- A chemical equation describes a reaction using formulas, symbols, and coefficients.
- A balanced equation uses coefficients to illustrate the law of conservation of mass, that mass is neither created nor destroyed during a chemical reaction.

Labs
Finding a Balance (p. 682)

SECTION 2

Vocabulary
- synthesis reaction (p. 358)
- decomposition reaction (p. 359)
- single-replacement reaction (p. 359)
- double-replacement reaction (p. 360)

Section Notes
- Many chemical reactions can be classified as one of four types by comparing reactants with products.
- In synthesis reactions, the reactants form a single product.
- In decomposition reactions, a single reactant breaks apart into two or more simpler products.

✓ Skills Check

Math Concepts

SUBSCRIPTS AND COEFFICIENTS A subscript is a number written below and to the right of a chemical symbol when writing the chemical formula of a compound. A coefficient is a number written in front of a chemical formula in a chemical equation. When you balance a chemical equation, you cannot change the subscripts in a formula; you can only add coefficients, as seen in the equation $2H_2 + O_2 \longrightarrow 2H_2O$.

Visual Understanding

REACTION TYPES It can be challenging to identify which type of reaction a particular chemical equation represents. Review four reaction types by studying Figures 14, 16, 17, and 19.

Lab and Activity Highlights

Finding a Balance PG 682

Putting Elements Together PG 684

Cata-what? Catalyst! PG 683

Speed Control PG 686

 Datasheets for LabBook
(blackline masters for these labs)

SECTION 2

- In single-replacement reactions, a more-reactive element takes the place of a less-reactive element in a compound. No reaction will occur if a less-reactive element is placed with a compound containing a more-reactive element.

- In double-replacement reactions, ions in two compounds switch places. A gas or precipitate is often formed.

Labs

Putting Elements Together (p. 684)

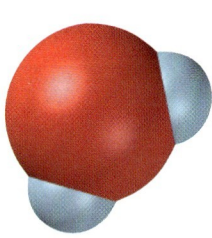

SECTION 3

Vocabulary
- **exothermic** (p. 361)
- **endothermic** (p. 362)
- **law of conservation of energy** (p. 362)
- **activation energy** (p. 362)
- **catalyst** (p. 365)
- **inhibitor** (p. 365)

Section Notes

- Energy is released in exothermic reactions. The energy released can be written as a product in a chemical equation.

- Energy is absorbed in endothermic reactions. The energy absorbed can be written as a reactant in a chemical equation.

- The law of conservation of energy states that energy is neither created nor destroyed.

- Activation energy is the energy needed to start a chemical reaction.

- Energy diagrams indicate whether a reaction is exothermic or endothermic by showing whether energy is given off or absorbed during the reaction.

- The rate of a chemical reaction is affected by temperature, concentration, surface area, and the presence of a catalyst or inhibitor.

- Raising the temperature, increasing the concentration, increasing the surface area, and adding a catalyst can increase the rate of a reaction.

Labs

Cata-what? Catalyst! (p. 683)
Speed Control (p. 686)

VOCABULARY DEFINITIONS, continued

SECTION 3

exothermic the term used to describe a physical or a chemical change in which energy is released or removed

endothermic the term used to describe a physical or a chemical change in which energy is absorbed

law of conservation of energy the law that states that energy is neither created nor destroyed

activation energy the minimum amount of energy needed for substances to react

catalyst a substance that speeds up a reaction without being permanently changed

inhibitor a substance that slows down or stops a chemical reaction

 Vocabulary Review Worksheet 14

 Blackline masters of these Chapter Highlights can be found in the **Study Guide**.

---

internetconnect

 **GO TO:** go.hrw.com

Visit the **HRW** Web site for a variety of learning tools related to this chapter. Just type in the keyword:

KEYWORD: HSTREA

 **GO TO:** www.scilinks.org

Visit the **National Science Teachers Association** on-line Web site for Internet resources related to this chapter. Just type in the *sci*LINKS number for more information about the topic:

TOPIC: Chemical Reactions	*sci*LINKS NUMBER: HSTP330
TOPIC: Chemical Formulas	*sci*LINKS NUMBER: HSTP335
TOPIC: Chemical Equations	*sci*LINKS NUMBER: HSTP340
TOPIC: Reaction Types	*sci*LINKS NUMBER: HSTP343
TOPIC: Exothermic and Endothermic Reactions	*sci*LINKS NUMBER: HSTP345

Lab and Activity Highlights

LabBank

 Inquiry Labs, Curses, Foiled Again! Lab 21

Labs You Can Eat, How to Fluff a Muffin, Lab 24

 Whiz-Bang Demonstrations, Fire and Ice, Demo 56

Long-Term Projects & Research Ideas, Fruitful Chemistry, Project 64

Chapter Review Answers

USING VOCABULARY

1. inhibitor
2. exothermic
3. synthesis reaction
4. subscript
5. reactants

UNDERSTANDING CONCEPTS

Multiple Choice

6. c
7. b
8. d
9. c
10. a

Short Answer

11. a. synthesis
    b. single-replacement
    c. double-replacement
12. raise the temperature, increase the concentration or the surface area of a reactant, add a catalyst
13. The reactants are acetic acid and baking soda. The products are carbon dioxide, water, and sodium acetate.

Chapter Review

USING VOCABULARY

To complete the following sentences, choose the correct term from each pair of terms listed below.

1. Adding a(n) ____ will slow down a chemical reaction. (*catalyst* or *inhibitor*)
2. A chemical reaction that gives off light is called ____. (*exothermic* or *endothermic*)
3. A chemical reaction that forms one compound from two or more substances is called a ____. (*synthesis reaction* or *decomposition reaction*)
4. The 2 in the formula Ag_2S is a ____. (*subscript* or *coefficient*)
5. The starting materials in a chemical reaction are ____. (*reactants* or *products*)

UNDERSTANDING CONCEPTS

Multiple Choice

6. Balancing a chemical equation so that the same number of atoms of each element is found in both the reactants and the products is an illustration of
   a. activation energy.
   b. the law of conservation of energy.
   c. the law of conservation of mass.
   d. a double-replacement reaction.

7. What is the correct chemical formula for calcium chloride?
   a. CaCl
   b. $CaCl_2$
   c. Ca_2Cl
   d. Ca_2Cl_2

8. In which type of reaction do ions in two compounds switch places?
   a. synthesis
   b. decomposition
   c. single-replacement
   d. double-replacement

9. Which is an example of the use of activation energy?
   a. plugging in an iron
   b. playing basketball
   c. holding a lit match to paper
   d. eating

10. Enzymes in your body act as catalysts. Thus, the role of enzymes is to
    a. increase the rate of chemical reactions.
    b. decrease the rate of chemical reactions.
    c. help you breathe.
    d. inhibit chemical reactions.

Short Answer

11. Classify each of the following reactions:
    a. $Fe + O_2 \longrightarrow Fe_2O_3$
    b. $Al + CuSO_4 \longrightarrow Al_2(SO_4)_3 + Cu$
    c. $Ba(CN)_2 + H_2SO_4 \longrightarrow BaSO_4 + HCN$

12. Name two ways that you could increase the rate of a chemical reaction.

13. Acetic acid, a compound found in vinegar, reacts with baking soda to produce carbon dioxide, water, and sodium acetate. Without writing an equation, identify the reactants and the products of this reaction.

368 Chapter 14 • Chemical Reactions

Concept Mapping

14. Use the following terms to create a concept map: chemical reaction, chemical equation, chemical formulas, reactants, products, coefficients, subscripts.

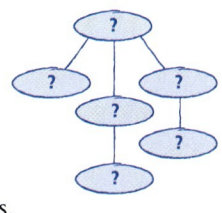

CRITICAL THINKING AND PROBLEM SOLVING

15. Your friend is very worried by rumors he has heard about a substance called dihydrogen monoxide. What could you say to your friend to calm his fears? (Be sure to write the formula of the substance.)

16. As long as proper safety precautions have been taken, why can explosives be transported long distances without exploding?

MATH IN SCIENCE

17. Calculate the number of atoms of each element shown in each of the following:
    a. $CaSO_4$
    b. $4NaOCl$
    c. $Fe(NO_3)_2$
    d. $2Al_2(CO_3)_3$

18. Write balanced equations for the following:
    a. $Fe + O_2 \longrightarrow Fe_2O_3$
    b. $Al + CuSO_4 \longrightarrow Al_2(SO_4)_3 + Cu$
    c. $Ba(CN)_2 + H_2SO_4 \longrightarrow BaSO_4 + HCN$

19. Write and balance chemical equations from each of the following descriptions:
    a. Bromine reacts with sodium iodide to form iodine and sodium bromide.
    b. Phosphorus reacts with oxygen gas to form diphosphorus pentoxide.
    c. Lithium oxide decomposes to form lithium and oxygen.

INTERPRETING GRAPHICS

20. What evidence in the photo supports the claim that a chemical reaction is taking place?

21. Use the energy diagram below to answer the questions that follow.

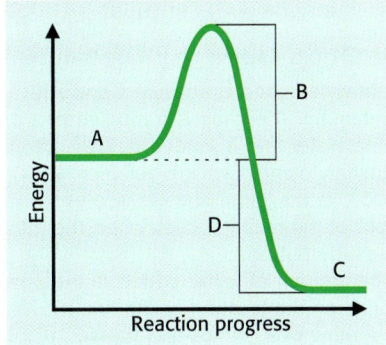

a. Which letter represents the energy of the products?
b. Which letter represents the activation energy of the reaction?
c. Is energy given off or absorbed by this reaction?

NOW What Do You Think?

Take a minute to review your answers to the ScienceLog questions on page 349. Have your answers changed? If necessary, revise your answers based on what you have learned since you began this chapter.

NOW WHAT DO YOU THINK?

1. gas formation, solid formation, color change, energy change
2. synthesis, decomposition, single-replacement, double-replacement
3. by changing the temperature, concentration, or surface area of reactants or by adding a catalyst or inhibitor

Concept Mapping

14. 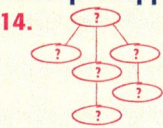 An answer to this exercise can be found at the end of this book.

CRITICAL THINKING AND PROBLEM SOLVING

15. The compound is water, H_2O.
16. Explosives need to absorb energy to begin the reaction. As long as precautions are taken to prevent the activation energy from being absorbed by the explosives, they should be safe to transport.

MATH IN SCIENCE

17. a. 1 calcium atom, 1 sulfur atom, 4 oxygen atoms
    b. 4 sodium atoms, 4 oxygen atoms, 4 chlorine atoms
    c. 1 iron atom, 2 nitrogen atoms, 6 oxygen atoms
    d. 4 aluminum atoms, 6 carbon atoms, 18 oxygen atoms

18. a. $4Fe + 3O_2 \longrightarrow 2Fe_2O_3$
    b. $2Al + 3CuSO_4 \longrightarrow Al_2(SO_4)_3 + 3Cu$
    c. $Ba(CN)_2 + H_2SO_4 \longrightarrow BaSO_4 + 2HCN$

19. a. $Br_2 + 2NaI \longrightarrow I_2 + 2NaBr$
    b. $4P + 5O_2 \longrightarrow 2P_2O_5$
    c. $2Li_2O \longrightarrow 4Li + O_2$

INTERPRETING GRAPHICS

20. Gas is produced, and light is given off.
21. a. C
    b. B
    c. given off

 Concept Mapping Transparency 14

 Blackline masters of this Chapter Review can be found in the **Study Guide**.

Chapter 14 • Chapter Review

EYE ON THE ENVIRONMENT

Slime That Fire!

Background

When wood burns, there are a lot of chemical reactions going on at once. As the long chains of molecules break down, the energy they release feeds the fire. Fire retardant works by increasing the activation energy for combustion. If the wood is smothered with retardant, the fire will be stopped. If the wood is not smothered, the fire will merely be slowed.

The active ingredients in fire retardant are ammonium sulfate and ammonium nitrate. These are common ingredients in agricultural fertilizer and do not harm the landscape. In general, fire retardant is used only to slow a fire down in order to give a ground crew more time to work on a fire line. However, if there are not enough ground crews to fight the fire, firefighters will try to contain the fire by using air tankers that drop water on the fire.

EYE ON THE ENVIRONMENT

Slime That Fire!

Once a fire starts in the hard-to-reach mountains of the western United States, it is difficult to stop. Trees, grasses, and brush can provide an overwhelming supply of fuel. In order to stop a fire, firefighters make a fire line. This is an area where all the burnable materials are removed from the ground. How would you slow down a fire to give a ground crew more time to build a fire line? Would you suggest dropping water from a plane? That is not a bad idea, but what if you had something even better than water—like some slimy red goop?

Red Goop Goes the Distance

The slimy red goop is actually a powerful fire retardant. The goop is a mixture of a powder and water that is loaded directly onto an old military plane. Carrying between 4,500 and 11,000 L of the slime, the plane drops it all in front of the raging flames when the pilot presses the button.

The amount of water added to the powder depends on the location of the fire. If a fire is burning over shrubs and grasses, more water is needed. In this form the goop actually rains down to the ground through the treetops. But if a fire is burning in tall trees, less water is used so the slime will glob onto the branches and ooze down very slowly.

Failed Flames

The burning of trees, grass, and brush is an exothermic reaction. A fire retardant slows or stops this self-feeding reaction. A fire retardant increases the activation energy for the materials it is applied to. Although a lot depends on how hot the fire is when it hits the area treated with the retardant and how much of the retardant

▲ *This plane is dropping fire retardant on a forest fire.*

is applied, firefighters on the ground can gain valuable time when a fire is slowed with a fire retardant. This extra time allows them to create a fire line that will ultimately stop the fire.

Neon Isn't Necessary

Once a fire is put out, the slimy red streaks left on the blackened ground can be an eyesore. To solve the problem, scientists have created special dyes for the retardant. These dyes make the goop neon colors when it is first applied, but after a few days in the sun, the goop turns a natural brown shade!

What Do They Study?

▶ Do some research to learn about a firefighter's training. What classes and exams are firefighters required to pass? How do they maintain their certifications once they become firefighters?

Answer to What Do They Study?

Student answers will vary according to state and local firefighting-training and certification requirements. Answers should include both the physical training firefighters receive and the academic classes they must take.

CAREERS

ARSON INVESTIGATOR

Once a fire dies down, you might see arson investigator **Lt. Larry McKee** on the scene. "After the fire is out, I can investigate the fire scene to determine where the fire started and how it started. If it was intentionally set and I'm successful at putting the arson case together, I can get a conviction. That's very satisfying," says Lt. McKee.

During a fire, fuel and oxygen combine in a chemical reaction called combustion. On the scene, Lt. Larry McKee questions witnesses and firefighters about what they saw. He knows, for example, that the color of the smoke can indicate certain chemicals.

McKee explains that fires usually burn "up and out, in a V shape." To find where the V begins, he says, "We work from the area with the least amount of damage to the one with the most damage. This normally leads us to the point of origin." Once the origin has been determined, it's time to call in the dogs!

An Accelerant-Sniffing Canine

"We have what we call an accelerant-sniffing canine. Our canine, Nikki, has been trained to detect approximately 11 different chemicals." When Nikki arrives on the scene, she sniffs for traces of chemicals, called accelerants, that may have been used to start the fire. When she finds one, she immediately starts to dig at it. At that point, McKee takes a sample from the area and sends it to the lab for analysis.

At the Lab

Once at the laboratory, the sample is treated so that any accelerants in it are dissolved in a liquid. A small amount of the liquid is then injected into an instrument called a *gas chromatograph*. The instrument heats the liquid, forming a mixture of gases. The gases then are passed through a flame. As each gas passes through the flame, it "causes a fluctuation in an electronic signal, which creates our graphs."

Solving the Case

If the laboratory report indicates that a suspicious accelerant has been found, McKee begins to search for arson suspects. By combining detective work with scientific evidence, fire investigators can successfully catch and convict arsonists.

Fascinating Fire Facts

▶ The temperature of a house fire can reach 980°C! At that temperature, aluminum window frames melt, and furniture goes up in flames. Do some research to discover three more facts about fires. Create a display with two or more classmates to illustrate some of your facts.

▲ *Nikki searches for traces of gasoline, kerosene, and other accelerants.*

Answers to Fascinating Fire Facts

Student answers will vary but may include facts about fire damage, fire fighting, fire detection, fire investigation, fire prevention, and fire safety.

CAREERS

Arson Investigator— Lt. Larry McKee

Background

In an arson investigator's laboratory, a mass spectrometer is sometimes used to test a vapor sample for accelerants. The spectrometer can provide detailed information about the chemical makeup of any accelerants present. Unlike the gas chromatograph, the mass spectrometer breaks down the chemical compounds in the vapor sample into their characteristic fragments, according to their chemical composition. The fragments are then checked against data in a computer to see how closely they match known accelerants. Turner explains, "We can't always identify everything. The sample may contain a lot of chemicals that come from the carpeting or the synthetic products that are present in the household. A lot of the time, there are so many chemicals in a sample that we can't make a conclusive statement about what is there."

Extension

Invite a firefighter, arson investigator, or fire chief to visit your classroom and to bring visual aids, such as household items found after a fire or some of the equipment used to detect how and where a fire started. Prepare the class to ask questions about the nature of fires, how fires start, how to prevent them, and how fire investigators use science to determine the cause of fires.

Chapter Organizer

CHAPTER ORGANIZATION	TIME MINUTES	OBJECTIVES	LABS, INVESTIGATIONS, AND DEMONSTRATIONS
Chapter Opener pp. 372–373	45	National Standards: UCP 1, 3, SAI 1, 2, ST 2, SPSP 5, HNS 1, 3, PS 1b	**Investigate!** Ionic Versus Covalent, p. 373
Section 1 Ionic and Covalent Compounds	90	▶ Describe the properties of ionic and covalent compounds. ▶ Classify compounds as ionic or covalent based on their properties. UCP 3, PS 1a, 1b, 3a, 3e	**Demonstration,** Observing Crystals, p. 375 in ATE
Section 2 Acids, Bases, and Salts	90	▶ Describe the properties and uses of acids and bases. ▶ Explain the difference between strong acids and bases and weak acids and bases. ▶ Identify acids and bases using the pH scale. ▶ Describe the properties and uses of salts. UCP 1, 3, SPSP 1, 3, 4, PS 1a, 1b; LabBook UCP 3, SAI 1, PS 1a, 1b	**Demonstration,** A Fruit Juice Indicator, p. 378 in ATE **Demonstration,** p. 379 in ATE **QuickLab,** pHast Relief! p. 380 **Demonstration,** Making Soap, p. 381 in ATE **Skill Builder,** Cabbage Patch Indicators, p. 688 **Datasheets for LabBook,** Cabbage Patch Indicators, Datasheet 44 **Skill Builder,** Making Salt, p. 690 **Datasheets for LabBook,** Making Salt, Datasheet 45 **Labs You Can Eat,** Can You Say Seviche? Lab 23 **EcoLabs & Field Activities,** Greener Cleaners, EcoLab 20
Section 3 Organic Compounds	90	▶ Explain why so many organic compounds are possible. ▶ Describe the characteristics of carbohydrates, lipids, proteins, and nucleic acids and their functions in the body. ▶ Describe and identify saturated, unsaturated, and aromatic hydrocarbons. UCP 1–5, SAI 2, ST 2, SPSP 1, 5, HNS 1, 3, PS 1c	**Demonstration,** Lipids and Water, p. 385 in ATE **Long-Term Projects & Research Ideas,** Project 65

See page **T20** *for a complete correlation of this book with the*

NATIONAL SCIENCE EDUCATION STANDARDS.

TECHNOLOGY RESOURCES

 Guided Reading Audio CD English or Spanish, Chapter 15

 One-Stop Planner CD-ROM with Test Generator

 CNN. Science, Technology & Society, Flavor Cells, Segment 3

Scientists in Action, Creating a Coat of Armor, Segment 22

371A Chapter 15 • Chemical Compounds

Chapter 15 • Chemical Compounds

CLASSROOM WORKSHEETS, TRANSPARENCIES, AND RESOURCES	SCIENCE INTEGRATION AND CONNECTIONS	REVIEW AND ASSESSMENT
Directed Reading Worksheet 15 **Science Puzzlers, Twisters & Teasers,** Worksheet 15	**Cross-Disciplinary Focus,** p. 373 in ATE	
Directed Reading Worksheet 15, Section 1		**Review,** p. 376 **Quiz,** p. 376 in ATE **Alternative Assessment,** p. 376 in ATE
Directed Reading Worksheet 15, Section 2 **Math Skills for Science Worksheet 24,** Creating Exponents **Transparency 259,** pH Values of Common Materials **Reinforcement Worksheet 15,** A Simple Solution **Critical Thinking Worksheet 15,** Battle of the Breads	**Multicultural Connection,** p. 378 in ATE **Math and More,** p. 380 in ATE **Biology Connection,** p. 381	**Homework,** pp. 379, 381 in ATE **Self-Check,** p. 381 **Review,** p. 382 **Quiz,** p. 382 in ATE **Alternative Assessment,** p. 382 in ATE
Directed Reading Worksheet 15, Section 3 **Transparency 260,** Structural Formulas **Transparency 5,** Phospholipid Molecule and Cell Membrane	**Connect to Life Science,** p. 385 in ATE **Biology Connection,** p. 386 **Multicultural Connection,** p. 386 in ATE **Math and More,** p. 388 in ATE **Across the Sciences:** Unique Compounds, p. 394 **Weird Science:** The Secrets of Spider Silk, p. 395	**Homework,** p. 386 in ATE **Review,** p. 387 **Review,** p. 389 **Quiz,** p. 389 in ATE **Alternative Assessment,** p. 389 in ATE

END-OF-CHAPTER REVIEW AND ASSESSMENT

Chapter Review in Study Guide
Vocabulary and Notes in Study Guide
Chapter Tests with Performance-Based Assessment, Chapter 15 Test
Chapter Tests with Performance-Based Assessment, Performance-Based Assessment 15
Concept Mapping Transparency 15

internetconnect

Holt, Rinehart and Winston On-line Resources
go.hrw.com
For worksheets and other teaching aids related to this chapter, visit the HRW Web site and type in the keyword: **HSTCMP**

National Science Teachers Association
www.scilinks.org
Encourage students to use the *sci*LINKS numbers listed in the internet connect boxes to access information and resources on the **NSTA** Web site.

Chapter 15 • Chapter Organizer

Chapter Resources & Worksheets

Visual Resources

TEACHING TRANSPARENCIES

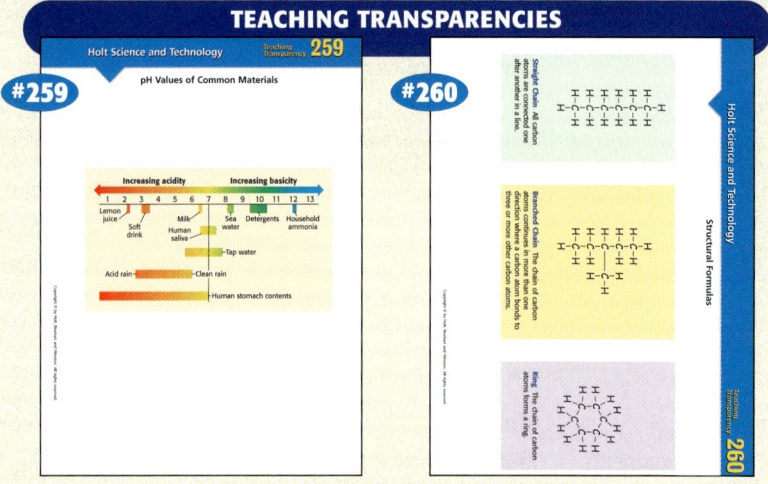

TEACHING TRANSPARENCIES

CONCEPT MAPPING TRANSPARENCY

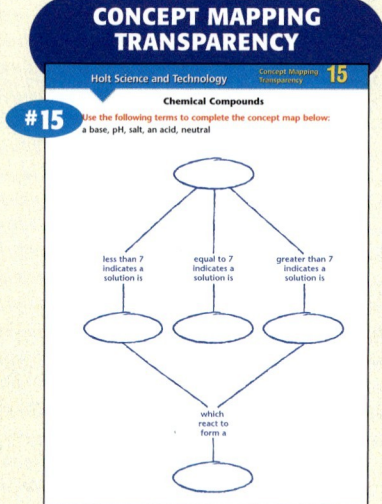

Meeting Individual Needs

DIRECTED READING

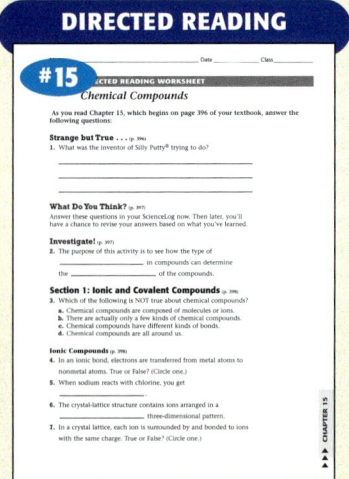

REINFORCEMENT & VOCABULARY REVIEW

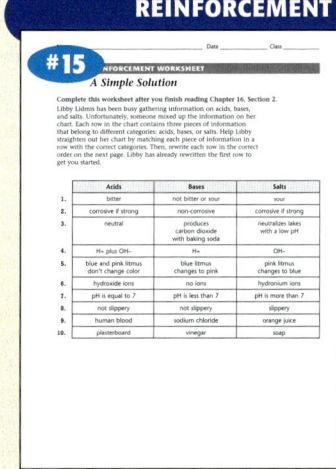

SCIENCE PUZZLERS, TWISTERS & TEASERS

Chapter 15 • Chemical Compounds

Chapter 15 • Chemical Compounds

Review & Assessment

STUDY GUIDE
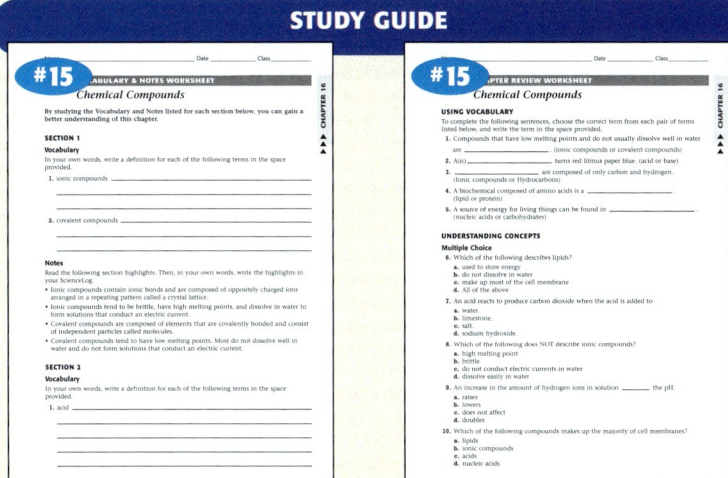

CHAPTER TESTS WITH PERFORMANCE-BASED ASSESSMENT
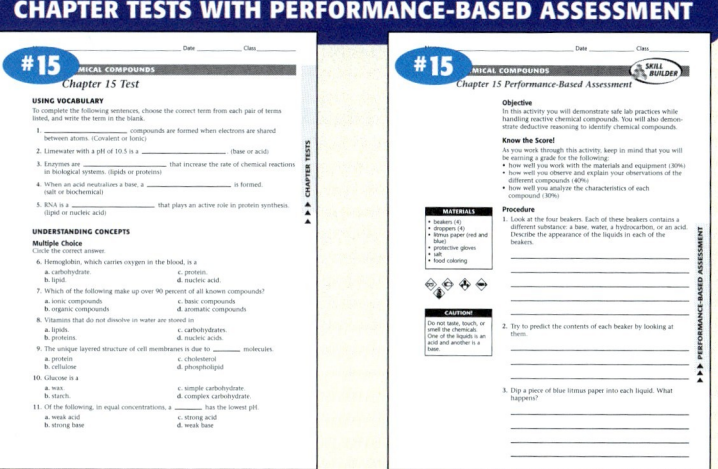

Lab Worksheets

LABS YOU CAN EAT
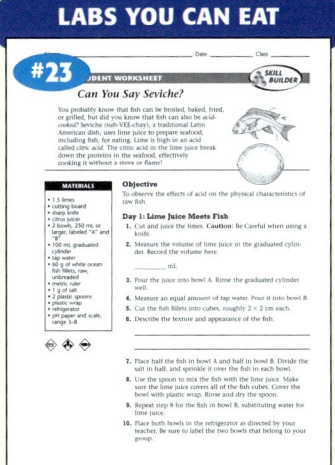

ECOLABS & FIELD ACTIVITIES
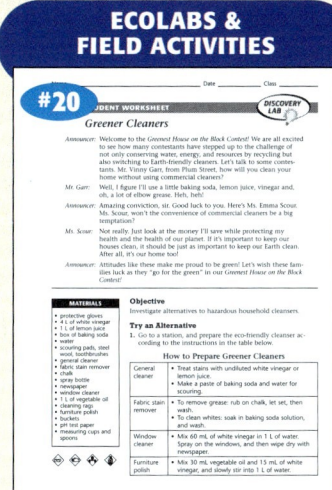

LONG-TERM PROJECTS & RESEARCH IDEAS
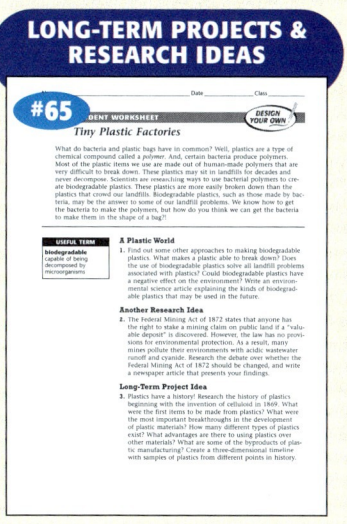

DATASHEETS FOR LABBOOK
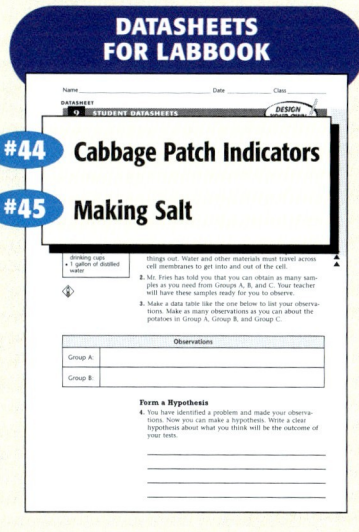

Applications & Extensions

CRITICAL THINKING & PROBLEM SOLVING
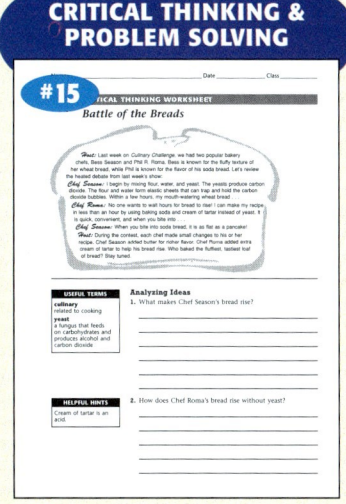

SCIENCE TECHNOLOGY
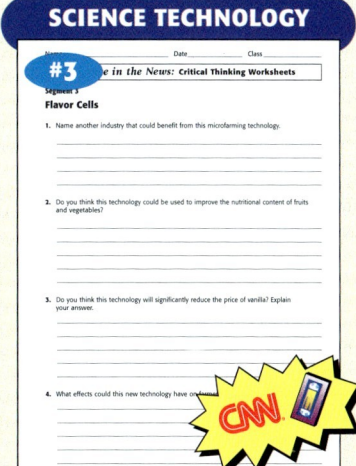

SCIENTISTS IN ACTION
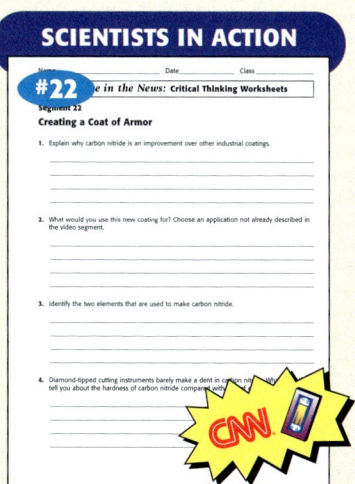

Chapter 15 • Chapter Resources & Worksheets **371D**

Chapter Background

SECTION 1

Ionic and Covalent Compounds

▶ **Network Crystals**
A crystal formed by covalent bonds between atoms becomes one large molecule, called a macromolecule or network crystal. Network crystals are usually nonmetallic. Diamonds are examples of network crystals. In a diamond, each carbon atom is covalently bonded to four other carbon atoms, forming a network crystal. Silicon carbide also forms a network crystal with covalent bonds between its atoms. Network crystals are very hard, have high melting points, and do not conduct electric current.

IS THAT A FACT!

◆ Water is the most common and most important compound on Earth. Each of a water molecule's hydrogen atoms shares its single electron with the molecule's oxygen atom, forming a covalent bond.

▶ **Diamonds**
Diamonds can be used in several different ways, not just as jewelry. Diamonds are composed of carbon atoms that are covalently bonded in a network of six-membered rings. This structure gives diamonds a unique combination of properties. Diamonds are very hard, have a hard melting point, and do not conduct electric current. As a result of these properties, industry uses diamonds in tools that drill, cut, or grind. Furthermore, manufacturers can use diamonds in semiconductor devices. Unfortunately, diamonds are too expensive and the demand for diamonds is too high for widespread use. To counteract the problems of diamonds' expense and scarcity, scientists are trying to devise inexpensive ways to make high-quality synthetic diamonds.

IS THAT A FACT!

◆ Not all ionic compounds are soluble in water. Silver chloride, zinc sulfide, copper(II) oxide, and magnesium phosphate are some ionic compounds that are not very water soluble.

SECTION 2

Acids, Bases, and Salts

▶ **Neutralizing Stings**
Bee venom is acidic, while wasp venom is basic. You can reduce the pain of bee and wasp stings by neutralizing the venom. To neutralize a bee's acidic venom, apply a paste of sodium bicarbonate (baking soda and water) or a weak ammonia solution. To neutralize a wasp's venom, apply vinegar. Of course, stinging insects inject their venom beneath the skin's outermost layer, so a topical salve will neutralize venom only on or near the skin's surface.

▶ **Indicators**
The pH scale was introduced by S.P.L. Sørensen (1868–1939) to measure the concentration of hydrogen ions in solution. The more hydrogen ions there are in solution, the more acidic a solution is.

• The percentage or number of hydrogen ions in solution affects the color of certain natural dyes. These dyes can be used as indicators of acidity and alkalinity. Litmus, an indicator obtained from lichens, is red in acids and blue in bases. Phenol red is yellow in acids and red in bases; methyl red is red in acids and yellow in bases; and thymol blue is yellow in acids and blue in bases. However, most indicators do not change color at pH 7. For example, methyl red changes color around pH 5.

• Universal indicator paper is made by combining different indicators. This paper tape, which comes with a comparative color scale, can be used to approximate the pH of almost any solution.

Chapter 15 • Chemical Compounds

Chapter 15 • Chemical Compounds

IS THAT A FACT!

- The antibiotic penicillin is produced by a mold. Microbiologists who help manufacture penicillin maintain the mold's environment at a pH between 6.8 and 7.4 by adding acidic and basic substances as needed.

Salt Crystals
The forces within a salt crystal hold the ions together in what is called a *crystal lattice.* Chemists define a crystal lattice as a repetitive, geometric packing arrangement. All of the ions in a crystal of table salt, NaCl, are part of one giant lattice. However, the smallest visible sodium chloride crystal still has more than a billion billion ions!

IS THAT A FACT!

- The mineral beryl is colorless. However, when beryl contains tiny amounts of the green salt chromium(III) oxide, the valuable green gemstone emerald is formed.

SECTION 3
Organic Compounds

Hodgkin and Vitamin B_{12}
In 1948, vitamin B_{12} was isolated as a red crystalline compound. Dorothy Hodgkin analyzed the vitamin's structure using X-ray crystallography. She won a Nobel Prize in 1964 for her work. Vitamin B_{12} is a complex, organic molecule containing 181 atoms.

Friedrich Wöhler
In 1828, while attempting to prepare ammonium cyanate from cyanic acid and ammonia, Friedrich Wöhler (1800–1882) accidentally synthesized urea. This was the first artificially synthesized organic compound. Wöhler's work proved that a compound naturally produced by animals could be made in the laboratory from inorganic chemicals.

Marcellin Berthelot
Marcellin Berthelot (1827–1907) further demonstrated that plants and animals are not the only sources of organic compounds. He synthesized many organic compounds from inorganic compounds and elements. In 1860, Berthelot synthesized acetylene from its elements, hydrogen and carbon. Berthelot also synthesized another commercially important organic compound, benzene.

IS THAT A FACT!

- Two compounds are considered structural isomers if they have the same molecular formula but different connections between atoms. Two compounds are stereoisomers if they have the same molecular formula and connections between atoms but different arrangements of atoms in three-dimensional space.

- An alkane containing 30 carbon atoms has 4,111,846,763 possible isomers.

For background information about teaching strategies and issues, refer to the *Professional Reference for Teachers.*

CHAPTER 15 Chemical Compounds

Chapter Preview

Section 1
Ionic and Covalent Compounds
- Ionic Compounds
- Covalent Compounds

Section 2
Acids, Bases, and Salts
- Acids
- Bases
- Acids and Bases Neutralize One Another
- Salts

Section 3
Organic Compounds
- Each Carbon Atom Forms Four Bonds
- Biochemicals: The Compounds of Life
- Hydrocarbons
- Other Organic Compounds

 Directed Reading Worksheet 15

 Science Puzzlers, Twisters & Teasers Worksheet 15

 Guided Reading Audio CD English or Spanish, Chapter 15

internetconnect

Smithsonian Institution®
Visit **www.si.edu/hrw** for additional on-line resources.

CHAPTER 15 Chemical Compounds

Strange but True . . .

During World War II, the United States could not obtain natural rubber from Asian suppliers, who gathered it from rubber trees as shown below. Faced with a shortage of raw material, American scientists searched for other materials to use in truck tires and soldiers' boots.

James Wright, an engineer at General Electric, was working with silicone oil—a clear, gooey compound composed of silicon bonded to several other elements. By substituting silicon for carbon, the main element in rubber, Wright hoped to create a new compound with all the flexibility and bounce of rubber.

In 1943, Wright made a surprising discovery. He mixed boric acid with silicone oil in a test tube. Instead of forming the hard rubber material he was looking for, the compound remained slightly gooey to the touch. Disappointed with the results, Wright tossed a gob of the material from the test tube onto the floor. To his surprise, the gob bounced right back at him.

Natural rubber is collected from a rubber tree as it flows from cuts made in the bark.

The new compound was very bouncy and could be stretched and pulled. However, it wasn't a good rubber substitute, so Wright and other General Electric scientists continued their search.

Seven years later, a toy seller named Peter Hodgson packaged some of Wright's creation in small plastic "eggs" and presented his new product at the 1950 International Toy Fair in New York. The material, called Silly Putty®, proved quite popular. Millions of eggs containing Silly Putty have been sold to kids of all ages since then.

Rubber and boric acid are substances with very different properties. In this chapter, you will learn about the properties that are used to classify many different compounds.

Strange but True . . .

In the late 1930s, there was another accidental chemical invention. A chemist named Roy Plunkett was researching nontoxic refrigerants at the DuPont Chemical Company when he accidentally discovered polytetrafluoroethylene (PTFE), better known as Teflon™. PTFE is an organic compound made of a carbon chain with fluorine atoms attached to it. The fluorine atoms are attracted only to other fluorines, and they repel all other molecules, even water. PTFE is used to make non-stick cookware and stain-resistant textiles. Some artificial body parts are also coated with PTFE to reduce the chance that the body will reject them.

What Do You Think?

In your ScienceLog, try to answer the following questions based on what you already know:

1. What is the difference between ionic compounds and covalent compounds?
2. What is an acid?
3. What is a hydrocarbon?

Ionic Versus Covalent

Compounds are often classified based on similarities in their structure or properties. For some compounds, differences in properties are a result of the type of chemical bonding present. In this activity, you will investigate the properties of two substances and relate the properties to the type of bonding in the compounds.

Procedure

1. Place a small amount of **paraffin wax** into a **test tube**. Place an equal amount of **table salt** into a **second test tube**.

2. Fill a **plastic-foam cup** halfway with **hot water**.

3. Place the test tubes into the water. After 3 minutes, remove the test tubes from the water. Observe the contents of the test tubes, and record your observations in your ScienceLog.

4. Add 10 mL of **water** to each test tube using a **graduated cylinder**.

5. Stir each test tube with a **stirring rod**. Record your observations in your ScienceLog.

Analysis

6. Summarize the properties you observed for each type of compound.

7. Ionic bonding is present in many compounds that have a high melting point and that will dissolve in water. Covalent bonding is present in many compounds that have a low melting point and that will not dissolve in water. Identify the type of bonding present in paraffin wax and in table salt.

CROSS-DISCIPLINARY FOCUS

History Table salt, or sodium chloride, is probably the most widely used ionic compound on Earth. It has been used to flavor and preserve foods since prehistoric times, and it was probably one of the first items traded by sea. In some areas, including Ethiopia and Tibet, salt was even used as a form of currency.

What Do You Think?

Accept all reasonable responses.

Students will have a chance to revise their answers in the Chapter Review under NOW What Do You Think?

Investigate!

MATERIALS

FOR EACH STUDENT:
- paraffin wax
- table salt
- 2 test tubes
- plastic-foam cup
- hot and cold water
- graduated cylinder
- stirring rod

Safety Caution: Remind students to review all safety cautions and icons before beginning this lab activity.

Teacher Notes: Remind students that only very small amounts (about half the size of a pea) of salt and paraffin wax should be used.

Answers to Investigate!

6. Paraffin wax has a low melting point and does not dissolve in water. Table salt has a high melting point and can dissolve in water.

7. Covalent bonding is present in paraffin wax. Ionic bonding is present in table salt.

Chapter 15 • Chemical Compounds   **373**

SECTION 1

Focus

Ionic and Covalent Compounds

In this section, students learn that chemical compounds can be classified by the bonds they contain: ionic bonds or covalent bonds. Students learn the distinguishing properties of each type of bond.

Bellringer

Give every student a rubber ball. Divide the class into two groups, and divide each group into pairs. Tell partners to stand and face each other. In Group 1, have one student from each pair give his or her ball to the other student. In Group 2, tell both students to hold both rubber balls, as in a tug of war. Explain that the students in Group 1 represent a compound formed by ionic bonding and that those in Group 2 represent a compound formed by covalent bonding. Ask students to write a paragraph in their ScienceLog explaining the differences between the two types of bonds. **Sheltered English**

Directed Reading Worksheet 15 Section 1

TOPIC: Ionic Compounds
GO TO: www.scilinks.org
*sci*LINKS NUMBER: HSTP355

Section 1

Terms to Learn
ionic compounds
covalent compounds

What You'll Do
- Describe the properties of ionic and covalent compounds.
- Classify compounds as ionic or covalent based on their properties.

Ionic and Covalent Compounds

The world around you is made up of chemical compounds. Chemical compounds are pure substances composed of ions or molecules. There are millions of different kinds of compounds, so you can imagine how classifying them might be helpful. One simple way to classify compounds is by grouping them according to the type of bond they contain.

Ionic Compounds

Compounds that contain ionic bonds are called **ionic compounds**. Remember that an ionic bond is the force of attraction between two oppositely charged ions. Ionic compounds can be formed by the reaction of a metal with a nonmetal. Electrons are transferred from the metal atoms (which become positively charged ions) to the nonmetal atoms (which become negatively charged ions). For example, when sodium reacts with chlorine, as shown in **Figure 1**, the ionic compound sodium chloride, or ordinary table salt, is formed.

Figure 1 An ionic compound is formed when the metal sodium reacts with the nonmetal chlorine. Sodium chloride is formed in the reaction, and energy is released as light and thermal energy.

Brittleness The forces acting between the ions that make up ionic compounds give these compounds certain properties. Ionic compounds tend to be brittle, as shown in **Figure 2**. The ions that make up an ionic compound are arranged in a repeating three-dimensional pattern called a crystal lattice. The ions that make up the crystal lattice are arranged as alternating positive and negative ions. Each ion in the lattice is surrounded by ions of the opposite charge, and each ion is bonded to the ions around it. When an ionic compound is struck with a hammer, the pattern of ions in the crystal lattice is shifted. Ions with the same charge line up and repel one another, causing the crystal to shatter.

Figure 2 Ionic compounds will shatter when hit with a hammer.

IS THAT A FACT!

The body's nerve cells contain a large number of sodium, potassium, and chloride ions. The movement of these ions into and out of the cells allows a type of electric current to exist in the nerve cells. This electric current allows "messages" to move very quickly through the body's nervous system.

High Melting Points Ionic compounds are almost always solid at room temperature, as shown in **Figure 3.** An ionic compound will melt only at temperatures high enough to overcome the strong ionic bonds between the ions. Sodium chloride, for instance, must be heated to 801°C before it will melt. This temperature is much higher than you can produce in your kitchen or even your school laboratory.

Magnesium oxide melts at 2,800°C.

Potassium dichromate melts at 398°C.

Nickel(II) oxide melts at 1,984°C.

Figure 3 Each of these ionic compounds has a high melting point and is solid at room temperature.

Solubility and Electrical Conductivity Many ionic compounds dissolve easily in water. Molecules of water attract each of the ions of an ionic compound and pull them away from one another. The solution created when an ionic compound dissolves in water can conduct an electric current, as shown in **Figure 4.** The ions are able to move past one another and conduct the electric current in the solution. Keep in mind that an undissolved crystal of an ionic compound does not conduct an electric current.

Pure water

Salt water

Figure 4 The pure water in the left beaker does not conduct an electric current. The solution of salt water in the right beaker conducts an electric current, and the bulb lights up.

Covalent Compounds

Compounds composed of elements that are covalently bonded are called **covalent compounds.** Remember that covalent bonds form when atoms share electrons. Gasoline, carbon dioxide, water, and sugar are well-known examples of covalent compounds.

IS THAT A FACT!

Some compounds contain both ionic and covalent bonds. For example, silver nitrate, $AgNO_3$, is made of Ag^+ (silver) and NO_3^- (nitrate) ions joined by ionic bonds. However, the atoms in the nitrate ion are held together by covalent bonds.

4) Close

Quiz

1. How are ionic compounds formed? (by the transfer of electrons from metal atoms to nonmetal atoms)

2. Give two examples of covalent compounds. (Answers will vary but may include sugar, water, and carbon dioxide.)

3. Potassium chloride is a crystalline solid at room temperature. Is it more likely to be ionic or covalent? (ionic)

Alternative Assessment

Writing Have students write a one- or two-page story that incorporates the ideas of ionic and covalent bonds. For example, the story could be a mystery that can be solved only by determining which of the two types of bonds a certain compound has.

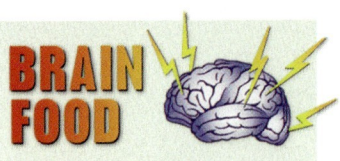

Molecules of covalent compounds can have anywhere from two atoms to hundreds or thousands of atoms! Small, lightweight molecules, like water or carbon dioxide, tend to form liquids or gases at room temperature. Heavier molecules, such as sugar or plastics, tend to form solids at room temperature.

Low Melting Points Covalent compounds exist as independent particles called molecules. The forces of attraction between molecules of covalent compounds are much weaker than the bonds between ions in a crystal lattice. Thus, covalent compounds have lower melting points than ionic compounds.

Solubility and Electrical Conductivity You have probably heard the phrase "oil and water don't mix." Oil, such as that used in salad dressing, is composed of covalent compounds. Many covalent compounds do not dissolve well in water. Water molecules have a stronger attraction for one another than they have for the molecules of most other covalent compounds. Thus, the molecules of the covalent compound get squeezed out as the water molecules pull together. Some covalent compounds do dissolve in water. Most of these solutions contain uncharged molecules dissolved in water and do not conduct an electric current, as shown in **Figure 5.** Some covalent compounds form ions when they dissolve in water. Solutions of these compounds, including compounds called acids, do conduct an electric current. You will learn more about acids in the next section.

Figure 5 This solution of sugar, a covalent compound, in water does not conduct an electric current because the individual molecules of sugar are not charged.

REVIEW

1. List two properties of ionic compounds.
2. List two properties of covalent compounds.
3. Methane is a gas at room temperature. What type of compound is this most likely to be?
4. **Comparing Concepts** Compare ionic and covalent compounds based on the type of particle that makes up each.

Answers to Review

1. Answers may include the following: brittle, high melting point, many can dissolve in water, and solutions can conduct an electric current.

2. Answers may include the following: low melting point, many do not dissolve in water, and solutions often do not conduct an electric current except for solutions of acids.

3. covalent

4. Ionic compounds are made up of ions, and covalent compounds are made up of molecules.

Chapter 15 • Chemical Compounds

Section 2

Acids, Bases, and Salts

Terms to Learn
- acid
- base
- pH
- salt

What You'll Do
- Describe the properties and uses of acids and bases.
- Explain the difference between strong acids and bases and weak acids and bases.
- Identify acids and bases using the pH scale.
- Describe the properties and uses of salts.

Have you ever noticed that when you squeeze lemon juice into tea, the color of the tea becomes lighter? Shown in **Figure 6,** lemon juice contains a substance called an acid that changes the color of a substance in the tea. The ability to change the color of certain chemicals is one property used to classify substances as acids or bases. A third category of substances, called salts, are formed by the reaction of an acid with a base.

Figure 6 Acids, like those found in lemon juice, can change the color of tea.

NEVER touch or taste a concentrated solution of a strong acid.

Acids

An **acid** is any compound that increases the number of hydrogen ions when dissolved in water, and whose solution tastes sour and can change the color of certain compounds.

Properties of Acids If you have ever had orange juice, you have experienced the sour taste of an acid. The taste of lemons, limes, and other citrus fruits is a result of citric acid. Taste, however, should NEVER be used as a test to identify an unknown chemical. Many acids are *corrosive,* meaning they destroy body tissue and clothing, and many are also poisonous.

Acids react with some metals to produce hydrogen gas, as shown in **Figure 7.** Adding an acid to baking soda or limestone produces a different gas, carbon dioxide.

Solutions of acids conduct an electric current because acids break apart to form ions in water. Acids increase the number of hydrogen ions, H^+, in a solution. However, the hydrogen ion does not normally exist alone. In a water solution, each hydrogen ion bonds to a water molecule, H_2O, to form a hydronium ion, H_3O^+.

Figure 7 Bubbles of hydrogen gas are produced when zinc metal reacts with hydrochloric acid.

Directed Reading Worksheet 15 Section 2

SECTION 2

Focus

Acids, Bases, and Salts

This section describes the properties and uses of acids, bases, and salts. Students learn the differences between strong and weak acids and bases, as well as how acids and bases neutralize one another. Students also learn how to identify acids and bases using the pH scale.

Bellringer

Show students a lemon and a tomato. Tell them that these fruits contain citric acid, which gives them a tangy flavor. Ask students to suggest other foods whose tanginess may be due to the presence of acids. (Responses might include dill pickles, grapefruits, strawberries, vinegar, and spoiled milk.)

1 Motivate

ACTIVITY

Tasting a Weak Acid Have groups of students taste samples of carbonated water and compare its flavor with that of regular water. Tell students to report their findings to the class. Students will probably report that carbonated water has a more sour or tangy flavor. Explain that carbonated water contains carbonic acid, a weak acid that forms when carbon dioxide dissolves in water. The acid is responsible for the sour flavor. Ask students if they can think of other foods that may be flavored with acids.
Sheltered English

2 Teach

RETEACHING

To reinforce the difference between strong and weak acids, place two Petri dishes on an overhead projector. In each dish, place a small piece of magnesium ribbon. Place several drops of 0.8 M HCl on one piece of magnesium and several drops of vinegar on the other piece. Emphasize to students that the concentrations of the two acids are the same. Have students compare the action of the strong acid with that of the weak acid.
Sheltered English

DEMONSTRATION

A Fruit Juice Indicator Place 1 mL of unsweetened purple grape juice and 9 mL of water into each of three test tubes. Instruct students to note the color of the diluted grape juice. Add a few drops of vinegar to the second test tube and a few drops of ammonia to the third test tube. Ask students to describe any color changes they observe. (In the second test tube, the color turns red. In the third test tube, the color turns blue.)

Finally, add ammonia to the second test tube and vinegar to the third test tube until they change color again. Tell students that by the end of this section, they will be able to explain what they observed in this activity.
Sheltered English

TOPIC: Acids and Bases
GO TO: www.scilinks.org
sciLINKS NUMBER: HSTP365

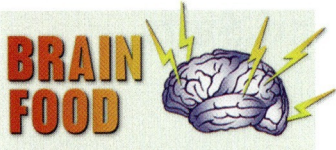
Some hydrangea plants act as indicators. Leaves on the plants change from pink to blue as the soil becomes more acidic.

Detecting Acids As mentioned earlier, a property of acids is their ability to change the color of a substance. An *indicator* is a substance that changes color in the presence of an acid or base. An indicator commonly used is litmus. Paper strips containing litmus are available in both blue and red. When an acid is added to blue litmus paper, the color of the litmus changes to red, as shown in **Figure 8**. (Red litmus paper is used to detect bases, as will be discussed shortly.) Many plant materials, such as red cabbage, contain compounds that are indicators.

Figure 8 *Vinegar turns blue litmus paper red because it contains acetic acid.*

Figure 9 *The label on this car battery warns you that sulfuric acid is found in the battery.*

Uses of Acids Acids are used in many areas of industry as well as in your home. Sulfuric acid is the most widely produced industrial chemical in the world. It is used in the production of metals, paper, paint, detergents, and fertilizers. It is also used in car batteries, as shown in **Figure 9**. Nitric acid is used to make fertilizers, rubber, and plastics. Hydrochloric acid is used in the production of metals and to help keep swimming pools free of algae. It is also found in your stomach, where it aids in digestion. Citric acid and ascorbic acid (vitamin C) are found in orange juice, while carbonic acid and phosphoric acid help give extra "bite" to soft drinks.

Strong Versus Weak As an acid dissolves in water, its molecules break apart and produce hydrogen ions. When all the molecules of an acid break apart in water to produce hydrogen ions, the acid is considered a strong acid. Strong acids include sulfuric acid, nitric acid, and hydrochloric acid.

When few molecules of an acid break apart in water to produce hydrogen ions, the acid is considered a weak acid. Acetic acid, citric acid, carbonic acid, and phosphoric acid are all weak acids.

Multicultural CONNECTION

What do sauerkraut and ketchup have in common? Both are food items from different cultures that are flavored and preserved with vinegar. Have students research the use of acids to flavor and preserve foods from different cultures. Encourage students to present their findings to the class.

IS THAT A FACT!

The proper way to use litmus paper is to dip a stirring rod into the solution to be tested and then touch the moist rod to the litmus paper. This procedure prevents the litmus from contaminating the solution and allows one piece of litmus paper to be used for three or four tests.

Bases

A **base** is any compound that increases the number of hydroxide ions when dissolved in water, and whose solution tastes bitter, feels slippery, and can change the color of certain compounds.

Properties of Bases If you have ever accidentally tasted soap, then you know the bitter taste of a base. Soap also demonstrates that a base feels slippery. However, NEVER use taste or touch as a test to identify an unknown chemical. Like acids, many bases are corrosive. If your fingers feel slippery when you are using a base in an experiment, you might have gotten the base on your hands. You should immediately rinse your hands with large amounts of water.

Solutions of bases conduct an electric current because bases increase the number of hydroxide ions, OH^-, in a solution. A hydroxide ion is actually a hydrogen atom and an oxygen atom bonded together. An extra electron gives the ion a negative charge.

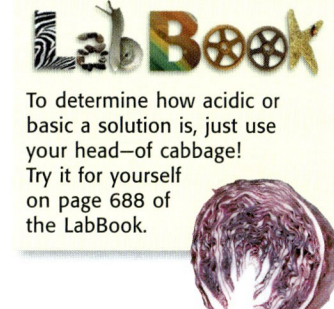

To determine how acidic or basic a solution is, just use your head—of cabbage! Try it for yourself on page 688 of the LabBook.

Detecting Bases Like acids, bases change the color of an indicator. Most indicators turn a different color for bases than they do for acids. For example, bases will change the color of red litmus paper to blue, as shown in **Figure 10**.

NEVER touch or taste a concentrated solution of a strong base.

Figure 10 Sodium hydroxide, a base, turns red litmus paper blue.

Uses of Bases Like acids, bases have many uses. Sodium hydroxide is used to make soap and paper. It is also in oven cleaners and in products that unclog drains, as shown in **Figure 11**. Remember, bases can harm your skin, so carefully follow the safety instructions when using these products. Calcium hydroxide is used to make cement, mortar, and plaster. Ammonia is found in many household cleaners and is also used in the production of fertilizers. Magnesium hydroxide and aluminum hydroxide are used in antacids to treat heartburn.

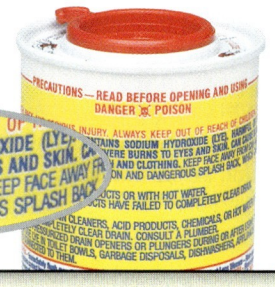

Figure 11 This drain cleaner contains sodium hydroxide to help dissolve grease that can clog the drain.

IS THAT A FACT!

Answer students' questions about how ammonia could be a base even though it does not have hydroxide in its chemical formula. Tell them that a solution of ammonia and water contains ammonium ions, NH_4^+, and hydroxide ions, OH^-.

Homework

Soap Making Before soap was made commercially, people made their own soap. They combined an oil or fat with a strong base, such as lye (sodium hydroxide). Have students research some aspect of soap making and compile their findings into a short report.

MEETING INDIVIDUAL NEEDS

Learners Having Difficulty Have students make a chart that compares the properties of acids and bases. Encourage them to refer to their chart as they read through this section.

Cabbage Patch Indicators

DEMONSTRATION

Safety Caution: Students should not look directly at the bright light produced by this reaction.

Explain to students that metal oxides react with water to form bases. Burn a few centimeters of magnesium ribbon. Explain to students that the residue left from the reaction is magnesium oxide. Place the residue in a test tube, and add several drops of water. Ask students what will form in the test tube. (magnesium hydroxide, a base)

Ask them what color of litmus paper they would use to test the solution. (red)

Then ask them to predict what will happen to the litmus paper. (The litmus paper will turn blue.)

Ask a volunteer to use litmus paper to check the predictions.

Section 2 • Acids, Bases, and Salts

2 Teach, continued

USING THE FIGURE

Direct students' attention to **Figure 13.** Ask what a pH of 7 indicates. (The solution is neither acidic nor basic; it is neutral.)

Ask what all acidic substances have in common. (a pH of less than 7)

MATH and MORE

Each one point step up or down the pH scale represents a tenfold difference in acidity. This means that a solution of pH 3 is 10 times more acidic than one of pH 4, and a solution of pH 9 is 10 times more basic than one of pH 8. Ask students the following question:

How much more acidic is a solution of pH 2 than one of pH 6? (6 − 2 = 4, and 10^4 = 10,000 times more acidic)

Math Skills Worksheet 24 "Creating Exponents"

MATERIALS

FOR EACH STUDENT:
- small plastic cup
- vinegar
- red and blue litmus paper
- antacid tablet

Safety Caution: Remind students to review all safety cautions and icons before beginning this lab activity.

Answers to QuickLab

3. The vinegar was more acidic before the reaction than the mixture was after the reaction.

Figure 12 Have heartburn? Take an antacid! Antacid tablets contain a base that neutralizes the acid in your stomach.

pHast Relief!

1. Fill a **small plastic cup** halfway with **vinegar.** Test the vinegar with **red** and **blue litmus paper.** Record your results in your ScienceLog.

2. Carefully crush an **antacid tablet,** and mix it with the vinegar. Test the mixture with litmus paper. Record your results in your ScienceLog.

3. Compare the acidity of the solution before and after the reaction.

380

Teaching Transparency 259 "pH Values of Common Materials"

Strong Versus Weak When all the molecules of a base break apart in water to produce hydroxide ions, the base is called a strong base. Strong bases include sodium hydroxide, calcium hydroxide, and potassium hydroxide.

When only a few of the molecules of a base produce hydroxide ions in water, the base is called a weak base. Ammonia, magnesium hydroxide, and aluminum hydroxide are all weak bases.

Acids and Bases Neutralize One Another

If you have ever suffered from an acid stomach, or heartburn, as shown in **Figure 12,** you might have taken an antacid. Antacids contain weak bases that soothe your heartburn by reacting with and neutralizing the acid in your stomach. Acids and bases neutralize one another because the H^+ of the acid and the $OH^−$ of the base react to form water, H_2O. Other ions from the acid and base are also dissolved in the water. If the water is evaporated, these ions join to form a compound called a salt. You'll learn more about salts later in this section.

The pH Scale Indicators such as litmus can identify whether a solution contains an acid or base. To describe how acidic or basic a solution is, the pH scale is used. The **pH** of a solution is a measure of the hydronium ion concentration in the solution. By measuring the hydronium ion concentration, the pH is also a measure of the hydrogen ion concentration. On the scale, a solution that has a pH of 7 is neutral, meaning that it is neither acidic nor basic. Pure water has a pH of 7. Basic solutions have a pH greater than 7, and acidic solutions have a pH less than 7. Look at **Figure 13** to see the pH values for many common materials.

Figure 13 pH Values of Common Materials

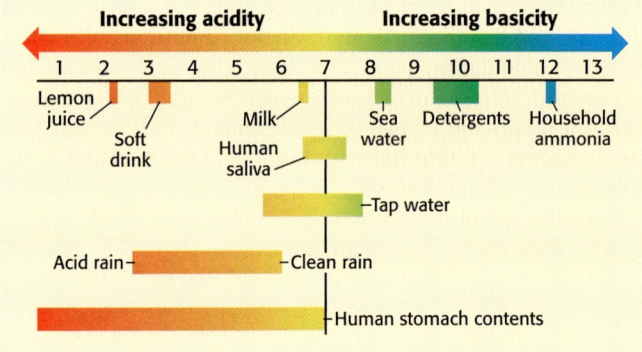

IS THAT A FACT!

Explain to students that the indicator litmus is actually a pigment derived from lichens. Lichens are organisms formed from the union of fungal and algal cells that appear as colored scales on trees and rocks. Litmus paper is paper that has been impregnated with litmus.

Chapter 15 • Chemical Compounds

Using Indicators to Determine pH A single indicator allows you to determine if a solution is acidic or basic, but a mixture of different indicators can be used to determine the pH of a solution. After determining the colors for this mixture at different pH values, the indicators can be used to determine the pH of an unknown solution, as shown in **Figure 14.** Indicators can be used as paper strips or solutions, and they are often used to test the pH of soil and of water in pools and aquariums. Another way to determine the acidity of a solution is to use an instrument called a pH meter, which can detect and measure hydrogen ions electronically.

Figure 14 *The paper strip contains several indicators. The pH of a solution is determined by comparing the color of the strip to the scale provided.*

 Self-Check

Which is more acidic, a soft drink or milk? (Hint: Refer to Figure 13 to find the pH values of these drinks.) *(See page 724 to check your answer.)*

pH and the Environment Living things depend on having a steady pH in their environment. Plants are known to have certain preferred growing conditions. Some plants, such as pine trees, prefer acidic soil with a pH between 4 and 6. Other plants, such as lettuce, require basic soil with a pH between 8 and 9. Fish require water near pH 7. As you can see in Figure 13, rainwater can have a pH as low as 3. This occurs in areas where compounds found in pollution react with water to make the strong acids sulfuric acid and nitric acid. As this acid precipitation collects in lakes, it can lower the pH to levels that may kill the fish and other organisms in the lake. To neutralize the acid and bring the pH closer to 7, a base can be added to the lakes, as shown in **Figure 15.**

 **Biology CONNECTION**

Human blood has a pH of between 7.38 and 7.42. If the pH is above 7.8 or below 7, the body cannot function properly. Sudden changes in blood pH that are not quickly corrected can be fatal.

Figure 15 *This helicopter is adding a base to an acidic lake. Neutralizing the acid in the lake might help protect the organisms living in the lake.*

3) Extend

DEMONSTRATION

Making Soap Place 40 g of lard or tallow in a beaker. Carefully add 10 mL of 20% sodium hydroxide solution (2 g sodium hydroxide dissolved in 10 mL of water) to the beaker. Warm the mixture gently on a hot plate for about 30 minutes. Stir it periodically with a wooden spoon to prevent spattering. Let the solution cool for a few minutes, then stir in 10 g of salt. Skim the soap off the top with the spoon, and rinse it well in very cold water. Place the soap on a paper towel to dry. Place a small amount of the soap in a test tube with 10 mL of distilled water. Stopper the test tube, and shake it to form suds. Sheltered English

Answer to Self-Check

a soft drink

Homework

 **Dissolving Marble** Have students research the effect of acid precipitation on statues, gravestones, and buildings. Tell them to make a small poster describing their findings and to display it to the class.

 Reinforcement Worksheet 15 "A Simple Solution"

 Critical Thinking Worksheet 15 "Battle of the Breads"

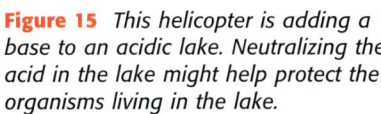

IS THAT A FACT!

The pH-sensitive compound cyanidin is present in many plants, including cornflowers, poppies, and rhubarb. Cornflowers are blue because their sap is basic, and cyanidin is blue in the presence of bases. Poppies have red flowers because their sap is acidic, and cyanidin is red in the presence of acids. The oxalic acid in rhubarb affects the cyanidin and is responsible for the vegetable's red color. Other plants that contain cyanidin include strawberries, raspberries, and cherries.

Section 2 • Acids, Bases, and Salts

④ Close

Making Salt   PG 690

Quiz

1. Is the compound H_3PO_4 an acid or a base? How do you know? (It is an acid because it will form hydrogen ions.)

2. Would you expect the pH of a sample of acid rain to be 4 or 9? Why? (4, because it is acidic)

3. What products would form when hydrochloric acid, HCl, and sodium hydroxide, NaOH, react? (The products would be water and the salt sodium chloride.)

ALTERNATIVE ASSESSMENT

Concept Mapping Have students use the following terms to make a concept map that compares the properties of acids and bases:

acid, neutral, base, bitter, sour, pH value greater than 7, pH value less than 7, salt, hydroxide ions, neutralize, hydrogen ions

---

internetconnect

TOPIC: Salts
GO TO: www.scilinks.org
*sci*LINKS NUMBER: HSTP370

Salts

When you hear the word *salt*, you probably think of the table salt you use to season your food. But the sodium chloride found in your salt shaker is only one example of a large group of compounds called salts. A **salt** is an ionic compound formed from the positive ion of a base and the negative ion of an acid. You may remember that a salt and water are produced when an acid neutralizes a base. However, salts can also be produced in other reactions, as shown in **Figure 16**.

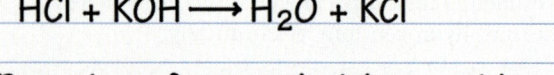

Figure 16 *The salt potassium chloride can be formed from several different reactions.*

Neutralization of an acid and a base:
$HCl + KOH \longrightarrow H_2O + KCl$

Reaction of a metal with an acid:
$2K + 2HCl \longrightarrow 2KCl + H_2$

Reaction of a metal and a nonmetal:
$2K + Cl_2 \longrightarrow 2KCl$

Figure 17 *Salts are used to help keep roads free of ice.*

internetconnect

TOPIC: Acids and Bases, Salts
GO TO: www.scilinks.org
*sci*LINKS NUMBER: HSTP365, HSTP370

Uses of Salts Salts have many uses in industry and in your home. You already know that sodium chloride is used to season foods. It is also used in the production of other compounds, including lye (sodium hydroxide), hydrochloric acid, and baking soda. The salt calcium sulfate is made into wallboard, or plasterboard, which is used in construction. Sodium nitrate is one of many salts used as a preservative in foods. Calcium carbonate is a salt that makes up limestone, chalk, and seashells. Another use of salts is shown in **Figure 17**.

REVIEW

1. What ion is present in all acid solutions?
2. What are two ways scientists can measure pH?
3. What products are formed when an acid and base react?
4. **Comparing Concepts** Compare the properties of acids and bases.
5. **Applying Concepts** Would you expect the pH of a solution of soap to be 4 or 9?

▼ **Answers to Review**

1. hydronium ion, H_3O^+
2. using indicators or a pH meter
3. a salt and water
4. Acids have a sour taste, produce hydronium ions in water, and turn blue litmus paper red. Bases have a bitter taste, feel slippery, produce hydroxide ions in water, and turn red litmus paper blue.
5. 9

Section 3

Terms to Learn

organic compounds
biochemicals   proteins
carbohydrates   nucleic acids
lipids   hydrocarbons

What You'll Do

- Explain why so many organic compounds are possible.
- Describe the characteristics of carbohydrates, lipids, proteins, and nucleic acids and their functions in the body.
- Describe and identify saturated, unsaturated, and aromatic hydrocarbons.

Organic Compounds

Of all the known compounds, more than 90 percent are members of a group of compounds called organic compounds. **Organic compounds** are covalent compounds composed of carbon-based molecules. Sugar, starch, oil, protein, nucleic acid, and even cotton and plastic are organic compounds. How can there be so many different kinds of organic compounds? The huge variety of organic compounds is explained by examining the carbon atom.

Each Carbon Atom Forms Four Bonds

Carbon atoms form the backbone of organic compounds. Because each carbon atom has four valence electrons (electrons in the outermost energy level of an atom), each atom can make four bonds. Thus, a carbon atom can bond to one, two, or even three other carbon atoms and still have electrons remaining to bond to other atoms. Three types of carbon backbones on which many organic compounds are based are shown in the models in **Figure 18.**

Some organic compounds have hundreds or even thousands of carbon atoms making up their backbone! Although the elements hydrogen and oxygen, along with carbon, make up many of the organic compounds, sulfur, nitrogen, and phosphorus are also important—especially in forming the molecules that make up all living things.

Figure 18 These models, called structural formulas, are used to show how atoms in a molecule are connected. Each line represents a pair of electrons shared in a covalent bond.

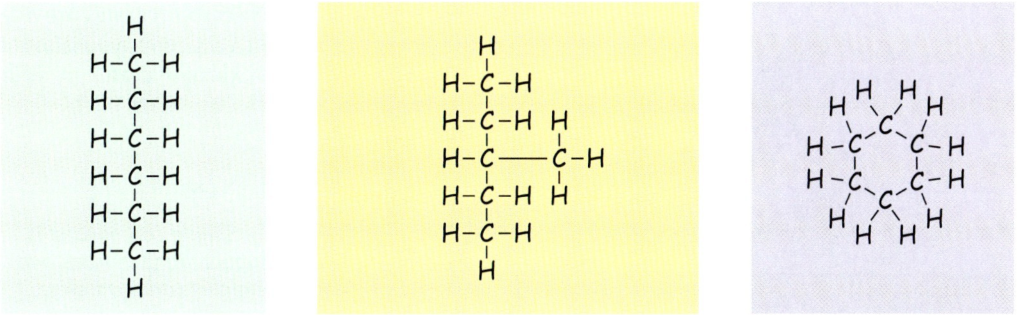

Straight Chain All carbon atoms are connected one after another in a line.

Branched Chain The chain of carbon atoms continues in more than one direction where a carbon atom bonds to three or more other carbon atoms.

Ring The chain of carbon atoms forms a ring.

IS THAT A FACT!

One reason so many organic compounds exist is that the same combination of atoms can be arranged to make more than one compound. For example, the formula C_4H_{10} represents two different compounds. Each compound has a different set of properties, but both compounds have the same number of carbon and hydrogen atoms. Different compounds that have the same chemical formulas are called *isomers*.

2) Teach

GUIDED PRACTICE

Give each student a photocopy of nutrition labels from several different foods, such as milk, cereal, and peanut butter. Ask each student to find and list the carbohydrate, lipid (fat), and protein content of each food.

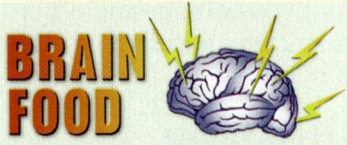

BRAIN FOOD

Tell students that carbohydrate molecules are composed of carbon, hydrogen, and oxygen atoms. Carbohydrates can be classified as simple or complex carbohydrates. Sugars are simple carbohydrates, while starches and cellulose are complex. Most of the fiber we get from plants is in the form of cellulose. The sugar units in cellulose are bonded together to form a structure that gives plants strength and shape. Because of the way the structure is formed, cellulose is impossible for humans to digest. However, high-fiber foods, such as plums and oatmeal, are healthy because they slow the absorption of calories and help move food through the digestive system.

TOPIC: Organic Compounds
GO TO: www.scilinks.org
sciLINKS NUMBER: HSTP375

Biochemicals: The Compounds of Life

Organic compounds made by living things are called **biochemicals**. The molecules of most biochemicals are very large. Biochemicals can be divided into four categories: carbohydrates, lipids, proteins, and nucleic acids. Each type of biochemical has important functions in living organisms.

Carbohydrates Starch and cellulose are examples of carbohydrates. **Carbohydrates** are biochemicals that are composed of one or more simple sugars bonded together; they are used as a source of energy and for energy storage. There are two types of carbohydrates: simple carbohydrates and complex carbohydrates. A single sugar molecule, represented using a hexagon, or a few sugar molecules bonded together are examples of simple carbohydrates, as illustrated in **Figure 19**. Glucose is a simple carbohydrate produced by plants through photosynthesis.

Figure 19 The sugar molecules in the left image are simple carbohydrates. The starch in the right image is a complex carbohydrate because it is composed of many sugar molecules bonded together.

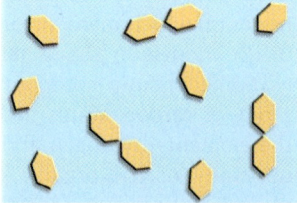
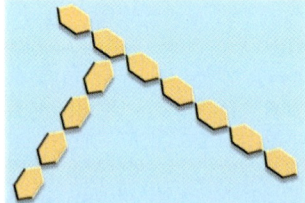

Sugar Storage System When an organism has more sugar than it needs, its extra sugar may be stored for later use in the form of complex carbohydrates, as shown in Figure 19. Molecules of complex carbohydrates are composed of hundreds or even thousands of sugar molecules bonded together. Because carbohydrates provide the energy you need each day, you should include sources of carbohydrates in your diet, such as the foods shown in **Figure 20**.

Figure 20 Simple carbohydrates include sugars found in fruits and honey. Complex carbohydrates, such as starches, are found in bread, cereal, and pasta.

MISCONCEPTION ALERT

When it comes to your health, sugar is sugar. Many packaged foods claim that they are healthful because they contain glucose or fructose (fruit sugar) instead of sucrose (refined table sugar). These are all concentrated sugars; all they provide is calories. It is much healthier to eat sugars in their truly natural form—as part of whole foods, such as fruits and vegetables.

Lipids Fats, oils, waxes, and steroids are examples of lipids. **Lipids** are biochemicals that do not dissolve in water and have many different functions, including storing energy and making up cell membranes. Although too much fat in your diet can be unhealthy, some fat is extremely important to good health. The foods in **Figure 21** are sources of lipids.

Figure 21 Vegetable oil, meat, cheese, nuts, and milk are sources of lipids in your diet.

Lipids store excess energy in the body. Animals tend to store lipids primarily as fats, while plants store lipids as oils. When an organism has used up most of its carbohydrates, it can obtain energy by breaking down lipids. Lipids are also used to store vitamins that dissolve in fat but not in water.

Lipids Make Up Cell Membranes Each cell is surrounded by a cell membrane. Much of the cell membrane is formed from molecules of phospholipids. The structure of these molecules plays an important part in the phospholipid's role in the cell membrane. The tail of a phospholipid molecule is a long, straight-chain carbon backbone composed only of carbon and hydrogen atoms. The tail is not attracted to water. The head of a phospholipid molecule is attracted to water because it is composed of phosphorus, oxygen, and nitrogen atoms in addition to carbon and hydrogen atoms. This results in the double layer of phospholipid molecules shown in the model in **Figure 22.** This arrangement of phospholipid molecules creates a barrier to help control the flow of chemicals into and out of the cell.

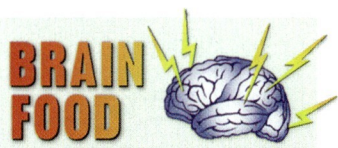

Deposits of the lipid cholesterol in the body have been linked to health problems such as heart disease. However, cholesterol is needed in nerve and brain tissue as well as to make certain hormones that regulate body processes such as growth.

Figure 22 A cell membrane is composed primarily of two layers of phospholipid molecules.

The **head** of each phospholipid molecule is attracted to water either inside or outside of the cell.

The **tail** of each phospholipid molecule is pushed against other tails because they are not attracted to water.

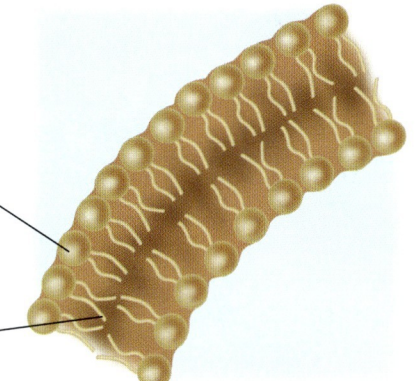

IS THAT A FACT!

The main difference between fats and oils is that fats are solid at room temperature, while oils are liquid at room temperature. Most fats, such as chicken fat and lard, come from animal sources. Most oils, such as olive oil and corn oil, come from plant sources.

Section 3 • Organic Compounds

Proteins Most of the biochemicals found in living things are proteins. In fact, after water, proteins are the most abundant molecules in your cells. **Proteins** are biochemicals that are composed of amino acids; they have many different functions, including regulating chemical activities, transporting and storing materials, and providing structural support.

Every protein is composed of small "building blocks" called *amino acids*. Amino acids are smaller molecules composed of carbon, hydrogen, oxygen, and nitrogen atoms. Some amino acids also include sulfur atoms. Amino acids chemically bond to form proteins of many different shapes and sizes. The function of a protein depends on the shape that the bonded amino acids adopt. If even a single amino acid is missing or out of place, the protein may not function correctly or at all. The foods shown in **Figure 23** provide amino acids that your body needs to make new proteins.

Figure 23 Meat, fish, cheese, and beans contain proteins, which are broken down into amino acids as they are digested.

All the proteins in your body are made from just 20 amino acids. Nine of these amino acids are called essential amino acids because your body cannot make them. You must get them from the food you eat.

Examples of Proteins Enzymes are proteins that regulate chemical reactions in the body by acting as catalysts to increase the rate at which the reactions occur. Some hormones are proteins. Insulin is a hormone that helps regulate the level of sugar in your blood. Oxygen is carried by the protein hemoglobin, allowing red blood cells to deliver oxygen throughout your body. There are also large proteins that extend through cell membranes and help control the transport of materials into and out of cells. Proteins that provide structural support often form structures that are easy to see, like those in **Figure 24**.

Figure 24 Hair and spider webs are made up of proteins that are shaped like long fibers.

Homework

Amino Acids and Vegetarians
Ask students to find out more about how people with vegetarian diets can get all the essential amino acids. Have students present their findings in the form of a poster.

Nucleic Acids The largest molecules made by living organisms are nucleic acids. **Nucleic acids** are biochemicals that store information and help to build proteins and other nucleic acids. Nucleic acids are sometimes called the "blueprints of life" because they contain all the information needed for the cell to make all of its proteins.

Like proteins, nucleic acids are long chains of smaller molecules joined together. These smaller molecules are composed of carbon, hydrogen, oxygen, nitrogen, and phosphorus atoms. Nucleic acids are much larger than proteins even though nucleic acids are composed of only five building blocks.

DNA and RNA There are two types of nucleic acids: DNA and RNA. DNA (**d**eoxyribo**n**ucleic **a**cid), like that shown in **Figure 25,** is the genetic material of the cell. DNA molecules can store an enormous amount of information because of their length. The DNA molecules in a single human cell have an overall length of about 2 m—that's over 6 ft long! When a cell needs to make a certain protein, it copies the important part of the DNA. The information copied from the DNA directs the order in which amino acids are bonded together to make that protein. DNA also contains information used to build the second type of nucleic acid, RNA (**r**ibo**n**ucleic **a**cid). RNA is involved in the actual building of proteins.

Nucleic acids store information—even about ancient peoples. Read more about these incredible biochemicals on page 394.

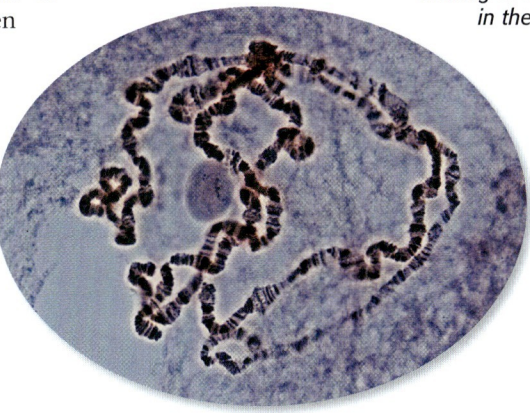

Figure 25 The DNA from a fruit fly contains all of the instructions for making proteins, nucleic acids . . . in fact, for making everything in the organism!

REVIEW

1. What are organic compounds?
2. What are the four categories of biochemicals?
3. What are two functions of proteins?
4. What biochemicals are used to provide energy?
5. **Inferring Relationships** Sickle-cell anemia is a condition that results from a change of one amino acid in the protein hemoglobin. Why is this condition a genetic disorder?

3 Extend

MAKING MODELS

Have students use toothpicks and two different colors of clay to make models of an alkane, an alkene, and an alkyne that each contain two carbon atoms. Ask students how many hydrogen atoms are in the alkane, how many are in the alkene, and how many are in the alkyne. **(6 in the alkane, 4 in the alkene, and 2 in the alkyne)**

MATH and MORE

Write the formulas for three saturated hydrocarbons— C_2H_6, C_3H_8, and C_4H_{10}—on the board. Ask students what relationship they see between the number of carbon atoms and the number of hydrogen atoms in each formula. **(They should conclude that the number of hydrogen atoms is equal to 2 times the number of carbon atoms plus 2.)**

Explain that the general formula for alkanes is C_nH_{2n+2}.

Hydrocarbons

Organic compounds that are composed of only carbon and hydrogen are called **hydrocarbons.** Hydrocarbons are an important group of organic compounds. Many fuels, including gasoline, methane, and propane, are hydrocarbons. Hydrocarbons can be divided into three categories: saturated, unsaturated, and aromatic.

Saturated Hydrocarbons Propane, like that used in the stove in **Figure 26,** is an example of a saturated hydrocarbon. A *saturated hydrocarbon* is a hydrocarbon in which each carbon atom in the molecule shares a single bond with each of four other atoms. A single bond is a covalent bond that consists of one pair of shared electrons. Hydrocarbons that contain carbon atoms connected only by single bonds are called saturated because no other atoms can be added without replacing an atom that is part of the molecule. Saturated hydrocarbons are also called *alkanes*.

Figure 26 *The propane in this camping stove is a saturated hydrocarbon.*

Unsaturated Hydrocarbons Each carbon atom forms four bonds. However, these bonds do not always have to be single bonds. An *unsaturated hydrocarbon* is a hydrocarbon in which at least two carbon atoms share a double bond or a triple bond. A double bond is a covalent bond that consists of two pairs of shared electrons. Compounds that contain two carbon atoms connected by a double bond are called *alkenes*.

A triple bond is a covalent bond that consists of three pairs of shared electrons. Hydrocarbons that contain two carbon atoms connected by a triple bond are called *alkynes*.

Hydrocarbons that contain double or triple bonds are called unsaturated because the double or triple bond can be broken to allow more atoms to be added to the molecule. Examples of unsaturated hydrocarbons are shown in **Figure 27**.

Figure 27 *Fruits produce ethene, which helps ripen the fruit. Ethyne, better known as acetylene, is burned in this miner's lamp and is also used in welding.*

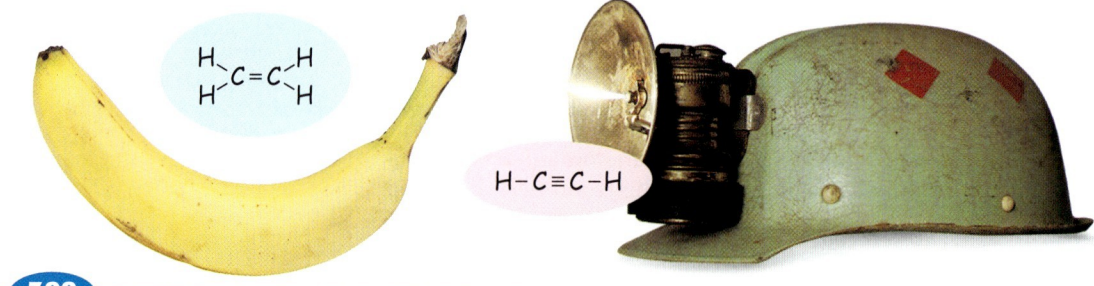

IS THAT A FACT!

Alkanes will burn and can be used as fuels. Natural gas is a mixture of alkanes. About 75 percent of natural gas is methane; the rest is a mixture of ethane, propane, and butane.

Aromatic Hydrocarbons Most aromatic compounds are based on benzene, the compound represented by the model in **Figure 28.** Look for this structure to help identify an aromatic hydrocarbon. As the name implies, aromatic hydrocarbons often have strong odors and are therefore used in such products as air fresheners and moth balls.

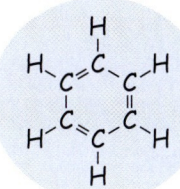

Figure 28 Benzene has a ring of six carbons with alternating double and single bonds. Benzene is the starting material for manufacturing many products, including medicines.

Other Organic Compounds

Many other types of organic compounds exist that have atoms of halogens, oxygen, sulfur, and phosphorus in their molecules. A few of these types of compounds and their uses are described in the chart below.

Types and Uses of Organic Compounds		
Type of compound	**Uses**	**Examples**
Alkyl halides	starting material for Teflon refrigerant (freon)	chloromethane (CH_3Cl) bromoethane (C_2H_5Br)
Alcohols	rubbing alcohol gasoline additive antifreeze	methanol (CH_3OH) ethanol (C_2H_5OH)
Organic acids	food preservatives flavorings	ethanoic acid (CH_3COOH) propanoic acid (C_2H_5COOH)
Esters	flavorings fragrances clothing (polyester)	methyl ethanoate (CH_3COOCH_3) ethyl propanoate ($C_2H_5COOC_2H_5$)

REVIEW

1. What is a hydrocarbon?
2. How many electrons are shared in a double bond? a triple bond?
3. **Comparing Concepts** Compare saturated and unsaturated hydrocarbons.

internetconnect

SC_{LINKS} NSTA

TOPIC: Organic Compounds
GO TO: www.scilinks.org
sciLINKS NUMBER: HSTP375

Chapter Highlights

VOCABULARY DEFINITIONS

SECTION 1

ionic compounds compounds that contain ionic bonds

covalent compounds compounds that are composed of elements that are covalently bonded

SECTION 2

acid any compound that increases the number of hydrogen ions when dissolved in water, and whose solution tastes sour and can change the color of certain compounds

base any compound that increases the number of hydroxide ions when dissolved in water, and whose solution tastes bitter, feels slippery, and can change the color of certain compounds

pH a measure of hydronium ion concentration in a solution

salt an ionic compound formed from the positive ion of a base and the negative ion of an acid

Chapter Highlights

SECTION 1

Vocabulary
ionic compounds (p. 374)
covalent compounds (p. 375)

Section Notes

- Ionic compounds contain ionic bonds and are composed of oppositely charged ions arranged in a repeating pattern called a crystal lattice.
- Ionic compounds tend to be brittle, have high melting points, and dissolve in water to form solutions that conduct an electric current.
- Covalent compounds are composed of elements that are covalently bonded and consist of independent particles called molecules.
- Covalent compounds tend to have low melting points. Most do not dissolve well in water and do not form solutions that conduct an electric current.

SECTION 2

Vocabulary
acid (p. 377)
base (p. 379)
pH (p. 380)
salt (p. 382)

Section Notes

- An acid is a compound that increases the number of hydrogen ions in solution. Acids taste sour, turn blue litmus paper red, react with metals to produce hydrogen gas, and react with limestone or baking soda to produce carbon dioxide gas.
- A base is a compound that increases the number of hydroxide ions in solution. Bases taste bitter, feel slippery, and turn red litmus paper blue.

- When dissolved in water, every molecule of a strong acid or base breaks apart to form ions. Few molecules of weak acids and bases break apart to form ions.
- When combined, an acid and a base neutralize one another to produce water and a salt.
- pH is a measure of hydronium ion concentration in a solution. A pH of 7 indicates a neutral substance. A pH of less than 7 indicates an acidic substance. A pH of greater than 7 indicates a basic substance.
- A salt is an ionic compound formed from the positive ion of a base and the negative ion of an acid.

Labs
Cabbage Patch Indicators (p. 688)
Making Salt (p. 690)

✓ Skills Check

Visual Understanding

LITMUS PAPER You can use the ability of acids and bases to change the color of indicators to identify a chemical as an acid or base. Litmus is an indicator commonly used in schools. Review Figures 8 and 10, which show how the color of litmus paper is changed by an acid and by a base.

pH SCALE Knowing whether a substance is an acid or a base can help explain some of the properties of the substance. The pH scale shown in Figure 13 illustrates the pH ranges for many common substances.

Lab and Activity Highlights

Cabbage Patch Indicators   PG 688

Making Salt   PG 690

 Datasheets for LabBook
(blackline masters for these labs)

SECTION 3

Vocabulary
- **organic compounds** (p. 383)
- **biochemicals** (p. 384)
- **carbohydrates** (p. 384)
- **lipids** (p. 385)
- **proteins** (p. 386)
- **nucleic acids** (p. 387)
- **hydrocarbons** (p. 388)

Section Notes

- Organic compounds are covalent compounds composed of carbon-based molecules.
- Each carbon atom forms four bonds with other carbon atoms or with atoms of other elements to form straight chains, branched chains, or rings.
- Biochemicals are organic compounds made by living things.
- Carbohydrates are biochemicals that are composed of one or more simple sugars bonded together; they are used as a source of energy and for energy storage.
- Lipids are biochemicals that do not dissolve in water and have many functions, including storing energy and making up cell membranes.
- Proteins are biochemicals that are composed of amino acids and have many functions, including regulating chemical activities, transporting and storing materials, and providing structural support.
- Nucleic acids are biochemicals that store information and help to build proteins and other nucleic acids.
- Hydrocarbons are organic compounds composed of only carbon and hydrogen.
- In a saturated hydrocarbon, each carbon atom in the molecule shares a single bond with each of four other atoms.
- In an unsaturated hydrocarbon, at least two carbon atoms share a double bond or a triple bond.
- Many aromatic hydrocarbons are based on the six-carbon ring of benzene.
- Other organic compounds, including alkyl halides, alcohols, organic acids, and esters, are formed by adding atoms of other elements.

VOCABULARY DEFINITIONS, continued

SECTION 3

organic compounds covalent compounds composed of carbon-based molecules

biochemicals organic compounds made by living things

carbohydrates biochemicals composed of one or more simple sugars bonded together that are used as a source of energy and for energy storage

lipids biochemicals that do not dissolve in water; their functions include storing energy and making up cell membranes

proteins biochemicals that are composed of amino acids; their functions include regulating chemical activities, transporting and storing materials, and providing structural support

nucleic acids biochemicals that store information and help to build proteins and other nucleic acids

hydrocarbons organic compounds that are composed of only carbon and hydrogen

 **internetconnect**

 GO TO: go.hrw.com

Visit the **HRW** Web site for a variety of learning tools related to this chapter. Just type in the keyword:

KEYWORD: HSTCMP

 GO TO: www.scilinks.org

Visit the **National Science Teachers Association** on-line Web site for Internet resources related to this chapter. Just type in the *sci*LINKS number for more information about the topic:

TOPIC: Ionic Compounds   *sci*LINKS NUMBER: HSTP355
TOPIC: Covalent Compounds *sci*LINKS NUMBER: HSTP360
TOPIC: Acids and Bases   *sci*LINKS NUMBER: HSTP365
TOPIC: Salts   *sci*LINKS NUMBER: HSTP370
TOPIC: Organic Compounds   *sci*LINKS NUMBER: HSTP375

 Vocabulary Review Worksheet 15

 Blackline masters of these Chapter Highlights can be found in the **Study Guide.**

Lab and Activity Highlights

LabBank

 Labs You Can Eat, Can You Say Seviche? Lab 23

EcoLabs & Field Activities, Greener Cleaners, EcoLab 20

Long-Term Projects & Research Ideas, Tiny Plastic Factories, Project 65

Chapter Review

USING VOCABULARY

To complete the following sentences, choose the correct term from each pair of terms listed below:

1. Compounds that have low melting points and do not usually dissolve well in water are __?__. (*ionic compounds* or *covalent compounds*)

2. A(n) __?__ turns red litmus paper blue. (*acid* or *base*)

3. __?__ are composed of only carbon and hydrogen. (*Ionic compounds* or *Hydrocarbons*)

4. A biochemical composed of amino acids is a __?__. (*lipid* or *protein*)

5. A source of energy for living things can be found in __?__. (*nucleic acids* or *carbohydrates*)

UNDERSTANDING CONCEPTS

Multiple Choice

6. Which of the following describes lipids?
   a. used to store energy
   b. do not dissolve in water
   c. make up most of the cell membrane
   d. all of the above

7. An acid reacts to produce carbon dioxide when the acid is added to
   a. water.
   b. limestone.
   c. salt.
   d. sodium hydroxide.

8. Which of the following does NOT describe ionic compounds?
   a. high melting point
   b. brittle
   c. do not conduct electric currents in water
   d. dissolve easily in water

9. An increase in the concentration of hydronium ions in solution __?__ the pH.
   a. raises
   b. lowers
   c. does not affect
   d. doubles

10. Which of the following compounds makes up the majority of cell membranes?
    a. lipids
    b. ionic compounds
    c. acids
    d. nucleic acids

11. The compounds that store information for building proteins are
    a. lipids.
    b. hydrocarbons.
    c. nucleic acids.
    d. carbohydrates.

Short Answer

12. What type of compound would you use to neutralize a solution of potassium hydroxide?

13. Explain why the reaction of an acid with a base is called *neutralization*.

14. What characteristic of carbon atoms helps to explain the wide variety of organic compounds?

15. Compare acids and bases based on the ion produced when each compound is dissolved in water.

Concept Mapping

16. Use the following terms to create a concept map: acid, base, salt, neutral, pH.

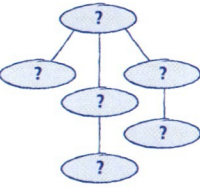

CRITICAL THINKING AND PROBLEM SOLVING

17. Fish give off the base ammonia, NH_3, as waste. How does the release of ammonia affect the pH of the water in the aquarium? What can be done to correct the problem?

18. Many insects, such as fire ants, inject formic acid, a weak acid, when they bite or sting. Describe the type of compound that should be used to treat the bite.

19. Organic compounds are also covalent compounds. What properties would you expect organic compounds to have as a result?

20. Farmers often can taste their soil to determine whether the soil has the correct acidity for their plants. How would taste help the farmer determine the acidity of the soil?

21. A diet that includes a high level of lipids is unhealthy. Why is a diet containing no lipids also unhealthy?

INTERPRETING GRAPHICS

Study the structural formulas below, and then answer the questions that follow.

a, **b**, **c**, **d** (structural formulas of hydrocarbons)

22. A saturated hydrocarbon is represented by which structural formula(s)?

23. An unsaturated hydrocarbon is represented by which structural formula(s)?

24. An aromatic hydrocarbon is represented by which structural formula(s)?

NOW What Do You Think?

Take a minute to review your answers to the ScienceLog questions on page 373. Have your answers changed? If necessary, revise your answers based on what you have learned since you began this chapter.

Concept Mapping

16. An answer to this exercise can be found at the end of this book.

CRITICAL THINKING AND PROBLEM SOLVING

17. The pH of the water will increase. An acid can be added to lower the pH and correct the problem.

18. A weak base should be used to treat the bite. It will neutralize the acid.

19. Organic compounds should have low melting and boiling points, should not dissolve well in water, and should not conduct an electric current in solution.

20. The taste of the soil can help a farmer determine if the soil is acidic or basic. If the soil tastes sour, it is acidic. If the soil tastes bitter, it is basic.

21. A diet containing no lipids is unhealthy because lipids are the major component of cell membranes and are important for storing energy and certain vitamins.

INTERPRETING GRAPHICS

22. *b* and *c*
23. *d*
24. *a*

Concept Mapping Transparency 15

Blackline masters of this Chapter Review can be found in the **Study Guide**.

NOW WHAT DO YOU THINK?

1. Ionic compounds contain ionic bonds and are made up of ions. Covalent compounds contain covalent bonds and are composed of molecules.
2. An acid is a substance that increases the number of hydrogen ions in solution. It has a sour taste and changes the color of indicators.
3. a covalent compound that is composed of only hydrogen and carbon

ACROSS THE SCIENCES
Unique Compounds

Background
Getting tissue samples from archaeological specimens isn't easy. Museum curators often won't give permission to study the DNA of a museum specimen because part of the specimen must be destroyed to study its genetic material. The mummies of people who lived in Egypt more than 4,400 years ago provided molecular archaeologists with their first look at ancient human DNA.

There are other problems with this type of investigation. The work is painstaking and often frustrating. Because there is so little DNA to work with, it is not always possible to repeat experiments in order to establish confidence in the results. Nevertheless, molecular archaeologists are excited about successes they have had with ancient plant and animal DNA. They are optimistic that their new field will add another dimension to the study of human origins.

ACROSS THE SCIENCES

PHYSICAL SCIENCE • LIFE SCIENCE

Unique Compounds

What makes you unique? Would you believe it's a complex pattern of information found on the deoxyribonucleic acid (DNA) in your cells? Well it is! And by analyzing how this information is arranged, scientists are finding clues about human ancestry.

Mummy Knows Best
If you compare the DNA from an older species and a more recent species, you can tell which traits were passed on. To consider the question of human evolution, scientists must use DNA from older humans—like mummies. Molecular archeologists study DNA from mummies in order to understand human evolution at a molecular level. Since well-preserved DNA fragments from mummies are scarce, you might be wondering why some ancient DNA fragments have been preserved better than others.

Neutralizing Acids
The condition of preserved DNA fragments depends on how the mummy was preserved. The tannic acid—commonly found in peat bogs—that is responsible for preserving mummies destroys DNA. But if there are limestone rocks nearby, the calcium carbonate from these rocks neutralizes the tannic acid, thereby preserving the DNA.

Molecular Photocopying
When scientists find well-preserved DNA, they make copies of it by using a technique called polymerase chain reaction (PCR). PCR takes advantage of *polymerases* to generate copies of DNA fragments. Polymerases are found in all living things, and their job is to make strands of genetic material using existing strands as templates. That is why PCR is also called molecular photocopying. But researchers who use this technique risk contaminating the ancient DNA with their own DNA. If even one skin cell falls into the PCR mixture, the results are ruined.

Mysteries Solved?
PCR has been used to research ancient civilizations and peoples. For example, scientists found an 8,000-year-old human brain in Florida. This brain was preserved well enough for scientists to analyze the DNA and to conclude that today's Native Americans are not direct descendants of this group of people.

PCR has also been used to analyze the culture of ancient peoples. When archeologists tested the pigments used in 4,000-year-old paintings on rocks along the Pecos River, in Texas, they found DNA that was probably from bison. This was an unexpected discovery because there were no bison along the Pecos River when the paintings were made. The archeologists have concluded, therefore, that the artists must have tried very hard to find this specific pigment for their paint. This leads the archeologists to believe that the paintings must have had some spiritual meaning.

On Your Own
▶ Research ways PCR is being used to detect diseases and infections in humans and animals.

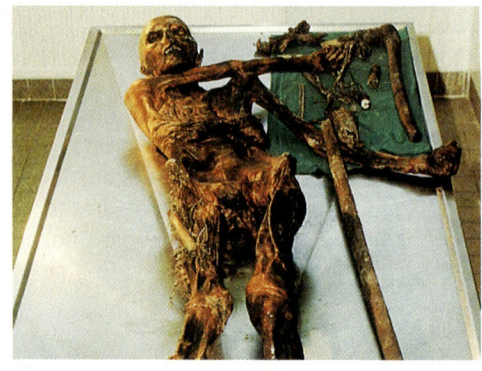

▲ *DNA from mummies like this one provides scientists with valuable information.*

Answers to On Your Own
Answers will vary. Possible answers include the following: PCR is being used to detect Lyme disease, breast cancer, and whooping cough.

WEIRD SCIENCE

THE SECRETS OF SPIDER SILK

What is as strong as steel, more elastic than a rubber band, and able to stop a speeding bullet? Spider silk! Spiders make this silk to weave their delicate but deadly webs.

▲ *A golden orb-weaving spider on its web*

The Tangled Web We Weave

If you've seen a spider web, you've probably noticed that it resembles a bicycle wheel. The "spokes" of the web are made of a silk thread called *dragline silk.* The sticky, stretchy part of the web is called *capture silk* because that's what spiders use to capture their prey. Spider silk is made of proteins, and these proteins are made of blocks of amino acids.

There are 20 naturally occurring amino acids, but spider silk has only seven of them. Until recently, scientists knew what the silk is made of, but they didn't know how these amino acids were distributed throughout the protein chains.

Scientists used a technique called nuclear magnetic resonance (NMR) to see the structure of dragline silk. The silk fiber is made of two tough strands of alanine–rich protein embedded in a glycine–rich substance. If you look at this protein even closer, it looks like tangled spaghetti. Scientists believe that this tangled part makes the silk springy and a repeating sequence of five amino acids makes the protein stretchy.

Spinning Tails

Scientists think they have identified the piece of DNA needed to make spider silk. Synthetic silk can be made by copying a small part of this DNA and inserting it into the bacterium *Escherichia coli.* The bacteria read the gene and make liquid silk protein. Biologists at the University of Wyoming, in Laramie, have come up with a way to spin spider silk into threads by pushing the liquid protein through fine tubes.

What Do You Think?

▶ Scientists seem to think that there are many uses for synthetic spider silk. Make a list in your ScienceLog of as many things as you can think of that this material would be good for.

▲ *Spiders use organs called spinnerets to spin their webs. This image of spinnerets was taken with a scanning electron microscope.*

Answers to What Do You Think?

Answers will vary but may include one or more of the following: clothing, tents, awnings, tarps, car covers, and furniture covers.

Chapter Organizer

CHAPTER ORGANIZATION	TIME MINUTES	OBJECTIVES	LABS, INVESTIGATIONS, AND DEMONSTRATIONS
Chapter Opener pp. 396–397	45	National Standards: UCP 1–3, SAI 1, ST 2, PS 3a, 3e	**Investigate!** Watch Your Headsium! p. 397
Section 1 Radioactivity	90	▶ Compare alpha, beta, and gamma decay. ▶ Describe the penetrating power of the three types of nuclear radiation. ▶ Calculate ages of objects using half-life. ▶ Identify uses of radioactive materials. UCP 1–3, SAI 2, ST 2, SPSP 1, 4, 5, HNS 1–3, PS 3a, 3e	**Demonstration**, p. 398 in ATE
Section 2 Energy from the Nucleus	90	▶ Describe the process of nuclear fission. ▶ Describe the process of nuclear fusion. ▶ Identify advantages and disadvantages of energy from the nucleus. UCP 2, 3, ST 1, 2, SPSP 3–5, HNS 1–3; LabBook UCP 2, 3, SAI 1, 2, PS 3a, 3e	**Demonstration**, p. 406 in ATE **QuickLab**, Gone Fission, p. 407 **Making Models**, Domino Chain Reactions, p. 692 **Datasheets for LabBook**, Domino Chain Reactions, Datasheet 46 **Long-Term Projects & Research Ideas**, Project 66

*See page **T20** for a complete correlation of this book with the*

NATIONAL SCIENCE EDUCATION STANDARDS.

TECHNOLOGY RESOURCES

 Guided Reading Audio CD English or Spanish, Chapter 16

One-Stop Planner CD-ROM with Test Generator

 CNN. Eye on the Environment, Fusion for Power? Segment 21

Chapter 16 • Atomic Energy

CLASSROOM WORKSHEETS, TRANSPARENCIES, AND RESOURCES	SCIENCE INTEGRATION AND CONNECTIONS	REVIEW AND ASSESSMENT
Directed Reading Worksheet 16 **Science Puzzlers, Twisters & Teasers,** Worksheet 16		**Homework,** p. 397 in ATE
Directed Reading Worksheet 16, Section 1 **Transparency 261,** Alpha Decay of Radium-226 **Transparency 261,** Beta Decay of Carbon-14 **Transparency 262,** The Penetrating Abilities of Nuclear Radiation **Math Skills for Science Worksheet 36,** Radioactive Decay and the Half-life **Transparency 263,** Radioactive Decay and Half-life **Reinforcement Worksheet 16,** The Decay of a Nucleus	**Geology Connection,** p. 399 **Real-World Connection,** p. 399 in ATE **Multicultural Connection,** p. 400 in ATE **Cross-Disciplinary Focus,** p. 401 in ATE **Environment Connection,** p. 402 **MathBreak,** How Old Is It? p. 404 **Math and More,** p. 404 in ATE **Connect to Life Science,** p. 405 in ATE	**Homework,** p. 399 in ATE **Self-Check,** p. 400 **Review,** p. 402 **Review,** p. 405 **Quiz,** p. 405 in ATE **Alternative Assessment,** p. 405 in ATE
Directed Reading Worksheet 16, Section 2 **Transparency 264,** Fission of a Uranium-235 Nucleus **Transparency 265,** How a Nuclear Power Plant Works **Critical Thinking Worksheet 16,** The Blue Flame **Transparency 190,** Fusion of Hydrogen in the Sun **Transparency 264,** Fusion of Hydrogen-1 Nuclei **Reinforcement Worksheet 16,** Fission or Fusion?	**Cross-Disciplinary Focus,** p. 407 in ATE **Cross-Disciplinary Focus,** p. 407 in ATE **Real-World Connection,** p. 408 in ATE **Apply,** p. 409 **Connect to Environmental Science,** p. 409 in ATE **Astronomy Connection,** p. 410 **Scientific Debate:** Wasting Yucca Mountain? p. 416 **Careers:** Materials Scientist–Dr. Michael Atzmon, p. 417	**Review,** p. 411 **Quiz,** p. 411 in ATE **Alternative Assessment,** p. 411 in ATE

END-OF-CHAPTER REVIEW AND ASSESSMENT

Chapter Review in Study Guide
Vocabulary and Notes in Study Guide
Chapter Tests with Performance-Based Assessment, Chapter 16 Test
Chapter Tests with Performance-Based Assessment, Performance-Based Assessment 16
Concept Mapping Transparency 16

 Holt, Rinehart and Winston On-line Resources

go.hrw.com

For worksheets and other teaching aids related to this chapter, visit the HRW Web site and type in the keyword: **HSTRAD**

 **National Science Teachers Association**

www.scilinks.org

Encourage students to use the sciLINKS numbers listed in the internet connect boxes to access information and resources on the **NSTA** Web site.

Chapter 16 • Chapter Organizer

Chapter Resources & Worksheets

Visual Resources

TEACHING TRANSPARENCIES

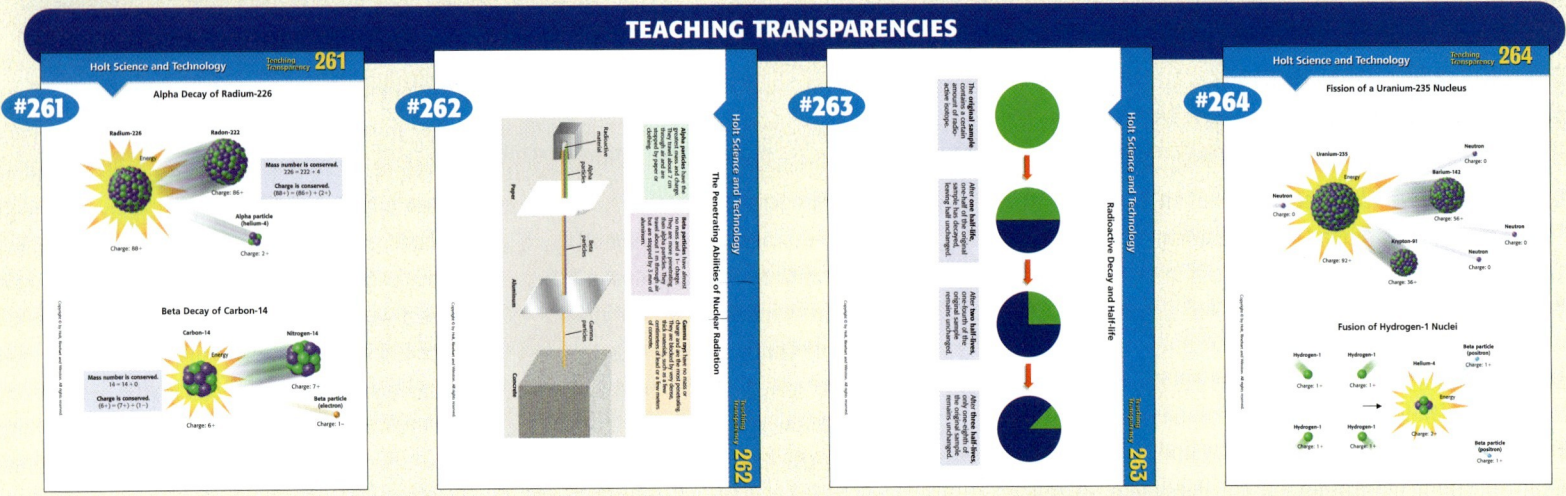

TEACHING TRANSPARENCIES

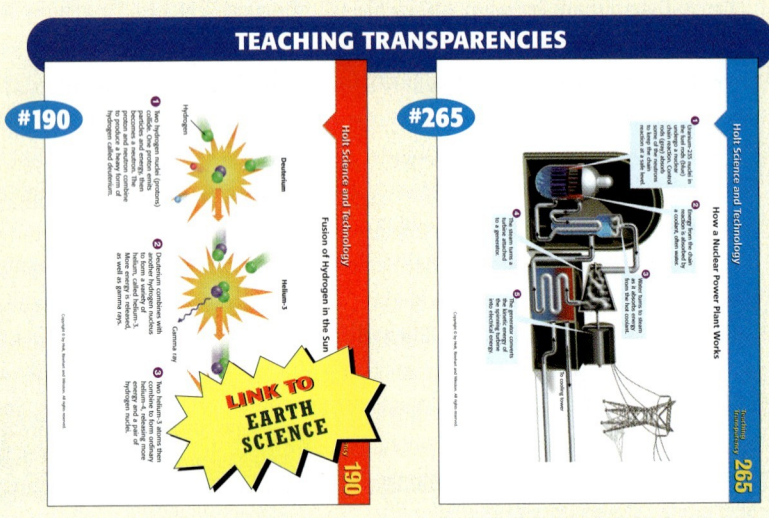

CONCEPT MAPPING TRANSPARENCY

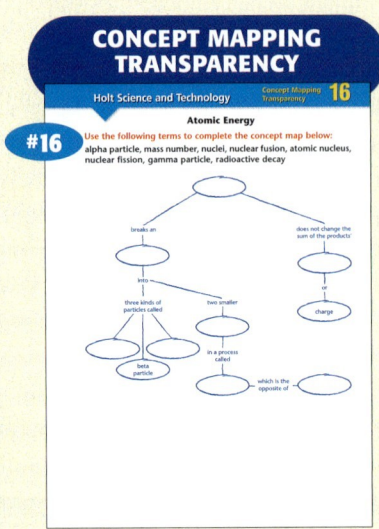

Meeting Individual Needs

DIRECTED READING

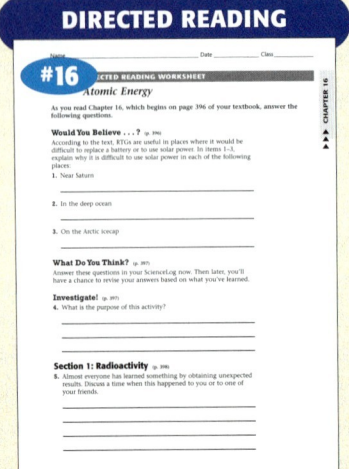

REINFORCEMENT & VOCABULARY REVIEW

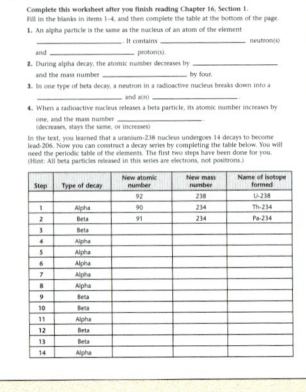

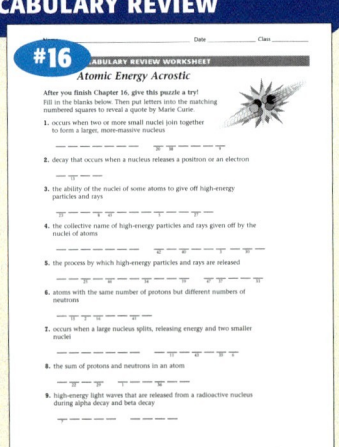

SCIENCE PUZZLERS, TWISTERS & TEASERS

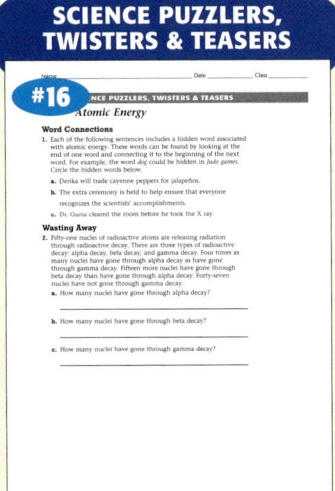

Chapter 16 • Atomic Energy

Chapter 16 • Atomic Energy

Review & Assessment

STUDY GUIDE

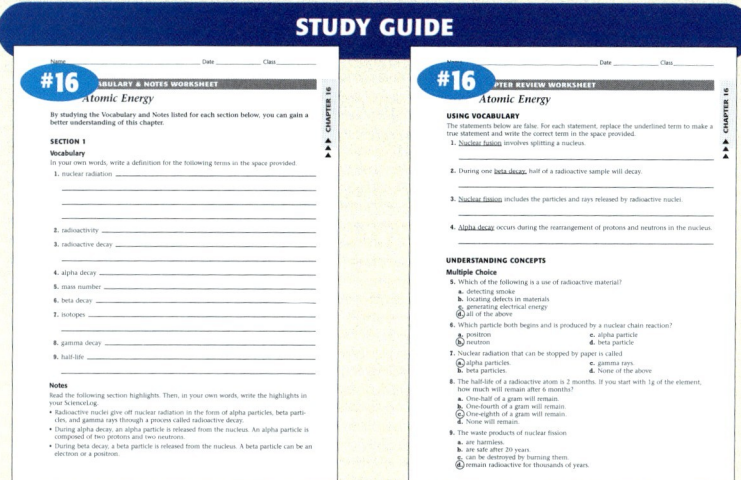

CHAPTER TESTS WITH PERFORMANCE-BASED ASSESSMENT

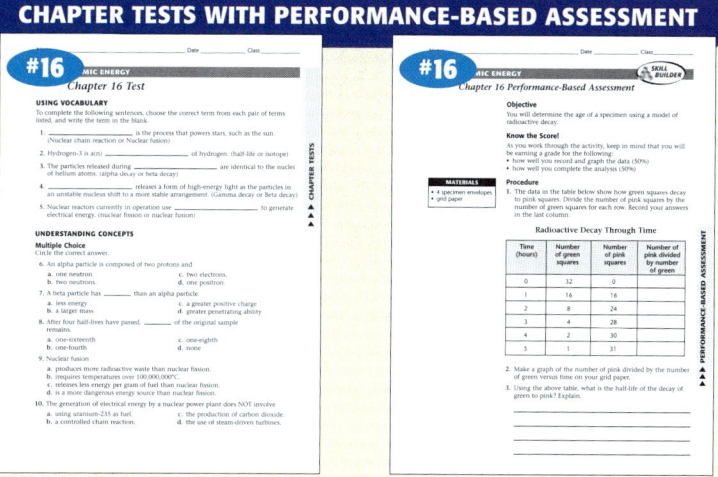

Lab Worksheets

LONG-TERM PROJECTS & RESEARCH IDEAS

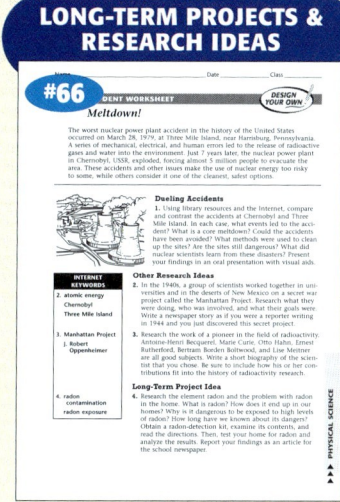

DATASHEETS FOR LABBOOK

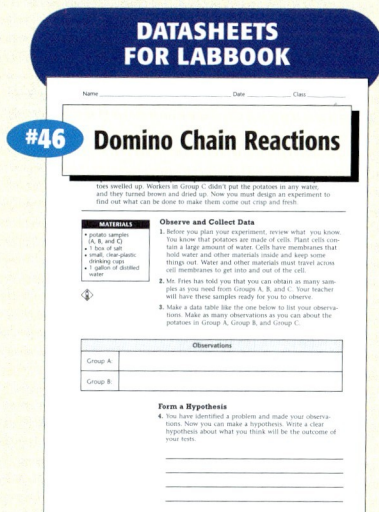

Applications & Extensions

CRITICAL THINKING & PROBLEM SOLVING

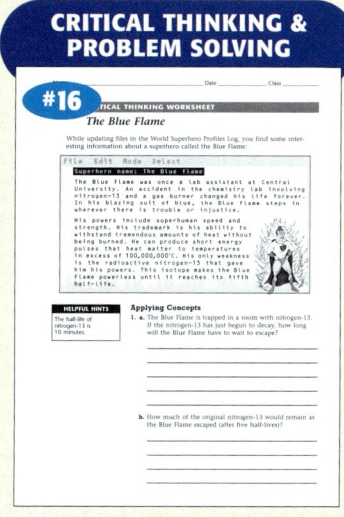

EYE ON THE ENVIRONMENT

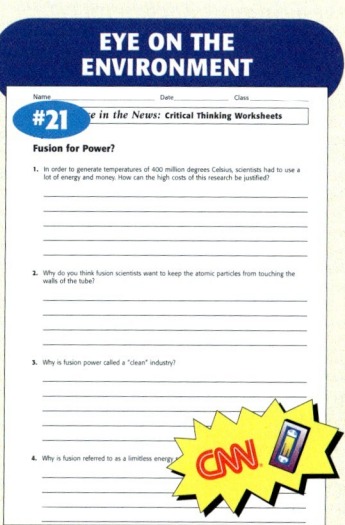

Chapter 16 • Chapter Resources & Worksheets

Chapter Background

SECTION 1

Radioactivity

Before and After Radioactivity

Radioactivity was discovered serendipitously by the French physicist Henri Becquerel (1852–1908) in 1896 while he was searching for evidence of X rays. X rays also had been discovered serendipitously by Wilhelm Conrad Roentgen (1845–1923) the previous year while he was studying cathode-ray tubes.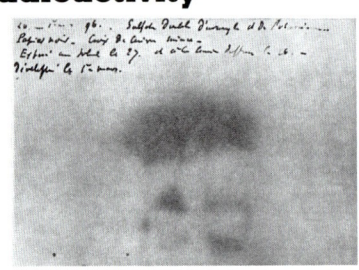

- Soon after Becquerel's discovery, Marie Curie (1867–1934) determined that the element thorium is radioactive. In 1898, Marie and her husband, Pierre (1859–1906), discovered polonium and radium, two new radioactive elements. Eventually, the Curies were able to quantify the amount of energy given off each hour by 1 g of radium—about 418 joules.

- In 1899, a French chemist named André-Louis Debierne (1874–1949) discovered the radioactive element actinium. In 1908, Ernest Rutherford (1871–1934) helped discover that alpha particles were helium nuclei.

IS THAT A FACT!

- Henri Becquerel came from a family of notable scientists. Antoine-César Becquerel (1788–1878), Henri's grandfather, was one of the founders of electrochemistry. Alexandre-Edmond Becquerel (1820–1891), Henri's father, studied light and phosphorescence and invented the phosphoroscope. In fact, Henri discovered radioactivity using the minerals his father had collected and studied.

Alpha, Beta, Gamma

Although there are many types of radiation, the three types discussed in this chapter are alpha particles, beta particles, and gamma rays.

- Alpha particles consist of two protons and two neutrons, which make their mass much greater than that of beta particles. Alpha particles are identical to helium nuclei. Because they have no electrons, they have a 2+ charge. The large size and 2+ charge of alpha particles make them easy to block. Alpha particles can be stopped by a rubber glove or thick paper.

- Beta particles can be positively charged (positrons) or negatively charged (electrons). They can be stopped by wood only a few centimeters thick and by thin sheets of aluminum, iron, and lead.

- Gamma rays are high-energy photons similar to X rays in their effect. They have no mass or charge. All but the highest-energy gamma rays are stopped by thick concrete or thin sheets of lead.

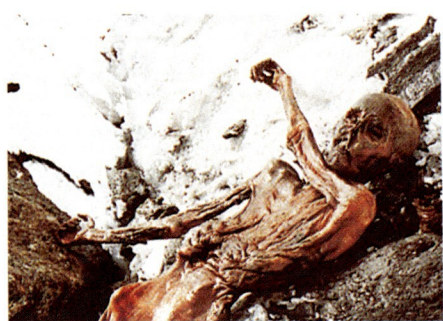

IS THAT A FACT!

- It is fortunate that alpha particles are so easily stopped because they are potentially the most damaging if they enter the body.

Radioactive Decay

The decay of naturally-occurring isotopes is used to date fossils and rocks. The decay of artificially-made isotopes has led to discoveries in nuclear energy, chemistry, and medicine.

- The decay of uranium-238 to lead-206 provides good examples of decay series in nature. Uranium-238 decays through both alpha and beta decays accompanied by gamma decay to its end product, a stable isotope of lead.

Chapter 16 • Atomic Energy

IS THAT A FACT!

▪ The alpha decay of radium-226 forms radon-222, the most abundant isotope of radon. Radon-222 undergoes alpha decay with a half-life of 3.8 days. The alpha particle and the radioactive polonium-198 produced by the decay of radon-222 create a serious lung cancer risk.

SECTION 2

Energy from the Nucleus

▶ **Fission**

The German chemists Otto Hahn (1879–1968) and Fritz Strassmann (1902–1980) were the first to demonstrate the splitting of a nucleus through fission when they bombarded a sample of uranium with neutrons and detected nuclei much smaller than uranium.

- In 1939, this process was identified as nuclear fission by Austrian physicist Lise Meitner (1878–1968) and her nephew Otto Frisch.

- An important characteristic of nuclear fission is the enormous amount of energy that can be produced from a continuous series of fissions called a chain reaction.

IS THAT A FACT!

▪ Controlled chain reactions occur in the reactors of nuclear power plants. Uncontrolled chain reactions occur during the detonation of atomic bombs.

▶ **Fusion**

Usually, two nuclei cannot collide because they are positively charged and repel each other. However, at very high temperature and pressure, nuclei not only collide but fuse together into a larger nucleus.

- Some of the energy released when nuclei fuse is in the form of electromagnetic waves, including visible light. The fusion of hydrogen nuclei to produce helium is the principal source of the energy that is released as light by the sun and other stars.

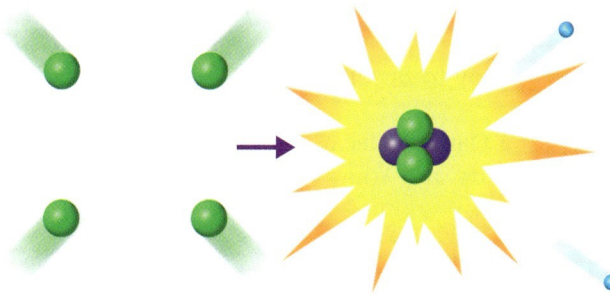

- Nuclear fusion releases less energy per nuclear reaction than does nuclear fission because less matter is converted into energy. However, the energy released per gram of fuel is far greater in the fusion process, because there are many more hydrogen atoms than uranium atoms in equal masses of the two fuels.

- Matter exists only in the plasma state at the extremely high temperatures required to make fusion occur. A chamber called a tokamak was invented in the 1960s to magnetically confine the plasma used for fusion reactions. The confinement prevents the plasma from destroying the tokamak.

IS THAT A FACT!

▪ In 1991, a controlled nuclear fusion reaction at the Joint European Torus Laboratory, in England, generated 1.7 million watts. In 1993, the Tokamak Fusion Test Reactor, at Princeton University, generated a controlled fusion reaction of 5.6 million watts. Unfortunately, both events required more energy than they produced, so fusion as an energy source is not yet practical.

For background information about teaching strategies and issues, refer to the *Professional Reference for Teachers*.

Chapter 16 • Chapter Background   **395F**

CHAPTER 16 Atomic Energy

Chapter Preview

Section 1
Radioactivity
- Discovering Radioactivity
- Nuclear Radiation Is Produced Through Decay
- The Penetrating Power of Radiation
- Nuclei Decay to Become Stable
- Finding a Date by Decay
- Radioactivity and Your World

Section 2
Energy from the Nucleus
- Nuclear Fission
- Nuclear Fusion

 Directed Reading Worksheet 16

 Science Puzzlers, Twisters & Teasers Worksheet 16

 Guided Reading Audio CD English or Spanish, Chapter 16

 Smithsonian Institution® Visit www.si.edu/hrw for additional on-line resources.

Would You Believe . . . ?

Replacing the battery in your camera can be a problem when you're traveling—especially 1.5 billion kilometers (932 million miles) from home! That's how far from Earth the *Cassini* spacecraft will be when it reaches Saturn in 2004. *Cassini*'s camera and other equipment need an energy source that will work after a trip of nearly 7 years. Otherwise, the trip to study the atmosphere and moons of Saturn would be wasted. The answer? the radioactive element plutonium!

The nuclei (plural of *nucleus*) of plutonium atoms are *radioactive,* meaning they are unstable. They become stable by giving off *radiation* in the form of particles and energy. This process heats the materials surrounding the plutonium, and the thermal energy of the materials is converted into electrical energy by a Radioisotope Thermoelectric Generator (RTG). Earlier spacecraft, including *Voyager, Galileo,* and *Ulysses,* have also depended on RTGs for electrical energy.

RTGs are also used on Earth. The deep ocean and the Arctic icecap are two places where RTGs are used in scientific equipment. Because electrical energy can be produced using a sample of plutonium for 10 or more years, RTGs provide energy longer than any battery known, as described below.

In this chapter you will learn more about the energy given off by radioactive materials. In addition, you will learn about the energy associated with the splitting and joining of atomic nuclei. Read on to continue your own journey!

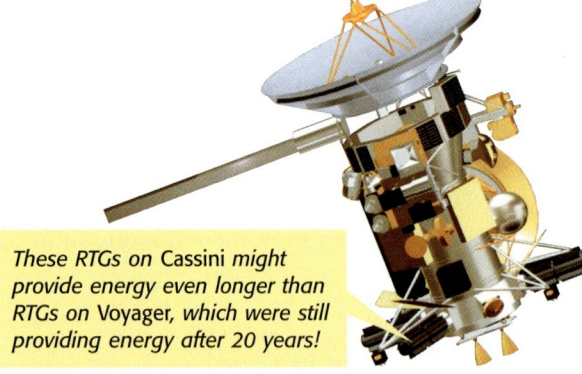

These RTGs on Cassini *might provide energy even longer than RTGs on* Voyager, *which were still providing energy after 20 years!*

Would You Believe . . . ?

The *Galileo* spacecraft, which is powered by a radioisotope thermoelectric generator, has studied Jupiter and its many satellites since 1995. Scientists have learned that one of Jupiter's moons, Ganymede, is covered by clouds of extremely fine dust. These thin clouds were apparently created when small interplanetary meteorites slammed into Ganymede's surface, creating small craters and sending up showers of fine dust. Scientists believe this process may be responsible for the formation of dust rings throughout the solar system, including some of Saturn's rings. Scientists will study information from the *Cassini* spacecraft to find further clues about how Saturn's rings were formed.

What Do You Think?

In your ScienceLog, try to answer the following questions based on what you already know:

1. What is nuclear radiation?
2. How are radioactive materials used?
3. What are two concerns about energy obtained from nuclear reactions?

Investigate!

Watch Your Headsium!

The nuclei of radioactive atoms are unstable. Therefore, they decay and change into different nuclei. In this activity, you will model the decay of unstable nuclei into stable nuclei.

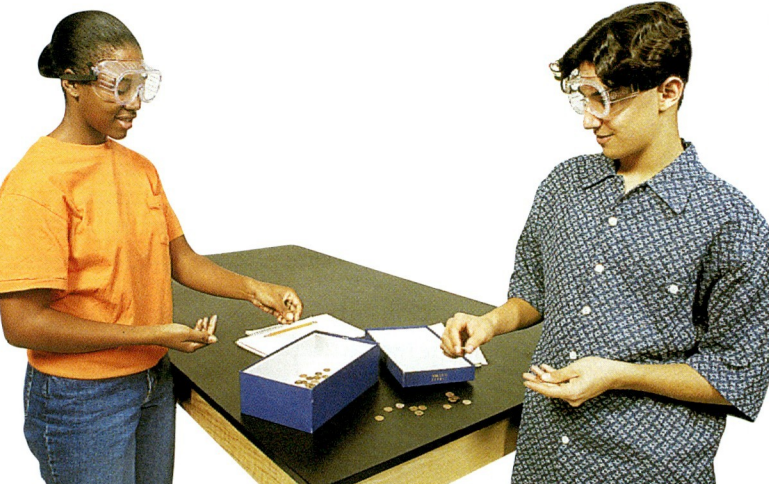

Procedure

1. Place **100 pennies** heads-up in a **box with a lid**. The pennies represent radioactive "headsium" nuclei. Record the 100 headsium nuclei present as Trial 0 in your ScienceLog.
2. Close the box, and shake it vigorously up and down for 5 seconds.
3. Open the box, and remove all of the "tailsium" nuclei, pennies that are tails-up. These pennies represent stable nuclei that result from decay. Count the number of headsium nuclei remaining, and record it in your ScienceLog as Trial 1.
4. Continue performing trials until you have no more pennies in the box or you have finished five trials, whichever comes first. Record all your results.

Analysis

5. On a piece of **graph paper**, graph your data by plotting "Number of headsium nuclei" on the *y*-axis and "Trial number" on the *x*-axis.
6. What trend do you see in the number of headsium nuclei over time?
7. Compare your graph with the graphs of other students in your class. How are the graphs similar? How are they different?

Going Further

In this activity, each trial represents the *half-life* of the unstable nuclei. Use reference books to find out more about half-life and how the length of time associated with the half-lives of unstable nuclei varies.

Homework

Have students research Henri Becquerel and his family or Marie Curie and her family. Becquerel's father and grandfather were scientists, and Curie's husband, Pierre, and her daughter, Irene, were scientists as well. Have students make a poster or a concept map to illustrate the contributions that the Becquerels or the Curies made to science.

What Do You Think?

Accept all reasonable responses. Students will have a chance to revise their answers in the Chapter Review under NOW What Do You Think?

Investigate!

MATERIALS

FOR EACH GROUP:
- 100 pennies
- a box with a lid
- graph paper
- pencil

Safety Caution: Remind students to review all safety cautions and icons before beginning this lab activity.

Teacher Notes: Because the process of radioactive decay modeled by this activity relies on the presence of a large number of nuclei, you might want students to enter their data into a class data table and graph the totals for the class.

Answers to Investigate!

5. Sample graph:

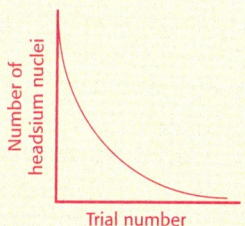

6. The number of headsium nuclei decreases over time. After each trial, the number of headsium nuclei is about half of the previous number.
7. The graphs have the same shape; however, the specific numbers of headsium nuclei at each trial are slightly different.

Chapter 16 • Atomic Energy **397**

SECTION 1

Focus

Radioactivity

In this section, students learn about alpha, beta, and gamma radiation and the penetrating ability of each. Students learn how to use an isotope's half-life to calculate the age of an object and other uses for radioactive materials.

Bellringer

On the board write the following:

> In a few sentences, write what you know about the term *nuclear radiation*. Include any benefits and any dangers you can think of.

1) Motivate

DEMONSTRATION

Display three items for students:
- piece of paper
- sheet of aluminum
- concrete cinder block

Explain to students that they are going to learn about three different types of radiation, and that one type can be stopped by paper, one by aluminum, and the third only by concrete or lead. Ask students what different characteristics of the radiation or of the barrier might be important.

Directed Reading Worksheet 16 Section 1

internetconnect
SCILINKS **TOPIC:** Discovering Radioactivity
GO TO: www.scilinks.org
sciLINKS NUMBER: HSTP380

398 Chapter 16 • Atomic Energy

Section 1

Terms to Learn
nuclear radiation
radioactivity
radioactive decay
alpha decay
mass number
beta decay
isotopes
gamma decay
half-life

What You'll Do
- Compare alpha, beta, and gamma decay.
- Describe the penetrating power of the three types of nuclear radiation.
- Calculate ages of objects using half-life.
- Identify uses of radioactive materials.

Radioactivity

When scientists perform experiments, they don't always get the results they expect. In 1896, a French scientist named Henri Becquerel did not get the results he expected, but he did discover a fascinating new area of science.

Discovering Radioactivity

Becquerel's hypothesis was that fluorescent minerals could give off X rays. (*Fluorescent* materials glow when exposed to light, as shown in **Figure 1.**) To test his hypothesis, Becquerel placed a fluorescent mineral on top of a photographic plate wrapped in paper. He placed the setup in bright sunlight. Becquerel predicted that an image of the mineral would appear on the plate. After developing the plate, he saw the image he expected.

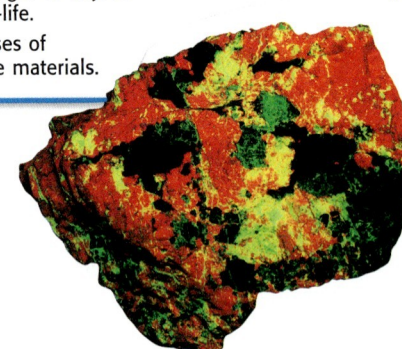

Figure 1 *The brightly colored portions of this sample are fluorescent in ultraviolet light.*

An Unexpected Result Becquerel tried to confirm his results, but cloudy weather delayed his plans. He placed his materials in a drawer. After several days, he developed the plate anyway. He was amazed to see a strong image, shown in **Figure 2.**

Becquerel's results showed that even without light, the mineral gave off energy that passed through paper and made an image on the plate. After more tests, Becquerel concluded that this energy comes from uranium, an element in the mineral.

Naming the Unexpected Scientists call this energy **nuclear radiation**, high-energy particles and rays that are emitted by the nuclei of some atoms. Marie Curie, a scientist working with Becquerel, named the ability of some elements to give off nuclear radiation **radioactivity**.

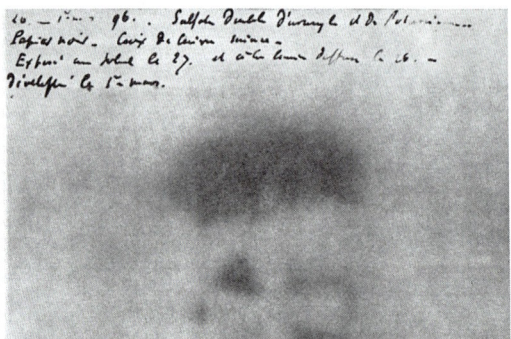

Figure 2 *The blurry image on this photographic plate surprised Becquerel.*

WEIRD SCIENCE

A thorough scientist makes sure the results of an experiment can be repeated. Although Becquerel tried to confirm his results, cloudy weather prevented him from repeating his experiment. So why did he develop the photographic plate anyway? One explanation is that he was scheduled to give a speech on his research the next night, and even a weak image would support his hypothesis. But when he saw a strong image, he realized that something strange and new had happened.

Nuclear Radiation Is Produced Through Decay

Radioactive decay is the process in which the nucleus of a radioactive atom releases nuclear radiation. Three types of radioactive decay are alpha decay, beta decay, and gamma decay.

Alpha Decay The release of an alpha particle from a nucleus is called **alpha decay**. An *alpha particle* consists of two protons and two neutrons, so it has a mass number of 4 and a charge of 2+. An alpha particle is identical to the nucleus of a helium atom. Many large radioactive nuclei give off alpha particles to become nuclei of atoms of different elements. One example is radium-226. (Remember that the number that follows the name of an element indicates the **mass number**—the sum of the protons and neutrons in an atom.)

Conservation in Decay Look at the model of alpha decay in **Figure 3**. This model illustrates two important features of all types of radioactive decay. First, the mass number is conserved. The sum of the mass numbers of the starting materials is always equal to the sum of the mass numbers of the products. Second, charge is conserved. The sum of the charges of the starting materials is always equal to the sum of the charges of the products.

Geology CONNECTION

Alpha particles emitted during alpha decay eventually gain two electrons from nearby atoms and become helium atoms. Almost all of the helium in Earth's atmosphere formed from alpha particles emitted by nuclei of radioactive atoms.

Figure 3 Alpha Decay of Radium-226

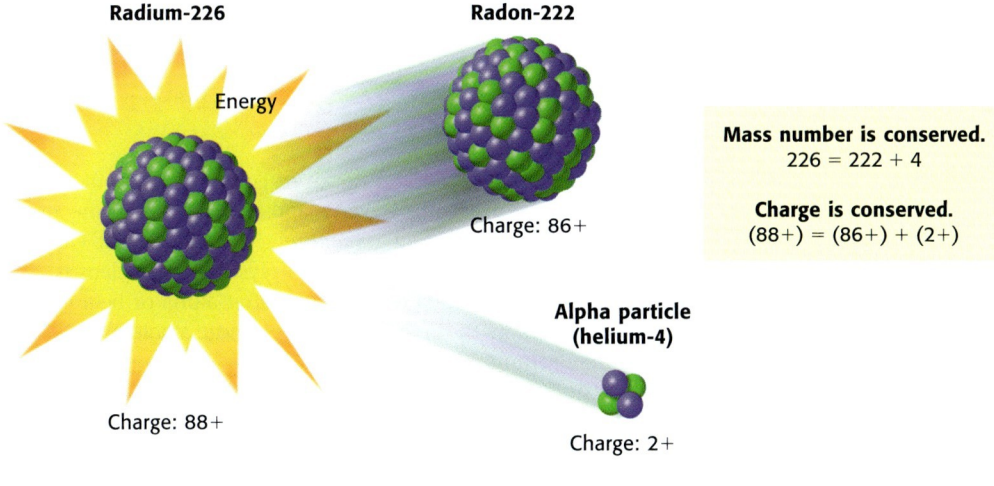

Mass number is conserved.
226 = 222 + 4

Charge is conserved.
(88+) = (86+) + (2+)

IS THAT A FACT!
A bacterium can withstand many more times the radiation dosage that would be fatal to a human.

SCIENCE HUMOR
Q: Why did the unstable nucleus use toothpaste?

A: It wanted to prevent decay.

---

2) Teach

READING STRATEGY

Prediction Guide Before students read this section, have them write a few sentences explaining what radioactive decay is. Ask students to write what they know about alpha particles, beta particles, and gamma rays. Discuss their ideas with them as they begin the section.

REAL-WORLD CONNECTION

Humans are exposed daily to radiation from many sources. The better part of this radiation is from natural sources, including radioactive elements in the Earth and radiation from space and from the sun. There are even radioactive elements in the human body! Only 18 percent of the radiation a person receives in a year comes from artificial sources, such as medical X rays.

Homework

Ask students to make models or posters representing alpha particles, beta particles, and gamma rays. They must show the differences between the three types of radiation. Encourage students to be creative in their choice of materials and in their method of display.

Teaching Transparency 261
"Alpha Decay of Radium-226"

TOPIC: Radioactive Isotopes
GO TO: www.scilinks.org
*sci*LINKS NUMBER: HSTP385

Section 1 • Radioactivity

2 Teach, continued

USING THE FIGURES

Concept Mapping Review **Figures 3, 4,** and **5** with students, and discuss the differences between alpha, beta, and gamma radiation. Have students create a concept map in their ScienceLog showing the differences between these three types of radiation. **Sheltered English**

MEETING INDIVIDUAL NEEDS

Learners Having Difficulty Ask a local radiology clinic for some sample X-ray images to show students. Remove identifying marks from the films before using them in class. Remind students that X rays are similar to gamma rays, but that gamma rays have higher penetrating ability and energy than X rays. Ask students why some structures appear brighter than others on an X-ray image. (Denser structures and tissues absorb more X rays and therefore appear brighter in the image.)

Answer to Self-Check
alpha particles

Teaching Transparency 261
"Beta Decay of Carbon-14"

BRAIN FOOD

Alpha and beta decay result in one element changing into another element, a process known as *transmutation*. Scientists can perform artificial transmutations by smashing particles into nuclei at high speeds. All elements with an atomic number greater than 94 were created through this process.

✓ **Self-Check**
Which type of nuclear radiation has the largest mass number? (See page 724 to check your answer.)

Beta Decay The release of a beta particle from a nucleus is called **beta decay**. A *beta particle* can be either an electron (having a charge of 1– and a mass of almost 0) or a *positron* (having a charge of 1+ and a mass of almost 0). Because electrons and positrons do not contain protons or neutrons, the mass number of a beta particle is 0.

Two Types of Beta Decay A carbon-14 nucleus undergoes beta decay as shown in the model in **Figure 4**. During this decay, a neutron breaks into a proton and an electron. Notice that the nucleus becomes a nucleus of a different element, and mass number and charge are conserved, similar to alpha decay.

Not all isotopes of an element decay in the same way. (Remember that **isotopes** are atoms that have the same number of protons but different numbers of neutrons.) A carbon-11 nucleus undergoes beta decay when a proton breaks into a positron and a neutron. However, the beta decay of carbon-11 still changes the nucleus into a nucleus of a different element while conserving both mass number and charge.

Figure 4 Beta Decay of Carbon-14

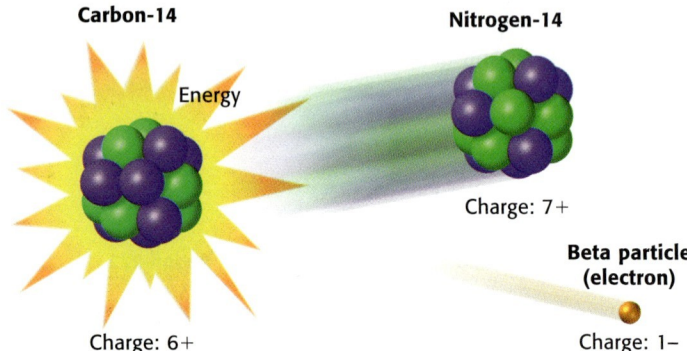

Mass number is conserved.
14 = 14 + 0

Charge is conserved.
(6+) = (7+) + (1–)

Gamma Decay Did you notice in Figures 3 and 4 that energy is released during alpha decay and beta decay? Some of this energy is in the form of *gamma rays*, a form of light with very high energy. The release of gamma rays from a nucleus is called **gamma decay**. Gamma decay occurs after alpha or beta decay as the particles in the nucleus shift to a more stable arrangement. Because gamma rays have no mass or charge, gamma decay alone does not cause one element to change into another as do alpha decay and beta decay.

 **Multicultural CONNECTION**

Early discoveries of radiation and nuclear energy were made by scientists all over the world. For example, Wilhelm Conrad Roentgen did his research in Germany; the Curies and Henri Becquerel worked in France; and Ernest Rutherford and Frederick Soddy experimented in England. Other discoveries were made in Canada, Sweden, New Zealand, Japan, and the United States.

The Penetrating Power of Radiation

The three forms of nuclear radiation differ in their ability to penetrate (go through) matter. This difference is due to the mass and charge associated with each type of radiation, as you can see in **Figure 5.**

Figure 5 The Penetrating Abilities of Nuclear Radiation

Alpha particles have the greatest charge and mass. They travel about 7 cm through air and are stopped by paper or clothing.

Beta particles have a 1– or 1+ charge and almost no mass. They are more penetrating than alpha particles. They travel about 1 m through air, but are stopped by 3 mm of aluminum.

Gamma rays have no charge or mass and are the most penetrating. They are blocked by very dense, thick materials, such as a few centimeters of lead or a few meters of concrete.

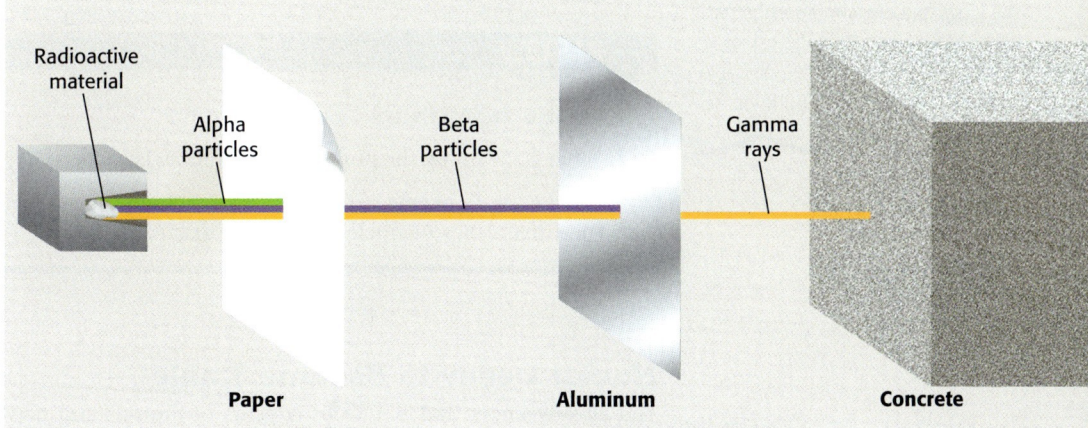

Effects of Radiation on Matter Nuclear radiation can "knock" electrons out of atoms and break chemical bonds between atoms. Both of these actions can cause damage to living and nonliving matter.

Damage to Living Matter When an organism absorbs radiation, its cells can be damaged, causing burns similar to those caused by touching a hot object. A single large exposure to radiation can lead to *radiation sickness*. Symptoms of this condition range from fatigue and loss of appetite to hair loss, destruction of blood cells, and even death. Exposure to radiation can also increase the risk of cancer because of the damage done to cells.

BRAIN FOOD

Marie and Irene Curie died of leukemia, a type of cancer in which abnormal white blood cells multiply and interfere with the body's immune system. It is thought that exposure to radiation caused their leukemia.

IS THAT A FACT!

Wilhelm Conrad Roentgen, Henri Becquerel, and the Curies all have units of radiation measurement named after them.

- A *curie* (Ci) equals 3.7×10^{10} decays per second—approximately the activity of 1 g of radium.
- The SI designation for the curie is the *becquerel* (Bq), which equals one disintegration per second.
- The *roentgen* or *radiation unit* (rad) is used to express the dose of energy absorbed from radiation per kilogram of material.

2) Teach, continued

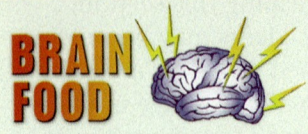

Natural radioactivity exists even in the food you eat. Potassium-40 and radium-226 are two radioactive isotopes found in food. Though these isotopes exist in extremely small amounts in foods, the variation between different foods is astounding; for example, 1 kg of fruit has an activity of 620–3,700 pCi of potassium-40. Brazil nuts have an activity of about 5,600 pCi of potassium-40 per kilogram!

SCIENTISTS AT ODDS

Most scientists think that the majority of lung cancer cases in the United States can be attributed to cigarette smoking. However, some scientists think that radon is responsible for some cases of lung cancer. Because some people are exposed to both cigarette smoke and radon, it may be impossible to determine exactly how many instances of lung cancer are caused by exposure to radon. Scientific estimates vary widely.

Environment CONNECTION

Radioactive radon-222 forms from the radioactive decay of uranium found in soil and rocks. Because radon is a gas, it can enter buildings through gaps in the walls and floors. If radon is inhaled, the alpha particles emitted through alpha decay can damage sensitive lung tissue. In addition, solid polonium forms as radon decays. The polonium stays in the lungs and emits more alpha particles, greatly increasing the risk of cancer. Radon detectors are available to monitor radon levels in the home.

Damage to Nonliving Matter Radiation can also damage nonliving matter. When radiation knocks electrons out of metal atoms, the metal is weakened. The metal structures of buildings, such as nuclear power plants, can become unsafe. High levels of radiation, such as gamma rays from the sun, can damage space vehicles.

Damage at Different Depths Because gamma rays are the most penetrating nuclear radiation, they can cause damage deep within an object. Beta particles cause damage closer to the surface, while alpha particles cause damage very near the surface. However, if a source of alpha particles enters an organism, alpha particles cause the most damage because they are the largest and most massive radiation.

REVIEW

1. What is radioactivity?
2. What is meant by the phrase "mass number is conserved"?
3. **Comparing Concepts** Compare the penetrating power of the three types of nuclear radiation discussed.

Nuclei Decay to Become Stable

You already know that a nucleus consists of protons and neutrons together in a very small space. Protons have a positive charge, so they repel one another. (Remember, opposite charges attract, but like charges repel.) Why don't the protons fly apart? Because of the *strong force*, an attractive force that holds the protons and neutrons together in the nucleus.

Polonium atomic number 84

Too Many Protons The strong force acts only at extremely short distances. As a result, a large nucleus, as modeled in **Figure 6**, is often radioactive. In fact, all nuclei composed of more than 83 protons are radioactive. There are simply too many protons. Although some of these nuclei can exist for billions of years before they decay, they do eventually decay and are therefore called *unstable*.

Figure 6 This nucleus is unstable, or radioactive, because the repulsion between the protons overcomes the strong force.

Answers to Review

1. Radioactivity is the ability of some elements to give off nuclear radiation.
2. Mass number is conserved when the sum of the mass numbers of the starting materials is equal to the sum of the mass numbers of the products.
3. Alpha particles are the least penetrating and are stopped by paper or clothing. Beta particles are more penetrating than alpha particles and are stopped by thin sheets of aluminum. Gamma rays are the most penetrating and are stopped by materials such as lead or concrete.

Ratio of Neutrons to Protons A nucleus can also be unstable if it contains too many or too few neutrons compared with protons. Nuclei with more than 60 protons are stable when the ratio of neutrons to protons is about 3 to 2. Nuclei with fewer than 20 protons only need a ratio of about 1 to 1 for stability. This explains the existence of small radioactive isotopes, like the ones modeled in **Figure 7.**

How Does a Nucleus Become Stable? An unstable nucleus will emit (give off) nuclear radiation until it has a stable number of neutrons and protons. An unstable nucleus doesn't always achieve stability through one decay. In fact, some nuclei are just the first in a series of radioactive isotopes formed as a result of alpha and beta decays. Eventually, a nonradioactive nucleus is formed. The nuclei of the most common isotope of uranium, uranium-238, forms the nonradioactive nuclei of lead-206 after a series of 14 decays.

Hydrogen-3
2 neutrons
1 proton

Beryllium-10
6 neutrons
4 protons

Figure 7 *The ratio of neutrons to protons in hydrogen-3 and beryllium-10 is greater than 1 to 1. Therefore, the nuclei of these isotopes are unstable.*

Finding a Date by Decay

Finding a date for someone can be challenging—especially if they are several thousand years old! When hikers in the Italian Alps found the remains shown in **Figure 8** in 1991, scientists were able to estimate the time of death—about 5,300 years ago! How did they do this? The decay of radioactive carbon was the key.

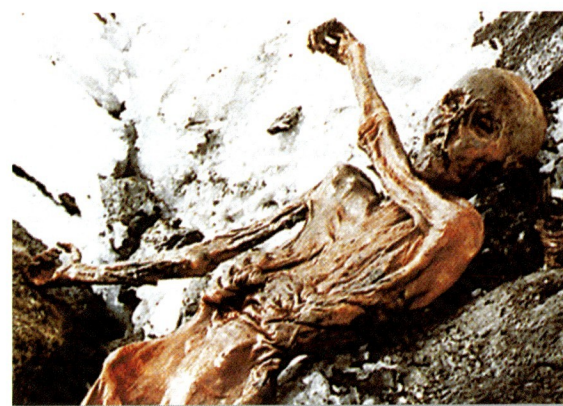

Figure 8 *The remains of the Iceman, a 5,300-year-old mummy, are the best preserved of a human from that time.*

Carbon-14—It's in You! Carbon atoms are found in all living things. A small percentage of these atoms are radioactive carbon-14 atoms. During an organism's life, the percentage of carbon-14 in the organism stays about the same because the atoms that decay are replaced by atoms taken in from the atmosphere by plants or from food by animals. But when an organism dies, the carbon-14 is no longer replaced. Over time, the level of carbon-14 in the remains drops through decay.

 **WEIRD SCIENCE**

The Iceman, shown in **Figure 8,** was frozen in a glacier in the European Alps at an altitude of 3,200 m and was preserved for 5,300 years in the ice. To continue to preserve the Iceman, the Institute for Anatomy, in Innsbruck, Austria, keeps the Iceman in a cooler that simulates the temperature and environmental conditions of the glacier. If the first cooler fails, a second one is ready as a backup. If the Iceman were allowed to warm up, he would begin to decompose.

3) Extend

MATH and MORE

Using the table on this page, present the following problem to students:

1. A 20 g nitrogen-13 sample is prepared for an experiment. If a scientist begins the experiment 20 min later, how many grams of nitrogen-13 remain? (5 grams)

2. At the end of the experiment, if only 2.5 g of nitrogen-13 remain, how much time has passed from the time the sample was prepared? (One-eighth of the original sample remains, so 3 half-lives have passed. The total time since the sample was prepared is 30 minutes (3 × 10 minutes).

 Math Skills Worksheet 36 "Radioactive Decay and the Half-life"

GOING FURTHER

Arrange a trip to a local history museum. Discuss the dating methods that might have been used to date the artifacts on exhibit. Alternatively, collect photographs from natural history magazines and discuss dating methods.

Answer to MATHBREAK
3 × 5,730 years = 17,190 years

Decay Occurs at a Steady Rate Scientists have determined that every 5,730 years, half of the carbon-14 in a sample decays. The rate of decay is constant and is not affected by other conditions, such as temperature or pressure. Each radioactive isotope has its own rate of decay, called half-life. A **half-life** is the amount of time it takes for one-half of the nuclei of a radioactive isotope to decay. **Figure 9** is a model of this process. The table below lists some radioactive isotopes with a wide range of half-lives.

Figure 9 Half of any radioactive sample decays during each half-life.

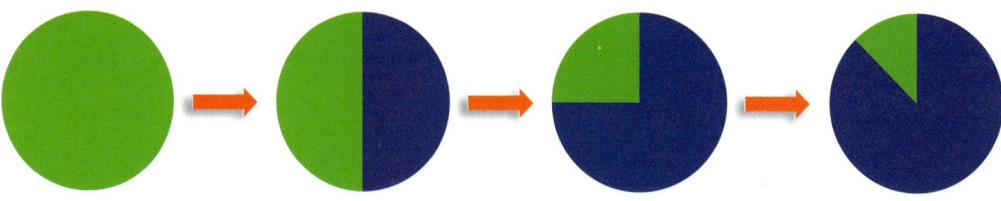

The **original sample** contains a certain amount of radioactive isotope.

After **one half-life**, one-half of the original sample has decayed, leaving half unchanged.

After **two half-lives**, one-fourth of the original sample remains unchanged.

After **three half-lives**, only one-eighth of the original sample remains unchanged.

MATH BREAK

How Old Is It?
An antler has one-fourth of its original carbon-14 unchanged. As shown in Figure 9, two half-lives have occurred. To determine the age of the antler, multiply the number of half-lives that have passed by the length of a half-life. The antler's age is two times the half-life of carbon-14:

2 × 5,730 years = 11,460 years

Now It's Your Turn
Determine the age of a spear containing one-eighth its original amount of carbon-14.

Examples of Half-lives

Isotope	Half-life	Isotope	Half-life
Uranium-238	4.5 billion years	Polonium-210	138 days
Oxygen-21	3.14 seconds	Nitrogen-13	10 minutes
Hydrogen-3	12.3 years	Calcium-36	0.1 second

Determining Age By measuring the number of decays each minute, scientists determined that a little less than half of the carbon-14 in the Iceman's body had decayed. This means that not quite one complete half-life (5,730 years) had passed since he died. You can try your hand at determining ages with the MathBreak at left.

Carbon-14 can be used to determine the age of objects up to 50,000 years old. To calculate the age of older objects, other elements must be used. For example, potassium-40, with a half-life of 1.3 billion years, is used to date dinosaur fossils.

 Teaching Transparency 263 "Radioactive Decay and Half-life"

 Reinforcement Worksheet 16 "The Decay of a Nucleus"

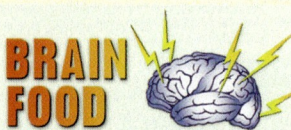

The half-life of some isotopes is only a few seconds. Some of these isotopes occur naturally as a result of the radioactive decay of other nuclei.

Radioactivity and Your World

Although radioactivity can be dangerous, it also has positive uses. Most medical and industrial uses involve small amounts of nuclei with very short half-lives, so human exposure is low. Keep in mind that there are risks involved, but often, the benefits outweigh the risks.

Uses of Radioactivity You have learned how radioactive isotopes are used to determine the age of objects. Some isotopes can be used as *tracers*—radioactive elements whose paths can be followed through a process or reaction. Tracers help farmers determine how well plants take in elements from fertilizers. Tracers also help doctors diagnose medical problems, as shown in **Figure 10**. Radiation detectors are needed to locate the radioactive material in the organism.

Radioactive isotopes can also help detect defects in structures. For example, radiation is used to test the thickness of metal sheets as they are made. Another structure-testing use of radioactive isotopes is shown in **Figure 11**. More uses of radioactive isotopes are listed in the chart below.

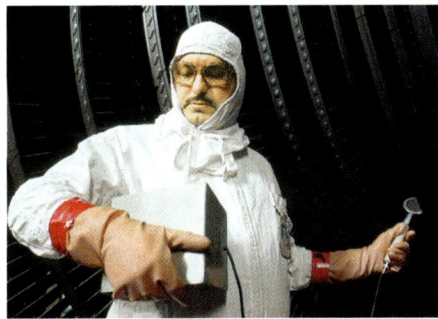

Figure 10 This scan of a thyroid was made using radioactive iodine-131. The dark area shows the location of a tumor.

Figure 11 Engineers can find weak spots in materials and leaks in pipes by detecting a tracer using a Geiger counter.

More Uses of Radioactive Isotopes	
■ Killing cancer cells	■ Detecting smoke
■ Sterilizing food and health-care products	■ Powering space probes

REVIEW

1. What is a half-life?
2. Give two examples each of how radioactivity is useful and how it is harmful.
3. How many half-lives have passed if a sample contains one-eighth of its original amount of radioactive material?
4. **Doing Calculations** A rock contains one-fourth of its original amount of potassium-40. Calculate the rock's age if the half-life of potassium-40 is 1.3 billion years.

internet connect

SC/LINKS NSTA

TOPIC: Discovering Radioactivity, Radioactive Isotopes
GO TO: www.scilinks.org
*sci*LINKS NUMBER: HSTP380, HSTP385

Section 2

Energy from the Nucleus

Terms to Learn
nuclear fission
nuclear chain reaction
nuclear fusion

What You'll Do
- Describe the process of nuclear fission.
- Describe the process of nuclear fusion.
- Identify advantages and disadvantages of energy from the nucleus.

From an early age, you were probably told not to play with fire. But fire itself is neither good nor bad, it simply has benefits and hazards. Likewise, getting energy from the nucleus has benefits and hazards. In this section you will learn about two methods used to get energy from the nucleus—fission and fusion. Gaining an understanding of their advantages and disadvantages is important for people who will make decisions regarding the use of this energy—people like you!

Nuclear Fission

Not all unstable nuclei decay by releasing an alpha or beta particle or gamma rays. The nuclei of some atoms decay by breaking into two smaller, more stable nuclei during a process called nuclear fission. **Nuclear fission** is the process in which a large nucleus splits into two smaller nuclei with the release of energy.

The nuclei of uranium atoms, as well as the nuclei of other large atoms, can undergo nuclear fission naturally. They can also be made to undergo fission by hitting them with neutrons, as shown by the model in **Figure 12**.

Figure 12 Fission of a Uranium-235 Nucleus

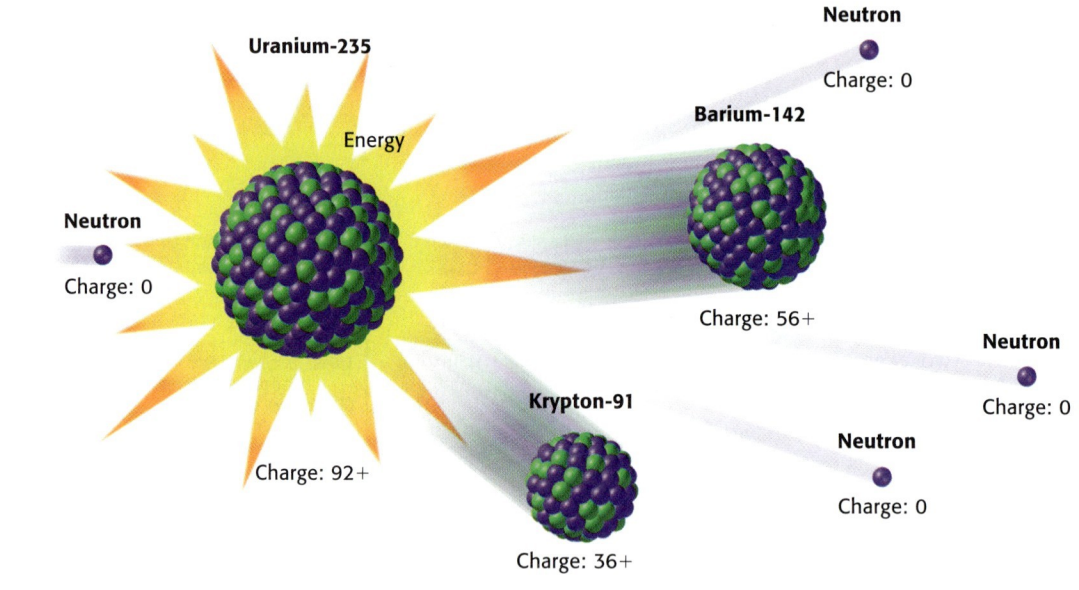

SCIENTISTS AT ODDS

Some scientists proposed that element 105, first synthesized in 1967, be named hahnium, in honor of Otto Hahn, a German chemist who helped to discover nuclear fission. Other scientists proposed other names for the element. The dispute has finally been resolved, and element 105 is now officially known as Dubnium (Db), after the Russian city of Dubna, where the element was first created.

Energy from Matter Did you know that matter can be changed into energy? It's true! If you could determine the total mass of the products in Figure 12 and compare it with the total mass of the reactants, you would find something strange. The products have a tiny bit less mass than the reactants. Why are the masses different? Some of the matter was converted into energy.

The amount of energy released when a single uranium nucleus splits is not very great. But, keep in mind that this energy comes from an incredibly tiny amount of matter—about one-fifth of the mass of a hydrogen atom, the smallest atom that exists. In **Figure 13** you'll see an example of how small amounts of matter can yield large amounts of energy through nuclear fission.

Figure 13 *The nuclear fission of the uranium nuclei in one fuel pellet releases as much energy as the chemical change of burning about 1,000 kg of coal!*

Nuclear Chain Reactions Look at Figure 12 again. Suppose that two or three of the neutrons produced split other uranium-235 nuclei, which released energy and some neutrons. And then suppose that two or three of *those* neutrons split other nuclei, and so on. This situation is one type of **nuclear chain reaction**—a continuous series of nuclear fission reactions. A model of an uncontrolled chain reaction is shown in **Figure 14**.

Figure 14 *A chain reaction results in the release of an enormous amount of energy.*

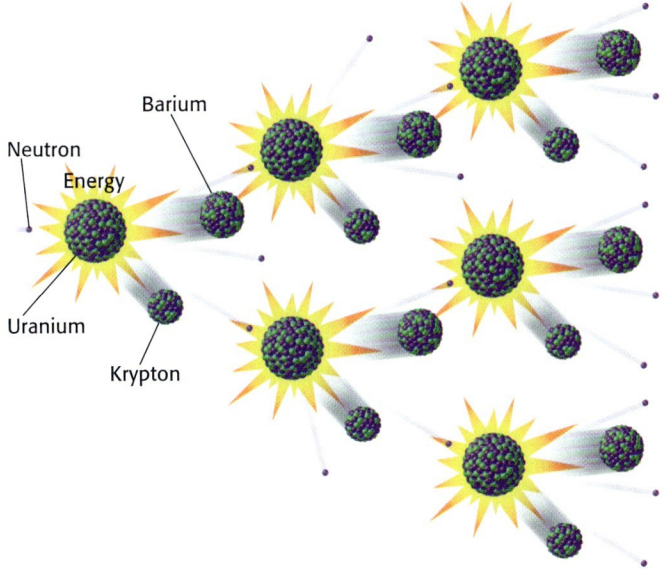

QuickLab

Gone Fission

1. Make two paper balls from a **sheet of paper.**
2. Stand in a group, arm's length apart, with your classmates.
3. Your teacher will gently toss one paper ball into the group. If you are touched by a ball, gently toss your paper balls into the group.
4. Explain how this activity is a model of a chain reaction. Be sure to explain what the students and the paper balls represent.

History The first uncontrolled nuclear chain reaction occurred on July 16, 1945, when the world's first atomic bomb was detonated in the desert of New Mexico. This explosion was a test to determine whether the atomic bombs designed by a group of scientists working on the top-secret Manhattan Project would work. In a blinding flash of light the uncontrolled fission reaction produced a blast that was equal to exploding 22,000 tons of TNT. Only a few weeks after this test, two atomic bombs were dropped on cities in Japan to end World War II.

2) Teach, continued

PG 692
Domino Chain Reactions

USING THE FIGURE

There are several types of nuclear reactors. The one shown in **Figure 15** is a pressurized water reactor. This reactor uses water under high pressure as a coolant. The pressure allows the water to become superheated without turning into steam. Another type of reactor uses water as a coolant but allows the water to boil and turn to steam.

REAL-WORLD CONNECTION

The waste produced in nuclear reactors consists of many different radioactive isotopes of different elements. Some of these isotopes have short half-lives, causing radiation levels to drop rapidly. However, other isotopes may have half-lives of hundreds or even thousands of years. These isotopes require long-term storage before the levels of radiation fall to acceptable levels.

Teaching Transparency 265
"How a Nuclear Power Plant Works"

internetconnect
TOPIC: Nuclear Reactors
GO TO: www.scilinks.org
sciLINKS NUMBER: HSTP395

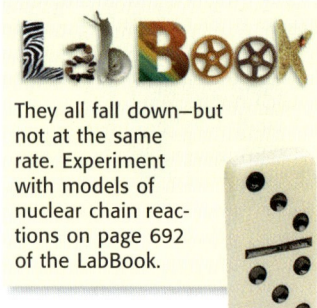
They all fall down—but not at the same rate. Experiment with models of nuclear chain reactions on page 692 of the LabBook.

Energy from a Chain Reaction In an uncontrolled chain reaction, huge amounts of energy are released very quickly. In fact, the tremendous energy of an atomic bomb is the result of an uncontrolled chain reaction. In contrast, nuclear power plants use controlled chain reactions. The energy released from the nuclei in the uranium fuel is used to generate electrical energy. **Figure 15** shows how a nuclear power plant works.

Nuclear Versus Fossil Fuel Although nuclear power plants are more expensive to build than power plants using fossil fuels, they are often less expensive to operate because less fuel is needed. Also, nuclear power plants do not release gases, such as carbon dioxide, into the atmosphere. The use of fission extends our supply of fossil fuels. However, the supply of uranium is limited. Many nations rely on nuclear power to supply their energy needs. Nuclear power plants provide about 20 percent of the electrical energy used in the United States.

Figure 15 How a Nuclear Power Plant Works

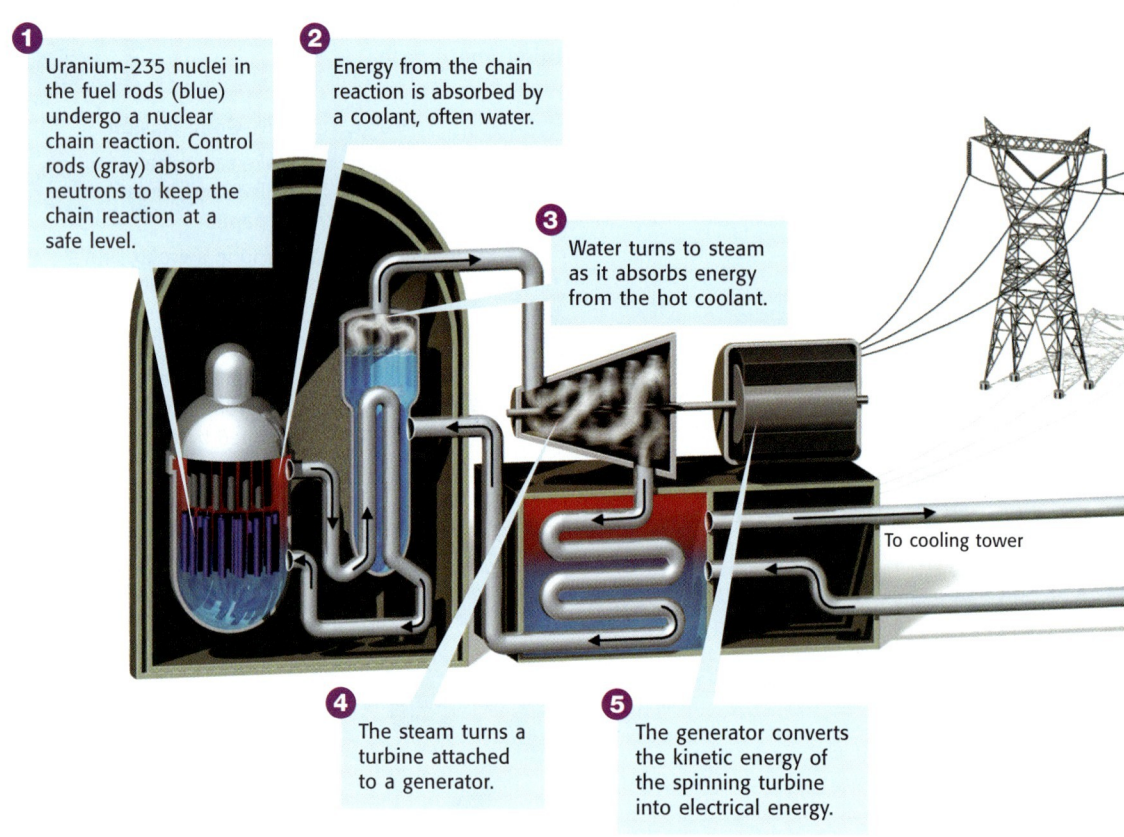

① Uranium-235 nuclei in the fuel rods (blue) undergo a nuclear chain reaction. Control rods (gray) absorb neutrons to keep the chain reaction at a safe level.

② Energy from the chain reaction is absorbed by a coolant, often water.

③ Water turns to steam as it absorbs energy from the hot coolant.

④ The steam turns a turbine attached to a generator.

⑤ The generator converts the kinetic energy of the spinning turbine into electrical energy.

To cooling tower

IS THAT A FACT!
The United States has the largest number of operational nuclear power plants in the world (more than 100). The country that comes closest to the United States is France, with 56 reactors; however, France is only about one-seventeenth the area of the United States.

SCIENCE HUMOR
Q: Why did the student bring a rod and reel to class?

A: The teacher said they would be studying fission.

408 Chapter 16 • Atomic Energy

Accidents Can Happen With the advantages described, why is fission not more widely used? Well, there are risks involved with generating electrical energy from fission. Probably the most immediate concern is the possibility of an accident. This fear was realized in Chernobyl, Ukraine, on April 26, 1986, as shown in **Figure 16.** An explosion released large amounts of radioactive uranium fuel and waste products into the atmosphere. The cloud of radioactive material spread over most of Europe and Asia and even reached as far as North America.

Figure 16 *During a test at the Chernobyl nuclear power plant, the emergency protection system was turned off. The reactor overheated, resulting in an explosion.*

What Waste! Another concern is nuclear waste, including used fuel rods, chemicals used to process uranium, and even shoe covers and overalls worn by workers. Although artificial fission has been carried out for only about 50 years, the waste will give off high levels of radiation for thousands of years. The rate of radioactive decay cannot be changed, so the waste must be stored until it becomes less radioactive. Most of the used fuel rods are stored in huge vats of water. Some of the liquid wastes are stored in underground tanks. However, scientists continue to look for more long-term storage solutions.

What would you say if a nuclear waste storage facility was planned near your town? Read about the debate over Yucca Mountain on page 416.

CONNECT TO ENVIRONMENTAL SCIENCE

Many environmentalists and ecologists share concerns for the flora and fauna in areas around nuclear power plants. Have students research the issues raised by ecologists regarding nuclear power plants. Encourage them to be creative in their presentations. **Sheltered English**

Answer to APPLY

Accept all reasonable answers. Student answers should address the need to keep the radioactive waste away from humans and protected from natural events such as floods, earthquakes, and extreme temperatures for thousands of years.

Critical Thinking Worksheet 16 "The Blue Flame"

Storage Site Selection

A law that passed in 1987 requires the United States government to build a large underground storage facility to store nuclear waste. Imagine that you are a scientist in charge of finding a location for the site. Describe the characteristics of a good location. Keep in mind that the waste will need to be stored for a very long time without escaping into the environment.

The first nuclear-powered submarine was the USS *Nautilus*. The *Nautilus* made its first sea run on January 17, 1955. Because a nuclear generator requires no oxygen, a nuclear-powered submarine can remain underwater for very long periods of time.

Section 2 • Energy from the Nucleus

2) Teach, continued

MEETING INDIVIDUAL NEEDS
Learners Having Difficulty
Have students model fission by breaking a piece of putty into smaller pieces, and fusion by combining small pieces of putty to make one larger piece.

3) Extend

RESEARCH

Have students research the work of Albert Einstein, Lise Meitner, the Curies, or Otto Hahn and prepare a poster, model, story, skit, or concept map to present their findings to the class.

DEBATE
Have students do research and hold a debate about the issue of using nuclear energy in spacecraft and satellites. Students on one side can defend the use of nuclear energy in space. The other side can point out the potential hazards associated with using nuclear energy in space.

CONNECT TO EARTH SCIENCE

Use Teaching Transparency 190 to show students a fusion reaction of other hydrogen isotopes.

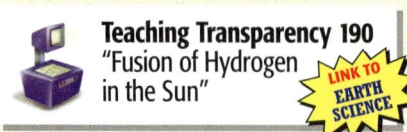

Astronomy CONNECTION

Hydrogen is not the only fuel stars use for fusion. As a star gets older, its supply of hydrogen runs low and it begins to fuse larger atoms, such as helium, carbon, and silicon.

Nuclear Fusion

Fusion is another nuclear reaction in which matter is converted into energy. In the process of **nuclear fusion,** two or more nuclei with small masses join together, or *fuse,* to form a larger, more massive nucleus.

In order for fusion to occur, the repulsion between positively charged nuclei must be overcome. That requires unbelievably high temperatures—over 100,000,000°C! But you already know a place where such temperatures are reached—the sun. In the sun's core, hydrogen nuclei fuse to form a helium nucleus, as shown in the model in **Figure 17.**

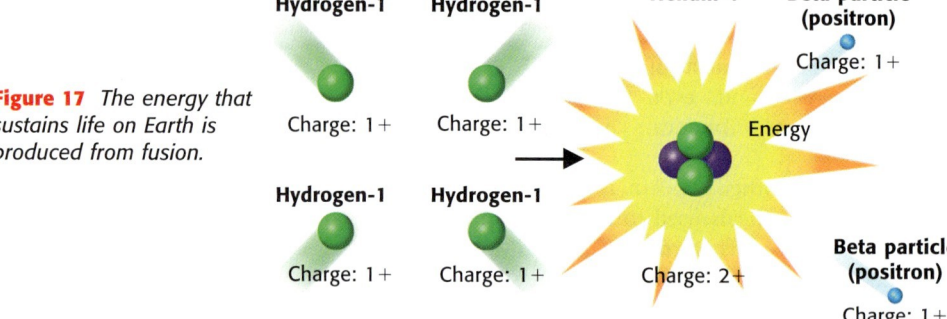

Figure 17 *The energy that sustains life on Earth is produced from fusion.*

Energy from Fusion? Energy for your home cannot yet be generated using nuclear fusion. First, incredibly high temperatures are needed. At these temperatures, hydrogen is a plasma, the state of matter in which electrons have been removed from atoms. No material on Earth can hold this plasma—imagine trying to bottle up plasma from the sun! **Figure 18** shows equipment used by researchers to try to contain plasma. Second, more energy is needed to create and contain the plasma than is produced by fusion. In spite of these problems, scientists predict that fusion will be used to provide electrical energy—possibly in your lifetime!

Figure 18 *Electric current in large coils of wire produces a strong magnetic field that can contain plasma.*

Science Bloopers

In 1989, two chemists at the University of Utah, B. Stanley Pons and Martin Fleischmann, announced that they had produced nuclear fusion at room temperature. Scientists around the world rushed to test the claim of what was called cold fusion. Results were varied, but no one has been able to duplicate the cold-fusion reaction claimed by Pons and Fleischmann. Many scientists have concluded that the original reports were incorrect and that further research would be a waste of time and money. Others continue looking for explanations of those results, which cannot be explained by current scientific understanding.

410 Chapter 16 • Atomic Energy

Oceans of Fuel Unlike nuclear fission, there is little concern about running out of fuel for nuclear fusion. Although the hydrogen-2 and hydrogen-3 isotopes used as fuel are much less common than hydrogen-1, there is still enough hydrogen in the waters of oceans and lakes to provide fuel for millions of years. In addition, a fusion reaction releases more energy than a fission reaction per gram of fuel, allowing for even greater savings of other resources, as shown in **Figure 19.**

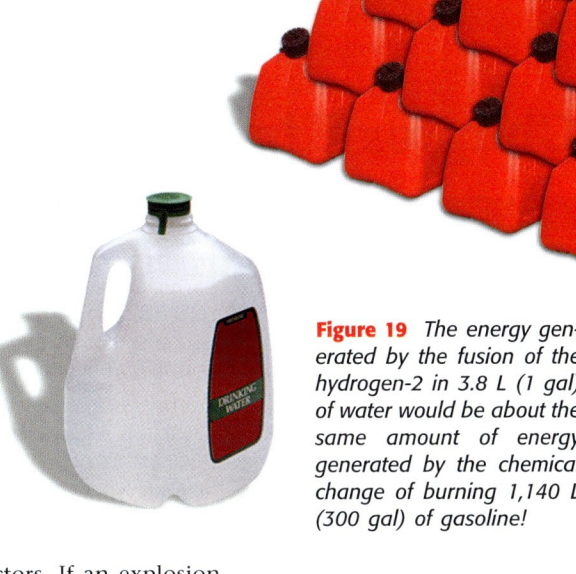

Figure 19 The energy generated by the fusion of the hydrogen-2 in 3.8 L (1 gal) of water would be about the same amount of energy generated by the chemical change of burning 1,140 L (300 gal) of gasoline!

Less Accident Prone The concern over an accident such as the one at Chernobyl is much lower for fusion reactors. If an explosion occurred, there would be very little release of radioactive materials. The radioactive hydrogen-3 used for fuel in experimental fusion reactors is much less radioactive than the uranium fuel used in fission reactors.

Less Waste In addition to the advantages mentioned above, the products of fusion reactions are not radioactive, so there would be much less radioactive waste to worry about. This would make fusion an even "cleaner" source of energy than fission. While fusion has many benefits over fission as an energy source, large amounts of money will be required to pay for the research to make fusion possible.

REVIEW

1. Which nuclear reaction is currently used to generate electrical energy?
2. Which nuclear reaction is the source of the sun's energy?
3. What particle is needed to begin a nuclear chain reaction?
4. In both fission and fusion, what is converted into energy?
5. **Comparing Concepts** Compare the processes of nuclear fission and nuclear fusion.

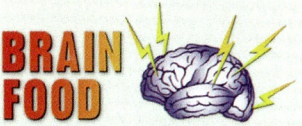

TOPIC: Nuclear Fission, Nuclear Fusion
GO TO: www.scilinks.org
sciLINKS NUMBER: HSTP390, HSTP400

4) Close

Quiz

1. Define *nuclear fission*. (the process in which a large nucleus splits into two smaller nuclei)
2. Define *nuclear fusion*. (the process in which two or more nuclei with small masses join together, or fuse, to form a larger, more massive nucleus)
3. What is the main product of nuclear fusion in the sun? (helium nuclei)

ALTERNATIVE ASSESSMENT

Concept Mapping Ask students to create concept maps to explain fission and fusion. Encourage students to label their diagrams carefully. Students should include where each type of reaction occurs. (fission: nuclear reactor, atomic bomb; fusion: stars, sun, hydrogen bomb)

BRAIN FOOD

Although Albert Einstein is considered one of the greatest scientists of the twentieth century, he did not begin to speak until the age of 3. In addition, most of his teachers considered him an academic failure because of his apparent lack of interest in classes.

Answers to Review

1. nuclear fission
2. nuclear fusion
3. a neutron
4. matter
5. Sample answer: In nuclear fission, a large nucleus is split into two smaller nuclei. In nuclear fusion, several small nuclei join together to form a larger, more massive nucleus. The products of fission are much more radioactive than the products of fusion. However, in both processes matter is converted into energy.

 Teaching Transparency 264 "Fusion of Hydrogen-1 Nuclei"

 Reinforcement Worksheet 16 "Fission or Fusion?"

Chapter Highlights

VOCABULARY DEFINITIONS

SECTION 1

nuclear radiation high-energy particles and rays that are emitted by the nuclei of some atoms; alpha particles, beta particles, and gamma rays are types of nuclear radiation

radioactivity the ability of some elements to give off nuclear radiation

radioactive decay the process in which the nucleus of a radioactive atom releases nuclear radiation

alpha decay the release of an alpha particle from a nucleus

mass number the sum of the protons and neutrons in an atom

beta decay the release of a beta particle from a nucleus

isotopes atoms that have the same number of protons but have different numbers of neutrons

gamma decay the release of gamma rays from a nucleus

half-life the amount of time it takes for one-half the nuclei of a radioactive isotope to decay

Chapter Highlights

SECTION 1

Vocabulary

nuclear radiation *(p. 398)*
radioactivity *(p. 398)*
radioactive decay *(p. 399)*
alpha decay *(p. 399)*
mass number *(p. 399)*
beta decay *(p. 400)*
isotopes *(p. 400)*
gamma decay *(p. 400)*
half-life *(p. 404)*

Section Notes

- Radioactive nuclei give off nuclear radiation in the form of alpha particles, beta particles, and gamma rays through a process called radioactive decay.

- During alpha decay, an alpha particle is released from the nucleus. An alpha particle is composed of two protons and two neutrons.

- During beta decay, a beta particle is released from the nucleus. A beta particle can be an electron or a positron.

- Gamma decay occurs with alpha decay and beta decay when particles in the nucleus rearrange and emit energy in the form of gamma rays.

- Gamma rays penetrate matter better than alpha or beta particles. Beta particles penetrate matter better than alpha particles.

- Nuclear radiation can damage living and nonliving matter.

- Half-life is the amount of time it takes for one-half of the nuclei of a radioactive isotope to decay. The age of some objects can be determined using half-lives.

- Uses of radioactive materials include detecting defects in materials, sterilizing products, tracing a plant's or animal's use of an element, diagnosing illness, and producing electrical energy.

✓ Skills Check

Math Concepts

HALF-LIFE Radioactive decay occurs at a steady rate. To calculate the time that has passed, multiply the number of half-lives by the length of a half-life. For example, a radioactive isotope has a half-life of 10 days. If one-eighth of the original sample remains, then three half-lives have passed. The time that has passed is:

$$3 \times 10 \text{ days} = 30 \text{ days}$$

Visual Understanding

FISSION VERSUS FUSION The changes that occur in nuclear fission and nuclear fusion are very different. Review Figure 12 on page 406 and Figure 17 on page 410 to better understand the starting materials, products, and process involved in fission and fusion.

Lab and Activity Highlights

Domino Chain Reactions PG 692

 Datasheets for LabBook
(blackline masters for this lab)

412 Chapter 16 • Atomic Energy

SECTION 2

Vocabulary
nuclear fission *(p. 406)*
nuclear chain reaction *(p. 407)*
nuclear fusion *(p. 410)*

Section Notes

- Nuclear fission occurs when a massive, unstable nucleus breaks into two less massive nuclei. Nuclear fission is used in power plants to generate electrical energy.

- Nuclear fusion occurs when two or more nuclei combine to form a larger nucleus. The sun's energy comes from the fusion of hydrogen to form helium.

- The energy released by nuclear fission and nuclear fusion is produced when matter is converted into energy.

- Nuclear power plants use nuclear fission to supply many homes with electrical energy without releasing carbon dioxide or other gases into the atmosphere. A limited fuel supply, radioactive waste products, and the possible release of radioactive material are disadvantages of fission.

- Fuel for nuclear fusion is plentiful, and only small amounts of radioactive waste products are produced. Fusion is not currently a practical energy source because of the large amount of energy needed to heat and contain the hydrogen plasma.

Labs
Domino Chain Reactions *(p. 692)*

VOCABULARY DEFINITIONS, continued

SECTION 2

nuclear fission the process in which a large nucleus splits into two smaller nuclei; during this process, matter is converted into energy

nuclear chain reaction a continuous series of nuclear fission reactions

nuclear fusion the process in which two or more nuclei with small masses join together, or fuse, to form a larger, more massive nucleus; during this process, matter is converted into energy

 Vocabulary Review Worksheet 16

 Blackline masters of these Chapter Highlights can be found in the **Study Guide**.

---

internet connect

GO TO: go.hrw.com

Visit the **HRW** Web site for a variety of learning tools related to this chapter. Just type in the keyword:

KEYWORD: HSTRAD

GO TO: www.scilinks.org

Visit the **National Science Teachers Association** on-line Web site for Internet resources related to this chapter. Just type in the *sci*LINKS number for more information about the topic:

TOPIC:	*sci*LINKS NUMBER:
Discovering Radioactivity	HSTP380
Radioactive Isotopes	HSTP385
Nuclear Fission	HSTP390
Nuclear Reactors	HSTP395
Nuclear Fusion	HSTP400

413

Lab and Activity Highlights

LabBank

 Long-Term Projects & Research Ideas, Meltdown! Project 66

Chapter 16 • Chapter Highlights **413**

Chapter Review Answers

USING VOCABULARY

1. Nuclear fission
2. half-life
3. Nuclear radiation
4. Gamma decay

UNDERSTANDING CONCEPTS

Multiple Choice

5. d
6. b
7. a
8. c
9. d
10. c

Short Answer

11. Having a very large number of protons or having too many or too few neutrons compared with protons could cause a nucleus to be unstable.
12. Two dangers associated with nuclear fission are the potential for an accident that could release radioactive material and the potential of radioactive waste leaking into the environment.
13. Two problems that need to be solved to make nuclear fusion a practical energy source are finding a way to contain the plasma and finding a process that generates more electrical energy than is needed to heat and contain the plasma.
14. Some matter is converted into energy during fission, so the mass of the products is less than the mass of the starting materials.

Concept Mapping

15. An answer to this exercise can be found at the end of this book.

Chapter Review

USING VOCABULARY

The statements below are false. For each statement, replace the underlined term to make a true statement.

1. <u>Nuclear fusion</u> involves splitting a nucleus.
2. During one <u>beta decay</u>, half of a radioactive sample will decay.
3. <u>Nuclear fission</u> includes the particles and rays released by radioactive nuclei.
4. <u>Alpha decay</u> occurs during the rearrangement of protons and neutrons in the nucleus.

UNDERSTANDING CONCEPTS

Multiple Choice

5. Which of the following is a use of radioactive material?
   a. detecting smoke
   b. locating defects in materials
   c. generating electrical energy
   d. all of the above

6. Which particle both begins and is produced by a nuclear chain reaction?
   a. positron
   b. neutron
   c. alpha particle
   d. beta particle

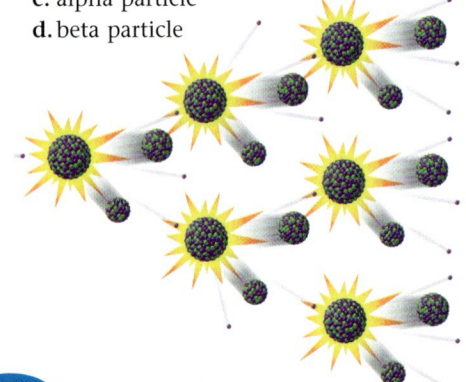

7. Nuclear radiation that can be stopped by paper is called
   a. alpha particles.   c. gamma rays.
   b. beta particles.   d. None of the above

8. The half-life of a radioactive atom is 2 months. If you start with 1g of the element, how much will remain after 6 months?
   a. One-half of a gram will remain.
   b. One-fourth of a gram will remain.
   c. One-eighth of a gram will remain.
   d. None will remain.

9. The waste products of nuclear fission
   a. are harmless.
   b. are safe after 20 years.
   c. can be destroyed by burning them.
   d. remain radioactive for thousands of years.

10. Which statement about nuclear fusion is false?
    a. Nuclear fusion occurs in the sun.
    b. Nuclear fusion is the joining of the nuclei of atoms.
    c. Nuclear fusion is currently used to generate electrical energy.
    d. Nuclear fusion uses hydrogen as fuel.

Short Answer

11. What conditions could cause a nucleus to be unstable?
12. What are two dangers associated with nuclear fission?
13. What are two of the problems that need to be solved in order to make nuclear fusion a practical energy source?
14. In fission, the products have less mass than the starting materials. Explain what happened.

 Concept Mapping Transparency 16

 Blackline masters of this Chapter Review can be found in the **Study Guide**.

414   Chapter 16 • Atomic Energy

Concept Mapping

15. Use the following terms to create a concept map: radioactive decay, alpha particle, beta particle, gamma ray, nuclear radiation.

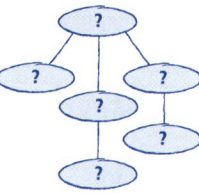

CRITICAL THINKING AND PROBLEM SOLVING

16. Smoke detectors often use americium-243 to detect smoke particles in the air. Americium-243 undergoes alpha decay. Do you think that these smoke detectors are safe to have in your home if used properly? Explain. (Hint: How penetrating are alpha particles?)

17. Explain how radiation can cause cancer.

18. Explain why nuclei of carbon, oxygen, and even iron can be found in stars.

19. If you could block all radiation from sources outside your body, explain why you would still be exposed to some radiation.

MATH IN SCIENCE

20. A scientist used 10 g of phosphorus-32 in a test on plant growth but forgot to record the date. When he measured the phosphorus-32 some time later, he found only 2.5 g remaining. If the half-life is 14 days, how many days ago did he start the experiment?

INTERPRETING GRAPHICS

21. Use the graph to answer the questions below:

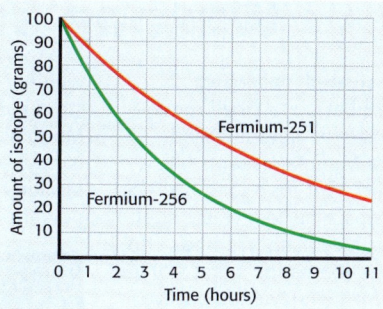

a. What is the half-life of fermium-256? of fermium-251?
b. Which of these isotopes is more stable? Explain.

22. The image of a small purse, shown below, was made in a similar manner as Becquerel's original experiment. What conclusions can be drawn about the penetrating power of radiation from this image?

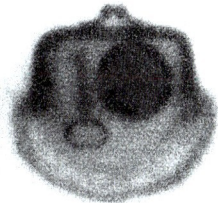

NOW What Do You Think?

Take a minute to review your answers to the ScienceLog questions on page 397. Have your answers changed? If necessary, revise your answers based on what you have learned since you began this chapter.

NOW WHAT DO YOU THINK?

1. Nuclear radiation is high-energy particles and rays that are emitted by the nuclei of some atoms.
2. Sample answer: Radioactive materials are used to diagnose medical problems, to detect defects in structures, to sterilize food and health-care products, to detect smoke, to kill cancer cells, and to power space probes.
3. Two concerns about energy obtained from nuclear reactions are the possibility of an accident releasing radioactive materials and the need to safely store the radioactive products of the reaction.

CRITICAL THINKING AND PROBLEM SOLVING

16. These smoke detectors should be safe to have in homes because alpha particles are not very penetrating and are stopped by about 7 cm of air.
17. Radiation can "knock" electrons out of atoms and break chemical bonds between atoms. If radiation breaks bonds in the DNA of a cell, the damage could cause the cell to divide uncontrollably. The cell is then cancerous.
18. Nuclear fusion in stars causes hydrogen nuclei to join together to form helium nuclei. If stars are hot enough, the hydrogen and helium nuclei could join together to form larger nuclei, such as carbon and oxygen. These nuclei can continue to join together and form even larger nuclei such as iron.
19. The food you eat contains some radioactive nuclei, such as carbon-14 nuclei. Atoms of carbon-14 have the same chemical properties as atoms of nonradioactive carbon-12, and are used by your body to build molecules, such as proteins. Thus, there is always some radiation being released by nuclei of atoms that are part of your body.

MATH IN SCIENCE

20. One-fourth of the original amount remains, so two half-lives have occurred. Thus, the experiment began 28 days ago (2×14 days = 28 days).

INTERPRETING GRAPHICS

21. a. 2.6 hours; 5.3 hours
    b. Fermium-251 is more stable because it has a longer half-life than fermium-256.
22. Sample answer: Radiation penetrates cloth more easily than it does metal. The darkness of the key and the round object (a compact) in the image demonstrate that they blocked more radiation than the cloth of the purse itself.

SCIENTIFIC DEBATE

Wasting Yucca Mountain?

Background

At present, most spent fuel rods are stored underwater at nuclear power plants. While most experts agree that underwater storage is an acceptable solution for the short term, everyone agrees that some safer way to store these dangerous materials must be found.

Wasting Yucca Mountain?

Isolated, unspoiled, quiet . . . a small mountain in Nevada called Yucca Mountain seems like a perfect spot for a long hike—or perhaps a nuclear waste site! Yucca Mountain has been chosen as the nation's first storage site for high-level radioactive waste. The plan is to seal 77,000 tons of radioactive waste in steel canisters and store them in a maze of underground tunnels.

Construction of the facility has already begun—Yucca Mountain is scheduled to receive its first shipment of nuclear waste by 2010. But the debate continues about whether it would be safer to store radioactive waste at Yucca Mountain or to keep it where it is now—in temporary storage facilities at various nuclear power plants.

▲ *Spent fuel rods are stored underwater at a nuclear power plant.*

Pros and Cons

Those who support construction of the Yucca Mountain facility point out that there are two major advantages to the plan. First, Yucca Mountain is far from any densely populated areas. Second, the climate is extremely dry. A dry climate means that rainfall is unlikely to cause the water table to rise and come in contact with the stored radioactive waste.

Many opponents fear that the highly toxic waste could eventually leak and contaminate the water in wells, springs, and streams. In time, the contamination could spread farther from the site and into the biosphere. The biosphere is the layer above and below the surface of the earth that supports life.

In addition, some scientific reports suggest that it is possible that the current dry climate could change over thousands of years into a rainy one, and the water table could rise dramatically.

Nevada residents argue that their economy is booming and they don't particularly need the construction jobs the facility would bring. Also their economy depends heavily on tourism, and residents worry that fears about Nevada being a dangerous place could cause the tourists to stay away.

Today construction at the Yucca Mountain facility continues. And existing storage sites expand with the waste generated by nuclear power plants. So, where should the waste go?

Have Waste, Will Travel

▶ What do you think? Jot down your initial thoughts. Then do research to find out whether any of the proposed routes from nuclear power plants to Yucca Mountain are near your town. Do your findings change your opinion? Why or why not?

▲ *Supporters of the Yucca Mountain storage facility think that this isolated spot in Nevada is a suitable place for permanent nuclear-waste disposal. Opponents of the site disagree.*

Answer to Have Waste, Will Travel

Students' answers will vary. Any change in the opinions held by students after researching the proposed routes will most likely depend on whether the students live near one of the routes.

CAREERS

MATERIALS SCIENTIST

Have you noticed that your forks, knives, and spoons don't tarnish easily? Most metal flatware is made of stainless steel. Because it doesn't tarnish easily, stainless steel is also used in nuclear reactors. **Dr. Michael Atzmon** studies radiation's effects on metals and other substances. He has a special interest in radiation's effect on stainless steel. He hopes that by understanding the changes that occur, scientists can prevent future radiation defects.

The damage to stainless steel is caused mainly by neutron and heavy ion radiation inside nuclear reactors. The radiation causes stress in the metal, which leads to corrosion and finally to cracking. Clearly this is not a desirable feature in parts of a nuclear reactor! Atzmon's goal is to try to understand how to make the metal more corrosion resistant. He also hopes that by studying the way radiation affects the atoms of metals, he can find a way to use the incoming radiation to make the surface stronger.

Training the Team

A large part of Atzmon's job is to train graduate students to assist him with his research. He happily reports that these creative new scientists "absolutely contribute" to the development of novel approaches. One interesting proposal is to use radiation effects to create crystal structures different from those that exist in nature. This could lead to the invention of new types of semiconductors, which are useful in modern electronic devices.

Always an Explorer

Atzmon spends time sharing ideas with other materials scientists. He also teaches at the University of Michigan. This very busy man recalls that as a young boy he became interested in experimenting with things to see how they work. He chose to play with toys that encouraged his exploration. This curiosity has remained with him and has been helpful in his profession.

▶ *Understanding material structures can help in the development of better semiconductors for microchips.*

Advice to Young People

Atzmon believes that students should choose to study a field that gives them the deepest background. This opens up many career opportunities and allows students to pursue what they eventually find interesting. Most important, he adds, "People should do what they love doing!"

CAREERS

Materials Scientist—Dr. Michael Atzmon

Background

Dr. Michael Atzmon is an associate professor at the University of Michigan. He earned his undergraduate degree in physics and mathematics at Hebrew University of Jerusalem, in Israel. He earned graduate degrees in applied physics at the California Institute of Technology.

Students might be interested in learning about the different principal alloys of iron and why stainless steel is commercially important.

Learning about semiconducting crystals will help students understand why Dr. Atzmon's work is useful in this area.

UNIT 6

TIMELINE
Electricity

Can you imagine a world without computers, motors, or even light bulbs? Your life would be very different indeed without electricity and the devices that depend on it. In this unit, you will learn how electricity results from tiny charged particles, how electricity and magnetism interact, and how electronic technology has revolutionized the world in a relatively short amount of time. This timeline includes some of the events leading to our current understanding of electricity, electromagnetism, and electronic technology.

1752
Benjamin Franklin flies a kite with a key attached to it in a thunderstorm to demonstrate that lightning is a form of electricity.

1911
Superconductivity is discovered. Superconductivity is the ability that some metals and alloys have under certain conditions to carry electric current without resistance.

1945
Grace Murray Hopper, a pioneer in computers and computer languages, coins the term "debugging the computer" after removing from the wiring of her computer a moth that caused the computer to fail.

1948
The transistor is invented.

1961
The invention of the integrated circuit, which uses millions of transistors, revolutionizes electronic technology.

1773
American colonists hold the "Boston Tea Party" and dump 342 chests of British tea into Boston Harbor.

1831
British scientist Michael Faraday and American physicist Joseph Henry separately demonstrate the principle of electromagnetic induction (using magnetism to generate electricity).

1876
The telephone is officially invented by Alexander Graham Bell, who beats Elisha Gray to the patent office by only a few hours.

1902
Dutch physician Willem Einthoven develops the first electrocardiograph machine to record the tiny electric currents that pass through the body's tissues.

1985
The first portable CD player is introduced.

1974
The first commercially successful microprocessor chip is introduced.

1997
Garry Kasparov, reigning world chess champion, loses a historic match to a computer named Deep Blue.

Electricity **419**

Chapter Organizer

CHAPTER ORGANIZATION	TIME MINUTES	OBJECTIVES	LABS, INVESTIGATIONS, AND DEMONSTRATIONS
Chapter Opener pp. 420–421	45	National Standards: UCP 5, SAI 1, 2, PS 3a	**Investigate!** Charge over Matter, p. 421
Section 1 Electric Charge and Static Electricity	135	▶ State and give examples of the law of electric charges. ▶ Describe three ways an object can become charged. ▶ Compare conductors with insulators. ▶ Give examples of static electricity and electric discharge. UCP 2, SPSP 3, 5, HNS 3, PS 2c, 3a; LabBook UCP 2, SAI 1, 2, PS 3a, 3d	**Demonstration,** Charging Objects, p. 424 in ATE **Interactive Explorations CD-ROM,** Tunnel Vision *A Worksheet is also available in the Interactive Explorations Teacher's Edition.* **Discovery Lab,** Stop the Static Electricity! p. 694 **Datasheets for LabBook,** Stop the Static Electricity! Datasheet 47 **Whiz-Bang Demonstrations,** Hoop It Up, Demo 57, Bending Water, Demo 58
Section 2 Electrical Energy	90	▶ Explain how a cell produces an electric current. ▶ Describe how the potential difference is related to electric current. ▶ Describe how photocells and thermocouples produce electrical energy. SPSP 5, PS 3a; LabBook UCP 2, SAI 1, 2, PS 3a	**Making Models,** Potato Power, p. 695 **Datasheets for LabBook,** Potato Power, Datasheet 48
Section 3 Electric Current	90	▶ Describe electric current. ▶ Identify the four factors that determine the resistance of an object. ▶ Explain how current, voltage, and resistance are related by Ohm's law. ▶ Describe how electric power is related to electrical energy. SPSP 1, 5, PS 3a	**Demonstration,** Current and Amps, p. 433 in ATE
Section 4 Electric Circuits	90	▶ Name the three essential parts of a circuit. ▶ Compare series circuits with parallel circuits. ▶ Explain how fuses and circuit breakers protect your home against short circuits and circuit overloads. SPSP 5, PS 3a; LabBook UCP 2, SAI 1, 2, PS 3a, 3d	**Demonstration,** p. 440 in ATE **QuickLab,** pp. 442, 443 **Skill Builder,** Circuitry 101, p. 696 **Datasheets for LabBook,** Circuitry 101, Datasheet 49 **Long-Term Projects & Research Ideas,** Project 67

See page T20 for a complete correlation of this book with the **NATIONAL SCIENCE EDUCATION STANDARDS.**

TECHNOLOGY RESOURCES

 Guided Reading Audio CD English or Spanish, Chapter 17

 **Science Discovery Videodiscs** Science Sleuths: The Crashing Computers

 Multicultural Connections, China's Solar Nomads, Segment 10

 Interactive Explorations CD-ROM CD 3, Exploration 5, Tunnel Vision

 One-Stop Planner CD-ROM with Test Generator

Chapter 17 • Introduction to Electricity

Chapter 17 • Introduction to Electricity

CLASSROOM WORKSHEETS, TRANSPARENCIES, AND RESOURCES	SCIENCE INTEGRATION AND CONNECTIONS	REVIEW AND ASSESSMENT
Science Puzzlers, Twisters & Teasers, Worksheet 17 **Directed Reading Worksheet 17**		
Directed Reading Worksheet 17, Section 1 **Transparency 266,** Structure of an Atom **Transparency 267,** Law of Electric Charges **Transparency 268,** How Lightning Forms **Reinforcement Worksheet 17,** Charge!	**Cross-Disciplinary Focus,** p. 423 in ATE **Multicultural Connection,** p. 428 in ATE **Across the Sciences:** Sprites and Elves, p. 451	**Self-Check,** p. 425 **Review,** p. 426 **Homework,** p. 427 in ATE **Review,** p. 429 **Quiz,** p. 429 in ATE **Alternative Assessment,** p. 429 in ATE
Directed Reading Worksheet 17, Section 2 **Transparency 90,** What's in a Nerve? **Transparency 269,** How a Cell Produces an Electric Current	**Connect to Life Science,** p. 430 in ATE **Cross-Disciplinary Focus,** p. 431 in ATE	**Review,** p. 432 **Quiz,** p. 432 in ATE **Alternative Assessment,** p. 432 in ATE
Directed Reading Worksheet 17, Section 3 **Math Skills for Science Worksheet 3,** Multiplying Whole Numbers **Critical Thinking Worksheet 17,** Potentially Shocking!	**Biology Connection,** p. 435 **Real-World Connection,** p. 436 in ATE **MathBreak,** Using Ohm's Law, p. 437 **Math and More,** p. 437 in ATE **Apply,** p. 439	**Self-Check,** p. 438 **Review,** p. 439 **Quiz,** p. 439 in ATE **Alternative Assessment,** p. 439 in ATE
Directed Reading Worksheet 17, Section 4 **Transparency 270,** Parts of a Circuit **Reinforcement Worksheet 17,** Electric Circuits	**Cross-Disciplinary Focus,** p. 440 in ATE **Biology Connection,** p. 441 **Science, Technology, and Society:** Riding the Electric Rails, p. 450	**Self-Check,** p. 441 **Homework,** pp. 442, 443 in ATE **Review,** p. 445 **Quiz,** p. 445 in ATE **Alternative Assessment,** p. 445 in ATE

 Holt, Rinehart and Winston On-line Resources
go.hrw.com

For worksheets and other teaching aids related to this chapter, visit the HRW Web site and type in the keyword: **HSTELE**

 **National Science Teachers Association**
www.scilinks.org

Encourage students to use the *sci*LINKS numbers listed in the internet connect boxes to access information and resources on the **NSTA** Web site.

END-OF-CHAPTER REVIEW AND ASSESSMENT

Chapter Review in Study Guide
Vocabulary and Notes in Study Guide
Chapter Tests with Performance-Based Assessment, Chapter 17 Test, Performance-Based Assessment 17
Concept Mapping Transparency 17

Chapter Resources & Worksheets

Visual Resources

TEACHING TRANSPARENCIES

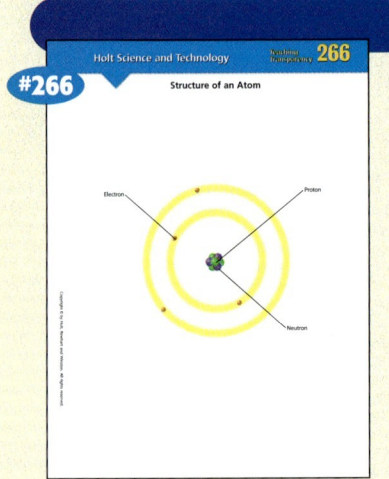
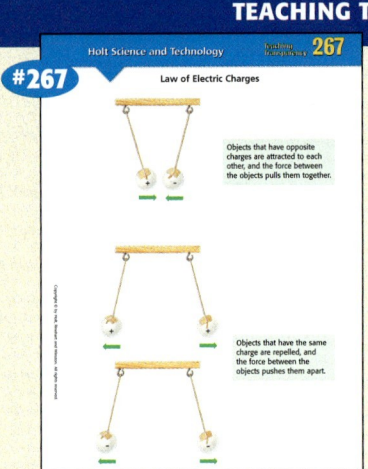

TEACHING TRANSPARENCIES

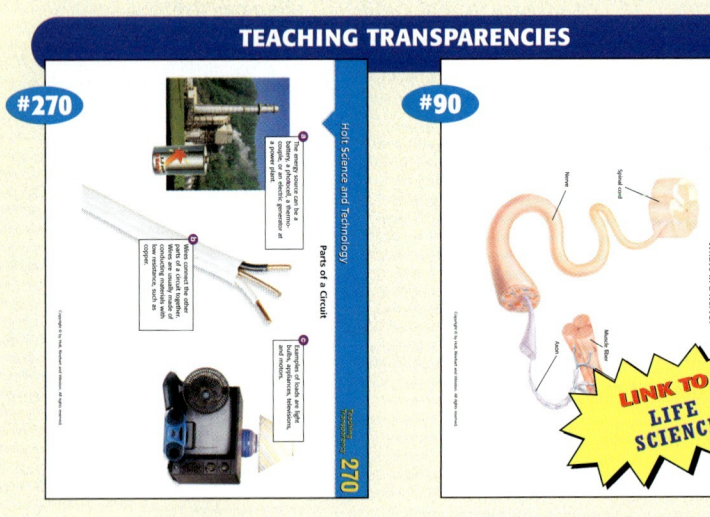

CONCEPT MAPPING TRANSPARENCY

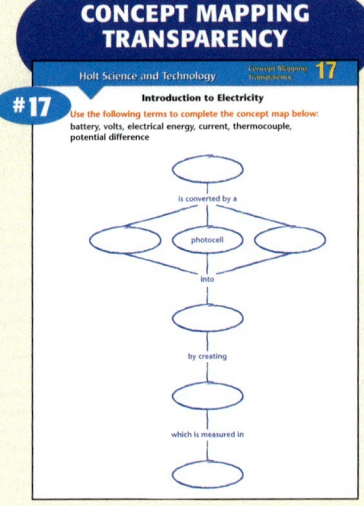

Meeting Individual Needs

DIRECTED READING

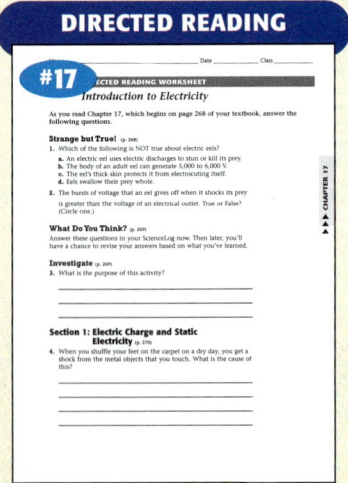

REINFORCEMENT & VOCABULARY REVIEW

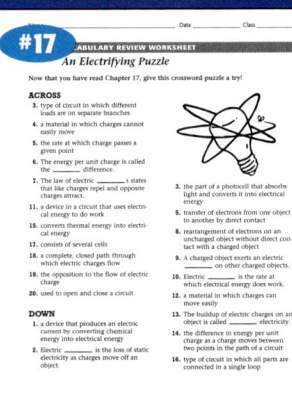

SCIENCE PUZZLERS, TWISTERS & TEASERS

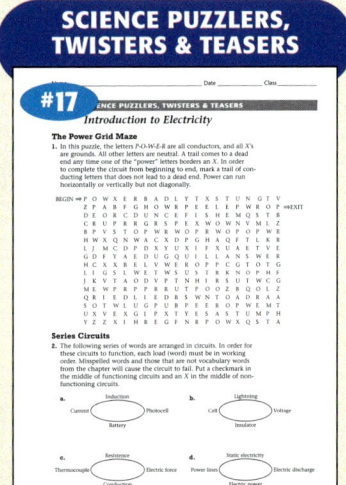

Chapter 17 • Introduction to Electricity

Chapter 17 • Introduction to Electricity

Review & Assessment

STUDY GUIDE

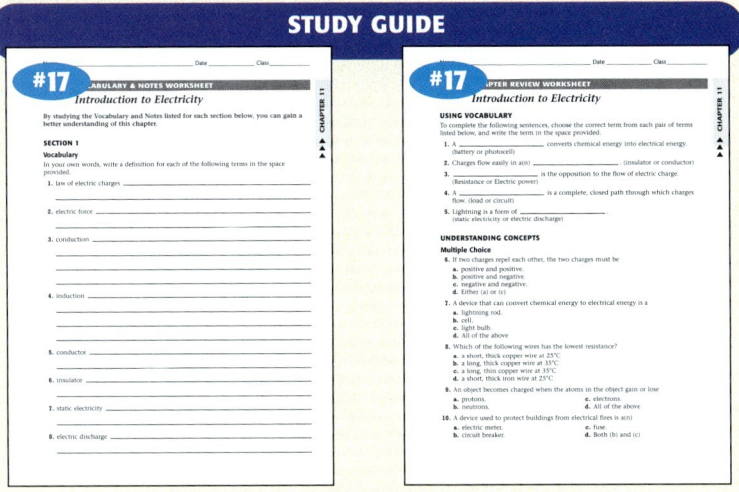

CHAPTER TESTS WITH PERFORMANCE-BASED ASSESSMENT

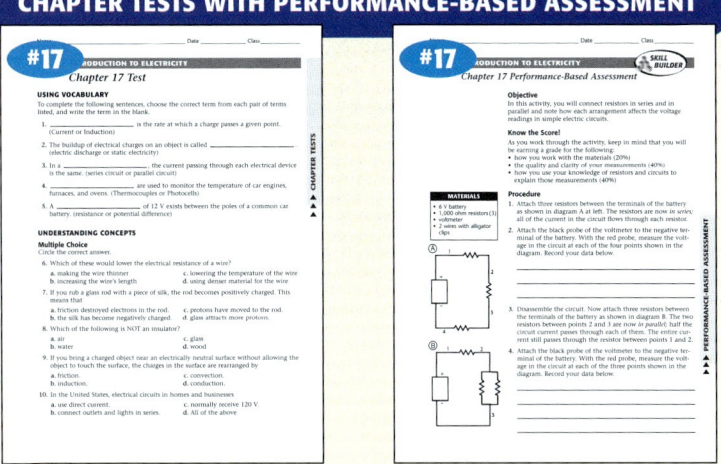

Lab Worksheets

WHIZ-BANG DEMONSTRATIONS

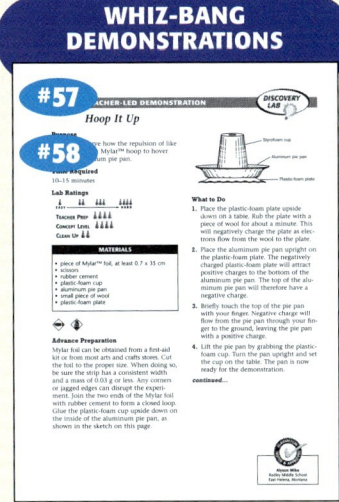

LONG-TERM PROJECTS & RESEARCH IDEAS

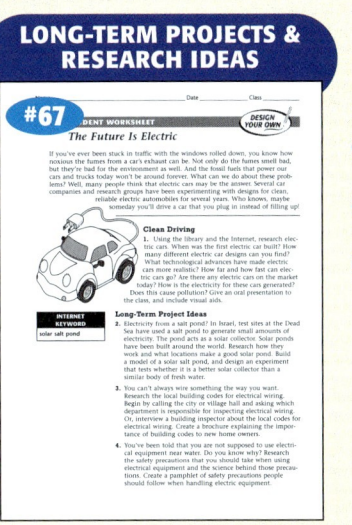

DATASHEETS FOR LABBOOK

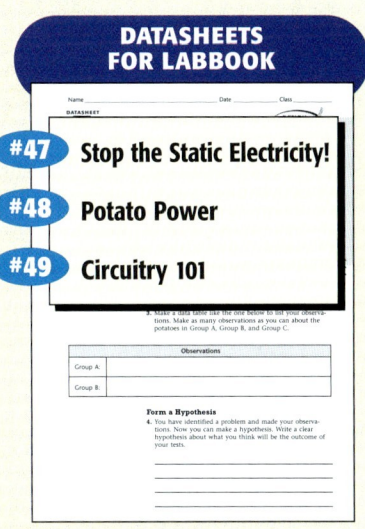

Applications & Extensions

CRITICAL THINKING & PROBLEM SOLVING

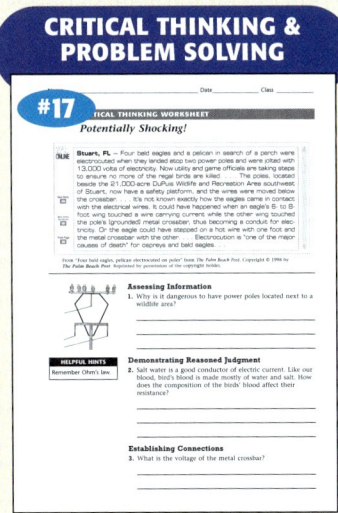

MULTICULTURAL CONNECTIONS

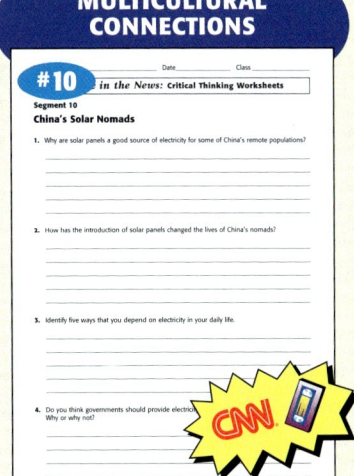

INTERACTIVE EXPLORATIONS

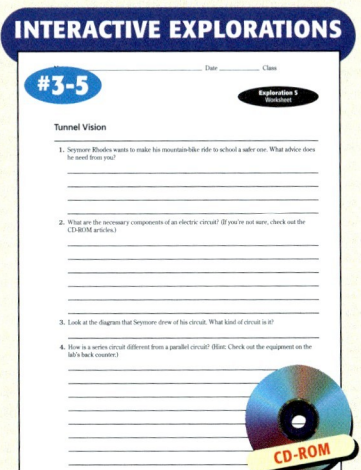

Chapter Background

SECTION 1

Electric Charge and Static Electricity

▶ **Electroscopes**
Although now out-of-date, the electroscope provided a simple method for measuring the amount of electric charge in an object. The distance between the two metal leaves (conductors) of an electroscope indicates the amount of charge being conducted.

- The British physicist and chemist Michael Faraday (1791–1867) was the first to detect electric charge using an electroscope. He made this observation in the early 1800s while he was a professor at England's Royal Institution.

IS THAT A FACT!

- To say that something is "charged" is not entirely accurate. Objects that we call charged actually have a charge imbalance; they have an unequal number of protons and electrons.

▶ **Photocopiers and Electric Charge**
One application of electric charges is the production of photocopied images. The ink on photocopies is actually composed of tiny black particles. The photocopier gives these particles a negative charge. When you put a document in the copier, it makes a positively charged image of the document on a rotating drum. The negatively charged toner particles stick to the positively charged image. Then the machine runs a charged sheet of paper alongside the drum, and the particles move to the paper. Finally, the machine thermally fuses the particles to the paper, and the copy is finished.

SECTION 2

Electrical Energy

▶ **Cells**
Cells can be classified into two broad categories: primary cells and secondary cells. Primary cells include the dry cell and the mercury cell. Secondary cells include the lead-acid battery, the nickel-iron cell, and the nickel-cadmium cell.

IS THAT A FACT!

- The electrolyte in a dry cell is a paste of ammonium chloride and zinc chloride. In the mercury battery, the electrolyte is a solution of potassium hydroxide.

▶ **Thermoelectricity and Thermocouples**
In 1821, a German physicist named Thomas Seebeck (1770–1831) observed that electrical energy was generated when the ends of two different kinds of wires were maintained at two different temperatures. A thermocouple measures the temperature change in such a situation.

IS THAT A FACT!

- Thermocouple wires are usually made of copper and iron. However, other pairs of metals, such as iron and constantan (a copper-nickel alloy) and copper and constantan, are also used.

▶ **Alternative Energy Sources**
Traditional methods of generating electrical energy have used fossil fuels, such as coal, as energy sources. But generating energy by burning fossil fuels releases carbon dioxide gas. Many scientists think that rising levels of atmospheric carbon dioxide are warming the Earth. This warming could have unwanted effects. A variety of alternatives to fossil fuels exists, including solar energy, wind energy, hydroelectric energy (energy from moving water), and geothermal energy (thermal energy from the Earth's interior).

Chapter 17 • Introduction to Electricity

SECTION 3

Electric Current

▶ **Superconductors**
Superconductors are materials that allow electric charges to flow with no resistance.

- In 1911, a Dutch physicist named Heike Kamerlingh Onnes (1853–1926) discovered superconductivity. He found that mercury chilled to very low temperatures (below −268.8°C) offered no electrical resistance. Because the chilled mercury conducted electric charges so well, it was called a *superconductor*.

IS THAT A FACT!

- Initially, liquid helium was used as a coolant for superconductors. Unfortunately, helium was both expensive and inefficient, making it impractical for widespread use.

- In the 1980s, researchers found new types of superconductors that worked at slightly higher temperatures. Therefore, liquid nitrogen, which is relatively inexpensive, could be used instead of liquid helium.

▶ **Superconducting Magnets**
Superconducting magnets generate magnetic fields with almost no energy loss from resistance. These magnets are used in advanced technological devices, such as particle accelerators.

▶ **Measuring Electricity**
An ohm (Ω) is a unit for expressing resistance. At a given voltage, the lower the resistance is, the higher the current.

- An ampere (A) is a unit for expressing current—the rate at which charges pass a given point. The more amps there are, the more charges pass the point each second.

- A watt (W) is a unit for expressing power. Electrical energy can be harnessed and used to do work. Watts are used to express the rate at which work is done at a given voltage and a given amperage.

SECTION 4

Electric Circuits

▶ **Household Circuits**
The blueprint of a house includes symbols that indicate where electric wiring belongs, where switches are located, and where light fixtures will be installed. Electricians follow the symbols in the blueprint as they help build the house.

- Closed circuits represent a continuous flow of charges. Open circuits represent a noncontinuous flow of charges. Short circuits are closed circuits in which a direct connection is made between terminals.

IS THAT A FACT!

- A typical water heater uses 4,800 kWh of electrical energy per year. By contrast, an electric toothbrush uses only 5 kWh of electrical energy per year.

For background information about teaching strategies and issues, refer to the *Professional Reference for Teachers*.

CHAPTER 17 Introduction to Electricity

Chapter Preview

Section 1
Electric Charge and Static Electricity
- Atoms and Charge
- Charge It!
- Moving Charges
- Static Electricity
- Lightning

Section 2
Electrical Energy
- Batteries Are Included
- Bring On the Potential
- Other Ways of Producing Electrical Energy

Section 3
Electric Current
- Current Revisited
- Voltage
- Resistance
- Ohm's Law: Putting It All Together
- Electric Power
- Measuring Electrical Energy

Section 4
Electric Circuits
- Parts of a Circuit
- Types of Circuits
- Household Circuits
- Circuit Safety

Science Puzzlers, Twisters & Teasers Worksheet 17

Guided Reading Audio CD
English or Spanish, Chapter 17

Strange but True!

The most shocking of all fish tales concerns the electric eel, a freshwater fish of Central America and South America that can produce powerful jolts of electrical energy. Electric discharges from this 2.5 m long creature are strong enough to stun and kill smaller fish and frogs in the water. The eel can then swallow its motionless prey whole. Early travelers to the Amazon River basin wrote that, in shallow pools, the eels' electric discharges could knock horses and humans over.

How does the electric eel perform its shocking feat? Within this fish's long body are a series of electroplates—modified muscle tissues that generate low voltages. The electricity produced by one wafer-thin electroplate is small. But eels have 5,000 to 6,000 electroplates connected

together and can therefore produce a high voltage. In laboratory experiments, the bursts of voltage from a fully grown eel have been measured at around 600 volts. That's five times the voltage of an electrical outlet—all from the cells of a single fish! The eel's thick, leathery skin prevents the eel from electrocuting itself while zapping prey.

Now that you know what one amazing fish can do with electricity, read on to learn what people have accomplished with this versatile form of energy.

Strange but True!
Other kinds of electric fish are the electric catfish, found in the larger rivers of tropical Africa, and the torpedo ray, found in warm, deep-sea water close to the shore. A species of torpedo ray that lives in the Atlantic Ocean has a mass up to 90 kg!

What Do You Think?

In your ScienceLog, try to answer the following questions based on what you already know:

1. What is static electricity, and how is it formed?
2. How is electrical energy produced?
3. What is a circuit, and what parts make up a circuit?

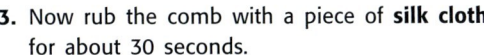

Charge over Matter

Because you don't have electroplates in your body, you cannot produce high voltages like an electric eel. However, you can make electrically charged objects and use them to pick up other objects.

Procedure

1. Cut **6–8 small squares of tissue paper.** Each square should be about 2 × 2 cm. Place the squares on your desk.
2. Hold a **plastic comb** close to the paper squares. Describe what, if anything, happens.
3. Now rub the comb with a piece of **silk cloth** for about 30 seconds.
4. Hold the comb close to the tissue-paper squares, but don't touch them. Describe what happens. If nothing happens, rub the comb for a little while longer and try again.
5. Now hold a **metal rod** close to the tissue-paper squares, and observe what happens.
6. Rub the rod with the silk cloth, and then hold the rod close to the tissue-paper squares. Describe what, if anything, happens.

Analysis

7. When you rub the comb with the cloth, you give the comb a negative electric charge. Why do you think this allowed you to pick up tissue-paper squares?
8. How were your results for steps 2 and 4 different? Why do you think they were different?
9. What other objects do you think you can use to pick up tissue-paper squares?

IS THAT A FACT!

Electric eels generate electrical energy using organs located on the sides of their long body. Modified muscle cells in the organs produce electric currents. The eels use electrical energy not only for stunning prey but also for self-defense and for communicating with other eels.

What Do You Think?

Accept all reasonable responses.

Students will have a chance to revise their answers in the Chapter Review under NOW What Do You Think?

Investigate!

MATERIALS

FOR EACH GROUP:
- 6–8 small squares of tissue paper
- plastic comb
- piece of silk cloth
- metal rod

Answers to Investigate!

Students may not be familiar with charge or electrical energy, so accept all reasonable answers to items 7–9.

7. The negative charge on the comb induced a positive charge on the paper. Since oppositely charged objects are attracted to one another, the paper was pulled toward the comb.
8. In step 2 the comb was not charged, so it could not pick up any tissue paper. The comb was charged during step 3, so it could pick up the paper.
9. Objects that are insulators can be charged and used to pick up tissue-paper squares.

Directed Reading Worksheet 17

SECTION 1

Focus

Electric Charge and Static Electricity

This section explains what electric charge is and how it works, and it explains the three ways that objects can become charged. Students learn about conductors and insulators. Finally, the section discusses static electricity and electric discharge.

**Bellringer**

Write the term *electric charge* on the board. Ask students how they would define this term. Students should write their definition in their ScienceLog.

1 Motivate

ACTIVITY

Balloons and Static Electricity
Distribute two inflated balloons and a piece of wool cloth to pairs of students. Instruct students to create static electricity by rubbing their balloons against the cloth. Ask them to describe what they observe when they hold the balloons close to their hair. (Their hair will move toward the balloon.)

Tell students that static electricity, which will be explained in this section, is responsible for their observation. Sheltered English

Section 1

Terms to Learn

law of electric charges
electric force
conduction
induction
conductor
insulator
static electricity
electric discharge

What You'll Do

- State and give examples of the law of electric charges.
- Describe three ways an object can become charged.
- Compare conductors with insulators.
- Give examples of static electricity and electric discharge.

Electric Charge and Static Electricity

Have you ever reached out to open a door and received a shock from the knob? You may have been surprised, and your finger or hand probably felt tingly afterward. On dry days, you can easily produce shocks by shuffling your feet on a carpet and then lightly touching a metal object. These shocks are a result of a buildup of static electricity. But what is static electricity, and how is it formed? To answer these questions, you need to learn about charge.

Atoms and Charge

To investigate charge, you must know a little about the nature of matter. All matter is composed of very small particles called atoms. Atoms are made of even smaller particles called protons, neutrons, and electrons, as shown in **Figure 1**. One important difference between protons, neutrons, and electrons is that protons and electrons are charged particles and neutrons are not.

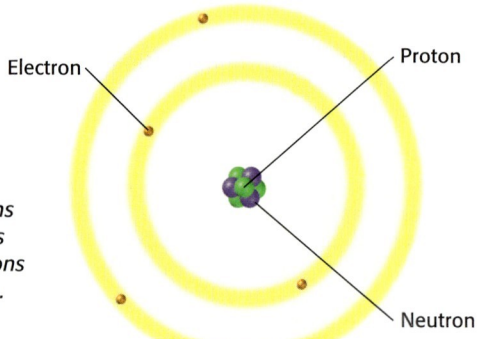

Figure 1 *Protons and neutrons make up the nucleus, which is the center of the atom. Electrons are found outside the nucleus.*

IS THAT A FACT!

The word *electricity* is derived from *elektron*, the Greek word for amber (fossilized tree sap). Thales, a Greek philosopher, observed that bits of straw were attracted to amber after the amber was rubbed with cloth.

Charges Can Exert Forces Charge is a physical property that is best understood by describing how charged objects interact with each other. A charged object exerts a force—a push or a pull—on other charged objects. There are two types of charge—positive and negative. The force between two charged objects varies depending on whether the objects have the same type of charge or opposite charges, as shown in **Figure 2**. The charged balls in Figure 2 illustrate the **law of electric charges,** which states that like charges repel and opposite charges attract.

Protons are positively charged, and electrons are negatively charged. Because protons and electrons are oppositely charged, protons and electrons are attracted to each other. If this attraction didn't exist, electrons would fly away from the nucleus of an atom.

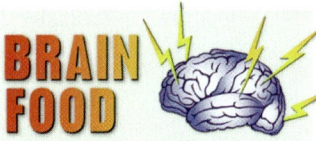

Car manufacturers take advantage of the law of electric charges when painting cars. The car bodies are given a positive charge. Then the paint droplets are given a negative charge as they exit the spray gun. The negatively charged paint droplets are attracted to the positively charged car body, so most of the paint droplets hit the car body and less paint is wasted.

Figure 2 *The law of electric charges states that like charges repel and opposite charges attract.*

Objects that have opposite charges are attracted to each other, and the force between the objects pulls them together.

Objects that have the same charge are repelled, and the force between the objects pushes them apart.

The Electric Force and the Electric Field The force between charged objects is an **electric force.** The strength of the electric force is determined by two factors. One factor is the size of the charges. The greater the charges are, the greater the electric force. The other factor that determines the strength of the electric force is the distance between the charges. The closer together the charges are, the greater the electric force.

The electric force exists because charged particles have electric fields around them. An *electric field* is a region around a charged particle that can exert a force on another charged particle. If a charged particle is in the electric field of another charged particle, the first particle is attracted or repelled by the electric force exerted on it.

2) Teach

ACTIVITY

MATERIALS

FOR EACH PAIR:
- 2 balloons
- piece of wool or silk cloth
- 1 m strings (2)

1. Have students inflate the balloons and tie a 1 m length of string to each one.
2. Tell one member of each pair to grasp one string in each hand about 0.5 m down the string from the balloons.
3. Instruct the other member to rub one of the balloons with the cloth about 10 times.
4. Release the rubbed balloon, and allow it hang freely next to the other balloon.
5. Ask students to share their observations. (The oppositely charged balloons move toward each other.)
6. Next have students rub both balloons with the cloth and observe what happens. (The balloons, which now have the same charge, move away from each other.)
7. Have students record their observations in their ScienceLog.

Teaching Transparency 267 "Law of Electric Charges"

Directed Reading Worksheet 17 Section 1

CROSS-DISCIPLINARY FOCUS

History Benjamin Franklin (1706-1790) is an important figure in the history of the United States. He signed the Declaration of Independence and the Constitution (both of which he helped to write), and he was integral to the development of our postal system. Franklin also made important contributions to science, including the study of electricity. For example, he introduced the terms *positive* and *negative* as they relate to electrical energy, and he invented the lightning rod.

Section 1 • Electric Charge and Static Electricity

2 Teach, continued

READING STRATEGY

Prediction Guide Before students read the passage about friction, conduction, and induction, ask them to explain what they think these terms mean. Encourage students to think of an example of each term. Then have them evaluate their responses after reading these pages.

DEMONSTRATION

Charging Objects As you read the corresponding text, demonstrate the three ways an object can become charged. Use the following materials:

- an inflated balloon to illustrate the effect of friction (Rub the balloon to show static electricity.)
- a glass stirring rod, a metal skewer, and a small bowl of rice cereal to illustrate the effect of conduction (Place the metal skewer in the cereal. Rub the glass rod to create a static charge, then touch the rod to the skewer in the cereal.)
- an inflated balloon to illustrate the effect of induction (Rub the balloon against a piece of clothing, and place the balloon against a wall.)

As you demonstrate each example, ask students to describe what is happening to each object. Remind them to think in terms of losing or gaining electrons. **Sheltered English**

Charge It!

Although an atom contains charged particles, the atom itself does not have a charge. Atoms contain an equal number of protons and electrons. Therefore, the positive and negative charges cancel each other out, and the atom has no overall charge. If the atoms of an object have no charge, how can the object become charged? Objects become charged because the atoms in the objects can gain or lose electrons. If the atoms of an object lose electrons, the object becomes positively charged. If the atoms gain electrons, the object becomes negatively charged. There are three common ways for an object to become charged—friction, conduction, and induction. When an object is charged by any method, no charges are created or destroyed. The charge on any object can be detected by a device called an electroscope.

Friction Rubbing two objects together can cause electrons to be "wiped" from one object and transferred to the other. If you rub a plastic ruler with a cloth, electrons are transferred from the cloth to the ruler. Because the ruler gains electrons, the ruler becomes negatively charged. Conversely, because the cloth loses electrons, the cloth becomes positively charged. **Figure 3** shows a fun example of objects becoming charged by friction.

Figure 3 When you rub a balloon against your hair, electrons from your hair are transferred to the balloon.

After the electrons are transferred, the balloon is negatively charged and your hair is positively charged.

Your hair and the balloon are attracted to each other because they are oppositely charged.

MISCONCEPTION ALERT

Students may think that atoms can gain or lose protons as well as electrons. Remind students that atoms can only lose or gain electrons, which are negatively charged. A net loss of electrons leaves an atom positively charged, whereas a net gain of electrons leaves an atom negatively charged.

Conduction Charging by **conduction** occurs when electrons are transferred from one object to another by direct contact. For example, if you touch an uncharged piece of metal with a positively charged glass rod, electrons from the metal will move to the glass rod. Because the metal loses electrons, it becomes positively charged. **Figure 4** shows what happens when you touch a negatively charged object to an uncharged object.

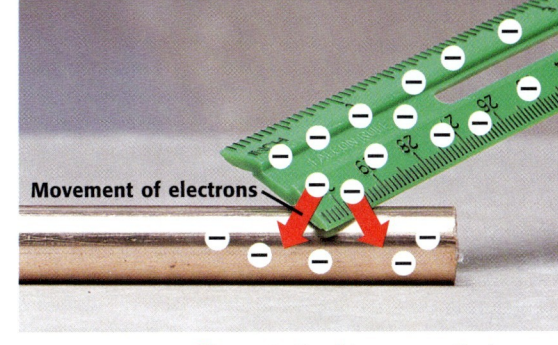

Figure 4 Touching a negatively charged plastic ruler to an uncharged metal rod causes the electrons in the ruler to travel to the rod. The rod becomes negatively charged by conduction.

Induction Charging by **induction** occurs when charges in an uncharged object are rearranged without direct contact with a charged object. For example, when a positively charged object is near a neutral object, the electrons in the neutral object are attracted to the positively charged object and move toward it. This movement produces a region of negative charge on the neutral object. **Figure 5** shows what happens when you hold a negatively charged balloon close to a neutral wall.

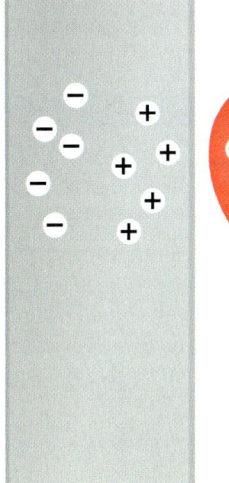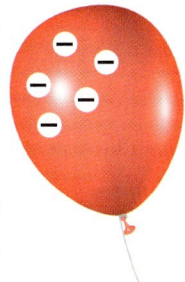

Figure 5 A negatively charged balloon induces a positive charge on a small section of a wall because the electrons in the wall are repelled and move away from the balloon.

Conservation of Charge When you charge objects by any method, no charges are created or destroyed. Electrons simply move from one atom to another, producing objects or regions with different charges. If you could count all the protons and all the electrons of all the atoms before and after charging an object, you would find that the numbers of protons and electrons do not change. Because charges are not created or destroyed, charge is said to be conserved.

Self-Check

Plastic wrap clings to food containers because the wrap has a charge. Explain how plastic wrap becomes charged. *(See page 724 to check your answer.)*

DISCUSSION

Charge and Insulation Lead students in a discussion about the role of insulation in maintaining an object in a charged state. Explain that a conductor must be insulated from other conductors in order to be charged. Otherwise, electrons will flow from one conductor to the next.

Ask students why the metal rod in **Figure 4** is able to hold a charge. (because it is insulated by the table under it)

Then ask what would happen if someone touched the metal rod. (It would become uncharged as the electrons flowed into the person.)

MEETING INDIVIDUAL NEEDS

Learners Having Difficulty Do the following demonstration to help students visualize the transfer of electrons between objects. Hold up a chalk eraser saturated with dust. Tell the class that the eraser represents a negatively charged object, the chalk particles represent electrons, and the (clean) board represents an uncharged object. Wipe the board with the eraser. Students will observe the "electron trail" that the chalk leaves behind. Sheltered English

Answer to Self-Check

Plastic wrap is charged by friction as it is pulled off the roll.

WEIRD SCIENCE

A Van de Graaff generator is a machine that continuously produces a positive charge on its domed metal surface. If you have your hands on the dome, electrons will be transferred from you to the dome by conduction, causing your hair to stand on end! Your hair becomes positively charged, and the like-charged strands of hair repel each other.

Detecting Charge To determine if an object has a charge, you can use a device called an *electroscope*. An electroscope is a glass flask that contains a metal rod inserted through a rubber stopper. There are two metal leaves at the bottom of the rod. The leaves hang straight down when the electroscope is not charged but spread apart when it is charged, as shown in **Figure 6**.

Figure 6 *When an electroscope is charged, the metal leaves have the same charge and repel each other.*

Electrons from a negatively charged plastic ruler move to the electroscope and travel down the rod. The metal leaves become negatively charged and spread apart.

A positively charged glass rod attracts the electrons in the metal rod, causing the electrons to travel up the rod. The metal leaves become positively charged and spread apart.

REVIEW

1. Describe how an object is charged by friction.
2. Compare charging by conduction and induction.
3. **Inferring Conclusions** Suppose you are conducting experiments using an electroscope. You touch an object to the top of the electroscope, the metal leaves spread apart, and you determine that the object has a charge. However, you cannot determine the type of charge (positive or negative) the object has. Explain why not.

Moving Charges

Have you ever noticed that the cords that connect electrical devices to outlets are always covered in plastic, while the prongs that fit into the socket are always metal? Both plastic and metal are used to make electrical cords because they differ in their ability to transmit charges. In fact, most materials can be divided into two groups based on how easily charges travel through the material. The two groups are conductors and insulators.

426 Chapter 17 • Introduction to Electricity

Conductors A **conductor** is a material in which charges can move easily. Most metals are good conductors because some of the electrons in metals are free to move about. Copper, silver, aluminum, and mercury are good conductors.

Conductors are used to make wires and other objects that transmit charges. For example, the prongs on a lamp's cord are made of metal so that charges can move in the cord and transfer energy to light the lamp.

Not all conductors are metal. Household, or "tap," water conducts charges very well. Because tap water is a conductor, you can receive an electric shock from charges traveling in it. Therefore, you should avoid using electrical devices (such as the one in **Figure 7**) near water unless they are specially designed to be waterproof.

Figure 7 Because tap water is a conductor, this hair dryer has a label that warns people not to use it near water.

Insulators An **insulator** is a material in which charges cannot easily move. Insulators do not conduct charges very well because electrons are tightly bound to the atoms of the insulator and cannot flow freely. Plastic, rubber, glass, wood, and air are all good insulators.

Wires used to conduct electric charges are usually covered with an insulating material. The insulator prevents charges from leaving the wire and protects you from electric shock.

Static Electricity

After taking your clothes out of the dryer, you sometimes find clothing stuck together. When this happens, you might say that the clothes stick together because of static electricity. **Static electricity** is the buildup of electric charges on an object.

When something is *static,* it is not moving. The charges that create static electricity do not move away from the object they are stuck to. Therefore, the object remains charged. For example, your clothes are charged by friction as they rub against each other inside a dryer. Positive charges build up on some clothes, and negative charges build up on other clothes. Because clothing is an insulator, the charges stay on each piece of clothing, creating static electricity. You can see the result of static electricity in **Figure 8**.

Figure 8 Opposite charges on pieces of clothing are caused by static electricity. The clothes stick together because their charges attract each other.

3 Extend

Research

Lightning comes in several different shapes and forms. Ball, forked, sheet, and bead lightning are a few examples. Have students research the many forms of lightning. Encourage them to be creative in the presentation of their results. Ask them to include photographs if possible.

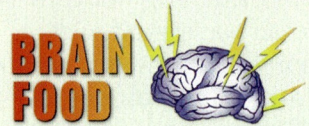

The electric discharge from a single stroke of lightning is caused by a voltage buildup of 10 million to 100 million volts between a cloud and the Earth. In July 1997, at a music festival in Haverhill, England, 45 people were simultaneously struck by lightning. To everyone's surprise, no one was killed or badly injured.

Going Further

Writing Have students research Benjamin Franklin's famous kite-flying experiment. Different sources may give different accounts of the incident. Encourage students to write their findings as a report or to make a model or a poster, and to share it with the class.

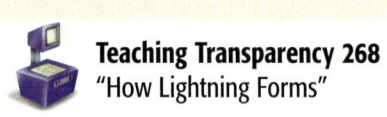
Teaching Transparency 268
"How Lightning Forms"

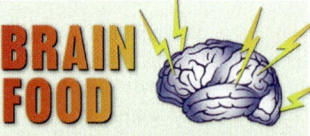
Although 70–80 percent of people struck by lightning survive, many suffer from long-term side effects such as memory loss, dizziness, and sleep disorders.

Electric Discharge Charges that build up as static electricity on an object eventually leave the object. The loss of static electricity as charges move off an object is called **electric discharge.** Sometimes electric discharge occurs slowly. For example, clothes stuck together by static electricity will eventually separate on their own because their electric charges are transferred to water molecules in the air over time.

Sometimes electric discharge occurs quickly and may be accompanied by a flash of light, a shock, or a cracking noise. For example, when you walk on a carpet with rubber-soled shoes, negative charges build up in your body. When you touch a metal doorknob, the negative charges in your body move quickly to the doorknob. Because the electric discharge happens quickly, you feel a shock.

Lightning

One of the most dramatic examples of electric discharge is lightning. Benjamin Franklin was the first to discover that lightning is a form of electricity. During a thunderstorm, Franklin flew a kite connected to a wire and successfully stored charge from a bolt of lightning. How does lightning form from a buildup of static electricity? **Figure 9** shows the answer.

Figure 9 How Lightning Forms

a During a thunderstorm, water droplets and air move within the storm cloud. As a result, negative charges build up at the bottom of the cloud and positive charges build up at the top.

c Because different parts of clouds have different charges, lightning can also occur within and between clouds.

b The negative charge at the bottom of the cloud induces a positive charge on the ground. The large charge difference causes a rapid electric discharge—called lightning.

428

Multicultural Connection
Different cultures have ascribed different meanings to lightning. In some African cultures, people struck by lightning were considered cursed.

Weird Science
Most lightning bolts move from a cloud to the ground. However, occasionally lightning bolts travel from the ground to a cloud! They usually start from the tips of mountain peaks, antenna towers, or very tall buildings.

Lightning Rods Benjamin Franklin also invented the lightning rod. A *lightning rod* is a pointed rod connected to the ground by a wire. Lightning usually strikes the highest point in a charged area because that point provides the easiest path for the charges to reach the ground. Therefore, lightning rods are always mounted so that they "stick out" and are the tallest point on a building, as shown in **Figure 10**.

Objects, such as a lightning rod, that are in contact with the Earth are *grounded*. Any object that is grounded provides a path for electric charges to travel to the Earth. Because the Earth is so large, it can give up or absorb electric charges without being damaged. When lightning strikes a lightning rod, the electric charges are carried safely to the Earth through the rod's wire. By directing the lightning's charge to the Earth, lightning rods prevent lightning damage to buildings.

Lightning Dangers Anything that sticks out in an area can provide a path for lightning. Trees and people in open areas are at risk of being struck by lightning. This is why it is particularly dangerous to be at the beach or on a golf course during a lightning storm. And standing under a tree during a storm is dangerous because the charge from lightning striking a tree can jump to your body.

Science CONNECTION

Sprites and elves aren't just creatures in fairy tales! Read about how they are related to lightning on page 451.

Figure 10 *Lightning strikes the lightning rod rather than the building because the lightning rod is the tallest point on the building.*

REVIEW

1. What is static electricity? Give an example of static electricity.
2. How is the shock you receive from a metal doorknob similar to a bolt of lightning?
3. **Applying Concepts** When you use an electroscope, you touch a charged object to a metal rod that is held in place by a rubber stopper. Why is it important to touch the object to the metal rod and not to the rubber stopper?

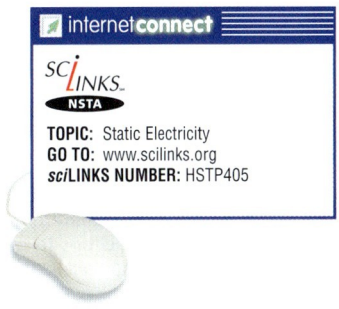

internetconnect

SC_**i**_**LINKS** NSTA

TOPIC: Static Electricity
GO TO: www.scilinks.org
***sci*LINKS NUMBER:** HSTP405

4) Close

Quiz

Ask students to answer the following questions:

1. Briefly explain the relationship between charge and force. (Charge is a physical property. Objects with a positive or negative charge exert a force on other charged objects.)
2. Discuss the difference between a conductor and an insulator. Give an example of each. (Charge moves easily in a conductor but has difficulty moving in an insulator. Most metals are conductors. Plastic, rubber, and glass are insulators.)

ALTERNATIVE ASSESSMENT

Concept Mapping Without naming them, demonstrate the three ways that an object can be charged (friction, conduction, and induction). Have students make a concept map that identifies and briefly explains the three methods of charging.

Reinforcement Worksheet 17 "Charge!"

Interactive Explorations CD-ROM "Tunnel Vision"

▼ Answers to Review

1. Static electricity is the buildup of electric charge on an object. Examples include clothes sticking together after being machine dried and hair sticking up after being brushed.
2. Both the shock you receive from a doorknob and a bolt of lightning are examples of electric discharge.
3. The metal rod is a conductor, so electrons can easily move down the rod to the metal leaves or up the rod from the metal leaves and confirm any charge present. The rubber stopper is an insulator. Electrons will not move through rubber, so the electroscope will not perform as intended.

Section 1 • Electric Charge and Static Electricity

SECTION 2

Focus

Electrical Energy

This section describes different ways to produce electric current. Students learn how cells and batteries convert chemical energy to electrical energy. They learn how potential difference is related to electric current. Students also learn how photocells and thermocouples convert light and thermal energy, respectively, into electrical energy.

Bellringer

Write the following question on the board:

What's inside a battery?

Display several kinds of batteries for students to see. Tell students to draw what they think the inside of a battery looks like in their ScienceLog.

1 Motivate

DISCUSSION

What's Inside? Show students a photo or illustration of the inside of a car battery or D cell. Ask them how they think a battery produces electrical energy, based on what they see. Tell them that they will learn the answer in this section.

Sheltered English

Directed Reading Worksheet 17 Section 2

Section 2

Terms to Learn

cell
battery
potential difference
photocell
thermocouple

What You'll Do

- Explain how a cell produces an electric current.
- Describe how the potential difference is related to electric current.
- Describe how photocells and thermocouples produce electrical energy.

Electrical Energy

Imagine living without electrical energy. You could not watch television or listen to a portable radio, and you could not even turn on a light bulb to help you see in the dark! *Electrical energy*—the energy of electric charges—provides people with many comforts and conveniences. A flow of charges is called an *electric current*. Electric currents can be produced in many ways. One common way to produce electric current is through chemical reactions in a battery.

Batteries Are Included

In science, energy is defined as the ability to do work. Energy cannot be created or destroyed; it can only be converted into other types of energy. A **cell** is a device that produces an electric current by converting chemical energy into electrical energy. A **battery** also converts chemical energy into electrical energy and is made of several cells.

Parts of a Cell Every cell contains a mixture of chemicals that conducts a current; the mixture is called an *electrolyte* (ee LEK troh LIET). Chemical reactions in the electrolyte convert chemical energy into electrical energy. Every cell also contains a pair of electrodes made from two different conducting materials that are in contact with the electrolyte. An *electrode* (ee LEK TROHD) is the part of a cell through which charges enter or exit. **Figure 11** shows how a cell produces an electric current.

Figure 11 *This cell has a zinc electrode and a copper electrode dipped in a liquid electrolyte.*

a A chemical reaction leaves extra electrons on the zinc electrode. Therefore, the zinc electrode has a negative charge.

b A different chemical reaction causes electrons to be pulled off the copper electrode, making the copper electrode positively charged.

c If the electrodes are connected by a wire, charges will flow from the negative zinc electrode through the wire to the positive copper electrode, producing an electric current.

CONNECT TO LIFE SCIENCE

We use electrolytes in our bodies as well. In biology, electrolytes are considered substances that can conduct an electric current when in solution. Electrolytes in the body include sodium ions and potassium ions in body fluids. Different concentrations of these ions inside and outside nerve cells enable nerve cells to conduct electrical impulses. Use Teaching Transparency 90, "What's in a Nerve?" to teach students more about nerves.

Teaching Transparency 90 "What's in a Nerve?"

430   Chapter 17 • Introduction to Electricity

Types of Cells Cells are divided into two groups—wet cells and dry cells. Wet cells, such as the cell shown in Figure 11, contain liquid electrolytes. A car battery is made of several wet cells that use sulfuric acid as the electrolyte.

Dry cells work in a similar way, but dry cells contain electrolytes that are solid or pastelike. The cells used in portable radios and flashlights are examples of dry cells.

You can make your own cell by inserting strips of zinc and copper into a lemon. The electric current produced when the metal strips are connected is strong enough to power a small clock, as shown in **Figure 12.**

Potatoes aren't just for eating anymore! Learn how to use a potato to produce an electric current on page 695 of the LabBook.

Figure 12 *This cell uses the juice of a lemon as an electrolyte and uses strips of zinc and copper as electrodes.*

Bring On the Potential

So far you have learned that cells and batteries can produce electric currents. But why does the electric current exist between the two electrodes? The electric current exists because a chemical reaction causes a difference in charge between the two electrodes. The difference in charge means that an electric current—a flow of electric charges—can be produced by the cell to provide energy. The energy per unit charge is called the **potential difference** and is expressed in volts (V).

As long as there is a potential difference between the electrodes of a cell and there is a wire connecting them, charges will flow through the cell and the wire, creating an electric current. The current depends on the potential difference. The greater the potential difference is, the greater the current. **Figure 13** shows batteries and cells with different potential differences.

Figure 13 *Batteries are made with different potential differences. The potential difference of a battery depends on the number of cells it contains.*

CROSS-DISCIPLINARY FOCUS

History The Italian physicist Count Alessandro Volta (1745–1827) probably developed the first battery in the late 1790s. His battery was a stack of pairs of silver and zinc disks separated by disks of cardboard moistened with salt solution. Napoleon bestowed the title of "Count" on Volta for his work on electricity. The volt is named after him.

---

2) Teach

LabBook   PG 695
Potato Power

ACTIVITY

Lemon Cells A variation of the lemon clock pictured in **Figure 12** can be constructed easily in the classroom. Divide students into small groups for this activity.

MATERIALS

FOR EACH GROUP:
- lemon
- strip of copper
- strip of zinc
- voltmeter
- two cables with alligator clips

1. Have students firmly roll the lemon on a hard surface to break up some of the juice sacs inside it.
2. Instruct students to stick the strips of copper and zinc into the lemon so that the strips are close together but not touching.
3. Tell students to fasten an alligator clip to each strip and plug the other end into the appropriate slot in the voltmeter.
4. Have students record their results in their ScienceLog.

Discuss the results with your students. **Sheltered English**

Teaching Transparency 269
"How a Cell Produces an Electric Current"

Section 2 • Electrical Energy   **431**

3 Close

Research

✏️ *Writing* Encourage students to research and write about one alternative way of producing electrical energy, such as using wind or water power. Tell them to include a basic explanation of the scientific principles involved.

Quiz

1. Explain what potential difference is and explain the difference between volts and potential difference. (**Electric charges flow between the electrodes of a cell or battery. Potential difference is the energy per unit charge. Volts are the units used to express the potential difference.**)
2. Explain the difference between wet cells and dry cells. (**Wet cells contain a liquid electrolyte such as sulfuric acid. Dry cells, such as flashlight cells, contain solid or pastelike electrolytes.**)

Alternative Assessment

Making Models Supply students with materials to construct a model of a cell. The materials could include colored construction paper, foam board, markers, and ice-cream sticks. Instruct students that their model should include all parts of a cell as well as labels for each part.

`Sheltered English`

Solar panel

Other Ways of Producing Electrical Energy

The conversion of chemical energy to electrical energy in batteries is not the only way electrical energy can be generated. Several technological devices have been developed to convert different types of energy into electrical energy for use every day. For example, generators convert kinetic energy into electrical energy. Two other devices that produce electrical energy are photocells and thermocouples.

Photocells Have you ever wondered how a solar-powered calculator works? If you look above the display of the calculator, you will see a dark strip called a solar panel. This panel is made of several photocells. A **photocell** is the part of a solar panel that converts light into electrical energy.

Photocells contain silicon atoms. When light strikes the photocell, electrons are ejected from the silicon atoms. If light continues to shine on the photocell, electrons will be steadily emitted. The ejected electrons are gathered into a wire to create an electric current.

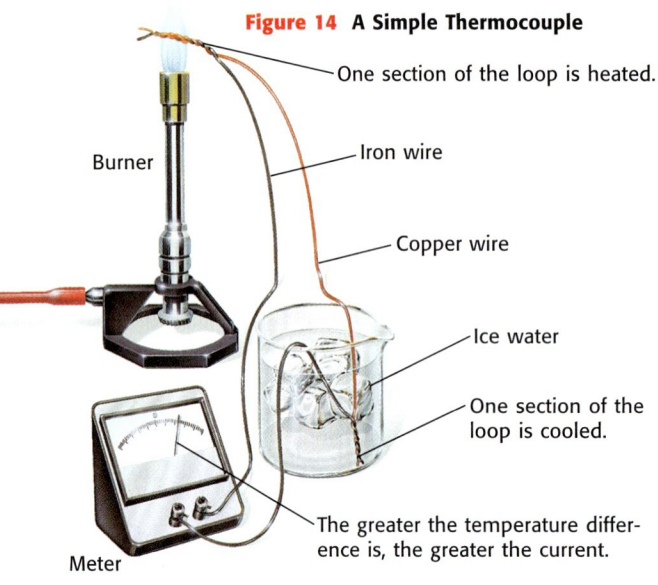

Figure 14 A Simple Thermocouple
- One section of the loop is heated.
- Burner
- Iron wire
- Copper wire
- Ice water
- One section of the loop is cooled.
- The greater the temperature difference is, the greater the current.
- Meter

Thermocouples Thermal energy can be converted to electrical energy by a **thermocouple.** A simple thermocouple is made by joining wires made of two different metals into a loop, as shown in **Figure 14.** The temperature difference within the loop causes charges to flow through the loop. Thermocouples are used to monitor the temperature of car engines, furnaces, and ovens.

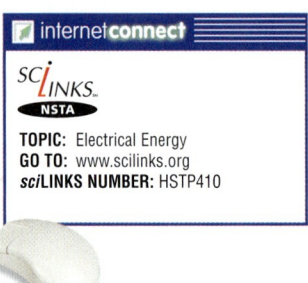

internetconnect
SCiLINKS NSTA
TOPIC: Electrical Energy
GO TO: www.scilinks.org
sciLINKS NUMBER: HSTP410

REVIEW

1. Name the parts of a cell, and explain how they work together to produce an electric current.
2. How do the currents produced by a 1.5 V flashlight cell and a 12 V car battery compare?
3. **Inferring Conclusions** Why do you think some solar calculators contain batteries?

Answers to Review

1. A cell is made of an electrolyte and two electrodes. Chemical reactions in the electrolyte leave extra electrons on one electrode and strip them from the other. If the charged electrodes are connected with a wire, electric charges will flow between them.

2. Under equal conditions, the current from a 12 V car battery is greater than the current from a 1.5 V flashlight cell. (Students will learn in the next section that resistance might change this comparison.)

3. Some solar calculators contain batteries as a backup power source, for when there is insufficient light.

Section 3

Electric Current

Terms to Learn

current
voltage
resistance
electric power

What You'll Do

- Describe electric current.
- Identify the four factors that determine the resistance of an object.
- Explain how current, voltage, and resistance are related by Ohm's law.
- Describe how electric power is related to electrical energy.

So far you have read how electrical energy can be generated by a variety of methods. A battery produces electrical energy very effectively, but electric power plants provide most of the electrical energy used every day. In this section, you will learn more about electric current and about the electrical energy you use at home.

Current Revisited

In the previous section, you learned that electric current is a continuous flow of charge. **Current** is more precisely defined as the rate at which charge passes a given point. The higher the current is, the more charge passes the point each second. The unit for current is the *ampere* (A), which is sometimes called amp for short. In equations, the symbol for current is the letter I.

Charge Ahead! When you flip a light switch, the light comes on instantly. Many people think that happens because electrons travel through the wire at the speed of light. In fact, it's because an electric field is created at close to the speed of light.

Flipping the light switch sets up an electric field in the wire that connects to the light bulb. The electric field causes the free electrons in the wire to move, as illustrated in **Figure 15.** Because the electric field is created so quickly, the electrons start moving through the wire at practically the same instant. You can think of the electric field as a kind of command to the electrons to "Charge ahead!" The light comes on instantly because the electrons simultaneously obey this command. So the current that causes the bulb to light up is established very quickly, even though individual electrons move quite slowly. In fact, it may take a single electron over an hour to travel 1 m through a wire.

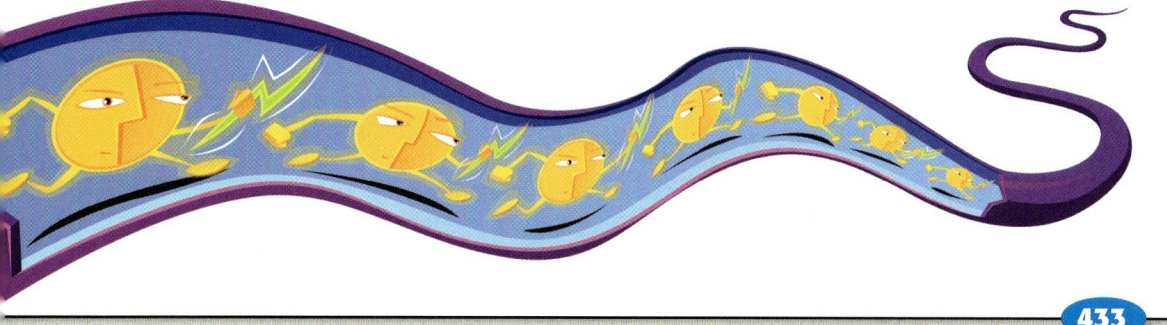

Figure 15 Electrons moving in a wire make up current, a continuous flow of charge.

Q: What part of the newspaper do electricians read first?

A: current events

MISCONCEPTION ALERT

Electrons do not travel single file in a straight line through a wire. Instead, electrons move through the spaces around atoms in the wire much like water would move through the spaces in a pipe filled with marbles. See **Figure 19** on page 436.

433

2) Teach

DISCUSSION

Invite a local electrician or electrical engineer to visit the classroom to talk about working with and around electric current. Ask your guest to discuss the safety aspects of his or her job. Before the speaker's visit, ask students to write down one or two questions to ask the speaker.

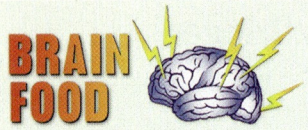

One of the major advantages of using the AC system is that it is easier to change the voltage between the producer of the electrical energy and the user of the electrical energy. Why does the voltage need to be changed? A generator at an electric power plant can produce up to 22,000 V, while the average home appliance in the United States requires only 120 V. The voltage is reduced at least three times as the electrical energy travels between the electric plant and your home.

TOPIC: Electric Current
GO TO: www.scilinks.org
sciLINKS NUMBER: HSTP415

Let's See, AC/DC . . . There are two different types of electric current—direct current (DC) and alternating current (AC). In *direct current* the charges always flow in the same direction. In *alternating current* the charges continually switch from flowing in one direction to flowing in the reverse direction. **Figure 16** illustrates the difference between DC and AC.

The electric current produced by batteries and cells is DC, but the electric current from outlets in your home is AC. Both types of electric current can be used to provide electrical energy. For example, if you connect a flashlight bulb to a battery, the light bulb will light. You can light a household light bulb by attaching it to a lamp and turning the lamp switch on.

Alternating current is used in homes because it is more practical for transferring electrical energy. In the United States, the alternating current provided to households changes directions 120 times each second.

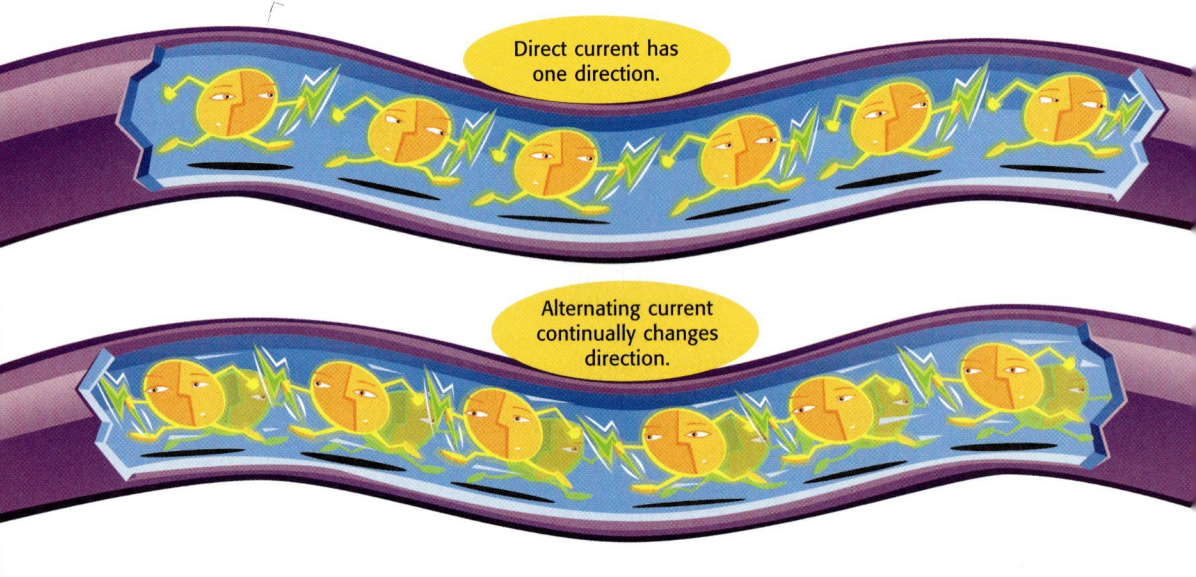

Figure 16 Unlike DC, charges continually change direction in AC.

Voltage

The current in a wire is determined by voltage. **Voltage** is the difference in energy per unit charge as a charge moves between two points in the path of a current. Voltage is another word for potential difference. Because voltage is the same as potential difference, voltage is expressed in volts. The symbol for voltage is the letter *V*. You can think of voltage as the amount of energy released as a charge moves between two points in the path of a current. The higher the voltage is, the more energy is released per charge. The current depends on the voltage. The greater the voltage is, the greater the current.

434

SCIENTISTS AT ODDS

Tesla and Edison In the late 1800s, a controversy brewed between advocates of alternating current and advocates of direct current. The Croatian-born inventor Nikola Tesla and the American inventor Thomas Edison championed their respective inventions. Eventually, the advantages of Tesla's AC system won out, and it was demonstrated to the public at the 1893 World's Columbian Exposition, in Chicago.

Voltage May Vary In the United States, electrical outlets usually supply a voltage of 120 V. Therefore, most electrical devices, such as televisions, toasters, lamps, and alarm clocks, are designed to run on 120 V. Devices that run on batteries or cells usually need a lower voltage. For example, a portable radio needs only 3 V. Compare this with the voltage created by the eel in **Figure 17.**

Pacemaker cells in the heart produce low electric currents at regular intervals to make the heart beat. During a heart attack, pacemaker cells do not work together and the heart beats irregularly. To correct this, doctors sometimes "jump start" the heart by creating a high voltage across a person's chest, which forces the pacemaker cells to act together, restoring a regular heartbeat.

Figure 17 *An electric eel can create a voltage of more than 600 V!*

Resistance

In addition to voltage, resistance also determines the current in a wire. **Resistance** is the opposition to the flow of electric charge. Resistance is expressed in ohms (Ω, the Greek letter *omega*). In equations, the symbol for resistance is the letter R.

You can think of resistance as "electrical friction." The higher the resistance of a material is, the lower the current is in it. Therefore, as resistance increases, current decreases if the voltage is kept the same. An object's resistance varies depending on the object's material, thickness, length, and temperature.

Material Good conductors, such as copper, have low resistance. Poorer conductors, such as iron, have higher resistance. The resistance of insulators is so high that electric charges cannot flow in them.

Materials with low resistance are used to make wires and other objects that are used to transfer electrical energy from place to place. For example, most of the electrical cords in your house contain copper wires. However, it is sometimes helpful to use a material with high resistance, as shown in **Figure 18.**

Figure 18 *Tungsten light bulb filaments have a high resistance. This property causes electrical energy to be converted to light and thermal energy.*

IS THAT A FACT!

Electrons moving in a conductor undergo collisions with the material's atoms. These collisions are responsible for the material's resistance; they slow the rate at which electrons flow. Anything that increases the number of collisions will tend to increase a material's resistance.

READING STRATEGY

Prediction Guide Before reading the passage on resistance, ask students to choose the correct term in the following statements:

1. If resistance in a material increases and the voltage is constant, current (increases, decreases). (decreases)
2. Assuming constant voltage, the (higher, lower) the resistance is, the higher the current. (lower)
3. Resistance depends on an object's material, thickness, length, and (color, temperature). (temperature)

GROUP ACTIVITY

Divide the class into groups of two or three. Instruct each group to create a model or a poster that illustrates the factors that affect resistance—material, thickness, length, and temperature. Encourage students to show clearly why a short, thick pipe, for example, has less resistance than a long, narrow one. Give students 2–3 days to complete their project. They can then make a short presentation about their poster or model to the class.

2) Teach, continued

RESEARCH

Writing In many animals, including humans, nerves transmit electric impulses to send messages to other nerves, to stimulate organs to perform various functions, and to stimulate muscles to contract. Have students research how nerves transmit electric impulses. Challenge them to find out how organisms, such as the giant squid, deal with the problem of resistance. (Hint: Some of the giant squid's nerve fibers are thick enough to see.) Have students compile their findings into a report or have them make a poster or a model.

REAL-WORLD CONNECTION

A few maglev (magnetically-levitated) trains use the "zero" resistance of superconductors to float above their tracks. Superconducting electromagnets keep a train elevated about 8 mm above the track while the train is moving. The main advantage of maglev trains over conventional trains is that they are not limited by friction between the train and its track. Therefore, they can travel very fast and make relatively little noise. Japanese prototype trains have reached speeds of more than 480 km per hour!

Thickness and Length To understand how the thickness and length of a wire affect the wire's resistance, consider the model in **Figure 19.** The pipe filled with gravel represents a wire, and the water flowing through the pipe represents electric charges. This analogy illustrates that thick wires have less resistance than thin wires and that long wires have more resistance than short wires.

Figure 19 *Gravel in a pipe is like resistance in a wire. Just as gravel makes it more difficult for water to flow through the pipe, resistance makes it more difficult for electric charges to flow in a wire.*

A thick pipe has less resistance than a thin pipe because there are more spaces between pieces of gravel in a thick pipe for water to flow through.

A short pipe has less resistance than a long pipe because the water in a short pipe does not have to work its way around as many pieces of gravel.

Temperature Resistance also depends somewhat on temperature. In general, the resistance of metals increases as temperature increases. This happens because atoms move faster at higher temperatures and get in the way of the flowing electric charges.

If you cool certain materials to an extremely low temperature, resistance will drop to nearly 0 Ω. Materials in this state are called *superconductors*. A small superconductor is shown in **Figure 20.** Superconductors can be useful because very little energy is wasted when electric charges travel in them. However, so much energy is necessary to cool them that superconductors are not practical for everyday use.

Figure 20 *One interesting property of superconductors is that they repel magnets. The superconductor in this photo is repelling the magnet so strongly that the magnet is floating.*

IS THAT A FACT!

An amazing characteristic of superconductors is that once a current is established in them, the current continues to exist *after* the potential difference is removed!

SCIENCE HUMOR

There was tin being electrically inducted
By current that it naturally conducted.
Then along came some fool,
Who said, "Let's make tin cool!"
And now the tin's superconducted!

Ohm's Law: Putting It All Together

So far, you have learned about current, voltage, and resistance. But how are they related? A German school teacher named Georg Ohm asked this very question. He determined that the relationship between current (I), voltage (V), and resistance (R) could be expressed with the equation shown at right. This equation, which is known as *Ohm's law*, shows that the units of current, voltage, and resistance are related in the following way:

$$\text{amperes (A)} = \frac{\text{volts (V)}}{\text{ohms }(\Omega)}$$

$$I = \frac{V}{R}$$

You can use Ohm's law to find the current in a wire if you know the voltage applied and the resistance of the wire. For example, if a voltage of 30 V is applied to a wire with a resistance of 60 Ω, the current is as follows:

$$I = \frac{V}{R} = \frac{30 \text{ V}}{60 \text{ }\Omega} = 0.5 \text{ A}$$

Electric Power

You probably hear the word *power* used in different ways. Power can be used to mean force, strength, or energy. In science, power is the rate at which work is done. **Electric power** is the rate at which electrical energy is used to do work. The unit for power is the watt (W), and the symbol for power is the letter *P*. Electric power is calculated with the following equation:

$$\text{power} = \text{voltage} \times \text{current}, \quad \text{or} \quad P = V \times I$$

For the units:

$$\text{watts (W)} = \text{volts (V)} \times \text{amperes (A)}$$

MATH BREAK

Using Ohm's Law

You can use Ohm's law to find voltage or resistance:

$$V = I \times R \qquad R = \frac{V}{I}$$

If a 2 A current flows through a resistance of 12 Ω, the voltage is calculated as follows.

$$V = I \times R$$
$$V = 2 \text{ A} \times 12 \text{ }\Omega$$
$$V = 24 \text{ V}$$

Now It's Your Turn

1. Find the resistance of an object if a voltage of 10 V produces a current of 0.5 A.
2. Find the current produced if a voltage of 36 V is applied to a resistance of 4 Ω.

MISCONCEPTION ALERT

Not all materials obey Ohm's law. Materials that do not obey Ohm's law are called nonohmic materials. Semiconductors are examples of nonohmic materials.

3) Extend

GOING FURTHER

Inform students that they are going to calculate the monthly cost of running their television set, a 100 W light, and a clock. Have them follow the steps below.

1. For 1 day, record how many hours each of the three electrical appliances are run in your home.
2. Multiply the hours of daily use by 30 to obtain the monthly usage.
3. Multiply the average number of watts used by each appliance (see below) by the monthly usage to get the monthly watt-hours.
   - television—200 W
   - 100 W light bulb—100 W
   - clock—3 W
4. Divide the monthly watt-hours by 1,000 to get the monthly kilowatt-hours.
5. Multiply the monthly kilowatt-hours for each appliance by the rate charged by the power company ($0.09 or the actual charge). This final result is the monthly cost of running the appliance.

Encourage students to share their results and to compare their monthly usage times. Were their results higher or lower than expected?

Watt Is a Power Rating?! If you have ever changed a light bulb, you are probably familiar with watts. Light bulbs have labels such as "60 W," "75 W," or "120 W." As electrical energy is supplied to a light bulb, the light bulb glows. As power increases, the bulb burns brighter because more electrical energy is converted to light energy. That is why a 120 W bulb burns brighter than a 60 W bulb.

Another common unit of power is the kilowatt (kW). One kilowatt is equal to 1,000 W. Kilowatts are used to express high values of power, such as the power needed to heat a house. The table shows the power ratings of some appliances you use every day.

Power Ratings of Household Appliances

Appliance	Power (W)
Clothes dryer	4,000
Toaster	1,100
Hair dryer	1,000
Refrigerator/freezer	600
Color television	200
Radio	100
Clock	3

 Self-Check

How much electrical energy is used by a color television that stays on for 2 hours? *(See page 724 to check your answer.)*

Measuring Electrical Energy

Electric power companies sell electrical energy to homes and businesses. Such companies determine how much a household or business has to pay based on power and time. For example, the amount of electrical energy used by a household depends on the power of the electrical devices in the house and how long those devices are on. The equation for electrical energy is as follows:

electrical energy = power × time, or $E = P \times t$

Answer to Self-Check

$E = P \times t$; $E = 200$ W $\times$ 2 h $= 400$ Wh
Students will have to use data from the table on page 438 to answer this question.

 **SCIENCE**

The longest span of electrical transmission line between two support structures stretches 5,379 m across the Ameralik Fjord, in Greenland. The line weighs 42 tons.

438 Chapter 17 • Introduction to Electricity

Measuring Household Energy Use Households use varying amounts of electrical energy during a day. Electric companies usually calculate electric energy by multiplying the power in kilowatts by the time in hours. The unit of electrical energy is usually kilowatt-hours (kWh). If a household used 2,000 W (2 kW) of power for 3 hours, it used 6 kWh of energy.

Electric power companies use electric meters such as the one shown at right to determine the number of kilowatt-hours of energy used by a household. Meters are often located outside houses and apartment buildings so someone from the power company can read them.

How to Save Energy

The amount of electrical energy used by an appliance depends on the power rating of the appliance and how long it is on. For example, a clock has a power rating of 3 W, and it is on 24 hours a day. Therefore, the clock uses 72 Wh (3 W × 24 hours), or 0.072 kWh, of energy a day. Using the information in the table on the previous page and an estimate of how long each appliance is on during a day, determine which appliances use the most energy and which use the least. Based on your findings, describe what you can do to use less energy.

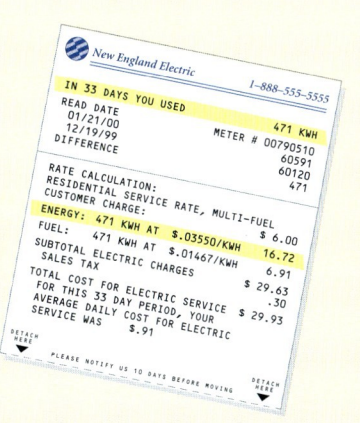

REVIEW

1. What is electric current?
2. How does increasing the voltage affect the current?
3. How does an electric power company calculate electrical energy from electric power?
4. **Making Predictions** Which wire would have the lowest resistance: a long, thin iron wire at a high temperature or a short, thick copper wire at a low temperature?
5. **Doing Calculations** Use Ohm's law to find the voltage needed to produce a current of 3 A in a device with a resistance of 9 Ω.

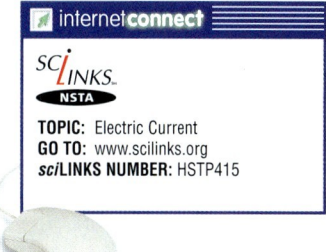

TOPIC: Electric Current
GO TO: www.scilinks.org
sciLINKS NUMBER: HSTP415

---

4) Close

Quiz

1. According to Ohm's law, what happens to the current if the voltage increases and the resistance stays constant? (current increases) If the current in a wire is 4 A, what is the ratio of the voltage applied to the wire to the wire's resistance in ohms? (You may wish to have students read the Math Refresher in the Appendix if they need help with ratios.) (4:1)

2. How do electric power companies keep track of how much electrical energy a household or business uses? (Usually they use electric meters that record the kilowatt-hours of energy used by a household or a business.)

ALTERNATIVE ASSESSMENT

Writing Have students write a paragraph about electric current. Tell them to include each of the units of measurement defined in this section (kilowatt-hours, volts, amperes, ohms, watts). Have them read their finished paragraph aloud.

Answer to APPLY

Answers will vary. Student answers should reflect an understanding of ways to use less energy, such as using appliances with high power ratings less often.

Critical Thinking Worksheet 17 "Potentially Shocking!"

Answers to Review

1. Electric current is a continuous flow of charge caused by the motion of electrons.
2. Current depends partially on voltage, so increasing the voltage increases the current.
3. Electric power companies calculate electrical energy by multiplying the power in kilowatts by the time in hours.
4. A short, thick copper wire at a low temperature would have a lower resistance than a long, thin iron wire at a high temperature.
5. $V = I \times R = 3\text{ A} \times 9\text{ Ω} = 27\text{ V}$

Section 3 • Electric Current

SECTION 4

Focus

Electric Circuits

In this section, students learn what an electric circuit is, the main parts of a circuit, and the difference between series and parallel circuits. The section also discusses circuits in the home and circuit safety.

Have the lights turned off as students enter the classroom. Write the following question on the chalkboard:

> What happens when you turn the lights on?

Encourage students to think beyond the obvious. Have them explain what allows lights to be turned on and off. Have students write down their answer or draw an explanatory picture in their ScienceLog for later reference.

1) Motivate

DEMONSTRATION

Create a circuit, and demonstrate how it works to the class. Connect a 6V battery to a small light bulb with copper wire. Students will observe that the bulb lights. Ask them to explain why this device constitutes a circuit. (When properly connected, the parts form a complete path through which electric charges flow.)

Directed Reading Worksheet 17 Section 4

Section 4

Electric Circuits

Terms to Learn
circuit
load
series circuit
parallel circuit

What You'll Do
- Name the three essential parts of a circuit.
- Compare series circuits with parallel circuits.
- Explain how fuses and circuit breakers protect your home against short circuits and circuit overloads.

Imagine that you are lost in a forest. You need to find your way back to camp, where your friends are waiting for you. Unfortunately, there are no trails to follow, so you don't know which way to go. Just as you need a trail to follow in order to return to camp, electric charges need a path to follow in order to travel from an outlet or a battery to the device it provides energy to. A path that charges follow is called a circuit.

A circuit, however, is not exactly the same as a trail in a forest. A trail may begin in one place and end in another. But a circuit always begins and ends in the same place, forming a loop. Because a circuit forms a loop, it is said to be a closed path. So an electric **circuit** is a complete, closed path through which electric charges flow.

Parts of a Circuit

All circuits consist of an energy source, a load, and wires to connect the other parts together. A **load** is a device that uses electrical energy to do work. All loads offer some resistance to electric currents and cause the electrical energy to change into other forms of energy such as light energy or kinetic energy. **Figure 21** shows some examples of the different parts of a circuit.

Figure 21 Parts of a Circuit

a The energy source can be a battery, a photocell, a thermocouple, or an electric generator at a power plant.

c Examples of loads are light bulbs, appliances, televisions, and motors.

b Wires connect the other parts of a circuit together. Wires are usually made of conducting materials with low resistance, such as copper.

CROSS-DISCIPLINARY FOCUS

Language Arts

Writing After students understand what a circuit is and what its parts are, have them write a short story that includes a circuit in some meaningful way. For example, a student could write about the role of a faulty circuit switch in solving a mystery or about a world where circuits behave differently than they do in this one. Have interested students read their story to the class.

440   Chapter 17 • Introduction to Electricity

Opening and Closing a Circuit Sometimes a circuit also contains a switch. A switch is used to open and close a circuit. Usually a switch is made of two pieces of conducting material, one of which can be moved, as shown in **Figure 22**. For charges to flow through a circuit, the switch must be closed, or "turned on." If a switch is open, or "off," the loop of the circuit is broken and no charges can flow through the circuit. Light switches, power buttons on radios, and even the keys on calculators and computers work this way.

Figure 22 *You can turn a light bulb on and off by using a switch to close and open a circuit.*

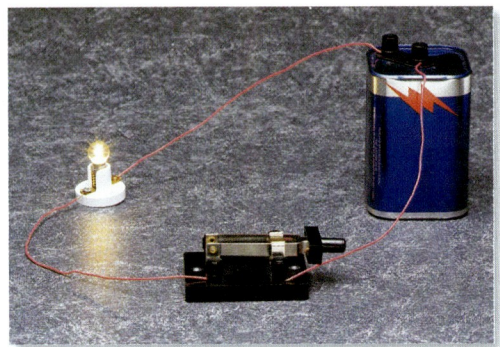

When the switch is **closed**, the two pieces of conducting material touch, allowing the electric charges to flow through the circuit.

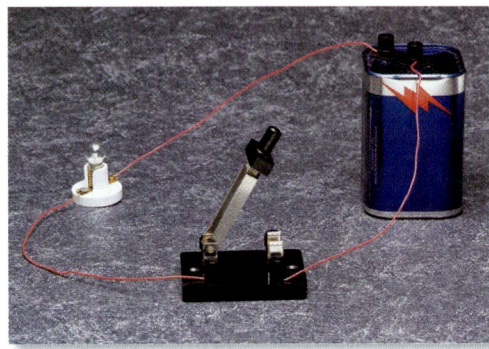

When the switch is **open**, the gap between the two pieces of conducting material prevents the electric charges from traveling through the circuit.

Biology CONNECTION

Believe it or not, your body is controlled by a large electric circuit. Electrical impulses from your brain control all the muscles and organs in your body. The food you eat is the energy source for your body's circuit, your nerves are the wires, and your muscles and organs are the loads.

Self-Check

Is a microwave oven an example of a load? Why or why not? *(See page 724 to check your answer.)*

Types of Circuits

Look around the room for a moment, and count the number of objects that use electrical energy. You probably found several objects, such as lights, a clock, and maybe a computer. All of the objects you counted are loads in a large circuit that may include several rooms in the building. In fact, most circuits contain more than one load. The loads in a circuit can be connected in two different ways—in series or in parallel.

WEIRD SCIENCE

Nikola Tesla, who developed the alternating-current system, was known as a brilliant but eccentric inventor. To dispel fears about the safety of his AC system, Tesla would light lamps using himself in place of the wires; the charges flowed through his body instead!

internetconnect

TOPIC: Electric Circuits
GO TO: www.scilinks.org
*sci*LINKS NUMBER: HSTP420

Section 4 • Electric Circuits   441

2 Teach, continued

QuickLab

MATERIALS

FOR EACH GROUP:
- 6 V battery
- 3 flashlight bulbs with holders
- 5 pieces of insulated copper wire with ends stripped
- burned-out flashlight bulb
- screwdriver
- tape

Safety Caution: Remind students not to touch the ends of the wire and to use only the screwdriver to connect the wire to the bulb holders. Also make sure that students do not connect the battery to itself (with no load), as this could create a short circuit. Have all students wear safety goggles.

Answers to QuickLab

1. The drawing of the circuit should show the light bulbs and the 6 V battery connected in a loop.
2. The light bulbs do not glow as brightly as they did when only two bulbs were attached.
3. The other light bulbs in the circuit do not glow.

MEETING INDIVIDUAL NEEDS

Learners Having Difficulty
Students may have difficulty remembering the parts of a series or parallel circuit. To help them, make flashcards with the words *battery, series, parallel,* and *bulb,* and make cards with arrows to show the direction charges flow. Help them arrange the cards in proper order, then ask them to make a concept map describing electric circuits.

Sheltered English

Series Circuits A **series circuit** is a circuit in which all parts are connected in a single loop. The charges traveling through a series circuit must flow through each part and can only follow one path. **Figure 23** shows an example of a series circuit.

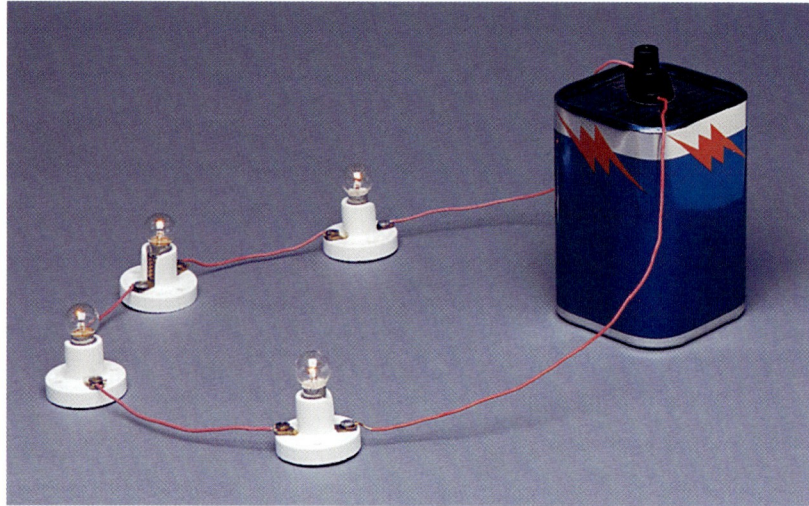

Figure 23 The charges flow from the battery through each light bulb (load) and finally back to the battery.

QuickLab

A Series of Circuits

1. Connect a **6 V battery** and **two flashlight bulbs** in a series circuit. Draw a picture of your circuit in your ScienceLog.
2. Add another **flashlight bulb** in series with the other two bulbs. How does the brightness of the light bulbs change?
3. Replace one of the light bulbs with a **burned-out light bulb**. What happens to the other lights in the circuit?

442

All the loads in a series circuit share the same current. Because the current in all the light bulbs in Figure 23 is the same, the light bulbs glow with the same brightness. However, if you add more light bulbs, the resistance of the entire circuit would increase and the current would decrease. Therefore, all the bulbs would be dimmer.

Uses for Series Circuits Some series circuits use a load as a switch. For example, the automatic door at the grocery store is operated by a series circuit with a motor that opens the door and a photoelectric device—an "electric eye"—that acts as an on-off switch. When no light hits the device, charges flow to the motor and the door opens.

For charges to flow in a series circuit, all the loads must be turned on and working. Charges pass through one load after another, in order, around the circuit. If one load is broken or missing, the other loads will not work. For example, if a television and a table lamp were connected in series and the lamp broke, your television would go off. This would be a problem at home, but it is useful in wiring bank alarms, some types of street lights, and certain computer circuits.

Homework

Circuit Drawings Have students draw two diagrams of series circuits in their ScienceLog, one with two bulbs and one with three bulbs. Remind students to label all parts of the circuits.

Students may think that charges are "used up" as they pass through a circuit. Reinforce that the current is the same everywhere in the circuit, as shown in **Figure 23.**

442 Chapter 17 • Introduction to Electricity

Parallel Circuits Think about what would happen if all the lights in your home were connected in series. If you needed a light on in your room, all the other lights in the house would have to be turned on too! Luckily, circuits in buildings are wired in parallel rather than in series. A **parallel circuit** is a circuit in which different loads are located on separate branches. Because there are separate branches, the charges travel through more than one path. **Figure 24** shows a parallel circuit.

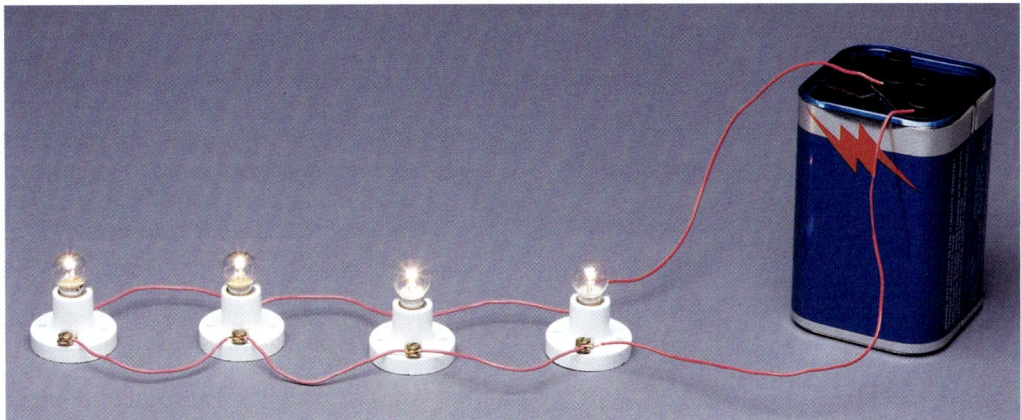

Figure 24 *The electric charges flow from the battery to each of the bulbs separately and then flow back to the battery.*

Unlike a series circuit, the loads in a parallel circuit do not have the same current in them. Instead, each load in a parallel circuit uses the same voltage. For example, the full voltage of the battery is applied to each bulb in Figure 24. As a result, each light bulb glows at full brightness, no matter how many bulbs are connected in parallel. You can connect loads that require different currents to the same parallel circuit. For example, you can connect a hair dryer, which requires a high current to operate, to the same circuit as a lamp, which requires less current.

Uses for Parallel Circuits In a parallel circuit, each branch of the circuit can function by itself. If one load is broken or missing, charges will still run through the other branches, and the loads on those branches will continue to work. In your home, each electrical outlet is usually on its own branch, with its own on-off switch. It would be inconvenient if each time a light bulb went out, your television or stereo stopped working. With parallel circuits, you can use one light or appliance at a time, even if another branch fails.

A Parallel Lab

1. Connect a **6 V battery** and **two flashlight bulbs** in a parallel circuit. Draw a picture of your circuit in your ScienceLog.

2. Add another **flashlight bulb** in parallel with the other two bulbs. How does the brightness of the light bulbs change?

3. Replace one of the light bulbs with a **burned-out light bulb**. What happens to the other lights in the circuit?

IS THAT A FACT!

A voltmeter is an instrument used in electrical work to measure the voltage between two conductors. Car mechanics, electricians, and industrial technicians routinely use voltmeters in their work.

3 Extend

USING THE FIGURE
Refer students to **Figure 25**, which explains more about short circuits and how they occur. Bring in examples of electric cords that are frayed or otherwise damaged. Make sure students understand the importance of using electrical cords that are in safe working condition.
Sheltered English

INDEPENDENT PRACTICE
Concept Mapping Have students create a concept map to describe what they have learned about electrical energy. Have the map begin with the topic *electrical energy*. Students should use the terms and concepts learned in this chapter to describe the many aspects of this broad topic. Encourage students to link as many terms as possible with appropriate phrases.

GOING FURTHER
Tell students to use Ohm's law to explore the math behind short circuits. During a short circuit, the current bypasses the load, so the resistance decreases dramatically. Have students show that at a constant voltage the current must increase if the resistance decreases.

Household Circuits

In every home, several circuits connect lights, major appliances, and outlets throughout the building. Most household circuits are parallel circuits that can have several loads attached to them. The circuits branch out from a breaker box or a fuse box that acts as the "electrical headquarters" for the building. Each branch receives a standard voltage, which is 120 V in the United States.

Mayday! Circuit Failure! Broken wires or water can cause electrical appliances to short-circuit. A short circuit occurs when charges bypass the loads in the circuit. When the loads are bypassed, the resistance of the circuit drops, and the current in the circuit increases. If the current increases too much, it can produce enough thermal energy to start a fire. **Figure 25** shows how a short circuit might occur.

Figure 25 *If the insulating plastic around a cord is broken, the two wires inside can touch. The charges can then bypass the load and travel from one wire to the other.*

Circuits also may fail if they are overloaded. A circuit is overloaded when too many loads, or electrical devices, are attached to it. Each time you add a load to a parallel circuit, the entire circuit draws more current. If too many loads are attached to one circuit, the current increases to an unsafe level that can cause the temperature of the wires to increase and cause a fire. **Figure 26** shows a situation that can cause a circuit overload.

Figure 26 *Plugging too many devices into one outlet can cause a circuit to overload.*

IS THAT A FACT!
Thomas Edison's famous quotation, "Genius is one percent inspiration, ninety-nine percent perspiration," is representative of his dedication and devotion to work. Edison and his assistants performed 1,200 experiments in an attempt to find the best material to use as a filament in light bulbs. Among the fibers he tested were baywood, boxwood, hickory, cedar, flax, and bamboo. Finally, in 1879, Edison discovered that carbonized cotton thread—cotton sewing thread that has been burned to an ash—worked well. The light bulb that used carbonized cotton filament burned for 2 days.

Circuit Safety

Because short circuits and circuit overloads can be so dangerous, safety features are built into the circuits in your home. The two most commonly used safety devices are fuses and circuit breakers, which are located in a fuse box or a breaker box.

Fuses A fuse contains a thin strip of metal through which the charges for a circuit flow. If the current in the circuit is too high, the metal in the fuse warms up and melts, as shown in **Figure 27.** A break or gap in the circuit is produced, and the charges stop flowing. This is referred to as blowing a fuse. After a fuse is blown, you must replace it with a new fuse in order for the charges to flow through the circuit again.

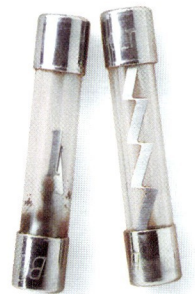

Figure 27 *The blown fuse on the left must be replaced with a new fuse, such as the one on the right.*

Circuit Breakers A circuit breaker is a switch that automatically opens if the current in the circuit is too high. If the current in a circuit is too high, a strip of metal in the circuit breaker warms up and bends away from the wires in the circuit. A break in the circuit results. Open circuit breakers can be closed easily by flipping a switch inside the breaker box once the problem has been corrected.

A device that acts like a miniature circuit breaker is a ground fault circuit interrupter (GFCI). A GFCI, like the one shown in **Figure 28,** provides protection by comparing the current in one side of an outlet with the current in the other side. If there is even a small difference, the GFCI opens the circuit. To close the circuit, you must push the RESET button.

Figure 28 *GFCI devices are usually found on outlets in bathrooms and kitchens to protect you from electric shock.*

REVIEW

1. Name and describe the three essential parts of a circuit.
2. Why are switches useful in a circuit?
3. What is the difference between series and parallel circuits?
4. How do fuses and circuit breakers protect your home against electrical fires?
5. **Developing Hypotheses** Whenever you turn on the portable heater in your room, the circuit breaker for the circuit in your room opens and all the lights go out. Propose two possible reasons for why this occurs.

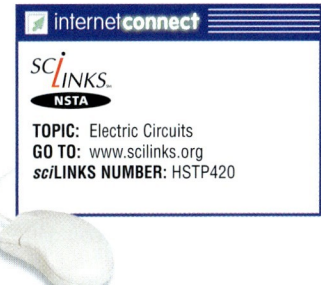

TOPIC: Electric Circuits
GO TO: www.scilinks.org
*sci*LINKS NUMBER: HSTP420

Chapter Highlights

VOCABULARY DEFINITIONS

SECTION 1

law of electric charges the law that states that like charges repel and opposite charges attract

electric force the force between charged objects

conduction a method of charging an object that occurs when electrons are transferred from one object to another by direct contact

induction a method of charging an object that occurs when charges in an uncharged object are rearranged without direct contact with a charged object

conductor a material in which charges can move easily

insulator a material in which charges cannot easily move

static electricity the buildup of electric charges on an object

electric discharge the loss of static electricity as charges move off an object

SECTION 2

cell a device that produces an electric current by converting chemical energy into electrical energy

battery a device that is made of several cells and that produces an electric current by converting chemical energy into electrical energy

potential difference energy per unit charge; specifically, the difference in energy per unit charge as a charge moves between two points in an electric circuit (same as voltage); expressed in volts (V)

photocell the part of a solar panel that converts light into electrical energy

thermocouple a device that converts thermal energy into electrical energy

Chapter Highlights

SECTION 1

Vocabulary
- law of electric charges (p. 423)
- electric force (p. 423)
- conduction (p. 425)
- induction (p. 425)
- conductor (p. 427)
- insulator (p. 427)
- static electricity (p. 427)
- electric discharge (p. 428)

Section Notes
- The law of electric charges states that like charges repel and opposite charges attract.
- The electric force varies depending on the size of the charges exerting the force and the distance between them.
- Objects become charged when they gain or lose electrons. Objects may become charged by friction, conduction, or induction.
- Charges are not created or destroyed and are said to be conserved.
- An electroscope can be used to detect charges.
- Charges move easily in conductors but do not move easily in insulators.
- Static electricity is the buildup of electric charges on an object. Static electricity is lost through electric discharge. Lightning is a form of electric discharge.
- Lightning rods work by directing the electric charge carried by lightning safely to the Earth.

Labs
Stop the Static Electricity! (p. 694)

SECTION 2

Vocabulary
- cell (p. 430)
- battery (p. 430)
- potential difference (p. 431)
- photocell (p. 432)
- thermocouple (p. 432)

Section Notes
- Batteries are made of cells that convert chemical energy to electrical energy.
- Electric currents can be produced when there is a potential difference.
- Photocells and thermocouples are devices used to produce electrical energy.

Labs
Potato Power (p. 695)

☑ Skills Check

Math Concepts

OHM'S LAW Ohm's law, shown on page 437, describes the relationship between current, voltage, and resistance. If you know two of the values, you can always calculate the third. For example, the current in a wire with a resistance of 4 Ω produced by a voltage of 12 V is calculated as follows:

$$I = \frac{V}{R} = \frac{12 \text{ V}}{4 \text{ Ω}} = 3 \text{ A}$$

Visual Understanding

SERIES AND PARALLEL CIRCUITS There are two types of circuits—series and parallel. The charges in a series circuit follow only one path, but the charges in a parallel circuit follow more than one path. Look at Figures 23 and 24 on pages 442–443 to review series and parallel circuits.

Lab and Activity Highlights

Stop the Static Electricity! **PG 694**

Potato Power **PG 695**

Circuitry 101 **PG 696**

Datasheets for LabBook
(blackline masters for these labs)

SECTION 3

Vocabulary
current (p. 433)
voltage (p. 434)
resistance (p. 435)
electric power (p. 437)

Section Notes
- Electric current is a continuous flow of charge caused by the motion of electrons.
- Voltage is the same as potential difference. As voltage increases, current increases.
- An object's resistance varies depending on the object's material, thickness, length, and temperature. As resistance increases, current decreases.
- Ohm's law describes the relationship between current, resistance, and voltage.
- Electric power is the rate at which electrical energy does work. It is expressed in watts or kilowatts.
- Electrical energy is electric power multiplied by time. It is usually expressed in kilowatt-hours.

SECTION 4

Vocabulary
circuit (p. 440)
load (p. 440)
series circuit (p. 442)
parallel circuit (p. 443)

Section Notes
- Circuits consist of an energy source, a load, wires, and sometimes a switch.
- All parts of a series circuit are connected in a single loop.
- The loads in a parallel circuit are on separate branches.
- Circuits can fail because of a short circuit or circuit overload.
- Fuses or circuit breakers protect your home against circuit failure.

Labs
Circuitry 101 (p. 696)

VOCABULARY DEFINITIONS, continued

SECTION 3

current the rate at which charge passes a given point; expressed in amperes (A)

voltage the difference in energy per unit charge as a charge moves between two points in an electric circuit (same as potential difference); expressed in volts (V)

resistance the opposition to the flow of electric charge; expressed in ohms (Ω)

electric power the rate at which electrical energy is used to do work; expressed in watts (W)

SECTION 4

circuit a complete, closed path through which electric charges flow

load a device that uses electrical energy to do work

series circuit a circuit in which all parts are connected in a single loop

parallel circuit a circuit in which different loads are located on separate branches

 Vocabulary Review Worksheet 17

 Blackline masters of these Chapter Highlights can be found in the **Study Guide**.

internet connect

GO TO: go.hrw.com

Visit the **HRW** Web site for a variety of learning tools related to this chapter. Just type in the keyword:

KEYWORD: HSTELE

GO TO: www.scilinks.org

Visit the **National Science Teachers Association** on-line Web site for Internet resources related to this chapter. Just type in the *sci*LINKS number for more information about the topic:

TOPIC: Static Electricity	*sci*LINKS NUMBER: HSTP405
TOPIC: Electrical Energy	*sci*LINKS NUMBER: HSTP410
TOPIC: Electric Current	*sci*LINKS NUMBER: HSTP415
TOPIC: Electric Circuits	*sci*LINKS NUMBER: HSTP420

Lab and Activity Highlights

LabBank

 Whiz-Bang Demonstrations
- Hoop It Up, Demo 57
- Bending Water, Demo 58

Long-Term Projects & Research Ideas
"The Future Is Electric," Project 67

Interactive Explorations CD-ROM

 CD 3, Exploration 5, "Tunnel Vision"

Chapter Review Answers

USING VOCABULARY

1. battery
2. conductor
3. Resistance
4. circuit
5. electric discharge

UNDERSTANDING CONCEPTS

Multiple Choice

6. d
7. b
8. a
9. c
10. d
11. a
12. b

Short Answer

13. The three essential parts of a circuit are an energy source, a load, and wires. The energy source provides electrical energy to do work. The load is a device that uses the electrical energy to do work. Loads cause electrical energy to be converted to other forms of energy. The wires are used to connect all the other parts of the circuit together. Wires are made of conductors.
14. One factor is the amount of the electric charge. The greater the charge is, the greater the force. The other factor is the distance between the charges. The closer the charges are to each other, the greater the force is.
15. The charges in direct current flow in one direction. In alternating current, the charges continually switch from flowing in one direction to flowing in the reverse direction.

Chapter Review

USING VOCABULARY

To complete the following sentences, choose the correct term from each pair of terms listed below:

1. A __?__ converts chemical energy into electrical energy. (*battery* or *photocell*)
2. Charges flow easily in a(n) __?__. (*insulator* or *conductor*)
3. __?__ is the opposition to the flow of electric charge. (*Resistance* or *Electric power*)
4. A __?__ is a complete, closed path through which charges flow. (*load* or *circuit*)
5. Lightning is a form of __?__. (*static electricity* or *electric discharge*)

UNDERSTANDING CONCEPTS

Multiple Choice

6. If two charges repel each other, the two charges must be
   a. positive and positive.
   b. positive and negative.
   c. negative and negative.
   d. Either (a) or (c)

7. A device that can convert chemical energy to electrical energy is a
   a. lightning rod.
   b. cell.
   c. light bulb.
   d. All of the above

8. Which of the following wires has the lowest resistance?
   a. a short, thick copper wire at 25°C
   b. a long, thick copper wire at 35°C
   c. a long, thin copper wire at 35°C
   d. a short, thick iron wire at 25°C

9. An object becomes charged when the atoms in the object gain or lose
   a. protons.   c. electrons.
   b. neutrons.   d. All of the above

10. A device used to protect buildings from electrical fires is a(n)
    a. electric meter.   c. fuse.
    b. circuit breaker.   d. Both (b) and (c)

11. In order to produce a current from a cell, the electrodes of the cell must
    a. have a potential difference.
    b. be in a liquid.
    c. be exposed to light.
    d. be at two different temperatures.

12. What type of current comes from the outlets in your home?
    a. direct current   c. electric discharge
    b. alternating current   d. static electricity

Short Answer

13. List and describe the three essential parts of a circuit.
14. Name the two factors that affect the strength of electric force, and explain how they affect electric force.
15. Describe how direct current differs from alternating current.

Concept Mapping Transparency 17

Blackline masters of this Chapter Review can be found in the **Study Guide**.

Chapter 17 • Introduction to Electricity

Concept Mapping

16. Use the following terms to create a concept map: electric current, battery, charges, photocell, thermocouple, circuit, parallel circuit, series circuit.

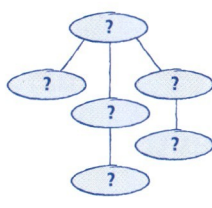

CRITICAL THINKING AND PROBLEM SOLVING

17. Your science classroom was rewired over the weekend. On Monday, you notice that the electrician may have made a mistake. In order for the fish-tank bubbler to work, the lights in the room must be on. And if you want to use the computer, you must turn on the overhead projector. Describe what mistake the electrician made with the circuits in your classroom.

18. You can make a cell using an apple, a strip of copper, and a strip of silver. Explain how you would construct the cell, and identify the parts of the cell. What type of cell is formed? Explain your answer.

19. Your friend shows you a magic trick. She rubs a plastic comb with a piece of silk and holds the comb close to a stream of water. When the comb is close to the water, the water bends toward the comb. Explain how this trick works. (Hint: Think about how objects become charged.)

MATH IN SCIENCE

Use Ohm's law to solve the following problems:

20. What voltage is needed to produce a 6 A current through a resistance of 3 Ω?

21. Find the current produced when a voltage of 60 V is applied to a resistance of 15 Ω.

22. What is the resistance of an object if a voltage of 40 V produces a current of 5 A?

INTERPRETING GRAPHICS

23. Classify the objects in the photograph below as conductors or insulators.

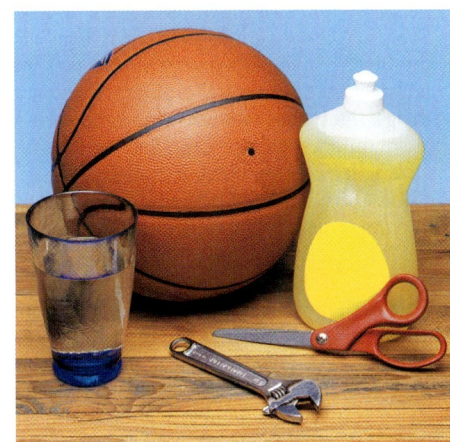

NOW What Do You Think?

Take a minute to review your answers to the ScienceLog questions on page 421. Have your answers changed? If necessary, revise your answers based on what you have learned since you began this chapter.

449

NOW WHAT DO YOU THINK?

1. Static electricity is the buildup of electric charges on an object. Static electricity may be created when an object is charged by friction or by induction.

2. Electrical energy can be converted from chemical energy by cells and batteries. Electrical energy can also be converted from light by photocells or from thermal energy by thermocouples.

3. A circuit is a complete, closed path through which electric charges flow. The parts of a circuit consist of an energy source, a load, wires, and sometimes a switch.

Concept Mapping

16. 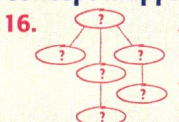 An answer to this exercise can be found at the end of this book.

CRITICAL THINKING AND PROBLEM SOLVING

17. The electrician must have wired the fish-tank bubbler in series with the lights and the computer in series with the overhead projector.

18. You would push the strip of copper and the strip of silver into the apple. The apple is the electrolyte, and the metal strips are the electrodes. Students may identify the cell as a dry cell because the apple is a solid or as a wet cell because the apple juice conducts the electric current.

19. When the comb is rubbed with a piece of silk, the comb is charged by friction. When the charged comb is held close to the stream of water, the charged comb induces a charge on the stream of water. The part of the stream closest to the comb has a charge opposite to that of the comb. Therefore, the stream is attracted by an electric force to the comb.

MATH IN SCIENCE

20. $V = I \times R = 6\,A \times 3\,\Omega = 18\,V$
21. $I = V/R = 60\,V/15\,\Omega = 4\,A$
22. $R = V/I = 40\,V/5\,A = 8\,\Omega$

INTERPRETING GRAPHICS

23. conductors: tap water in glass, wrench, metal part of scissors, liquid soap in plastic bottle; insulators: basketball, glass, plastic bottle, plastic scissors handles, wooden table

Chapter 17 • Chapter Review

SCIENCE, TECHNOLOGY, AND SOCIETY

Riding the Electric Rails

Background
The first modern light-rail transit (LRT) systems were developed in the 1980s. LRTs have since been established in more than 18 cities in the United States, including Los Angeles, Philadelphia, Cleveland, and Portland, Oregon.

In addition to their more streamlined look, LRT vehicles differ from earlier trolleys in several ways. The LRT vehicles can operate singly, in short trains of two or three cars, or as a longer series of units hinged together to allow for sharp turns. They operate at higher speeds, are quieter, and can carry up to 16,000 more passengers per track per hour than conventional streetcars. Most of the vehicles also rely on computers to control acceleration and braking. In addition, the new LRT tracks now run along the roadside instead of down the middle of the street. As a result, LRT vehicles are more accessible to passengers and interfere less with automobile traffic.

Science, Technology, and Society

Riding the Electric Rails

For more than 100 years, the trolley, or streetcar, was a popular way to travel around a city. Then, beginning in the 1950s, most cities ripped up their trolley tracks to make way for automobiles. Today, trolleys are making a comeback around the world.

From Horse Power to Electric Power

In 1832, the first trolleys, called *horsecars*, were pulled by horses through the streets of New York. Soon horsecars were used in most large cities in the United States. However, using horses for power presented several problems. Among other things, the horses were slow and required special attention and constant care. So inventors began looking for other sources of power.

In 1888, Frank J. Sprague developed a way to operate trolleys with electrical energy. These electric trolleys ran on a metal track and were connected by a pole to an overhead power line. Electric charges flowed down the pole to motors in the trolley. A wheel at the top of the pole, called a *shoe*, rolled along the power line, allowing the trolley to move along its track without losing contact with its power source. The charges passed through the motor and then returned to a power generator by way of the metal track.

Taking It to the Streets

By World War I, more than 40,000 km of electric-trolley tracks were in use in the United States. The trolley's popularity helped shape American cities because businesses were built along the trolley lines. But competition from cars and buses grew over the next decade, and many trolley lines were abandoned.

By the 1980s, nearly all of the trolley lines had been shut down. But by then, people were looking for new ways to cut down on the pollution, noise, and traffic problems caused by automobiles and buses. Trolleys provided one possible solution. Because they run on electrical energy, they create little pollution, and because many people can ride on a single trolley, they cut down on traffic.

Today, a new form of trolley is being used in a number of major cities. These light-rail transit vehicles are quieter, faster, and more economical than the older trolleys. They usually run on rails alongside the road and contain new systems, such as automated brakes and speed controls.

Think About It!
▶ Because trolleys operate on electrical energy, does this mean that they don't create any pollution? Explain your answer.

▲ *The horsecar was a popular mode of travel in many cities during the early 1900s.*

▲ *Many cities across the country now use light-rail systems for public transportation.*

Answers to Think About It!
Running electric-powered vehicles is a clean process, but the production of electrical energy is often not. Electrical energy is often generated by burning fossil fuels, which pollutes the atmosphere. So pollution is produced at another location, such as a power plant, rather than at street level. (You may wish to point out that this concern applies to electric cars as well.)

Across the Sciences

PHYSICAL SCIENCE • EARTH SCIENCE

Sprites and Elves

Imagine you are a pilot flying a plane on a moonless night. About 80 km away, you notice a powerful thunderstorm and see the lightning move *between* the clouds and the Earth. This makes sense because you know that all weather activity takes place in the lowest layer of Earth's atmosphere, which is called the troposphere. But all of a sudden, a ghostly red glow stretches many kilometers *above* the storm clouds and *into* the stratosphere!

Capturing Sprites

In 1989, scientists at the University of Minnesota followed the trail of many such reports. They captured the first image of this strange, red-glowing lightning using a video camera. Since then, photographs from space shuttles, airplanes, telescopes, and observers on the ground have identified several types of wispy electrical glows. Two of these types were named sprites and elves because, like the mythical creatures, they last only a few thousandths of a second and disappear just as the eye begins to see them.

Photographs show that sprites and elves occur only when ordinary lightning is discharged from a cloud. Sprites are very large, extending from the cloud tops at an altitude of about 15 km to as high as 95 km. They are up to 50 km wide. Elves are expanding disks of red light, probably caused by an electromagnetic pulse from lightning or sprites. Elves can be 200 km across, and they appear at altitudes above 90 km.

What Took So Long?

It is likely that sprites and elves have been occurring for thousands of years but went unrecorded. This is because they are produced with only about 1 percent of lightning flashes. They also last for a short period of time and are very faint. Since they occur above thunderclouds, where few people can see, observers are more often distracted by the brighter lightning below.

▲ *Sprites (left) and elves (right) are strange electric discharges in the atmosphere.*

Still, scientists are not surprised to learn that electric discharges extend up from clouds. There is a large potential difference between thunderclouds and the ionosphere, an atmospheric level above the clouds. The ionosphere is electrically conductive and provides a path for these electric discharges.

Search and Find

▶ Would you like to find sprites on your own? (Elves disappear too quickly.) Go with an adult, avoid being out in a thunderstorm, and remember:
- It must be completely dark, and your eyes must adjust to the total darkness.
- Viewing is best when a large thunderstorm is 48 to 97 km away, with no clouds in between.
- Block out the lightning below the clouds with dark paper so that you can still see above the clouds.
- Be patient.

Report sightings to a university geophysical department. Scientists need more information to fully understand how these discharges affect the chemical and electrical workings of our atmosphere.

Across the Sciences

Sprites and Elves

Background

This feature highlights the interdisciplinary nature of current scientific investigations. Earth scientists, geophysicists, atmospheric scientists, astronomers, pilots, and astronauts are all contributing to the research. Researchers are studying diverse aspects of these phenomena, including causes and possible effects. For example, researchers might investigate the impact of these events on atmospheric chemistry.

Students may need additional background on the layers of the atmosphere and their characteristics to understand the relationship between electrical events and atmospheric science.

Teaching Strategy

A research project on the Internet is an ideal way to generate student interest in current atmospheric research. It also gives students the opportunity to monitor and perhaps even contribute to the scientific community's ongoing work.

Information for Search and Find

Tell students that they are most likely to observe sprites and elves while they are watching storms more than 150 km wide with many cloud-to-ground lightning strikes. Advise students to look for sprites at a height four to five times that of the cloud tops. Because of the nature of night vision, students are most likely to observe sprites out of the corners of their eyes. The actual color of a sprite is pinkish orange, but because of the low light level, students might see the color as green, orange, or white. A hazy or polluted atmosphere will make observing these phenomena more difficult.

Chapter Organizer

CHAPTER ORGANIZATION	TIME MINUTES	OBJECTIVES	LABS, INVESTIGATIONS, AND DEMONSTRATIONS
Chapter Opener pp. 452–453	45	National Standards: UCP 2, SAI 1, 2, HNS 1	**Investigate!** Magnetic Attraction, p. 453
Section 1 Magnets and Magnetism	90	▶ Describe the force between two magnetic poles. ▶ Explain why some materials are magnetic and some are not. ▶ Describe four different categories of magnets. ▶ Give two examples of the effect of Earth's magnetic field. UCP 1, 2, SPSP 1, 3, 5, HNS 1, 3, PS 3a; LabBook UCP 2, SAI 1	**QuickLab,** Model of Earth's Magnetic Field, p. 459 **Skill Builder,** Magnetic Mystery, p. 698 **Datasheets for LabBook,** Magnetic Mystery, Datasheet 50 **Inquiry Labs,** An Attractive Way to Navigate, Lab 22
Section 2 Magnetism from Electricity	90	▶ Identify the relationship between an electric current and a magnetic field. ▶ Compare solenoids, electromagnets, and magnets. ▶ Describe how electromagnetism is involved in the operation of doorbells, electric motors, and galvanometers. SPSP 5, HNS 1, 3; LabBook UCP 2, ST 1, 2, PS 3a	**Demonstration,** Electromagnets, p. 462 in ATE **QuickLab,** Electromagnets, p. 464 **Whiz-Bang Demonstrations,** Magnetic Nails, Demo 59 **Making Models,** Build a DC Motor, p. 700 **Datasheets for LabBook,** Build a DC Motor, Datasheet 52
Section 3 Electricity from Magnetism	90	▶ Explain how a magnetic field can produce an electric current. ▶ Explain how electromagnetic induction is used in a generator. ▶ Compare step-up and step-down transformers. SPSP 5, HNS 1, 3, PS 3a; LabBook UCP 3, SAI 1, PS 3a	**Discovery Lab,** Electricity from Magnetism, p. 699 **Datasheets for LabBook,** Electricity from Magnetism, Datasheet 51 **EcoLabs & Field Activities,** A Light Current of Air, EcoLab 21 **Long-Term Projects & Research Ideas,** Project 68

*See page **T20** for a complete correlation of this book with the* **NATIONAL SCIENCE EDUCATION STANDARDS.**

TECHNOLOGY RESOURCES

 Guided Reading Audio CD English or Spanish, Chapter 18

 One-Stop Planner CD-ROM with Test Generator

 CNN Science, Technology & Society, Building a Supercollider, Segment 20

Chapter 18 • Electromagnetism

CLASSROOM WORKSHEETS, TRANSPARENCIES, AND RESOURCES	SCIENCE INTEGRATION AND CONNECTIONS	REVIEW AND ASSESSMENT
Science Puzzlers, Twisters & Teasers, Worksheet 18 **Directed Reading Worksheet 18**	**Connect to Earth Science,** p. 453 in ATE	
Directed Reading Worksheet 18, Section 1 **Transparency 109,** Special Properties of Some Minerals **Transparency 271,** Magnetic Force Between Magnets **Science Skills Worksheet 18,** Finding Useful Sources **Transparency 272,** Earth as a Magnet **Reinforcement Worksheet 18,** Planet Lodestone	**Connect to Earth Science,** p. 455 in ATE **Real-World Connection,** p. 457 in ATE **Connect to Earth Science,** p. 457 in ATE **Cross-Disciplinary Focus,** p. 457 in ATE **Real-World Connection,** p. 459 in ATE **Biology Connection,** p. 460 **Connect to Earth Science,** p. 460 in ATE **Math and More,** p. 460 in ATE **Connect to Earth Science,** p. 461 in ATE **Across the Sciences:** Geomagnetic Storms, p. 478 **Health Watch:** Magnets in Medicine, p. 479	**Review,** p. 458 **Homework,** p. 459 in ATE **Review,** P. 461 **Quiz,** p. 461 in ATE **Alternative Assessment,** p. 461 in ATE
Directed Reading Worksheet 18, Section 2 **Transparency 273,** The Discovery of Electromagnetism **Science Skills Worksheet 6,** Boosting Your Memory **Critical Thinking Worksheet 18,** Magic Magnet Misfortune	**Apply,** p. 463 **Real-World Connection,** p. 463 in ATE **Connect to Life Science,** p. 463 in ATE **Real-World Connection,** p. 465 in ATE **Multicultural Connection,** p. 465 in ATE	**Self-Check,** p. 464 **Review,** p. 467 **Quiz,** p. 467 in ATE **Alternative Assessment,** p. 467 in ATE
Directed Reading Worksheet 18, Section 3 **Transparency 274,** Electromagnetic Induction **Transparency 275,** Parts of a Simple Generator **Transparency 275,** How a Generator Works **Math Skills for Science Worksheet 17,** Using Proportions and Cross-Multiplication **Reinforcement Worksheet 18,** A Magnetic Time	**Connect to Earth Science,** p. 470 in ATE **Math and More,** p. 471 in ATE **Math and More,** p. 472 in ATE **Real-World Connection,** p. 472 in ATE **Multicultural Connection,** p. 473 in ATE	**Review,** p. 473 **Quiz,** p. 473 in ATE **Alternative Assessment,** p. 473 in ATE

END-OF-CHAPTER REVIEW AND ASSESSMENT

Chapter Review in Study Guide
Vocabulary and Notes in Study Guide
Chapter Tests with Performance-Based Assessment, Chapter 18 Test
Chapter Tests with Performance-Based Assessment, Performance-Based Assessment 18
Concept Mapping Transparency 18

internet connect

 Holt, Rinehart and Winston On-line Resources
go.hrw.com

For worksheets and other teaching aids related to this chapter, visit the HRW Web site and type in the keyword: **HSTEMG**

 **National Science Teachers Association**
www.scilinks.org

Encourage students to use the *sci*LINKS numbers listed in the internet connect boxes to access information and resources on the **NSTA** Web site.

Chapter 18 • Chapter Organizer   **451B**

Chapter Resources & Worksheets

Visual Resources

TEACHING TRANSPARENCIES

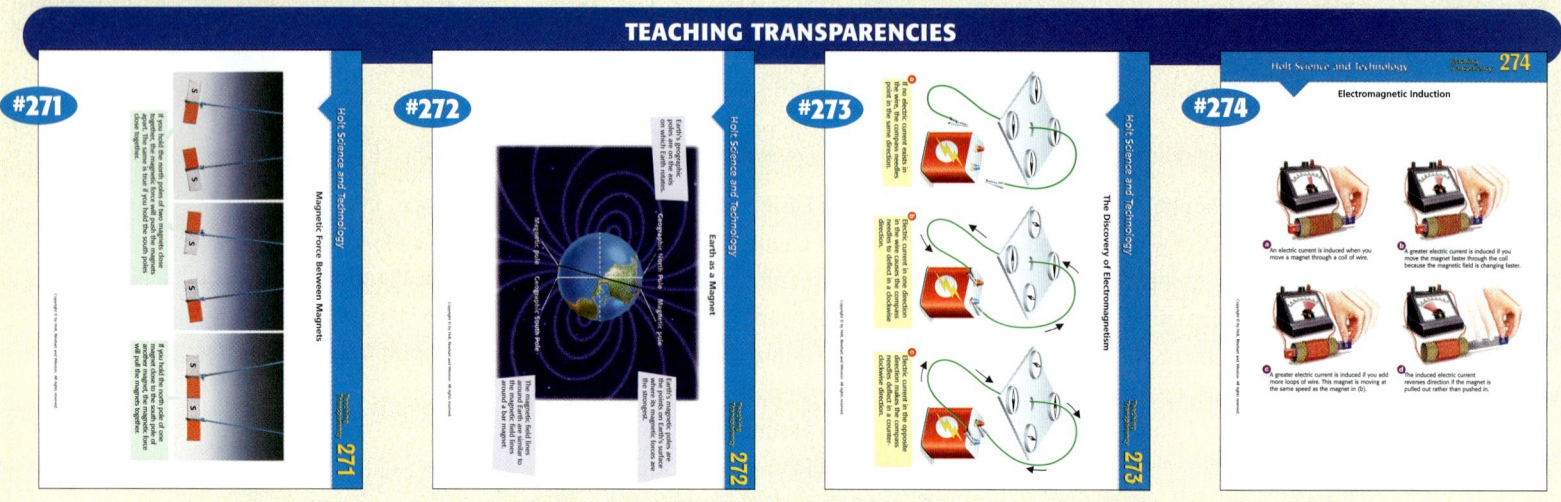

TEACHING TRANSPARENCIES

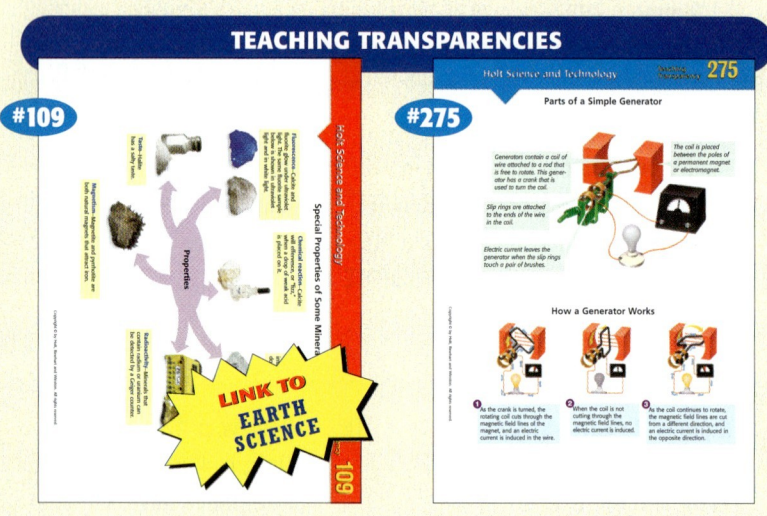

CONCEPT MAPPING TRANSPARENCY

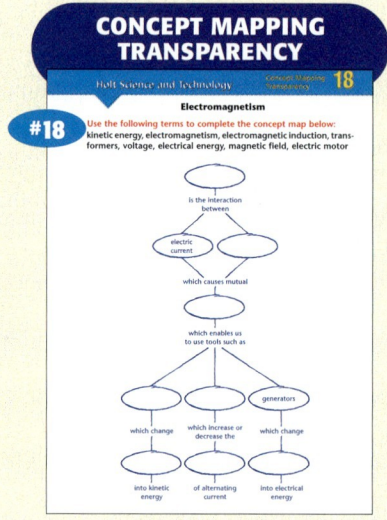

Meeting Individual Needs

DIRECTED READING

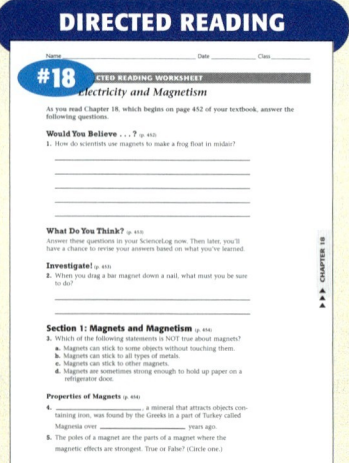

REINFORCEMENT & VOCABULARY REVIEW

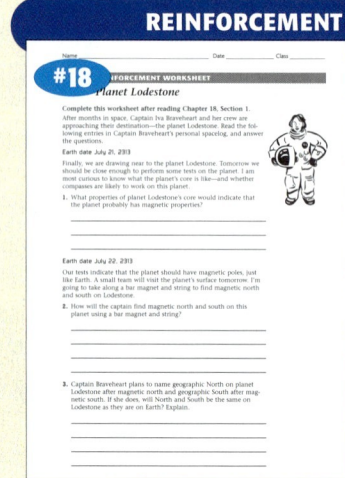
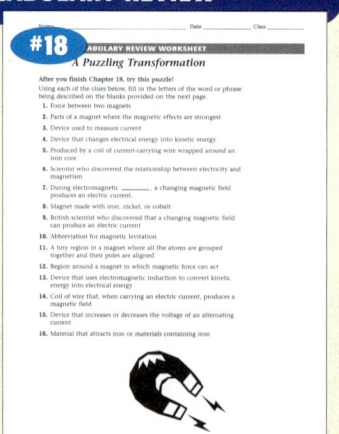

SCIENCE PUZZLERS, TWISTERS & TEASERS

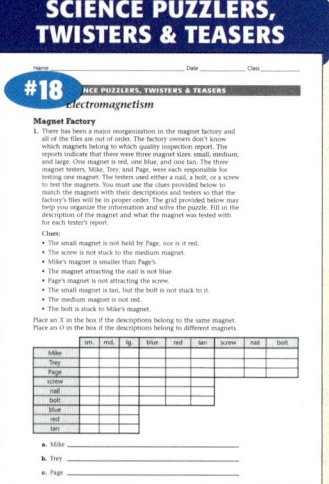

451C Chapter 18 • Electromagnetism

Chapter 18 • Electromagnetism

Review & Assessment

STUDY GUIDE

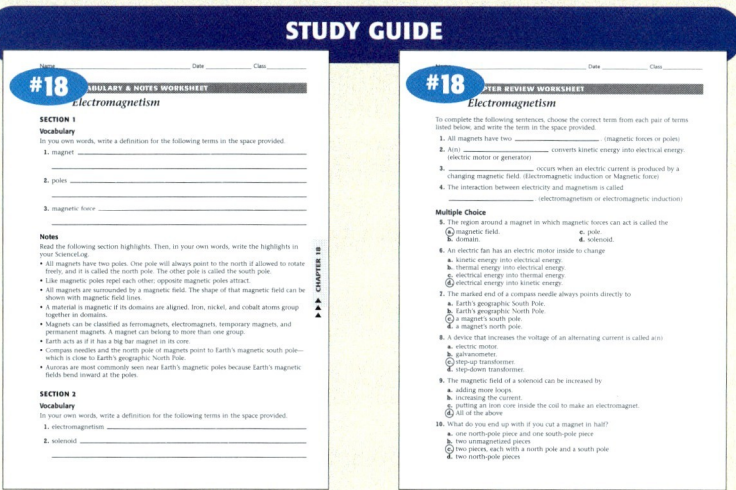

CHAPTER TESTS WITH PERFORMANCE-BASED ASSESSMENT

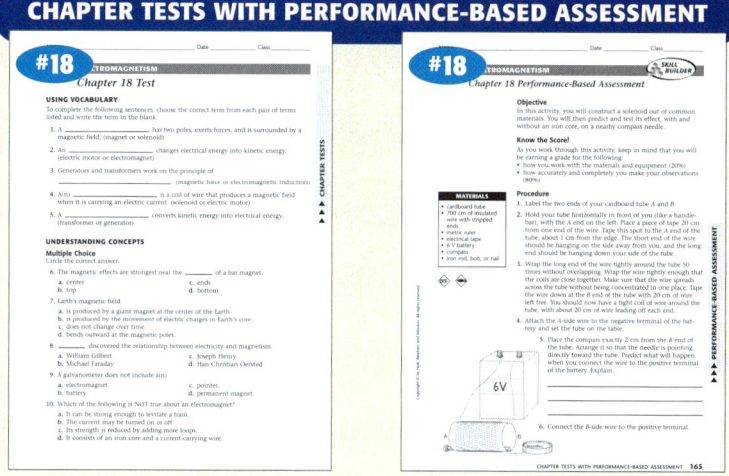

Lab Worksheets

INQUIRY LABS

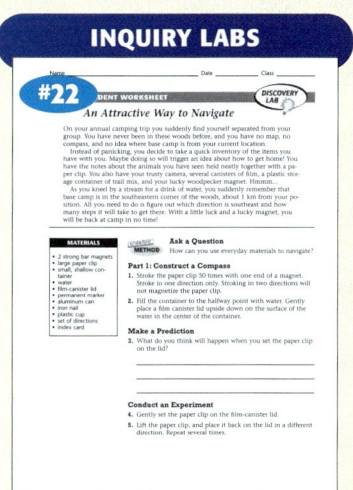

WHIZ-BANG DEMONSTRATIONS

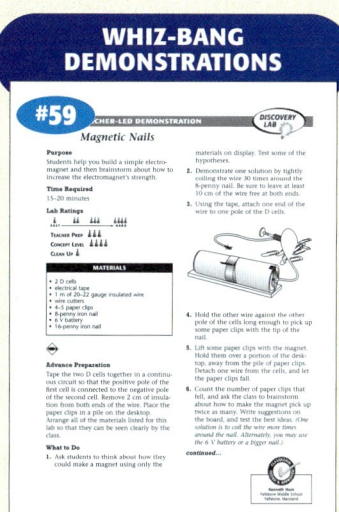

ECOLABS & FIELD ACTIVITIES

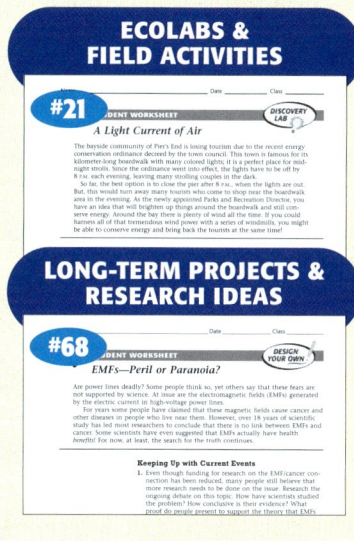

LONG-TERM PROJECTS & RESEARCH IDEAS

DATASHEETS FOR LABBOOK

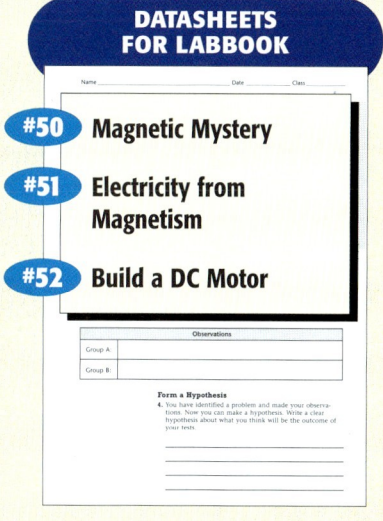

Applications & Extensions

CRITICAL THINKING & PROBLEM SOLVING

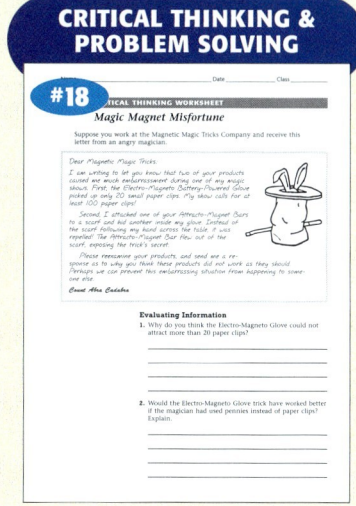

SCIENCE, TECHNOLOGY & SOCIETY

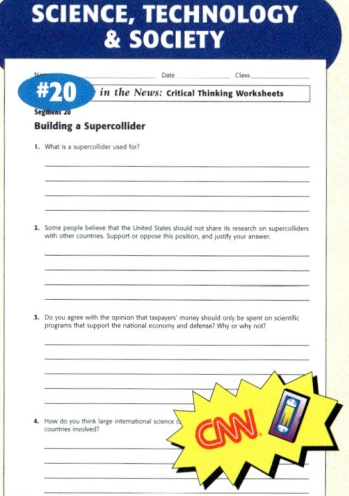

Chapter Background

SECTION 1

Magnets and Magnetism

▶ **The First Magnets**
In ancient times, the Greeks and Chinese discovered a stone with the unusual property that it attracted iron or objects containing iron. The stone was the natural magnet lodestone, or magnetite.

- The Chinese observed three characteristics of magnetite: first, it attracted iron; second, when set afloat in water, magnetite aligned in a north–south direction; third, magnetite could transfer its magnetic force to an iron needle.

- William Gilbert (1544–1603), an English physician, is considered to be the father of magnetism. In 1600, Gilbert comprehensively described the magnetic properties of lodestone.

- In 1820, Danish physicist Hans Christian Oersted (1777–1851) discovered the connection between magnetism and electricity.

IS THAT A FACT!

- The ancient Chinese name for lodestone translates into "the stone that picks up iron."

- The ancient Greeks told of a mythical island made of lodestone that pulled the iron nails out of passing ships, causing them to sink.

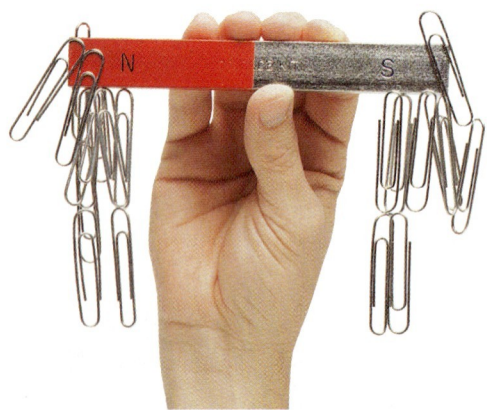

▶ **Poles, Forces, and Fields**
The lines used to map the strength of a magnetic field are called flux lines. The direction of the magnetic field is the same as the direction of the flux lines. The spacing between flux lines indicates the strength of the magnetic field. The closer the lines are to one another, the stronger the magnetic field.

- The SI unit of magnetism is the tesla (T). A refrigerator-door magnet has a magnetic force of 0.00002 T. By comparison, the strongest superconducting electromagnet has a magnetic force of 13.5 T.

- Earth's magnetic and geographic poles are located in different places. The difference in degrees between the magnetic pole and the geographic pole is called the angle of declination.

IS THAT A FACT!

- Even if a magnet is divided into smaller sections, each section will still have two poles. Magnetic monopoles may exist, but scientists have yet to find one.

▶ **Domains**
Ferromagnetic materials are made of atoms that act like individual magnets. Electrons in the atoms create a magnetic field in each atom. A *domain* is a region in a substance where most of these fields are aligned in the same direction. A magnet's strength is greatest when the maximum number of domains is aligned.

- The domains in lodestones, which originally formed from magma, remained aligned even after the magma had cooled and the rock had formed. Because the domains lined up parallel to Earth's magnetic field, lodestones were magnetized.

Chapter 18 • Electromagnetism

Chapter 18 • Electromagnetism

SECTION 2

Magnetism from Electricity

▶ **History of Electromagnetism**
Hans Christian Oersted's discovery made a formal connection between magnetism and electricity. His finding was quickly followed by the works of André-Marie Ampère (1755–1836), Dominique Arago (1786–1853), and Michael Faraday (1791–1867). The scientific culmination came when James Clerk Maxwell (1831–1879) described all of the electromagnetic phenomena known at that time with one theory.

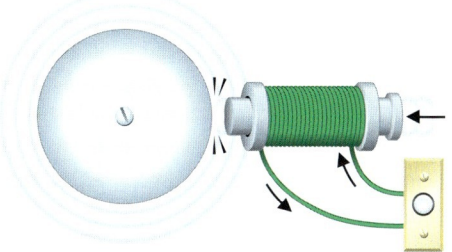

▶ **The First Electromagnet**
In 1825, just 5 years after Oersted's discovery, an English electrician named William Sturgeon (1783–1850) invented the first electromagnet.

- Four years later, in 1829, American physicist Joseph Henry (1797–1878) was credited for making the first practical electromagnet.

- Electromagnets have numerous applications. Doorbells, scrap-metal removal, MRI (magnetic resonance imaging) machines, electric motors, and maglev (magnetic levitation) trains are just a few examples.

IS THAT A FACT!

▶ Electromagnets are useful because they can be turned on and off. In this way, doorbells can ring more than once, scrap-metal magnets can remove and release scrap, and door latches can be opened and closed.

SECTION 3

Electricity from Magnetism

▶ **Complementary Discoveries**
Hans Oersted discovered that a magnetic field was produced from an electric current. In the early 1830s, English physicist Michael Faraday and American physicist Joseph Henry each discovered the inverse: an electric current could be produced by a magnetic field.

- Faraday's and Henry's work laid the foundation for the later development of the electric generator, or dynamo, and the transformer.

▶ **Electromagnetic Induction**
The basis of electromagnetic induction is the generation of electrical energy when magnetic fields are changed.

- Magnetic fields can be changed by moving a wire near a magnet, by moving a magnet near a wire, or by increasing or decreasing the magnetic field.

IS THAT A FACT!

▶ Because electromagnetic induction depends on changes in the magnetic field, only an alternating current system can produce such a phenomenon. A direct current system would induce electric current only at the moment the magnetic field is turned on.

For background information about teaching strategies and issues, refer to the *Professional Reference for Teachers*.

CHAPTER 18 Electromagnetism

Chapter Preview

Section 1
Magnets and Magnetism
- Properties of Magnets
- What Makes Materials Magnetic?
- Types of Magnets
- Earth as a Magnet

Section 2
Magnetism from Electricity
- The Discovery of Electromagnetism
- Using Electromagnetism
- Magnetic Force and Electric Current
- Applications of Electromagnetism

Section 3
Electricity from Magnetism
- Electric Current from a Magnetic Field
- Applications of Electromagnetic Induction

Science Puzzlers, Twisters & Teasers Worksheet 18

Guided Reading Audio CD
English or Spanish, Chapter 18

Smithsonian Institution®
Visit www.si.edu/hrw for additional on-line resources.

Would You Believe . . . ?

Frogs have been seen floating in midair! No, it's not a magic trick that relies on mirrors to fool your eyes. It's part of an experiment by Dutch scientists Andrey Geim and Jan Maan. They are doing experiments using magnets to levitate, or lift, objects. They have successfully levitated drops of liquids, nuts, flowers, and live grasshoppers and frogs—without harming them.

How do they do it? Every object, living or nonliving, contains atoms that can act like magnets. These atomic magnets are millions of times weaker than common household magnets. But they can be influenced by stronger magnets. If a frog—or any object— is placed near a very strong magnet, the magnetic force acting on the frog can lift it and hold it in midair!

Andrey Geim (pictured) and Jan Maan used this device to levitate a frog.

To produce such a strong magnet, the scientists use a large solenoid. A solenoid consists of a coil of wire that acts like a magnet when electric charges flow in the wire. When objects are placed inside the solenoid, where the magnetic effects are the strongest, they float!

The research of Geim and Maan is based on the close relationship between electricity and magnetism. In this chapter you will learn how electricity produces magnetism, and how magnetism produces electricity, for your use every day.

Would You Believe . . . ?

The electromagnet that Geim and Maan used to levitate the frog produces a magnetic field that is up to 1,000 times stronger than the field produced by a household magnet. The power supply for the magnet—6,000,000 W—could light sixty thousand 100 W light bulbs. That amount of electrical energy produces quite a bit of thermal energy, so the magnet must be cooled with water while it is in operation. By the way, the floating frog healthily and happily rejoined the other frogs after being levitated.

What Do You Think?

In your ScienceLog, try to answer the following questions based on what you already know:

1. What are the properties of magnets?
2. How does electricity produce magnetism?
3. How does magnetism produce electricity?

Magnetic Attraction

You just read about a frog that was lifted with a magnet. In this activity, you will investigate different ways you can use a magnet to lift steel paper clips.

Procedure

1. Place **5 or 6 small steel paper clips** on your desk. Touch the clips with an **unmagnetized iron nail,** and then lift the nail. In your ScienceLog, record the number of paper clips that stick to the nail.

2. Touch the clips with the end of a **strong bar magnet.** Record the number of clips that stick to the magnet.

3. While holding the magnet against the head of the nail, touch the tip of the nail to the paper clips. Count the number of paper clips that stick to the nail.

4. Remove the magnet from the end of the nail, and observe what happens. Record the number of paper clips you counted in step 3 and your observations from step 4.

5. Hold the nail by the head, and drag one end of the bar magnet 50 times down the nail. Be sure to drag the magnet in only one direction.

6. Set the magnet aside, and touch the nail to the paper clips. Record the number of paper clips that stick to the nail.

Analysis

7. What caused the difference between the number of paper clips you picked up in step 1 and the number you picked up in step 2?

8. Why do you think there was a difference between the number of paper clips you picked up in step 1 and the number you picked up in step 3?

9. What effect did the magnet have on the nail in step 5?

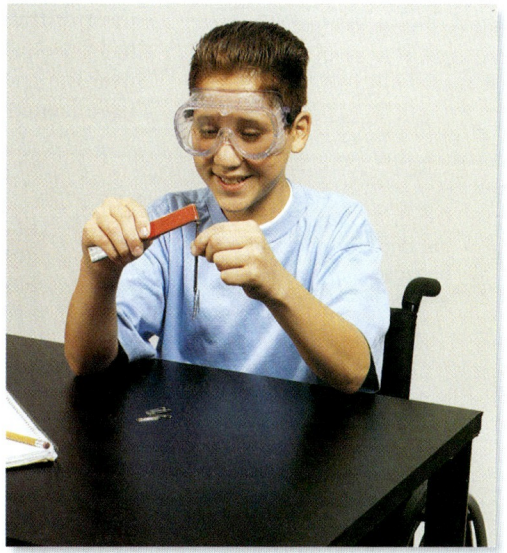

What Do You Think?

Accept all reasonable responses.

Students will have a chance to revise their answers in the Chapter Review under NOW What Do You Think?

Investigate!

MATERIALS

FOR EACH GROUP:
- 5 or 6 small steel paper clips
- 1 unmagnetized iron nail
- 1 strong bar magnet

Safety Caution: Remind students that the end of the nail is sharp and should be handled carefully. Caution students to wear goggles when doing this activity.

Teacher Notes: Use new nails for each class period. After the students magnetize the nails (in step 5), the nails may remain magnetic for days or weeks. Very strong magnets or horseshoe magnets are required for step 3. Test your magnets before students do the activity to make sure the magnets are strong enough to produce the results for step 3.

CONNECT TO EARTH SCIENCE

Neutron stars are probably the strongest magnets in the universe: they have magnetic fields a million million times more powerful than Earth's.

Directed Reading Worksheet 18

Answers to Investigate!

1. No paper clips should stick to the nail.
2. All paper clips should stick to the magnet.
3. One or more paper clips should stick to the nail.
4. Paper clips stuck to the nail should drop.
6. One or more paper clips should stick to the nail. (If no paper clips stick, repeat step 5 with the same nail.)
7. The nail picked up no paper clips because it was not magnetic; the magnet, being magnetic, picked up paper clips.
8. Accept all reasonable answers. Sample answer: The magnet aligned the magnetic domains of the nail slightly, making the nail a temporary magnet.
9. The magnet magnetized the nail.

Section 1

Focus

Magnets and Magnetism

This section describes the properties and characteristics of magnets, magnetic fields, and magnetic poles. The section also explains why some materials are magnetic and others are not. Finally, the section discusses four types of magnets and the fact that the Earth is a giant magnet.

Display the following objects to students:

a piece of aluminum foil, a nickel, a plastic object, a wooden object, a glass object, and some paper clips

Write the question, "Attracted or Not Attracted?" on the board. Ask students to predict which objects will be attracted to a magnet. (only paper clips)

1 Motivate

GROUP ACTIVITY

Place students together in groups. Give each group two bar magnets, a variety of small metal objects, and a variety of small nonmetallic objects such as plastic beads or even dried beans. Explain to students that their task is to describe as many properties of magnets as they can discover. Encourage groups to manipulate the magnets and to manipulate the small objects using the magnets. Have each group record their observations about the magnets and report their results to the class. Students should use their magnets and compasses for the prediction activity on page 455.

454   Chapter 18 • Electromagnetism

Section 1

Terms to Learn

magnet
poles
magnetic force

What You'll Do

- Describe the force between two magnetic poles.
- Explain why some materials are magnetic and some are not.
- Describe four different categories of magnets.
- Give two examples of the effect of Earth's magnetic field.

Magnets and Magnetism

You've probably seen magnets like the ones at right and below, stuck to a refrigerator door. These magnets might have been used to hold up notes or pictures or might have been used just for decoration. If you have ever played with magnets, you know that they stick to each other and to some types of metals. You also know that magnets can stick to objects without directly touching them—like when one is used to hold a piece of paper to a refrigerator door. How do magnets work? Read on to find out.

Properties of Magnets

More than 2,000 years ago, the Greeks discovered a mineral that attracted objects containing iron. Because this mineral was found in a part of Turkey called Magnesia, the Greeks called it magnetite. Today any material that attracts iron or materials containing iron is called a **magnet.** All magnets have certain properties. For example, all magnets have two poles, exert forces, and are surrounded by a magnetic field.

Magnetic Poles   The magnetic effects of a magnet are not evenly distributed throughout the magnet. For example, if you dip a bar magnet into a box of paper clips, you will find that most of the paper clips stick to the ends of the bar, as shown in **Figure 1.** As you can see, the magnetic effects are strongest near the ends of the bar magnet. The parts of a magnet where the magnetic effects are strongest are called **poles.**

Figure 1 *More paper clips stick to the ends, or poles, of a magnet because that's where the magnetic effects are strongest.*

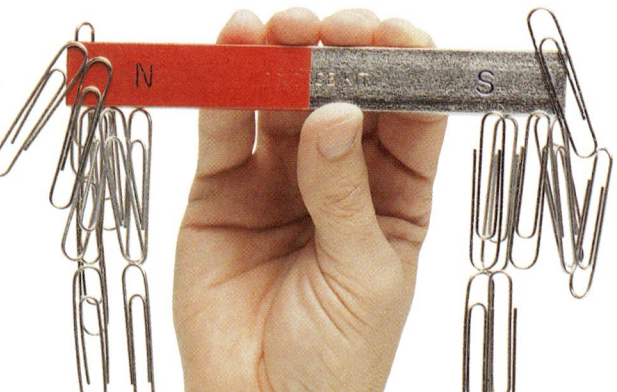

Directed Reading Worksheet 18 Section 1

TOPIC: Magnetism
GO TO: www.scilinks.org
sciLINKS NUMBER: HSTP430

WEIRD SCIENCE

The "Magnet Lady," Louise J. Greenfarb of Henderson, Nevada, reportedly has the world's largest collection of refrigerator magnets—almost 30,000. Greenfarb has collected magnets for more than 30 years. Many of her magnets are on display in a museum in Las Vegas.

North and South If you attach a magnet to a string so that the magnet is free to rotate, you will see that one end of the magnet always ends up pointing to the north, as shown in **Figure 2**. The pole of a magnet that points to the north is called the magnet's north pole. The opposite end of the magnet points to the south and is therefore called the magnet's south pole. Magnetic poles always occur in pairs; you will never find a magnet with only a north pole or only a south pole.

Figure 2 The needle in a compass is a magnet that is free to rotate.

Magnetic Forces When you bring two magnets close together, the magnets each exert a force that can either push the magnets apart or pull them together. The force of repulsion or attraction between the poles of magnets is called the **magnetic force**. The magnetic force between a pair of magnets depends on how the poles of the magnets line up, as shown in **Figure 3**. As you can see, magnetic poles are similar to electric charges in that like poles repel and opposite poles attract.

Figure 3 Magnetic Force Between Magnets

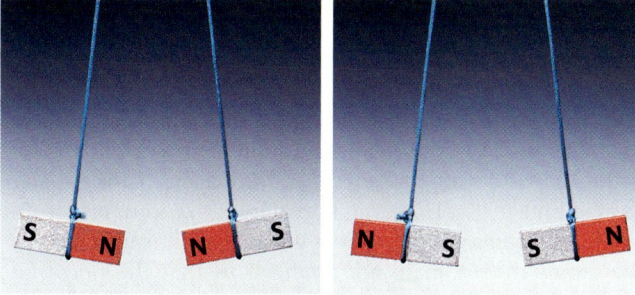
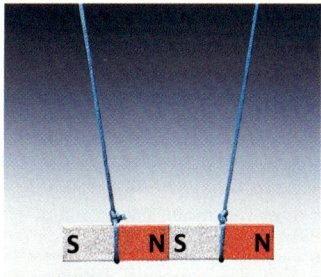

If you hold the north poles of two magnets close together, the magnetic force will push the magnets apart. The same is true if you hold the south poles close together.

If you hold the north pole of one magnet close to the south pole of another magnet, the magnetic force will pull the magnets together.

IS THAT A FACT!
The record for the strongest steady magnetic field produced in a laboratory is more than 38.7 T and was achieved in 1994 at the Massachusetts Institute of Technology.

2) Teach

READING STRATEGY

Prediction Guide As students read this page and manipulate their magnets and compasses, ask them to speculate why magnets attract or repel each other.

RESEARCH

History The ancient Chinese are generally credited with discovering how to make a compass out of a piece of lodestone floating in water. Have students research that discovery and see if they can replicate it with a model or a poster to show the class.

CONNECT TO EARTH SCIENCE

Magnetite is actually a common ore of the metal iron. It is an iron oxide, a chemical compound consisting of iron and oxygen (Fe_3O_4). It is sometimes called lodestone. Use Teaching Transparency 109, "Special Properties of Some Minerals," to show students that many minerals have unusual or unique properties.

Teaching Transparency 109 "Special Properties of Some Minerals" LINK TO EARTH SCIENCE

Teaching Transparency 271 "Magnetic Force Between Magnets"

Science Skills Worksheet 18 "Finding Useful Sources"

Section 1 • Magnets and Magnetism

2) Teach, continued

USING THE FIGURE
Have students compare the drawing of a bar magnet in **Figure 4** with the photograph. The solid field lines in the drawing represent both the direction and the strength (the closer together the lines, the stronger the field) of a bar magnet's magnetic field. The iron filings in the photograph show the size and shape of that magnet's magnetic field. Ask students which model makes it easier for them to understand a magnetic field and why. Students can create a model of Earth's magnetic field in the QuickLab on page 459. **Sheltered English**

Magnetic Mystery PG 698

READING STRATEGY
Prediction Guide As part of the Using the Figure, above, ask students to predict what would happen if two bar magnets were placed side by side or end to end. Discuss the predictions. Demonstrate what happens when the like poles and then the opposite poles of two magnets are brought together.

MEETING INDIVIDUAL NEEDS
Learners Having Difficulty
Some students may have difficulty understanding magnetic poles. Provide each student with a compass and a magnet. Help the students to see the magnetic needle of the compass pointing north. Have them observe the effect of the north and south poles of a magnet on the compass needle. **Sheltered English**

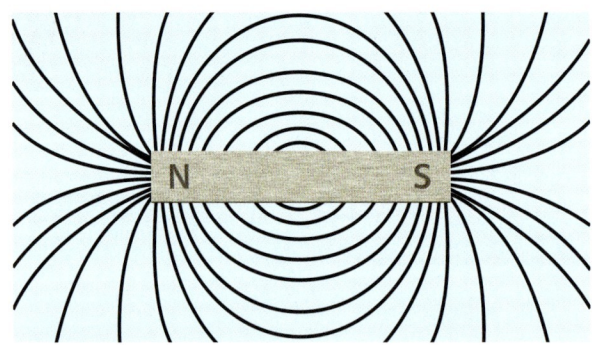

Magnetic Fields A *magnetic field* exists in the region around a magnet in which magnetic forces can act. The shape of a magnetic field can be shown with lines drawn from the north pole of a magnet to the south pole, as shown in **Figure 4**. These lines map the strength of magnetic force and are called *magnetic field lines*. The closer together the field lines are, the stronger the magnetic field is. Magnetic field lines around a magnet are closest together at the poles, showing that the magnetic force is strongest at these two places.

Figure 4 Magnetic field lines show the shape of a magnetic field around a magnet. You can model magnetic field lines by sprinkling iron filings around a magnet.

What Makes Materials Magnetic?
Some materials are magnetic, and some are not. For example, a magnet can pick up objects such as paper clips and iron nails, but it cannot pick up paper, plastic, pennies, or aluminum foil. What causes the difference? Whether a material is magnetic depends on the atoms in the material.

Atoms and Domains All matter is composed of atoms. In the atoms, electrons are the negatively charged particles that move around the nucleus. Moving electrons produce magnetic fields that can give an atom a north and a south pole. In most materials, such as copper and aluminum, the magnetic fields of the individual atoms cancel each other out, so the materials aren't magnetic. However, in materials like iron, nickel, and cobalt, the atoms group together in tiny regions called *domains*. The atoms in a domain are arranged so that the north and south poles of all the atoms line up and create a strong magnetic field. Domains are like tiny magnets of different sizes within an object. **Figure 5**, on the next page, shows how domains affect the magnetic properties of an object.

BRAIN FOOD
Grazing cows sometimes eat pieces of metal that have fallen on the ground. To protect their cows, ranchers have them swallow special cow magnets. These magnets stay in one of the cow's stomachs and attract any metal objects containing iron that the cow eats. This keeps the metal from traveling through the rest of the cow's digestive system.

In the chapter opener, students learned about a magnetic field so strong it can levitate objects, such as a frog, that are not normally magnetic. Yet, in this section, students learn that there are many materials that are not magnetic because the magnetic fields of their individual atoms cancel each other out. Explain that the magnet that levitated the frog has an extremely strong magnetic field, up to 1,000 times stronger than household magnets. The powerful magnetic field influenced the magnetic fields of individual atoms in normally nonmagnetic materials. This caused even a frog to become temporarily magnetic.

Figure 5 *The arrangement of domains in an object determines whether the object is magnetic.*

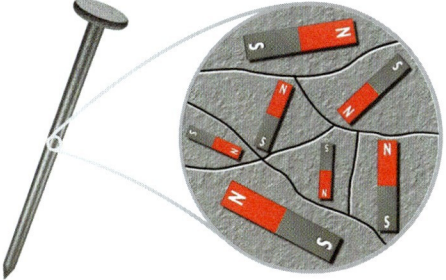

If the domains in an object are randomly arranged, the magnetic fields of the individual domains cancel each other out, and the object overall has no magnetic properties.

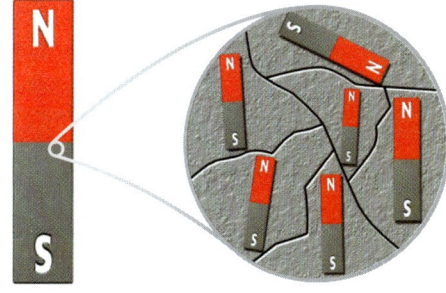

If most of the domains in an object are aligned, the magnetic fields of the individual domains combine to make the whole object magnetic.

Losing Alignment The domains of a magnet may not always stay aligned. Dropping a magnet or striking it too hard can jostle the domains out of alignment, causing the magnet to lose its magnetic properties. Increasing the temperature of a magnet can also demagnetize it. At higher temperatures, atoms in the magnet vibrate faster and lose their alignment within the domains.

Making Magnets A magnet can be made from an unmagnetized object made of iron, cobalt, or nickel by aligning the domains in the object. For example, you can magnetize an iron nail if you rub it in one direction with one pole of a magnet. The magnetic field of the magnet will cause the domains in the nail to rotate and align with the domains in the magnet. As more domains become aligned, the overall magnetic field of the nail will strengthen, and the nail will become a magnet, as shown in **Figure 6.**

The process of making a magnet also explains how a magnet can pick up an unmagnetized object, such as a paper clip. When you hold a magnet close to a paper clip, the magnetic field of the magnet causes the domains in the paper clip to align slightly, creating a temporary magnet. The domains align such that the north pole of the paper clip points toward the south pole of the magnet. The paper clip is therefore attracted to the magnet. The domains of the paper clip return to a random arrangement after the magnet is removed.

Figure 6 *This nail was magnetized by rubbing it with a magnet.*

MEETING INDIVIDUAL NEEDS

Advanced Learners Electrons have a property called "spin" that produces a small magnetic field. Have students research spin and whether magnetic fields or magnetism would be possible if all motion, including the motion of electrons, could be stopped. (Remind students that stopping all motion at the subatomic level is not theoretically possible.) Their research may include topics such as absolute zero, electrons, domains, and spin.

REAL-WORLD CONNECTION

Magnets are made by placing a material with good magnetic properties, such as iron, nickel, or steel, in a strong magnetic field. The strong external field aligns the domains in the material. Depending on the material, many of the domains remain aligned when the material is removed from the external magnetic field, leaving it magnetized.

CONNECT TO EARTH SCIENCE

How does magnetite become magnetized? Earth's magnetic field does it. Iron is found in igneous rocks, which form from magma. While the iron is molten, the domains in iron align themselves with Earth's magnetic field like tiny compass needles. When the iron cools and solidifies into magnetite, its domains remain aligned and it is magnetized.

CROSS-DISCIPLINARY FOCUS

Language Arts Legends (stories or popular beliefs handed down from earlier times) are often used to explain the origins of things or events when the actual origin is unknown. One legend about the discovery of magnets tells that a Greek shepherd named Magnes discovered magnetite. Magnes was herding his sheep in the area known as Magnesia when nails in his shoes and the metal tip of his staff became stuck to a rock. This rock was named magnetite after Magnes or Magnesia. Students may want to research this and other legends. Have them present a legend they have learned in a story, a report, or a skit.

2 Teach, continued

ACTIVITY

MATERIALS

FOR EACH PAIR:
- strong bar magnet
- test tube filled with iron filings and closed securely with a rubber stopper
- compass

Have students move the compass close to the tube and record their observations. Next have them drag one pole of the bar magnet along the tube several times in one direction. Then have students gently shake the filings inside the tube. Discuss how the iron filings simulated magnetic domains. **(The filings behave as a magnet only when they are aligned, like magnetic domains.)**

Ask students why they had to drag the magnet along the test tube. **Sheltered English**

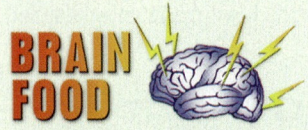

BRAIN FOOD

You cannot create a single magnetic pole, or *monopole*, by cutting a magnet in pieces. Some scientists think that monopoles do exist and that they played a part in the formation of the universe. Scientists are trying to find magnetic monopoles, but they have so far been unsuccessful.

MISCONCEPTION ALERT

Ferromagnets do not have to be made of iron. Ferromagnetism is a property of several different elements. The word *ferromagnet* comes from the Latin word for iron, *ferrum*, because ferromagnets have magnetic properties like those of iron.

458 Chapter 18 • Electromagnetism

Half a Magnet? What do you think would happen if you cut a magnet in half? You might predict that you would end up with one north-pole piece and one south-pole piece. But that's not what happens. When you cut a magnet in half, you end up with two magnets, each with its own north pole and south pole, as shown in **Figure 7**. Each domain within a magnet is like a tiny magnet with a north and south pole, so even the smallest pieces of a magnet have two poles.

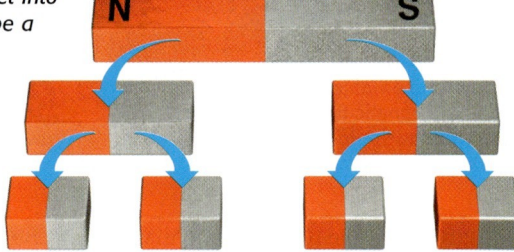

Figure 7 If you cut a magnet into pieces, each piece will still be a magnet with two poles.

REVIEW

1. Name three properties of magnets.
2. Why are some iron objects magnetic and others not magnetic?
3. **Applying Concepts** Suppose you have two bar magnets. One has its north and south poles marked, but the other one does not. Describe how you could use the first magnet to identify the poles of the second magnet.

Figure 8 Magnetite attracts objects containing iron and is a ferromagnet.

Types of Magnets

There are different ways to describe magnets. The magnets you may be most familiar with are those made of iron, nickel, cobalt, or alloys of those metals. Magnets made with these metals have strong magnetic properties and are called *ferromagnets*. The mineral magnetite, which you read about at the beginning of this section and which is shown in **Figure 8**, is an example of a naturally occurring ferromagnet. Another type of magnet is the *electromagnet*. An electromagnet is a magnet, usually with an iron core, produced by an electric current. You will learn more about electromagnets in the next section.

Answers to Review

1. All magnets have two poles, exert magnetic forces, and are surrounded by a magnetic field.
2. Iron objects are magnetic if most of their domains are aligned. If their domains are randomly arranged, they aren't magnetic.
3. Hold one end of the unmarked magnet close to the marked north pole. If the two magnets attract each other, that end of the unmarked magnet is its south pole. If the magnets repel each other, that end of the unmarked magnet is its north pole.

Temporary and Permanent Magnets Magnets can also be described as temporary magnets or permanent magnets. *Temporary magnets* are made from materials that are easy to magnetize but tend to lose their magnetization easily. Soft iron (iron that is not mixed with any other materials) can be made into temporary magnets. *Permanent magnets,* on the other hand, are difficult to magnetize but tend to retain their magnetic properties better. Strong permanent magnets are made with alnico (AL ni кон)—an alloy of aluminum, nickel, and cobalt.

Earth as a Magnet

Recall that one end of every magnet points to the north if the magnet is allowed to rotate freely. For more than 2,000 years, travelers and explorers have relied on this to help them navigate. In fact, you take advantage of this property any time you use a compass, because a compass contains a freely rotating magnet. But why do magnets point to the north? Read on to find out.

One Giant Magnet In 1600, an English physician named William Gilbert suggested that magnets point to the north because Earth itself is one giant magnet. In fact, Earth behaves as if it has a bar magnet running through its center. The poles of this imaginary magnet are located near Earth's geographic poles, as shown in **Figure 9.**

Figure 9 The magnetic poles of Earth are close to—but not the same as—the geographic poles.

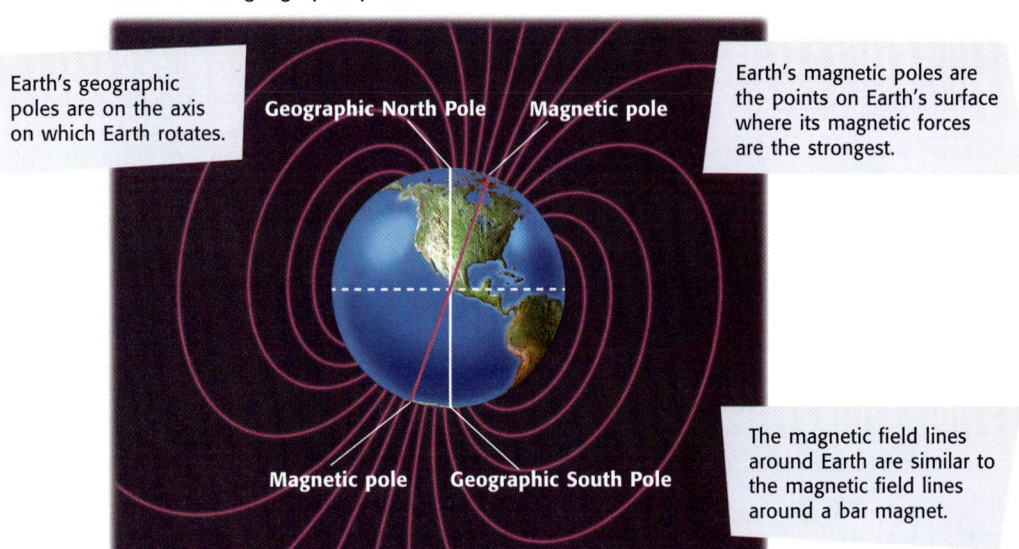

Earth's geographic poles are on the axis on which Earth rotates.

Geographic North Pole   Magnetic pole

Earth's magnetic poles are the points on Earth's surface where its magnetic forces are the strongest.

Magnetic pole   Geographic South Pole

The magnetic field lines around Earth are similar to the magnetic field lines around a bar magnet.

QuickLab

Model of Earth's Magnetic Field

1. On a **sheet of butcher paper,** draw a circle with a diameter larger than a bar magnet. This represents the surface of the Earth. Label Earth's North and South Poles.

2. Place a **bar magnet** under the butcher paper and line it up with the poles.

3. Sprinkle some **iron filings** lightly around the perimeter of the circle. In your ScienceLog, describe and sketch the pattern you see.

Homework

Concept Mapping Have students make concept maps in their ScienceLog using the terms *magnet, pole, ferromagnet, magnetic force, temporary magnet,* and *permanent magnet.*

SCIENCE HUMOR

In a lab where there wasn't much action,
Two magnets supplied some distraction.
So with similar goals,
They matched opposite poles.
And now they're quite an attraction!

REAL-WORLD CONNECTION

Magnetic declination, the angle between true north and magnetic north, depends on where the observer is with respect to the north magnetic pole. For example, in Victoria, British Columbia, on the west coast of Canada, the magnetic declination is about 20° E—a compass will point 20° east of true north. In St. John's, Newfoundland, on the east coast of Canada, the magnetic declination is about 23° W.

QuickLab

MATERIALS

FOR EACH STUDENT OR PAIRS OF STUDENTS:
- piece of butcher paper
- bar magnet
- iron filings

Answers to Quicklab

3. Students should see that the iron filings form a pattern similar to the one surrounding the photograph of the magnet on page 456.

MEETING INDIVIDUAL NEEDS

Advanced Learners Data gathered with ground telescopes and from spacecraft have revealed that most planets have magnetic fields. For example, Saturn's magnetic field is 1,000 times stronger than Earth's! Have students find information about the magnetic fields of other planets and present their findings to the class.

 Teaching Transparency 272 "Earth as a Magnet"

TOPIC: Types of Magnets
GO TO: www.scilinks.org
*sci*LINKS NUMBER: HSTP435

Section 1 • Magnets and Magnetism   **459**

3 Extend

CONNECT TO EARTH SCIENCE

On a globe or a wall map, point out the present locations of Earth's magnetic north and south poles. The north magnetic pole is located about 1,600 km south of the geographic north pole near Bathurst Island in northern Canada. It was discovered in 1831 by Sir James Clark Ross (1800–1862). Since 1831, magnetic north has been moving northward at a rate of about 10 km per year. The south magnetic pole is now about 2,600 km from the geographic South Pole near the Adélie Coast of Antarctica.

MATH and MORE

If the north magnetic pole has moved on average about 10 km per year in the twentieth century, approximately how many kilometers has it moved since 1900? **(approximately 1,000 km)**

MEETING INDIVIDUAL NEEDS

Advanced Learners The Earth's poles also show daily elliptical movement around their average positions. On any given day, the poles can be as much as 80 km away from their average position. Have students research this phenomenon and share what they have learned with the class. Encourage them to make a model or other creative display to help their presentation.

Biology CONNECTION

Scientists think that birds may use the Earth's magnetic field to help them navigate. Tiny pieces of magnetite have been found in the brains of birds, which could help them sense which direction is north as they fly.

North or South? Try this simple experiment. Place a compass on a bar magnet that has its north and south poles marked. Which pole of the magnet did the marked end of the needle of the compass point to? If your compass is working properly, the marked end should have pointed to the south pole of the magnet, as shown in **Figure 10.** Does that surprise you? Think about what you have already learned about magnets.

Figure 10 The marked end of a compass needle always points to the south pole of a magnet.

One property of magnets is that opposite poles attract each other. That means that the north pole of one magnet is attracted to the south pole of another magnet. A compass needle is a small magnet, and the tip that points to the north is the needle's north pole. Therefore, the point of a compass needle will be attracted to the south pole of a bar magnet.

North Is South! So why does the needle of a compass point north? The answer is that the magnetic pole of Earth that is closest to the geographic North Pole is actually a magnetic *south* pole! So a compass needle points to the north because its north pole is attracted to a very large magnetic south pole.

The Core of the Matter Although you can think of Earth as having a giant bar magnet in its center, as shown in **Figure 11,** there isn't really a magnet there. The temperature of Earth's core (or center) is so high that atoms in it move too violently to remain aligned in domains. Scientists think that the Earth's magnetic field is produced by the movement of electric charges in the Earth's core. The Earth's core is made mostly of iron and nickel. The inner core is solid because it is under such great pressure. In the outer core, the pressure is less and the metals are in a liquid state. As Earth rotates, the liquid in the core flows and causes electric charges to move, creating a magnetic field.

Figure 11 The Earth acts like a giant magnet.

WEIRD SCIENCE

In the 1500s, people believed that compasses pointed north because there was a large mountain of magnetite at the North Pole. This mountain, they believed, caused Earth's magnetic field.

Science Bloopers

Scientists originally thought that the sun and stars were the only navigational devices used by migrating birds and other animals. They ridiculed a theory that animals might also use Earth's magnetic field to navigate. More recent research shows that some animals do, in fact, use Earth's magnetic fields to aid their navigation.

460 Chapter 18 • Electromagnetism

A Magnetic Light Show One of the most spectacular effects caused by the Earth's magnetic field is a curtain of light called an *aurora*, like the one shown in **Figure 12.** An aurora is formed when charged particles from the sun interact with oxygen and nitrogen atoms in Earth's atmosphere. When charged particles from the sun strike these atoms, the atoms emit light of different colors.

Figure 12 The photo at left shows what an aurora looks like from the ground.

Earth's magnetic field acts like a barrier to most charged particles from the sun, so the particles cannot strike the atmosphere in most places. But because Earth's magnetic field bends inward at the magnetic poles, the charged particles can crash into the atmosphere at and near the poles. Therefore, auroras are most often seen in areas near the north and south magnetic poles. Auroras seen near the north magnetic pole are called aurora borealis (ah ROHR uh BOHR ee AL is), the northern lights, and auroras seen near the south magnetic pole are called aurora australis (ah ROHR uh ah STRAY lis), the southern lights.

Auroras are a result of geomagnetic storms. Read more about these storms on page 478.

REVIEW

1. Name the metals used to make ferromagnets.
2. How are temporary magnets different from permanent magnets?
3. **Applying Concepts** Why are auroras more commonly seen in places like Alaska and Australia than in places like Florida and Mexico?

TOPIC: Magnetism, Types of Magnets
GO TO: www.scilinks.org
sciLINKS NUMBER: HSTP430, HSTP435

---

4 Close

CONNECT TO EARTH SCIENCE

Scientists know that Earth's magnetic poles have reversed more than once. When certain kinds of molten rocks cool, their crystals line up with the Earth's magnetic field. By studying the magnetic orientation of these rocks, scientists have determined that Earth's poles have reversed several times in the past 5 million years.

Quiz

Ask students to identify what is described by each of the following statements:

1. All magnets have two areas where the magnetic effects are strongest. (poles)
2. Within an object are tiny magnetic areas that can be either aligned or misaligned. (domains)
3. Some magnets retain their magnetic properties well but are difficult to magnetize. (permanent magnets)

ALTERNATIVE ASSESSMENT

In a short paragraph or with diagrams or other illustrations, have students explain how Earth is like a giant bar magnet and how it is different. Students should include and explain the difference between the Earth's geographic poles and its magnetic poles.

Reinforcement Worksheet 18
"Planet Lodestone"

Answers to Review

1. Ferromagnets are made from iron, nickel, cobalt, or alloys of those metals.
2. Temporary magnets are easy to magnetize but lose their magnetization easily. Permanent magnets are difficult to magnetize but retain their magnetic properties for a long time.
3. Auroras are most commonly seen near Earth's magnetic poles. Because Alaska and Australia are close to the Earth's magnetic poles, people living there are more likely to see auroras than are people living in Florida and Mexico, which are far away from the Earth's magnetic poles.

SECTION 2

Focus

Magnetism from Electricity

This section explains the relationship between electricity and magnetism, known as electromagnetism. Students will learn about electromagnets and solenoids. The section also describes several applications of electromagnetism.

 **Bellringer**

Tell students the following:

Recall the opener about the floating frog at the beginning of this chapter. Suppose you had a machine that could levitate heavy objects with the flick of a switch. In your ScienceLog, write a paragraph about how this machine would make your life easier.

1) Motivate

DEMONSTRATION

Electromagnets You will need a compass, a 6 V battery, and some insulated copper wire. Connect one end of the wire to the positive battery terminal. Wrap the wire around the compass. Connect the other end of the wire to the negative battery terminal to start the flow of electric charges. The electric current in the wire will cause the magnetic compass needle to move. Review with students what they learned about magnetic fields in the previous section. Ask students what kinds of forces could cause the compass needle to move.

Directed Reading Worksheet 18 Section 2

Section 2

Terms to Learn

electromagnetism
solenoid
electromagnet
electric motor

What You'll Do

- Identify the relationship between an electric current and a magnetic field.
- Compare solenoids, electromagnets, and magnets.
- Describe how electromagnetism is involved in the operation of doorbells, electric motors, and galvanometers.

Magnetism from Electricity

Most of the trains you see roll on wheels on top of a track. But engineers have developed trains that have no wheels and actually float above the track. These trains are able to levitate because of magnetic forces between the track and the train cars. Such trains are called maglev trains. The name *maglev* is short for magnetic levitation. To levitate, maglev trains use a type of magnet called an electromagnet, which can produce a strong magnetic field. In this section you will learn how electricity and magnetism are related and how electromagnets are made.

The Discovery of Electromagnetism

Danish physicist Hans Christian Oersted discovered the relationship between electricity and magnetism in 1820. During a lecture, he held a compass near a wire carrying an electric current. Oersted noticed that when the compass was close to the wire, the compass needle no longer pointed to the north. This result surprised Oersted because a compass needle is a magnet and only moves from its usual north-south orientation when it is in a magnetic field different from Earth's magnetic field. Oersted tried a few experiments with the compass and the wire and found the results shown in **Figure 13**.

Figure 13 *Oersted's experiments show that an electric current can move a compass needle.*

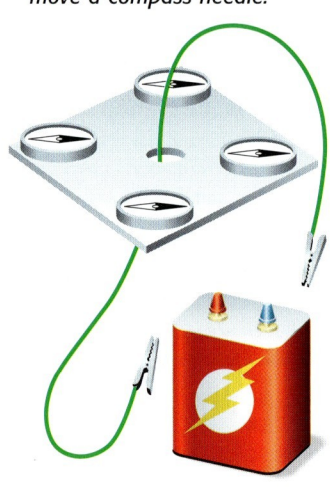
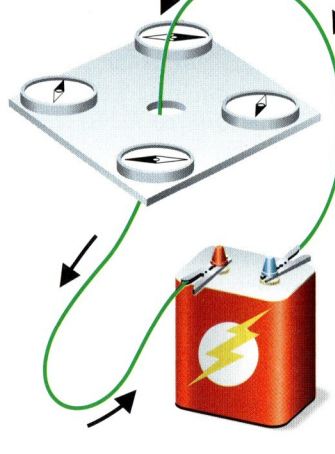
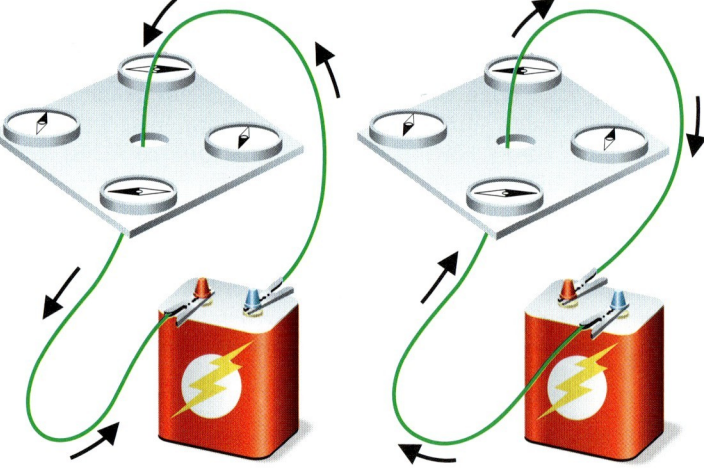

a If no electric current exists in the wire, the compass needles point in the same direction.

b Electric current in one direction in the wire causes the compass needles to deflect in a clockwise direction.

c Electric current in the opposite direction makes the compass needles deflect in a counterclockwise direction.

IS THAT A FACT!

Hans Christian Oersted was also the first person to isolate the element aluminum. Although the ancient Greeks and Romans used alum in dyeing processes and as an astringent, it wasn't until 1825 that Oersted isolated the metal by reacting aluminum chloride with a potassium-mercury alloy and heating the resulting aluminum-mercury amalgam.

462   Chapter 18 • Electromagnetism

More Research From his experiments, Oersted concluded that an electric current produces a magnetic field and that the direction of the magnetic field depends on the direction of the current. The French scientist André-Marie Ampère heard about Oersted's findings and did more research with electricity and magnetism. Together, their work was the first research conducted on electromagnetism. **Electromagnetism** is the interaction between electricity and magnetism.

Compasses Near Magnets

If you try to use a compass near devices that have strong magnets, electromagnets, or electric motors, such as stereo speakers, radios, and televisions, you might notice that the needle of the compass does not always point to the north. Use the results from Oersted's experiments to explain why this occurs. Why do you think it is important for a boater to keep the navigation compass away from the boat's radio?

Using Electromagnetism

Although the magnetic field created by an electric current in a wire may deflect a compass needle, it is not strong enough to be very useful. However, two devices, the solenoid and the electromagnet, strengthen the magnetic field created by a current-carrying wire. Both devices make electromagnetism more useful for practical applications.

Solenoids The scientists mentioned at the beginning of this chapter used a solenoid to levitate a frog. A **solenoid** is a coil of wire that produces a magnetic field when carrying an electric current. A single loop of wire carrying a current does not have a very strong magnetic field. However, if many loops are used to form a coil, the magnetic fields of the individual loops can combine to produce a much stronger magnetic field. In fact, the magnetic field around a solenoid is very similar to the magnetic field of a bar magnet, as shown in **Figure 14.** The strength of the magnetic field produced by a solenoid increases as more loops are added and as the current in the wire is increased.

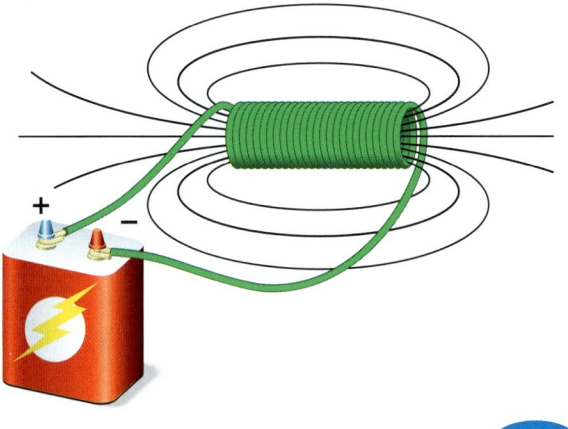

Figure 14 The ends of the solenoid are like the poles of a magnet.

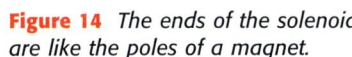

CONNECT TO LIFE SCIENCE

Magnetic resonance imaging (MRI; also referred to as nuclear magnetic resonance) can reveal details of the human body never before visible without surgery. MRI machines use strong electromagnetic fields to detect energy given off by the nuclei of some cells under certain conditions. Doctors can diagnose injuries, conditions, and diseases that are not apparent using standard X rays. Interested students should read the feature "Magnets in Medicine" on page 479.

2 Teach, continued

Meeting Individual Needs

Learners Having Difficulty
Use markers and index cards to make a name card for each component in the QuickLab. Make two additional cards with the terms *magnetic field* and *electric current* on them. Discuss the activity with students. Have them place each card close to the appropriate component. Then have them place the two additional cards where the electric current exists and where a magnetic field is produced.
Sheltered English

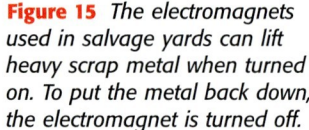

MATERIALS

For Each Group:
- 1 m of insulated copper wire
- 1 large iron nail
- electrical tape
- 1 D-cell
- paper clips

Safety Caution: Have students wear goggles during this activity.

Teacher Notes: Instead of the D-cell, 6 V lantern batteries or 9 V batteries can be used. If they are used, make sure the students know the correct places to attach the ends of the wire. To save time, the ends of the wire can be stripped before the activity.

Answers to QuickLab

3. Students should be able to pick up several paper clips.
4. After one wire is detached from the cell, the paper clips should fall off.

Electromagnets

1. Tightly wrap an **insulated copper wire** around a **large iron nail**, leaving 10 cm of wire loose at each end.
2. Remove the insulation from the ends of the wire, and use **electrical tape** to attach the ends against the top and bottom of a **D-cell**.
3. Hold the end of the nail near some **paper clips**, and try to lift them up.
4. While holding the clips up with your electromagnet, remove the wires from the cell.
5. Record your observations in your ScienceLog.

Figure 15 The electromagnets used in salvage yards can lift heavy scrap metal when turned on. To put the metal back down, the electromagnet is turned off.

Self-Check

Can you make an electromagnet by wrapping a coil of wire around a wooden core? Explain your answer.
(See page 724 to check your answer.)

Answer to Self-Check
No; an electromagnet is produced when the magnetic field of the coil of wire causes the domains in the core line up. Wood does not contain domains and therefore cannot be the core of an electromagnet.

Electromagnets An **electromagnet** is a magnet that consists of a solenoid wrapped around an iron core. The magnetic field produced by the solenoid causes the domains inside the iron core to become better aligned. The magnetic field for the entire electromagnet is the field produced by the solenoid plus the field produced by the magnetized iron core. As a result, the magnetic field produced by an electromagnet may be hundreds of times stronger than the magnetic field produced by just a solenoid with the same number of loops.

The strength of an electromagnet can be made even stronger by increasing the number of loops in the solenoid, by increasing the size of the iron core, and by increasing the electric current in the wire. Some electromagnets are strong enough to lift a car or levitate a train!

Heavy Lifting Do you remember the maglev trains discussed at the beginning of this section? Those trains levitate because there are strong magnets on the cars that are repelled by powerful electromagnets in the rails. Electromagnets are particularly useful because they can be turned on and off as needed. Electromagnets attract objects containing iron only when a current exists in the wire. When there is no current in the wire, the electromagnet is turned off. **Figure 15** shows an example of how this property can be useful.

IS THAT A FACT!
An average American car built in the early 1990s used about 880 kg of steel and iron and about 300 kg of other materials. Cars can be recycled; they are shredded, and electromagnets remove the steel and iron so those materials can be reused.

Magnetic Force and Electric Current

At the beginning of this section you learned that an electric current can cause a compass needle to move. The needle, a small magnet, moves because the electric current in a wire creates a magnetic field that exerts a force on the needle. If a current-carrying wire causes a magnet to move, can a magnet cause a current-carrying wire to move? **Figure 16** shows that the answer is yes.

Figure 16 *A magnet exerts a force on a current-carrying wire.*

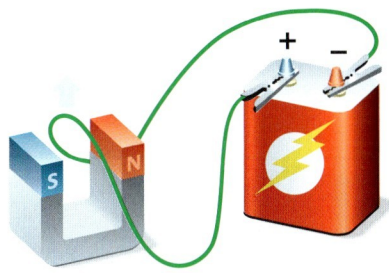

a When a current-carrying wire is placed between two poles of a magnet, the wire will jump up.

b If the direction of the electric current in the wire is reversed, the wire is pushed down instead of up.

Applications of Electromagnetism

Electromagnetism is useful in your everyday life. You already know that electromagnets can be used to lift heavy objects containing iron. But did you know that you use a solenoid whenever you ring a doorbell or that there are electromagnets in motors? Keep reading to learn how electromagnetism makes these devices work.

Doorbells Many doorbells contain a solenoid with an iron rod inserted part way in it. The electric current in the solenoid is controlled by the doorbell button. When you press the button, a switch in the solenoid circuit closes, creating an electric current in the solenoid. What happens next is shown in **Figure 17**.

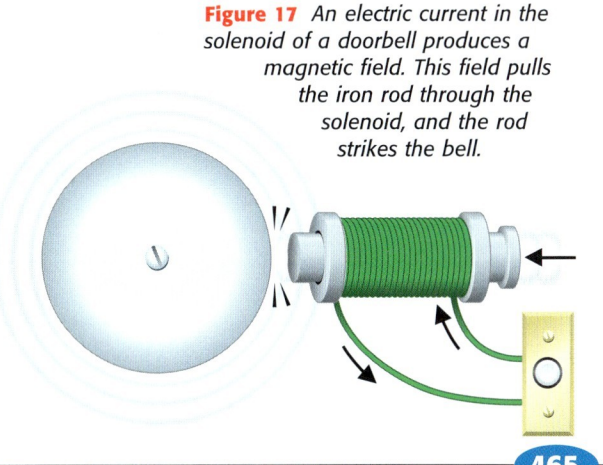

Figure 17 *An electric current in the solenoid of a doorbell produces a magnetic field. This field pulls the iron rod through the solenoid, and the rod strikes the bell.*

USING THE FIGURE

Making Models With **Figure 17** as a guide, provide students with the following steps in the operation of a doorbell:

1. The button of a doorbell is pushed, completing (or closing) the electric circuit.
2. An electric current is created in the coil.
3. The coil becomes an electromagnet.
4. A permanent magnet inside the coil is repelled.
5. The magnet moves against a chime, creating the sound of the doorbell.

Tell students that their assignment is to construct a model (it doesn't have to work) of a doorbell. Encourage them to be creative in their choice of materials, but emphasize the importance of clarity and accuracy. Finished models can be presented and then displayed in the classroom. **Sheltered English**

REAL-WORLD CONNECTION

Solenoids have many more uses in everyday life. For instance, starters in automobile engines use a solenoid, and some race car engines use solenoids to control the mix and flow of fuels such as nitrous oxide. Much quieter, but just as important, most washing machines use a solenoid to control the flow of water into the machine.

Multicultural CONNECTION

Maglev ("magnetic levitation") train systems have been tested in Germany and Japan, and a short maglev shuttle has been installed in Birmingham, England. The German and Japanese experimental trains carry passengers at speeds between 400 and 540 km/h. Maglev trains use powerful electromagnets to lift them a few centimeters above a central monorail and to drive them down the track at high speeds. There is very little friction between the track and the train, which greatly reduces wear and tear on both.

3) Extend

DEBATE

Alternating or Direct? Have students research the War of the Currents to see how Edison and Westinghouse each fought to have his system of generating electric energy adopted. Then have a class debate; choose students to advocate for either the AC or the DC electric system. At the end of the debate, conduct a secret ballot among the class to see which side presented its case most convincingly. (See the "Scientists at Odds" below.)

RETEACHING

Students may confuse the terms *machine, motor,* and *generator*. To help clarify the difference, show students that Electrical Energy → Mechanical Energy = Motor (or "E-E-M-E-M," which resembles the sound a motor makes). Next, show students that Mechanical Energy → Electrical Energy = Generator (or "M-E-E-E-Generation"). Create a poster for each of these, and display them for this section and the next.

Build a DC Motor PG 700

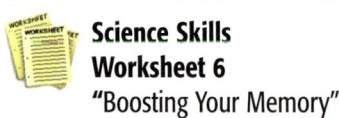
Science Skills Worksheet 6 "Boosting Your Memory"

Electric Motors An **electric motor** is a device that changes electrical energy into kinetic energy. All electric motors have an *armature*—a loop or coil of wire that can rotate. The armature is mounted between the poles of a permanent magnet or electromagnet.

In electric motors that use direct current, a device called a *commutator* is attached to the armature to reverse the direction of the electric current in the wire. A commutator is a ring that is split in half and connected to the ends of the armature. Electric current enters the armature through brushes that touch the commutator. Every time the armature and the commutator make a half-turn, the direction of the current is reversed. **Figure 18** shows how a direct-current motor works.

Figure 18 A Direct-Current Electric Motor

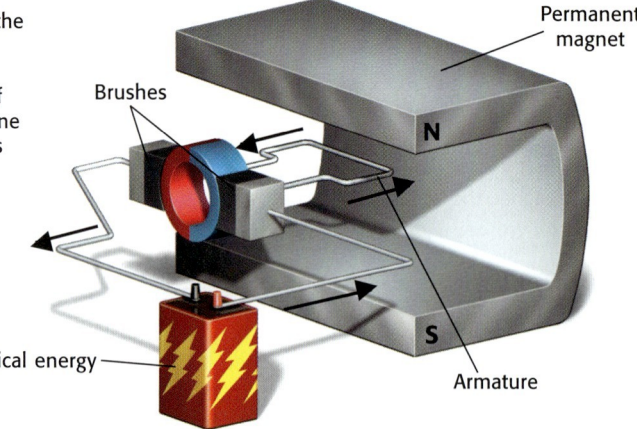

Getting Started An electric current in the armature causes the magnet to exert a force on the armature. Because of the direction of the current on either side of the armature, the magnet pulls up on one side and down on the other. This makes the armature rotate.

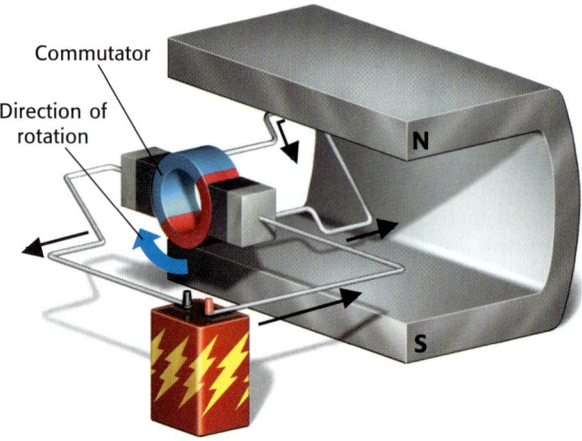

Running the Motor As the armature rotates, the commutator causes the electric current in the coil to change directions. When the electric current is reversed, the side of the coil that was pulled up is pulled down, and the side that was pulled down is pulled up. This keeps the armature rotating.

SCIENTISTS AT ODDS

In the late 1880s, a fully charged battle sparked between George Westinghouse (1846–1914), owner of the Westinghouse Electric alternating-current system, and Thomas Edison (1847–1931), renowned inventor and owner of a direct-current electrical system. What began as two different methods of generating electrical energy became a full-blown power struggle. It was called the "War of the Currents," and it raged until 1893 when Westinghouse was awarded the contract to light the entire World Columbian Exposition in Chicago with his AC system. Soon afterward, alternating current became the system of choice throughout the country.

Galvanometers A galvanometer is a device used to measure current through the interaction of an electromagnet and a permanent magnet. Galvanometers are sometimes found in equipment used by electricians, such as ammeters and voltmeters. Galvanometers contain an electromagnet placed between the poles of a permanent magnet. The electromagnet is free to rotate and is attached to a pointer. The pointer moves along a scale that shows the size and direction of the current. When there is a current in the coil of the electromagnet, the poles of the electromagnet are repelled by the poles of the permanent magnet. **Figure 19** shows how the parts of a galvanometer work.

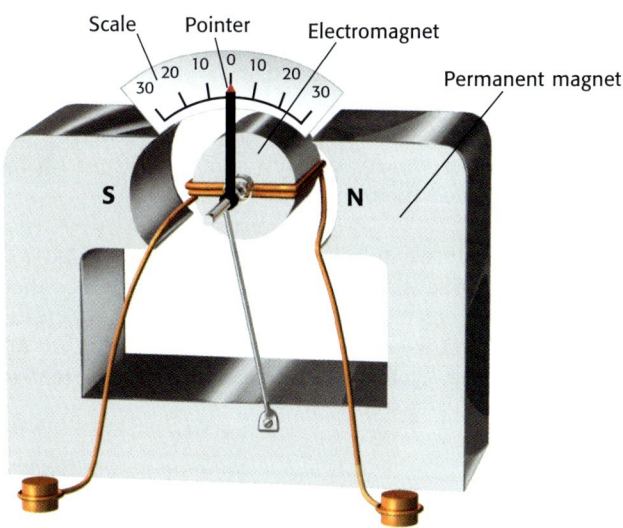

Figure 19 *The pointer will move farther when there is a large current in the electromagnet than when there is a small current.*

REVIEW

1. Describe what happens when you hold a compass close to a wire carrying a current.
2. How is a solenoid like a bar magnet?
3. What makes the armature in an electric motor rotate?
4. Explain how a solenoid works to make a doorbell ring.
5. **Applying Concepts** What do Hans Christian Oersted's experiments have to do with a galvanometer? Explain your answer.

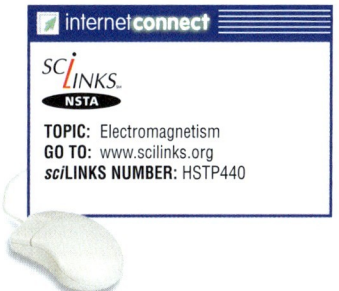

TOPIC: Electromagnetism
GO TO: www.scilinks.org
*sci*LINKS NUMBER: HSTP440

4) Close

Quiz

1. Explain Oersted's 1820 discovery. (Oersted discovered that electric current produces a magnetic field and that the direction of the magnetic field is dependent on the direction of the current.)
2. Explain how an electromagnet works. (An iron core has current-carrying wire wrapped around it. The current causes the iron core to become magnetic. The entire coil-wrapped mechanism becomes an electromagnet.)

ALTERNATIVE ASSESSMENT

Ask students to diagram and explain how an ordinary doorbell works. Each part of the mechanism should be labeled and described.

Critical Thinking Worksheet 18 "Magic Magnet Misfortune"

TOPIC: Electromagnetism
GO TO: www.scilinks.org
*sci*LINKS NUMBER: HSTP440

▼ Answers to Review

1. The needle may deflect and not point north.
2. A solenoid has a magnetic field similar to the magnetic field around a bar magnet.
3. The motor's magnet exerts a force (up on one side, down on the other) on the armature, causing the armature to rotate.
4. When the doorbell button is pushed, an electric current in the wire of the solenoid creates a magnetic field in and around the solenoid. The magnetic field pulls the iron rod through the solenoid and the rod strikes the bell.
5. Oerstedt's work (that an electric current produces a magnetic field) led to electromagnets. A galvanometer measures the interaction between the magnetic field produced by an electromagnet and the magnetic field of a permanent magnet.

SECTION 3

Focus

Electricity from Magnetism

In this section, students learn how a magnetic field can produce an electric current. They also learn about the application of electromagnetic induction in the use of generators and transformers.

Bellringer

Ask students the following:

Have you ever discovered something by accident? Maybe you looked in a dictionary for the definition of an unknown word, only to find the definition of another word you didn't know. In your ScienceLog, write a short paragraph describing how you have discovered something by accident.

1) Motivate

DISCUSSION

Discuss with students why it might be acceptable for a scientist not to get the results he or she was looking for when doing a scientific experiment. Might something useful be learned from the experiment? Could what the scientist learned lead to a discovery? Help students understand that science is a dynamic, ongoing process and not a set of facts, and that scientific experiments are not a failure if they do not give the answer the scientist was expecting.

Directed Reading Worksheet 18 Section 3

Section 3

Electricity from Magnetism

Terms to Learn
electromagnetic induction
generator
transformer

What You'll Do
- Explain how a magnetic field can produce an electric current.
- Explain how electromagnetic induction is used in a generator.
- Compare step-up and step-down transformers.

When you use an electric appliance or turn on a light in your home, you probably don't think about where the electrical energy comes from. For most people, an electric power company supplies their home with electrical energy. In this section, you'll learn how a magnetic field can produce an electric current and how power companies use this process to supply electrical energy.

Electric Current from a Magnetic Field

After Oersted discovered that an electric current could produce a magnetic field, scientists began to wonder if a magnetic field could produce an electric current. In 1831, two scientists—Michael Faraday, from Great Britain, and Joseph Henry, from the United States—independently solved this problem. Although Henry was the first to make the discovery, Faraday's results are better known because Faraday published his results first and reported them in greater detail.

Faraday's Failure? In his experiments, Faraday used a setup similar to the one shown in **Figure 20.** Faraday hoped that the magnetic field created by the electromagnet would create—or induce—an electric current in the second wire. But no matter how strong the electromagnet was, no electric current could be produced in the second wire.

Figure 20 Faraday's Setup

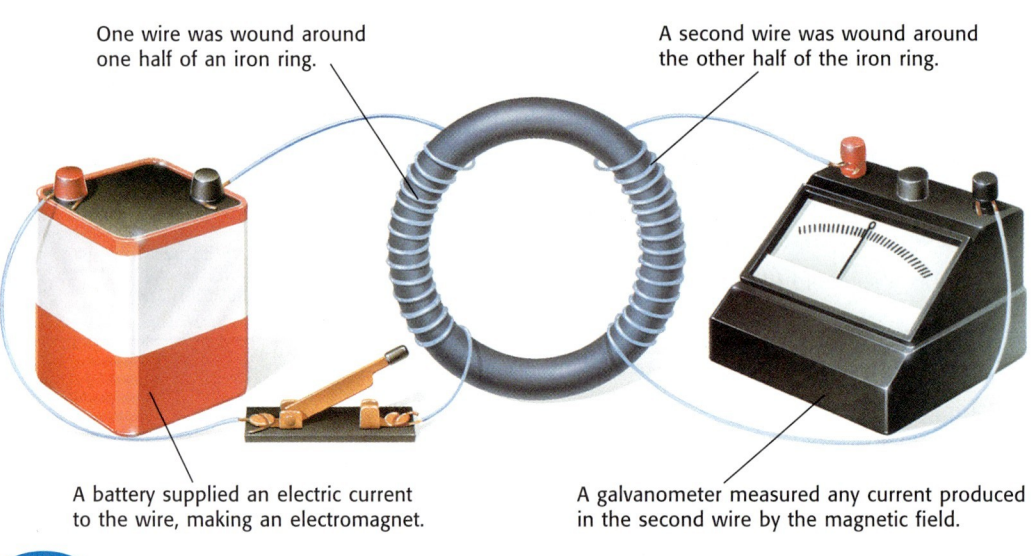

One wire was wound around one half of an iron ring.

A second wire was wound around the other half of the iron ring.

A battery supplied an electric current to the wire, making an electromagnet.

A galvanometer measured any current produced in the second wire by the magnetic field.

468

IS THAT A FACT!

As a chemist, Michael Faraday (1791–1867) worked to improve the quality of steel and was the first to liquefy chlorine gas. As a physicist, Faraday discovered a number of phenomena in the field of electromagnetism, starting with electromagnetic rotation (the principle behind the electric motor) in 1821 and including the theory of electromagnetic induction, the magneto-optical effect, diamagnetism, and field theory. Faraday was also a professor, a lecturer, and a consultant to the British government on a variety of matters.

468   Chapter 18 • Electromagnetism

Success for an Instant As Faraday experimented with this electromagnetic ring, he noticed something interesting. At the instant he connected the wires of the electromagnet to the battery, the galvanometer pointer moved, indicating that an electric current was present. The pointer moved again at the instant he disconnected the electromagnet. But as long as the electromagnet was fully connected to the battery, the galvanometer measured no electric current.

Faraday realized that electric current in the second wire was produced only when the magnetic field was changing—in this case, when the magnetic field was turned on and off as the battery was connected and disconnected. The process by which an electric current is produced by a changing magnetic field is called **electromagnetic induction.** Faraday did many more experiments on electromagnetic induction. Some of his results are summarized in **Figure 21.**

You too can have instant success with the activity on page 699 of the LabBook.

Figure 21 *The size and direction of the electric current induced by a changing magnetic field depends on several factors.*

a An electric current is induced when you move a magnet through a coil of wire.

b A greater electric current is induced if you move the magnet faster through the coil because the magnetic field is changing faster.

c A greater electric current is induced if you add more loops of wire. This magnet is moving at the same speed as the magnet in (b).

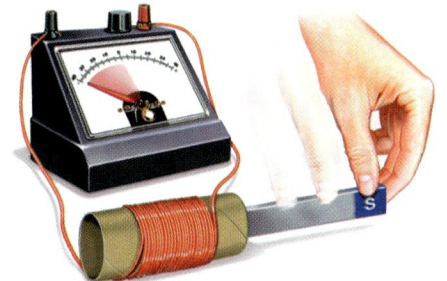

d The induced electric current reverses direction if the magnet is pulled out rather than pushed in.

2 Teach

USING THE FIGURE

Use **Figures 20** and **21** to help students understand why Faraday's initial experimental setup failed and why his realization of what was happening at the moment he turned his apparatus on or off was so important.
Sheltered English

ACTIVITY

MATERIALS

FOR EACH SMALL GROUP:
- a magnetic compass
- a cardboard or plastic box
- 1–3 m of insulated copper wire
- a broom handle
- a strong bar magnet

Have students place the compass in the box and wind one end of the wire around the box 20 times. At the wire's other end, they should make a 50-turn coil by winding the wire around the broom handle. Tell them to remove the handle. The coil should be placed as far away from the compass as possible. Instruct students to move the north pole of the bar magnet back and forth in the coil. Have them record what they observe about the compass needle. Repeat the procedure using the south pole. Discuss the results. Ask students what they could do to move the needle more. (increase the number of coils)
Sheltered English

BRAIN FOOD

If you look around your house, you may find as many as 50 electric motors. Where are they? You can find motors in the kitchen (electric can opener, refrigerator, microwave oven, garbage disposal), bathroom (fan, hairdryer, electric toothbrush), car (windshield-wiper motors, starter motor, electric windows), laundry room (washer, dryer, vacuum cleaner, electric drill), and other places (VCR, CD player, computer, toys, electric clocks, aquarium pump).

LabBook PG 699
Electricity from Magnetism

Teaching Transparency 274 "Electromagnetic Induction"

Section 3 • Electricity from Magnetism   **469**

2) Teach, continued

READING STRATEGY

Prediction Guide Before reading the passage about generators, ask students the following questions:

1. What does it mean to *generate* something? (to produce or make something)
2. What is a generator? (a device that converts kinetic energy into electrical energy)
3. How can a generator do this? (Refer students back to Faraday's experiment in which electric current was induced. Have students name the principal parts of this experiment—the wire coil, the magnet, and some source of movement.)

Some students may think that both motors and generators produce electrical energy. Review with students that although a motor and a generator are made of the same parts, they do different things. A motor changes electrical energy into mechanical energy (as in an electric fan). A generator changes mechanical energy into electrical energy (as occurs at a power plant).

Teaching Transparency 275
"Parts of a Simple Generator"
"How a Generator Works"

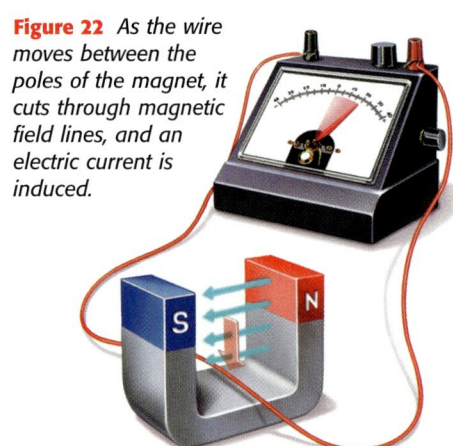

Figure 22 As the wire moves between the poles of the magnet, it cuts through magnetic field lines, and an electric current is induced.

Inducing Electric Current Faraday's experiments also showed that the magnetic field around a wire can be changed by moving either the magnet or the wire. Therefore, an electric current could be induced by moving a magnet in a coil of wire or by moving a wire between the poles of a magnet.

One way to remember when an electric current is produced by electromagnetic induction is to consider the magnetic field lines between the poles of the magnet. An electric current is induced only when a wire cuts through, or crosses, the magnetic field lines, as shown in **Figure 22**. This is because the magnetic force causes electric charges to move through the wire as the wire moves through the magnetic field.

Applications of Electromagnetic Induction

Electromagnetic induction is very important for the production of electrical energy at an electric power plant, and it is important for the transmission of energy from the plant to your home. Generators and transformers work on the principle of electromagnetic induction and are used by power plants to provide the electrical energy that you need every day.

Generators A **generator** is a device that uses electromagnetic induction to convert kinetic energy into electrical energy. **Figure 23** shows the parts of a simple generator, and **Figure 24**, on the next page, explains how the generator works.

Figure 23
Parts of a Simple Generator

Generators contain a **coil of wire** attached to a rod that is free to rotate. This generator has a crank that is used to turn the coil.

Slip rings are attached to the ends of the wire in the coil.

The coil is placed between the poles of a **permanent magnet** or electromagnet.

Electric current leaves the generator when the slip rings touch a pair of **brushes**.

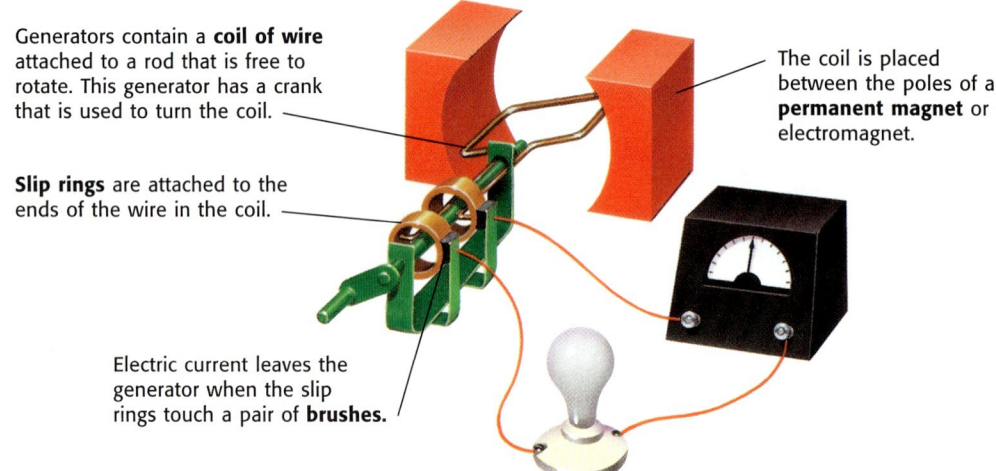

CONNECT TO EARTH SCIENCE

Another energy source for generators in an electric power plant is geothermal energy. Geothermal energy comes from hot magma deep within the Earth. In some areas, magma rises near the Earth's surface. Ground water may be heated by magma to form hot springs, geysers, and steam vents. Geothermal power plants capture steam created by magma and use it to generate electrical energy.

470 Chapter 18 • Electromagnetism

Figure 24 How a Generator Works

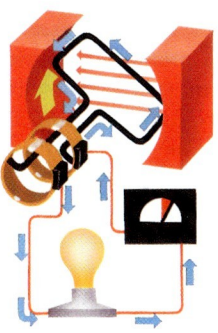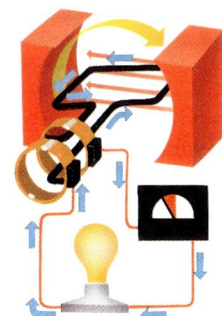

① As the crank is turned, the rotating coil cuts through the magnetic field lines of the magnet, and an electric current is induced in the wire.

② When the coil is not cutting through the magnetic field lines, no electric current is induced.

③ As the coil continues to rotate, the magnetic field lines are cut from a different direction, and an electric current is induced in the opposite direction.

Alternating Current The electric current produced by the generator shown in Figure 24 changes direction each time the coil makes a half-turn. Because the electric current continually changes direction, the electric current is an alternating current. Generators in power plants also produce alternating current. But generators in power plants are much larger and contain many coils of wire instead of just one. In most large generators, the magnet is turned instead of the coils.

Generating Electrical Energy The energy that generators convert to electrical energy comes from different sources. In nuclear power plants, thermal energy from a nuclear reaction boils water to produce steam, which turns a turbine. The turbine turns the magnet of the generator, inducing an electric current and generating electrical energy. **Figure 25** shows a similar process in a hydroelectric power plant.

Figure 25 As water flows down a chute, it turns a turbine. The turbine spins the magnet of the generator, inducing an electric current.

IS THAT A FACT!
The largest turbines in an electric power plant measure about 9.8 m in diameter and are found at the Grand Coulee Third Powerplant in Washington State.

internet connect
TOPIC: Electromagnetic Induction
GO TO: www.scilinks.org
sciLINKS NUMBER: HSTP445

MEETING INDIVIDUAL NEEDS
Learners Having Difficulty If possible, obtain some used (but cleaned up) generators from a local car mechanic. Help students disassemble the generator to reveal the internal structure. Have students diagram and identify as many of the internal parts as possible. Ask students to compare what they discover in the generator to **Figure 24**.
Sheltered English

MATH and MORE
The voltage of alternating current is constantly rising and falling; it increases to a maximum, or peak value, before it decreases again. The voltage that most homes receive falls somewhere between the peak value and the lowest value. This effective value is called the rms voltage. The rms value is calculated by multiplying 0.707 by the peak value. Have students calculate the rms value (in volts) for the United States and Canada (peak = 156 V) versus most other countries (peak = 339 V). (rms value for United States is 0.707 x 156 V = 110 V; rms value for other countries is 0.707 x 339 V = 240 V)

BRAIN FOOD
Both Michael Faraday and Joseph Henry have units of measurement named after them. The *farad* (F) expresses capacitance (the ability of a material to store electric charges). The *henry* (H) expresses inductance (the ability of a material to produce an electromotive force).

Section 3 • Electricity from Magnetism

3) Extend

MATH and MORE

The resulting voltage in a step-up or step-down transformer can be calculated using the formula:

$$\frac{\text{no. turns on primary coil}}{\text{no. turns on secondary coil}} = \frac{\text{primary coil voltage}}{\text{secondary coil voltage}}$$

Have students calculate the voltage that results in the following transformer problem:

A step-up transformer has 80 turns on its primary coil and 1,200 turns on its secondary coil. The primary coil receives 120 V of AC. What is the voltage across the secondary coil?

$$\frac{80 \text{ turns}}{1{,}200 \text{ turns}} = \frac{120 \text{ V}}{? \text{ V}} = 1{,}800 \text{ V}$$

 Math Skills Worksheet 17 "Using Proportions and Cross-Multiplication"

REAL-WORLD CONNECTION

The step-up and step-down power transformers that hang on utility poles must be efficient: power companies cannot afford to lose energy when voltages are transformed. Most transformers used by utility companies are at least 99 percent efficient, which means that one percent or less of the energy passing through the transformer is lost as thermal energy. Some high current transformers have cooling radiators filled with oil to dissipate the thermal energy.

Transformers Another device that relies on electromagnetic induction is a transformer. A **transformer** increases or decreases the voltage of an alternating current. A simple transformer consists of two coils of wire wrapped around an iron ring.

Alternating current from an electrical energy source is supplied to one coil, called the primary coil. The electric current makes the ring an electromagnet. But the electric current in the primary coil is alternating, so the magnetic field of the electromagnet changes with every change in electric current direction. The changing magnetic field in the iron ring induces an electric current in the other coil, called the secondary coil.

Step-Up, Step-Down The number of loops in the primary and secondary coils of a transformer determines whether it increases or decreases the voltage. If a transformer increases voltage, it is a step-up transformer. If a transformer decreases voltage, it is a step-down transformer. Both kinds of transformers are shown in **Figure 26**.

Figure 26 Transformers can either increase or decrease voltage.

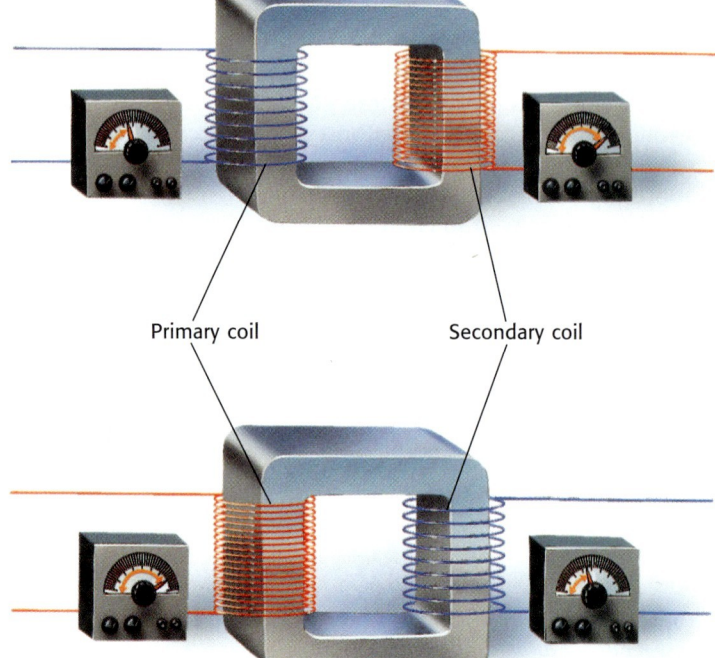

The primary coil of a **step-up transformer** has fewer loops than the secondary coil. So the voltage of the electric current in the secondary coil is higher than the voltage of the electric current in the primary coil. Therefore, voltage is increased.

The primary coil of a **step-down transformer** has more loops than the secondary coil. So the voltage of the electric current in the secondary coil is lower than the voltage of the electric current in the primary coil. Therefore, voltage is decreased.

 **SCIENCE HUMOR**

Q: Why do transformers hum?

A: Because they don't know the words!

IS THAT A FACT!

Model-train enthusiasts use step-down transformers to run their trains. In order for the trains to operate, the 110–120 V in the electrical outlet must be reduced to 12 V. This is accomplished by using a step-down transformer.

Chapter 18 • Electromagnetism

Electrical Energy for Your Home The electric current that provides your home with electrical energy is usually transformed three times before it reaches your home. Generators at the power plants produce electric current with high voltage. To decrease the loss of power that occurs during transmission over long distance, the voltage is increased thousands of times with a step-up transformer. Of course, the voltage must be decreased before it is distributed to households. Two different step-down transformers are used before the electric current reaches consumers. **Figure 27** shows how electric current is transformed on its way to your home.

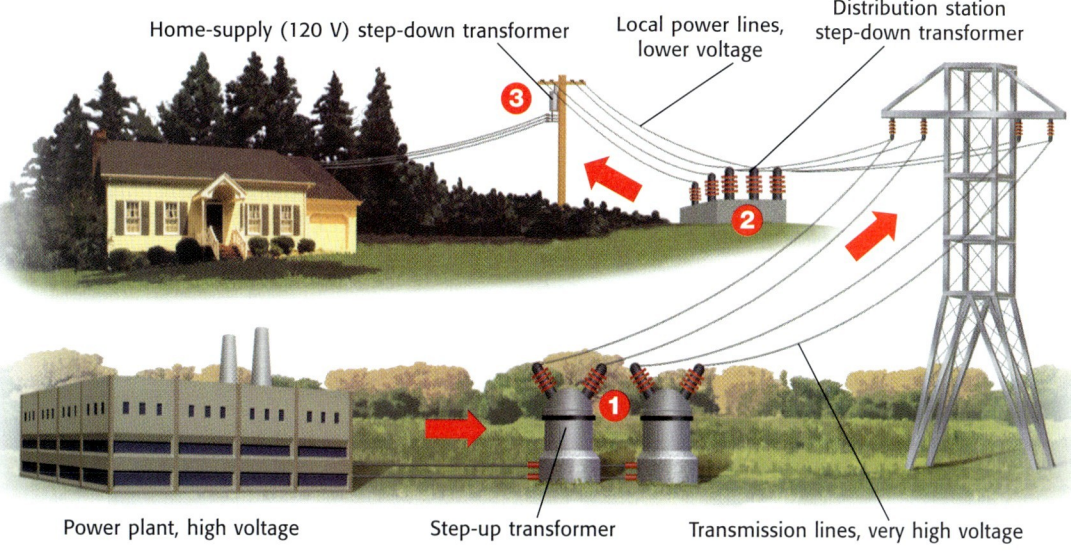

Figure 27 Electric current is transformed three times before reaching your home.

REVIEW

1. How does a generator produce an electric current?
2. Explain why rotating either the coil or the magnet induces an electric current in a generator.
3. **Inferring Conclusions** One reason why electric power plants do not distribute electrical energy as direct current is that direct current cannot be transformed. Explain why not.

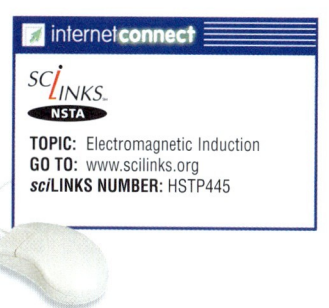

TOPIC: Electromagnetic Induction
GO TO: www.scilinks.org
sciLINKS NUMBER: HSTP445

Chapter Highlights

Vocabulary Definitions

SECTION 1

magnet any material that attracts iron or materials containing iron

poles the parts of a magnet where the magnetic effects are strongest

magnetic force the force of attraction or repulsion between the poles of magnets

SECTION 2

electromagnetism the interaction between electricity and magnetism

solenoid a coil of wire that produces a magnetic field when carrying an electric current

electromagnet a magnet that consists of a solenoid wrapped around an iron core

electric motor a device that changes electrical energy into kinetic energy

Chapter Highlights

SECTION 1

Vocabulary
- magnet (p. 454)
- poles (p. 454)
- magnetic force (p. 455)

Section Notes
- All magnets have two poles. One pole will always point to the north if allowed to rotate freely, and it is called the north pole. The other pole is called the south pole.
- Like magnetic poles repel each other; opposite magnetic poles attract.
- All magnets are surrounded by a magnetic field. The shape of that magnetic field can be shown with magnetic field lines.
- A material is magnetic if its domains are aligned. Iron, nickel, and cobalt atoms group together in domains.
- Magnets can be classified as ferromagnets, electromagnets, temporary magnets, and permanent magnets. A magnet can belong to more than one group.
- Earth acts as if it has a big bar magnet in its core.
- Compass needles and the north pole of magnets point to Earth's magnetic south pole—which is close to Earth's geographic North Pole.
- Auroras are most commonly seen near Earth's magnetic poles because Earth's magnetic fields bend inward at the poles.

Labs
Magnetic Mystery (p. 698)

SECTION 2

Vocabulary
- electromagnetism (p. 463)
- solenoid (p. 463)
- electromagnet (p. 464)
- electric motor (p. 466)

Section Notes
- Oersted discovered that a wire carrying an electric current produces a magnetic field.
- Electromagnetism is the interaction between electricity and magnetism.
- A solenoid is a coil of current-carrying wire that produces a magnetic field.
- An electromagnet is a solenoid with an iron core. The electromagnet has a stronger magnetic field than a solenoid of the same size does.
- Increasing the current in a solenoid or an electromagnet increases the magnetic field.

✓ Skills Check

Visual Understanding

ELECTROMAGNETISM The two important concepts in electromagnetism were discovered by Oersted and Faraday. Figure 13 on page 462 summarizes Oersted's work, which showed that an electric current can produce a magnetic field.

ELECTROMAGNETIC INDUCTION Faraday's work showed that a changing magnetic field can induce an electric current in a wire. His results are summarized in Figure 21 on page 469.

Lab and Activity Highlights

Magnetic Mystery PG 698

Electricity from Magnetism PG 699

Build a DC Motor PG 700

Datasheets for LabBook
(blackline masters for these labs)

SECTION 2

- Increasing the number of loops on a solenoid or an electromagnet increases the magnetic field.
- A magnet can exert a force on a wire carrying a current.
- In a doorbell, the magnetic field of a solenoid pulls an iron rod, and the iron rod strikes the bell.
- The magnetic force between a magnet and wires carrying an electric current makes an electric motor turn.
- An electric motor converts electrical energy into kinetic energy.
- A galvanometer measures current by using the magnetic force between an electromagnet and a permanent magnet.

Labs
Build a DC Motor (p. 700)

SECTION 3

Vocabulary
electromagnetic induction (p. 469)
generator (p. 470)
transformer (p. 472)

Section Notes
- Faraday discovered that a changing magnetic field can create an electric current in a wire. This is called electromagnetic induction.
- Generators use electromagnetic induction to convert kinetic energy into electrical energy.

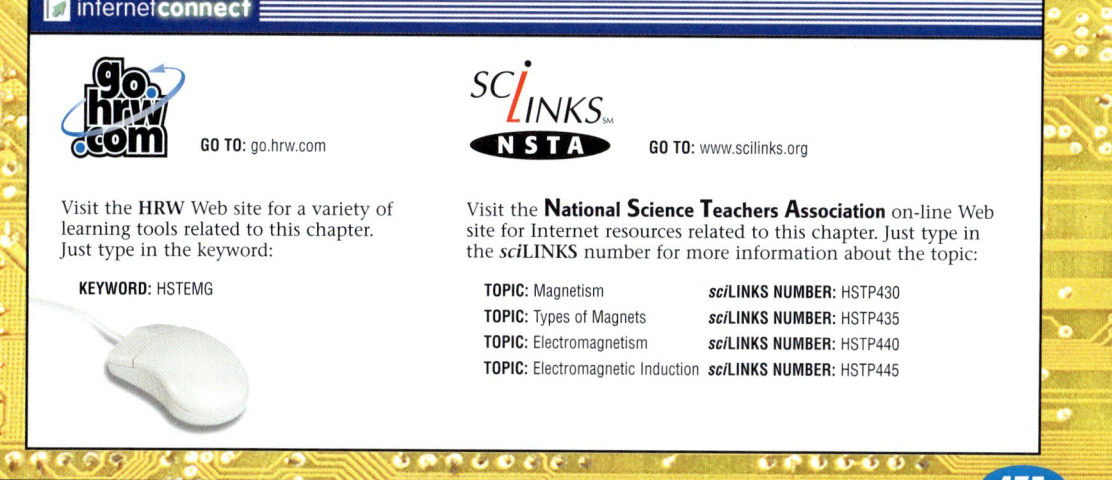

- Kinetic energy can be supplied to a generator in different ways.
- Transformers increase or decrease the voltage of an alternating current using electromagnetic induction.
- A step-up transformer increases the voltage of an alternating current. Its primary coil has fewer loops than its secondary coil.
- A step-down transformer decreases the voltage of an alternating current. Its primary coil has more loops than its secondary coil.

Labs
Electricity from Magnetism (p. 699)

VOCABULARY DEFINITIONS, continued

SECTION 3

electromagnetic induction the process by which a current is produced by a changing magnetic field

generator a device that uses electromagnetic induction to convert kinetic energy to electrical energy

transformer a device that increases or decreases the voltage of an alternating current

 Vocabulary Review Worksheet 18

 Blackline masters of these Chapter Highlights can be found in the **Study Guide**.

---

internet connect

GO TO: go.hrw.com

Visit the **HRW** Web site for a variety of learning tools related to this chapter. Just type in the keyword:

KEYWORD: HSTEMG

GO TO: www.scilinks.org

Visit the **National Science Teachers Association** on-line Web site for Internet resources related to this chapter. Just type in the *sci*LINKS number for more information about the topic:

TOPIC:		*sci*LINKS NUMBER:
Magnetism		HSTP430
Types of Magnets		HSTP435
Electromagnetism		HSTP440
Electromagnetic Induction		HSTP445

475

Lab and Activity Highlights

LabBank

 Inquiry Labs,
An Attractive Way to Navigate, Lab 22

Whiz-Bang Demonstrations,
Magnetic Nails, Demo 59

 Long-Term Projects & Research Ideas,
EMFs–Peril or Paranoia? Project 68

EcoLabs & Field Activities,
A Light Current of Air, EcoLab 21

Chapter Review Answers

USING VOCABULARY

1. poles
2. generator
3. Electromagnetic induction
4. electromagnetism

UNDERSTANDING CONCEPTS

Multiple Choice

5. a
6. d
7. c
8. c
9. d
10. c

Short Answer

11. Auroras are usually seen near Earth's magnetic poles. Earth's magnetic poles are located near Earth's geographic North and South Poles.
12. The function of a generator is opposite of the function of an electric motor. A generator converts kinetic energy to electrical energy and an electric motor converts electrical energy to kinetic energy.
13. Some pieces of iron are more magnetic than others because the domains of the magnetic pieces are more aligned, while the domains of the less-magnetic pieces are randomly arranged.

Chapter Review

USING VOCABULARY

To complete the following sentences, choose the correct term from each pair of terms listed below:

1. All magnets have two __?__. (*magnetic forces* or *poles*)
2. A(n) __?__ converts kinetic energy into electrical energy. (*electric motor* or *generator*)
3. __?__ occurs when an electric current is produced by a changing magnetic field. (*Electromagnetic induction* or *Magnetic force*)
4. The interaction between electricity and magnetism is called __?__. (*electromagnetism* or *electromagnetic induction*)

UNDERSTANDING CONCEPTS

Multiple Choice

5. The region around a magnet in which magnetic forces can act is called the
   a. magnetic field.
   b. domain.
   c. pole.
   d. solenoid.

6. An electric fan has an electric motor inside to change
   a. kinetic energy into electrical energy.
   b. thermal energy into electrical energy.
   c. electrical energy into thermal energy.
   d. electrical energy into kinetic energy.

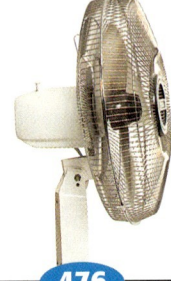

7. The marked end of a compass needle always points directly to
   a. Earth's geographic South Pole.
   b. Earth's geographic North Pole.
   c. a magnet's south pole.
   d. a magnet's north pole.

8. A device that increases the voltage of an alternating current is called a(n)
   a. electric motor.
   b. galvanometer.
   c. step-up transformer.
   d. step-down transformer.

9. The magnetic field of a solenoid can be increased by
   a. adding more loops.
   b. increasing the current.
   c. putting an iron core inside the coil to make an electromagnet.
   d. All of the above

10. What do you end up with if you cut a magnet in half?
    a. one north-pole piece and one south-pole piece
    b. two unmagnetized pieces
    c. two pieces, each with a north pole and a south pole
    d. two north-pole pieces

Short Answer

11. Explain why auroras are seen mostly near the North and South Poles.
12. Compare the function of a generator with the function of an electric motor.
13. Explain why some pieces of iron are more magnetic than others.

Concept Mapping

14. Use the following terms to create a concept map: electromagnetism, electricity, magnetism, electromagnetic induction, generator, transformer.

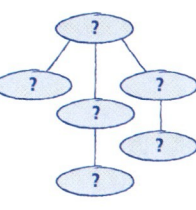

CRITICAL THINKING AND PROBLEM SOLVING

15. You win a hand-powered flashlight as a prize in your school science fair. The flashlight has a clear plastic case so you can look inside to see how it works. When you press the handle, a gray ring spins between two coils of wire. The ends of the wire are connected to the light bulb. So when you press the handle, the light bulb glows. Explain how an electric current is produced to light the bulb. (Hint: Paper clips are attracted to the gray ring.)

16. Fire doors are doors that can slow the spread of fire from room to room when they are closed. In some buildings, fire doors are held open by electromagnets. The electromagnets are controlled by the building's fire alarm system. If a fire is detected, the doors automatically shut. Explain why electromagnets are used instead of permanent magnets.

INTERPRETING GRAPHICS

17. Study the solenoids and electromagnets shown below. Rank them in order of strongest magnetic field to weakest magnetic field. Explain your ranking.

a

Current = 2 A

b

Current = 2 A

c

Current = 4 A

d

Current = 4 A

NOW What Do You Think?

Take a minute to review your answers to the ScienceLog questions on page 453. Have your answers changed? If necessary, revise your answers based on what you have learned since you began this chapter.

477

NOW WHAT DO YOU THINK?

1. All magnets have two poles, exert forces, and are surrounded by a magnetic field.
2. An electric current produces a magnetic field around the wire. Solenoids and electromagnets are examples of devices that use electricity to produce magnetism.
3. A changing magnetic field can induce an electric current.

Concept Mapping

14. An answer to this exercise can be found at the end of this book.

CRITICAL THINKING AND PROBLEM SOLVING

15. The electric current is produced by electromagnetic induction. The gray ring is a magnet, and when it spins, it creates a changing magnetic field around the coils of wire. An electric current is induced in the wire and is used to illuminate the light bulb.

16. Electromagnets are used instead of permanent magnets because electromagnets can be easily turned off. When the electromagnets are turned off, the fire doors are no longer held open, and they close.

INTERPRETING GRAPHICS

17. Rank from strongest to weakest magnetic field: (c), (b), (d), (a). Electromagnet (c) is strongest because it has an iron core and 4 A of current. Electromagnet (b) is next strongest because, even though it has a weaker current, it has an iron core. Solenoid (d) is next because it has a stronger current than (a). Solenoid (a) is weakest.

Concept Mapping Transparency 18

Blackline masters of this Chapter Review can be found in the **Study Guide.**

ACROSS THE SCIENCES
Geomagnetic Storms

Background

Each solar cycle is really only half of a longer 22-year cycle called the Hale Cycle. This cycle lasts 22 years because it takes that long for the sun's poles to reverse and then return again. The last half of the latest Hale Cycle, solar cycle 23, began in 1986.

The number of sunspots has been linked to climate conditions. There is a theory that the very low occurrence of sunspots between 1645 and 1715 caused a "Little Ice Age" in Europe when temperatures were colder than average.

Many communication systems depend on a tranquil magnetic field around the Earth. Satellites in the Earth's lower earth orbital carry an ever-increasing amount of global voice and data communications. Disruption of these satellite systems can cause costly communication delays or interference. Solar flare particles may become imbedded in a satellite and cause drag that can change the satellite's orbital path slightly. This may hasten the satellite's fall toward Earth where it will burn up in the atmosphere.

There are some benefits from geomagnetic storms. Auroras, one of the effects of these storms, are used by some geologists to help them locate subsurface oil and mineral deposits.

ACROSS THE SCIENCES

PHYSICAL SCIENCE • EARTH SCIENCE

Geomagnetic Storms

On March 13, 1989, a storm hit Montreal, Quebec. But this wasn't an ordinary storm. This was a geomagnetic storm that caused an electrical blackout. About 6 million people went without electricity for 9 hours.

What Is a Geomagnetic Storm?

To understand a geomagnetic storm, you must first know a few things about the sun. By looking closely at the surface of the sun, scientists have discovered that it has cycles of very violent activity. Powerful eruptions called solar flares occur periodically, sending charged particles outward at almost the speed of light and with the energy of millions of hydrogen bombs. As particles explode away from the solar surface, they create a solar wind of charged particles that travels several million kilometers per hour through space between the sun and the Earth. A geomagnetic storm occurs when the solar wind sweeps across Earth's atmosphere, causing a variety of disturbances.

Grids and Pipelines

Geomagnetic storms happen frequently, especially in the north. As the people of Quebec found out in 1989, such storms can interfere with systems used to operate power grids. They can also cause heavy static in long-distance radio reception and can affect the orbit of satellites. Geomagnetic storms can even cause corrosion in the metal of petroleum pipelines. In fact, scientists are not sure that they know of all the systems and materials that are affected by geomagnetic storms.

Knowledge Is the First Line of Defense

Solar flares are not well understood and are difficult to predict. There may be nothing that can be done to stop geomagnetic storms, but understanding them better is the first step toward protecting valuable systems from an eruption's effects. Scientists prepared several satellites to study the sun's activity and solar flares in 2000 and 2001. By studying solar eruptions, scientists think they can predict a geomagnetic storm 50 to 70 hours in advance. This could give industries affected by these storms time to protect their systems.

Solar Sails for Solar Wind

▶ Do research on solar flares and geomagnetic storms. Government agencies and universities have a number of programs, including satellites, to study and predict solar events. Create a model or a poster to explain something you learned from your research.

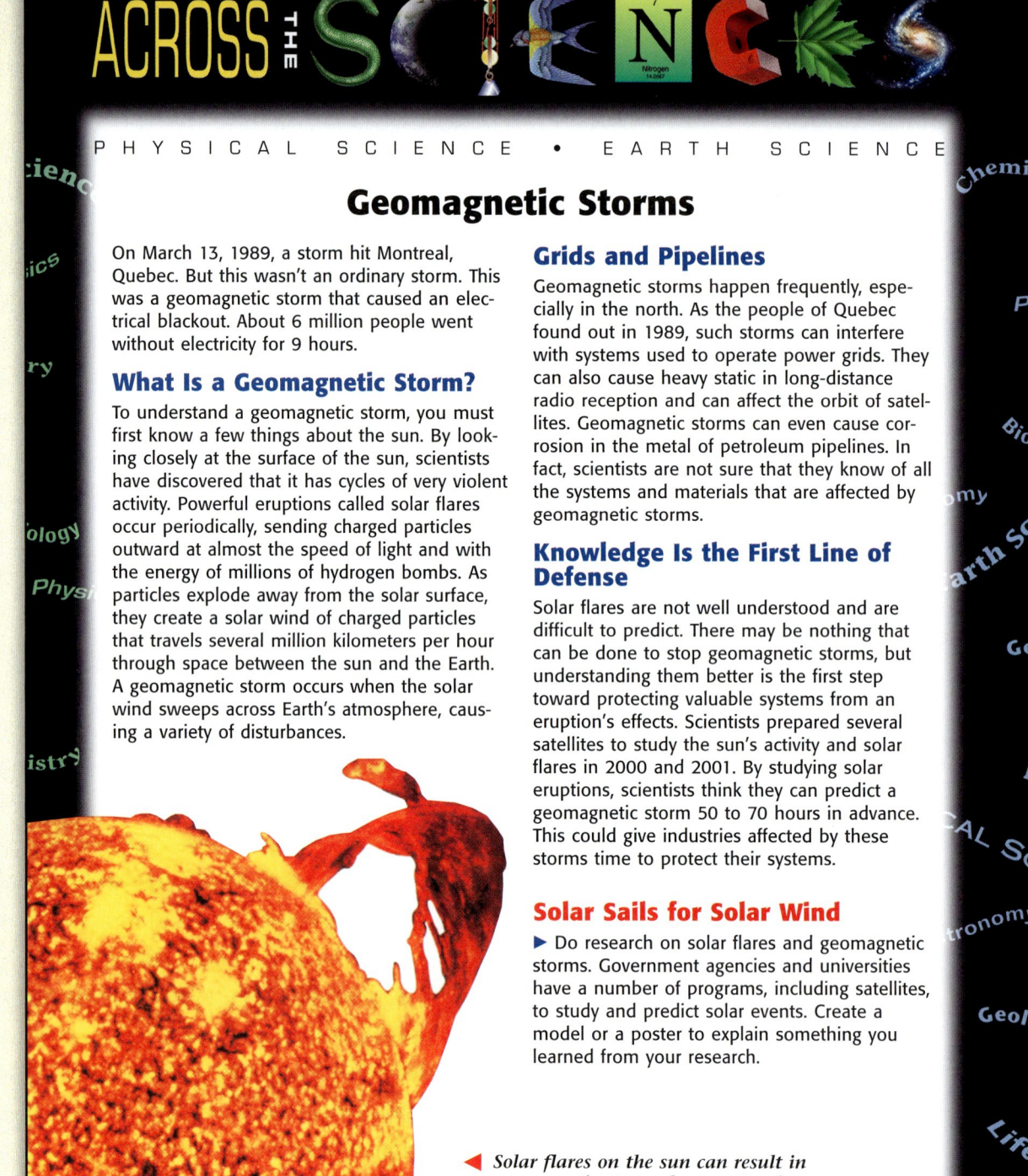

◀ *Solar flares on the sun can result in geomagnetic storms here on Earth.*

Answers for Solar Sails for Solar Wind

Using *HESSI, SMEI,* and *geomagnetic storms* as keywords, students should be able to find a considerable amount of information about HESSI, SMEI, and other programs for predicting these storms. Because of the solar flare activity in or about 2000, students may find very recent information about the storms and their effects. Students can build models of the detectors or of the sun and solar flares and the process of detecting the particles.

Magnets in Medicine

Think about what it would be like to peer inside the human body to locate a tumor, find tiny blockages in blood vessels, or even identify damage to the brain. Medical technology known as magnetic resonance imaging (MRI) gives doctors a quick and painless way to see and diagnose these problems and more.

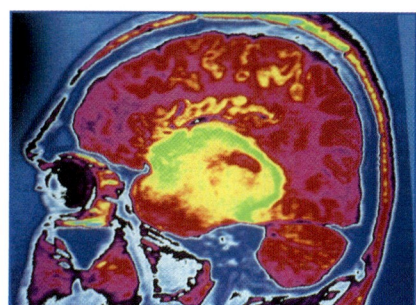

▲ *This color-enhanced MRI image of a brain shows a tumor (tinted yellow). The tumor was removed, and the patient resumed a healthy life.*

Magnetic Images

Like X rays, MRI creates pictures of a person's internal organs and skeleton. But MRI produces clearer pictures than X rays do, and MRI does not expose the body to the potentially harmful radiation of X rays. Instead, MRI uses powerful electromagnets and radio waves to create images.

The patient is placed in a large machine. An electric current in the electromagnet creates a powerful magnetic field around the patient. Because the human body is composed mostly of fat and water, there are many hydrogen atoms in the body. The magnetic field causes the nuclei of the hydrogen atoms to align in the direction of the magnetic field. Then another, weaker magnetic signal is sent out to the cells. The energy in this signal causes some hydrogen nuclei to change their position. As the signal's energy is absorbed and then released by the hydrogen nuclei, the MRI machine collects the signals and its computer converts the information into an image.

A Diagnostic Device

MRI is particularly useful for locating small tumors, revealing subtle changes in the brain, pinpointing blockages in blood vessels, and showing damage to the spinal cord. This technology also allows doctors to observe the function of specific body parts, such as the ears, heart, muscles, tendons, and blood vessels.

Researchers are experimenting with more-powerful magnets that work on other types of atoms. This technology is known as magnetic resonance spectroscopy (MRS). One current use of MRS is to monitor the effectiveness of chemotherapy in cancer patients. Doctors analyze MRS images to find chemical changes that might indicate whether the therapy is successful.

Picture This

▶ You may be familiar with X rays, but procedures like CAT or CT scans and MRI may be new to you. Research the different imaging tools—including X-ray tomography, CT or CAT scans, and MRI—that doctors can use to diagnose and treat injuries and disease. Select one of the imaging processes and make a model of how it works to demonstrate to the class. Be sure to include the procedure's advantages and disadvantages and the types of injuries or diseases for which it is used.

Answers to Picture This

Students will be able to find a great deal of information about the various medical imaging processes and devices. Students can make models of one or more of the machines or they could make posters or models of the imaging process itself.

HEALTH WATCH
Magnets in Medicine

Background

MRI has been a diagnostic tool since the early 1980s. An MRI scan is usually done as an outpatient procedure. During the scan, the patient must lie very still inside a large, hollow tube for approximately half an hour. (Newer MRI machines are open on the sides, so patients do not feel so closed in.) The patient is exposed to an extremely powerful (but harmless) magnetic field.

One of the advantages of MRI is that it can provide clear images of parts of the body that are surrounded by dense bone tissue. As a result, MRI is particularly valuable for studying the brain and spinal cord. MRI is also useful for examining joints, soft tissues, the heart, blood vessels, eyes, and ears.

Both MRI and X-ray imaging form pictures by sending electromagnetic radiation into a patient's body. MRI is safer than X-ray imaging because it uses radio waves, which do not cause any known damage to human tissue. An overdose of X rays, on the other hand, can cause cancer or can damage or even destroy body tissue.

One advantage of X-ray imaging is that it is less expensive than MRI. X rays are used to treat some types of cancer and are also used to sterilize medical equipment.

Chapter Organizer

CHAPTER ORGANIZATION	TIME MINUTES	OBJECTIVES	LABS, INVESTIGATIONS, AND DEMONSTRATIONS
Chapter Opener pp. 480–481	45	National Standards: UCP 2, SAI 1, ST 2	**Investigate!** Talking Long Distance, p. 481
Section 1 Electronic Components	90	▶ Describe semiconductors and how their conductivity can be modified. ▶ Identify diodes, transistors, and integrated circuits as electronic components. ▶ Explain how integrated circuits have influenced electronic technology. ▶ Compare vacuum tubes and transistors. ST 2, SPSP 5, PS 3a	
Section 2 Communication Technology	90	▶ Describe how signals transmit information. ▶ Explain how a telephone works. ▶ Compare analog and digital signals. ▶ Describe how radios and televisions transmit information. ST 2, SPSP 1, 5; LabBook UCP 2	**Demonstration,** p. 490 in ATE **Making Models,** Tune In! p. 702 **Datasheets for LabBook,** Tune In! Datasheet 53
Section 3 Computers	90	▶ List the basic functions of a computer. ▶ Identify the main components of computer hardware. ▶ Describe what computer software allows a computer to do. ▶ Describe how the Internet works. ST 2, SPSP 5	**Demonstration,** p. 494 in ATE **Long-Term Projects & Research Ideas,** Project 69

*See page **T20** for a complete correlation of this book with the*

NATIONAL SCIENCE EDUCATION STANDARDS.

TECHNOLOGY RESOURCES

 Guided Reading Audio CD English or Spanish, Chapter 19

 One-Stop Planner CD-ROM with Test Generator

 CNN Science, Technology & Society, Brain Cell Visuals, Segment 23

Multicultural Connections, The Internet in Asia, Segment 11

Chapter 19 • Electronic Technology

Chapter 19 • Electronic Technology

CLASSROOM WORKSHEETS, TRANSPARENCIES, AND RESOURCES	SCIENCE INTEGRATION AND CONNECTIONS	REVIEW AND ASSESSMENT
Directed Reading Worksheet 19 **Science Puzzlers, Twisters & Teasers,** Worksheet 19		
Directed Reading Worksheet 19, Section 1 **Transparency 276,** Types of Doped Semiconductors **Transparency 277,** A Transistor as an Amplifier **Transparency 277,** A Transistor as a Switch **Reinforcement Worksheet 19,** Semiconductors' Conductivity	**Connect to Life Science,** p. 483 in ATE **Connect to Earth Science,** p. 485 in ATE **Cross-Disciplinary Focus,** p. 485 in ATE **Connect to Life Science,** p. 486 in ATE **Holt Anthology of Science Fiction,** *There Will Come Soft Rains*	**Homework,** p. 485 in ATE **Review,** p. 487 **Quiz,** p. 487 in ATE **Alternative Assessment,** p. 487 in ATE
Directed Reading Worksheet 19, Section 2 **Transparency 132,** Finding an Earthquake's Epicenter **Transparency 278,** How Radio Works **Transparency 279,** Images on a Color Television **Critical Thinking Worksheet 19,** Building a Better Mousetrap	**Cross-Disciplinary Focus,** p. 488 in ATE **Geology Connection,** p. 489 **Real-World Connection,** p. 489 in ATE **Connect to Earth Science,** p. 489 in ATE **Math and More,** p. 490 **Health Watch:** Listening Lower, p. 504	**Homework,** p. 492 in ATE **Review,** p. 493 **Quiz,** p. 493 in ATE **Alternative Assessment,** p. 493 in ATE
Directed Reading Worksheet 19, Section 3 **Reinforcement Worksheet 19,** The Ins and Outs of Computing	**MathBreak,** Computer Memory, p. 497 **Real-World Connection,** p. 497 in ATE **Math and More,** p. 497 in ATE **Cross-Disciplinary Focus,** p. 498 in ATE	**Homework,** p. 494 in ATE **Review,** p. 499 **Quiz,** p. 499 in ATE **Alternative Assessment,** p. 499 in ATE

END-OF-CHAPTER REVIEW AND ASSESSMENT

Chapter Review in Study Guide
Vocabulary and Notes in Study Guide
Chapter Tests with Performance-Based Assessment, Chapter 19 Test
Chapter Tests with Performance-Based Assessment, Performance-Based Assessment 19
Concept Mapping Transparency 19

 Holt, Rinehart and Winston On-line Resources
go.hrw.com
For worksheets and other teaching aids related to this chapter, visit the HRW Web site and type in the keyword: **HSTELT**

 **National Science Teachers Association**
www.scilinks.org
Encourage students to use the *sci*LINKS numbers listed in the internet connect boxes to access information and resources on the **NSTA** Web site.

Chapter 19 • Chapter Organizer **479B**

Chapter Resources & Worksheets

Visual Resources

TEACHING TRANSPARENCIES

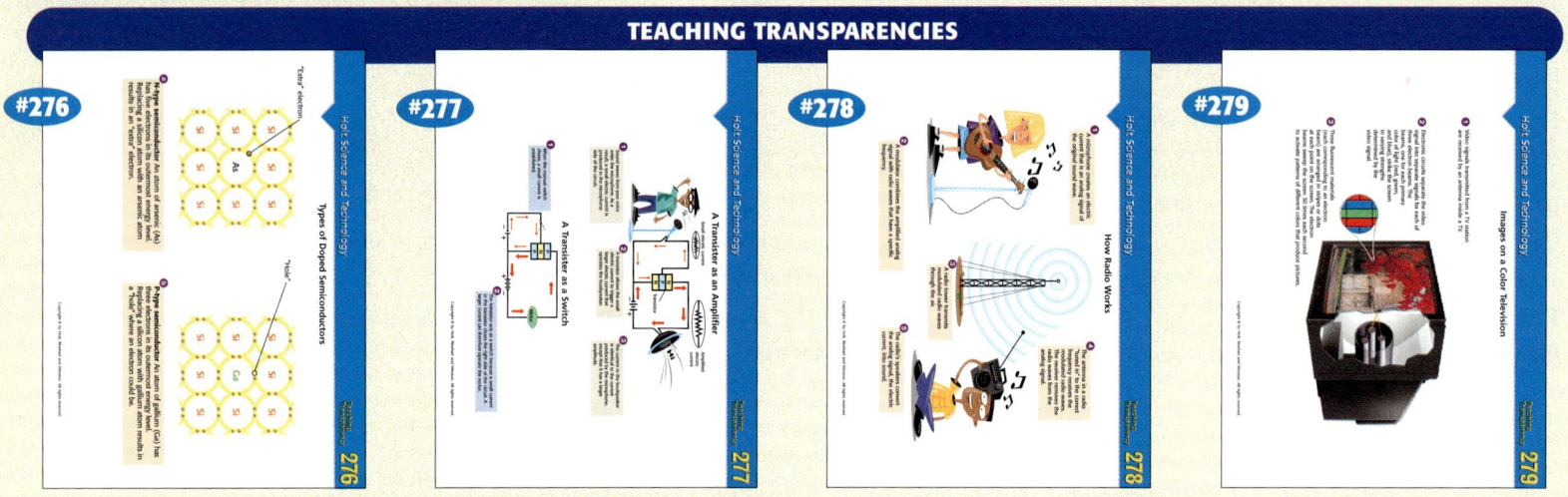

TEACHING TRANSPARENCIES

CONCEPT MAPPING TRANSPARENCY

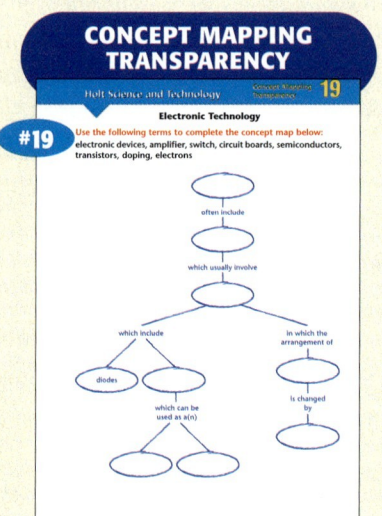

Meeting Individual Needs

DIRECTED READING

REINFORCEMENT & VOCABULARY REVIEW

SCIENCE PUZZLERS, TWISTERS & TEASERS

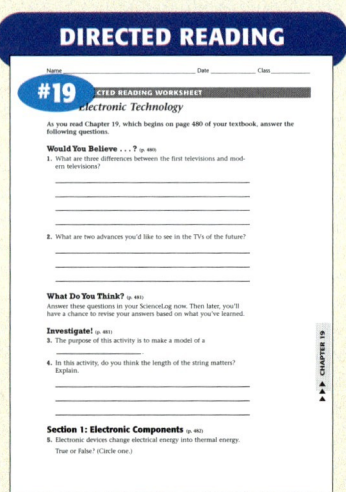

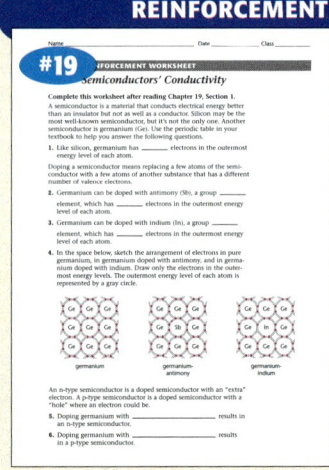

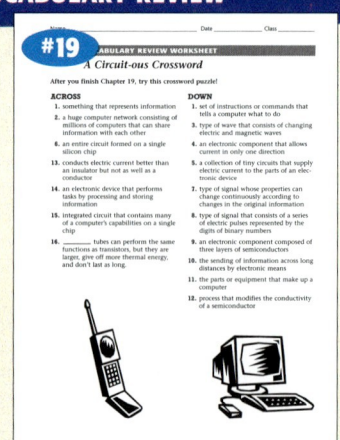

Chapter 19 • Electronic Technology

Chapter 19 • Electronic Technology

Review & Assessment

STUDY GUIDE

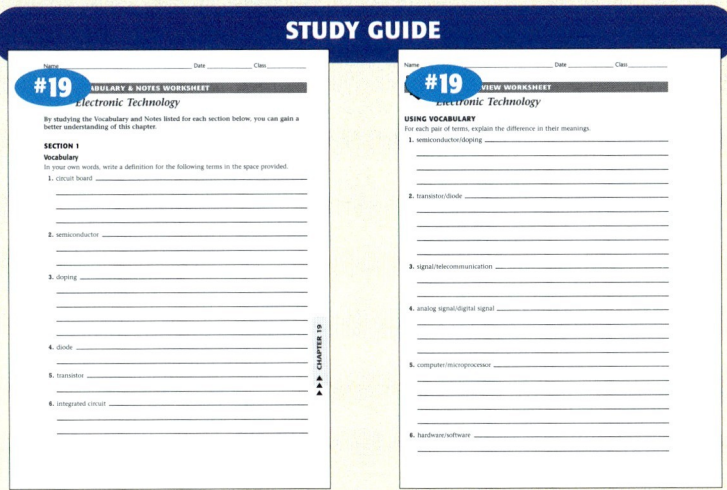

CHAPTER TESTS WITH PERFORMANCE-BASED ASSESSMENT

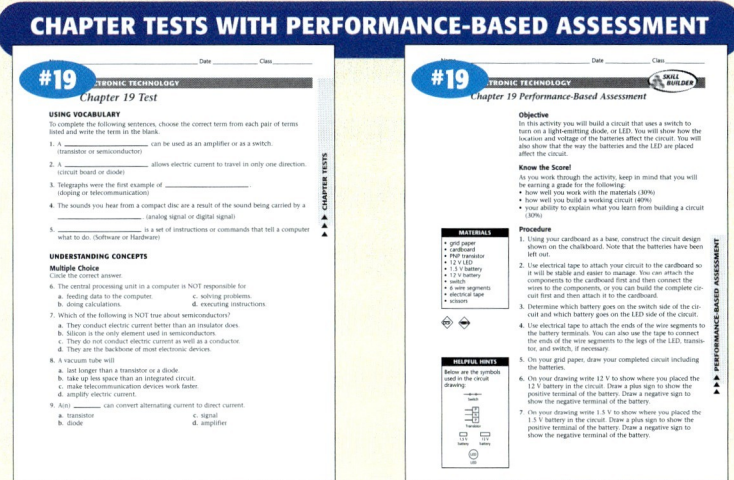

Lab Worksheets

LONG-TERM PROJECTS & RESEARCH IDEAS

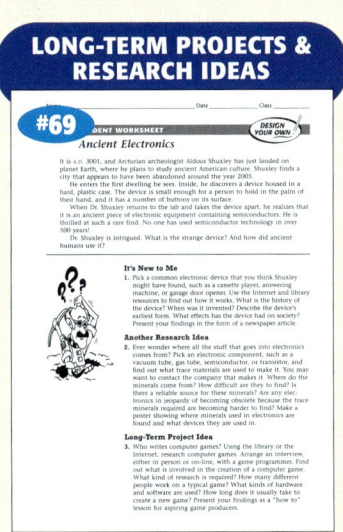

DATASHEETS FOR LABBOOK

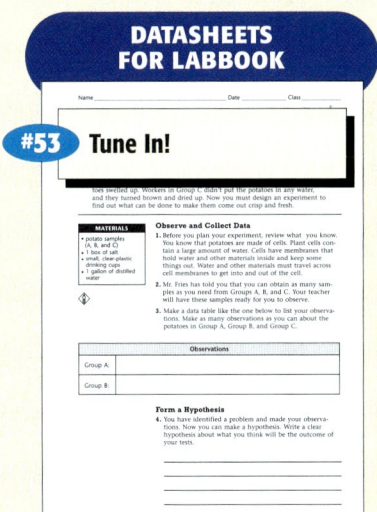

Applications & Extensions

CRITICAL THINKING & PROBLEM SOLVING

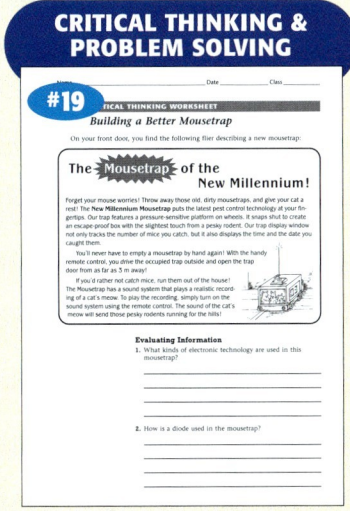

MULTICULTURAL CONNECTIONS

SCIENCE, TECHNOLOGY & SOCIETY

Chapter 19 • Chapter Resources & Worksheets

Chapter Background

SECTION 1

Electronic Components

▶ **Before Transistors, Vacuum Tubes**
Modern electronics began with the development of the vacuum tube. Thomas Edison apparently invented an early vacuum tube but decided not to develop the invention any further. Sir John Ambrose Fleming, an English engineer, is credited with formally inventing the vacuum-tube diode in 1904.

- It wasn't long before vacuum tubes had a wide variety of applications. For example, although telegraph and telephone circuits could transmit and receive radio signals, the vacuum tube made it possible to manipulate them.

▶ **Transistors and Diodes**
Three American physicists—Walter Houser Brattain, John Bardeen, and William Bradford Shockley—working together, invented the transistor. For their combined efforts, they received the 1956 Nobel Prize in physics.

- Transistors are electronic components used as amplifiers or switches in electric circuits. They are used extensively in control, communications, and computer systems.

- The semiconductor diode is an electronic component that rectifies electric current. Some special diodes are light-emitting diodes (LEDs), which give off light, and photodiodes, which are sensitive to light.

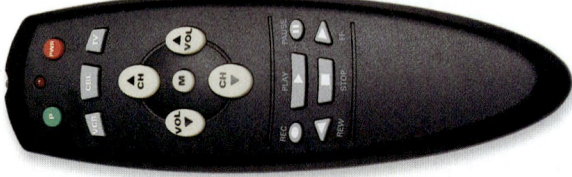

IS THAT A FACT!

◆ Both transistors and vacuum tubes can amplify signals up to about 1,000 MHz. But transistors have significant advantages over vacuum tubes: Transistors use less electrical energy, cost less, produce less thermal energy, weigh less, and are more reliable. Today, the transistor has all but replaced the vacuum tube.

▶ **A Replacement for Transistors?**
In the late 1960s, a new application of transistor technology emerged. The integrated circuit, a piece of silicon measuring about 2–4 mm^2, was able to perform the function of 15 to 20 transistors.

- Photolithography (the process of transferring a pattern to a surface) makes it possible to put thousands, or even millions, of transistors on one microchip.

SECTION 2

Communication Technology

▶ **Telecommunication**
The basic elements of any telecommunication device are the transmitter, the signal, the medium, and the receiver. These parts are connected by the source and destination of a given message.

- Modern telecommunication devices are able to incorporate signals for voice, sound, text, graphics, images, calculations, and moving-image messages in a single carrier.

Chapter 19 • Electronic Technology

IS THAT A FACT!

- With the invention of the electric telegraph in 1837, messages could be sent at the speed of light. The speed of the fastest nontelegraph system was around 40 km/h.

Analog Vs. Digital
Until the 1980s, sound wave signals were transmitted only in analog form. The telephone, radio, and television are examples of analog devices.

- The primary advantage of a digital device is the elimination of unwanted information, or noise, in the transmission. Examples of digital devices include compact discs, videodiscs, and digital computers.

- Modern telephone systems are now able to perform digitally using fiber-optic technology.

Television Transmission
Television images can be transmitted in several ways. Three familiar examples are the typical over-the-air transmission of electromagnetic waves, cable transmission that uses either metallic or fiber-optic cores, and satellite transmission of electromagnetic waves.

IS THAT A FACT!

- More than 93 million households in the United States receive electromagnetic television signals.

SECTION 3

Computers

History of Computer Technology
The origins of electronic computers can be traced back to mechanical calculating devices. More than 2,000 years ago, ancient civilizations in Rome and Greece used the abacus for calculations.

- The first "digital calculating machine" was built in 1642 by Blaise Pascal to help his father, who was a tax official.

- In the 1830s, Charles Babbage designed a mechanical computer device with the ability to store results and perform multiple tasks. The machine was never completed because the engineering of the time was not advanced enough.

- To help tabulate the U.S. Census of 1890, Herman Hollerith invented a machine that electronically processed information coded onto punched cards. The machine could add and multiply, sort, and feed out cards with results punched on them.

- The first large-scale electronic digital computer, ENIAC (Electronic Numerical Integrator and Computer), was built at the Moore School of Electrical Engineering at the University of Pennsylvania between 1943 and 1946. ENIAC is considered the first modern computer.

IS THAT A FACT!

- In 1986, the first complete encyclopedia, The Academic American Encyclopedia, was recorded on CD-ROM (compact disc read-only memory). Early CD-ROMs could store 500 megabytes (MB) of data.

- In the late 1990s, DVD-ROM discs were developed with storage capacities of 4,482 MB (or 4.7 gigabytes; 1,024 MB is equal to 1 gigabyte). The technology continues to improve.

For background information about teaching strategies and issues, refer to the *Professional Reference for Teachers*.

Chapter 19 • Chapter Background

CHAPTER 19
Electronic Technology

Chapter Preview

Section 1
Electronic Components
- Inside an Electronic Device
- Semiconductors
- Diodes
- Transistors

Section 2
Communication Technology
- Communicating with Signals
- Analog Signals
- Digital Signals
- Radio and Television

Section 3
Computers
- What Is a Computer?
- Historic Developments
- Computer Hardware
- Computer Software
- The Internet—A Global Network

 Directed Reading Worksheet 19

 Science Puzzlers, Twisters & Teasers Worksheet 19

 Guided Reading Audio CD
English or Spanish, Chapter 19

 internetconnect
Smithsonian Institution®
Visit www.si.edu/hrw for additional on-line resources.

CHAPTER 19 Electronic Technology

Would You Believe . . . ?

Now you can buy big screen TVs that are cable-ready and have remote controls. Some TVs are small enough to hold in your hand. You can even get a TV with a built-in videotape player or with theater-quality sound. But even these improvements may seem outdated in 20 years because of advances in electronic technology.

In this chapter you will learn about the world of electronic technology. You'll learn about electronic devices like televisions, CD players, and computers. You'll also find out about some major breakthroughs that helped make electronic devices smaller, faster, and more powerful. So stay tuned!

The first television sets hit the market in the late 1930s. They were big, bulky, and expensive. Many models cost about $500 in 1939, which is roughly the same as $5,000–$6,000 in recent times. Although the actual TV sets, like the one above, were big, the screens were small. Some were only 25–35 cm (10–14 in.) across. Their pictures were fuzzy and were in black and white. And even if your family could afford one of these early TVs, you could choose from only a few television shows.

Today's TVs consist of a variety of electronic components, including transistors, integrated circuits, and printed circuit boards. They have much bigger screens and a much sharper picture—in full color. In addition, many TVs today cost less than half what a TV cost in the 1940s, and that's not accounting for inflation.

Would you Believe . . .

One of the largest television sets is the 25 × 45 m Sony JumboTron™ color TV exhibited at the 1985 Tsukuba International Exposition near Tokyo. In the late 1990s, a new 18.3 × 47.5 m JumboTron™ was installed in AllTel Stadium in Jacksonville, Florida.

What Do You Think?

In your ScienceLog, try to answer the following questions based on what you already know:

1. What is an electronic device?
2. What are some electronic devices used for communication?
3. What are the parts of a computer?

Talking Long Distance

Using a telephone allows you to communicate with someone from a distance. In this activity you'll construct a model of a telephone.

Procedure

1. Collect two **empty coffee cans** and a piece of **string** from your teacher. Each can will have a small hole in the bottom of it.
2. Thread one end of the string through the hole.
3. Tie a knot in the end of the string inside the can. The knot should be large enough to keep the string in place. The rest of the string should be coming out of the bottom of the can.
4. Repeat with the other can and the other end of the string.
5. Hold one can and have a classmate hold the other. Walk away from each other until the string is pulled fairly taut.
6. Speak into your can while your classmate holds the other can at his or her ear. Switch roles.

Analysis

7. In your ScienceLog, describe what you heard.
8. How is your apparatus similar to a real telephone? How is it different?
9. How are signals sent back and forth along the string?
10. Why do you think it was important to pull the string taut?

What Do You Think?

Accept all reasonable responses. Students will have a chance to revise their answers in the Chapter Review under NOW What Do You Think?

Investigate!

MATERIALS

FOR EACH PAIR:
- 2 empty coffee cans
- string

Teacher Notes: Prior to beginning this activity, you will have to punch a small hole in the bottom of each coffee can for the string. A nail and a hammer may be used to punch the hole.

Answers to Investigate!

8. Answers may vary. Sample answer: similarities include the transmission of signals, and that the signals represent sound waves; differences include that the model is nonelectronic and that it does not work at very long distances.
9. Signals are sent as vibrations of the string.
10. The vibrations travel better through taut string.

IS THAT A FACT!

The Scottish-born inventor Alexander Graham Bell (1847–1922) was a professor of voice physiology at Boston University and spent much of his life trying to find ways to help the deaf. Bell believed that "when one door closes, another door opens." Such an "open door" appeared June 2, 1874, as Thomas Watson, Bell's assistant, adjusted a reed on an experimental telegraph. This adjustment produced an unexpected transmission of sound. Bell realized that voices could be transmitted over long distances in a similar way.

Chapter 19 • Electronic Technology   **481**

SECTION 1

Focus

Electronic Components

In this section, students will learn about semiconductors and how their conductivity can be modified. They will learn about electronic components made from semiconductors, such as diodes, transistors, and integrated circuits—and how these components have affected electronic technology. Finally, they will compare vacuum tubes and transistors.

🔔 Bellringer

Write the word *technology* on the board for students to see. Ask students to try to define the word. (the application of knowledge, tools, and materials to accomplish tasks and solve problems; also refers to the objects used to accomplish tasks)

Have students describe in their ScienceLog ways that technology affects them. (Answers will vary. Accept all reasonable answers.)

1) Motivate

DISCUSSION

Circuit Boards Try to obtain circuit boards for two different electronic devices, such as a remote control and a small radio or a computer and a television set. Allow students to study the circuit boards, then ask them to list as many differences and similarities as possible.

Section 1

Terms to Learn
circuit board   diode
semiconductor   transistor
doping   integrated circuit

What You'll Do

- Describe semiconductors and how their conductivity can be modified.
- Identify diodes, transistors, and integrated circuits as electronic components.
- Explain how integrated circuits have influenced electronic technology.
- Compare vacuum tubes and transistors.

Electronic Components

Electronic devices rely on electrical energy, but not in the same way that appliances and machines do. Some machines can convert electrical energy into light, thermal, and mechanical energy in order to do work. Electronic devices use electrical energy to transmit information.

Inside an Electronic Device

A TV remote control is an example of an electronic device. It transmits information to a TV about volume levels and what channel to display. Have you ever looked inside of a TV remote control? If so, you would have seen something similar to **Figure 1.** A remote control contains a **circuit board**, a collection of hundreds of tiny circuits that supply electric current to the various parts of an electronic device.

To change channels or adjust the volume on the TV, you push buttons on the remote control. When you push a button, a tiny bulb called a light-emitting diode (DIE ohd), or LED, sends information to the TV in the form of infrared light. The components of the circuit board you see in Figure 1 control the electric current within the remote control in order to send the correct information to the TV. In this section you'll learn about some components of electronic devices and how they control electric current.

Figure 1 Each part of a remote control has a role in transmitting information.

MISCONCEPTION ALERT

Students may think that the red LED on a TV remote control is what sends signals to the television. The remote control shown in **Figure 1** has 2 LEDs—one clear, the other red. When a button on the remote control is pushed, the clear LED sends signals to the television. At the same time, the red LED flashes to indicate that the remote control is working.

482 Chapter 19 • Electronic Technology

Semiconductors

Many electronic components are made from semiconductors (SEM i kuhn DUHK tuhrz). A **semiconductor** is a substance that conducts an electric current better than an insulator but not as well as a conductor. The use of semiconductors has resulted in some incredible advances in electronic technology.

How Do Semiconductors Work? The way a semiconductor conducts electric current is based on how its electrons are arranged. Silicon (Si) is a widely used semiconductor in electronic technology. When silicon atoms bond, they share their valence electrons, as shown in **Figure 2**. Because all the valence electrons are shared, there are no electrons free to create much electric current in the semiconductor. So why are semiconductors like silicon used in electronic devices? Because their conductivity can be modified.

Figure 2 *Each silicon atom shares its four valence electrons with other silicon atoms.*

Doping In order to modify the conductivity of a semiconductor, its arrangement of electrons must be altered. This is done through **doping** (DOHP eeng), the process of replacing a few atoms of a semiconductor with a few atoms of another substance that have a different number of valence electrons. Two types of doped semiconductors are shown in **Figure 3**.

Figure 3 Types of Doped Semiconductors

N-type semiconductor An atom of arsenic (As) has five electrons in its outermost energy level. Replacing a silicon atom with an arsenic atom results in an "extra" electron.

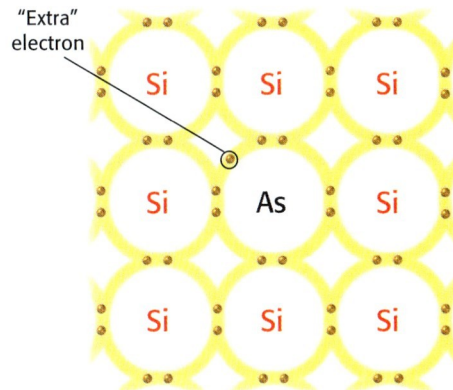

P-type semiconductor An atom of gallium (Ga) has three electrons in its outermost energy level. Replacing a silicon atom with a gallium atom results in a "hole" where an electron could be.

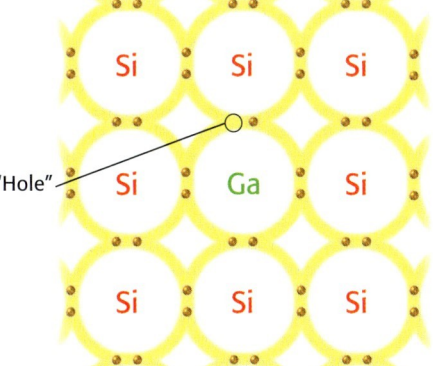

IS THAT A FACT!

An n-type semiconductor is also known as a negative-type semiconductor, because its charge carriers are electrons. Likewise, a p-type semiconductor is also known as a positive-type semiconductor because "holes" can be thought of as positive charge carriers. However, both n-type semiconductors and p-type semiconductors are neutral materials because they are made of atoms, which have no net charge.

2) Teach

ACTIVITY

MATERIALS

FOR EACH GROUP:
- 9 small plastic-foam balls
- toothpicks
- about 60 small, single-colored, round beads
- colored stickers

Using **Figures 2** and **3** as references, have students create a model of an n-type and a p-type semiconductor. Students should use the small plastic-foam balls to represent atoms of arsenic, gallium, or silicon. The colored stickers can be used to designate one atom from another. The toothpicks and beads can be used to model the valence electrons surrounding each atom to create "holes" or "extra" electrons. Make sure each model is properly labeled with "n-type" or "p-type." Models can be shared, then displayed in the classroom. **Sheltered English**

CONNECT TO LIFE SCIENCE

Electronic technology has produced the Scanning Tunneling Microscope (STM), an instrument that records the electronic structure of conductive surfaces with a conducting probe. A computer uses the information from the probe to produce a three-dimensional image of the electronic structure of the surface.

Teaching Transparency 276 "Types of Doped Semiconductors"

Directed Reading Worksheet 19 Section 1

Section 1 • Electronic Components **483**

2) Teach, continued

USING THE FIGURE

Use **Figures 5, 7,** and **8** to help students understand how electrons move in diodes and transistors. Have students copy these figures in their ScienceLog while you draw them on an overhead projector. Discuss each part of the figure as you draw it. Be sure students understand that the red arrows in Figures 5, 7, and 8 show the flow of electrons. The red arrows do NOT show the electric current. Conventional current and the flow of electrons are in the opposite directions.

MEETING INDIVIDUAL NEEDS

Learners Having Difficulty
To strengthen students' understanding of the difference between n-type and p-type semiconductors, reproduce **Figure 5** as a small poster. Use removable pieces to represent the electrons and the "plus" and "minus" terminal indicators.

RETEACHING

If students are having trouble understanding the difference between AC and DC, refer them to Chapter 17.

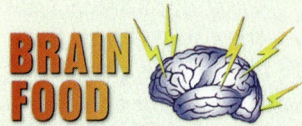

In electronic devices where size and weight are considerations, transistors have become irreplaceable. For example, transistors have improved the quality and feasibility of hearing aids (imagine wearing a hearing aid made with vacuum tubes).

Diodes

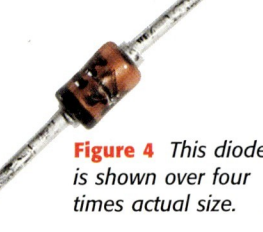

Figure 4 *This diode is shown over four times actual size.*

Layers of semiconductors can be put together like sandwiches to make electronic components. For example, joining one layer of an n-type semiconductor and one layer of a p-type semiconductor creates a semiconductor diode, like the one shown in **Figure 4**. A **diode** is an electronic component that allows electric current in only one direction.

Diodes in Circuits The way in which a diode works has to do with its semiconductor layers. Where the p-type and n-type layers meet, some "extra" electrons move from the n-type layer to fill some "holes" in the p-type layer. This gives the p-type layer a negative charge and the n-type layer a positive charge. If a diode is connected to a source of electrical energy so that the positive terminal is closest to the p-type layer, a current is established. However, if the terminals are reversed so that the negative terminal is closest to the p-type layer, there will be no current. **Figure 5** illustrates how a diode works.

Figure 5 How a Diode Works

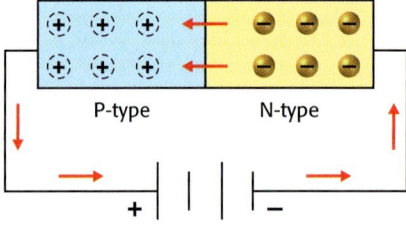

a Electrons move from the negatively charged p-type layer toward the positive terminal. As a result, electrons from the n-type layer can move to fill the newly created "holes" in the p-type layer, and a current is established.

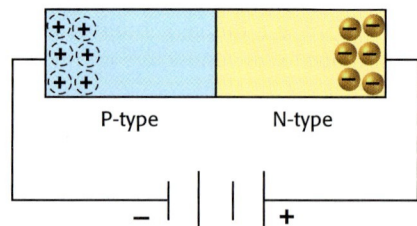

b Electrons in the negatively charged p-type layer are repelled by the negative terminal. No new "holes" are created, so no electrons can move from the n-type layer to the p-type layer. As a result, there is no current.

Using Diodes to Change AC to DC

Power plants supply electrical energy to homes by means of AC (alternating current). Many electronic systems, however, such as radios, require DC (direct current). Because diodes allow current in only one direction, they can convert AC to pulses of DC. An AC adapter contains a diode.

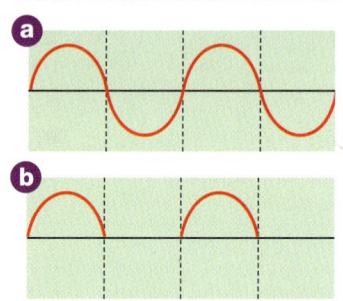

a Alternating current, which periodically changes direction, is supplied to the diode.

b The diode blocks the current in one direction, resulting in pulsed direct current.

MISCONCEPTION ALERT

Some students may think that n-type semiconductors always have a positive charge and p-type semiconductors always have a negative charge. However, both n- and p-type semiconductors are uncharged materials because they are made of atoms, which have no charge. N- and p-type semiconductors become charged after they are joined and some electrons move from the n-type semiconductor to the p-type semiconductor.

Transistors

What do you get when you sandwich three layers of semiconductors together? A transistor! A **transistor** is an electronic component that can be used as an amplifier or as a switch. Transistors, such as the one shown in **Figure 6,** can be NPN or PNP transistors. An NPN transistor consists of one layer of a p-type semiconductor between two layers of an n-type semiconductor. A PNP transistor consists of one layer of an n-type semiconductor between two layers of a p-type semiconductor. When connected in a circuit, the transistor's "legs" conduct electric current into and out of the transistor's layers.

Figure 6 *This transistor is smaller than a pencil eraser!*

Transistors as Amplifiers To see how a transistor is used as an amplifier, look at the circuit shown in **Figure 7.** A microphone does not supply a large enough current to operate a loudspeaker. But if a transistor is used, the small electric current in the microphone side of the circuit can trigger a larger electric current in the loudspeaker side of the circuit. The electric current can be larger because of the large source of electrical energy in the loudspeaker side of the circuit.

Figure 7 A Transistor as an Amplifier

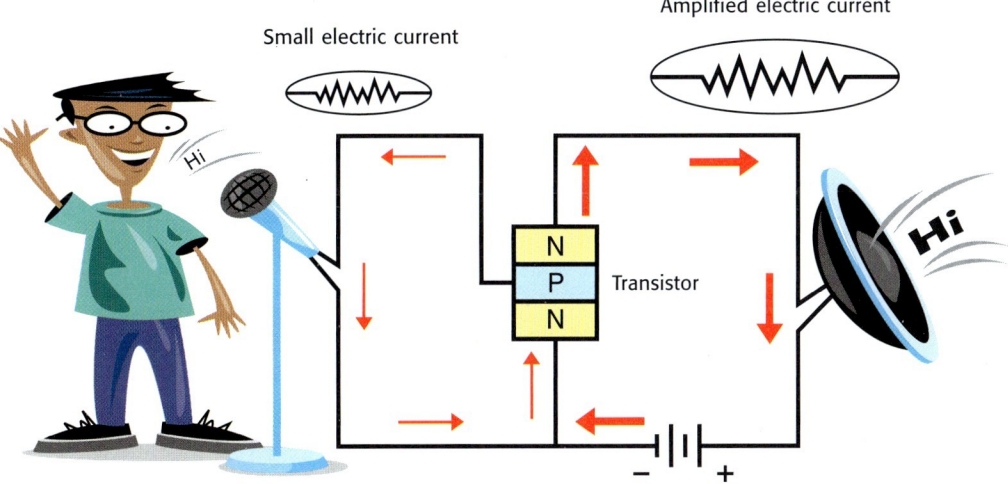

① Sound waves from your voice enter the microphone. As a result, a small electric current is produced in the microphone side of the circuit.

② A transistor allows the small electric current to trigger a larger electric current that operates the loudspeaker.

③ The current in the loudspeaker is identical to the current produced by the microphone, except that it has a larger amplitude.

WEIRD SCIENCE

Although silicon chips use small amounts of electrical energy, some energy is wasted as thermal energy. Researchers are trying to develop an optical chip that uses light energy instead of electrical energy. The optical chip would produce very little thermal energy.

 **Teaching Transparency 277** "A Transistor as an Amplifier"

3) Extend

CONNECT TO LIFE SCIENCE

Many people owe their lives to transistors. Astronauts in space have their heart, respiratory, and other physiological data monitored by devices that use transistors, and all their life support, navigation, and control systems use transistors. People with some diseases, such as diabetes, cancer, or AIDS, now wear transistor-controlled portable pumps that pump medicine into their veins.

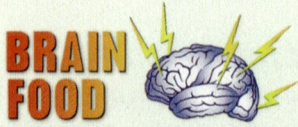

The first integrated circuits and microprocessors, created in the early 1970s, contained just a few transistors wired together. In the summer of 1999, a computer chip for use in personal computers was introduced that contained more than 22 million transistors. And the predictions are that in the near future, computer chips will contain 2 to 3 times that number of transistors.

USING THE FIGURE

In the Electronic Technology feature on the next page, the transistor and vacuum tube are shown at almost actual size. Pointing this out to students will help them understand that devices made with vacuum tubes would have to be much larger than similar devices made with transistors.

Teaching Transparency 277
"A Transistor as a Switch"

Transistors as Switches A transistor can also be used as an electronic on-off switch in a circuit. When the manual switch in **Figure 8** is closed, a small current is established in the left side of the circuit. The small current causes the transistor to close the right side of the circuit. As a result, a larger current, which operates a small motor, is established in the right side of the circuit. Basically, you switch on a small current, and the transistor switches on a larger current. If the manual switch is opened, there will no longer be a current in the left side of the circuit. As a result, the transistor will switch off the current that operates the motor. Circuits similar to the one in Figure 8 can be found in remote-controlled toy cars and in windshield wipers.

Figure 8 A Transistor as a Switch

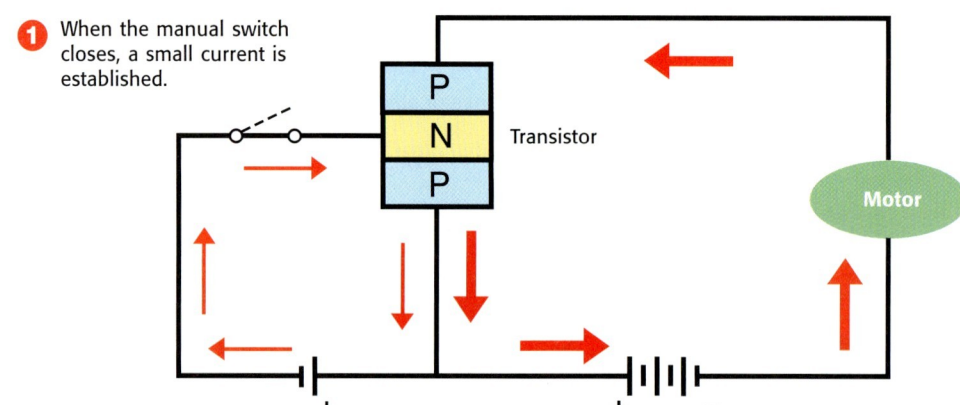

① When the manual switch closes, a small current is established.

② The transistor acts as a switch because a small current in the transistor closes the right side of the circuit. A larger current can therefore operate the motor.

Integrated Circuits Look at the electronic device shown in **Figure 9.** This is an **integrated** (IN tuh GRAYT ed) **circuit,** an entire circuit containing many transistors and other electronic components formed on a single silicon chip. The components of the circuit are constructed on the silicon layer by doping the silicon at specific places.

Integrated circuits and circuit boards, such as the one in the TV remote control at the beginning of this section, have helped shrink electronic systems. Because several complete circuits can fit into one integrated circuit, complicated electronic systems can be made very small. In addition, integrated circuit devices can operate at high speeds because the electric charges traveling through them do not have to travel very far.

Figure 9 This integrated circuit contains thousands of electronic components, yet its dimensions are only about 1×3 cm!

In 1999, a group of electrical engineering students at the University of Pennsylvania re-created the circuitry of the original ENIAC computer (as much as possible) on a single computer chip! Some changes were necessary: transistors replaced vacuum tubes and electrical switches replaced mechanical ones. ENIAC filled a 10×15.25 m room; the ENIAC-on-a-chip occupies a space of 7.44×5.29 mm.

Electronic Technology of Yesterday . . .

Before the invention of transistors and semiconductor diodes, electronic devices used vacuum tubes, like the one shown here. Vacuum tubes can amplify electric current and convert AC to DC. However, vacuum tubes are much larger, give off more thermal energy, and don't last as long as transistors and semiconductor diodes. Early radios were very bulky because they were made with vacuum tubes. Another reason the radios had to be so big was so that the vacuum tubes had space to give off thermal energy.

. . . and Today

Modern radios are built with transistors and semiconductor diodes. Frequently, a radio comes with other features, such as a clock or a tape deck, all packaged in less space than a radio made with vacuum tubes. Modern electronic components have enabled electronic devices to become much smaller and perform more functions.

REVIEW

1. Describe how p-type and n-type semiconductors are made.
2. Explain how a diode changes AC to DC.
3. What two purposes do transistors serve?
4. **Comparing Concepts** How might an electronic system that uses vacuum tubes be different from one that uses integrated circuits?

internetconnect

TOPIC: Transistors
GO TO: www.scilinks.org
sciLINKS NUMBER: HSTP455

4) Close

Quiz

Ask students to answer the following questions:

1. What is the purpose of doping a semiconductor? (to alter the conductivity of a semiconductor so electric charges will flow)
2. How does a transistor act as an amplifier? (The small electric current in the transistor circuit can trigger a larger electric current in another circuit in the device.)
3. Describe an imaginary electronic device using the vocabulary words learned in this section. (Answers will vary, but must reflect an understanding of the vocabulary words.)

ALTERNATIVE ASSESSMENT

Give students the following list of activities that involve the use of transistors:

- announcing the play-by-play at an athletic event
- conducting experiments in space
- working on a computer
- listening to music on the bus or as you walk around

Ask students to choose any two of these activities and discuss how they would be different if transistors did not exist.

Answers to Review

1. N- and p-type semiconductors are both made by doping. An n-type semiconductor is made by replacing a semiconductor atom with an atom that has more than four electrons in its outermost energy level. A p-type semiconductor is made by replacing a semiconductor atom with an atom that has less than four electrons in its outermost energy level.

2. A diode allows current in only one direction. The direction of alternating current (AC) reverses, but the diode blocks the current in one direction. The result is pulses of direct current (DC).

3. Transistors can be used to amplify an electric current or as a switch in a circuit.

4. An electronic system that uses a vacuum tube would be much larger than one that uses integrated circuits.

Reinforcement Worksheet 19 "Semiconductors' Conductivity"

internetconnect

TOPIC: Transistors
GO TO: www.scilinks.org
sciLINKS NUMBER: HSTP455

Section 1 • Electronic Components

SECTION 2

Focus

Communication Technology

This section explains how signals transmit information. Students learn about the difference between analog and digital signals. Finally, students learn how some electronic devices transmit information.

**Bellringer**

Give each student a copy of the International Morse Code (that you have prepared ahead of time). On the board, write three or four questions (such as, "What is your first name?") in Morse code and have the students decipher the questions, and then answer them in Morse code. **Sheltered English**

1 Motivate

DISCUSSION

Have students think of several different methods of sending messages. Examples might include: telegram, letter, E-mail, telephone, and beeper. Then ask students to compare the equipment needed and the cost, speed, and reliability of each method. How has technology changed the transmission of information?

CROSS-DISCIPLINARY FOCUS

History The telegraph was invented concurrently in two countries by three different inventors. In 1837, Samuel Morse invented the device in the United States. In Great Britain, Sir Charles Wheatstone and Sir William F. Cooke were credited with the same accomplishment.

488 Chapter 19 • Electronic Technology

Section 2

Terms to Learn
telecommunication
signal
analog signal
digital signal

What You'll Do
- Describe how signals transmit information.
- Explain how a telephone works.
- Compare analog and digital signals.
- Describe how radios and televisions transmit information.

Communication Technology

One of the first electronic communication devices was the telegraph, which was invented in the 1830s. **Figure 10** shows the telegraph key invented by Samuel Morse. The telegraph used an electric current to send messages between two devices connected by wires. Telegraph operators sent messages in Morse code by tapping the telegraph key to close an electric circuit, causing "clicks" at the recieving end of the telegraph. Although telegraphs are not used much today, they served as the first example of **telecommunication,** the sending of information across long distances by electronic means. In this section you'll learn about some electronic devices that are used for communication.

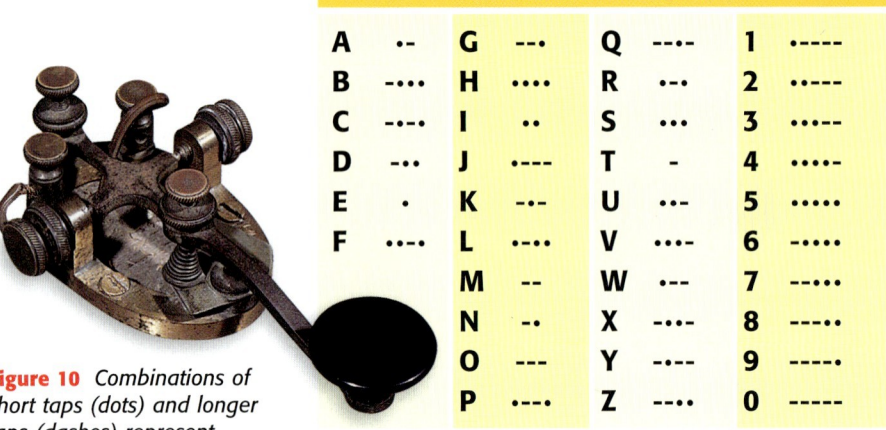

Figure 10 *Combinations of short taps (dots) and longer taps (dashes) represent numbers and letters.*

International Morse Code

A	·—	G	——·	Q	——·—	1	·————
B	—···	H	····	R	·—·	2	··———
C	—·—·	I	··	S	···	3	···——
D	—··	J	·———	T	—	4	····—
E	·	K	—·—	U	··—	5	·····
F	··—·	L	·—··	V	···—	6	—····
		M	——	W	·——	7	——···
		N	—·	X	—··—	8	———··
		O	———	Y	—·——	9	————·
		P	·——·	Z	——··	0	—————

Communicating with Signals

Electronic communication devices transmit information by using signals. A **signal** is something that represents information. A signal can be a command, a sound, or a series of numbers and letters. Often a signal travels better when contained in another form of energy, called a *carrier*. For example, in a telegraph, electric current is the carrier of the signals created by tapping the telegraph key. Two types of signals that carry information in electronic communication devices are analog signals and digital signals.

Activity

Write out a message to a friend using Morse code.

···· · ·—·· ·—·· ———
H E L L O

IS THAT A FACT!

In Morse Code, the international call for help is SOS (···———···). The three letters do not stand for any other words or phrases. SOS is used because it is easy to remember and can be sent quickly.

SCIENCE HUMOR

Q: How do you telephone from an airplane?

A: The airplane's the one with the wings.

Analog Signals

The signals that carry the information through telephone lines are analog signals. An **analog** (AN uh LAHG) **signal** is a signal whose properties, such as amplitude and frequency, can change continuously according to changes in the original information. For example, when you talk on the phone, the sound of your voice is converted into changing electric current in the form of a wave. This wave is an analog signal that is similar in frequency and amplitude to the original sound wave. Just remember that the analog signal is not a sound wave—it is a wave of electric current.

Talking on the Phone Look at the telephone in **Figure 11.** The part you talk into is called the transmitter, and the part you listen to is called the receiver. The transmitter converts the sound waves produced when you speak into the analog signal that travels through phone wires to the receiver of another phone. The receiver converts the analog signal back into the sound of your voice.

Geology CONNECTION

A seismograph is a device geologists use to record earthquakes. A seismograph produces a seismogram—wavy lines on paper that represent earthquake waves. A seismogram is an example of an analog signal. The waves on a seismogram are similar in amplitude and frequency to the waves produced by an earthquake. As the earthquake changes in magnitude, the lines change accordingly.

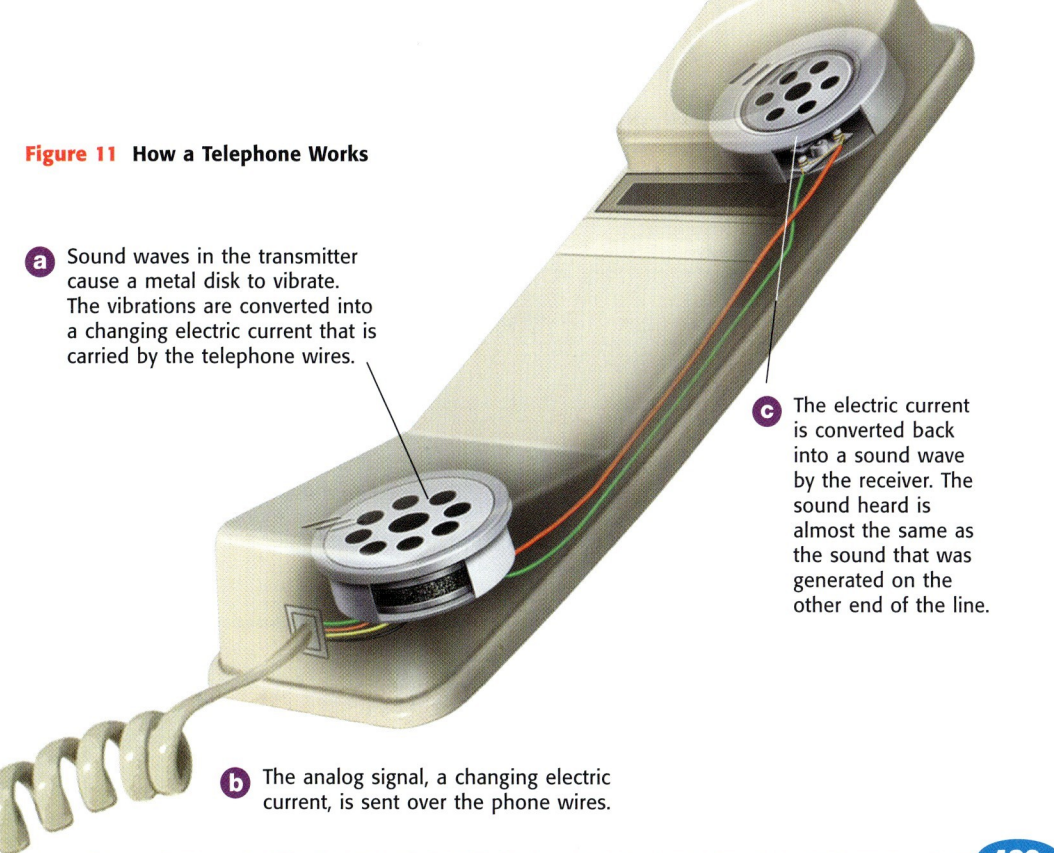

Figure 11 How a Telephone Works

a Sound waves in the transmitter cause a metal disk to vibrate. The vibrations are converted into a changing electric current that is carried by the telephone wires.

b The analog signal, a changing electric current, is sent over the phone wires.

c The electric current is converted back into a sound wave by the receiver. The sound heard is almost the same as the sound that was generated on the other end of the line.

Science Bloopers

While attending the University of London, Alexander Graham Bell read *On the Sensations of Tone* by the German physicist Hermann Von Helmholtz. Bell wasn't fluent in German, and he mistranslated part of the thesis as saying that vowel sounds could be transmitted over a wire. Later Bell said that he might never have begun experimenting with electricity if he had been able to read German.

2) Teach

REAL-WORLD CONNECTION

History Morse code was used for more than a century as a means of communication over the telegraph wire and over radio waves. As communication technology improved, starting with the spread of telephones, better ways to send information, such as satellites and fiber-optic networks, largely replaced the telegraph. Have students research the variety of methods people now use to send and receive information and compare them to what was available 100 years ago. Encourage students to make models or posters to show what they have learned.

CONNECT TO EARTH SCIENCE

Use Transparency 132 to show students how scientists can use seismograms to find the epicenter of an earthquake.

 Teaching Transparency 132 "Finding an Earthquake's Epicenter"

 **Directed Reading Worksheet 19** Section 2

TOPIC: Telephone Technology
GO TO: www.scilinks.org
sciLINKS NUMBER: HSTP460

Section 2 • Communication Technology **489**

2 Teach, continued

DEMONSTRATION

Analog Versus Digital Discuss with students the differences and similarities between the analog recording of a cassette tape and the digital recording of a CD. Most students will comment on the superior sound quality of a CD. Bring in a cassette tape and a CD of the same recording and a CD/cassette player. Cover or shield the CD/cassette player so that the students cannot see whether you are playing the tape or the CD. See if students can hear the difference.

MATH and MORE

Binary Numbers Some students may want to know more about binary numbers. Remind students that in the base 10, or decimal, system the columns are ones (10^0), tens (10^1), hundreds (10^2), etc. In the binary system, as shown in the table below, the columns are ones (2^0), twos (2^1), fours (2^2), eights (2^3), etc. In the decimal system, the number 11 stands for "one *ten* plus one *one*". In binary, the number 11 stands for "one *two* plus one *one*", which is the same as the decimal number 3. Give students an unfinished version of the table below to complete.

Base 10 number	Binary number			
	eights	fours	twos	ones
1	0	0	0	1
2	0	0	1	0
3	0	0	1	1
4	0	1	0	0
5	0	1	0	1
6	0	1	1	0
7	0	1	1	1
8	1	0	0	0
9	1	0	0	1
10	1	0	1	0

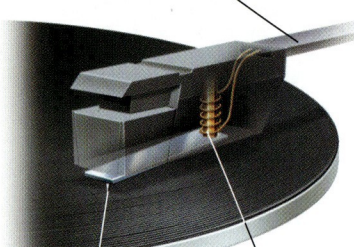

Figure 12 As the stylus rides in the record's grooves, it causes an electromagnet to vibrate.

Analog Recording One way to reproduce sound is by storing an analog signal of the sound wave. In vinyl records, the analog signal is carved into a grooved plastic disk. The frequency and loudness of the sound are represented by the number and depth of the contours carved into the grooved disk.

Playing a Record **Figure 12** shows how a record player's needle, called a stylus (STIE luhs), creates vibrations in an electromagnet. The vibrating electromagnet creates an electric current that is used to produce sound. Although analog recording produces sound that is very similar to the original sound, it has some drawbacks. First, undesirable sounds are sometimes recorded and are difficult to filter out. Also, because the stylus physically touches the record to play it, records can wear out, so the sound can be changed over time.

Digital Signals

A **digital signal** is a series of electric pulses that represents the digits of binary (BIE neh ree) numbers. *Binary* means two. A series of digits, which are composed of only two numbers—1 and 0—represent binary numbers. Each pulse in a digital signal stands for a 1, and each missing pulse is a 0.

Digital Storage on a CD You've probably listened to the digital sound from a compact disc, or CD. Sound is recorded onto a CD by means of a digital signal. A CD stores digital signals in a thin layer of aluminum. As shown in **Figure 13,** the aluminum layer has a series of pits. Each pit is a 0, and each nonpitted region, called a land, is a 1.

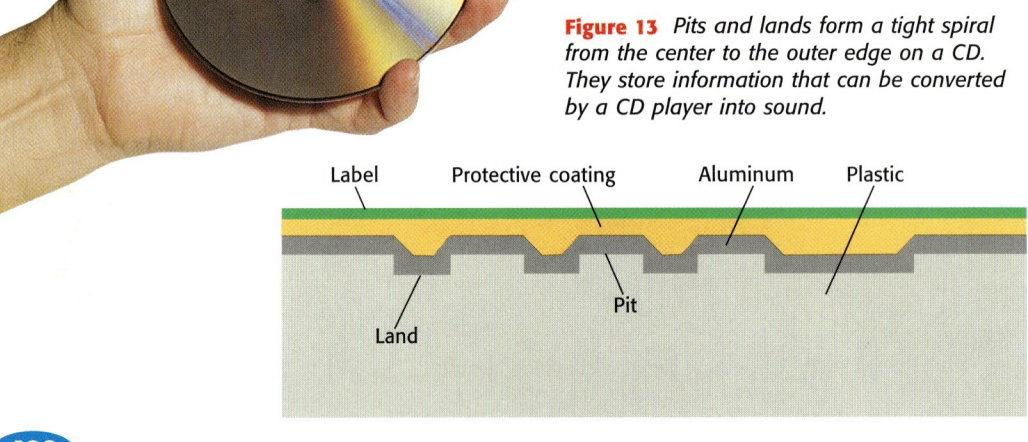

Figure 13 Pits and lands form a tight spiral from the center to the outer edge on a CD. They store information that can be converted by a CD player into sound.

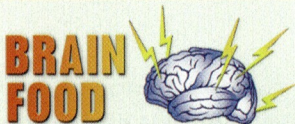

In addition to the sound recording application of the compact disc, the CD-ROM (compact disc read-only memory) can store over 600 megabytes of text, graphics, and sound information.

IS THAT A FACT!

Digital audio tapes (DAT), a development in magnetic recording, produce sound reproduction so similar to the original that the human ear is unable to tell the difference.

Digital Recording In a digital recording, the amplitude of the sound wave is sampled many times per second. From the samples, numbers are generated that are equal to the amplitude of the sound at each instant. **Figure 14** shows how these sample values represent the original sound signal. These numbers are then represented in binary as 1s and 0s and stored as pits and lands on a CD. Undesirable sample values can be filtered out, resulting in a cleaner sound.

The drawback to digital recording is that the sample values don't exactly match the original sound wave. To improve the reproduction of sound, a higher sampling rate can be used. A higher sampling rate means that there will be more sample values taken each second (narrower bars), and the resulting digital sound will be closer to the original sound.

Playing a CD In a CD player, the CD spins around while a laser scans it from underneath. As shown in **Figure 15,** the detector in a CD player receives light reflected from the surface of the CD. The detector converts the pattern of reflected light into a digital signal. The digital signal is changed into an analog signal, which is used to generate a sound wave. Because only light touches the CD, the CD doesn't wear out even after it has been played many times.

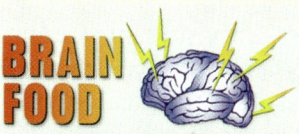

Figure 14 *Each bar represents a digital sample of the sound wave.*

Figure 15 *Different sequences and sizes of pits and lands will register different patterns of numbers that are converted into different sounds.*

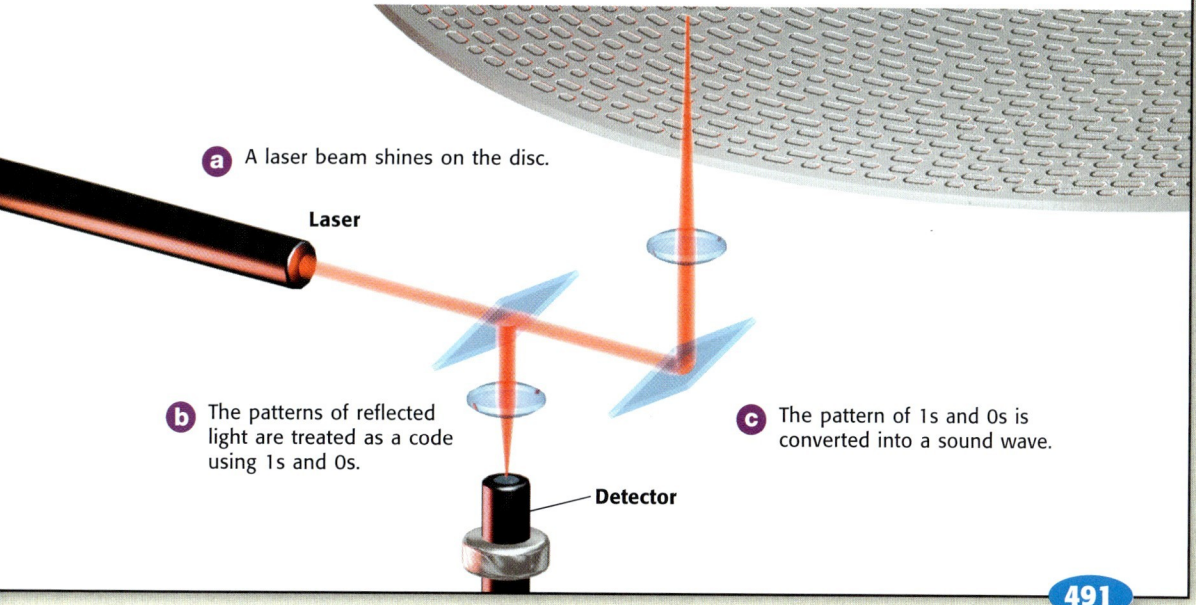

a A laser beam shines on the disc.

Laser

b The patterns of reflected light are treated as a code using 1s and 0s.

c The pattern of 1s and 0s is converted into a sound wave.

Detector

As reported in the 1999 *Old Farmer's Almanac*, a survey conducted by the Timex corporation revealed that more than two-thirds of all watches purchased every year are analog watches—watches with hands for hours, minutes, and seconds. A retired physicist claimed that he prefers the analog face because the circular path of the watch hand better represents the passage of time.

3 Extend

Tune In! PG 702

MEETING INDIVIDUAL NEEDS

Advanced Learners Encourage students to construct a photographic report on the history of the radio and the television. Students can create a photomontage to illustrate the changes that have taken place in television and radio design.

USING THE FIGURE

 Have students study **Figures 12, 15,** and **16.** Ask students to work in pairs to create a poster or other model of how music played at a radio station ultimately reaches their ears. Remind them to show how the sound information (music) is "stored" on a record or a disc, and to explain when the information is converted from one form of energy to another.
Sheltered English

 **Teaching Transparency 278** "How Radio Works"

 Teaching Transparency 279 "Images on a Color Television"

 Critical Thinking Worksheet 19 "Building a Better Mousetrap"

TOPIC: Television Technology
GO TO: www.scilinks.org
sciLINKS NUMBER: HSTP465

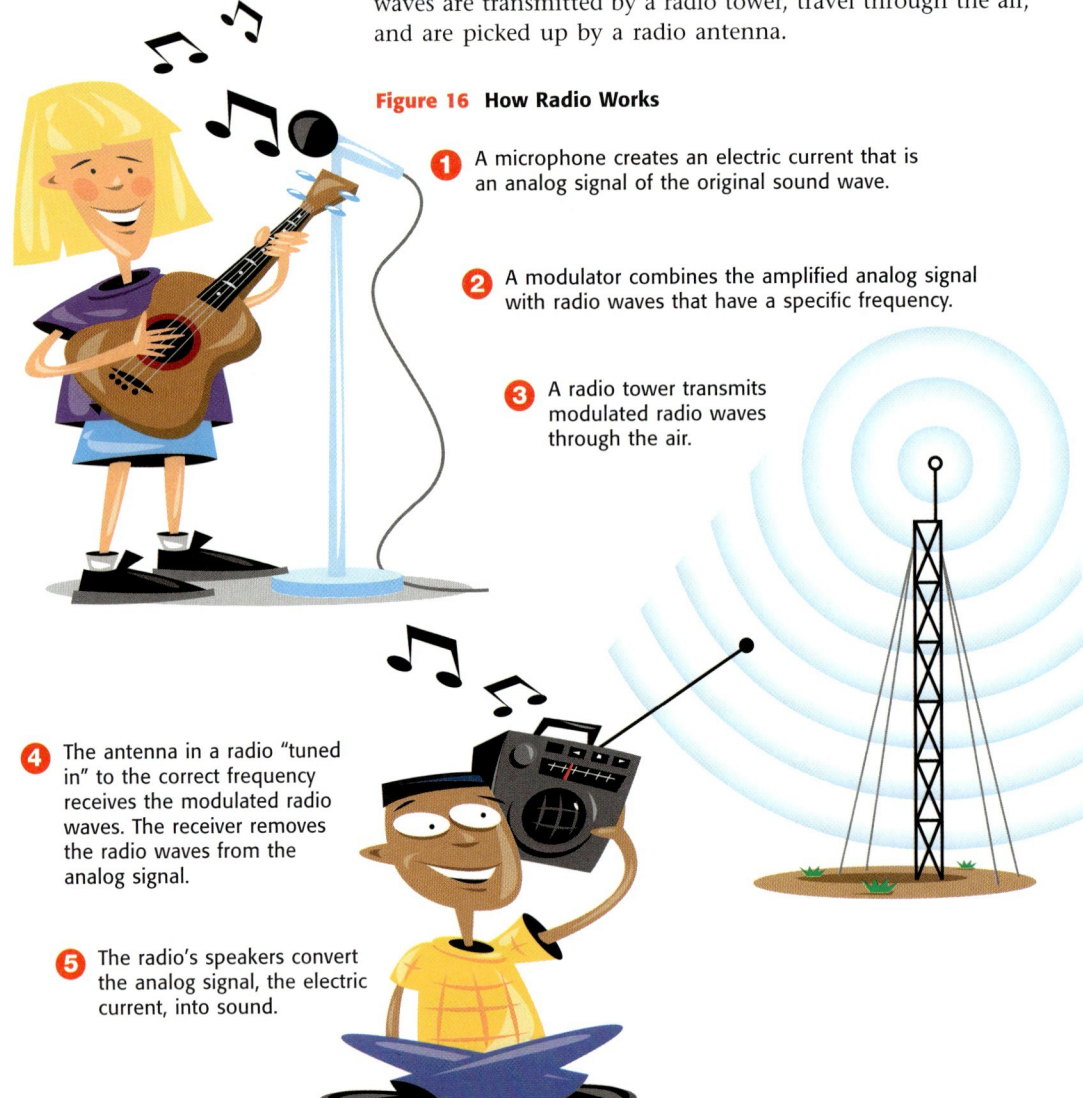

Get tuned in! Turn to page 702 in the LabBook, and build your own radio-wave receiver.

Radio and Television

When you turn on your radio or television, you can hear or see programs broadcast from a radio or TV station that may be many kilometers away. Radio and television use electromagnetic waves. An *electromagnetic wave* is a wave that consists of changing electric and magnetic fields.

Radio Radio waves are one type of electromagnetic wave. The basic operation of a radio involves using radio waves to carry signals that represent sound. As shown in **Figure 16,** radio waves are transmitted by a radio tower, travel through the air, and are picked up by a radio antenna.

Figure 16 How Radio Works

① A microphone creates an electric current that is an analog signal of the original sound wave.

② A modulator combines the amplified analog signal with radio waves that have a specific frequency.

③ A radio tower transmits modulated radio waves through the air.

④ The antenna in a radio "tuned in" to the correct frequency receives the modulated radio waves. The receiver removes the radio waves from the analog signal.

⑤ The radio's speakers convert the analog signal, the electric current, into sound.

Homework

Research Now that students know the basics of how a radio station works, have them research how the signals sent by AM (amplitude modulation) and FM (frequency modulation) radio stations differ. Have them create a poster illustrating the advantages and disadvantages of each.

IS THAT A FACT!

The first radio broadcast of a presidential election was that of the Harding-Cox election on November 2, 1920. That broadcast came from Westinghouse station KDKA in Pittsburgh, Pennsylvania.

492 Chapter 19 • Electronic Technology

Television The images you see on your television are produced by beams of electrons projected onto a screen. Three beams of electrons are produced within a cathode-ray tube, or CRT. The screen is coated with special fluorescent (FLOO uh RES uhnt) materials that glow when hit by electrons. Video signals, which contain the information that produces an image, are carried by electromagnetic waves. Electromagnetic waves also carry the audio signals that produce sound from the speakers. **Figure 17** illustrates how a color television works.

Activity

Use a magnifying lens to look at a television screen. How are the fluorescent materials arranged? Hold the lens at various distances from the screen. What effects do you see? How does the screen's changing picture affect what you see?

TRY at HOME

Figure 17 Images on a Color Television

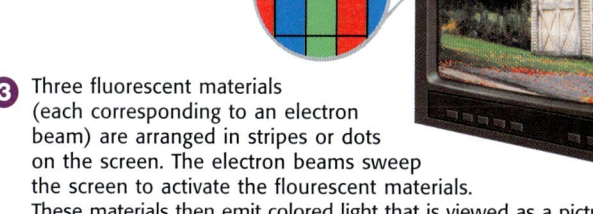

① Video signals transmitted from a TV station are received by the antenna of a TV receiver.

② Electronic circuits separate the video signal into separate signals for each of three electron beams. The beams, one for each primary color of light (red, green, and blue), strike the screen in varying strengths determined by the video signal.

③ Three fluorescent materials (each corresponding to an electron beam) are arranged in stripes or dots on the screen. The electron beams sweep the screen to activate the flourescent materials. These materials then emit colored light that is viewed as a picture.

REVIEW

1. How are analog signals different from digital signals?
2. Compare how a telephone and a radio tower transmit information.
3. **Making Predictions** How could a digital signal be corrupted?

internet connect

SCILINKS
NSTA

TOPIC: Telephone Technology, Television Technology
GO TO: www.scilinks.org
sciLINKS NUMBER: HSTP460, HSTP465

4) Close

GOING FURTHER

Have students create an old-time radio show using only their voices and sound effects. If possible, arrange for students to perform the broadcast schoolwide using the main sound system. **Sheltered English**

Answer to Activity

Students will see stripes or dots of red, blue, and green fluorescent materials. Moving the lens will cause the stripes to appear to change size or become distorted. As the screen changes pictures, different stripes of color will glow with different intensities.

Quiz

1. Name three electronic telecommunication devices and the type of signal associated with each. (telephone—analog signal; compact disc—digital signal; radio—analog signal)
2. Compare the sound produced by analog and digital recording processes. (Analog recordings are true to the original sound, but records wear out over time. Digital recordings can be played many times more than analog records. Noise can be easily removed from digital recordings.)

ALTERNATIVE ASSESSMENT

Concept Mapping Have students create a concept map that uses all the new terms in this section. The map should emphasize the difference between analog signals and digital signals, and should explain how both can be converted to electromagnetic waves. **Sheltered English**

Answers to Review

1. An analog signal has properties that can change with the original information. Digital signals are a series of electric pulses that represent binary numbers.
2. Both a telephone and a radio tower use analog signals to transmit information. However, telephone signals are sent over wires as electric current, while radio signals are sent out through the air as electromagnetic waves.
3. To corrupt a digital signal, information must be lost. A scratch on a CD, for example, could cause bits of information to be lost or misread, which could affect the sound.

Section 2 • Communication Technology

SECTION 3

Focus
Computers
This section covers the basic functions and major parts of a computer. Students learn about computer software and what it can do. Finally, students learn how the Internet works.

 **Bellringer**

Give students the definition of "computer" found on this page. Ask students to list in their ScienceLog all the times in their daily lives they think they use a computer.

1) Motivate

DEMONSTRATION
Computers were developed to do calculations of complicated problems faster than a person could do them by hand. If possible, obtain an abacus and a slide rule, two mechanical counting machines. Demonstrate to students how the abacus is used to add and subtract numbers and the slide rule is used to multiply and divide numbers. (You may want to invite a guest to the classroom who is familiar with each of these machines to demonstrate them.) Discuss with the class the differences between these two earlier calculating machines and today's desktop computers.

 **Directed Reading Worksheet 19** Section 3

Section 3

Terms to Learn
computer
microprocessor
hardware
software
Internet

What You'll Do
- List the basic functions of a computer.
- Identify the main components of computer hardware.
- Describe what computer software allows a computer to do.
- Describe how the Internet works.

Computers

Did you use a computer to wake up this morning? You might think of a computer as something you use to send e-mail or surf the Net, but computers are around you all the time. Computers are in automobiles, VCRs, and telephones. Even an alarm clock is a computer! An alarm clock, like the one in **Figure 18,** lets you program the time you want to wake up, and will wake you up at that time.

Figure 18 *Believe it or not, this alarm clock is a computer!*

What Is a Computer?
A **computer** is an electronic device that performs tasks by processing and storing information. A computer performs a task when it is given a command and has the instructions necessary to carry out that command. Computers do not operate by themselves, or "think."

Basic Functions The basic functions a computer performs are shown in **Figure 19.** The information you give to a computer is called *input.* Setting your alarm clock is a type of input. To perform a task, a computer *processes* the input, changing it to a desirable form. Processing could mean adding a list of numbers, executing a drawing, or even moving a piece of equipment. Input doesn't have to be processed immediately; it can also be stored until it is needed. Computers store information in their *memory.* For example, your alarm clock stores the time you want to wake up. It can then process this stored information by going off when it is the programmed time. *Output* is the final result of the task performed by the computer. What's the output of an alarm clock? The sound that wakes you up!

Figure 19
The Functions of a Computer

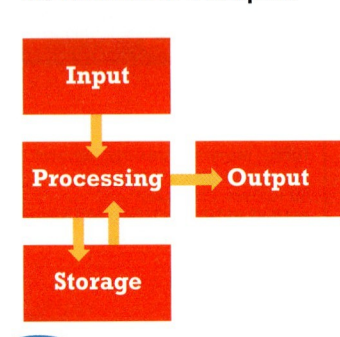

Homework
Have students research the history of calculating devices, including the abacus, "Napier's bones," and early devices invented by Blaise Pascal (1623–1662) and Gottfried von Leibniz (1646–1716). Have them make a model of at least one of the devices to demonstrate and explain to the class. Each explanation should include the role the device played in the evolution of computers. (This project can extend through this section.) **Sheltered English**

494   Chapter 19 • Electronic Technology

Historic Developments

Your pocket calculator is a simple example of a computer. But computers weren't always so small and efficient. The first computers were massive systems consisting of large pieces of electronic equipment that could fill up an entire room.

The First Computers The first general-purpose computer is shown in **Figure 20**. This monstrous collection of equipment is the ENIAC (Electronic Numerical Integrator and Computer), developed in 1946 by the U.S. Army. The ENIAC consisted of thousands of vacuum tubes and, as a result, produced a lot of excess thermal energy. It was also extremely expensive to build and maintain.

When the ENIAC was built, transistors and integrated circuits did not exist. Instead, it used 18,000 vacuum tubes, filled a 10 × 15.25 m room, had a mass of more than 23,500 kg, and used as much electrical energy as 150 ordinary light bulbs!

Figure 20 Fast for its time, the ENIAC could add 5,000 numbers per second.

Modern Computers With the invention of transistors and integrated circuits, the size of computers could be greatly reduced. Computers today use microprocessors, like the one shown in **Figure 21**. A **microprocessor** is an integrated circuit that contains many of a computer's capabilities on a single silicon chip. The first commercially available microprocessor contained only 4,800 transistors, but microprocessors made today may contain more than 3 million transistors. As a result, computers can now be made so small and lightweight that we can carry them around like a notebook!

Figure 21 This microprocessor is about 4 × 4 cm.

WEIRD SCIENCE

Computer viruses, worms, and logic bombs pose serious concerns among computer users. A virus replicates itself within programs and can destroy files but requires human intervention (such as sharing files or sending E-mail) to spread. Worms are designed to destroy data, replicate, and spread without assistance. Logic bombs are programmed to destroy files when triggered by a specific event. Several anti-virus software programs have been developed to guard against or eliminate these computer invaders.

2 Teach, continued

READING STRATEGY

Activity Before students read this page about computer hardware, make large name tags for each of the hardware components described (input device, CPU, monitor, keyboard, mouse). Display each name tag and ask students to identify and describe which part of the computer the name tag corresponds to. (This is a good review activity for students familiar with computer components.)

DISCUSSION

Computer Health People who spend long hours working at a computer terminal may face health hazards. Discuss with students some of the health problems associated with prolonged computer use, such as eyestrain, headache, backache, and repetitive motion syndrome. Ask students if they know of anyone who has computer-related illnesses and what solutions those people found. Discuss ways to prevent some of these hazards.

RESEARCH

Ask students the following questions: "Who wrote the first computer program, and when was it written?" After students have thought about an answer, disclose to them that many people consider the daughter of poet Lord Byron, Augusta Ada Byron, Countess of Lovelace (1815–1852), to have been the first computer programmer. Have students research her life and work, and ask them to create a mobile, write a poem, or find some other creative way to present what they have learned.

Computer Hardware

For each function of a computer, there is a corresponding part of the computer where each function occurs. **Hardware** refers to the parts or equipment that make up a computer. As you read about each piece of hardware, refer to **Figure 22**.

Input Devices Instructions given to a computer are called input. An *input device* is the piece of hardware that feeds information to the computer. You can enter information into a computer using a keyboard, a mouse, a scanner, a digitizing pad and pen—even your own voice!

Central Processing Unit A computer performs tasks within an area called the *central processing unit,* or CPU. In a personal computer, the CPU is a microprocessor. Input goes through the CPU for immediate processing or for storage in memory. The CPU is where the computer does calculations, solves problems, and executes the instructions given to it.

Figure 22 Computer Hardware

MISCONCEPTION ALERT

Some students may believe that computers are more intelligent than people. Remind students that although computers are capable of functioning at extremely high speeds, they can only perform functions that have been programmed by people. Remind students of the computer rule GIGO (garbage in—garbage out). It's not *what* computers do, it's *how fast* they do it that makes them such a valuable tool.

Memory Information can be stored in the computer's memory until it is needed. Hard disks inside a computer and floppy disks or CD-ROMs inserted into a computer have memory to store information. Two other types of memory are *ROM* (read-only memory) and *RAM* (random-access memory).

ROM is permanent. It handles functions such as computer start-up, maintenance, and hardware management. ROM normally cannot be added to or changed, and it cannot be lost when the computer is turned off. On the other hand, RAM is temporary. It stores information only while that information is being used. RAM is sometimes called working memory. Large amounts of RAM allow more information to be input, which makes for a more powerful computer.

Output Devices Once a computer performs a task, it shows the results on an *output device*. Monitors, printers, and speaker systems are all examples of output devices.

Modems One piece of computer hardware that serves as an input device as well as an output device is a *modem*. Modems allow computers to communicate. One computer can input information into another computer over a telephone line, as long as each computer has its own modem. As a result, modems permit computers to "talk" with other computers.

MATH BREAK

Computer Memory

Computers operate using binary numbers. Each digit in a binary number is called a *bit*. Computers store and process information in chunks called *bytes*. A byte is eight bits of information in a computer's memory. A kilobyte is 1,024 bytes, and a gigabyte is 1,073,741,824 bytes.

1. Some computer memory is expressed in gigabytes. How many bits can a 1.5 gigabyte hard disk store?

2. Suppose you download a document from the Internet that uses 25 kilobytes of memory. How many of those documents could you fit on a disk containing 1 gigabyte of memory?

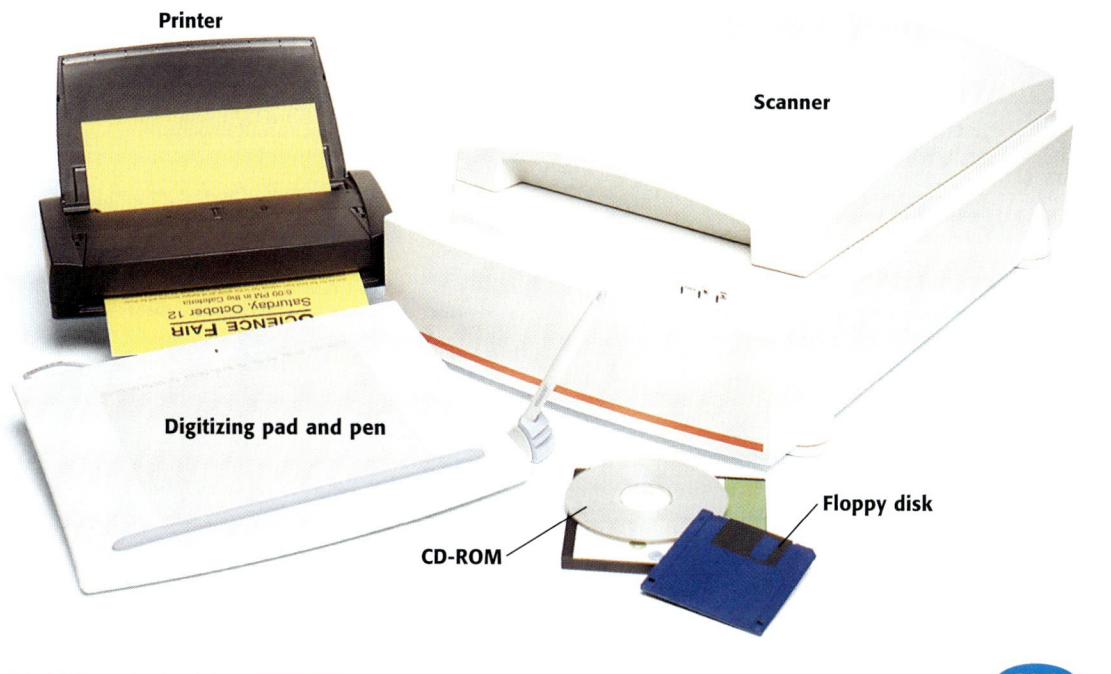

Printer

Scanner

Digitizing pad and pen

CD-ROM

Floppy disk

Answers to MATHBREAK

1. $1.5 \text{ gigabytes} \times \frac{1{,}073{,}741{,}824 \text{ bytes}}{1 \text{ gigabyte}} \times \frac{8 \text{ bits}}{1 \text{ byte}} = 12{,}884{,}901{,}888$ bits

2. 1 gigabyte = 1,073,741,824 bytes;

   $25 \text{ kilobytes} \times \frac{1{,}024 \text{ bytes}}{1 \text{ kilobyte}} = 25{,}600$ bytes;

   $\frac{1{,}073{,}741{,}824 \text{ bytes}}{25{,}600 \text{ bytes}} = 41{,}943$ documents

REAL-WORLD CONNECTION

Have students go through a newspaper to find sale advertisements for computers. Students should cut out several advertisements that give computer specifications (amount of RAM, speed in megahertz, size of hard drive, amount of ROM, size of monitor, inclusion of modem). Have a discussion about the wide variety of configurations available and how to decide which components to select.

MEETING INDIVIDUAL NEEDS

Learners Having Difficulty There may be some students who do not operate a computer frequently. They may be intimidated by the skills of others. Try to arrange a separate time and place, perhaps with the school's computer teacher, for these students to practice turning the computer on and off, opening and closing applications, and performing one or two tasks.

MATH and MORE

Have students do the following problem for additional practice:

Scientists estimate that to create a three-dimensional model of the human brain would require about 15 gigabytes of memory. How many bytes is that? (about 16 billion bytes)

MISCONCEPTION ALERT

Normally, the prefix *giga-* stands for 1,000,000,000 and the prefix *kilo-* stands for 1,000. Kilobyte and gigabyte are different because computers operate using binary numbers. So a kilobyte is 1,024 (2^{10}) bytes and a gigabyte is 1,073,741,824 (2^{30}) bytes.

Section 3 • Computers

3 Extend

CROSS-DISCIPLINARY FOCUS

Language Arts Have students write a short story that describes a futuristic application of computers. Encourage students to be creative and imaginative in their stories. Finished stories can be read aloud to the class.

DEBATE

Computers and Privacy With the use of computers increasing so much over the past 20 years, there has been increasing concern about computer users' right to privacy. Exposing personal information to computer hackers, advertisers, businesses, police, insurance companies, governmental agencies, and others may pose a serious threat to an individual's personal privacy. Have students debate the issue of computers and privacy. One side can represent businesses that rely on access to personal data (such as health or financial information) now available over the Internet. The other side should support the protection of individual rights, stiffer regulations, and new laws that would tighten computer security.

TOPIC: Computer Technology
GO TO: www.scilinks.org
sciLINKS NUMBER: HSTP470

Computer Software

Computers need a set of instructions before they can perform any given task. **Software** is a set of instructions, or commands, that tells a computer what to do. A computer program is an example of software.

Kinds of Software Software can be classified into two categories: operating system software and application software. Operating system software manages basic operations required by the computer and supervises all interactions between software and hardware. It interprets commands from the input device, such as locating programming instructions on a hard disk to be loaded into memory.

Application software contains instructions ordering the computer to operate a utility, such as a word processor, spreadsheet, or even a computer game. The pages in this book were created using a variety of application software! Some examples of application software are shown in **Figure 23.**

Figure 23 Computer software allows a computer to perform all kinds of tasks, such as word processing, video games, interactive tutoring, and graphics.

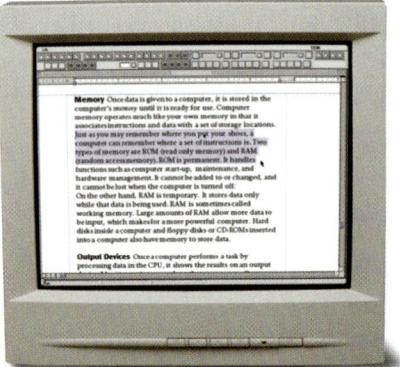

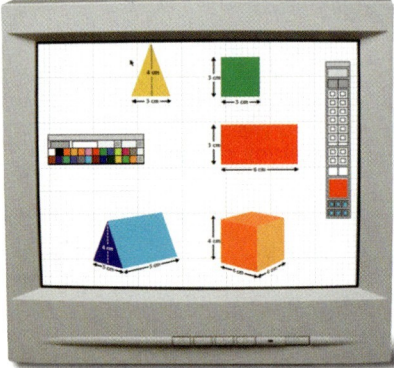

Q: What do you get when you cross a computer with a rubber band?

A: I don't know what it's called, but it makes very snappy decisions!

The Internet—A Global Network

Thanks to modems and computer software, it is possible to connect many computers and allow them to communicate with one another. That's what the **Internet** is—a huge computer network consisting of millions of computers that can all share information with one another.

How the Internet Works Computers can connect to one another on the Internet by using modems to dial into an Internet Service Provider, or ISP. A home computer connects to an ISP over a normal phone line. A school, business, or other group can have a Local Area Network (LAN) that connects to an ISP using one phone line. As depicted in **Figure 24,** ISPs are connected globally by satellite. And that's how computers go global!

Figure 24 Through a series of connections like this, every computer on the Internet can share information.

REVIEW

1. Using the terms *input, output, processing,* and *memory,* explain how you use a pocket calculator to add numbers.
2. What is the difference between hardware and software?
3. **Analyzing Relationships** Could something like the Internet exist without modems and telephone lines? Explain.

TOPIC: Computer Technology, Internet
GO TO: www.scilinks.org
sciLINKS NUMBER: HSTP470, HSTP475

499

Answers to Review

1. Sample answer: I use the buttons on the calculator to *input* the numbers and the addition symbol into the calculator. The calculator accesses its *memory* to execute the addition command. *Processing* occurs when the calculator adds the numbers. The calculator shows the sum on its screen as *output*.
2. Hardware is the parts and equipment that make up the computer. Software is a set of instructions that tells a computer what to do.
3. Accept all reasonable answers. Sample answer: Yes; something like the Internet could exist using only satellites or radio to transmit signals from computer to computer. However, it would still require signals being sent, and something to receive the signals.

4) Close

Quiz

1. Discuss the changes in computers that have occurred since the development of ENIAC in 1946. (Answers should include the changes in size brought about with the invention of the transistor and integrated circuits.)
2. Explain the difference between application software and operating system software. (Application software involves a utility, like a computer game, word processor, or spreadsheet. Operating system software manages basic operations required by the computer and supervises software-to-hardware interactions.)

ALTERNATIVE ASSESSMENT

Concept Mapping Have students create a concept map to explain each of the vocabulary terms in this section. Ask them to include a digital alarm clock or other electronic device to help identify and explain the basic functions of a computer.

Reinforcement Worksheet 19 "The Ins and Outs of Computing"

TOPIC: Internet
GO TO: www.scilinks.org
sciLINKS NUMBER: HSTP475

Section 3 • Computers

Chapter Highlights

VOCABULARY DEFINITIONS

SECTION 1

circuit board a collection of hundreds of tiny circuits that supply electric current to the various parts of an electronic device

semiconductor a substance that conducts electric current better than an insulator but not as well as a conductor

doping the process of replacing a few atoms of a semiconductor with a few atoms of another substance that have a different number of valence electrons. Doping changes the arrangement of electrons in the semiconductor.

diode an electronic component that allows electric current in only one direction

transistor an electronic component that can be used as an amplifier or a switch

integrated circuit an entire circuit containing many transistors and other electronic components formed on a single silicon chip

SECTION 2

telecommunication the sending of information across long distances by electronic means

signal something that represents information, such as a command, a sound, or a series of numbers and letters

analog signal a signal whose properties, such as amplitude and frequency, can change continuously according to changes in the original information

digital signal a series of electric pulses that represents the digits of binary numbers

Chapter Highlights

SECTION 1

Vocabulary
circuit board (p. 482)
semiconductor (p. 483)
doping (p. 483)
diode (p. 484)
transistor (p. 485)
integrated circuit (p. 486)

Section Notes
- Electronic devices use electrical energy to transmit information.
- Many electronic components are made of semiconductors. Two types of semiconductors result from a process called doping. They are n-type and p-type semiconductors.
- The two types of semiconductors can be sandwiched together to produce diodes and transistors.
- Diodes allow electric current in only one direction.
- Transistors can be used as amplifiers or as switches.
- Integrated circuits can contain many electronic components. They allow electronic systems to be smaller.

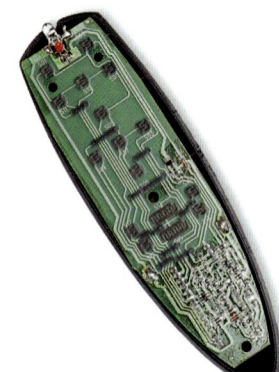

SECTION 2

Vocabulary
telecommunication (p. 488)
signal (p. 488)
analog signal (p. 489)
digital signal (p. 490)

Section Notes
- Electronic devices use signals to transmit information. The signals are usually contained in another form of energy, such as radio waves or electric current.
- The properties of analog signals change continuously according to changes in the original signal. Telephones use analog signals.
- A digital signal is a series of electrical pulses that represents the digits of binary numbers. CD players use digital signals.

✓ Skills Check

Visual Understanding

DIODES Sandwiching an n-type semiconductor and a p-type semiconductor together produces a diode. Charges can pass through a diode in only one direction.

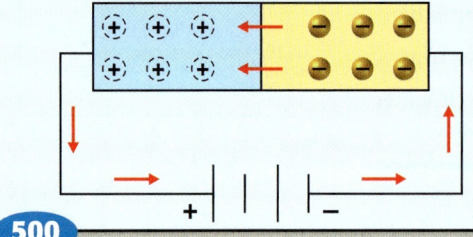

TRANSMITTING SIGNALS BY RADIO Electronic devices transmit information through signals. Look at Figure 16 on page 492 to see how electromagnetic waves can transmit radio signals.

COMPUTERS In order for a computer to perform a task, it must be given information. Look at the diagram on page 494 to learn about the steps a computer takes to perform various tasks.

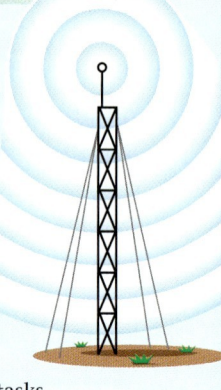

Lab and Activity Highlights

Tune In! PG 702

 Datasheets for LabBook
(blackline masters for this lab)

SECTION 2

- Sound can be recorded digitally or as an analog signal.
- Radio and television rely on electromagnetic waves.
- In radio, signals that represent sound are combined with radio waves and sent through the air. Radios can pick up the radio waves and convert them back to sound waves.
- A color television image is produced by three electron beams that scan the screen of a cathode-ray tube, or CRT. Fluorescent materials on the screen glow to create the picture.

Labs
Tune In! (p. 702)

SECTION 3

Vocabulary
computer (p. 494)
microprocessor (p. 495)
hardware (p. 496)
software (p. 498)
Internet (p. 499)

Section Notes
- The basic functions of a computer involve input, processing, memory, and output. A computer cannot perform a task without a set of commands.

- The first computers were very large and could not perform many tasks.
- Because microprocessors contain many computer capabilities on a single chip, computers have been reduced in size.
- Computer hardware refers to the parts or the equipment that make up a computer.
- Computer software is a set of instructions or commands that tells a computer what to do.
- Modems allow millions of computers to connect with one another and share information on the Internet.

VOCABULARY DEFINITIONS, continued

SECTION 3

computer an electronic device that performs tasks by processing and storing information

microprocessor an integrated circuit that contains many of a computer's capabilities on a single silicon chip

hardware the parts or equipment that make up a computer

software a set of instructions or commands that tells a computer what to do; a computer program

Internet a huge computer network consisting of millions of computers that can all share information with one another

 Vocabulary Review Worksheet 19

 Blackline masters of these Chapter Highlights can be found in the **Study Guide.**

internetconnect

GO TO: go.hrw.com

Visit the **HRW** Web site for a variety of learning tools related to this chapter. Just type in the keyword:

KEYWORD: HSTELT

GO TO: www.scilinks.org

Visit the **National Science Teachers Association** on-line Web site for Internet resources related to this chapter. Just type in the *sci*LINKS number for more information about the topic:

TOPIC: Transistors	*sci*LINKS NUMBER: HSTP455
TOPIC: Telephone Technology	*sci*LINKS NUMBER: HSTP460
TOPIC: Television Technology	*sci*LINKS NUMBER: HSTP465
TOPIC: Computer Technology	*sci*LINKS NUMBER: HSTP470
TOPIC: Internet	*sci*LINKS NUMBER: HSTP475

Lab and Activity Highlights

LabBank

Long-Term Projects & Research Ideas
Ancient Electronics, Project 69

Chapter Review

USING VOCABULARY

For each pair of terms, explain the difference in their meanings.

1. semiconductor/doping
2. transistor/diode
3. signal/telecommunication
4. analog signal/digital signal
5. computer/microprocessor
6. hardware/software

UNDERSTANDING CONCEPTS

Multiple Choice

7. All electronic devices transmit information using
   a. signals.
   b. electromagnetic waves.
   c. radio waves.
   d. modems.

8. Semiconductors are used to make
   a. transistors.
   b. integrated circuits.
   c. diodes.
   d. All of the above

9. Which of the following is an example of a telecommunication device?
   a. vacuum tube
   b. telephone
   c. radio
   d. Both (b) and (c)

10. A monitor, printer, and speaker are examples of
    a. input devices.   c. computers.
    b. memory.   d. output devices.

11. Record players play sounds that were recorded in the form of
    a. digital signals.
    b. electric current.
    c. analog signals.
    d. radio waves.

12. Memory in a computer that is permanent and cannot be added to is called
    a. RAM.
    b. ROM.
    c. CPU.
    d. None of the above

13. Cathode-ray tubes are used in
    a. telephones.
    b. telegraphs.
    c. televisions.
    d. radios.

Short Answer

14. How is an electronic device different from a machine that uses electrical energy?

15. How does a diode allow current to flow in one direction?

16. In one or two sentences, describe how a TV works.

17. Give three examples of how computers are used in your everyday life.

18. Explain the advantages that transistors have over vacuum tubes.

502 Chapter 19 • Electronic Technology

Concept Mapping

19. Use the following terms to create a concept map: electronic devices, radio waves, electric current, signals, information.

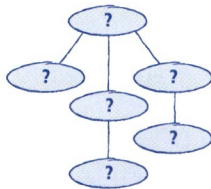

CRITICAL THINKING AND PROBLEM SOLVING

20. Your friend is preparing an oral report on the history of radio and finds the photograph shown below. "Why is this radio so huge?" he asks you. Using what you know about electronic devices, how do you explain the size of this vintage radio?

21. Using what you know about the differences between analog and digital signals, explain how the sound from a record player is different from the sound from a CD player.

22. What do Morse code and digital signals have in common?

23. Computers can process a lot of information, but they cannot think. Explain why this is true.

24. Based on what you learned in the chapter, how do you think an automatic garage door opener works?

INTERPRETING GRAPHICS

Look at the diagram below, and answer the questions that follow.

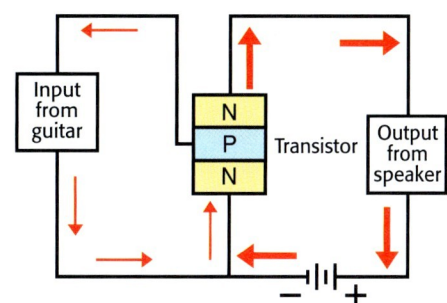

25. What purpose does the transistor serve in this situation?

26. How does the current in the left side of the circuit compare with the current in the right side of the circuit?

27. How does the sound from the speaker compare with the sound from the guitar?

NOW What Do You Think?

Take a minute to review your answers to the ScienceLog questions on page 481. Have your answers changed? If necessary, revise your answers based on what you have learned since you began this chapter.

NOW WHAT DO YOU THINK?

1. An electronic device is a device that uses electrical energy to transmit information.
2. Answers will vary. Television, radio, telephone, telegraph, and computers with modems are all electronic devices used for communication.
3. The parts of a computer are input devices, the central processing unit, memory, output devices, and modems.

Concept Mapping Transparency 19

Blackline masters of this Chapter Review can be found in the **Study Guide**.

Concept Mapping

19. 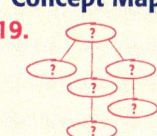 An answer to this exercise can be found at the end of this book.

CRITICAL THINKING AND PROBLEM SOLVING

20. This radio was built before the invention of semiconductors. It was built with vacuum tubes instead of transistors. Vacuum tubes are much larger than transistors, so the radio is much larger than a modern radio.
21. The sound produced by a record player comes from an analog signal of the sound stored on the record. The sound from a CD player comes from a digital signal of the sound stored on a CD. It is easier to remove noise from a recording on a CD.
22. Sample answer: Digital signals are represented by a combination of pulses and missing pulses of electric current. Likewise, Morse code signals are represented by combinations of dots and dashes.
23. Computers can only process the information that is given to them. They can also only perform the functions for which they are programmed.
24. Sample answer: The remote control sends a signal to the garage door opener. The signal activates a small motor, and the garage door opens.

INTERPRETING GRAPHICS

25. This transistor is an amplifier in the circuit.
26. The current in the right side of the circuit varies in the same pattern as the current in the left side of the circuit; the current in the right side of the circuit is larger.
27. The sound from the speaker is the same as the sound from the guitar, except the sound from the speaker is louder.

Chapter 19 • Chapter Review

HEALTH WATCH
Listening Lower

Background

Students may enjoy researching Alexander Graham Bell and his work with human speech. Bell invented the telephone as part of his work to improve communications with people who could not hear. The decibel bears his name, as does the Alexander Graham Bell Association for the Deaf, which provides information and support to the hard-of-hearing and to educators.

Students will gain important background from a decibel table relating common sounds to decibel levels. In addition, an explanation of the exponential nature of the decibel scale will help them comprehend why damage to hearing can occur with little notice. Every 10 decibels is a factor of 10 increase in sound intensity, but is not perceived that way. For example, a perceived doubling of sound from 60 dB (normal conversation) to 120 dB (pneumatic drill) is actually a 10^6 increase in intensity.

Health Watch

Listening Lower

Do you ever listen to your favorite music on headphones? Many people like to use headphones while they exercise. Terrific! But doctors believe that this habit may be putting people's hearing at risk.

The Blood Brain Drain

▲ *How high should the volume be when listening to music on headphones?*

Aerobic exercise, including walking, jogging, skating, dancing, and competitive sports, is an important part of a healthy lifestyle. However, when you exercise, more blood is sent to your arms and legs than is sent to your ears. The inner ear is more easily damaged when the blood flow is lowered. Once the cells of the inner ear are damaged, they cannot be replaced. A study in Sweden showed that hearing loss doubles when loud noise and aerobic exercise are combined!

How Loud Is Too Loud?

The federal Occupational Safety and Health Administration (OSHA) requires hearing protection for workers exposed to 95 decibels for 4 hours. A lawn mower emits 95 decibels. If workers are exposed to 100 decibels for 3 hours, they must wear hearing protection. People generally listen to headphones at levels between 90 and 115 decibels.

Why So Loud?

Most people turn the volume up as they continue to listen to music because their ears adapt to the volume. However, permanent hearing loss can occur at well below painful or even uncomfortable levels. Another concern is that hearing loss is often gradual, starting at high frequencies. The loss goes unnoticed until the damage is quite extensive. Generally, more problems occur when noise is louder, lasts longer, or occurs frequently.

What to Do

How can you protect your hearing and still use those headphones? Keep the volume of your headphones as low as possible, and try not to raise the volume once it is set. Then always remember this: If a person 1 m away has to shout in order for you to hear, the volume is too high. However, this test does not work for headphones with muffs that fit around the ear. The volume is probably too high if your hearing is dulled after you remove your headphones. This usually goes away quickly, but it may become permanent if you keep the volume high.

Sound It Out

► Obtain a sound meter, and survey the sound levels around your school. Measure the levels at dances and other noisy locations. Report your findings to your class, and discuss ways to lower your exposure to loud sounds. You may just save someone's hearing!

On Your Own

For the On Your Own activity, demonstrate the use of a sound level meter. Sound level meters can be purchased from a scientific supply house. Explain the difference between emitted and perceived sound, as sound dissipates with the inverse square of the distance, and that students should be concerned about the level they hear. Escort students if they are going to test areas such as factories, airports, crowded malls, sports events, or locations near highways. They should have ear protection in any area where sound levels require it.

Encourage students to share their results and to raise awareness of this problem. Perhaps an assembly can be held in which different sound levels are demonstrated.

Science Fiction

"There Will Come Soft Rains"

by Ray Bradbury

Ticktock, seven o'clock, time to get up, time to get up, seven o'clock. The voice clock in the living room sends out the wake-up message, gently calling to the family to get up and begin their new day.

It is August 4, 2026, in Allandale, California. The house is attractive, in an attractive neighborhood, just right for a mother, father, two children, and a dog. And it is state of the art: automatic kitchen, extremely sensitive fire-detection and fire-protection systems, walls that look like walls but become video display screens—everything a family could want.

A few minutes after the wake-up call, the automatic stove in the kitchen begins the family breakfast—toast, eggs (sunny side up), and bacon. While the breakfast is cooking, the voice in the kitchen ceiling lists the reminders for the day: a birthday, an anniversary, the bills that are due.

About an hour after the wake-up message, the ceiling voice speaks again, this time to remind anyone listening that it is time to go to school. A soft rain is falling outside, so the weather box by the front door suggests that raincoats are necessary today.

But something has happened. No family sounds come from the house. The house goes on talking to itself and carrying on its routine as if it were keeping itself company. Why doesn't anyone answer? Find out when you read Ray Bradbury's "There Will Come Soft Rains" in the *Holt Anthology of Science Fiction*.

Further Reading Bradbury's best-known books include the short-story collections *The Martian Chronicles* (Bantam) and *The Illustrated Man* (Bantam), and the novel *Fahrenheit 451* (Ballantine).

SCIENCE FICTION

"There Will Come Soft Rains"
by Ray Bradbury

It's the start of a new day, but where is everybody?

Teaching Strategy

Reading Level This story is of moderate difficulty, but most middle-school students should be able to read and enjoy it.

Background

About the Author At the age of twelve, Ray Bradbury (1920–) wrote his first short stories, about the planet Mars, in pencil on brown wrapping paper. He's been writing stories—and novels, poems, plays, and screenplays—ever since. Their settings range from Mars and Venus, to Ireland and Greentown, a fictional town based on his birthplace, Waukegan, Illinois. Much of Bradbury's writing, like "There Will Come Soft Rains," expresses his belief that advances in science and technology should never come at the expense of human beings.

UNIT 7

TIMELINE
Waves, Sound, and Light

When you hear the word *waves,* you probably think of waves in the ocean. But waves that you encounter every day have a much bigger effect on your life than do water waves! In this unit, you will learn about different types of waves, how waves behave and interact, and how sound energy and light energy travel in waves. This timeline shows some events and discoveries that have occurred throughout history as scientists have sought to learn more about the energy of waves.

Around 1600
Italian astronomer and physicist Galileo Galilei attempts to calculate the speed of light by using lanterns and shutters. He writes that the speed is "extraordinarily rapid."

1929
American astronomer Edwin Hubble uses the Doppler effect of light to determine that the universe is expanding.

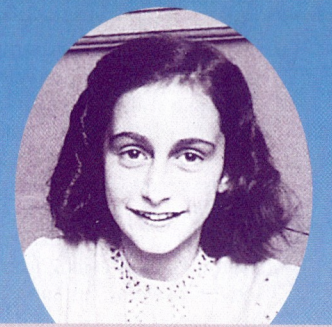

1947
The *Diary of Anne Frank* is published. The book is an edited version of the diary kept by a Jewish teenager while in hiding during World War II.

1960
The first working laser is demonstrated.

1971
Hungarian physicist Dennis Gabor wins the Nobel Prize in Physics for his invention of holography, the method used to make holograms.

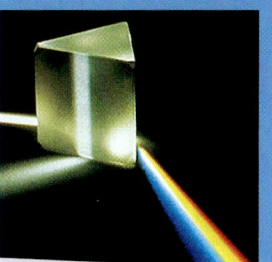

1704
Sir Isaac Newton publishes his book *Optiks*, which contains his theories about light and color.

1711
The tuning fork—an instrument that produces a single-frequency note—is invented by English trumpeter John Shore.

1801
British scientist Thomas Young is the first to provide experimental data showing that light behaves as a wave.

1905
Physicist Albert Einstein suggests that light sometimes behaves as a particle.

1903
The popularity of an early movie called *The Great Train Robbery* leads to the establishment of permanent movie theaters.

1984
A "mouse" is first used on personal computers.

1983
The exact speed of light is determined to be 299,792,458 m/s.

1997
British pilot Andy Green drives a jet-powered car at 341 m/s, making him the first person to travel faster than the speed of sound on land.

Waves, Sound, and Light

Chapter Organizer

CHAPTER ORGANIZATION	TIME MINUTES	OBJECTIVES	LABS, INVESTIGATIONS, AND DEMONSTRATIONS
Chapter Opener pp. 508–509	45	National Standards: SAI 1, SPSP 3, PS 3a	**Investigate!** Making Waves, p. 509
Section 1 The Nature of Waves	90	▶ Describe how waves transfer energy without transferring matter. ▶ Distinguish between waves that require a medium and waves that do not. ▶ Explain the difference between transverse and longitudinal waves. UCP 1, 2, SAI 1, PS 3a, 3f	**QuickLab,** Energetic Waves, p. 510 **Demonstration,** p. 510 in ATE **Demonstration,** p. 514 in ATE
Section 2 Properties of Waves	90	▶ Identify and describe four wave properties. ▶ Explain how amplitude and frequency are related to the energy of a wave. UCP 3, 5, SAI 1, ST 2, HNS 2, PS 3a; LabBook UCP 5, SAI 1, 2, PS 3a	**Demonstration,** p. 516 in ATE **QuickLab,** Springy Waves, p. 518 **Discovery Lab,** Wave Energy and Speed, p. 706 **Datasheets for LabBook,** Wave Energy and Speed, Datasheet 54 **Skill Builder,** Wave Speed, Frequency, and Wavelength, p. 708 **Datasheets for LabBook,** Wave Speed, Frequency, and Wavelength, Datasheet 55
Section 3 Wave Interactions	90	▶ Describe reflection, refraction, diffraction, and interference. ▶ Compare destructive interference with constructive interference. ▶ Describe resonance, and give examples. UCP 3, ST 2, PS 3c	**Demonstration,** p. 521 in ATE **Whiz-Bang Demonstrations,** Pitch Forks, Demo 60 **Long-Term Projects & Research Ideas,** Project 70

*See page **T20** for a complete correlation of this book with the*

NATIONAL SCIENCE EDUCATION STANDARDS.

TECHNOLOGY RESOURCES

 Guided Reading Audio CD English or Spanish, Chapter 20

One-Stop Planner CD-ROM with Test Generator

 CNN. Science, Technology & Society, Harnessing Sound Energy, Segment 24

Chapter 20 • The Energy of Waves

CLASSROOM WORKSHEETS, TRANSPARENCIES, AND RESOURCES	SCIENCE INTEGRATION AND CONNECTIONS	REVIEW AND ASSESSMENT
Directed Reading Worksheet 20 **Science Puzzlers, Twisters & Teasers,** Worksheet 20	**Multicultural Connection,** p. 508 in ATE	
Directed Reading Worksheet 20, Section 1 **Transparency 131,** Primary and Secondary Waves **Transparency 280,** Transverse Waves **Transparency 280,** Longitudinal Waves	**Astronomy Connection,** p. 512 **Real-World Connection,** p. 512 in ATE **MathBreak,** Perpendicular Lines, p. 513 **Multicultural Connection,** p. 513 in ATE **Connect to Earth Science,** p. 513 in ATE **Connect to Life Science,** p. 514 in ATE **Real-World Connection,** p. 515 in ATE	**Self-Check,** p. 512 **Homework,** p. 514 in ATE **Review,** p. 515 **Quiz,** p. 515 in ATE **Alternative Assessment,** p. 515 in ATE
Directed Reading Worksheet 20, Section 2 **Transparency 281,** Wavelength **Transparency 281,** Frequency **Transparency 282,** Wave Speed, Wavelength, and Frequency **Reinforcement Worksheet 20,** Getting on the Same Frequency **Math Skills for Science Worksheet 5,** Dividing Whole Numbers with Long Division	**MathBreak,** Wave Calculations, p. 519 **Across the Sciences:** Sounds of Silence, p. 531	**Review,** p. 519 **Quiz,** p. 519 in ATE **Alternative Assessment,** p. 519 in ATE
Directed Reading Worksheet 20, Section 3 **Transparency 283,** Constructive and Destructive Interference **Reinforcement Worksheet 20,** Makin' Waves **Critical Thinking Worksheet 20,** The Case of the Speeding Ticket	**Real-World Connection,** p. 522 in ATE **Apply,** p. 523 **Multicultural Connection,** p. 524 in ATE **Science, Technology, and Society:** The Ultimate Telescope, p. 530	**Self-Check,** p. 521 **Homework,** p. 524 in ATE **Review,** p. 525 **Quiz,** p. 525 in ATE **Alternative Assessment,** p. 525 in ATE

internet connect

 Holt, Rinehart and Winston On-line Resources
go.hrw.com

For worksheets and other teaching aids related to this chapter, visit the HRW Web site and type in the keyword: **HSTWAV**

 **National Science Teachers Association**
www.scilinks.org

Encourage students to use the sciLINKS numbers listed in the internet connect boxes to access information and resources on the **NSTA** Web site.

END-OF-CHAPTER REVIEW AND ASSESSMENT

Chapter Review in Study Guide
Vocabulary and Notes in Study Guide
Chapter Tests with Performance-Based Assessment, Chapter 20 Test
Chapter Tests with Performance-Based Assessment, Performance-Based Assessment 20
Concept Mapping Transparency 20

Chapter Resources & Worksheets

Visual Resources

TEACHING TRANSPARENCIES

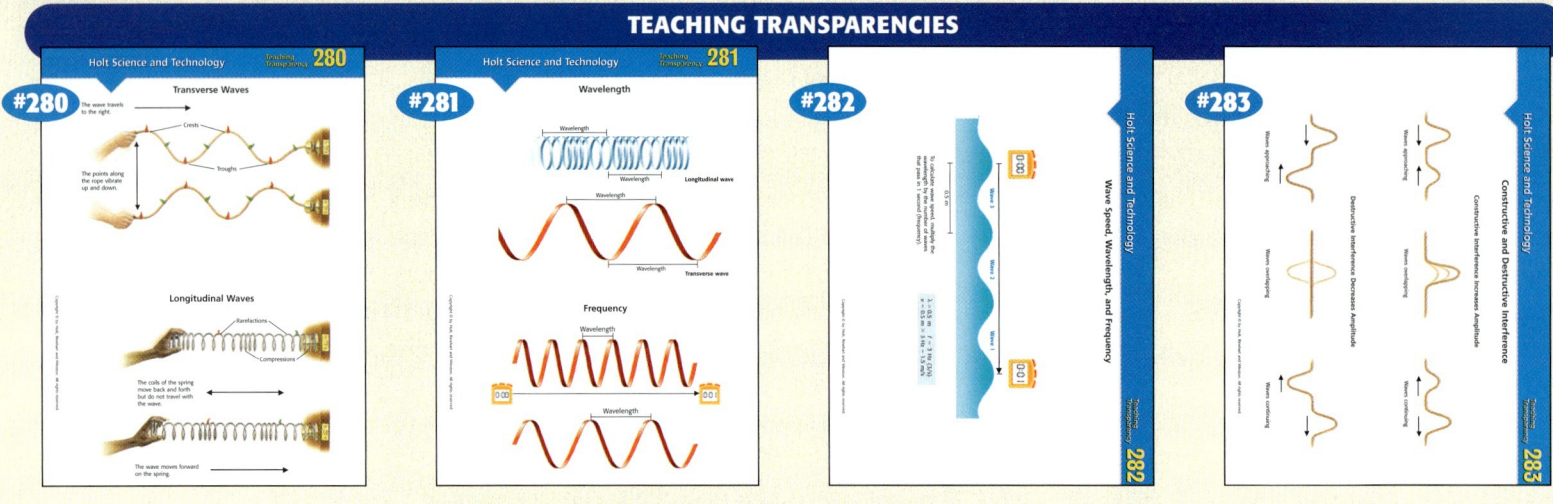

TEACHING TRANSPARENCIES

CONCEPT MAPPING TRANSPARENCY

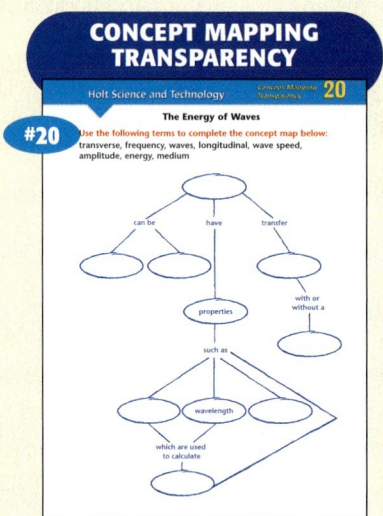

Meeting Individual Needs

DIRECTED READING

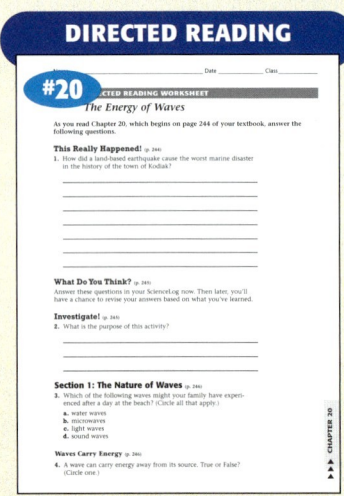

REINFORCEMENT & VOCABULARY REVIEW

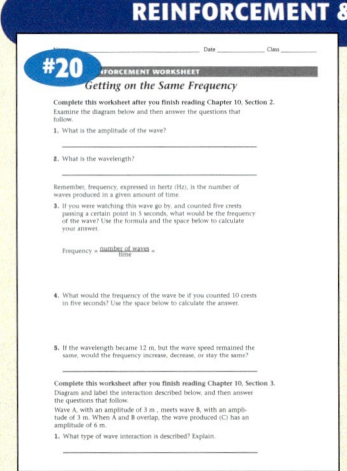

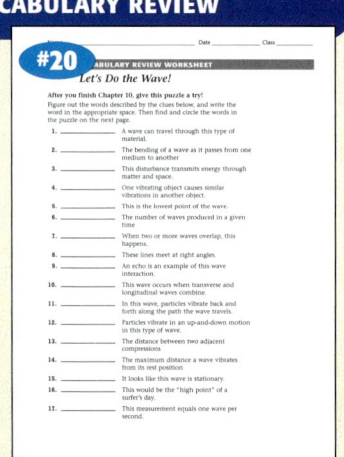

SCIENCE PUZZLERS, TWISTERS & TEASERS

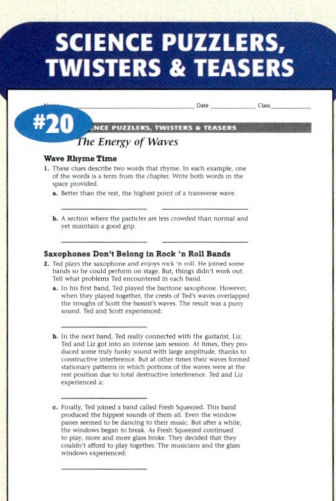

Chapter 20 • The Energy of Waves

Review & Assessment

STUDY GUIDE

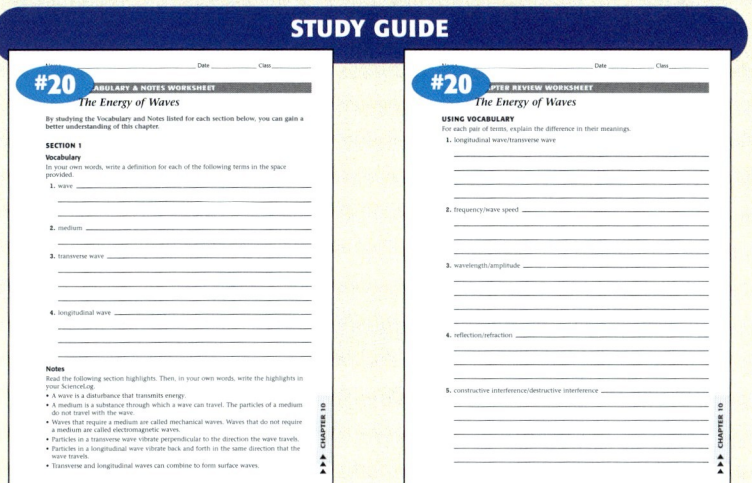

CHAPTER TESTS WITH PERFORMANCE-BASED ASSESSMENT

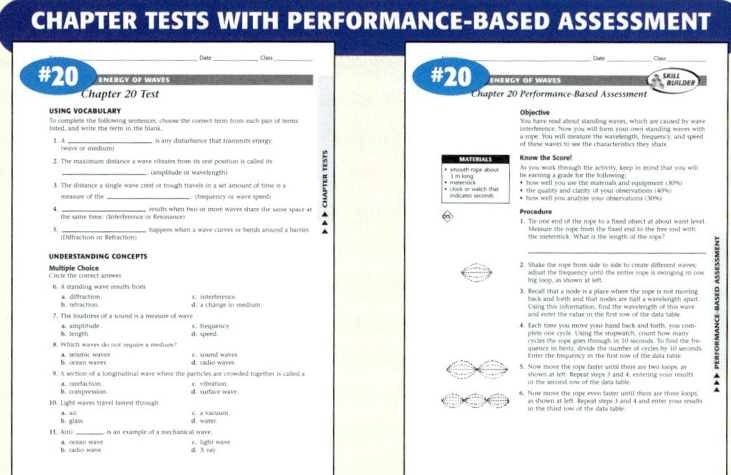

Lab Worksheets

WHIZ-BANG DEMONSTRATIONS

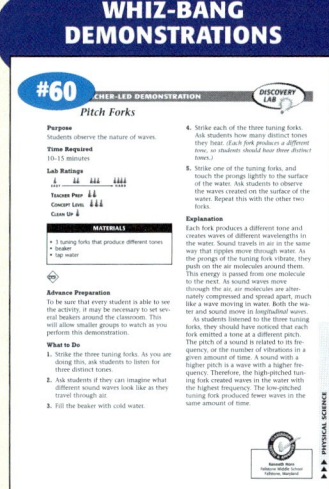

LONG-TERM PROJECTS & RESEARCH IDEAS

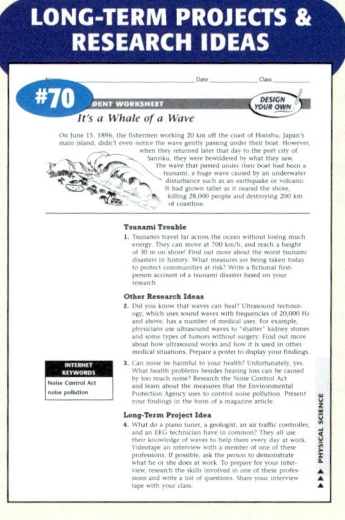

DATASHEETS FOR LABBOOK

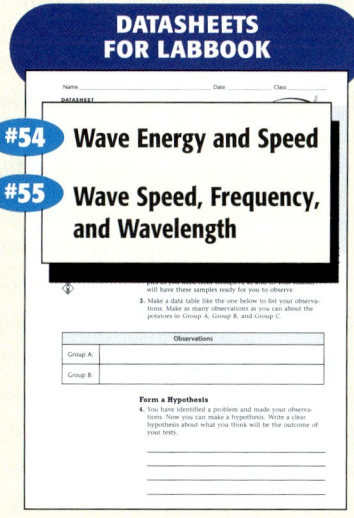

Applications & Extensions

CRITICAL THINKING & PROBLEM SOLVING

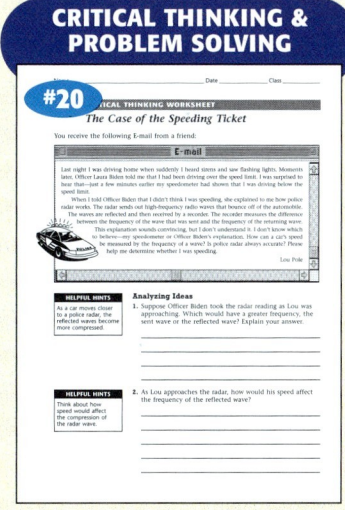

SCIENCE TECHNOLOGY

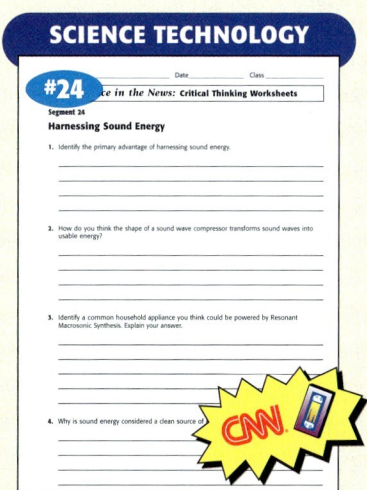

Chapter 20 • Chapter Resources & Worksheets

Chapter Background

SECTION 1

The Nature of Waves

▶ **Tsunamis**

What many people call tidal waves are not caused by the tides. They are usually caused by undersea earthquakes, volcanic eruptions, landslides, or violent windstorms that occur over the open sea. A large wave produced by any of these phenomena is called a *tsunami*.

- Tsunamis often begin as a series of small waves no larger than 1 m high but traveling at great speed (188 m/s) over deep water. In deep water, a tsunami may not even be seen. However, when the depth of the water becomes less than the height of the wave, the wave builds into a wall of water that can reach a height of 30 m.

▶ **Mechanical Waves**

Some scientists call waves "a wiggle in time and space." Mechanical waves are periodic disturbances that pass through matter. As a wave passes through matter, the material's particles vibrate about their rest positions and only the energy moves through. Some of the wave's energy is used to do work on the particles. Mechanical waves eventually die out as their energy is dissipated.

▶ **Electromagnetic Waves**

An electromagnetic wave is a transverse wave comprising vibrating electric and magnetic fields at right angles to each other. Electromagnetic waves, like mechanical waves, are described in terms of wavelength and frequency. Types of electromagnetic waves (from longest wavelength to shortest) include radio waves, microwaves, infrared waves, visible light, ultraviolet light, X rays, and gamma rays.

SECTION 2

Properties of Waves

▶ **Waves**

A wave is produced by a vibrating object. For example, music is produced by vibrating strings or by vibrating columns of air.

- The frequency of the wave is equal to the frequency of the vibrating object. The square of the amplitude of the wave is proportional to the energy used to produce the wave.

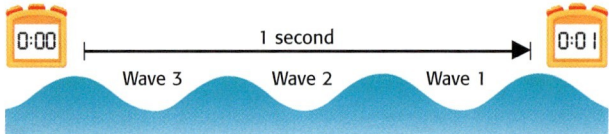

- The speed of a wave depends on the medium through which it travels. For mechanical waves, the density, elasticity, and temperature of the medium affect the speed. A mechanical wave's speed increases with elasticity and decreases with density. For example, the speed of sound at 0°C is 331.5 m/s in air and 5,200 m/s in steel.

Chapter 20 • The Energy of Waves

IS THAT A FACT!

- Heinrich Hertz (1857–1894) was a German physicist. The unit for describing frequency is named in his honor. Hertz's goal was to prove Maxwell's theory of electromagnetic radiation. While Hertz was performing his experiments, he discovered radio waves. This discovery led to the development of radio, radar, and television.

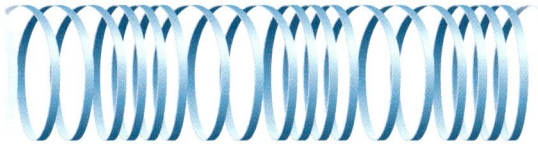

▶ Longitudinal Waves and Wavelength

Longitudinal waves do not have high and low points, but they do have regions of high pressure (compressions) and regions of low pressure (expansions). Sound waves are an example of longitudinal waves. When you strike a tuning fork, the prongs vibrate back and forth. Like a drum, the tuning fork sends out compressions when the prongs vibrate out and rarefactions when the prongs vibrate back. The compressions of the sound waves correspond to crests. Rarefactions of sound waves correspond to troughs. Therefore, the wavelength of a sound wave is the distance between adjacent compressions or adjacent expansions.

IS THAT A FACT!

- If you are listening to your favorite radio station, whose frequency is 96.1 MHz (96,100,000 Hz), the electrons in the radio antenna are vibrating at the same frequency—96,100,000 vibrations/second.

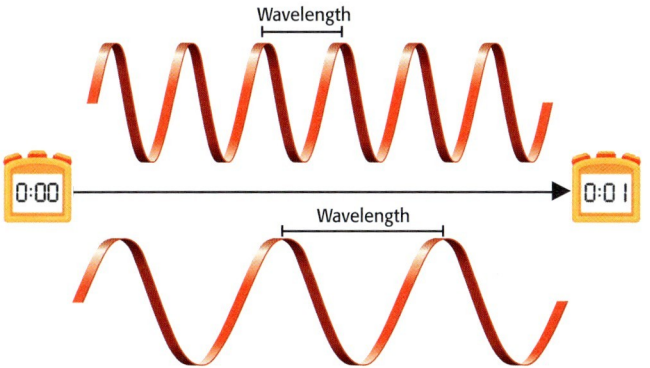

SECTION 3

Wave Interactions

▶ Christiaan Huygens

Christiaan Huygens (1629–1695) was a Dutch mathematician, astronomer, and physicist. His life overlapped that of Galileo (1564–1642) and of Newton (1642–1727). Many historians believe that Huygens's contributions to science were much broader than those of either Newton or Galileo.

- Huygens invented the pendulum clock and developed the first wave theory. Huygens's theory states that any point on a wave can be a source of a new disturbance.

▶ Lasers

In 1960, T. H. Maiman and others built the first successful laser. They used a large ruby crystal doped with chromium-ion impurities as the source of light. The electrons of the chromium ions were excited by a special flash lamp. The excited ions dropped to a lower energy level almost immediately and emitted photons of a single wavelength.

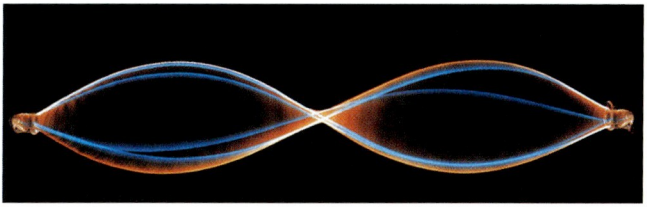

IS THAT A FACT!

- The word *refraction* comes from the Latin prefix *re-*, meaning "back," and *frangere*, meaning "to break."

For background information about teaching strategies and issues, refer to the *Professional Reference for Teachers*.

CHAPTER 20
The Energy of Waves

Chapter Preview

Section 1
The Nature of Waves
- Waves Carry Energy
- Types of Waves

Section 2
Properties of Waves
- Amplitude
- Wavelength
- Frequency
- Wave Speed

Section 3
Wave Interactions
- Reflection
- Refraction
- Diffraction
- Interference

The word *tsunami* is a Japanese word that is represented by two characters in the Japanese language. The first character, *tsu*, translates as "harbor." The second character, *nami*, translates as "wave." The literal English translation of *tsunami* is "harbor wave." The Japanese islands are susceptible to tsunamis generated by earthquakes and undersea volcanoes anywhere around the rim of the Pacific Ocean.

Science Puzzlers, Twisters & Teasers Worksheet 20

Guided Reading Audio CD
English or Spanish, Chapter 20

CHAPTER 20 The Energy of Waves

This Really Happened!

On March 27, 1964, the most powerful earthquake ever recorded on the North American continent rocked Alaska. The quake started on land near the city of Anchorage, but the seismic waves spread quickly in all directions, toppling buildings and ripping up roads.

The earthquake created a series of waves called tsunamis (tsoo NAH mees) in the Gulf of Alaska. In the deep water of the Gulf, the tsunamis were short and widely separated. But as these waves entered the shallow water surrounding Kodiak Island, off the coast of Alaska, they became taller and closer together. One of the tsunamis rose to a height of nearly 30 m! That's as tall as an eight-story building.

The powerful tsunamis pounded everything in their path. Eighty-one fishing boats were destroyed, and 86 others were damaged in the town of Kodiak. The destructive forces of the earthquake and tsunamis killed 21 people and caused $10 million in damage to Kodiak, making this the worst marine disaster in the town's 200-year history.

A tsunami is a dramatic example of the energy of waves. But waves affect your life in many common and less harmful ways. In fact, whenever you listen to music, talk with your friends, or watch a sunrise, you are experiencing the energy of waves. Read on to find out more about waves and how they affect your life every day.

This Really Happened!

Some scientists believe that a series of earthquakes near New Madrid, Missouri, in 1811 and 1812 may have been more powerful than the 1964 earthquake in Alaska. The first quake in New Madrid happened at around 2:00 A.M. on December 16, 1811. These quakes rang church bells as far away as Boston and were felt in Charleston, South Carolina. The quakes caused giant waves to move up the Mississippi river, making the river appear to flow backward. Loss of life was minimal because the area was sparsely populated in 1811. Seismographs didn't exist in 1811, so scientists will never know whether these quakes were actually stronger than the 1964 quake in Alaska.

What Do You Think?

In your ScienceLog, try to answer the following questions based on what you already know:

1. What is a wave?
2. What properties do all waves have?
3. What can happen when waves interact?

Making Waves

There are many types of waves, but you are probably most familiar with water waves. All waves behave in similar ways, so you can use water waves to predict what might happen with other types of waves.

Procedure

1. Spread **newspapers** on a table, and place a **wide pan** in the center of the table.
2. Fill the pan with **water** to a depth of 3 cm.
3. When the water is still, tap the surface of the water with the eraser end of a **pencil**. In what direction do the waves travel?
4. Tap the water again with the pencil, and watch what happens to a wave when it hits the side of the pan. Try this several times. Write your observations in your ScienceLog.
5. Place a **cork** in the center of the pan. Try to move the cork to the edge of the pan by making waves with the pencil.
6. Carefully empty the pan, and clean up any spilled water.

Analysis

7. The source of the energy of the water waves you observed was your hand. In what direction was the energy transmitted?
8. In step 4, you observed the *reflection* of water waves. How is this similar to the reflection of light off a mirror?
9. Describe the motion of the cork in step 5. Did the cork move with the wave? Explain your observations.

What Do You Think?

Accept all reasonable responses.

Students will have a chance to revise their answers in the Chapter Review under NOW What Do You Think?

Investigate!

MATERIALS

FOR EACH GROUP:
- newspaper
- wide pan
- water
- pencil
- cork

Safety Caution: Students should wear aprons for this activity.

It is best to use a 23 × 30 cm baking pan with sides 5 to 8 cm tall. The sides must be tall so that the water can be at least 3 cm deep. (Waves in shallow water may be difficult to observe).

This activity can also be done in a glass pan on an overhead projector.

Directed Reading Worksheet 20

Visit www.si.edu/hrw for additional on-line resources.

Answers to Investigate

3. The waves travel in all directions.
4. Students will see the reflection of the water waves bouncing off the side of the pan. If the pan does not have smooth sides, students will not see a smooth reflection. You can provide a smooth surface by propping a flat ruler up in the pan with some clay or by leaning a piece of glass against the side of the pan.
5. The cork should not move to the edge of the pan.
7. The energy, like the waves, travels away from the source (hand) in all directions.
8. Light bounces off mirrors just as the water waves bounced off the side of the pan.
9. The cork bobbed up and down (or moved in small circles). The waves traveled horizontally. (Students may indicate directions such as "forward" or "left/right".)

Chapter 20 • The Energy of Waves **509**

SECTION 1

Focus

The Nature of Waves

In this section, students learn that waves are a means of transmitting energy. Students learn about different types of waves and their properties.

Bellringer

Have students answer the following question:

What do you think of when you hear the word *wave*? In your ScienceLog, write a brief description of what you think a wave is. Then write a short paragraph describing a time you might have experienced waves.

Discuss with students some of their answers.

1) Motivate

DEMONSTRATION

Show students a video or photographs of people surfing the giant waves of California, Hawaii, South Africa, or Australia. Explain that this section introduces basic concepts about waves but that the waves that "break" as surfers ride them are not covered—scientists still do not fully understand why waves break. Remind students that there are still natural phenomena that scientists do not fully understand. Studying waves around the world might make a fun career!

Directed Reading Worksheet 20 Section 1

Section 1

Terms to Learn
wave
medium
transverse wave
longitudinal wave

What You'll Do

- Describe how waves transfer energy without transferring matter.
- Distinguish between waves that require a medium and waves that do not.
- Explain the difference between transverse and longitudinal waves.

QuickLab

Energetic Waves

1. Tie one end of a piece of **rope or string** to the back of a **chair**.
2. Hold the other end in one hand, and stand away from the chair so that the rope is almost straight but is not pulled tight.
3. Move the rope up and down quickly to create a single wave. Try this several times.
4. Which way does the wave move? How does the rope move compared with the movement of the wave?
5. Where does the energy of the wave come from?
6. Record your observations and answers in your ScienceLog.

TRY at HOME

The Nature of Waves

Imagine that your family has just returned home from a day at the beach. You had fun, but you are hungry from playing in the ocean under a hot sun. You put some leftover pizza in the microwave for dinner, and you turn on the radio. Just then, the phone rings. It's your best friend calling to find out if you've done your math homework yet.

In the events described above, how many different waves were present? Believe it or not, at least five can be identified! Can you name them? Here's a hint: A **wave** is any disturbance that transmits energy through matter or space. Okay, here are the answers: water waves in the ocean; microwaves inside the microwave oven; light waves from the sun; radio waves transmitted to the radio; and sound waves from the radio, telephone, and voices. Don't worry if you didn't get very many. You will be able to name them all after you read this section.

Waves Carry Energy

Energy can be carried away from its source by a wave. However, the material through which the wave travels does not move with the energy. For example, sound waves often travel through air, but the air does not travel with the sound. If air were to travel with sound, you would feel a rush of air every time you heard the phone ring! **Figure 1** illustrates how waves carry energy but not matter.

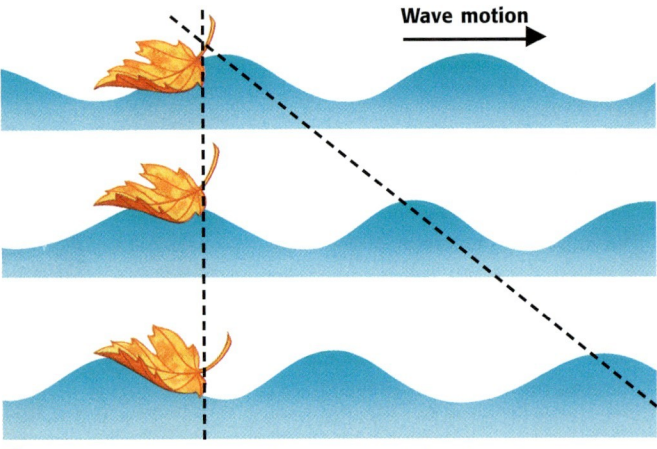

Figure 1 *Waves on a pond move toward the shore, but the water and the leaf floating on the surface do not move with the wave.*

QuickLab

This QuickLab works best if rope is used rather than string.

Answers to QuickLab

4. The wave moves from one end of the rope to the other. Each piece of rope moves up and down, that is, in a direction different from the wave. (If students have difficulty observing this, tie a piece of yarn to the rope, and have students watch only the yarn while waves are being made. The yarn will clearly move only up and down.)

5. The energy of the wave comes from the students shaking the rope.

As a wave travels, it uses its energy to do work on everything in its path. For example, the waves in a pond do work on the water to make it move up and down. The waves also do work on anything floating on the water's surface—for example, boats and ducks bob up and down with waves.

Energy Transfer Through a Medium Some waves transfer energy by the vibration of particles in a medium. A **medium** is a substance through which a wave can travel. A medium can be a solid, a liquid, or a gas. The plural of *medium* is *media*.

When a particle vibrates (moves back and forth, as in **Figure 2**), it can pass its energy to a particle next to it. As a result, the second particle will vibrate in a way similar to the first particle. In this way, energy is transmitted through a medium.

Sound waves require a medium. Sound energy travels by the vibration of particles in liquids, solids, and gases. If there are no particles to vibrate, no sound is possible. For example, if you put an alarm clock inside a jar and remove all the air from the jar to create a vacuum, you will not be able to hear the alarm.

Other waves that require a medium include ocean waves, which travel through water, and waves on guitar and cello strings. Waves that require a medium are called *mechanical waves*. **Figure 3** shows the effect of another mechanical wave.

Figure 2 *A vibration is one complete back-and-forth motion of an object.*

Figure 3 *Seismic waves travel through the ground. The 1964 earthquake in Alaska changed the features of this area.*

2 Teach

READING STRATEGY

Prediction Guide Before students read this section, ask them whether the following statements are true or false:

- Light waves are mechanical waves because they must travel in a medium. (false)
- In space, no one can hear an explosion. (true)
- Water waves are a combination of longitudinal and transverse waves. (true)

USING THE FIGURE

Discussion Encourage students to imagine that they are on the leaf shown in **Figure 1.** Ask them to describe their motions. Ask them how they could get to shore. (They would have to paddle.) Would the waves carry them to shore? (no)

Teacher Note: Explain to students that in **Figure 1** the diagonal line shows the motion of a wave as it travels across a pond, and the vertical line shows that the leaf does not move with the wave. Sheltered English

---

MISCONCEPTION ALERT

Students may believe that sounds can be heard in a vacuum. In many science-fiction movies, explosions and other sounds are heard in outer space. This is scientifically inaccurate.

Section 1 • The Nature of Waves **511**

2 Teach, continued

REAL-WORLD CONNECTION

Microwave Ovens Microwave ovens use electromagnetic waves to heat food. When the microwave energy penetrates a food item in a microwave oven, some of the energy from the waves causes water molecules to vibrate rapidly. The vibrating molecules are converting kinetic energy to thermal energy, which warms the rest of the particles in the food by conduction.

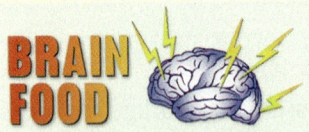

Albert Einstein, perhaps the world's most famous scientist, proposed that electromagnetic radiation could be viewed as a stream of particles, rather than as a wave of energy. He called these particles photons. In fact, Einstein proposed that energy has mass and that an electromagnetic wave can be viewed as a stream of particles that have mass. Experiments have proved that Einstein was right.

Answer to Self-Check

Mechanical waves require a medium; electromagnetic waves do not.

You can see distant objects in space using electromagnetic waves. Turn to page 530 to learn how.

Light waves from some stars and galaxies travel distances so great that they can be expressed only in light-years. A light-year is the distance that light travels in a year. Some of the light waves from these stars have traveled billions of light-years before reaching Earth. This means that the light that we see today from some distant stars left the star's surface before the Earth was formed.

Energy Transfer Without a Medium Some waves can transfer energy without traveling through a medium. Visible light is an example of a wave that doesn't require a medium. Other examples include microwaves produced by microwave ovens, TV and radio signals, and X rays used by dentists and doctors. Waves that do not require a medium are called *electromagnetic waves.*

Although electromagnetic waves do not require a medium, they can travel through substances such as air, water, and glass. However, they travel fastest through empty space. Light from the sun is a type of electromagnetic wave. **Figure 4** shows that light waves from the sun can travel through both space and matter to support life on Earth.

Figure 4 Light waves from the sun travel more than 100 million kilometers through nearly empty space, then more than 300 km through the atmosphere, and then another 10 m through water to support life in and around a coral reef.

 Self-Check

How do mechanical waves differ from electromagnetic waves? *(See page 724 to check your answer.)*

Types of Waves

Waves can be classified based on the direction in which the particles of the medium vibrate compared with the direction in which the waves travel. The two main types of waves are transverse waves and longitudinal (LAHN juh TOOD nuhl) waves. In certain conditions, a transverse wave and a longitudinal wave can combine to form another type of wave, called a surface wave.

Transverse Waves Waves in which the particles vibrate with an up-and-down motion are called **transverse waves.** *Transverse* means "moving across." The particles in a transverse wave move across, or perpendicular to, the direction that the wave is traveling. To be *perpendicular* means to be "at right angles." Try the MathBreak to practice identifying perpendicular lines.

A wave moving on a rope is an example of a transverse wave. In **Figure 5,** you can see that the points along the rope vibrate perpendicular to the direction the wave is traveling. The highest point of a transverse wave is called a *crest,* and the lowest point between each crest is called a *trough.* Although electromagnetic waves do not travel by vibrating particles in a medium, all electromagnetic waves are classified as transverse waves.

MATH BREAK

Perpendicular Lines

If the angle between two lines is 90°, the lines are said to be perpendicular. The figure below shows a set of perpendicular lines.

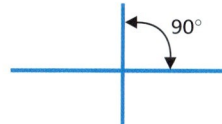

Look at the objects around you. Identify five objects with perpendicular lines or edges and five objects that do not have perpendicular lines. Sketch these objects in your ScienceLog.

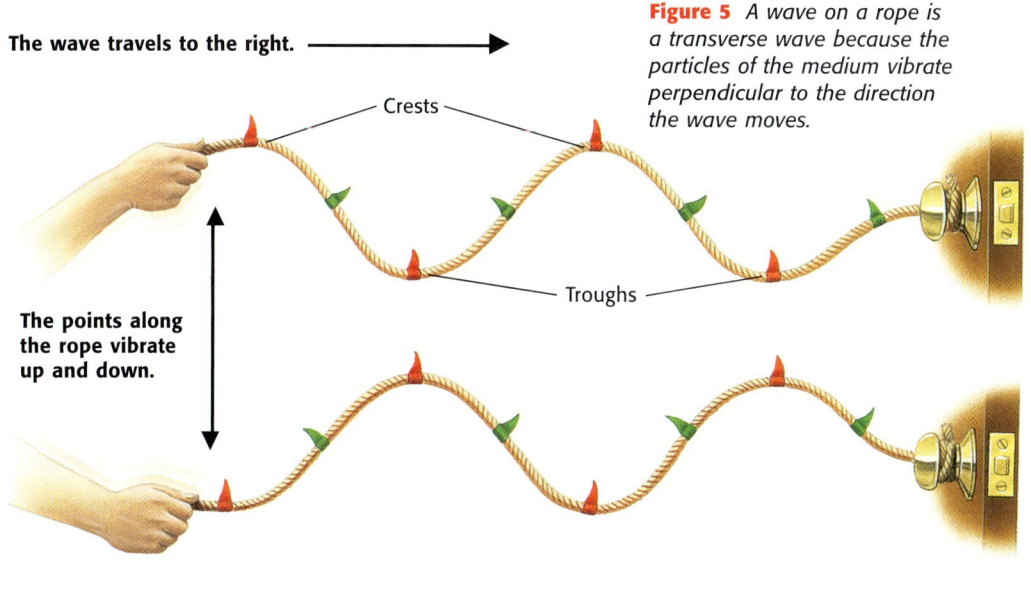

The wave travels to the right. ⟶

The points along the rope vibrate up and down.

Crests

Troughs

Figure 5 *A wave on a rope is a transverse wave because the particles of the medium vibrate perpendicular to the direction the wave moves.*

Multicultural CONNECTION

Hertha Marks Ayrton (1854–1923) was a British physicist. Her first accomplishment was inventing and patenting the line divider, a tool for architects. Her primary interests were the electric arc and certain sand ripples found on beaches. The ripples form as a result of wave action along the shore. The electric arc was widely used for lighting. Ayrton was the first woman to read a research paper to the Royal Society. Although Ayrton could not become a member of the society because she was a woman, she was awarded the Hughes Medal for her research on the electric arc and sand ripples. Have interested students write a research paper about Ayrton's life and research.

Answers to MATHBREAK

Accept all reasonable answers. Some possible answers:

perpendicular lines: corners of books, paper, the room, desks, and tiles on floors

no perpendicular lines: cups, globe, fruit, balls, plates

CONNECT TO EARTH SCIENCE

Use Teaching Transparency 131 to show students how earthquakes generate waves similar to transverse waves (called *secondary waves*) and longitudinal waves (called *primary waves*).

MISCONCEPTION ALERT

In this chapter, transverse waves are often represented as moving up and down. However, students should understand that not all transverse waves move in a vertical plane. A transverse wave is any wave in which the particles of the medium vibrate perpendicularly to the direction the wave moves.

Teaching Transparency 280 "Transverse Waves"

Teaching Transparency 131 "Primary and Secondary Waves" LINK TO EARTH SCIENCE

3) Extend

USING THE FIGURE

Ask the students to look at **Figures 5** and **6.** Have them try to describe the similarities between a trough and a rarefaction and between a crest and compression. (A trough is the low point of a transverse wave, and a rarefaction is the area of least density in a longitudinal wave. A crest is the high point of a transverse wave, and a compression is the area of greatest density in a longitudinal wave.) **Sheltered English**

CONNECT TO LIFE SCIENCE

Ears are pretty amazing. Sound waves (a type of longitudinal wave) travel down the ear canal, where they strike the eardrum, causing it to vibrate. Use the demonstration below to show what a longitudinal wave is.

DEMONSTRATION

1. Secure one end of a coiled spring toy. Either tape the end to a vertical surface or have a student hold it. Tie small pieces of yarn to a few of the coils (to make the wave motion more apparent).
2. Stretch the spring across a horizontal surface, such as a counter top.
3. Move the free end of the toy back and forth in a regular rhythm toward the secured end. Students should see compressions and rarefactions traveling down the spring.

Teaching Transparency 280
"Longitudinal Waves"

Longitudinal Waves In a **longitudinal wave**, the particles of the medium vibrate back and forth along the path that the wave travels. You can create a longitudinal wave on a spring, as shown in **Figure 6.**

When you push on the end of the spring, the coils of the spring are crowded together. A section of a longitudinal wave where the particles are crowded together is called a *compression*. When you pull back on the end of the spring, the coils are less crowded than normal. A section where the particles are less crowded than normal is called a *rarefaction* (RER uh FAK shuhn).

Compressions and rarefactions travel along a longitudinal wave much in the way the crests and troughs of a transverse wave move from one end to the other, as shown in **Figure 7.**

Figure 6 Pushing a spring back and forth creates a longitudinal wave.

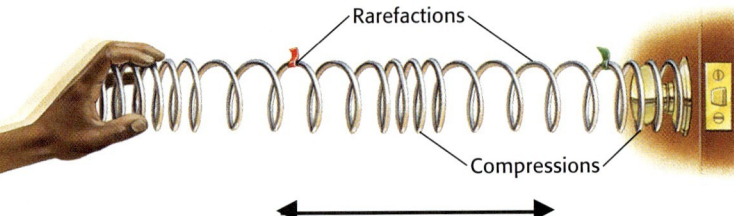

The coils of the spring move back and forth but do not travel with the wave.

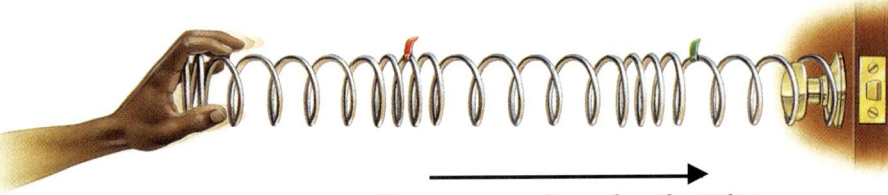

The wave moves forward on the spring.

Figure 7 The compressions of a longitudinal wave are like the crests of a transverse wave, and the rarefactions are like troughs.

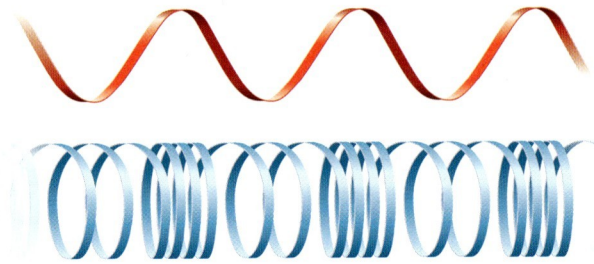

Homework

Concept Mapping Have students create and label a concept map of longitudinal waves and transverse waves. Students should include the terms *compressions*, *rarefactions*, *crests*, and *troughs* in their concept map.

internetconnect
TOPIC: Types of Waves
GO TO: www.scilinks.org
*sci*LINKS NUMBER: HSTP490

A sound wave is an example of a longitudinal wave. Sound waves travel by compressions and rarefactions of air particles. **Figure 8** shows how a vibrating drumhead creates these compressions and rarefactions.

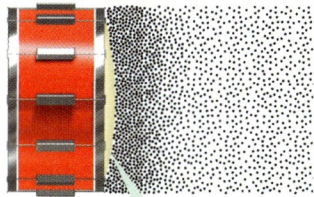
When the drumhead moves out after being hit, a compression is created in the air particles.

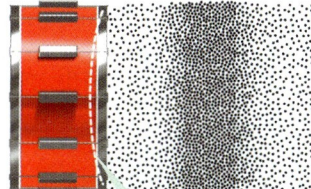
When the drumhead moves back in, a rarefaction is created.

Figure 8 Sound energy is carried away from a drum in a longitudinal wave.

Combinations of Waves When waves occur at or near the boundary between two media, a transverse wave and a longitudinal wave can combine to form a *surface wave*. An example is shown in **Figure 9**. Surface waves look like transverse waves, but the particles of the medium in a surface wave move in circles rather than up and down. The particles move forward at the crest of each wave and move backward at the trough. The arrows in Figure 9 show the movement of particles in a surface wave.

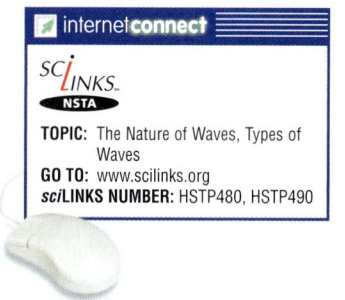

Figure 9 Ocean waves are surface waves because they travel at the water's surface, where the water meets the air. A floating bottle shows the motion of particles in a surface wave.

REVIEW

1. Describe how transverse waves differ from longitudinal waves.
2. Why can't you cause a floating leaf to move to the edge of a pond by throwing stones behind it?
3. Explain why supernova explosions in space can be seen but not heard on Earth.
4. **Applying Concepts** Sometimes people at a sports event do "the wave." Do you think this is a real example of a wave? Why or why not?

internetconnect
SC*LINKS*
NSTA
TOPIC: The Nature of Waves, Types of Waves
GO TO: www.scilinks.org
*sci*LINKS NUMBER: HSTP480, HSTP490

---

4) Close

Quiz

1. A wave is a disturbance that travels through _____ or _____. (space, matter)
2. A wave carries _____. (energy)
3. Waves that require a medium are called _____ waves. (mechanical)
4. Waves that do not require a medium are called _____ waves. (electromagnetic)
5. Waves produced by a combination of longitudinal and transverse waves are called _____ waves. (surface)

ALTERNATIVE ASSESSMENT

Provide students with markers, construction paper, yarn, glue, and scissors. Have students use these materials to illustrate the following three wave types: longitudinal, transverse, and surface. Students should label their waves and the medium (if any) through which the wave is moving and should indicate compressions, rarefactions, crests, and troughs.

REAL-WORLD CONNECTION

Seismic waves consist of longitudinal, transverse, and surface waves. Geophysicists searching for oil and gas deposits use seismic waves to study underground rock formations. A mechanical device produces seismic shock waves that reflect off the various layers of rock. These reflections produce a profile of the different layers. From the profiles, geophysicists can locate formations where oil and gas are usually found.

▼ Answers to Review

1. As a transverse wave moves through a medium, the particles vibrate at right angles to the direction of the wave. In longitudinal waves, the particles vibrate back and forth along the wave's path.
2. Waves transfer energy but not matter. The leaf would just bob up and down; it would not move with the wave toward the shore.
3. Sound waves are mechanical waves and therefore cannot travel through space. However, visible light is an electromagnetic wave and therefore can travel through space.
4. No; the people stand up on their own and then sit down again. No energy is transmitted from one person to the next.

SECTION 2

Focus

Properties of Waves

This section introduces properties common to all types of waves. Students explore frequency, wavelength, amplitude, energy content, and speed of waves.

 **Bellringer**

Before class, draw a longitudinal wave and a transverse wave on the board or the overhead projector. Have students draw the waves and label the parts of each.

1) Motivate

DEMONSTRATION

Pluck a rubber band so that it makes a tone. Then change the length of the rubber band so that the tone changes pitch. Ask students to explain what caused the pitch change. Have them observe the wave (the vibration) in the rubber band as you repeat the demonstration. Lead students to the conclusion that the tone changes as the frequency of the wave changes. Explain that the frequency is the number of waves produced in a given amount of time. (You can also use a guitar for this demonstration.)

 **Directed Reading Worksheet 20** Section 2

Section 2

Properties of Waves

Terms to Learn
amplitude frequency
wavelength wave speed

What You'll Do
◆ Identify and describe four wave properties.
◆ Explain how amplitude and frequency are related to the energy of a wave.

Imagine that you are canoeing on a lake. You decide to stop paddling for a while and relax in the sunshine. The breeze makes small waves on the water. These waves are short and close together, and they have little effect on the canoe. Then a speedboat roars past you. The speedboat creates tall, widely spaced waves that cause your canoe to rock wildly. So much for relaxation!

Waves have properties that are useful for description and comparison. In this example, you could compare properties such as the height of the waves and the distance between the waves. In this section, you will learn about the properties of waves and how to measure them.

Amplitude

If you tie one end of a rope to the back of a chair, you can create waves by moving the other end up and down. If you move the rope a small distance, you will make a short wave. If you move the rope a greater distance, you will make a tall wave.

The property of waves that is related to the height of a wave is known as amplitude. The **amplitude** of a wave is the maximum distance the wave vibrates from its rest position. The rest position is where the particles of a medium stay when there are no disturbances. The larger the amplitude is, the taller the wave is. **Figure 10** shows how the amplitude of a transverse wave is measured.

Figure 10 *The amplitude of a transverse wave is measured from the rest position to the crest or to the trough of the wave.*

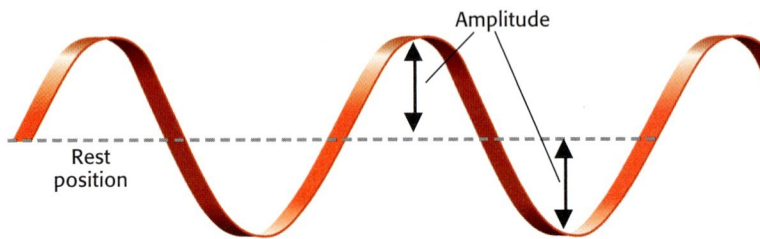

MISCONCEPTION ALERT

The amplitude of a longitudinal wave is usually measured as a difference in pressure (air pressure or otherwise) between the compressions and rarefactions. Longitudinal waves are not discussed in terms of pressure in the text, so this method of measuring amplitude is not discussed.

516 Chapter 20 • The Energy of Waves

Larger Amplitude Means More Energy When using a rope to make waves, you have to work harder to create a wave with a large amplitude than to create one with a small amplitude. This is because it takes more energy to move the rope farther from its rest position. Therefore, a wave with a large amplitude carries more energy than a wave with a small amplitude, as shown in **Figure 11.**

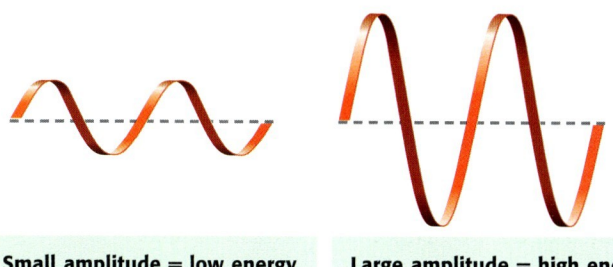

Figure 11 *The amplitude of a wave depends on the amount of energy.*

Small amplitude = low energy   Large amplitude = high energy

Wavelength

Another property of waves is wavelength. A **wavelength** is the distance between any two adjacent crests or compressions in a series of waves. The distance between two adjacent troughs or rarefactions is also a wavelength. In fact, the wavelength can be measured from any point on one wave to the corresponding point on the next wave. All of the measurements will be equal, as shown in **Figure 12.**

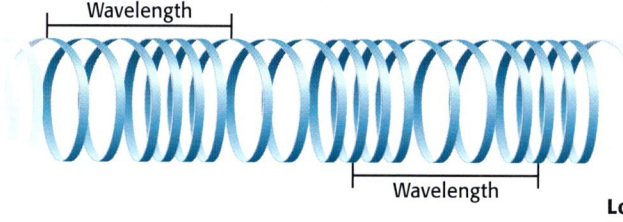

Figure 12 *Wavelengths measured from any two corresponding points are the same for a given wave.*

Longitudinal wave

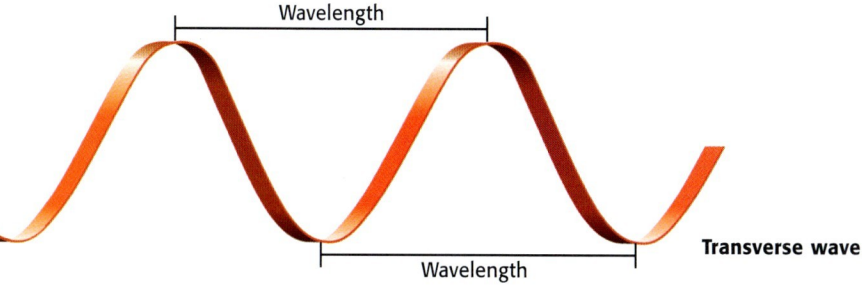

Transverse wave

IS THAT A FACT!

The wavelength of visible light is in the range of 10^{-7} m. For X rays and gamma rays, wavelengths are 10^{-9} m to 10^{-12} m. Radio waves are much longer and have wavelengths from 3,000 m to 30 cm.

2) Teach

READING STRATEGY

Prediction Guide Before students read this page, ask them:

Based on your experiences with water waves and from pictures of tsunamis, what do you think the height of a wave indicates?

Ask the students to explain their predictions.

MEETING INDIVIDUAL NEEDS

Learners Having Difficulty Provide students with yarn and tape. Have them use the yarn to construct a transverse wave similar to the one on these two pages. Ask them to increase the amplitude of the wave while keeping the frequency constant. (Students will need excess yarn for this step.) Have them explain what increasing the amplitude represents. Then have them change the frequency, and ask them what happened to the wavelength when they changed the frequency. (The wavelength decreased with an increase in frequency, and it increased with a decrease in frequency.)
Sheltered English

Teaching Transparency 281
"Wavelength"

TOPIC: Properties of Waves
GO TO: www.scilinks.org
*sci*LINKS NUMBER: HSTP485

Section 2 • Properties of Waves   **517**

3) Extend

QuickLab

MATERIAL

For Each Group:
- coiled spring toy or piece of rope

Answers to QuickLab

3. To increase the amplitude of the wave, the spring must be shaken farther with bigger motions. That is, the student must provide more energy to the wave. There should be no effect on wavelength when amplitude increases. (It may be difficult to increase amplitude without increasing frequency. If students increase frequency significantly, wavelength will change.)

4. The wavelength should become shorter as the frequency is increased.

MISCONCEPTION ALERT

One hertz is often defined as one cycle per second. In this chapter, one hertz is defined as one wave per second. However, the unit expression is written 1 Hz = 1/s instead of 1 Hz = 1 wave/s to make the cancellation of units easier.

Going Further

Write the frequencies of local radio stations on the board. For example, 90.5 MHz is equal to 90,500,000 Hz. Ask students to calculate the wavelength of their favorite stations. Students will need to know the speed of light, $c = 3 \times 10^8$ m/s. The formula becomes $c = \lambda \times f$, where students know c and f and calculate λ. Have students rank the stations from lowest frequency to highest frequency and from longest wavelength to shortest wavelength.

QuickLab

Springy Waves

1. Hold a **coiled spring toy** on the floor between you and a classmate so that the spring is straight. This is the rest position.

2. Move one end of the spring from side to side at a constant rate. The number of times you move it in a complete cycle (back and forth) each second is the frequency.

3. Keeping the frequency the same, increase the amplitude. What did you have to do? How did the change in amplitude affect the wavelength?

4. Now shake the spring back and forth about twice as fast (to double the frequency). What happens to the wavelength?

5. Record your observations and answers in your ScienceLog.

Spring into action! Find the speed of waves on a spring toy. Turn to page 708 of the LabBook.

LabBook PG 706
Wave Energy and Speed

Teaching Transparency 281
"Frequency"

Frequency

Think about making rope waves again. The number of waves that you can make in 1 second depends on how quickly you move the rope. If you move the rope slowly, you make only a small number of waves each second. If you move it quickly, you make a large number of waves. The number of waves produced in a given amount of time is the **frequency** of the wave.

Measuring Frequency You can measure frequency by counting either the number of crests or the number of troughs that pass a point in a certain amount of time. If you were measuring the frequency of a longitudinal wave, you would count the number of compressions or rarefactions. Frequency is usually expressed in *hertz* (Hz). For waves, one hertz equals one wave per second (1 Hz = 1/s). The frequency of a wave is related to its wavelength, as shown in **Figure 13**.

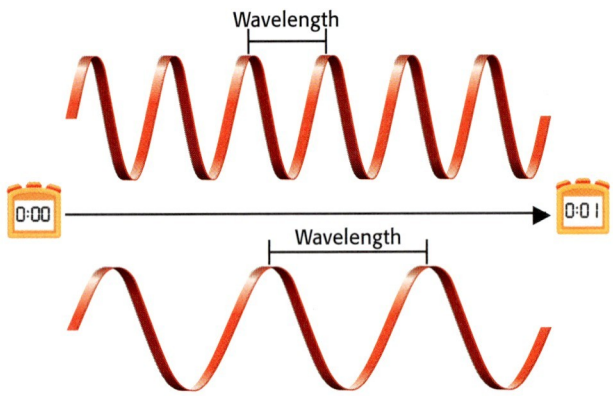

Figure 13 At a given speed, the higher the frequency is, the shorter the wavelength.

Higher Frequency Means More Energy It takes more energy to vibrate a rope quickly than to vibrate a rope slowly. If the amplitudes are equal, high-frequency waves carry more energy than low-frequency waves. In Figure 13, the top wave carries more energy than the bottom wave.

Because frequency and wavelength are so closely related, you can also relate the amount of energy carried by a wave to the wavelength. In general, a wave with a short wavelength carries more energy than a wave with a long wavelength.

IS THAT A FACT!

Humans normally hear sounds with frequencies from 20 to 20,000 Hz.

Wave Speed

Another property of waves is **wave speed**—the speed at which a wave travels. Speed is the distance traveled over time, so wave speed can be found by measuring the distance a single crest or compression travels in a given amount of time.

The speed of a wave depends on the medium in which the wave is traveling. For example, the wave speed of sound in air is about 340 m/s, but the wave speed of sound in steel is about 5,200 m/s.

Calculating Wave Speed Wave speed can be calculated using wavelength and frequency. The relationship between wave speed (v), wavelength (λ, the Greek letter lambda), and frequency (f) is expressed in the following equation:

$$v = \lambda \times f$$

You can see in **Figure 14** how this equation can be used to determine wave speed. Try the MathBreak to practice using this equation.

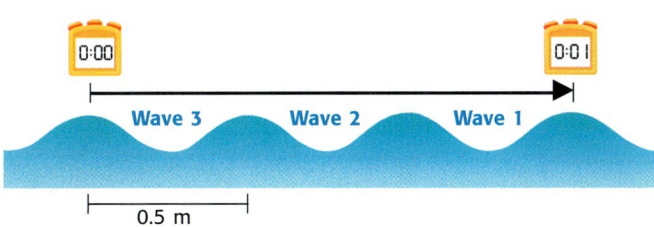

$\lambda = 0.5$ m $f = 3$ Hz (3/s)
$v = 0.5$ m $\times$ 3 Hz $= 1.5$ m/s

Figure 14 To calculate wave speed, multiply the wavelength by the number of waves that pass in 1 second (frequency).

MATH BREAK

Wave Calculations

The equation for wave speed can be rearranged to determine wavelength (λ) or frequency (f).

$$\lambda = \frac{v}{f} \qquad f = \frac{v}{\lambda}$$

You can determine the wavelength of a wave with a speed of 20 m/s and a frequency of 4 Hz like this:

$\lambda = \frac{v}{f}$

$\lambda = 20$ m/s $\div$ 4 Hz

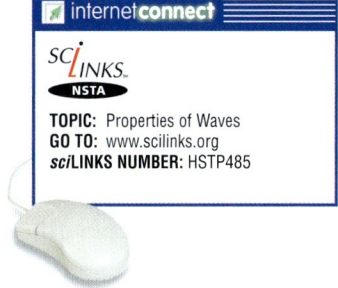

$\lambda = 5$ m

Now It's Your Turn

1. What is the frequency of a wave if it has a speed of 12 cm/s and a wavelength of 3 cm?
2. A wave has a frequency of 5 Hz and a wave speed of 18 m/s. What is its wavelength?

REVIEW

1. Draw a transverse wave, and identify its amplitude and wavelength.
2. What is the speed (v) of a wave that has a wavelength (λ) of 2 m and a frequency (f) of 6 Hz?
3. **Inferring Conclusions** Compare the amplitudes and frequencies of the two types of waves discussed at the beginning of this section, and infer which type of wave carried the most energy. Explain your answer.

internet connect

SC_**LINKS**_
NSTA

TOPIC: Properties of Waves
GO TO: www.scilinks.org
sciLINKS NUMBER: HSTP485

---

4) Close

Quiz

1. If wave speed is constant, as frequency increases, the _____ decreases. (wavelength)
2. _____ is the number of vibrations per second. (Frequency)
3. The distance between two corresponding points on consecutive waves is one _____. (wavelength)
4. As frequency increases, the _____ of the wave also increases. (energy)

ALTERNATIVE ASSESSMENT

Concept Mapping Have students make a concept map explaining how amplitude and frequency are related to the energy of a wave.

LabBook PG 708
Wave Speed, Frequency, and Wavelength

Answers to MATHBREAK

1. $f = \frac{v}{\lambda} = \frac{12 \text{ cm/s}}{3 \text{ cm}} = 4/s = 4$ Hz

2. $\lambda = \frac{v}{f} = \frac{18 \text{ m/s}}{5 \text{ Hz}} = \frac{18 \text{ m/s}}{5/s}$
   $= 3.6$ m

 Teaching Transparency 282
"Wave Speed, Wavelength, and Frequency"

 Reinforcement Worksheet 20
"Getting on the Same Frequency"

 Math Skills Worksheet 5
"Dividing Whole Numbers with Long Division"

Section 2 • Properties of Waves

Answers to Review

1.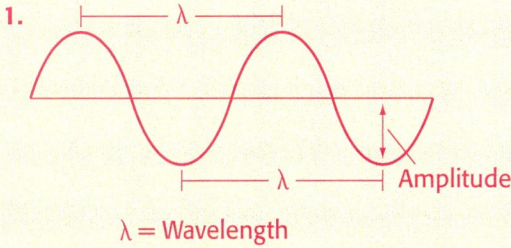
   λ = Wavelength

2. $v = \lambda \times f = 2$ m $\times$ 6 Hz $= 12$ m/s

3. The amplitude of the speedboat waves was larger than that of the breeze waves. The frequency of the speedboat waves was lower than that of the breeze waves. However, the speedboat waves had more effect on the boat, so they most likely had more energy.

SECTION 3

Focus

Wave Interactions

In this section, students explore how waves reflect, refract, or diffract when interacting with a different medium or barrier. Students also learn how waves interfere with other waves.

Bellringer

Write *v*, *f*, and λ on the board. Have students write each symbol, what each symbol stands for, and how each symbol relates to the other two.

1) Motivate

ACTIVITY

Use two different types of spring. A long, tightly coiled spring, often called a snake, and a large, coiled spring toy are ideal. Using a strong cord, tie one end of each spring together, forming a "spring rope." Have two volunteers sit about 3 m apart on the floor. Have one student hold the spring rope on the floor while the other creates transverse waves by moving the spring from side to side. Ask the class to observe what happens at the boundary between the two springs when a wave passes from one spring to the other spring. (Students should see a change in the wave's speed and wavelength.)

Directed Reading Worksheet 20 Section 3

Section 3

Terms to Learn

reflection   interference
refraction   standing wave
diffraction   resonance

What You'll Do

◆ Describe reflection, refraction, diffraction, and interference.
◆ Compare destructive interference with constructive interference.
◆ Describe resonance, and give examples.

Wave Interactions

Imagine that you wake up early one morning before the sun has risen and go outside. You look up and notice that a full moon is high in the sky, and the stars are twinkling brilliantly, as shown in **Figure 15.** The sky is so clear you can find constellations (groupings of stars), such as the Big Dipper and Cassiopeia, and planets, such as Venus and Mars.

All stars, including the sun, produce light. But planets and the moon do not produce light. So why do they shine so brightly? Light from the sun *reflects* off the planets and the moon. Reflection is one of the wave interactions that you will learn about in this section.

Figure 15 A wave interaction is responsible for this beautiful morning scene.

Figure 16 These water waves are reflecting off the side of the container.

Reflection

Reflection occurs when a wave bounces back after striking a barrier. All waves—including water, sound, and light waves—can be reflected. The reflection of water waves is shown in **Figure 16.** Reflected sound waves are called *echoes*, and light waves reflecting off an object allow you to see that object. For example, light waves from the sun are reflected when they strike the surface of the moon. These reflected waves allow us to enjoy moonlit nights.

IS THAT A FACT!

The reflection of sound is called an *echo*. If you are closer than 15 m to a reflecting wall, you cannot hear an echo. The brain requires a 0.1 second delay to perceive an echo, and at less than 15 m, the sound wave would be reflected back from the wall in less than 0.1 second.

---

520 Chapter 20 • The Energy of Waves

Refraction

Try this simple experiment: place a pencil in a half-filled glass of water. Now look at the pencil from the side. The pencil appears to be broken into two pieces! But when you take the pencil out of the water, it is perfectly fine.

What you observed in this experiment was the result of the refraction of light waves. **Refraction** is the bending of a wave as it passes at an angle from one medium to another.

Remember that the speed of a wave varies depending on the medium in which the wave is traveling. So when a wave moves from one medium to another, the wave's speed changes. When a wave enters a new medium at an angle, the part of the wave that enters first begins traveling at a different speed from the rest of the wave. This causes the wave to bend, as shown in **Figure 17.**

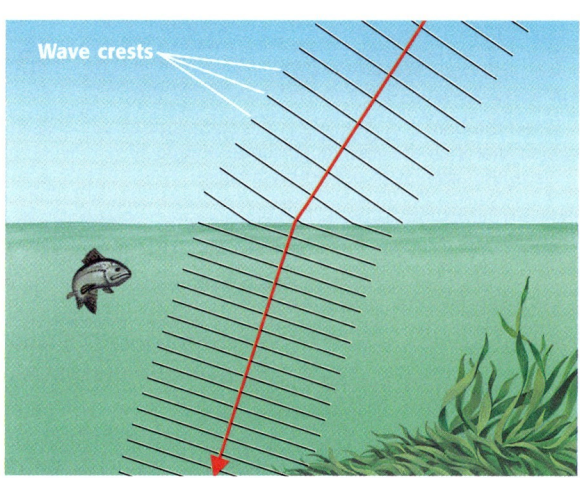

Figure 17 Light waves passing at an angle into a new medium—such as water—are refracted because the speed of the waves changes.

Self-Check

Will a light wave refract if it enters a new medium perpendicular to the surface? Explain. *(See page 724 to check your answer.)*

Diffraction

Suppose you are walking down a city street and you hear music. The sound seems to be coming from around the corner, but you cannot see who is playing the music because the building on the corner blocks your view. Why is it that sound waves travel around a corner better than light waves do?

Most of the time, waves travel in straight lines. For example, a beam of light from a flashlight is fairly straight. But in some circumstances, waves curve or bend when they reach the edge of an object. The bending of waves around a barrier or through an opening is known as **diffraction.**

Activity

Light waves diffract around corners of buildings much less than sound waves. Imagine what would happen if light waves diffracted around corners much more than sound waves. Write a paragraph describing how this would change what you see and hear as you walk around your neighborhood.

TRY at HOME

2 Teach, continued

REAL-WORLD CONNECTION
In some occupations, workers are exposed to noise with amplitudes or frequencies that can be harmful. Now there are headphones available that create destructive interference to cancel the dangerous noise. These headphones receive the noise that the wearer hears, process the sounds, and then produce destructive interference to reduce or cancel the outside noise.

Have students think of and discuss situations in which these headphones would be useful.

Food heated in a microwave oven sometimes has hot spots and cold spots. This problem may be caused by *interference.* Constructive interference, which increases the amplitude of the microwaves, can cause hot spots. Destructive interference, which decreases the amplitude of the waves, can cause cold spots.

MEETING INDIVIDUAL NEEDS
Advanced Learners Have students research AM and FM radio waves. What are the differences between them? In terms of wave interactions, why is it harder to receive FM broadcasts in some places? Why can AM broadcasts be heard for great distances under certain conditions?

Figure 18 Diffraction of Waves

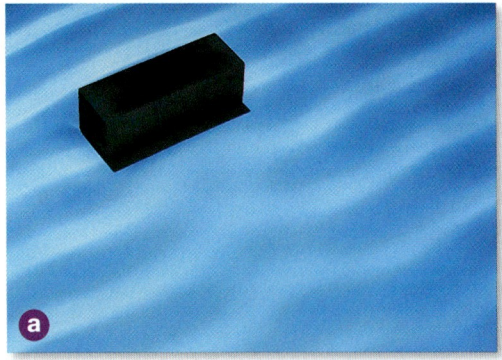

a When the barrier or opening is the same size as or is smaller than the wavelength of an approaching wave, the amount of diffraction is large.

b If the barrier or opening is larger than the wavelength of the wave, there is only a small amount of diffraction.

The amount of diffraction a wave experiences depends on its wavelength and the size of the barrier or opening the wave encounters, as shown in **Figure 18.** You can hear music around the corner of a building because sound waves have long wavelengths and are able to diffract around corners. However, you cannot see who is playing the music because the wavelengths of light waves are much smaller than the building, so light is not diffracted very much.

Interference
You know that all matter has volume. Therefore, objects cannot occupy the same space at the same time. But because waves are energy and not matter, more than one wave can exist in the same place at the same time. In fact, two waves can meet, share the same space, and pass through each other! When two or more waves share the same space, they overlap. The result of two or more waves overlapping is called **interference. Figure 19** shows one situation where waves occupy the same space.

Figure 19 *When sound waves from several instruments combine through interference, the result is a wave with a larger amplitude, which means a louder sound.*

MISCONCEPTION ALERT

Interference occurs only in the region where the waves overlap. After the waves pass through this region, they continue on as if they never met.

522 Chapter 20 • The Energy of Waves

Constructive Interference Increases Amplitude *Constructive interference* occurs when the crests of one wave overlap the crests of another wave or waves. The troughs of the waves also overlap. An example of constructive interference is shown in **Figure 20.** When waves combine in this way, the result is a new wave with higher crests and deeper troughs than the original waves. In other words, the resulting wave has a larger amplitude than the original waves had.

Figure 20 When waves combine by constructive interference, the resulting wave has an amplitude that is larger than those of the original waves. After the waves interfere, they continue traveling in their original directions.

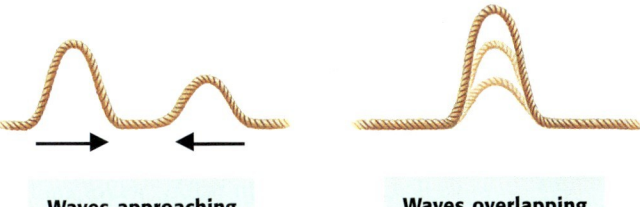
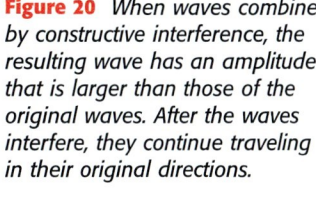
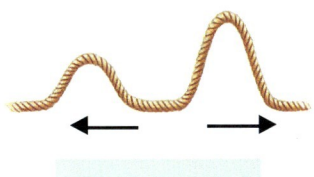

Destructive Interference Decreases Amplitude *Destructive interference* occurs when the crests of one wave and the troughs of another wave overlap. The resulting wave has a smaller amplitude than the original waves had. What do you think happens when the waves involved in destructive interference have the same amplitude? Find out in **Figure 21.**

Figure 21 When two waves with the same amplitude combine by destructive interference, they cancel each other out. This is called total destructive interference.

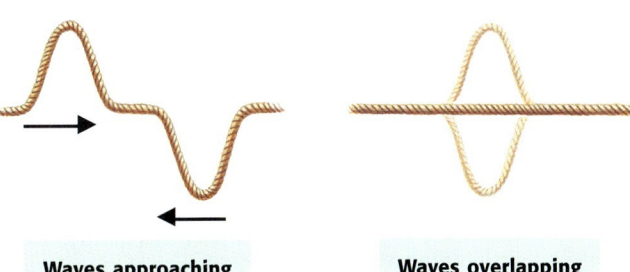
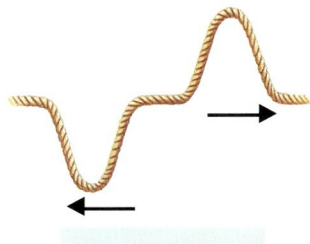

Sound Waves in Movie Theaters

Movie theaters use large screens and several speakers to make your moviegoing experience exciting. Theater designers know that increasing the amplitude of sound waves increases the volume of the sound. In terms of interference, how do you think the positioning of the speakers adds to the excitement?

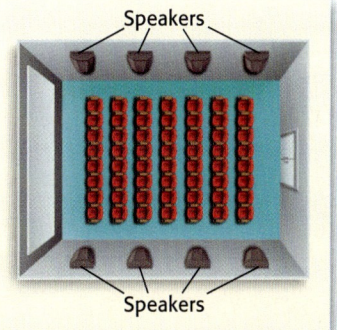

IS THAT A FACT!

In 1962, New York City's Avery Fisher Hall opened, but there were problems with the hall's acoustics. There were too many echoes and dead spots caused by the interfering sound waves. In 1976, the hall's interior was removed and was replaced with an interior that produced better acoustics.

3) Extend

RESEARCH

Encourage students to use the Internet or library sources to research holograms and to prepare a report on their findings. Their reports should include who invented the hologram, how holograms are made using the interference of light, and how to view them.

Homework

Research Resonance is a very important concept in music. Have students conduct research to learn how resonance affects the sounds produced by different musical instruments. Students can share their results by writing a report, by making a poster, or by playing a musical instrument.

Multicultural CONNECTION

The marimba is an instrument of African origin that is similar to a xylophone.

MISCONCEPTION ALERT

The destruction of the Tacoma Narrows Bridge, as shown in **Figure 24,** is often given as an example of simple resonance. (The bridge's nickname was Galloping Gertie because it moved up and down in winds of just 5–7 km/h.) However, the destruction was actually caused by a much more complicated combination of vertical waves and twisting motions.

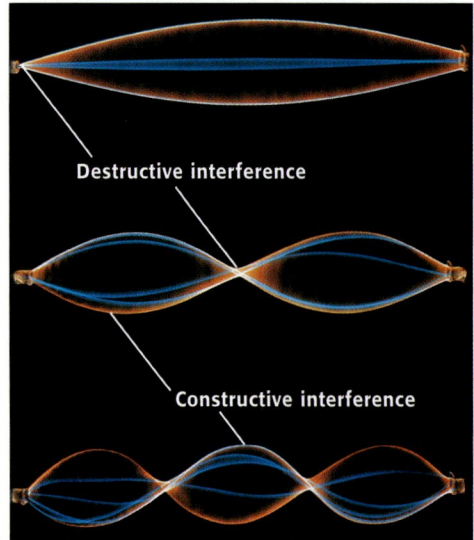

Figure 22 When you move a rope at certain frequencies, you can create different standing waves.

Interference Can Create Standing Waves

If you tie one end of a rope to the back of a chair and move the other end up and down, the waves you create travel down the rope and are reflected back. If you move the rope at certain frequencies, the rope appears to vibrate in loops, as shown in **Figure 22.** The loops result from the interference between the wave you created and the reflected wave. The resulting wave is called a standing wave. A **standing wave** is a wave that forms a stationary pattern in which portions of the wave are at the rest position due to total destructive interference and other portions have a large amplitude due to constructive interference. However, it only *looks* as if the wave is standing still. In reality, waves are traveling in both directions. Standing waves can be formed with transverse waves, as shown here, as well as with longitudinal waves.

One Object Causes Another to Vibrate During Resonance

As shown above, standing waves can occur at more than one frequency. The frequencies at which standing waves are produced are called *resonant frequencies*. When an object vibrating at or near the resonant frequency of a second object causes the second object to vibrate, **resonance** occurs. A resonating object absorbs energy from the vibrating object and therefore vibrates, too. An example of resonance is shown in **Figure 23.**

a The marimba bars are struck with a mallet, causing the bars to vibrate.

b The vibrating bars cause the air in the columns to vibrate.

Figure 23 A marimba produces notes through the resonance of air columns.

c The lengths of the columns have been adjusted so that the resonant frequency of the air column matches the frequency of the bar.

d The air column resonates with the bar, increasing the amplitude of the vibrations to produce a loud note.

IS THAT A FACT!

Earthquakes send out waves that cause Earth's surface to vibrate. In 1985, a severe earthquake occurred in Mexico City. The earthquake was especially destructive because the frequency of the waves matched the natural frequency of many buildings, causing them to vibrate and collapse.

The Tacoma Narrows Bridge Resonance was partially responsible for the destruction of the Tacoma Narrows Bridge, in Washington. The bridge opened in July 1940 and soon earned the nickname Galloping Gertie because of its wavelike motions. These motions were created by wind that blew across the bridge. The wind caused vibrations that were close to a resonant frequency of the bridge. Because the bridge was in resonance, it absorbed a large amount of energy from the wind, which caused it to vibrate with a large amplitude.

On November 7, 1940, a supporting cable slipped, and the bridge began to twist. The twisting of the bridge, combined with high winds, further increased the amplitude of the bridge's motion. Within hours, the amplitude became so great that the bridge collapsed, as shown in **Figure 24**. Luckily, all the people on the bridge that day were able to escape before it crashed into the river below.

BRAIN FOOD

Resonance caused the collapse of a bridge near Manchester, England, in 1831. Cavalry troops marched across the bridge in rhythm with its resonant frequency. This caused the bridge to vibrate with a large amplitude and eventually to fall. Since that time, all troops are ordered to "break step" when they cross a bridge.

Figure 24 The twisting motion that led to the destruction of the bridge was partially caused by resonance.

REVIEW

1. Name two wave interactions that can occur when a wave encounters a barrier.
2. Describe what happens when a wave is refracted.
3. **Inferring Relationships** Sometimes when music is played loudly, you can feel your body shake. Explain what is happening in terms of resonance.

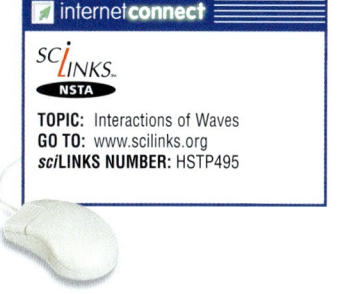

TOPIC: Interactions of Waves
GO TO: www.scilinks.org
*sci*LINKS NUMBER: HSTP495

4) Close

Quiz

1. When a wave bounces back from a barrier, _____ has occurred. (reflection)
2. _____ occurs when a wave bends as it passes at an angle from one medium to a different medium. (Refraction)
3. _____ happens when two or more waves overlap. (Interference)

ALTERNATIVE ASSESSMENT

Concept Mapping Have students create a concept map using as many vocabulary words from this chapter as they can. Then provide groups of students with yarn, poster board, glue, tape, and scissors. Each group should construct a model for the concepts on their map.

Reinforcement Worksheet 20
"Makin' Waves"

Critical Thinking Worksheet 20
"The Case of the Speeding Ticket"

TOPIC: Interactions of Waves
GO TO: www.scilinks.org
*sci*LINKS NUMBER: HSTP495

▼ Answers to Review

1. Reflection and diffraction can occur when a wave encounters a barrier.
2. When a wave enters a new medium at an angle, the part of the wave that enters first changes speed before the rest of the wave. This causes the wave to bend and is called refraction.
3. The frequency of the sound waves is near one of your body's resonant frequencies. This causes your body to vibrate. In other words, your body is in resonance with the music.

Chapter Highlights

Vocabulary Definitions

SECTION 1

wave a disturbance that transmits energy through matter or space

medium a substance through which a wave can travel

transverse wave a wave in which the particles of the wave's medium vibrate perpendicularly to the direction the wave is traveling

longitudinal wave a wave in which the particles of the medium vibrate back and forth along the path that the wave travels

SECTION 2

amplitude the maximum distance a wave vibrates from its rest position

wavelength the distance between one point on a wave and the corresponding point on an adjacent wave in a series of waves; for example, the distance between two adjacent crests or compressions

frequency the number of waves produced in a given amount of time

wave speed the speed at which a wave travels

Chapter Highlights

SECTION 1

Vocabulary
- **wave** (p. 510)
- **medium** (p. 511)
- **transverse wave** (p. 513)
- **longitudinal wave** (p. 514)

Section Notes
- A wave is a disturbance that transmits energy.
- A medium is a substance through which a wave can travel. The particles of a medium do not travel with the wave.
- Waves that require a medium are called mechanical waves. Waves that do not require a medium are called electromagnetic waves.
- Particles in a transverse wave vibrate perpendicular to the direction the wave travels.
- Particles in a longitudinal wave vibrate back and forth in the same direction that the wave travels.
- Transverse and longitudinal waves can combine to form surface waves.

SECTION 2

Vocabulary
- **amplitude** (p. 516)
- **wavelength** (p. 517)
- **frequency** (p. 518)
- **wave speed** (p. 519)

Section Notes
- Amplitude is the maximum distance the particles in a wave vibrate from their rest position. Large-amplitude waves carry more energy than small-amplitude waves.
- Wavelength is the distance between two adjacent crests (or compressions) of a wave.
- Frequency is the number of waves that pass a given point in a given amount of time. High-frequency waves carry more energy than low-frequency waves.

✓ Skills Check

Math Concepts

WAVE-SPEED CALCULATIONS The relationship between wave speed (v), wavelength (λ), and frequency (f) is expressed by the equation:

$$v = \lambda \times f$$

For example, if a wave has a wavelength of 1 m and a frequency of 6 Hz (6/s), the wave speed is calculated as follows:

$$v = 1 \text{ m} \times 6 \text{ Hz} = 1 \text{ m} \times 6/\text{s}$$
$$v = 6 \text{ m/s}$$

Visual Understanding

TRANSVERSE AND LONGITUDINAL WAVES Two common types of waves are transverse waves (shown below) and longitudinal waves. Study Figure 5 on page 513 and Figure 6 on page 514 to review the differences between these two types of waves.

Lab and Activity Highlights

Wave Energy and Speed PG 706

Wave Speed, Frequency, and Wavelength PG 708

 Datasheets for LabBook (blackline masters for these labs)

SECTION 2

- Wave speed is the speed at which a wave travels. Wave speed can be calculated by multiplying the wavelength by the wave's frequency.

Labs

Wave Energy and Speed (p. 706)

Wave Speed, Frequency, and Wavelength (p. 708)

SECTION 3

Vocabulary
reflection (p. 520)
refraction (p. 521)
diffraction (p. 521)
interference (p. 522)
standing wave (p. 524)
resonance (p. 524)

Section Notes

- Waves bounce back after striking a barrier during reflection.
- Refraction is the bending of a wave when it passes at an angle from one medium to another.
- Waves bend around barriers or through openings during diffraction. The amount of diffraction depends on the wavelength of the waves and the size of the barrier or opening.
- The result of two or more waves overlapping is called interference.
- Amplitude increases during constructive interference and decreases during destructive interference.
- Standing waves are waves in which portions of the wave do not move and other portions move with a large amplitude.
- Resonance occurs when a vibrating object causes another object to vibrate at one of its resonant frequencies.

VOCABULARY DEFINITIONS, continued

SECTION 3

reflection the bouncing back of a wave after it strikes a barrier or an object

refraction the bending of a wave as it passes at an angle from one medium to another

diffraction the bending of waves around a barrier or through an opening

interference a wave interaction that occurs when two or more waves overlap

standing wave a wave that forms a stationary pattern in which portions of the wave do not move and other portions move with a large amplitude

resonance what occurs when an object vibrating at or near a resonant frequency of a second object causes the second object to vibrate

 Vocabulary Review Worksheet 20

 Blackline masters of these Chapter Highlights can be found in the **Study Guide.**

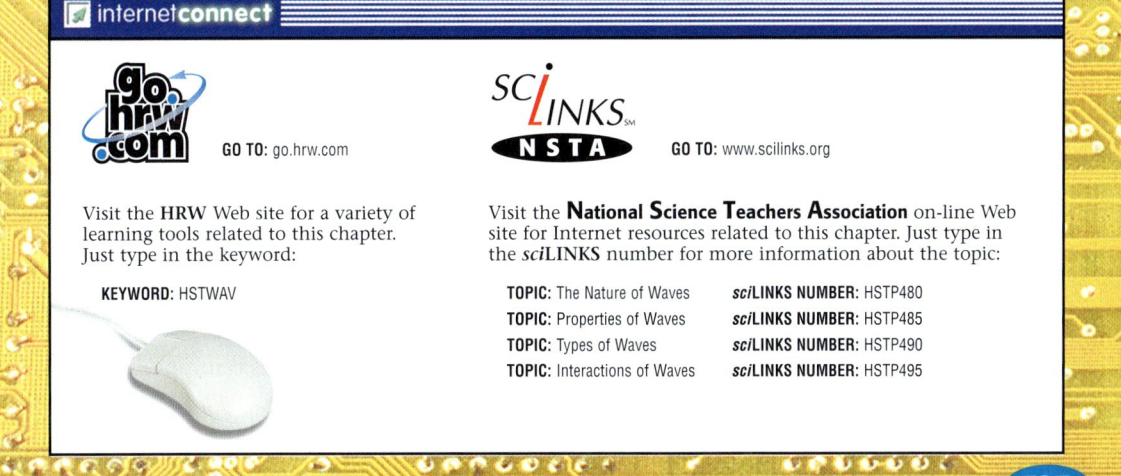

internetconnect

GO TO: go.hrw.com

Visit the **HRW** Web site for a variety of learning tools related to this chapter. Just type in the keyword:

KEYWORD: HSTWAV

GO TO: www.scilinks.org

Visit the **National Science Teachers Association** on-line Web site for Internet resources related to this chapter. Just type in the *sci*LINKS number for more information about the topic:

TOPIC	*sci*LINKS NUMBER
TOPIC: The Nature of Waves	*sci*LINKS NUMBER: HSTP480
TOPIC: Properties of Waves	*sci*LINKS NUMBER: HSTP485
TOPIC: Types of Waves	*sci*LINKS NUMBER: HSTP490
TOPIC: Interactions of Waves	*sci*LINKS NUMBER: HSTP495

527

Lab and Activity Highlights

LabBank

 Whiz-Bang Demonstrations, Pitch Forks, Demo 60

Long-Term Projects & Research Ideas, It's a Whale of a Wave, Project 70

Chapter 20 • Chapter Highlights **527**

Chapter Review

USING VOCABULARY

For each pair of terms, explain the difference in their meanings.

1. longitudinal wave/transverse wave
2. frequency/wave speed
3. wavelength/amplitude
4. reflection/refraction
5. constructive interference/destructive interference

UNDERSTANDING CONCEPTS

Multiple Choice

6. As the wavelength increases, the frequency
   a. decreases.
   b. increases.
   c. remains the same.
   d. increases, then decreases.

7. Which wave interaction explains why sound waves can be heard around corners?
   a. reflection
   b. refraction
   c. diffraction
   d. interference

8. Refraction occurs when a wave enters a new medium at an angle because
   a. the frequency changes.
   b. the amplitude changes.
   c. the wave speed changes.
   d. None of the above

9. The speed of a wave with a frequency of 2 Hz (2/s), an amplitude of 3 m, and a wavelength of 10 m is
   a. 0.2 m/s.
   b. 5 m/s.
   c. 12 m/s.
   d. 20 m/s.

10. Waves transfer
    a. matter.
    b. energy.
    c. particles.
    d. water.

11. A wave that is a combination of longitudinal and transverse waves is a
    a. sound wave.
    b. light wave.
    c. rope wave.
    d. surface wave.

12. The wave property that is related to the height of a wave is the
    a. wavelength.
    b. amplitude.
    c. frequency.
    d. wave speed.

13. During constructive interference,
    a. the amplitude increases.
    b. the frequency decreases.
    c. the wave speed increases.
    d. All of the above

14. Waves that don't require a medium are
    a. longitudinal waves.
    b. electromagnetic waves.
    c. surface waves.
    d. mechanical waves.

Short Answer

15. Draw a transverse and a longitudinal wave. Label a crest, a trough, a compression, a rarefaction, and wavelengths. Also label the amplitude on the transverse wave.

16. What is the relationship between frequency, wave speed, and wavelength?

17. Explain how two waves can cancel each other out.

Chapter Review Answers

USING VOCABULARY

1. The particles in a longitudinal wave vibrate back and forth along the direction the wave is traveling. The particles of a transverse wave vibrate perpendicularly to the direction the wave is traveling.
2. Frequency is the number of waves that pass by in a given amount of time. Wave speed is the distance a wave travels in a given amount of time.
3. Wavelength is the distance between any two adjacent crests (or compressions) in a series of waves. Amplitude is the maximum distance particles travel from their rest position.
4. Waves bounce off barriers during reflection. Waves bend when entering a new medium at an angle during refraction.
5. Interference occurs when two or more waves overlap. Constructive interference occurs when the resulting wave has a larger amplitude than the starting waves. Destructive interference occurs when the resulting wave has a smaller amplitude than the starting waves.

UNDERSTANDING CONCEPTS

Multiple Choice
6. a
7. c
8. c
9. d
10. b
11. d
12. b
13. a
14. b

Short Answer
15. (An example of a transverse wave can be found on page 513. An example of a longitudinal wave can be found on page 514.)
16. Wave speed is the frequency times the wavelength ($v = f \times \lambda$).
17. When two waves with the same amplitude overlap so that the crests of one wave overlap the troughs of the other, they cancel each other out through destructive interference. This results in a "flat" wave.

Chapter 20 • The Energy of Waves

Concept Mapping

18. Use the following terms to create a concept map: wave, refraction, transverse wave, longitudinal wave, wavelength, wave speed, diffraction.

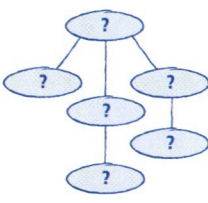

CRITICAL THINKING AND PROBLEM SOLVING

19. After you set up stereo speakers in your school's music room, you notice that in certain areas of the room the sound from the speakers is very loud and in other areas the sound is very soft. Explain how interference causes this.

20. You have lost the paddles for the canoe you rented, and the canoe has drifted to the center of the pond. You need to get the canoe back to shore, but you do not want to get wet by swimming in the pond. Your friend on the shore wants to throw rocks behind the canoe to create waves that will push the canoe toward shore. Will this solution work? Why or why not?

21. Some opera singers have voices so powerful they can break crystal glasses! To do this, they sing one note very loudly and hold it for a long time. The walls of the glass move back and forth until the glass shatters. Explain how this happens in terms of resonance.

MATH IN SCIENCE

22. A fisherman in a rowboat notices that one wave crest passes his fishing line every 5 seconds. He estimates the distance between the crests to be 2 m and estimates the crests of the waves to be 0.4 m above the troughs. Using these data, determine the amplitude and wave speed of the waves. Remember that wave speed is calculated with the formula $v = \lambda \times f$.

INTERPRETING GRAPHICS

23. Rank the waves below from highest energy to lowest energy, and explain your reasoning.

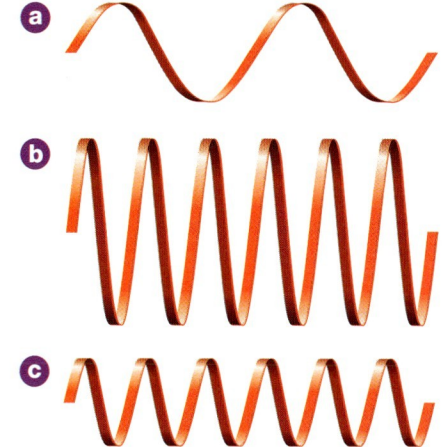

NOW What Do You Think?

Take a minute to review your answers to the ScienceLog questions on page 509. Have your answers changed? If necessary, revise your answers based on what you have learned since you began this chapter.

529

NOW What Do You Think?
1. A wave is a disturbance that transmits energy through matter or space.
2. All waves have amplitude, wavelength, frequency, and wave speed.
3. Waves can reflect off barriers, can refract when passing into a new medium at an angle, can diffract around barriers or through openings, or can overlap and combine by interference.

Concept Mapping Transparency 20

Blackline Masters of this Chapter Review can be found in the **Study Guide**.

Concept Mapping

18. An answer to this exercise can be found at the end of this book.

CRITICAL THINKING AND PROBLEM SOLVING

19. With constructive interference, the crest of one wave overlaps with the crest of another wave, making a new wave with a higher crest and greater amplitude, or loudness. With destructive interference, the crest of one wave overlaps with the trough of another wave, decreasing the amplitude and making the sound softer.

20. Waves carry energy, not matter. So waves will make the canoe bob up and down in the pond but will not push the canoe closer to the shore.

21. The vibrations from the singer's voice cause the glass to vibrate at one of its resonant frequencies. It does not take much energy to make it vibrate with a large amplitude. But the glass is not very flexible, so it shatters.

MATH IN SCIENCE

22. wavelength is 2 m, frequency is 1 wave/5 s = 0.2 Hz, so $v = 2 \text{ m} \times 0.2 \text{ Hz} = 0.4 \text{ m/s}$

Amplitude is half the distance between the crests and troughs. The amplitude is 0.4 m/2 = 0.2 m.

INTERPRETING GRAPHICS

23. rank: *b*, *c*, *a*

Wave *b* has a high frequency and a large amplitude. Wave *c* has a high frequency and a small amplitude. Wave *a* has a low frequency and a small amplitude.

high frequency and large amplitude = more energy
low frequency and small amplitude = less energy

Chapter 20 • Chapter Review **529**

SCIENCE, TECHNOLOGY, AND SOCIETY

The Ultimate Telescope

Background

A radio telescope collects radio waves, just as an optical telescope collects visible light. However, to bring radio waves into sharp focus, a radio telescope must be much larger than an optical telescope because radio waves have much longer wavelengths than wavelengths of visible light.

While some objects that give off relatively few radio waves are best observed by optical telescopes, objects that produce more radio waves are best observed by radio telescopes. However, objects that produce both visible light and radio waves are best observed with radio telescopes, which produce images with higher resolution than those produced by optical telescopes.

Radio telescopes do have one disadvantage. They create images from only one wavelength at a time. Using a radio telescope is like looking at an object through a lens that allows you to see only green light. If you want to see the object in another color, such as red or blue, you have to change the lens. This is exactly what astronomers have to do with radio telescopes.

Science, Technology, and Society

The Ultimate Telescope

The largest telescopes in the world don't depend on visible light, lenses, or mirrors. Instead, they collect radio waves from the far reaches of outer space. One radio telescope, called the Very Large Array (VLA), is located in a remote desert in New Mexico.

From Radio Waves to Computer Images

Objects in space give off radio waves that radio telescopes collect. A bowl-shaped dish called a reflector focuses the radio waves onto a small radio antenna hung over the center of the dish. The antenna converts the waves into electric signals. The signals are relayed to a radio receiver, where they are amplified and recorded on tape that can be read by a computer. The computer combines the signals to create an image of the source of the radio waves.

▲ *Only a few of the 27 radio telescopes of the VLA, near Datil, New Mexico, can be seen in this photograph.*

A Marvel at "Seeing"

Radio telescopes have some distinct advantages over optical telescopes. They can "see" objects that are as far as 13 billion light-years away. They can even detect objects that don't release any light at all. Radio telescopes can be used in any kind of weather, can receive signals through atmospheric pollution, and can even penetrate the cosmic dust and gas clouds that occupy vast areas of space. However, radio telescopes must be large in order to be accurate.

Telescope Teamwork

The VLA is an array of 27 separate radio telescopes mounted on railroad tracks and electronically linked by computers. Each of the 27 reflectors is 25 m in diameter. When they operate together, they work like a single telescope with a diameter of 47 km! Using the VLA, astronomers have been able to explore distant galaxies, pulsars, quasars, and possible black holes.

A system of telescopes even larger than the VLA has been used. In the Very Long Baseline Array (VLBA), radio telescopes in different parts of the world all work together. The result is a telescope that is almost as large as the Earth itself!

What Do They See?

▶ Find out about some of the objects "seen" by the VLA, such as pulsars, quasars, and possible black holes. Prepare a report or create a model of one of the objects, and make a presentation to your class. Use diagrams and photographs to make your presentation more interesting.

Information for What Do They See?
Provide students with some popular astronomy books and magazines. You may wish to contact NASA's Space Science Institute, which operates the Hubble Space Telescope. The telescope takes numerous photographs daily that are eventually released to the public.

Across the Sciences

PHYSICAL SCIENCE • LIFE SCIENCE

Sounds of Silence

It's morning on the African savanna. Suddenly, without a sound, a family of elephants stops eating and begins to move off. At the same moment, about 6 km away, other members of the same family move off in a direction that will reunite them with the first group. How did the groups know when it was time to go?

Do You Hear What I Hear?

Elephants do much of their communicating by infrasound. This is sound energy with a frequency too low to be heard by humans. These infrasonic conversations take place through deep, soft rumblings produced by the animals. Though humans can't hear the sounds, elephants as far as 10 km away respond quickly to the messages.

Because scientists couldn't hear the elephant "conversations," they couldn't understand how the animals coordinated their activities. Of course, the elephants, which have superb low-frequency hearing, heard the messages clearly. It turns out that much elephant behavior is affected by infrasonic messages. For instance, one kind of rumble from a mother to her calf tells the calf it is all right to nurse. Another rumble, from the group's leader, is the "time to move on" message. Still another infrasonic message may be sent to other elephant groups in the area, warning them of danger.

Radio Collars

Once scientists learned about elephants' infrasonic abilities, they devised ways to study the sounds. Researchers developed radio collars for individual animals to wear. The collars are connected to a computer that helps researchers identify which elephant sent the message. The collars also record the messages. This information helps scientists understand both the messages and the social organization of the group.

Let's Talk

Elephants have developed several ways to "talk" to each other. For example, they greet each other by touching trunks and tusks. And elephants have as many as 25 vocal calls, including the familiar bellowing trumpet call (a sign of great excitement). In other situations, they use chemical signals.

▲ *Two elephants greeting each other*

Recently, researchers recording elephant communications found that when elephants vocalize their low-frequency sounds, they create seismic waves. Elephant messages sent by these underground energy waves may be felt more than 8 km away. Clearly, there is a lot more to elephant conversations than meets the ear!

On Your Own

▶ Elephants are very intelligent and highly sociable. Find out more about the complex social structure of elephant groups. Why is it important for scientists to understand how elephants communicate with each other? How can that understanding help elephants?

Across the Sciences
Sounds of Silence

Background

Elephants are highly intelligent and very social animals. Each herd or family has a highly complex social arrangement. The family is usually led by the oldest female, the matriarch of the group. She is responsible for leading the family to the best feeding grounds and away from danger. The family group usually consists of the matriarch, her female relatives of all ages, and young males. When males reach sexual maturity (at about age 14), they leave (or are nudged out of) the family and go off on their own or join all-male bachelor herds.

Sample Answer to On Your Own

Elephant herds need large amounts of food and water and large areas in which to roam. Humans kill elephants for a variety of reasons, such as to obtain the ivory in the elephants' tusks or to protect farmland from being trampled by elephants. Humans are also occupying more and more of the natural habitat of elephants. If scientists learn to understand elephant communication and behavior, they can devise plans that use those natural behaviors to protect and preserve elephant herds and habitats from human destruction. For instance, scientists might broadcast sounds that elephants recognize as danger signals to warn the animals away from a particular location.

Chapter Organizer

CHAPTER ORGANIZATION	TIME MINUTES	OBJECTIVES	LABS, INVESTIGATIONS, AND DEMONSTRATIONS
Chapter Opener pp. 532–533	45	National Standards: UCP 2, SAI 1, HNS 1, 3	**Investigate!** A Homemade Guitar, p. 533
Section 1 What Is Sound?	90	▶ Describe how sound is caused by vibrations. ▶ Explain how sound is transmitted through a medium. ▶ Explain how the human ear works, and identify its parts. UCP 1, 2, SAI 1, ST 2, SPSP 1, 5, HNS 1, PS 3a	**QuickLab,** Good Vibrations, p. 534 **Demonstration,** p. 534 in ATE **Whiz-Bang Demonstrations,** Hear Ye, Hear Ye, Demo 63 **Whiz-Bang Demonstrations,** Jingle Bells, Silent Bells, Demo 62
Section 2 Properties of Sound	90	▶ Compare the speed of sound in different media. ▶ Explain how frequency and pitch are related. ▶ Describe the Doppler effect, and give examples of it. ▶ Explain how amplitude and loudness are related. UCP 1, 3, SAI 1, ST 2, SPSP 5, HNS 1, 3, PS 3a; LabBook UCP 2, SAI 1, 2	**Demonstration,** p. 542 in ATE **QuickLab,** Sounding Board, p. 543 **Discovery Lab,** Easy Listening, p. 710 **Datasheets for LabBook,** Easy Listening, Datasheet 56 **Whiz-Bang Demonstrations,** The Sounds of Time, Demo 64
Section 3 Interactions of Sound Waves	90	▶ Explain how echoes are produced, and describe their use in locating objects. ▶ Give examples of constructive and destructive interference of sound waves. ▶ Identify three sound-wave interactions, and give examples of each. UCP 1–3, ST 2, SPSP 5; LabBook UCP 2, 3, SAI 1, 2, PS 3a	**Demonstration,** p. 545 in ATE **Skill Builder,** Tuneful Tube, p. 713 **Design Your Own,** The Speed of Sound, p. 712 **Skill Builder,** The Energy of Sound, p. 714 **Datasheets for LabBook,** Datasheets 57, 58, 59 **Whiz-Bang Demonstrations,** A Hot Tone, Demo 61
Section 4 Sound Quality	90	▶ Define sound quality. ▶ Describe how each family of musical instruments produces sound. ▶ Explain how noise is different from music. UCP 1, 2, 5, SPSP 1–3	**Demonstration,** pp. 552, 553 in ATE **Interactive Explorations CD-ROM,** Sound Bite! A **Worksheet** is also available in the **Interactive Explorations Teacher's Edition.** **EcoLabs & Field Activities,** An Earful of Sounds, Field Activity 22 **Long-Term Projects & Research Ideas,** Project 71

See page T20 for a complete correlation of this book with the

NATIONAL SCIENCE EDUCATION STANDARDS.

TECHNOLOGY RESOURCES

 Guided Reading Audio CD
English or Spanish, Chapter 21

 Science Discovery Videodiscs:
Image and Activity Bank with Lesson Plans: Making a Pitch
Science Sleuths: Noises in School

 Science, Technology & Society,
Salmon Sound Barriers, Segment 25
Learning from Frog Ears, Segment 26

 Interactive Explorations CD-ROM,
CD 3, Exploration 6, Sound Bite!

 One-Stop Planner CD-ROM with Test Generator

Chapter 21 • The Nature of Sound

Chapter 21 • The Nature of Sound

CLASSROOM WORKSHEETS, TRANSPARENCIES, AND RESOURCES	SCIENCE INTEGRATION AND CONNECTIONS	REVIEW AND ASSESSMENT
Directed Reading Worksheet 21 **Science Puzzlers, Twisters & Teasers,** Worksheet 21	**Cross-Disciplinary Focus,** p. 533 in ATE	
Directed Reading Worksheet 21, Section 1 **Transparency 284,** Sounds from a Stereo Speaker **Transparency 285,** How the Human Ear Works	**Biology Connection,** p. 535 **Connect to Life Science,** p. 535 in ATE **Astronomy Connection,** p. 536 **Science, Technology, and Society:** Jurassic Bark, p. 560 **Holt Anthology of Science Fiction,** Ear	**Homework,** p. 536 in ATE **Review,** p. 538 **Quiz,** p. 538 in ATE **Alternative Assessment,** p. 538 in ATE
Directed Reading Worksheet 21, Section 2 **Transparency 286,** Pitch Depends on Frequency **Transparency 286,** Frequencies Heard by Different Animals **Transparency 287,** The Doppler Effect **Reinforcement Worksheet 21,** Doppler Dan's Dump Truck	**MathBreak,** Speed of Sound, p. 540 **Connect to Earth Science,** p. 540 in ATE **Math and More,** p. 540 in ATE **Biology Connection,** p. 541 **Connect to Life Science,** p. 542 in ATE	**Review,** p. 544 **Quiz,** p. 544 in ATE **Alternative Assessment,** p. 544 in ATE
Directed Reading Worksheet 21, Section 3 **Transparency 154,** How Sonar Works **Transparency 288,** Echolocation	**Cross-Disciplinary Focus,** p. 546 in ATE **Connect to Earth Science,** p. 546 in ATE **Apply,** p. 547 **Real-World Connection,** p. 547 in ATE **Cross-Disciplinary Focus,** p. 548 in ATE **Real-World Connection,** p. 549 in ATE	**Review,** p. 547 **Self-Check,** p. 549 **Review,** p. 551 **Quiz,** p. 551 in ATE **Alternative Assessment,** p. 551 in ATE
Directed Reading Worksheet 21, Section 4 **Critical Thinking Worksheet 21,** The Noise Police	**Multicultural Connection,** p. 554 in ATE **Environment Connection,** p. 555	**Self-Check,** p. 553 **Homework,** p. 553 in ATE **Review,** p. 555 **Quiz,** p. 555 in ATE **Alternative Assessment,** p. 555 in ATE

END-OF-CHAPTER REVIEW AND ASSESSMENT

Chapter Review in Study Guide
Vocabulary and Notes in Study Guide
Chapter Tests with Performance-Based Assessment, Chapter 21 Test
Chapter Tests with Performance-Based Assessment, Performance-Based Assessment 21
Concept Mapping Transparency 21

internet connect

Holt, Rinehart and Winston On-line Resources
go.hrw.com
For worksheets and other teaching aids related to this chapter, visit the HRW Web site and type in the keyword: **HSTSND**

National Science Teachers Association
www.scilinks.org
Encourage students to use the *sci*LINKS numbers listed in the internet connect boxes to access information and resources on the **NSTA** Web site.

Chapter Resources & Worksheets

Visual Resources

TEACHING TRANSPARENCIES

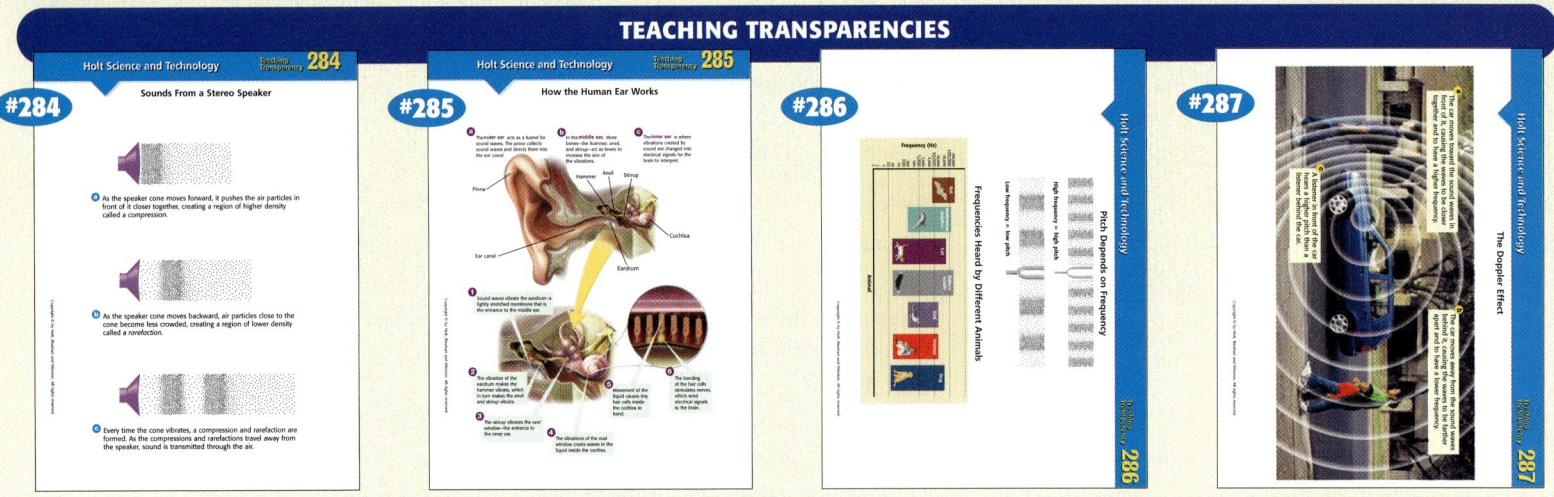

TEACHING TRANSPARENCIES

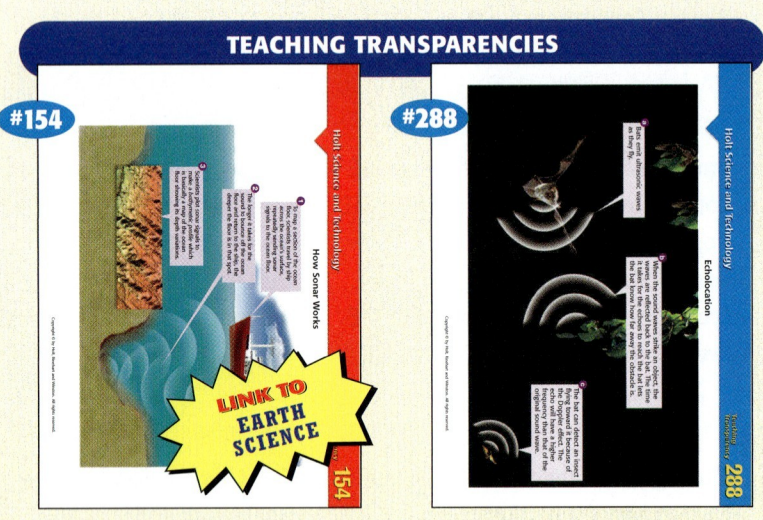

CONCEPT MAPPING TRANSPARENCY

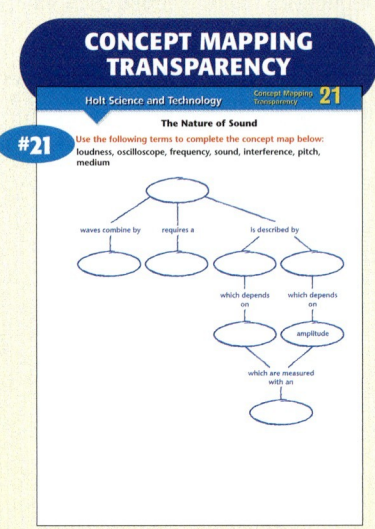

Meeting Individual Needs

DIRECTED READING

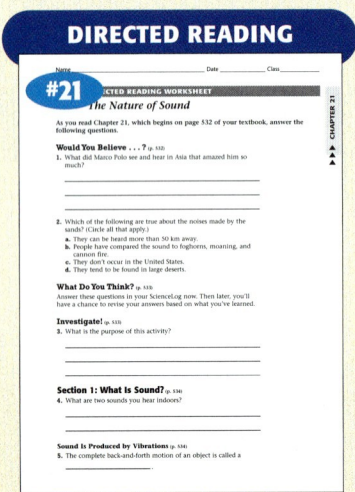

REINFORCEMENT & VOCABULARY REVIEW

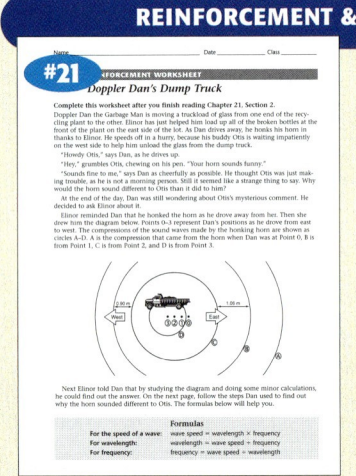

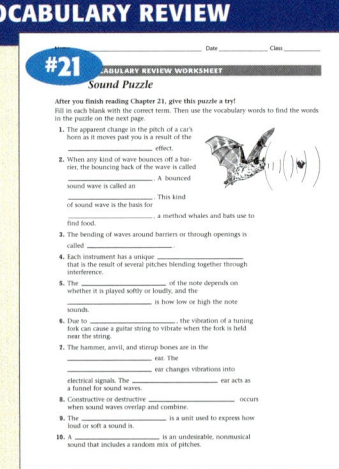

SCIENCE PUZZLERS, TWISTERS & TEASERS

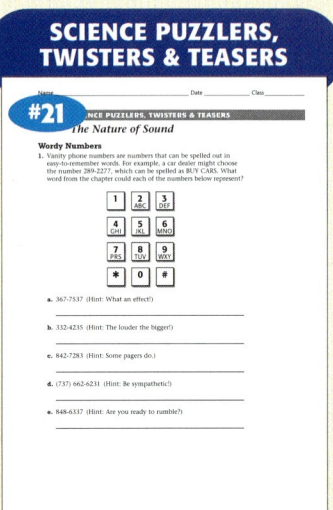

Chapter 21 • The Nature of Sound

Chapter 21 • The Nature of Sound

Review & Assessment

STUDY GUIDE

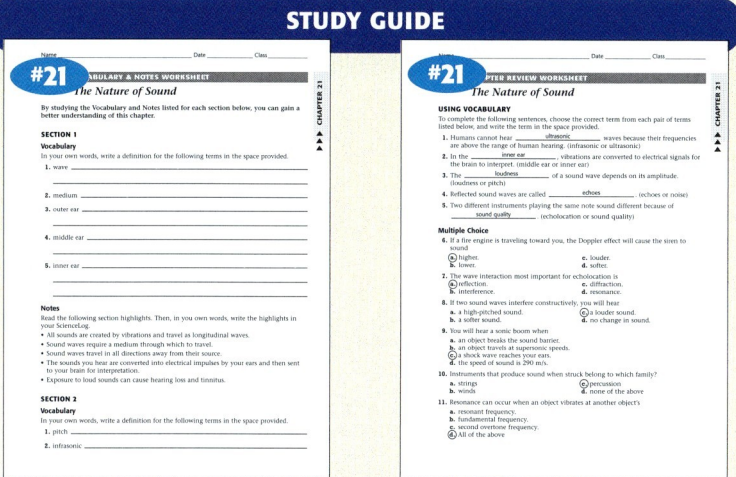

CHAPTER TESTS WITH PERFORMANCE-BASED ASSESSMENT

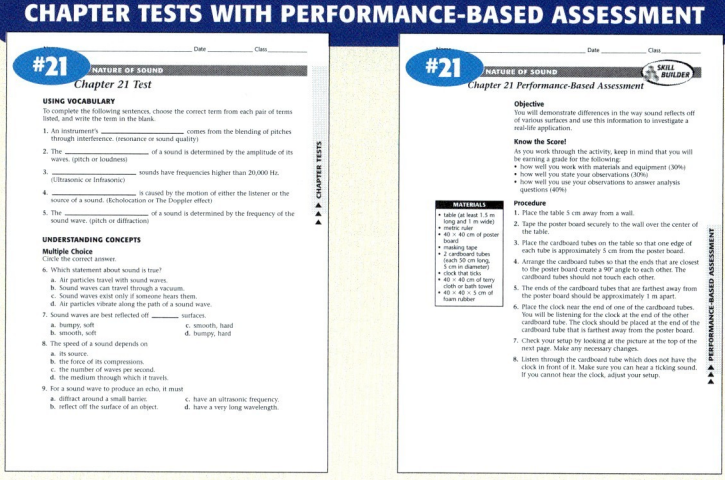

Lab Worksheets

WHIZ-BANG DEMONSTRATIONS

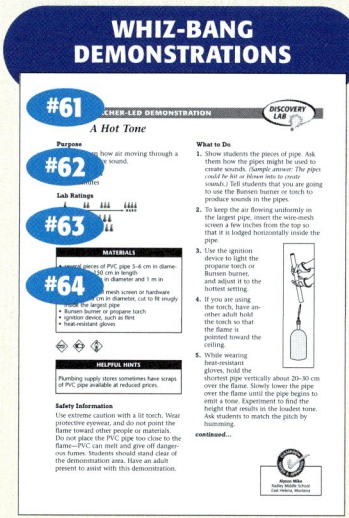

ECOLABS & FIELD ACTIVITIES

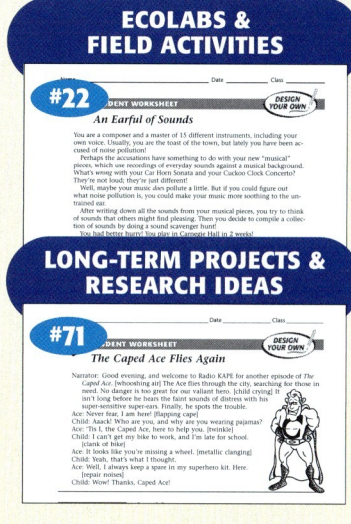

DATASHEETS FOR LABBOOK

Applications & Extensions

CRITICAL THINKING & PROBLEM SOLVING

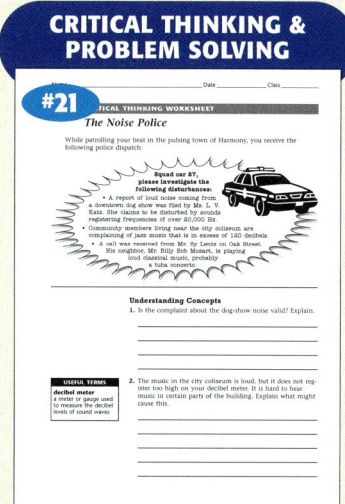

SCIENCE, TECHNOLOGY & SOCIETY

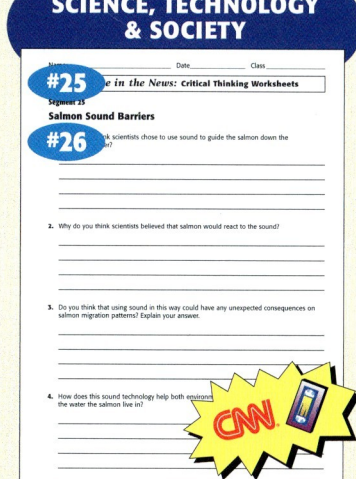

INTERACTIVE EXPLORATIONS

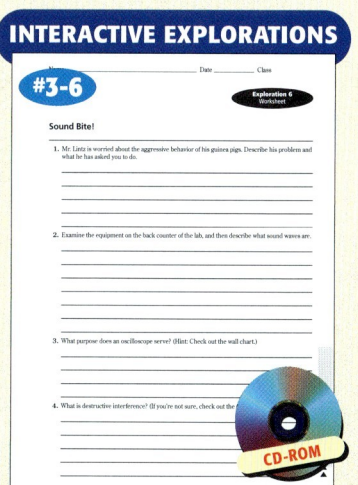

Chapter Background

SECTION 1

What Is Sound?

▶ **Doppler Effect**
In 1842, the Doppler effect was explained by the Austrian physicist Christian Doppler (1803–1853). He noted that there is a change in wavelength of both light and sound when either the source or the receiver (or both, if they move at different velocities) moves. If the wavelength becomes shorter and the frequency of the sound becomes higher, it is known as blue shift. If the wavelength increases and the frequency becomes lower, it is known as red shift.

- In acoustical Doppler effects, the frequency depends on the speed of the observer relative to the speed of the source.

IS THAT A FACT!

- Singing sand dunes can make two very different sounds: some dunes "whistle" or "squeak" in the 500–2500 Hz range, while others "boom" at frequencies of 50–300 Hz. Interestingly, the booming sands can be felt as well; the dune trembles noticeably as it booms.

- Only sand grains with certain sizes and shapes whistle or squeal. Sands in many locations, including beach sands in a variety of places, can be induced to whistle. Scientists are less certain what factors create "booming" dunes, although grains of a certain size and shape seem to be required.

SECTION 2

Properties of Sound

▶ **Loudness**
Loudness is expressed in decibels. An increase of 10 dB multiplies the intensity of a sound by 10 times. An increase of 20 dB is 10 × 10, or 100 times louder.

▶ **Robert Boyle (1627–1691)**
Robert Boyle, a British scientist who lived in Ireland, performed a famous experiment in 1660. When a bell was suspended in a vacuum, the clapper could be seen striking the bell, but no sound was heard. This demonstration proved that sound is dependent on a medium.

IS THAT A FACT!

- The longest distance traveled by any audible sound in air is about 4,600 km. The volcanic explosion on the Indonesian island of Krakatau, in 1883, propelled a column of smoke and ash more than 80 km into the air. The explosion sounded like distant cannon fire to people in Australia, Singapore, and Rodriguez Island—4,600 km away in the Indian Ocean. Waves reached the Pacific coastline of Colombia, 19 hours later, and tsunamis were recorded in other parts of South America. Remnants of the giant tsunamis were detected in the English Channel, halfway around the Earth from where the eruption took place.

- Sound travels 1.7 km in about 5 seconds in air that is 20°C. Sound travels the same distance (1.7 km) in just over 1 second underwater and in only three-tenths of a second in steel.

Chapter 21 • The Nature of Sound

SECTION 3

Interactions of Sound Waves

▶ **Bat Sonar Beats Human Technology**
Experiments conducted at Brown University found that bat sonar can detect the difference between echoes just two- to three-millionths of a second apart. The best naval sonar could differentiate between echoes about 5 to 10 millionths of a second apart.

IS THAT A FACT!

- Nikola Tesla, a Croatian inventor, once created a man-made earthquake by making a steam-driven oscillator vibrate at the same frequency as the ground. Tesla had accurately determined the resonant frequency of the Earth! In a similar experiment, Tesla proved theories of seismic wave activity by sending waves of energy through the Earth. As these waves of energy returned, Tesla added electric current to them and thereby created a man-made bolt of lightning that measured 40 m. The accompanying thunder was heard for more than 35 km!

SECTION 4

Sound Quality

▶ **Recording Sound**
The two basic methods of recording sound are analog and digital recording. In analog recording, the recording medium varies continuously with the incoming signal. In digital recording, the signal is recorded as a rapid sequence of coded measurements.

- Both methods preserve the varying voltage of the sound signal, but digital recording eliminates the hiss or electrical noise. Analog recordings can be improved by a noise reduction system, such as the Dolby® system.

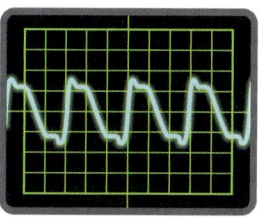

Piano   Violin

IS THAT A FACT!

- Notes on a musical scale are set by exact frequencies. Although humans can hear frequencies as low as 20 Hz, the lowest frequency heard as a note is about 30 Hz. The highest frequency audible to humans is about 20,000 Hz. Middle C on the piano has a frequency of 263 Hz.

- Little was known about the science of sound until the 1600s. The Greeks were more interested in music than in the scientific aspects of sound. However, the Greek philosopher and mathematician Pythagoras (c. 580–500 B.C.) discovered that doubling the frequency of a pitch produces a pitch one octave higher.

For background information about teaching strategies and issues, refer to the *Professional Reference for Teachers*.

CHAPTER 21

The Nature of Sound

Chapter Preview

Section 1
What Is Sound?
- Sound Is Produced by Vibrations
- Creating Sound Vs. Detecting Sound
- Sound Waves Require a Medium
- How You Detect Sound

Section 2
Properties of Sound
- The Speed of Sound Depends on the Medium
- Pitch Depends on Frequency
- Loudness Is Related to Amplitude

Section 3
Interactions of Sound Waves
- Reflection of Sound Waves
- Interference of Sound Waves
- Diffraction of Sound Waves

Section 4
Sound Quality
- What Is Sound Quality?
- Sound Quality of Instruments
- Music or Noise?

Directed Reading Worksheet 21

Science Puzzlers, Twisters & Teasers Worksheet 21

Guided Reading Audio CD
English or Spanish, Chapter 21

CHAPTER 21 The Nature of Sound

Marco Polo

Would You Believe . . . ?

In 1271, the Italian explorer Marco Polo began his historic journey to China with his father and uncle. He was only 17 years old. Though he didn't know it at the time, 24 years would pass before he and his companions would return home to Venice, Italy.

Upon his return, Marco Polo wrote of the many incredible things he had observed while in Asia. One such thing was the booming sand dunes of the Asian desert. Marco Polo wrote how the sands actually made noises, filling the air with sounds of music, drums, and weapons of war.

Although they were a mystery during Marco Polo's time, much has been learned about these booming sands. For example, they are most often found in the middle of large deserts. The loud, low-pitched sounds—which have been compared to foghorns, cannon fire, and moaning—can last from a few seconds to 15 minutes and can be heard more than 10 km away! Booming sands have been discovered all over the world, including the United States.

Scientists have learned that the loud sounds are caused by avalanches of sand within a dune. As the top layers of sand slip over the layers below, vibrations are produced that create the strange sounds. However, scientists are still not sure why these sands make noise and other sands do not.

Although there is still much to learn about booming sands, the nature of sound is well understood. In this chapter, you will learn about sound, its properties, and how sound waves interact to influence your life.

Sand Mountain, in Nevada, makes low droning sounds.

Would You Believe . . . ?

Scientists have identified more than 30 sites around the world, including Africa, Asia, the Arabian Peninsula, North and South America, and the Hawaiian Islands, where booming dunes are found. Although scientists know where these sands are, they do not completely understand why some sands make sounds! Scientific investigations have revealed that booming sand grains are usually fairly smooth and rounded. Scientists have also noted that water and humidity can stop the booming effect. In fact, adding just 5–10 drops of water to a 1 L bag of booming sand can silence it. Booming sands usually do not produce sound for 3 weeks after a rainfall. Humidity can also stop the booming, apparently by creating a surface of water on sand grains.

What Do You Think?

In your ScienceLog, try to answer the following questions based on what you already know:

1. How does sound travel from one place to another?
2. What determines a sound's pitch and loudness?
3. What can happen when sound waves interact with each other?

TRY at HOME

A Homemade Guitar

In this chapter you will learn about sound. You can start by making yourself a guitar. It won't sound as good as a real guitar, but it will help you explore the nature of sound.

Procedure

1. Stretch a **rubber band** lengthwise around an empty **shoe box**, and gently pluck the rubber band with your finger. In your ScienceLog, describe what you see and hear.
2. Stretch **another rubber band of a different thickness** around the box, and pluck both rubber bands. Describe the difference in the two sounds.
3. Put a **pencil** across the top of the box and under the rubber bands, and pluck again. Compare the sound with the sound you heard before the pencil was used.
4. Move the pencil closer to one end of the shoe box, and pluck on both sides of the pencil. Describe the difference in the sounds you hear.

Analysis

5. Describe what happened to the rubber band after you plucked it in step 1. Did it move differently during steps 3 and 4? If so, describe how it moved differently.
6. How did the thickness of the rubber bands affect their sound?
7. In steps 3 and 4, the pencil was used to shorten the part of the rubber band that was vibrating. What is the relationship between the shortened length and the sound you heard?

What Do You Think?

Accept all reasonable responses.

Students will have a chance to revise their answers in the Chapter Review under NOW What Do You Think?

Investigate!

MATERIALS

FOR EACH GROUP:
- thin rubber band
- thick rubber band
- shoe box
- pencil

The photo on the page shows how the rubber band should be wrapped around the box. The photo also shows how to position the pencil as described in step 3.

Teacher Notes:

1. Students should hear a sound and see the rubber band vibrate.
2. Students should hear a higher pitch or note from the thinner rubber band. They may not use the words *pitch* or *note* at this point, but they should be able to notice and describe the differences between the two sounds.
3. When the pencil is used, the pitch of the sound is higher.
4. A high pitch is produced by the short part of the rubber band, and a low pitch is produced by the longer part of the rubber band.

Visit www.si.edu/hrw for additional on-line resources.

CROSS-DISCIPLINARY FOCUS

Psychoacoustics is the branch of science that deals with the mental and auditory aspects of sound communication. A psychoacoustician might address the issues of how the brain can determine the pitch of a musical instrument or how the brain can separate sounds occurring simultaneously, as in two speakers speaking at once.

Answers to Investigate!

5. The rubber band moved back and forth (or vibrated) after it was plucked. It vibrated faster in steps 3 and 4 than it did in step 1.
6. The thicker the rubber band is, the lower the pitch.
7. The shorter the rubber band is, the higher the pitch.

Chapter 21 • The Nature of Sound

SECTION 1

Focus

What Is Sound?
This section introduces sound and how it is produced. Students learn how sound waves travel, and how the human ear works.

Bellringer
If you've ever been near a large fireworks display, you may have *felt* the sound of the explosions. Think of other instances when you might feel sound and describe them in your ScienceLog.

1) Motivate

DEMONSTRATION
Set up a stereo system with speakers (these must have woofers that reproduce low-frequency sounds) in the classroom, and remove the outer cover of the speakers. Play music that has a strong bass beat or bass chords. Students will be able to see the woofers vibrating with the bass sounds. Challenge them to explain why the vibrations of the woofers can be seen but the vibrations of the tweeters are almost imperceptible.

QuickLab
MATERIALS
FOR EACH GROUP:
- tuning fork
- rubber eraser
- small plastic cup of water

Safety Caution: Remind students that the tuning forks should not touch their eyes or eyeglasses.

Section 1

Terms to Learn
- wave
- medium
- outer ear
- middle ear
- inner ear

What You'll Do
- Describe how sound is caused by vibrations.
- Explain how sound is transmitted through a medium.
- Explain how the human ear works, and identify its parts.

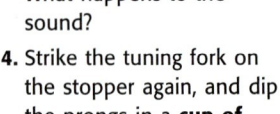

QuickLab
Good Vibrations
1. Gently strike a **tuning fork** on a **rubber eraser.** Watch the prongs, and listen for a sound. Describe what you see and hear.
2. Lightly touch the fork with your fingers. What do you feel?
3. Grasp the prongs of the fork firmly with your hand. What happens to the sound?
4. Strike the tuning fork on the stopper again, and dip the prongs in a **cup of water.** Describe what happens to the water.
5. Record your observations in your ScienceLog.

What Is Sound?

Think about all the sounds you hear every day. Indoors, you might hear people talking, the radio blaring, or dishes clattering in the kitchen sink. Outdoors, you might hear birds singing, cars driving by, or a mosquito buzzing in your ear. That's a lot of different sounds! In this section, you'll explore some common characteristics of the different sounds you hear.

Sound Is Produced by Vibrations

As different as they are, all sounds have some things in common. One characteristic of sound is that it is created by vibrations. A *vibration* is the complete back-and-forth motion of an object. **Figure 1** shows an example of how sound is created by vibrations.

Figure 1 Sounds from a Stereo Speaker

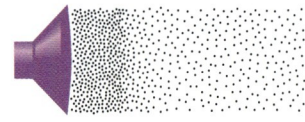

a As the speaker cone moves forward, it pushes the air particles in front of it closer together, creating a region of higher density and pressure called a *compression.*

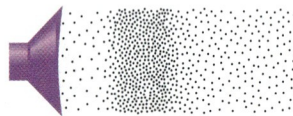

b As the speaker cone moves backward, air particles close to the cone become less crowded, creating a region of lower density and pressure called a *rarefaction.*

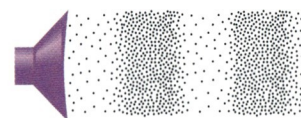

c Every time the cone vibrates, compression and rarefaction are formed. As the compressions and rarefactions travel away from the speaker, sound is transmitted through the air.

Answers to QuickLab
1. Students should hear a faint sound coming from the tuning fork. They may or may not see the prongs of the tuning fork vibrate—this will depend on how hard the fork was struck and on the size of the fork.
2. Students should feel that the prongs are vibrating.
3. After the students grasp the prongs, the sound will immediately stop.
4. The vibrations of the prongs will create waves in the water in the cup.

Sound Travels as Longitudinal Waves A **wave** is a disturbance that transmits energy through matter or space. In a longitudinal wave, particles vibrate back and forth along the path that the wave travels. Longitudinal (LAHN juh TOOD nuhl) waves consist of compressions and rarefactions. Sound is transmitted through the vibrations and collisions of particles of matter, such as air particles. Because the particles vibrate back and forth along the paths that sound travels, sound travels as longitudinal waves.

Sound waves travel in all directions away from their source as illustrated in **Figure 2**. However, air or other matter does not travel with the sound waves. The particles of air only vibrate back and forth in place. If air did travel with sound, wind gusts from music speakers would blow you over at a school dance!

Biology CONNECTION

The vibrations that produce your voice are made inside your throat. When you speak, laugh, or sing, your lungs force air up your windpipe, causing your vocal cords to vibrate.

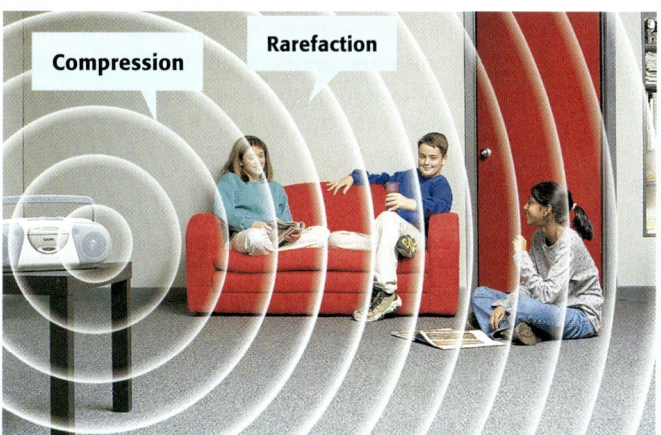

Figure 2 You can't actually see sound waves, but they can be represented by spheres that spread out in all directions.

Creating Sound Vs. Detecting Sound

Have you heard this riddle before?
If a tree falls in the forest and no one is around
to hear it, does the tree make a sound?

Think about this situation for a minute. When a tree falls and hits the ground, the tree and the ground vibrate. These vibrations create compressions and rarefactions in the surrounding air. So, yes, there would be a sound!

Making sound is separate from detecting sound. The fact that no one heard the tree fall doesn't mean that there wasn't a sound. A sound was created—it just wasn't detected.

2) Teach

READING STRATEGY

Activity Have students write in their ScienceLog all the different sounds they hear during a typical day. Have students describe which sounds they enjoy and which are unpleasant to the ear and why.

CONNECT TO LIFE SCIENCE

The vocal cords are located in an organ in the throat called the larynx. Besides producing sound, the larynx controls the flow of air during breathing. The vocal cords are located in the center of the larynx. They are made of thin strips of muscle. They form a V-shaped opening in the airway. Other small muscles stretch and loosen the vocal cords to produce different sounds as air moves across them.

 Teaching Transparency 284 "Sounds from a Stereo Speaker"

 Directed Reading Worksheet 21 Section 1

TOPIC: What Is Sound?
GO TO: www.scilinks.org
*sci*LINKS NUMBER: HSTP505

IS THAT A FACT!

Imagine the sound that is created when a giant sequoia falls! The most massive living organisms in the world are giant sequoia trees, which can grow to more than 85 m tall and can be more than 9 m in diameter at the base. Scientists estimate that some of the largest giant sequoias can have masses up to 2,500 metric tons. Some of the oldest giant sequoias are more than 3,000 years old.

Section 1 • What Is Sound?

2 Teach, continued

DISCUSSION

Some science fiction movies are full of scenes of roaring spacecraft, drilling on asteroids, or deafening explosions during fictional space battles. Discuss with students why these movies are not scientifically accurate.

GROUP ACTIVITY

Have groups of students search the school and grounds to record a variety of sounds. If possible, use a tape recorder or video camera.

Instruct them to find the following sounds:
- high-pitched sound
- sound from above or overhead
- repeating sound
- sound that would startle
- irritating sound
- sound made by an animal
- sound made by wind
- sound made by something moving

Students should record what the sound is and where it was made. Compare and discuss what different groups found.

Figure 3 You can still hear traffic sounds when you are in a car because sound waves can travel through the glass windows and metal body of the car.

Astronomy CONNECTION

The moon has no atmosphere, so there is no air through which sound can travel. The astronauts who walked on the moon had to use radios to talk to each other even when they were standing side by side. Radio waves could travel between the astronauts because they are electromagnetic waves, which don't require a medium. The radio speakers were inside the astronauts' helmets, which were filled with air for the astronauts to breathe.

Sound Waves Require a Medium

Another characteristic of sound is that all sound waves require a medium. A **medium** is a substance through which a wave can travel. In the example of a falling tree on the previous page, the medium is air. Most of the sounds that you hear travel through air at least part of the time. But sound waves can also travel through other materials, such as water, glass, and metal, as shown in **Figure 3**.

What would happen if a tree fell in a vacuum? No sound would be created because in a vacuum, there are no air particles to vibrate. Sound cannot travel in a vacuum. This helps to explain the effect described in **Figure 4**. Sound must travel through air or some other medium to reach your ears and be detected.

Figure 4 Tubing is connected to a pump that is removing air from the jar. As the air is removed, the ringing alarm clock gets quieter and quieter.

How You Detect Sound

Imagine you are watching a suspenseful movie. Just before a door is opened, the background music becomes louder. You know that there is something scary behind that door! Now imagine watching the same scene without the sound. It's hard to figure out what's going on without sound to help you understand what you see. Your ears play an important role in this understanding. On the next page, you will see how your ears convert sound waves into electrical signals, which are then sent to your brain for interpretation.

Homework

Because so many young people listen to very loud music through headphones, one of the next major industries may be the manufacturing of hearing aids. Have students research the different kinds of hearing aids available, how they work, and their costs.

WEIRD SCIENCE

A cricket hears through its front legs and produces a series of chirps, or trills, by rubbing its two front wings together. And the pistol shrimp makes a sound much like a gunshot by snapping shut its enlarged claw.

536 Chapter 21 • The Nature of Sound

How the Human Ear Works

a The **outer ear** acts as a funnel for sound waves. The *pinna* collects sound waves and directs them into the *ear canal*.

b In the **middle ear,** three bones—the *hammer, anvil,* and *stirrup*—act as levers to increase the size of the vibrations.

c The **inner ear** is where vibrations created by sound are changed into electrical signals for the brain to interpret.

Labels on diagram: Pinna, Ear canal, Hammer, Anvil, Stirrup, Cochlea, Eardrum

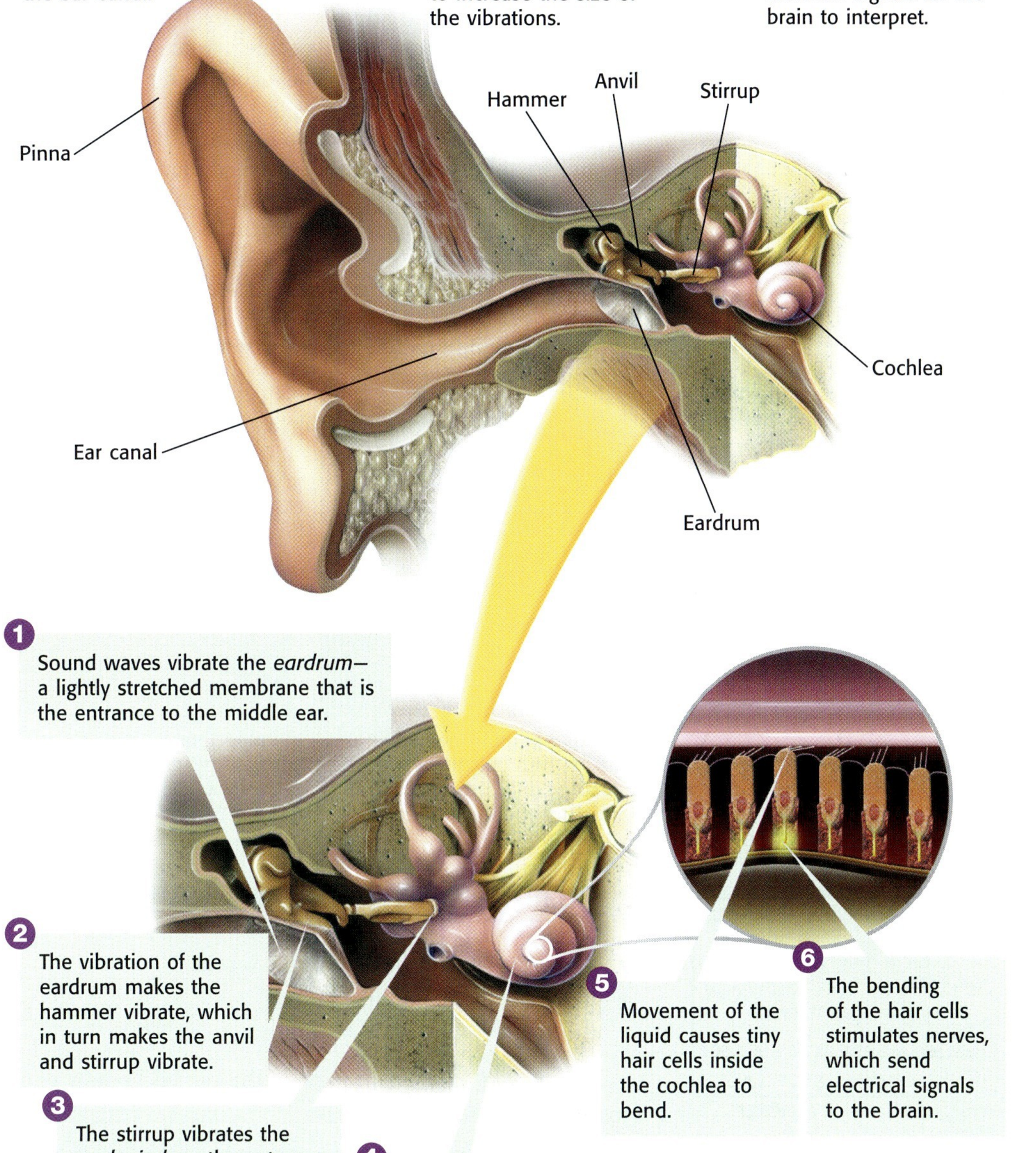

1 Sound waves vibrate the *eardrum*—a lightly stretched membrane that is the entrance to the middle ear.

2 The vibration of the eardrum makes the hammer vibrate, which in turn makes the anvil and stirrup vibrate.

3 The stirrup vibrates the *oval window*—the entrance to the inner ear.

4 The vibrations of the oval window create waves in the liquid inside the *cochlea*.

5 Movement of the liquid causes tiny hair cells inside the cochlea to bend.

6 The bending of the hair cells stimulates nerves, which send electrical signals to the brain.

537

Teaching Transparency 285 "How the Human Ear Works"

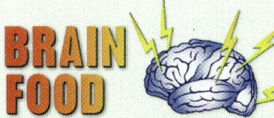

BRAIN FOOD

The inner ear contains the organs that are responsible for maintaining balance. These organs are located in a hollow region called the *vestibule*. Therefore, the sense of balance is sometimes referred to as the *vestibular sense*.

3) Extend

GUIDED PRACTICE

Have students read the information with the pictures on this page and ask these questions:

What is the function of the outer ear? (to collect sound waves and direct them into the ear canal) the bones in the middle ear? (The three bones act as levers to increase the size of vibrations.) the inner ear? (to convert vibrations into electrical signals for the brain to interpret)

DISCUSSION

Discuss the following with students to help them realize how remarkable the ear is:

- One part of the ear is not labeled in this diagram: the semicircular canals. The canals are located in the inner ear, but they do not contribute to the hearing process. The canals help you keep your balance by allowing you to determine which way is up.

- The bones in the middle ear, which are the smallest bones in the body, act as levers to increase the amplitude of the vibrations. Review *levers* from Chapter 8, "Work and Machines."

MEETING INDIVIDUAL NEEDS

Learners Having Difficulty
Using colored pencils, have students draw and label the parts of the ear. They can trace the diagram in the book or draw it freehand. Have students write short descriptions of how the ear works. Be sure students understand how sound waves are collected, amplified, and converted into electrical signals.
Sheltered English

Section 1 • What Is Sound?

4 Close

Quiz

1. Name the three bones in the ear that act as levers. (hammer, stirrup, anvil)

2. Suppose you had hearing loss or tinnitus. How might it affect your daily life, and what changes would you make? (Accept all reasonable answers.)

3. What is necessary for sound to travel from its source to a listener? (a medium through which the sound waves can travel)

ALTERNATIVE ASSESSMENT

Have students write letters to a fictional boss explaining that they are having a hearing problem at work. They should explain the problem, what it is, and what corrections could be made in the workplace for the benefit of everyone who works there.

TOPIC: The Ear
GO TO: www.scilinks.org
sciLINKS NUMBER: HSTP510

Could a dinosaur have played a horn? Check it out on page 560.

Hearing Loss and Deafness The many parts of the ear must work together for you to hear sounds. If any part of the ear is damaged or does not work properly, hearing loss or deafness may result.

One of the most common types of hearing loss is called *tinnitus* (ti NIE tuhs), which results from long-term exposure to loud sounds. Loud sounds can cause damage to the hair cells and nerve endings in the cochlea. Damage to the cochlea or any part of the inner ear usually results in permanent hearing loss.

People who have tinnitus often complain about hearing a ringing in their ears. They also have difficulties understanding other people and hearing the difference between words that sound very similar. Tinnitus can affect people of any age. Fortunately, tinnitus can be prevented. **Figure 5** shows some ways that you can protect yourself from hearing loss.

Figure 5 *Reducing exposure to loud sounds will protect your ears.*

Wearing ear protection while working with machinery blocks out some of the sounds that can injure your ears.

Turning your radio down will prevent hearing loss, especially when you use headphones.

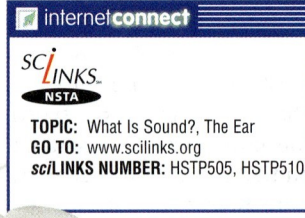
TOPIC: What Is Sound?, The Ear
GO TO: www.scilinks.org
sciLINKS NUMBER: HSTP505, HSTP510

REVIEW

1. Describe how a bell produces sound.

2. Explain why a person at a rock concert will not feel gusts of wind coming out of the speakers.

3. Name the three main parts of the ear, and briefly explain the function of each part.

4. **Inferring Conclusions** If a meteorite crashed on the moon, would you be able to hear it on Earth? Why or why not?

▼ **Answers to Review**

1. When a bell swings back and forth, the clapper strikes the side of the bell and causes the bell to vibrate. The vibrations of the bell produce the sound.

2. A person will not feel gusts of wind coming from speakers at a rock concert because air and other matter does not travel with sound waves. The air particles only vibrate back and forth in place.

3. The outer ear directs sound into the middle ear, where the amplitude of the sound is increased. In the inner ear, vibrations created by the sound are changed into electrical signals for the brain to interpret.

4. From Earth, you would not be able to hear a meteor crash on the moon because there is no medium between the moon and Earth through which sound can travel.

Section 2

Properties of Sound

Terms to Learn

pitch
infrasonic
ultrasonic
Doppler effect
loudness
decibel

What You'll Do

- Compare the speed of sound in different media.
- Explain how frequency and pitch are related.
- Describe the Doppler effect, and give examples of it.
- Explain how amplitude and loudness are related.

Imagine you are swimming in a neighborhood pool. You hear many different sounds as you float on the water. Some are high, like the laughter of small children, and some are low, like the voices of men. Some sounds are loud, like the *BOING* of the diving board, and some are soft, like the sound of water lapping on the sides of the pool. The differences between the sounds—how high or low and how loud or soft they are—depend on the properties of the sound waves. In this section, you will learn about properties of sound.

The Speed of Sound Depends on the Medium

If two people at the other end of the pool shout at you at the same time, will you hear one person's voice before the other? No—the sounds of their voices will reach you at the same time. The time it takes for the sounds to reach you does not depend on who shouted or how loudly the person shouted. The speed of sound depends only on the medium through which the sound is traveling. Assuming that your head is above water, the sounds of the voices traveled through air to your ears and therefore traveled at the same speed.

Speed Changes When the Medium Changes The speed of sound through any medium is constant if the properties of the medium do not change. The chart at left shows the speed of sound in different media. If the properties of a medium change, the speed of sound through that medium will change. On the next page, you will explore how a change in one property—temperature—affects the speed of sound through air.

Speed of Sound in Different Media at 20°C

Medium	Speed (m/s)
Air	343
Helium	1,005
Water	1,482
Sea water	1,522
Wood (oak)	3,850
Glass	4,540
Steel	5,200

IS THAT A FACT!

In some western movies, a character would be shown putting an ear to the hard ground to find out if someone was coming. This technique actually works because sound travels faster and with less loss of energy through the ground than through air.

Directed Reading Worksheet 21 Section 2

SECTION 2

Focus

Properties of Sound

In this section, students learn about properties of sound, what affects the speed of sound, and how pitch and frequency are related. Students also learn about the Doppler effect and how volume and amplitude are related.

🔔 Bellringer

Ask students the following question:

You are the commander of a space station located about halfway between Earth and the moon. You are in the Command Center, and your chief of security tells you that sensors have just detected an explosion 61.054 km from the station. How long will it be before you hear the sound of the explosion? (You won't hear it. Sound waves will not travel in the vacuum of space.)

1) Motivate

ACTIVITY

MATERIALS

FOR EACH PAIR OF STUDENTS:
- 2 paper cups
- several types of string, 6 m each

Have students punch a hole in the bottom of each cup, insert one end of the string into each cup, and tie a knot in the string. Have one student from each pair talk quietly into the cup while the other listens through the second cup. Have each pair experiment with the types of string, the tension of the strings, and lengths of the strings to see which combination works best.

Section 2 • Properties of Sound

2) Teach

CONNECT TO EARTH SCIENCE

Weather has been found to have an influence on the movement of sound waves. Wind and temperature gradients can refract sound waves. Turbulence in the atmosphere scatters sound waves and can change the amplitude of sound waves. Depending on the humidity, temperature, and atmospheric pressure, the atmosphere can even absorb some of the energy of sound waves.

Answers to MATHBREAK

air: 1,715 m; water: 7,410 m, steel: 26,000 m

MATH and MORE

The temperature is 20°C. You are standing next to a railing located in a national park. The railing is 7,700 m long. One-half of the railing is solid oak. The other half of the railing is made of steel. Your friend is at the other end of the railing, and she hits the railing with a hammer. How long will it take for the sound to get to you through the railing? Less than 1 second? Between 1 and 2 seconds? More than 2 seconds? Explain your answer. (between 1 and 2 seconds; Sound travels 3,850 m through oak and 5,200 m through steel in 1 second. Therefore, sound will take between 1 and 2 seconds to travel through the 7,700 m rail.)

How long will it take the sound to reach you through the air? (between 22 and 23 seconds)

MATH BREAK

Speed of Sound

The speed of sound depends on the medium through which sound is traveling and the medium's temperature. Sound travels at 343 m/s through air that has a temperature of 20°C. How far will sound travel in 3 seconds through air at 20°C?

distance = speed × time

distance = 343 $\frac{m}{\cancel{s}}$ × 3 $\cancel{s}$

distance = 1,029 m

Now It's Your Turn

How far does sound travel in 5 seconds through air, water, and steel at 20°C? Use the speeds given in the chart on the previous page.

Easy Listening — LabBook PG 710

Teaching Transparency 286
"Pitch Depends on Frequency"
"Frequencies Heard by Different Animals"

The Speed of Sound Depends on Temperature

In 1947, American pilot Chuck Yeager became the first person to travel faster than the speed of sound. But he was flying at a speed of only 293 m/s! If the speed of sound in air is 343 m/s (as shown in the chart on the previous page), how did Yeager fly faster than the speed of sound? The answer has to do with the temperature of the air.

In general, the cooler the medium, the slower the speed of sound. This happens because particles in cool materials move slower than particles in warmer materials. When the particles move slower, they transmit energy more slowly. Therefore, sound travels more slowly in cold air than in hot air.

Chuck Yeager flew at 12,000 m above sea level. At that height the temperature of the air is so low that the speed of sound is only 290 m/s. So when he flew at 293 m/s, he was flying 3 m/s faster than the speed of sound.

Pitch Depends on Frequency

Think about the guitar you made at the beginning of this chapter. You used two rubber bands of different thicknesses as strings. You probably noticed that the thicker rubber band made a lower sound than the thinner rubber band made. How low or high you perceive a sound to be is the **pitch** of that sound.

The pitch of a sound is determined by the frequency of the sound wave, as shown in **Figure 6**. The *frequency* of a wave is the number of waves produced in a given time. Frequency is expressed in *hertz* (Hz), where 1 Hz = 1 wave per second.

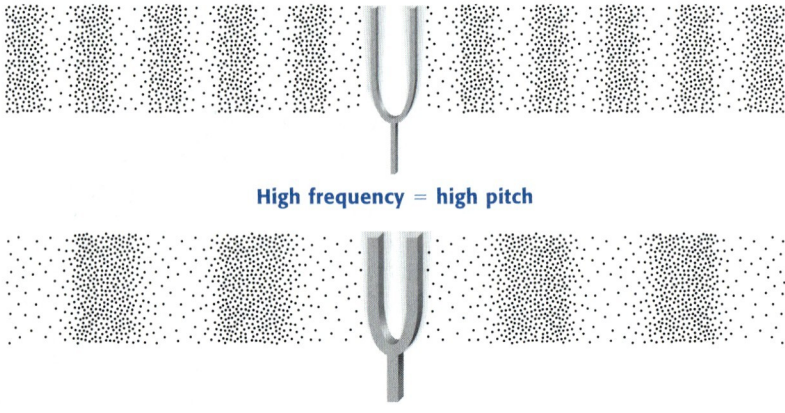

Figure 6 *The thicker tuning fork vibrates at a lower frequency. Therefore, it creates a sound with a lower pitch.*

High frequency = high pitch

Low frequency = low pitch

Science Bloopers

In 1742, the freezing point of water was set by the Swedish astronomer Anders Celsius (1701–1744) at 100°C and the boiling point was set at 0°C. Carolus Linnaeus (1707–1778) reversed the scale, but a textbook gave Celsius the credit and his name continues to be associated with this temperature scale.

Frequency and Hearing Some people use dog whistles to call their dog. But when you see someone blow a dog whistle, the whistle seems silent to you. That's because the frequency of the sound wave is out of the range of human hearing. But the dog hears a very high pitch from the whistle and comes running! The graph below compares the range of frequencies that humans and animals can hear.

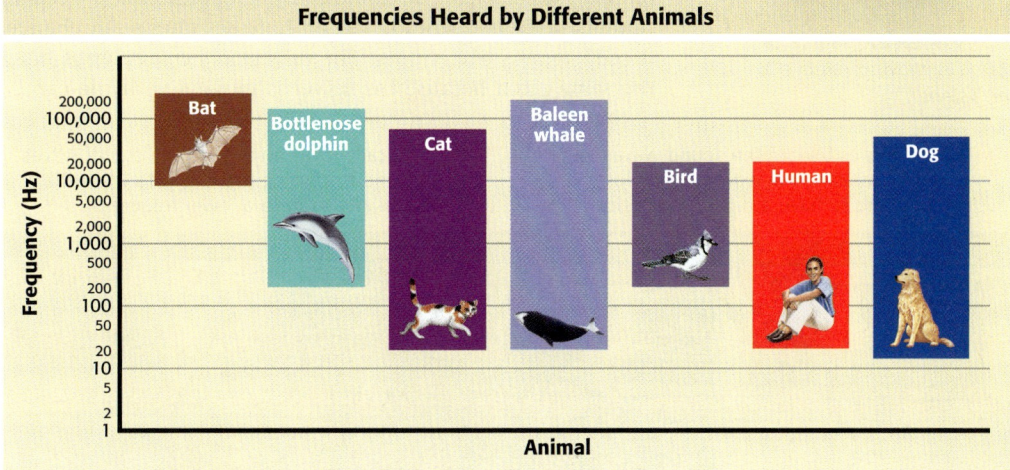

Frequencies You Can Hear The average human ear can detect sounds that have frequencies between 20 Hz and 20,000 Hz. Examples of sounds within this range include the lowest sound a pipe organ can make (about 40 Hz) and the screech of a bat (10,000 Hz or higher). The range of hearing varies from person to person. Young children can often hear sounds with frequencies above this range, while many elderly people have difficulty hearing sounds higher than 8,000 Hz.

Frequencies You Can't Hear Sounds that are outside the range of human hearing have special names. Sounds with frequencies that are lower than 20 Hz are described as **infrasonic.** Sounds with frequencies that are higher than 20,000 Hz are described as **ultrasonic.** The sounds are given these names because *sonic* refers to sound, *infra* means "below," and *ultra* means "beyond."

Ultrasonic waves have a variety of applications. For example, ultrasonic waves are used to clean jewelry and to remove ice from metal. Scientists hope to use this technology to remove ice from airplane wings, car windshields, and freezers. You will learn about other uses of ultrasonic waves in the next section.

Biology CONNECTION

Kidney stones—deposits of calcium salts that form inside kidneys—can cause a great deal of pain. Sometimes they are so large that they have to be removed by a doctor. Surgery was once the primary way to remove kidney stones, but now ultrasonic waves can be used to break kidney stones into smaller pieces that can pass out of the body with urine.

Because of prolonged exposure to loud noises, some people suffer from a type of hearing loss called sensorineural hearing loss. Often, they lose only the ability to hear high-frequency sounds. Middle- and low-frequency hearing in these people are usually unaffected. Thus, people who have sensorineural hearing loss may complain that people mumble. They can hear a person talking, but because of their hearing loss they cannot understand what is being said.

USING THE GRAPH

Tell students that in a normal conversation the human voice ranges from about 110 Hz to 500 Hz. Ask which animals on the chart would be able to hear this range of frequencies.

Point out that the bar graph on this page has a logarithmic scale. It looks like the ranges of hearing for the different animals do not differ by very much, but if the students look at the numbers on the *y*-axis, they will see that there are large differences. Have the students find the ranges of frequencies heard by humans and by dogs and compare the numbers.

CONNECT TO LIFE SCIENCE

Elephants are highly social animals that use vision, scent, and sounds to communicate with each other. Scientists have learned that some of those sounds are infrasonic (below the range of human hearing) and that these sounds can travel as far as 10 km. Read or review the feature "Sounds of Silence," on page 531.

IS THAT A FACT!

Studies now show that regions of hair cells within the inner ear are actually "tuned" to specific frequencies. Because of their differences in size and shape, hair cells have a specific resonance at which they vibrate. This means that certain frequencies will activate some hair cells but not others.

Section 2 • Properties of Sound 541

2 Teach, continued

MEETING INDIVIDUAL NEEDS

Learners Having Difficulty
Have students use colored pencils to draw a diagram showing the Doppler effect. Have them include a listener, a vehicle, and lines depicting sound waves.

DEMONSTRATION

Find a noisemaker that produces a constant sound (a small buzzer or something similar). Attach the noisemaker to the end of a string or rope approximately 70–90 cm long. (It may be necessary to do this demonstration outside.)

Let students hear the noise from the noisemaker. Stand away from the students and away from any walls. Swing the noisemaker by the string in a wide circle over your head. Ask students to explain what they hear in terms of the Doppler effect. (When the noisemaker is coming toward them, they will hear a higher pitch because the sound waves are closer together. When it is moving away from them, they will hear a lower pitch because the sound waves are farther apart.)

CONNECT TO LIFE SCIENCE

The loudest bird in North America is the whooping crane. Its call can be heard from about 5 km away.

Teaching Transparency 287
"The Doppler Effect"

The Doppler Effect Have you ever been passed by a car with its horn honking? If so, you probably noticed the sudden change in pitch—sort of an *EEEEEOOooooowwn* sound—as the car sped past you. The pitch you heard was higher while the car was approaching than it was after the car passed. This is a result of the Doppler effect. For sound waves, the **Doppler effect** is the apparent change in the frequency of a sound caused by the motion of either the listener or the source of the sound. **Figure 7** explains the Doppler effect. Keep in mind that the frequency of the car horn does not really change; it only sounds like it does. The driver of the car always hears the same pitch because the driver is moving with the car.

Figure 7 The Doppler effect occurs when the source of a sound is moving relative to the listener.

a The car moves toward the sound waves in front of it, causing the waves to be closer together and to have a higher frequency.

b The car moves away from the sound waves behind it, causing the waves to be farther apart and to have a lower frequency.

c A listener in front of the car hears a higher pitch than a listener behind the car.

Loudness Is Related to Amplitude

If you gently tap a bass drum, you will hear a soft rumbling. But if you strike the drum with a large force, you will hear a loud *BOOM*! By changing the force you use to strike the drum, you change the loudness of the sound that is created. **Loudness** is how loud or soft a sound is perceived to be.

Energy and Vibration The harder you strike a drum, the louder the boom. As you strike the drum harder, you transfer more energy to the drum. The drum moves with a larger vibration and transfers more energy to the surrounding air. This increase in energy causes air particles to vibrate farther from their rest positions.

BRAIN FOOD

The sounds made by booming sands are sometimes so loud that scientists working on the dunes have to shout to hear each other.

542

CROSS-DISCIPLINARY FOCUS

History The Doppler effect is named after the Austrian mathematician Christian Doppler (1803–1853), who first proposed it in 1842 in a paper describing the colored light of double stars. In 1845, Doppler applied his theory to sound waves and tested it with trumpet players on a train.

In 1929, astronomer Edwin Hubble (1889–1953) used Doppler's theory to interpret his measurements and show that the farther away from Earth a galaxy is, the faster it is moving away from Earth and the more the light from that galaxy is "shifted" toward the red end of the spectrum.

Increasing Amplitude When you strike a drum harder, you are increasing the amplitude of the sound waves being created. The *amplitude* of a wave is the maximum distance the particles in a wave vibrate from their rest positions. The larger the amplitude, the louder the sound, and the smaller the amplitude, the softer the sound. **Figure 8** shows one way to increase the loudness of a sound. Do the QuickLab on this page to investigate the loudness and pitch of sounds.

Figure 8 *An amplifier increases the amplitude of the sound generated by an electric guitar.*

Measuring Loudness The most common unit used to express loudness is the **decibel (dB).** The faintest sounds an average human ear can hear are at a level of 0 dB. The level of 120 dB is sometimes called the threshold of pain because sounds at that level and higher can cause your ears to hurt. Continued exposure to sounds above 85 dB causes gradual hearing loss by permanently damaging the hair cells in your inner ear. The chart below shows the decibel levels of some common sounds.

Some Common Decibel Levels

Sound	Decibel level
The softest sounds you can hear	0
Whisper	20
Purring cat	25
Normal conversation	60
Lawn mower, vacuum cleaner, truck traffic	80
Chain saw, snowmobile	100
Sandblaster, loud rock concert, automobile horn	115
Threshold of pain	120
Jet engine 30 m away	140
Rocket engine 50 m away	200

QuickLab

Sounding Board

1. With one hand, hold a **metric ruler** on your desk so that one end of it hangs over the edge.
2. With your other hand, pull the free end of the ruler up a few centimeters and let go.
3. Try pulling the ruler up different distances. How does the distance affect the sounds you hear? What property of the sound wave are you changing?
4. Try changing the length of the part that hangs over the edge. What property of the sound wave is affected?
5. Record your answers and observations in your ScienceLog.

IS THAT A FACT!

The decibel is one-tenth of a Bel, which is a unit of measurement used to compare two levels of sound intensity. The Bel is named for Alexander Graham Bell (1847–1922), the inventor of the telephone.

 Reinforcement Worksheet 21 "Doppler Dan's Dump Truck"

TOPIC: Properties of Sound
GO TO: www.scilinks.org
sciLINKS NUMBER: HSTP515

QuickLab

Safety Caution: Remind students to wear safety goggles when doing this lab.

Teacher Notes:
Any stiff wooden or plastic ruler will work for this lab.

Answers to QuickLab

3. The farther up they pull the ruler, the louder the sound will be. Amplitude is changing.
4. The shorter the length of the ruler hanging off the edge of the table, the higher the pitch will be. Changing the length of the ruler hanging off the edge changes the frequency of the sound wave.

3) Extend

REAL-WORLD CONNECTION

Listening to loud music and attending loud concerts can be harmful to your hearing. Loudness is expressed in *decibels* (dB). Long-term exposure to sounds above 85 dB is considered hazardous to your hearing. Sounds louder than 85 dB take less time to cause hearing damage. Music concerts are often 110 dB or louder, so the potential for hearing damage is very real.

RESEARCH

 Have students select one of the topics they read about in this section (speed of sound, Doppler effect, or loudness) and find ways that the topic is relevant to their everyday lives. They may wish to research supersonic flight, Doppler radar, or hearing damage due to exposure to louds sounds. Students can share their findings in a variety of ways. Sheltered English

Section 2 • Properties of Sound **543**

4 Close

Multicultural CONNECTION

An oscilloscope is a device that visually represents sound as an electric wave. The first oscilloscope, a modification of the cathode ray, was invented in 1897 by a German physicist named Karl Ferdinand Braun (1850–1918).

Quiz

1. Name three properties of sound. (The speed of sound depends on the medium; pitch depends on frequency; and loudness depends on amplitude.)

2. Explain how a person can observe the Doppler effect. (When a loud noise is moving toward or away from an observer, the sound appears to change pitch because the sound waves are moving closer together or farther apart.)

3. What is the difference between ultrasonic and infrasonic waves? (Ultrasonic waves are waves above 20,000 Hz, and infrasonic waves are those below 20 Hz.)

ALTERNATIVE ASSESSMENT

Concept Mapping Have students create a concept map showing the properties of sound. Concept maps should include the vocabulary terms from this section and examples illustrating the terms.

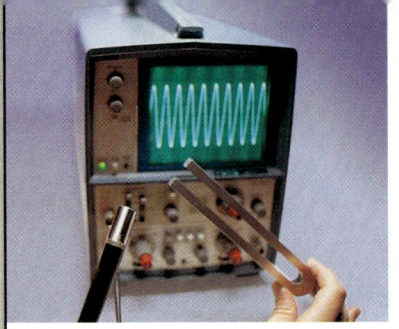

Figure 9 An oscilloscope can be used to represent sounds.

Figure 10 "Seeing" Sounds

The graph on the right has a **larger amplitude** than the graph on the left. Therefore, the sound represented on the right is **louder** than the one on the left.

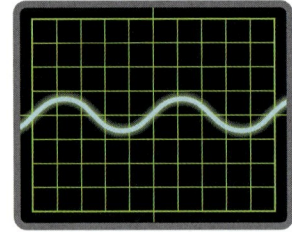 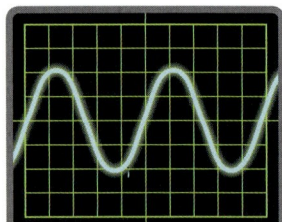

The graph on the right has a **lower frequency** than the one on the left. So the sound represented on the right has a **lower pitch** than the one on the left.

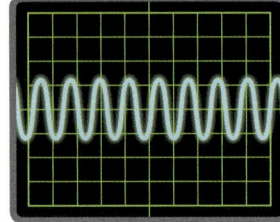 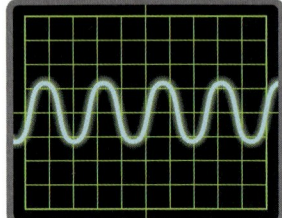

internetconnect

SC_**LINKS**_
NSTA

TOPIC: Properties of Sound
GO TO: www.scilinks.org
sci**LINKS NUMBER:** HSTP515

"Seeing" Sounds Because sound waves are invisible, their amplitude and frequency is impossible to measure directly. However, technology can provide a way to "see" sound waves. A device called an *oscilloscope* (uh SIL uh SKOHP), shown in **Figure 9,** is used to graph representations of sound waves.

A microphone first converts the sound wave into an electric current. The oscilloscope then converts the electric current into graphs such as the ones shown in **Figure 10**. Notice that the graphs look like transverse waves instead of longitudinal waves. The highest points (crests) of these waves represent compressions, and the lowest points (troughs) represent rarefactions. By looking at the displays on the oscilloscope, you can quickly see the difference in both amplitude and frequency of sound waves.

REVIEW

1. In general, how does changing the temperature of a medium affect the speed of sound through that medium?

2. What properties of waves affect the pitch and loudness of sound?

3. **Inferring Conclusions** Will a listener notice the Doppler effect if he or she and the source of the sound are traveling toward each other? Explain your answer.

Answers to Review

1. In general, increasing the temperature of a medium will increase the speed of sound through that medium. Likewise, decreasing the temperature will decrease the speed of sound.

2. The frequency of the sound wave affects the pitch of the sound, and the amplitude of the sound wave affects the loudness of the sound.

3. Yes; the sound waves in front of the source will become closer together as the source moves forward. Also, the listener will "meet" the sound waves more rapidly by moving toward the source. The movements of both the source and the listener will make the pitch of the sound higher.

Section 3

Interactions of Sound Waves

Terms to Learn
reflection
echo
echolocation
interference
sonic boom
standing wave
resonance
diffraction

What You'll Do
- Explain how echoes are produced, and describe their use in locating objects.
- Give examples of constructive and destructive interference of sound waves.
- Identify three sound-wave interactions, and give examples of each.

Beluga whales, such as those shown in **Figure 11,** communicate by using a wide variety of sounds, including clicks, chirps, whistles, trills, screeches, and moos. The sounds they make can be heard above and below water. Because of the wide range of sounds they make, belugas have been nicknamed "sea canaries." But belugas use sound for more than just communication—they also use reflected sound waves to find fish, crabs, and shrimp to eat. In this section you'll learn about reflection and other interactions of sound waves.

Figure 11 Beluga whales depend on sound interactions for survival.

Reflection of Sound Waves

Reflection is the bouncing back of a wave after it strikes a barrier. You're probably already familiar with a reflected sound wave, otherwise known as an **echo.** The amount a sound wave will reflect depends on the reflecting surface. Sound waves reflect best off smooth, hard surfaces. That's why a shout in an empty gymnasium can produce an echo, but a shout in an empty auditorium usually does not, as shown in **Figure 12.**

Figure 12
Sound Reflection and Absorption

Sound waves easily reflect off the smooth, hard walls of a gymnasium. That's why you hear an echo.

In well-designed auditoriums, echoes are reduced by soft materials that absorb sound waves and by irregular shapes that scatter sound waves.

IS THAT A FACT!
According to Greek mythology, echoes originated when the angry goddess Hera placed a curse on the wood nymph Echo that caused her to repeat whatever was said to her.

 Directed Reading Worksheet 21 Section 3

2) Teach

CROSS-DISCIPLINARY FOCUS

Language Arts The power of sound is so strong that stories have been written about it. In Homer's epic poem *The Odyssey* the war hero Odysseus makes his journey home after the Trojan War. Odysseus and his crew sail near an island where beautiful women sing so sweetly that men are lured to their death. While his men put wax in their ears, Odysseus chooses to be lashed to the mast so that he can hear the beautiful music but not be lured onto the rocks. Have students write a story in which the plot depends on a sound. Students must include science concepts learned in this chapter.

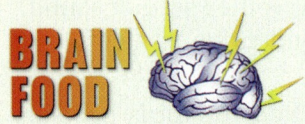

Can people learn echolocation? Many blind people know how to locate items by clicking their fingers or listening to their own footsteps.

CONNECT TO EARTH SCIENCE

Use Teaching Transparency 154 to show students how scientists use sound waves to map the ocean floor.

Teaching Transparency 154 "How Sonar Works"

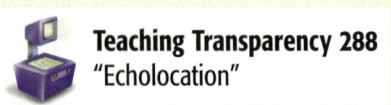
Teaching Transparency 288 "Echolocation"

Figure 13 *Bats use echolocation to navigate around barriers and to find insects to eat.*

Echolocation Beluga whales use echoes to find food. The process of using reflected sound waves to find objects is called **echolocation**. Other animals—such as dolphins, bats, and some species of birds—also use echolocation to hunt food and detect objects in their paths. **Figure 13** shows how echolocation works.

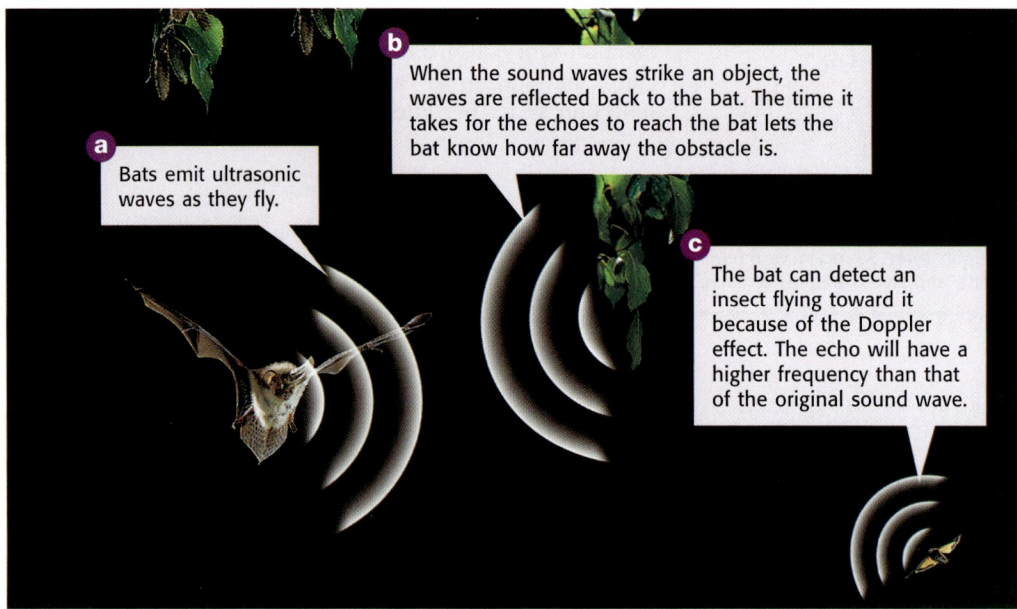

a. Bats emit ultrasonic waves as they fly.

b. When the sound waves strike an object, the waves are reflected back to the bat. The time it takes for the echoes to reach the bat lets the bat know how far away the obstacle is.

c. The bat can detect an insect flying toward it because of the Doppler effect. The echo will have a higher frequency than that of the original sound wave.

Echolocation Technology Humans use echoes to locate objects underwater and underground by using sonar (**so**und **na**vigation **a**nd **r**anging). *Sonar* is a type of electronic echolocation. **Figure 14** shows how sonar works. Ultrasonic waves are used because their short wavelengths provide more details about the objects they reflect off. Sonar can also help navigators on ships detect icebergs and can help oceanographers map the ocean floor.

Figure 14 *A depth finder sends ultrasonic waves down into the water. The time it takes for the echo to return helps the fishermen determine the location of the fish.*

IS THAT A FACT!

Dolphins use echolocation by emitting rapid, high-pitched clicks and listening for the returning echo. The closer a dolphin gets to an object, the faster the clicks return. As a dolphin moves its head side to side to scan, it detects both distance and shape. Dolphins can detect an object that is 2 cm in diameter more than 70 m away in open water.

546 Chapter 21 • The Nature of Sound

APPLY

Insightful Technology

Many people who are blind use a cane to help them detect obstacles while they are walking. Now engineers have developed a sonar cane, shown at right, to help blind people even more. The cane emits and detects sound waves. Based on your knowledge of echolocation, explain how you think this cane works.

Ultrasonography Another type of electronic echolocation is used in a medical procedure called *ultrasonography*. Ultrasonography uses echoes to "see" inside a patient's body without performing surgery. A device called a transducer produces ultrasonic waves, which reflect off the patient's internal organs. These echoes are then converted into images that can be seen on a television monitor, as shown in **Figure 15.** Ultrasonography is used to examine kidneys, gallbladders, and other abdominal organs and to check the development of an unborn baby in a mother's body. Ultrasonic waves are safer than X rays because sound waves are less harmful to human tissue.

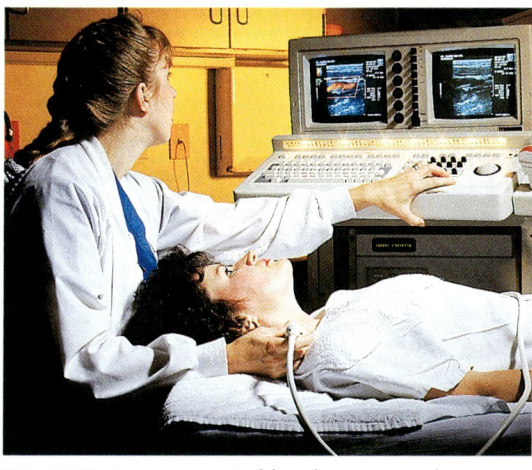

Figure 15 Images created by ultrasonography are fuzzy, but they are a safe way to see inside a patient's body.

REVIEW

1. Describe a place in which you would expect to hear echoes.
2. How do bats use echoes to find insects to eat?
3. **Comparing Concepts** Explain how sonar and ultrasonography are similar when used to locate objects.

2) Teach, continued

MEETING INDIVIDUAL NEEDS

Advanced Learners Destructive interference can make it hard to hear in some parts of a theater or auditorium. To reduce the effects of destructive interference, sounds are usually amplified electronically and speakers are located in different places. But sound waves from the many speakers can also produce destructive interference. Also, sound waves reflected from the walls and other surfaces can interfere with waves from the speakers. Have students find out how theaters, concert halls, and recording studios are designed and built to reduce destructive interference. Encourage them to use models or posters to show their results.

CROSS-DISCIPLINARY FOCUS

Music In 1962, New York City's Avery Fisher Hall opened, but there were problems with the hall's acoustics. There were too many echoes and dead spots caused by sound waves interfering with one another. In 1976, the hall's interior was removed and was replaced with an interior that produced better acoustics.

REAL-WORLD CONNECTION

Some livestock ranchers use machines that are similar to medical ultrasound devices to measure the fat layers in their cattle and pigs. These devices use frequencies of sound that are far above the range of human hearing to determine the amount of body fat in the animals.

Interference of Sound Waves

Another interaction of sound waves is interference. **Interference** is the result of two or more waves overlapping. **Figure 16** shows how two sound waves can combine by both constructive and destructive interference.

Figure 16 Sound waves from two speakers producing sound of the same frequency combine by both constructive and destructive interference.

Constructive Interference
As the compressions of one wave overlap the compressions of another wave, the sound will be louder because the amplitude is increased.

Destructive Interference
As the compressions of one wave overlap the rarefactions of another wave, the sound will be softer because the amplitude is decreased.

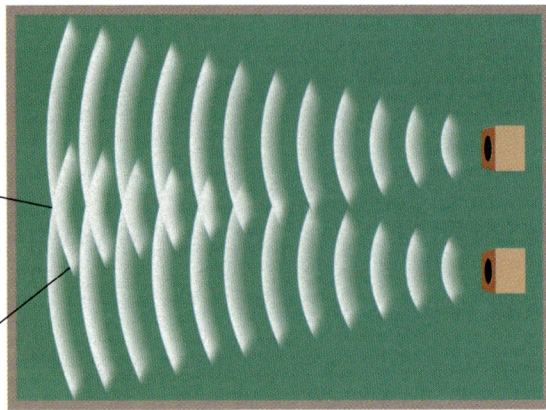

Orchestras and bands take advantage of constructive interference when several instruments play the same notes. The sound waves from the instruments combine by constructive interference to produce a louder sound. But destructive interference may keep you from hearing the concert. "Dead spots" are areas in an auditorium where sound waves reflecting off the walls interfere destructively with the sound waves from the stage. If you are at a concert and you can't hear the orchestra very well, try changing seats before you decide to get your ears checked!

The Sound Barrier As the source of a sound—such as a jet plane—accelerates to the speed of sound, the sound waves in front of the jet plane compress closer and closer together. **Figure 17** shows what happens as a jet plane reaches the speed of sound.

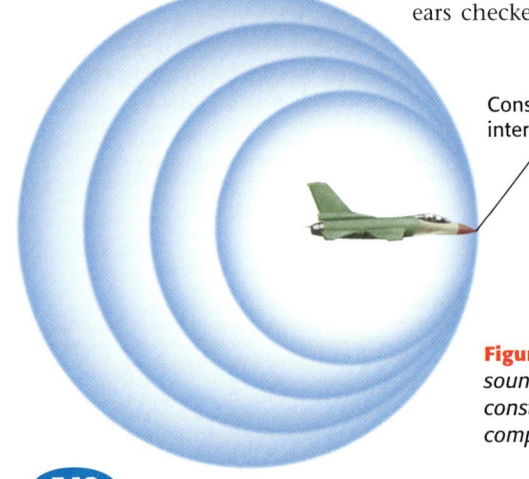

Constructive interference

Figure 17 When a jet plane reaches the speed of sound, the sound waves in front of the jet combine by constructive interference. The result is a high-density compression that is called the sound barrier.

548

IS THAT A FACT!

Mach number is not a speed. It is the ratio between the speed of an object, usually an airplane, and the speed of sound in the medium in which the object is traveling. A plane traveling at Mach 3.0 is traveling at three times whatever the speed of sound is at the plane's altitude.

WEIRD SCIENCE

The speed of sound is about 343 m/s at sea level at 20°C and is known as Mach 1. As a plane passes through the sound barrier created at this speed, the resulting shock wave increases the drag on the plane. The plane has to be equipped to control this change in airflow.

548   Chapter 21 • The Nature of Sound

Shock Waves and Sonic Booms For the jet in Figure 17 to travel faster than the speed of sound, it must overcome the pressure of the compressed sound waves. **Figure 18** shows what happens as soon as the jet achieves supersonic speeds—speeds faster than the speed of sound. At these speeds, the sound waves trail off behind the jet and combine at their outer edges to form a shock wave.

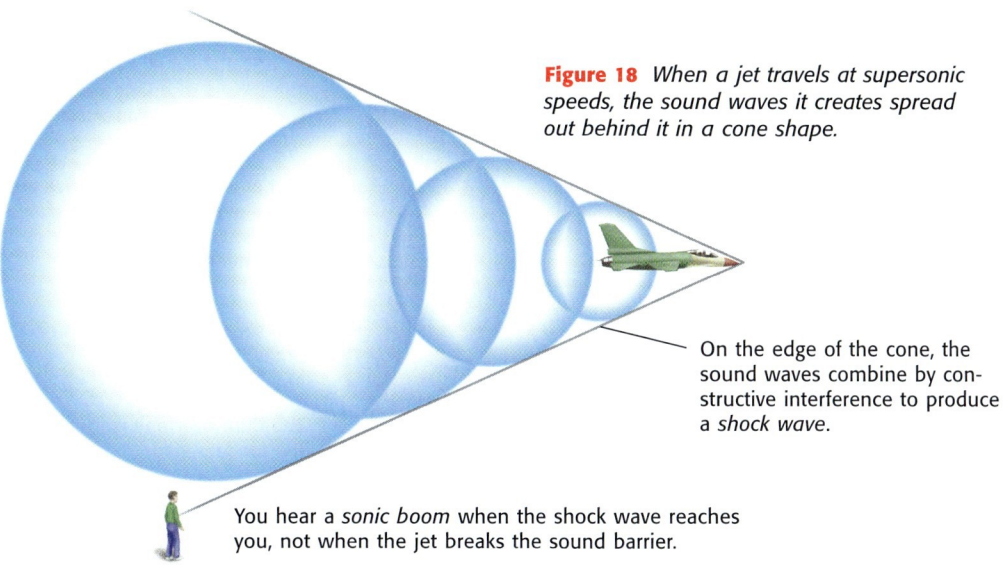

Figure 18 *When a jet travels at supersonic speeds, the sound waves it creates spread out behind it in a cone shape.*

On the edge of the cone, the sound waves combine by constructive interference to produce a *shock wave*.

You hear a *sonic boom* when the shock wave reaches you, not when the jet breaks the sound barrier.

A **sonic boom** is the explosive sound heard when a shock wave reaches your ears. Sonic booms can be so loud that they can hurt your ears and break windows. They can even make the ground shake as it does during an earthquake.

 **Self-Check**

Explain why two people will not hear a sonic boom at the same time if they are standing a block or two apart. *(See page 724 to check your answer.)*

The cracking sound made by a whip is actually a miniature sonic boom caused by the shock wave formed as the tip of the whip travels faster than the speed of sound!

Standing Waves When you play a guitar, you can make some pleasing sounds and maybe even play a tune. But have you ever watched a guitar string after you've plucked it? You may have noticed that the string vibrates as a standing wave. A **standing wave** is a result of interference in which portions of the wave are at the rest position and other portions have a large amplitude.

IS THAT A FACT!

A double sonic boom occurs when the space shuttle enters the atmosphere. Whenever a craft exceeds Mach 1, one shock wave is formed at the nose and another shock wave is formed at the tail. If the shock waves are more than 0.10 s apart, you hear two sonic booms.

REAL-WORLD CONNECTION

The sound transmission class (STC) rating tells how well building materials insulate sound. The higher the number, the more the material blocks sound.

STC #	What can be heard
25	Normal speech can be heard.
30	Loud speech can be heard.
35	Loud speech is audible but not intelligible.
42	Loud speech is audible as a murmur.
45	A person must strain to hear loud speech.
48	Some loud speech is barely audible.
50	Loud speech is inaudible.

Have students research what sort of building materials have the STC ratings given above. Then, have students design a house and use this rating system to determine what building materials to use. Ask them to explain why they put the materials where they did.

Answer to Self-Check

A person hears a sonic boom when a shock wave reaches his or her ears. If two people are standing a block or two apart, the shock wave will reach them at different times, so they will hear a sonic boom at different times.

3) Extend

Research

For more than a century, people have been recording and playing sound. Have students research the history and development of sound recording, including the latest stereo systems used in theaters. Encourage them to find creative ways, such as recordings, to present their findings.

Meeting Individual Needs

Advanced Learners Have students research active noise control (ANC), which reduces or eliminates low-frequency sounds through destructive interference. The system broadcasts sound waves through speakers that are 180° out of phase with the noise. Encourage students to create models or posters to demonstrate their findings.

When overtones are exact multiples of the fundamental, they are often called "harmonics." However, confusion sometimes results because harmonics are numbered to include the fundamental, but overtones are not. As a result, the first overtone is the second harmonic, the second overtone is the third harmonic, and so on.

Tuneful Tube

TOPIC: Interactions of Sound Waves
GO TO: www.scilinks.org
sciLINKS NUMBER: HSTP520

Resonant Frequencies Although you can see only one standing wave, the guitar string actually creates several standing waves of different frequencies at the same time. The frequencies at which standing waves are made are called *resonant frequencies*. Resonant frequencies are sometimes called by special names, as shown in **Figure 19**.

Figure 19 *A plucked string vibrates at several resonant frequencies.*

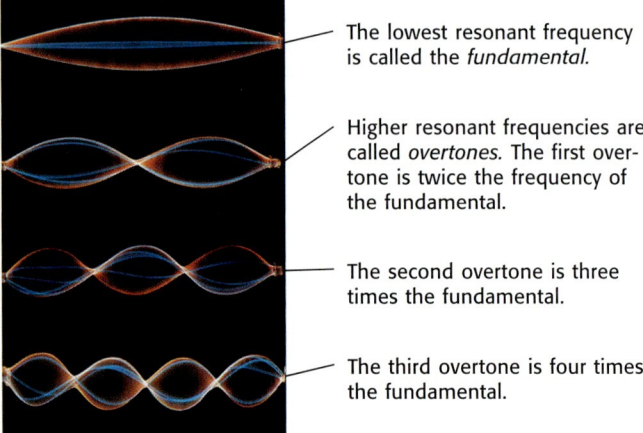

- The lowest resonant frequency is called the *fundamental.*
- Higher resonant frequencies are called *overtones.* The first overtone is twice the frequency of the fundamental.
- The second overtone is three times the fundamental.
- The third overtone is four times the fundamental.

A tuning fork and a plastic tube make beautiful music together on page 713 of the LabBook.

Resonance Would you believe that you can make a guitar string make a sound without touching it? You can do this if you have a tuning fork, shown in **Figure 20,** that vibrates at one of the resonant frequencies of the guitar string. Strike the tuning fork, and hold it close to the string. The string will start to vibrate and produce a sound. The effect is the greatest when the resonant frequency of the tuning fork matches the fundamental frequency of the string.

Using the vibrations of the tuning fork to make the string vibrate is an example of resonance. **Resonance** occurs when an object vibrating at or near a resonant frequency of a second object causes the second object to vibrate.

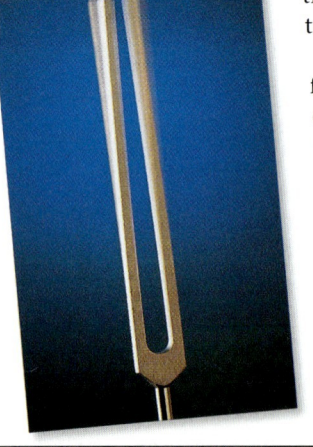

Figure 20 *When struck, a tuning fork can make certain objects vibrate.*

Diffraction of Sound Waves

Have you ever noticed the different sounds of thunder? From a distance, thunder sounds like a low rumbling. From nearby, thunder sounds like a loud *CRACK*! A type of wave interaction called diffraction causes this difference. **Diffraction** is the bending of waves around barriers or through openings. It is how sound waves travel around the corners of buildings and through doorways. The amount of diffraction is greatest when the size of the barrier or the opening is the same size or smaller than the wavelength of the sound waves, as shown in **Figure 21**.

Figure 21 Determining the Amount of Diffraction

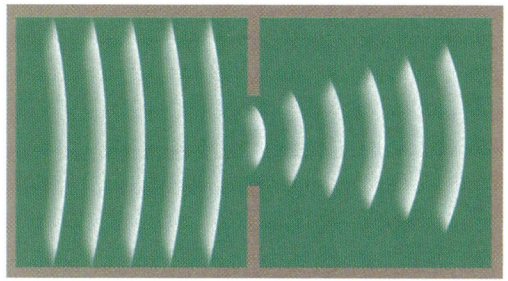
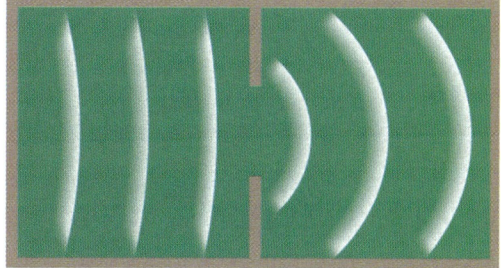

High-frequency sound waves have short wavelengths and do not diffract very much when they travel through a doorway. Therefore, high pitches can be hard to hear when you are in the next room.

Low-frequency sound waves have longer wavelengths, so they diffract more through doorways. Therefore, you can hear lower pitches better when you are in the next room.

So what about thunder? Thunder consists of both high- and low-frequency sound waves. When lightning strikes nearby, you hear all the sound waves together as a loud cracking noise. But when the lightning strikes far away, buildings, trees, hills, and other barriers stop most of the high-frequency waves. Only the low-frequency waves can diffract around these large objects, and thus you hear only a low rumbling.

REVIEW

1. How is a sound barrier formed?
2. When you are in a classroom, why can you hear voices from the hallway even when you cannot see who is talking?
3. **Inferring Conclusions** Your friend is playing a song on a piano. Whenever your friend hits a certain key, the lamp on top of the piano rattles. Explain why this happens.

TOPIC: Interactions of Sound Waves
GO TO: www.scilinks.org
*sci*LINKS NUMBER: HSTP520

4) Close

Quiz

1. Why does everything seem so quiet after a snowfall? (Snow does not reflect sound waves; it absorbs them.)
2. Have you ever sung in the shower? Why does your voice sound so much better there? (The hard, smooth walls of the shower reflect sound waves, and the interactions of the waves, make your voice sound fuller.)
3. In some places, like on the Colorado River, deep in the Grand Canyon gorge, a motorboat can be heard 15 minutes before the boat comes into view. Why? (The sound waves from the boat's motor travel faster than the boat. These sound waves are trapped and reflected by the canyon's wall, and this keeps the waves from spreading out and losing intensity, as they would in a flat, open area.)

ALTERNATIVE ASSESSMENT

Have students write fictional articles for a tabloid newspaper about a strange phenomenon caused by an interaction of sound waves they have learned about in this chapter. Remind them that the science must be accurate but that they can be creative and exaggerate the effects of the sound waves.

Answers to Review

1. A sound barrier is formed by constructive interference of sound waves. The sound waves produced by a plane traveling at the speed of sound will combine by constructive interference to form a high-density compression. This high-density compression is the sound barrier.
2. The sound waves of the people's voices diffract around the opening of the door.
3. The lamp is in resonance with the sound made by the piano key. Because it is in resonance, the lamp vibrates and rattles.

The Speed of Sound

The Energy of Sound

SECTION 4

Focus

Sound Quality

This section defines *sound quality* and explains how the three main musical-instrument families (wind, percussion, and string) produce sound. Students learn the difference between music and noise.

Bellringer

Ask the following questions:

- Which strings on a piano have lower pitch? (the longer and thicker strings)
- Why does a tuba have a lower pitch than a trumpet? (Sample answer: A tuba has a longer and larger air column.)
- Why are some sounds pleasing to hear and some sounds not? Explain your answer. (Accept all reasonable answers.)

1 Motivate

DEMONSTRATION

This should be a brief demonstration just to show students the variety of ways that musical instruments can make sounds. Ask two or three different volunteers who play musical instruments to demonstrate them for the class. Without discussing the different families of instruments, have students compare the sound quality of instruments within a family and from different families. Tell the band or orchestra members that they will have a chance to perform later in the lesson. A more extensive demonstration is found on page 553.

Directed Reading Worksheet 21 Section 4

552   Chapter 21 • The Nature of Sound

Section 4

Terms to Learn
sound quality
noise

What You'll Do
- Define sound quality.
- Describe how each family of musical instruments produces sound.
- Explain how noise is different from music.

Sound Quality

Have you ever been told that some music you really like is just a lot of noise? If you have, you know that people sometimes disagree about the difference between noise and music. You probably think of noise as sounds you don't like and think of music as sounds that are interesting and pleasant to hear. But there is actually a difference between music and noise, and the difference has to do with sound quality.

What Is Sound Quality?

If the same note is played with the same loudness on a piano and on a violin, could you tell the instruments apart without looking? Although the notes played are identical, you probably could tell them apart because the sounds the instruments produce are not the same. The notes sound different because each instrument actually produces several different pitches: the fundamental and several overtones. These pitches are modeled in **Figure 22.** The result of several pitches blending together through interference is **sound quality.** Each instrument has a unique sound quality. **Figure 23** shows how the sound quality differs when two instruments play the same note.

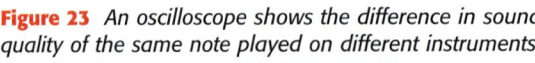

Figure 22 *The top three diagrams represent three different pitches played at the same time. The bottom diagram shows the result when the pitches blend through interference.*

Figure 23 *An oscilloscope shows the difference in sound quality of the same note played on different instruments.*

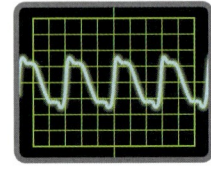
Piano

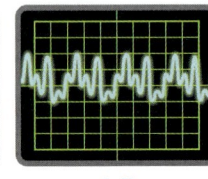
Violin

IS THAT A FACT!

Many cultures write and play music on a basic eight-tone scale, although the notes or tones may vary greatly from scale to scale. Other cultures use a five-tone, or *pentatonic*, scale. Whichever scale is used, each note has a characteristic frequency and the notes span a frequency range called an octave.

Sound Quality of Instruments

When you listen to an orchestra play you can hear many different kinds of instruments. The difference in sound quality among the instruments comes from the structural differences of the instruments. All instruments produce sound with vibrations. But the part of the instrument that vibrates and how the vibrations are made vary from instrument to instrument. Even so, all instruments fall within three main families: string instruments, wind instruments, and percussion instruments.

String Instruments Violins, guitars, and banjos are examples of string instruments. They produce sound when their strings vibrate after being plucked or bowed. **Figure 24** shows how two different string instruments produce sounds.

> **Self-Check**
>
> Which wave interaction is most important in determining sound quality? *(See page 724 to check your answer.)*

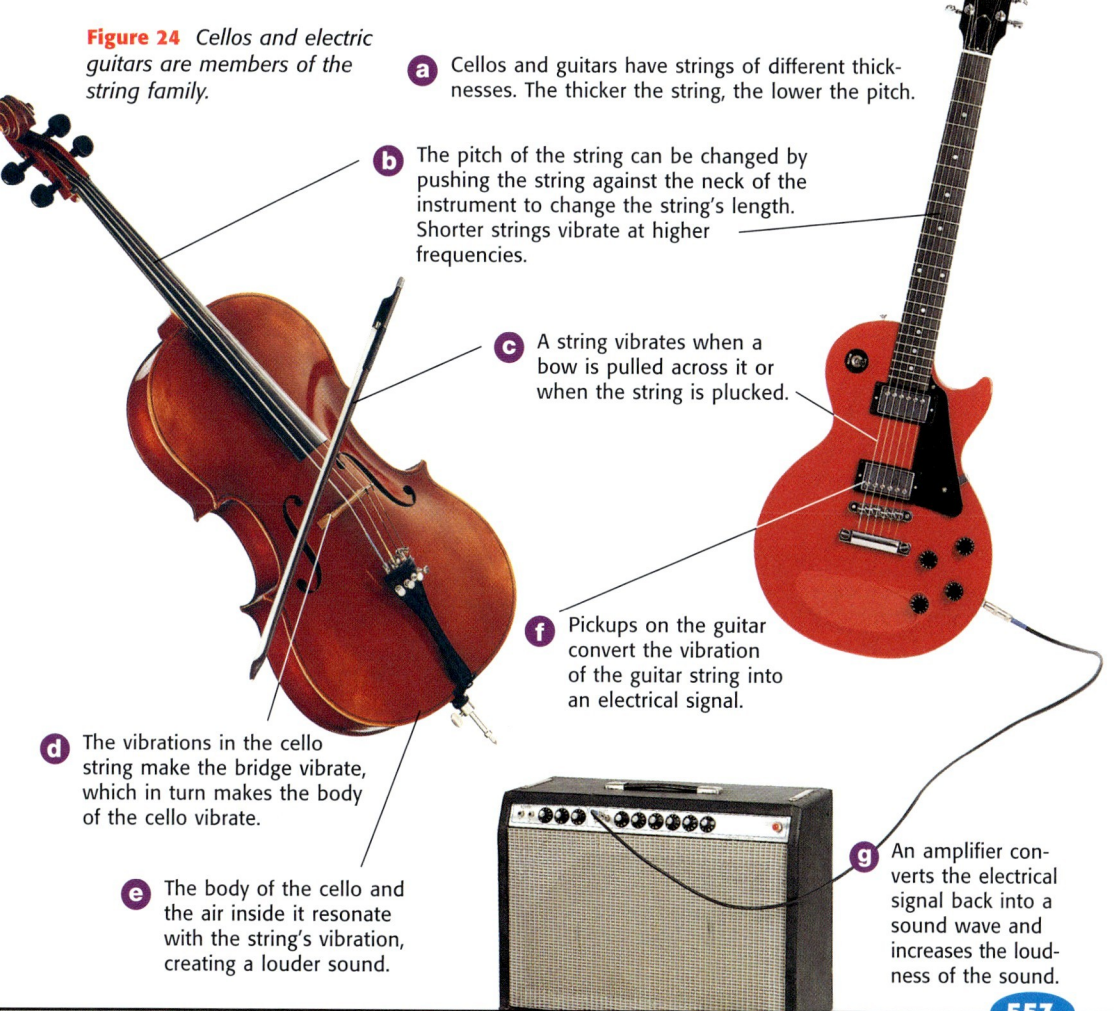

Figure 24 Cellos and electric guitars are members of the string family.

a Cellos and guitars have strings of different thicknesses. The thicker the string, the lower the pitch.

b The pitch of the string can be changed by pushing the string against the neck of the instrument to change the string's length. Shorter strings vibrate at higher frequencies.

c A string vibrates when a bow is pulled across it or when the string is plucked.

d The vibrations in the cello string make the bridge vibrate, which in turn makes the body of the cello vibrate.

e The body of the cello and the air inside it resonate with the string's vibration, creating a louder sound.

f Pickups on the guitar convert the vibration of the guitar string into an electrical signal.

g An amplifier converts the electrical signal back into a sound wave and increases the loudness of the sound.

IS THAT A FACT!

The pickup on an electric guitar is a set of magnets wrapped by thousands of turns of wire. The vibrations of the guitar strings create disturbances in the magnetic fields. These disturbances produce electrical impulses in the coils of wire, and these impulses are transmitted to an amplifier, where they are converted into sounds.

3) Extend

ACTIVITY

Making Models Have pairs of students design and make a model of a simple musical instrument. They may use rubber bands, boxes, cans, yarn, paper, scissors, tacks, and wire. Have them present their instrument and explain the type of instrument they have made and the portion that produces the sound.

DEBATE

Noise Pollution at Airports: Who Has the Right? Should people in a neighborhood have a say in whether airplanes can fly over their homes? Should taxpayers pay to have an airport moved to a less populated location? Students can check the regulations at their local airport to find out what the restrictions are. Have students research and debate advantages to adding runways to crowded airports versus maintaining quiet neighborhoods.

Wind Instruments A wind instrument produces sound when a vibration is created at one end of its air column. The vibration creates standing waves in the air column. Wind instruments are sometimes divided into two groups—woodwinds and brass. Examples of woodwinds are saxophones, oboes, and recorders. Brass instruments include French horns, trombones, and tubas. A woodwind instrument and a brass instrument are shown in **Figure 25.**

Figure 25 Clarinets are woodwind instruments, and trumpets are brass instruments.

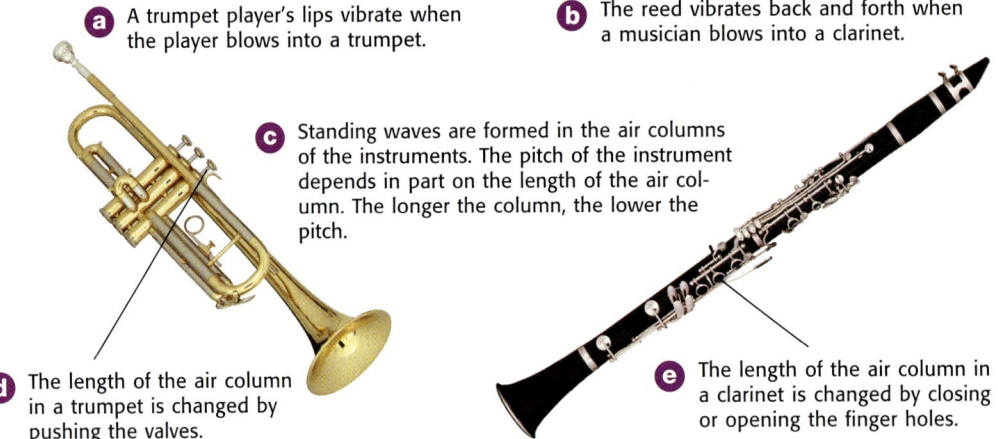

a A trumpet player's lips vibrate when the player blows into a trumpet.

b The reed vibrates back and forth when a musician blows into a clarinet.

c Standing waves are formed in the air columns of the instruments. The pitch of the instrument depends in part on the length of the air column. The longer the column, the lower the pitch.

d The length of the air column in a trumpet is changed by pushing the valves.

e The length of the air column in a clarinet is changed by closing or opening the finger holes.

Percussion Instruments Drums, bells, and cymbals are examples of percussion instruments. They produce sound when struck. Different-sized instruments are used to get different pitches. Usually, the larger the instrument, the lower the pitch. **Figure 26** shows examples of percussion instruments.

Figure 26 Drums and cymbals in a trap set are examples of percussion instruments.

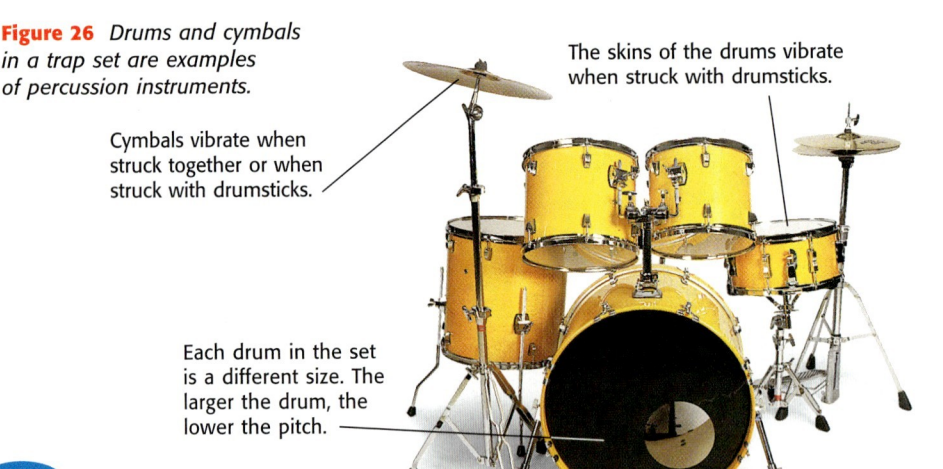

The skins of the drums vibrate when struck with drumsticks.

Cymbals vibrate when struck together or when struck with drumsticks.

Each drum in the set is a different size. The larger the drum, the lower the pitch.

Multicultural CONNECTION

Drums, the most common percussion instruments, have been around since at least 6000 B.C. Drums are found in almost every culture and have been used for a number of purposes, including music. In some African cultures, drums were used to transmit messages over many miles. In Europe, infantry regiments once used snare drums to transmit coded orders to soldiers.

Music or Noise?

Most of the sounds we hear are noises. The sound of a truck roaring down the highway, the slamming of a door, and the jingle of keys falling to the floor are all noises. **Noise** can be described as any undesired sound, especially a nonmusical sound, that includes a random mix of pitches. **Figure 27** shows the difference between a musical sound and noise on an oscilloscope.

Figure 27 *A note from a French horn produces a sound wave with a repeating pattern, but noise from a clap produces complex sound waves with no pattern.*

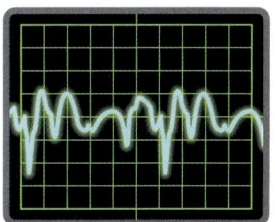
French horn

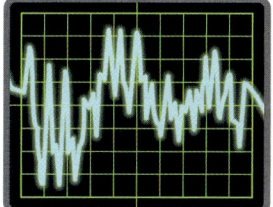
A sharp clap

Noise Pollution The amount of noise around you can become so great that it is not only bothersome but can cause health problems. When noise reaches a level that causes pain or damages the body, it is considered *noise pollution*.

Noise pollution can damage the inner ear, causing permanent hearing loss. Noise pollution can also contribute to sleeplessness, high blood pressure, and stress. Because of these health concerns, the federal government has set noise exposure limits for people who work in areas with loud noises. Noise pollution also makes the environment less livable for humans as well as wildlife.

Environment CONNECTION

The Los Angeles International Airport was built next to the main habitat of an endangered butterfly species called the El Segundo blue. The noise pollution from the airport has driven people and other animals from the area, but the butterflies are not affected because they have no ears!

REVIEW

1. What is the role of interference in determining sound quality?
2. Name the three families of musical instruments, and describe how vibrations are created in each family.
3. **Interpreting Graphics** Look at the oscilloscope screen at right. Do you think the sound represented by the wave on the screen was noise or music? Explain your answer.

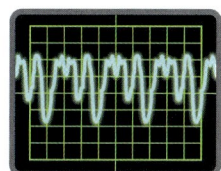

internetconnect
TOPIC: Sound Quality
GO TO: www.scilinks.org
*sci*LINKS NUMBER: HSTP525

Chapter Highlights

VOCABULARY DEFINITIONS

SECTION 1

wave a disturbance that transmits energy through matter or space

medium a substance through which a wave can travel

outer ear the part of the ear that acts as a funnel to direct sound waves into the middle ear

middle ear the part of the ear where the amplitude of sound vibrations is increased

inner ear the part of the ear where vibrations created by sound are changed into electrical signals for the brain to interpret

SECTION 2

pitch how high or low a sound is perceived to be

infrasonic the term describing sounds with frequencies lower than 20 Hz

ultrasonic the term describing sounds with frequencies higher than 20,000 Hz

Doppler effect the apparent change in the frequency of a sound caused by the motion of either the listener or the source of the sound (refers to sound only)

loudness how loud or soft a sound is perceived to be

decibel the most common unit used to express loudness

Chapter Highlights

SECTION 1

Vocabulary
- **wave** (p. 535)
- **medium** (p. 536)
- **outer ear** (p. 537)
- **middle ear** (p. 537)
- **inner ear** (p. 537)

Section Notes
- All sounds are created by vibrations and travel as longitudinal waves.
- Sound waves require a medium through which to travel.
- Sound waves travel in all directions away from their source.
- The sounds you hear are converted into electrical impulses by your ears and then sent to your brain for interpretation.
- Exposure to loud sounds can cause hearing loss and tinnitus.

SECTION 2

Vocabulary
- **pitch** (p. 540)
- **infrasonic** (p. 541)
- **ultrasonic** (p. 541)
- **Doppler effect** (p. 542)
- **loudness** (p. 542)
- **decibel** (p. 543)

Section Notes
- The speed of sound depends on the medium through which the sound is traveling. Changes in temperature of the medium can affect the speed of sound.
- The pitch of a sound depends on frequency. High-frequency sounds are high-pitched, and low-frequency sounds are low-pitched.
- Humans can hear sounds with frequencies between 20 Hz and 20,000 Hz.
- The Doppler effect is the apparent change in frequency of a sound caused by the motion of either the listener or the source of the sound.
- The loudness of a sound increases as the amplitude increases. Loudness is expressed in decibels.
- An oscilloscope can be used to "see" sounds.

Labs
Easy Listening (p. 710)

✓ Skills Check

Math Concepts

THE SPEED OF SOUND The speed of sound depends on the medium through which the sound waves are traveling. The speed of sound through wood at 20°C is 3,850 m/s. The distance sound will travel through wood in 5 seconds can be calculated as follows:

$$\text{distance} = \text{speed} \times \text{time}$$
$$= 3{,}850 \, \tfrac{\text{m}}{\cancel{\text{s}}} \times 5 \, \cancel{\text{s}}$$
$$= 19{,}250 \text{ m}$$

Visual Understanding

HOW THE HUMAN EAR WORKS The human ear has several parts that are divided into three regions—the outer ear, the middle ear, and the inner ear. Study the diagram on page 537 to review how the ear works.

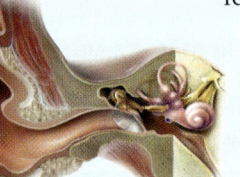

Lab and Activity Highlights

Easy Listening PG 710

The Speed of Sound PG 712

Tuneful Tube PG 713

The Energy of Sound PG 714

 Data Sheets for LabBook (blackline masters for these labs)

556 Chapter 21 • The Nature of Sound

SECTION 3

Vocabulary
- reflection (p. 545)
- echo (p. 545)
- echolocation (p. 546)
- interference (p. 548)
- sonic boom (p. 549)
- standing wave (p. 549)
- resonance (p. 550)
- diffraction (p. 551)

Section Notes
- Echoes are reflected sound waves.
- Some animals use echolocation to find food or navigate around objects. Sonar and ultrasonography are types of echolocation.
- Sound barriers and shock waves are created by interference. You hear a sonic boom when a shock wave reaches your ears.
- Standing waves form at an object's resonant frequencies.
- Resonance occurs when a vibrating object causes a second object to vibrate at one of its resonant frequencies.
- The bending of sound waves around barriers or through openings is called diffraction. The amount of diffraction depends on the wavelength of the waves as well as the size of the opening.

Labs
- The Speed of Sound (p. 712)
- Tuneful Tube (p. 713)
- The Energy of Sound (p. 714)

SECTION 4

Vocabulary
- sound quality (p. 552)
- noise (p. 555)

Section Notes
- Different instruments have different sound qualities.
- The three families of instruments are strings, winds, and percussion.
- The sound quality of noise is not pleasing because it is a random mix of frequencies.

VOCABULARY DEFINITIONS, continued

SECTION 3

reflection the bouncing back of a wave after it strikes a barrier or an object

echo a reflected sound wave

echolocation the process of using reflected sound waves to find objects

interference a wave interaction that occurs when two or more waves overlap and combine

sonic boom the explosive sound heard when a shock wave from an object traveling faster than the speed of sound reaches a person's ears

standing wave a wave that forms a pattern in which portions of the wave do not move and other portions move with a large amplitude

resonance what occurs when an object vibrating at or near a resonant frequency of a second object causes the second object to vibrate

diffraction the bending of waves around barriers or through openings

SECTION 4

sound quality the result of several pitches blending together through interference

noise any undesired sound, especially a nonmusical sound, that includes a random mix of pitches

---

 **internet connect**

 GO TO: go.hrw.com

Visit the **HRW** Web site for a variety of learning tools related to this chapter. Just type in the keyword:

KEYWORD: HSTSND

 GO TO: www.scilinks.org

Visit the **National Science Teachers Association** on-line Web site for Internet resources related to this chapter. Just type in the sciLINKS number for more information about the topic:

TOPIC:	sciLINKS NUMBER:
What Is Sound?	HSTP505
The Ear	HSTP510
Properties of Sound	HSTP515
Interactions of Sound Waves	HSTP520
Sound Quality	HSTP525

 Vocabulary Review Worksheet 21

 Blackline masters of these Chapter Highlights can be found in the **Study Guide**.

Lab and Activity Highlights

LabBank

 EcoLabs & Field Activities, An Earful of Sounds, Field Activity 22

Whiz-Bang Demonstrations,
- A Hot Tone, Demo 61
- Jingle Bells, Silent Bells, Demo 62
- Hear Ye, Hear Ye, Demo 63
- The Sounds of Time, Demo 64

 Long-Term Projects & Research Ideas, The Caped Ace Flies Again, Project 71

Interactive Explorations CD-ROM

 CD 3, Exploration 6, "Sound Bite!"

Chapter Review Answers

USING VOCABULARY

1. ultrasonic
2. inner ear
3. loudness
4. echoes
5. sound quality

UNDERSTANDING CONCEPTS

Multiple Choice

6. a
7. a
8. c
9. c
10. c
11. d
12. d
13. a

Short Answer

14. If a fish is moving away from the whale, the echo off the fish that the whale hears will have a lower pitch than the original sound. If the fish is moving toward the whale, the echo off the fish heard by the whale will have a higher pitch than the original sound.
15. When a jet is traveling at supersonic speeds, the sound waves trail behind it in a cone shape. On the edge of the cone, the sound waves combine by constructive interference and form a shock wave.
16. The outer ear acts like a funnel and directs sound waves into the middle ear. In the middle ear, the hammer, the anvil, and the stirrup work as levers to increase the amplitude of the vibrations. In the inner ear, the vibrations are translated into electrical signals for the brain to interpret.

Chapter Review

USING VOCABULARY

To complete the following sentences, choose the correct term from each pair of terms listed below:

1. Humans cannot hear __?__ waves because their frequencies are above the range of human hearing. (*infrasonic* or *ultrasonic*)
2. In the __?__, vibrations are converted to electrical signals for the brain to interpret. (*middle ear* or *inner ear*)
3. The __?__ of a sound wave depends on its amplitude. (*loudness* or *pitch*)
4. Reflected sound waves are called __?__. (*echoes* or *noise*)
5. Two different instruments playing the same note sound different because of __?__. (*echolocation* or *sound quality*)

UNDERSTANDING CONCEPTS

Multiple Choice

6. If a fire engine is traveling toward you, the Doppler effect will cause the siren to sound
   a. higher.
   b. lower.
   c. louder.
   d. softer.
7. The wave interaction most important for echolocation is
   a. reflection.
   b. interference.
   c. diffraction.
   d. resonance.
8. If two sound waves interfere constructively, you will hear
   a. a high-pitched sound.
   b. a softer sound.
   c. a louder sound.
   d. no change in sound.
9. You will hear a sonic boom when
   a. an object breaks the sound barrier.
   b. an object travels at supersonic speeds.
   c. a shock wave reaches your ears.
   d. the speed of sound is 290 m/s.
10. Instruments that produce sound when struck belong to which family?
    a. strings
    b. winds
    c. percussion
    d. none of the above
11. Resonance can occur when an object vibrates at another object's
    a. resonant frequency.
    b. fundamental frequency.
    c. second overtone frequency.
    d. All of the above
12. The amount of diffraction that a sound wave undergoes depends on
    a. the frequency of the wave.
    b. the amplitude of the wave.
    c. the size of the barrier.
    d. Both (a) and (c)
13. A technological device that can be used to "see" sound waves is a(n)
    a. oscilloscope.
    b. sonar.
    c. transducer.
    d. amplifier.

Short Answer

14. Describe how the Doppler effect helps a beluga whale determine whether a fish is moving away from it or toward it.
15. How is interference involved in forming a shock wave?
16. Briefly describe how the three parts of the ear work.

558

Concept Mapping Transparency 21

558 Chapter 21 • The Nature of Sound

Concept Mapping

17. Use the following terms to create a concept map: sound, sound wave, pitch, loudness, decibel, hertz, frequency, amplitude.

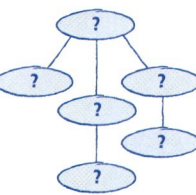

CRITICAL THINKING AND PROBLEM SOLVING

18. An anechoic chamber is a room where there is almost no reflection of sound waves. Anechoic chambers are often used to test sound equipment, such as stereos. The walls of such chambers are usually covered with foam triangles. Explain why this design eliminates echoes in the room.

19. Suppose you are sitting in the passenger seat of a parked car. You hear sounds coming from the stereo of another car parked on the opposite side of the street. You can easily hear the low-pitched bass sounds but cannot hear any high-pitched sounds coming from the parked car. Explain why you think this happens.

20. After working in a factory for a month, a man you know complains about a ringing in his ears. What might be wrong with him? What do you think may have caused his problem? What can you suggest to prevent further hearing loss?

MATH IN SCIENCE

21. How far does sound travel in 4 seconds through water at 20°C and glass at 20°C? Refer to the chart on page 539 for the speed of sound in different media.

INTERPRETING GRAPHICS

Use the oscilloscope screens below to answer the following questions:

22. Which sound is probably noise?
23. Which represents the softest sound?
24. Which represents the sound with the lowest pitch?
25. Which two sounds were produced by the same instrument?

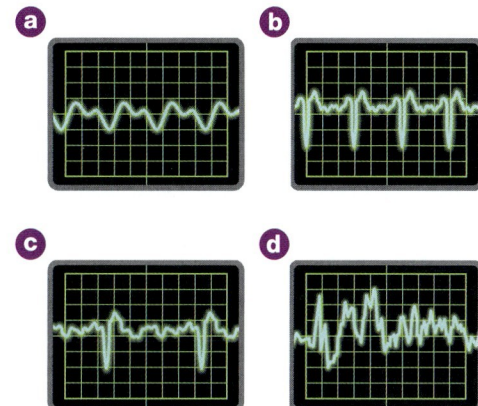

NOW What Do You Think?

Take a minute to review your answers to the ScienceLog questions on page 533. Have your answers changed? If necessary, revise your answers based on what you have learned since you began this chapter.

Concept Mapping

17. 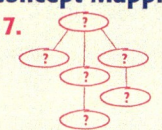 An answer to this exercise can be found at the end of this book.

CRITICAL THINKING AND PROBLEM SOLVING

18. The foam triangles reduce echoes in two ways. The soft foam absorbs the sound waves, and the irregular shapes of the triangles sticking out from the walls scatter the sound waves.

19. Sample answer: Low frequency sounds diffract more than high frequency sounds. Therefore, low frequency bass sounds coming from the car are more likely to reach your ears than high frequency sounds.

20. The man is probably suffering from tinnitus. His condition was probably caused by exposure to loud sounds in the factory where he works. To prevent further hearing loss, you could tell him to wear earplugs or earmuffs while at work.

MATH IN SCIENCE

21. water: 5,928 m; glass: 18,160 m

INTERPRETING GRAPHICS

22. d
23. a
24. c
25. b and c

 Blackline masters of this Chapter Review can be found in the **Study Guide.**

NOW WHAT DO YOU THINK?

1. Sound travels from one place to another by vibrations of particles in a medium.
2. The frequency of a sound wave determines the sound's pitch, and the amplitude of the sound wave determines the sound's loudness.
3. Sound waves can reflect off a barrier or can diffract around it. Sound waves can interfere with one another, and they sometimes form standing waves.

Chapter 21 • Chapter Review

SCIENCE, TECHNOLOGY, AND SOCIETY

Jurassic Bark

Background

Computed axial tomography (CAT scanning), which has been used for many years in medicine, is now being used by paleontologists to study the internal structure of fossils. CAT scanning can provide interior views of a fossil without even touching the fossil's surface.

To understand how CAT scanning works, imagine moving an object through the center of a circle. The CAT scan looks at the object and takes an X-ray picture of it from every point around the circle. A computer then re-creates a two-dimensional picture, using each of the X-ray points around the circle. In this way, the CAT scan shows what you would see if you had taken a slice out of the object and were looking at the cross section.

If a paleontologist needs to reconstruct an entire skull, a series of two-dimensional "slice" shots are taken and combined through computer imaging to produce a three-dimensional image of the skull—inside and out!

Science, Technology, and Society

Jurassic Bark

Imagine you suddenly hear an incredibly loud honking sound, like a trombone or a tuba. "Must be band tryouts," you think. You turn to find the noise and find yourself face to face with a 10 m long, 2,800 kg dinosaur with a huge tubular crest extending back more than 2 m from its snout. Do you run? No—your musical friend, *Parasaurolophus,* is a vegetarian.

Now there's no way you'll bump into this extinct hadrosaur, a duck-billed dinosaur that existed about 75 million years ago in the late Cretaceous period. But through recent advances in computer technology, you can hear how *Parasaurolophus* might have sounded.

A Snorkel or a Trombone?

Parasaurolophus's crest contained a network of tubes connected to the animal's breathing passages. Some scientists believe the dinosaurs used the distinctive crest to make sounds. Other scientists theorize that the crest allowed *Parasaurolophus* to stay underwater and feed, that it was used to regulate body temperature, or that it allowed the animals to communicate with each other by exhaling strongly through the crest.

The study of the *Parasaurolophus*'s potential sound-making ability really began after a 1995 expedition in northwestern New Mexico uncovered an almost-complete fossil skull of an adult. With this nearly complete skull and some modern technology, scientists tested the noise-making qualities of the crest.

Dino Scan

In Albuquerque, New Mexico, Dr. Carl Diegert of Sandia National Laboratories and Dr. Tom Williamson of the New Mexico Museum of Natural History and Science teamed up to use CT (Computed Tomography). With this scanning system, they created three-dimensional images of the crest's internal structure. The results

▶ *Aside from a role in the* Jurassic Park *movies, the Parasaurolophus dinosaur's biggest claim to fame is the enormous crest that extends back from its snout.*

showed that the crest had more tubes than previously thought as well as additional chambers.

Sound That Funky Horn

Once the crest's internal structure was determined, Diegert used powerful computers and special software to produce a sound that *Parasaurolophus* might have made. Since it is not known whether *Parasaurolophus* had vocal cords, Diegert made different versions of the sound by simulating the movement of air through the crest in several ways. Intrigued by Diegert's results, other researchers are trying to reproduce the sounds of other dinosaurs. In time, *Parasaurolophus* might be just one of a band of musical dinosaurs.

On Your Own

▶ *Parasaurolophus* is just one type of hadrosaur recognized for the peculiar bony crest on top of its head. On your own, research other hadrosaurs that had a bony crest similar to that of the *Parasaurolophus*. What are the names of these dinosaurs?

Answer to On Your Own

Parasaurolophus is only one of a number of crested hadrosaurs, also referred to as lambeosaurs. Other lambeosaurs include *Corythosaurus* and *Lambeosaurus*.

Science Fiction

"Ear"
by Jane Yolen

"Jily put on her Ear and sighed. The world went from awful silence to the pounding rhythms she loved. Without the Ear she was locked into her own thoughts and the few colors her eyes could pick out. But with the Ear she felt truly connected to the world."

Jily and her friends, Sanya and Feeny, live in a time not too far in the future. It is a time when everyone's hearing is damaged. People communicate using sign language—unless they put on their Ear. Then the whole world is filled with sounds. Of course, there are rules. No Ears allowed in school. Ears are only to be worn on the street, at night. Life is so much richer with an Ear, a person would have to be crazy to go without one.

The Low Down, the first club Jily and her friends visit, is too quiet for Jily's tastes. She wants to leave and tries to find Sanya and Feeny. But Sanya is dancing by herself, even though there is no music. When Jily finds Feeny, they notice some Earless kids their own age. Earless people never go to clubs, and Jily finds their presence offensive. But Feeny is intrigued.

Everyone is given an Ear at the age of 12 but has to give it up at the age of 30. Why would these kids want to go out without their Ears before the age of 30? Jily thinks the idea is ridiculous and doesn't stick around to find out the answer to such a question. But, it is an answer that will change her life by the end of the next day.

Read the rest of Jily's story, "Ear" by Jane Yolen, in the *Holt Anthology of Science Fiction*.

Further Reading If you liked this story, you can read more by Jane Yolen. Some of her other works include:

- *The Devil's Arithmetic,* Viking, 1988
- *Dragon's Blood: A Fantasy,* Delacorte, 1982
- *The Emperor and the Kite,* Philomel, 1997

SCIENCE FICTION
"Ear"
by Jane Yolen

And they say kids don't listen . . .

Teaching Strategy
Reading Level This is a relatively short story that should not be difficult for the average student to read and comprehend.

Background
About the Author As a Caldecott award winner, National Book nominee, and Nebula finalist, Jane Yolen knows how to write successful stories. Her work spans a wide range of topics—from imaginative alphabet books for the youngest reader to serious novels for the young adult and adult audience.

Jane Yolen was born in 1939. She attended Smith College and received a master's in education. Since the 1960s, she has earned critical acclaim as a writer, especially for stories and novels written for young people. In fact, her love for children's literature has led her to sit on the board of directors for the Society of Children's Book Writers since the 1970s. The inspiration for much of her work comes from folktales and stories with rich histories. She has written with references to such familiar works as *Cinderella* and ancient Greek mythology, as well as more unusual folktales such as those of rural Scotland.

Chapter Organizer

CHAPTER ORGANIZATION	TIME MINUTES	OBJECTIVES	LABS, INVESTIGATIONS, AND DEMONSTRATIONS
Chapter Opener pp. 562–563	45	National Standards: UCP 2, SAI 1, 2, ST 2, SPSP 5, HNS 1, PS 3c	**Investigate!** Colors of Light, p. 563
Section 1 What Is Light?	90	▶ Explain why electromagnetic waves are transverse waves. ▶ Describe how electromagnetic waves are produced. ▶ Calculate distances traveled by light using the value for speed of light. UCP 1, 2, SPSP 5, PS 3a	**Demonstration,** p. 564 in ATE
Section 2 The Electromagnetic Spectrum	90	▶ Identify how EM waves differ from each other. ▶ Describe some uses for radio waves and microwaves. ▶ Give examples of how infrared waves and visible light are important in your life. ▶ Explain how ultraviolet light, X rays, and gamma rays can be both helpful and harmful. UCP 2, SAI 1, 2, SPSP 1, 3–5, HNS 1, PS 3a, 3f	
Section 3 Interactions of Light Waves	90	▶ Compare regular reflection with diffuse reflection. ▶ Describe absorption and scattering of light. ▶ Explain how refraction can create optical illusions and separate white light into colors. ▶ Describe diffraction and interference of light. UCP 2, PS 3c	**QuickLab,** Scattering Milk, p. 577 **Demonstration,** p. 579 in ATE
Section 4 Light and Color	135	▶ Name and describe the three ways light interacts with matter. ▶ Explain how the color of an object is determined. ▶ Compare the primary colors of light and the primary pigments. PS 3c; LabBook UCP 2, 3, SAI 1, 2, PS 3a–3c	**Demonstration,** pp. 581, 584 in ATE **Discovery Lab,** What Color of Light Is Best for Green Plants? p. 716 **Datasheets for LabBook,** Datasheets 60, 61, 62 **Discovery Lab,** Which Color Is Hottest? p. 717 **QuickLab,** Rose-Colored Glasses? p. 584 **Skill Builder,** Mixing Colors, p. 718 **Long-Term Projects & Research Ideas,** Project 72

TECHNOLOGY RESOURCES

See page **T20** for a complete correlation of this book with the **NATIONAL SCIENCE EDUCATION STANDARDS.**

 Guided Reading Audio CD English or Spanish, Chapter 22

 One-Stop Planner CD-ROM with Test Generator

 CNN Scientists in Action, Slow Light Scientist, Segment 28

 Interactive Explorations CD-ROM, CD 3, Exploration 7, In the Spotlight

Chapter 22 • The Nature of Light

CLASSROOM WORKSHEETS, TRANSPARENCIES, AND RESOURCES	SCIENCE INTEGRATION AND CONNECTIONS	REVIEW AND ASSESSMENT
Directed Reading Worksheet 22 **Science Puzzlers, Twisters & Teasers,** Worksheet 22		
Directed Reading Worksheet 22, Section 1 **Transparency 289,** Electromagnetic Waves **Transparency 290,** The Production of Light	**Multicultural Connection,** p. 565 in ATE **MathBreak,** p. 566 **Science, Technology, and Society:** Fireflies Light the Way, p. 590	**Review,** p. 566 **Quiz,** p. 566 in ATE **Alternative Assessment,** p. 566 in ATE
Directed Reading Worksheet 22, Section 2 **Transparency 291,** The Electromagnetic Spectrum	**Astronomy Connection,** p. 567 **Cross-Disciplinary Focus,** p. 568 in ATE **Connect to Earth Science,** p. 571 in ATE **Biology Connection,** p. 572 **Apply,** p. 573 **Eureka!** It's a Heat Wave! p. 591	**Homework,** p. 568 in ATE **Review,** p. 571 **Review,** p. 574 **Quiz,** p. 574 in ATE **Alternative Assessment,** p. 574 in ATE
Directed Reading Worksheet 22, Section 3 **Transparency 292,** Reflection **Transparency 293,** White Light Is Separated by a Prism **Reinforcement Worksheet 22** **Transparency 294,** Constructive and Destructive Interference **Critical Thinking Worksheet 22,** Now You See It, Now You Don't	**Multicultural Connection,** p. 575 in ATE **Multicultural Connection,** p. 576 in ATE **Connect to Life Science,** p. 578 in ATE **Cross-Disciplinary Focus,** p. 578 in ATE **Real-World Connection,** p. 578 in ATE **Real-World Connection,** p. 579 in ATE **Connect to Life Science,** p. 579 in ATE	**Homework,** p. 576 in ATE **Review,** p. 580 **Quiz,** p. 580 in ATE **Alternative Assessment,** p. 580 in ATE
Directed Reading Worksheet 22, Section 4 **Transparency 196,** The H-R Diagram: A **Transparency 197,** The H-R Diagram: B	**Connect to Life Science,** p. 582 in ATE **Connect to Earth Science,** p. 583 in ATE **Multicultural Connection,** p. 583 in ATE **Geology Connection,** p. 585 **Cross-Disciplinary Focus,** p. 585 in ATE	**Homework,** pp. 581, 582 in ATE **Self-Check,** p. 583 **Review,** p. 585 **Quiz,** p. 585 in ATE **Alternative Assessment,** p. 585 in ATE

END-OF-CHAPTER REVIEW AND ASSESSMENT

Chapter Review in Study Guide
Vocabulary and Notes in Study Guide
Chapter Tests with Performance-Based Assessment, Chapter 22 Test, Performance-Based Assessment 22
Concept Mapping Transparency 22

 Holt, Rinehart and Winston On-line Resources
go.hrw.com
For worksheets and other teaching aids related to this chapter, visit the HRW Web site and type in the keyword: **HSTLGT**

 **National Science Teachers Association**
www.scilinks.org
Encourage students to use the *sci*LINKS numbers listed in the internet connect boxes to access information and resources on the **NSTA** Web site.

Chapter Resources & Worksheets

Visual Resources

TEACHING TRANSPARENCIES

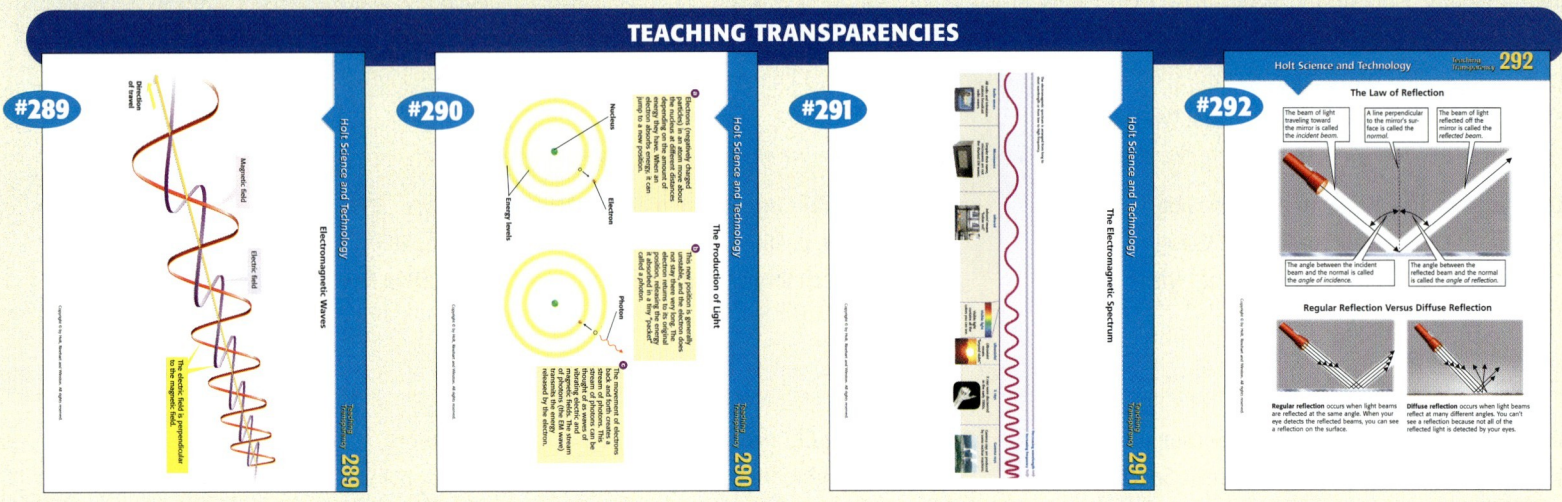

TEACHING TRANSPARENCIES

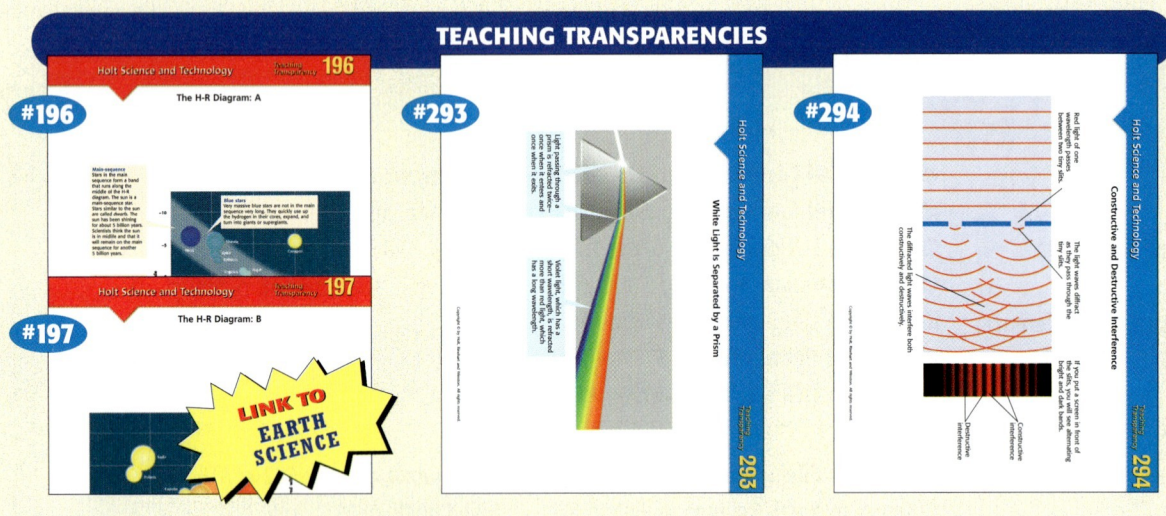

CONCEPT MAPPING TRANSPARENCY

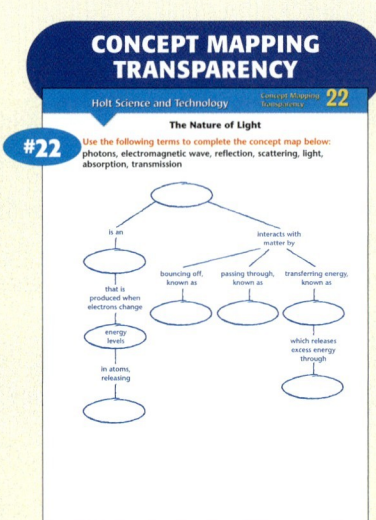

Meeting Individual Needs

DIRECTED READING

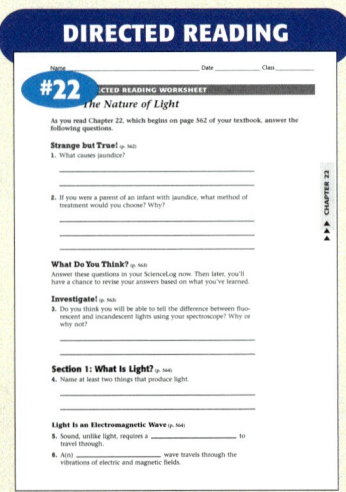

REINFORCEMENT & VOCABULARY REVIEW

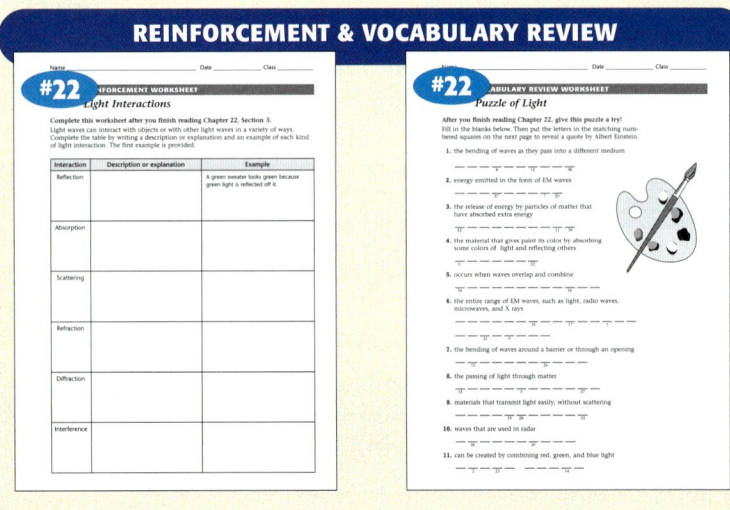

SCIENCE PUZZLERS, TWISTERS & TEASERS

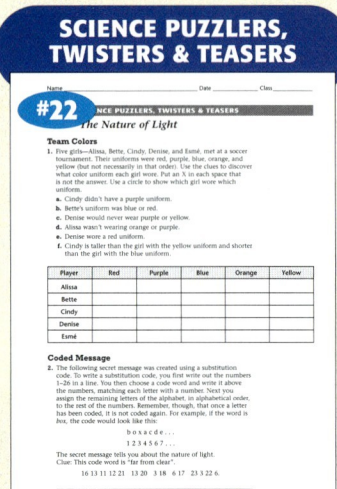

561C Chapter 22 • The Nature of Light

Chapter 22 • The Nature of Light

Review & Assessment

STUDY GUIDE

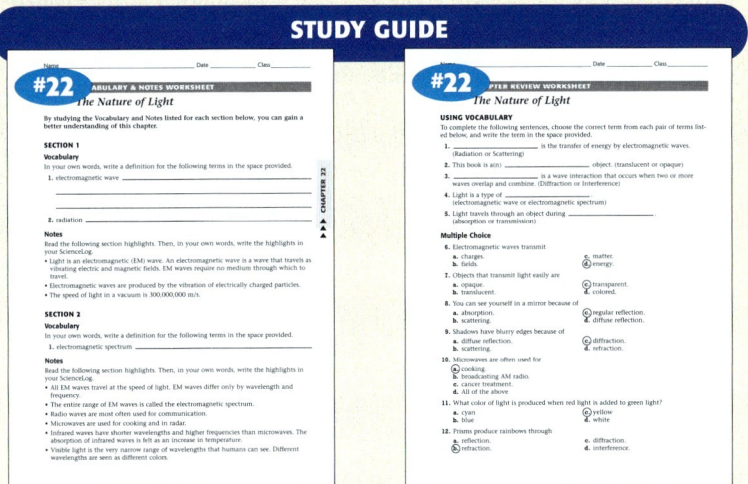

CHAPTER TESTS WITH PERFORMANCE-BASED ASSESSMENT

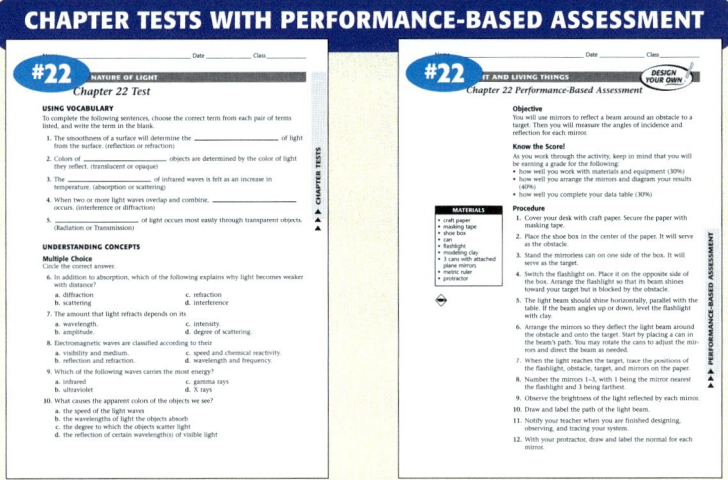

Lab Worksheets

LONG-TERM PROJECTS & RESEARCH IDEAS

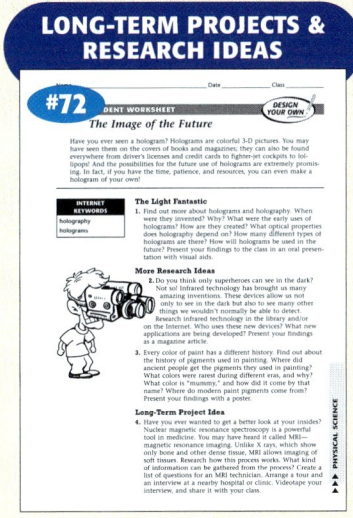

DATASHEETS FOR LABBOOK

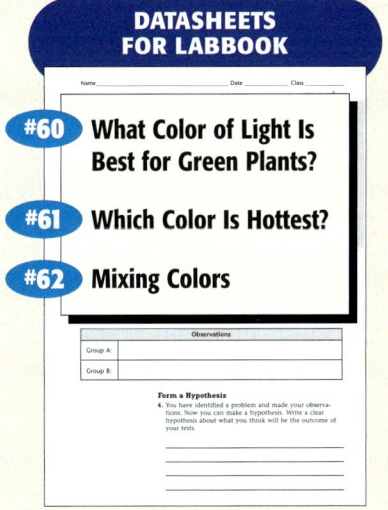

Applications & Extensions

CRITICAL THINKING & PROBLEM SOLVING

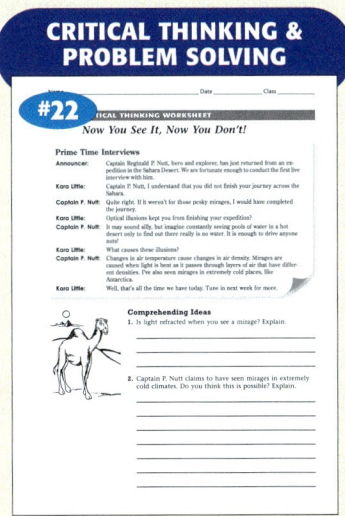

SCIENTISTS IN ACTION

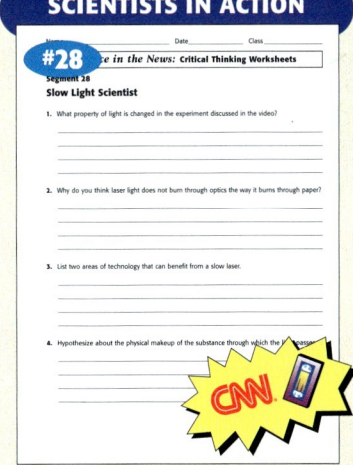

INTERACTIVE EXPLORATIONS

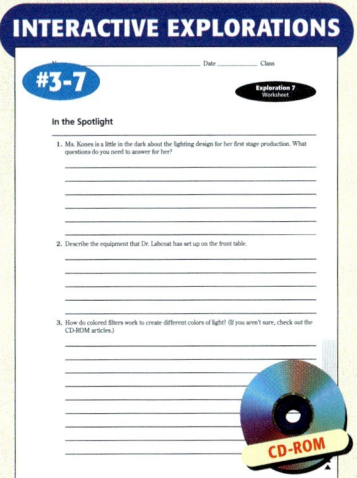

Chapter 22 • Chapter Resources & Worksheets

Chapter Background

SECTION 1

▶ **What Is Light?**
The nature of light has been debated for thousands of years. The argument about how light travels—as a wave or as a particle—began with the Greek mathematician and philosopher Pythagoras (c. 580–500 B.C.). Pythagoras and his followers believed that light is emitted from a source in the form of tiny particles.

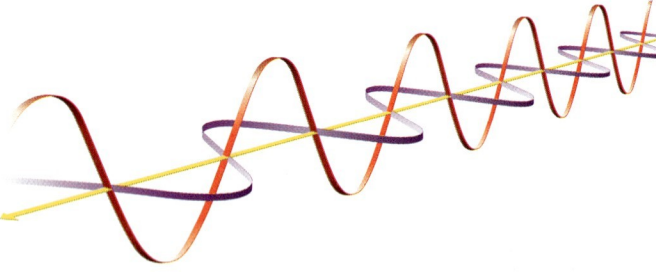

- However, Empedocles (c. 490–430 B.C.), another Greek philosopher, taught that light travels from its source as waves.

- In the fifth century B.C., the Greek philosophers Socrates (c. 470–399 B.C.) and Plato (c. 428–348 B.C.) thought that the eyes emitted streamers, or filaments, and that sight occurred when these streamers made contact with objects.

- Even as late as the 1600s, René Descartes (1596–1650), the great French mathematician and philosopher, held beliefs similar to those of Socrates and Plato.

IS THAT A FACT!

▶ Galileo Galilei (1564–1642) once tried to measure the speed of light from a lantern from one hilltop to another. He soon realized that light traveled very fast.

SECTION 2

▶ **The Electromagnetic Spectrum**
- In 1865, James Clerk Maxwell (1831–1879), a Scottish physicist, developed a theory stating that certain waves are propagated through space at the speed of light. In fact, his equations predicted that energy of the waves was equally divided between an electric field and a magnetic field. He called the waves electromagnetic waves.

- In 1886, Heinrich Hertz (1859–1894) was trying to prove Maxwell's equations experimentally. His experimentation was very fruitful: Not only did he prove Maxwell correct, but he also discovered radio waves. The unit for frequency was named in his honor.

IS THAT A FACT!

▶ The infrared portion of the spectrum was discovered by William Herschel (1738–1822), a famous British astronomer. In 1800, he was investigating the heat produced by certain waves located just below the red part of the visible spectrum. He named the waves *infrared*. *Infra* is a Latin word meaning "below."

▶ In 1895, Wilhelm Roentgen (1845–1923) serendipitously discovered X rays. While working with a barium ore, he discovered that the ore glowed when placed near a tube in which an electric current was passing. He experimented and found that the ore would glow even if placed behind substances that would block ordinary light.

▶ Roentgen didn't know the source of the radiation that caused the barium to glow, so he called the source X rays. He received the first Nobel Prize in physics for his discovery of X rays.

Chapter 22 • The Nature of Light

SECTION 3

▶ Interactions of Light Waves

Thomas Young (1773–1829) was a medical doctor born in Milverton, England. But Young had a variety of interests and wrote important papers in Egyptology and physics.

- Young aided in the translation of the Rosetta stone (1812–1813).

- In physics and the study of solid materials, the Young modulus (a measure of the strength and elasticity of a solid) is named after him for his work with solids.

- Young was the first to propose the three-primary-color model for vision.

- Young discovered the phenomenon of interference of light using an apparatus with a double slit. From his experiments, Young was able to measure the wavelengths of red and blue light. However, it was his revival of the wave theory of light that aided others in their search for the nature of light.

IS THAT A FACT!

▶ In the 1960s, earthquake lights were photographed in Japan. Earthquake lights are beams, columns, or fireballs of light seen just before the Earth begins to shake. This phenomenon has not been explained; however, one theory states that the cause may be the piezoelectric effect. This effect refers to the generation of an electrostatic voltage that occurs when great pressure is placed on quartz or other types of crystals.

SECTION 4

▶ Light and Color

In humans, light rays pass through the lens onto the retina. This back part of the eye contains two types of nerve cells, *rods* and *cones,* that respond to light energy.

- The visual system can be divided into two categories: *photopic vision* and *scotopic vision.* Photopic vision primarily utilizes cones, which detect light under high illumination. Scotopic vision involves rods, which detect light under low illumination.

- Rods are most sensitive to movement and to changes in light and dark. Rods do not respond to different frequencies of light, so they do not perceive color.

- Cones, on the other hand, come in three types and are sensitive to different frequencies and intensities of light. One type is triggered by light energy at the blue end of the spectrum, the second responds to the red end of the spectrum, and the third type is stimulated by the middle of the spectrum, or the greens.

- When light energy stimulates the cones, they send signals to the brain. The brain interprets these signals as colors, depending on how many of each type of cone has been stimulated.

IS THAT A FACT!

▶ Experiments have shown that the human eye can *detect* a single photon of light. However, neural filters will only trigger a conscious response when between five and ten photons arrive within a certain period of time. This is so we won't see visual "noise" in low light!

▶ In 1932, John Logie Baird developed the first commercially viable electromechanical television system and sold over 10,000 sets!

For background information about teaching strategies and issues, refer to the *Professional Reference for Teachers.*

CHAPTER 22
The Nature of Light

Chapter Preview

Section 1
What Is Light?
- Light Is an Electromagnetic Wave
- How Light Is Produced
- The Speed of Light

Section 2
The Electromagnetic Spectrum
- Characteristics of EM Waves
- Radio Waves
- Microwaves
- Infrared Waves
- Visible Light
- Ultraviolet Light
- X Rays and Gamma Rays

Section 3
Interactions of Light Waves
- Reflection
- Absorption and Scattering
- Refraction
- Diffraction
- Interference

Section 4
Light and Color
- Light and Matter
- Colors of Objects
- Mixing Colors of Light
- Mixing Colors of Pigment

Directed Reading Worksheet 22

Science Puzzlers, Twisters & Teasers Worksheet 22

Guided Reading Audio CD
English or Spanish, Chapter 22

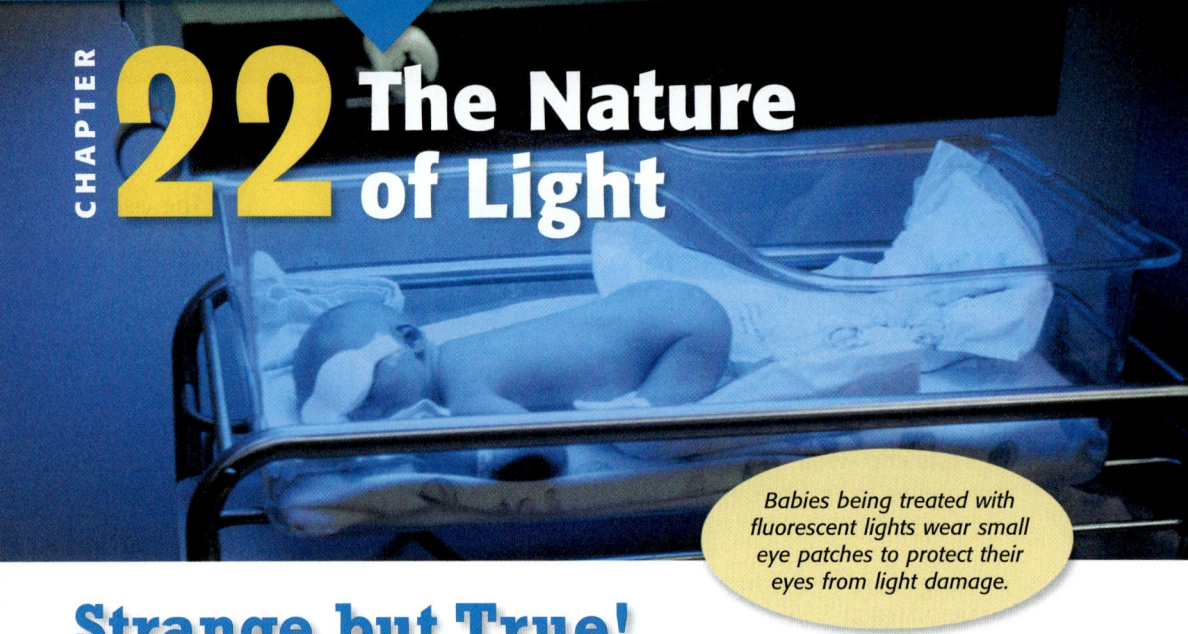

Babies being treated with fluorescent lights wear small eye patches to protect their eyes from light damage.

Strange but True!

What would you think if you walked into a hospital and saw the baby in the picture shown above? It looks like the baby is in a tanning booth! But this baby isn't getting a tan—he is being treated for a condition called jaundice (JAWN dis).

Jaundice occurs in some infants when bilirubin (BIL i ROO bin)—a pigment in healthy red blood cells—builds up in the bloodstream as blood cells break down. This excess bilirubin is deposited in the skin, giving the skin a yellowish hue. Jaundice is not dangerous if treated quickly. If left untreated, it can lead to brain damage.

The excess bilirubin in the skin is best broken down by bright blue light. For this reason, hospitals hang special blue fluorescent lamps above the cribs of newborns needing treatment. The blue light is sometimes balanced with light of other colors so that doctors and nurses can be sure the baby is not blue from a lack of oxygen.

A more convenient form of treatment is offered by the "bili blanket," a soft pad made of fiber-optic materials connected to a light box that produces blue light. This special light-emitting blanket can be wrapped around the infant, and the newborn can even be picked up and cuddled during treatment.

Light treatment for babies with jaundice is just one of the important uses of light. In this chapter you will learn about the nature of light, how light waves interact, and other ways that light is important to your life.

Strange but True!

Lighting is very important in hospitals and operating rooms. In fact, some medical lighting companies have developed special reflectors that reflect visible light toward the patient and transmit heat away from the patients and physicians. These reflectors are called dichroic reflectors or *cold mirrors*. Dichroic reflectors filter out infrared and UV rays and reflect only rays of the visible spectrum. This property keeps patients and physicians from overheating during long surgical procedures and provides the visible light needed in an operating room.

What Do You Think?

In your ScienceLog, try to answer the following questions based on what you already know:

1. What is light?
2. How do light waves interact?
3. Why are you able to see different colors?

Colors of Light

When a baby is under blue light, it is difficult to see whether the baby is blue from a lack of oxygen or from the reflected blue lighting. To solve this problem, the blue light is mixed with other colors of light to produce white light. With this white light, doctors and nurses can see the baby's true color. In this activity you will study two types of white light.

Procedure

1. Using **scissors,** carefully cut a narrow slit in the center of a piece of **black construction paper.** Use **tape** to attach the paper to one end of a **paper-towel tube** so that the paper covers the opening of the tube.

2. Turn on an **incandescent light bulb.** Holding the open end of the tube to your eye, look through the tube at the light bulb. If no light passes through the slit in the paper, make the slit a little wider.

3. Hold a **diffraction grating** against the open end of the tube. Look at the light bulb through the grating, as shown below. Make sure the slit in the paper is vertical. Rotate the diffraction grating until you see colors inside the tube to the left and right sides of the slit. Use **tape** to attach the diffraction grating to the tube in this position. You have now made your own spectroscope.

4. Hold the spectroscope up to one eye and look at the light bulb. Describe what you see.

5. Repeat step 4 using a **fluorescent light bulb.** Describe what you see. How does it compare with what you saw when you looked at the incandescent light bulb?

Analysis

6. Both incandescent light bulbs and fluorescent light bulbs produce white light. What did you learn about white light using the spectroscope?

7. Light from the sun is also white light. What would you expect to see if you used a spectroscope to look at sunlight?
   Caution: Do not use the spectroscope you made to look at the sun. It does not provide enough protection against bright sunlight.

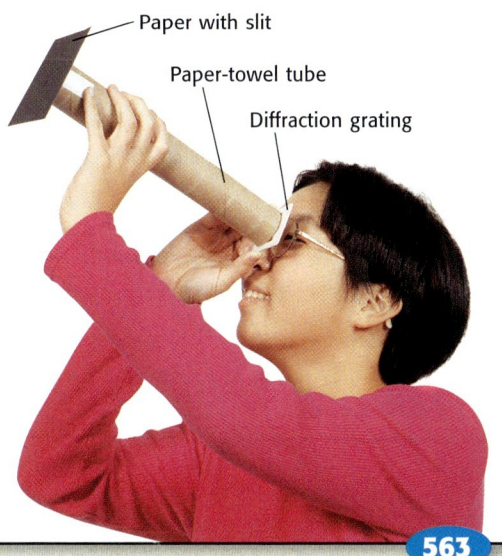

Paper with slit
Paper-towel tube
Diffraction grating

IS THAT A FACT!

Diffraction can separate white light into colors. Diffraction gratings are pieces of glass, metal, or plastic with many slits, sometimes thousands per centimeter. When light passes through the slits, each color of light travels at a different angle. The degree of the angle depends on the wavelength of the light. Instead of bright and dark bands, you see colored lines separated by dark bands. Thus, white light passing through a grating can produce the entire visible spectrum.

What Do You Think?

Accept all reasonable responses. Students will have a chance to revise their answers in the Chapter Review under NOW What Do You Think?

Investigate!

MATERIALS

FOR EACH GROUP:
- clear incandescent light bulb
- fluorescent light bulb
- diffraction grating
- tape
- black construction paper
- paper-towel tube

Safety Caution: Students should avoid handling the hot bulbs.

Teacher Notes: Toilet-paper tubes will also work for this experiment. Diffraction gratings are often sold as small squares held in plastic slide holders.

Answers to Investigate!

4. Students should see a solid, continuous spectrum of colors (rainbow colors) on both sides of the tube. All colors should have about the same brightness.

5. Students should see a spectrum of colors again. However, there will be bright bands and faint bands within the spectrum.

6. White light is made up of different colors of light.

7. Students should expect to see a solid continuous spectrum of colors that resembles the spectrum of the light bulb.

 Smithsonian Institution®
Visit **www.si.edu/hrw** for additional on-line resources.

Chapter 22 • The Nature of Light

SECTION 1

Focus

What Is Light?
Students will learn what EM waves are, how they are produced, and how they differ from other waves. Students will also learn about the speed of light.

Bellringer
Draw a transverse wave with a wavelength of 1 m on the board. Label each part of the wave, such as the wavelength, crest, and trough. Have students copy the wave in their ScienceLog and label their drawing carefully. Ask them to explain in their own words what wavelength and frequency are and how the two are related. (Remind them that these are concepts they studied in Chapter 20.)

1 Motivate

DEMONSTRATION
Using tongs to hold one end of a small piece of copper wire, place the other end into the flame of a Bunsen burner. (Any source of thermal energy, such as a lighter, will work.) A green, luminous glow will be produced. Ask students to explain the source of the green glow. Guide the discussion to help students realize that atoms in the copper wire emit a green light when thermal energy is added.

Teaching Transparency 289 "Electromagnetic Waves"

Directed Reading Worksheet 22 Section 1

Section 1

Terms to Learn
electromagnetic wave
radiation

What You'll Do
- Explain why electromagnetic waves are transverse waves.
- Describe how electromagnetic waves are produced.
- Calculate distances traveled by light using the value for speed of light.

What Is Light?

We rely on light from the sun and from electric bulbs to help us see. But what exactly is light? Scientists are still studying light to learn more about its makeup and characteristics. Fortunately, much has already been discovered about light, as you will soon find out. You may even become enlightened!

Light Is an Electromagnetic Wave
Like sound, light is a type of energy that travels as a wave. But unlike sound, light does not require a medium through which to travel. Light is an **electromagnetic wave** (EM wave). An EM wave is a wave that can travel through space or matter and consists of changing electric and magnetic fields. A *field* is a region around an object that can exert a force, a push or pull, on another object without actually touching that object. For example, a magnet is surrounded by a magnetic field that can pull a paper clip toward it. But keep in mind that this field, like all fields, is not made of matter.

Figure 1 shows a diagram of an electromagnetic wave. Notice that the electric and magnetic fields are at right angles—or *perpendicular*—to each other. These fields are also perpendicular to the direction of the wave motion. Because of this arrangement, electromagnetic waves are transverse waves.

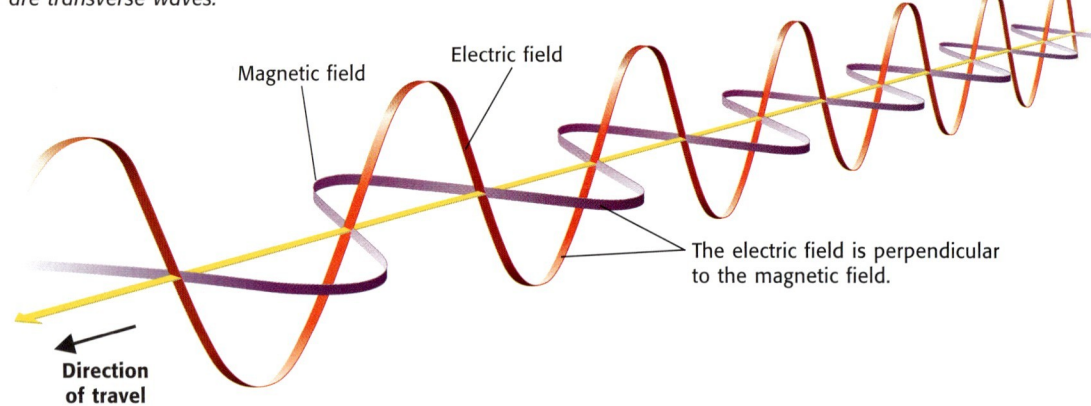

Figure 1 *Electromagnetic waves are transverse waves.*

SCIENTISTS AT ODDS
Sir Isaac Newton (1642–1727) thought that a particle model best described the properties of light that he observed. Christian Huygens (1629–1695), a Dutch mathematician and scientist, disagreed with Newton's theory because Newton's particle model could not explain the diffraction of light. This argument was continued by other scientists for nearly 200 years, until the early 1900s. It was finally settled when Albert Einstein (1879–1955) and Maurice de Broglie (1875–1960) each arrived at the conclusion that EM waves are best described by a particle-wave model.

564 Chapter 22 • The Nature of Light

How Light Is Produced

An EM wave is produced by the vibration of an electrically charged particle. A particle with an electric charge is surrounded by an electric field. When the particle vibrates, or moves back and forth, the electric field around it vibrates too. When the electric field starts vibrating, a vibrating magnetic field is created. The vibration of an electric field and a magnetic field together produces an EM wave that carries energy released by the original vibration of the particle. The emission of energy in the form of EM waves is called **radiation**.

Sounds complicated, right? To better understand how light is produced, think about the following example. When you turn on a lamp, the electrical energy supplied to the filament in the bulb causes the atoms in the filament to vibrate. Charged particles inside the atoms then vibrate, and light is produced, as shown in **Figure 2**.

Extra! Extra! Read all about how light-producing fireflies save people's lives! Turn to page 590.

Figure 2 The Production of Light

a Electrons (negatively charged particles) in an atom move about the nucleus at different distances depending on the amount of energy they have. When an electron absorbs energy, it can jump to a new position.

b This new position is generally unstable, and the electron may not stay there very long. The electron returns to its original position, releasing the energy it absorbed in a tiny "packet" called a *photon*.

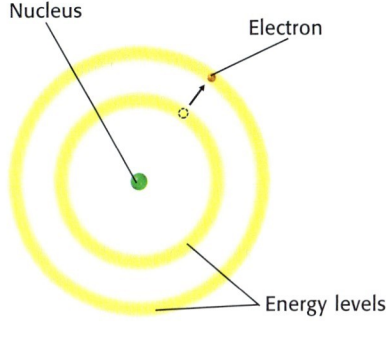

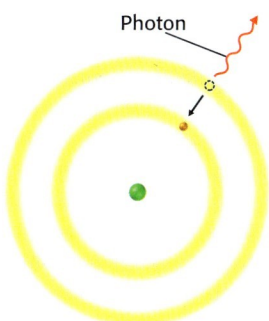

c The movement of electrons back and forth creates a stream of photons. This stream of photons can be thought of as waves of vibrating electric and magnetic fields. The stream of photons (the EM wave) carries the energy released by the electrons.

The Split Personality of Light

The fact that light is a wave explains certain behaviors of light, but not others. These puzzling behaviors of light are easier to explain if light is thought to consist of particles instead of waves. Scientists think that light has the properties of both a particle and a wave. Albert Einstein was one of many scientists who researched the dual nature of light. The idea that light can act as either particles or waves is known as the *particle-wave theory of light*.

Is That A Fact!

Galileo was perhaps the first scientist to suggest a method for measuring the speed of light. In 1675, the Danish astronomer Ole Roemer (1644–1710) was the first to demonstrate that the speed of light is finite by observing the eclipses of Jupiter's satellites.

Multicultural Connection

Indian physicist Satyendra Nath Bose (1894–1974) published a paper in 1924 dealing with quantum mechanics. Albert Einstein read Bose's paper and praised it. Einstein then generalized Bose's theory into quantum statistics and described certain subatomic particles. When later experiments found the particles, they were named *bosons* in honor of Bose.

2) Teach

Using the Figure

Using **Figure 2**, discuss with students the difficult concept that there are two different transverse waves vibrating perpendicular to one another. One wave is a vibrating electric field; the other is a vibrating magnetic field. Remind students that a vibrating electric field generates a magnetic field and a vibrating magnetic field generates an electric field. Together they form a single EM wave traveling in a particular direction. **Sheltered English**

Discussion

Physicist Paul Hewitt has stated that all that we see, even our own reflection, is from the past. Have students write about whether they think that this statement is true, and why or why not. Have students discuss what they have written.

3) Extend

Research

Have students research either Isaac Newton's, Christiaan Huygens's, or Albert Einstein's theories on the nature of light. Encourage students to hold a class debate about the positions of the scientists they research. As an alternative, have interested students research the history of how the speed of light was determined. **Sheltered English**

Teaching Transparency 290
"The Production of Light"

Section 1 • What Is Light? **565**

4) Close

Quiz

1. If the circumference of Earth is 40,100 km, how many times can light travel around Earth in 1 second? (about 7 times)
2. Tiny packets of energy are called photons. (true)
3. EM radiation is produced by the vibrations of charged particles. (true)
4. In your own words, explain what light is and how it is produced. (Answers will vary but should discuss EM waves, transverse waves, electric and magnetic fields vibrating perpendicularly to each other, electrons, photons, and the particle-wave nature of light.)

ALTERNATE ASSESSMENT

Concept Mapping Have students prepare a concept map showing the properties of light. Their concept map should in some way illustrate which property or properties are described by the wave model of light and which are described by the particle model.

Answer to MATHBREAK

time = $\frac{distance}{speed}$

time = $\frac{150,000,000,000 \text{ m}}{300,000,000 \text{ m/s}}$

time = 500 seconds

TOPIC: Using Light
GO TO: www.scilinks.org
sciLINKS NUMBER: HSTP528

TOPIC: Light Energy
GO TO: www.scilinks.org
sciLINKS NUMBER: HSTP529

MATH BREAK

Just How Fast Is Light?

To give you an idea of how fast light travels, calculate the time it takes for light to travel from Earth to the moon. The distance from Earth to the moon is 382,000,000 m.

$$speed = \frac{distance}{time}$$

This equation can be rearranged to solve for time:

$$time = \frac{distance}{speed}$$

$$time = \frac{382,000,000 \text{ m}}{300,000,000 \text{ m/s}}$$

time = 1.27 seconds

Now It's Your Turn

The distance from the sun to Earth is 150,000,000,000 m. Calculate the time it takes for light to travel that distance.

The Speed of Light

Scientists have yet to discover anything in the universe that travels faster than light. In the near-vacuum of space, the speed of light is about 300,000,000 m/s. Light travels slightly slower in air, glass, and other types of matter. (Keep in mind that even though EM waves do not require a medium, they can travel through many substances.) Believe it or not, light can travel more than 880,000 times faster than sound! This explains the phenomenon described in **Figure 3**. And if you could run at the speed of light, you could travel around Earth 7.5 times in 1 second.

Figure 3 Although thunder and lightning are produced at the same time, you usually see lightning before you hear thunder. That's because light travels much faster than sound.

REVIEW

1. Why are electromagnetic waves transverse waves?
2. How is a sound wave different from an EM wave?
3. How does a charged particle produce an EM wave?
4. **Making Inferences** Explain why EM waves do not require a medium through which to travel.
5. **Doing Calculations** The distance from the sun to Jupiter is 778,000,000,000 m. How long does it take for light from the sun to reach Jupiter?

Answers to Review

1. EM waves are transverse waves because the electric and magnetic fields vibrate perpendicularly to the direction the wave is traveling.
2. A sound wave requires a medium through which to travel and an EM wave does not.
3. A vibrating charged particle produces a vibrating electric field that, in turn, produces a vibrating magnetic field. The two vibrating fields make up an electromagnetic wave.
4. EM waves travel through the vibrations of electric and magnetic fields. These fields are not made of matter. Therefore, EM waves can travel without passing through a medium.
5. time = 2,593 seconds (or 43.2 minutes)

Section 2

The Electromagnetic Spectrum

Terms to Learn

electromagnetic spectrum

What You'll Do

- Identify how EM waves differ from each other.
- Describe some uses for radio waves and microwaves.
- Give examples of how infrared waves and visible light are important in your life.
- Explain how ultraviolet light, X rays, and gamma rays can be both helpful and harmful.

When you look around, you can see objects because light reflects off them. But if a bee looked at the same objects, it would see them differently, as shown in **Figure 4.** This is because bees can see a kind of light that you can't see. This type of light is called ultraviolet light.

It might seem strange to you to call something you can't see *light,* because the light you are most familiar with is visible light. But ultraviolet light is very similar to visible light. Both visible light and ultraviolet light are types of EM waves. In this section you will learn about many other types of EM waves, including X rays, radio waves, and microwaves.

Figure 4 The petals of the flower on the right look solid yellow to you. But a bee may see dark ultraviolet markings that make the same flower appear quite different to the bee.

Astronomy CONNECTION

Scientists know that all electromagnetic waves in empty space travel at the same speed. If EM waves traveled at different speeds, planets, stars, and galaxies would appear to be in different places depending upon which EM wave was used to view them. For example, using X rays to view a star might make the star appear to be in a different place than if radio waves were used.

Characteristics of EM Waves

Even though there are many types of EM waves, each type of wave travels at the same speed in a vacuum—300,000,000 m/s. How is this possible? Well, the speed of a wave is determined by multiplying its wavelength by its frequency. So EM waves having different wavelengths can travel at the same speed as long as their frequencies are also different. The entire range of EM waves is called the **electromagnetic spectrum.** Categories of waves in the EM spectrum include radio waves, microwaves, and visible light.

IS THAT A FACT!

Photoelectric cells, often found in alarm systems, change light energy of a given frequency into an electric voltage. The electric current stops when the beam of light is broken, and this closes a default circuit. When the default circuit is triggered, it sets off an alarm.

 Teaching Transparency 291 "The Electromagnetic Spectrum"

 Directed Reading Worksheet 22 Section 2

2) Teach

MEETING INDIVIDUAL NEEDS

Learners Having Difficulty Have students create in their ScienceLog an electromagnetic spectrum chart similar to the one found across the bottom of pages 568 and 569. As they read about each category of electromagnetic wave, have students write one or two facts about the category on their chart.
Sheltered English

CROSS-DISCIPLINARY FOCUS

History Have students find out about the lives and accomplishments of these pioneers in the study of EM waves.

- James Clerk Maxwell
- Heinrich Hertz
- Guglielmo Marconi
- Nikolai Tesla

(Maxwell introduced the theory of electromagnetic waves in 1865; Hertz created electromagnetic waves with a spark generator and reported that they could be transmitted over a distance; Marconi made the first wireless transmission across the Atlantic Ocean; Tesla developed the alternating current electrical system and some of the first electric motors.)

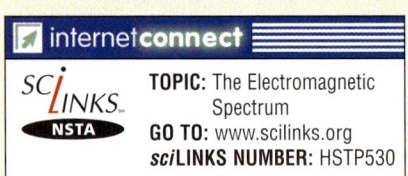
TOPIC: The Electromagnetic Spectrum
GO TO: www.scilinks.org
sciLINKS NUMBER: HSTP530

Radio Waves

Radio waves cover a wide range of waves in the EM spectrum. Radio waves have some of the longest wavelengths and the lowest frequencies of all EM waves. Therefore, radio waves are low energy waves. They carry enough energy, however, to be used for broadcasting radio signals. **Figure 5** shows how this process works.

Radio stations encode sound information into radio waves by varying either the waves' amplitude or their frequency. Changing amplitude or frequency is called modulation. You probably know that there are AM radio stations and FM radio stations. The abbreviation AM stands for amplitude modulation, and the abbreviation FM stands for frequency modulation. AM radio waves have longer wavelengths than FM radio waves.

Figure 5 *Radio waves cannot be heard, but they carry energy that can be converted into sound.*

① A radio station converts sound into an electric current. The current produces radio waves that are sent out in all directions by the antenna.

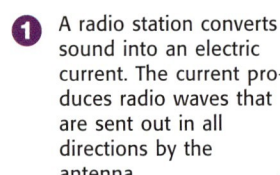

② A radio receives radio waves and then converts them into an electric current, which is then converted to sound.

Electromagnetic Spectrum
The electromagnetic spectrum is arranged from long to short wavelength or from low to high frequency.

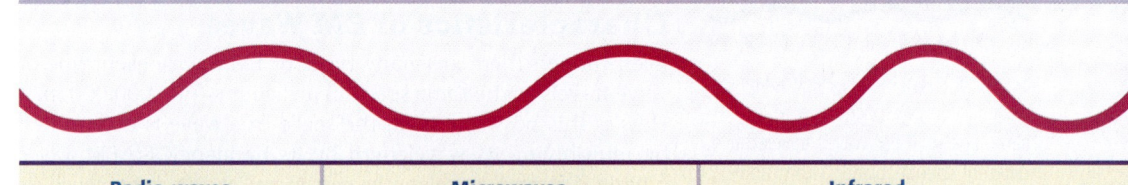

Radio waves	Microwaves	Infrared
All radio and television stations broadcast radio waves.	Despite their name, microwaves are not the shortest EM waves.	*Infrared* means "below red." |//

Homework

Concept Mapping Have students use the diagram of the EM spectrum on this page and page 569 to make a concept map of the different parts of the spectrum. Students should include one or more examples of how we use each part of the spectrum. Encourage them to be creative and to illustrate their concept map with drawings, photos, or images from magazines or newspapers.

AM and FM Radio Waves Although AM radio waves can travel farther than FM waves, as shown in **Figure 6,** many stations—especially those that broadcast mostly music—use FM waves. That's because more information can be encoded by using frequency modulation than by using amplitude modulation. Because FM waves carry more information, music broadcast from FM stations sounds better.

Figure 6 The difference in the wavelengths of AM and FM radio waves affects how the waves interact with a layer of the atmosphere called the ionosphere.

AM radio waves can reflect off the ionosphere. This helps AM waves travel long distances.

FM radio waves pass through the ionosphere. Therefore, FM waves cannot travel as far as AM waves.

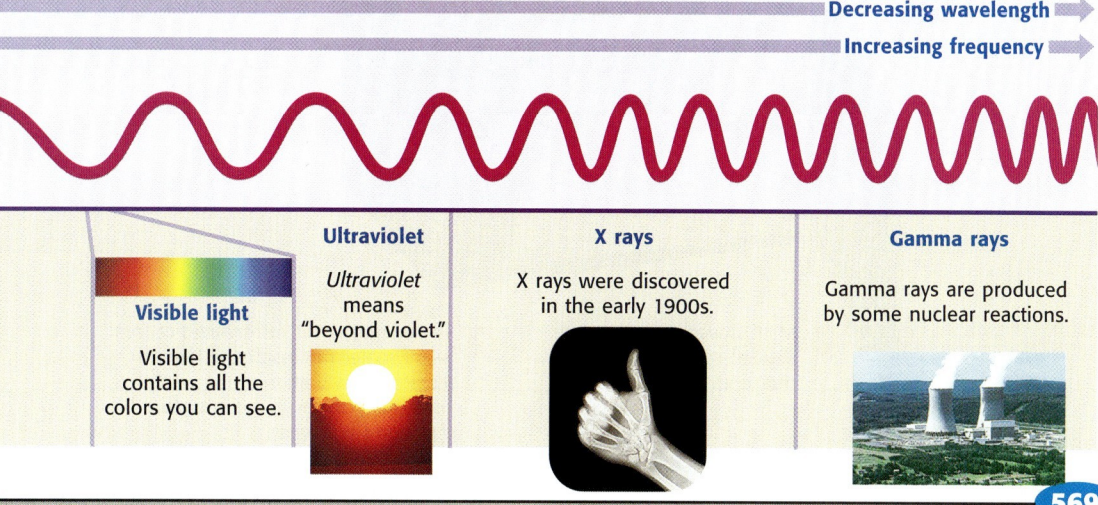

> **MEETING INDIVIDUAL NEEDS**
>
> **Learners Having Difficulty**
> Write some frequencies on the board. Ask students which EM wave corresponds to each frequency. For example, 4.3×10^{14} Hz is the frequency of red light, and the frequency of microwaves is about 10^9 Hz. Students should understand the relationship between wavelength and frequency. **Sheltered English**
>
> **ACTIVITY**
>
> **Blocked Ultraviolet Rays**
> Divide students into groups. Give each group a few coins and a piece of construction paper. Each group's piece of paper should be a different color. Have each group place the coins on their paper and set the paper outside in direct sunlight. (Glass in a window will block the UV rays.) Have students wait a couple of days and compare the amounts of fading among the different colored papers. Explain to students that the UV rays break down different types of dye at different rates.

WEIRD SCIENCE

Scientists recently conducted experiments that slowed down a beam of laser light to 17 m/s (38 mph)! This incredible phenomena was achieved by firing a laser beam through a gas cloud of sodium atoms cooled to only a fraction of a degree above absolute zero.

SCIENCE HUMOR

Q: How many actors does it take to change a light bulb?

A: Only one. They don't like to share the spotlight!

2) Teach, continued

READING STRATEGY

Prediction Guide Before students read this page, ask them:

- If you were going to buy a radio station that would play mostly music, would you apply for an AM station license or an FM station license? Why? What if your station broadcast mostly news and sports? Which license would you apply for, and why?

Have students record their answers in their ScienceLog and have them evaluate their answers after reading this page.

RESEARCH

No one person is credited with the invention of television. Some pioneers of television technology include the German scientist Paul Nipkow (1860–1940), the American scientist and inventor Charles F. Jenkins (1867–1934), the Scottish inventor John Logie Baird (1888–1946), the Russian-born Vladymir Zworykin (1889–1982), the Japanese engineer Kenjiro Takayanagi (1899–1990), and American Philo T. Farnsworth (1906–1971). Have students research one or more of these developers of television technology. Encourage them to be creative with their presentations. Some students may want to build models of early television devices.

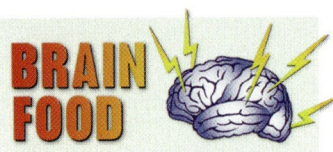

BRAIN FOOD

The frequencies at which radio and television stations broadcast in the United States are assigned by the Federal Communications Commission (FCC). In fact, the FCC has assigned frequencies for all devices that use radio waves. Such devices include garage door openers, baby monitors, radio controlled toys, and wildlife tracking collars.

Television and Radio Waves Television signals are also carried by radio waves. Most television stations broadcast radio waves that have shorter wavelengths and higher frequencies than those broadcast by radio stations. However, television signals are still broadcast using amplitude modulation and frequency modulation. Television stations use frequency-modulated waves to carry sound and amplitude-modulated waves to carry pictures.

Some waves carrying television signals are transmitted to satellites around the Earth. The waves are amplified and relayed back to ground antennae and then travel through cables to televisions in homes. This is how cable television works.

Microwaves

Microwaves have shorter wavelengths and higher frequencies than radio waves. Therefore, microwaves carry more energy than radio waves. You are probably familiar with microwaves—they are created in a microwave oven, like the model illustrated in **Figure 7**.

Figure 7 How a Microwave Oven Works

a A device called a magnetron produces microwaves by accelerating charged particles.

b The microwaves reflect off a metal fan and are directed into the cooking chamber.

c Microwaves can penetrate several centimeters into the food.

d The energy of the microwaves causes water molecules inside the food to vibrate. The vibration of the water molecules causes the temperature of the food to increase.

IS THAT A FACT!
One of the first public radio broadcast in the United States occurred in 1910—a live concert of an opera featuring the great tenor Enrico Caruso.

 **SCIENCE**

When food is cooked in a microwave oven, the dish holding the food may get warm. But the microwave is not heating the dish. The dish is warmed by heat dissipating from the cooking food.

570 Chapter 22 • The Nature of Light

Radar Microwaves are also used in radar. Radar (**ra**dio **d**etection **a**nd **r**anging) is used to detect the speed and location of objects. **Figure 8** shows a police officer using radar to determine the speed of a car. The officer points the radar device at a car and presses a button. The device emits short pulses of microwaves that reflect off the car and return to the device. The rate at which the waves are reflected is used to calculate the speed of the car. Radar is also used to monitor the movement of airplanes and to help ship captains navigate at night or in foggy weather.

Figure 8 Police officers use radar to detect cars going faster than the speed limit.

Infrared Waves

Infrared waves have shorter wavelengths and higher frequencies than microwaves. So infrared waves can carry more energy than microwaves and radio waves carry.

When you sit outside on a sunny summer day, you feel warm because of *infrared waves* emitted by the sun. Infrared waves are absorbed by your skin when they strike your body. The energy of the waves causes the particles in your skin to vibrate faster, and you feel the increased vibration as an increase in temperature.

The sun is not the only source of infrared waves. Objects that emit infrared waves include stars, planets, buildings, trees, and you! The amount of infrared radiation emitted by an object varies depending on the object's temperature. Warmer objects give off more infrared radiation than cooler objects.

Your eyes can't see infrared waves, but there are devices that can detect infrared radiation. For example, infrared binoculars convert infrared radiation into light you can see. Such binoculars can be used to observe animals at night. **Figure 9** shows how certain photographic films are sensitive to infrared radiation.

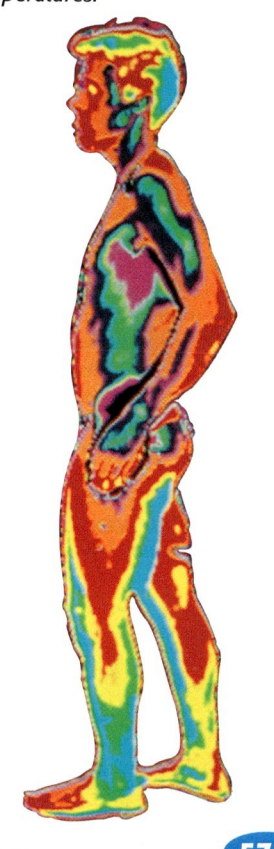

Figure 9 In this photograph, brighter colors indicate higher temperatures.

REVIEW

1. How do infrared waves differ from radio waves in terms of frequency and wavelength?
2. Describe two ways that radio waves are used for transmitting information.
3. **Inferring Relationships** Why do the frequencies of EM waves increase as the wavelengths decrease?

CONNECT TO
EARTH SCIENCE

Scientists can detect mineral deposits, underground fires, diseased vegetation, and a variety of other things using infrared film. For instance, rocks and minerals vary in color because they are at slightly different temperatures. They appear a different color from each other on IR film. In this way, geologists are able to chart the mineral content of the soil from the air. This technique lets scientists analyze soil on the moon and planets from spacecraft.

CONNECT TO
LIFE SCIENCE

More than 140 species of snakes belong to the family known as pit vipers. The rattlesnake, cottonmouth, and copperhead are common North American pit vipers, and the bushmaster and fer-de-lance are pit vipers found in Central and South America. Pit vipers are unique in that they have a pair of organs called pits between the eyes and nostrils. The pits are very sensitive to infrared radiation up to 20 cm away. Nerve impulses from the pits and eyes are interpreted by the brain as a single picture. The pits allow pit vipers to see prey even at night.

Answers to Review

1. Infrared waves have shorter wavelengths and higher frequencies than radio waves, and they can carry more energy than radio waves.
2. Radio waves can transmit information by either AM (amplitude modulation) or FM (frequency modulation). Students may also say that radio waves can be used to transmit television and radio signals.
3. All electromagnetic waves that travel through the same medium travel at the same speed. Wave speed is frequency times wavelength. Because wave speed is constant, the frequencies of EM waves must increase as the wavelengths decrease.

2) Teach, continued

MISCONCEPTION ALERT

The range of the electromagnetic spectrum that humans can see is called the visible spectrum. However, other animals are able to see electromagnetic radiation with wavelengths outside of the visible spectrum. For example, bees and other insects use ultraviolet light (see page 573), and pit vipers can detect infrared radiation.

MEETING INDIVIDUAL NEEDS

Advanced Learners Ask students, "What is a rainbow?" Basically, a rainbow is sunlight spread out into its spectrum of colors. The colors are directed toward the viewer by raindrops or other water droplets in the air. But rainbows are more complex than this. Challenge students to research how rainbows are formed and why we see them as we do. Encourage students to be creative; presentations might include models of rainbows, photographs of rainbows, or creating a rainbow in the school parking lot.

REAL-WORLD CONNECTION

Therapy involving exposure to certain kinds of light has become an accepted treatment of a mood disorder known as *seasonal affective disorder*. Seasonal affective disorder, or SAD, is characterized by feelings of depression that typically occur during the fall and winter months. Researchers believe that the reduction in the amount of light that passes through the eyes during these months affects the release of important brain chemicals. The treatment, known as phototherapy, involves a 20–30 minute daily exposure to a specific kind of light.

572 Chapter 22 • The Nature of Light

Biology CONNECTION

Visible light provides the energy necessary for photosynthesis—the process by which plants make their own food. Photosynthesis is important to you for two reasons. First, during photosynthesis, plants produce oxygen for you to breathe. Second, the food produced by plants provides your body with energy. When you eat plants, or eat meat from animals that ate plants, you get energy to live from the food produced through photosynthesis.

Visible Light

Visible light is the very narrow range of wavelengths and frequencies in the electromagnetic spectrum that humans can see. Humans see the different wavelengths as different colors, as shown in **Figure 10**. The longest wavelengths are seen as red light, and the shortest wavelengths are seen as violet light. Because violet light has the shortest wavelength, it carries the most energy of the visible light waves.

Figure 10 *White light, such as light from the sun, is actually visible light of all wavelengths combined. You see all the colors of visible light in a rainbow.*

Colors of Light The range of colors is called the *visible spectrum*. When you list the colors, you might use the imaginary name "Roy G. Biv" to help you remember their order. The letters in Roy's name represent the first letter of each color of visible light: **r**ed, **o**range, **y**ellow, **g**reen, **b**lue, **i**ndigo, and **v**iolet. When all the colors of visible light are combined, you see the light as white light. Sunlight and light from incandescent light bulbs and fluorescent light bulbs are examples of white light. You can see the visible spectrum in **Figure 11**.

Figure 11 *The visible spectrum contains all colors of light.*

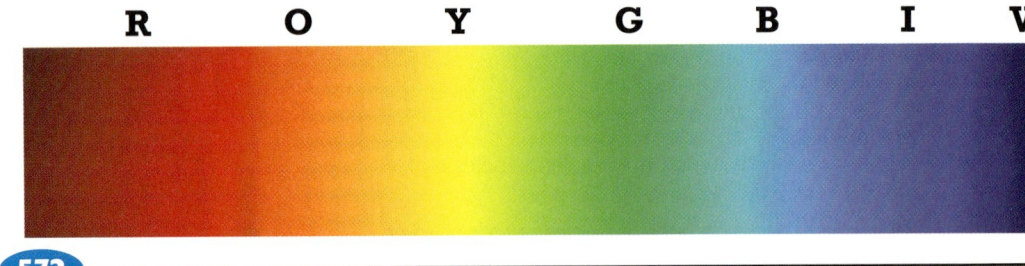

IS THAT A FACT!

John Dalton (1766–1844), an English chemist and researcher of matter, suffered from colorblindness. Because he suffered from this malady, he was the first to study it and perform preliminary tests. In 1794, Dalton presented a paper on colorblindness before the Manchester Literary and Philosophical Society. Dalton's paper was the first known description of this vision phenomenon, and for many years colorblindness was called Daltonism.

Ultraviolet Light

Ultraviolet light is another type of electromagnetic wave produced by the sun. Ultraviolet waves have shorter wavelengths and higher frequencies than visible light. Therefore, ultraviolet waves carry more energy than visible light carries. This greater amount of energy affects us in both positive and negative ways.

Positive Effects On the positive side, ultraviolet waves produced artificially by ultraviolet lamps are used to kill bacteria on food and surgical instruments. In addition, limited exposure to ultraviolet light is beneficial to your body. When exposed to ultraviolet light, skin cells produce vitamin D, a substance necessary for the absorption of calcium by the intestines. Without calcium, your teeth and bones would be very weak.

Negative Effects On the negative side, overexposure to ultraviolet light can cause sunburn, skin cancer, damage to the eyes, wrinkles, and premature aging of the skin. Fortunately, much of the ultraviolet light from the sun does not reach the surface of the Earth. But you should still protect yourself against the ultraviolet light that does reach you. To do so, you should use sunscreen with a high SPF (**S**un **P**rotection **F**actor) and wear sunglasses that block out ultraviolet light, like the person on the left in **Figure 12.** You need this protection even on overcast days because ultraviolet light can travel through clouds.

Figure 12 *Sunscreen offers protection against a painful sunburn.*

Blocking the Sun

Sunscreens contain a chemical that prevents ultraviolet light from penetrating your skin. When you look at a bottle of sunscreen, you will see the abbreviation SPF followed by a number. The number is a guide to how long you can stay in the sun without getting a sunburn. For example, if you use a sunscreen with SPF 15 and you normally burn after being in the sun for 10 minutes, you will be able to stay in the sun for 150 minutes without getting burned. Why do you think people who burn easily need a higher SPF?

3 Extend

CONNECT TO LIFE SCIENCE

Our bodies can make vitamin D if the skin is exposed to ultraviolet light in sunlight for certain periods of time. Many people are not exposed to sunlight long enough for their bodies to produce enough vitamin D. However, vitamin D is available in some foods. Good dietary sources of vitamin D are milk and dairy products, butter, eggs, liver, cod-liver oil, and oily fish, such as salmon.

Answer to APPLY

People who burn easily also tend to burn quickly. Therefore, they need a higher SPF in order to be able to stay in the sun for a long time without getting burned.

RETEACHING

Remind students that the EM spectrum is continuous and that one segment blends into the next. On the board, write the following range of frequencies for each of the segments. Do not write the name of the segment next to its frequency. Help students use what they know about the relationship between frequency and wavelength to match the frequencies with the correct wavelengths and names. (radio waves: 10^4 Hz to 10^8 Hz; microwaves: 10^9 Hz to 10^{11} Hz; infrared: 10^{12} Hz to 10^{14} Hz; visible light: 4×10^{14} Hz to 7.9×10^{15} Hz; ultraviolet light: 10^{15} Hz to 5×10^{16} Hz; X rays: 1×10^{17} Hz to 1×10^{18} Hz; gamma rays: 1×10^{18} Hz and beyond.) **Sheltered English**

IS THAT A FACT!

Ordinary window glass, which is made of silicon, is opaque to ultraviolet light. Suntanning lamps are made of quartz glass. Quartz glass transmits the ultraviolet rays needed for tanning.

Q: Why did the beam of light look sad after meeting with the prism?

A: It was all broken up inside!

4) Close

Quiz

1. Why are X ray machines used in some manufacturing processes? (X rays can detect flaws, cracks, or other defects inside an object that cannot be seen from the outside.)

2. Why are infrared sensors more useful at night? (Infrared sensors detect thermal energy given off by an object. During the daytime, temperature differences may not be as noticeable as they are at night.)

3. True or false: FM radio waves can travel greater distances than AM radio waves. (false)

ALTERNATIVE ASSESSMENT

Writing Have students write a short story in which the characters use or are affected by each of the different types of EM radiation.

SCIENTISTS AT ODDS

Some scientists consider cosmic photons to be EM waves. These photons have greater frequencies and shorter wavelengths than gamma rays. The incredible energy required to create these cosmic photons may come from supernovas or other astrophysical phenomena. Refer to Teaching Transparencies 196 and 197 to help students understand supernovas.

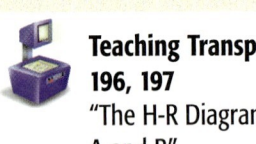

Teaching Transparencies 196, 197
"The H-R Diagram: A and B"

LINK TO EARTH SCIENCE

X Rays and Gamma Rays

X rays and gamma rays have some of the shortest wavelengths and highest frequencies of all EM waves. X rays carry a great deal of energy and easily penetrate a variety of materials. This characteristic makes X rays useful in the medical field, as shown in **Figure 13.** However, too much exposure to X rays can damage or kill living cells. Patients receiving X-ray examinations often wear a lead-lined apron to protect the parts of the body that do not need X-ray exposure.

Figure 13 *If you fall and hurt your arm, a doctor might use an X-ray machine to check for broken bones.*

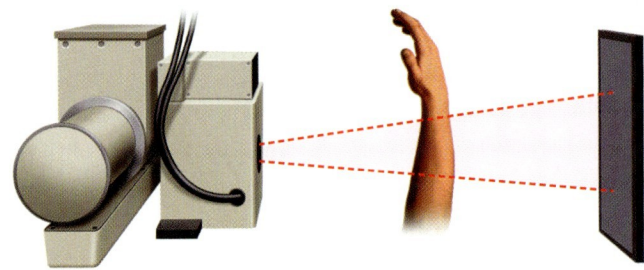 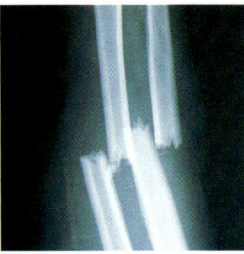

X rays travel easily through skin and muscle but are absorbed by bones.

The X rays that are not absorbed strike the film.

Bright areas appear on the film where X rays are absorbed by the bones.

Gamma rays carry large amounts of energy and can penetrate materials very easily. Every day you are exposed to small amounts of gamma rays that do not harm you. Because of their high energy, gamma rays are used to treat some forms of cancer. Radiologists focus the rays on tumors inside the body to kill the cancer cells. While this treatment can have positive effects, it often has negative side effects because some healthy cells are also killed.

internetconnect

SCILINKS NSTA
TOPIC: The Electromagnetic Spectrum
GO TO: www.scilinks.org
sciLINKS NUMBER: HSTP530

REVIEW

1. Explain why ultraviolet light, X rays, and gamma rays can be both helpful and harmful.

2. Describe how three different types of electromagnetic waves have been useful to you today.

3. **Comparing Concepts** Compare the wavelengths and frequencies of infrared, ultraviolet, and visible light. How does the energy carried by each type of wave compare with the others?

Answers to Review

1. Ultraviolet light is useful because it can kill bacteria and help the human body produce vitamin D. But overexposure to ultraviolet waves can cause sunburn, wrinkles, and skin cancer. X rays and gamma rays are used in medicine to check for broken bones and to treat cancer. Because X rays and gamma rays carry so much energy, they can kill healthy, living cells. Therefore, exposure to both X rays and gamma rays should be limited.

2. Accept all reasonable answers.

3. wavelengths (longest to shortest): IR, visible light, UV light; frequencies (lowest to highest): IR, visible light, UV; energy (lowest to highest): IR, visible, UV. Light waves with shorter wavelengths and higher frequencies will carry greater amounts of energy.

Section 3

Interactions of Light Waves

Terms to Learn

reflection
law of reflection
absorption
scattering
refraction
diffraction
interference

What You'll Do

- Compare regular reflection with diffuse reflection.
- Describe absorption and scattering of light.
- Explain how refraction can create optical illusions and separate white light into colors.
- Describe diffraction and interference of light.

Have you ever seen a cat's eyes glow in the dark when light shines on them? Cats have a special layer of cells in the back of their eyes that reflects light. This layer helps the cat see better by giving the eyes another chance to detect the light. Reflection is just one way light waves interact. All types of EM waves interact in several ways. Because we can see visible light, it is easier to explain interactions involving visible light.

Reflection

Reflection occurs when light or any other wave bounces off an object. When you see yourself in a mirror, you are actually seeing light that has been reflected twice—first from you and then from the mirror. Reflection allows you to see objects that don't produce their own light. When light strikes an object, some of the light reflects off of it and is detected by your eyes.

But if light is reflecting off you and off the objects around you, why can't you see your reflection on a wall? To answer this question, you must first learn about the law of reflection.

The Law of Reflection Light reflects off surfaces the same way that a ball bounces off the ground. If you throw the ball straight down against a smooth surface, it will bounce straight up. If you bounce it at an angle, it will bounce away at an angle. The **law of reflection** states that the angle of incidence is equal to the angle of reflection. *Incidence* is the falling of a beam of light on a surface. **Figure 14** illustrates this law.

Figure 14 The Law of Reflection

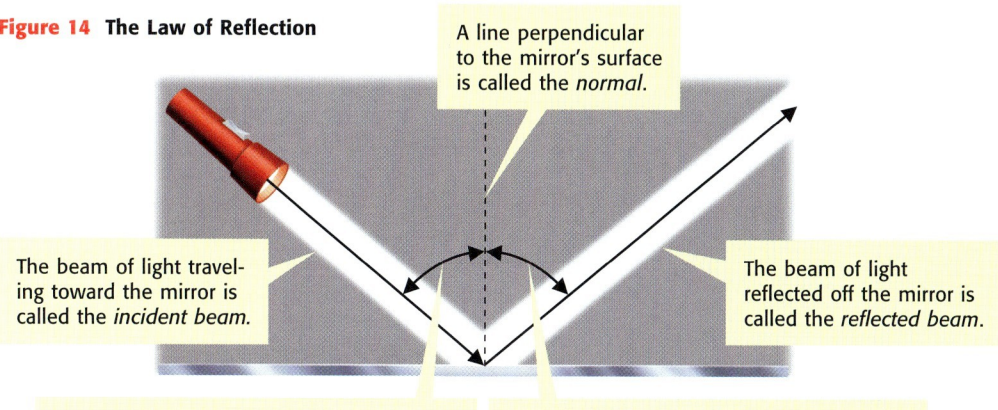

- A line perpendicular to the mirror's surface is called the *normal*.
- The beam of light traveling toward the mirror is called the *incident beam*.
- The beam of light reflected off the mirror is called the *reflected beam*.
- The angle between the incident beam and the normal is called the *angle of incidence*.
- The angle between the reflected beam and the normal is called the *angle of reflection*.

Multicultural CONNECTION

Greek philosophers Hero and Ptolemy believed that eyes emitted rays that were reflected back by objects. However, an Iraqi scientist named Abu 'Ali al-Hasan ibn al-Haytham (c. 965–1039) believed differently. His theory of vision was very similar to today's: Objects are seen because of the light they reflect or emit.

Teaching Transparency 292 "The Law of Reflection"

Directed Reading Worksheet 22 Section 3

2 Teach

READING STRATEGY

Predicting Students have already studied mechanical waves, so ask them to predict some of the ways in which light waves might interact with each other. (Students should predict that light waves can be reflected, refracted, or diffracted and that they may interfere with each other.)

MEETING INDIVIDUAL NEEDS

Learners Having Difficulty
Provide each pair of students with a flashlight, a comb, a protractor, and a mirror. Have them stand the mirror on one edge with the reflecting side facing them. Have students place a sheet of paper on the table in front of the mirror and lay the protractor on top of the paper with the straight edge of the protractor against the mirror. Next, have them place the flashlight pointed toward the mirror at an angle and turn it on. The comb should be placed in front of the light. Have students trace the path of one of the beams and note the angle at which the beam strikes the mirror. Have students compare that angle with the angle of reflection.
Sheltered English

Teaching Transparency 292
"Regular and Diffuse Reflection"

Types of Reflection So back to the question, "Why can you see your reflection in a mirror but not in a wall?" The answer has to do with the differences between the two surfaces. If the reflecting surface is very smooth, like a mirror or polished metal, light beams reflect off all points of the surface at the same angle. This is called *regular reflection*. If the reflecting surface is slightly rough, like a wall, light beams will hit the surface and reflect at many different angles. This is called *diffuse reflection*. **Figure 15** illustrates the difference between the two types of reflection.

Figure 15 Regular Reflection Vs. Diffuse Reflection

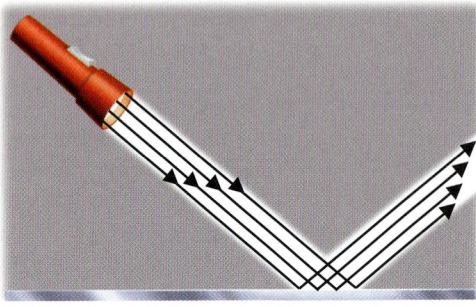
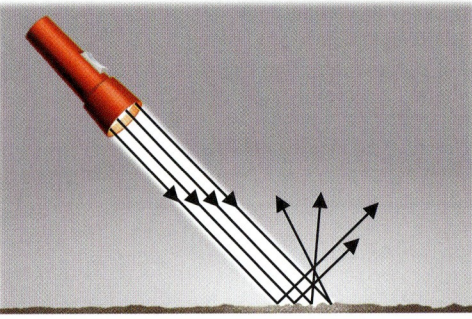

Regular reflection occurs when light beams are reflected at the same angle. When your eye detects the reflected beams, you can see a reflection on the surface.

Diffuse reflection occurs when light beams reflect at many different angles. You can't see a reflection because not all of the reflected light is directed toward your eyes.

Absorption and Scattering

You have probably noticed that when you use a flashlight, objects that are closer to you appear brighter than objects that are farther away. The light appears to weaken the farther it travels from the flashlight. This happens partially because the beam spreads out and partially because of absorption and scattering.

Absorption of Light The transfer of energy carried by light waves to particles of matter is called **absorption**. When you shine a flashlight in the air, the air particles absorb some of the energy from the light. This causes the light to become dim, as shown in **Figure 16**. The farther the light travels from the flashlight, the more it is absorbed by air particles.

Figure 16 A beam of light becomes dimmer partially because of absorption and scattering.

 **Multicultural CONNECTION**

The French scientist Hippolyte-Louis Fizeau was the first person to measure the speed of light using a laboratory experiment. Fizeau used mirrors and a rotating toothed-wheel to break a beam of light into a series of pulses and then measure the speed of those pulses.

Homework

Have students determine the length and the placement of the shortest possible flat mirror in which a 2 m tall person could see his/her entire body. (1 m long; the top of the mirror should be placed slightly above eye level—one half the distance between the eyes and the top of the head)

Scattering of Light The release of light energy by particles of matter that have absorbed energy is called **scattering**. When the light is released, it scatters in all directions. Light from a flashlight is scattered out of the beam by air particles. This scattered light allows you to see objects outside of the beam, as shown in Figure 16 on the previous page. However, because light is scattered out of the beam, the beam becomes dimmer.

Scattering makes the sky blue. Light with shorter wavelengths is scattered more than light with longer wavelengths. Sunlight is made up of many different colors of light, but blue light (which has a very short wavelength) is scattered more than any other color. So when you look at the sky, you see a background of blue light. You can learn more about the scattering of light by doing the QuickLab at right.

Refraction

Imagine that you and a friend are at a lake. Your friend wades into the water. You look at her and are startled to see that her feet look like they are separated from her legs! You know her feet did not come off, so how can you explain what you see? The answer has to do with refraction.

Refraction is the bending of a wave as it passes at an angle from one medium to another. Refraction of light waves occurs because the speed of light varies depending on the material through which the waves are traveling. In a vacuum, light travels at 300,000,000 m/s, but it travels more slowly through matter. When a wave enters a new medium at an angle, the part of the wave that enters first begins traveling at a different speed from the rest of the wave. **Figure 17** shows how a light beam is bent by refraction.

QuickLab

Scattering Milk

1. Fill a clear **2 L plastic bottle** with **water**.
2. Turn the lights off, and shine a **flashlight** through the water. Look at the water from all sides of the bottle. Describe what you see in your ScienceLog.
3. Add a few drops of **milk** to the water, and shake the bottle to mix it up.
4. Repeat step 2. Describe any color changes. If you don't see any, add more milk until you do.
5. How is the water-and-milk mixture like air particles in the atmosphere? Write your answer in your ScienceLog.

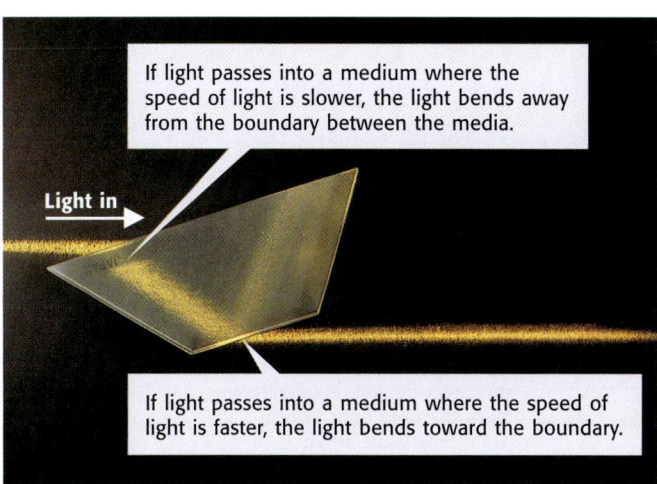

Figure 17 Light travels more slowly through glass than it does through air. Therefore, light refracts as it passes at an angle from air to glass or from glass to air.

IS THAT A FACT!
A blue jay's feathers are not really blue. The air molecules on the surface barbs of the feathers scatter the red-and-green light of the visible spectrum, leaving blue light to reflect to our eyes.

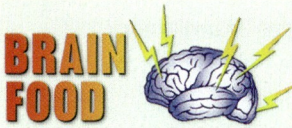

The earliest mirrors date back to 6000 B.C. and were discovered in areas around Turkey and Egypt. These mirrors were about 90 mm in diameter and were made from flat pieces of polished igneous rock called obsidian.

QuickLab

MATERIALS

FOR EACH GROUP:
- 2 L clear plastic bottle
- water
- flashlight
- milk

Answers to QuickLab

2. Students should see the light of the flashlight beam shining straight through the water. They may also see the beam from the sides because some of the light is scattered to the side.

4. When students view the bottle from the side, they should see a bluish color from blue light being scattered to the sides. If they look through the water straight toward the flashlight, the light will appear reddish.

5. The milk particles scatter the light traveling through the water just like air particles scatter sunlight as it travels through the air.

MEETING INDIVIDUAL NEEDS

Advanced Learners Have students do research into why the sky appears blue. Wrong answers to this question are quite common. Students should find that when visible light from the sun passes through the atmosphere, air molecules scatter light waves with shorter wavelengths. Blue happens to be the most affected wavelength. Encourage students to create posters or demonstrations to explain their findings.

TOPIC: Reflection and Refraction
GO TO: www.scilinks.org
sciLINKS NUMBER: HSTP545

2) Teach, continued

CONNECT TO LIFE SCIENCE

Natural rainbows are visible only when the sun is lower than 42° above the horizon. This is because of the way water refracts through raindrops. It is unlikely that you will see a rainbow at noon!

CROSS-DISCIPLINARY FOCUS

Mathematics The first person to explain how rainbows form was René Descartes (1596–1650), a famous French mathematician and scientist. His explanation was published in 1637 in his book *Discours de la Methode*. Descartes reasoned that because rainbows also appear in waterfalls and water fountains, as well as in the sky, rainbows must be a result of drops of water affecting light waves.

REAL-WORLD CONNECTION

In recent decades, fiber optic technology has become a standard for the telecommunication industry. This technology utilizes information encoded into light beams that travel through small, pliable glass cables. These glass, or fiberoptic, cables are composed of two different types of optically conducting materials. The center, or *core*, is the glass through which the light travels. The *clad*, which surrounds the core, has a lower index of refraction and totally reflects light, thereby containing the light within the core regions.

Figure 18 Refraction can create the illusion that the feet of the person in the water are separated from her legs. Try this for yourself!

Figure 19 A prism is a piece of glass that separates white light into the colors of visible light by refraction.

Light passing through a prism is refracted twice—once when it enters and once when it exits.

Violet light, which has a short wavelength, is refracted more than red light, which has a long wavelength.

Optical Illusions Normally when you look at an object, the light reflecting off the object travels in a straight line from the object to your eye. Your brain always interprets light as traveling in straight lines. However, when you look at an object that is underwater, the light reflecting off the object does *not* travel in a straight line. Instead, it refracts. **Figure 18** shows how refraction creates an optical illusion.

Refraction and Color Separation You have already learned that white light is actually composed of all the colors of visible light. You also know that the different colors correspond to different wavelengths. When white light is refracted, the amount that the light bends depends on its wavelength. Light waves with short wavelengths bend more than light waves with long wavelengths. Because of this, white light can be separated into different colors during refraction, as shown in **Figure 19**. Color separation during refraction is responsible for the formation of rainbows. Rainbows are created when sunlight is refracted by water droplets.

Teaching Transparency 293 "White Light is Separated by a Prism"

IS THAT A FACT!

Some light bulbs and mirrors are frosted or etched to reduce glare or to create interesting visual effects. This process involves applying hydrofluoric acid, a powerful and toxic acid, directly to the glass. This acid reacts with silicon atoms in the glass to produce this effect.

578 Chapter 22 • The Nature of Light

Diffraction

Refraction isn't the only way light waves are bent. **Diffraction** is the bending of waves around barriers or through openings. The diffraction of light waves is not always easy to see. The diffraction of water waves, shown in **Figure 20,** is easier to see. The amount a wave diffracts depends on its wavelength and the size of the barrier or the opening. The greatest amount of diffraction occurs when the barrier or opening is the same size or smaller than the wavelength.

The wavelength of light is very small—about 100 times smaller than the thickness of a human hair! So in order for light to diffract very much, light has to be passing through a slit or some other opening that is very narrow.

Light waves cannot diffract very much around large obstacles, such as buildings. That's why you can't see around corners. But light waves always diffract a small amount. You can observe light waves diffracting if you examine the edges of a shadow. Diffraction causes the edges of shadows to be blurry.

Figure 20 Water waves are often used to model the behavior of light waves.

Interference

Interference is a wave interaction that occurs when two or more waves overlap. Overlapping waves can combine by constructive or destructive interference.

Constructive Interference When waves combine by *constructive interference,* the resulting wave has a greater amplitude than the individual waves had. Constructive interference of light waves can be observed when light of one wavelength shines through two small slits onto a screen. The light on the screen will appear as a series of alternating bright and dark bands. The bright bands result from light waves combining through constructive interference to create a light wave with a greater amplitude.

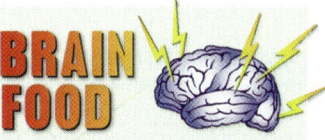

BRAIN FOOD

Two lamps are brighter than one, but it's not because of constructive interference. It's because two lamps produce more energy in the form of photons than one lamp. As a result, the light has a greater intensity, which makes the room brighter.

3) Extend

DEMONSTRATION

Obtain a piece of diffraction grating and a laser. Darken the room, and point the laser at a wall. Ask the students to describe what they see on the wall. (a single red dot)

Place the diffraction grating in front of the laser light, and aim the beam at the same wall. Ask students what they see on the wall. (a series of small red dots)

Have students look at the dots carefully and describe what they see. (The dots aren't really round like the single dot.)

Pass out small pieces of diffraction grating and magnifying lenses. Encourage students to look carefully at the grating and to describe what they see. (lines)

Discuss diffraction with students and how diffracted laser light causes the series of flattened circles of light instead of a single dot.

REAL-WORLD CONNECTION

A common use of light interference is using laser light to create a hologram. Students will learn more about how holograms are produced in Chapter 23, "Light and Our World."

Reinforcement Worksheet 22
"Fiona, Private Eye"

Reinforcement Worksheet 22
"Light Interactions"

CONNECT TO LIFE SCIENCE

Archerfish *(Toxotes jaculator)* have the ability to correct for the refraction of light between air and water, and they have the ability to judge the distance to their prey. There are six species of archerfish that live in estuaries, wetlands, and fresh water in Southeast Asia, the western Pacific, and Australia. Archerfish can grow to 23 cm in length. Archerfish knock insects and other small prey from overhanging vegetation by spitting jets of water at them. Archerfish have a groove in the roof of their mouth. When the tongue is pressed against the groove and the gills are squeezed shut, a jet of water is produced. These fish can hit prey more than 1.5 m away!

4 Close

Quiz

1. The moon does not produce light of its own. So where does moonlight come from? (Moonlight is sunlight that is reflected off of the moon to the Earth.)

2. Archerfish shoot jets of water at insects sitting on vegetation above the water, so they must adjust for refraction. Where is the ideal place for an archerfish to be in relation to its prey? Why? (The archerfish should be directly below its prey. Light entering the water perpendicular to the surface is not refracted.)

3. Explain how colors are separated in a rainbow. (Rainbows form when water droplets refract sunlight. Light of shorter wavelengths, such as violet, is refracted more than light of longer wavelengths, such as red.)

ALTERNATIVE ASSESSMENT

Concept Mapping Have students make a concept map that shows the following properties of light:

reflection, refraction, scattering, diffraction, and interference

Concept maps should include examples.

Teaching Transparency 294
"Constructive and Destructive Interference"

Critical Thinking Worksheet 22
"Now You See It, Now You Don't"

Destructive Interference When waves combine by *destructive interference*, the resulting wave has a smaller amplitude than the individual waves had. Therefore, when light waves interfere destructively, the result will be dimmer light.

You do not see constructive or destructive interference of white light. To understand why, remember that white light is composed of waves with many different wavelengths. The waves rarely line up to combine in total destructive interference. However, if light of only one wavelength is used, both constructive and destructive interference are easily observed, as illustrated in **Figure 21**.

Figure 21 Constructive and Destructive Interference

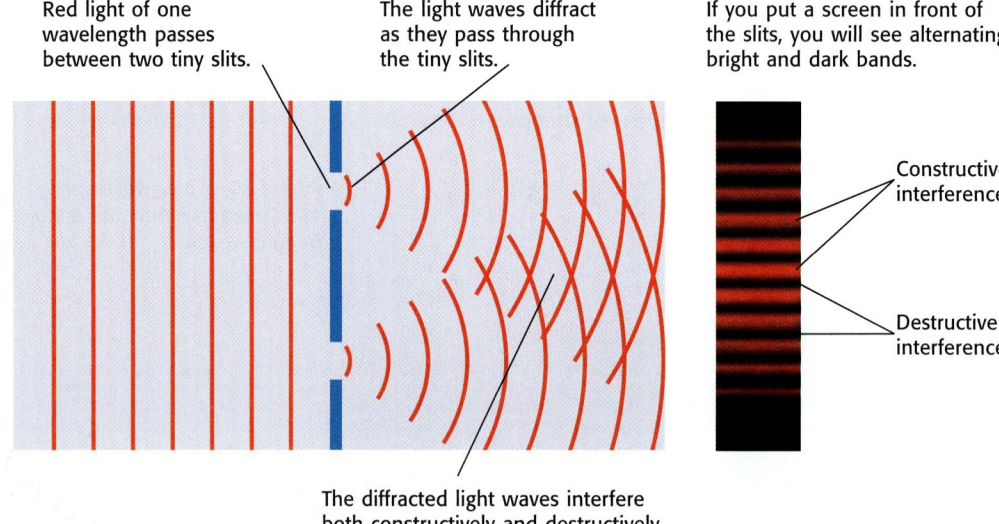

Red light of one wavelength passes between two tiny slits.

The light waves diffract as they pass through the tiny slits.

If you put a screen in front of the slits, you will see alternating bright and dark bands.

Constructive interference

Destructive interference

The diffracted light waves interfere both constructively and destructively.

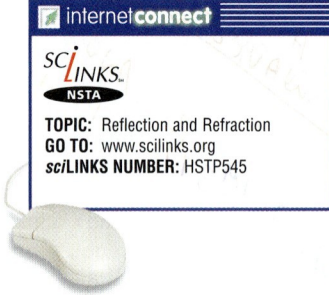

TOPIC: Reflection and Refraction
GO TO: www.scilinks.org
sciLINKS NUMBER: HSTP545

REVIEW

1. Explain the difference between absorption and scattering.
2. Why does a straw look bent in a glass of water?
3. Why do the edges of shadows seem blurry? Explain your answer.
4. **Applying Concepts** Explain why you can see your reflection on a spoon but not on a piece of cloth.

Answers to Review

1. Absorbtion is the transfer of energy carried by light waves to particles of matter. Scattering is the release of light energy by particles that have absorbed energy.

2. A straw looks bent in a glass of water because of the refraction of light waves.

3. The edge of shadows seem blurry because light waves diffract around objects.

4. Light reflects off of a spoon by regular reflection, so you can see your image in the spoon. But light reflects off of a piece of cloth by diffuse reflection. Thus, you can see the cloth, but not your image.

Section 4

Light and Color

Terms to Learn

transmission
transparent
translucent
opaque
pigment

What You'll Do

- Name and describe the three ways light interacts with matter.
- Explain how the color of an object is determined.
- Compare the primary colors of light and the primary pigments.

Have you ever wondered what gives an object its color? You already know that white light is made of all the colors of light. But when you see fruit in white light, you see color. For example, strawberries are red and bananas are yellow. Why aren't they all white? And how can a soda bottle be green and let you see through it at the same time? To answer these questions, you must first learn how light interacts with matter. Then you will understand why objects have different colors.

Light and Matter

When light strikes any form of matter, it can interact with the matter in three different ways—it can be reflected, absorbed, or transmitted. You learned about reflection and absorption in the previous section. **Transmission** is the passing of light through matter. You see the transmission of light all the time. All of the light that reaches your eyes is transmitted through air. Light can interact with matter in several ways at the same time, as shown in **Figure 22**.

Figure 22 *Light is transmitted, reflected, and absorbed when it strikes the glass in a window.*

You can see the glass and your reflection in it because light is **reflected** off the glass.

You can see objects outside because light is **transmitted** through the glass.

The glass feels warm when you touch it because some light is **absorbed** by the glass.

Q: How many magicians does it take to change a light bulb?

A: Depends on what you want to change it into!

Homework

Challenge students to write a short explanation of why it is fortunate that some materials and objects transmit light. Why is it fortunate that some things are translucent or opaque? Accept all reasonable answers.

Section 4

Focus

Light and Color

Students will learn how light interacts with matter. Students will also learn what determines the color of an object and will learn about the primary colors of light and the primary pigments. Students will explore what happens when colors of light or pigments are mixed.

🔔 Bellringer

Ask students the following:

What is your favorite color? It is a simple question, but have you ever thought about why you like a particular color more than others? In a short paragraph, explain why you like your favorite color. Also explain how certain colors affect your mood.

1) Motivate

DEMONSTRATION

Cover one lens of a high-intensity flashlight with a green filter and a second flashlight lens with a red filter. In a darkened room, turn the "green" light on, and shine it on a white sheet, white wall, or overhead screen. Turn the "red" light on, and shine it on a different area of the screen. Ask the students what colors they see. Ask students to predict what color they will see if you overlap the green and red light. The students will probably answer "brown." Slowly overlap the two colors. (Yellow will appear.)

Directed Reading Worksheet 22 Section 4

② Teach

CONNECT TO LIFE SCIENCE

Although the lens of the human eye is usually transparent, some conditions, such as cataracts, and injuries can make the lens translucent or even opaque. Most cataracts are the result of aging or long-term exposure to ultraviolet light. While you cannot stop the aging process, you can minimize exposure to UV light by wearing a hat and sunglasses.

GROUP ACTIVITY

Up to 1 in 12 men are reported to be colorblind. This does not mean that they see only in black and white. In fact, most colorblind people can't distinguish between red and green. Some people who are colorblind can't distinguish between red and yellow colors. With this in mind, consider the color of traffic lights. Have students design a traffic light or a flashing caution light that would be better suited for people who are colorblind.

Types of Matter Matter through which visible light is easily transmitted is said to be **transparent.** Air, glass, and water are examples of transparent matter. You can see objects clearly when you view them through transparent matter.

Sometimes windows in bathrooms are made of frosted glass. If you try to look through one of these types of windows, you will see only blurry shapes. You can't see clearly through a frosted window because it is translucent. **Translucent** matter transmits light but also scatters the light as it passes through the matter. Wax paper is an example of translucent matter.

Matter that does not transmit any light is said to be **opaque.** You cannot see through opaque objects. Metal, wood, and this book are examples of opaque objects. You can compare transparent, translucent, and opaque matter in **Figure 23.**

Figure 23 What's for Lunch?

Transparent plastic makes it easy to see what you are having for lunch.

Translucent wax paper makes it a little harder to see exactly what's for lunch.

Opaque aluminum foil makes it impossible to see your lunch without unwrapping it.

Colors of Objects

What's a bean's favorite color? It's not a riddle, it's an experiment on page 716 of the LabBook.

How does the interaction of light with matter determine an object's color? You already know that the color of light is determined by the wavelength of the light wave. Red has the longest wavelength, violet has the shortest wavelength, and other colors have wavelengths in between.

The color that an object appears to be is determined by the wavelengths of light that reach your eyes. Light reaches your eyes after being reflected off an object or after being transmitted through an object. After reaching your eyes, light is converted into electrical impulses and interpreted by your brain as colors.

Homework

Cone cells in our eyes react to wavelengths of light that we call red, green, and blue. Humans can detect a tremendous range of colors, hues, tints, and shades. Have students look around at home and make a table or chart of all the different colors they see. The title of the table is "colors," and the four main headings are "red," "green," "blue," and "others." Have students describe as many different colors, shades, and tints as they can.

Colors of Opaque Objects When white light strikes a colored opaque object, some colors of light are absorbed and some are reflected. Only the light that is reflected reaches your eyes and is detected. Therefore, the colors of light that are reflected by an opaque object determine the color you see. For example, if your sweater reflects blue light and absorbs all other colors, you will see that the sweater is blue. Another example is shown in **Figure 24.**

Figure 24 *When white light shines on a strawberry, only red light is reflected. All other colors of light are absorbed. Therefore, the strawberry looks red to you.*

If green objects reflect green light and red objects reflect red light, what colors of light are reflected by the cow shown at right? Remember that white light includes all colors of light. So white objects—such as the white hair in the cow's hide—appear white because all the colors of light are reflected. On the other hand, black is the absence of color. When light strikes a black object, all the colors are absorbed.

Colors of Transparent and Translucent Objects

The color of transparent and translucent objects is determined differently from the color of opaque objects. Ordinary window glass is colorless in white light because it transmits all the colors that strike it. However, some transparent objects are colored. When you look through colored transparent or translucent objects, you see the color of light that was transmitted through the material. All the other colors were absorbed, as shown in **Figure 25.**

Figure 25 *This bottle is green because the plastic transmits only green light.*

✓ Self-Check

If blue light shines on a white sheet of paper, what color does the paper appear to be?
(Turn to page 724 to check your answer.)

CONNECT TO EARTH SCIENCE

Astronomers use starlight to calculate the temperature of stars. Because of its size and temperature, our sun is listed as a yellow dwarf. Interested students can do some research to find out more about how scientists use light to study stars and other objects in space.

What Color of Light Is Best for Green Plants?

Which Color Is Hottest?

READING STRATEGY

Prediction Guide Before students read the section about colors of opaque objects, ask them whether they would rather sit on a black bench or a white bench if both benches have been exposed to direct sunlight on a hot day. Ask students to explain their answer. Have students read the section and discuss it with them to make sure they understand why the black bench would be warmer. Ask them whether they would make the same choice if the same two benches were made of transparent or translucent plastic.
Sheltered English

Answer to Self-Check
The paper will appear blue because only blue light is reflected from the paper.

Multicultural CONNECTION

Colors are used as symbols in many human cultures. For example, red often represents warning or danger, while green can represent safety or safe passage. In the Ukraine, there is a long tradition of egg art—the coloring and decorating of eggs—to express emotions and to send messages. Choosing the right color is important. Egg decorators know, for instance, that red stands for love, green for growth, pink for success, and black for remembrance.

Interactive Explorations CD-ROM In the Spotlight

TOPIC: Colors
GO TO: www.scilinks.org
*sci*LINKS NUMBER: HSTP550

Section 4 • Light and Color   **583**

3) Extend

DEMONSTRATION

Take three small, high-intensity flashlights or slide projectors, and cover one light with a red filter (or colored cellophane), one with a green filter, and one with a blue filter. Darken the room as much as possible. Shine the lights on a white screen without mixing any colors. Then, mix two or more colors from the lights. Before each combination, ask students to predict what color will be produced.

Mixing Colors   PG 718

GOING FURTHER

Divide the class into small groups. Distribute a page from the Sunday comics to each group and ask students to list the colors they see on the page. Then give each group one or more magnifying lenses, and instruct students to look very carefully at the different colors. Ask them to list the colors they see under the magnifying lens. Have them list the colors of dots necessary to make a colored image. For instance, "What colors of dots produce a true green in a cartoon image?" (yellow and cyan)

MATERIALS

FOR EACH STUDENT:
- 4 plastic filters

Teacher Notes: Used but still functioning filters can be obtained from your school's theater department.

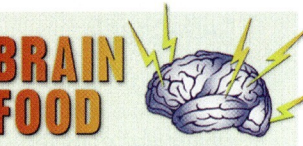

The colors you see on a color television are produced by color addition of the primary colors of light. A television screen is made up of groups of tiny red, green, and blue dots. These dots are made of chemicals called phosphors. Each phosphor dot will glow red, green, or blue—depending on the type of phosphor it is—when the dot is hit by an electron beam. The colors emitted by the glowing phosphor dots add together to produce all the different colors you see on the screen.

QuickLab

Rose-Colored Glasses?

1. Obtain **four plastic filters**—red, blue, yellow, and green.
2. Look through one filter at an object across the room. Describe the object's color.
3. Repeat step 2 with each of the filters.
4. Repeat step 2 with two or three filters together.
5. Why do you think the colors change when you use more than one filter?
6. Write your observations and answers in your ScienceLog.

Answers to QuickLab

2–4. The answers will vary depending on the object chosen by the student and the order in which the different filters are used. Students should notice that a colored object seems to change colors when viewed through different filters or combinations of filters.

5. The colors changed because different colors of light are allowed to pass through the different filters. If you use more than one filter, fewer colors are allowed to pass through.

Mixing Colors of Light

In order to get white light, you need to combine all colors of light, right? Well, that's one way of doing it. You can also get white light by adding just three colors of light together—red, blue, and green—as shown in **Figure 26.** In fact, these three colors can be combined in different ratios to produce all colors of visible light. Red, blue, and green are therefore called the *primary colors of light.*

Color Addition   When colors of light combine, more wavelengths of light are present. Therefore, combining colors of light is called color addition. When two primary colors are added together, a *secondary color* is produced. The secondary colors are cyan (blue plus green), magenta (blue plus red), and yellow (red plus green).

Figure 26   Primary colors—written in white—combine to produce white light. Secondary colors—written in black—are the result of two primary colors added together.

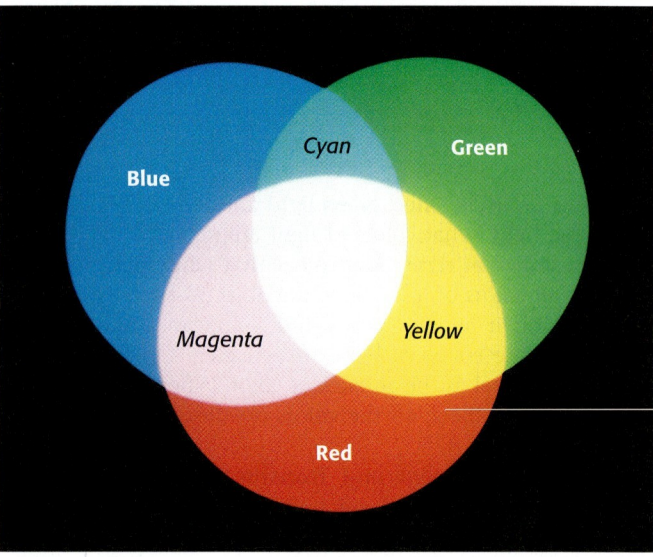

Mixing Colors of Pigment

If you have ever tried mixing paints in art class, you know that you can't make white paint by mixing red, blue, and green paint. The difference between mixing paint and mixing light is due to the fact that paint contains pigments. A **pigment** is a material that gives a substance its color by absorbing some colors of light and reflecting others.

584   Chapter 22 • The Nature of Light

Almost everything contains pigments. In fact, pigments give objects color. Chlorophyll and melanin are two examples of pigments. Chlorophyll gives plants a green color, and melanin gives your skin its color.

Color Subtraction Each pigment absorbs at least one color of light. When you mix pigments together, more colors of light are absorbed, or subtracted. Therefore, mixing colors of pigments is called color subtraction.

The *primary pigments* are yellow, cyan, and magenta. They can be combined to produce any other color. In fact, all the colors in this book were produced by using just the primary pigments and black ink. The black ink was used to provide contrast to the images. **Figure 27** shows how the four pigments combine to produce many different colors.

Geology CONNECTION

Minerals are naturally occurring crystalline solids. A blue mineral called azurite was once used by European painters as a pigment in paint. But these painters didn't realize that azurite changes into another mineral over time. The new mineral, malachite, is green. So some paintings that once had beautiful blue skies now have skies that look greenish.

Figure 27 *The picture of the balloon on the left was made by overlapping yellow ink, cyan ink, magenta ink, and black ink.*

Yellow
Cyan
Magenta
Black

REVIEW

1. Describe three different ways light interacts with matter.
2. What are the primary colors of light, and why are they called primary colors?
3. Describe the difference between the primary colors of light and the primary pigments.
4. **Applying Concepts** Explain what happens to the different colors of light when white light shines on a violet object.

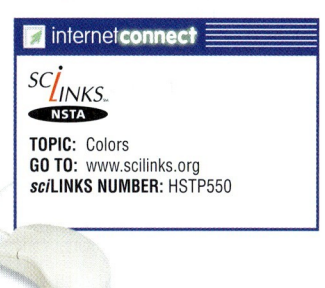

internetconnect

SCLINKS NSTA
TOPIC: Colors
GO TO: www.scilinks.org
*sci*LINKS NUMBER: HSTP550

585

Chapter Highlights

Vocabulary Definitions

Section 1

electromagnetic wave a wave that can travel through space or matter and consists of changing electric and magnetic fields.

radiation the emission of energy in the form of electromagnetic waves

Section 2

electromagnetic spectrum the entire range of electromagnetic waves

Chapter Highlights

SECTION 1

Vocabulary
electromagnetic wave *(p. 564)*
radiation *(p. 565)*

Section Notes

- Light is an electromagnetic (EM) wave. An electromagnetic wave is a wave that travels as vibrating electric and magnetic fields. EM waves require no medium through which to travel.
- Electromagnetic waves are produced by the vibration of electrically charged particles.
- The speed of light in a vacuum is 300,000,000 m/s.

SECTION 2

Vocabulary
electromagnetic spectrum *(p. 567)*

Section Notes

- All EM waves travel at the speed of light. EM waves differ only by wavelength and frequency.
- The entire range of EM waves is called the electromagnetic spectrum.
- Radio waves are most often used for communication.
- Microwaves are used for cooking and in radar.
- Infrared waves have shorter wavelengths and higher frequencies than microwaves. The absorption of infrared waves is felt as an increase in temperature.

- Visible light is the very narrow range of wavelengths that humans can see. Different wavelengths are seen as different colors.
- Ultraviolet light is useful for killing bacteria and for producing vitamin D in the body, but overexposure can cause health problems.
- X rays and gamma rays are EM waves that are often used in medicine. Overexposure to these EM waves can damage or kill living cells.

✓ Skills Check

Math Concepts

DISTANCE To calculate the distance that light travels in space, multiply the amount of time light travels by the speed of light in a vacuum. The speed of light in a vacuum is 300,000,000 m/s. If light from a star travels for 192 seconds before reaching a planet, then the distance the light traveled can be calculated as follows:

distance = speed of light × time
distance = 300,000,000 m/s × 192 s
distance = 57,600,000,000 m

Visual Understanding

THE PRODUCTION OF LIGHT Light is produced by the vibration of electrically charged particles. Repeated vibrations of these particles, or electrons, release tiny "packets" of energy called photons. Review Figure 2 on page 565 to see how light and other electromagnetic waves are the result of electron movement.

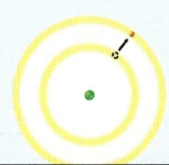 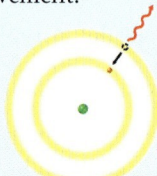

Lab and Activity Highlights

What Color of Light Is Best for Green Plants? PG 716

Which Color Is Hottest? PG 717

Mixing Colors PG 718

 Datasheets for LabBook
(blackline masters for these labs)

586 Chapter 22 • The Nature of Light

SECTION 3

Vocabulary

reflection *(p. 575)*
law of reflection *(p. 575)*
absorption *(p. 576)*
scattering *(p. 577)*
refraction *(p. 577)*
diffraction *(p. 579)*
interference *(p. 579)*

Section Notes

- Two types of reflection are regular and diffuse reflection.
- Absorption and scattering cause light beams to become dimmer with distance.
- How much a light beam bends during refraction depends on the light's wavelength.
- Light waves diffract more when traveling through a narrow opening.
- Interference of light waves can cause bright and dark bands.

SECTION 4

Vocabulary

transmission *(p. 581)*
transparent *(p. 582)*
translucent *(p. 582)*
opaque *(p. 582)*
pigment *(p. 584)*

Section Notes

- Objects are classified as transparent, translucent, or opaque depending on their ability to transmit light.
- Colors of opaque objects are determined by the color of light they reflect. White opaque objects reflect all colors and black opaque objects absorb all colors.
- Colors of transparent and translucent objects are determined by the color of light they transmit. All other colors are absorbed.
- White light is a mixture of all colors of light. The primary colors of light are red, blue, and green.
- Pigments give objects color. The primary pigments are magenta, cyan, and yellow.

Labs

What Color of Light Is Best for Green Plants? *(p. 716)*
Which Color Is Hottest? *(p. 717)*
Mixing Colors *(p. 718)*

VOCABULARY DEFINITIONS, continued

SECTION 3

reflection what happens when light or any other wave bounces off an object

law of reflection the law that states that the angle of incidence is equal to the angle of reflection

absorption the transfer of energy carried by light waves to particles of matter

scattering the release of light energy by particles of matter that have absorbed energy

refraction the bending of a wave as it passes at an angle from one medium to another

diffraction the bending of waves around barriers or through openings

interference a wave interaction that occurs when two or more waves overlap and combine

SECTION 4

transmission the passing of light through matter

transparent describes matter through which light is easily transmitted

translucent describes matter that transmits light but also scatters the light as it passes through the matter

opaque describes matter that does not transmit any light

pigment a material that gives a substance its color by absorbing some colors of light and reflecting others

---

internet connect

GO TO: go.hrw.com

Visit the **HRW** Web site for a variety of learning tools related to this chapter. Just type in the keyword:

KEYWORD: HSTLGT

GO TO: www.scilinks.org

Visit the **National Science Teachers Association** on-line Web site for Internet resources related to this chapter. Just type in the *sci*LINKS number for more information about the topic:

TOPIC: Using Light	*sci*LINKS NUMBER: HSTP528
TOPIC: Light Energy	*sci*LINKS NUMBER: HSTP529
TOPIC: The Electromagnetic Spectrum	*sci*LINKS NUMBER: HSTP530
TOPIC: Reflection and Refraction	*sci*LINKS NUMBER: HSTP545
TOPIC: Colors	*sci*LINKS NUMBER: HSTP550

587

Lab and Activity Highlights

LabBank

Long-Term Projects & Reseach Ideas,
The Image of the Future, Project 72

Interactive Explorations CD-ROM

CD3, Exploration 7, "In the Spotlight"

Vocabulary Review Worksheet 22

Blackline masters of these Chapter Highlights can be found in the **Study Guide.**

Chapter 22 • Chapter Highlights   **587**

Chapter Review

USING VOCABULARY

To complete the following sentences, choose the correct term from each pair of terms listed below:

1. __?__ is the transfer of energy by electromagnetic waves. (*Radiation* or *Scattering*)

2. This book is a(n) __?__ object. (*translucent* or *opaque*)

3. __?__ is a wave interaction that occurs when two or more waves overlap and combine. (*Diffraction* or *Interference*)

4. Light is a type of __?__. (*electromagnetic wave* or *electromagnetic spectrum*)

5. Light travels through an object during __?__. (*absorption* or *transmission*)

UNDERSTANDING CONCEPTS

Multiple Choice

6. Electromagnetic waves transmit
   a. charges.
   b. fields.
   c. matter.
   d. energy.

7. Objects that transmit light easily are
   a. opaque.
   b. translucent.
   c. transparent.
   d. colored.

8. You can see yourself in a mirror because of
   a. absorption.
   b. scattering.
   c. regular reflection.
   d. diffuse reflection.

9. Shadows have blurry edges because of
   a. diffuse reflection.
   b. scattering.
   c. diffraction.
   d. refraction.

10. Microwaves are often used for
    a. cooking.
    b. broadcasting AM radio.
    c. cancer treatment.
    d. All of the above

11. What color of light is produced when red light is added to green light?
    a. cyan
    b. blue
    c. yellow
    d. white

12. Prisms produce rainbows through
    a. reflection.
    b. refraction.
    c. diffraction.
    d. interference.

13. Which type of electromagnetic wave travels the fastest in a vacuum?
    a. radio waves
    b. visible light
    c. gamma rays
    d. They all travel at the same speed.

14. Electromagnetic waves are made of
    a. vibrating particles.
    b. vibrating charged particles.
    c. vibrating electric and magnetic fields.
    d. electricity and magnetism.

Short Answer

15. Name two ways EM waves differ from one another.

16. Describe how an electromagnetic wave is produced.

17. Why is it difficult to see through glass that has frost on it?

Chapter Review Answers

USING VOCABULARY

1. Radiation
2. opaque
3. Interference
4. electromagnetic wave
5. transmission

UNDERSTANDING CONCEPTS

Multiple Choice

6. d
7. c
8. c
9. c
10. a
11. c
12. b
13. d
14. c

Short Answer

15. Electromagnetic waves differ by their wavelength and frequency (and by the amount of energy they carry).

16. An electromagnetic wave is produced when a charged particle vibrates. This creates a vibrating electric field, which creates a vibrating magnetic field. The two vibrating fields make up an electromagnetic wave.

17. Frost is translucent, so the light traveling through it is scattered as it passes through.

Concept Mapping

18. Use the following terms to create a concept map: light, matter, reflection, absorption, scattering, transmission.

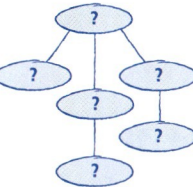

CRITICAL THINKING AND PROBLEM SOLVING

19. A tern is a type of bird that dives underwater to catch fish. When a young tern begins learning to catch fish, it is rarely successful. The tern has to learn that when a fish appears to be in a certain place underwater, the fish is actually in a slightly different place. Explain why the tern sees the fish in the wrong place.

20. Radio waves and gamma rays are both types of electromagnetic waves. Exposure to radio waves does not harm the human body, whereas exposure to gamma rays can be extremely dangerous. What is the difference between these types of EM waves? Why are gamma rays more dangerous?

21. If you look around a parking lot during the summer, you might notice sun shades set up in the windshields of cars. Explain how the sun shades help keep the inside of a car cool.

MATH IN SCIENCE

22. Calculate the time it takes for light from the sun to reach Mercury. Mercury is 54,900,000,000 m away from the sun.

INTERPRETING GRAPHICS

23. Each of the pictures below shows the effects of a wave interaction of light. Identify the interaction involved.

a

b

c

NOW What Do You Think?

Take a minute to review your answers to the ScienceLog questions on page 563. Have your answers changed? If necessary, revise your answers based on what you have learned since you began this chapter.

589

Concept Mapping

18. An answer to this exercise can be found at the end of this book.

CRITICAL THINKING AND PROBLEM SOLVING

19. The tern sees the fish in the wrong place because light refracts as it passes from the water to the air. This creates an optical illusion for the tern—the fish appears to be in a different place than it is.

20. Radio waves carry a lot less energy than gamma rays, so radio waves are not dangerous. However, the energy carried by gamma rays is so high that gamma rays can kill healthy living cells in your body.

21. Sunshades keep the interiors of cars from getting very hot because they reflect light that is transmitted through the glass windows of the car. The light reflects back out the window, so the light cannot warm the air or seats inside the car.

MATH IN SCIENCE

22. $\text{time} = \dfrac{\text{distance}}{\text{speed}}$

$\text{time} = \dfrac{54{,}900{,}000{,}000 \text{ m}}{300{,}000{,}000 \text{ m/s}}$

$\text{time} = 183$ seconds (or 3.05 minutes)

INTERPRETING GRAPHICS

23. a. refraction
    b. diffusion and scattering
    c. reflection

NOW WHAT DO YOU THINK?

1. Light can be thought of as a stream of photons that are produced by the movements of electrons between energy levels.
2. Light waves can interact through reflection, refraction, diffraction, interference, absorption, and scattering.
3. Colors of light are determined by the wavelength of a light wave. The different colors we see are determined by the wavelengths of light that reach our eyes.

 Concept Mapping Transparency 22

 Blackline masters of this Chapter Review can be found in the **Study Guide.**

SCIENCE, TECHNOLOGY, AND SOCIETY

Fireflies Light the Way

Background

Luciferase assays have a number of relevant uses in medicine as well. Bacterial infections can be deadly. Researchers have developed luciferase assays to measure bacteria in the urine and blood. Antibiotics, the medicines used to treat bacterial infections, are not always effective. Luciferase tests can be used to evaluate the effectiveness of antibiotic therapy on particular patients.

ATP is one of the most significant sources of energy in biological compounds. ATP has three phosphate bonds; when these bonds are broken, they give off energy. If one phosphate is cleaved off the ATP molecule, it yields ADP, or adenosine diphosphate. This converts chemical energy into light energy by exciting the electrons in luciferin.

Science, Technology, and Society

Fireflies Light the Way

Just as beams of light from coastal lighthouses warn boats of approaching danger, scientists are using the light of an unlikely source—fireflies—to warn food inspectors of life-threatening bacterial contamination! Thousands of people die each year from meat contaminated with bacteria. The light from fireflies is being used to study several diseases, waste-water treatment, and environmental protection as well!

Nature's Guiding Light

A number of organisms, including some fishes, squids, beetles, and bacteria, emit light. Fireflies, in particular, use this light to attract mates. How do these organisms use energy to emit light?

Remarkably, all of these organisms use one enzyme to make light, an enzyme called *luciferase*. This enzyme breaks down *adenosine triphosphate* (ATP) to create energy. This energy is used to excite electrons to produce light in the form of a glow or flash. Fireflies are very effective light bulbs. Nearly 100 percent of the energy they get from ATP is given off as light. Only 10 percent of energy given off by electrical light bulbs is in the form of light; the other 90 percent is thermal energy!

Harnessing Life's Light

How have scientists harnessed the firefly's ability to produce light to find bacteria? Researchers have found the gene responsible for making luciferase. Scientists have taken the gene from fireflies that makes luciferase and inserted it into a virus that preys on bacteria. The virus isn't harmful to humans and can be mixed into meat to help scientists detect bacteria. When the virus infects the bacteria, it transfers the gene into the genetic machinery of the bacteria. This bacteria then produces luciferase and glows!

▲ *The firefly (Photuris pyralis) is helping food inspectors save thousands of lives each year!*

This process is being used to find a number of dangerous bacteria that contaminate foods, including *Salmonella* and *Escherichia coli*. These bacteria are responsible for thousands of deaths each year. Not only is the test effective, it is fast. Before researchers developed this test, it took up to 3 days to determine whether food was contaminated by bacteria. By that time, the food was already at the grocery store!

Think About It!

▶ What color of light would you hypothesize gives plants the most energy? Investigate, and see if your hypothesis is right!

Answer to "Think About It!"

Given the information on light energy in this chapter, students may hypothesize that light toward the blue end of the spectrum will provide the most energy to plants. Students will find out that photosynthesis is much more complex than this and requires a variety of light.

Eureka!

It's a Heat Wave!

Percy L. Spencer never stopped looking for answers. In fact, he patented 120 inventions in his 39 years with the company Raytheon. During a routine visit to one of the Raytheon laboratories in 1946, Spencer found that a candy bar had melted inside his coat pocket. He could have just chalked this up to body heat, but he didn't. Instead, he took a closer look at his surroundings and noticed a nearby magnetron—a tube he designed to produce microwaves for radar systems.

A Popping Test

This made Spencer curious. Did the microwaves from the magnetron melt the candy bar, and if so, could microwaves be used to heat other things? Spencer answered his questions by putting a bag of unpopped corn kernels next to a magnetron. The kernels popped! Spencer had just made the first "microwave" popcorn! The test was a huge success. This simple experiment showed that a magnetron could heat foods with microwaves, and it could heat them quickly. When Spencer patented his invention in 1953, he called it a "High Frequency Dielectric Heating Apparatus."

Perfect Timing!

Spencer originally designed magnetrons for radar machines used in World War II. Discovering another use for them was well timed. After the war, the military had little use for the 10,000 magnetrons a week that Raytheon could manufacture. So Raytheon decided to use the magnetrons to power Spencer's "High Frequency Dielectric Heating Apparatus." But first the company had to come up with a simpler name! The winning entry in the renaming contest was "Radar Range," which later became one word, *Radarange*.

▲ *The first microwave oven, known as a "Radarange," 1953*

An Inconvenient Convenience

The first Radaranges had a few drawbacks. For one thing, they were very expensive. They also weighed over 340 kg and were 1.6 m tall. Try fitting that on your kitchen counter! Because the Radarange was so large and expensive, only restaurants, railroad companies, and cruise ships used them. By 1967, improvements in the design made the Radarange compact and affordable, similar to the microwave ovens of today.

Now You're Cooking!

Just how do microwave ovens cook food? It just so happens that microwaves are absorbed by water molecules in the food being cooked. When water molecules throughout the food absorb microwaves, they start to move faster. As a result, the food's temperature increases. Leftovers anyone?

Find Out for Yourself

▶ Microwaves make water molecules in food move faster. This is what increases the temperature of food that is cooked in a microwave. But did you know that most dishes will not heat up in a microwave oven if there is no food on them? To discover why, find out what most dishes are made of. Then infer why empty dishes do not heat up in a microwave.

Eureka!
It's a Heat Wave!

Background

Microwave radiation is very different from radioactive radiation. The radiation that microwave ovens use is called *nonionizing radiation*. This is not to be confused with the ionizing radiation of X rays, gamma rays, and cosmic rays that can cause damage to living cells (including genetic mutations and tissue damage) and alter the molecular structure of matter. Examples of nonionizing radiation are radio waves, infrared radiation, and visible light. These waves have lower frequencies and less energy than ionizing radiation.

Answer to Find Out for Yourself

Most dishes are made of materials that do not have water molecules. If the dishes have no water molecules to absorb microwaves, the dishes will not get hot.

Chapter Organizer

CHAPTER ORGANIZATION	TIME MINUTES	OBJECTIVES	LABS, INVESTIGATIONS, AND DEMONSTRATIONS
Chapter Opener pp. 592–593	45	National Standards: UCP 2, 3, SAI 1, ST 1, SPSP 5, HNS 1, 3	**Investigate!** Mirror, Mirror, p. 593
Section 1 Light Sources	90	▶ Compare luminous and illuminated objects. ▶ Name four ways light can be produced. UCP 1, 2, SPSP 5, HNS 1, 3, PS 3a, 3c, 3e, 3f	**Demonstration,** Neon Light, p. 596 in ATE
Section 2 Mirrors and Lenses	90	▶ Illustrate how mirrors and lenses form images using ray diagrams. ▶ Explain the difference between real and virtual images. ▶ Compare plane mirrors, concave mirrors, and convex mirrors. ▶ Explain how concave and convex lenses form images. UCP 2, SPSP 5, PS 3c; LabBook UCP 3, PS 3c	**Skill Builder,** Mirror Images, p. 720 **Datasheets for LabBook,** Mirror Images, Datasheet 63 **Discovery Lab,** Images from Convex Lenses, p. 722 **Datasheets for LabBook,** Images from Convex Lenses, Datasheet 64 **Inquiry Labs,** Eye Spy, Lab 23
Section 3 Light and Sight	90	▶ Identify the parts of the human eye, and describe their functions. ▶ Describe some common vision problems, and explain how they can be corrected. UCP 2, SPSP 1, PS 3c	**Whiz-Bang Demonstrations,** Light Humor, Demo 65
Section 4 Light Technology	90	▶ Explain how optical instruments use lenses and mirrors to form images. ▶ Explain how lasers work and what makes laser light different from non-laser light. ▶ Identify uses for lasers. ▶ Describe how optical fibers and polarizing filters work. UCP 5, ST 2, SPSP 2, 5, PS 3c	**Demonstration,** p. 608 in ATE **QuickLab,** Now You See, Now You Don't, p. 613 **Labs You Can Eat,** Fiber-Optic Fun, Lab 25 **EcoLabs & Field Activities,** Photon Drive, EcoLab 23 **Long-Term Projects & Research Ideas,** Project 73

*See page **T20** for a complete correlation of this book with the* **NATIONAL SCIENCE EDUCATION STANDARDS.**

TECHNOLOGY RESOURCES

 Guided Reading Audio CD English or Spanish, Chapter 23

 One-Stop Planner CD-ROM with Test Generator

 CNN Science, Technology & Society, Correcting Colorblindness, Segment 2

 Science Discovery Videodiscs: Image and Activity Bank with Lesson Plans: Light Fantastic
 Science Sleuths: The Fogged Photos

Chapter 23 • Light and Our World

CLASSROOM WORKSHEETS, TRANSPARENCIES, AND RESOURCES	SCIENCE INTEGRATION AND CONNECTIONS	REVIEW AND ASSESSMENT
Directed Reading Worksheet 23 **Science Puzzlers, Twisters & Teasers,** Worksheet 23		
Directed Reading Worksheet 23, Section 1	**Connect to Earth Science,** p. 593 in ATE **Astronomy Connection,** p. 594 **Cross-Disciplinary Focus,** p. 595 in ATE **Science, Technology, and Society:** Traffic Lights, p. 618	**Homework,** p. 596 in ATE **Review,** p. 597 **Quiz,** p. 597 in ATE **Alternative Assessment,** p. 597 in ATE
Directed Reading Worksheet 23, Section 2 **Transparency 295,** How a Mirror Works **Transparency 296,** The Optical Axis, Focal Point, and Focal Length **Transparency 297,** Creating Virtual Images and Real Images with a Concave Mirror **Transparency 298,** Thick and Thin Convex Lenses **Transparency 298,** A Concave Lens **Reinforcement Worksheet 23,** Mirror, Mirror	**Real-World Connection,** p. 599 in ATE **Real-World Connection,** p. 601 in ATE **Apply,** p. 602 **Math and More,** p. 602 in ATE **Cross-Disciplinary Focus,** p. 604 in ATE	**Homework,** pp. 599, 601 in ATE **Review,** p. 602 **Review,** p. 604 **Quiz,** p. 604 in ATE **Alternative Assessment,** p. 604 in ATE
Directed Reading Worksheet 23, Section 3 **Transparency 299,** How Your Eyes Work	**Connect to Life Science,** p. 605 in ATE **Cross-Disciplinary Focus,** p. 606 in ATE **Biology Connection,** p. 607	**Review,** p. 607 **Quiz,** p. 607 in ATE **Alternative Assessment,** p. 607 in ATE
Directed Reading Worksheet 23, Section 4 **Transparency 299,** How a Camera Works **Transparency 300,** How Telescopes Work **Transparency 2,** Compound Light Microscope **Critical Thinking Worksheet 23,** Light That Heals	**Cross-Disciplinary Focus,** p. 608 in ATE **Connect to Life Science,** p. 609 in ATE **Cross-Disciplinary Focus,** p. 609 in ATE **Multicultural Connection,** p. 611 in ATE **Connect to Life Science,** p. 611 in ATE **Real-World Connection,** p. 612 in ATE **Eye on the Environment:** Light Pollution, p. 619	**Self-Check,** p. 609 **Homework,** p. 610 in ATE **Review,** p. 613 **Quiz,** p. 613 in ATE **Alternative Assessment,** p. 613 in ATE

END-OF-CHAPTER REVIEW AND ASSESSMENT

Chapter Review in Study Guide
Vocabulary and Notes in Study Guide
Chapter Tests with Performance-Based Assessment, Chapter 23 Test
Chapter Tests with Performance-Based Assessment, Performance-Based Assessment 23
Concept Mapping Transparency 23

 Holt, Rinehart and Winston On-line Resources
go.hrw.com
For worksheets and other teaching aids related to this chapter, visit the HRW Web site and type in the keyword: **HSTLOW**

 **National Science Teachers Association**
www.scilinks.org
Encourage students to use the *sci*LINKS numbers listed in the internet connect boxes to access information and resources on the **NSTA** Web site.

Chapter Resources & Worksheets

Visual Resources

TEACHING TRANSPARENCIES

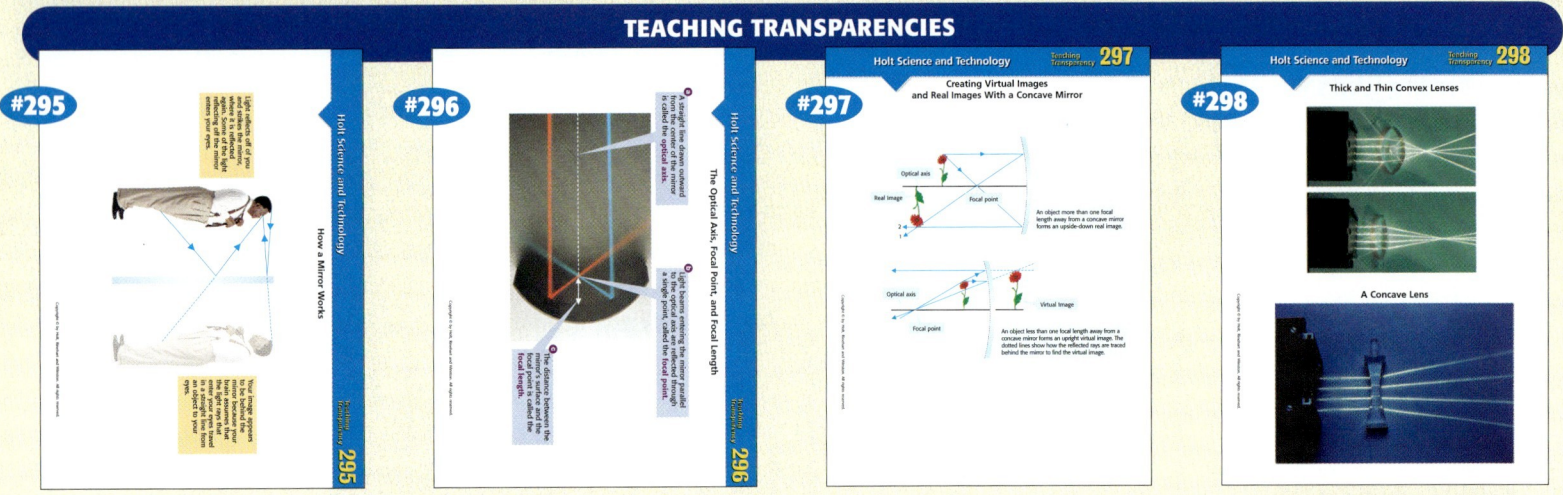

TEACHING TRANSPARENCIES

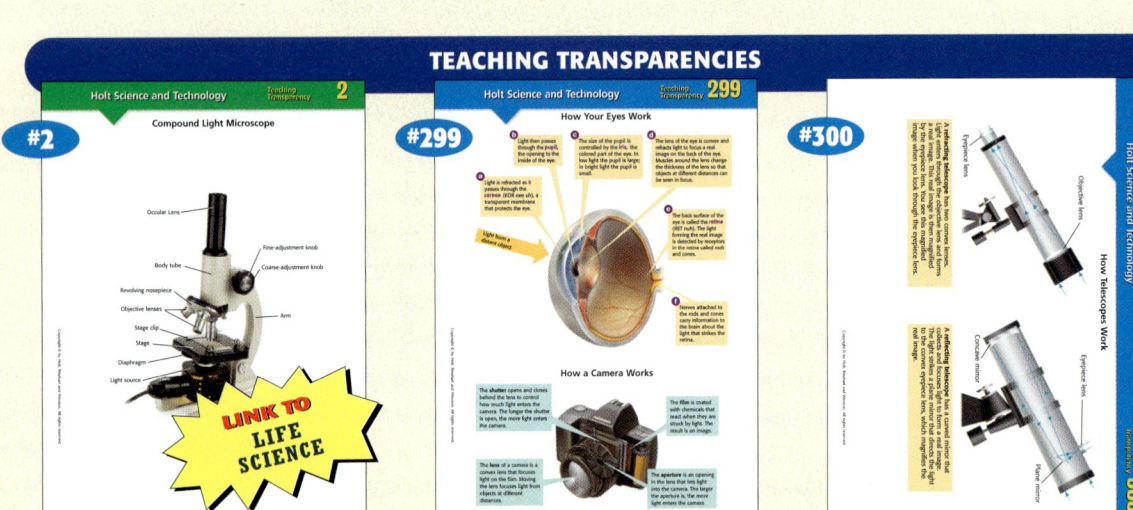

CONCEPT MAPPING TRANSPARENCY

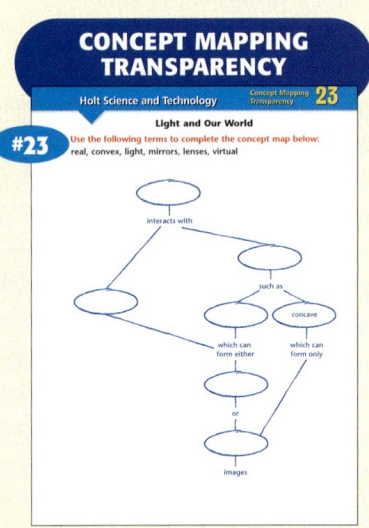

Meeting Individual Needs

DIRECTED READING

REINFORCEMENT & VOCABULARY REVIEW

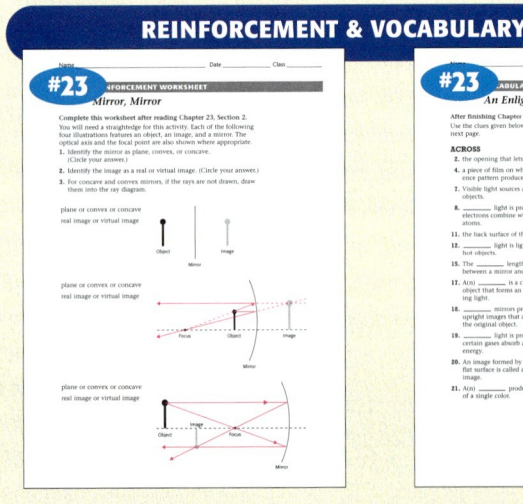

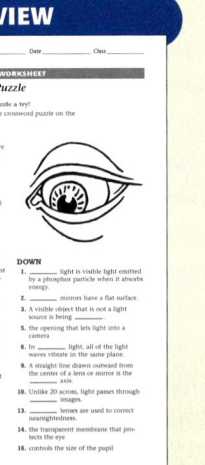

SCIENCE PUZZLERS, TWISTERS & TEASERS

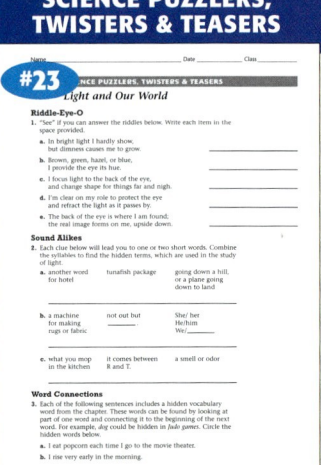

591C Chapter 23 • Light and Our World

Chapter 23 • Light and Our World

Review & Assessment

STUDY GUIDE

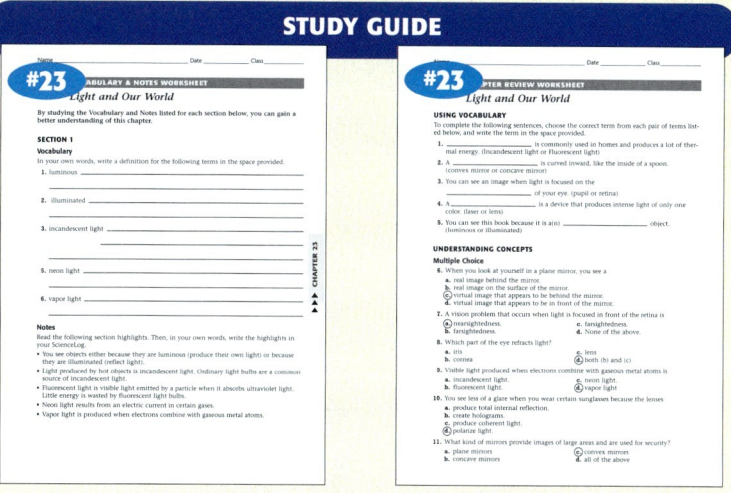

CHAPTER TESTS WITH PERFORMANCE-BASED ASSESSMENT

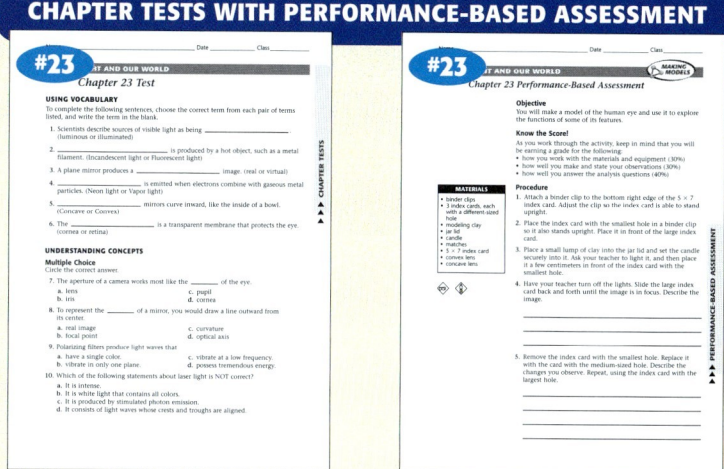

Lab Worksheets

INQUIRY LABS

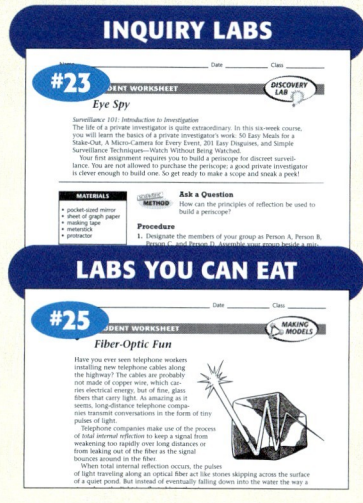

#23 Eye Spy

LABS YOU CAN EAT

#25 Fiber-Optic Fun

ECOLABS & FIELD ACTIVITIES

#23 Photon Drive

LONG-TERM PROJECTS & RESEARCH IDEAS

#73 Island Vacation

WHIZ-BANG DEMONSTRATIONS

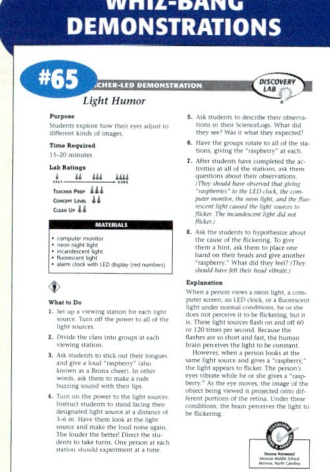

#65 Light Humor

DATASHEETS FOR LABBOOK

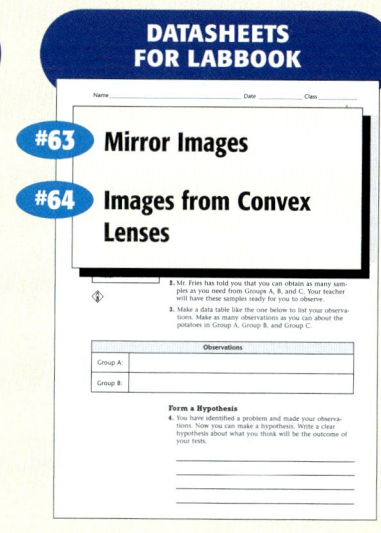

#63 Mirror Images

#64 Images from Convex Lenses

Applications & Extensions

CRITICAL THINKING & PROBLEM SOLVING

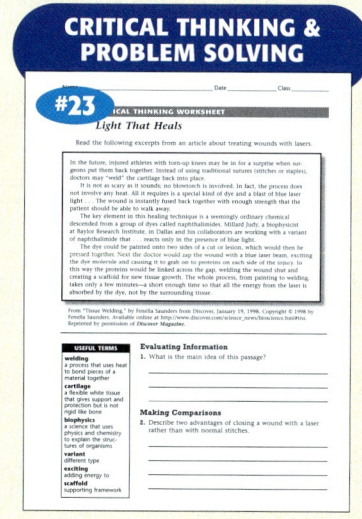

#23 Light That Heals

SCIENCE, TECHNOLOGY & SOCIETY

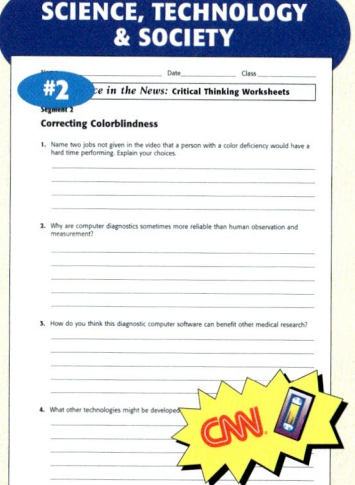

#2 Correcting Colorblindness

Chapter 23 • Chapter Resources & Worksheets   **591D**

Chapter Background

SECTION 1

Light Sources

▶ **Photons**
Light is produced when an electron in an atom shifts from an excited or energized energy level back to its unexcited level. The electron emits a quantum of energy called a *photon*.

▶ **Artificial Light Sources**
There are two basic ways to produce light from artificial sources. Both methods use electrons to increase the energy of electrons in other materials.

- One way is to use electrons to excite the electrons in a solid filament until they begin to emit photons. We say that the filament is so hot that it glows. This is the principle behind incandescent and fluorescent light bulbs.

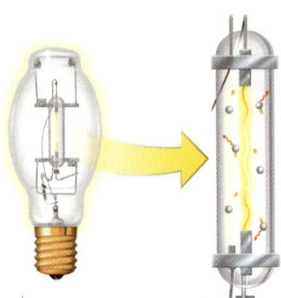

- The second method is to pass electrons through a gas so that the electrons in the atoms of the gas are excited to the point that they begin to emit photons. This is the principle behind neon lights and mercury and sulfur lamps.

▶ **Street Lights**
The color of street lights depends on the material inside the tube. Sodium lights contain sodium vapor, which glows a bright yellow-orange when electrons pass through it. Mercury vapor lights give off a bluish white light.

IS THAT A FACT!

- Light bulb filaments are made of long spirals of tungsten that glow white-hot and will not melt at 2,500°C. The bulbs also contain an inert gas, such as argon, to keep the metal from combining with the oxygen in the air and burning up.

- Fluorescent lights were developed in 1939 by General Electric.

SECTION 2

Mirrors and Lenses

▶ **History of Mirrors**
Natural mirrors made of obsidian were used in Turkey 7,500 years ago. Bronze mirrors were used in Egypt as early as 3500 to 3000 B.C. Later, polished mirrors of copper, brass, bronze, tin, and silver were used.

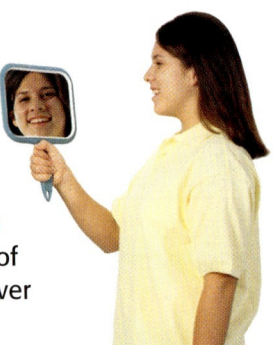

- Metal mirrors were luxury items because it was difficult to make a flat, highly polished metal surface that would reflect light well enough to form images.

- The Venetians found a way to use polished silver to make mirrors in the 1200s, but the silvering process used on mirrors today was founded by a German chemist, Justus von Liebig (1803–1873), in 1835.

IS THAT A FACT!

- The Keck and Keck II telescopes, in Mauna Kea, Hawaii, are 10 m in diameter. They are the largest reflecting telescopes in the world today. Each uses 36 mirror segments fitted together so seamlessly that they act as one large mirror. The segments are realigned about 1,000 times a second by computers to counteract the effects of gravity and other distortions.

▶ **Early Uses of Lenses**
The use of lenses is first known from references to the Roman emperor Nero. As Nero watched performances in the arena, he used a piece of emerald that happened to be the perfect shape to correct his poor eyesight. Convex lenses in eyeglasses came into use in Italy in about 1287.

Chapter 23 • Light and Our World

SECTION 3

Light and Sight

▶ **Correcting Vision**
Adapting lasers for medical use enables doctors to correct previously untreatable eye problems. Laser surgery can repair the retina and is used in cataract surgery, cornea replacement, and vision corrective surgery. Most of these treatments have been developed in just the last 20–30 years.

▶ **Stereoscopic Vision**
Having two eyes allows humans to judge depth, distance, and speed effectively. Each eye receives a slightly different view of the same object, and the brain combines these views to give a three-dimensional interpretation. People who suffer from strabismus, a defect in which the eyes are not used together, often have difficulty judging distances to objects.

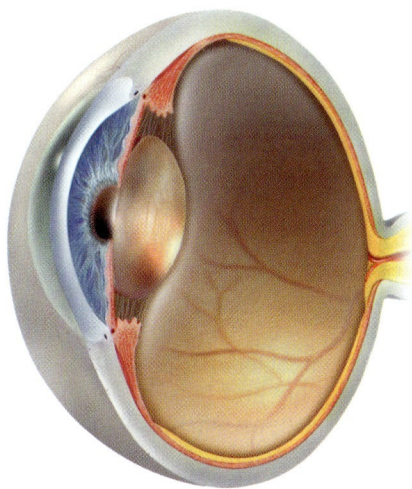

IS THAT A FACT!

- The human eye is so sensitive to light that in the dark it can see a lighted candle 1.6 km away.

- The human body needs vitamin A to produce the light-sensitive protein *rhodopsin* in the rods of the eye. The structure of the rods and rhodopsin enable the eyes to see in dim light. Carrots are an excellent source of vitamin A, which helps prevent night blindness.

SECTION 4

Light Technology

▶ **Holograms**
The word hologram is a compound word derived from two Greek words. *Holo* is Greek for "whole," and *gram* is Greek for "message."

- In 1948, Dennis Gabor (1900–1979) invented the process for making holograms. The first holograms were of poor quality because a good source of coherent light was not available. When lasers were perfected in the 1960s, holography surged in popularity.

- If a hologram is made from a source with a short wavelength, such as ultraviolet rays, then viewed in visible light with its longer wavelengths, the image produced appears greatly magnified. The amount of magnification is proportional to the ratio of the increase in wavelengths.

▶ **Endoscopes**
In use since 1958, endoscopes are medical tools used to look inside the body with fiber optics. The long, thin tubes carry light without distortion to and from the area being observed. Observation is made through an eyepiece. Fiber optic threads can be thinner than human hair.

IS THAT A FACT!

- In fiber optics, total internal reflection depends on the shallow angle (critical angle) at which the light waves reflect off the walls of the optical fiber. The critical angle when water acts as the prism is 49°; for crown glass (a type of optical glass), it is 41.1°.

For background information about teaching strategies and issues, refer to the *Professional Reference for Teachers*.

CHAPTER 23
Light and Our World

Chapter Preview

Section 1
Light Sources
- Light Source or Reflection?
- Producing Light

Section 2
Mirrors and Lenses
- Rays Show the Path of Light Waves
- Mirrors Reflect Light
- Lenses Refract Light

Section 3
Light and Sight
- How You Detect Light
- Common Vision Problems

Section 4
Light Technology
- Optical Instruments
- Lasers and Laser Light
- Fiber Optics
- Polarized Light

Directed Reading Worksheet 23

Science Puzzlers, Twisters & Teasers Worksheet 23

Guided Reading Audio CD
English or Spanish, Chapter 23

Smithsonian Institution®
Visit www.si.edu/hrw for additional on-line resources.

CHAPTER 23 Light and Our World

Imagine . . .

When *Apollo 11* astronauts Neil Armstrong and Edwin "Buzz" Aldrin completed the first moonwalk in 1969, they left more than footprints on the moon. Armstrong and Aldrin also left a small panel called a retroreflector that consists of 100 light-reflecting cubes.

Ever since, scientists on Earth have been aiming light beams at the retroreflector—more than 370,000 km away. The beams come from a laser, which is a device that produces intense light of only one wavelength. The laser light is directed through a telescope, reflected off a mirror inside the telescope, and aimed toward the retroreflector. By the time the laser beam reaches the retroreflector, its light has spread to cover an area more than 6 km wide.

The retroreflector, which is about 46 cm on a side, reflects a portion of the laser beam back to Earth. Scientists record the time it takes for the light to return to the laboratory.

Scientists say that striking the retroreflector with a laser beam is like hitting a moving dime with a bullet from a rifle—from 3 km away!

Using these data, scientists have been able to measure the distance between Earth and the moon to within 3 cm!

Researchers around the world continue to bounce laser beams off the retroreflector and continue to learn more about the moon. For example, scientists have determined that the moon is slowly moving away from Earth and that the length of an Earth day changes slightly over the course of a year.

In this chapter you will learn more about light sources, such as lasers, and the mirrors and lenses that are used to build telescopes. All these things are not just useful to scientists; they are a part of *your* world!

Imagine . . .

Entire libraries can be sent around the world at the speed of light—using light. Surgery is performed on one of the most delicate organs—the eye—using light. Some types of cancer cells can be killed with light. Light from the sun powers all life on Earth. Scientists believe that exposure to light adjusts the internal clock that most animals, including humans, seem to have. And movies, television, books, theater, clothing—anything with color—depend on light and mixing wavelengths of light. Light is everywhere!

What Do You Think?

In your ScienceLog, try to answer the following questions based on what you already know:

1. Name three sources of light.
2. How do mirrors and lenses form images?
3. How does the human eye detect light?

Mirror, Mirror

The mirrors you are most familiar with are flat, or plane, mirrors. In this activity, you will explore properties of images formed by plane mirrors.

Procedure

1. Tape a piece of **graph paper** on your desk. Stand a **plane mirror** straight up on top of the paper, about halfway down from the top. Hold the mirror in place with small pieces of **modeling clay**.

2. Count off four grid squares from the mirror, and place a **pencil** on the paper at that spot. Look at the image in the mirror. How many squares behind the mirror is the image of the pencil? Move the pencil farther away from the mirror. How did the image change?

3. Replace the mirror with a piece of **colored glass**. Like the mirror, the glass reflects light but the glass also lets you see through it. Look for the image of the pencil in the glass. How does it compare with the image you saw in the mirror?

4. Use a pencil to draw a square on the graph paper in front of the glass. Looking through the glass, trace the image of the square on the paper behind the glass. Using a **metric ruler**, measure and compare the sides of the two squares. Record this data in your ScienceLog.

Analysis

5. In general, how does the distance from an object to a plane mirror compare with the apparent distance from the mirror to the object's image behind the mirror?

6. Images formed in the colored glass are similar to images formed in a plane mirror. In general, how does the size of an object compare with that of its image in a plane mirror?

What Do You Think?

Accept all reasonable responses.

Students will have a chance to revise their answers in the Chapter Review under NOW What Do You Think?

Investigate!

MATERIALS

For Each Group:
- graph paper, 1 cm squares
- plane mirror
- clay
- pencil
- colored glass
- metric ruler

Safety Caution: Caution students to wear safety goggles while doing this activity. Also caution students to handle the mirrors and pieces of colored glass very carefully. Tape the edges of the glass with masking tape.

Answers to Investigate!

2. The pencil should be four squares behind the mirror. The pencil should appear farther behind the mirror than before.
3. The image in the glass should be the same size and same distance behind the glass as the image was in the mirror.
4. The length of the sides of both squares should be identical.
5. In general, the distance from an object to a plane mirror and the distance from the mirror to the image is the same.
6. In general, the size of an object and the size of its image in a plane mirror are identical.

CONNECT TO EARTH SCIENCE

The moon is not always the same distance from Earth. The moon's orbit is elliptical, which means it is not a perfect circle—it is shaped more like an oval. The mean distance to the moon is about 384,400 km. The closest the moon comes to Earth, its *perigee*, is about 356,375 km. At its farthest point from Earth, its *apogee*, the moon is about 406,395 km from Earth. The mean distance is not exactly between the perigee and apogee because the sun's gravity affects the moon's orbit, causing it to vary from a true ellipse.

Chapter 23 • Light and Our World

Section 1

Focus

Light Sources

Students learn the difference between luminous objects and illuminated objects. Students also learn how incandescent, fluorescent, neon, and vapor light are produced and how these different types of light may be used.

🔔 Bellringer

Give students the following:

Most people use some sort of light from the moment they wake up until they go to bed at night. In your ScienceLog, list the many different sources of light you use in a typical day. Explain why you need each source of light.

1) Motivate

DISCUSSION

Ask students to think about how different light sources can be used to create different moods. Ask them to imagine that they are the lighting director for a movie or a play. Have them describe a scene and explain what kind of light source they would use to create the proper mood. Ask them to share their ideas with the class.

Directed Reading Worksheet 23 Section 1

Section 1

Terms to Learn

luminous
illuminated
incandescent light
fluorescent light
neon light
vapor light

What You'll Do

- Compare luminous and illuminated objects.
- Name four ways light can be produced.

Astronomy CONNECTION

Sometimes the moon shines so brightly that you might think there is a lot of "moonlight." But did you know that moonlight is actually sunlight? The moon does not give off light. You can see the moon because it is illuminated by light from the sun. You see different phases of the moon because light from the sun shines only on the part of the moon that faces the sun.

Light Sources

Although visible light represents only a small portion of the electromagnetic spectrum, it has a huge effect on your life. Visible light from the sun gives plants the energy necessary for growth and reproduction. Without plants at the base of the food chain, few other life-forms could exist. And of course, without visible light, you could not see anything. Your eyes are totally useless without sources of visible light.

Light Source or Reflection?

If you look at a television in a bright room, you see the cabinet around the television as well as the image on the screen. But if you look at the same television in the dark, only the image on the screen shows up. The difference is that the screen is a light source, while the cabinet around the television isn't.

You can see a light source even in the dark because its light passes directly into your eyes. Flames, light bulbs, fireflies, and the sun are all light sources. Scientists describe objects that produce visible light as being **luminous** (LOO muh nuhs). **Figure 1** shows examples of luminous objects.

Most of the objects around you are not light sources. But you can still see them because light from a light source reflects off the objects and then travels to your eyes. Scientists describe a visible object that is not a light source as being **illuminated** (i LOO muh NAYT ed).

Figure 1 Television screens, fires, and fireflies are luminous objects.

🧪 WEIRD SCIENCE

There are about 175 species of fireflies in the United States and perhaps 2,000 species worldwide. Fireflies (really a type of beetle) are luminous animals. They produce flashes of light by means of a chemical reaction that happens inside photocytes (special cells in their abdomen). Inside the photocytes, two chemicals, luciferin (named after Lucifer, the fallen angel of light) and the enzyme luciferase, combine with oxygen, ATP, and magnesium to produce energy in the form of light. Read the feature about fireflies at the end of Chapter 22.

Producing Light

Light sources produce light in many ways. For example, if you heat a piece of metal enough, it will visibly glow red hot. Light can also be produced chemically, like the light produced by a firefly. Light can even be produced by sending an electric current through certain gases.

Incandescent Light If you have ever looked inside a toaster while toasting a piece of bread, you may have seen thin wires or bars glowing red. The wires give off energy as light when heated to a high temperature. Light produced by hot objects is called **incandescent** (IN kuhn DES uhnt) **light**. **Figure 2** shows a source of incandescent light that you have in your home.

Sources of incandescent light also release a large amount of thermal energy. Sometimes this thermal energy is useful because it can be used to cook food or to warm a room. But often this thermal energy is not used for anything. For example, the thermal energy given off by a light bulb is not very useful.

Halogen lights are another type of incandescent light. They were originally developed for use on the wings of airplanes, but they are now used in homes and in car headlights. **Figure 3** shows how halogen lights work.

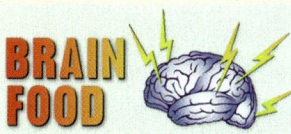

Figure 2 Light bulbs produce incandescent light.

ⓐ Wires and the filament carry an electric current.

ⓑ Electric current in the tungsten filament causes the filament's temperature to increase.

ⓒ The hot filament gives off visible light and thermal energy.

Figure 3 The way in which the tungsten from the filament can be used over and over again prevents the bulb from burning out too quickly.

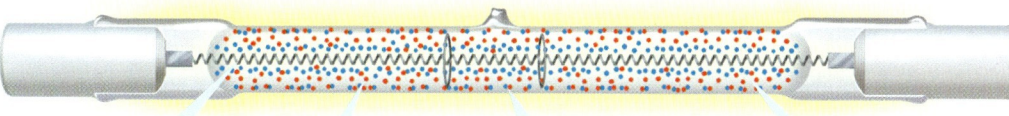

A tungsten filament, heated to about 3,000°C, glows very brightly and vaporizes.

The tungsten vapor (red particles) travels to the glass wall, where it cools to about 800°C.

At the lower temperature, tungsten combines with a halogen gas (blue particles) to form a new compound.

The new compound travels back to the filament, where it breaks down because of the high temperature. Tungsten from the compound is deposited on the filament and can be used again.

IS THAT A FACT!

Thomas Edison (1847–1931) is usually credited with the invention of the electric light bulb in 1879. However, in 1860, almost 20 years before Edison, British chemist and physicist Joseph Swan (1828–1914) demonstrated a carbon-filament incandescent bulb in London. Swan improved his bulb in 1878. The next year, Edison independently created a carbon-filament incandescent vacuum light bulb that burned for nearly 50 hours. Swan's 1878 improved bulb was better than Edison's, and Edison subsequently bought the rights to Swan's design.

2 Teach

READING STRATEGY

Predicting Before students read this section, discuss with them the many kinds of artificial lighting that humans use. Most artificial lighting involves electrical energy. But are all electric lights the same? Have students identify some different types of artificial light. Are the lights in the classroom the same kind as the ones at home? Are street lamps or lights at sports stadiums different from other types of artificial lights?

BRAIN FOOD

The moon's *albedo*, or reflectivity, is about the same as a piece of coal. Both reflect only about 7 percent of the sunlight that strikes them. Yet the moon is often the brightest object in the night sky, and a full moon is sometimes almost bright enough to read by. Imagine what life would be like if the moon were twice as bright as it is?

CROSS-DISCIPLINARY FOCUS

History A Greek scientist, Hipparchus (147–126 B.C.), is considered the father of astronomy. Hipparchus measured the distance from the Earth to the moon and calculated the coordinates of stars. His catalog of 850 stars, the first such list ever compiled, gave each star's coordinates and approximate brightness relative to other stars.

Section 1 • Light Sources

Fluorescent Light The light that comes from the long, cylindrical bulbs in your classroom is called fluorescent light. **Fluorescent** (FLOO uh RES uhnt) **light** is visible light emitted by a phosphor particle when it absorbs energy such as ultraviolet light. Fluorescent light is sometimes called cool light because less thermal energy is produced than with incandescent light. **Figure 4** shows how a fluorescent light bulb works.

Figure 4 Fluorescent Light

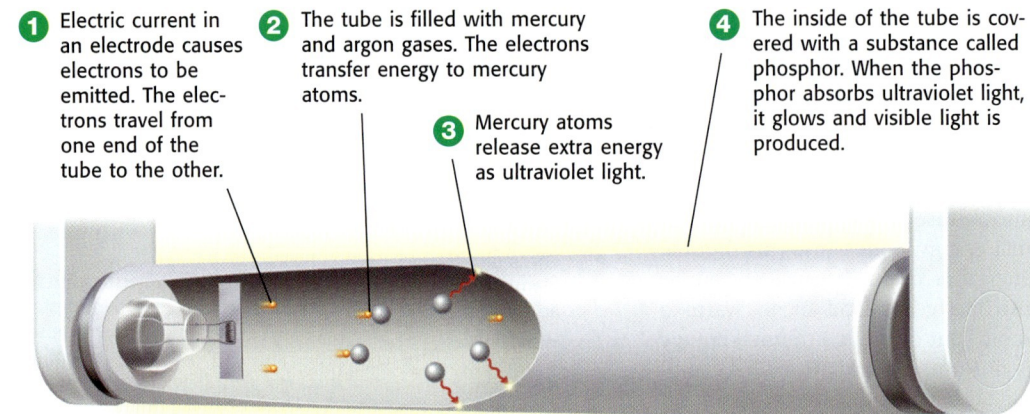

① Electric current in an electrode causes electrons to be emitted. The electrons travel from one end of the tube to the other.

② The tube is filled with mercury and argon gases. The electrons transfer energy to mercury atoms.

③ Mercury atoms release extra energy as ultraviolet light.

④ The inside of the tube is covered with a substance called phosphor. When the phosphor absorbs ultraviolet light, it glows and visible light is produced.

Neon Light The visible light emitted by atoms of certain gases, such as neon, when they absorb and then release energy is called **neon light**. **Figure 5** shows how neon light is produced.

A true neon light—one in which the tube is filled with neon gas—glows red. Other colors are produced when the tubes are filled with different gases. For example, sodium gas produces yellow light, and krypton gas produces purple light. A mixture of argon gas and mercury gas produces blue light.

Figure 5 Neon Light

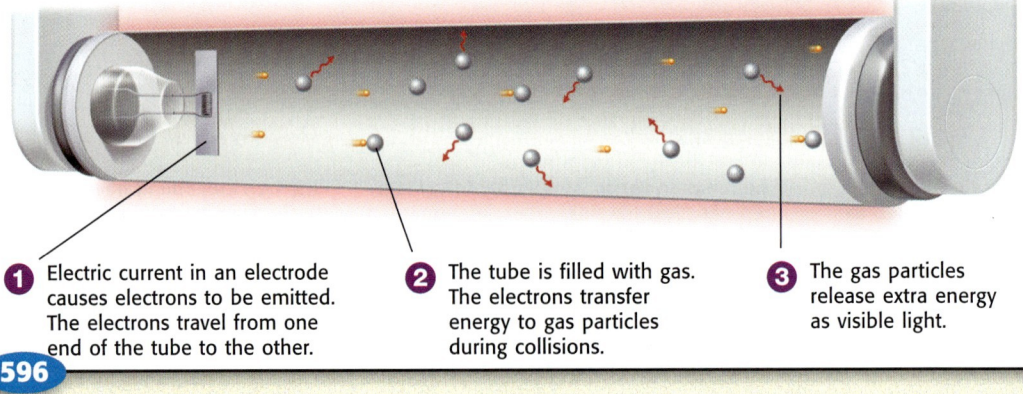

① Electric current in an electrode causes electrons to be emitted. The electrons travel from one end of the tube to the other.

② The tube is filled with gas. The electrons transfer energy to gas particles during collisions.

③ The gas particles release extra energy as visible light.

IS THAT A FACT!

Combustible gases have been known since the seventeenth century. The use of gas for heat and light was pioneered by French chemist Philippe Lebon (1767–1804). Lebon demonstrated gas lighting to the public in 1801 when he used flammable gas derived from wood.

Q: Where was Edison when the lights went out?

A: in the dark

---

2 Teach, continued

MEETING INDIVIDUAL NEEDS

Advanced Learners Have students compare incandescent lighting and fluorescent lighting for home use and for use in business, commercial, school, and manufacturing buildings. Encourage them to be creative in presenting their findings; some students may want to create models to demonstrate the advantages and disadvantages of each type of lighting. **Sheltered English**

DEMONSTRATION

Neon Light You will need a screwdriver-type circuit tester (available in hardware stores) with a small neon bulb. Remove the neon light from the handle. Hold one end of the bulb in your hand, and rub the other end against a piece of Styrofoam™ or hard foam insulation. The bulb will light due to static electricity.

Homework

Have students research the history of neon lighting or the making of neon signs. The basic principles of neon lighting go back to 1675 and the French astronomer Jean Picard. Georges Claude (1870–1960), a French inventor, engineer, and chemist, was the first to make a neon lamp in about 1902. Eight years later, Claude presented his lamp to the public, and the neon sign industry was born. Neon signs today are made in much the same way as they were 90 years ago.

Vapor Light Another type of incandescent light, called **vapor light,** is produced when electrons combine with gaseous metal atoms. Street lamps usually contain either mercury vapor or sodium vapor. You can tell the difference by the color of the light. If the light is bluish, the lamp contains mercury vapor. If the light is orange, the lamp contains sodium vapor. Both kinds of vapor lamps produce light in similar ways, as described in **Figure 6**.

Stop! and go read about the invention of traffic lights on page 618.

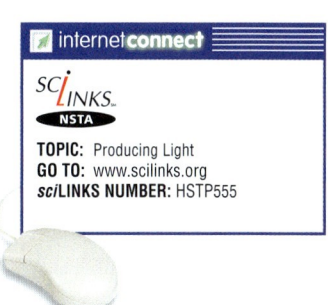

Figure 6 *Sodium vapor lights are very bright and do not produce much glare.*

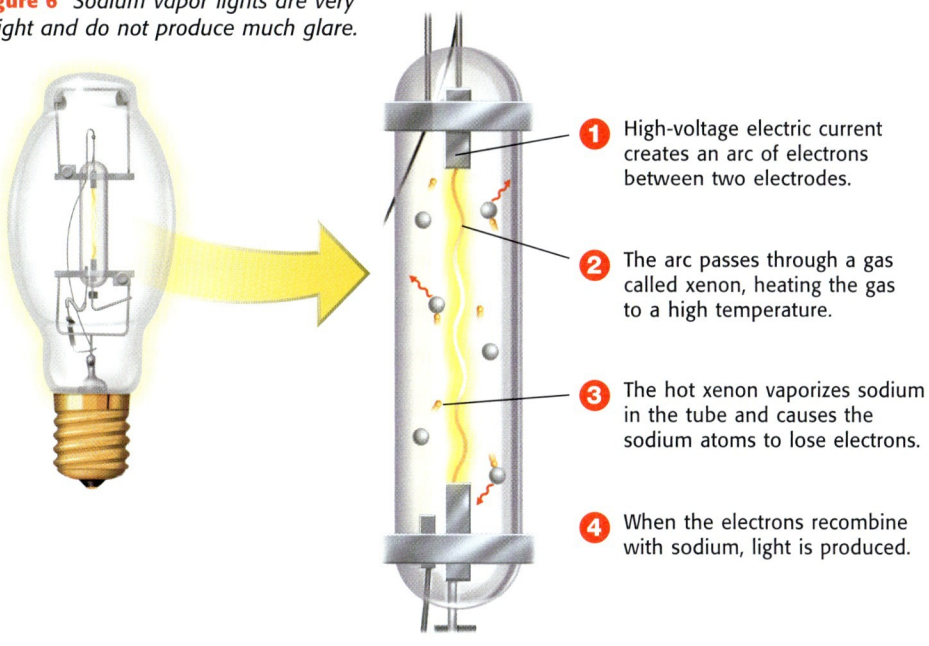

1. High-voltage electric current creates an arc of electrons between two electrodes.
2. The arc passes through a gas called xenon, heating the gas to a high temperature.
3. The hot xenon vaporizes sodium in the tube and causes the sodium atoms to lose electrons.
4. When the electrons recombine with sodium, light is produced.

REVIEW

1. Identify five illuminated objects in your classroom, and name the luminous object (or objects) providing the light.
2. Describe places where you might use incandescent light, fluorescent light, neon light, and vapor light.
3. Describe how fluorescent light is similar to neon light.
4. **Applying Concepts** Halogen bulbs emit bright light from small bulbs. They also emit thermal energy. Would you use a halogen bulb to study by? Why or why not?

internet connect

TOPIC: Producing Light
GO TO: www.scilinks.org
sciLINKS NUMBER: HSTP555

SECTION 2

Focus

Mirrors and Lenses

In this section, students learn how mirrors and lenses form images and how ray diagrams are used to determine where the images are. This section covers plane mirrors, concave mirrors, convex mirrors, convex lenses, and concave lenses. Students learn uses for the different kinds of mirrors and lenses.

 **Bellringer**

Ask students:

What is the difference between a mirror and a lens? What is the difference between a convex mirror and a concave mirror? Can you think of one common use for convex and concave lenses? Write your answers in your ScienceLog.

1) Motivate

ACTIVITY

MATERIALS

For each small group:
- flashlight
- 1 or 2 small hand mirrors

Give each group of students one or two small hand mirrors and a flashlight. Allow students to experiment with the mirrors and flashlights to find out how light waves travel and what mirrors do to light waves. Dim the classroom lights so students can see the beams from their flashlight better. Students should discover that light waves seem to travel in straight lines, and that they continue to travel in straight lines after they have been reflected by a mirror.

Section 2

Mirrors and Lenses

Terms to Learn

plane mirror
concave mirror
focal point
convex mirror
lens
convex lens
concave lens

What You'll Do

- Illustrate how mirrors and lenses form images using ray diagrams.
- Explain the difference between real and virtual images.
- Compare plane mirrors, concave mirrors, and convex mirrors.
- Explain how concave and convex lenses form images.

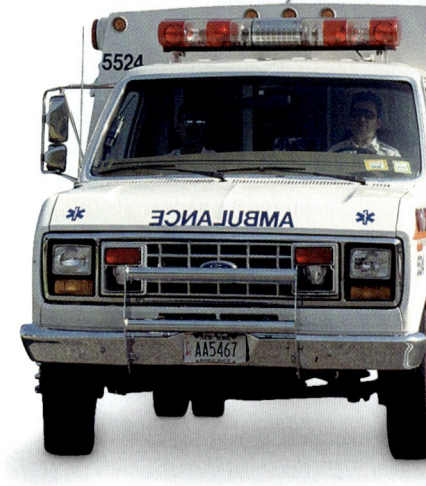

Look at the letters on the front of the ambulance shown at right. Do you notice anything strange about them? Some of the letters are backward, and they don't seem to spell a word.

The letters spell the word AMBULANCE when viewed in a mirror. Images in mirrors are reversed left to right. The word *ambulance* is spelled backward so that people driving cars can read it when they see the ambulance in their rearview mirror. To understand how images are formed in mirrors, you must first learn how to use rays to trace the path of light waves.

Rays Show the Path of Light Waves

Light is an electromagnetic wave. Light waves travel from their source in all directions. If you could trace the path of one wave as it travels away from a light source, you would find that the path is a straight line. Because light waves travel in straight lines, you can use an arrow called a *ray* to show the path and the direction of a light wave. **Figure 7** shows some rays coming from a light bulb.

Rays can also be used to show the path of light waves after the waves have been reflected or refracted. Therefore, rays in ray diagrams are often used to show changes in the direction light travels after being reflected by mirrors or refracted by lenses. You'll learn more about ray diagrams a little later in this section.

Figure 7 *Rays from this light bulb show the path and direction of some light waves produced by the bulb.*

SCIENTISTS AT ODDS

Sir Isaac Newton (1642–1727) did not accept the theory of his colleague Robert Hooke (1635–1703) that light is a wave. Newton believed that white light was composed of particles, or "corpuscles."

Newton knew that if light were a wave, it should bend around corners. When Newton could not prove that light bends around corners, he disagreed with Hooke.

598 Chapter 23 • Light and Our World

Mirrors Reflect Light

Have you ever looked at your reflection in a metal spoon? The polished metal of the spoon acts like a mirror, but not like the mirror in your bathroom! If you look on one side of the spoon, your face is upside down. But if you look on the other side, your face is right side up. Why?

The shape of a reflecting surface affects the way light reflects from it. Therefore, the image you see in your bathroom mirror differs from the image you see in a spoon. Mirrors are classified by their shape. The different shapes are called plane, concave, and convex.

Plane Mirrors Most mirrors, such as the one in your bathroom, are plane mirrors. A **plane mirror** is a mirror with a flat surface. When you look in a plane mirror, your reflection is upright and is the same size as you are. Images in plane mirrors are reversed left to right, as shown in **Figure 8**.

Figure 8 Rearview mirrors in cars are plane mirrors.

When you look in a plane mirror, your image appears to be the same distance behind the mirror as you are in front of it. Why does your image seem to be behind the mirror? Because mirrors are opaque objects, light does not travel through them. But when light reflects off the mirror, your brain interprets the reflected light as if it travels in a straight line from behind the mirror. A *virtual image* is an image through which light does not actually travel. The image formed by a plane mirror is a virtual image. The ray diagram in **Figure 9** explains how light travels when you look into a mirror.

Figure 9 The rays show how light reaches your eyes. The dotted lines show where the light appears to come from.

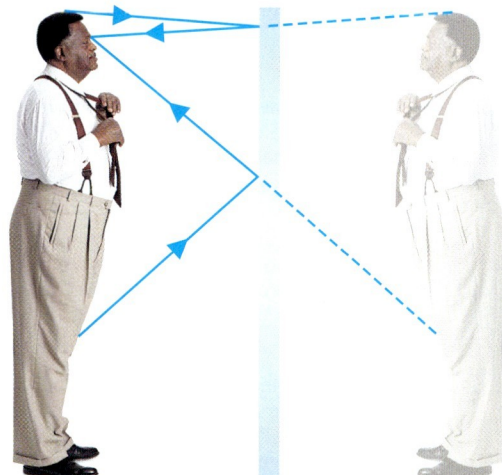

Light reflects off of you and strikes the mirror, where it is reflected again. Some of the light reflecting off the mirror enters your eyes.

Your image appears to be behind the mirror because your brain assumes that the light rays that enter your eyes travel in a straight line from an object to your eyes.

Teaching Transparency 295 "How a Mirror Works"

Directed Reading Worksheet 23 Section 2

2) Teach

MEETING INDIVIDUAL NEEDS
Advanced Learners Have students use what they know about reflection to explain why a plane mirror must be at least half a person's height for the person to see his or her full image in the mirror. Have students use diagrams or mirrors in their explanations. (The angle of incidence equals the angle of reflection, so a person can see the top of his or her head by looking at a point on the mirror halfway between his or her eyes and the top of his or her head. A person can see his or her feet by looking at a point on the mirror halfway between his or her eyes and feet. Together, these two images add up to half the person's height.)

REAL-WORLD CONNECTION
Up to 40 percent of the summertime heat that builds up in a house is a direct result of sunlight that shines through the windows. Special coatings can be applied to windows that reflect up to 80 percent of the incoming sunlight. These coatings are partially reflective, much like a plane mirror. They do transmit enough light that a person can still see through the window. Adding a reflective coating to windows that receive direct sunlight can reduce the amount of energy needed to cool a home.

Homework
Have students make periscopes using materials of their choice. Each student should draw a diagram explaining how his or her periscope works. Challenge students to think of ways in which periscopes can be used.

Section 2 • Mirrors and Lenses

2 Teach, continued

READING STRATEGY

Mnemonics Students are learning about concave and convex mirrors and lenses and about the types of images each produces. Have students create mnemonic devices to help them recall the differences between concave and convex. For example: Concave curves inward because it has caved in.

ACTIVITY

MATERIALS
For Each Student: • shiny metal spoon

Before handing out spoons to students, have them predict what type of image they will see when they look at themselves in the front of the spoon. Ask them to draw in their ScienceLog the image they predict they will see. Then give students the spoons, and have them look at their reflection. Have them draw what they actually see. Then have students move the spoon closer and closer to their eye and describe what they see. Ask them if they can explain how the spoon reflects light rays.

Repeat the activity with the back of the spoon. Sheltered English

USING THE FIGURE

After students have done the activity above, use **Figure 10** to help them understand how the image in the front (concave) part of the spoon is formed.

Mirror Images PG 720

Concave Mirrors Mirrors that are curved inward, such as the inside of a spoon, are called **concave mirrors**. Because the surfaces of concave mirrors are curved, the images formed by concave mirrors differ from the images formed by plane mirrors. To understand how concave mirrors form images, you must learn the terms illustrated in **Figure 10**.

Figure 10 *The image formed by a concave mirror depends on its optical axis, its focal point, and its focal length.*

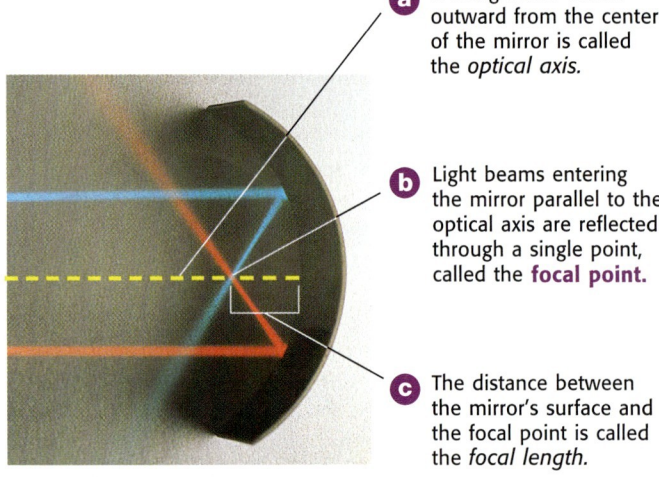

a A straight line drawn outward from the center of the mirror is called the *optical axis*.

b Light beams entering the mirror parallel to the optical axis are reflected through a single point, called the **focal point**.

c The distance between the mirror's surface and the focal point is called the *focal length*.

You already learned that plane mirrors can form only virtual images. Concave mirrors also form virtual images, but they can form *real images* too. A real image is an image through which light actually passes. A real image can be projected onto a screen; a virtual image cannot. To find out what kind of image a concave mirror forms, you can create a ray diagram. Just remember the following three rules when drawing ray diagrams for concave mirrors:

Is an image real or virtual? Turn to page 720 in the LabBook to see the difference.

1 Draw a ray from the top of the object parallel to the optical axis. This ray will reflect through the focal point.

2 If the object is more than one focal length away from the mirror, draw a ray from the top of the object through the focal point. This ray will reflect parallel to the optical axis.

3 If the object is less than one focal length away from the mirror, draw a ray through the top of the object as if it came from the focal point. This ray will reflect parallel to the optical axis.

600

IS THAT A FACT!

In 1663, Scottish astronomer James Gregory (1638–1675) was the first to describe using a concave mirror to focus light rays in a telescope. In 1688, Isaac Newton used Gregory's idea to build the first reflecting telescope. Astronomers found that reflecting telescopes were much more powerful than refracting telescopes. Today's most powerful telescopes use giant concave mirrors.

600 Chapter 23 • Light and Our World

Real or Virtual For each ray diagram, you need to draw only two rays from the top of the object to find what kind of image is formed. If the reflected rays cross in front of the mirror, a real image is formed. The point where the rays cross is the top of the image. If the reflected rays do not cross, trace the reflected rays in straight lines behind the mirror. Those lines will cross to show where a virtual image is formed. Study **Figure 11** to better understand ray diagrams.

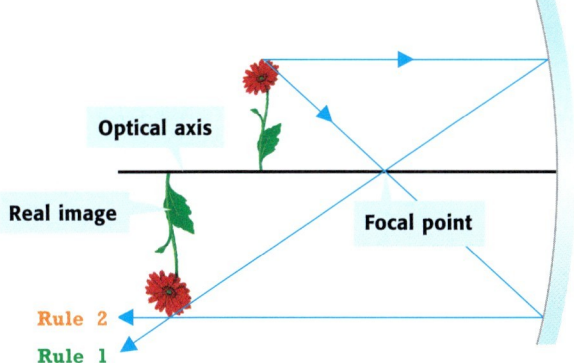

Figure 11 *The type of image formed by a concave mirror depends on the distance between the object and the mirror as well as the focal length.*

An object more than one focal length away from a concave mirror forms an upside-down real image.

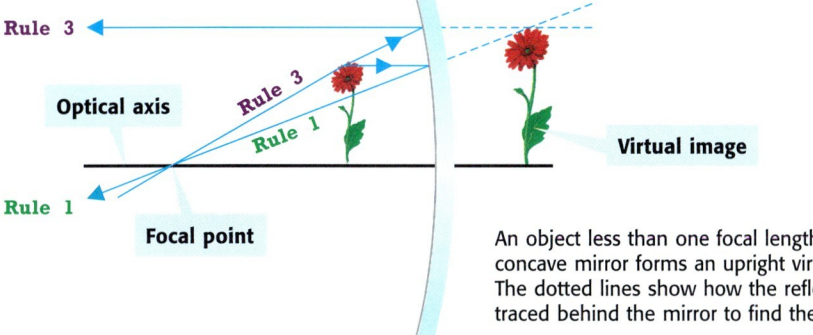

An object less than one focal length away from a concave mirror forms an upright virtual image. The dotted lines show how the reflected rays are traced behind the mirror to find the virtual image.

Neither Real Nor Virtual If an object is placed at the focal point of a concave mirror, no image will form. Rule 2 explains why this happens—all rays that pass through the focal point on their way to the mirror will reflect parallel to the optical axis. Because all the reflected rays are parallel, they will never cross in front of or behind the mirror. If you place a light source at the focal point of a concave mirror, the light will reflect outward in a powerful light beam. Therefore, concave mirrors are used in car headlights and flashlights.

REAL-WORLD CONNECTION

Concave mirrors are often used instead of lenses in optical equipment where accurate color is important. For example, mirrors are often used in spectrometers that divide light into its component colors for analysis. A hardware store may have such a spectrometer in a paint color-matching machine. These machines use the reflected light from a sample of paint to mix a new can of paint to the same color.

MISCONCEPTION ALERT

Be sure students understand that the focal point and focal length for any mirror or lens depends on the curvature of the mirror or lens.

MEETING INDIVIDUAL NEEDS

Learners Having Difficulty Discuss with students the three rules for making ray diagrams (previous page). Help students make three ray diagrams using a ruler and a compass. Ask them to show an object:

- reflected in a plane mirror
- reflected in a concave mirror less than one focal length away
- reflected in a concave mirror more than one focal length away **Sheltered English**

Homework

Some lighthouses use a strong light source placed at or near the focal point of a concave mirror. Ask students to research both ancient and modern lighthouses. Have them make a poster or do a presentation showing a particular lighthouse and how it operates.

internetconnect

TOPIC: Mirrors
GO TO: www.scilinks.org
*sci*LINKS NUMBER: HSTP560

 Teaching Transparency 296 "The Optical Axis, Focal Point, and Focal Length"

 **Teaching Transparency 297** "Creating Virtual Images and Real Images with a Concave Mirror"

Section 2 • Mirrors and Lenses

2 Teach, continued

DISCUSSION

Concept Mapping As a class, make a concept map and ray diagrams for mirrors on the board. Help students classify mirrors and the types of images they make. Then have students copy the completed concept map and ray diagrams in their ScienceLog to use as a study aid.
Sheltered English

MATH and MORE

An object is one half the focal length away from a concave mirror. Will the image be virtual or real? Draw a ray diagram to find the answer. (The image is upright and virtual. The diagram should look like the bottom image in Figure 11 on page 601.)

MEETING INDIVIDUAL NEEDS

Learners Having Difficulty Help students make a ray diagram by using a ruler and a compass to show an object reflected in a convex mirror.
Sheltered English

Answer to APPLY

The images in convex mirrors are always smaller than the original objects. Because the images are smaller than the original objects, the objects look like they are farther away. It is important for drivers to remember that approaching cars are actually closer than they appear. This warning helps drivers to remember and to avoid accidents.

Convex Mirrors If you look at your reflection in the back of a spoon, you will notice that your image is right side up and small. The back of a spoon is a **convex mirror**—a mirror that curves out toward you. **Figure 12** shows how an image is formed by a convex mirror. All images formed by convex mirrors are virtual, upright, and smaller than the original object. Convex mirrors are useful because they produce images of a large area. This is the reason convex mirrors are often used for security in stores and factories. Convex mirrors are also used as side mirrors in cars and trucks.

Figure 12 All images formed by convex mirrors are formed behind the mirror. Therefore, all images formed by convex mirrors are virtual.

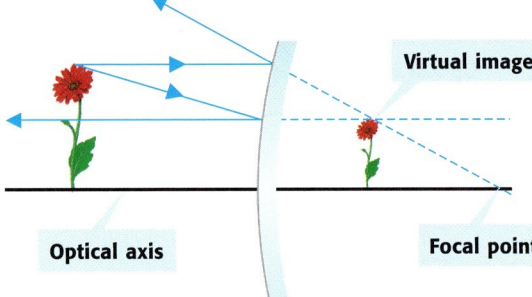

Convex Mirrors Help Drivers

The passenger side mirrors of most cars and trucks are convex mirrors. Convex mirrors are used because they help the driver see more of the traffic around the car than a plane mirror would. However, these mirrors are often stamped with the words "Objects in Mirror Are Closer Than They Appear." What property of convex mirrors makes this warning necessary? Why do you think the warning is important for drivers?

internetconnect

SCILINKS NSTA
TOPIC: Mirrors
GO TO: www.scilinks.org
sciLINKS NUMBER: HSTP560

REVIEW

1. How is a concave mirror different from a convex mirror?
2. Draw a ray diagram showing how a concave mirror forms a real image.
3. **Applying Concepts** Plane mirrors, concave mirrors, and convex mirrors are useful at different times. Describe a situation in which you would use each type of mirror.

Answers to Review

1. A concave mirror is curved inward like the inside of a spoon. A concave mirror can form a real image, a virtual image, or no image at all, depending on the mirror's focal length and the distance from the object to the mirror. A convex mirror is curved outward like the back of a spoon, and can form only a virtual image.
2. Students' diagrams should look like the top image in Figure 11 on page 601.
3. Accept all reasonable answers. Possible answers: Plane mirrors are useful when you comb your hair or as rearview mirrors in cars. Concave mirrors are useful to create strong beams of light, such as in car headlights and flashlights. Convex mirrors are useful for security purposes in stores and as side mirrors on cars.

602 Chapter 23 • Light and Our World

Lenses Refract Light

What do cameras, binoculars, telescopes, and movie projectors have in common? They all use lenses to create images. A **lens** is a curved, transparent object that forms an image by refracting, or bending, light. Like mirrors, lenses are classified by their shape. There are two types of lenses—convex and concave.

Convex Lenses A **convex lens** is thicker in the middle than at the edges. When light rays enter a convex lens, they refract toward the center. Light rays that enter a convex lens parallel to the optical axis are refracted so that they go through a focal point. The amount of refraction and the focal length depend on the curvature of the lens, as shown in **Figure 13**. Light rays that pass through the center of a lens are not refracted.

Convex lenses form many different kinds of images, depending on the focal length of the lens and the position of the object. For example, whenever you use a magnifying glass, you are using a convex lens to form an enlarged, virtual image. **Figure 14** illustrates how a magnifying lens works.

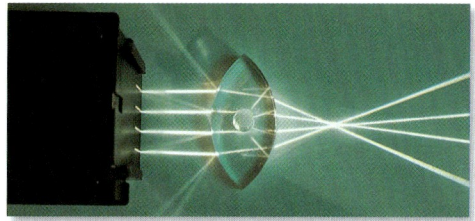
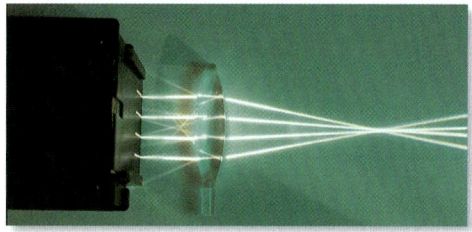

Figure 13 Light rays refract more through convex lenses with greater curvature than through convex lenses with less curvature.

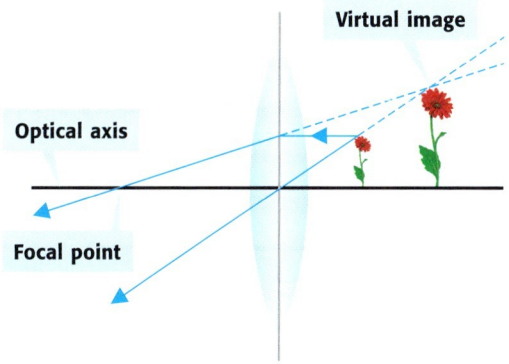

Figure 14 If an object is less than one focal length away from a convex lens, a virtual image is formed. The image is larger than the object and can be seen only by looking into the lens.

MISCONCEPTION ALERT

The amount that a lens refracts light, and therefore its focal point and focal length, depends mostly on the curvature of the lens and not its thickness. If the thin lens in **Figure 13** had the same curvature as the thick lens, it would refract light just as much as the thick lens. The material of which a lens is made may also affect the amount it refracts light.

LabBook PG 722
Images from Convex Lenses

 Teaching Transparency 298
"Thick and Thin Convex Lenses"
"A Concave Lens"

3) Extend

MEETING INDIVIDUAL NEEDS

Advanced Learners Glass lenses are made from a high-quality type of glass known as optical glass. Have students research the history of grinding glass to make lenses, the development of optical glass, and the way lenses are made, ground, and polished. Have them compare and contrast making lenses with making mirrors. Encourage students to be creative with their presentations.

ACTIVITY

Each group of students will need a small comb, some tape, a flashlight, a small index card, a piece of white paper on top of a textbook, a convex lens, a concave lens (eyeglass lens), and a pair of scissors.

Have students cut a 2 cm hole in the card and tape the comb to it. Then have students stand the card up and shine the light through the card and the comb onto the sheet of paper. Have them place the convex lens in front of the paper and observe what happens to the light. Ask students to draw their observations in their ScienceLog. Then have students remove the convex lens and put the concave lens in front of the paper. Ask them to observe the difference in the light pattern. Have students again draw their observations in their ScienceLog.

GUIDED PRACTICE

Have students use a ruler and a compass to make simple ray diagrams for a magnifying glass, a movie projector, camera, and a plain convex lens.
Sheltered English

Section 2 • Mirrors and Lenses

4) Close

CROSS-DISCIPLINARY FOCUS

Mathematics In 1610, Johannes Kepler (1571–1630), a German mathematician and astronomer, was the first scientist to describe the properties of lenses. A year later, he presented a new design for the telescope using two convex lenses.

Quiz

1. What is the difference between a real image and a virtual image? (Light actually passes through a real image, and a real image can be projected onto a screen. Neither is true of a virtual image.)
2. What is the difference between a mirror and a lens? (Mirrors reflect light; lenses refract light.)
3. Use ray diagrams to explain the difference between convex lenses and concave lenses. (Students' ray diagrams should look like the diagrams on pages 603 and 604.)

ALTERNATIVE ASSESSMENT

Concept Mapping Have students make a concept map explaining the properties of lenses and the images they form.

Reinforcement Worksheet 23 "Mirror, Mirror"

TOPIC: Lenses
GO TO: www.scilinks.org
sciLINKS NUMBER: HSTP565

Convex lenses can also form real images. Movie projectors use convex lenses to focus real images on a screen. Cameras use convex lenses to focus real images on a piece of film. Both types of images are shown in **Figure 15**.

Figure 15 Convex lenses can also form real images.

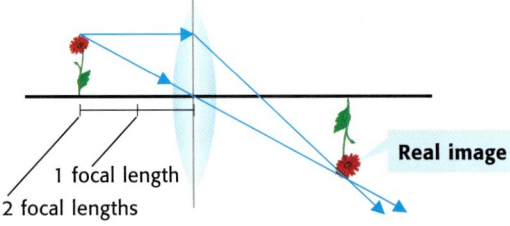

a If the object is located between one and two focal lengths away from the lens, a real, enlarged image is formed far away from the lens. This is how movie projectors produce images on large screens.

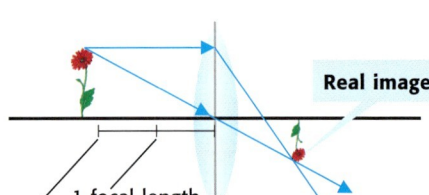

b If the object is located more than two focal lengths away from the lens, a real, reduced image is formed close to the lens. This is how the lens of a camera forms images on the film.

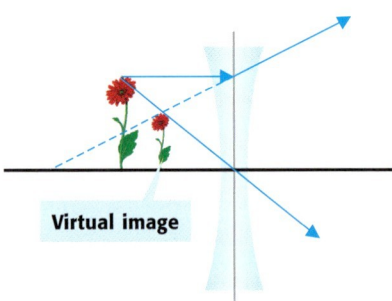

Figure 16 Concave lenses form reduced virtual images. If you trace the refracted rays in a straight line behind a concave lens, you can determine where the virtual image is formed.

Concave Lenses A **concave lens** is thinner in the middle than at the edges. Light rays entering a concave lens parallel to the optical axis always bend away from each other toward the edges of the lens; the rays never meet. Therefore, concave lenses can never form a real image. Instead, they form virtual images, as shown in **Figure 16**. Concave lenses are sometimes combined with other lenses in telescopes. The combination of lenses produces clearer images of distant objects. You will read about another, more common use for concave lenses in the next section.

TOPIC: Lenses
GO TO: www.scilinks.org
sciLINKS NUMBER: HSTP565

REVIEW

1. Draw a ray diagram showing how a magnifying glass forms a virtual image.
2. Explain why a concave lens cannot form a real image.
3. **Applying Concepts** Your teacher sometimes uses an overhead projector to show transparencies on a screen. What type of lens does an overhead projector use?

Answers to Review

1. Students' ray diagrams should look like the one in Figure 14 at the bottom of page 603.
2. A concave lens cannot form real images because light rays passing through it bend away from each other and never meet.
3. Overhead projectors must use convex lenses because real images that can be projected onto a screen can only be formed by convex lenses.

Section 3

Light and Sight

Terms to Learn

cornea   iris
pupil   retina

What You'll Do

- Identify the parts of the human eye, and describe their functions.
- Describe some common vision problems, and explain how they can be corrected.

When you look around, you can see objects both near and far. You can also see the different colors of the objects. You see luminous objects because they produce their own light, which is detected by your eyes. You see all other objects (illuminated objects) because light reflecting off the objects enters your eyes. But how do your eyes work, and what causes people to have problems with their vision? Read on to find out.

How You Detect Light

Visible light is the part of the electromagnetic spectrum that can be detected by your eyes. The process by which your eye gathers light to form the images that you see involves several steps, as shown in **Figure 17.**

Figure 17 How Your Eyes Work

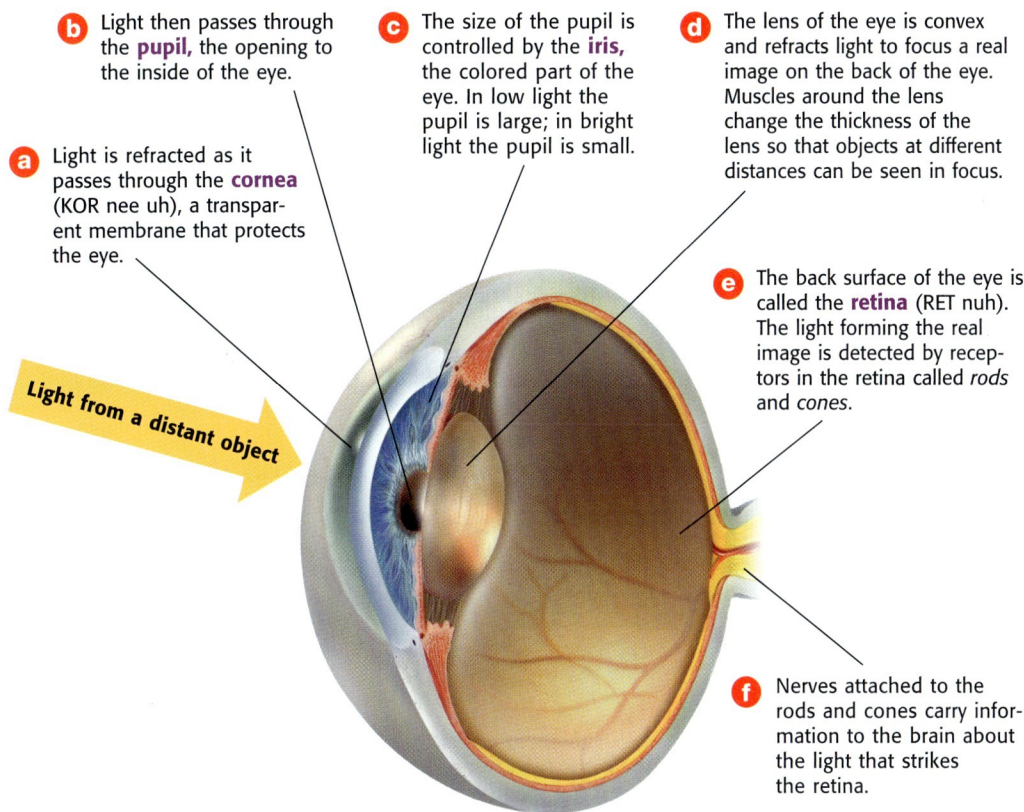

a Light is refracted as it passes through the **cornea** (KOR nee uh), a transparent membrane that protects the eye.

b Light then passes through the **pupil,** the opening to the inside of the eye.

c The size of the pupil is controlled by the **iris,** the colored part of the eye. In low light the pupil is large; in bright light the pupil is small.

d The lens of the eye is convex and refracts light to focus a real image on the back of the eye. Muscles around the lens change the thickness of the lens so that objects at different distances can be seen in focus.

e The back surface of the eye is called the **retina** (RET nuh). The light forming the real image is detected by receptors in the retina called *rods* and *cones*.

f Nerves attached to the rods and cones carry information to the brain about the light that strikes the retina.

Light from a distant object

CONNECT TO LIFE SCIENCE

In some people, the lens of the eye gets cloudy. This is called a cataract. Eye surgeons correct cataracts by making a tiny incision in the eye and inserting a slender instrument that uses sound waves to break up the cloudy lens. The surgeon then vacuums out the pieces. Once the cataract is removed, a new, clear-plastic implant lens is inserted through the incision and positioned inside the eye. The surgery takes about an hour, and the patient can go home the same day.

SECTION 3

Focus

Light and Sight

This section identifies the parts of the human eye and explains how they function. It also describes some common vision problems and how they are corrected.

Bellringer

Ask students the following:

If you were going to design a camera, would you make it work like the human eye? Why or why not? Explain your answer.

1) Motivate

ACTIVITY

Have pairs of students observe one another's eyes. Turn off the lights, and have them observe what happens to the pupils. Then turn the lights on, and have students observe the pupils. Ask students why the pupils change size. Sheltered English

BRAIN FOOD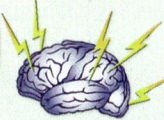

In 1604, Johannes Kepler (1571–1630) gave the first correct explanation of how the human eye works, including why the image formed on the retina is upside down. Kepler's interest in light and optics led to his study of the eye.

 Teaching Transparency 299 "How Your Eyes Work"

 Directed Reading Worksheet 23 Section 3

Section 3 • Light and Sight

3) Extend

ACTIVITY

To simulate normal vision, have students focus an image from an overhead projector onto a screen. Have them measure and record the distance from the projector to the screen. Then, to simulate a nearsighted eye, have students increase the distance between the projector and the screen. The image becomes blurry because it is focused in front of the screen. Then have students move the projector closer to the screen than the original distance. This simulates farsightedness: the image is now focused behind the screen, making it blurry. **Sheltered English**

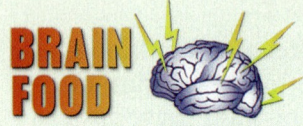

One explanation offered as to why red contacts reduce chickens' aggressiveness is that when chickens see a spot of blood on another chicken, they will peck that chicken, and even kill it. Red contact lenses keep chickens from seeing blood on other chickens and thereby reduce aggressive behavior.

GOING FURTHER

Some animals' eyes seem to glow in the dark, while other animals have highly specialized eyes. Have students research unusual eyes in the animal kingdom. Encourage students to find creative ways to present the results of their research.

BRAIN FOOD

Some chickens wear red contact lenses. The lenses don't improve the chickens' vision—they just make the chickens see everything in red! Chickens that see in red are less aggressive and produce more eggs. But it is difficult to fit a chicken for contact lenses properly, and chickens often lose their contacts quickly.

606

internetconnect

SCLINKS **TOPIC:** The Eye
GO TO: www.scilinks.org
NSTA **sciLINKS NUMBER:** HSTP570

Common Vision Problems

A person with normal vision can clearly see objects both close up and far away and can distinguish all colors of visible light. However, because the eye is complex, it's no surprise that many people have defects in their eyes that affect their vision. Luckily, some common vision problems can be easily corrected.

Nearsightedness and Farsightedness The lens of a properly working eye focuses light on the retina, so the images formed are always clear. Two common vision problems—nearsightedness and farsightedness—occur when light is not focused on the retina. A nearsighted person can see objects clearly only if the objects are nearby. Objects that are farther away look blurry. A farsighted person can see faraway objects clearly, but objects nearby look blurry. **Figure 18** explains how nearsightedness and farsightedness occur and how they can be corrected.

Figure 18 *Nearsightedness and farsightedness are common vision problems that can be corrected easily with glasses or contact lenses.*

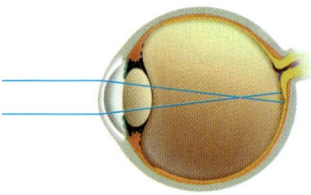 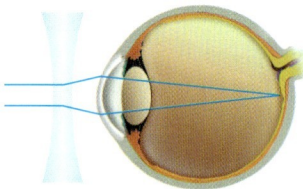

Nearsightedness occurs when the eye is too long and the lens focuses light in front of the retina.

A **concave lens** placed in front of the eye refracts the light outward. The lens in the eye can then focus the light on the retina.

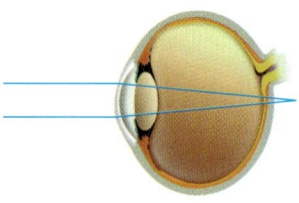 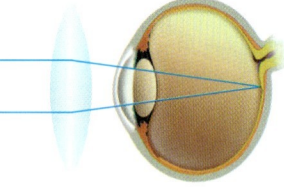

Farsightedness occurs when the eye is too short and the lens focuses light behind the retina.

A **convex lens** placed in front of the eye refracts the light and focuses it slightly. The lens in the eye can then focus the light on the retina.

CROSS-DISCIPLINARY FOCUS

Language Arts French author Antoine de Saint-Exupéry (1900–1944), in his book *The Little Prince*, wrote, "It is only with the heart one can see rightly; what is essential is invisible to the eye." Have students write an explanation of what they think this quote means. Ask students to discuss their ideas.

606 Chapter 23 • Light and Our World

Color Deficiency Roughly 5 to 8 percent of men and 0.5 percent of women in the world have *color deficiency*, often referred to as colorblindness. True colorblindness, in which a person can see only in black and white, is very rare. The majority of people with color deficiency have trouble distinguishing shades of red and green, or distinguishing red from green.

Color deficiency occurs when the cones in the retina do not receive the right instructions. The three types of cones are named for the colors they detect most—red, green, and blue. Each type of cone reacts to a range of wavelengths of light. A person with normal color vision can see all colors. But in some people, the cones get the wrong instructions and respond to the wrong wavelengths. That person may have trouble seeing certain colors. For example, he or she may see too much red or too much green, and not enough of the other color. **Figure 19** shows one type of test for color deficiency.

Biology CONNECTION

Whether a person is colorblind depends on his or her genes. Certain genes give instructions to the cones for detecting certain wavelengths of light. If the genes give the wrong instructions, the person will have a color deficiency. A person needs one set of the genes that give the right instructions. Genes for color vision are on the X chromosome. Women have two X chromosomes, but men have only one. Therefore, men are more likely to be lacking a set of these genes and are more likely than women to be colorblind.

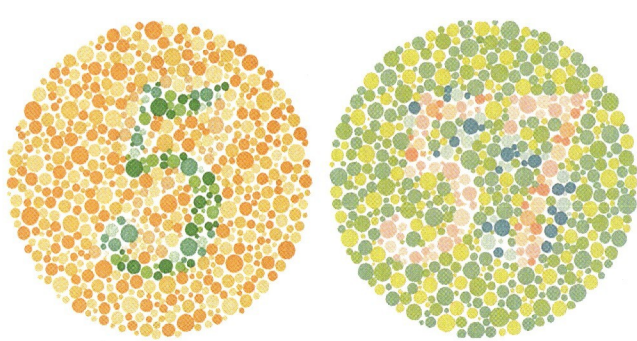

Figure 19 Doctors use images like these to detect red-green color deficiency. Can you see a number in each image?

REVIEW

1. Name the parts of the human eye, and describe what each part does.
2. What kind of lens would help a person who is nearsighted? What kind would help someone who is farsighted?
3. **Inferring Conclusions** Why do you think colorblindness cannot be corrected?
4. **Applying Concepts** Sometimes people are both nearsighted and farsighted. They wear glasses with two different kinds of lenses. Why are two lenses necessary?

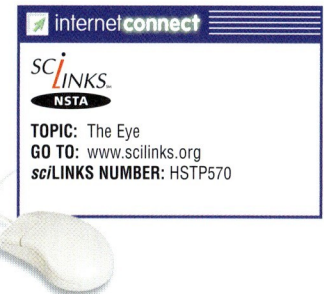

internet connect

SC*i*LINKS
NSTA

TOPIC: The Eye
GO TO: www.scilinks.org
*sci*LINKS NUMBER: HSTP570

SECTION 4

Focus

Light Technology

This section describes some optical instruments that make use of lenses and mirrors. It also explains how lasers work and discusses some uses for lasers. Students also learn about fiber optics and polarized light.

 **Bellringer**

Ask students if they have ever taken or seen a blurry photograph. Ask them what they think might have caused the problem.

1) Motivate

DEMONSTRATION

If you have them, demonstrate a Polaroid™ camera and a classroom laser. Ask students what the two items have in common and how they are different. Display other optical instruments, especially a microscope and a telescope, where students can see them. Discuss each instrument with students. Ask them what they know about each instrument and if they can explain how each one works.

 Teaching Transparency 299 "How a Camera Works"

 Directed Reading Worksheet 23 Section 4

Section 4

Terms to Learn
laser   hologram

What You'll Do
- Explain how optical instruments use lenses and mirrors to form images.
- Explain how lasers work and what makes laser light different from non-laser light.
- Identify uses for lasers.
- Describe how optical fibers and polarizing filters work.

Light Technology

So far in this chapter, you have learned some ways light can be produced, how mirrors and lenses affect light, and some ways that people use mirrors and lenses. In this section, you will learn how different technological devices rely on mirrors and lenses and how mirrors help produce a type of light called laser light.

Optical Instruments

Optical instruments are devices that use arrangements of mirrors and lenses to help people make observations. Some optical instruments help you see objects that are very far away, and some help you see objects that are very small. Some optical instruments record images. The optical instrument that you are probably most familiar with is the camera.

Cameras The way a camera works is similar to the way your eye works. A camera has a lens that focuses light and has an opening that lets in light. The main difference between a camera and the eye is that the film in a camera permanently stores the images formed on it, but the images formed on the retina disappear when you stop looking at an object. **Figure 20** shows the parts of a camera and their functions.

Figure 20 The Parts of a Camera

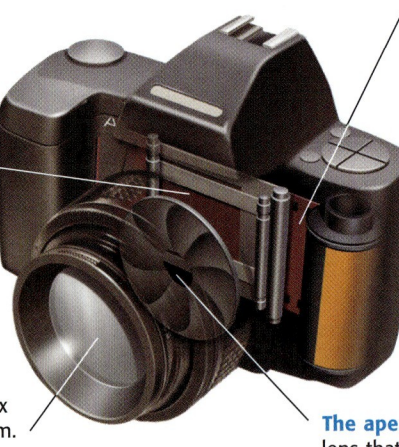

The shutter opens and closes behind the lens to control how much light enters the camera. The longer the shutter is open, the more light enters the camera.

The film is coated with chemicals that react when they are struck by light. The result is an image stored on the film.

The lens of a camera is a convex lens that focuses light on the film. Moving the lens focuses light from objects at different distances.

The aperture is an opening in the lens that lets light into the camera. The larger the aperture is, the more light enters the camera.

608

CROSS-DISCIPLINARY FOCUS

Math (Challenging) Two numbers are very important to photographers: shutter speed and f-stop. Have students research both, and have them make a concept map, diagram, or other presentation to explain their findings to the class. Encourage them to be creative.

608 Chapter 23 • Light and Our World

Telescopes Astronomers use telescopes to study objects in space, such as the moon, planets, and stars. Telescopes are classified as either refracting or reflecting. Refracting telescopes use lenses to collect light, while reflecting telescopes use mirrors. **Figure 21** illustrates how simple refracting and reflecting telescopes work.

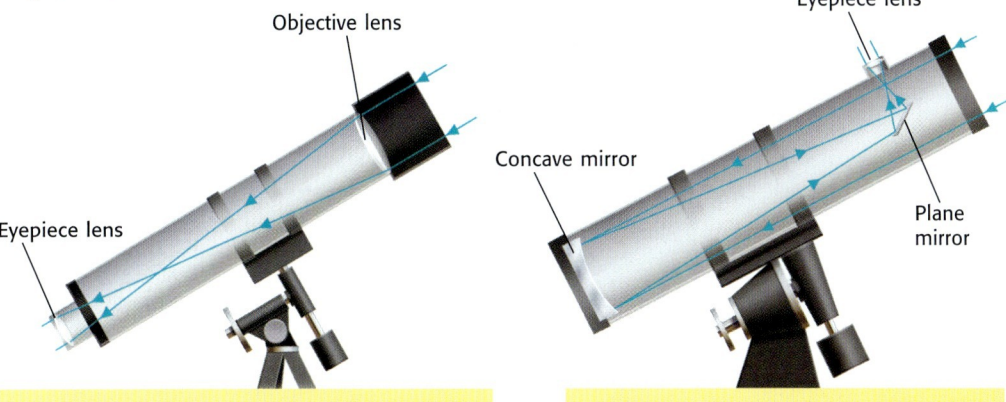

Figure 21 Both refracting and reflecting telescopes are used to see objects that are far away.

A **refracting telescope** has two convex lenses. Light enters through the objective lens and forms a real image. This real image is then magnified by the eyepiece lens. You see this magnified image when you look through the eyepiece lens.

A **reflecting telescope** has a concave mirror that collects and focuses light to form a real image. The light strikes a plane mirror that directs the light to the convex eyepiece lens, which magnifies the real image.

Light Microscopes Simple light microscopes are similar to refracting telescopes. They have two convex lenses—an objective lens, which is close to the object being studied, and an eyepiece lens, which you look through. The difference between microscopes and telescopes is that microscopes are used to see magnified images of tiny, nearby objects rather than images of large, distant objects.

Self-Check

Explain why the objective lens of a telescope cannot be a concave lens. *(See page 724 to check your answer.)*

Lasers and Laser Light

Have you ever seen a laser light show? Laser light beams flash through the air and sometimes form pictures on surfaces. A **laser** is a device that produces intense light of only one color and wavelength. Laser light is different from non-laser light in many ways. One important difference is that laser light is *coherent*. When light is coherent, light waves move together as they travel away from their source. The crests and troughs of coherent light waves line up, and the individual waves behave as one single wave. Other differences between laser light and non-laser light are shown in **Figure 22,** on the next page.

CROSS-DISCIPLINARY FOCUS

Art Photography is a combination of art and science. A photographer must understand how film, light, and lenses work together to produce images. And a good photographer must know how light will interact with the subject of a photograph, what the camera lens will do to the light, and how the light will affect the film.

Answer to Self-Check

Concave lenses do not form real images. Only a real image can be magnified by another lens, such as the eyepiece lens.

---

2) Teach

CONNECT TO EARTH SCIENCE

The Dutch lensmaker Hans Lippershey (c.1570–1619) is thought to have invented the first telescope. However, it was Italian scientist Galileo (1564–1642) who first used a telescope to study the sky. With his telescope, Galileo discovered the craters of the moon, the four largest moons of Jupiter, and what were later identified as the rings of Saturn.

RESEARCH

Ask students to find images from the world's largest optical (reflecting and refracting) telescopes, such as the Keck Observatory, European Southern Observatory, and Yerkes Observatory. Encourage students to be creative in displaying their images, and discuss with the class some of the results.

MEETING INDIVIDUAL NEEDS

Learners Having Difficulty Ask students to research the life and work of either Robert Hooke (1635–1702) or Anton van Leeuwenhoek (1632–1723). Have students create a poster, a mobile, or a model showing what they learned. Use Teaching Transparency 2 to get them started. **Sheltered English**

Teaching Transparency 2 "Compound Light Microscope" LINK TO LIFE SCIENCE

Teaching Transparency 300 "How Telescopes Work"

Section 4 • Light Technology

2 Teach, continued

USING THE FIGURE

Use **Figure 23** to explain the two special properties of laser light: it is light of a single wavelength and color, and it is *coherent*. Light is coherent when the peaks and troughs of light waves are aligned through interference. This causes the individual light waves to act as a single wave. Soon the laser light has enough energy to escape through the partially coated mirror in an intense and concentrated beam. Non-laser light sources emit light waves of many different wavelengths and colors whose peaks are not aligned.

MEETING INDIVIDUAL NEEDS

Learners Having Difficulty Have students make a model of a laser by using construction paper for the tube and aluminum foil for the mirrors. They can use fishing weights for neon atoms and red holes from a hole punch for the photons. Have students explain their model.

Homework

Have students research the many ways argon, carbon dioxide, helium-neon, and other lasers are used for medical diagnosis and treatment.

internetconnect
TOPIC: Lasers
GO TO: www.scilinks.org
sciLINKS NUMBER: HSTP575

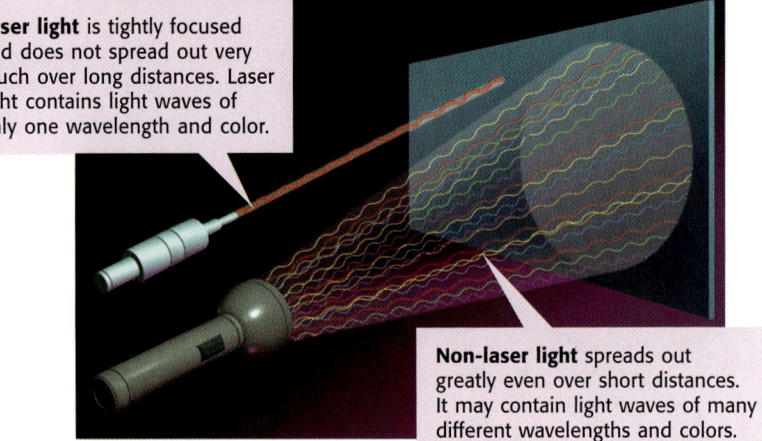

Figure 22 Laser Light Versus Non-laser Light

Laser light is tightly focused and does not spread out very much over long distances. Laser light contains light waves of only one wavelength and color.

Non-laser light spreads out greatly even over short distances. It may contain light waves of many different wavelengths and colors.

How Lasers Produce Light The word *laser* stands for **l**ight **a**mplification by **s**timulated **e**mission of **r**adiation. You already know what light and radiation are. *Amplification* is the increase in the brightness of the light.

What is stimulated emission? In an atom, an electron can move from one energy level to another. A photon is released when an electron moves from a higher energy level to a lower energy level. This process is called *emission. Stimulated emission* occurs when a photon strikes an atom in an excited state and makes that atom emit another photon. The newly emitted photon is identical to the first photon, and they travel away from the atom together. **Figure 23** shows how stimulated emission works to produce laser light.

Figure 23 A Helium-Neon Laser

a The inside of the laser is filled with helium and neon gases. An electric current in the gases excites the atoms of the gases.

b Excited neon atoms release photons of red light. When these photons strike other excited neon atoms, stimulated emission occurs.

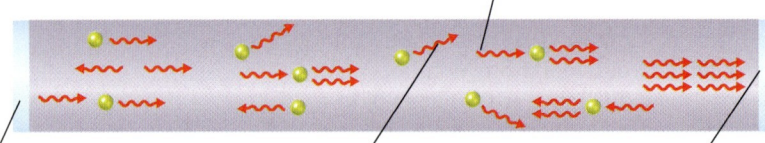

c Plane mirrors on both ends of the laser reflect photons traveling the length of the laser back and forth along the tube.

d Because the photons travel back and forth many times, many stimulated emissions occur, making the laser light brighter.

e One mirror is only partially coated, so some of the photons "leak" out and form a laser light beam.

WEIRD SCIENCE

Laser light can be produced in a variety of ways. Gas lasers, such as the one in **Figure 23,** produce laser light from excited gas atoms. Solid-state lasers have a solid, rather than a gas, between the two mirrors to produce photons for the laser beam. Semiconductor lasers use the same material that is found in computer chips to produce laser light. Most CD and DVD players use semiconductor lasers.

Holograms Lasers are used to produce holograms. A **hologram** is a piece of film on which an interference pattern produces a three-dimensional image of an object. You have probably seen holograms on magazine covers or baseball cards. **Figure 24** shows how light from a laser is split into two beams. These two beams combine to form an interference pattern on the film, which results in a hologram.

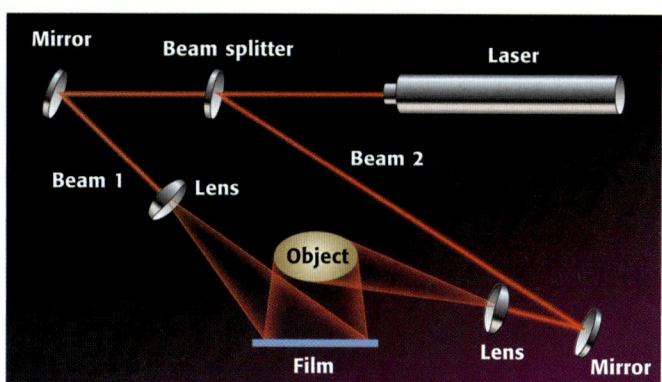

Figure 24 Light from one beam shines directly on the film, and light from the other beam shines on an object and is reflected onto the film.

Holograms, like the one shown in **Figure 25,** are similar to photographs because they are images permanently recorded on film. However, unlike photographs, the images you see are not on the surface of the film. They appear either in front of or behind the film. And if you move the image around, you will see it from different angles.

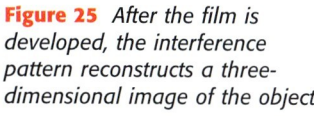

Figure 25 After the film is developed, the interference pattern reconstructs a three-dimensional image of the object.

Other Uses for Lasers In addition to making holograms, lasers are used for a wide variety of tasks. For example, lasers are used to cut materials such as metal and cloth. Surgeons sometimes use lasers to cut through human tissue. Laser surgery on the cornea of the eye can correct nearsightedness and farsightedness. And, as you read at the beginning of this chapter, lasers can also be used as extremely accurate rulers. You even use a laser when you listen to music from a CD player.

SCIENTISTS AT ODDS

Two American physicists, Arthur Schawlow and Charles Townes, received a patent for the working principles of a laser in 1958. But Gordon Gould claimed that he not only had discovered how to produce laser light but also had named the process in 1957. Finally, in 1987, after many bitter court battles, Gould's claim was upheld.

CONNECT TO LIFE SCIENCE

Biologists use laser devices called optical tweezers to handle organisms without damaging them. Biologists also use optical tweezers to manipulate organelles within living cells without breaking the cell membrane, to move chromosomes within a cell nucleus, and to manipulate single strands of DNA.

3) Extend

REAL-WORLD CONNECTION

Although many systems that transmit information now use fiber optic cables, these thin threads are not perfect. The advantages of fiber optics—that they carry more data, are less susceptible to interference, are thinner and lighter than copper wires, and transmit data digitally—must be weighed against the disadvantages. Fiber optics are more expensive to install and are much more fragile than copper wires.

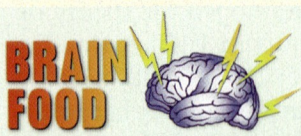

Polarized light is used in liquid crystal displays. When the polarized light passes through the liquid crystal material, the liquid crystals cause the polarized light to twist. When a weak electric voltage is applied to the liquid crystals, it no longer twists or affects the polarized light. This lets part of the display go dark and leaves a segment to form a number or letter.

ACTIVITY

Place a polarizing filter over the face of a liquid-crystal display calculator. An overhead calculator gives excellent results. Rotate the filter; have students observe what happens. Ask students to speculate on what causes these changes. (As the filter is rotated, the display blacks out. This means there must be another polarizing filter inside the device because two polarizing filters are needed to block out light.)

Fiber Optics

Imagine a glass thread as thin as a human hair that can transmit more than 1,000 telephone conversations at the same time with only flashes of light. It might sound impossible, but such glass threads are at work all over the world. These threads, called *optical fibers,* are thin, flexible glass wires that can transmit light over long distances. Some optical fibers are shown at left. The use of optical fibers is called *fiber optics*. The transmission of information through telephone cables is the most common use of fiber optics. Optical fibers carry information faster and more clearly than older copper telephone cables. Optical fibers are also used to network computers and to allow doctors to see inside patients' bodies without performing major surgery.

Light in a Pipe Optical fibers transmit light over long distances because they act like pipes for light. Just as a good water pipe doesn't let water leak out, a good light pipe doesn't let light leak out. Light stays inside an optical fiber because of total internal reflection. *Total internal reflection* is the complete reflection of light along the inside surface of the medium through which it travels. **Figure 26** shows total internal reflection in an optical fiber.

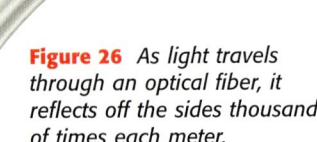

Figure 26 As light travels through an optical fiber, it reflects off the sides thousands of times each meter.

Polarized Light

Next time you go shopping for sunglasses, look for those that have lenses that polarize light. Sunglasses that contain polarizing lenses reduce glare better than sunglasses that do not. *Polarized light* consists of light waves that vibrate in only one plane. **Figure 27** illustrates how light is polarized.

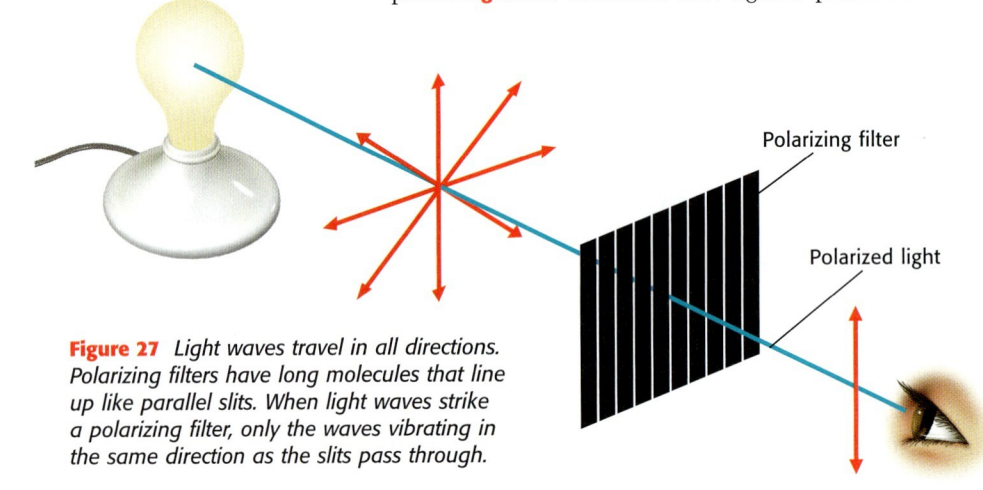

Figure 27 Light waves travel in all directions. Polarizing filters have long molecules that line up like parallel slits. When light waves strike a polarizing filter, only the waves vibrating in the same direction as the slits pass through.

Critical Thinking Worksheet 23, "Light That Heals"

IS THAT A FACT!

Have you used a laser today? If you've played a CD or DVD, the answer is yes. And you probably used a laser the last time you picked up the phone. Many phone lines are now made of fiber optic cables, and lasers are the source of the light that transmits information through fiber optic cables.

When light reflects at a certain angle from a smooth surface, it is completely polarized parallel to that surface. If the surface is parallel to the ground, the light is polarized horizontally. This is what causes the bright glare from bodies of water and car hoods.

Polarizing sunglasses reduce glare from horizontal surfaces because the sunglasses have lenses with vertically polarized filters. These filters allow only vertically vibrating light waves to pass through them. So when you wear polarizing sunglasses, the reflected light that is horizontally polarized does not reach your eyes. Polarizing filters are also used by photographers to reduce glare and reflection in their photographs. Examine **Figure 28** to see the effect of a polarizing filter on a camera.

QuickLab

Now You See, Now You Don't

1. Hold a **lens from a pair of polarizing sunglasses** up to your eye, and look through it. Describe your observations in your ScienceLog.
2. Put a **second polarizing lens** over the first lens. Make sure both lenses are right side up. Look through both lenses, and describe your observations in your ScienceLog.
3. Rotate one lens slowly as you look through both lenses, and describe what happens.
4. Why can't you see through the lenses when they are lined up a certain way? Record your answer in your ScienceLog.

Try at Home

Figure 28 *These two photos were taken by the same camera from the same angle. There is less reflected light in the photo at right because a polarizing filter was placed over the lens of the camera.*

REVIEW

1. How is a camera similar to the human eye?
2. What is the difference between a refracting telescope and a reflecting telescope?
3. How is a beam of laser light different from non-laser light?
4. Why are fiber optics useful for transmitting information?
5. **Applying Concepts** Why do you think lasers are used to cut cloth and metal and to perform surgery?

internetconnect

SCiLINKS NSTA
TOPIC: Lasers
GO TO: www.scilinks.org
sciLINKS NUMBER: HSTP575

4) Close

QuickLab

MATERIALS

FOR EACH GROUP:
• 2 polarizing lenses

Answers to QuickLab

3. As one lens is rotated, the room becomes progressively darker until, when one lens is rotated 90° relative to the other lens, students will not be able to see the room.
4. The first lens polarizes light so that only waves vibrating in, for example, the vertical plane are able to pass through. When the second lens is rotated 90° from the first lens, it polarizes light in the horizontal plane (90° from the first lens). The vertically polarized light from the first lens can't pass through the second (horizontal) lens. No light gets through, and the room looks completely dark.

Quiz

1. Name three optical instruments that use lenses or mirrors. (microscopes, telescopes, cameras)
2. What is one use of fiber optics? (endoscopy; computer networking)
3. How do polarized sunglass lenses work? (They have filters that allow only vertical waves to pass through, reducing the amount of glare.)

ALTERNATIVE ASSESSMENT

Have each student write seven questions with answers from this section. Play a game with the class. Each student should answer at least one question.

Answers to Review

1. Answers will vary; they should cover the information from Figure 17 on page 605.
2. refracting telescope—two convex lenses; reflecting telescope—one concave mirror and one convex lens
3. Laser light is coherent, has only one color and wavelength, and stays focused over long distances. Non-laser light is not coherent and may have light waves of many different colors and wavelengths.
4. Fiber optics transmit information faster and more clearly than older metal cables.
5. Accept all reasonable answers. Possible answers: Lasers produce tightly focused beams of light that can deliver a large amount of energy to a small space.

Chapter Highlights

VOCABULARY DEFINITIONS

SECTION 1

luminous describes objects that are visible light sources

illuminated describes visible objects that are not light sources

incandescent light light produced by hot objects

fluorescent light visible light emitted by a phosphor particle when it absorbs energy, such as ultraviolet light

neon light visible light emitted by atoms of certain gases when they absorb and then release energy

vapor light light produced when electrons combine with gaseous metal atoms

SECTION 2

plane mirror a mirror with a flat surface

concave mirror a mirror that is curved inward like the inside of a spoon

focal point the point on the axis of a mirror or lens through which light beams entering the mirror or lens parallel to the axis are focused

convex mirror a mirror that curves out toward you, like the back of a spoon

lens a curved, transparent object that forms an image by refracting light; the part of the eye that refracts light to focus an image on the retina

convex lens a lens that is thicker in the middle than at the edges

concave lens a lens that is thinner in the middle than at the edges

Chapter Highlights

SECTION 1

Vocabulary
- **luminous** (p. 594)
- **illuminated** (p. 594)
- **incandescent light** (p. 595)
- **fluorescent light** (p. 596)
- **neon light** (p. 596)
- **vapor light** (p. 597)

Section Notes
- You see objects either because they are luminous (produce their own light) or because they are illuminated (reflect light).
- Light produced by hot objects is incandescent light. Ordinary light bulbs are a common source of incandescent light.
- Fluorescent light is visible light emitted by a particle when it absorbs ultraviolet light. Little energy is wasted by fluorescent light bulbs.
- Neon light results from an electric current in certain gases.
- Vapor light is produced when electrons combine with gaseous metal atoms.

SECTION 2

Vocabulary
- **plane mirror** (p. 599)
- **concave mirror** (p. 600)
- **focal point** (p. 600)
- **convex mirror** (p. 602)
- **lens** (p. 603)
- **convex lens** (p. 603)
- **concave lens** (p. 604)

Section Notes
- Rays are arrows that show the path and direction of a single light wave. Ray diagrams can be used to determine where images are formed by mirrors and lenses.
- Plane mirrors produce virtual images that are the same size as the objects. These images are reversed left to right.

✓ Skills Check

Visual Understanding

OPTICAL AXIS, FOCAL POINT, AND FOCAL LENGTH To understand how concave and convex mirrors and lenses work, you need to know what the terms *optical axis*, *focal point*, and *focal length* mean. Figure 10 on page 600 explains these terms.

LASERS Laser light is different from ordinary non-laser light in several ways. Look back at Figure 22 on page 610 to review some differences between the two types of light.

THE EYE Study Figure 17 on page 605 to review the parts of the eye and review the process by which your eye gathers light to form the images that you see.

Lab and Activity Highlights

Mirror Images `PG 720`

Images from Convex Lenses `PG 722`

 Datasheets for LabBook (blackline masters for these labs)

614 Chapter 23 • Light and Our World

SECTION 2

- Concave mirrors can produce real images and virtual images. They can also be used to produce a powerful light beam.
- Convex mirrors produce only virtual images.
- Convex lenses can produce real images and virtual images. A magnifying glass is an example of a convex lens.
- Concave lenses produce only virtual images.

Labs

Mirror Images (p. 720)
Images from
Convex Lenses (p. 722)

SECTION 3

Vocabulary

cornea (p. 605)
pupil (p. 605)
iris (p. 605)
retina (p. 605)

Section Notes

- Your eye has several parts, such as the cornea, the pupil, the iris, the lens, and the retina.
- Nearsightedness and farsightedness occur when light is not focused on the retina. Both problems can be corrected with glasses or contact lenses.
- Color deficiency is a genetic condition in which cones in the retina are given the wrong instructions. Color deficiency cannot be corrected.

SECTION 4

Vocabulary

laser (p. 609)
hologram (p. 611)

Section Notes

- Optical instruments, such as cameras, telescopes, and microscopes, are devices that use mirrors and lenses to help people make observations.
- Lasers are devices that produce intense, coherent light of only one wavelength and color. Lasers produce light by a process called stimulated emission.
- Optical fibers can transmit light over long distances because of total internal reflection.
- Polarized light contains light waves that vibrate in only one direction.

VOCABULARY DEFINITIONS, continued

SECTION 3

cornea a transparent membrane that protects the eye and refracts light

pupil the opening to the inside of the eye

iris the colored part of the eye

retina the back surface of the eye

SECTION 4

laser a device that produces intense light of only one wavelength and color

hologram a piece of film on which an interference pattern produces a three-dimensional image of an object

Vocabulary Review Worksheet 23

Blackline masters of these Chapter Highlights can be found in the **Study Guide**.

---

internet connect

GO TO: go.hrw.com

Visit the **HRW** Web site for a variety of learning tools related to this chapter. Just type in the keyword:

KEYWORD: HSTLOW

GO TO: www.scilinks.org

Visit the **National Science Teachers Association** on-line Web site for Internet resources related to this chapter. Just type in the sciLINKS number for more information about the topic:

TOPIC:	Producing Light	sciLINKS NUMBER: HSTP555
TOPIC:	Mirrors	sciLINKS NUMBER: HSTP560
TOPIC:	Lenses	sciLINKS NUMBER: HSTP565
TOPIC:	The Eye	sciLINKS NUMBER: HSTP570
TOPIC:	Lasers	sciLINKS NUMBER: HSTP575

Lab and Activity Highlights

LabBank

Labs You Can Eat,
Fiber-Optic Fun, Lab 25

EcoLabs and Field Activities,
Photon Drive, EcoLab 23

Whiz-Bang Demonstrations,
Light Humor, Demo 65

Inquiry Labs, Eye Spy, Lab 23

Long-Term Projects & Research Ideas,
Island Vacation, Project 73

Chapter Review Answers

USING VOCABULARY

1. Incandescent light
2. concave mirror
3. retina
4. laser
5. illuminated

UNDERSTANDING CONCEPTS

Multiple Choice

6. c
7. a
8. d
9. d
10. d
11. c
12. c
13. c

Short Answer

14. Convex lenses should be prescribed. Convex lenses focus light slightly before it enters the eye so that the lens of the eye can focus the light properly on the retina.
15. Holograms produce three-dimensional images that appear in front of or behind the hologram. Photographs have two-dimensional images on the surface of the film.
16. The North Pole is covered with snow that reflects a great deal of light. The reflected light is polarized and can be eliminated by using sunglasses with polarized lenses.

Chapter Review

USING VOCABULARY

To complete the following sentences, choose the correct term from each pair of terms listed below:

1. __?__ is commonly used in homes and produces a lot of thermal energy. (*Incandescent light* or *Fluorescent light*)

2. A __?__ is curved inward, like the inside of a spoon. (*convex mirror* or *concave mirror*)

3. You can see an object when light is focused on the __?__ of your eye. (*pupil* or *retina*)

4. A __?__ is a device that produces coherent, intense light of only one color. (*laser* or *lens*)

5. You can see this book because it is a(n) __?__ object. (*luminous* or *illuminated*)

UNDERSTANDING CONCEPTS

Multiple Choice

6. When you look at yourself in a plane mirror, you see a
   a. real image behind the mirror.
   b. real image on the surface of the mirror.
   c. virtual image that appears to be behind the mirror.
   d. virtual image that appears to be in front of the mirror.

7. A vision problem that occurs when light is focused in front of the retina is
   a. nearsightedness.
   b. farsightedness.
   c. color deficiency.
   d. None of the above

8. Which part of the eye refracts light?
   a. iris   c. lens
   b. cornea   d. both (b) and (c)

9. Visible light produced when electrons combine with gaseous metal atoms is
   a. incandescent light.
   b. fluorescent light.
   c. neon light.
   d. vapor light.

10. You see less of a glare when you wear certain sunglasses because the lenses
    a. produce total internal reflection.
    b. create holograms.
    c. produce coherent light.
    d. polarize light.

11. What kind of mirrors provide images of large areas and are used for security?
    a. plane mirrors   c. convex mirrors
    b. concave mirrors   d. all of the above

12. A simple refracting telescope has
    a. a convex lens and a concave lens.
    b. a concave mirror and a convex lens.
    c. two convex lenses.
    d. two concave lenses.

13. Light waves in a laser beam interact and act as one wave. This light is called
    a. red.   c. coherent.
    b. white.   d. emitted.

Short Answer

14. What type of lens should be prescribed for a person who cannot focus on nearby objects? Explain.

15. How is a hologram different from a photograph?

16. Why might a scientist at the North Pole need polarizing sunglasses?

Concept Mapping

17. Use the following terms to create a concept map: lens, telescope, camera, real image, virtual image, optical instrument.

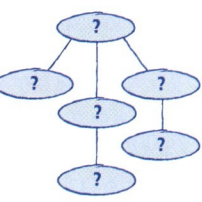

CRITICAL THINKING AND PROBLEM SOLVING

18. Stoplights are usually mounted so that the red light is on the top and the green light is on the bottom. Explain why it is important for a person who has red-green color deficiency to know this arrangement.

19. Some companies are producing fluorescent light bulbs that will fit into sockets on lamps designed for incandescent light bulbs. Although fluorescent bulbs are more expensive, the companies hope that people will use them because they are better for the environment. Explain why fluorescent light bulbs are better for the environment than incandescent light bulbs.

20. Imagine you are given a small device that produces a beam of red light. You want to find out if the device is producing laser light or if it is just a red flashlight. To do this, you point the beam of light against a wall across the room. What would you expect to see if the device is producing laser light? Explain.

INTERPRETING GRAPHICS

21. Examine the ray diagrams below, and identify the type of mirror or lens that is being used and the kind of image that is being formed.

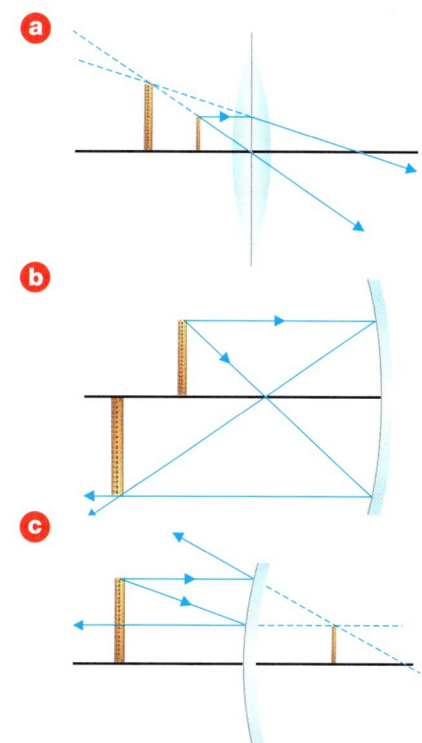

a

b

c

NOW What Do You Think?

Take a minute to review your answers to the ScienceLog questions on page 593. Have your answers changed? If necessary, revise your answers based on what you have learned since you began this chapter.

617

Concept Mapping

17. An answer to this exercise can be found at the end of this book.

CRITICAL THINKING AND PROBLEM SOLVING

18. People who are red-green color-blind cannot distinguish between red and green. If they do not know the arrangement of lights on stoplights, they can't use the stoplight to determine when it is safe to cross an intersection or when they need to stop.

19. Fluorescent lights are better than incandescent lights for the environment because they waste less thermal energy, and less energy is needed to make fluorescent light bulbs glow.

20. You would expect to see a small dot of light because focused laser light does not spread out very much over long distances.

INTERPRETING GRAPHICS

21. a. convex lens; a virtual image
    b. concave mirror; a real image
    c. convex mirror; a virtual image

Concept Mapping Transparency 23

Blackline masters of this Chapter Review can be found in the **Study Guide.**

NOW WHAT DO YOU THINK?

1. Accept all reasonable answers. Possible answers include incandescent light, fluorescent light, neon light, and vapor light.
2. Mirrors and lenses form images by focusing light or by making it appear that light is focused.
3. Light is refracted as it passes through the cornea and enters the eye through the pupil. The size of the pupil is controlled by the iris. The lens of the eye focuses light on the retina. Light is detected by the rods and cones in the retina. Nerves attached to the rods and cones carry information to the brain, where an image is formed.

Chapter 23 • Chapter Review   **617**

SCIENCE, TECHNOLOGY, AND SOCIETY
Traffic Lights

Background
Traffic lights are crucial to modern transportation because in most situations they are far more effective at regulating traffic than other methods of traffic control. And although color-blind drivers cannot distinguish the color of each light, they can respond to the signal by memorizing the position of each color.

In addition to the traffic light, Morgan also invented a woman's hat fastener, a friction-drive clutch, and a safety hood—a gas mask—that protected the wearer from dangerous airborne materials.

Morgan's safety hood was tested in 1916 when an explosion in a Cleveland tunnel left 32 men trapped amid smoke and toxic gases. Morgan and his brother heard of the disaster, raced to the scene, donned their gas masks, and went into the tunnel. Although not all of the men survived, Morgan and his brother retrieved every single man from the tunnel. For his actions, Morgan received a medal from a group of Cleveland citizens as well as an award from the International Association of Fire Engineers.

Science, Technology, and Society
Traffic Lights

One day in the 1920s, an automobile collided with a horse and carriage. The riders were thrown from their carriage, the driver of the car was knocked unconscious, and the horse was fatally injured. A man named Garrett Morgan (1877–1963) witnessed this scene, and the accident gave him an idea.

A Bright Idea
Morgan's idea was a signal that included signs to direct traffic at busy intersections. The signal could be seen from a distance and could be clearly understood.

Morgan patented the first traffic signal in 1923. His signal looked very different from those used today. Unlike the small, three-bulb signal boxes that now hang over most busy intersections, the early versions were T-shaped, with the words *stop* and *go* printed on them.

Morgan's traffic signal was operated by a preset timing system. An electric motor turned a system of gears that operated a timing dial. As the timing dial rotated, it turned the switches on and off.

Morgan's invention was an immediate success, and he sold the patent to General Electric Corporation for $40,000—quite a large sum in those days. Since then, later versions of Morgan's traffic signal have been the mainstay of urban traffic control.

Light Technology
The technology of traffic lights continues to improve. For example, in some newer models the timing can be changed, depending on the traffic needs for a particular time of day. Some models have sensors installed in the street to monitor traffic flow. In other models, sensors can be triggered from inside an ambulance so that the light automatically turns green, allowing the ambulance to pass.

More About Morgan
Garrett Morgan, the son of former slaves, was born in Paris, Kentucky. He was one of 11 children, and his formal education ended at the sixth grade. At age 14, with no money and few skills, Morgan left home to work in Cincinnati, Ohio. He soon moved to Cleveland and quickly taught himself enough about sewing machines to get a job repairing them. Morgan saw how important the rest of his education was, so he taught himself and he hired tutors to help him complete his education. By 1907, Morgan opened his own sewing-machine repair shop. He was on his way!

Not only was Morgan an inventor, he was a hero. Gas masks that Morgan invented in 1912 were used in WWI to protect soldiers from chlorine gas fumes. Morgan himself, wearing one of his masks, later helped save several men trapped in a tunnel after a gas explosion.

Think About It
▶ Traffic control is not the only system in which light is used as a signal. What are some other systems that do so, and what makes light so useful for communication?

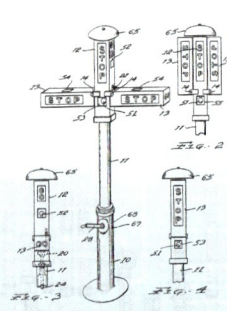

▲ *Morgan's patent for the first traffic light*

Answer to Think About It
Other systems that use light for communication include Morse code (such as when ships communicate with flashing lights), spotlights, lighthouses, crosswalk signals, and advertisements. In addition, aisles in theaters and airplanes are often equipped with lights to guide foot traffic. Light is a good method of communication because it is not affected by noise, it works well in all lighting conditions, and it is fairly inexpensive.

EYE ON THE ENVIRONMENT

Light Pollution

At night, large cities are often visible from far away. Soft light from windows outlines buildings. Bright lights from stadiums and parking lots shine like beacons. Scattered house lights twinkle like jewels. The sight is stunning!

Unfortunately, astronomers consider all these lights a form of pollution. Around the world, light pollution is reducing astronomers' ability to see beyond our atmosphere.

Sky Glow

Twenty years ago, stars were very visible above even large cities. The stars are still there, but now they are obscured by city lights. This glow, called sky glow, is created when light reflects off dust and other particles suspended in the atmosphere. Sky glow affects the entire atmosphere to some degree. Today, even remote locations around the globe are affected by light pollution.

The majority of light pollution comes from outdoor lights such as headlights, street lights, porch lights, and bright parking-lot and stadium lights. Other sources include forest fires and gas burn-offs in oil fields. Air pollution makes the situation worse, adding more particles to the air so that reflection is even greater.

A Light of Hope

Unlike other kinds of pollution, light pollution has some simple solutions. In fact, light pollution can be reduced in as little time as it takes to turn off a light! While turning off most city lights is impractical, several simple strategies can make a surprising difference. For example, using covered outdoor lights keeps the light angled downward, preventing most of the light from reaching particles in the sky. Also, using motion-sensitive lights and timed lights helps eliminate unnecessary light.

▲ *Lights from cities can be seen from space, as shown in this photograph taken from the space shuttle* Columbia. *Bright, uncovered lights (inset) create a glowing haze in the night sky above most cities in the United States.*

Many of these strategies also save money by saving energy.

Astronomers hope that public awareness will help improve the visibility of the night sky in and around major cities. Some cities, including Boston and Tucson, have already made some progress in reducing light pollution. Scientists have projected that if left unchecked, light pollution will affect every observatory on Earth within the next decade.

See for Yourself

▶ With your parents' permission, go outside at night and find a place where you can see the sky. Count the number of stars you can see. Now turn on a flashlight or porch light. How many stars can you see now? Compare your results. How much was your visibility reduced?

Contents

Safety First! 622

Chapter 1 The World of Physical Science
Exploring the Unseen 626
Off to the Races! 627
Measuring Liquid Volume 628
Coin Operated 629

Chapter 2 The Properties of Matter
Volumania! 630
Determining Density 632
Layering Liquids 633
White Before Your Eyes 634

Chapter 3 States of Matter
Full of Hot Air! 636
Can Crusher 637
A Hot and Cool Lab 638

Chapter 4
Elements, Compounds, and Mixtures
Flame Tests 640
A Sugar Cube Race! 642
Making Butter 643
Unpolluting Water 644

Chapter 5 Matter in Motion
Built for Speed 646
Detecting Acceleration 647
Science Friction 650
Relating Mass and Weight 651

Chapter 6 Forces in Motion
A Marshmallow Catapult 652
Blast Off! 653
Inertia-Rama! 654
Quite a Reaction 656

Chapter 7 Forces in Fluids
Fluids, Force, and Floating 658
Density Diver 660
Taking Flight 661

Chapter 8 Work and Machines
A Powerful Workout 662
Inclined to Move 664
Building Machines 665
Wheeling and Dealing 666

Chapter 9 Energy and Energy Resources
Finding Energy 668
Energy of a Pendulum 670
Eggstremely Fragile 671

Chapter 10 Heat and Heat Technology
Feel the Heat 672
Save the Cube! 674
Counting Calories 675

Chapter 11 Introduction to Atoms
Made to Order 676

Chapter 12 The Periodic Table
Create a Periodic Table 678

Chapter 13 Chemical Bonding
Covalent Marshmallows 680

Chapter 14 Chemical Reactions
Finding a Balance 682
Cata-what? Catalyst! 683
Putting Elements Together 684
Speed Control 686

Chapter 15 Chemical Compounds
Cabbage Patch Indicators 688
Making Salt 690

Chapter 16 Atomic Energy
Domino Chain Reactions 692

Chapter 17 Introduction to Electricity
Stop the Static Electricity! 694
Potato Power 695
Circuitry 101 696

Chapter 18 Electromagnetism
Magnetic Mystery 698
Electricity from Magnetism 699
Build a DC Motor 700

Chapter 19 Electronic Technology
Tune In! 702

Chapter 20 The Energy of Waves
Wave Energy and Speed 706
Wave Speed, Frequency, and Wavelength . . 708

Chapter 21 The Nature of Sound
Easy Listening 710
The Speed of Sound 712
Tuneful Tube 713
The Energy of Sound 714

Chapter 22 The Nature of Light
What Color of Light Is Best
  for Green Plants? 716
Which Color Is Hottest? 717
Mixing Colors 718

Chapter 23 Light and Our World
Mirror Images 720
Images from Convex Lenses 722

LabBook **621**

Exploring, inventing, and investigating are essential to the study of science. However, these activities can also be dangerous. To make sure that your experiments and explorations are safe, you must be aware of a variety of safety guidelines.

You have probably heard of the saying, "It is better to be safe than sorry." This is particularly true in a science classroom where experiments and explorations are being performed. Being uninformed and careless can result in serious injuries. Don't take chances with your own safety or with anyone else's.

Following are important guidelines for staying safe in the science classroom. Your teacher may also have safety guidelines and tips that are specific to your classroom and laboratory. Take the time to be safe.

Safety Rules!

Start Out Right

Always get your teacher's permission before attempting any laboratory exploration. Read the procedures carefully, and pay particular attention to safety information and caution statements. If you are unsure about what a safety symbol means, look it up or ask your teacher. You cannot be too careful when it comes to safety. If an accident does occur, inform your teacher immediately, regardless of how minor you think the accident is.

Safety Symbols

All of the experiments and investigations in this book and their related worksheets include important safety symbols to alert you to particular safety concerns. Become familiar with these symbols so that when you see them, you will know what they mean and what to do. It is important that you read this entire safety section to learn about specific dangers in the laboratory.

Eye protection · Clothing protection · Hand safety
Heating safety · Electric safety · Chemical safety
Animal safety · Sharp object · Plant safety

If you are instructed to note the odor of a substance, wave the fumes toward your nose with your hand. Never put your nose close to the source.

Eye Safety

Wear safety goggles when working around chemicals, acids, bases, or any type of flame or heating device. Wear safety goggles any time there is even the slightest chance that harm could come to your eyes. If any substance gets into your eyes, notify your teacher immediately, and flush your eyes with running water for at least 15 minutes. Treat any unknown chemical as if it were a dangerous chemical. Never look directly into the sun. Doing so could cause permanent blindness.

Avoid wearing contact lenses in a laboratory situation. Even if you are wearing safety goggles, chemicals can get between the contact lenses and your eyes. If your doctor requires that you wear contact lenses instead of glasses, wear eye-cup safety goggles in the lab.

Safety Equipment

Know the locations of the nearest fire alarms and any other safety equipment, such as fire blankets and eyewash fountains, as identified by your teacher, and know the procedures for using them.

Be extra careful when using any glassware. When adding a heavy object to a graduated cylinder, tilt the cylinder so the object slides slowly to the bottom.

Neatness

Keep your work area free of all unnecessary books and papers. Tie back long hair, and secure loose sleeves or other loose articles of clothing, such as ties and bows. Remove dangling jewelry. Don't wear open-toed shoes or sandals in the laboratory. Never eat, drink, or apply cosmetics in a laboratory setting. Food, drink, and cosmetics can easily become contaminated with dangerous materials.

Certain hair products (such as aerosol hair spray) are flammable and should not be worn while working near an open flame. Avoid wearing hair spray or hair gel on lab days.

Sharp/Pointed Objects

Use knives and other sharp instruments with extreme care. Never cut objects while holding them in your hands. Place objects on a suitable work surface for cutting.

Safety First! LabBook **623**

Heat

Wear safety goggles when using a heating device or a flame. Whenever possible, use an electric hot plate as a heat source instead of an open flame. When heating materials in a test tube, always angle the test tube away from yourself and others. In order to avoid burns, wear heat-resistant gloves whenever instructed to do so.

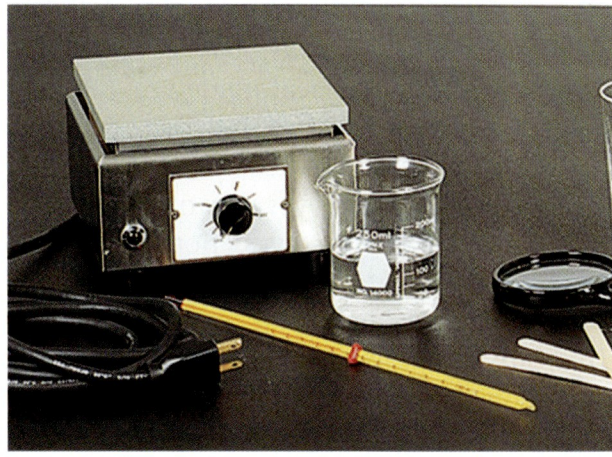

Electricity

Be careful with electrical cords. When using a microscope with a lamp, do not place the cord where it could trip someone. Do not let cords hang over a table edge in a way that could cause equipment to fall if the cord is accidentally pulled. Do not use equipment with damaged cords. Be sure your hands are dry and that the electrical equipment is in the "off" position before plugging it in. Turn off and unplug electrical equipment when you are finished.

Chemicals

Wear safety goggles when handling any potentially dangerous chemicals, acids, or bases. If a chemical is unknown, handle it as you would a dangerous chemical. Wear an apron and safety gloves when working with acids or bases or whenever you are told to do so. If a spill gets on your skin or clothing, rinse it off immediately with water for at least 5 minutes while calling to your teacher.

Never mix chemicals unless your teacher tells you to do so. Never taste, touch, or smell chemicals unless you are specifically directed to do so. Before working with a flammable liquid or gas, check for the presence of any source of flame, spark, or heat.

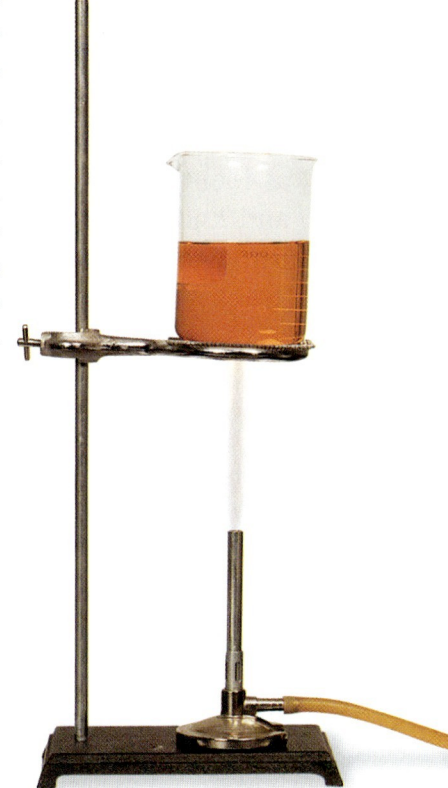

624 LabBook

Animal Safety

Always obtain your teacher's permission before bringing any animal into the school building. Handle animals only as your teacher directs. Always treat animals carefully and with respect. Wash your hands thoroughly after handling any animal.

Plant Safety

Do not eat any part of a plant or plant seed used in the laboratory. Wash hands thoroughly after handling any part of a plant. When in nature, do not pick any wild plants unless your teacher instructs you to do so.

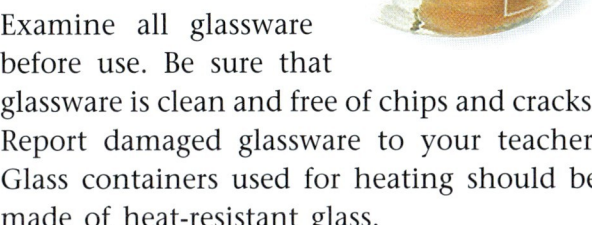

Glassware

Examine all glassware before use. Be sure that glassware is clean and free of chips and cracks. Report damaged glassware to your teacher. Glass containers used for heating should be made of heat-resistant glass.

Exploring the Unseen
Teacher's Notes

Time Required
One 45-minute class period

Lab Ratings

EASY → HARD

- TEACHER PREP 🧪🧪🧪
- STUDENT SET-UP 🧪
- CONCEPT LEVEL 🧪🧪
- CLEAN UP 🧪

Prepare boxes ahead of time. There should be one box for each group of 2–4 students. The box may be a shoe box, a pencil box, or a cigar box. Inside, create a division (such as blocking one corner of the box) out of cardboard. The divisions you create should not be too complex but should include some differences in complexity to allow for different levels of student ability. Tape the division in place. Put a marble in the box, and secure the box with tape or with rubber bands.

 Datasheets for LabBook
Datasheet 1

Larry Tackett
Andrew Jackson Middle School
Cross Lanes, West Virginia

Using Scientific Methods

Exploring the Unseen

Your teacher will give you a box in which a special divider has been created. Your task is to describe this divider as precisely as possible—without opening the box! Your only aid is a marble that is also inside the box. This task will allow you to demonstrate your understanding of the scientific method. Good luck!

Materials
- a sealed mystery box

Ask a Question

1. In your ScienceLog, record the question that you are trying to answer by doing this experiment. (Hint: Read the introductory paragraph again if you are not sure what your task is.)

Form a Hypothesis

2. Before you begin the experiment, think about what's required. Do you think you will be able to easily determine the shape of the divider? What about its texture? its color? In your ScienceLog, write a hypothesis that states how much you think you will be able to determine about the divider during the experiment. (Remember, you can't open the box!)

Test the Hypothesis

3. Using all the methods you can think of (except opening the box), test your hypothesis. Make careful notes about your testing and observations in your ScienceLog.

Analyze the Results

4. What characteristics of the divider were you able to identify? Draw or write your best description of the interior of the box.

5. Do your observations support your hypothesis? Explain. If your results do not support your hypothesis, write a new hypothesis and test it.

6. With your teacher's permission, open the box and look inside. Record your observations in your ScienceLog.

Communicate Results

7. Write a paragraph summarizing your experiment. Be sure to include your methods, whether your results supported your hypothesis, and how you could improve your methods.

Answers

1. Questions should relate to identifying the shape of the divider.
2. Answers will vary. Students may hypothesize that they cannot easily determine very much about the divider without looking inside.
4. Accept all reasonable responses. Characteristics may include the shape, size, and texture of the divider.
5. Accept all reasonable responses. Students may find that they were able to determine more about the divider than they first anticipated.
7. Answers will vary. Accept all reasonable responses.

Off to the Races!

Scientists often use models—representations of objects or systems. Physical models, such as a model airplane, are generally a different size than the objects they represent. In this lab you will build a model car, test its design, and then try to improve the design.

Procedure

1. Using the materials listed, design and build a car that will carry the load (the eraser or block of wood) down the ramp as quickly as possible. Your car must be no wider than 8 cm, it must have room to carry the load, and it must roll.

2. As you test your design, do not be afraid to rebuild or redesign your car. Improving your methods is an important part of scientific progress.

3. When you have a design that works well, measure the time required for your car to roll down the ramp. Record this time in your ScienceLog. Repeat this step several times.

4. Try to improve your model. Find one thing that you can change to make your model car roll faster down the ramp. In your ScienceLog, write a description of the change.

5. Repeat step 3.

Analysis

6. Why is it important to have room in the model car for the eraser or wood block? (Hint: Think about the function of a real car.)

7. Before you built the model car, you created a design for it. Do you think this design is also a model? Explain.

8. Based on your observations in this lab, list three reasons why it is helpful for automobile designers to build and test small model cars rather than immediately building a full-size car.

9. In this lab you built a model that was smaller than the object it represented. Some models are larger than the objects they represent. List three examples of larger models that are used to represent objects. Why is it helpful to use a larger model in these cases?

Materials

- 2 sheets of typing paper
- glue
- 16 cm clothes-hanger wire
- pliers or wire cutters
- metric ruler
- rubber eraser or wooden block
- ramp (board and textbooks)
- stopwatch

Terry Rakes
Elmwood Junior High
Rogers, Arkansas

Datasheets for LabBook
Datasheet 2

Science Skills Worksheet 10
"Doing a Lab Write-up"

Off to the Races!
Teacher's Notes

Time Required
One or two 45-minute class periods

Lab Ratings

TEACHER PREP — easy
STUDENT SET-UP — medium
CONCEPT LEVEL — medium
CLEAN UP — easy

MATERIALS
The materials listed for this lab are for each group of 2–3 students.

Safety Caution
Remind students to review all safety cautions and icons before beginning this lab activity.

Lab Notes
Encourage students to share design hints, but make sure there are a number of different designs created.

Answers

6. A real car should have room inside for passengers.

7. The design is a model because it represents the car to be built.

8. Accept any reasonable answers. Sample answer: It is faster, cheaper, and easier to make changes to a smaller model.

9. Accept all reasonable answers. Some examples include atomic models, cell diagrams, and models of computer circuits. Large models can be helpful when objects are too small to observe directly or easily.

Measuring Liquid Volume
Teacher's Notes

Time Required
One 45-minute class period

Lab Ratings

TEACHER PREP 🧪🧪
STUDENT SET-UP 🧪
CONCEPT LEVEL 🧪🧪
CLEAN UP 🧪🧪

MATERIALS
The materials listed for this lab are for each group of 2–4 students. Each lab group should have one 30 mL beaker each of red, yellow, and blue water. The large test tubes must have a capacity of at least 14 mL.

Safety Caution
Remind students to review all safety cautions and icons before beginning this lab activity.

Preparation Notes
On the board, set up a chart with one row for each group and six columns, one for each test tube.

Answers
11. Groups may have different results because of measuring inaccuracy. Have students discuss how these inaccuracies might have resulted. Remind students that the purpose of this lab is to practice a skill, not necessarily to get the same results.

12. The graduated cylinder should not be filled to the top because the scale does not go all the way to the top, so accurate measurements would not be possible.

Measuring Liquid Volume

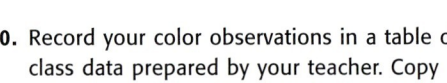

In this lab you will use a graduated cylinder to measure and transfer precise amounts of liquids. Remember, in order to accurately measure liquids in a graduated cylinder, you should read the level at the bottom of the meniscus, the curved surface of the liquid.

Materials
- masking tape
- marker
- 6 large test tubes
- test-tube rack
- 10 mL graduated cylinder
- 3 beakers filled with colored liquid
- small funnel

Procedure

1. Using the masking tape and marker, label the test tubes A, B, C, D, E, and F. Place them in the test-tube rack. Be careful not to confuse the test tubes.

2. Using the 10 mL graduated cylinder and the funnel, pour 14 mL of the red liquid into test tube A. (To do this, first pour 10 mL of the liquid into the test tube and then add 4 mL of liquid.)

3. Rinse the graduated cylinder and funnel between uses.

4. Measure 13 mL of the yellow liquid, and pour it into test tube C. Then measure 13 mL of the blue liquid, and pour it into test tube E.

5. Transfer 4 mL of liquid from test tube C into test tube D. Transfer 7 mL of liquid from test tube E into test tube D.

6. Measure 4 mL of blue liquid from the beaker, and pour it into test tube F. Measure 7 mL of red liquid from the beaker, and pour it into test tube F.

7. Transfer 8 mL of liquid from test tube A into test tube B. Transfer 3 mL of liquid from test tube C into test tube B.

Collect Data

8. Make a data table in your ScienceLog, and record the color of the liquid in each test tube.

9. Use the graduated cylinder to measure the volume of liquid in each test tube, and record the volumes in your data table.

10. Record your color observations in a table of class data prepared by your teacher. Copy the completed table into your ScienceLog.

Analysis

11. Did all of the groups report the same colors? Explain why the colors were the same or different.

12. Why should you not fill the graduated cylinder to the very top?

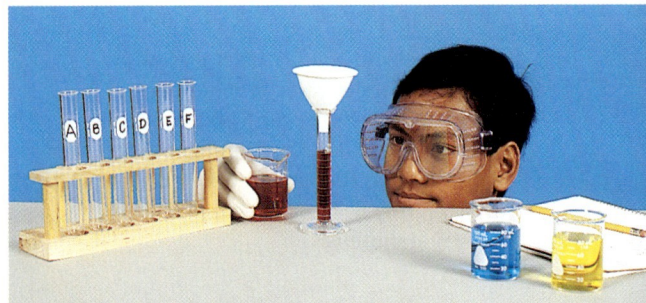

 Datasheets for LabBook
Datasheet 3

 Science Skills
Worksheet 15 "Measuring"

Norman Holcomb
Marion Elementary School
Maria Stein, Ohio

Coin Operated

All pennies are exactly the same, right? Probably not! After all, each penny was made in a certain year at a specific mint, and each has traveled a unique path to reach your classroom. But all pennies *are* similar. In this lab you will investigate differences and similarities among a group of pennies.

Procedure

1. Write the numbers 1 through 10 on a page in your ScienceLog, and place a penny next to each number.
2. Use the metric balance to find the mass of each penny to the nearest 0.1 g. Record each measurement in your ScienceLog.
3. On a table that your teacher will provide, make a mark in the correct column of the table for each penny you measured.
4. Separate your pennies into piles based on the class data. Place each pile on its own sheet of paper.
5. Measure and record the mass of each pile. Write the mass on the paper you are using to identify the pile.
6. Fill a graduated cylinder about halfway with water. Carefully measure the volume, and record it.
7. Carefully place the pennies from one pile in the graduated cylinder. Measure and record the new volume.
8. Carefully remove the pennies from the graduated cylinder, and dry them off.
9. Repeat steps 6 through 8 for each pile of pennies.

Analyze the Results

10. Determine the volume of the displaced water by subtracting the initial volume from the final volume. This amount is equal to the volume of the pennies. Record the volume of each pile of pennies.
11. Calculate the density of each pile. To do this, divide the total mass of the pennies by the volume of the pennies. Record the density in your ScienceLog.

Draw Conclusions

12. How is it possible for the pennies to have different densities?
13. What clues might allow you to separate the pennies into the same groups without experimentation? Explain.

Materials

- 10 pennies
- metric balance
- few sheets of paper
- 100 mL graduated cylinder
- water
- paper towels

Coin Operated
Teacher's Notes

Time Required
One 45-minute class period

Lab Ratings

TEACHER PREP 🧪🧪
STUDENT SET-UP 🧪
CONCEPT LEVEL 🧪🧪
CLEAN UP 🧪

MATERIALS
The materials listed for this lab are for each group of 2–4 students. Be sure each group has both pre-1982 and post-1982 pennies. (1982 was the year the U.S. Department of the Treasury changed the penny's composition from copper to zinc with copper coating.)

Safety Caution
Remind students to review all safety cautions and icons before beginning this lab activity.

Procedure Note
3. Create the table (step 3) with one row for each group and 11 columns in 0.1 g increments. A twelfth column should be added for density. Record the number of pennies in the appropriate columns.

Answers

4. Students should have two piles of pennies based on the mass of the pennies.
11. The density of the copper pennies is approximately 8.85 g/cm³; of the zinc-and-copper pennies, 7.14 g/cm³.
12. The pennies can have different densities if they are made with different materials.
13. Pennies can be sorted by their dates. (Encourage students to examine the pennies closely for clues and to compare their piles with the piles of other students.)

 **Datasheets for LabBook** Datasheet 4

Paul Boyle
Perry Heights Middle School
Evansville, Indiana

Chapter 1 • LabBook **629**

Volumania!
Teacher's Notes

Time Required
One 45-minute class period

Lab Ratings

TEACHER PREP 🧪
STUDENT SET-UP 🧪🧪
CONCEPT LEVEL 🧪🧪
CLEAN UP 🧪

Part A: Finding the Volume of Small Objects

MATERIALS

The materials listed are for each group of 2–3 students. The objects used must fit in the graduated cylinders but be large enough to make a measurable change in volume. Rock or mineral samples, hardware (such as bolts or screws), and fishing weights work well.

Safety Caution

To avoid breaking glass graduated cylinders, caution students to tilt the graduated cylinder so objects can slide in gently. Remind students to read the volume when the meniscus is at eye level. Caution students to wear goggles during this lab.

Answers

6. The units of milliliters should be changed to cubic centimeters because you are measuring the volume of a solid object.

7. No; sometimes a heavier object will have a smaller volume than a lighter object because the matter is more tightly packed.

Volumania!

You have learned how to measure the volume of a solid object that has square or rectangular sides. But there are lots of objects in the world that have irregular shapes. In this lab activity, you'll learn some ways to find the volume of objects that have irregular shapes.

Part A: Finding the Volume of Small Objects

Procedure

1. Fill a graduated cylinder half full with water. Read the volume of the water, and record it in your ScienceLog. Be sure to look at the surface of the water at eye level and to read the volume at the bottom of the meniscus, as shown below.

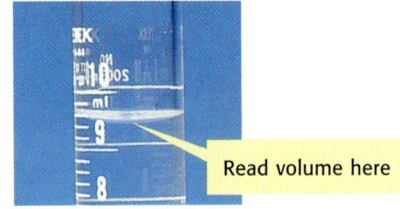
Read volume here

2. Carefully slide one of the objects into the tilted graduated cylinder, as shown below.

3. Read the new volume, and record it in your ScienceLog.

4. Subtract the old volume from the new volume. The resulting amount is equal to the volume of the solid object.

5. Use the same method to find the volume of the other objects. Record your results in your ScienceLog.

Analysis

6. What changes do you have to make to the volumes you determine in order to express them correctly?

7. Do the heaviest objects always have the largest volumes? Why or why not?

Materials

Part A
- graduated cylinder
- water
- various small objects supplied by your teacher

Part B
- bottom half of a 2 L plastic bottle or similar container
- water
- aluminum pie pan
- paper towels
- funnel
- graduated cylinder

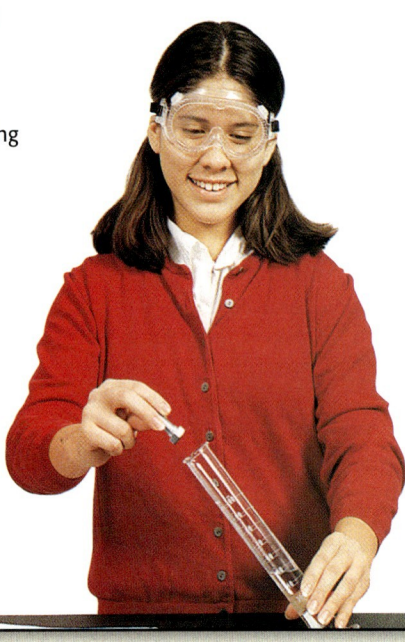

 Datasheets for LabBook Datasheet 5

Alyson Mike
Radley Middle School
East Helena, Montana

Part B: Finding the Volume of Your Hand

Procedure

8. Completely fill the container with water. Put the container in the center of the pie pan. Be sure not to spill any of the water into the pie pan.

9. Make a fist, and put your hand into the container up to your wrist.

10. Remove your hand, and let the excess water drip into the container, not the pie pan. Dry your hand with a paper towel.

11. Use the funnel to pour the overflow water into the graduated cylinder. Measure the volume. This is the volume of your hand. Record the volume in your ScienceLog. (Remember to use the correct unit of volume for a solid object.)

12. Repeat this procedure with your other hand.

Analysis

13. Was the volume the same for both of your hands? If not, were you surprised? What might account for a person's hands having different volumes?

14. Would it have made a difference if you had placed your open hand into the container instead of your fist? Explain your reasoning.

15. Compare the volume of your right hand with the volume of your classmates' right hands. Create a class graph of right-hand volumes. What is the average right-hand volume for your class?

Going Further

- Design an experiment to determine the volume of a person's body. In your plans, be sure to include the materials needed for the experiment and the procedures that must be followed. Include a sketch that shows how your materials and methods would be used in this experiment.

- Using an encyclopedia, the Internet, or other reference materials, find out how the volumes of very large samples of matter—such as an entire planet—are determined.

Science Skills Worksheet 18 "Finding Useful Sources"

Science Skills Worksheet 19 "Researching on the Web"

Part B: Finding the Volume of Your Hand

MATERIALS

Plastic containers from whipped toppings and the like can also be used. Containers should be deep enough so students' fists can be submerged. Remind students that their container must be completely filled with water so that it overflows as their hand enters. The pie pan should be dry at the start. When students remove their hand from the container, they should allow the water cupped in their hand to drip back into the container and not into the pie pan. This water was not displaced and should not be measured.

Answers

13. Answers will vary. Often the preferred hand will be slightly larger due to greater muscle development.

14. It would not make a difference; a hand's volume remains the same regardless of its shape.

15. Answers will vary by class. Check for correct graphing technique and interpretation.

Going Further

- Designs should center on finding the volume of the body through water displacement. The equipment designed should be large enough to perform the experiment and allow for overflow.

- Accept all reasonable answers and findings.

Determining Density
Teacher's Notes

Time Required

One 45-minute class period

Lab Ratings

- TEACHER PREP 🧪
- STUDENT SET-UP 🧪
- CONCEPT LEVEL 🧪🧪
- CLEAN UP 🧪

Safety Caution

Caution students to tilt the graduated cylinder so marbles can slide in gently.

Answers

8. The total mass increases. The volume of the marbles increases. The density of the marbles remains the same.

9. The graph is a straight line (see graph below).

10. No; the density is independent of the amount of substance. The density is the same for one marble as it is for several marbles.

Going Further

To calculate the slope of the graph, pick two points on the line. The slope is the difference between the y-values of the points divided by the difference between the x-values of the points. The slope of the graph should be equal to the density of the marbles because the graph shows mass versus volume, which means the slope is mass divided by volume—in other words, density.

Datasheets for LabBook
Datasheet 6

632 Chapter 2 • LabBook

Determining Density

The density of an object is its mass divided by its volume. But how does the density of a small amount of a substance relate to the density of a larger amount of the same substance? In this lab, you will calculate the density of one marble and of a group of marbles. Then you will confirm the relationship between the mass and volume of a substance.

Collect Data

1. Copy the table below in your ScienceLog. Include one row for each marble.

Mass of marble, g	Total mass of marbles, g	Total volume, mL	Volume of marbles, mL (total volume minus 50.0 mL)	Density of marbles, g/mL (total mass of marbles divided by volume of marbles)
DO NOT WRITE IN BOOK			DO NOT WRITE IN BOOK	

2. Fill the graduated cylinder with 50.0 mL of water. If you put in too much water, twist one of the paper towels and use its end to absorb excess water.

3. Measure the mass of a marble as accurately as you can (to at least one-tenth of a gram). Record the marble's mass in the table.

4. Carefully drop the marble in the tilted cylinder, and measure the total volume. Record the volume in the third column.

5. Measure and record the mass of another marble. Add the masses of the marbles together, and record this value in the second column of the table.

6. Carefully drop the second marble in the graduated cylinder. Complete the row of information in the table.

7. Repeat steps 5 and 6, adding one marble at a time. Stop when you run out of marbles, the water no longer completely covers the marbles, or the graduated cylinder is full.

Analyze the Results

8. Examine the data in your table. As the number of marbles increases, what happens to the total mass of the marbles? What happens to the volume of the marbles? What happens to the density of the marbles?

9. Graph the total mass of the marbles (y-axis) versus the volume of the marbles (x-axis). Is the graph a straight line or a curved line?

Draw Conclusions

10. Does the density of a substance depend on the amount of substance present? Explain how your results support your answer.

Going Further

Calculate the slope of the graph. How does the slope compare with the values in the column titled "Density of marbles"? Explain.

SKILL BUILDER

Materials

- 100 mL graduated cylinder
- water
- paper towels
- 8 to 10 glass marbles
- metric balance
- graph paper

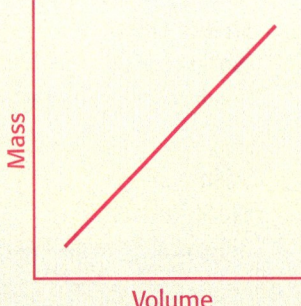

Alyson Mike
Radley Middle School
East Helena, Montana

Using Scientific Methods

Layering Liquids

You have learned that liquids form layers according to their densities. In this lab, you'll discover whether it matters in which order you add the liquids.

Make a Prediction

1. Does the order in which you add liquids of different densities to a container affect the order of the layers formed by those liquids?

Conduct an Experiment

2. Using the graduated cylinders, add 10 mL of each liquid to the clear container. Remember to read the volume at the bottom of the meniscus, as shown below. In your ScienceLog, record the order in which you added the liquids.

3. Observe the liquids in the container. In your ScienceLog, sketch what you see. Be sure to label the layers and the colors.

4. Add 10 mL more of liquid C. Observe what happens, and write your observations in your ScienceLog.

5. Add 20 mL more of liquid A. Observe what happens, and write your observations in your ScienceLog.

Analyze Your Results

6. Which of the liquids has the greatest density? Which has the least density? How can you tell?

7. Did the layers change position when you added more of liquid C? Explain your answer.

8. Did the layers change position when you added more of liquid A? Explain your answer.

Materials

- liquid A
- liquid B
- liquid C
- beaker or other small, clear container
- 10 mL graduated cylinders (3)
- 3 funnels

Communicate Your Results

9. Find out in what order your classmates added the liquids to the container. Compare your results with those of a classmate who added the liquids in a different order. Were your results different? In your ScienceLog, explain why or why not.

Draw Conclusions

10. Based on your results, evaluate your prediction from step 1.

Layering Liquids
Teacher's Notes

Time Required
One 45-minute class period

Lab Ratings

EASY ──────────▶ HARD

- **TEACHER PREP** 🧪🧪🧪
- **STUDENT SET-UP** 🧪
- **CONCEPT LEVEL** 🧪🧪
- **CLEAN UP** 🧪🧪

Preparation Notes
Liquid A is red-colored water, liquid B is vegetable oil, and liquid C is dark corn syrup.

Disposal Information
To keep the oil out of the drains, have students empty their containers into several disposable containers. These can be capped, refrigerated, and thrown in the trash. It might be interesting to let these waste bottles stand overnight to see if the layers are visible the following day.

Datasheets for LabBook
Datasheet 7

Science Skills Worksheet 12
"Working with Hypotheses"

Alyson Mike
Radley Middle School
East Helena, Montana

Answers

1. Accept all reasonable predictions.

6. Liquid C has the greatest density. Liquid B has the least density. The liquids form layers with the least dense on top and the most dense on bottom.

7. The position of the layers did not change. Adding more of liquid C does not change its density, so its position stays the same.

8. The position of the layers did not change. Adding more of liquid A does not change its density, so its position stays the same.

9. All results should be identical. Liquid B is the top layer, liquid A is the middle layer, and liquid C is the bottom layer.

10. Answers will vary, depending on the original prediction. The order in which the liquids are added does not affect the order of the layers formed.

White Before Your Eyes
Teacher's Notes

Time Required

One or two 45-minute class periods

Lab Ratings

TEACHER PREP 🧪🧪
STUDENT SET-UP 🧪
CONCEPT LEVEL 🧪🧪
CLEAN UP 🧪🧪

MATERIALS

Use an iodine solution that contains no more than 1.0% iodine in water. Instead of using an egg carton, you may wish to use a 24-well spot plate or test tubes. The containers used for the solids can be baby food jars or even plastic film canisters. Canisters may be available from a local film processing store. If you do not have small medicine-dropper bottles, you can use small soft-drink bottles for liquids and solutions. A small test tube taped to the bottle makes a great holder for a dropper or pipette and decreases the chance of contamination. A drinking straw cut in half at an angle works well as a spatula; the pointed end is a great scoop, and its large size makes it easy to handle.

Safety Caution

When iodine is being used, be certain that a functioning eye-wash is available in case of a splash. Caution students that iodine can stain skin and clothes. Students should wash their face and hands when finished. Clean up any spills immediately to avoid slips and falls.

White Before Your Eyes

You have learned how to describe matter based on its physical and chemical properties. You have also learned some clues that can help you determine whether a change in matter is a physical change or a chemical change. In this lab, you'll use what you have learned to describe four substances based on their properties and the changes they undergo.

Procedure

1. Copy Table 1 and Table 2, shown on the next page, into your ScienceLog. Be sure to leave plenty of room in each box to write down your observations.

2. Use a spatula to place a small amount (just enough to cover the bottom of the cup) of baking powder into three cups of your egg carton. Look closely at the baking powder, and record observations of its color, texture, etc., in the column of Table 1 titled "Unmixed."

3. Use an eyedropper to add 60 drops of water to the baking powder in the first cup, as shown below. Stir with the stirring rod. Record your observations in Table 1 in the column titled "Mixed with water." Clean your stirring rod.

4. Use a clean dropper to add 20 drops of vinegar to the second cup of baking powder. Stir. Record your observations in the column titled "Mixed with vinegar." Clean your stirring rod.

Materials

- 4 spatulas
- baking powder
- plastic-foam egg carton
- 3 eyedroppers
- water
- stirring rod
- vinegar
- iodine solution
- baking soda
- cornstarch
- sugar

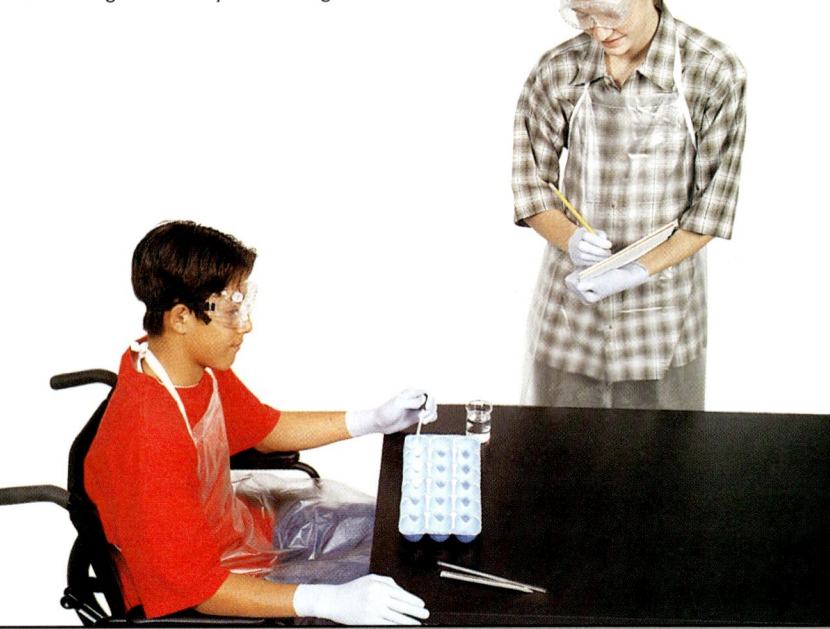

Datasheets for LabBook
Datasheet 8

Joseph Price
H. M. Browne Junior High
Washington, D.C.

5. Use a clean dropper to add five drops of iodine solution to the third cup of baking powder. Stir. Record your observations in the column in Table 1 titled "Mixed with iodine solution." Clean your stirring rod.

   Caution: Be careful when using iodine. Iodine will stain your skin and clothes.

6. Repeat steps 2–5 for each of the other substances. Use a clean spatula for each substance.

Analysis

7. In Table 2, write the type of change you observed, and state the property that the change demonstrates.

8. What clues did you use to identify when a chemical change happened?

Table 1 Observations

Substance	Unmixed	Mixed with water	Mixed with vinegar	Mixed with iodine solution
Baking powder				
Baking soda				
Cornstarch				
Sugar				

Table 2 Changes and Properties

Substance	Mixed with water		Mixed with vinegar		Mixed with iodine solution	
	Change	Property	Change	Property	Change	Property
Baking powder						
Baking soda						
Cornstarch						
Sugar						

LabBook

Answers

7. See the table at the bottom of the page.
8. color change, fizzing

Lab Notes

Remind students that vinegar is an acid.

Disposal Information

Dispose of any unreacted iodine solution by combining all student solutions. Decolorize if necessary by adding 1.0 M $Na_2S_2O_3$ while stirring until the dark color disappears. Dilute the mixture with at least 10 times its volume of water. Then pour down the drain.

Science Skills Worksheet 2 "Using Your Senses"

Teacher's Note

Although Table 2 states that baking powder reacts with water, baking powder is actually not reactive with water. Baking powder can contain baking soda (a base), a weak acid, and a starch. The baking soda and the weak acid in baking powder will react with each other when the baking powder is dissolved in water. This reaction produces the bubbles that students observe in this experiment.

Answer

7.

Substance	Mixed with water		Mixed (vinegar)		Mixed (iodine solution)	
	Change	Property	Change	Property	Change	Property
Baking powder	chemical	reactivity with water	chemical	reactivity with acid	physical	solubility
Baking soda	physical	solubility	chemical	reactivity with acid	physical	solubility
Cornstarch	physical	solubility	physical	solubility	chemical	reactivity with iodine
Sugar	physical	solubility	physical	solubility	physical	solubility

Full of Hot Air!
Teacher's Notes

Time Required
One 45-minute class period

Lab Ratings

TEACHER PREP
STUDENT SET-UP
CONCEPT LEVEL
CLEAN UP

Safety Caution
Remind students to review all safety cautions and icons before beginning this lab activity. Keep all power cords away from the beakers and pans of hot water. Be careful—hot plates may stay hot for a long time. Students should wear heat-resistant gloves when handling the hot beaker.

Answers

1. Accept all reasonable hypotheses.

9. When the balloon cooled, it contracted. When heated, it expanded. These observations confirm Charles's law.

10. Answers will vary, depending on the original hypothesis. Sample supported hypothesis: Increasing temperature increases the volume of a balloon, while decreasing temperature decreases the volume of a balloon.

11. As the temperature increased, volume increased and mass remained constant. Therefore the density decreased. Conversely, density increases when temperature decreases.

Using Scientific Methods

Full of Hot Air!

Why do hot-air balloons float gracefully above Earth, while balloons you blow up fall to the ground? The answer has to do with the density of the air inside the balloon. Density is mass per unit volume, and volume is affected by changes in temperature. In this experiment, you will investigate the relationship between the temperature of a gas and its volume. Then you will be able to determine how the temperature of a gas affects its density.

Form a Hypothesis

1. How does an increase or decrease in temperature affect the volume of a balloon? Write your hypothesis in your ScienceLog.

Test the Hypothesis

2. Fill an aluminum pan with water about 4 to 5 cm deep. Put the pan on the hot plate, and turn the hot plate on.

3. While the water is heating, fill the other pan 4 to 5 cm deep with ice water.

4. Blow up a balloon inside the 500 mL beaker, as shown. The balloon should fill the beaker but should not extend outside the beaker. Tie the balloon at its opening.

5. Place the beaker and balloon in the ice water. Observe what happens. Record your observations in your ScienceLog.

6. Remove the balloon and beaker from the ice water. Observe the balloon for several minutes. Record any changes.

12. When you heat the air, it expands and becomes less dense than the surrounding air. The balloon begins to float.

 Datasheets for LabBook
Datasheet 9

DISCOVERY LAB

Materials
- 2 aluminum pans
- water
- metric ruler
- hot plate
- ice water
- balloon
- 250 mL beaker
- heat-resistant gloves

7. Put on heat-resistant gloves. When the hot water begins to boil, put the beaker and balloon in the hot water. Observe the balloon for several minutes, and record your observations.

8. Turn off the hot plate. When the water has cooled, carefully pour it into a sink.

Analyze the Results

9. Summarize your observations of the balloon. Relate your observations to Charles's law.

10. Was your hypothesis for step 1 supported? If not, revise your hypothesis.

Draw Conclusions

11. Based on your observations, how is the density of a gas affected by an increase or decrease in temperature?

12. Explain in terms of density and Charles's law why heating the air allows a hot-air balloon to float.

Sharon L. Woolf
Langston Hughes Middle School
Reston, Virginia

Can Crusher

Condensation can occur when gas particles come near the surface of a liquid. The gas particles slow down because they are attracted to the liquid. This reduction in speed causes the gas particles to condense into a liquid. In this lab, you'll see that particles that have condensed into a liquid don't take up as much space and therefore don't exert as much pressure as they did in the gaseous state.

Materials

- water
- 2 empty aluminum cans
- heat-resistant gloves
- hot plate
- tongs
- 1 L beaker

Conduct an Experiment

1. Place just enough water in an aluminum can to slightly cover the bottom.
2. Put on heat-resistant gloves. Place the aluminum can on a hot plate turned to the highest temperature setting.
3. Heat the can until the water is boiling. Steam should be rising vigorously from the top of the can.
4. Using tongs, quickly pick up the can and place the top 2 cm of the can upside down in the 1 L beaker filled with room-temperature water.
5. Describe your observations in your ScienceLog.

Analyze the Results

6. The can was crushed because the atmospheric pressure outside the can became greater than the pressure inside the can. Explain what happened inside the can to cause this.

Draw Conclusions

7. Inside every popcorn kernel is a small amount of water. When you make popcorn, the water inside the kernels is heated until it becomes steam. Explain how the popping of the kernels is the opposite of what you saw in this lab. Be sure to address the effects of pressure in your explanation.

Going Further

Try the experiment again, but use ice water instead of room-temperature water. Explain your results in terms of the effects of temperature.

Lee Yassinski
Sun Valley Middle School
Sun Valley, California

Going Further

The can was crushed more quickly because the ice water made the steam condense more quickly. So the pressure inside the can decreased further.

Can Crusher
Teacher's Notes

Time Required
One 45-minute class period

Lab Ratings

- TEACHER PREP ▲
- STUDENT SET-UP ▲
- CONCEPT LEVEL ▲▲
- CLEAN UP ▲

Safety Caution

Remind students to review all safety cautions and icons before beginning this lab activity. To prevent spills, caution students to keep all power cords away from beakers and pans of hot water. Heat-resistant gloves may not be necessary if tongs are properly used.

Answers

6. The steam inside the can cooled and condensed. The volume of water (condensed steam) is smaller than the volume of the steam, so the pressure inside the can was reduced.

7. When the water inside the kernel becomes steam, it expands about 100 times. The pressure inside the kernel increases. The pressure outside is unchanged, so the pressure inside forces the kernel to "explode."

 Datasheets for LabBook
Datasheet 10

A Hot and Cool Lab
Teacher's Notes

Time Required
One or two 45-minute class periods

Lab Ratings

EASY → HARD

TEACHER PREP 🧪🧪🧪
STUDENT SET-UP 🧪🧪
CONCEPT LEVEL 🧪🧪🧪
CLEAN UP 🧪🧪

MATERIALS
The materials listed are for a group of 3–4 students.

Safety Cautions
Remind students to review all safety cautions and icons before beginning this lab activity. Hot plates should have flat metal surfaces and not metal coils. To prevent spills, caution students to keep all power cords away from the beakers and pans of hot water.

Answer
1. Accept all reasonable predictions.

C. John Graves
Monforton Middle School
Bozeman, Montana

A Hot and Cool Lab

When you add energy to a substance through heating, does the substance's temperature always go up? When you remove energy from a substance through cooling, does the substance's temperature always go down? In this lab you'll investigate these important questions with a very common substance—water.

Part A: Boiling Water

Make a Prediction
1. What happens to the temperature of boiling water when you continue to add energy through heating?

Procedure
2. Fill the beaker about one-third to one-half full with water.
3. Put on heat-resistant gloves. Turn on the hot plate, and put the beaker on the burner. Put the thermometer in the beaker. **Caution:** Be careful not to touch the burner.

Collect Data
4. In a table like the one below, record the temperature of the water every 30 seconds. Continue doing this until about one-fourth of the water boils away. Note the first temperature reading at which the water is steadily boiling.

Time (s)	30	60	90	120	150	180	210	etc.
Temperature (°C)				DO NOT WRITE IN BOOK				

5. Turn off the hot plate.
6. While the beaker is cooling, make a graph of temperature (y-axis) versus time (x-axis). Draw an arrow pointing to the first temperature at which the water was steadily boiling.
7. After you finish the graph, use heat-resistant gloves to pick up the beaker. Pour the warm water out, and rinse the warm beaker with cool water. **Caution:** Even after cooling, the beaker is still too warm to handle without gloves.

Materials

Part A
- 250 or 400 mL beaker
- water
- heat-resistant gloves
- hot plate
- thermometer
- stopwatch
- graph paper

Part B
- 100 mL graduated cylinder
- water
- large coffee can
- crushed ice
- rock salt
- thermometer
- wire-loop stirring device
- stopwatch
- graph paper

638

Preparation Notes
To construct the wire-loop stirring device, make a loop slightly smaller than the inside of the graduated cylinder at one end of a straightened 25 cm piece of copper wire. The loop should easily fit into the graduated cylinder with the thermometer in place. Angle the loop so that it is perpendicular to the rest of the wire.

At the other end of the wire, make a handle that extends in the opposite direction of the loop. Students will use this device to stir the contents of the graduated cylinder by placing the loop around the thermometer and using the handle to move the device up and down.

638   Chapter 3 • LabBook

Part B: Freezing Water

Make Another Prediction

8. What happens to the temperature of freezing water when you continue to remove energy through cooling?

Procedure

9. Put approximately 20 mL of water in the graduated cylinder.

10. Put the graduated cylinder in the coffee can, and fill in around the graduated cylinder with crushed ice. Pour rock salt on the ice around the graduated cylinder. Place the thermometer and the wire-loop stirring device in the graduated cylinder.

11. As the ice melts and mixes with the rock salt, the level of ice will decrease. Add ice and rock salt to the can as needed.

Collect Data

12. In a new table, record the temperature of the water in the graduated cylinder every 30 seconds. Stir the water with the stirring device.
    Caution: Do not stir with the thermometer.

13. Once the water begins to freeze, stop stirring. Do not try to pull the thermometer out of the solid ice in the cylinder.

14. Note the temperature when you first notice ice crystals forming in the water. Continue taking readings until the water in the graduated cylinder is completely frozen.

15. Make a graph of temperature (*y*-axis) versus time (*x*-axis). Draw an arrow to the temperature reading at which the first ice crystals form in the water in the graduated cylinder.

Analyze the Results (Parts A and B)

16. What does the slope of each graph represent?

17. How does the slope when the water is boiling compare with the slope before the water starts to boil? Why is the slope different for the two periods?

18. How does the slope when the water is freezing compare with the slope before the water starts to freeze? Why is the slope different for the two periods?

Draw Conclusions (Parts A and B)

19. Addition or subtraction of energy leads to changes in the movement of particles that make up solids, liquids, and gases. Use this idea to explain why the temperature graphs of the two experiments look the way they do.

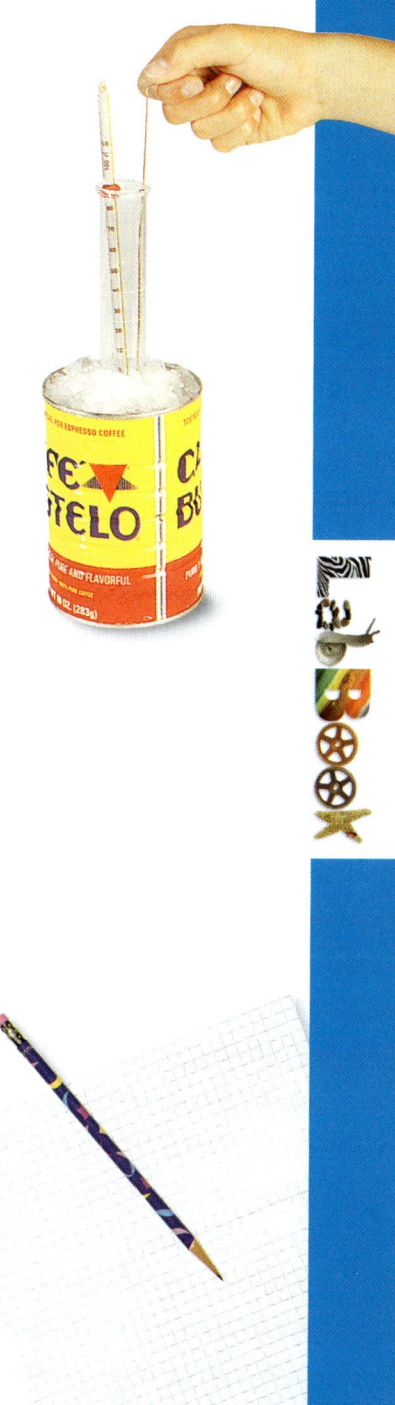

Datasheets for LabBook
Datasheet 11

Science Skills Worksheet 26
"Grasping Graphing"

Answers

8. Accept all reasonable predictions.

16. The slope of each graph represents the rate of temperature change.

17. The slope is less steep (line should be horizontal) when the water starts to boil. The slope is different because the energy added to the water through heating is making steam rather than increasing the temperature.

18. The slope is less steep (the line should be horizontal) when the water starts to freeze. The slope is different because the removal of energy from the water allows crystal structures (ice) to form rather than decreasing the temperature.

19. Adding energy to liquid water makes the particles speed up, thereby increasing the temperature. When the particles speed up enough, water can become gas (steam), which has more energy at the same temperature. Even though energy is being added the whole time, the temperature stops rising when the liquid starts changing into a gas. This explains the part of the graph that levels off. When energy is removed, the temperature stops falling, and the liquid turns to solid. At this point, the particles have less energy, but the temperature of the water stays the same. This explains the part of the graph that levels off.

Flame Tests
Teacher's Notes

Time Required
One or two 45-minute class periods

Lab Ratings

TEACHER PREP 🧪🧪🧪
STUDENT SET-UP 🧪🧪
CONCEPT LEVEL 🧪🧪🧪🧪
CLEAN UP 🧪🧪🧪

MATERIALS
The materials listed are for each group of 2–3 students. The unknown solution should be clear. Use only dilute hydrochloric acid—concentrations lower than 1.0 M. When diluting an acid, always add the acid to the water.

Preparation Notes
Prepare three chloride solutions, such as KCl, $CaCl_2$, and NaCl. Make enough of one of the three solutions to serve as the "unknown" solution. Prepare a mild concentration (approximately 10 g per 500 mL) of each test solution. You will need 5 to 10 mL of each solution per group. Make the wire holder with Nichrome® wire or paper clips and ice-cream sticks or corks. Bend one end of the wire into a small loop like a bubble wand. Tape the other end of the wire to the stick, or insert it into the cork.

 **Datasheets for LabBook**
Datasheet 12

Using Scientific Methods

Flame Tests

 DISCOVERY LAB

Fireworks produce fantastic combinations of color when they are ignited. The different colors are the results of burning different compounds. Imagine that you are the lead chemist for a fireworks company. The label has fallen off one box filled with a compound, and you must identify the unknown compound so that it may be used in the correct fireworks display. To identify the compound, you will use your knowledge that every compound has a unique set of properties.

Make a Prediction
1. Can you identify the unknown compound by heating it in a flame? Explain.

Conduct an Experiment
Caution: Be very careful in handling all chemicals. Tell your teacher immediately if you spill a chemical.

2. Arrange the test tubes in the test-tube rack. Use masking tape to label the tubes with the following names: calcium chloride, potassium chloride, sodium chloride, and unknown.

3. Copy the table below into your ScienceLog. Then ask your teacher for your portions of the solutions.

Test Results	
Compound	Color of flame
Calcium chloride	
Potassium chloride	
Sodium chloride	
Unknown	

Materials
- 4 small test tubes
- test-tube rack
- masking tape
- 4 chloride test solutions
- spark igniter
- Bunsen burner
- wire and holder
- dilute hydrochloric acid in a small beaker
- distilled water in a small beaker

Safety Caution
Remind students to review all safety cautions and icons before beginning this lab activity. Students should touch only the wooden handle of the wire holder device because the wire will become hot and could cause burns. Students should be careful with the dilute hydrochloric acid. If contact occurs, they should flush their skin immediately with water. Long hair and loose clothing should be restricted around an open flame. Remind students to keep wooden sticks away from the open flame. In case of an acid spill, first dilute the spill with water. Then mop up the spill with wet cloths or a wet mop while wearing disposable plastic gloves.

4. Light the burner. Clean the wire by dipping it into the dilute hydrochloric acid and then into distilled water. Holding the wooden handle, heat the wire in the blue flame of the burner until the wire is glowing and it no longer colors the flame. **Caution:** Use extreme care around an open flame.

Collect Data

5. Dip the clean wire into the first test solution. Hold the wire at the tip of the inner cone of the burner flame. In the table, record the color given to the flame.

6. Clean the wire by repeating step 4.

7. Repeat steps 5 and 6 for the other solutions.

8. Follow your teacher's instructions for cleanup and disposal.

Analyze the Results

9. Is the flame color a test for the metal or for the chloride in each compound? Explain your answer.

10. What is the identity of your unknown solution? How do you know?

Draw Conclusions

11. Why is it necessary to carefully clean the wire before testing each solution?

12. Would you expect the compound sodium fluoride to produce the same color as sodium chloride in a flame test? Why or why not?

13. Each of the compounds you tested is made from chlorine, which is a poisonous gas at room temperature. Why is it safe to use these compounds without a gas mask?

Answers

9. The flame test is a test for the metal in each compound. Because each compound contains chloride, the color difference must be due to the different metals. Any color contribution from the chloride would be the same in each trial.

10. Answers will depend on the teacher's choice for the unknown compound. Students will know its identity because it will produce the same color flame as one of the other three solutions.

11. The wire must be cleaned so the color observed is from the solution being tested, not from a mixture of two solutions.

12. Yes; the sodium fluoride compound would likely burn the same color as the sodium chloride compound because the flame test is a test for the metal in a compound and both compounds contain sodium.

13. Compounds have chemical and physical properties that are different from those of the elements the compounds are formed from.

Science Skills Worksheet 5 "Using Logic"

Disposal Information

Hydrochloric acid: Titrate with 0.1 M NaOH as required until the pH is between 6 and 8, and pour the liquid down the drain.

Calcium chloride solution: Adjust the pH of the waste liquid with 1.0 M acid or base until the pH is between 5 and 9. Pour the neutralized liquid down the drain.

Potassium chloride and sodium chloride solutions: These can be washed down the sink with plenty of water, provided your school drains are connected to a sanitary sewer system with a treatment plant.

Kenneth J. Horn
Fallston Middle School
Fallston, Maryland

Chapter 4 • LabBook

A Sugar Cube Race!
Teacher's Notes

Time Required

One 45-minute class period

Lab Ratings

TEACHER PREP 🧪
STUDENT SET-UP 🧪
CONCEPT LEVEL 🧪🧪
CLEAN UP 🧪

Preparation Notes

Materials listed are for each student. Remind students not to eat the sugar cube. Have hot water or hot plates and heat-resistant gloves ready for students who want to test temperature. Have paper towels on hand for students to wrap their cube in as they crush it. Caution students to wear goggles.

Answers

1. Accept all reasonable predictions. Variables include water temperature, surface area of cube, motion of water due to stirring, and time. Sample predictions: Increasing the temperature of the water will make the sugar cube dissolve faster.

5. Answers will vary, depending on the original prediction.

6. Observing the sugar cube dissolving on its own provides a control so that you can measure the effect of the variable.

7. Changing two variables that each increase the dissolving rate should increase the rate of dissolving even more, but it would be difficult to determine which variable had the greater effect.

Using Scientific Methods

A Sugar Cube Race!

DISCOVERY LAB

If you drop a sugar cube into a glass of water, how long will it take to dissolve? Will it take 5 minutes, 10 minutes, or longer? What can you do to speed up the rate at which it dissolves? Should you change something about the water, the sugar cube, or the process? In other words, what variable should you change? Before reading further, make a list of variables that could be changed in this situation. Record your list in your ScienceLog.

Materials

- water
- graduated cylinder
- 2 sugar cubes
- 2 beakers or other clear containers
- clock or stopwatch
- other materials approved by your teacher

Make a Prediction

1. Choose one variable to test. In your ScienceLog, record your choice, and predict how changing your variable will affect the rate of dissolving.

Conduct an Experiment

2. Pour 150 mL of water into one of the beakers. Add one sugar cube, and use the stopwatch to measure how long it takes for the sugar cube to dissolve. You must not disturb the sugar cube in any way! Record this time in your ScienceLog.

3. Tell your teacher how you wish to test the variable. Do not proceed without his or her approval. You may need additional equipment.

4. Prepare your materials to test the variable you have picked. When you are ready, start your procedure for speeding up the dissolving of the sugar cube. Use the stopwatch to measure the time. Record this time in your ScienceLog.

Analyze the Results

5. Compare your results with the results obtained in step 2. Was your prediction correct? Why or why not?

Draw Conclusions

6. Why was it necessary to observe the sugar cube dissolving on its own before you tested the variable?

7. Do you think that changing more than one variable would speed up the rate of dissolving even more? Explain your reasoning.

Communicate Results

8. Discuss your results with a group that tested a different variable. Which variable had a greater effect on the rate of dissolving?

8. Accept all reasonable answers based on class data.

 Datasheets for LabBook
Datasheet 13

Kenneth J. Horn
Fallston Middle School
Fallston, Maryland

Making Butter

A colloid is an interesting substance. It has properties of both solutions and suspensions. Colloidal particles are not heavy enough to settle out, so they remain evenly dispersed throughout the mixture. In this activity, you will make butter—a very familiar colloid—and observe the characteristics that classify butter as a colloid.

Materials

- marble
- small, clear container with lid
- heavy cream
- clock or stopwatch

Procedure

1. Place a marble inside the container, and fill the container with heavy cream. Put the lid tightly on the container.

2. Take turns shaking the container vigorously and constantly for 10 minutes. Record the time when you begin shaking in your ScienceLog. Every minute, stop shaking the container and hold it up to the light. Record your observations.

3. Continue shaking the container, taking turns if necessary. When you see, hear, or feel any changes inside the container, note the time and change in your ScienceLog.

4. After 10 minutes of shaking, you should have a lump of "butter" surrounded by liquid inside the container. Describe both the butter and the liquid in detail in your ScienceLog.

5. Let the container sit for about 10 minutes. Observe the butter and liquid again, and record your observations in your ScienceLog.

Analysis

6. When you noticed the change in the container, what did you think was happening at that point?

7. Based on your observations, explain why butter is classified as a colloid.

8. What kind of mixture is the liquid that is left behind? Explain.

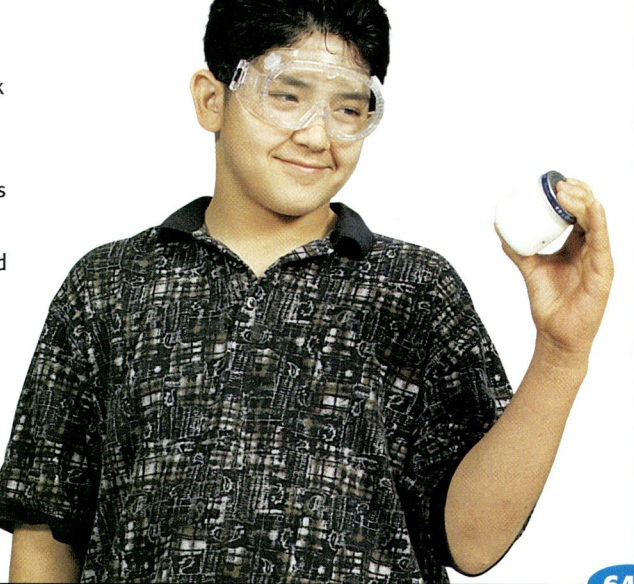

Kenneth J. Horn
Fallston Middle School
Fallston, Maryland

 Datasheets for LabBook
Datasheet 14

Making Butter
Teacher's Notes

Time Required
One 45-minute class period

Lab Ratings
EASY ——→ HARD

- **Teacher Prep** ♦♦
- **Student Set-Up** ♦
- **Concept Level** ♦♦
- **Clean Up** ♦♦

MATERIALS
Materials listed are for each pair of students. If using glass containers, students should shake the container vigorously but not violently because it might break. Be sure each lid fits tightly. A small or medium-sized ball bearing may be substituted for the marble. For best results, the cream should be room temperature, not cold.

Safety Caution
Caution students to wear safety goggles while performing this activity.

Answers

6. Answers may vary. Students should mention that the suspended materials were starting to settle out.

7. The butter appears to have characteristics of both a solution and a suspension.

8. The liquid left behind appears to be a suspension.

Chapter 4 • LabBook   **643**

Unpolluting Water
Teacher's Notes

Time Required
One or two 45-minute class periods

Lab Ratings

TEACHER PREP 🧪🧪
STUDENT SET-UP 🧪🧪🧪
CONCEPT LEVEL 🧪🧪🧪
CLEAN UP 🧪🧪

MATERIALS
Materials listed are for each group of 2–3 students. Use large filter paper for part D, or place filter paper in a funnel.

Special notes on supplies:

1. Sand must be thoroughly washed to eliminate as much dust as possible. Put the sand in a bowl and run water into it while stirring until the water runs clear. The finer the sand, the better the filtering action.

2. Use activated charcoal, available from pet-supply stores. This charcoal can be washed by quickly running water through the charcoal in a sieve or colander. Do not allow the charcoal to remain in water too long or it will lose its adsorbing power.

Safety Caution
Remind students to review all safety cautions and icons before beginning this lab activity. Make sure all spills are cleaned up immediately.

Unpolluting Water

In many cities, the water supply comes from a river, lake, or reservoir. This water may include several mixtures, including suspensions (with suspended dirt, oil, or living organisms) and solutions (with dissolved chemicals). To make the water safe to drink, your city's water supplier must remove impurities. In this lab, you will model the procedures used in real water-treatment plants.

Part A: Untreated Water

Procedure

1. Measure 100 mL of "polluted" water into a graduated cylinder. Be sure to shake the bottle of water before you pour so your sample will include all the impurities.

2. Pour the contents of the graduated cylinder into one of the beakers.

3. Copy the table below into your ScienceLog, and record your observations of the water in the "Before treatment" row.

Materials
- "polluted" water
- graduated cylinder
- 250 mL beakers (4)
- 2 plastic spoons
- small nail
- 8 oz plastic-foam cup (2)
- scissors
- 2 pieces of filter paper
- washed fine sand
- metric ruler
- washed activated charcoal
- rubber band

	Observations					
	Color	Clearness	Odor	Any layers?	Any solids?	Water volume
Before treatment						
After oil separation						
After sand filtration						
After charcoal						

Part B: Settling In

If a suspension is left standing, the suspended particles will settle to the top or bottom. You should see a layer of oil at the top.

Procedure

4. Separate the oil by carefully pouring the oil into another beaker. You can use a plastic spoon to get the last bit of oil from the water. Record your observations.

Preparation Notes

Make "polluted water" as follows: Put the following into a half-gallon milk jug:

    1 cup cooking oil

    3/4 to 1 cup of dirt

    1 or 2 drops of food coloring (yellow or red works best)

Fill the jug with water, put the cap on, and shake the jug well. It is important that students shake the mixture well before pouring their 100 mL sample. Students can estimate the water volume after parts B–D using the approximate volume markings on the side of the beaker. In part D, have students use a clean graduated cylinder to measure the volume of treated water.

Part C: Filtration

Cloudy water can be a sign of small particles still in suspension. These particles can usually be removed by filtering. Water-treatment plants use sand and gravel as filters.

Procedure

5. Make a filter as follows:
   a. Use the nail to poke 5 to 10 small holes in the bottom of one of the cups.
   b. Cut a circle of filter paper to fit inside the bottom of the cup. (This will keep the sand in the cup.)
   c. Fill the cup to 2 cm below the rim with wet sand. Pack the sand tightly.
   d. Set the cup inside an empty beaker.

6. Pour the polluted water on top of the sand, and let it filter through. Do not pour any of the settled mud onto the sand. (Dispose of the mud as instructed by your teacher.) In your table, record your observations of the water collected in the beaker.

Part D: Separating Solutions

Something that has been dissolved in a solvent cannot be separated using filters. Water-treatment plants use activated charcoal to absorb many dissolved chemicals.

Procedure

7. Place activated charcoal about 3 cm deep in the unused cup. Pour the water collected from the sand filtration into the cup, and stir for a minute with a spoon.

8. Place a piece of filter paper over the top of the cup, and fasten it in place with a rubber band. With the paper securely in place, pour the water through the filter paper and back into a clean beaker. Record your observations in your table.

Analysis (Parts A–D)

9. Is your unpolluted water safe to drink? Why or why not?
10. When you treat a sample of water, do you get out exactly the same amount of water that you put in? Explain your answer.
11. Some groups may still have cloudy water when they finish. Explain a possible cause for this.

Joseph Price
H. M. Browne Junior High
Washington, D.C.

Datasheets for LabBook
Datasheet 15

Answers

9. Students will have different opinions, depending on their results. Many will likely say that unpolluted water is safe to drink because it goes through so many filtering processes, but some may say it is unsafe because their samples still look cloudy after the experiment. (Students should be discouraged from tasting the water. This activity does not include treatment with chlorine that takes place at most water treatment plants to kill bacteria.)

10. No; some of the water is lost in the treatment processes.

11. Accept all reasonable answers. Students may note that dust came from the charcoal and sand or that bacteria in the water caused it to appear cloudy.

Disposal Information

1. Solid charcoal should be dried and buried in a landfill that is approved for chemical disposal. You may want to consider drying and reusing the charcoal, although it will eventually lose its absorbing power.

2. Pour cooking oil into disposable containers, refrigerate (if possible) until the oil congeals, and put in the trash.

3. The sand can be reused if it is washed after this activity.

4. Spoon or pour the mud into disposable containers and put them in the trash.

Built for Speed
Teacher's Notes

Time Required
One or two 45-minute class periods

Lab Ratings

TEACHER PREP
STUDENT SET-UP
CONCEPT LEVEL
CLEAN UP

MATERIALS
Students may be able to supply toy vehicles from home. The toy vehicles should be self-propelled, either battery-operated or wind-up.

Preparation Notes
If you are using battery-operated cars, ensure that the batteries are fresh and that spare batteries are available. You may wish to discuss the use of correct units (m/s) before students begin.

Answers
1. Goals and procedures will vary, but students should outline a procedure for measuring their car's speed.
4. Answers will vary.
5. Answers will vary. Students should show some critical analysis of their procedure and that of others.
6. Answers will vary. Students should consider factors such as battery life and the age of the spring in wind-up vehicles. They may mention other factors, such as the testing surface or the wheels of the vehicle.

Built for Speed

Imagine that you are an engineer at GoCarCo, a toy-vehicle company. GoCarCo is trying to beat the competition by building a new toy vehicle. Several new designs are being tested. Your boss has given you one of the new toy vehicles and instructed you to measure its speed as accurately as possible with the tools you have. Other engineers (your classmates) are testing the other designs. Your results could decide the fate of the company!

DESIGN YOUR OWN

Materials
- toy vehicle
- meterstick
- masking tape
- stopwatch

Procedure
1. How will you accomplish your goal? Write a paragraph in your ScienceLog to describe your goal and your procedure for this experiment. Be sure that your procedure includes several trials.
2. Show your plan to your boss (teacher). Get his or her approval to carry out your procedure.
3. Perform your stated procedure. Record all data in your ScienceLog. Be sure to express all data in the correct units.

Analysis
4. What was the average speed of your vehicle? How does your result compare with the results of the other engineers?
5. Compare your technique for determining the speed of your vehicle with the techniques of the other engineers. Which technique do you think is the most effective?
6. Was your toy vehicle the fastest? Explain why or why not.

Going Further
Think of several conditions that could affect your vehicle's speed. Design an experiment to test your vehicle under one of those conditions. Write a paragraph in your ScienceLog to explain your procedure. Be sure to include an explanation of how that condition changes your vehicle's speed.

Going Further
Procedures will vary but should show a clear understanding of how the condition could affect the vehicle's speed.

 Datasheets for LabBook
Datasheet 16

Elsie Waynes
Terrell Junior High
Washington, D.C.

Detecting Acceleration

Have you ever noticed that you can "feel" acceleration? In a car or in an elevator you notice the change in speed or direction—even with your eyes closed! Inside your ears are tiny hair cells. These cells can detect the movement of fluid in your inner ear. When you accelerate, the fluid does, too. The hair cells detect this acceleration in the fluid and send a message to your brain. This allows you to sense acceleration.

In this activity you will build a device that detects acceleration. Even though this device is made with simple materials, it is very sensitive. It registers acceleration only briefly. You will have to be very observant when using this device.

Materials

- scissors
- string
- 1 L container with water-tight lid
- pushpin
- small cork or plastic-foam ball
- modeling clay
- water

Procedure

1. Cut a piece of string that is just long enough to reach three quarters of the way inside the container.
2. Use a pushpin to attach one end of the string to the cork or plastic-foam ball.
3. Use modeling clay to attach the other end of the string to the center of the *inside* of the container lid. Be careful not to use too much string—the cork (or ball) should hang no farther than three-quarters of the way into the container.
4. Fill the container to the top with water.
5. Put the lid tightly on the container with the string and cork (or ball) on the inside.
6. Turn the container upside down (lid on the bottom). The cork should float about three-quarters of the way up inside the container, as shown at right. You are now ready to use your accelerometer to detect acceleration by following the steps on the next page.

 **Datasheets for LabBook**
Datasheet 17

Elsie Waynes
Terrell Junior High
Washington, D.C.

Detecting Acceleration
Teacher's Notes

Time Required
One or two 45-minute class periods

Lab Ratings

EASY ——————→ HARD

- **TEACHER PREP** 🧪
- **STUDENT SET-UP** 🧪🧪
- **CONCEPT LEVEL** 🧪🧪🧪
- **CLEAN UP** 🧪🧪

MATERIALS

The materials listed are for each student or each small group of 2–3 students. Instead of using modeling clay to secure the thread to the bottle cap, students can cut the thread long enough so that it hangs out while the lid is screwed on tightly.

Safety Caution

Remind students to review all safety cautions and icons before beginning this lab activity.

Preparation Notes

You may wish to build an accelerometer before class to show students.

Chapter 5 • LabBook

7. Put the accelerometer lid side down on a tabletop. Notice that the cork floats straight up in the water.

8. Now gently start pushing the accelerometer across the table at a constant speed. Notice that the cork quickly moves in the direction you are pushing then swings backward. If you did not see this happen, try the same thing again until you are sure you can see the first movement of the cork.

9. Once you are familiar with how to use your accelerometer, try the following changes in motion, and record your observations of the cork's first motion for each change in your ScienceLog.

   a. While moving the device across the table, push a little faster.
   b. While moving the device across the table, slow down.
   c. While moving the device across the table, change the direction that you are pushing. (Try changing both to the left and to the right.)
   d. Make any other changes in motion you can think of. You should only change one part of the motion at a time.

648 Chapter 5 • LabBook

Analysis

10. The cork moves forward (in the direction you were pushing the bottle) when you speed up but backward when you slow down. Why? (Hint: Think about the direction of acceleration.)

11. When you push the bottle at a constant speed, why does the cork quickly swing back after it shows you the direction of acceleration?

12. Imagine you are standing on a corner, watching a car that is waiting at a stoplight. A passenger inside the car is holding some helium balloons. Based on what you observed with your accelerometer, what do you think will happen to the balloons when the car begins moving?

Going Further

If you move the bottle in a circle at a constant speed, what do you predict the cork will do? Try it, and check your answer.

Answers

10. The cork will move opposite to the motion of the water. As the bottle accelerates forward, the water sloshes backward, which makes the cork move forward. The cork will always move in the direction of acceleration.

11. The bottle stops accelerating (it is moving with a constant speed), so the cork shows zero acceleration.

12. As the car begins accelerating forward, the balloons will move forward because the air in the car moves backward. When the car reaches a steady speed, the balloons will move back to stand straight up.

Going Further

The cork will also travel in a circle, staying closest to the side of the bottle nearest the center of the circle.

Science Friction
Teacher's Notes

Time Required

One 45-minute class period

Lab Ratings

TEACHER PREP △
STUDENT SET-UP △
CONCEPT LEVEL △△
CLEAN UP △

MATERIALS

The rollers may be made from ring-stand poles or wooden dowels.

Safety Caution

Remind students to review all safety cautions and icons before beginning this lab activity.

Preparation Notes

If the spring scale is not very sensitive, students may record a force of zero for rolling friction. Encourage students to discuss whether this is realistic and what could be causing them to get such a result. For best results, students should keep the spring scale parallel to the table and should pull gradually, as a quick pull will give an incorrect reading.

Answers

2. Accept all reasonable hypotheses.
8. Static friction was the largest. Rolling friction was the smallest.
9. Answers will vary. Students may mention conducting more trials, using different objects or surfaces, or using the spring scale more carefully.

650   Chapter 5 • LabBook

Using Scientific Methods

Science Friction

DISCOVERY LAB

In this experiment, you will investigate three types of friction—static, sliding, and rolling—to determine which is the largest force and which is the smallest force.

Ask a Question

1. Which type of friction is the largest force—static, sliding, or rolling? Which is the smallest?

Form a Hypothesis

2. In your ScienceLog, write a statement or statements that answer the questions above. Explain your reasoning.

Test the Hypothesis/Collect Data

3. Cut a piece of string, and tie it in a loop that fits in the textbook, as shown below. Hook the string to the spring scale.
4. Practice the next three steps several times before you collect data.
5. To measure the static friction between the book and the table, pull the spring scale very slowly. Record the largest force on the scale before the book starts to move.
6. After the book begins to move, you can determine the sliding friction. Record the force required to keep the book sliding at a slow, constant speed.
7. Place two or three rods under the book to act as rollers. Make sure the rollers are evenly spaced. Place another roller in front of the book so that the book will roll onto it. Pull the force meter slowly. Measure the force needed to keep the book rolling at a constant speed.

Materials

- scissors
- string
- textbook (covered)
- spring scale (force meter)
- 3 to 4 wooden or metal rods

Analyze the Results

8. Which type of friction was the largest? Which was the smallest?
9. Do the results support your hypothesis? If not, how would you revise or retest your hypothesis?

Communicate Results

10. Compare your results with those of another group. Are there any differences? Working together, design a way to improve the experiment and resolve possible differences.

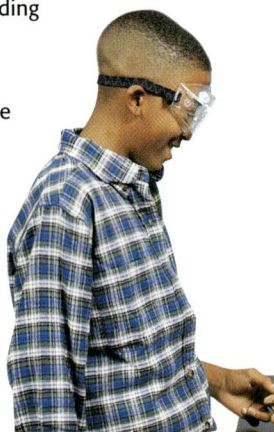

650

10. Answers will vary but should show consideration of the experimental procedure.

 Datasheets for LabBook
Datasheet 18

Barry L. Bishop
San Rafael Junior High
Ferron, Utah

Relating Mass and Weight

Why do objects with more mass weigh more than objects with less mass? All objects have weight on Earth because their mass is affected by Earth's gravitational force. Because the mass of an object on Earth is constant, the relationship between the mass of an object and its weight is also constant. You will measure the mass and weight of several objects to verify the relationship between mass and weight on the surface of Earth.

Materials

- metric balance
- small classroom objects
- spring scale (force meter)
- string
- scissors
- graph paper

Collect Data

1. Copy the table below into your ScienceLog.

Mass and Weight Measurements		
Object	Mass (g)	Weight (N)

DO NOT WRITE IN BOOK

2. Using the metric balance, find the mass of five or six small classroom objects designated by your teacher. Record the masses in your ScienceLog.

3. Using the spring scale, find the weight of each object. Record the weights in your ScienceLog. (You may need to use the string to create a hook with which to hang some objects from the spring scale, as shown at right.)

Analyze the Results

4. Using your data, construct a graph of weight (y-axis) versus mass (x-axis). Draw a line that best fits all your data points.

5. Does the graph confirm the relationship between mass and weight on Earth? Explain your answer.

651

Answers

4. The graph should be a straight or almost straight line. (If the line is not straight, encourage students to check their data or remeasure the weights and masses of the objects.)

5. Weight is a measure of the gravitational force on an object. Weight depends on mass. Because an object's mass never changes, its weight on Earth never changes. The straight line of the graph illustrates the direct relationship between mass and weight.

 **Datasheets for LabBook Datasheet 19**

Relating Mass and Weight
Teacher's Notes

Time Required
One 45-minute class period

Lab Ratings

EASY ——————→ HARD

TEACHER PREP 🧪
STUDENT SET-UP 🧪
CONCEPT LEVEL 🧪🧪
CLEAN UP 🧪

MATERIALS
The materials listed are for each group of 2–3 students. A set of metric masses may be used as objects, but at least one random object should be included. Objects must be measurable with the spring scales and metric balances.

Safety Caution
Remind students to review all safety cautions and icons before beginning this lab activity.

Preparation Notes
If metric masses are used, put a small piece of opaque tape over the stamped value for mass. Ensure all objects are easily picked up with the spring scales. Use string to create a "handle." Choose at least five objects for each group.

Barry L. Bishop
San Rafael Junior High
Ferron, Utah

Chapter 5 • LabBook

A Marshmallow Catapult
Teacher's Notes

Time Required
One or two 45-minute classes

Lab Ratings

TEACHER PREP 🧪🧪
STUDENT SET-UP 🧪
CONCEPT LEVEL 🧪🧪🧪
CLEAN UP 🧪

MATERIALS

The materials listed are for each group of 1–3 students. Marshmallows may be dusted with alum (a harmless but bitter kitchen spice) to discourage students from eating all the supplies. You may wish to leave the marshmallows out overnight to harden, so they will be easier to launch.

Safety Caution
Remind students to review all safety cautions and icons before beginning this lab activity.

Preparation Notes
Some ceilings may be too low and some classrooms too crowded for this lab. Move to the hallway or outdoors to give students plenty of room.

Answers
1. Accept all reasonable hypotheses.
8. The catapult should launch farthest at a 40–50° angle.
9. The path of the projectile does depend on the angle because different angles resulted in different distances.

652 Chapter 6 • LabBook

Using Scientific Methods

A Marshmallow Catapult

DISCOVERY LAB

Catapults use projectile motion to launch objects across distances. A variety of factors can affect the distance an object can be launched, such as the weight of the object, how far the catapult is pulled back, and the catapult's strength. In this lab, you will build a simple catapult and determine the angle at which the catapult will launch an object the farthest.

Materials
- plastic spoon
- block of wood, 3.5 cm × 3.5 cm × 1 cm
- duct tape
- miniature marshmallows
- protractor
- meterstick

Form a Hypothesis
1. At what angle, from 10° to 90°, will a catapult launch a marshmallow the farthest?

Test the Hypothesis
2. Copy the table below into your ScienceLog. In your table, add one row each for 20°, 30°, 40°, 50°, 60°, 70°, 80°, and 90° angles.

Angle	Distance 1 (cm)	Distance 2 (cm)	Average distance (cm)
10°	DO NOT WRITE IN BOOK		

3. Attach the plastic spoon to the 1 cm side of the block with duct tape. Use enough tape so that the spoon is attached securely.

4. Place one marshmallow in the center of the spoon, and tape it to the spoon. This serves as a ledge to hold the marshmallow that will be launched.

5. Line up the bottom corner of the block with the bottom center of the protractor, as shown in the photograph. Start with the block at 10°.

6. Place a marshmallow in the spoon, on top of the taped marshmallow. Pull back lightly, and let go. Measure and record the distance from the catapult that the marshmallow lands. Repeat the measurement, and calculate an average.

7. Repeat step 6 for each angle up to 90°.

Analyze the Results
8. At what angle did the catapult launch the marshmallow the farthest? Compare this with your hypothesis. Explain any differences.

Draw Conclusions
9. Does the path of an object's projectile motion depend on the catapult's angle? Support your answer with your data.

10. At what angle should you throw a ball or shoot an arrow so that it will fly the farthest? Why? Support your answer with your data.

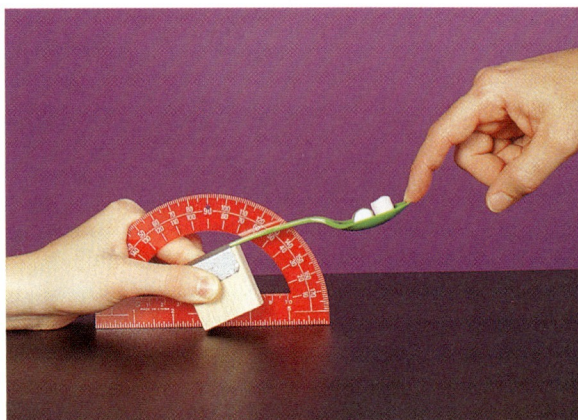

652

10. An angle of approximately 45° is best because it gives the best combination of distance and height. The evidence is that the marshmallow traveled farthest at 40–50°.

Datasheets for LabBook
Datasheet 20

Vicky Farland
Crane Junior High
Yuma, Arizona

Blast Off!

You have been hired as a rocket scientist for NASA. Your job is to design a rocket that will have a controlled flight while carrying a payload. Keep in mind that Newton's laws will have a powerful influence on your rocket.

Procedure

1. When you begin your experiment, your teacher will tape one end of the fishing line to the ceiling.
2. Use a pencil to poke a small hole in each side of the cup near the top. Place a 15 cm piece of string through each hole, and tape down the ends inside.
3. Inflate the balloon, and use the twist tie to hold it closed.
4. Tape the free ends of the strings to the sides of the balloon near the bottom. The cup should hang below the balloon. Your model rocket should look like a hot-air balloon.
5. Thread the fishing line that is hanging from the ceiling through the straw. Tape the balloon securely to the straw.
6. Tape the loose end of the fishing line to the floor.

Collect Data

7. Untie the twist tie while holding the end of the balloon closed. When you are ready, release the end of the balloon. Mark and record the maximum height of the rocket.
8. Repeat the procedure, adding a penny to the cup each time until your rocket cannot lift any more pennies.

Analysis

9. In a paragraph, describe how all three of Newton's laws influenced the flight of your rocket.
10. Draw a diagram of your rocket. Label the action and reaction forces.

Going Further

Brainstorm ways to modify your rocket so that it will carry the most pennies to the maximum height. Select the best design. When your teacher has approved all the designs, each team will build and launch their rocket. Which variable did you modify? How did this variable affect your rocket's flight?

Materials

- tape
- 3 m fishing line
- pencil
- small paper cup
- 15 cm pieces of string (2)
- long, thin balloon
- twist tie
- drinking straw
- meterstick
- pennies

Vicky Farland
Crane Junior High
Yuma, Arizona

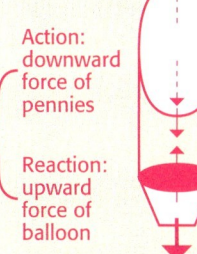

Action: downward force of pennies

Reaction: upward force of released air pushing balloon

Action: downward force of air being squeezed out of balloon

Reaction: upward force of balloon

Action: downward gravitational force of the Earth on the rocket (rocket's weight)

Reaction: upward gravitational force of the rocket on Earth.

Blast Off!
Teacher's Notes

Time Required
One or two 45-minute class periods

Lab Ratings

EASY —— HARD

TEACHER PREP 🧪🧪
STUDENT SET-UP 🧪🧪🧪
CONCEPT LEVEL 🧪🧪🧪🧪
CLEAN UP 🧪

MATERIALS
You need 100 pennies per group. Use two balloons for more force.

Answers

9. Newton's first law: The rocket remains at rest until a force is exerted on it. Newton's second law: The rocket's acceleration depends on the force (which is constant) and the mass (which increases with each penny). Newton's third law: The force of the air leaving the balloon on the rocket is equal and opposite to the force of the balloon on the air.

10. See the sample diagram at left. You may wish to point out the less obvious force pairs.

Going Further
Answers will vary but should show a clear understanding of how the variable affects the rocket's flight.

 Datasheets for LabBook
Datasheet 21

Chapter 6 • LabBook

Inertia-Rama!
Teacher's Notes

Time Required
Two 45-minute class periods

Lab Ratings

- TEACHER PREP 🧪🧪
- STUDENT SET-UP 🧪
- CONCEPT LEVEL 🧪🧪
- CLEAN UP 🧪

MATERIALS

1. Be sure to have a few extra raw and hard-boiled eggs on hand in case of breakage. Having students spin their eggs in a box may reduce the chance that an egg will break.
2. Use a relatively large coin, such as a quarter or 50-cent piece. Or you may have students try the Station 2 procedure with coins of different sizes and compare the results.
3. The mass used at Station 3 should be at least 1 kg. A larger mass will give better results.

Safety Caution
Remind students to review all safety cautions and icons before beginning this lab activity.

Preparation Notes
This lab may be done in one class period if enough supplies are available to avoid changing stations.

 Datasheets for LabBook Datasheet 22

Inertia-Rama!

Inertia is a property of all matter, from small particles of dust to enormous planets and stars. In this lab, you will investigate the inertia of various shapes and types of matter. Keep in mind that each investigation requires you to either overcome or use the object's inertia.

Station 1: Magic Eggs

Procedure

1. There are two eggs at this station—one is hard-boiled (solid all the way through) and the other is raw (liquid inside). The masses of the two eggs are about the same. The eggs are marked so that you can tell them apart.
2. You will spin each egg and then stop it from spinning by placing a finger on its center. Before you do anything to either egg, write some predictions in your ScienceLog: Which egg will be the easiest to spin? Which egg will be the easiest to stop?
3. Spin the hard-boiled egg. Then place your finger on it to make it stop spinning. Record your observations in your ScienceLog.
4. Repeat step 3 with the raw egg.
5. Compare your predictions with your observations. (Repeat steps 3 and 4 if necessary.)

Analysis

6. Explain why the eggs behave differently when you spin them even though they should have the same inertia. (Hint: Think about what happens to the liquid inside the raw egg.)
7. In terms of inertia, explain why the eggs react differently when you try to stop them.

Station 2: Coin in a Cup

Procedure

8. At this station, you will find a coin, an index card, and a cup. Place the card over the cup. Then place the coin on the card over the center of the cup, as shown at right.

Answers

6. The liquid inside the raw egg sloshes; it doesn't spin smoothly like the hard-boiled egg.
7. When you stop the eggs, the hard-boiled egg stops as a whole, while the shell of the raw egg can be stopped and the liquid inside keeps spinning.

SKILL BUILDER

Materials

Station 1
- hard-boiled egg
- raw egg

Station 2
- coin
- index card
- cup

Station 3
- spool of thread
- suspended mass
- scissors
- meterstick

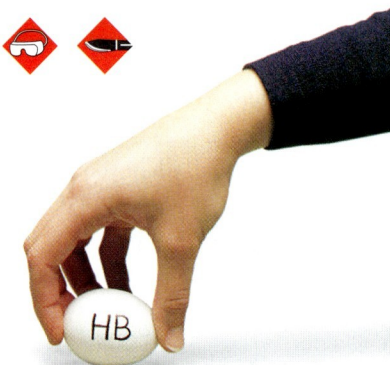

9. In your ScienceLog, write down a method for getting the coin into the cup without touching the coin and without lifting the card.

10. Try your method. If it doesn't work, try again until you find a method that does work. When you are done, place the card and coin on the table for the next group.

Analysis

11. Use Newton's first law of motion to explain why the coin falls into the cup when your method is used.

12. Explain why pulling on the card slowly will not work, even though the coin has inertia. (Hint: Friction is a force.)

Station 3: The Magic Thread

Procedure

13. At this station, you will find a spool of thread and a mass hanging from a strong string. Cut a piece of thread about 40 cm long. Tie the thread around the bottom of the mass, as shown at right.

14. Pull gently on the end of the thread. Observe what happens, and record your observations in your ScienceLog.

15. Stop the mass from moving. Now hold the end of the thread so that there is a lot of slack between your fingers and the mass.

16. Give the thread a quick, hard pull. You should observe a very different event. Record your observations in your ScienceLog. Throw away the thread.

Analysis

17. Use Newton's first law of motion to explain why the results of a gentle pull are so different from the results of a hard pull.

Draw Conclusions

18. Remember that both moving and nonmoving objects have inertia. Explain why it is hard to throw a bowling ball and why it is hard to catch a thrown bowling ball.

19. Why is it harder to run with a backpack full of books than with an empty backpack?

Answers

11. The coin tends to remain at rest, so when the card is removed quickly, there is not enough friction to move the coin.

12. When you pull slowly, there is enough time for the friction between the card and the coin to move the coin.

17. The mass tends to stay at rest. A gentle pull exerts a small force over a longer time and moves the mass, but a hard pull breaks the thread before the mass moves.

18. It is just as hard to catch the bowling ball as it is to throw the bowling ball because the bowling ball has the same inertia in both cases.

19. Accept all reasonable answers that take into account the added inertia of the objects in the backpack. Sample answer: Starting and stopping will be harder because the extra mass increases your inertia. In addition, the books in the backpack act like the liquid inside a raw egg. As you bounce up, they resist your upward movement. As you bounce down, they are still moving upward.

Vicky Farland
Crane Junior High
Yuma, Arizona

Quite a Reaction
Teacher's Notes

Time Required
One to two 45-minute class periods

Lab Ratings

TEACHER PREP 🧪🧪
STUDENT SET-UP 🧪🧪🧪
CONCEPT LEVEL 🧪🧪🧪
CLEAN UP 🧪

MATERIALS
The materials listed are for groups of 1–3 students. Thick pieces of poster board work well. One piece of corrugated cardboard will work as a substitute. A large marble will produce more-dramatic results than a small marble. Also, be sure to give students enough time for the glue to dry.

Safety Caution
Remind students to review all safety cautions and icons before beginning this lab activity.

Pick up any marbles, pins, or other materials that fall on uncarpeted floors immediately. This helps prevent slips and falls. Give students plenty of space to do this lab.

Vicky Farland
Crane Junior High
Yuma, Arizona

656 Chapter 6 • LabBook

Quite a Reaction

Catapults have been used for centuries to throw objects great distances. You may already be familiar with catapults after doing the marshmallow catapult lab. According to Newton's third law of motion (whenever one object exerts a force on a second object, the second object exerts an equal and opposite force on the first), when an object is launched, something must also happen to the catapult. In this activity, you will build a kind of catapult that will allow you to observe the effects of Newton's third law of motion and the law of conservation of momentum.

Conduct an Experiment

1. Glue the cardboard rectangles together to make a stack of three.
2. Push two of the pushpins into the cardboard stack near the corners at one end, as shown below. These will be the anchors for the rubber band.
3. Make a small loop of string.
4. Put the rubber band through the loop of string, and then place the rubber band over the two pushpin anchors. The rubber band should be stretched between the two anchors with the string loop in the middle.
5. Pull the string loop toward the end of the cardboard stack opposite the end with the anchors, and fasten the loop in place with the third pushpin.
6. Place the six straws about 1 cm apart on a tabletop or on the floor. Then carefully center the catapult on top of the straws.
7. Put the marble in the closed end of the V formed by the rubber band.

Materials
- glue
- 10 cm × 15 cm rectangles of cardboard (3)
- 3 pushpins
- string
- rubber band
- 6 plastic straws
- marble
- scissors
- meterstick

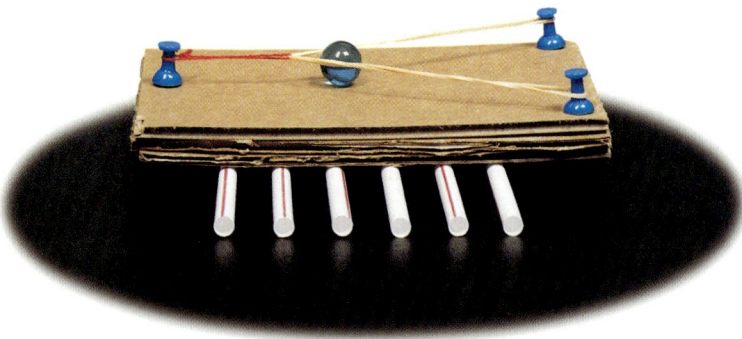

 Datasheets for LabBook
Datasheet 23

8. Use scissors to cut the string holding the rubber band, and observe what happens. (Be careful not to let the scissors touch the cardboard catapult when you cut the string.)

9. Reset the catapult with a new piece of string. Try launching the marble several times to be sure that you have observed everything that happens during a launch. Record all your observations in your ScienceLog.

Analyze the Results

10. Which has more mass, the marble or the catapult?

11. What happened to the catapult when the marble was launched?

12. How far did the marble fly before it landed?

13. Did the catapult move as far as the marble did?

Draw Conclusions

14. Explain why the catapult moved backward.

15. If the forces that made the marble and the catapult move apart are equal, why didn't the marble and the catapult move apart the same distance? (Hint: The fact that the marble can roll after it lands is not the answer.)

16. The momentum of an object depends on the mass and velocity of the object. What is the momentum of the marble before it is launched? What is the momentum of the catapult? Explain your answers.

17. Using the law of conservation of momentum, explain why the marble and the catapult move in opposite directions after the launch.

Going Further
How would you modify the catapult if you wanted to keep it from moving backward as far as it did? (It still has to rest on the straws.) Using items that you can find in the classroom, design a catapult that will move backward less than the original design.

Answers

10. Answers will depend on the type of marble and the type of cardboard. It is likely that the catapult will have more mass.

11. The catapult moved backward.

12. Answers will vary depending on the mass of the marble, the type of cardboard, and the size of the straws.

13. Answers will vary, but the marble will likely go farther than the catapult.

14. The catapult moved backward due to Newton's third law. The catapult exerted a force on the marble that made it move forward. The marble exerted an equal and opposite force on the catapult, making it move backward.

15. More friction acts on the cardboard because it is in contact with the straws. Some students may also note that the marble and the cardboard have different masses. The acceleration (and, therefore, the velocity) of each is different as a result of Newton's second law, $F = ma$.

16. The momentum of both the marble and the catapult is zero because both have zero velocity.

17. Because the initial momentum of the system is zero, the catapult has to move backward with a momentum equal to that of the marble moving forward. The momenta of the catapult and marble have to be in opposite directions so they will cancel out.

Going Further

Accept all reasonable designs.

Fluids, Force, and Floating
Teacher's Notes

Time Required
One to two 45-minute class periods

Lab Ratings

TEACHER PREP 🧪
STUDENT SET-UP 🧪🧪
CONCEPT LEVEL 🧪🧪🧪
CLEAN UP 🧪

MATERIALS
The supplies listed are for one group of 3–4 students. The tank or tub should have vertical sides. A small or medium-sized tub works best so that changes in volume can be observed easily. Masses should be added near the center of the baking pan. A fish tank or aquarium works well for this activity.

Preparation Notes
Before you begin this lab, review the concept of buoyant force with students. Make sure students wear an apron when doing this lab activity.

If you use a tub or pan without vertical sides, the buoyant force and the weight of the pans and masses will not be equal. In most cases the buoyant force will be greater than the weight.

Have students measure the side of the baking pan and mark the one-quarter, one-half, and three-quarter levels.

Fluids, Force, and Floating

Why do some objects sink in fluids but others float? In this lab, you'll get a sinking feeling as you determine that an object floats when its weight is less than the buoyant force exerted by the surrounding fluid.

Procedure

1. Copy the table below into your ScienceLog.

Measurement	Trial 1	Trial 2
Length (l), cm		
Width (w), cm		
Initial height (h_1), cm		
Initial volume (V_1), cm³ $V_1 = l \times w \times h_1$		
New height (h_2), cm		
New volume (V_2), cm³ $V_2 = l \times w \times h_2$		
Displaced volume (ΔV), cm³ $\Delta V = V_2 - V_1$		
Mass of displaced water, g $m = \Delta V \times 1 \text{ g/cm}^3$		
Weight of displaced water, N (buoyant force)		
Weight of pan and masses, N		

2. Fill the tank or tub half full with water.

3. Measure (in centimeters) the length, width, and initial height of the water. Record your measurements in the table.

4. Using the equation given in the table, determine the initial volume of water in the tank. Record your results in the table.

5. Place the pan in the water, and place masses in the pan, as shown on the next page. Keep adding masses until the pan sinks to about three-quarters of its height. This will cause the water level in the tank to rise. Record the new height of the water in the table. Then use this value to determine and record the new volume of water.

Materials
- large rectangular tank or plastic tub
- water
- metric ruler
- small rectangular baking pan
- labeled masses
- metric balance
- paper towels

 Datasheets for LabBook
Datasheet 24

Sharon L. Woolf
Langston Hughes Middle School
Reston, Virginia

6. Determine the volume of the water that was displaced by the pan and masses, and record this value in the table. The displaced volume is equal to the new volume minus the initial volume.

7. Determine the mass of the displaced water by multiplying the displaced volume by its density (1 g/cm^3). Record the mass in the table.

8. Divide the mass by 100. The value you get is the weight of the displaced water in newtons (N). This is equal to the buoyant force. Record the weight of the displaced water in the table.

9. Remove the pan and masses, and determine their total mass (in grams) using the balance. Convert the mass to weight (N), as you did in step 8. Record the weight of the masses and pan in the table.

10. Place the empty pan back in the tank. Perform a second trial by repeating steps 5–9. This time add masses until the pan is just about to sink.

Analysis

11. In your ScienceLog, compare the buoyant force (the weight of the displaced water) with the weight of the pan and masses for both trials.

12. How did the buoyant force differ between the two trials? Explain.

13. Based on your observations, what would happen if you were to add even more mass to the pan than you did in the second trial? Explain your answer in terms of the buoyant force.

14. What would happen if you put the masses in the water without the pan? What difference does the pan's shape make?

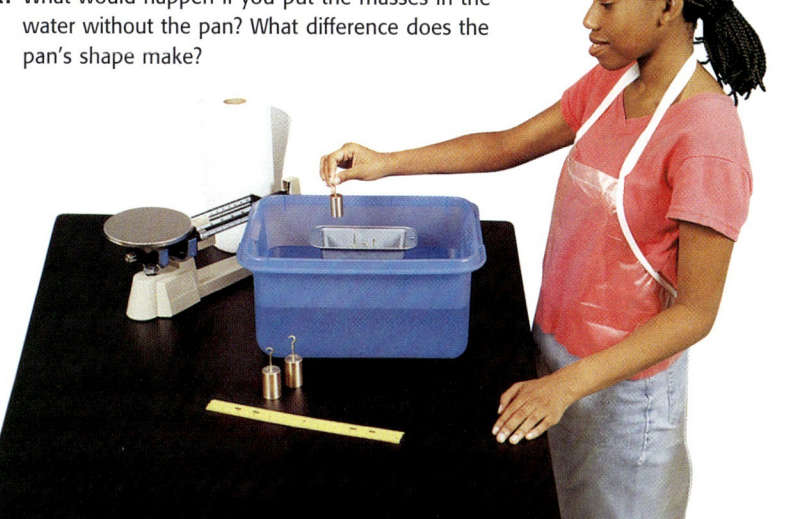

Answers

11. In each trial, the buoyant force and the weight should be the same.

12. The buoyant force is larger in the second trial because more water is displaced.

13. The pan would sink because its weight would be larger but the buoyant force (the weight of the water displaced) would be about the same.

Before students answer item 14, review "The Mystery of Floating Steel," on page 171, for a hint.

14. The masses would sink because the shape of the pan would allow the masses to displace more water than the masses alone displace.

Lab Notes

Volumes of liquids are usually expressed in milliliters (mL). Here the volume measurements for the water displaced are based on a rectangular container (the tank or tub), so cubic centimeters (cm^3) are used.

Math Skills Worksheet 2 "Subtraction Review"

Chapter 7 • LabBook

Density Diver
Teacher's Notes

Time Required
One 45-minute class period

Lab Ratings

TEACHER PREP 🧪
STUDENT SET-UP 🧪🧪
CONCEPT LEVEL 🧪🧪
CLEAN UP 🧪

Lab Notes
If there is any air in the bottle, students will have to squeeze harder to make the diver move.

Answers
1. Accept all reasonable hypotheses.

7. When the water level inside the diver rises, the diver starts sinking. When the level decreases, the diver floats.

8. Higher water level corresponds to higher density. Adding more water to the diver results in more mass in the same volume, so the density is greater.

9. When the density is higher, the diver starts to sink. When it is low, the diver floats. When it is just right, the diver hovers without sinking or rising.

10. Controlling the water level inside the diver is similar to controlling the water level inside a submarine.

11. Squeezing the bottle increases the water pressure. This increase is transmitted equally throughout the bottle to the diver (Pascal's principle). The air inside the diver is compressed and water enters the diver. This increases the density of the diver.

Using Scientific Methods

Density Diver

Crew members of a submarine can control the submarine's density underwater by allowing water to flow into and out of special tanks. These changes in density affect the submarine's position in the water. In this lab, you'll control a "density diver" to learn for yourself how the density of an object affects its position in a fluid.

Materials
- 2 L plastic bottle with screw-on cap
- water
- medicine dropper

Form a Hypothesis
1. How does the density of an object determine whether the object floats, sinks, or maintains its position in a fluid? Write your hypothesis in your ScienceLog.

Test the Hypothesis
2. Completely fill the 2 L plastic bottle with water.

3. Fill the diver (medicine dropper) approximately halfway with water, and place it in the bottle. The diver should float with only part of the rubber bulb above the surface of the water. If the diver floats too high, carefully remove it from the bottle and add a small amount of water to the diver. Place the diver back in the bottle. If you add too much water and the diver sinks, empty out the bottle and diver and go back to step 2.

4. Put the cap on the bottle tightly so that no water leaks out.

5. Apply various pressures to the bottle. Carefully watch the water level inside the diver as you squeeze and release the bottle. Record what happens in your ScienceLog.

6. Try to make the diver rise, sink, or stop at any level. Record your technique and your results.

Analyze the Results
7. How do the changes inside the diver affect its position in the surrounding fluid?

8. What is the relationship between the water level inside the diver and the diver's density? Explain.

Draw Conclusions
9. What relationship did you observe between the diver's density and the diver's position in the fluid?

10. Explain how your density diver is like a submarine.

11. Explain how pressure on the bottle is related to the diver's density. Be sure to include Pascal's principle in your explanation.

12. What was the variable in this experiment? What factors were controlled?

12. The variable is the amount of pressure put on the bottle by squeezing. Factors controlled include the amount of water, the type of bottle, and the size of the medicine droppers.

Datasheets for LabBook
Datasheet 25

C. John Graves
Monforton Middle School
Bozeman, Montana

Taking Flight

When air moves above and below the wing of an airplane, the air pressure below the wing is higher than the air pressure above the wing. This creates lift. In this activity, you will build a model airplane to help you identify how wing size and thrust (forward force provided by the engine) affect the lift needed for flight.

Procedure

1. Fold the paper in half lengthwise and open it again, as shown at right. Make sure to crease all folds well.
2. Fold the right- and left-hand corners toward the center crease.
3. Fold the entire sheet in half along the center crease.
4. With the plane lying on its side, fold the top front edge down so that it meets the bottom edge, as shown.
5. Fold the top wing down again, bringing the top edge to the bottom edge.
6. Turn the plane over, and repeat steps 4 and 5.
7. Raise both wings away from the body to a position slightly above horizontal. Your plane is ready!

Collect Data

8. Point the plane slightly upward, and gently throw it. Repeat several times. Describe your observations in your ScienceLog. **Caution:** Be sure to point the plane away from people.
9. Make the wings smaller by folding them one more time. Gently throw the plane overhand. Repeat several times. Describe your observations in your ScienceLog.
10. Try to achieve the same flight path you saw when the plane's wings were bigger. Record your technique.

Analysis

11. What happened to the plane's flight when you reduced the size of its wings? Explain.
12. What provided your airplane's thrust?
13. From your observations, how does changing the thrust affect the lift?

Materials

- sheet of paper

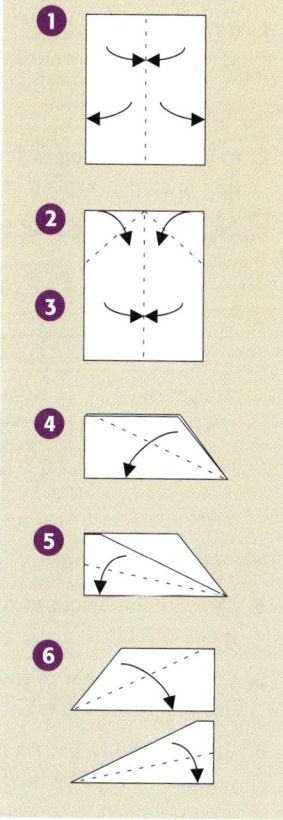

 Datasheets for LabBook Datasheet 26

Answers

11. Lift was reduced. If you didn't throw harder, the flight was shorter. To get a longer flight, you had to throw much harder.
12. You provided the thrust by throwing the plane.
13. More thrust results in more lift. When you throw harder, the plane stays in the air longer.

Taking Flight
Teacher's Notes

Time Required
One 45-minute class period

Lab Ratings

TEACHER PREP 🔬
STUDENT SET-UP 🔬
CONCEPT LEVEL 🔬🔬
CLEAN UP 🔬

MATERIALS

The supplies listed are for each student. Standard copier paper and notebook paper work well. Avoid paper with ragged edges, such as paper from a spiral notebook.

Preparation Notes

Before beginning this lab, review the concepts of lift and thrust. Remind students that this activity is an exception to the usual rules about flying paper planes. Encourage students to be precise in folding the plane. Straight, sharp creases work best. Contests for maximum distance or maximum time aloft encourage active participation. Give students enough time to make and test a couple of airplanes before beginning the competition. Bonus points can be given to the winners.

Lee Yassinski
Sun Valley Middle School
Sun Valley, California

Chapter 7 • LabBook **661**

A Powerful Workout
Teacher's Notes

Time Required
One or two 45-minute class periods

Lab Ratings

- TEACHER PREP
- STUDENT SET-UP
- CONCEPT LEVEL
- CLEAN UP

MATERIALS
The materials listed for this lab are for the entire class or for smaller groups. Students in wheelchairs can use a ramp instead of a flight of stairs.

Safety Caution
Make sure that students use caution when climbing the stairs. Students with asthma or any other respiratory problems should not do this lab. Any student who becomes winded should sit down and take deep breaths. Caution students that this is not a race to see who can get the fastest time.

Answer
2. Answers will vary. Accept all reasonable hypotheses.

 Datasheets for LabBook
Datasheet 27

Using Scientific Methods

A Powerful Workout

DISCOVERY LAB

Does the amount of work you do depend on how fast you do it? No! But doing work in a shorter amount of time does affect your power—the rate at which work is done. In this lab, you'll calculate your work and power when climbing a flight of stairs at different speeds. Then you'll compare your power with that of an ordinary household object—a 100 W light bulb.

Materials
- flight of stairs
- metric ruler
- stopwatch

TRY at HOME

Ask a Question
1. How does your power when climbing a flight of stairs compare with the power of a 100 W light bulb?

Form a Hypothesis
2. In your ScienceLog, write a hypothesis that answers the question in step 1. Explain your reasoning.
3. Copy Table 1 into your ScienceLog.

Table 1 Data Collection				
Height of step (cm)	Number of steps	Height of stairs (m)	Time for slow walk (s)	Time for quick walk (s)
		DO NOT WRITE IN BOOK		

Test the Hypothesis
4. Measure the height of one stair step. Record the measurement in Table 1.
5. Count the number of stairs, including the top step, and record this number in Table 1.
6. Calculate the height (in meters) of the stairs by multiplying the number of steps by the height of one step. Record your answer. (You will need to convert from centimeters to meters.)
7. Using a stopwatch, measure how many seconds it takes you to walk slowly up the flight of stairs. Record your measurement in Table 1.
8. Now measure how many seconds it takes you to walk quickly up the flight of stairs. Be careful not to overexert yourself.

Analyze the Results

9. Copy Table 2 into your ScienceLog.

Table 2 Work and Power Calculations			
Weight (N)	Work (J)	Power for slow walk (W)	Power for quick walk (W)
	DO NOT WRITE IN BOOK		

10. Determine your weight in newtons by multiplying your weight in pounds (lb) by 4.45 N/lb. Record it in Table 2.

11. Calculate and record your work done to climb the stairs using the following equation:

$$\text{Work} = \text{Force} \times \text{distance}$$

Remember that 1 N•m is 1 J. (Hint: Remember that force is expressed in newtons.)

12. Calculate and record your power for each trial (the slow walk and the quick walk) using the following equation:

$$\text{Power} = \frac{\text{Work}}{\text{time}}$$

Remember that the unit for power is the watt (1 W = 1 J/s).

Draw Conclusions

13. In step 11 you calculated your work done in climbing the stairs. Why didn't you calculate your work for each trial?

14. Look at your hypothesis in step 2. Was your hypothesis supported? Write a statement in your ScienceLog that describes how your power in each trial compares with the power of a 100 W light bulb.

15. The work done to move one electron in a light bulb is very small. Write down two reasons why the power is large. (Hints: How many electrons are in the filament of a light bulb? Why was more power used in your second trial?)

Communicate Results

16. Write your average power in a class data table. Calculate the average power for the class. How many light bulbs would it take to equal the power of one student?

Where is work done in a light bulb? Electrons in the filament move back and forth very quickly. These moving electrons do work by heating up the filament and making it glow.

Answers

10. Answers will vary. For reference, 100 lb = 445 N.

11. Answers will vary, based on the weight calculation from step 10. For reference, 445 N × 4 m = 1,780 J.

12. Answers will vary. For reference, $\frac{1,780 \text{ J}}{10 \text{ s}} = 178$ W; $\frac{1,780 \text{ J}}{5 \text{ s}} = 356$ W

13. The work is the same, no matter how long it takes.

14. Answers will vary, based on original hypotheses. The statement should reflect a comparison between the student's power calculations and the power of a 100 W light bulb.

15. The power of a light bulb is large because there are millions of electrons moving in the filament and the electrons are moving very quickly.

16. Answers will vary, depending on the average power calculated by the class. Sample answer: The average power for the class was 250 W, so it would take two and a half 100 W bulbs to equal the power of one student.

Lab Notes

To help calculate averages, set up a class data table on the board. The table should have four columns: Student; Power S (for Power, Slow Walk); Power Q (for Power, Quick Walk); and Average (each student's average power). Remind students how to calculate their average power and the average power for the whole class. To find their individual average power, they add the power for their slow walk plus the power for their quick walk and divide by two. To calculate the class average power, they add all the individual averages together and divide by the number of students in the class.

Terry Rakes
Elmwood Junior High
Rogers, Arkansas

Inclined to Move
Teacher's Notes

Time Required
One 45-minute class period

Lab Ratings

TEACHER PREP 🧪🧪
STUDENT SET-UP 🧪🧪🧪
CONCEPT LEVEL 🧪🧪🧪
CLEAN UP 🧪

Safety Caution
Remind students to review all safety cautions and icons before beginning this lab activity.

Answers

6. The amount of work done should increase as ramp height increases (line A).

7. The amount of work done should increase as ramp height increases (line B).

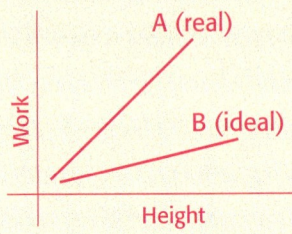

8. It requires less force but more work to raise the book using the ramp. At each height, more work must be done to overcome friction between the book and the ramp.

9. The higher the inclined plane is, the greater the input force.

10. The slope of ideal work versus height will always be less than the slope of real work versus height. That's because there is no friction in ideal work, but

Inclined to Move

In this lab, you will examine a simple machine—an inclined plane. Your task is to compare the work done with and without the inclined plane and to analyze the effects of friction.

Collect Data

1. Copy the table below into your ScienceLog.

2. Tie a piece of string around a book. Attach the spring scale to the string. Use the spring scale to slowly lift the book to a height of 50 cm. Record the output force (the force needed to lift the book). The output force is constant throughout the lab.

3. Use the board and blocks to make a ramp 10 cm high at the highest point. Measure and record the ramp length.

4. Keeping the spring scale parallel to the ramp, as shown below, slowly raise the book. Record the input force (the force needed to pull the book up the ramp).

5. Increase the height of the ramp by 10 cm. Repeat step 4. Repeat this step for each ramp height up to 50 cm.

Analyze the Results

6. The *real* work done includes the work done to overcome friction. Calculate the real work at each height by multiplying the ramp length (converted to meters) by the input force. Graph your results, plotting work (*y*-axis) versus height (*x*-axis).

7. The *ideal* work is the work you would do if there were no friction. Calculate the ideal work at each height by multiplying the ramp height (m) by the output force. Plot the data on your graph.

SKILL BUILDER

Materials
- string
- small book
- spring scale
- meterstick
- wooden board
- blocks
- graph paper

Force vs. Height

Ramp height (cm)	Output force (N)	Ramp length (cm)	Input force (N)
10			
20			
30			
40			
50			

DO NOT WRITE IN BOOK

Draw Conclusions

8. Does it require more or less force and work to raise the book using the ramp? Explain, using your calculations and graphs.

9. What is the relationship between the height of the inclined plane and the input force?

10. Write a statement that summarizes why the slopes of the two graphs are different.

real work includes the work done to overcome the friction between the book and the ramp.

 Datasheets for LabBook
Datasheet 28

Jennifer Ford
North Ridge Middle School
North Richland Hills, Texas

Building Machines

You are surrounded by machines. Some are simple machines, such as ramps for wheelchair access to a building. Others are compound machines, like elevators and escalators, that are made of two or more simple machines. In this lab, you will design and build several simple machines and a compound machine.

Procedure

1. Use the listed materials to build a model of each simple machine: inclined plane, lever, wheel and axle, pulley, screw, and wedge. Describe and draw each model in your ScienceLog.

2. In your ScienceLog, design a compound machine using the materials listed. You may design a machine that already exists, or you may invent your own machine—be creative!

3. After your teacher approves your design, build your compound machine.

Analysis

4. List a possible use for each of your simple machines.

5. Compare your simple machines with those created by your classmates.

6. How many simple machines are in your compound machine? List them.

7. Compare your compound machine with those created by your classmates.

8. What is a possible use for your compound machine? Why did you design it as you did?

9. A compound machine is listed in the Materials list. What is it?

Going Further

Design a compound machine that has all the simple machines in it. Explain what the machine will do and how it will make work easier. With your teacher's approval, build your machine.

Materials

- bottle caps
- cardboard
- craft sticks
- empty thread spools
- glue
- modeling clay
- paper
- pencils
- rubber bands
- scissors
- shoe boxes
- stones
- straws
- string
- tape
- other materials available in your classroom that are approved by your teacher

Answer to Going Further

Accept all reasonable designs. Check all materials for safety and availability.

Datasheets for LabBook
Datasheet 29

Norman Holcomb
Marion Elementary School
Maria Stein, Ohio

Building Machines
Teacher's Notes

Time Required
One or two 45-minute class periods

Lab Ratings

EASY ——————→ HARD

- **TEACHER PREP** 🔬🔬
- **STUDENT SET-UP** 🔬🔬
- **CONCEPT LEVEL** 🔬🔬
- **CLEAN UP** 🔬

MATERIALS

The materials listed for this lab should be available in quantities sufficient for the entire class. You may provide different materials for students to use. Be sure students work carefully with the supplied materials. Students should work in groups of 2–4. Be sure to approve designs before students begin building their compound machines.

Safety Caution
Remind students to review all safety cautions and icons before beginning this lab activity.

Answers

4. Accept all reasonable answers.
5. Accept all reasonable answers.
6. Answers will vary, based on machine design.
7. Accept all reasonable answers.
8. Accept all reasonable answers.
9. The compound machine listed in the Materials List is the pair of scissors.

Chapter 8 • LabBook **665**

Wheeling and Dealing
Teacher's Notes

Time Required
Two 45-minute class periods

Lab Ratings

EASY ———→ HARD

TEACHER PREP 🧪🧪🧪🧪
STUDENT SET-UP 🧪🧪
CONCEPT LEVEL 🧪🧪🧪🧪
CLEAN UP 🧪

MATERIALS

The materials listed in this lab are for each group of 2–4 students. The materials listed below are what you will need in order to prepare each wheel and axle assembly.

- 30 cm of 1 in. dowel
- 70 cm of 0.5 in. dowel for handles (cut into 4 pieces of 10 cm, 15 cm, 20 cm, and 25 cm)
- wheel
- small screw
- 1.5 in. PVC pipe

Safety Caution

Remind students to review all safety cautions and icons before beginning this lab activity.

Lab Notes

The wheel and axle assembly must be constructed before class. Use a marker to number the handles 1 through 4 (shortest to longest). Drill a 0.5 in. diameter hole half way through the large dowel near one end. The handles will be inserted into the hole. A small screw should be inserted into the large dowel near the handle attachment point, on the side away from the end. This will be the attachment point for the string. The 1.5 in. PVC pipe should have an inside diameter slightly larger than the large dowel. The clamps are the most expensive pieces and are optional. If students work in groups, one student may act as the clamp and hold the PVC pipe firmly against the tabletop. Use a 500 g or 1 kg mass for the large mass.

It takes a fair amount of time and materials to build the wheel and axle assemblies, but once you have built them, they will be available to use in subsequent years.

Students should review the sections on work input, work output, mechanical efficiency, mechanical advantage, and a wheel and axle before beginning this lab. Demonstrate the assembly for students. Remind students that they can measure the axle radius and the wheel radius in centimeters and then convert to meters.

666 Chapter 8 • LabBook

Wheeling and Dealing

A wheel and axle is one type of simple machine. A crank handle, such as that used in pencil sharpeners, ice-cream makers, and water wells is one kind of wheel and axle. In this lab, you will use a crank handle to find out how a wheel and axle helps you do work. You will also determine what effect the length of the handle has on the operation of the machine.

Procedure

1. Copy Table 1 into your ScienceLog.
2. Measure the radius (in meters) of the large dowel in the wheel and axle assembly. Record this in Table 1 as the axle radius, which remains constant throughout the lab. (Hint: Measure the diameter and divide by two.)
3. Using the spring scale, measure the weight of the large mass. Record this in Table 1 as the output force, which remains constant throughout the lab.
4. Use two C-clamps to secure the wheel and axle assembly to the table, as shown at right.

Collect Data

5. Measure the length (in meters) of handle 1. Record this as a wheel radius in Table 1.
6. Insert the handle into the hole in the axle. Attach one end of the string to the large mass and the other end to the screw in the axle. The mass should hang down and the handle should turn freely.
7. Turn the handle to lift the mass off the floor. Hold the spring scale upside down, and attach it to the end of the handle. Measure the force (in newtons) as the handle pulls up on the spring scale. Record this as the input force.

666

SKILL BUILDER

Materials

- wheel and axle assembly
- meterstick
- large mass
- spring scale
- handles
- 0.5 m string
- 2 C-clamps

Table 1 Data Collection				
Handle	Axle radius (m)	Output force (N)	Wheel radius (m)	Input force (N)
1				
2				
3				
4				

DO NOT WRITE IN BOOK

8. Remove the spring scale, and lower the mass to the floor. Remove the handle.

9. Repeat steps 5 through 8 with the other three handles. Record all data in Table 1.

Analyze the Results

10. Copy Table 2 into your ScienceLog.

		Table 2 Calculations				
Handle	Axle distance (m)	Wheel distance (m)	Work input (J)	Work output (J)	Mechanical efficiency (%)	Mechanical advantage
1						
2						
3						
4						

DO NOT WRITE IN BOOK

11. Calculate the following for each handle using the equations given. Record your answers in Table 2.

   a. Distance axle rotates = $2 \times \pi \times$ axle radius

   Distance wheel rotates = $2 \times \pi \times$ wheel radius

   (Use 3.14 for the value of π.)

   b. Work input = input force × wheel distance

   Work output = output force × axle distance

   c. Mechanical efficiency = $\frac{\text{work output}}{\text{work input}} \times 100$

   d. Mechanical advantage = $\frac{\text{wheel radius}}{\text{axle radius}}$

Draw Conclusions

12. What happens to work output and work input as the handle length increases? Why?

13. What happens to mechanical efficiency as the handle length increases? Why?

14. What happens to mechanical advantage as the handle length increases? Why?

15. What will happen to mechanical advantage if the handle length is kept constant and the axle radius gets larger?

16. What factors were controlled in this experiment? What was the variable?

Datasheets for LabBook
Datasheet 30

Larry Tackett
Andrew Jackson Middle School
Cross Lanes, West Virginia

Safety Caution

Remind students not to stand too close to the handle after the string is wound on the axle. If the spring scale comes off the handle, the handle may spin around and hit someone.

Answers

11a. Axle distance = 2 π (0.012 m) = 0.075 m

Wheel distance = 2 π × (handle length: 0.10 m, 0.15 m, 0.20 m, 0.25 m) = 0.63 m, 0.94 m, 1.3 m, 1.6 m

b. Answers will depend on the mass used. Check calculations for accuracy.

c. Mechanical efficiency will depend on the materials used. Check calculations for accuracy.

d. Mechanical advantages are 8.3, 12.5, 16.7, and 20.8 for the handles (10 cm, 15 cm, 20 cm, and 25 cm).

12. As the handle length increases, work output stays the same, but work input gets slightly larger because the machine becomes less efficient.

13. The mechanical efficiency decreases as the handle length increases because the large dowel rotates within the PVC pipe more, creating more friction. More friction leads to lower mechanical efficiency.

14. Mechanical advantage increases as handle length increases because the input force for a large handle (wheel) is less.

15. The mechanical advantage will decrease.

16. Controlled factors include the axle radius and the mass used. The variable was the wheel radius (the length of the handle).

Chapter 8 • LabBook 667

Finding Energy
Teacher's Notes

Time Required
Two 45-minute class periods

Lab Ratings

TEACHER PREP
STUDENT SET-UP
CONCEPT LEVEL
CLEAN UP

MATERIALS
The materials listed for this lab are enough for each group of 2–3 students. Rolling carts are available from suppliers of science classroom materials. The ramp should be at least 1 m long.

Procedure Notes
Use one day to set up and collect data. Use the second day for calculations, or assign the calculations as homework.

Answers
1. Accept all reasonable hypotheses.

 Datasheets for LabBook Datasheet 31

Using Scientific Methods

Finding Energy

DISCOVERY LAB

When you coast down a big hill on a bike or skateboard, you may notice that you pick up speed. Because you are moving, you have kinetic energy—the energy of motion. Where does that energy come from? In this lab you will find out!

Materials
- 2 or 3 books
- wooden board
- masking tape
- meterstick
- metric balance
- rolling cart
- stopwatch

Form a Hypothesis
1. Where does the kinetic energy come from when you roll down a hill? Write your hypothesis in your ScienceLog.

Conduct an Experiment
2. Copy Table 1 into your ScienceLog.

Table 1 Data Collection						
Height of ramp (m)	Length of ramp (m)	Mass of cart (kg)	Weight of cart (N)	Time of trial (s)			Average time (s)
				1	2	3	
DO NOT WRITE IN BOOK						

3. Make a ramp with the books and board.
4. Use masking tape to make a starting line. Be sure the starting line is far enough from the top so the cart can be placed behind the line.
5. Place a strip of masking tape at the bottom of the ramp to mark the finish line.
6. Determine the height of the ramp by measuring the height of the starting line and subtracting the height of the finish line. Record the height of the ramp in meters in Table 1.
7. Measure the distance in meters between the starting and the finish lines. Record this distance as the length of the ramp in Table 1.
8. Use the metric balance to find the mass of the cart in grams. Convert this to kilograms by dividing by 1,000. Record the mass in kilograms in Table 1.
9. Multiply the mass by 10 to get the weight of the cart in newtons. Record the weight in Table 1.

Collect Data
10. Set the cart behind the starting line, and release it. Use the stopwatch to time how long it takes for the cart to reach the finish line. Record the time in Table 1.
11. Repeat step 10 twice more, and average the results. Record the average time in Table 1.

Rebecca Ferguson
North Ridge Middle School
North Richland Hills, Texas

Analyze the Results

12. Copy Table 2 into your ScienceLog.

Table 2 Calculations			
Average speed (m/s)	Final speed (m/s)	Kinetic energy at bottom (J)	Gravitational potential energy at top (J)
DO NOT WRITE IN BOOK			

13. Calculate and record the following quantities for the cart in Table 2 using your data and the equations below:

   a. Average speed = $\dfrac{\text{length of ramp}}{\text{average time}}$

   b. Final speed = 2 × average speed
   (This equation works because the cart accelerates smoothly from 0 m/s.)

   c. Kinetic energy = $\dfrac{\text{mass} \times (\text{final speed})^2}{2}$
   (Remember that 1 kg · m²/s/s = 1 J, the unit used to express energy.)

   d. Gravitational potential energy = weight × height
   (Remember that 1 N = 1 kg · m/s/s, so 1 N × 1 m = 1 kg · m²/s/s = 1 J.)

Draw Conclusions

14. How does the cart's gravitational potential energy at the top of the ramp compare with its kinetic energy at the bottom? Does this support your hypothesis? Explain your answer.

15. You probably found that the gravitational potential energy of the cart at the top of the ramp was close but not exactly equal to the kinetic energy of the cart at the bottom. Explain this finding.

16. While riding your bike, you coast down both a small hill and a large hill. Compare your final speed at the bottom of the small hill with your final speed at the bottom of the large hill. Explain your answer.

Answers

14. The cart's gravitational potential energy at the top of the ramp is very close to its kinetic energy at the bottom of the ramp. Whether this finding supports the original hypothesis will depend on the original hypothesis.

15. The cart's gravitational potential energy at the top of the ramp is slightly greater than its kinetic energy at the bottom of the ramp because some of the energy is used to do work against friction. Without friction, the two energy measurements would be the same.

16. You would have a greater final speed at the bottom of the large hill than at the bottom of the small hill. The amount of gravitational potential energy depends on height. Starting from a greater height means starting with more gravitational potential energy, which is converted into kinetic energy as you coast down the hill.

Science Skills Worksheet 12
"Working with Hypotheses"

Energy of a Pendulum
Teacher's Notes

Time Required

One 45-minute class period

Lab Ratings

TEACHER PREP 🔥
STUDENT SET-UP 🔥🔥
CONCEPT LEVEL 🔥🔥
CLEAN UP 🔥

MATERIALS

The materials listed are for each student.

Safety Caution

Caution students to swing the pendulum gently. Students should be a reasonable distance from one another and from classroom equipment. Students should wear safety goggles.

Answers

5. Accept all reasonable answers.

6. slowest when it is first released and when it is at the top of the opposite side; fastest at the bottom of its swing during each trial

7. greatest potential energy at the greatest height on either side; smallest potential energy at the bottom of its swing

8. greatest kinetic energy at the bottom of its swing (moving fastest); smallest kinetic energy at the top of its swing (moving slowest)

9. The pendulum's kinetic energy increases on its way down (as the pendulum speeds up). As the pendulum moves from its highest point to its lowest point, potential energy decreases.

10. Accept all reasonable answers.

Energy of a Pendulum

A pendulum clock is a compound machine that uses stored energy to do work. A spring stores energy, and with each swing of the pendulum, some of that stored energy is used to move the hands of the clock. In this lab you will take a close look at the energy conversions that occur as a pendulum swings.

SKILL BUILDER

Materials
- 1 m of string
- 100 g hooked mass
- marker
- meterstick

Collect Data

1. Make a pendulum by tying the string around the hook of the mass. Use the marker and the meterstick to mark points on the string that are 50 cm, 70 cm, and 90 cm away from the mass.

2. Hold the string at the 50 cm mark. Gently pull the mass to the side, and release it without pushing it. Observe at least 10 swings of the pendulum.

3. In your ScienceLog, record your observations. Be sure to note how fast and how high the pendulum swings.

4. Repeat steps 2 and 3 while holding the string at the 70 cm mark and again while holding the string at the 90 cm mark.

Analyze the Results

5. In your ScienceLog, list similarities and differences in the motion of the pendulum during all three trials.

6. At which point (or points) of the swing was the pendulum moving the slowest? the fastest?

Draw Conclusions

7. In each trial, at which point (or points) of the swing did the pendulum have the greatest potential energy? the smallest potential energy? (Hint: Think about your answers to question 6.)

8. At which point (or points) of the swing did the pendulum have the greatest kinetic energy? the smallest kinetic energy? Explain your answers.

9. Describe the relationship between the pendulum's potential energy and its kinetic energy on its way down. Explain.

10. What improvements might reduce the amount of energy used to overcome friction so that the pendulum would swing for a longer period of time?

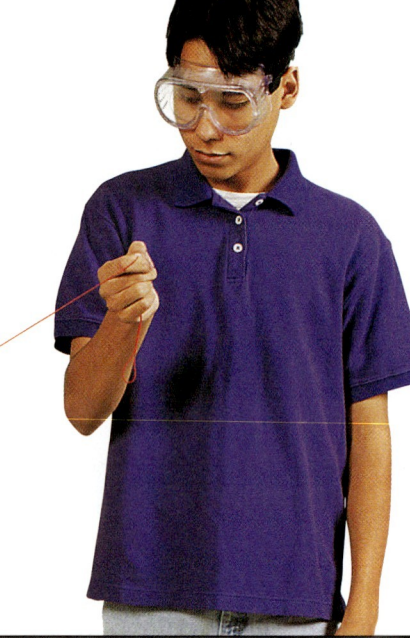

 Datasheets for LabBook
Datasheet 32

Edith C. McAlanis
Socorro Middle School
El Paso, Texas

Eggstremely Fragile

All moving objects have kinetic energy. The faster an object is moving, the more kinetic energy it has. When a falling object hits the floor, the law of conservation of energy requires that the energy be transferred to another object or changed into another form of energy.

When an unprotected egg hits the ground from a height of 1 m, most of the kinetic energy of the falling egg is transferred to the pieces of the shell—with messy results. In this lab you will design a protection system for an egg.

Materials

- raw egg
- empty half-pint milk carton
- assorted materials provided by your teacher

Conduct an Experiment

1. Using the materials provided by your teacher, design a protection system that will prevent the egg from breaking when it is dropped from heights of 1, 2, and 3 m. Keep the following points in mind while developing your egg-protection system:
   a. The egg and its protection system must fit inside the closed milk carton. (Note: The milk carton will not be dropped with the egg.)
   b. The protective materials don't have to be soft.
   c. The protective materials can surround the egg or can be attached to the egg at various points.
2. In your ScienceLog, explain why you chose your materials.
3. You will perform the three trials at a time and location specified by your teacher. Record your results for each trial in your ScienceLog.

Analyze the Results

4. Did your egg survive all three trials? If it did not, why did your egg-protection system fail? If your egg did survive, what features of your egg-protecting system transferred or absorbed the energy?

Draw Conclusions

5. How do egg cartons like those you find in a grocery store protect eggs from mishandling?

Answers

4. Answers will depend on the results of the trials. Possible reasons for failure include thin protection or the protection falling off. Features that enable the egg to survive might include those that slow the egg down so that it lands gently or those that pad the egg so that the protective material, rather than the egg, absorbs the energy of the impact.

5. The cardboard or plastic foam provides padding, and the shape of the carton directs energy away from the egg instead of into the shell.

Datasheets for LabBook
Datasheet 33

Eggstremely Fragile
Teacher's Notes

Time Required
One or two 45-minute class periods

Lab Ratings

Teacher Prep 🧪🧪
Student Set-Up 🧪🧪🧪
Concept Level 🧪🧪🧪
Clean Up 🧪🧪🧪

Safety Caution
Students should wear safety goggles and an apron when doing this lab. Caution students not to throw the eggs. Students should wash their hands thoroughly after handling the eggs.

Procedure Notes
The more types of materials you provide, the more creative students' solutions will be. Good materials include cotton balls, plastic straws, modeling clay, wooden craft sticks, newspaper, glue, and Silly Putty™. Try to provide both hard and soft materials. Place the egg and protection system in a plastic bag; wrap the egg and protective system in plastic wrap; or spread a large plastic sheet on the ground at the drop point.

John Zambo
E. Ustach Middle School
Modesto, California

Feel the Heat
Teacher's Notes

Time Required
One or two 45-minute class periods

Lab Ratings

- TEACHER PREP 🧪🧪🧪
- STUDENT SET-UP 🧪🧪
- CONCEPT LEVEL 🧪🧪🧪
- CLEAN UP 🧪🧪

MATERIALS
Materials listed are for each group of 2–4 students.

Safety Caution
Caution students to review all safety cautions and icons before beginning this activity. Remind students that a thermometer should never be used for stirring. The container of hot water should be located where it cannot spill on students. Caution students to handle the nails carefully.

Procedure Notes
Heat water before class. Do not let the water temperature exceed 60°C. You may want to keep a large container of water heating on a hot plate. For step 4, the nails are set aside for about 5 minutes so that they will warm up to the same temperature as the water.

Answer
1. Accept all reasonable predictions.

Using Scientific Methods

DISCOVERY LAB

Feel the Heat

Heat is the transfer of energy between objects at different temperatures. Energy moves from objects at higher temperatures to objects at lower temperatures. If two objects are left in contact for a while, the warmer object will cool down, and the cooler object will warm up until they eventually reach the same temperature. In this activity, you will combine equal masses of water and iron nails at different temperatures to determine which has a greater effect on the final temperature.

Materials
- rubber band
- 10–12 nails
- metric balance
- 30 cm of string
- 9 oz plastic-foam cups (2)
- hot water
- 100 mL graduated cylinder
- cold water
- thermometer
- paper towels

Make a Prediction
1. When you combine substances at two different temperatures, will the final temperature be closer to the initial temperature of the warmer substance or of the colder substance, or halfway in between? Write your prediction in your ScienceLog.

Conduct an Experiment/Collect Data
2. Copy the table below into your ScienceLog.

Data Collection Table					
Trial	Mass of nails (g)	Volume of water that equals mass of nails (mL)	Initial temp. of water and nails (°C)	Initial temp. of water to which nails will be transferred (°C)	Final temp. of water and nails combined (°C)
1					
2					

DO NOT WRITE IN BOOK

3. Use the rubber band to bundle the nails together. Find and record the mass of the bundle. Tie a length of string around the bundle, leaving one end of the string 15 cm long.

4. Put the bundle of nails into one of the cups, letting the string dangle outside the cup. Fill the cup with enough hot water to cover the nails, and set it aside for at least 5 minutes.

5. Use the graduated cylinder to measure enough cold water to exactly equal the mass of the nails (1 mL of water = 1 g). Record this volume in the table.

6. Measure and record the temperature of the hot water with the nails and the temperature of the cold water.

 Datasheets for LabBook
Datasheet 34

Dennis Hanson
Big Bear Middle School
Big Bear Lake, California

7. Use the string to transfer the bundle of nails to the cup of cold water. Use the thermometer to monitor the temperature of the water-nail mixture. When the temperature stops changing, record this final temperature in the table.

8. Empty the cups, and dry the nails.

9. For Trial 2, repeat steps 3 through 8, but switch the hot and cold water. Record all of your measurements.

Analyze the Results

10. In Trial 1, you used equal masses of cold water and nails. Did the final temperature support your initial prediction? Explain.

11. In Trial 2, you used equal masses of hot water and nails. Did the final temperature support your initial prediction? Explain.

12. In Trial 1, which material—the water or the nails—changed temperature the most after you transferred the nails? What about in Trial 2? Explain your answers.

Draw Conclusions

13. The cold water in Trial 1 gained energy. Where did the energy come from?

14. How does the energy gained by the nails in Trial 2 compare with the energy lost by the hot water in Trial 2? Explain.

15. Which material seems to be able to hold energy better? Explain your answer.

16. Specific heat capacity is a property of matter that indicates how much energy is required to change the temperature of 1 kg of a material by 1°C. Which material in this activity has a higher specific heat capacity (changes temperature less for the same amount of energy)?

17. Would it be better to have pots and pans made from a material with a high specific heat capacity or a low specific heat capacity? Explain your answer. (Hint: Do you want the pan or the food in the pan to absorb all of the energy from the stove?)

Communicate Results

18. Share your results with your classmates. Discuss how you would change your prediction to include your knowledge of specific heat capacity.

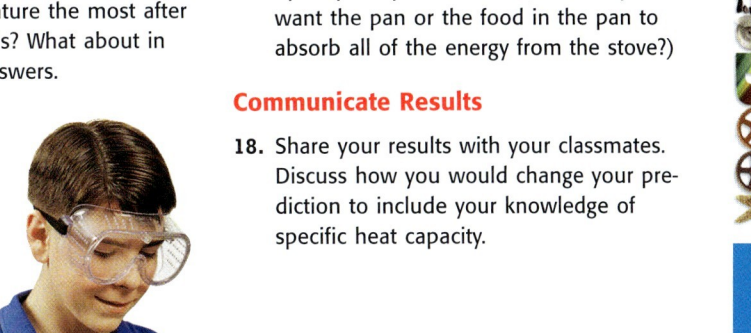

Answers

10. Answers will vary depending on the initial prediction.
11. Answers will vary depending on the initial prediction.
12. The nails changed temperature more in both trials. Explanations should include references to initial and final temperatures.
13. from the heated nails
14. The energy gained by the nails should be about the same as the energy lost by the hot water (there might be some difference due to energy transfer to the cup and air). The energy changes are the same because energy is conserved. Any energy gained by the nails must come from somewhere—in this case, from the water.
15. The water appears to hold energy better. Students' explanations should include that the temperature of the water changed less than the temperature of an equal mass of iron.
16. water
17. Pots and pans should be made from a material with a low specific heat capacity so that more energy from the stove will be transferred to the food than to the pots and pans.
18. Accept all reasonable answers. Sample revised prediction: The final temperature would be closer to the original temperature of the substance that has the higher specific heat capacity.

Save the Cube!
Teacher's Notes

Time Required
One or two 45-minute class periods

Lab Ratings

TEACHER PREP	🧪🧪🧪
STUDENT SET-UP	🧪🧪
CONCEPT LEVEL	🧪🧪🧪
CLEAN UP	🧪

MATERIALS
Use incandescent lights, a hair dryer, or hot plates (low setting) to prepare a "thermal zone." Use the lowest setting on the hot plate so the plastic bags do not melt. Provide a large assortment of materials to protect the ice cubes, including white paper, cotton balls, plastic-foam packing peanuts, bubble wrap, tape, aluminum foil, and rubber bands.

Safety Caution
Caution students to wear heat-resistant gloves if working near a hot plate.

Procedure Notes
Set up the thermal zone before class. Have students find and record the masses of the empty cup and empty bag before they obtain their ice cubes.

 Datasheets for LabBook
Datasheet 35

Save the Cube!

The biggest enemy of an ice cube is the transfer of thermal energy—heat. Energy can be transferred to an ice cube in three ways: conduction (the transfer of energy through direct contact), convection (the transfer of energy by the movement of a liquid or gas), and radiation (the transfer of energy through matter or space). Your challenge in this activity is to design a way to protect an ice cube as much as possible from all three types of energy transfer.

Materials
- small plastic bag
- ice cube
- assorted materials provided by your teacher
- empty half-pint milk carton
- metric balance
- small plastic or paper cup

Procedure

1. Follow these guidelines: Use a plastic bag to hold the ice cube and any water from its melting. You may use any of the materials to protect the ice cube. The ice cube, bag, and protection must all fit inside the milk carton.

2. Describe your proposed design in your ScienceLog. Explain how your design protects against each type of energy transfer.

3. Find the mass of the empty cup, and record it in your ScienceLog. Then find and record the mass of an empty plastic bag.

4. Place an ice cube in the bag. Quickly find and record their mass together.

5. Quickly wrap the bag (and the ice cube inside) in its protection. Remember that the package must fit in the milk carton.

6. Place your protected ice cube in the "thermal zone" set up by your teacher. After 10 minutes, remove the package from the zone and remove the protective material from the plastic bag and ice cube.

7. Open the bag. Pour any water into the cup. Find and record the mass of the cup and water together.

8. Find and record the mass of the water by subtracting the mass of the empty cup from the mass of the cup and water.

9. Use the same method to find and record the mass of the ice cube.

10. Find the percentage of the ice cube that melted using the following equation:

$$\% \text{ melted} = \frac{\text{mass of water}}{\text{mass of ice cube}} \times 100$$

11. Record this percentage in your ScienceLog and on the board.

Analysis

12. Compared with other designs in your class, how well did your design protect against each type of energy transfer? How could you improve your design?

13. Why is a white plastic-foam cooler so useful for keeping ice frozen?

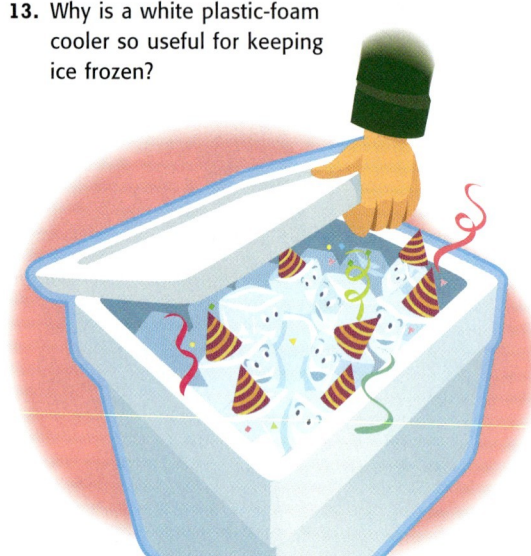

Answers

12. Answers will vary but should provide an accurate assessment of results and reasonable ideas for design improvement.

13. Answers should address how the cooler minimizes the effects of all three types of energy transfer (radiation, convection, and conduction).

David Sparks
Redwater Junior High
Redwater, Texas

Counting Calories

Energy transferred by heat is often expressed in units called calories. In this lab, you will build a model of a device called a calorimeter. Scientists often use calorimeters to measure the amount of energy that can be transferred by a substance. In this experiment, you will construct your own calorimeter and test it by measuring the energy released by a hot penny.

Procedure

1. Copy the table below into your ScienceLog.

Data Collection Table									
Seconds	0	15	30	45	60	75	90	105	120
Water temp. (°C)									

DO NOT WRITE IN BOOK

Materials

- small plastic-foam cup with lid
- thermometer
- large plastic-foam cup
- water
- 100 mL graduated cylinder
- tongs
- heat source
- penny
- stopwatch

2. Place the lid on the small plastic-foam cup, and insert a thermometer through the hole in the top of the lid. (The thermometer should not touch the bottom of the cup.) Place the small cup inside the large cup to complete the calorimeter.

3. Remove the lid from the small cup, and add 50 mL of room-temperature water to the cup. Measure the water's temperature, and record the value in the first column (0 seconds) of the table.

4. Using tongs, heat the penny carefully. Add the penny to the water in the small cup, and replace the lid. Start your stopwatch.

5. Every 15 seconds, measure and record the temperature. Gently swirl the large cup to stir the water, and continue recording temperatures for 2 minutes (120 seconds).

Analysis

6. What was the total temperature change of the water after 2 minutes?

7. The number of calories absorbed by the water is the mass of the water (in grams) multiplied by the temperature change (in °C) of the water. How many calories were absorbed by the water? (Hint: 1 mL of water = 1 g of water)

8. In terms of heat, explain where the calories to change the water temperature came from.

John Zambo
E. Ustach Middle School
Modesto, California

Answers

6. Answers should be the final temperature (at 120 seconds) minus the initial temperature (at 0 seconds).

7. The number of calories absorbed by the water equals temperature change (step 6) times the mass of the water (50 g).

8. The calories came from the penny. The penny increased the temperature of the water by transferring energy to it.

Counting Calories
Teacher's Notes

Time Required
One 45-minute class period

Lab Ratings

EASY ——————→ HARD

- TEACHER PREP 🧪🧪
- STUDENT SET-UP 🧪
- CONCEPT LEVEL 🧪🧪
- CLEAN UP 🧪

MATERIALS
The materials listed are for each group of 2–3 students.

Safety Caution
Caution students to wear goggles and an apron and to use care when working near the heat source. Remind students never to use a thermometer for stirring.

Preparation Notes
You may wish to model the procedure for making the calorimeter and the proper method of heating the penny before students begin the lab. Remind students that a calorie is the amount of energy needed to raise the temperature of 1 g of water by 1°C. All students should heat the penny for the same amount of time.

 Datasheets for LabBook
Datasheet 36

Made to Order
Teacher's Notes

Time Required

One 45-minute class period

Lab Ratings

- TEACHER PREP — 🧪🧪
- STUDENT SET-UP — 🧪
- CONCEPT LEVEL — 🧪🧪🧪
- CLEAN UP — 🧪

MATERIALS

The supplies listed are for a pair of students. Foam balls of any color are acceptable as long as there are two colors. Flexible pipe cleaners may be used instead of toothpicks.

Safety Caution

Remind students to review all safety cautions and icons before beginning this lab activity.

Preparation Notes

Before you begin this lab, review the concepts of isotopes, atomic number, and mass number.

To create colored balls, use colored markers or spray paint. Alternatively, you can label white balls with "N" or "P." If you prefer to make two-dimensional models, use colored dots (from an office-supply store) to represent the different particles. Reinforce the idea that the particles should be compact—the strong force binds the particles together as tightly as possible.

Made to Order

MAKING MODELS

Imagine that you are a new employee at the Elements-4-U Company, which custom builds elements. Your job is to construct the atomic nucleus for each element ordered by your clients. You were hired for the position because of your knowledge about what a nucleus is made of and your understanding of how isotopes of an element differ from each other. Now it's time to put that knowledge to work!

Materials

- 4 protons (white plastic-foam balls, 2–3 cm in diameter)
- 6 neutrons (blue plastic-foam balls, 2–3 cm in diameter)
- 20 strong-force connectors (toothpicks)
- periodic table

Procedure

1. Copy the table below into your ScienceLog. Be sure to leave room to expand the table to include more elements.

	Hydrogen-1	Hydrogen-2	Helium-3	Helium-4	Lithium-7	Beryllium-9	Beryllium-10
No. of protons							
No. of neutrons							
Atomic number							
Mass number							

DO NOT WRITE IN BOOK

2. Your first assignment: the nucleus of hydrogen-1. Pick up one proton (a white plastic-foam ball). Congratulations! You have just built a hydrogen-1 nucleus, the simplest nucleus possible.

3. Count the number of protons and neutrons in the nucleus, and fill in rows 1 and 2 for this element in the table.

4. Use the information in rows 1 and 2 to determine the atomic number and mass number of the element. Record this information in the table.

5. Draw a picture of your model in your ScienceLog.

6. Hydrogen-2 is an isotope of hydrogen that has one proton and one neutron. Using a strong-force connector, add a neutron to your hydrogen-1 nucleus. (Remember that in a nucleus, the protons and neutrons are held together by the strong force, which is represented in this activity by the toothpicks.) Repeat steps 3–5.

 Datasheets for LabBook
Datasheet 37

Sharon L. Woolf
Langston Hughes Middle School
Reston, Virginia

7. Helium-3 is an isotope of helium that has two protons and one neutron. Add one proton to your hydrogen-2 nucleus to create a helium-3 nucleus. Each particle should be connected to the other two particles so they make a triangle, not a line. Protons and neutrons always form the smallest arrangement possible because the strong force pulls them together. Repeat steps 3–5.

8. For the next part of the lab, you will need to use information from the periodic table of the elements. Look at the illustration at right. It shows the periodic table entry for carbon, one of the most abundant elements on Earth. For your job, the most important information in the periodic table is the atomic number. You can find the atomic number of any element at the top of its entry on the table. In the example, the atomic number of carbon is 6.

9. Use the information in the periodic table to build models of the following isotopes of elements: helium-4, lithium-7, beryllium-9, and beryllium-10. Remember to put the protons and neutrons as close together as possible—each particle should attach to at least two others. Repeat steps 3–5 for each isotope.

Atomic number

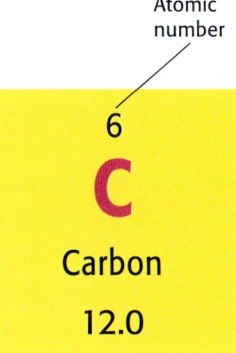

Analyze the Results

10. What is the relationship between the number of protons and the atomic number?

11. If you know the atomic number and the mass number of an isotope, how could you figure out the number of neutrons in its nucleus?

12. Look up uranium on the periodic table.
    a. What is the atomic number of uranium?
    b. How many neutrons does the isotope uranium-235 have?

Communicate Results

13. Compare your model with the models of other groups. How are they similar? How are they different?

Going Further
Working with another group, combine your models. Identify the element (and isotope) you have created.

Answers
10. The number of protons is the same as the atomic number.
11. The number of neutrons equals the mass number minus the atomic number.
12. a. 92
    b. 143 neutrons
    (235 − 92 = 143)
13. Accept all reasonable answers.

Going Further
If all of the protons and neutrons are used, the isotope created will be oxygen-20.

Science Skills Worksheet 24 "Using Models to Communicate"

Chapter 11 • LabBook **677**

Create a Periodic Table
Teacher's Notes

Time Required
One to two 45-minute class periods

Lab Ratings

TEACHER PREP 🔺🔺🔺
STUDENT SET-UP 🔺
CONCEPT LEVEL 🔺🔺🔺
CLEAN UP 🔺

MATERIALS
The materials listed for this lab are for each group of 2–4 students. For each group of students, assemble a collection of 20 objects (five sets of four objects). You should provide a bag containing 19 of these objects. A recommended collection of objects includes sets of coins (penny, nickel, dime, quarter), sets of buttons that are similar but vary in diameter, and washers that vary in diameter. Other objects, such as nuts, bolts, and paper circles, will work and are easily obtainable. The difference in masses should be large enough for a beam balance to detect. Ideally, each set (one column on the table) should be of the same material and thickness and vary only in diameter.

Preparation Note
You may have students prepare the 20 squares of paper, but the lab will go faster if the squares are prepared ahead of time.

Datasheets for LabBook
Datasheet 38

Create a Periodic Table

You probably have classification systems for many things in your life, such as your clothes, your books, and your CDs. One of the most important classification systems in science is the periodic table of the elements. In this lab you will develop your own classification system for a collection of ordinary objects. You will analyze trends in your system and compare your system with the periodic table of the elements.

Materials
- bag of objects
- 20 squares of paper, each 3 × 3 cm
- metric balance
- metric ruler
- 2 sheets of graph paper

Procedure

1. Your teacher will give you a bag of objects. Your bag is missing one item. Examine the items carefully. Describe the missing object in as many ways as you can in your ScienceLog. Be sure to include the reasons why you think the missing object has these characteristics.

2. Lay the paper squares out on your desk or table so that you have a grid of five rows of four squares each.

3. Arrange your objects on the grid in a logical order. (You must decide what order is logical!) You should end up with one blank square for the missing object.

4. In your ScienceLog, describe the basis for your arrangement.

5. Measure the mass (g) and diameter (mm) of each object, and record your results in the appropriate square. Each square (except the empty one) should have one object and two written measurements on it.

Answer
4. Answers will vary. One basis is increasing size from left to right and increasing diameter from top to bottom. This places similar objects in a vertical group or family, like the groups of the periodic table.

Norman Holcomb
Marion Elementary School
Maria Stein, Ohio

6. Examine your pattern again. Does the order in which your objects are arranged still make sense? Explain.

7. Rearrange the squares and their objects if necessary to improve your arrangement. Describe the basis for the new arrangement in your ScienceLog.

8. Working across the rows, number the squares 1 to 20. When you get to the end of a row, continue numbering in the first square of the next row.

9. Copy your grid into your ScienceLog. In each square, be sure to list the type of object and label all measurements with appropriate units.

Analyze the Results

10. Make a graph of mass (y-axis) versus object number (x-axis). Label each axis, and title the graph.

11. Now make a graph of diameter (y-axis) versus object number (x-axis).

Communicate Results

12. Discuss each graph with your classmates. Try to identify any important features of the graph. For example, does the graph form a line or a curve? Is there anything unusual about the graph? What do these features tell you? Write your answers in your ScienceLog.

Draw Conclusions

13. How is your arrangement of objects similar to the periodic table of the elements found in this textbook? How is your arrangement different from that periodic table?

14. Look back at your prediction about the missing object. Do you think it is still accurate? Try to improve your description by estimating the mass and diameter of the missing object. Record your estimates in your ScienceLog.

15. Mendeleev created a periodic table of elements and predicted characteristics of missing elements. How is your experiment similar to Mendeleev's work?

Science Skills Worksheet 26 "Grasping Graphing"

7. The primary difference many students will note is in rearranging the columns so that the mass (rather than size) increases across a row. More information (the mass of each object) allows students to create a more organized chart.

10. Graphs should be similar to sample graph A.

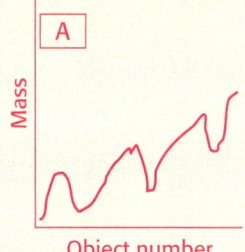

11. Graphs should be similar to sample graph B.

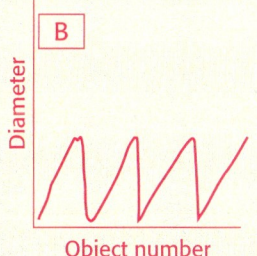

12. Answers will vary. The primary feature is the repeating pattern of increases. This pattern in the first graph indicates the periodic nature of the mass of the items. This pattern in the second graph indicates the periodic nature of the diameter of the items.

13. Answers may vary. Similarities include repeating patterns (such as mass) across the table. Differences may include no consistent family traits and no chemical properties associated with position in the table.

14. Answers will vary, depending on the student's original prediction. Accept all reasonable answers. (You may wish to provide the students with the missing object so they can further evaluate their prediction.)

15. This experiment is similar in that a pattern was identified that helped to identify characteristics of a missing object.

LabBook

Covalent Marshmallows
Teacher's Notes

Time Required
One 45-minute class period

Lab Ratings

- TEACHER PREP 🧪🧪
- STUDENT SET-UP 🧪
- CONCEPT LEVEL 🧪🧪
- CLEAN UP 🧪

MATERIALS

Materials listed are for each one to two students. Colored marshmallows are available in some grocery stores. To create different colored marshmallows, "paint" the marshmallows lightly with diluted food coloring. To discourage students from eating the marshmallows, dust them lightly with alum, a bitter spice that can be purchased at a grocery store. An alternative method of coloring the marshmallows is to spray them lightly with hair spray, and sprinkle them with different colors of glitter. Be sure students do not eat the marshmallows!

Safety Caution

Remind students to review all safety cautions and icons before beginning this lab activity.

Rebecca Ferguson
North Ridge Middle School
North Richland Hills, Texas

Covalent Marshmallows

A hydrogen atom has one electron in its outer energy level, but two electrons are required to fill its outer level. An oxygen atom has six electrons in its outer energy level, but eight electrons are required to fill its outer level. In order to fill their outer energy levels, two atoms of hydrogen and one atom of oxygen can share electrons, as shown below. Such a sharing of electrons to fill the outer level of atoms is called covalent bonding. When hydrogen and oxygen bond in this manner, a molecule of water is formed. In this lab you will build a three-dimensional model of water in order to better understand the covalent bonds formed in a water molecule.

Materials
- marshmallows (2 of one color, 1 of another color)
- toothpicks

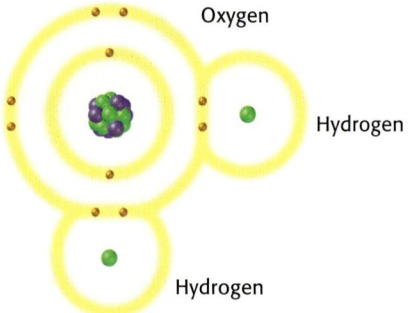

A Model of a Water Molecule

Procedure

1. Using the marshmallows and toothpicks, create a model of a water molecule. Use the diagram above for guidance in building your model.
2. Draw a sketch of your model in your ScienceLog. Be sure to label the hydrogen and oxygen atoms on your sketch.
3. Draw an electron-dot diagram of the water molecule in your ScienceLog. (Refer to the chapter text if you need help drawing an electron-dot diagram.)

Analysis

4. What do the marshmallows represent? What do the toothpicks represent?
5. Why are the marshmallows different colors?
6. Compare your model with the picture above. How might your model be improved to more accurately represent a water molecule?

Answers

4. The marshmallows represent atoms. The toothpicks represent the pairs of electrons that create the covalent bonds.
5. Marshmallows are different colors to represent atoms of different elements.
6. Accept all reasonable answers. Sample answers: Use marshmallows of different sizes to show the difference in size between the atoms. Use different substances to represent hydrogen and oxygen because they are different elements.

7. Hydrogen in nature can covalently bond to form hydrogen molecules, H$_2$. How could you model this using the marshmallows and toothpicks?

8. Draw an electron-dot diagram of a hydrogen molecule in your ScienceLog.

9. Which do you think would be more difficult to create—a model of an ionic bond or a model of a covalent bond? Explain your answer.

Going Further

Create a model of a carbon dioxide molecule, which consists of two oxygen atoms and one carbon atom. The structure is similar to the structure of water, although the three atoms bond in a straight line instead of at angles. The bond between each oxygen atom and the carbon atom in a carbon dioxide molecule is a "double bond," so use two connections. Do the double bonds in carbon dioxide appear stronger or weaker than the single bonds in water? Explain your answer.

7. A hydrogen molecule could be modeled by using a toothpick to connect the two hydrogen marshmallows together without the oxygen marshmallow.

8. An electron-dot diagram of the hydrogen molecule should look like the following: H : H.

9. Students will likely answer that a model of an ionic bond would be more difficult to create because it involves the transfer of electrons. That would be like breaking off a little piece of one marshmallow and gluing it to another marshmallow, but then there is no way to hold the marshmallows together.

Going Further

The double bonds appear stronger than single bonds because there is more "attraction" (there are more toothpicks) holding the atoms together. It is more difficult to separate two shared pairs of electrons (break two toothpicks) than to separate one shared pair of electrons (break one toothpick).

Datasheets for LabBook
Datasheet 39

Science Skills Worksheet 23
"Science Drawing"

Procedure Notes

To extend this activity, you may use additional colors to create marshmallow models of various molecules. In addition, different-sized marshmallows can be used to represent the relative sizes of atoms of different elements.

Finding a Balance
Teacher's Notes

Time Required
One 45-minute class period

Lab Ratings

- TEACHER PREP 🧪🧪
- STUDENT SET-UP 🧪
- CONCEPT LEVEL 🧪🧪
- CLEAN UP 🧪

MATERIALS

Create at least two envelopes per group. Label each envelope with an unbalanced chemical equation. In each envelope place one paper arrow, some reactant molecules, and some product molecules. Include extra reactants and products so students do not just put the reactants on one side of the arrow and the products on the other. To create molecule models, draw squares onto a sheet of paper, and label them. Color the squares so that each element has a unique color. Hint: Draw the molecule models on a sheet of paper, make enough photocopies for all your groups, color the squares (or have students do it), laminate the pages, then cut out the squares.

Sample unbalanced equations:

$Na + Cl_2 \rightarrow NaCl$

$C_2H_4 + O_2 \rightarrow CO_2 + H_2O$

$Fe + O_2 \rightarrow FeO$

$Al + CuSO_4 \rightarrow Al_2(SO_4)_3 + Cu$

$Ba(CN)_2 + H_2SO_4 \rightarrow BaSO_4 + HCN$

Datasheets for LabBook
Datasheet 40

Finding a Balance

 MAKING MODELS

Usually, balancing a chemical equation involves just writing in your ScienceLog. But in this activity, you will use models to practice balancing chemical equations, as shown below. By following the rules, you will soon become an expert equation balancer!

Materials
- envelopes, each labeled with an unbalanced equation

Example

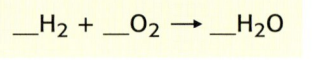

$\_\_H_2 + \_\_O_2 \rightarrow \_\_H_2O$

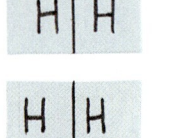

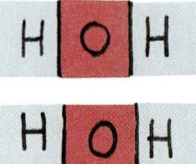

Balanced Equation

$2H_2 + O_2 \rightarrow 2H_2O$

Procedure

1. The rules:
   a. Reactant-molecule models may be placed only to the left of the arrow.
   b. Product-molecule models may be placed only to the right of the arrow.
   c. You may use only complete molecule models.
   d. At least one of each of the reactant and product molecules shown in the equation must be included in the model when you are finished.

2. Select one of the labeled envelopes. Copy the unbalanced equation written on the envelope into your ScienceLog.

3. Open the envelope, and pull out the molecule models and the arrow. Place the arrow in the center of your work area.

4. Put one model of each molecule that is a reactant on the left side of the arrow and one model of each product on the right side.

5. Add one reactant-molecule or product-molecule model at a time until the number of each of the different-colored squares on each side of the arrow is the same. Remember to follow the rules.

6. When the equation is balanced, count the number of each of the molecule models you used. Write these numbers as coefficients, as shown in the balanced equation above.

7. Select another envelope, and repeat the steps until you have balanced all of the equations.

Analysis

8. The rules specify that you are only allowed to use complete molecule models. How is this similar to what occurs in a real chemical reaction?

9. In chemical reactions, energy is either released or absorbed. In your ScienceLog, devise a way to improve the model to show energy being released or absorbed.

Answers

8. Chemical reactions cannot involve partial molecules.

9. Accept all reasonable answers. One possible answer is for students to create a symbol for energy that can be used with the reaction models.

Laura Fleet
Alice B. Landrum Middle School
Ponte Vedra Beach, Florida

Using Scientific Methods

Cata-what? Catalyst!

Catalysts increase the rate of a chemical reaction without being changed during the reaction. In this experiment, hydrogen peroxide, H_2O_2, decomposes into oxygen, O_2, and water, H_2O. An enzyme present in liver cells acts as a catalyst for this reaction. You will investigate the relationship between the amount of the catalyst and the rate of the decomposition reaction.

Ask a Question

1. How does the amount of a catalyst affect reaction rate?

Form a Hypothesis

2. In your ScienceLog, write a statement that answers the question above. Explain your reasoning.

Test the Hypothesis

3. Put a small piece of masking tape near the top of each test tube, and label the tubes 1, 2, and 3.
4. Create a hot-water bath by filling the beaker half-full with hot water.
5. Using the funnel and graduated cylinder, measure 5 mL of the hydrogen peroxide solution into each test tube. Place the test tubes in the hot-water bath for 5 minutes.
6. While the test tubes warm up, grind one liver cube with the mortar and pestle.
7. After 5 minutes, use the tweezers to place the cube of liver in test tube 1. Place the ground liver in test tube 2. Leave test tube 3 alone.

Make Observations

8. Observe the reaction rate (the amount of bubbling) in all three test tubes, and record your observations in your ScienceLog.

Materials

- 10 mL test tubes (3)
- masking tape
- 600 mL beaker
- hot water
- funnel
- 10 mL graduated cylinder
- hydrogen peroxide solution
- 2 small liver cubes
- mortar and pestle
- tweezers

Analyze Your Results

9. Does liver appear to be a catalyst? Explain your answer.
10. Which type of liver (whole or ground) produced a faster reaction? Why?
11. What is the purpose of test tube 3?

Draw Conclusions

12. How do your results support or disprove your hypothesis?
13. Why was a hot-water bath used? (Hint: Look in your book for a definition of activation energy.)

Cata-what? Catalyst!
Teacher's Notes

Time Required
One 45-minute class period

Lab Ratings

EASY ——— HARD

- TEACHER PREP 🧪🧪🧪
- STUDENT SET-UP 🧪
- CONCEPT LEVEL 🧪🧪🧪
- CLEAN UP 🧪🧪

MATERIALS

Materials listed are for each group of 2–3 students. Liver cubes should be about 1 cm^3. Hot water can be obtained from the tap.

Safety Caution

Remind students to review all safety cautions and icons before beginning this lab activity. Use hydrogen peroxide solutions with concentrations of less than 3 percent.

Disposal Information

Solutions may be washed down the sink if your school drains are connected to a sanitary sewer system with a treatment plant. Students should clean the lab area and wash their hands thoroughly.

Answers

9. Yes; the more-vigorous bubbling in the test tubes with liver indicates a faster reaction rate.
10. ground liver; grinding released more catalyst (enzyme) from the liver cells
11. Test tube 3 is a control test tube, used to compare the rate of bubbling with liver to the rate without liver.
12. Accept all reasonable explanations.
13. The bath provides activation energy to start the reaction. The higher temperature also allows the reaction to happen faster.

 **Datasheets for LabBook** Datasheet 41

Rodney A. Sandefur
Naturita Middle School
Naturita, Colorado

Putting Elements Together
Teacher's Notes

Time Required

One to two 45-minute class periods

Lab Ratings

- TEACHER PREP 🧪🧪
- STUDENT SET-UP 🧪🧪
- CONCEPT LEVEL 🧪🧪
- CLEAN UP 🧪

Safety Caution

Remind students to review all safety cautions and icons before beginning this lab activity. Caution students to be careful around the open flame. All loose hair or clothing should be tied back. Students should wear protective gloves when working with the copper powder and use tongs properly when working near the flame. Caution students not to touch the hot evaporating dish with their bare hands.

Procedure Notes

Set up the ring stand so that the ring will be about 5 cm above the flame.

Putting Elements Together

A synthesis reaction is a reaction in which two or more substances combine to form a single compound. The resulting compound has different chemical and physical properties than the substances from which it is composed. In this activity, you will synthesize, or create, copper(II) oxide from the elements copper and oxygen.

Conduct an Experiment/Collect Data

1. Copy the table below into your ScienceLog.

Data Collection Table	
Object	Mass (g)
Evaporating dish	
Copper powder	
Copper + evaporating dish after heating	
Copper(II) oxide	

DO NOT WRITE IN BOOK

2. Use the metric balance to measure the mass (to the nearest 0.1 g) of the empty evaporating dish. Record this mass in the table.

3. Place a piece of weighing paper on the metric balance, and measure approximately 10 g of copper powder. Record the mass (to the nearest 0.1 g) in the table.
   Caution: Wear protective gloves when working with copper powder.

4. Use the weighing paper to place the copper powder in the evaporating dish. Spread the powder over the bottom and up the sides as much as possible. Discard the weighing paper.

Materials

- metric balance
- evaporating dish
- weighing paper
- copper powder
- ring stand and ring
- wire gauze
- Bunsen burner or portable burner
- spark igniter
- tongs

Datasheets for LabBook
Datasheet 42

Paul Boyle
Perry Heights Middle School
Evansville, Indiana

684   Chapter 14 • LabBook

5. Set up the ring stand and ring. Place the wire gauze on top of the ring. Carefully place the evaporating dish on the wire gauze.

6. Place the Bunsen burner under the ring and wire gauze. Use the spark igniter to light the Bunsen burner.
   Caution: Use extreme care when working near an open flame.

7. Heat the evaporating dish for 10 minutes.

8. Turn off the burner, and allow the evaporating dish to cool for 10 minutes. Use tongs to remove the evaporating dish and place it on the balance to determine the mass. Record the mass in the table.

9. Determine the mass of the reaction product—copper(II) oxide—by subtracting the mass of the evaporating dish from the mass of the evaporating dish and copper powder after heating. Record this mass in the table.

Analyze the Results

10. What evidence of a chemical reaction did you observe after the copper was heated?

11. Explain why a change in mass occurred.

12. How does the change in mass support the idea that this is a synthesis reaction?

Draw Conclusions

13. Why was powdered copper used rather than a small piece of copper? (Hint: How does surface area affect the rate of the reaction?)

14. Why was the copper heated? (Hint: Look in your book for the discussion of *activation energy*.)

15. The copper bottoms of cooking pots can turn black when used. How is that similar to the results you obtained in this lab?

Going Further
Rust, shown below, is iron(III) oxide—the product of a synthesis reaction between iron and oxygen. How does painting a car help prevent this type of reaction?

Disposal Information
Any leftover copper powder can be thrown in the trash. Students should wash their hands thoroughly after completing this lab. Dispose of the copper(II) oxide by letting it cool thoroughly, wrapping it in newspaper or paper towels, and then putting it in the trash.

Answers

10. The copper changed color, and the mass changed.

11. A change in mass occurred because the copper combined with oxygen from the air. The resulting copper(II) oxide has more mass than the original copper alone.

12. A synthesis reaction is one in which two or more substances join to form a new substance. The mass of the copper(II) oxide is greater than the mass of the copper alone, so a synthesis reaction, in which the copper combined with oxygen from the air, must have occurred, resulting in the change in mass.

13. Powdered copper has a larger surface area than a piece of copper. More surface area increases the rate of the reaction because more copper is exposed to oxygen.

14. The copper was heated because the formation of copper(II) oxide requires a large activation energy.

15. The copper(II) oxide synthesized in this experiment is the same black powder that appears on copper pots.

Going Further
Painting a car helps prevent rust from forming on it by creating a barrier between the iron of the car and the oxygen. If the iron and oxygen are not in contact, they cannot react to form rust.

Speed Control
Teacher's Notes

Time Required

One to two 45-minute class periods

Lab Ratings

TEACHER PREP 🧪🧪🧪
STUDENT SET-UP 🧪🧪
CONCEPT LEVEL 🧪🧪
CLEAN UP 🧪🧪

MATERIALS

Materials listed are for groups of 2–3 students. Use hydrochloric acid with a concentration between 0.5 and 1.0 M for acid A. Use 0.1 M hydrochloric acid for acid B. When making a solution of acid, it is important always to add the acid to the water. If aluminum strips are not available, substitute strips cut from aluminum cans or aluminum foil.

Safety Caution

Review all safety cautions and icons before beginning this lab activity. Only hydrochloric acid of concentrations less than 1.0 M should be used. Students should not handle concentrated hydrochloric acid. Everyone should wear safety goggles, protective gloves, and an apron. Avoid contact with skin and eyes, and avoid breathing vapors. In case of an acid spill, dilute the spill first with water. Then, wearing disposable plastic gloves, mop up the spill with wet cloths designated for spill cleanup. A wet cloth mop can be rinsed out and used until it falls apart. Work with another person nearby who can call for help in case of an emergency, and work near (no more than a few seconds away from) a safety shower and eyewash station known to be in operating condition.

Using Scientific Methods

Speed Control

DISCOVERY LAB

The reaction rate (how fast a chemical reaction happens) is an important factor to control. Sometimes you want a reaction to take place rapidly, such as when you are removing tarnish from a metal surface. Other times you want a reaction to happen very slowly, such as when you are depending on a battery as a source of electrical energy. In this lab, you will discover how changing the surface area and concentration of the reactants affects reaction rate. In this lab, you can estimate the rate of reaction by observing how fast bubbles form.

Part A—Surface Area

Ask a Question

1. How does changing the surface area of a metal affect reaction rate?

Form a Hypothesis

2. In your ScienceLog, write a statement that answers the question above. Explain your reasoning.

Test the Hypothesis

3. Use three identical strips of aluminum. Put one strip into a test tube. Place the test tube in the test-tube rack.
   Caution: The strips of metal may have sharp edges.

4. Carefully fold a second strip in half and then in half again. Use a text book or other large object to flatten the folded strip as much as possible. Place the strip in a second test tube in the test-tube rack.

5. Use scissors to cut a third strip of aluminum into the smallest possible pieces. Place all of the pieces into a third test tube, and place the test tube in the test-tube rack.

Materials

- 30 mL test tubes (6)
- 6 strips of aluminum, approximately 5 × 1 cm each
- test-tube rack
- scissors
- 2 funnels
- 10 mL graduated cylinders (2)
- acid A
- acid B

6. Use a funnel and a graduated cylinder to pour 10 mL of acid A into each of the three test tubes.
   Caution: Hydrochloric acid is corrosive. If any acid should spill on you, immediately flush the area with water and notify your teacher.

Make Observations

7. Observe the rate of bubble formation in each test tube. Record your observations in your ScienceLog.

Analyze the Results

8. Which form of aluminum had the greatest surface area? Which had the smallest?

9. In the three test tubes, the amount of aluminum and the amount of acid were the same. Which form of the aluminum seemed to react the fastest? Which form reacted the slowest? Explain your answers.

10. Do your results support the hypothesis you made in step 2? Explain.

Procedure Notes

You may need to assist students with folding and cutting the aluminum strips. Sharp scissors will work best. The folded aluminum may actually react *faster* because folding may break open the oxide that coats the aluminum. Sandpaper the metal first or have students sandpaper each strip before they begin the lab.

Draw Conclusions

11. Would powdered aluminum react faster or slower than the forms of aluminum you used? Explain your answer.

Part B—Concentration

Ask a Question

12. How does changing the concentration of acid affect the reaction rate?

Form a Hypothesis

13. In your ScienceLog, write a statement that answers the question above. Explain your reasoning.

Test the Hypothesis

14. Place one of the three remaining aluminum strips in each of the three clean test tubes. (Note: Do not alter the strips.) Place the test tubes in the test-tube rack.

15. Using the second funnel and graduated cylinder, pour 10 mL of water into one of the test tubes. Pour 10 mL of acid B into the second test tube. Pour 10 mL of acid A into the third test tube.

Make Observations

16. Observe the rate of bubble formation in the three test tubes. Record your observations in your ScienceLog.

Analyze the Results

17. In this set of test tubes, the strips of aluminum were the same, but the concentration of the acid was different. Acid A is more concentrated than acid B. Was there a difference between the test tube with water and the test tubes with acid? Which test tube formed bubbles the fastest? Explain your answers.

18. Do your results support the hypothesis you made in step 13? Explain.

Draw Conclusions

19. Explain why spilled hydrochloric acid should be diluted with water before it is wiped up.

Disposal Information

For disposal, titrate all hydrochloric acid with 0.1 M NaOH as required until the pH is between 6 and 8, and pour down the drain. Aluminum strips that cannot be reused can be placed in the trash.

Tracy Jahn
Berkshire Union Free School
Canaan, New York

Answers

2. Accept all reasonable hypotheses.

8. The strip of aluminum cut into pieces had the greatest surface area. The folded strip of aluminum had the smallest surface area.

9. The cut-up strip reacted fastest, and the folded strip reacted slowest. The cut-up strip had more surface area with which to react with the acid.

10. Answers will vary, depending on hypotheses, but students should understand that increased surface area leads to a faster reaction.

11. Powdered aluminum would react faster than the other forms of aluminum because it has more surface area.

13. Accept all reasonable hypotheses.

17. The test tube with water showed no signs of reaction. The test tubes with acid were bubbling. Acid A caused the most bubbling because it has the greatest concentration of acid.

18. Answers will depend on student hypotheses, but students should state that a higher acid concentration produces a faster reaction.

19. Diluting acid with water will decrease the acid's concentration and slow down any reaction between the acid and a surface.

 Datasheets for LabBook
Datasheet 43

Cabbage Patch Indicators
Teacher's Notes

Time Required

One 45-minute class period

Lab Ratings

TEACHER PREP 🧪🧪
STUDENT SET-UP 🧪🧪
CONCEPT LEVEL 🧪🧪
CLEAN UP 🧪🧪

MATERIALS

Materials listed are for groups of 2–3 students. Choose a wide variety of sample liquids, including bleach, ammonia, clear soda pop, lemon juice, milk, and baking soda (dissolved in water). Either red or blue litmus paper (or both) will work.

Safety Caution

Remind students to review all safety cautions and icons before beginning this lab activity. Caution students to use care when using the hot plate. Have students use tongs when handling the beaker with the hot water. Tell students that even dilute acids and bases can irritate the skin. Students should wash immediately if any sample liquid contacts their skin.

Dennis Hanson
Big Bear Middle School
Big Bear Lake, California

Cabbage Patch Indicators

Indicators are weak acids or bases that change color due to the pH of the substance to which they are added. Red cabbage contains a natural indicator that turns specific colors at specific pHs. In this lab you will extract the indicator from red cabbage and use it to determine the pH of several liquids.

Procedure

1. Copy the table below into your ScienceLog. Be sure to include one line for each sample liquid.

Data Collection Table			
Liquid	Color with indicator	pH	Effect on litmus paper
Control			

DO NOT WRITE IN BOOK

2. Put on protective gloves. Place 100 mL of distilled water in the beaker. Tear the cabbage leaf into small pieces, and place the pieces in the beaker.

3. Use the hot plate to heat the cabbage and water to boiling. Continue boiling until the water is deep blue. **Caution:** Use extreme care when working near a hot plate.

688

 Datasheets for LabBook
Datasheet 44

 **SKILL BUILDER**

Materials

- distilled water
- 250 mL beaker
- red cabbage leaf
- hot plate
- beaker tongs
- masking tape
- test tubes
- test-tube rack
- eyedropper
- sample liquids provided by teacher
- litmus paper

4. Use tongs to remove the beaker from the hot plate, and turn the hot plate off. Allow the solution to cool for 5–10 minutes.

5. While the solution is cooling, use masking tape and a pen to label the test tubes for each sample liquid. Label one test tube as the control. Place the tubes in the rack.

6. Use the eyedropper to place a small amount (about 5 mL) of the indicator (cabbage juice) in the test tube labeled as the control. Pour a small amount (about 5 mL) of each sample liquid into the appropriate test tube.

7. Using the eyedropper, place several drops of the indicator into each test tube and swirl gently. Record the color of each liquid in the table. Use the chart below to determine and record the pH for each sample.

pH 1 2 3 4 5 6 7 8 9 10 11 12 13 14

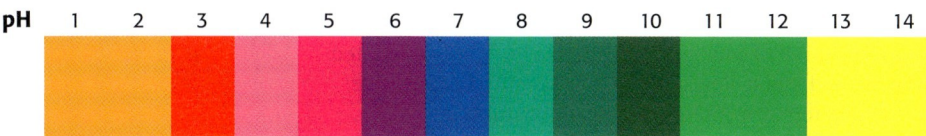

8. Litmus paper is an indicator that turns red in an acid and blue in a base. Test each liquid with a strip of litmus paper, and record the results.

Analysis

9. What purpose does the control serve? What is the pH of the control?

10. What colors are associated with acids? with bases?

11. Why is red cabbage juice considered a good indicator?

12. Which do you think would be more useful to help identify an unknown liquid—litmus paper or red cabbage juice? Why?

Going Further

Unlike distilled water, rainwater has some carbon dioxide dissolved in it. Is rainwater acidic, basic, or neutral? To find out, place a small amount of the cabbage juice indicator (which is water-based) in a clean test tube. Use a straw to gently blow bubbles in the indicator. Continue blowing bubbles until you see a color change. What can you conclude about the pH of your "rainwater?" What is the purpose of blowing bubbles in the cabbage juice?

Answers

9. The control serves as a color comparison for test tubes containing the sample liquids. The control is reddish blue, which indicates that it is neutral.

10. reddish colors—acids, bluish colors—bases

11. Red cabbage juice is a good indicator because its color can indicate many pH values. It can be used to identify the relative strengths of acids and bases if their concentrations are the same.

12. Red cabbage juice—it would give you an approximate idea of the pH of the unknown liquid. The pH could then be used to help identify the substance. Litmus paper can only indicate whether the unknown liquid is acidic or basic.

Going Further

Students should find that rainwater is slightly acidic. Blowing bubbles dissolves carbon dioxide in the cabbage juice.

Disposal Information

Use the appropriate disposal technique for each sample liquid.

Chapter 15 • LabBook

Making Salt
Teacher's Notes

Time Required
One 45-minute class period, plus 10 minutes the following day

Lab Ratings

TEACHER PREP 🧪🧪
STUDENT SET-UP 🧪🧪
CONCEPT LEVEL 🧪🧪
CLEAN UP 🧪🧪

Safety Caution
Review all proper safety precautions with your students. Students should wear safety goggles, protective gloves, and an apron. In case of an acid or a base spill, dilute the spill first with water. Then, while wearing disposable plastic gloves, mop up the spill with wet cloths designated for spill cleanup. A wet cloth mop can be rinsed out a few times and used until it falls apart. Work with another person nearby who can call for help in case of an emergency, and work near (no more than a few seconds away from) a safety shower and eyewash station known to be in operating condition.

Procedure Notes
You may wish to do this lab as a demonstration or class activity if time or materials are limited.

Datasheets for LabBook
Datasheet 45

Making Salt

A neutralization reaction between an acid and a base produces water and a salt. In this lab, you will react an acid with a base and then let the water evaporate. You will then examine what is left for properties that tell you that it is indeed a salt.

Procedure

1. Put on protective gloves. Carefully measure 25 mL of hydrochloric acid in a graduated cylinder, then pour it into the beaker. Carefully rinse the graduated cylinder with distilled water to clean out any leftover acid.
   Caution: Hydrochloric acid is corrosive. If any should spill on you, immediately flush the area with water and notify your teacher.

2. Add three drops of phenolphthalein indicator to the acid in the beaker. You will not see anything happen yet because this indicator won't show its color unless too much base is present.

3. Measure 20 mL of sodium hydroxide (base) in the graduated cylinder, and add it slowly to the beaker with the acid. Use the stirring rod to mix the substances completely.
   Caution: Sodium hydroxide is also corrosive. If any should spill on you, immediately flush the area with water and notify your teacher.

4. Use an eyedropper to add more base to the acid-base mixture in the beaker a few drops at a time. Be sure to stir the mixture after each few drops. Continue adding drops of base until the mixture remains colored after stirring.

5. Use another eyedropper to add acid to the beaker, one drop at a time, until the color just disappears after stirring.

Materials
- hydrochloric acid
- 100 mL graduated cylinder
- 100 mL beaker
- distilled water
- phenolphthalein solution in a dropper bottle
- sodium hydroxide
- glass stirring rod
- 2 eyedroppers
- evaporating dish
- magnifying lens

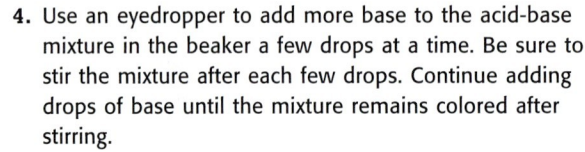

Safety Caution

Hydrochloric acid Use only concentrations of hydrochloric acid below 1.0 M. Students should not handle concentrated solutions. Avoid contact with skin and eyes, and avoid breathing vapors. When making a solution, it is important always to add the acid to the water so that if something splashes out, it will most likely be water.

Sodium hydroxide Use only concentrations of sodium hydroxide below 1.0 M. Students should not handle concentrated solutions. Avoid contact with skin and eyes. You should wear goggles, a face shield, impermeable gloves, and a lab apron if you must prepare a solution of NaOH.

6. Pour the mixture carefully into an evaporating dish, and place the dish where your teacher tells you to allow the water to evaporate overnight.

7. The next day, examine your evaporating dish and study the crystals that were left with a magnifying lens. Identify the color, shape, and other properties that the crystals have.

Analysis

8. The equation for the reaction above is:

   HCl + NaOH ⟶ H_2O + NaCl.

   NaCl is ordinary table salt and forms very regular cubic crystals that are white. Did you find white cubic crystals?

9. The phenolphthalein indicator changes color in the presence of a base. Why did you add more acid in step 5 until the color disappeared?

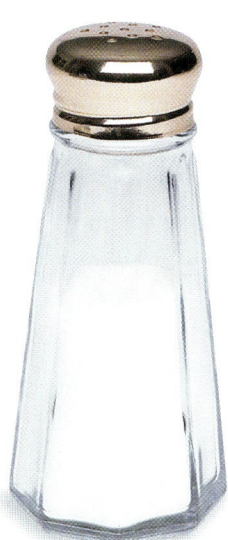

Going Further

Another neutralization reaction occurs between hydrochloric acid and potassium hydroxide, KOH. The equation for this reaction is as follows:

HCl + KOH ⟶ H_2O + KCl

What are the products of this neutralization reaction? How do they compare with those you discovered in this experiment?

MATERIALS

The magnifying lens is not needed until day 2.

Safety Caution

Phenolphthalein Students should use only pre-mixed solutions (2 g in 100 mL 95 percent ethanol, add 100 mL water) Phenolphthalein solutions are flammable, and the vapors can explode when mixed with air. Ensure that there are no flames or sources of ignition, such as sparks, when you are using the phenolphthalein solution. Restrict the amount of phenolphthalein in the room to 100 mL.

Caution students not to taste the salt they create—it will have phenolphthalein in it.

Answers

8. Students should observe white cubic crystals.

9. When the phenolphthalein changed color in step 4, that meant too much base was present. Acid was added to bring the solution back to neutral.

Going Further

The products are water and a salt, KCl (potassium chloride).

Disposal Information

Hydrochloric acid Titrate with 0.1 M NaOH as required until the pH is between 6 and 8; pour down the drain.

Sodium hydroxide Titrate with 0.1 M HCl as required until the pH is between 5 and 9; pour down the drain.

Phenolphthalein Set out a container for any used indicator solutions that are left over at the end of the procedure. Titrate the mixture with 0.1 M HCl or 0.1 M NaOH as required until the pH is between 6 and 8; pour down the drain. Unused indicators should be tightly covered and returned to the storage shelf.

Rodney A. Sandefur
Naturita Middle School
Naturita, Colorado

Domino Chain Reactions
Teacher's Notes

Time Required
One or two 45-minute class periods

Lab Ratings

- TEACHER PREP
- STUDENT SET-UP
- CONCEPT LEVEL
- CLEAN UP

Lab Notes
In the chapter titled "Atomic Energy," images of fission reactions show three neutrons produced when a uranum-235 nucleus splits. However, there are fissions that release only two neutrons. In this activity, each "fission" releases only two neutrons, with each neutron being represented by a domino.

 Datasheets for LabBook
Datasheet 46

Larry Tackett
Andrew Jackson Middle School
Cross Lanes, West Virginia

Domino Chain Reactions

MAKING MODELS

Fission of uranium-235 is a process that relies on neutrons. When a uranium-235 nucleus splits into two smaller nuclei, it releases two or three neutrons that can cause neighboring nuclei to undergo fission. This can result in a nuclear chain reaction. In this lab you will build two models of nuclear chain reactions using dominoes.

Materials
- 15 dominoes
- stopwatch

Conduct an Experiment

1. For the first model, set up the dominoes as shown below. Each domino should hit two dominoes in the next row when pushed over.

2. Measure the time it takes for all of the dominoes to fall. To do this, start the stopwatch as you tip over the front domino. Stop the stopwatch when the last domino falls. Record this time in your ScienceLog.

3. If some of the dominoes do not fall, repeat steps 1 and 2. You may have to adjust the setup a few times.

4. For the second model, set up the dominoes as shown at right. The domino in the first row should hit both of the dominoes in the second row. Beginning with the second row, only one domino from each row should hit both of the dominoes in the next row.

5. Repeat step 2. Again, you may have to adjust the setup a few times to get all the dominoes to fall.

692 Chapter 16 • LabBook

Analyze Your Results

6. Which model represents an uncontrolled chain reaction? Which represents a controlled chain reaction? Explain your answers.

7. Imagine that each domino releases a certain amount of energy as it falls. Compare the total amount of energy released in the two models.

8. Compare the time needed to release the energy in the models. Which model was longest? Which model was shortest?

Draw Conclusions

9. In a nuclear power plant, a chain reaction is controlled by using a material that absorbs neutrons. Only enough neutrons to continue the chain reaction are allowed to produce further fission of uranium-235. Explain how your model of a controlled nuclear chain reaction modeled this process.

10. Why must uranium nuclei be close to each other in order for a nuclear chain reaction to occur? (Hint: What would happen in your model if the dominoes were too far apart?)

Answers

6. The first model represents an uncontrolled reaction. The second model represents a controlled reaction. The number of fission reactions doubles in each step of the first model and would quickly get out of control. Only one fission reaction occurs in each step of the second model, so the reaction happens at a steady, controlled rate.

7. The same amount of energy was released in each model because the same number of dominoes fell in each model.

8. The second model was the longest. The first model was the shortest.

9. In the second model, the dominoes were set up so that only one of each falling pair would knock down another pair of dominoes. So only a few dominoes were used to continue the "reaction," just as only some neutrons may continue a chain reaction.

10. The nuclei must be close to each other so that a neutron produced in one fission has a greater chance of hitting another nucleus and causing it to split.

Chapter 16 • LabBook

Stop the Static Electricity!
Teacher's Notes

Time Required
One 45-minute class period

Lab Ratings

TEACHER PREP 🧪
STUDENT SET-UP 🧪
CONCEPT LEVEL 🧪🧪
CLEAN UP 🧪

Procedure Notes

This lab works best on cold, dry days. If you live in an area with high humidity, use a dehumidifier or substitute a piece of PVC pipe for the rubber rod.

Answers

2. Accept all reasonable hypotheses.

8. Step 4—the rod induced an opposite charge in the peanut; step 5—the charge was transferred by touching.

9. Yes; the peanut was initially attracted and then repelled by the rods.

10. The peanut was repelled by the rod in step 5. It was attracted to the rod in step 7. The peanut's charge must have changed due to the charge on the glass rod.

11. New answers should include that charges build up through friction as clothes rub together.

12. Rubbing the rods builds up a charge on the rod, causing the peanut to be attracted or repelled (depending on the peanut's charge and the charge on the rod).

Using Scientific Methods

Stop the Static Electricity!

DISCOVERY LAB

Imagine this scenario: Some of your clothes cling together when they come out of the dryer. This annoying problem is caused by static electricity—the buildup of electric charges on an object. In this lab, you'll discover how this buildup occurs.

Materials

- 30 cm thread
- plastic-foam packing peanut
- tape
- rubber rod
- wool cloth
- glass rod
- silk cloth

Ask a Question

1. How do electric charges build up on clothes in a dryer?

Form a Hypothesis

2. Write a statement that answers the question above. Explain your reasoning.

Test the Hypothesis

3. Tie a piece of thread approximately 30 cm in length to a packing peanut. Hang the peanut by the thread from the edge of a table. Tape the thread to the table.

4. Rub the rubber rod with the wool cloth for 10–15 seconds. Bring the rod near, but do not touch, the peanut. Observe the peanut and record your observations. If nothing happens, repeat this step.

5. Touch the peanut with the rubber rod. Pull the rod away from the peanut, and then bring it near again. Record your observations.

6. Repeat steps 4 and 5 with the glass rod and silk cloth.

7. Now rub the rubber rod with the wool cloth, and bring the rod near the peanut again. Record your observations.

Analyze the Results

8. What caused the peanut to act differently in steps 4 and 5?

9. Did the glass rod have the same effect on the peanut as the rubber rod did? Explain how the peanut reacted in each case.

10. Was the reaction of the peanut the same in steps 5 and 7? Explain.

Draw Conclusions

11. Based on your results, was your hypothesis correct? Explain your answer, and write a new statement if necessary.

Communicate Results

12. Explain why the rubber rod and the glass rod affected the peanut.

Going Further
Do some research to find out how a dryer sheet helps stop the buildup of electric charges in the dryer.

Going Further
Dryer sheets leave a layer of soap on clothes, and this soap attracts moisture from the air. This allows built-up charges to dissipate.

 Datasheets for LabBook
Datasheet 47

Laura Fleet
Alice B. Landrum Middle School
Ponte Vedra Beach, Florida

Potato Power

Have you ever wanted to look inside a D cell from a flashlight or an AA cell from a portable radio? All cells include the same basic components, as shown below. There is a metal "bucket," some electrolyte (a paste), and a rod of some other metal (or solid) in the middle. Even though the construction is simple, companies that manufacture cells are always trying to make a product with the highest voltage possible from the least expensive materials. Sometimes they try different pastes, and sometimes they try different combinations of metals. In this lab, you will make your own cell. Using inexpensive materials, you will try to produce the highest voltage you can.

Materials

- labeled metal strips
- potato
- metric ruler
- voltmeter

Procedure

1. Choose two metal strips. Carefully push one of the strips into the potato at least 2 cm deep. Insert the second strip the same way, and measure how far apart the two strips are. (If one of your metal strips is too soft to push into the potato, push a harder strip in first, remove it, and then push the soft strip into the slit.) Record the two metals you have used and the distance between the strips in your ScienceLog. **Caution:** The strips of metal may have sharp edges.

2. Connect the voltmeter to the two strips, and record the voltage.

3. Move one of the strips closer to or farther from the other. Measure the new distance and voltage. Record your results.

4. Repeat steps 1 through 3, using different combinations of metal strips and distances until you find the combination that produces the highest voltage.

Analysis

5. What combination of metals and distance produced the highest voltage?

6. If you change only the distance but use the same metal strips, what is the effect on the voltage?

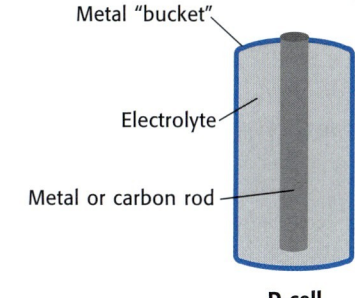

D cell

7. One of the metal strips tends to lose electrons, while the other tends to gain electrons. What do you think would happen if you used two strips of the same metal?

Datasheets for LabBook
Datasheet 48

Answers

5. Answers will depend on the metals used.
6. As distance increases, voltage decreases.
7. If you used two strips of the same metal, there would be no voltage because each strip has the same tendency to gain or lose electrons.

Potato Power
Teacher's Notes

Time Required
One 45-minute class period

Lab Ratings

TEACHER PREP 🧪
STUDENT SET-UP 🧪
CONCEPT LEVEL 🧪
CLEAN UP 🧪

MATERIALS

Provide each group of 2–3 students with at least three metal strips (0.5 × 2 cm) of dissimilar metals. Metal strips that work well are zinc, copper, aluminum, and iron. If metal strips are difficult to obtain, copper wires, zinc screws, and other pieces of iron and aluminum may be used. A voltmeter with a range of 0–5 V works best. Students may also need 2 wires to connect the meter to the metal strips.

Safety Caution

Remind students to review all safety cautions and icons before beginning this lab activity. Caution students that the metal strips may have sharp edges. Students should wash their hands thoroughly after handling the potatoes.

Susan Gorman
North Ridge Middle School
North Richland Hills, Texas

Circuitry 101
Teacher's Notes

Time Required
Two 45-minute class periods

Lab Ratings

TEACHER PREP 🧪🧪
STUDENT SET-UP 🧪🧪
CONCEPT LEVEL 🧪🧪🧪
CLEAN UP 🧪

MATERIALS
Materials listed are for each group of 3–5 students. Use a series of three 1.5 V cells or a 6 V battery as a power source. If you use a series of 1.5 V cells, create a single battery by taping the cells together (positive to negative). Use only regular dry cell or alkaline batteries. Do not use nicad or lithium batteries.

Safety Caution
Remind students to review all safety cautions and icons before beginning this lab activity. Caution students that connecting either meter improperly can result in ruining the meter.

Procedure Notes
Explain or demonstrate how to construct a circuit properly before students begin. Demonstrate the proper way to use an ammeter and a voltmeter. You may wish to perform this lab as a demonstration if materials are limited.

Circuitry 101

You have learned that there are two basic types of electrical circuits. A series circuit connects all the parts in a single loop, and a parallel circuit connects each of the parts on separate branches to the power source. If you want to control the whole circuit, the loads and the switch must be wired in series. If you want parts of the circuit to operate independently, the loads must be wired in parallel.

No matter how simple or complicated a circuit may be, Ohm's law (current equals voltage divided by resistance) applies. In this lab, you will construct both a series circuit and a parallel circuit. You will use an ammeter to measure current and a voltmeter to measure voltage. With each circuit, you will test and apply Ohm's law.

Part A—Series Circuit

Procedure

1. Construct a series circuit with a power source, a switch, and three light bulbs. **Caution:** Always leave the switch open when constructing or changing the circuit. Close the switch only when you are testing or taking a reading.

2. Draw a diagram of your circuit in your ScienceLog.

3. Test your circuit. Do all three bulbs light up? Are they all the same brightness? What happens if you carefully unscrew one light bulb? Does it make any difference which bulb you unscrew? Record your observations in your ScienceLog.

4. Connect the ammeter between the power source and the switch. Close the switch, and record the current with a label on your diagram in your ScienceLog. Be sure to show where you measured the current and what the value was.

5. Reconnect the circuit so the ammeter is between the first and second bulbs. Record the current, as you did in step 4.

6. Move the ammeter so it is between the second and third bulbs, and record the current again.

7. Remove the ammeter from the circuit, and connect the voltmeter to the two ends of the power source. Record the voltage with a label on your diagram.

8. Use the voltmeter to measure the voltage across each bulb. Label the voltage across each bulb on your diagram.

Part B—Parallel Circuit

Procedure

9. Take apart your series circuit, and reassemble the same power source, switch, and three light bulbs so that the bulbs are wired in parallel. (Note: The switch must remain in series with the power source to be able to control the whole circuit.)

Materials
- power source—dry cell(s)
- switch
- 3 light-bulb holders
- 3 light bulbs
- insulated wire, cut into 15 cm lengths with both ends stripped
- ammeter
- voltmeter

Datasheets for LabBook
Datasheet 49

David Sparks
Redwater Junior High
Redwater, Texas

10. Draw a diagram of your parallel circuit in your ScienceLog.

11. Test your circuit, and record your observations, as you did in step 3.

12. Connect the ammeter between the power source and the switch. Record the reading on your diagram.

13. Reconnect the circuit so that the ammeter is right next to one of the three bulbs. Record the current on your diagram.

14. Repeat step 13 for the two remaining bulbs.

15. Remove the ammeter from your circuit, and connect the voltmeter to the two ends of the power source. Record this voltage.

16. Measure and record the voltage across each light bulb.

Analysis—Parts A and B

17. Was the current the same at all places in the series circuit? Was it the same everywhere in the parallel circuit?

18. For each circuit, compare the voltage at each light bulb with the power source.

19. What is the relationship between the voltage at the power source and the voltages at the light bulbs in a series circuit?

20. Use Ohm's law and the readings for current (I) and voltage (V) at the power source for both circuits to calculate the total resistance (R) in both the series and parallel circuits.

21. Was the total resistance for both circuits the same? Explain your answer.

22. Why did the bulbs differ in brightness?

23. Based on your results, what do you think might happen if too many electric appliances are plugged into the same series circuit? the same parallel circuit?

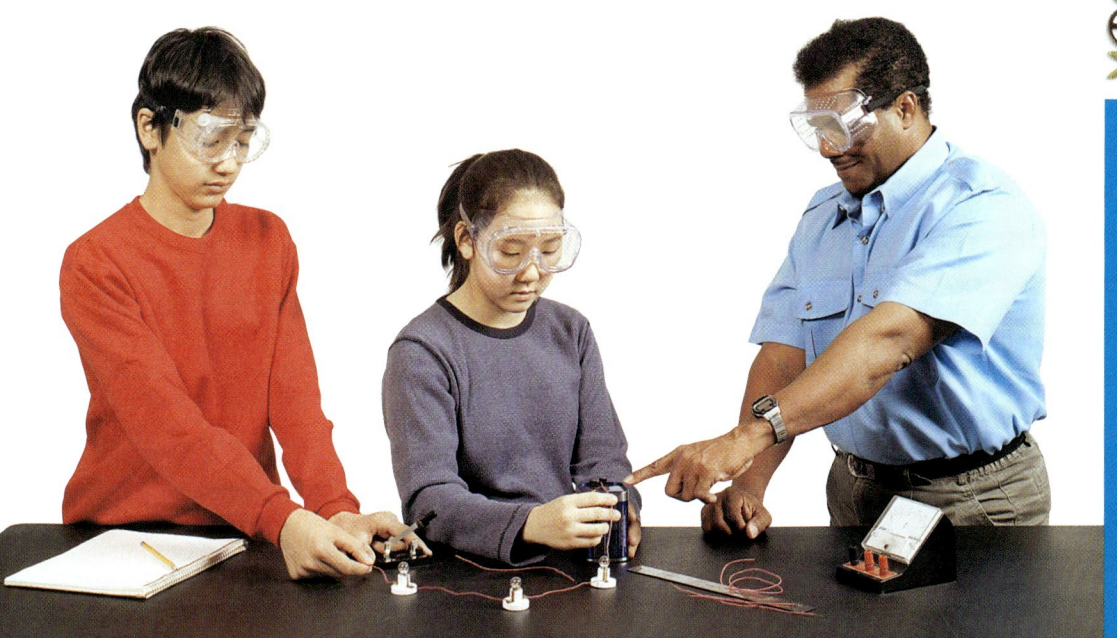

Disposal Information

Regular dry cell or alkaline flashlight batteries (or regular 6 V batteries) can be disposed of in normal trash containers. Nicad and lithium batteries are toxic and should not be used.

Answers

17. The current was the same at all points in the series circuit. The current was not the same at all points in the parallel circuit.

18. The voltage at each light bulb in the series circuit was about the same and less than the voltage of the power source. The voltage at each light bulb in the parallel circuit was the same as the voltage at the power source.

19. The voltage at the power source is the sum of the voltages at the light bulbs in a series circuit.

20. Answers will depend on the bulbs used. Check for correct calculations.

21. No. The series circuit had a much higher resistance than the parallel circuit. The resistance is less in a parallel circuit because the electric current has more than one path to follow.

22. The parallel circuit had brighter bulbs because the voltage across each bulb was greater than in the series circuit.

23. Too many appliances on the same series circuit would cause each appliance to get very little voltage, so they may not receive enough electric current to work. Too many appliances on the same parallel circuit could cause too much electric current to flow through the circuit (because all loads in a parallel circuit draw the same voltage), leading to a short circuit or fire.

Magnetic Mystery
Teacher's Notes

Time Required
One 45-minute class period

Lab Ratings

- TEACHER PREP 🧪
- STUDENT SET-UP 🧪
- CONCEPT LEVEL 🧪
- CLEAN UP 🧪🧪

MATERIALS
Materials listed are for each group of 2–3 students. Have students bring in shoe boxes from home. Bar magnets and horseshoe magnets work better than disk magnets for this lab. White paper can be used instead of the acetate sheet.

Safety Caution
Caution students to wear safety goggles and an apron when doing this lab. Have students wash their hands thoroughly after handling iron filings.

Disposal Information
Iron filings should be collected and reused. If it becomes necessary to dispose of them, filings should be buried in a landfill approved for chemical disposal.

 Datasheets for LabBook Datasheet 50

Magnetic Mystery

Every magnet is surrounded by a magnetic field. Magnetic field lines show the shape of the magnetic field. These lines can be modeled by using iron filings. The iron filings are affected by the magnetic field, and they fall into lines showing the field. In this lab, you will first learn about magnetic fields, and then you will use this knowledge to identify a mystery magnet's shape and orientation based on observations of the field lines.

Collect Data

1. Lay one of the magnets flat on a table.
2. Place a sheet of clear acetate over the magnet. Sprinkle some iron filings on the acetate to see the magnetic field lines.
3. In your ScienceLog, draw the magnet and the magnetic field lines.
4. Remove the acetate, and pour the iron filings back into the container.
5. Place your magnet so that one end is pointing up. Repeat steps 2 through 4.
6. Place your magnet on its side. Repeat steps 2 through 4.
7. Repeat steps 1 through 6 with the other magnet.

Conduct an Experiment

8. Create a magnetic mystery for another lab team by removing the lid from a shoe box, and taping a magnet underneath the lid. Orient the magnet so that determining the shape of the magnetic field and the orientation of the magnet will be challenging. Once the magnet is secure, place the lid on the box.
9. Exchange boxes with another team.
10. Without opening the box, use the sheet of acetate and the iron filings to determine the shape of the magnetic field of the magnet in the box.
11. Make a drawing of the magnetic field lines in your ScienceLog.

SKILL BUILDER

Materials
- 2 magnets, different shapes
- sheet of clear acetate
- iron filings
- shoe box
- masking tape

Draw Conclusions

12. Use your drawings from steps 1 through 7 to identify the shape and orientation of the magnet in your magnetic mystery box. Draw a picture of your conclusion.

Going Further
Examine your drawings. Can you identify the north and south poles of a magnet from the shape of the magnetic field lines? Design a procedure that would allow you to determine the poles of a magnet.

Answer
12. Drawings will vary. Placement of the magnet should match the field lines.

Going Further
The poles of a magnet cannot be identified by looking at the field lines. A navigation compass or a magnet with labeled poles could be used to identify the magnet's poles.

Paul Boyle
Perry Heights Middle School
Evansville, Indiana

Using Scientific Methods

Electricity from Magnetism

You use electricity every day. But did you ever wonder where it comes from? Some of the electrical energy you use is converted from chemical energy in cells or batteries. But what about when you plug a lamp into a wall outlet? In this lab, you will see how electricity can be generated from magnetism.

Ask a Question

1. How can electricity be generated from magnetism?

Form a Hypothesis

2. Write a statement to answer question 1.

Test the Hypothesis

3. Sand the enamel off of the last 2 or 3 cm of each end of the magnet wire. Wrap the magnet wire around the tube to make a coil as illustrated below. Attach the bare ends of the wire to the galvanometer using the insulated wires.

4. While watching the galvanometer, move a bar magnet into the coil, hold it there for a moment, and then remove it. Record your observations in your ScienceLog.

5. Repeat step 4 several times, moving the magnet at different speeds. Observe the galvanometer carefully.

6. Hold the magnet still, and pass the coil over the magnet. Record your observations.

Analyze the Results

7. How does the speed of the magnet affect the size of the electric current?

Materials

- sandpaper
- 150 cm of magnet wire
- cardboard tube
- commercial galvanometer
- 2 insulated wires with alligator clips, each approximately 30 cm long
- strong bar magnet

8. How is the direction of the electric current affected by the motion of the magnet?

9. Examine your hypothesis. Is your hypothesis accurate? Explain. If necessary, write a new hypothesis to answer question 1.

Draw Conclusions

10. Would an electric current still be generated if the wire were broken? Why or why not?

11. Could a stationary magnet be used to generate an electric current? Explain.

12. What energy conversions occur in this investigation?

Communicate Results

13. Write a short paragraph that explains the requirements for generating electricity from magnetism.

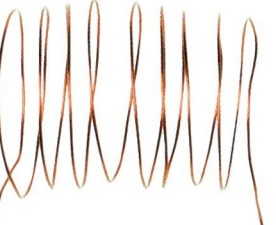

Electricity from Magnetism
Teacher's Notes

Time Required
One to two 45-minute class periods

Lab Ratings

TEACHER PREP
STUDENT SET-UP
CONCEPT LEVEL
CLEAN UP

MATERIALS
Materials listed are for each group of 2–3 students.

Safety Caution
Caution students to wear safety goggles when doing this lab.

 Datasheets for LabBook
Datasheet 51

Answers

7. The faster the magnet moves, the greater the electric current is.

8. When the direction of the magnet's motion is reversed, so is the direction of the current.

9. Answers will depend on the hypothesis created in step 2.

10. Electric current would not be generated because the circuit is not complete.

11. A stationary magnet could produce an electric current if the wire moves, as in step 6.

12. The kinetic energy of the moving wire or magnet is converted into electrical energy.

13. Sample paragraph: The three requirements for generating electricity from magnetism are a magnet, a complete circuit, and motion between the two.

Bert Sherwood
Socorro Middle School
El Paso, Texas

Chapter 18 • LabBook

Build a DC Motor
Teacher's Notes

Time Required

One to two 45-minute class periods

Lab Ratings

EASY ——————→ HARD

- TEACHER PREP ▲
- STUDENT SET-UP ▲▲▲
- CONCEPT LEVEL ▲▲▲
- CLEAN UP ▲

MATERIALS

Materials listed are for each group of 2–3 students.

Safety Caution

Caution students to wear safety goggles when doing this lab.

Procedure Notes

You may want to have students spend one class period building their motors and a second class period troubleshooting and analyzing their motors. You may want to do this activity as a demonstration or a class project.

Build a DC Motor

 MAKING MODELS

Electric motors can be used for many things. Hair dryers, CD players, and even some cars and buses are powered by electric motors. In this lab, you will build a direct current electric motor—the basis for the electric motors you use every day.

Procedure

1. To make the armature for the motor, wind the wire around the cardboard tube to make a coil like the one shown below. Wind the ends of the wire around the loops on each side of the coil. Leave about 5 cm free on each end.

2. Hold the coil on its edge. Sand the enamel from only the top half of each end of the wire. This acts like a commutator, except that it blocks the electric current instead of reversing it during half of each rotation.

3. Partially unfold the two paper clips from the middle. Make a hook in one end of each paper clip to hold the coil, as shown at right.

4. Place two disk magnets in the bottom of the cup, and place the other magnets on the outside of the bottom of the cup. The magnets should remain in place when the cup is turned upside down.

5. Tape the paper clips to the sides of the cup. The hooks should be at the same height, and should keep the coil from hitting the magnet.

6. Test your coil. Flick the top of the coil lightly with your finger. The coil should spin freely without wobbling or sliding to one side.

7. Make adjustments to the ends of the wire and the hooks until your coil spins freely.

8. Use the alligator clips to attach one wire to each paper clip.

9. Attach the free end of one wire to one terminal of the battery.

Materials

- 100 cm of magnet wire
- cardboard tube
- sandpaper
- 2 large paper clips
- 4 disk magnets
- plastic-foam cup
- tape
- 2 insulated wires with alligator clips, each approximately 30 cm long
- 4.5 V battery
- permanent marker

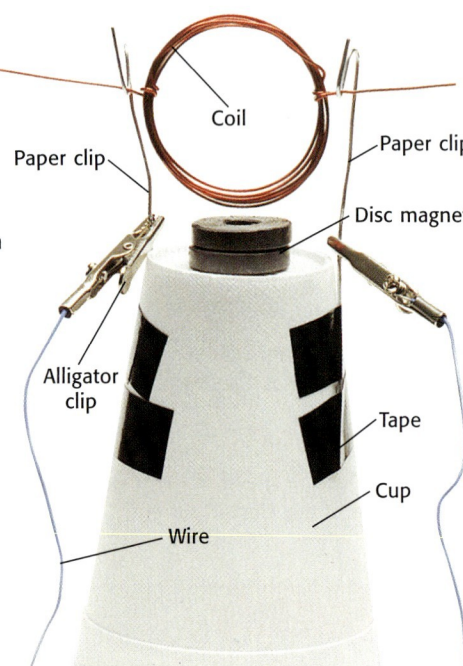

 Datasheets for LabBook Datasheet 52

Tracy Jahn
Berkshire Junior–Senior High School
Canaan, New York

Collect Data

10. Connect the free end of the other wire to the second battery terminal and give your coil a gentle spin. Record your observations.
11. Stop the coil and give it a gentle spin in the opposite direction. Record your observations.
12. If the coil does not keep spinning, check the ends of the wire. Bare wire should touch the paper clips during half of the spin, and only enamel should touch the paper clips for the other half of the spin.
13. If you removed too much enamel, color half of the wire with a permanent marker.
14. Switch the connections to the battery and repeat steps 10 and 11.

Analyze the Results

15. Did your motor always spin in the direction you started it? Explain.
16. Why was the motor affected by switching the battery connections?
17. Some electric cars run on solar power. Which part of your model would be replaced by the solar panels?

Draw Conclusions

18. Some people claim that electric-powered cars are cleaner than gasoline-powered cars. Explain why this might be true.
19. List some reasons that electric cars are not ideal. (Hint: What happens to batteries?)
20. How could your model be used to help design a hair dryer?
21. Make a list of at least three other items that could be powered by an electric motor like the one you built.

Answers

15. The motor did not always continue to spin in the direction it was started. Switching the battery connections caused it to spin in the opposite direction.
16. The motor was affected by switching the battery connections because the direction of the electric current in the coil was reversed. This reversed the magnetic field, which caused the motor to spin in the opposite direction.
17. Solar panels would replace the battery as the energy source.
18. Electric cars do not burn gasoline, so they do not produce exhaust gases that are components of air pollution.
19. Electric cars are not ideal because the batteries run down and have to be replaced (which means more waste) or recharged (which requires more electrical energy). Also, batteries don't produce much energy for their weight, so electric cars aren't very powerful.
20. Accept all reasonable answers. Sample answer: The model could be used to help design a hair dryer by attaching various fans to the armature (spinning part) to see how well they work. Also, different combinations of batteries and coils could be tested to see if a battery-powered hair dryer would be powerful enough.
21. Answers will vary. Accept all reasonable answers that include items that use a spinning motion.

Tune In!
Teacher's Notes

Time Required

Two to three 45-minute class periods

Lab Ratings

TEACHER PREP 🧪🧪🧪
STUDENT SET-UP 🧪🧪🧪🧪
CONCEPT LEVEL 🧪🧪🧪
CLEAN UP 🧪

MATERIALS
Materials listed are for each group of 2–3 students.

Safety Caution

Students should be instructed to clean earphones between uses, especially if there are not enough earphones for each student to have his or her own.

The ground wire needs to be attached to an available ground in the classroom, such as a plumbing fixture.

Tune In!

You probably have listened to radios many times in your life. Modern radios are complicated electronic devices. However, radios do not have to be so complicated. The basic parts of all radios include: a diode, an inductor, a capacitor, an antenna, a ground wire, and an earphone (or a speaker and amplifier on a large radio). In this activity, you will examine each of these components one at a time as you build a working model of a radio-wave receiver.

Procedure

1. Examine the diode. Describe it in your ScienceLog.
2. A diode carries current in only one direction. Draw the inside of a diode in your ScienceLog, and illustrate how this might occur.
3. An inductor controls the amount of electric current due to the resistance of the wire. Make an inductor by winding the insulated wire around a cardboard tube approximately 100 times. Wind the wire so that all the turns of the coil are neat and in an orderly row, as shown below. Leave about 25 cm of wire on each end of the coil. The coil of wire may be held on the tube using tape.

Materials

- diode
- 2 m of insulated wire
- 2 cardboard tubes
- tape
- scissors
- aluminum foil
- sheet of paper
- 7 connecting wires, 30 cm each
- 3 paper clips
- cardboard, 20 × 30 cm
- antenna
- ground wire
- earphone

4. Now you will construct the variable capacitor. A capacitor stores electrical energy when an electric current is applied. A variable capacitor is a capacitor in which the amount of energy stored can be changed. Cut a piece of aluminum foil to go around the tube but only half the length of the tube, as shown on the next page. Keep the foil as wrinkle-free as possible as you wrap it around the tube, and tape the foil to itself. Now tape the foil to the tube.

5. Use the sheet of paper and tape to make a sliding cover on the tube. The paper should completely cover the foil on the tube with about 1 cm extra.

 Datasheets for LabBook
Datasheet 53

Rodney A. Sandefur
Naturita Middle School
Naturita, Colorado

6. Cut another sheet of aluminum foil to wrap completely around the paper. Leave approximately 1 cm of paper showing at each end of the foil. Tape this foil sheet to the paper sleeve. If you have done this correctly, you have a paper/foil sheet which will slide up and down the tube over the stationary foil. The two pieces of foil should not touch.

7. Stand your variable capacitor on its end so that the stationary foil is at the bottom. The amount of stored energy is greater when the sleeve is down than when the sleeve is up.

8. Use tape to attach one connecting wire to the stationary foil at the end of the tube. Use tape to attach another connecting wire to the sliding foil sleeve. Be sure that the metal part of the wire touches the foil.

9. Hook three paper clips on one edge of the cardboard, as shown below. Label one paper clip A, another B, and the third one C.

10. Lay the inductor on the piece of cardboard, and tape it to the cardboard.

11. Stand the capacitor next to the inductor, and tape the tube to the cardboard. Be sure not to tape the sleeve—it must be free to slide.

Capacitor

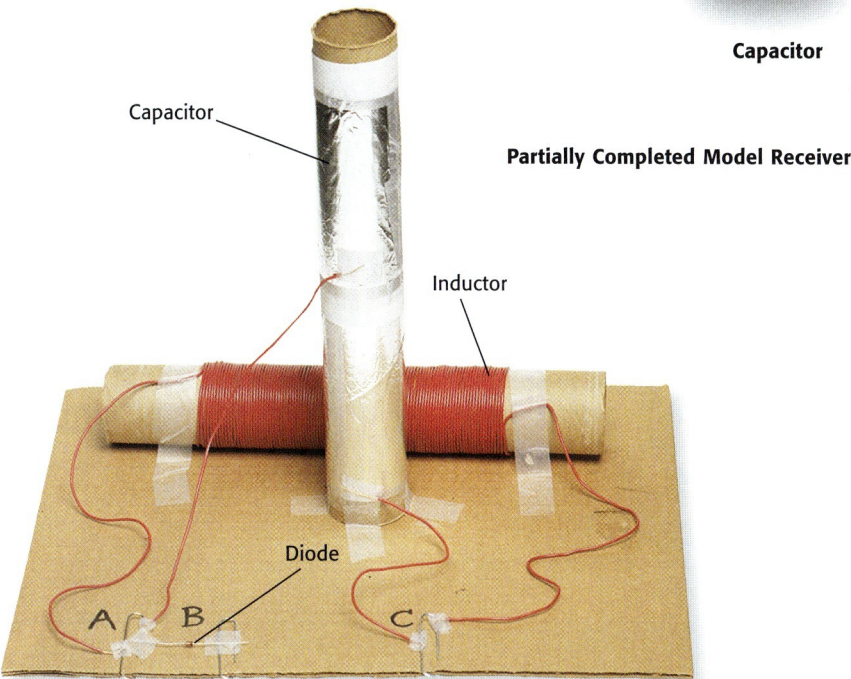

Partially Completed Model Receiver

Lab Notes

Diodes may be available through your school or a science supply house. They are relatively inexpensive and can also be purchased at electronics stores. Many things may be used as an antenna: the rim and spokes of a bicycle wheel, a long wire, or the antenna from an old stereo. Inexpensive antennas can also be purchased at electronics stores. Use a large-gauge wire (one with a small diameter) for the 2 m insulated copper wire.

The ground wire must be long enough to attach to a plumbing fixture or other available ground.

Chapter 19 • LabBook   **703**

Procedure Notes

Remind students that this is a long lab. Encourage them to be patient while making and troubleshooting their setup. If materials or time are limited, you may wish to do this lab as a special class project or as a demonstration.

Remind students that this radio is not very sophisticated and that they probably won't be able to receive music or voices. Let students know that even hearing static demonstrates that their receiver is working.

12. Use tape to connect the diode to paper clips A and B. The cathode should be closest to paper clip B. (The cathode end of the diode is the one with the dark band.) Make sure that all connections have good metal-to-metal contact.

13. Connect one end of the inductor to paper clip A, and the other end to paper clip C. Use tape to hold the wires in place.

14. Connect the wire from the sliding part of the capacitor to paper clip A. Connect the other wire (from the stationary foil) to paper clip C.

15. The antenna receives radio waves transmitted by a radio station. Tape a connecting wire to your antenna. Then connect this wire to paper clip A.

16. Use tape to connect one end of the ground wire to paper clip C. The other end of the ground wire should be connected to an object specified by your teacher.

A Completed Model Receiver!
Earphone
Antenna
Ground wire

17. The earphone will allow you to detect the radio waves you receive. Connect one wire from the earphone to paper clip B and the other wire to paper clip C.

18. You are now ready to begin listening. With everything connected, and the earphone in your ear, slowly slide the paper/foil sheet of the capacitor up and down. Listen for a very faint sound. You may have to troubleshoot many of the parts to get your receiver to work. As you troubleshoot, check to be sure there is good contact between all the connections.

Analysis

19. Describe the process of operating your receiver.

20. Considering what you have learned about a diode, why is it important to have the diode connected the correct way?

21. A function of the inductor on a radio is to "slow the current down." Why does the inductor you made slow the current down more than does a straight wire the length of your coil?

22. A capacitor consists of any two conductors separated by an insulator. For your capacitor, list the two conductors and the insulator.

23. Explain why the amount of stored energy is increased when you slide the foil sleeve down and decreased when the sleeve is up.

24. In your ScienceLog, make a list of ways that your receiver is similar to a modern radio. Make a second list of ways that your receiver is different from a modern radio.

Answers

19. Accept all reasonable answers. Sample answer: The process of operating the receiver involved sliding the variable capacitor up and down slowly until a noise was heard. Then the capacitor was moved very slightly back and forth to fine tune the reception.

20. The diode allows electric current in only one direction, so no current would exist in the circuit if the diode were connected in the wrong way.

21. A wire much longer than the length of the tube was used to make the inductor. The longer the wire is, the greater the resistance is.

22. The two conductors are the two sheets of aluminum foil. They are separated by the sheet of paper, which acts as an insulator.

23. The amount of energy stored in the capacitor is increased when the sleeve is lowered because the area where the conductors overlap is increased. The reverse is true when the sleeve is raised.

24. Accept all reasonable answers. Sample answers: The receiver is similar to a modern radio because it is tunable, it has electronic components (the diode, capacitor, and inductor), and it has an antenna to receive the signal from the radio station. The receiver is different from a modern radio because it has no battery or speakers, it has no volume control, and it has no FM capabilities.

Wave Energy and Speed

Teacher's Notes

Time Required
One 45-minute class period

Lab Ratings

- TEACHER PREP 🧪🧪
- STUDENT SET-UP 🧪🧪
- CONCEPT LEVEL 🧪🧪🧪
- CLEAN UP 🧪🧪

MATERIALS
The materials listed are for each group of 2–4 students.

Safety Caution
Remind students to review all safety cautions and icons before beginning this lab activity.

Procedure Notes
Finding enough stopwatches for all students may be difficult. Students may have watches that can serve as timers or stopwatches.

Lab Notes
You may wish to do this lab as a teacher demonstration using a glass pan and an overhead projector.

Using Scientific Methods

Wave Energy and Speed

DISCOVERY LAB

If you threw a rock into a pond, waves would carry energy away from the point of origin. But if you threw a large rock into a pond, would the waves carry more energy away from the point of origin than waves created by a small rock? And would a large rock create waves that move faster than waves created by a small rock? In this lab you'll answer these questions.

Ask a Question

1. In this lab you will answer the following questions: Do waves created by a large disturbance carry more energy than waves created by a small disturbance? Do waves created by a large disturbance travel faster than waves created by a small disturbance?

Form a Hypothesis

2. In your ScienceLog, write a few sentences that answer the questions above.

Test the Hypothesis

3. Place the pan on a few sheets of newspaper. Using the small beaker, fill the pan with water.

4. Make sure that the water is still. Tap the surface of the water near one end of the pan with the eraser end of one pencil. This represents the small disturbance. In your ScienceLog, record your observations about the size of the waves that are created and the path they take.

5. Repeat step 4. This time, use the stopwatch to measure the time it takes for one of the waves to reach the other side of the pan. Record your data in your ScienceLog.

6. Repeat steps 4 and 5 using two pencils at once. This represents the large disturbance. (Try to use the same amount of force to tap the water as you did with just one pencil.)

Materials

- shallow pan, approximately 20 × 30 cm
- newspaper
- small beaker
- water
- 2 pencils
- stopwatch

 Datasheets for LabBook Datasheet 54

 Science Skills Worksheet 27 "Interpreting Your Data"

Answer

2. Answers will vary but should address each question in step 1.

706 Chapter 20 • LabBook

Analyze the Results

7. Compare the appearance of the waves created by one pencil with that of the waves created by two pencils. Were there any differences in amplitude (wave height)?

8. Compare the amount of time required for the waves to reach the side of the pan. Did the waves travel faster when two pencils were used?

Draw Conclusions

9. Do waves created by a large disturbance carry more energy than waves created by a small disturbance? Explain your answer using your results to support your answer. (Hint: Remember the relationship between amplitude and energy.)

10. Do waves created by a large disturbance travel faster than waves created by a small disturbance? Explain your answer.

Going Further

A tsunami is a giant ocean wave that can reach a height of 30 m. Tsunamis that reach land can cause injury and enormous property damage. Using what you learned in this lab about wave energy and speed, explain why tsunamis are so dangerous. How do you think scientists can predict when tsunamis will reach land?

Answers

7. The waves created by two pencils had a larger amplitude than the waves created by one pencil.

8. The amount of time it took for the waves to reach the side of the pan was the same for both trials. The waves appeared to travel at the same rate.

9. Yes; the large disturbance creates waves with a large amplitude. Because amplitude is related to energy, waves created by a large disturbance carry more energy.

10. No; all the waves appear to travel at the same speed because the times recorded for both trials were the same.

Answer to Going Further

Tsunamis have large amplitudes, so they carry a lot of energy that can cause injury and property damage. All waves in the ocean travel at the same speed. Therefore, scientists can determine when a tsunami will reach land.

Jennifer Ford
North Ridge Middle School
North Richland Hills, Texas

Wave Speed, Frequency, and Wavelength
Teacher's Notes

Time Required
One or two 45-minute class periods

Lab Ratings

- TEACHER PREP 🧪
- STUDENT SET-UP 🧪
- CONCEPT LEVEL 🧪🧪
- CLEAN UP 🧪

MATERIALS
The materials listed for this lab are for each group of 3 students. This lab can also be done as a teacher demonstration if space or materials are limited.

Safety Caution
Remind all students to review all safety cautions and icons before beginning this lab activity.

Lab Notes
You may need to demonstrate step 3 in Part A. Do all of Part A before beginning Part B.

Wave Speed, Frequency, and Wavelength

Wave speed, frequency, and wavelength are three related properties of waves. In this lab you will make observations and collect data to determine the relationship among these properties.

Materials
- coiled spring toy
- meterstick
- stopwatch

Part A—Wave Speed

Procedure
1. Copy Table 1 into your ScienceLog.

Table 1 Wave Speed Data			
Trial	Length of spring (m)	Time for wave (s)	Speed of wave (m/s)
1			
2			
3			
Average			

DO NOT WRITE IN BOOK

2. On the floor or a table, two students should stretch the spring to a length of 2 to 4 m. A third student should measure the length of the spring. Record the length in Table 1.

3. One student should pull part of the spring sideways with one hand, as shown at right, and release the pulled-back portion. This will cause a wave to travel down the spring.

4. Using a stopwatch, the third student should measure how long it takes for the wave to travel down the length of the spring and back. Record this time in Table 1.

5. Repeat steps 3 and 4 two more times.

Analyze Your Results
6. Calculate and record the wave speed for each trial. (Hint: Speed equals distance divided by time; distance is twice the spring length.)

7. Calculate and record the average time and the average wave speed.

 Datasheets for LabBook
Datasheet 55

Part B—Wavelength and Frequency

Procedure

8. Keep the spring the same length that you used in Part A.
9. Copy Table 2 into your ScienceLog.

Table 2 Wavelength and Frequency Data			
Trial	Length of spring (m)	Time for 10 cycles (s)	Wave frequency (Hz)	Wavelength (m)
1				
2				
3				
Average				

DO NOT WRITE IN BOOK

10. One of the two students holding the spring should start shaking the spring from side to side until a wave pattern appears that resembles one of those shown below.
11. Using the stopwatch, the third group member should measure and record how long it takes for 10 cycles of the wave pattern to occur. (One back-and-forth shake is one cycle.) Keep the pattern going so that measurements for three trials can be made.

Analyze Your Results

12. Calculate the frequency for each trial by dividing the number of cycles (10) by the time. Record the answers in Table 2.
13. Determine the wavelength using the equation at right that matches your wave pattern. Record your answer in Table 2.
14. Calculate and record the average time and frequency.

Draw Conclusions—Parts A and B

15. To discover the relationship among speed, wavelength, and frequency, try multiplying or dividing any two of them to see if the result equals the third. (Use the average speed, wavelength, and average frequency from your data tables.) In your ScienceLog, write the equation that shows the relationship.
16. Reread the definitions for *frequency* and *wavelength* in the chapter titled "The Energy of Waves." Use these definitions to explain the relationship that you discovered.

Wave Patterns

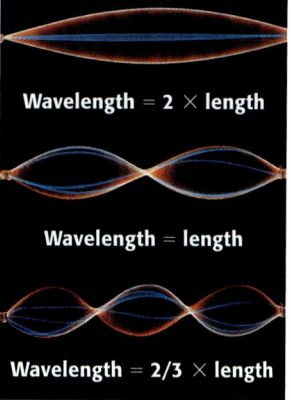

Wavelength = 2 × length

Wavelength = length

Wavelength = 2/3 × length

Answers

15. Accept all answers with correct calculations. Correct forms of the equation are: speed = wavelength × frequency; wavelength = speed/frequency; or frequency = speed/wavelength.

Lab Notes

In answer 15, students will be using numbers from their data to do the calculations. However, when students write their equation, they should use the terms, not their numbers.

16. Sample answer: The frequency of a wave is the number of waves that pass a certain point in a given amount of time. The wavelength is how long a wave is. So the speed of a wave must be wavelength (how long it is) times frequency (how many pass by per second).

Kevin McCurdy
Elmwood Junior High
Rogers, Arkansas

Easy Listening
Teacher's Notes

Time Required

One or two 45-minute class periods

Lab Ratings

TEACHER PREP 🧪
STUDENT SET-UP 🧪
CONCEPT LEVEL 🧪🧪
CLEAN UP 🧪

MATERIALS

FOR EACH GROUP OF 3 TO 4 STUDENTS:
- 4 tuning forks of different frequencies
- pink rubber eraser (or tuning fork mallet)
- meterstick
- graph paper

Answer

2. Answers will vary. Accept all reasonable hypotheses.

 Datasheets for LabBook
Datasheet 56

Terry Rakes
Elmwood Junior High
Rogers, Arkansas

Using Scientific Methods

Easy Listening

Pitch describes how low or high a sound is. A sound's pitch is related to its frequency—the number of waves per second. Frequency is expressed in hertz (Hz), where 1 Hz equals one wave per second. Most humans can hear frequencies from 20 Hz to 20,000 Hz. However, not everyone detects all pitches equally well at all distances. In this activity you will collect data to see how well you and your classmates hear different frequencies at different distances.

Materials
- 4 tuning forks of different frequencies
- pink rubber eraser
- meterstick
- graph paper

Ask a Question

1. Do students in your classroom hear low-, mid-, or high-frequency sounds better?

Form a Hypothesis

2. In your ScienceLog, write a hypothesis that answers the question above. Explain your reasoning.

Test the Hypothesis

3. Choose one member of your group to be the sound maker. The others will be the listeners.

4. Copy the data table below into your ScienceLog. Be sure to include a column for every listener in your group.

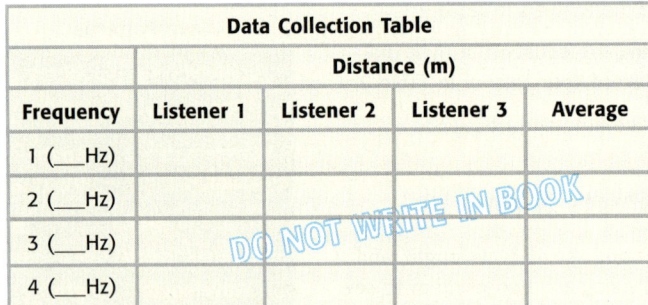

Data Collection Table				
	Distance (m)			
Frequency	Listener 1	Listener 2	Listener 3	Average
1 (___Hz)				
2 (___Hz)				
3 (___Hz)				
4 (___Hz)				

DO NOT WRITE IN BOOK

5. Record the frequency of one of the tuning forks in the top row of the first column of the data table.

710

Chapter 21 • LabBook

6. The listeners should stand in front of the sound maker with their backs turned.

7. The sound maker will create a sound by striking the tip of the tuning fork gently with the eraser.

8. The listeners who hear the sound should take one step away from the sound maker. The listeners who do not hear the sound should stay where they are.

9. Repeat steps 7 and 8 until none of the listeners can hear the sound or the listeners reach the edge of the room.

10. Using the meterstick, the sound maker should measure the distance from his or her position to each of the listeners. All group members should record this data in their tables.

11. Repeat steps 5 through 10 with a different tuning fork.

12. Continue until all four tuning forks have been tested.

Analyze the Results

13. Calculate the average distance for each frequency. Share your group's data with the rest of the class to make a data table for the whole class.

14. Calculate the average distance for each frequency for the class.

15. Make a graph of the class results, plotting average distance (*y*-axis) versus frequency (*x*-axis).

Draw Conclusions

16. Was everyone in the class able to hear all frequencies equally? (Hint: Was the average distance for each frequency the same?)

17. If the answer to question 16 is no, which frequency had the largest average distance? Which frequency had the smallest average distance?

18. Based on your graph, do your results support your hypothesis? Explain your answer.

19. Do you think your class sample is large enough to confirm your hypothesis for all humans of all ages? Explain your answer.

Lab Notes

You may wish to use the classroom graph to have students practice interpreting a graph. For instance, you could ask students to try and pinpoint the distances at which other frequencies might be heard based on the graph.

Answers

13. You may wish to provide a table on the board or on an overhead transparency for students to record their data. The table should include a column for each group and a row for the distance measurement for each tuning fork.

14. Calculate the class average for each frequency. All students should have the same averages.

15. The graph will vary depending on what frequencies are used, surrounding noise levels, and individual hearing abilities. See the sample graph below:

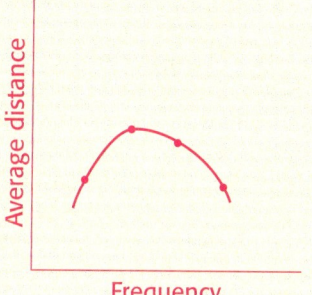

16. The average distance for each frequency should be different.

17. Answers will depend on which frequencies were used. Accept all answers that agree with class data.

18. Answers will vary depending on hypotheses. Accept all reasonable responses.

19. The class sample is not enough to confirm the hypothesis for all humans of all ages, because most people in the classroom are the same age. In addition, the number of students in an average classroom is just too small to provide results that can be extended to the general population.

The Speed of Sound
Teacher's Notes

Time Required
One 45-minute class period

Lab Ratings

EASY → HARD

- TEACHER PREP 🔺🔺
- STUDENT SET-UP 🔺🔺
- CONCEPT LEVEL 🔺🔺
- CLEAN UP 🔺

MATERIALS
Students will need stopwatches, measuring tapes, and various types of noise makers (cymbals, wood blocks, drums, horns, etc.). You will need an area where students can hear an echo. A long hall will do, but this lab generally works better outside. To make this lab even more interesting, you might have a contest with awards for the most creative experiment, the most accurate experiment, and the experiment with the least spread in the data for multiple measurements.

Safety Caution
Be sure that you have approved all experimental designs before students proceed.

Answers
4. Answers may vary. Factors that could cause a different value include air temperature and accuracy of distance and time measurements.
5. Several trials are necessary in order to confirm results and to rule out the possibility of reporting an error with just one measurement.
6. Answers will vary. Accept all reasonable responses.

712 Chapter 21 • LabBook

DESIGN YOUR OWN

The Speed of Sound

In the chapter titled "The Nature of Sound," you learned that the speed of sound in air is 343 m/s at 20°C (approximately room temperature). In this lab you'll design an experiment to measure the speed of sound yourself—and you'll determine if you're "up to speed"!

Materials
- materials of your choice, approved by your teacher

Procedure

1. Brainstorm with your teammates to come up with a way to measure the speed of sound. Consider the following as you design your experiment:

   a. You must have a method of making a sound. Some simple examples include speaking, clapping your hands, and hitting two boards together.

   b. Remember that speed is equal to distance divided by time. You must devise methods to measure the distance that a sound travels and to measure the amount of time it takes for that sound to travel that distance.

   c. Sound travels very rapidly. A sound from across the room will reach your ears almost before you can start recording the time! You may wish to have the sound travel a long distance.

   d. Remember that sound travels in waves. Think about the interactions of sound waves. You might be able to include these interactions in your design.

2. Discuss your experimental design with your teacher, including any equipment you need. Your teacher may have questions that will help you improve your design.

Conduct an Experiment

3. Once your design is approved, carry out your experiment. Be sure to perform several trials. Record your results in your ScienceLog.

Draw Conclusions

4. Was your result close to the value given in the introduction to this lab? If not, what factors may have caused you to get such a different value?

5. Why was it important for you to perform several trials in your experiment?

Communicate Your Results

6. Compare your results with those of your classmates. Determine which experimental design provided the best results. In your ScienceLog, explain why you think this design was so successful.

712

 Datasheets for LabBook
Datasheet 57

Paul Boyle
Perry Heights Middle School
Evansville, Indiana

Tuneful Tube

If you have seen a singer shatter a crystal glass simply by singing a note, you have seen an example of resonance. For this to happen, the note has to match the resonant frequency of the glass. A column of air within a cylinder can also resonate if the air column is the proper length for the frequency of the note. In this lab you will investigate the relationship between the length of an air column, the frequency, and the wavelength during resonance.

Procedure

1. Copy the data table below into your ScienceLog.

Data Collection Table				
Frequency (Hz)				
Length (cm)				

Materials

- 100 mL graduated cylinder
- water
- plastic tube, supplied by your teacher
- metric ruler
- 4 tuning forks of different frequencies
- pink rubber eraser
- graph paper

2. Fill the graduated cylinder with water.
3. Hold a plastic tube in the water so that about 3 cm is above the water.
4. Record the frequency of the first tuning fork. Gently strike the tuning fork with the eraser, and hold it so that the prongs are just above the tube, as shown at right. Slowly move the tube and fork up and down until you hear the loudest sound.
5. Measure the distance from the top of the tube to the water. Record this length in your data table.
6. Repeat steps 3–5 using the other three tuning forks.

Analysis

7. Calculate the wavelength (in centimeters) of each sound wave by dividing the speed of sound in air (343 m/s at 20°C) by the frequency and multiplying by 100.
8. Make the following graphs: air column length versus frequency and wavelength versus frequency. On both graphs, plot the frequency on the *x*-axis.
9. Describe the trend between the length of the air column and the frequency of the tuning fork.
10. How are the pitches you heard related to the wavelengths of the sounds?

Jennifer Ford
North Ridge Middle School
North Richland Hills, Texas

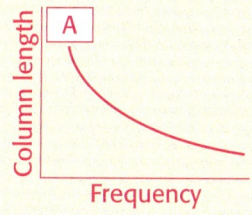
A — Column length vs Frequency

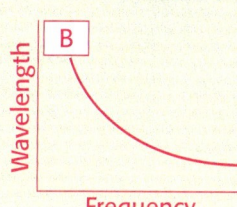
B — Wavelength vs Frequency

Datasheets for LabBook
Datasheet 58

Tuneful Tube
Teacher's Notes

Time Required
One 45-minute class period

Lab Ratings

EASY → HARD

- TEACHER PREP: 🧪🧪🧪
- STUDENT SET-UP: 🧪
- CONCEPT LEVEL: 🧪🧪🧪
- CLEAN UP: 🧪🧪

MATERIALS
The length of tube needed (PVC pipe works well) equals 25 times the speed of sound in air (343 m/s at 20°C) divided by the lowest frequency of the tuning forks used. (The answer is one-fourth the wavelength of the sound wave expressed in centimeters.) Cut each tube at least 5 cm longer than the calculated length. You may want to demonstrate the resonance point so students can hear the change in volume.

Answers

7. Answers will depend on the frequency of the tuning forks.
8. Graphs will depend on results. Sample graphs are shown at left.
9. As the frequency decreases, the length of the air column increases.
10. The pitches (which are determined by the frequencies) are inversely related to the wavelengths of the sounds. As the pitch gets lower (when the frequency decreases), the wavelength increases.

Chapter 21 • LabBook

The Energy of Sound
Teacher's Notes

Time Required
One or two 45-minute class periods

Lab Ratings

TEACHER PREP 🧪🧪
STUDENT SET-UP 🧪
CONCEPT LEVEL 🧪🧪🧪🧪
CLEAN UP 🧪

Safety Caution
Make sure students are at a safe distance before you perform the Part D exercise. You might wish to take the class outside.

Answers

2. The water begins to move. Vibrations from the tuning fork caused the water's movement.

6. The vibrating tuning fork causes the air to vibrate at a certain frequency. The energy of the vibrations is transferred through the air to the second tuning fork, which starts to resonate (vibrate at the same frequency).

7. Hitting the first tuning fork harder causes a larger amount of energy to be transferred from the tuning fork to the air. However, the vibration of the air particles is not at the same frequency as the second tuning fork and will therefore not cause the second tuning fork to make a sound.

The Energy of Sound

In the chapter titled "The Nature of Sound," you learned about various properties and interactions of sound. In this lab you will perform several activities that will demonstrate that the properties and interactions of sound all depend on one thing—the energy carried by sound waves.

Part A—Sound Vibrations

Procedure

1. Lightly strike a tuning fork with the eraser. Slowly place the prongs of the tuning fork in the plastic cup of water. Record your observations in your ScienceLog.

Analysis

2. How do your observations demonstrate that sound waves are carried through vibrations?

Part B—Resonance

Procedure

3. Strike a tuning fork with the eraser. Quickly pick up a second tuning fork in your other hand and hold it about 30 cm from the first tuning fork.

4. Place the first tuning fork against your leg to stop its vibration. Listen closely to the second tuning fork. Record your observations, including the frequencies of the two tuning forks.

5. Repeat steps 3 and 4, using the remaining tuning fork as the second tuning fork.

Analysis

6. Explain why you can hear a sound from the second tuning fork when the frequencies of the tuning forks used are the same.

7. When using tuning forks of different frequencies, would you expect to hear a sound from the second tuning fork if you strike the first tuning fork harder? Explain your reasoning.

Materials
- 2 tuning forks of the same frequency and one of a different frequency
- pink rubber eraser
- small plastic cup filled with water
- rubber band
- 50 cm string

 Datasheets for LabBook
Datasheet 59

Kevin McCurdy
Elmwood Junior High
Rogers, Arkansas

Part C—Interference

Procedure

8. Using the two tuning forks with the same frequency, place a rubber band tightly over the prongs near the base of one tuning fork. Strike both tuning forks at the same time against the eraser. Hold a tuning fork 3 to 5 cm from each ear. If you cannot hear any differences, move the rubber band down further on the prongs. Strike again. Record your observations in your ScienceLog.

Analysis

9. Did you notice the sound changing back and forth between loud and soft? A steady pattern like this is called a beat frequency. Explain this changing pattern of loudness and softness in terms of interference (both constructive and destructive).

Part D—The Doppler Effect

Procedure

10. Your teacher will tie the piece of string securely to the base of one tuning fork. Your teacher will then strike the tuning fork and carefully swing the tuning fork in a circle overhead. Record your observations in your ScienceLog.

Analysis

11. Did the tuning fork make a different sound when your teacher was swinging it than when he or she was holding it? If yes, explain why.

12. Is the actual pitch of the tuning fork changing? Explain.

Draw Conclusions— Parts A–D

13. Explain how your observations from each part of this lab verify that sound waves carry energy from one point to another through a vibrating medium.

14. Particularly loud thunder can cause the windows of your room to rattle. How is this evidence that sound waves carry energy?

Answers

9. The loudness corresponds to constructive interference (when the crests of the sound waves overlap, increasing the amplitude), and the softness corresponds to destructive interference (when the crests and troughs of sound waves overlap, decreasing the amplitude).

11. Yes. As the tuning fork swings toward the listeners, the pitch is higher because the sound waves in front of it are closer together and therefore have a higher frequency. As the tuning fork swings away from the listeners, the pitch is lower because the sound waves are farther apart and therefore have a lower frequency.

12. Yes. The pitch you hear changes because of the Doppler effect, but the actual frequency of the tuning fork does not change.

13. Part A shows that the vibrations of the tuning fork have energy that does work on the water. Part B shows that the energy from one vibrating tuning fork can be passed by vibrations through the air to cause another tuning fork to vibrate. Part C shows that the energy from each vibrating tuning fork can travel through the air as waves that can interfere with each other. Part D shows that the vibrations from a tuning fork travel through the air to your ears, and the amount of energy being carried by the vibration determines what is heard (higher pitch = higher frequency = higher energy).

14. It takes energy to move the windows to cause them to rattle. Therefore, energy from the thunder's sound waves must be transferred through the air to the windows.

What Color of Light Is Best for Green Plants?
Teacher's Notes

Time Required
One 45-minute class period, plus 5 minutes/day for 5 days

Lab Ratings

- TEACHER PREP 🔺🔺🔺
- STUDENT SET-UP 🔺🔺
- CONCEPT LEVEL 🔺🔺🔺🔺
- CLEAN UP 🔺

MATERIALS
Seeds may be purchased at a garden store and should be germinated several days before this activity. At least green and red lights should be used. Colored bulbs or bulbs with theatrical gels can be used. For best results, give seedlings light of only one color.

Safety Caution
Caution students to use care when working near hot bulbs.

Answers
2. Accept all reasonable hypotheses.
8. Other than natural light, red light is the best, and green light is the worst.
9. Green plants reflect green light and use other colors to grow. Red is best because it is reflected the least.
10. Purple plants do not grow well under purple light because all the light is reflected.
11. Accept all reasonable summaries.

716 Chapter 22 • LabBook

Using Scientific Methods

What Color of Light Is Best for Green Plants?

DISCOVERY LAB

Plants grow well outdoors under natural sunlight. However, some plants are grown indoors under artificial light. A wide variety of colored lights are available for helping plants grow indoors. In this experiment, you'll test several colors of light to discover which color best meets the energy needs of green plants.

Ask a Question
1. What color of light is the best for growing green plants?

Form a Hypothesis
2. In your ScienceLog, write a hypothesis that answers the question above. Explain your reasoning.

Test the Hypothesis
3. Use the masking tape and marker to label the side of each Petri dish with your name and the type of light you will place the dish under.
4. Place a moist paper towel in each Petri dish. Place five seedlings on top of the paper towel. Cover each dish.
5. Record your observations of the seedlings, such as length, color, and number of leaves, in your ScienceLog.
6. Place each dish under the appropriate light.
7. Observe the Petri dishes every day for at least 5 days. Record your observations in your ScienceLog.

Analyze the Results
8. Based on your results, which color of light is the best for growing green plants? Which color of light is the worst?

Materials
- masking tape
- marker
- Petri dishes and covers
- water
- paper towels
- bean seedlings
- variety of colored lights, supplied by your teacher

Draw Conclusions
9. Remember that the color of an opaque object (such as a plant) is determined by the colors the object reflects. Use this information to explain your answer to question 8.
10. Would a purple light be good for growing purple plants? Explain.

Communicate Results
11. Write a short paragraph summarizing your conclusions.

716

 Datasheets for LabBook
Datasheet 60

Edith C. McAlanis
Socorro Middle School
El Paso, Texas

Which Color Is Hottest?

Will a navy blue hat or a white hat keep your head warmer in cool weather? Colored objects absorb energy, which can make the objects warmer. How much energy is absorbed depends on the object's color. In this experiment you will test several colors under a bright light to determine which colors absorb the most energy.

Materials

- tape
- squares of colored paper
- thermometer
- light source
- cup of room-temperature water
- paper towels
- graph paper
- colored pencils or pens

Procedure

1. Copy the table below into your ScienceLog. Be sure to have one column for each color of paper you have and enough rows to end at 3 minutes.

Data Collection Table

Time (s)	White	Red	Blue	Black
0				
15				
30				
45				
etc.				

DO NOT WRITE IN BOOK

2. Tape a piece of colored paper around the bottom of a thermometer and hold it under the light source. Record the temperature every 15 seconds for 3 minutes.

3. Cool the thermometer by removing the piece of paper and placing the thermometer in the cup of room-temperature water. After 1 minute, remove the thermometer, and dry it with a paper towel.

4. Repeat steps 2 and 3 with each color, making sure to hold the thermometer at the same distance from the light source.

Analyze the Results

5. Prepare a graph of temperature (*y*-axis) versus time (*x*-axis). Plot all data on one graph using a different colored pencil or pen for each set of data.

6. Rank the colors you used in order from hottest to coolest.

Draw Conclusions

7. Compare the colors based on the amount of energy each absorbs.

8. In this experiment a white light was used. How would your results be different if you used a red light? Explain.

9. Use the relationship between color and energy absorbed to explain why different colors of clothing are used for different seasons.

Which Color Is Hottest?
Teacher's Notes

Time Required
One or two 45-minute class periods

Lab Ratings

EASY ————→ HARD

- TEACHER PREP 🧪🧪
- STUDENT SET-UP 🧪🧪
- CONCEPT LEVEL 🧪🧪🧪🧪
- CLEAN UP 🧪

MATERIALS

A 75 W or 100 W incandescent bulb is a good light source. For best results, a single type of paper should be used. Each group needs one square of each color. Be sure to use at least black, blue, red, and white.

Safety Caution

Caution students to wear safety goggles and aprons while performing this activity.

Procedure Notes

To conserve class time, prepare 2 × 2 cm squares of colored paper in advance.

Answers

5. A sample graph is shown at right. (Red and blue may be reversed.)

6. Black, red, blue, and white.

7. Black absorbs the most energy. Red absorbs more energy than blue. White absorbs the least energy.

8. The red and white papers would be coolest because they reflect red light.

9. Sample answer: Black clothes absorb energy and can help keep a person warm in winter. White clothes reflect energy and can help keep a person cool in summer.

 Datasheets for LabBook Datasheet 61

Tracy Jahn
Berkshire Junior–Senior High School
Canaan, New York

Chapter 22 • LabBook

Mixing Colors
Teacher's Notes

Time Required
One or two 45-minute class periods

Lab Ratings

EASY ———→ HARD

Teacher Prep 🧪🧪
Student Set-Up 🧪🧪🧪
Concept Level 🧪🧪
Clean Up 🧪🧪

MATERIALS

Materials listed are for each group of 2–4 students. If a sufficient number of flashlights is not available, consider using the spotlights on the school stage or portable floodlight holders instead. Each group should have a set of watercolors that includes red, blue, and green.

Safety Caution

Students should wear aprons when doing Part B of this lab.

Answers

6. Mixing two colors of light together results in a color that is brighter than the original colors.

7. Mixing three colors of light results in a color that is much brighter than the color produced by mixing two colors because more wavelengths are present.

8. The result would be bright, white light because all the wavelengths of light would be combined.

Mixing Colors

When you mix two colors, like red and green, you create a different color. But what color do you create? And is that new color brighter or darker? The color and brightness you see depend on the light that reaches your eye, and that depends on whether you are performing color addition (combining wavelengths by mixing colors of light) or color subtraction (absorbing light by mixing colors of pigments). In this experiment, you will try both types of color formation and see the results firsthand!

Part A—Color Addition

Procedure

1. Place a colored filter over each flashlight lens. Use masking tape to hold the filters in place.

2. In a darkened room, shine the red light on a sheet of clean white paper. Then shine the blue light next to the red light. You should see two circles of light, one red and one blue, next to each other.

3. Move the flashlights so that the circles overlap by about half their diameter. Examine the three areas of color, and record your observations. What color is formed in the mixed area? Is the mixed area brighter or darker than the single-color areas?

4. Repeat steps 2 and 3 with the red and green lights.

5. Now shine all three lights at the same point on the sheet of paper. Examine the results, and record your observations.

Analysis

6. In general, when you mixed two colors, was the result brighter or darker than the original colors?

7. In step 5, you mixed all three colors. Was the resulting color brighter or darker than mixing two colors? Explain your answer in terms of color addition. (Hint: Read the definition of color addition in the introduction.)

8. Based on your results, what do you think would happen if you mixed all the colors of light? Explain.

 Datasheets for LabBook
Datasheet 62

SKILL BUILDER

Materials

Part A
- 3 flashlights
- colored filters—red, green, and blue
- masking tape
- white paper

Part B
- masking tape
- 2 small plastic or paper cups
- water
- paintbrush
- watercolor paints
- white paper
- metric ruler

Barry Bishop
San Rafael Junior High
Ferron, Utah

Part B—Color Subtraction

Procedure

9. Place a piece of masking tape on each cup. Label one cup "Clean" and the other cup "Dirty." Fill both cups approximately half full with water.

10. Wet the paintbrush thoroughly in the "Clean" cup. Using the watercolor paints, paint a red circle on the white paper. The circle should be approximately 4 cm in diameter.

11. Clean the brush by rinsing it first in the "Dirty" cup and then in the "Clean" cup.

12. Paint a blue circle next to the red circle. Then paint half the red circle with the blue paint.

13. Examine the three areas: red, blue, and mixed. What color is the mixed area? Does it appear brighter or darker than the red and blue areas? Record your observations in your ScienceLog.

14. Clean the brush. Paint a green circle 4 cm in diameter, and then paint half the blue circle with green paint.

15. Examine the green, blue, and mixed areas. Record your observations.

16. Now add green paint to the mixed red-blue area, so that you have an area that is a mixture of red, green, and blue paint. Clean your brush.

17. Record your observations of this new mixed area.

Analysis

18. In general, when you mixed two colors, was the result brighter or darker than the original colors?

19. In step 16, you mixed all three colors. Was the result brighter or darker than mixing two colors? Explain your answer in terms of color subtraction. (Hint: Read the definition of color subtraction in the introduction.)

20. Based on your results, what do you think would happen if you mixed all the colors of paint? Explain.

Procedure Notes

For further reinforcement in Part B, students can continue to mix colors to confirm their findings about color subtraction (provided their watercolor sets include more than the three required colors).

Answers

18. Mixing two colors of paint together results in a color that is darker than the original colors.

19. Mixing three colors of paint results in a color that is darker than the color that results from mixing two colors. Because each color of paint absorbs some light, colors that have been mixed together absorb even more light.

20. If you mixed all the colors of paint, all colors of light would be absorbed, and a black spot would result.

Disposal Information

Have plenty of paper towels on hand to wipe up water and paint spills. Make sure students clean their brushes thoroughly. Students should use soap and water to clean any water color smudges off their lab tables.

Mirror Images
Teacher's Notes

Time Required
One or two 45-minute class periods

Lab Ratings

- TEACHER PREP
- STUDENT SET-UP
- CONCEPT LEVEL
- CLEAN UP

MATERIALS
Mirrors with a focal length around 50 cm work well.

Safety Caution
Caution students about working near an open flame. Any loose hair or clothing should be tied back before beginning the experiment.

Kevin McCurdy
Elmwood Junior High
Rogers, Arkansas

Mirror Images

When light actually passes through an image, the image is a real image. When light does not pass through the image, the image is a virtual image. Recall that plane mirrors produce only virtual images because the image appears to be behind the mirror where no light can pass through it.

In fact, all mirrors can form virtual images, but only some mirrors can form real images. In this experiment, you will explore the virtual images formed by concave and convex mirrors, and you will try to find a real image using both types of mirrors.

Part A—Finding Virtual Images

Make Observations

1. Hold the convex mirror at arm's length away from your face. Observe the image of your face in the mirror.
2. Slowly move the mirror toward your face, and observe what happens to the image. Record your observations in your ScienceLog.
3. Move the mirror very close to your face. Record your observations in your ScienceLog.
4. Slowly move the mirror away from your face, and observe what happens to the image. Record your observations.
5. Repeat steps 1 through 4 with the concave mirror.

Analyze Your Results

6. For each mirror, did you find a virtual image? How can you tell?
7. Describe the images you found. Were they smaller, larger, or the same size as your face? Were they upright or inverted?

Draw Conclusions

8. Describe at least one use for each type of mirror. Be creative, and try to think of inventions that might use the properties of the two types of mirrors.

Materials

- convex mirror
- concave mirror
- candle
- jar lid
- modeling clay
- matches
- index card

Answers

6. Students should find a virtual image for both kinds of mirrors. The virtual image appears to be behind the mirror, where no light rays can pass through the image.
7. Images in a convex mirror will be smaller and upright. Images in a concave mirror will be larger and upright when the mirror is close and smaller and inverted when the mirror is farther from the student's face.
8. Accept all reasonable answers. Convex mirrors are used for wide-angle views in side-view mirrors on cars and to see around corners in busy hallways. Concave mirrors are used for make-up and shaving mirrors. Concave mirrors are also used in telescopes.

Part B—Finding a Real Image

Make Observations

9. In a darkened room, place a candle in a jar lid near one end of a table. Use modeling clay to hold the candle in place. Light the candle.
   Caution: Use extreme care around an open flame.

10. Use more modeling clay to make a base to hold the convex mirror upright. Place the mirror at the other end of the table, facing the candle.

11. Hold the index card between the candle and the mirror but slightly to one side so that you do not block the candlelight, as shown below.

12. Move the card slowly from side to side and back and forth to see whether you can focus an image of the candle on it. Record your results in your ScienceLog.

13. Repeat steps 10–12 with the concave mirror.

Analyze Your Results

14. For each mirror, did you find a real image? How can you tell?

15. Describe the real image you found. Was it smaller, larger, or the same size as the object? Was it upright or inverted?

Draw Conclusions

16. Astronomical telescopes use large mirrors to reflect light to form a real image. Based on your results, would a concave or convex mirror be better for this instrument? Explain your answer.

14. A real image can be observed with the concave mirror but not with the convex mirror. The real image is "real" because the light reflects off the mirror and forms a visible image on the card.

15. The image is smaller and inverted.

16. A concave mirror would be better than a convex mirror. A real image cannot be formed with a convex mirror.

Datasheets for LabBook
Datasheet 63

Images from Convex Lenses
Teacher's Notes

Time Required
One or two 45-minute class periods

Lab Ratings

TEACHER PREP 🧪
STUDENT SET-UP 🧪
CONCEPT LEVEL 🧪🧪🧪
CLEAN UP 🧪

MATERIALS
Lenses with a focal length of around 25 cm work well.

Safety Caution
Caution students about working near an open flame. Any loose hair or clothing should be tied back before beginning the experiment.

Lab Notes
Image 1 forms when the distance between the candle and the card is 4 times the focal length of the lens. However, students do NOT need to know the focal length of the lens to perform the procedure.

Using Scientific Methods

Images from Convex Lenses

A convex lens is thicker in the center than at the edges. Light rays passing through a convex lens come together at a point. Under certain conditions, a convex lens will create a real image of an object. This image will have certain characteristics, depending on the distance between the object and the lens. In this experiment you will determine the characteristics of real images created by a convex lens—the kind of lens used as a magnifying lens.

Materials
- index card
- modeling clay
- candle
- jar lid
- matches
- convex lens
- meterstick

Ask a Question
1. What are the characteristics of real images created by a convex lens? How do these characteristics depend on the location of the object and the lens?

Conduct an Experiment
2. Copy the table below into your ScienceLog.

Data Collection				
Image	Orientation (upright/inverted)	Size (larger/smaller)	Image distance (cm)	Object distance (cm)
1				
2				
3				

DO NOT WRITE IN BOOK

3. Use some modeling clay to make a base for the lens. Place the lens and base in the middle of the table.

 Datasheets for LabBook
Datasheet 64

Patricia McFarlane Soto
George Washington Carver Middle School
Miami, Florida

4. Stand the index card upright in some modeling clay on one side of the lens.

5. Place the candle in the jar lid, and anchor it with some modeling clay. Place the candle on the table so that the lens is halfway between the candle and the card. Light the candle.
Caution: Use extreme care around an open flame.

Collect Data

6. In a darkened room, slowly move the card and the candle away from the lens while keeping the lens exactly halfway between the card and the candle. Continue until you see a clear image of the candle flame on the card. This is image 1.

7. Measure and record the distance between the lens and the card (image distance) and between the lens and the candle (object distance).

8. Is image 1 upright or inverted? Is it larger or smaller than the candle? Record this information in the table.

9. Slide the lens toward the candle to get a new image (image 2) of the candle on the card. Leave the lens in this position.

10. Repeat steps 7 and 8 for image 2.

11. Move the lens back to the middle, and then move the lens toward the card to get a third image (image 3).

12. Repeat steps 7 and 8 for image 3.

Analyze Your Results

13. Describe the trend between image distance and image size.

14. What are the similarities between the real images formed by a convex lens?

Draw Conclusions

15. The lens of your eye is a convex lens. Use the information you collected to describe the image projected on the back of your eye when you look at an object.

16. Convex lenses are used in film projectors. Explain why your favorite movie stars are truly "larger than life" on the screen in terms of the image distance and the object distance.

Communicate Your Results

17. Write a paragraph to summarize your answer to the question in step 1. Be sure to include the roles that image distance and object distance have in determining the characteristics of the images.

Answers

13. When the image distance gets larger, the image size gets larger.

14. The images are inverted.

15. The image projected on the back of your eye is a real image that is smaller than the object and inverted.

16. The object distance (from the film to the lens) is much smaller than the image distance (from the lens to the screen). Thus, the image projected on the screen will be very large compared with the size of the image on the film itself.

17. Accept all reasonable answers. Sample summary: At certain combinations of object distance and image distance, a convex lens will form a real image. The image size varies with the distances. When the image distance is small (and the object distance is large) the image size is small. When the image distance is large, the image size is large. When the image distance and object distance are the same, the image is the same size as the object. All of the real images were inverted, which did not depend on distance at all.

Self-Check Answers

Chapter 1—The World of Physical Science
Page 16: flapping rate

Chapter 2—The Properties of Matter
Page 41: approximately 30 N

Chapter 3—States of Matter
Page 64: The pressure would increase.
Page 70: endothermic

Chapter 4—Elements, Compounds, and Mixtures
Page 87: No, the properties of pure water are the same no matter what its source is.
Page 93: Copper and silver are solutes. Gold is the solvent.

Chapter 5—Matter in Motion
Page 110: Numbers 1 and 3 are examples of velocity.
Page 117: 2 N north
Page 122: sliding friction
Page 126: Gravity is a force of attraction between objects that is due to the masses of the objects.

Chapter 6—Forces in Motion
Page 140: A leaf is more affected by air resistance.
Page 147: This can be answered in terms of either Newton's first law or inertia.

Newton's first law: When the bus is still, both you and the bus are at rest. The bus started moving, but no unbalanced force acted on your body, so your body stayed at rest.

Inertia: You have inertia, and that makes you difficult to move. As a result, when the bus started to move, you didn't move with it.

Chapter 7—Forces in Fluids
Page 175: Air travels faster over the top of a wing.

Chapter 8—Work and Machines
Page 189: Pulling a wheeled suitcase is doing work because the force applied and the motion of the suitcase are in the same direction.

Chapter 9—Energy and Energy Resources

Page 223: A roller coaster has the greatest potential energy at the top of the highest hill (usually the first hill) and the greatest kinetic energy at the bottom of the highest hill.

Chapter 10—Heat and Heat Technology

Page 259: Two substances can have the same temperature but different amounts of thermal energy because temperature, unlike thermal energy, does not depend on mass. A small amount of a substance at a particular temperature will have less thermal energy than a large amount of the substance at the same temperature.

Page 261: Steam can cause a more severe burn than boiling water because steam contains more energy per unit mass than does boiling water.

Chapter 11—Introduction to Atoms

Page 285: The particles Thomson discovered had negative charges. Because an atom has no charge, it must contain positively charged particles to cancel the negative charges.

Chapter 12—The Periodic Table

Page 312: It is easier for atoms of alkali metals to lose one electron than for atoms of alkaline-earth metals to lose two electrons. Therefore, alkali metals are more reactive than alkaline-earth metals.

Chapter 13—Chemical Bonding

Page 333: neon

Page 337: 1. 6   **2.** In a covalent bond, electrons are shared between atoms. In an ionic bond, electrons are transferred from one atom to another.

Chapter 14—Chemical Reactions

Page 353: 2 sodium atoms, 1 sulfur atom, and 4 oxygen atoms

Page 355: $CaBr_2 + Cl_2 \rightarrow Br_2 + CaCl_2$

reactants: $CaBr_2$ and Cl_2

products: Br_2 and $CaCl_2$

Chapter 15—Chemical Compounds

Page 381: a soft drink

Chapter 16—Atomic Energy

Page 400: alpha particles

Self-Check Answers

Chapter 17—Introduction to Electricity

Page 425: Plastic wrap is charged by friction as it is pulled off the roll.

Page 438: $E = P \times t$; $E = 200 \text{ W} \times 2 \text{ h} = 400 \text{ Wh}$

Students will have to use data from the table on page 438 to answer this question.

Page 441: Yes; a microwave oven is an example of a load because it uses electrical energy to do work.

Chapter 18—Electromagnetism

Page 464: No; an electromagnet is produced when the magnetic field of the coil of wire causes the domains in the core to line up. Wood does not contain domains and therefore cannot be the core of an electromagnet.

Chapter 19—Electronic Technology

No self-check question for this chapter.

Chapter 20—The Energy of Waves

Page 512: Mechanical waves require a medium; electromagnetic waves do not.

Page 521: A light wave will not refract if it enters a new medium perpendicular to the surface because the entire wave enters the new medium at the same time.

Chapter 21—The Nature of Sound

Page 549: A person hears a sonic boom when a shock wave reaches his or her ears. If two people are standing a block or two apart, the shock wave will reach them at different times, so they will hear sonic booms at different times.

Page 553: Interference is the most important wave interaction for determining sound quality.

Chapter 22—The Nature of Light

Page 583: The paper will appear blue because only blue light is reflected from the paper.

Chapter 23—Light and Our World

Page 602: Concave lenses do not form real images. Only a real image can be magnified by another lens, such as the eyepiece lens.

Appendix

CONTENTS

Concept Mapping **728**
SI Measurement **729**
Temperature Scales **730**
Measuring Skills **731**
Scientific Method **732**
Making Charts and Graphs **735**
Math Refresher **738**
Physical Science Refresher **742**
Periodic Table of the Elements **744**
Physical Science Laws and Principles **746**

Concept Mapping: A Way to Bring Ideas Together

What Is a Concept Map?

Have you ever tried to tell someone about a book or a chapter you've just read and found that you can remember only a few isolated words and ideas? Or maybe you've memorized facts for a test and then weeks later discovered you're not even sure what topics those facts covered.

In both cases, you may have understood the ideas or concepts by themselves but not in relation to one another. If you could somehow link the ideas together, you would probably understand them better and remember them longer. This is something a concept map can help you do. A concept map is a way to see how ideas or concepts fit together. It can help you see the "big picture."

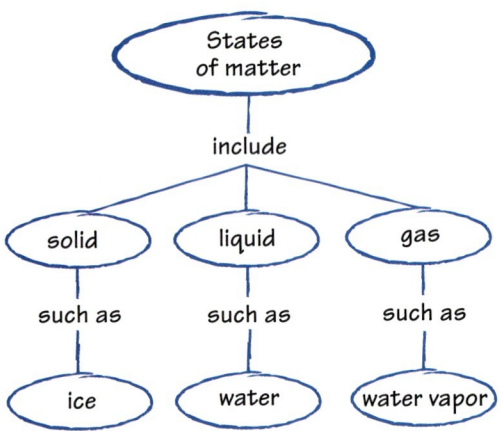

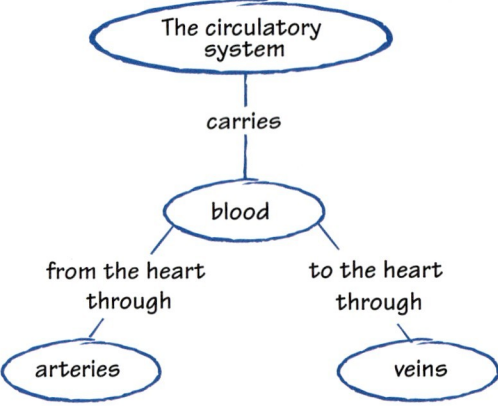

How to Make a Concept Map

1 **Make a list of the main ideas or concepts.**

It might help to write each concept on its own slip of paper. This will make it easier to rearrange the concepts as many times as necessary to make sense of how the concepts are connected. After you've made a few concept maps this way, you can go directly from writing your list to actually making the map.

2 **Arrange the concepts in order from the most general to the most specific.**

Put the most general concept at the top and circle it. Ask yourself, "How does this concept relate to the remaining concepts?" As you see the relationships, arrange the concepts in order from general to specific.

3 **Connect the related concepts with lines.**

4 **On each line, write an action word or short phrase that shows how the concepts are related.**

Look at the concept maps on this page, and then see if you can make one for the following terms:

plants, water, photosynthesis, carbon dioxide, sun's energy

One possible answer is provided at right, but don't look at it until you try the concept map yourself.

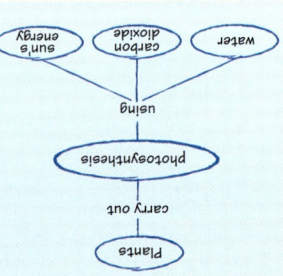

728 Appendix

SI Measurement

The International System of Units, or SI, is the standard system of measurement used by many scientists. Using the same standards of measurement makes it easier for scientists to communicate with one another.

SI works by combining prefixes and base units. Each base unit can be used with different prefixes to define smaller and larger quantities. The table below lists common SI prefixes.

SI Prefixes			
Prefix	**Abbreviation**	**Factor**	**Example**
kilo-	k	1,000	kilogram, 1 kg = 1,000 g
hecto-	h	100	hectoliter, 1 hL = 100 L
deka-	da	10	dekameter, 1 dam = 10 m
		1	meter, liter
deci-	d	0.1	decigram, 1 dg = 0.1 g
centi-	c	0.01	centimeter, 1 cm = 0.01 m
milli-	m	0.001	milliliter, 1 mL = 0.001 L
micro-	µ	0.000 001	micrometer, 1 µm = 0.000 001 m

SI Conversion Table		
SI units	**From SI to English**	**From English to SI**
Length		
kilometer (km) = 1,000 m	1 km = 0.621 mi	1 mi = 1.609 km
meter (m) = 100 cm	1 m = 3.281 ft	1 ft = 0.305 m
centimeter (cm) = 0.01 m	1 cm = 0.394 in.	1 in. = 2.540 cm
millimeter (mm) = 0.001 m	1 mm = 0.039 in.	
micrometer (µm) = 0.000 001 m		
nanometer (nm) = 0.000 000 001 m		
Area		
square kilometer (km^2) = 100 hectares	1 km^2 = 0.386 mi^2	1 mi^2 = 2.590 km^2
hectare (ha) = 10,000 m^2	1 ha = 2.471 acres	1 acre = 0.405 ha
square meter (m^2) = 10,000 cm^2	1 m^2 = 10.765 ft^2	1 ft^2 = 0.093 m^2
square centimeter (cm^2) = 100 mm^2	1 cm^2 = 0.155 in.^{2}	1 in.^{2} = 6.452 cm^2
Volume		
liter (L) = 1,000 mL = 1 dm^3	1 L = 1.057 fl qt	1 fl qt = 0.946 L
milliliter (mL) = 0.001 L = 1 cm^3	1 mL = 0.034 fl oz	1 fl oz = 29.575 mL
microliter (µL) = 0.000 001 L		
Mass		
kilogram (kg) = 1,000 g	1 kg = 2.205 lb	1 lb = 0.454 kg
gram (g) = 1,000 mg	1 g = 0.035 oz	1 oz = 28.349 g
milligram (mg) = 0.001 g		
microgram (µg) = 0.000 001 g		

Temperature Scales

Temperature can be expressed using three different scales: Fahrenheit, Celsius, and Kelvin. The SI unit for temperature is the kelvin (K). Although 0 K is much colder than 0°C, a change of 1 K is equal to a change of 1°C.

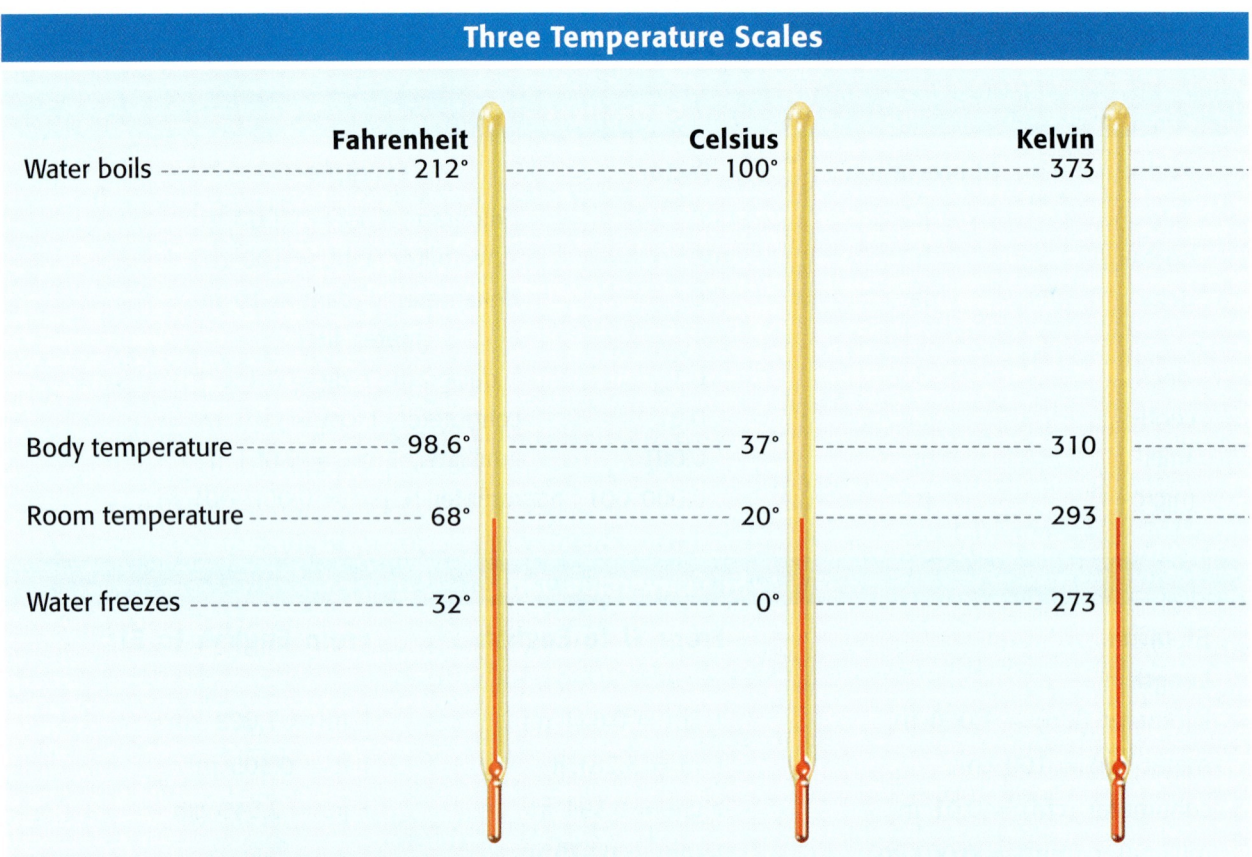

Three Temperature Scales

	Fahrenheit	Celsius	Kelvin
Water boils	212°	100°	373
Body temperature	98.6°	37°	310
Room temperature	68°	20°	293
Water freezes	32°	0°	273

Temperature Conversions Table

To convert	Use this equation:	Example
Celsius to Fahrenheit °C ⟶ °F	$°F = \left(\frac{9}{5} \times °C\right) + 32$	Convert 45°C to °F. $°F = \left(\frac{9}{5} \times 45°C\right) + 32 = 113°F$
Fahrenheit to Celsius °F ⟶ °C	$°C = \frac{5}{9} \times (°F - 32)$	Convert 68°F to °C. $°C = \frac{5}{9} \times (68°F - 32) = 20°C$
Celsius to Kelvin °C ⟶ K	$K = °C + 273$	Convert 45°C to K. $K = 45°C + 273 = 318 K$
Kelvin to Celsius K ⟶ °C	$°C = K - 273$	Convert 32 K to °C. $°C = 32 K - 273 = -241°C$

Measuring Skills

Using a Graduated Cylinder

When using a graduated cylinder to measure volume, keep the following procedures in mind:

1. Make sure the cylinder is on a flat, level surface.
2. Move your head so that your eye is level with the surface of the liquid.
3. Read the mark closest to the liquid level. On glass graduated cylinders, read the mark closest to the center of the curve in the liquid's surface.

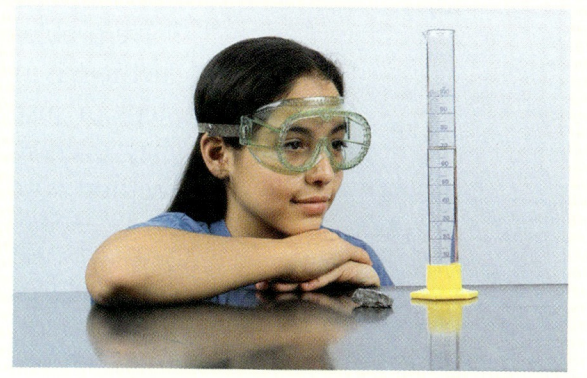

Using a Meterstick or Metric Ruler

When using a meterstick or metric ruler to measure length, keep the following procedures in mind:

1. Place the ruler firmly against the object you are measuring.
2. Align one edge of the object exactly with the zero end of the ruler.
3. Look at the other edge of the object to see which of the marks on the ruler is closest to that edge. **Note:** Each small slash between the centimeters represents a millimeter, which is one-tenth of a centimeter.

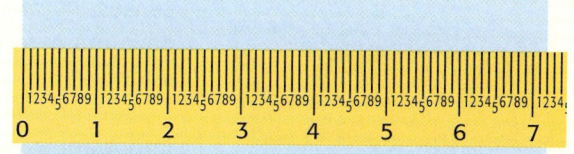

Using a Triple-Beam Balance

When using a triple-beam balance to measure mass, keep the following procedures in mind:

1. Make sure the balance is on a level surface.
2. Place all of the countermasses at zero. Adjust the balancing knob until the pointer rests at zero.
3. Place the object you wish to measure on the pan. **Caution:** Do not place hot objects or chemicals directly on the balance pan.
4. Move the largest countermass along the beam to the right until it is at the last notch that does not tip the balance. Follow the same procedure with the next-largest countermass. Then move the smallest countermass until the pointer rests at zero.
5. Add the readings from the three beams together to determine the mass of the object.
6. When determining the mass of crystals or powders, use a piece of filter paper. First find the mass of the paper. Then add the crystals or powder to the paper and re-measure. The actual mass of the crystals or powder is the total mass minus the mass of the paper. When finding the mass of liquids, first find the mass of the empty container. Then find the mass of the liquid and container together. The mass of the liquid is the total mass minus the mass of the container.

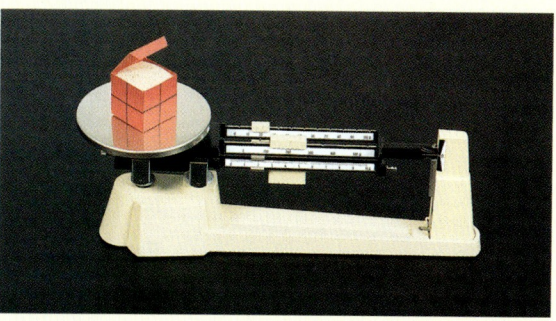

Scientific Method

The series of steps that scientists use to answer questions and solve problems is often called the **scientific method.** The scientific method is not a rigid procedure. Scientists may use all of the steps or just some of the steps of the scientific method. They may even repeat some of the steps. The goal of the scientific method is to come up with reliable answers and solutions.

Six Steps of the Scientific Method

1 Ask a Question Good questions come from careful **observations.** You make observations by using your senses to gather information. Sometimes you may use instruments, such as microscopes and telescopes, to extend the range of your senses. As you observe the natural world, you will discover that you have many more questions than answers. These questions drive the scientific method.

Questions beginning with *what, why, how,* and *when* are very important in focusing an investigation, and they often lead to a hypothesis. (You will learn what a hypothesis is in the next step.) Here is an example of a question that could lead to further investigation.

Question: How does acid rain affect plant growth?

2 Form a Hypothesis After you come up with a question, you need to turn the question into a **hypothesis.** A hypothesis is a clear statement of what you expect the answer to your question to be. Your hypothesis will represent your best "educated guess" based on your observations and what you already know. A good hypothesis is testable. If observations and information cannot be gathered or if an experiment cannot be designed to test your hypothesis, it is untestable, and the investigation can go no further.

Here is a hypothesis that could be formed from the question, "How does acid rain affect plant growth?"

Hypothesis: Acid rain causes plants to grow more slowly.

Notice that the hypothesis provides some specifics that lead to methods of testing. The hypothesis can also lead to predictions. A **prediction** is what you think will be the outcome of your experiment or data collection. Predictions are usually stated in an "if . . . then" format. For example, **if** meat is kept at room temperature, **then** it will spoil faster than meat kept in the refrigerator. More than one prediction can be made for a single hypothesis. Here is a sample prediction for the hypothesis that acid rain causes plants to grow more slowly.

Prediction: If a plant is watered with only acid rain (which has a pH of 4), then the plant will grow at half its normal rate.

3 **Test the Hypothesis** After you have formed a hypothesis and made a prediction, you should test your hypothesis. There are different ways to do this. Perhaps the most familiar way is to conduct a **controlled experiment**. A controlled experiment tests only one factor at a time. A controlled experiment has a **control group** and one or more **experimental groups**. All the factors for the control and experimental groups are the same except for one factor, which is called the **variable**. By changing only one factor, you can see the results of just that one change.

Sometimes, the nature of an investigation makes a controlled experiment impossible. For example, dinosaurs have been extinct for millions of years, and the Earth's core is surrounded by thousands of meters of rock. It would be difficult, if not impossible, to conduct controlled experiments on such things. Under such circumstances, a hypothesis may be tested by making detailed observations. Taking measurements is one way of making observations.

4 **Analyze the Results** After you have completed your experiments, made your observations, and collected your data, you must analyze all the information you have gathered. Tables and graphs are often used in this step to organize the data.

5 **Draw Conclusions** Based on the analysis of your data, you should conclude whether or not your results support your hypothesis. If your hypothesis is supported, you (or others) might want to repeat the observations or experiments to verify your results. If your hypothesis is not supported by the data, you may have to check your procedure for errors. You may even have to reject your hypothesis and make a new one. If you cannot draw a conclusion from your results, you may have to try the investigation again or carry out further observations or experiments.

6 **Communicate Results** After any scientific investigation, you should report your results. By doing a written or oral report, you let others know what you have learned. They may want to repeat your investigation to see if they get the same results. Your report may even lead to another question, which in turn may lead to another investigation.

Appendix **733**

Scientific Method in Action

The scientific method is not a "straight line" of steps. It contains loops in which several steps may be repeated over and over again, while others may not be necessary. For example, sometimes scientists will find that testing one hypothesis raises new questions and new hypotheses to be tested. And sometimes, testing the hypothesis leads directly to a conclusion. Furthermore, the steps in the scientific method are not always used in the same order. Follow the steps in the diagram below, and see how many different directions the scientific method can take you.

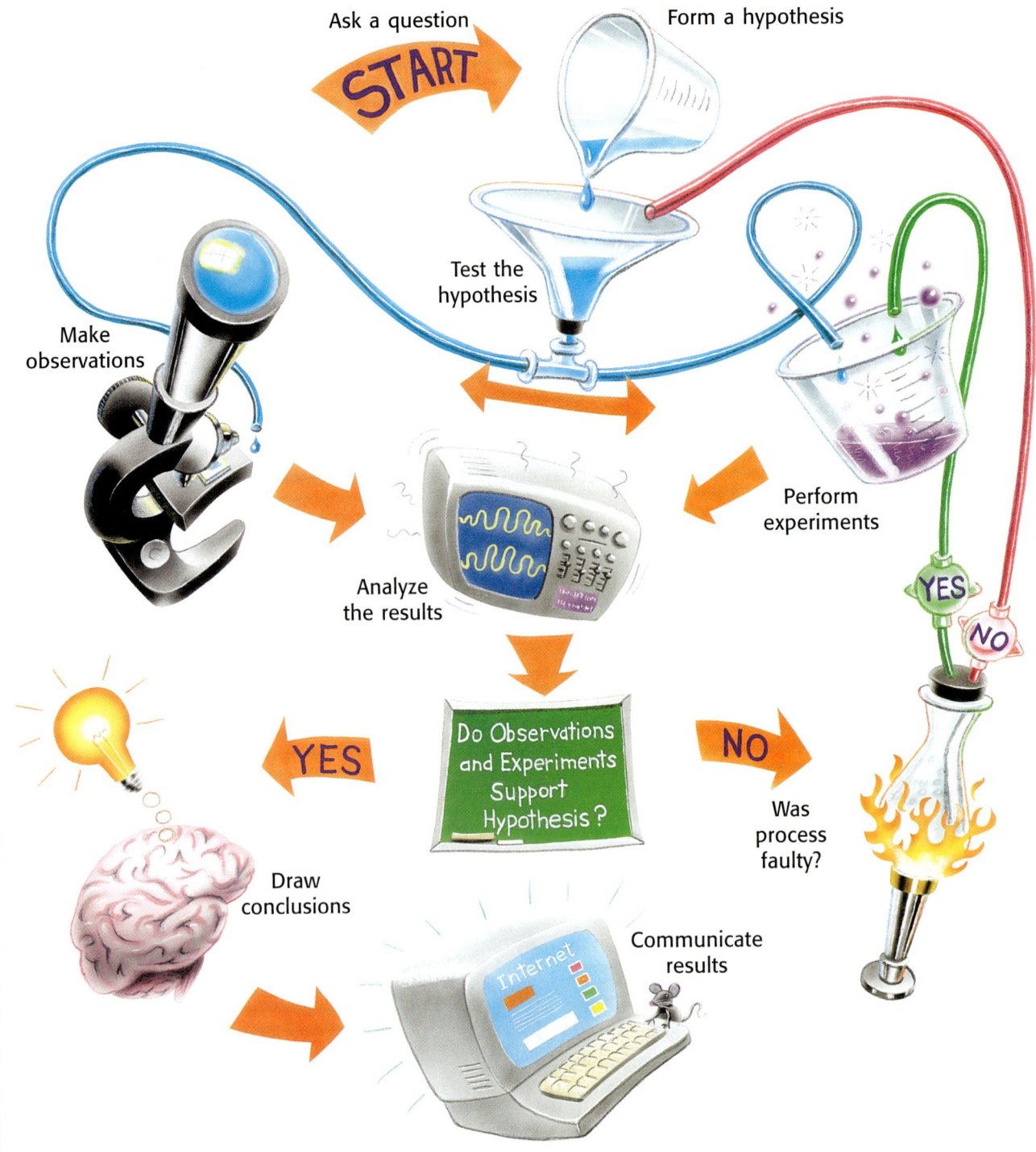

Making Charts and Graphs

Circle Graphs

A circle graph, or pie chart, shows how each group of data relates to all of the data. Each part of the circle represents a category of the data. The entire circle represents all of the data. For example, a biologist studying a hardwood forest in Wisconsin found that there were five different types of trees. The data table at right summarizes the biologist's findings.

Wisconsin Hardwood Trees	
Type of tree	**Number found**
Oak	600
Maple	750
Beech	300
Birch	1,200
Hickory	150
Total	3,000

How to Make a Circle Graph

1 In order to make a circle graph of this data, first find the percentage of each type of tree. To do this, divide the number of individual trees by the total number of trees and multiply by 100.

$$\frac{600 \text{ oak}}{3{,}000 \text{ trees}} \times 100 = 20\%$$

$$\frac{750 \text{ maple}}{3{,}000 \text{ trees}} \times 100 = 25\%$$

$$\frac{300 \text{ beech}}{3{,}000 \text{ trees}} \times 100 = 10\%$$

$$\frac{1{,}200 \text{ birch}}{3{,}000 \text{ trees}} \times 100 = 40\%$$

$$\frac{150 \text{ hickory}}{3{,}000 \text{ trees}} \times 100 = 5\%$$

2 Now determine the size of the pie shapes that make up the chart. Do this by multiplying each percentage by 360°. Remember that a circle contains 360°.

$20\% \times 360° = 72°$ $25\% \times 360° = 90°$
$10\% \times 360° = 36°$ $40\% \times 360° = 144°$
$5\% \times 360° = 18°$

3 Then check that the sum of the percentages is 100 and the sum of the degrees is 360.

$20\% + 25\% + 10\% + 40\% + 5\% = 100\%$
$72° + 90° + 36° + 144° + 18° = 360°$

4 Use a compass to draw a circle and mark its center.

5 Then use a protractor to draw angles of 72°, 90°, 36°, 144°, and 18° in the circle.

6 Finally, label each part of the graph, and choose an appropriate title.

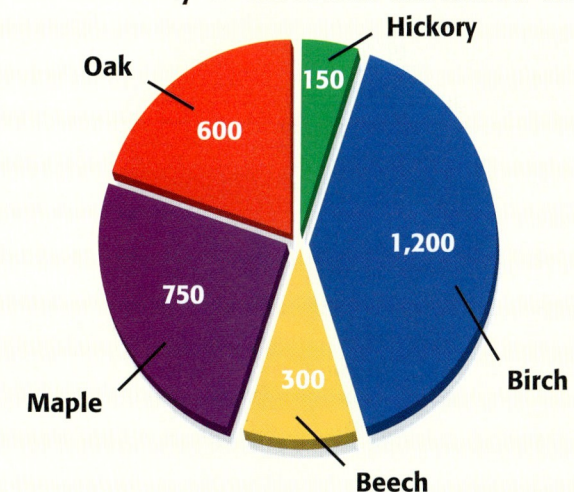

A Community of Wisconsin Hardwood Trees

Appendix **735**

Line Graphs

Line graphs are most often used to demonstrate continuous change. For example, Mr. Smith's science class analyzed the population records for their hometown, Appleton, between 1900 and 2000. Examine the data at left.

Because the year and the population change, they are the *variables*. The population is determined by, or dependent on, the year. Therefore, the population is called the **dependent variable**, and the year is called the **independent variable**. Each set of data is called a **data pair**. To prepare a line graph, data pairs must first be organized in a table like the one at left.

Population of Appleton, 1900–2000

Year	Population
1900	1,800
1920	2,500
1940	3,200
1960	3,900
1980	4,600
2000	5,300

How to Make a Line Graph

1. Place the independent variable along the horizontal (x) axis. Place the dependent variable along the vertical (y) axis.
2. Label the x-axis "Year" and the y-axis "Population." Look at your largest and smallest values for the population. Determine a scale for the y-axis that will provide enough space to show these values. You must use the same scale for the entire length of the axis. Find an appropriate scale for the x-axis too.
3. Choose reasonable starting points for each axis.
4. Plot the data pairs as accurately as possible.
5. Choose a title that accurately represents the data.

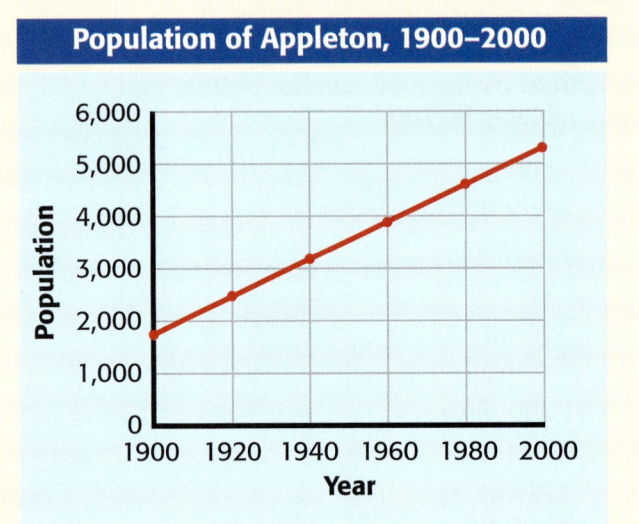

How to Determine Slope

Slope is the ratio of the change in the y-axis to the change in the x-axis, or "rise over run."

1. Choose two points on the line graph. For example, the population of Appleton in 2000 was 5,300 people. Therefore, you can define point *a* as (2000, 5,300). In 1900, the population was 1,800 people. Define point *b* as (1900, 1,800).
2. Find the change in the y-axis.
   (y at point *a*) − (y at point *b*)
   5,300 people − 1,800 people = 3,500 people
3. Find the change in the x-axis.
   (x at point *a*) − (x at point *b*)
   2000 − 1900 = 100 years
4. Calculate the slope of the graph by dividing the change in y by the change in x.

$$\text{slope} = \frac{\text{change in } y}{\text{change in } x}$$

$$\text{slope} = \frac{3{,}500 \text{ people}}{100 \text{ years}}$$

slope = 35 people per year

In this example, the population in Appleton increased by a fixed amount each year. The graph of this data is a straight line. Therefore, the relationship is **linear**. When the graph of a set of data is not a straight line, the relationship is **nonlinear**.

Using Algebra to Determine Slope

The equation in step 4 may also be arranged to be:

$$y = kx$$

where y represents the change in the y-axis, k represents the slope, and x represents the change in the x-axis.

$$\text{slope} = \frac{\text{change in } y}{\text{change in } x}$$

$$k = \frac{y}{x}$$

$$k \times x = \frac{y \times x}{x}$$

$$kx = y$$

Bar Graphs

Bar graphs are used to demonstrate change that is not continuous. These graphs can be used to indicate trends when the data are taken over a long period of time. A meteorologist gathered the precipitation records at right for Hartford, Connecticut, for April 1–15, 1996, and used a bar graph to represent the data.

Precipitation in Hartford, Connecticut April 1–15, 1996

Date	Precipitation (cm)	Date	Precipitation (cm)
April 1	0.5	April 9	0.25
April 2	1.25	April 10	0.0
April 3	0.0	April 11	1.0
April 4	0.0	April 12	0.0
April 5	0.0	April 13	0.25
April 6	0.0	April 14	0.0
April 7	0.0	April 15	6.50
April 8	1.75		

How to Make a Bar Graph

1. Use an appropriate scale and a reasonable starting point for each axis.
2. Label the axes, and plot the data.
3. Choose a title that accurately represents the data.

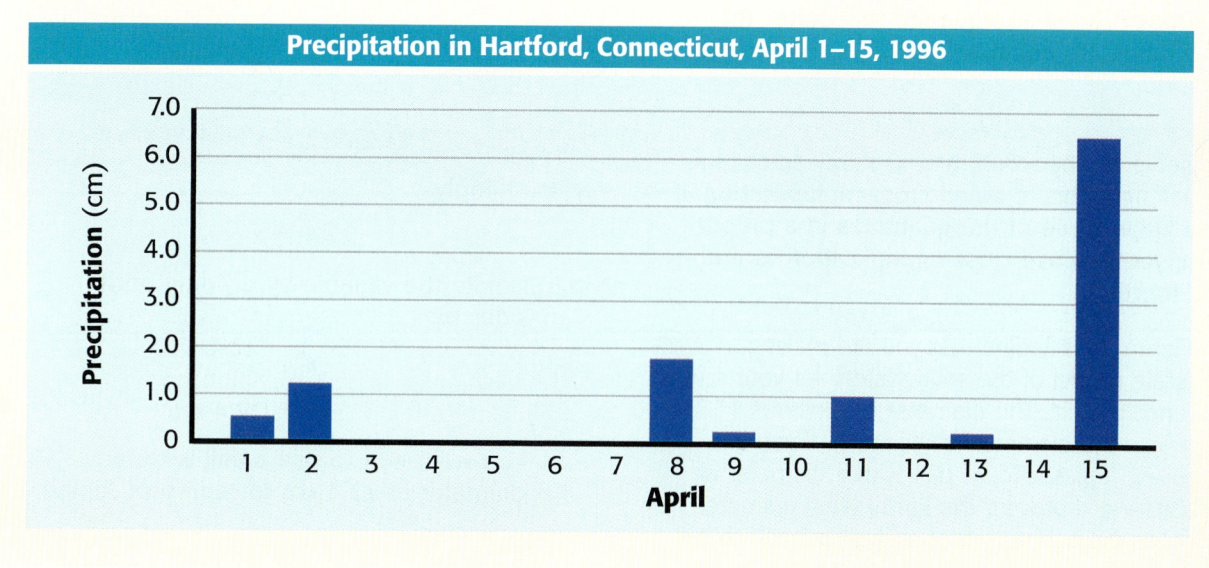

Appendix **737**

Math Refresher

Science requires an understanding of many math concepts. The following pages will help you review some important math skills.

Averages

An **average,** or **mean,** simplifies a list of numbers into a single number that *approximates* their value.

Example: Find the average of the following set of numbers: 5, 4, 7, and 8.

Step 1: Find the sum.

$$5 + 4 + 7 + 8 = 24$$

Step 2: Divide the sum by the amount of numbers in your set. Because there are four numbers in this example, divide the sum by 4.

$$\frac{24}{4} = 6$$

The average, or mean, is **6.**

Ratios

A **ratio** is a comparison between numbers, and it is usually written as a fraction.

Example: Find the ratio of thermometers to students if you have 36 thermometers and 48 students in your class.

Step 1: Make the ratio.

$$\frac{36 \text{ thermometers}}{48 \text{ students}}$$

Step 2: Reduce the fraction to its simplest form.

$$\frac{36}{48} = \frac{36 \div 12}{48 \div 12} = \frac{3}{4}$$

The ratio of thermometers to students is **3 to 4,** or $\frac{3}{4}$. The ratio may also be written in the form 3:4.

Proportions

A **proportion** is an equation that states that two ratios are equal.

$$\frac{3}{1} = \frac{12}{4}$$

To solve a proportion, first multiply across the equal sign. This is called cross-multiplication. If you know three of the quantities in a proportion, you can use cross-multiplication to find the fourth.

Example: Imagine that you are making a scale model of the solar system for your science project. The diameter of Jupiter is 11.2 times the diameter of the Earth. If you are using a plastic-foam ball with a diameter of 2 cm to represent the Earth, what diameter does the ball representing Jupiter need to be?

$$\frac{11.2}{1} = \frac{x}{2 \text{ cm}}$$

Step 1: Cross-multiply.

$$\frac{11.2}{1} \diagdown\!\!\!\!\diagup \frac{x}{2}$$

$$11.2 \times 2 = x \times 1$$

Step 2: Multiply.

$$22.4 = x \times 1$$

Step 3: Isolate the variable by dividing both sides by 1.

$$x = \frac{22.4}{1}$$

$$x = 22.4 \text{ cm}$$

You will need to use a ball with a diameter of **22.4 cm** to represent Jupiter.

Appendix

Percentages

A **percentage** is a ratio of a given number to 100.

Example: What is 85 percent of 40?

Step 1: Rewrite the percentage by moving the decimal point two places to the left.

.85

Step 2: Multiply the decimal by the number you are calculating the percentage of.

$0.85 \times 40 = 34$

85 percent of 40 is **34.**

Decimals

To **add** or **subtract decimals,** line up the digits vertically so that the decimal points line up. Then add or subtract the columns from right to left, carrying or borrowing numbers as necessary.

Example: Add the following numbers: 3.1415 and 2.96.

Step 1: Line up the digits vertically so that the decimal points line up.

$$\begin{array}{r} 3.1415 \\ + \ 2.96 \ \ \\ \hline \end{array}$$

Step 2: Add the columns from right to left, carrying when necessary.

$$\begin{array}{r} 1\ 1 \\ 3.1415 \\ + \ 2.96 \\ \hline 6.1015 \end{array}$$

The sum is **6.1015.**

Fractions

Numbers tell you how many; **fractions** tell you *how much of a whole.*

Example: Your class has 24 plants. Your teacher instructs you to put 5 in a shady spot. What fraction does this represent?

Step 1: Write a fraction with the total number of parts in the whole as the denominator.

$\frac{?}{24}$

Step 2: Write the number of parts of the whole being represented as the numerator.

$\frac{5}{24}$

$\frac{5}{24}$ of the plants will be in the shade.

Reducing Fractions

It is usually best to express a fraction in simplest form. This is called *reducing* a fraction.

Example: Reduce the fraction $\frac{30}{45}$ to its simplest form.

Step 1: Find the largest whole number that will divide evenly into both the numerator and denominator. This number is called the greatest common factor (GCF).

factors of the numerator 30: 1, 2, 3, 5, 6, 10, **15,** 30

factors of the denominator 45: 1, 3, 5, 9, **15,** 45

Step 2: Divide both the numerator and the denominator by the GCF, which in this case is 15.

$$\frac{30}{45} = \frac{30 \div 15}{45 \div 15} = \frac{2}{3}$$

$\frac{30}{45}$ reduced to its simplest form is $\frac{2}{3}$.

Adding and Subtracting Fractions

To **add** or **subtract fractions** that have the **same denominator,** simply add or subtract the numerators.

Examples:
$$\frac{3}{5} + \frac{1}{5} = ? \text{ and } \frac{3}{4} - \frac{1}{4} = ?$$

Step 1: Add or subtract the numerators.
$$\frac{3}{5} + \frac{1}{5} = \frac{4}{} \text{ and } \frac{3}{4} - \frac{1}{4} = \frac{2}{}$$

Step 2: Write the sum or difference over the denominator.
$$\frac{3}{5} + \frac{1}{5} = \frac{4}{5} \text{ and } \frac{3}{4} - \frac{1}{4} = \frac{2}{4}$$

Step 3: If necessary, reduce the fraction to its simplest form.
$$\frac{4}{5} \text{ cannot be reduced, and } \frac{2}{4} = \frac{1}{2}.$$

To **add** or **subtract fractions** that have **different denominators,** first find the least common denominator (LCD).

Examples:
$$\frac{1}{2} + \frac{1}{6} = ? \text{ and } \frac{3}{4} - \frac{2}{3} = ?$$

Step 1: Write the equivalent fractions with a common denominator.
$$\frac{3}{6} + \frac{1}{6} = ? \text{ and } \frac{9}{12} - \frac{8}{12} = ?$$

Step 2: Add or subtract.
$$\frac{3}{6} + \frac{1}{6} = \frac{4}{6} \text{ and } \frac{9}{12} - \frac{8}{12} = \frac{1}{12}$$

Step 3: If necessary, reduce the fraction to its simplest form.
$$\frac{4}{6} = \frac{2}{3}, \text{ and } \frac{1}{12} \text{ cannot be reduced.}$$

Multiplying Fractions

To **multiply fractions,** multiply the numerators and the denominators together, and then reduce the fraction to its simplest form.

Example:
$$\frac{5}{9} \times \frac{7}{10} = ?$$

Step 1: Multiply the numerators and denominators.
$$\frac{5}{9} \times \frac{7}{10} = \frac{5 \times 7}{9 \times 10} = \frac{35}{90}$$

Step 2: Reduce.
$$\frac{35}{90} = \frac{35 \div 5}{90 \div 5} = \frac{7}{18}$$

Dividing Fractions

To **divide fractions,** first rewrite the divisor (the number you divide *by*) upside down. This is called the reciprocal of the divisor. Then you can multiply and reduce if necessary.

Example:
$$\frac{5}{8} \div \frac{3}{2} = ?$$

Step 1: Rewrite the divisor as its reciprocal.
$$\frac{3}{2} \rightarrow \frac{2}{3}$$

Step 2: Multiply.
$$\frac{5}{8} \times \frac{2}{3} = \frac{5 \times 2}{8 \times 3} = \frac{10}{24}$$

Step 3: Reduce.
$$\frac{10}{24} = \frac{10 \div 2}{24 \div 2} = \frac{5}{12}$$

Scientific Notation

Scientific notation is a short way of representing very large and very small numbers without writing all of the place-holding zeros.

Example: Write 653,000,000 in scientific notation.

Step 1: Write the number without the place-holding zeros.

653

Step 2: Place the decimal point after the first digit.

6.53

Step 3: Find the exponent by counting the number of places that you moved the decimal point.

6.53000000

The decimal point was moved eight places to the left. Therefore, the exponent of 10 is positive 8. Remember, if the decimal point had moved to the right, the exponent would be negative.

Step 4: Write the number in scientific notation.

6.53×10^8

Area

Area is the number of square units needed to cover the surface of an object.

Formulas:
Area of a square = side × side
Area of a rectangle = length × width
Area of a triangle = $\frac{1}{2}$ × base × height

Examples: Find the areas.

Triangle
Area = $\frac{1}{2}$ × base × height
Area = $\frac{1}{2}$ × 3 cm × 4 cm
Area = **6 cm²**

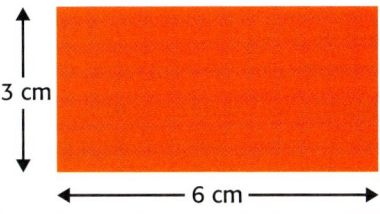

Rectangle
Area = length × width
Area = 6 cm × 3 cm
Area = **18 cm²**

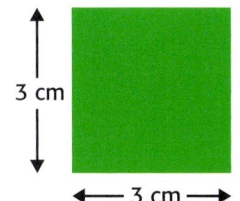

Square
Area = side × side
Area = 3 cm × 3 cm
Area = **9 cm²**

Volume

Volume is the amount of space something occupies.

Formulas:
Volume of a cube = side × side × side

Volume of a prism = area of base × height

Examples: Find the volume of the solids.

Cube
Volume = side × side × side
Volume = 4 cm × 4 cm × 4 cm
Volume = **64 cm³**

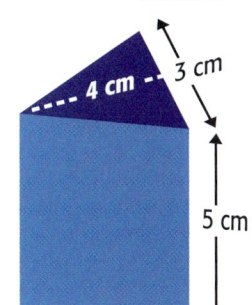

Prism
Volume = area of base × height
Volume = (area of triangle) × height
Volume = $\left(\frac{1}{2} \times 3 \text{ cm} \times 4 \text{ cm}\right) \times 5 \text{ cm}$
Volume = 6 cm² × 5 cm
Volume = **30 cm³**

Physical Science Refresher

Atoms and Elements

Every object in the universe is made up of particles of some kind of matter. **Matter** is anything that takes up space and has mass. All matter is made up of elements. An **element** is a substance that cannot be separated into simpler components by ordinary chemical means. This is because each element consists of only one kind of atom. An **atom** is the smallest unit of an element that has all of the properties of that element.

Atomic Structure

Atoms are made up of small particles called subatomic particles. The three major types of subatomic particles are **electrons, protons,** and **neutrons.** Electrons have a negative electric charge, protons have a positive charge, and neutrons have no electric charge. The protons and neutrons are packed close to one another to form the **nucleus.** The protons give the nucleus a positive charge. Electrons are most likely to be found in regions around the nucleus called **electron clouds.** The negatively charged electrons are attracted to the positively charged nucleus. An atom may have several energy levels in which electrons are located.

Atomic Number

To help in the identification of elements, scientists have assigned an **atomic number** to each kind of atom. The atomic number is the number of protons in the atom. Atoms with the same number of protons are all the same kind of element. In an uncharged, or electrically neutral, atom there are an equal number of protons and electrons. Therefore, the atomic number equals the number of electrons in an uncharged atom. The number of neutrons, however, can vary for a given element. Atoms of the same element that have different numbers of neutrons are called **isotopes.**

Periodic Table of the Elements

In the periodic table, the elements are arranged from left to right in order of increasing atomic number. Each element in the table is in a separate box. An atom of each element has one more electron and one more proton than an atom of the element to its left. Each horizontal row of the table is called a **period.** Changes in chemical properties of elements across a period correspond to changes in the electron arrangements of their atoms. Each vertical column of the table, known as a **group,** lists elements with similar properties. The elements in a group have similar chemical properties because their atoms have the same number of electrons in their outer energy level. For example, the elements helium, neon, argon, krypton, xenon, and radon all have similar properties and are known as the noble gases.

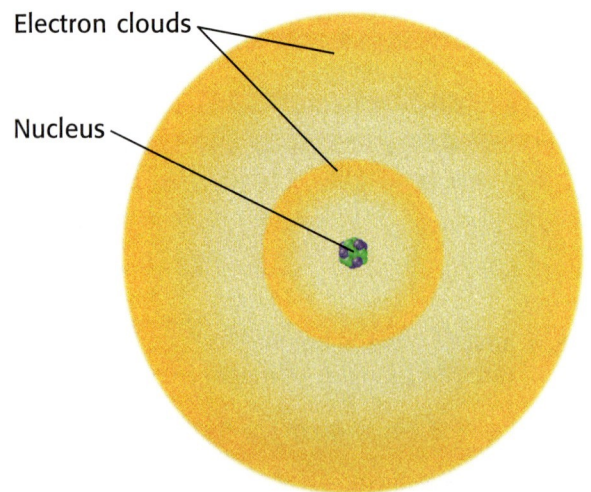

Electron clouds

Nucleus

742 Appendix

Molecules and Compounds

When two or more elements are joined chemically, the resulting substance is called a **compound**. A compound is a new substance with properties different from those of the elements that compose it. For example, water, H_2O, is a compound formed when hydrogen (H) and oxygen (O) combine. The smallest complete unit of a compound that has the properties of that compound is called a **molecule**. A chemical formula indicates the elements in a compound. It also indicates the relative number of atoms of each element present. The chemical formula for water is H_2O, which indicates that each water molecule consists of two atoms of hydrogen and one atom of oxygen. The subscript number is used after the symbol for an element to indicate how many atoms of that element are in a single molecule of the compound.

Acids, Bases, and pH

An ion is an atom or group of atoms that has an electric charge because it has lost or gained one or more electrons. When an acid, such as hydrochloric acid, HCl, is mixed with water, it separates into ions. An **acid** is a compound that produces hydrogen ions, H^+, in water. The hydrogen ions then combine with a water molecule to form a hydronium ion, H_3O^+. A **base**, on the other hand, is a substance that produces hydroxide ions, OH^-, in water.

To determine whether a solution is acidic or basic, scientists use pH. The **pH** is a measure of the hydronium ion concentration in a solution. The pH scale ranges from 0 to 14. The middle point, pH = 7, is neutral, neither acidic nor basic. Acids have a pH less than 7; bases have a pH greater than 7. The lower the number is, the more acidic the solution. The higher the number is, the more basic the solution.

Chemical Equations

A chemical reaction occurs when a chemical change takes place. (In a chemical change, new substances with new properties are formed.) A chemical equation is a useful way of describing a chemical reaction by means of chemical formulas. The equation indicates what substances react and what the products are. For example, when carbon and oxygen combine, they can form carbon dioxide. The equation for the reaction is as follows: $C + O_2 \longrightarrow CO_2$.

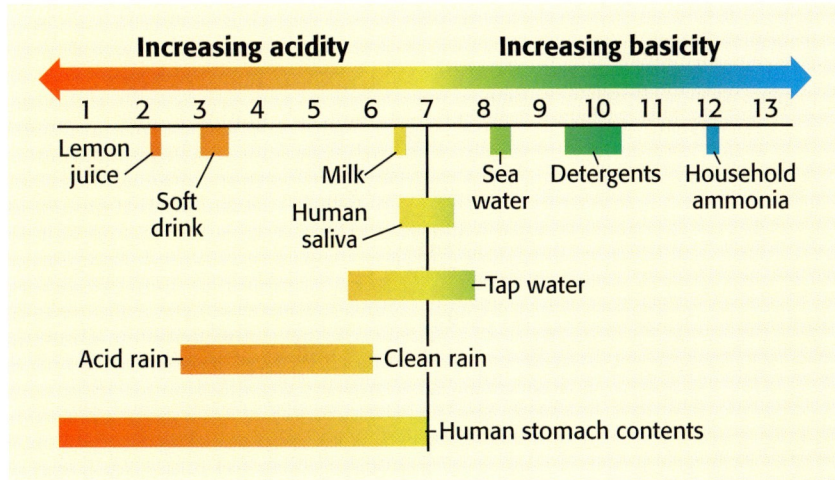

Appendix

Periodic Table of the Elements

Each square on the table includes an element's name, chemical symbol, atomic number, and atomic mass.

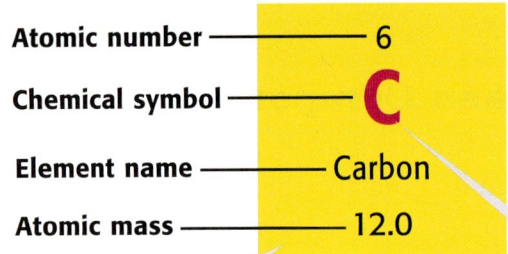

- Atomic number — 6
- Chemical symbol — C
- Element name — Carbon
- Atomic mass — 12.0

The background color indicates the type of element. Carbon is a nonmetal.

The color of the chemical symbol indicates the physical state at room temperature. Carbon is a solid.

Background
- Metals
- Metalloids
- Nonmetals

Chemical symbol
- Solid
- Liquid
- Gas

Period 1
- 1 H Hydrogen 1.0

Period 2
- Group 1: 3 Li Lithium 6.9
- Group 2: 4 Be Beryllium 9.0

Period 3
- 11 Na Sodium 23.0
- 12 Mg Magnesium 24.3

Period 4
- 19 K Potassium 39.1
- 20 Ca Calcium 40.1
- 21 Sc Scandium 45.0
- 22 Ti Titanium 47.9
- 23 V Vanadium 50.9
- 24 Cr Chromium 52.0
- 25 Mn Manganese 54.9
- 26 Fe Iron 55.8
- 27 Co Cobalt 58.9

Period 5
- 37 Rb Rubidium 85.5
- 38 Sr Strontium 87.6
- 39 Y Yttrium 88.9
- 40 Zr Zirconium 91.2
- 41 Nb Niobium 92.9
- 42 Mo Molybdenum 95.9
- 43 Tc Technetium (97.9)
- 44 Ru Ruthenium 101.1
- 45 Rh Rhodium 102.9

Period 6
- 55 Cs Cesium 132.9
- 56 Ba Barium 137.3
- 57 La Lanthanum 138.9
- 72 Hf Hafnium 178.5
- 73 Ta Tantalum 180.9
- 74 W Tungsten 183.8
- 75 Re Rhenium 186.2
- 76 Os Osmium 190.2
- 77 Ir Iridium 192.2

Period 7
- 87 Fr Francium (223.0)
- 88 Ra Radium (226.0)
- 89 Ac Actinium (227.0)
- 104 Rf Rutherfordium (261.1)
- 105 Db Dubnium (262.1)
- 106 Sg Seaborgium (263.1)
- 107 Bh Bohrium (262.1)
- 108 Hs Hassium (265)
- 109 Mt Meitnerium (266)

A row of elements is called a period.

A column of elements is called a group or family.

Lanthanides
- 58 Ce Cerium 140.1
- 59 Pr Praseodymium 140.9
- 60 Nd Neodymium 144.2
- 61 Pm Promethium (144.9)
- 62 Sm Samarium 150.4

Actinides
- 90 Th Thorium 232.0
- 91 Pa Protactinium 231.0
- 92 U Uranium 238.0
- 93 Np Neptunium (237.0)
- 94 Pu Plutonium 244.1

These elements are placed below the table to allow the table to be narrower.

This zigzag line reminds you where the metals, nonmetals, and metalloids are.

Group 10	Group 11	Group 12	Group 13	Group 14	Group 15	Group 16	Group 17	Group 18
								2 **He** Helium 4.0
			5 **B** Boron 10.8	6 **C** Carbon 12.0	7 **N** Nitrogen 14.0	8 **O** Oxygen 16.0	9 **F** Fluorine 19.0	10 **Ne** Neon 20.2
			13 **Al** Aluminum 27.0	14 **Si** Silicon 28.1	15 **P** Phosphorus 31.0	16 **S** Sulfur 32.1	17 **Cl** Chlorine 35.5	18 **Ar** Argon 39.9
28 **Ni** Nickel 58.7	29 **Cu** Copper 63.5	30 **Zn** Zinc 65.4	31 **Ga** Gallium 69.7	32 **Ge** Germanium 72.6	33 **As** Arsenic 74.9	34 **Se** Selenium 79.0	35 **Br** Bromine 79.9	36 **Kr** Krypton 83.8
46 **Pd** Palladium 106.4	47 **Ag** Silver 107.9	48 **Cd** Cadmium 112.4	49 **In** Indium 114.8	50 **Sn** Tin 118.7	51 **Sb** Antimony 121.8	52 **Te** Tellurium 127.6	53 **I** Iodine 126.9	54 **Xe** Xenon 131.3
78 **Pt** Platinum 195.1	79 **Au** Gold 197.0	80 **Hg** Mercury 200.6	81 **Tl** Thallium 204.4	82 **Pb** Lead 207.2	83 **Bi** Bismuth 209.0	84 **Po** Polonium (209.0)	85 **At** Astatine (210.0)	86 **Rn** Radon (222.0)
110 **Uun** Ununnilium (271)	111 **Uuu** Unununium (272)	112 **Uub** Ununbium (277)						

The names and symbols of elements 110–112 are temporary. They are based on the atomic number of the element. The official name and symbol will be approved by an international committee of scientists.

63 **Eu** Europium 152.0	64 **Gd** Gadolinium 157.3	65 **Tb** Terbium 158.9	66 **Dy** Dysprosium 162.5	67 **Ho** Holmium 164.9	68 **Er** Erbium 167.3	69 **Tm** Thulium 168.9	70 **Yb** Ytterbium 173.0	71 **Lu** Lutetium 175.0
95 **Am** Americium (243.1)	96 **Cm** Curium (247.1)	97 **Bk** Berkelium (247.1)	98 **Cf** Californium (251.1)	99 **Es** Einsteinium (252.1)	100 **Fm** Fermium (257.1)	101 **Md** Mendelevium (258.1)	102 **No** Nobelium (259.1)	103 **Lr** Lawrencium (262.1)

A number in parentheses is the mass number of the most stable isotope of that element.

Physical Science Laws and Principles

Law of Conservation of Energy

> The **law of conservation of energy** states that energy can be neither created nor destroyed.

The total amount of energy in a closed system is always the same. Energy can be changed from one form to another, but all the different forms of energy in a system always add up to the same total amount of energy, no matter how many energy conversions occur.

Law of Universal Gravitation

> The **law of universal gravitation** states that all objects in the universe attract each other by a force called gravity. The size of the force depends on the masses of the objects and the distance between them.

The first part of the law explains why a bowling ball is much harder to lift than a table-tennis ball. Because the bowling ball has a much larger mass than the table-tennis ball, the amount of gravity between the Earth and the bowling ball is greater than the amount of gravity between the Earth and the table-tennis ball.

The second part of the law explains why a satellite can remain in orbit around the Earth. The satellite is carefully placed at a distance great enough to prevent the Earth's gravity from immediately pulling it down but small enough to prevent it from completely escaping the Earth's gravity and wandering off into space.

Newton's Laws of Motion

> **Newton's first law of motion** states that an object at rest remains at rest and an object in motion remains in motion at constant speed and in a straight line unless acted on by an unbalanced force.

The first part of the law explains why a football will remain on a tee until it is kicked off or until a gust of wind blows it off.

The second part of the law explains why a bike's rider will continue moving forward after the bike tire runs into a crack in the sidewalk and the bike comes to an abrupt stop until gravity and the sidewalk stop the rider.

> **Newton's second law of motion** states that the acceleration of an object depends on the mass of the object and the amount of force applied.

The first part of the law explains why the acceleration of a 4 kg bowling ball will be greater than the acceleration of a 6 kg bowling ball if the same force is applied to both.

The second part of the law explains why the acceleration of a bowling ball will be larger if a larger force is applied to it.

The relationship of acceleration (a) to mass (m) and force (F) can be expressed mathematically by the following equation:

$$\text{acceleration} = \frac{\text{force}}{\text{mass}}, \text{ or } a = \frac{F}{m}$$

This equation is often rearranged to the form:

$$\text{force} = \text{mass} \times \text{acceleration},$$
$$\text{or}$$
$$F = m \times a$$

> **Newton's third law of motion** states that whenever one object exerts a force on a second object, the second object exerts an equal and opposite force on the first.

This law explains that a runner is able to move forward because of the equal and opposite force the ground exerts on the runner's foot after each step.

Appendix

Law of Reflection

The law of reflection states that the angle of incidence is equal to the angle of reflection. This law explains why light reflects off of a surface at the same angle it strikes the surface.

A line perpendicular to the mirror's surface is called the *normal*.

The beam of light reflected off the mirror is called the *reflected beam*.

The beam of light traveling toward the mirror is called the *incident beam*.

The angle between the incident beam and the normal is called the *angle of incidence*.

The angle between the reflected beam and the normal is called the *angle of reflection*.

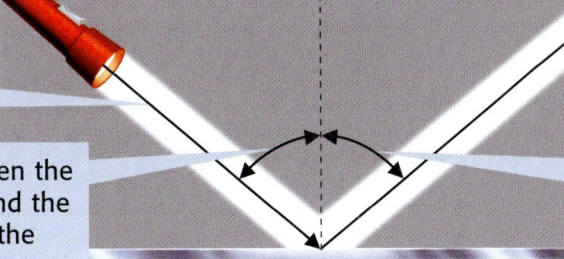

Charles's Law

Charles's law states that for a fixed amount of gas at a constant pressure, the volume of the gas increases as its temperature increases. Likewise, the volume of the gas decreases as its temperature decreases.

If a basketball that was inflated indoors is left outside on a cold winter day, the air particles inside of the ball will move more slowly. They will hit the sides of the basketball less often and with less force. The ball will get smaller as the volume of the air decreases. If a basketball that was inflated outdoors on a cold winter day is brought indoors, the air particles inside of the ball will move more rapidly. They will hit the sides of the basketball more often and with more force. The ball will get larger as the volume of the air increases.

Boyle's Law

Boyle's law states that for a fixed amount of gas at a constant temperature, the volume of a gas increases as its pressure decreases. Likewise, the volume of a gas decreases as its pressure increases.

This law explains why the pressure of the gas in a helium balloon decreases as the balloon rises from the Earth's surface.

Pascal's Principle

Pascal's principle states that a change in pressure at any point in an enclosed fluid will be transmitted equally to all parts of that fluid.

When a mechanic uses a hydraulic jack to raise an automobile off the ground, he or she increases the pressure on the fluid in the jack by pushing on the jack handle. The pressure is transmitted equally to all parts of the fluid-filled jacking system. The fluid presses the jack plate against the frame of the car, lifting the car off the ground.

Archimedes' Principle

Archimedes' principle states that the buoyant force on an object in a fluid is equal to the weight of the volume of fluid that the object displaces.

A person floating in a swimming pool displaces 20 L of water. The weight of that volume of water is about 200 N. Therefore, the buoyant force on the person is 200 N.

Appendix **747**

Bernoulli's Principle

Bernoulli's principle states that as the speed of a moving fluid increases, its pressure decreases.

Bernoulli's principle explains how a wing gives lift to an airplane or even how a Frisbee® can fly through the air. Because of the shape of the Frisbee, the air moving over the top of the Frisbee must travel farther than the air below the Frisbee in the same amount of time. In other words, the air above the Frisbee is moving faster than the air below it. This faster-moving air above the Frisbee exerts less pressure than the slower-moving air below it. The resulting increased pressure below exerts an upward force, pushing the Frisbee up.

Useful Equations

Average speed

$$\text{Average speed} = \frac{\text{total distance}}{\text{total time}}$$

Example: A bicycle messenger traveled a distance of 136 km in 8 hours. What was the messenger's average speed?

$$\frac{136 \text{ km}}{8 \text{ h}} = 17 \text{ km/h}$$

The messenger's average speed was **17 km/h**.

Average acceleration

$$\text{Average acceleration} = \frac{\text{final velocity} - \text{starting velocity}}{\text{time it takes to change velocity}}$$

Example: Calculate the average acceleration of an Olympic 100 m dash sprinter who reaches a velocity of 20 m/s south at the finish line. The race was in a straight line and lasted 10 s.

$$\frac{20 \text{ m/s} - 0 \text{ m/s}}{10 \text{ s}} = 2 \text{ m/s/s}$$

The sprinter's average acceleration is **2 m/s/s south**.

Net force

Forces in the Same Direction

When forces are in the same direction, add the forces together to determine the net force.

Example: Calculate the net force on a stalled car that is being pushed by two people. One person is pushing with a force of 13 N northwest and the other person is pushing with a force of 8 N in the same direction.

$$13 \text{ N} + 8 \text{ N} = 21 \text{ N}$$

The net force is **21 N northwest**.

Forces in Opposite Directions

When forces are in opposite directions, subtract the smaller force from the larger force to determine the net force.

Example: Calculate the net force on a rope that is being pulled on each end. One person is pulling on one end of the rope with a force of 12 N south. Another person is pulling on the opposite end of the rope with a force of 7 N north.

$$12 \text{ N} - 7 \text{ N} = 5 \text{ N}$$

The net force is **5 N south**.

Work

Work is done by exerting a force through a distance. Work has units of joules (J), which are equivalent to Newton-meters.

$$W = F \times d$$

Example: Calculate the amount of work done by a man who lifts a 100 N toddler 1.5 m off the floor.

$$W = 100 \text{ N} \times 1.5 \text{ m} = 150 \text{ N} \cdot \text{m} = 150 \text{ J}$$

The man did **150 J** of work.

Power

Power is the rate at which work is done. Power is measured in watts (W), which are equivalent to joules per second.

$$P = \frac{W}{t}$$

Example: Calculate the power of a weightlifter who raises a 300 N barbell 2.1 m off the floor in 1.25 s.

$$W = 300 \text{ N} \times 2.1 \text{ m} = 630 \text{ N} \cdot \text{m} = 630 \text{ J}$$

$$P = \frac{630 \text{ J}}{1.25 \text{ s}} = 504 \text{ J/s} = 504 \text{ W}$$

The weightlifter has **504 W** of power.

Pressure

Pressure is the force exerted over a given area. The SI unit for pressure is the pascal, which is abbreviated Pa.

$$\text{Pressure} = \frac{\text{force}}{\text{area}}$$

Example: Calculate the pressure of the air in a soccer ball if the air exerts a force of 10 N over an area of 0.5 m^2.

$$\text{Pressure} = \frac{10 \text{ N}}{0.5 \text{ m}^2} = 20 \text{ N/m}^2 = 20 \text{ Pa}$$

The pressure of the air inside of the soccer ball is **20 Pa.**

Density

$$\text{Density} = \frac{\text{mass}}{\text{volume}}$$

Example: Calculate the density of a sponge with a mass of 10 g and a volume of 40 mL.

$$\frac{10 \text{ g}}{40 \text{ mL}} = 0.25 \text{ g/mL}$$

The density of the sponge is **0.25 g/mL.**

Concentration

$$\text{Concentration} = \frac{\text{mass of solute}}{\text{volume of solvent}}$$

Example: Calculate the concentration of a solution in which 10 g of sugar is dissolved in 125 mL of water.

$$\frac{10 \text{ g of sugar}}{125 \text{ mL of water}} = 0.08 \text{ g/mL}$$

The concentration of this solution is **0.08 g/mL.**

Glossary

A

absolute zero the lowest possible temperature (0 K, −273°C) (249)

absorption the transfer of energy carried by light waves to particles of matter (576)

acceleration (ak SEL uhr AY shuhn) the rate at which velocity changes; an object accelerates if its speed changes, if its direction changes, or if both its speed and its direction change (112)

acid any compound that increases the number of hydrogen ions when dissolved in water and whose solution tastes sour and can change the color of certain compounds; acids turn blue litmus red, react with metals to produce hydrogen gas, and react with limestone or baking soda to produce carbon dioxide gas (377)

activation energy the minimum amount of energy needed for substances to react (362)

active solar heating a solar-heating system consisting of solar collectors and a network of pipes that distributes energy from the sun throughout a building (265)

alkali (AL kuh LIE) **metals** the elements in Group 1 of the periodic table; they are the most reactive metals; their atoms have one electron in their outer level (310)

alkaline-earth metals the elements in Group 2 of the periodic table; they are reactive metals but are less reactive than alkali metals; their atoms have two electrons in their outer level (311)

alloys solid solutions of metals or nonmetals dissolved in metals (93)

alpha decay the release of an alpha particle from a nucleus (399)

alpha particle a type of nuclear radiation consisting of two protons and two neutrons emitted by the nucleus of a radioactive atom; identical to the nucleus of a helium atom (399)

alternating current (AC) electric current in which the charges continually switch from flowing in one direction to flowing in the reverse direction (434)

amplitude the maximum distance a wave vibrates from its rest position (516, 543)

analog (AN uh LAHG) **signal** a signal whose properties, such as amplitude and frequency, can change continuously according to changes in the original information (489)

Archimedes' (ahr kuh MEE deez) **principle** the principle that states that the buoyant force on an object in a fluid is an upward force equal to the weight of the volume of fluid that the object displaces (168)

area a measure of how much surface an object has (26)

atmospheric pressure the pressure caused by the weight of the atmosphere (163)

atom the smallest particle into which an element can be divided and still be the same substance (280)

atomic mass the weighted average of the masses of all the naturally occurring isotopes of an element (292)

atomic mass unit (amu) the SI unit used to express the masses of particles in atoms (288)

atomic number the number of protons in the nucleus of an atom (290)

average speed the overall rate at which an object moves; average speed can be calculated by dividing total distance by total time (109)

B

balanced forces forces on an object that cause the net force to be zero; balanced forces do not cause a change in motion or acceleration (118)

base any compound that increases the number of hydroxide ions when dissolved in water and whose solution tastes bitter, feels slippery, and can change the color of certain compounds; bases turn red litmus blue (379)

battery a device that is made of several cells and that produces an electric current by converting chemical energy into electrical energy (430)

Bernoulli's (buhr NOO leez) **principle** the principle that states that as the speed of a moving fluid increases, its pressure decreases (173)

beta decay the release of a beta particle from a nucleus (400)

beta particle an electron or positron emitted by the nucleus of a radioactive atom (400)

bimetallic (BIE muh TAL ik) **strip** a strip made by stacking two different metals in a long thin strip; because the different metals expand at different rates, a bimetallic strip can coil and uncoil with changes in temperature; bimetallic strips are used in devices such as thermostats (250)

binary (BIE neh ree) two; binary numbers contain only the digits 1 and 0 (490)

750 Glossary

biochemicals organic compounds made by living things (384)

biomass organic matter, such as plants, wood, and waste, that contains stored energy (236)

bit the name for each of the digits in a binary number (497)

block and tackle a fixed pulley and a movable pulley used together; it can have a large mechanical advantage if several pulleys are used (204)

boiling vaporization that occurs throughout a liquid (70)

boiling point the temperature at which a liquid boils and becomes a gas (70)

Boyle's law the law that states that for a fixed amount of gas at a constant temperature, the volume of a gas increases as its pressure decreases (65)

buoyant force the upward force that fluids exert on all matter; buoyant force opposes gravitational force (168)

byte a unit in which computers store and process information; equal to eight bits (497)

C

calorie the amount of energy needed to change the temperature of 0.001 kg of water by 1°C; 1 calorie is equivalent to 4.184 J (258)

calorimeter (KAL uh RIM uht uhr) a device used to determine the specific heat capacity of a substance (258)

carbohydrates biochemicals composed of one or more simple sugars bonded together that are used as a source of energy and for energy storage (384)

catalyst (KAT uh LIST) a substance that speeds up a reaction without being permanently changed (365)

cathode-ray tube (CRT) a special vacuum tube in which a beam of electrons is projected onto a screen (493)

cell a device that produces an electric current by converting chemical energy into electrical energy (430)

central processing unit (CPU) the physical area in which a computer performs tasks (496)

centripetal (sen TRIP uht uhl) **acceleration** the acceleration that occurs in circular motion; an object traveling in a circle is constantly changing directions, so acceleration occurs continuously (114)

change of state the conversion of a substance from one physical form to another (68, 261)

characteristic property a property of a substance that is always the same whether the sample observed is large or small (48)

Charles's law the law that states that for a fixed amount of gas at a constant pressure, the volume of a gas increases as its temperature increases (66)

chemical bond a force of attraction that holds two atoms together (328)

chemical bonding the joining of atoms to form new substances (328)

chemical change a change that occurs when one or more substances are changed into entirely new substances with different properties; cannot be reversed using physical means (49, 262)

chemical energy the energy of a compound that changes as its atoms are rearranged to form a new compound; chemical energy is a form of potential energy (218)

chemical equation a shorthand description of a chemical reaction using chemical formulas and symbols (354)

chemical formula a shorthand notation for a compound or a diatomic element using chemical symbols and numbers (352)

chemical property a property of matter that describes a substance based on its ability to change into a new substance with different properties (47)

chemical reaction the process by which one or more substances undergo change to produce one or more different substances (350)

circuit a complete, closed path through which electric charges flow (440)

circuit board a collection of hundreds of tiny circuits that supply electric current to the various parts of an electronic device (482)

coefficient (KOH uh FISH uhnt) a number placed in front of a chemical symbol or formula; used to balance a chemical equation (356)

colloid (KAWL OYD) a mixture in which the particles are dispersed throughout but are not heavy enough to settle out (97)

combustion the burning of fuel; specifically, the process in which fuel combines with oxygen in a chemical change that produces thermal energy (266)

compound a pure substance composed of two or more elements that are chemically combined (86)

compound machine a machine that is made of two or more simple machines (204)

compression a region of higher density or pressure in a wave (514, 534)

computer an electronic device that performs tasks by processing and storing information (494)

Glossary **751**

concave lens a lens that is thinner in the middle than at the edges (604)

concave mirror a mirror that is curved inward like the inside of a spoon (600)

concentration a measure of the amount of solute dissolved in a solvent (94, 364)

condensation the change of state from a gas to a liquid (71)

condensation point the temperature at which a gas becomes a liquid (71)

conduction (electrical) a method of charging an object that occurs when electrons are transferred from one object to another by direct contact (425)

conduction (thermal) the transfer of thermal energy from one substance to another through direct contact; conduction can also occur within a substance (253)

conductor (electrical) a material in which charges can move easily (427)

conductor (thermal) a substance that conducts thermal energy well (254)

constructive interference interference that results in a wave that has a greater amplitude than that of the individual waves (523, 548, 579)

convection the transfer of thermal energy by the movement of a liquid or a gas (254)

convection current the circular motion of liquids or gases due to density differences that result from temperature differences (254)

convex lens a lens that is thicker in the middle than at the edges (603)

convex mirror a mirror that is curved outward like the back of a spoon (602)

cornea a transparent membrane that protects the eye and refracts light (605)

covalent (KOH VAY luhnt) **bond** the force of attraction between the nuclei of atoms and the electrons shared by the atoms (336)

covalent compounds compounds that are composed of elements that are covalently bonded; these compounds are composed of independent molecules, tend to have low melting and boiling points, do not usually dissolve in water, and form solutions that do not conduct an electric current when they do dissolve (375)

crest the highest point of a transverse wave (513)

crystal lattice (LAT is) a repeating three-dimensional pattern of ions (335)

current a continuous flow of charge caused by the motion of electrons; the rate at which charge passes a given point; expressed in amperes (A) (433)

D

data any pieces of information acquired through experimentation (16)

decibel (dB) the most common unit used to express loudness (543)

decomposition reaction a reaction in which a single compound breaks down to form two or more simpler substances (359)

density the amount of matter in a given space; mass per unit volume (27, 44, 165)

destructive interference interference that results in a wave that has a smaller amplitude than that of the individual waves (523, 548, 579)

diffraction the bending of waves around a barrier or through an opening (521, 551, 579)

digital signal a series of electrical pulses that represents the digits of binary numbers (490)

diode (DIE OHD) an electronic component that allows electric current in only one direction (484)

direct current (DC) electric current in which the charges always flow in the same direction (434)

doping (DOHP eeng) the process of replacing a few atoms of a semiconductor with a few atoms of another substance that have a different number of valence electrons (483)

Doppler effect the apparent change in the frequency of a sound caused by the motion of either the listener or the source of the sound (refers to sound only) (542)

double-replacement reaction a reaction in which ions in two compounds switch places (360)

drag the force that opposes or restricts motion in a fluid; drag opposes thrust (176)

ductility (duhk TIL uh tee) the ability of a substance to be drawn or pulled into a wire (44, 340)

E

echo a reflected sound wave (520, 545)

echolocation the process of using reflected sound waves to find objects (546)

electrical energy the energy of electric charges (219, 430)

electric discharge the loss of static electricity as charges move off an object (428)

electric field the region around a charged particle that can exert a force on another charged particle (423)

electric force the force between charged objects (423)

electric motor a device that changes electrical energy into kinetic energy (466)

electric power the rate at which electrical energy is used to do work; expressed in watts (W) (437)

electrode the part of a cell through which charges enter or exit (430)

electrolyte in a cell, a mixture of chemicals that carries an electric current (430)

electromagnet a magnet that consists of a solenoid wrapped around an iron core (464)

electromagnetic induction the process by which an electric current is produced by a changing magnetic field (469)

electromagnetic spectrum the entire range of electromagnetic waves (567)

electromagnetic wave a wave that can travel through space or matter and consists of changing electric and magnetic fields (492, 512, 564)

electromagnetism the interaction between electricity and magnetism (463)

electron clouds the regions inside an atom where electrons are likely to be found (286)

electrons the negatively charged particles found in all atoms; electrons are involved in the formation of chemical bonds (283)

element a pure substance that cannot be separated or broken down into simpler substances by physical or chemical means (82)

endothermic the term used to describe a physical or a chemical change in which energy is absorbed (69, 362)

energy the ability to do work (214)

energy conversion a change from one form of energy into another (222)

energy efficiency (e FISH uhn see) a comparison of the amount of energy before a conversion and the amount of useful energy after a conversion (228)

energy resource a natural resource that can be converted by humans into other forms of energy in order to do useful work (232)

evaporation (ee VAP uh RAY shuhn) vaporization that occurs at the surface of a liquid below its boiling point (70)

exothermic the term used to describe a physical or a chemical change in which energy is released or removed (69, 361)

external combustion engine a heat engine that burns fuel outside the engine, such as a steam engine (266)

F

fiber optics the use of optical fibers (thin, flexible glass wires) to transmit light over long distances (612)

fixed pulley a pulley that is attached to something that does not move; fixed pulleys change the direction of a force but do not increase the force (203)

fluid any material that can flow and that takes the shape of its container (162)

fluorescent light visible light emitted by a phosphor particle when it absorbs energy such as ultraviolet light (596)

focal length the distance between a mirror or lens and its focal point (600)

focal point the point on the axis of a mirror or lens through which all incident parallel light rays are focused (600)

force a push or a pull; all forces have both size and direction (115)

fossil fuels nonrenewable energy resources that form in the Earth's crust over millions of years from the buried remains of once-living organisms (232)

free fall the condition an object is in when gravity is the only force acting on it (141)

freezing the change of state from a liquid to a solid (69)

freezing point the temperature at which a liquid changes into a solid (69)

frequency the number of waves produced in a given amount of time (518, 540)

friction a force that opposes motion between two surfaces that are touching (119, 229)

fulcrum the fixed point about which a lever pivots (198)

fundamental the lowest resonant frequency (550)

G

gamma decay the release of gamma rays from a nucleus (400)

gamma rays EM waves with very high energy and no mass or charge; they are emitted by the nucleus of a radioactive atom (400, 574)

gas the state in which matter changes in both shape and volume (63)

generator a device that uses electromagnetic induction to convert kinetic energy into electrical energy (470)

geothermal energy energy resulting from the heating of the Earth's crust (236)

gravitational potential energy energy due to an object's position above the Earth's surface (216)

gravity a force of attraction between objects that is due to their masses (39, 125)

greenhouse effect the natural heating process of a planet, such as the Earth, by which gases in the atmosphere trap thermal energy (255)

group a column of elements on the periodic table (309)

H

half-life the amount of time it takes for one-half of the nuclei of a radioactive isotope to decay (404)

halogens the elements in Group 17 of the periodic table; they are very reactive nonmetals, and their atoms have seven electrons in their outer level (316)

hardware the parts or equipment that make up a computer (496)

heat the transfer of energy between objects that are at different temperatures; energy is always transferred from higher-temperature objects to lower-temperature objects until thermal equilibrium is reached (251); *also* the amount of energy that is transferred between objects that are at different temperatures (257)

heat engine a machine that uses heat to do work (266)

hertz (Hz) the unit used to express frequency; one hertz is one cycle per second (518, 540)

heterogeneous (HET uhr OH JEE nee uhs) **mixture** a combination of substances in which different components are easily observed (96)

hologram a piece of film on which an interference pattern produces a three-dimensional image of an object (611)

homogeneous (HOH moh JEE nee uhs) **mixture** a combination of substances in which the appearance and properties are the same throughout (92)

hydraulic (hie DRAW lik) **device** a device that uses liquids to transmit pressure from one point to another (167)

hydrocarbons organic compounds that are composed of only carbon and hydrogen (388)

hypothesis a possible explanation or answer to a question (14)

I

ideal machine a machine that has 100 percent mechanical efficiency (197)

illuminated the term describing visible objects that are not a light source (594)

incandescent light light produced by hot objects (595)

inclined plane a simple machine that is a straight, slanted surface; a ramp (200)

induction a method of charging an object that occurs when charges in an uncharged object are rearranged without direct contact with a charged object (425)

inertia the tendency of all objects to resist any change in motion (42, 147)

infrared waves EM waves that are between microwaves and visible light in the electromagnetic spectrum (571)

infrasonic the term describing sounds with frequencies lower than 20 Hz (541)

inhibitor a substance that slows down or stops a chemical reaction (365)

inner ear the part of the ear where vibrations created by sound are changed into electrical signals for the brain to interpret (537)

input the information given to a computer (494)

input device a piece of hardware that feeds information to the computer (496)

input force the force applied to a machine (193)

insulation a substance that reduces the transfer of thermal energy (264)

insulator (electrical) a material in which charges cannot easily move (427)

insulator (thermal) a substance that does not conduct thermal energy well (254)

integrated (IN tuh GRAYT ed) **circuit** an entire circuit containing many transistors and other electronic components formed on a single silicon chip (486)

interference a wave interaction that occurs when two or more waves overlap (522, 548, 579)

internal combustion engine a heat engine that burns fuel inside the engine; for example, an automobile engine (267)

Internet a huge computer network consisting of millions of computers that can all share information with one another (499)

ionic (ie AHN ik) **bond** the force of attraction between oppositely charged ions (332)

ionic compounds compounds that contain ionic bonds; composed of ions arranged in a crystal lattice, they tend to have high melting and boiling points, are solid at room temperature, and dissolve in water to form solutions that conduct an electric current (374)

ions charged particles that form during chemical changes when one or more valence electrons transfer from one atom to another (332)

iris the colored part of the eye (605)

isotopes atoms that have the same number of protons but have different numbers of neutrons (290, 400)

J

joule (J) the unit used to express work and energy; equivalent to the newton-meter (N•m) (190)

K

kilocalorie the unit of energy equal to 1,000 calories; the kilocalorie can also be referred to as the Calorie, which is the unit of energy listed on food labels (258)

kinetic (ki NET ik) **energy** the energy of motion; kinetic energy depends on speed and mass (215)

L

laser a device that produces intense light of only one wavelength and color (609)

law a summary of many experimental results and observations; a law tells how things work (19)

law of conservation of energy the law that states that energy is neither created nor destroyed (230, 362)

law of conservation of mass the law that states that mass is neither created nor destroyed in ordinary chemical and physical changes (357)

law of electric charges the law that states that like charges repel and opposite charges attract (423)

law of reflection the law that states that the angle of incidence is equal to the angle of reflection (575)

law of universal gravitation the law that states that all objects in the universe attract each other through gravitational force; the size of the force depends on the masses of the objects and the distance between them (126)

lens a curved, transparent object that forms an image by refracting light (603); also the part of the eye that refracts light to focus an image on the retina (605)

lever a simple machine consisting of a bar that pivots at a fixed point, called a fulcrum; there are three classes of levers, based on where the input force, output force, and fulcrum are placed in relation to the load: first class levers, second class levers, and third class levers (198)

lift an upward force on an object (such as a wing) that opposes the downward pull of gravity; differences in pressure above and below the object contribute to lift (174)

light energy the energy produced by the vibrations of electrically charged particles (220)

lipids biochemicals that do not dissolve in water; their functions include storing energy and making up cell membranes; waxes, fats, and oils (385)

liquid the state in which matter takes the shape of its container and has a definite volume (62)

load a device that uses electrical energy to do work (440)

longitudinal wave a wave in which the particles of the medium vibrate back and forth along the path that the wave travels (514)

loudness how loud or soft a sound is perceived to be (542)

lubricant (LOO bri kuhnt) a substance applied to surfaces to reduce the friction between them (123)

luminous the term describing objects that produce visible light (594)

M

machine a device that helps make work easier by changing the size or direction (or both) of a force (192)

magnet any material that attracts iron or materials containing iron (454)

magnetic field the region around a magnet in which magnetic forces can act (456)

magnetic force the force of repulsion or attraction between the poles of magnets (455)

malleability (MAL ee uh BIL uh tee) the ability of a substance to be pounded into thin sheets (44, 340)

mass the amount of matter that something is made of (26, 38, 129)

mass number the sum of the protons and neutrons in an atom (291, 399)

matter anything that has volume and mass (7, 36)

mechanical advantage a number that tells how many times a machine multiplies force; can be calculated by dividing the output force by the input force (196)

mechanical efficiency (e FISH uhn see) a comparison—expressed as a percentage—of a machine's work output with the work input; can be calculated by dividing work output by work input and then multiplying by 100 (197)

mechanical energy the total energy of motion and position of an object (217)

medium a substance through which a wave can travel (511, 536)

melting the change of state from a solid to a liquid (69)

melting point the temperature at which a substance changes from a solid to a liquid (69)

memory the location where a computer stores information (494)

meniscus (muh NIS kuhs) the curve at a liquid's surface by which you measure the volume of the liquid (37)

metallic bond the force of attraction between a positively charged metal ion and the electrons in a metal (339)

metalloids elements that have properties of both metals and nonmetals; sometimes referred to as semiconductors (85)

metals elements that are shiny and are good conductors of thermal energy and electric current; most metals are malleable and ductile (85)

meter (m) the basic unit of length in the SI system (25)

microprocessor an integrated circuit that contains many of a computer's capabilities on a single silicon chip (495)

microwaves EM waves that are between radio waves and infrared waves in the electromagnetic spectrum (570)

middle ear the part of the ear where the amplitude of sound vibrations is increased (537)

mixture a combination of two or more substances that are not chemically combined (90)

model a representation of an object or system (20, 283)

modem a piece of computer hardware that allows computers to communicate over telephone lines (497)

molecule (MAHL i KYOOL) a neutral group of atoms held together by covalent bonds (336)

momentum a property of a moving object that depends on the object's mass and velocity (152)

motion an object's change in position over time when compared with a reference point (108)

movable pulley a pulley attached to the object being moved; movable pulleys increase force (203)

N

negative acceleration acceleration in which velocity decreases; also called deceleration (113)

neon light light emitted by atoms of certain gases, such as neon, when they absorb and then release energy (596)

net force the force that results from combining all the forces exerted on an object (116)

neutrons the particles of the nucleus that have no charge (288)

newton (N) the SI unit of force (41, 115)

noble gases the unreactive elements in Group 18 of the periodic table; their atoms have eight electrons in their outer level (except for helium, which has two electrons) (316)

noise any undesired sound, especially nonmusical sound, that includes a random mix of pitches (555)

nonmetals elements that are dull and are poor conductors of thermal energy and electric current (85)

nonrenewable resource a natural resource that cannot be replaced or that can be replaced only over thousands or millions of years (232)

nuclear (NOO klee uhr) **chain reaction** a continuous series of nuclear fission reactions (407)

nuclear energy the form of energy associated with changes in the nucleus of an atom (221)

nuclear fission the process in which a large nucleus splits into two smaller nuclei (235, 406)

nuclear fusion the process in which two or more nuclei with small masses join together, or fuse, to form a larger, more massive nucleus (410)

Glossary

nuclear radiation high-energy particles and rays that are emitted by the nuclei of some atoms; alpha particles, beta particles, and gamma rays are types of nuclear radiation (398)

nucleic acids biochemicals that store information and help to build proteins and other nucleic acids; made up of subunits called nucleotides (387)

nucleus (NOO klee uhs) the tiny, extremely dense, positively charged region in the center of an atom; made up of protons and neutrons (285)

O

observation any use of the senses to gather information (12)

Ohm's law the law that states the relationship between current (I), voltage (V), and resistance (R); expressed by the equation $I = \dfrac{V}{R}$ (437)

opaque the term describing matter that does not transmit any light (582)

optical axis a straight line drawn outward from the center of a mirror or lens (600)

organic compounds covalent compounds composed of carbon-based molecules (383)

oscilloscope (uh SIL uh SKOHP) a device used to graph representations of sound waves (544)

outer ear the part of the ear that acts as a funnel to direct sound waves into the middle ear (537)

output the result of processing that is the final result or the proof of the task performed by a computer (494)

output device a piece of hardware on which a computer shows the results of performing a task (497)

output force the force applied by a machine (193)

overtones resonant frequencies that are higher than the fundamental (550)

P

parallel circuit a circuit in which different loads are on separate branches (443)

pascal (Pa) the SI unit of pressure; equal to the force of 1 N exerted over an area of one square meter (162)

Pascal's principle the principle that states that a change in pressure at any point in an enclosed fluid is transmitted equally to all parts of that fluid (167)

passive solar heating a solar-heating system that relies on thick walls and large windows to use energy from the sun as a means of heating (265)

period a horizontal row of elements on the periodic table (309)

periodic having a regular, repeating pattern (302)

periodic law the law that states that the chemical and physical properties of elements are periodic functions of their atomic numbers (303)

perpendicular at right angles (513, 564)

perpetual (puhr PECH oo uhl) **motion machine** a machine that runs forever without any additional energy input; perpetual motion machines are impossible to create (231)

pH a measure of hydronium ion concentration in a solution; a pH of 7 is neutral; a pH less than 7 is acidic; a pH greater than 7 is basic (380)

photocell the part of a solar panel that converts light into electrical energy (432)

photon a tiny "packet" of energy that is released by an electron that moves to a lower energy level in an atom (565)

physical change a change that affects one or more physical properties of a substance; many physical changes are easy to undo (48, 261)

physical property a property of matter that can be observed or measured without changing the identity of the matter (43)

physical science the study of matter and energy (7)

pigment a material that gives a substance its color by absorbing some colors of light and reflecting others (584)

pitch how high or low a sound is perceived to be (540)

plane mirror a mirror with a flat surface (599)

plasma the state of matter that does not have a definite shape or volume and whose particles have broken apart; plasma is composed of electrons and positively charged ions (67)

polarized light consists of light waves that vibrate in only one plane (one direction) (612)

poles the parts of a magnet where the magnetic effects are strongest (454)

positive acceleration acceleration in which velocity increases (113)

positron a beta particle with a charge of 1+ and a mass of almost 0 (400)

potential difference energy per unit charge; specifically, the difference in energy per unit charge as a charge moves between two points in an electric circuit (same as voltage); expressed in volts (V) (431)

Glossary

potential energy the energy of position or shape (216)

power the rate at which work is done (191)

pressure the amount of force exerted on a given area; expressed in pascals (Pa) (64, 162)

primary colors of light red, blue, and green; these colors of light can be combined in different ratios to produce all colors of light (584)

primary pigments yellow, cyan, and magenta; these pigments can be combined to produce any other pigment (585)

products the substances formed from a chemical reaction (354)

projectile (proh JEK tuhl) **motion** the curved path an object follows when thrown or propelled near the surface of the Earth (143)

proteins biochemicals that are composed of amino acids; their functions include regulating chemical activities, transporting and storing materials, and providing structural support (386)

protons the positively charged particles of the nucleus; the number of protons in a nucleus is the atomic number that determines the identity of an element (288)

pulley a simple machine consisting of a grooved wheel that holds a rope or a cable (203)

pupil the opening to the inside of the eye (605)

pure substance a substance in which there is only one type of particle; includes elements and compounds (82)

R

radiation the transfer of energy through matter or space as electromagnetic waves, such as visible light and infrared waves (255, 565)

radioactive decay the process in which the nucleus of a radioactive atom releases nuclear radiation (399)

radioactivity the ability of some elements to give off nuclear radiation (398)

radio waves EM waves with long wavelengths and low frequencies (568)

RAM (random-access memory) computer memory that stores information only while that information is being used (497)

rarefaction (RER uh FAK shuhn) a region of lower density or pressure in a wave (514, 534)

reactants (ree AK TUHNTS) the starting materials in a chemical reaction (354)

real image an image through which light passes (600)

reference point an object that appears to stay in place in relation to an object being observed for motion (108)

reflection the bouncing back of a wave after it strikes a barrier or an object (520, 545, 575)

refraction the bending of a wave as it passes at an angle from one medium to another (521, 577)

renewable resource a natural resource that can be used and replaced over a relatively short time (235)

resistance the opposition to the flow of electric charge; expressed in ohms (Ω) (435)

resonance what occurs when an object vibrating at or near a resonant frequency of a second object causes the second object to vibrate (524, 550)

resonant frequencies the frequencies at which standing waves are made (524, 550)

resultant velocity the combination of two or more velocities (111)

retina the back surface of the eye (605)

ROM (read-only memory) computer memory that cannot be added to or changed (497)

S

salt an ionic compound formed from the positive ion of a base and the negative ion of an acid (382)

saturated hydrocarbon a hydrocarbon in which each carbon atom in the molecule shares a single bond with each of four other atoms; an alkane (388)

saturated solution a solution that contains all the solute it can hold at a given temperature (94)

scattering the release of light energy by particles of matter that have absorbed energy (577)

scientific method a series of steps that scientists use to answer questions and solve problems (11)

screw a simple machine that is an inclined plane wrapped in a spiral (201)

secondary color cyan, magenta, and yellow; a color of light produced when two primary colors of light are added together (584)

semiconductor (SEM i kuhn DUHK tor) a substance that conducts electric current better than an insulator but not as well as a conductor (483)

series circuit a circuit in which all parts are connected in a single loop (442)

signal something that represents information, such as a command, a sound, or a series of numbers and letters (488)

simple machines the six machines from which all other machines are constructed: a lever, an inclined plane, a wedge, a screw, a wheel and axle, and a pulley (198)

single-replacement reaction a reaction in which an element takes the place of another element in a compound; this can occur only when a more-reactive element takes the place of a less-reactive one (359)

software a set of instructions or commands that tells a computer what to do; a computer program (498)

solenoid a coil of wire that produces a magnetic field when carrying an electric current (463)

solid the state in which matter has a definite shape and volume (61)

solubility (SAHL yoo BIL uh tee) the ability to dissolve in another substance; more specifically, the amount of solute needed to make a saturated solution using a given amount of solvent at a certain temperature (44, 94)

solute the substance that is dissolved to form a solution (92)

solution a mixture that appears to be a single substance but is composed of particles of two or more substances that are distributed evenly amongst each other (92)

solvent the substance in which a solute is dissolved to form a solution (92)

sonar (**so**und **na**vigation and **r**anging) a type of electronic echolocation (546)

sonic boom the explosive sound heard when a shock wave from an object traveling faster than the speed of sound reaches a person's ears (549)

sound energy the energy caused by an object's vibrations (220)

sound quality the result of several pitches blending together through interference (552)

specific heat capacity the amount of energy needed to change the temperature of 1 kg of a substance by 1°C (256)

speed the rate at which an object moves; speed depends on the distance traveled and the time taken to travel that distance (109)

standing wave a wave that forms a stationary pattern in which portions of the wave do not move and other portions move with a large amplitude (524, 549)

states of matter the physical forms in which a substance can exist; states include solid, liquid, gas, and plasma (60, 260)

static electricity the buildup of electric charges on an object (427)

sublimation (SUHB luh MAY shuhn) the change of state from a solid directly into a gas (72)

subscript a number written below and to the right of a chemical symbol in a chemical formula (352)

surface tension the force acting on the particles at the surface of a liquid that causes the liquid to form spherical drops (63)

surface wave a wave that occurs at or near the boundary of two media and that is a combination of transverse and longitudinal waves (515)

suspension a mixture in which particles of a material are dispersed throughout a liquid or gas but are large enough that they settle out (96)

synthesis (SIN thuh sis) **reaction** a reaction in which two or more substances combine to form a single compound (358)

T

technology the application of knowledge, tools, and materials to solve problems and accomplish tasks; technology can also refer to the objects used to accomplish tasks (11)

telecommunication the sending of information across long distances by electronic means (488)

temperature a measure of how hot (or cold) something is; specifically, a measure of the average kinetic energy of the particles in an object (26, 246)

terminal velocity the constant velocity of a falling object when the size of the upward force of air resistance matches the size of the downward force of gravity (140)

theory a unifying explanation for a broad range of hypotheses and observations that have been supported by testing (19, 280, 328)

thermal energy the total energy of the particles that make up an object (218, 252)

thermal equilibrium the point at which two objects reach the same temperature (252)

thermal expansion the increase in volume of a substance due to an increase in temperature (248)

thermal pollution the excessive heating of a body of water (269)

thermocouple a device that converts thermal energy into electrical energy (432)

thrust the forward force produced by an airplane's engines; thrust opposes drag (175)

tinnitus hearing loss resulting from damage to the hair cells and nerve endings in the cochlea (538)

tracer a radioactive element whose path can be followed through a process or reaction (405)

transformer a device that increases or decreases the voltage of alternating current (472)

transistor an electronic component that can be used as an amplifier or a switch (485)

translucent the term describing matter that transmits light but also scatters the light as it passes through the matter (582)

transmission the passing of light through matter (581)

transparent the term describing matter through which light is easily transmitted (582)

transverse wave a wave in which the particles of the wave's medium vibrate perpendicular to the direction the wave is traveling (513)

trough the lowest point of a transverse wave (513)

turbulence an irregular or unpredictable flow of fluids that can cause drag; lift is often reduced by turbulence (176)

U

ultrasonic the term describing sounds with frequencies higher than 20,000 Hz (541)

ultrasonography a medical procedure that uses echoes from ultrasonic waves to "see" inside a patient's body without performing surgery (547)

ultraviolet light EM waves that are between visible light and X rays in the electromagnetic spectrum (573)

unbalanced forces forces on an object that cause the net force to be other than zero; unbalanced forces produce a change in motion or acceleration (117)

unsaturated hydrocarbon a hydrocarbon in which at least two carbon atoms share a double bond (an alkene) or a triple bond (an alkyne) (388)

V

valence (VAY luhns) **electrons** the electrons in the outermost energy level of an atom; these electrons are involved in forming chemical bonds (329)

vapor light light produced when electrons combine with gaseous metal atoms (597)

vaporization the change of state from a liquid to a gas; includes boiling and evaporation (70)

velocity (vuh LAHS uh tee) the speed of an object in a particular direction (110)

vibration the complete back-and-forth motion of an object (534)

virtual image an image through which light does not actually pass (599)

viscosity (vis KAHS uh tee) a liquid's resistance to flow (63)

visible light the very narrow range of wavelengths and frequencies in the electromagnetic spectrum that humans can see (572)

voltage the difference in energy per unit charge as a charge moves between two points in an electric circuit (same as potential difference); expressed in volts (V) (434)

volume the amount of space that something occupies or the amount of space that something contains (25, 36)

W

watt (W) the unit used to express power; equivalent to joules per second (J/s) (191)

wave a disturbance that transmits energy through matter or space (510, 535)

wavelength the distance between one point on a wave and the corresponding point on an adjacent wave in a series of waves (517)

wave speed the speed at which a wave travels (519)

wedge a simple machine that is a double inclined plane that moves; a wedge is often used for cutting (201)

weight a measure of the gravitational force exerted on an object, usually by the Earth (40, 128)

wheel and axle a simple machine consisting of two circular objects of different sizes; the wheel is the larger of the two circular objects (202)

work the action that results when a force causes an object to move in the direction of the force (188)

work input the work done on a machine; the product of the input force and the distance through which it is exerted (193)

work output the work done by a machine; the product of the output force and the distance through which it is exerted (193)

X

X rays high-energy EM waves that are between ultraviolet light and gamma rays in the electromagnetic spectrum (574)

Index

A **boldface** number refers to an illustration on that page.

A

absolute zero, 249, 274
absorption, **576,** 576–577
acceleration, 112–114, **113**
   calculation of, 112–113
   centripetal, 114, **114**
   defined, 112
   force and, 148–149
   gravitational, 138–139, **139,** 144, **144,** 149
   negative, 113
   Newton's second law and, 148–149
   positive, 113, **114**
   units, 112
acid precipitation, 51, 381
acids
   defined, 377, 743
   hydrogen ions and, 377
   neutralization, 380–381, **381**
   organic, 389
   pH scale and, **380,** 380–381
   properties of, 377–378
   strong versus weak, 378
   tannic, 394
   uses of, 378
action force, **150,** 150–151, **151**
activation energy, 348, 362, **363,** 365
active solar heating, 265
air, 92, **96,** 170, 174–177, 264
air bags, 348, **348**
aircraft, 136, 174, **174**
airplanes, 62, 136, 174–176, **174–176**
air pressure, 162. See also atmospheric pressure
air resistance, 139–141, **141**
   terminal velocity and, 140
alcohols, 48, 59, 389
Alexander the Great, 281
alkali metals, **310,** 310–311
alkaline-earth metals, 311
alloys, 93
alpha particles, 399, **399, 401,** 402
alternating current (AC), 434, **434**
aluminum, 88–89, 256, 287, **287,** 314, 333, **333**
amber, 283
amino acids, 346, 386, 395
ammonia, 89, 379
amorphous solids, 61, **61**
Ampère, André-Marie, 463
amperes, 433, 437
amplitude, **516,** 516–517
   of sound waves, 542–544, **544**
amplitude modulation (AM), 568–569, **569**
analog signals, 488–490, **489, 490, 492**
angle of incidence, 575, **575,** 747
angle of reflection, 575, **575, 576,** 747
Archimedes' principle, 104, 168–169, 747
area
   calculation of, 26, **26,** 741
   force, pressure, and, 162
argon, 291, 316, **317**
Aristotle, 281
armature, 466, **466**
ascorbic acid, 378
astronomy, **9**
atmospheric pressure, 71, 162–164, **164,** 166
atomic mass, 292, 302–303
atomic mass unit (amu), 288
atomic nucleus, 276, 285, 288, **288**
atomic number, 290, 303, 742
atomic theory, **23,** 280–286, **286**
atoms, 276–293, 742
   in chemical bonds, 328
   defined, 280, 742
   electrical energy and, 219
   electric charge and, 422–423
   forces in, 293
   size of, 287, **288**
   structure of, **288,** 288–289
Atzmon, Michael, 417, **417**
auroras, **67,** 461, **461**
automobiles. See cars
average acceleration, 748
averages, 738
average speed, 109
   calculation of, 109, 748
azurite, 585

B

baking soda, 48, 348, **348**
balanced forces, 118
ball bearings, 123
bar graphs, 737, **737**
barium, **406**
baseball, **177**
bases
   defined, 379, 743
   hydroxide ions and, 379
   neutralization, 380–381, **381**
   pH scale and, **380,** 380–381
   properties of, 379, **379**
   strong versus weak, 380
   uses of, 379, **379**
batteries, 225, 430, **430,** 431, **431,** 434–435
Becquerel, Henri, 325, 398
Bell, Alexander Graham, 419
beluga whales, 545, **545**
benzene, 389
Bernoulli, Daniel, 173
Bernoulli's principle, **173,** 173–177, 748
beta particles, 400, **400, 401,** 402
bicycles, **226**
big bang theory, **19**
bilirubin, 562
bimetallic strips, 250, **250**
binary numbers, 490
biochemicals, 384–387
biochemistry, 384–387
biology, **9**
biomass, **236,** 237
birds, 175, 460
bits, 497
black holes, 127
bleach, 48, **48**

Index **761**

Index

block and tackle, 203–204, **204**
blood, 96
   pH of, 381
blood pressure, 162
body temperature, **248**
Bohr, Niels, 286
boiling, 70, **70**
boiling point, 70–71, 73
   pressure and, 71
bonds. *See* chemical bonds
booming sands, 532, **532,** 542
boric acid, 372
boron, **291,** 307
Boron group, 314
botany, **9**
Boyle, Robert, 2, 65
Boyle's law, 65, **65,** 747
brake fluid, 62
brakes, 167, **167**
branched chain structures, **383**
breaker boxes, 444–445
breathing, 166, **166**
bridges
   collapse of, 525, **525**
   Golden Gate (San Francisco), 117, 135, **135**
bromine, **309, 316**
bubbles, 163, **163**
buckyballs, 323, **323**
buoyant force, 168–172
bytes, 497

C

calcium, 311
   in bones, 40
calcium carbonate, 382, 394
calcium hydroxide, 379
calcium phosphate, 86
calcium sulfate, 382
calories, 258, 262
calorimeters, 258, **258,** 262, 271
cameras, 608, **608**
carbohydrates, 384
   simple and complex, 384
carbon
   beta decay, 400, **400**
   bonding, 323, 324, 383, **383**
   carbon-14 dating, 403–404
   compounds of, 315, 346, **346, 383,** 383–389

electron-dot diagrams, 337, **337**
   isotopes, 292
carbonated drinks, 88, **88**
carbon dioxide
   composition of, 86
   gas formation and, **350,** 351
   properties of, **355**
   sublimation, 72, **72**
Carbon group, 314–315
carbonic acid, **88,** 378
carbon monoxide, 86, **355**
careers, 10, **10**
   arson investigator, 371
   electronics engineer, 32
   experimental physicist, 299
   mechanical engineer, 159
   power-plant manager, 243
cars
   air bags, 348
   batteries, **431**
   brake fluid, 62
   coolants, 123
   crash tests, **146,** 348
   energy conversions in, **227**
   engines, 267, **267**
   fuel combustion, **350**
   hydraulic brakes, 62, 167, **167**
   maintenance of, 47, **47**
   mass production, 185
   motor oil, 197
   painting, 423
   pollution from, 148
   side mirrors, 602
   spoilers, 176
   tires, **124,** 162
Cassini spacecraft, 396, **396**
catalysts, 365
catalytic converters, **365**
cathode-ray tubes (CRT), 282, **282,** 493
Cavendish, Henry, 3
CD players, 419, **419, 490,** 490–491, **491**
CDs (compact discs), **490,** 490–491
cell diagrams, **20**
cell membranes, **385,** 385–386
cells, electric, **430,** 430–431
Celsius scale, 26, **26, 248,** 249, 730
central processing unit (CPU), 496, **496**

centrifuges, 91
centripetal acceleration, 114
centripetal force, 142, **142**
cerium sulfate, **95**
Chadwick, James, 276
chain reactions, 325, **407,** 407–408
changes of state, 68–73, 261
   boiling, 70
   chart, 72
   condensation, 71
   defined, 68, **68**
   endothermic, 69
   evaporation, 70
   exothermic, 69
   freezing, 69, **69**
   graph of, 73
   melting, 69, **69**
   sublimation, 72
   temperature and, 73
   vaporization, 70, **70**
characteristic properties, 48, 69–70, 83
charge. *See* electric charge
Charles's law, 66, 747
chemical bonding, 328–341
chemical bonds, 328. *See also* compounds
   covalent, 336–339
   defined, 328
   double, 388, **388**
   ionic, 332–335
   making and breaking, 352, **352**
   metallic, 339–341, **340, 341**
   triple, 388, **388**
chemical changes, 49–51, 262
   clues to, **50,** 50–51
chemical energy
   in chemical reactions, **351, 361,** 361–363, **363**
   conversions, **223,** 223–224, **224, 226, 227**
   overview, 218, **219**
chemical equations, 354–357, **356,** 743
chemical formulas, **352,** 352–353, **353,** 355
chemical properties, 47–49
chemical reactions, 348–365, 743
   energy and, **361,** 361–363, **363**

762   Index

equations for, 354–357, **356**
overview, 350–352
rates of, 363–365
types of, 358–360
chemical symbols, 308, 354–355
chemistry, 8
Chernobyl nuclear accident, 409, **409**, 411
chloride ion, 334, **334**
chlorine
   atoms, **329**, 334, **334**
   bleach, **351**
   hydrogen and, **352**
   properties of, **87**, 316
chlorophyll, 224, 350, 585
cholesterol, 385
circle graph, **735**
circuit boards, 482, **482**
circuit breakers, 444–445, **445**
circuits, 440–445. *See also* electric circuits
   integrated, 486, **486**
citric acid, 378
closed systems, **230**, 230–231
coal, 184, **232**, 232–233
cobalt, **83**, 355
coefficients, 356
Coleman, Bessie, 104, **104**
colloids, 97, **97**, 99
color, 43, **351, 572**, 577–578, **578**, 582–585, **584, 585**. *See also* light
   mixing of, **584**, 584–585, **585**
   of objects, 582–583, **583**
   separation, 578, **578**
color deficiency, 607, **607**
combustion, 266, 371
comets, 71, 298
   Halley's, 104
communication technology
   analog signals, 488–490, **489, 490**, 492
   CDs (compact discs), 490, **490**
   digital signals, **490**, 490–491, **491**
   radio, 492, **492**
   records, 490, **490**
   telegraph, 488, **488**
   telephone, 489, **489**
   television, 493, **493**
commutator, 466, **466**
compasses, 459, 460, **460, 462**, 463

compound machines, 204–205
compounds
   breakdown of, 88, **88**
   covalent, 336–339, **337, 338**, 353, **353**, 375–376
   defined, 86, 743
   formation of, 83, 86, **86**, 743
   ionic, 335, **335**, 353, **353, 374**, 374–375, **375**
   in nature, 89, **89**
   organic, **383**, 383–389
   properties of, 87
compression, 135, 514, **514, 534, 535**
compressors, 268, **268**
computers, 494–499
   basic functions, 494, **494**
   defined, 494
   hardware, **496**, 496–497, **497**
   history, 495
   Internet, 499, **499**
   software, 498, **498**
concave lenses, 604, **604, 606**
concave mirrors, **600**, 600–601, **601**
concentration, 94, 364
   calculation of, 94, 749
concept mapping
   defined, 728
condensation, **68**, 71–72
condensation point, 71
conduction
   of charge, 425, **425**, 435
   of electric current, **375**, 375–377, **376**, 379
   of thermal energy, **253**, 253–254
conductivity
   electrical, 306–307, **375**, 375–377, **376**, 379
   thermal, 44, 306–307
conductors, 254, 375, 377, 379, 427
conservation
   of charge, 425, 446
   of energy, **19, 229**, 229–231, 362
   of mass, 357, **357**
   of momentum, **152**, 152–153, **153**
constructive interference, **523**, 523–524, **524**, 579, **580**
contact lenses, 347, **347**

control group, 15, 733
controlled experiment, 15, 733
convection, 254, **254**
convection currents, 254
conversion tables
   SI, 729
   temperature, 730
convex lenses, **603**, 603–604, **606**
convex mirrors, 602, **602**
cooling systems, 267–268, **268**, 271
copper, 256, 292, **292, 306**, 322
   density of, 45
copper carbonate, **50**
cornea, 605, **605**
corrosivity, 377, 379
covalent bonds, 336–339, **337, 338**
covalent compounds
   formulas for, 353, **353**
   organic compounds, **383**, 383–389, **388, 389**
   properties of, 375–376, **376**
CPU (central processing unit), 496, **496**
crest, 513
CRT (cathode-ray tube), 282, **282**, 493
cryogenics, 274
crystal lattice, 335. *See also* ionic bonds
crystalline solids, 61, **61**, 335, 374, **374**
Curie, Irene, 401
Curie, Marie, 325, **325**, 398, 401
Curie, Pierre, 325
current, 433. *See also* amperes; electric current
Czarnowski, James, 4, **12**, 12–17

D

Dallos, Joseph, 347
Dalton, John, 277, **281**, 281–283
dark matter, 56
data, 16
deafness, 538
deceleration, 113

decibels, 543
decimals, 739
decomposition reactions, 359, **359**
Deep Flight, 160
Democritus, 276, **276,** 280–281
density
    buoyant force and, 170–171
    calculation of, 27, 45, 170, 749
    defined, 27, 44–45, 53, 749
    identifying substances using, 45
    liquid layers and, 46, **46**
    of pennies, 45
    units, 27
    water pressure and, 165
deoxyribonucleic acid (DNA), 387, **387,** 394
derived quantities, 26–27
destructive interference, 523, **523, 524,** 580, **580**
diamond, **315**
DiAPLEX®, 275, **275**
diatomic molecules, **338,** 338–339
Diegert, Carl, 560
diffraction, 521–522, **522,** 551, **551,** 579, **579**
diffuse reflection, 576, **576**
digital signals, **490,** 490–491, **491**
dimension, 38
dinosaurs, 278, 560
diodes, 484, **484**
direct current (DC), 434, **434,** 484
dissolution, 92, 95, 375–376
distillation, 91
DNA (deoxyribonucleic acid), 387, **387,** 394
domains, 456–458, **457**
doorbells, 465, **465**
doping, 483
Doppler effect, 506, 542, **542**
double-replacement reactions, 360, **360**
drag, 158, 176
drums, 554, **554**
dry cells, 431
dry ice, 72, **72.** *See also* carbon dioxide
ductility, 44, 85, 306, 340
dynamite, 325

E

E. coli, 395, 590
ears, 504, **537,** 561. *See also* hearing
Earth
    core, 460
    gravity and, 126–129, **128**
    magnetic field, 459, **459,** 460–461
    rotational velocity, 111
    rotation of, 22
earthquakes, 489, 508, 515
Earthships, **244,** 244–245, 264
echoes, 520, 545, **545**
echolocation, **546,** 546–547
ecology, **9**
effervescent tablets, **50**
efficiency
    energy, 12–13, **13,** 16, **16,** 228
    mechanical, 197, 205
Egypt, 186
Einstein, Albert, 33, 104, **104,** 507, 565, **565**
Einthoven, Willem, 419, **419**
elastic force, 135
electrical energy
    alternative sources of, 432
    atoms and, 422–423
    from chemical reactions, **361**
    electric charge and, 282–283, 422–429, 446
    from fossil fuels, 234, **234,** 237
    generating, 471, 473, **473**
    household use of, 219, **219,** 225, **225**
    measurement of, 438–439, 447
    nuclear fission and, 235, **408,** 408–409
    nuclear fusion and, **410,** 410–411, **411**
    power plants and, 243, **243**
    resistance and, 435–437, 447
    from water, 235, **235**
    from wind, 228, **228,** 236, **236**
electrical storms, **428,** 428–429, 446
electric cells, 430, 430–431
electric charge, 282, 423–427
    conduction, 425
    conservation of, 425
    detecting, 426
    friction and, 424, **424**
    induction, 425
    law of, 423, **423**
    static electricity and, 427, **427**
electric circuits, 440–445
    defined, 440
    failures, **444,** 444–445, **445,** 447
    household, 444–445
    parts of, **440,** 440–441, **441,** 447
    types of, 441–443, **442, 443,** 446
electric current, 430–431, 433–439, 447
    alternating, 434, **434,** 471–472, 484
    covalent compounds and, 376, **376**
    diodes and, **484**
    direct, 434, **434,** 484
    ionic compounds and, 375, **375**
    magnetic force and, 465, **465, 466,** 466–467, **467, 468,** 468–470, **469, 470**
    transistors, **485,** 485–486, **486**
electric discharge, 428
electric eels, 420, **435**
electric fields, 423, 433
electric force, 423, 446
electric generators, 234, **234, 470,** 470–471, **471**
electricity, 418, 420. *See also* electrical energy; electric current
    from magnetism, 419, 468–473
    from ocean temperature differences, 266
electric motors, 466, **466**
electric power, 437–438, 447. *See also* electrical energy
electrocardiograph machine, 419
electrodes, 430, **430**
electrolysis, 88, **359**
electrolytes, 430
electromagnetic force, 293
electromagnetic induction, 469, **469,** 470, **470**

applications, **470,** 470–473, **471, 472, 473**
electromagnetic spectrum, 567–574, **568–569.** See also light
electromagnetic wave, 255, **255,** 564, **564**
electromagnetism, 452–479. See also magnets
　applications, 465–467
　discovery of, **462,** 462–463
　electric current and, 465, **465,** 466, **466,** 467, **467, 468,** 468–470, **469, 470**
　light waves, **564,** 564–565, 567
　uses of, 463–467
electromagnets, 458, 464
electron clouds, 286, **286,** 742, **742**
electron-dot diagrams, **337**
electronic components, 482–487
　circuit boards, 482, **482**
　diodes, 484, **484**
　integrated circuits, 486, **486,** 500
　semiconductors and, 483, **483**
　transistors, **485,** 485–486, **486,** 500
　vacuum tubes, 487, **487**
electrons
　in atomic models, 283, **283, 285,** 285–286, **286,** 742
　chemical bonding and, 328–331
　discovery of, 277, 283
　electrical energy and, 219, **219, 422,** 433, **433**
　in electric cells, **430**
　electric charge, 423–427, **425, 426**
　in energy levels, 329, **329**
　magnetic fields and, 456
　in metals, **340,** 340–341, **341**
　overview, 283, **288,** 289
　valence, **329,** 329–331, **330, 331**
electroscopes, 426, **426**
elements, 82–85. See also periodic table

chemical symbols for, 308, 354–355
classes of, 84, **85,** 98, 306–307
defined, 82, 742
groups of, 310–317
pattern of arrangement, 83, 302–309
elephants, 300, **300,** 531, **531**
endothermic, 69, 362
endothermic reactions, 69, 72, 362–363, **363**
energy, 212–237. See also chemical energy; electrical energy; gravitational potential energy; kinetic energy; mechanical energy; nuclear energy; thermal energy
　change of state and, 68
　conservation of, **19, 229,** 229–231, **230,** 362
　conversions, **222,** 222–228, **223, 228, 234**
　defined, 7, 214
　diagrams, **363**
　efficiency, 12–13, **13,** 16, 228
　electron loss/gain and, 333–334
　in food, 262
　light, 220, **220**
　nonrenewable resources, **232,** 232–235, 237
　renewable resources, **235,** 235–236, **236,** 237, 432
　resources, 232–237
　sound, 220, **220**
　transfer of, 257
　units, 214
　in waves, 510–512, 517–518
　work and, **214,** 214–217
engines, **266,** 266–267, **267**
ENIAC (Electronic Numerical Integrator and Computer), 495, **495**
enzymes, 365, 386
equations, 354–357, **356**
Erie, Lake, 37
Escherichia coli, 395, 590
esters, 389
ethene, **388**
ethyne, **388**
europium, **313**

evaporation, 70, **70**
exothermic, 69, 361
exothermic reactions, 69, 71, 361, **361, 363**
experimental group, 733
external combustion engines, 266, **266**
eyes, **605,** 605–607, **606**

F

Fahrenheit scale, 26, **26, 248,** 249, 728
falling objects
　acceleration of, 138–139
　free fall, **141,** 141–142
　Newton's second law and, 149
　orbits, 141–142, **142**
　projectile motion, **143,** 143–144, **144**
　terminal velocity, 140
Faraday, Michael, 468–470, 474
farsightedness, 606, **606**
fats, dietary, 385
Feinbloom, William, 347
ferromagnets, 458
fertilizers, 89, 315
fiber optics, 612
fields
　electric, 423
　electromagnetic waves and, 564
　magnetic, 456, **456,** 457, 463, 469
Fields, Julie, **10**
filtration, 91, 96
fireflies, 590
fire retardant, 370, **370**
fireworks, 322, **322**
first class lever, 198, **198.** See also levers
fish, swim bladders in, 172, **172**
fission, 221, **221,** 235, 237, **406,** 406–411, **410**
fixed pulley, 203, **203**
flammability, 47
flashbulbs, **357,** 358
Fleming, Alexander, 3
floating (buoyant force), 168–172

fluid friction, 122
fluids, 122, 160–177. *See also* gases; liquids
   Bernoulli's principle, **173,** 173–177
   buoyant force, 168–172
   defined, 162
   drag, 176
   flow, 166
   pressure, 162–167
   turbulence, 176
fluorescence, 398, **398,** 614, 617
fluorescent light, 596, **596**
fluorine, **338**
focal length, **600,** 601
focal point, **600, 602, 603**
fool's gold (iron pyrite), **34,** 34–35,
   density of, 45
force
   acceleration and, **148,** 148–149
   action/reaction pairs, **150,** 150–151, **151,** 153, **153**
   in atoms, 293
   balanced, 117–118
   buoyant, 168–172
   centripetal, 142
   defined, 115
   distance and, 194, **195**
   electric, 423, 446
   electromagnetic, 293
   friction, 119–124, **120**
   gravitational, **39,** 39–40, 125–129
   input, **193,** 193–194, **194, 195,** 196, **196**
   magnetic, 455, **455**
   motion and, 117–118
   net, **116,** 116–117, **117,** 748
   output, 193, **193,** 195, 196, **196**
   strong/weak, 293, 402
   unbalanced, 117–118
   units, 41, 115
   work and, 188–190, **189, 190**
fossil fuels, 51, **232,** 232–234, **233, 234,** 237
fractions, 739–740
Franklin, Benjamin, 418, **418,** 428–429
Franklin, Melissa, **284,** 299, **299**

Franscioni, Warren, 182
free fall, **141,** 141–142. *See also* projectile motion
freezing, **68,** 69, 72
freezing point, 69
frequency, 518
   of light, 567–574
   of sound, 540–541, **541**
frequency modulation (FM), 568–569, **569**
friction, 119–124
   as activation energy, 362
   defined, 119
   effects of, **123,** 123–124
   efficiency and, 197
   electric charge and, 424, **424**
   energy conservation and, 229
   force and, **120,** 120–122
   Newton's first law and, 146
   resistance and, 435
   sources of, 119–120
   types of, 121–122
fuels
   fossil, 51, **232,** 232–234, **233, 234,** 237
   hydrogen gas, 317, 355
   uranium, **235**
fulcrum, 198
fulgurite, 58, **58**
Fuller, Buckminster, 323. *See also* buckyball
fuses, 445, **445**
fusion, nuclear, 221, 410–411

G

Galileo Galilei, 138, 506
gallium, 69, **69**
galvanometers, 467, **467**
gamma rays, 400, **401,** 402, 569, **569,** 574
gases
   formation of, **351**
   as lubricants, 123
   model of, **60**
   natural, 232, **232,** 233
   pressure of, 64–66, 74
   in solution, 93
   states of matter and, **260,** 262
   volume of, 38, 63, **63,** 65–66

gas hydrates, 212, **212**
gas laws
   Boyle's law, 65, **65**
   Charles's law, 66, **66**
gas masks, 618
Geim, Andrey, 452
General Electric, 372
generators, 234, **234,** 470, 470–471, **471**
geology, **9**
geomagnetic storms, 478
geothermal energy, **236,** 237
germanium, 303, **309,** 314
geysers, **236**
GFCI (ground fault circuit interrupters), 445, **445**
Gilbert, William, 459
glass, 256
glass making, 59
gliders, 175
glucose, **352,** 362, 384
Goddard, Robert, 184, **184**
gold, **34,** 34–35, 93, 277, 312, **312,** 340
   density of, 45
   specific heat capacity of, 256
Golden Gate Bridge, 117, 135, **135**
gold foil experiment, **284,** 284–285
graduated cylinders, 25, **25,** 37, 731
grams, **24,** 26, 41
granite, **90,** 92
graphite, 123
graphs, 16, **16,** 66, **109,** 114, **233,** 735–737
gravitational force, 125–129
gravitational potential energy, **216,** 216–217
gravity, 125–129
   acceleration due to, 138–139, **139,** 144, **144,** 149
   air resistance and, 139–141
   within atoms, 293
   defined, 39, 125
   distance and, **127,** 128, **128**
   on Earth, 126–129
   law of universal gravitation, 105, 126–128, **127,** 746
   mass and, **39,** 39–40, **127,** 127–129, **129**

matter and, 56, 125
orbits and, 141–142, **142**
projectile motion and, **143,** 143–144, **144**
terminal velocity and, 140
Great Pyramid of Giza (Egypt), 186, **186,** 200
green buildings, 242
greenhouse effect, 255, **255**
ground fault circuit interrupters (GFCI), 445, **445**
groups, elements in, 309–317, 330, 742

H

half-life
   carbon-14 dating, 403–404, **404**
   examples of, 404
halogen lights, 595, **595**
halogens, 316, 334
headphones, 504, **538**
health
   food contamination, 590
   hearing problems, 504, 538, 555
   jaundice, 562
   kidney stones, 541
   leukemia, 401
   magnets in, 479
   radiation in medicine, 405, 574
   radiation sickness, 401–402
   ultrasound, 547, **547**
   vision problems, **606,** 606–607, **607**
   vitamin D, 573
   X rays, 574, **574**
hearing, 504, **537,** 538, 541, **541,** 555
heat, 251–259, 361. *See also* temperature; thermal conductivity; thermal energy
   calculation of, 257
   changes of state and, 261
   chemical changes and, 262
   cooling systems, 267–268, **268**
   heating methods, 253–255

heating systems, **263,** 263–265, **264, 265**
   specific heat capacity, 256–258
   thermal energy and, 259
   thermal pollution, 269
heat engines, **266,** 266–267, **267**
heat island effect, 269
Heisenberg, Werner, 286
helium
   from alpha decay, 399, **399**
   density of, 45
   from nuclear fusion, **410**
   properties of, 45, 48, **48,** 170, **170**
   uses of, 317, **317**
   valence electrons, 330–331
hemoglobin, 386
Henry, Joseph, 468
Hensler, Mike, 211, **211**
Hero, 60
hertz, 518
heterogeneous mixtures, 96
Hindenburg, 3, **3**
Hodgson, Peter, 372
holograms, 506, **506,** 611, **611**
homogeneous mixtures, 92
Hopper, Grace Murray, 418, **418**
hormones, 386
hot-water heating, 263, **263**
household appliances, 438–439
household circuits, 444–445
Hubble, Edwin, 506
Huygens, Christiaan, 185
hydraulic devices, 167, **167**
hydrocarbons, 388–389
hydrochloric acid, 351, **377,** 377–378
hydroelectricity, **235,** 471, **471**
hydrogen. *See also* nuclear fusion
   chlorine and, **352**
   electron-dot diagrams, **337**
   gas, 355, **364, 377**
   isotopes, **289,** 289–290, **290,** 292
   molecules, 336, **336**
   nuclear fusion, **410,** 410–411
   properties of, 317
   radioactive isotope, **403,** 404
hydrogen peroxide, 86, 88, 363
hypotheses, 14–17, 22

I

ideal machine, 197
illuminated objects, 594. *See also* light
incandescent light, 595, **595**
incidence, angle of, 575, 747
inclined planes, 186, 200, **200**
induction, 419, 425, **425, 469,** 469–473, 475
inertia, 42, 52, 147, **147, 149**
infrared waves, 255, **255,** 346, **568,** 571, **571**
infrasonic frequencies, 531, 541
infrasound, 531
inhibitors, 365
inner ear, **537**
input devices, 496, **496–497**
input force, 193. *See also* force
   distance and, 194, **194, 195**
   inclined planes and, 200, **200**
   levers and, **198,** 198–199, **199**
   mechanical advantage and, 196, **196**
   pulleys and, **203,** 203–204, **204**
   screws and, 201, **201**
   wedges and, 201, **201**
   wheel and axle and, 202, **202**
insulation, thermal, 244
insulators, electric, 427, 435
insulators, thermal, 254
insulin, 386
integrated circuits, 418, 486, **486**
interference, **522,** 522–525, **548,** 548–550, 579–580, **580**
internal combustion engines, 267, **267**
International System of Units, 24–26
   conversion chart, 729
   SI prefixes, 729
Internet, 499, **499**
iodine, 316, **316**
ionic bonds, 332–335
ionic compounds, 335, 353, **353, 374,** 374–375, **375**
ions, 289, 332–335, **333, 334,** 340–341, **341,** 743

iris, **605**
iron, **47,** 47–48, **83,** 256, 312, **312**
iron pyrite, **34,** 34–35
  density of, 45
isotopes, **290,** 290–292, **291,** 400, 403

J

Jackson, Shirley Ann, **10**
jaundice, 562
joules, 190, 214
Joyce, James, 276
jumping beans, 152

K

Kekulé, Friedrich August, 324
Kelvin scale, 26, **248,** 249, 730
Kemph, Martine, 211
kidney stones, 541
kilocalories, 258, 262
kilograms, **24,** 26, 41
kilowatt-hours, 439
kilowatts, 437–439
kinetic energy
  calculation of, 215
  conversions, 222, **222,** 223, **223, 225–230,** 234
  machines and, **226, 227**
  mass and, 215, **215**
  mechanical energy and, 217
  potential energy and, **222,** 222–223, **223**
  speed and, 215, **215**
  thermal energy and, 218, **218**
King, Martin Luther, Jr., 324
knife, as wedge, **201**
Kodiak Island, 508
krypton, 83, 277, **337, 406**

L

Lake Erie, volume of, 37
lanthanides, 313
La Paz, Bolivia, **164**
lasers, 32, 78, 274, 506
  in CD players, 491, **491**
  in holograms, 611, **611**
  operation of, 609–610, **610**
  retroreflectors and, 592, **592**
Lavoisier, Antoine, 357
law, scientific, 19
law of conservation of energy, **19, 230,** 230–231, 362, 746
law of conservation of mass, 357, **357**
law of conservation of momentum, **152,** 152–153, **153**
law of electric charges, 423, **423**
law of reflection, 575, **575,** 746
law of universal gravitation, 105, 126–128, **127,** 746
lead, 256, 308
  density of, 45
LED (light-emitting diode), 482
length, 24–25
lenses, **603,** 603–604, **604, 605, 606, 608**
leukemia, 401
levers, 186, **198,** 198–199, **199**
Lidar, 32
lift, 174, 182
light. *See also* lasers; light bulbs; waves
  absorption and scattering, **576,** 576–577
  from chemical reactions, 351, 361
  coherent, 609
  colors, **572,** 577–578, **578,** 581–584, **584**
  diffraction, 579, **579**
  energy, 220, **220,** 224
  fiber optics, 612
  fluorescent, 596, **596**
  frequencies of, 567–574
  infrared, 346, 482, **568,** 571, **571**
  matter and, 581–582
  neon, **317,** 596, **596**
  optical instruments, **608,** 608–609, **609**
  polarized, 612–613, **613**
  pollution, 619
  production of, 565
  rays, 598, **598,** 600
  scattering, 93, **93,** 96
  sight and, 575, **605,** 605–607, **606**
  speed of, 506–507, 566, 567, **577**
  transmission of, 581
  ultraviolet, 346, **569,** 573
  visible, **569,** 572
  waves, 512, **521,** 564, 567–574
light bulbs
  argon in, 291, 317
  in circuits, **442,** 442–443, **443**
  energy conservation in, 225, 230, **230**
  tungsten filaments in, **435**
  types of, **595, 596,** 596–597, **597**
light-emitting diode (LED), 482
lightning, 78, 418, **428,** 428–429, **429,** 446, 451, 551, **566**
lightning rods, 429, **429,** 446
Lim, Drahoslav, 347
line graphs, 736, **736**
lipids, 385, **385**
liquids. *See also* fluids
  density of, 46, **46**
  model of, **60**
  particles in, **62,** 62–63
  in solutions, 93
  states of matter and, 260
  surface tension and viscosity, 63, **63**
  volume of, 25, 37, **37**
liters, **24,** 25
litmus paper, **378,** 378–379, **379**
loads, 440, **440**
longitudinal waves, **514,** 514–515, **517,** 535, **535**
loudness, 542–544
lubricants, 123
luminous objects, 594, 614. *See also* light

M

Maan, Jan, 452
machines, 192–205
  compound, 204–205
  defined, 192
  energy and, **226,** 226–227, **227**
  ideal, 197
  mechanical advantage, 196, **196,** 198–204
  mechanical efficiency, 197, 205
  simple, 198–204
  work and, 193–194, **195**
MACHOs (MAssive Compact Halo Objects), 56
Magellan, Ferdinand, 105
maglev trains, 464
magnesium, **86,** 311, 322, **331, 357, 358**
magnesium oxide, **358, 375**
magnetic fields, 456, **456**
magnetic force, 455, **455**
magnetic resonance imaging (MRI), 479
magnetic resonance spectroscopy (MRS), 479
magnetism, electricity from, 468–473
magnetite, 454, 458, **458,** 460
magnetrons, 591
magnets, 91, **436.** *See also* electromagnetism
  atomic, 452
  in cows, 456
  cut in half, 458, **458**
  domains in, 456–457, **457**
  Earth as, **459,** 459–461, **460**
  electromagnets, 458, 464
  magnetic materials, 456–458, **457**
  properties of, **454,** 454–456, **456**
  types of, 458–459
  uses of, 463–464
magnifying glasses, **603**
malachite, 585
malleability, 44, 85, 306–307, 340
marimba, **524**
Marshall, James, 277

mass
  acceleration and, 148–149, **149**
  atomic, 292, 302–303
  conservation of, 357, **357**
  defined, 26, 38, **41**
  gravity and, **127,** 127–129, **129**
  heat and, 257
  inertia and, 42, 147
  kinetic energy and, 215
  measurement of, 41, **41**
  number, **291,** 291–292, 399–400
  units, **24,** 26
  weight and, 39–41, **41,** 129, **129**
Massachusetts Institute of Technology (MIT), 4, 12
mass number, **291,** 291–292, 399–400
matches, **315,** 362, **362**
math refresher, 738–741
matter, 2, 36–51
  defined, 7, 36, 742
  effects of radiation on, 401–402
  energy from, 407, **407, 410**
  gravity and, 125–126
  light and, 581–582
  overview, 36–42
  properties of, 43–51
  states of, 58–73, 260, 261
  volume of, 36–38
McKee, Larry, 371, **371**
measurement units, 24–27, 729
measuring skills, 731
mechanical advantage, 196, **196,** 198–204
  calculation of, 196
mechanical efficiency, 197, 205
  calculation of, 197
  compound machines and, 205
mechanical energy, 217, **217, 226,** 226–227, **227**
medicines, **96**
medium, 511, 577
  sound and, 536, 539–540
Mele, Cheryl, 243, **243**
melting, 49, **49, 68,** 69, 72
melting point, 69, **73, 375,** 375–376

memory, computer, 497
Mendeleev, Dmitri, 277, 300, **302,** 302–303
meniscus, 37, **37**
mercury, 70, **88,** 256, **312**
  density of, 45
mercury(II) oxide, **88**
metallic bonds, 339–341, **340, 341**
metalloids, 84–85, 307, 314–315
metals
  alkali, 310–311
  alkaline-earth, 311
  as conductors, 306, 340, 427
  properties of, 84–85, 306, **306,** 340–341, **341**
  transition, 312–313
meteorites, 82, 325, **325**
meteorology, **9**
meters, **24,** 25
meterstick, 731
methane, 77, **262**
micromachine, 210, **210**
microprocessors, 419, 495, **495**
microscopes, 609
  scanning tunneling, 277
microwave ovens, **570,** 591
microwaves, **220, 568,** 570–571
middle ear, **537**
milk, **50,** 385
mirrors, 593, **599,** 599–602, **600, 601, 602**
mixtures, 90–97
  colloids, 97, **97**
  heterogeneous, 96
  homogenous, 92
  properties of, 90–93
  separation of, 91, 96
  solutions, 92–95
  suspensions, 96
models
  atomic theory, 280–286, **283, 285–286**
  defined, 20
  Earth, sun, moon, **22**
  electron-dot diagrams, 337, **337**
  electrons, 283, **283,** 286, **286**
  overview, **20,** 20–23
  size of, 22
  of solids, liquids, and gases, **60**

space-filling, **338, 339**
structural formulas, **383**
theories and, 23
modems, 497
modulation of radio waves, 568–569, **569**, 570
molecules, 336–339, **337, 338,** 743
momentum, **152,** 152–153, **153**
monopoles, 458
moon
   distance to Earth, 592
   gravity and, 125, **125**
   motion of, **22, 142**
Morgan, Garrett, 618
Morrison, Fred, 182
Morse code, 488, **488**
Moseley, Henry, 303
motion
   circular, 114
   forces and, 117–118
   inertia, 147
   measuring, 108–114
   Newton's first law and, 145–147
   Newton's second law and, 148–149
   Newton's third law and, 150–151, 153
   observing, 108
   pendulum, 223, **223**
   perpetual, 231, **231**
   projectile, **143,** 143–144, **144**
   reference points, 108
motors, electric, 466, **466**
movable pulley, 203, **203**
Mozart, Wolfgang Amadeus, 105, **105**
music, 555, **555**
musical instruments, **552,** 552–554, **553, 554**

N

Napoleon, 200
Napoleon III, **314**
NASA, 32, 105, 136
natural gas, 212, 232, **232, 233, 262**
nearsightedness, 606, **606**
negative acceleration, 113
neon, 277, **317**
neon light, **596,** 596–597
neutralization, 380–381, **381,** 382
neutrons, **246,** 276, **288,** 288–293, **290,** 403, **406,** 406–408, 742
neutron spectrometer, 298
Newcomen, Thomas, 2, 79
Newton, Sir Isaac, 105, 126, **126,** 145, 507
newtons, 41, 115, 128
Newton's first law of motion, 145–147, 746
Newton's second law of motion, 148–149, 746
Newton's third law of motion, 150–151, 153, 746
   action force, 150
   reaction force, 150
nickel, **83**
nickel(II) oxide, **375**
Nimbus III, 324
nitric acid, 378
nitrogen, 89, 315
nitrogen-fixing bacteria, **89**
Nitrogen group, 315
nitroglycerin, 325
Nobel, Alfred, 325
noble gases, 316–317, 330
noise, 555, **555**
noise pollution, 555
nonmetals, 84–85
   properties of, 307, **307,** 316–317
nonrenewable resources, 232–235
normal, 575, **575,** 747
n-type semiconductor, 483, **483**
nuclear energy, 221, **221,** 235, 237, **406,** 406–411, **410**
nuclear fission, 221, 235, **406,** 406–409, **407**
nuclear fusion, 221, **410,** 410–411
nuclear magnetic resonance (NMR), 395
nuclear power, **408,** 408–409
nuclear radiation, 398–402, **401**
nuclear waste, 409, 411, 416, **416**
nucleic acids, 387, **387**
nucleus, 285, **285,** 286, **286,** 288, 402–403, 742

O

observations, 12
oceanography, **9**
ocean thermal energy conversion (OTEC), 266
ocean waves, **515**
odor, 43
Oersted, Hans Christian, 462–463
Ohm, Georg, **437**
ohms (units), 435, 437
Ohm's law, 437, 446–447
Okamoto, Steve, 159, **159**
opaque materials, **582,** 582–583
optical axis, 600, **600, 601, 602, 603**
optical fibers, 612, **612**
optical illusions, 578
orbits, 141–142, **142**
organic compounds, 325, **383,** 383–389, **388, 389**
   biochemicals, 384–387
   carbohydrates, 384
   lipids, 385
   nucleic acids, 387, **387**
   proteins, 386
Orion, 346
oscilloscopes, 544, **544,** 552, **555**
outer ear, **537**
output devices, **496–497,** 497
output force, 193. *See also* force
   distance and, **194,** 194–195, **195**
   inclined planes and, 200, **200**
   levers and, **198,** 198–199, **199**
   mechanical advantage and, 196, **196**
   pulleys and, **203,** 203–204, **204**
   screws and, **201,** 201–202, **202**
   wedges and, 201, **201**
   wheel and axle and, 202, **202,** 203
overtones, **550,** 552, **552**
oxide ion, 334, **334**
oxygen
   atoms, **329,** 334, **334**

chemical formula, **352**
density of, 45
electron-dot diagrams, **337**
in light bulbs, 291
properties of, 291, 315
Oxygen group, 315

P

pacemaker cells, 435
Papin, Denis, 79
parachutes, 140
parallel circuits, 443, **443**, 446
Parasaurolophus, 560
particle accelerators, **299**
particles
   alpha, 399, **399**
   beta, 400, **400**
   light as, 565
   light scattering, 93, **93**, 96
   in solution, 93
   states of matter and, **60, 61**
   in waves, 513–515
Pascal, Blaise, 167
pascals, **71,** 162
Pascal's principle, 167, 747
passive solar heating, 265, **265**
Pasteur, Louis, 346
pendulum motion, 15, 223, **223**
penguins, 4, **4**, 14, **14**
pennies, 45, 287
percentages, 739
percussion instruments, 554, **554**
period, 309, **309,** 742
periodic, 302
periodic law, 303
periodic table, **304–305, 744–745**
   classes, 306–308
   development of, 277, 302–303
   groups, 309
   periods, 309
   valence electrons and, **330,** 330–331
periods of elements, 309
perpendicular, defined, 513
perpetual motion machines, 231
perspiration, 70
petroleum, 232, **232, 233**

pH, **380,** 380–381, **381,** 743
   values, 380, **380**
phospholipids, 385, **385**
phosphor, 569
phosphorus, 315, 415
photocell, 432. See also solar energy
photons, **565**
photosynthesis, 224, **224,** 262, 362, 572
physical changes, 48–49, 261
physical properties, 43–46
physical science, 6–8, **9,** 10
physics, 8
pigments, 584–585. See also color
pitch, 540–542
plane mirrors, 599, **599**
plasma (blood), 96
plasma channel, 78
plasmas, 60, 67, **67,** 410
plum-pudding model, 283, **283**
plutonium, 396
polarized light, **612,** 612–613, **613**
poles, magnetic, 454–456, **455, 456, 459,** 459–460
pollution
   noise, 555
   thermal, 269
Polo, Marco, 532
polonium, 402, **402**
polymerase chain reaction (PCR), 394
polymers, 347
positive acceleration, 113, **114**
potassium bromide, **95,** 311
potential difference (voltage), 431, **431,** 434–435, 437
potential energy, **216,** 216–217, **222,** 222–223
   calculation of, 217
   conversions involving, 222, **222,** 223, **223,** 229, **229**
power, 191, 437–438, 749
   calculating, 191
   hydroelectric, 471, **471**
   nuclear, **408,** 408–409
power plants, 269
precipitates, **351.** See also solids
prefixes, 353, **353**
   SI, 729

pressure, 162, **162,** 749
   atmospheric, 71, **163,** 163–164, **164,** 166
   boiling point and, 71
   calculation of, 162
   depth and, 164–165
   fluids and, **162,** 162–167, 173
   gases and, 64–66
   Pascal's principle, 167, 747
   units, 71, 162
   water, 165, **165**
primary colors, 584, **584**
products, 354, **354, 356.** See also chemical reactions
projectile motion, **143,** 143–144, **144**
propane, 388, **388**
propellers, **13**
properties
   characteristic, 69–70, 83
   chemical, 47–49, 53
   of matter, 43–51
   physical, 43–46
proportions, defined, 738
propulsion systems, 4, 12–17
proteins, 339, 346, 386, 395
Proteus (boat), 4, **4,** 12, **15,** 16–17, 22–23
protons
   discovery of, 284
   electric charge, 423, 742
   nuclear decay and, 402–403
   overview, 288, **288,** 290, **422**
p-type semiconductor, 483, **483**
pulleys, **203,** 203–204, **204**
pupil, **605**
pure substance, 82
pyrotechnics, 322, **322**

Q

quarks, 276, 299

R

radar, 571, **571**
radiation, 255, 565
radiation sickness, 401–402
radioactive decay, 399–404

radioactivity, 291, 313, 325, 398–405. *See also* nuclear radiation
  alpha particles, 399, **399, 401,** 401–402
  atomic nucleus and, 402–403
  beta particles, **400,** 400–402, **401**
  carbon-14 dating, 403–405
  discovery of, 398
  gamma rays, 400–402, **401, 569,** 574
  penetrating power of, **401,** 401–402
  stainless steel and, 417
  types of decay, 399–400
  uses of, 396, 405
radio broadcasting, 492, **492**
radioisotope thermoelectric generator (RTG), 396, **396**
radios, 487, **487**
radio waves, 492, **492,** 536, **568,** 568–570, **569**
radium, 399, **399**
radius, 203, **203**
radon, 399, **399,** 402
rainbows, 578
RAM (random-access memory), **496,** 497
ramps, 194, **194,** 200, **200**
Ramsay, William, 277
rarefaction, 514, **514, 534, 535**
ratios
  defined, 738
ray diagrams, **600,** 600–604, **601, 602, 603, 604**
reactants, 354, **354, 356.** *See also* chemical reactions
reaction force, 150, **150,** 151
reactivity, 47
real images, 600–601, **601,** 604, **604**
record players, 490, **490**
reducing fractions, 739
reference points, 108, **108**
reflected beam, 747
reflection, 520, **520, 545,** 545–547, **575,** 575–576, **576,** 599, 602, 612
refraction, 521, **521, 577,** 577–578, **578, 603,** 603–604, **604**

refrigerators, 268, **268**
remote controls, 482, **482**
renewable resources, **235,** 235–236, **236**
resistance, 435–437, 447
resonance, 524–525, 550
resonant frequencies, 550, **550**
resultant velocity, 111, **111**
retina, **605**
retroreflector, 592, **592**
Reynolds, Michael, 244
ring structures, **383**
RNA (ribonucleic acid), 387
rocket, 184
roller coasters, **8,** 159, **159,** 229, **229**
rolling friction, 121, **121**
ROM (read-only memory), 497
rubber, 372
rust, 47, **47**
Rutan, Richard, 326
Rutherford, Ernest, 276, 284–285

S

safety
  acids and, 377
  bases and, 379
  electrical, 444, 445
  guidelines, 622
  symbols, 27, **27,** 622, **622**
Salmonella, 590
salt. *See* sodium chloride
salts, 382, **382**
sampling rates, 491
Sand Mountain, **542**
sands, booming, 532, 542
Santibanez, Roberto, **10**
saturated hydrocarbons, 388, **388**
saturation in solutions, 94
Sauerbrun, Karl von Drais de, 185
Savery, Thomas, 79
scattering, **576,** 576–577
Schrödinger, Erwin, 286
science, 6
  branches of, 9, **9**
  careers in, **10**
  models in, 20–23
  technology and, 11

scientific knowledge, 18–19, 22–23
scientific method, 11–19, **18,** 22–23, 732–734
scientific notation, 741
screws, **201,** 201–202, **202**
Seawise Giant, 171
second class lever, 199, **199.** *See also* levers
seeds, gravity and, 125
seismographs, 489
semiconductors, 307, 483, **483**
separation techniques, 91, 96
series circuits, 442, **442,** 446–447
short circuit, 444
SI (Système International d'Unités), 24
  conversion chart, 729
  prefixes, 729
  units, **24,** 24–26
sight, 575, **605,** 605–607, **606**
signals
  analog, **489,** 489–490, **490, 492**
  audio, 493, **493**
  defined, 488
  digital, **490,** 490–491, **491**
  television, 570, 584
  video, 493, **493**
silica, 58
silicon, 307, 314, 483, **483**
Silly Putty, 2, **2,** 372, **372**
silver
  density of, 45
  specific heat capacity of, 256
simple machines, 198–203
  in compound machines, 204–205
  mechanical advantage of, 198–203
  types of, 198–203
single-replacement reactions, **359,** 359–360, **360**
sky glow, 619
sliding friction, 121, **121**
slope, 736
sodium, **87, 329,** 333, **333**
sodium chlorate, **95**
sodium chloride
  crystal lattices, **22,** 335, **335**
  properties of, 69, **87, 95,** 311, 332

salt water, 92
synthesis, **87, 358**
uses of, 382
sodium hydroxide, 311, **379**
sodium nitrate, **95,** 382
sodium vapor lights, 597, **597**
solar cells, 235, **235**
solar energy, **235,** 237, 432
solar flares, 478
solar heating, 265, **265**
solar wind, 478
solenoids, 452, **463,** 463–465, **464, 465**
solids. *See also* compounds
formation of, **351**
model of, **60**
particles in, 60
in solutions, 93
states of matter and, **260**
types of, 61, **61**
volume of, 25, 37–38, **38**
solubility, 44, 94–95, **95,** 375–376
solutes, 92, 94
solutions, 92–95. *See also* dissolution; liquids; solubility
solvents, 92
sonar, **546,** 546–547
sonic booms, 549, **549**
sound. *See also* waves
amplitude, 542–544, **544**
detecting, 535–536, **537**
diffraction, 551, **551**
frequency, **540,** 540–541, **541, 544**
interference, **548,** 548–550
loudness, 542–544, **544**
pitch, **540,** 540–541, **541, 544**
production of, **534,** 534–535
quality, 552–555
reflection of, **545,** 545–547
resonance, 550
resonant frequencies, 550, **550**
speed of, 104, 507, 519, 539–540
waves, 21, **21,** 511, 515, **515,** 520, 535, **535,** 549–550
sound barrier, 540, **548,** 548–549, **549**
sound energy, 220

spacecraft, exploratory, 396, **396**
space shuttle, **50,** 111, 136, **136, 142, 151, 317**
space travel, 141, **141**
specific heat capacity, 256–258
speed
average, 109
fluid pressure and, 173
kinetic energy and, 215
of light, 566–567, **577**
of sound, 539–540
velocity and, 110
wave, 519, **519,** 521, **521**
wing shape and, 175
Spencer, Percy, 591
spider silk, **386, 395, 395**
spider webs, 386, **386**
spoilers, 176
Sprague, Frank J., 450
Sputnik I, 2, **2**
stainless steel, 417
standing wave, 524, **524,** 549–550. *See also* waves
starches, **384**
states of matter, 58–73, 260. *See also* matter
change of state, 68–73, 261
defined, 44, 60, **60,** 260
static cling, 335, **335**
static electricity, **427,** 427–429, 446
static friction, 122, **122**
Statue of Liberty, **50,** 292, **292**
steam engines, 60, **60,** 79, 266, **266**
steam-heating systems, 263
steel, 47, **171,** 171
stimulated emission, 610
straight chain structures, **383**
streetcars, 450, **450**
string instruments, 553, **553**
strong force, 293, 402
strontium, 322
stylus, 490, **490**
sublimation, 68, **68,** 72
submarines, 172
subscripts, 352, **352,** 743
substances, pure, 82
sucrose, **339**
sugar, 48, **219,** 339, **339, 352,** 362, 384, **384**
sulfur, 80, **307,** 315, 322, **331**
sulfur dioxide, 51

sulfuric acid, 51, 378
sun
energy from, 221, **221, 235,** 237, 432
gravity and, 128, **128**
nuclear fusion in, 221
solar heating systems, 265, **265**
volume of, **36**
sunscreens, 573
superconductors, 274, 418, 436, **436**
superglue, 326
surface area, 365
surfaces, **119,** 119–120, 124
surface tension, 63, **63**
surface waves, 515, **515**
suspensions, 96, 99
swim bladders, 172, **172**
switches, 441, **441**
symbols, 27, **27,** 308, 354–355
synthesis reactions, 358, **358.** *See also* chemical reactions

T

Tacoma Narrows Bridge, collapse of, 525, **525**
technology, 11–12
telecommunication, 488. *See also* communication technology
telegraphs, 488, **488**
telephones, 419, **419,** 489, **489**
telescopes, 609, **609**
radio, 530, **530**
television, 480, **480,** 493, **493,** 570, 584
Telkes, Maria, 184, **184**
tellurium, **307**
temperature
change of state and, 68, 73
conversions, 249
defined, 246
of gases, 65–66
infrared waves and, 571
kinetic energy and, 247, **247**
measurement, 248–249
nuclear fusion and, 410
overview, 246–247

Index **773**

reaction rates and, 364
resistance and, 436
scales, **248,** 249
solubility and, 95, **95**
speed of sound and, 540
thermal energy and, 259
thermal equilibrium, 252, **252**
units, **24,** 26, **248,** 248–249, 730
volume and, 250
tension, 135
terminal velocity, 140
theories, scientific, 19, 23, 280, 328
thermal conductivity, 44, 306–307
thermal energy. See also heat; temperature
  calculations, 257
  from chemical reactions, **361**
  conversions, **223, 225, 227,** 229, 231
  defined, 218
  heat and, 252–253, 259
  heat engines, 266
  kinetic energy and, 218, **218**
  matter and, 260
  particles and, 218, **218**
  from solar cells, 235, **235**
thermal equilibrium, 252, **252**
thermal expansion, 248, 250, **250**
thermal pollution, 269
thermocouples, 432, **432**
thermometers, **26, 248,** 248–249
thermostats, 250, **250**
third class lever, 199, **199.** See also levers
Thomson, J. J., 277, 282–283
threads, of screw, **202**
Three Mile Island, 324
thrust, 175, 182
thunderstorms, **428,** 428–429, 446
thyroid, **405**
tin, 48, 314
tinnitus, 538
tire pressure, 67, 162
Titanic, 80, **80, 165**
titanium, **309,** 312, **312**
  as bone replacement, 57, 312, **312**

total internal reflection, 612
tracers, 405
traffic lights, 618
transformers, 472, **472, 473**
transistors, 418, **418, 485,** 485–487, **486, 487**
transition metals, 312–313
translucent materials, **582,** 582–583
transmission of light, **581,** 581–582
transmutation, 400
transparent materials, **582,** 582–583
transverse waves, 513, **513,** 515, **516–517**
Travers, Morris W., 277
Triantafyllou, Michael, 4, **12,** 12–17
Trieste, **165**
triple-beam balance, 731
trolley, 450, **450**
troughs, 513, **513**
tsunamis, 508
tungsten filaments, 435, **595**
tuning fork, 507
turbine
  steam, **234**
  water, **235**
  wind, 228, **228, 236**
turbulence, 176
Tyrannosaurus rex, 278

U

ultrasonic frequencies, 541, **546**
ultrasonography, 547, **547**
ultraviolet (UV) light, 346, **569,** 573
unbalanced forces, 117–118
United Nations, 276
universal gravitation, law of, 105, 126–128, **127**
universal solvent, water as, 92
unsaturated hydrocarbons, 388, **388**
ununnilium, 308
uranium, **235,** 402, 404, **406,** 406–407
Uranus, 105, **105**
urea, 324

urine, 324
useful equations, 748

V

vacuum tubes, 487, **487**
valence electrons, **329,** 329–331, **330, 331.** See also electrons
vaporization, **68, 70,** 70–72
variables, 15
velocity, 110–112, **111**
  of falling objects, 139
  terminal, 140
Venus, 105, **128**
vibrations, 220, 511, **511**
  sound and, **534,** 534–535, 553, 554
vinegar, 348, **348**
  as an acid, 378, **378**
viper fish, **165**
virtual images, 599, **599,** 600–601, **601, 602, 603, 604**
virtual reality devices, 134
viscosity, 63
visible light, 572, **572**
vision problems, **606,** 606–607, **607.** See also sight
vitamin D, 573
vocal chords, 535
voltage, 431, **431,** 434–435, 437, 447, 472, **473**
volts, 434–435, 437
volume
  calculation of, 25, 38, 45
  defined, 741
  gases and, 38, 63, **63,** 65–66
  measurement of, 36–38
  units, **24,** 25, **25,** 729

W

warm-air heating, 264
waste thermal energy, 231
water
  alkali metals in, 311, **311**
  boiling point of, **248**
  change of state, **68,** 68–72,

261, **261**
composition of, 86, 352
as conductor, 375–376, 427
decomposition reaction, **359**
density of, 45
energy from, **235**, 237
freezing point of, **248**
heating systems, 263, **263**
molecules, **337, 338**
pH of, 380
pressure, 162, 165, **165**
specific heat capacity, 256–258
as a universal solvent, 92
Watt, James, 79
watts, 191, 437–439
wavelength, **517,** 517–518, **518,** 564–574, 579
waves, 508–525. *See also* light; sound
  absorption and scattering, **576,** 576–577
  amplitude, **516,** 516–517, 542–544, **544**
  calculations, 519
  compressions, 514, **514**
  crests, 513, **513**
  defined, 510
  diffraction, 521–522, **522,** 551, **551,** 579, **579**
  electromagnetic, 492, **492,** 512–513, **564,** 564–565, 567–574
  energy in, 510–512
  frequency of, 518, **540,** 540–541, **541, 544**
  infrared, 482, **568,** 571, **571**
  interactions, 520–525
  interference and, 522–524, **548,** 548–550, 579–580, **580**
  longitudinal, **514,** 514–515, **515, 517,** 535, **535**
  mechanical, 511
  medium and, 511
  microwaves, **568,** 570–571
  properties of, 516–519
  radio, 492, **492,** 536, 567–570, **568, 569**
  rarefactions, 514, **514**
  reflection, 520, **520, 545,** 545–547, **575,** 575–576, **576**
  refraction, 521, **521, 577,** 577–578, **578**
  resonance, 524–525
  seismic, 511
  sound, 515, **515**
  standing, 524, **524,** 549–550
  surface, 515
  transverse, 513, **513,** 515, **516–517,** 564, **564**
  troughs, 513, **513**
  units, 518
  wavelength, **517,** 517–518, **518,** 572, 579
  wave speed, 519, **519,** 521, **521**
weak force, 293
weather, 71
  models and, 21, **21**
weather balloons, 66
Webb, Gene, **10**
wedges, 201, **201**
weight
  buoyant force and, 169, **169**
  in free fall, 141, **141**
  gravity and, 128–129, **129, 216,** 216–217
  mass and, 39–41, **41,** 129
wet cells, 431
wheel and axle, **202,** 202–203, **203**
Wichterle, Otto, 347
Williams-Byrd, Julie, 32, **32**
Williamson, Tom, 560
WIMPs (Weakly Interacting Massive Particles), 56
wind energy, **228, 236,** 237
wind instruments, 554, **555**
wing shape, **174,** 174–176, **175**
wiring, 436, **436,** 440, 447
work
  calculation of, 190, **190,** 749
  defined, 188, 749
  energy and, **214,** 214–217
  input/output, **193,** 193–194, **195,** 197
  machines and, 192–194
  overview, 188–189, **189**
  power and, 191
  units, 190
World's Fair, 3
Wright, Orville, 174

X

xenon, 277, **317**
X rays, 569, **569,** 574, **574**

Y

Yeager, Chuck, 104, 540
Yeager, Jeana, 326
Young, Thomas, 507
Yucca Mountain, 416

Z

zinc, 45, **377**
zinc chloride, **359**
zipper, 185, **185,** 205, **205**

Credits

Credits

Abbreviations used: (t) top, (c) center, (b) bottom, (l) left, (r) right, (bkgd) background

ILLUSTRATIONS

All illustrations, unless noted below, by Holt, Rinehart and Winston.

Table of Contents Page v(bl), Kristy Sprott; vii(tl), ix(tr), Stephen Durke/Washington Artists; ix(bl), Keith Locke/Suzanne Craig; xi(tr), Stephen Durke/Washington Artists; xi(tl), Terry Kovalcik; xii(tl), Stephen Durke/Washington Artists; xii(bl), Blake Thornton/Rita Marie; xiii(bl), Stephen Durke/Washington Artists; xiv(tl), Blake Thornton/Rita Marie; xv(cr), Sidney Jablonski; xv(bl), Marty Roper/Planet Rep; xvi(t), Annie Bissett.

Chapter One Page 6, 9, Rainey Kirk/The Neis Group; 13, John Huxtable/Black, Inc.; 14, Will Nelson/Sweet Reps; 16, Preface, Inc.; 17, Terry Guyer; 18(b), Brian White; 20(tr), Kristy Sprott; 20(bl) Morgan Cain & Associates; 21(t), Stephen Durke/Washington Artists; 21(c), Keith Locke/Suzanne Craig; 21(b) Gary Antonetti/Ortelius Design; 22(cl), Kristy Sprott; 22(b), Blake Thornton/Rita Marie; 23(t), Stephen Durke/Washington Artists and Preface, Inc.; 24(all), Stephen Durke/Washington Artists; 26(t), Morgan Cain & Associates; 29, Blake Thornton/Rita Marie; 31(tl), David Merrell/Suzanne Craig.

Chapter Two Page 38(t), 39, Stephen Durke/Washington Artists; 42(l), Gary Locke/Suzanne Craig; 43, Blake Thornton/Rita Marie; 50, 51, 53, Marty Roper/Planet Rep; 55(lc), Terry Kovalcik; 57(tc), Daniels & Daniels.

Chapter Three Page 60(t), Mark Heine; 60(b), 61, 62, 63, 64, 65, 66(cl,cr), Stephen Durke/ Washington Artists; 66(bl), Preface, Inc.; 68, David Schleinkofer/ Mendola Ltd.; 70(t), Marty Roper/ Planet Rep; 70(b), Mark Heine; 73, David Schleinkofer/Mendola Ltd. and Preface, Inc., 74(t), Stephen Durke/Washington Artists; 74(b), Preface, Inc.; 75, Marty Roper/Planet Rep; 77(cr), Preface, Inc.

Chapter Four Page 82, Marty Roper/Planet Rep; 84(b), Preface, Inc.; 88, Blake Thornton/Rita Marie; 95, Preface, Inc.

Chapter Five Page 109, Preface, Inc.; 111, Marty Roper/Planet Rep; 112, Gary Locke/Suzanne Craig; 113(t), Mike Carroll/Steve Edsey & Sons; 114(cr), Preface, Inc.; 119(t), Blake Thornton/Rita Marie; 119(b), 120, 122, Gary Ferster; 126, Doug Henry/ American Artists; 127, Stephen Durke/Washington Artists; 128, Craig Attebery/Jeff Lavaty; 129, Terry Guyer; 130(br), Stephen Durke/Washington Artists; 131, Terry Guyer; 133(r), Preface, Inc.

Chapter Six Page 139, 140, Gary Ferster; 142, Craig Attebery/Jeff Lavaty; 144(tl), Mike Carroll/Steve Edsey & Sons; 146, Marty Roper/Planet Rep; 148, Charles Thomas; 151(tr), Gary Ferster; 154(br), Craig Attebery/Jeff Lavaty; 155, Marty Roper/Planet Rep; 158, James Pfeffer.

Chapter Seven Page 160, Rainey Kirk/The Neis Group; 162, 163, Stephen Durke/ Washington Artists; 164, 165, Rainey Kirk/The Neis Group; 166, Christy Krames; 167, Mark Heine; 168, Preface, Inc.; 169, Will Nelson/Sweet Reps; 171, Preface, Inc.; 172, Sam Collins/Art & Science, Inc.; 174(c), Craig Attebery/Jeff Lavaty; 174(bl), Will Nelson/Sweet Reps; 176(l), Marty Roper/Planet Rep; 177, Terry Guyer; 178, Craig Attebery/Jeff Lavaty; 181(tr), Jared Schneidman/ Wilkinson Studios; 181(bl), Keith Locke/Suzanne Craig.

Chapter Eight Page 189(tr), Blake Thornton/Rita Marie; 190, John White/The Neis Group; 195(l), Annie Bissett; 195(r), John White/The Neis Group; 196, Keith Locke/ Suzanne Craig; 198(l), 199(tl, bl), Annie Bissett; 201(cl), Preface, Inc.; 203(t), Gary Ferster; 203(c,b), 204, John White/The Neis Group; 206, Blake Thornton/Rita Marie.

Chapter Nine Page 215(b), Dave Joly; 216, John White/The Neis Group; 218, Stephen Durke/Washington Artists; 219(t), Kristy Sprott; 219(b), Stephen Durke/Washington Artists; 220(t), Gary Ferster; 224, Will Nelson/Sweet Reps; 225, Dan Stuckenschneider/ Uhl Studios Inc.; 226(t), Blake Thornton/Rita Marie; 227, Dan Stuckenschneider/Uhl Studios Inc.; 229, Dan McGeehan/ Koralik Associates; 230(t), Marty Roper/Planet Rep; 230(b), 232(b), Dan Stuckenschneider/Uhl Studios Inc.; 233(r), Preface, Inc.; 234, Patrick Gnan/Deborah Wolfe; 235(br), Michael Moore; 236(cr), Dan Stuckenschneider/ Uhl Studios Inc.; 237(b), Preface, Inc.; 241(r), Dave Joly.

Chapter Ten Page 246, Blake Thornton/Rita Marie; 247, Stephen Durke/Washington Artists; 248, Terry Guyer; 249(tr), Dave Joly; 250, Dan Stuckenschneider/Uhl Studios Inc.; 252, 253, Stephen Durke/Washington Artists; 254(bl), Mark Heine; 255, Jared Schneidman/Wilkinson Studios; 258, 260, Stephen Durke/Washington Artists; 261, Preface, Inc.; 263, 264, 265, 266, 268, 269, Dan Stuckenschneider/Uhl Studios Inc.; 270(c), Dave Joly; 272(br), Dan Stuckenschneider/Uhl Studios Inc.; 273(cr), Preface, Inc.; 275, Stephen Durke/Washington Artists.

Unit Four Page 276(cr), Stephen Durke/Washington Artists.

Chapter Eleven Page 281(c), Preface, Inc.; 282, Mark Heine; 283, Stephen Durke/ Washington Artists; 284(c), Mark Heine; 284(b), Preface, Inc.; 285(t), Stephen Durke/Washington Artists; 285(br), Preface, Inc.; 286, 288, 289(t,b), Stephen Durke/Washington Artists; 289(cr), Terry Kovalcik; 290, 291(b), 293, 294(br), Stephen Durke/Washington Artists; 295, Terry Kovalcik; 296, Mark Heine; 297(r), Stephen Durke/Washington Artists.

Chapter Twelve Page 302, Michael Jaroszko/American Artists; 304, 305, Kristy Sprott; 306(tr), 307, Stephen Durke/Washington Artists; 309, 310(bc), 311(bl), 312(t), 313(t), 314(tc, b), Preface, Inc.; 314(l), Gary Locke/Suzanne Craig; 315, 316, 317(lc), Preface, Inc.; 319, Gary Locke/Suzanne Craig; 321(tr), Preface, Inc.; 321(bl), Keith Locke/Suzanne Craig; 321(br), Annie Bissett; 323(l), Dan Stuckenschneider/Uhl Studios Inc.

Unit Five Page 324(cr), Kristy Sprott.

Chapter Thirteen Page 329, Stephen Durke/Washington Artists; 330, Preface, Inc.; 331, 333, 334, Stephen Durke/Washington Artists; 335(t), Keith Locke/Suzanne Craig; 335(br), Kristy Sprott; 336(c), 337(tl), Stephen Durke/Washington Artists; 337(tr,c), Preface, Inc.; 338(tr,br), Kristy Sprott; 338(bl), Stephen Durke/Washington Artists; 339, Kristy Sprott; 340(cl), 341(tc), Kristy Sprott; 341(br), Preface, Inc.; 342(t), Keith Locke/Suzanne Craig; 342(b), Stephen Durke/Washington Artists; 343, Kristy Sprott; 344(b), Stephen Durke/Washington Artists; 346, Kristy Sprott.

Chapter Fourteen Page 352(t), 356, Kristy Sprott; 358(b), 359(c,b), 360(b), Blake Thornton/Rita Marie; 363(t), 365(b), Preface, Inc.; 366, Blake Thornton/Rita Marie; 367, Kristy Sprott; 369(cr), Preface, Inc.

Chapter Fifteen Page 380(t), Dave Joly; 380(b), 383, Preface, Inc.; 384, 385(b), Morgan Cain & Associates; 388, 389(t), 393(tr), Preface, Inc.

Chapter Sixteen Page 399, 400, Stephen Durke/Washington Artists; 401, Gary Ferster; 402, 403, Stephen Durke/Washington Artists; 404, Preface, Inc.; 406, 407, Stephen Durke/Washington Artists; 408, Patrick Gnan/Deborah Wolfe Ltd.; 410(c), 412(br), 414, Stephen Durke/Washington Artists; 415(tr), Preface, Inc.

Chapter Seventeen Page 422(t), Blake Thornton/Rita Marie; 422(b), Stephen Durke/Washington Artists; 423, John White/The Neis Group; 425(l), Stephen Durke/Washington Artists; 428, Dan Stuckenschneider/Uhl Studios Inc.; 430, 432, Mark Heine; 433, 434, Geoff Smith/Scott Hull; 436, Will Nelson/Sweet Reps; 439(cr), Boston Graphics; 444, Dan McGeehan/Koralik Associates.

Chapter Eighteen Page 456, 457, 458, Stephen Durke/Washington Artists; 459, Mark Persyn; 460(b), Stephen Durke/Washington Artists; 462, 463, 465, Sidney Jablonski; 466, Patrick Gnan/Deborah Wolfe Ltd.; 467, Stephen Durke/Washington Artists; 468, Mark Heine; 469, 470(t), Mark Persyn; 470(b), 471(t), David Fischer; 471(b), John Francis, 472, Tony Randazzo; 473, Dan Stuckenschneider/Uhl Studios Inc.; 474(l), Sidney Jablonski; 474(r), Mark Persyn; 475, David Fischer; 477, Stephen Durke/Washington Artists.

Chapter Nineteen Page 483, 484(c), Stephen Durke/Washington Artists; 484(b), Gary Ferster; 485, Blake Thornton/Rita Marie; 486, Gary Ferster; 489, 490(tl), Dan Stuckenschneider/Uhl Studios Inc.; 490(b), 491(tr), Gary Ferster; 491(b), Stephen Durke/Washington Artists; 492, Blake Thornton/Rita Marie; 493, Dan Stuckenschneider/Uhl Studios Inc.; 494, Preface, Inc.; 499, Blake Thornton/Rita Marie; 500(b), Stephen Durke/Washington Artists; 500(br), Blake Thornton/Rita Marie; 502(cl), 503(tr), Gary Ferster.

Chapter Twenty Page 508(t), Gary Antonetti/Ortelius Design; 510, Will Nelson/Sweet Reps; 513(tr), Preface, Inc.; 513(b), 514(t,c), John White/The Neis Group; 514(b), Sidney Jablonski; 515(tl), Stephen Durke/Washington Artists; 515(r), Jared Schneidman/Wilkinson Studios; 516(t), Marty Roper/Planet Rep; 516(b), 517, 518, Sidney Jablonski; 518(cl, cr), 519(cl,cr), Mike Carroll/Steve Edsey & Sons; 519, 521, Will Nelson/Sweet Reps; 523(tl,tc,tr,cl,c,cr), John White/The Neis Group; 523(br), Terry Guyer; 526(b), John White/The Neis Group; 529(r), Sidney Jablonski.

Chapter Twenty-one Page 534, Annie Bissett; 535(l), Gary Ferster; 535(br), Terry Kovalcik; 536(tl), David Merrell/Suzanne Craig; 537, Keith Kasnot; 538 (tl), Terry Kovalcik; 539, Keith Locke/Suzanne Craig; 540, Annie Bissett, 541, Will Nelson/Sweet Reps (dolphin, cat, dog), Rob Wood (whale), Michael Woods (bat, bird), John White/ The Neis Group (girl), and Preface, Inc.; 542, Gary Ferster; 544, Annie Bissett; 545(b), John White/The Neis Group; 546(t), Gary Ferster; 546(b), Terry Guyer; 548(t), Gary Ferster; 548(b), 549, Terry Guyer; 551, 552(c), Gary Ferster; 552(b), 555, Annie Bissett; 556(br), Keith Kasnot; 559(r), Annie Bissett; 560, Barbara Hoopes-Ambler.

Chapter Twenty-two Page 564, Sidney Jablonski; 565(tr), Blake Thornton/Rita Marie; 565(b), Stephen Durke/Washington Artists; 568(t), Blake Thornton/Rita Marie; 568(b), Preface, Inc.; 569(tl,tr), Terry Guyer; 569 (b), Preface, Inc.; 570, Dan Stuckenschneider/Uhl Studios Inc.; 572, Preface, Inc.; 573, Blake Thornton/Rita Marie; 574, 575, 576, Dan Stuckenschneider/Uhl Studios Inc.; 578, Stephen Durke/ Washington Artists; 580, Preface, Inc.; 582, Dave Joly; 583, Preface, Inc.; 586, Stephen Durke/Washington Artists.

Chapter Twenty-three Page 595, 596, 597, Dan Stuckenschneider/Uhl Studios Inc.; 598, Stephen Durke/Washington Artists; 599, Preface, Inc.; 601, 602, 603, 604, Will Nelson/Sweet Reps (flowers) and Preface, Inc.; 605, Keith Kasnot; 606, Keith Kasnot and Preface Inc.; 608, 609, Dan Stuckenschneider/Uhl Studios Inc.; 610(t), Digital Art; 610(b), Stephen Durke/ Washington Artists; 611, Digital Art; 612, Stephen Durke/ Washington Artists; 614(t), Dan Stuckenschneider/Uhl Studios Inc.; 614(b), Keith Kasnot; 617, Stephen Durke/Washington Artists (rulers) and Preface, Inc.

LabBook Page 642, Blake Thornton/Rita Marie; 661, Preface, Inc.; 665(l), John White/The Neis Group; 669, Dan McGeehan/Koralik Associates; 671, Marty Roper/ Planet Rep.; 674, Dave Joly; 677(t), Preface, Inc.; 680, Stephen Durke/Washington Artists; 689, Preface, Inc.; 695(tr), Gary Ferster; 695(br), Dave Joly; 712, Blake Thornton/Rita Marie; 716, Terry Guyer; 718, Stephen Durke/Washington Artists; 721, 722, John White/The Neis Group.

Appendix Page 727, Blake Thornton/Rita Marie; 730(t), Terry Guyer; 734(b), Mark Mille/Sharon Langley Artist Rep.; 735, 736, 737, Preface, Inc.; 742, Stephen Durke/ Washington Artists; 743(tl,c), Kristy Sprott; 743(b), Bruce Burdick; 744, 745, Kristy Sprott; 747(t), Dan Stuckenschneider/Uhl Studios Inc.

PHOTOGRAPHY

Front Cover (tl) Ed Young/Science Photo Library/Photo Researchers, Inc.; (tr) FPG International; (bl) Henry Kaiser/Leo de Wys; (br) Firefly Productions/The Stock Market (also on title page); (cr) Stephen Dalton/Photo Researchers, Inc.; owl (front cover, back cover, spine and title page) Kim Taylor/Bruce Coleman, Inc.

Table of Contents Page v(tr), Robert Daemmrich/Tony Stone Images; (br), Peter Van Steen/HRW Photo; vi(cl), Richard Megna/Fundamental Photographs; (bl), Joseph Drivas/Image Bank; vii(bl), Richard Megna/Fundamental Photographs; viii(tr), James Balog/Tony Stone Images; (cl), Sergio Purtell/FOCA; (bl) NASA; ix(tl), T. Mein/N&M Mischler/Tony Stone Images; x(tr), NASA; xiii(br), Dr. E.R. Degginger/Color-Pic, Inc.; xiv(t), Stephanie Morris/HRW Photo; xv(inset), Archive Photos; xvi(bl), Leonard Lessin/Peter Arnold, Inc.; xvii(tr), Harry Rogers/Photo Researchers, Inc.; (tl), Robert Wolf; xxi(br), Superstock.

Feature Borders Unless otherwise noted below, all images ©2001 PhotoDisc/HRW: "Across the Sciences" Pages 56, 135, 242, 267, 322, 370, 418, 448, all images by HRW; "Careers" 32, 159, 243, 323, 395, 509, sand bkgd and saturn, Corbis Images, DNA, Morgan Cain & Associates, scuba gear, ©1997 Radlund & Associates for Artville; "Eureka" 79, 158, 182, 211, 371, ©2001 PhotoDisc/HRW; "Eye on the Environment" 394, clouds and sea in bkgd, HRW, bkgd grass and red eyed frog, Corbis Images, hawks and pelican, Animals Animals/Earth Scenes, rat, John Grelach/Visuals Unlimited, endangered flower, Dan Suzio/Photo Researchers, Inc.; "Health Watch" 57, dumbell, Sam Dudgeon/ HRW Photo, aloe vera and EKG, Victoria Smith/ HRW Photo, basketball, ©1997 Radlund & Associates for Artville, shoes and Bubbles, Greg Geisler; "Scientific Debate" 449, 480, Sam Dudgeon/HRW Photo; "Science Fiction" 33, 103, 183, 481, saucers, Ian Christopher/Greg Geisler, book, HRW, bkgd, Stock Illustration Source; "Science, Technology, and Society" 78, 102, 134, 210, 266, 298, 346, robot, Greg Geisler; "Weird Science" 299, 347, 419, 508, mite, David Burder/Tony Stone, atom balls, J/B Woolsey Associates, walking stick and turtle, EclectiCollection.

Unit One Page 2(t), Corbis-Bettman; 2(cl), Photosource; 2(b), Enrico Tedeschi; 3(tl), Sam Shere/ Corbis Bettmann; 3(tr), Brown Brothers/HRW Photo Library; 3(bl), Natalie Fobes/Tony Stone Images; 3(br), Noble Proctor/Science Source/Photo Researchers, Inc.

Chapter One Page 4(t), David Lawrence/The Stock Market; 4(b), Donna Coveney/MIT News; 7(t), Jeff Hunter/The Image Bank; 7(b), Scala/Art Resource, NY; 8(b), Gunnar Kullengerg/Stock Connection/ PNI; 9(tr), Chris Madley/Science Photo Library/ Photo Researchers, Inc.; 9(bkgd), Joseph Nettis/Photo Researchers, Inc.; 9(cl), Stuart Westmorland/Photo Researchers, Inc.; 9(br), M.H. Sharp/Photo Researchers, Inc.; 9(cr), David R. Frazier Photolibrary; 9(b), Norbert Wu; 10 (tl), John Langford/HRW Photo; 10(tr), courtesy of the U.S. Nuclear Regulatory Commission; 10(cr), Michele Forman; 12(br), HRW photo by Stephen Maclone; 12(bl), Barry Chin/Boston Globe; 15, Donna Coveney/MIT News; 19(t), Chris Butler/Science Photo Library/Photo Researchers, Inc.; 19(b), Richard Megna/Fundamental

Photographs; 20(br), Rosenfeld Images LTD/Science Photo Library/Photo Researchers, Inc.; 23(b), courtesy of FHWA/NHTSA National Crash Analysis/The George Washington University; 25(bl,r), HRW photo by Peter Van Steen; 27, Image ©2001 PhotoDisc, Inc.; 28(c), Tom McHugh/Steinhart Aquarium/Photo Researchers, Inc.; 31(cr), HRW photo by Victoria Smith; 32(all), HRW photos by Art Louis.

Chapter Two Page 34(l), Hartmann/Sachs/Phototake, NY; 34(c), Ken Lucas/Visuals Unlimited; 34(r), The Granger Collection, NY; 34(tr), Image ©2001 PhotoDisc, Inc.; 36(b), NASA, Media Services Corp.; 40(all), John Morrison/Morrison Photography; 41(t), HRW photo by Michelle Bridwell; 43-44(all), John Morrison/Morrison Photography; 45, Neal Nishler/Tony Stone Images; 46(all), John Morrison/Morrison Photography; 47, Rob Boudreau/Tony Stone Images; 48(t), Brett H. Froomer/The Image Bank; 48(cl,cr), John Morrison/Morrison Photography; 49, HRW photo by Lance Schriner; 50(tl,tr), John Morrison/Morrison Photography; 50(bl), Joseph Drivas/The Image Bank; 50(br), SuperStock; 52(r), HRW photo by Michelle Bridwell; 55, HRW photo by Lance Schriner; 56, David Malin/©Anglo-Austrialian Observatory/ Royal Observatory, Edinburgh.

Chapter Three Page 58(r), Tony Stone Images; 58(l), Peter Menzel; 61(t), Gilbert J. Charbonneau; 63(t), Dr. Harold E. Edgerton/©The Harold E. Edgerton 1992 Trust/courtesy Palm Press, Inc.; 67(b), Pekka Parviainen/Science Photo Library/Photo Researchers, Inc.; 68, Union Pacific Museum Collection; 69(t), Richard Megna/Fundamental Photographs; 76(t), Myrleen Ferguson/PhotoEdit; 77, Charles D. Winters/Photo Researchers, Inc.; 78(l), Kennan Ward Photography; 78(r), Dr. Jean-Claude Diels/University of New Mexico; 79, Union Pacific Museum Collection.

Chapter Four Page 80(l), Fr. Browne S.J. Collection; 80(r), RMS Titanic Inc.; 82(r), David R. Frazier Photolibrary; 82(l), Jonathan Blair/Woodfin Camp & Associates; 83(b), Russ Lappa/Photo Researchers, Inc.; 83(t,c), Charles D. Winters/Photo Researchers, Inc.; 84(t,l), Walter Chandoha; 84(r), Zack Burris; 84(b), Yann Arthus-Bertrand/Corbis; 85(tc), HRW photo by Victoria Smith; 85(cl), Dr. E.R. Degginger/Color-Pic, Inc.; 85(cr), Runk/Schoenberg/Grant Heilman Photography Inc.; 85(br), Joyce Photographics/Photo Researchers, Inc.; 85(l), Russ Lappa/Photo Researchers, Inc.; 85(bc), Charles D. Winters/Photo Researchers, Inc.; 86(c), Runk/Schoenberger/Grant Heilman; 87(l), Runk/Shoenberger/ Grant Heilman Photography; 87(b), Richard Megna/Fundamental Photographs; 88, Runk/Schoenberg/Grant Heilman Photography Inc.; 88, Richard Megna/Fundamental Photographs; 89(t), John Kapriellan/Photo Researchers, Inc.; 90(l), HRW photo by Victoria Smith; 91(t), Charles D. Winters/Timeframe Photography; 91(c), Charles Winters/Photo Researchers, Inc.; 91(cr), Klaus Guldbrandsen/Science Photo Library/Photo Researchers, Inc.; 93(b), HRW photo by Richard Haynes; 93(c), Image ©2001 PhotoDisc, Inc.; 94(c), Dr. E.R. Degginger/Color-Pic, Inc.; 96(c), HRW photo by Michelle Bridwell; 97(t), HRW photo by Lance Schriner; 97(b), Dr. E.R. Degginger/Color-Pic, Inc.; 98(b), HRW photo by Victoria Smith; 98(t), David R. Frazier Photolibrary; 100(t), Yann Arthus-Bertrand/Corbis; 101(t), Richard Megna/ Fundamental Photographs; 102(l), Anthony Bannister/Photo Researchers, Inc.; 102(r), Richard Steedman/The Stock Market.

Unit Two Page 104(tl), Archive Photos; 104(tr), Image ©1998 PhotoDisc, Inc.; 104(bl), Photo Researchers, Inc.; 104(br), Underwood & Underwood/Corbis-Bettman; 105(tl), The Vittoria, colored line engraving, 16th century/The Granger Collection, NY; 105(tr), Stock Montage, Inc.; 105(cl), NASA/Science Source/Photo Researchers, Inc.; 105(cr), W.A. Mozart at the age of 7: oil on canvas, 1763, by P.A. Lorenzoni/The Granger Collection, NY; 105(b), NASA.

Chapter Five Page 106(c), George Catlin, Ball of Play of the Choctaw/National Museum of American Art, Washington D.C./Art Resource, NY; 106(b), Lawrence Migdale; 108(all), SuperStock; 110(t), Tom Tietz/Tony Stone Images; 110(b), Robert Ginn/PhotoEdit; 113, Sergio Putrell/Foca; 114(t), Gene Peach/The Picture Cube; 115, 116(b), HRW photos by Michelle Bridwell; 117, HRW photo by Daniel Schaefer; 118(t), David Young-Wolff/PhotoEdit; 118(b), Arthur C. Smith/Grant Heilman Photography; 121(all), HRW photos by Michelle Bridwell; 121(insets), HRW photos by Stephanie Morris; 122, Tony Freedman/PhotoEdit; 124(cl), HRW photo by Michelle Bridwell; 125, NASA; 128, Image ©2001 PhotoDisc; 130(c), Superstock; 133, HRW photo by Mavournea Hay; 134, Hunter Hoffman; 135, Bruce Hands/Tony Stone Images.

Chapter Six Page 136(b), David R. Frazier Photography; 136(all), 137(t), NASA; 138, Richard Megna/Fundamental Photographs; 139, Doug Armand/Tony Stone Images; 140, Robert Daemmrich/Tony Stone Photography; 141(t), James Sugar/Black Star; 141(b), NASA; 143(b), James Balog/Tony Stone Images; 143(l), Michelle Bridwell/Frontera Fotos; 143(r), Image ©2001 PhotoDisc, Inc.; 144(t), Richard Megna/Fundamental Photographs; 146, Marc Asnin/SABA Press Photos, Inc.; 147(l), HRW photo by Mavournea Hay; 147(r), Michelle Bridwell/Frontera Fotos; 149(all), Image ©2001 PhotoDisc, Inc.; 150, David Madison; 151(tl), Gerard Lacz/Animals Animals/Earth Sciences; 151(tc), HRW photo by Coronado Rodney Jones; 151(tr), Image ©2001 PhotoDisc, Inc.; 151(bl), NASA; 151(br), HRW photo by Lance Schriner; 152(all), HRW photos by Michelle Bridwell; 153(t), Zigy Kaluzny/Tony Stone Images; 153(b), HRW Photo by Michelle Bridwell; 154, Robert Daemmrich/Tony Stone Photography; 156(t), James Balog/Tony Stone Images; 156(b), David Madison/Tony Stone Images; 157(l), NASA; 158(t), courtesy of Steve Okamoto; 158(b), Lee Schwabe; 159, R.N. Metheny/The Christian Science Monitor.

Chapter Seven Page 159(t), courtesy of Steve Okamoto; 159(b), Lee Schwabe; 164(t), I. M. House/Tony Stone Images; 164(tc), David R. Frazier Photolibrary, Inc.; 164(c), Deiter and Mary Plage/Bruce Coleman; 164(bc), Wolfgang Kaeler/Corbis; 164(b), Martin Barraud/Tony Stone Images; 165(t), SuperStock; 165(tc), Daniel A. Nord; 165(c), Ken Marschall/Madison Press Books; 165(bc), Bassot/Photo Researchers Inc.; 165(b), Bettmann Archive; 168, HRW photo by Michelle Bridwell; 170, Bruno P. Zehnder/Peter Arnold, Inc.; 173, Richard Megna/Fundamental Photographs; 175(t), Larry L. Miller/Photo Researchers, Inc.; 175(c), Richard Neville/Check Six; 175(bl), T. Mein/N&M Mishler/Tony Stone Images; 175(t), Larry L. Miller/Photo Researchers, Inc.; 176 (t), Ron Kimball/Ron Kimball Photography, Inc.; 176(t), HRW Photo by Michelle Bridwell; 177(b), George Hall/Check Six; 179(t), Ron Kimball/Ron Kimball Photography, Inc.; 182 (t), Victor Malafronte.

Unit Three Page 184(t); The Granger Collection, New York; 184(b); Conley Photography, Inc./American Solar Energy Society; 184(c); The Granger Collection, NY; 185(tl); Phil Degginger/Color-Pic, Inc.; 185(tr); Corbis-Bettmann; 185(cr); Robert Wolf; 185(cl); The Granger Collection, NY; 185(b); David Madison.

Chapter Eight Page 186(b), Yoram Lehman/Peter Arnold Inc., NY; 186, 187(t), Erich Lessing/Art Resource/NY ; 192(cl,cr,bc,br,t) Robert Wolf; 192(bl), image copyright 2001 PhotoDisc, Inc.; 197, 198(l,r), 199 (c), Robert Wolf; 200, Lisa Davis; 201(b,c), 202(t,b), Robert Wolf; 204(t), HRW photo by Russell Dian; 204(b), Robert Wolf; 205(tl), Image copyright1998 PhotoDisc, Inc.; 205(tc), 208(t), Robert Wolf; 209(l), Helmut Gritscher/Peter Arnold, Inc.; 209(br), HRW photo by Stephanie Morris; 210, courtesy of IBM Corp., Research Division, Almaden Research; 211, A.W. Stegmeyer/Upstream.

Chapter Nine Page 212, courtesy of L. Stern and J. Pinkston, US Geological Survey; 214, Al Bello/Allsport; 216, Earl Kowall/Corbis; 218(c), Paul A. Souders/Corbis; 218(r), Tony Freeman/Photo Edit; 221(t), NASA; 221(b), Mark C. Burnett/Photo Researchers, Inc.; 222(l,cl,cr,r), HRW photo by Peter Van Steen; 223(t), Richard Megna/Fundamental Photographs; 228, Morton Beebe/Corbis; 231, HRW photo byVictoria Smith; 232, Ted Clutter/Photo Researchers, Inc.; 233(t), Tom Carroll/ Phototake; 233(cl), Mark E. Gibson ; 233(br), John Kaprielian/Photo Researchers, Inc.; 234(t), Robert Wolf; 235(t), D.O.E./Science Source/Photo Researchers, Inc.; 235(cl), H.P. Merton/The Stock Market; 235(b), Tom Carroll/Phototake; 235(bl), HRW photo by Coronado Rodney Jones; 235 (br), Kevin R. Morris/Corbis; 236(tl), Bob Gomel/The Stock Market; 236(tr), Ed Young/Corbis; 236(c), Richard Nowitz/ Phototake; 239, Ed Young/Corbis; 240(b), Ted Clutter/Photo Researchers, Inc.; 241(bl), Mike Powell/Allsport; 242, Solar Survival Architecture; 243(t,b), Robert Wolf.

Chapter Ten Page 244(t), Solar Survival Architecture; 250, Mark Burnett/Photo Researchers, Inc.; 259, L.D. Gordon/The Image Bank; 262, HRW Photo by Peter Van Steen; 267(t), Dorling Kindersley LTD; 267(b), Peter Arnold Inc., NY; 272, Dorling Kindersley LTD; 273, Kees van den Berg/Photo Researchers, Inc.; 274, Dan Winters/ Discover Magazine.

Unit Four Page 276(t), The Granger Collection, New York; 277(t), SuperStock; 277(b), Reuters/Mark Cardwell/Archive Photos.

Chapter Eleven Page 278, Universal City Studios; 278(t), Copyright 2001 by Universal City Studios, Inc. Courtesy of Universal Studios Licensing, Inc. All rights reserved.; 280(t), Dr. Mitsuo Ohtsuki/Photo Researchers, Inc.; 280(b), Nawrocki Stock Photography; 281, Corbis-Bettmann; 284, Stephen Maclone; 285(l), John Zoiner; 285(r), HRW photo by Mavournea Hay; 287(t), Lawrence Berkeley National Lab; 291, Charles D. Winters/Timeframe Photography Inc./Photo Researchers, Inc.; 292, Superstock; 294, Nawrocki Stock Photography; 297, Fermilab National Laboratory; 298, NASA Ames ; 299(t), Stephen Maclone; 299(b), Fermi National Lab/Corbis.

Chapter Twelve Page 300(tl), B.G. Murray Jr./Animals Animals/Earth Scenes; 300(tr), Joe McDonald/Animals Animals/Earth Scenes; 300(bl), Dr. E.R. Degginger/Color-Pic, Inc.; 300(br), Richard Megna/Fundamental Photographs; 301(bl), IBM/Visuals Unlimited; 301(br), Bisson/Sygma ; 307(r), Richard Megna/Fundamental Photographs; 307(bl), Russ Lappa/Photo Researchers, Inc.; 307(br), Lester V. Bergman/Corbis-Bettman; 309(l,c), Dr. E.R. Degginger/Color-Pic, Inc.; 309(r), Richard Megna/Fundamental Photography; 310, Charles D. Winters/Photo Researchers, Inc.; 311(l,c,r), Richard Megna/Fundamental Photographs; 312(tr), P. Petersen/Custom Medical Stock Photo; 312(tc), HRW photo by Victoria Smith; 313, David Parker/ Science Photo Library/Photo Researchers, Inc.; 315(t), Phillip Hayson/Photo Researchers; 316(t,c), Richard Megna/Fundamental Photographs; 316(b), Dr. E.R. Degginger/Color-Pic, Inc.; 317(t), Michael Dalton/Fundamental Photographers; 317(b), NASA; 318(b), 320, Richard Megna/Fundamental Photographs; 323, Image copyright 2001 PhotoDisc, Inc.

Unit Five Page 324(b), Wally McNamee/Corbis; 324(b), Reuters/NASA/Archive; 324(t), Archive France/Archive Photos; 325(t), James Foote/Photo Researchers, Inc.; 325(r), Sygma; 325(l), Argonne National Laboratory/Corbis-Bettman.

Chapter Thirteen Page 326(b), Photri; 326(t), Jim Sugar Photography/Corbis; 332(t), Kevin Schafer/Peter Arnold, Inc.; 332(l), HRW Photo by Peter Van Steen; 335(r), Paul Silverman/Fundamental Photographs; 339(r), Calder Sculpture, National Museum in Washington D.C. Photo © Ted Mahiec/The Stock Market; 340, 344, HRW photo by Victoria Smith.

Chapter Fourteen Page 348(t), Romilly Lockyer/The Image Bank; 350(t), Rob Matheson/The Stock Market; 350(br), Dorling Kindersley, LTD.; 351(tl), Charles D. Winters/Timeframe Photography Inc.; 351(tr), Richard Megna/Fundamental Photographs; 351(br), Dr. E.R. Degginger/Color-Pic, Inc.; 354(b), HRW Photo by Richard Haynes; 355(r), Charles D. Winters/Photo Researchers, Inc.; 355(l), Mark C. Burnett/Photo Researchers, Inc.; 357(l,r), Michael Dalton/ Fundamental Photographs; 358, Richard Megna/Fundamental Photographs; 359, Charles D. Winters/Photo Researchers, Inc.; 360(l), Peticolas/Megna/Fundamental Photographs; 360(r), Richard Megna/Fundamental Photographs; 361(c), HRW Photo by Peter Van Steen; 361(r), Tom Stewart/The Stock Market; 361(l), HRW photo by Victoria Smith; 364(t), 364(bl), 364(br), Richard Megna/Fundamental Photographs; 365, Dorling Kindersley, LTD, courtesy of the Science Museum, London; 368(t), 369, Richard Megna/Fundamental Photographs.

Chapter Fifteen Page 372(b), SuperStock; 374(t), Yoav Levy/Phototake; 375(t,bl,br), 376, Richard Megna/Fundamental Photographs; 377(b), Charles D. Winters/Timeframe Photography Inc.; 381(t), Runk/Schoenberger/Grant Heilman Photography Inc.; 381(b), Peter Arnold Inc., NY; 382, Miro Vinton/Stock Boston/PNI; 382(b), John Deeks/Photo Researchers, Inc.; 386(br), Hans Reinhard/Bruce Coleman Inc.; 387, David M. Phillips/ Visuals Unlimited; 388(br), Charles D. Winters/Timeframe Photography Inc.; 390, Runk Schoenberger/Grant Heilman Photography; 392(b), Charles D. Winters/Timeframe Photography Inc.; 392(t), Richard Megna/Fundamental Photographs; 394, Sygma; 395(t), Tom McHugh/Photo Researchers, Inc.; 395(b), Dennis Kunkel, University of Hawaii.

Chapter Sixteen Page 396(b), Dave Steel/NASA; 396(t), NASA; 398(b), Henri Becquerel/The Granger Collection; 398(t), Dr. E.R. Degginger/Color-Pic, Inc.; 403, Sygma; 405(b), Tim Wright/Corbis; 405(t), Custom Medical Stock Photo; 407, Emory Kristof/National Geographic Image Collection; 409(t), Shone/Liaison International; 409(b), Michael Melford/The Image Bank; 410, Roger Rossmeyer/Corbis Bettmann; 412(c), Dr. E.R. Degginger/Color-Pic, Inc.; 413, Emory Kristof/National Geographic Image Collection; 415(r), Science Photo Library/Photo Researchers, Inc.; 416(b), Sauder/Gamma Liason; 416(t), Cameramann International; 417(b), Charles O'Rear/ Corbis ; 417(t), Courtesy of Micheal Atzmon.

Unit Six Page 418(b), Enrico Tedeschi; 418(t), AKG London; 418(c), Peter Southwick/AP Wide World; 419(b), Ilkka Uimonen/Sygma; 419(c), Enrico Tedeschi; 419(tl), Hulton Getty; 419(tr), property of AT&T Archives. Printed with permission of AT&T.

Chapter Seventeen Page 420(t), Norbert Wu; 420(b), Norbert Wu; 421(tr), NASA; 421(tl), Corbis ; 421(br), ESA/Sygma; 421(bl), Anglo-Australian Observatory ; 424(l,r), HRW photo by Victoria Smith; 426(b), HRW photo by Stephanie Morris; 427(b), HRW Photo by Peter Van Steen; 429, Jack "Thunderhead" Corso; 435(t), Patricia Ceisel/Visuals Unlimited; 435(b), David R. Frazier Photolibrary; 436, Takeshi Takahara/Photo Researchers, Inc.; 437, Science Photo Library/Photo Researchers, Inc.; 438(br), HRW photo by Richard Hanes; 439, Visuals Unlimited; 440(l), Richard T. Nowitz/Photo Researchers, Inc.; 445(t), Paul Silverman/Fundamental Photographs; 448(t), HRW photo by Victoria Smith; 450(t), Corbis-Bettmann; 450(b), Bill Ross/ Corbis; 451(l), Daniel Osborne, University of Alaska/Detlev Ban Ravenswaay/Science Photo Library/Photo Researchers, Inc.; 451(r), STARLab, Stanford University.

Chapter Eighteen Page 452(t), Photo Researchers, Inc.; 452(b), Courtesy Dr. Andre Geim; 453, HRW photo by Victoria Smith; 455(bl,bc,br), 456, Richard Megna/ Fundamental Photographs; 461(l), Pekka Parviainen/Photo Researchers Inc; 463, SuperStock; 464, Tom Tracy/The Stock Shop; 478, The Image Bank; 479, Howard Sochurek.

Chapter Nineteen Page 480(t), MZTV; 480(inset), Archive Photos; 488, Dr. E.R. Degginger/Color-Pic, Inc.; 489, Yoav Levy/PhotoTake; 493 (inset), Corbis Images; 495(l), Corbis/Bettmann; 495(r), 501, SuperStock; 504, HRW Photo by Peter Van Steen.

Unit Seven Page 506(t), Fotos International/Archive Photos; 506(b), courtesy of Hughes Research Laboratories; 507(tl), David Parker/Science Photo Library/Photo Researchers; 507(tr), Dr. E.R. Degginger/Color-Pic, Inc.; 507(c), Photofest; 507(br), HRW Photo by Victoria Smith; 507(bl), Brook/Gamma Liaison.

Chapter Twenty Page 508, AP/Wide World Photos; 511(t), Phil Degginger/Color-Pic, Inc.; 511(b), Emil Muench/Photo Researchers, Inc.; 512, Norbert Wu; 520(b), Erich Schrempp/Photo Researchers, Inc. ; 520, Don Spiro/Tony Stone Images; 522(tl,tr,), Richard Megna/Fundamental Photographs; 522(b), Richard Hamilton Smith/Corbis-Bettmann; 524(t), Richard Megna/Fundamental Photographs; 525,

777

AP/Wide World Photos; 526, Norbert Wu; 528, Richard Megna/Fundamental Photographs; 529, Martin Bough/Fundamental Photographs; 530, Pete Saloutos/The Stock Market; 531, Betty K. Bruce/Animals Animals/Earth Scenes.

Chapter Twenty-one Page 532(c), SuperStock; 532(t), The Granger Collection, NY; 532(b), Mark Newman/Photo Researchers, Inc.; 538(c), Michael A. Keller/The Picture Cube; 543(cl), Art Wolfe/ Tony Stone Images; 543(b), Tom Hannon/Picture Cube; 544, Charles D. Winters/Timeframe Photography Inc.; 545, Dr. E.R. Degginger/Color-Pic, Inc.; 546, Stephen Dalton/Photo Researchers, Inc.; 547(b), Matt Meadows/Photo Researchers, Inc.; 547(t), courtesy of Johann Borenstein; 550(b,c), Richard Megna/ Fundamental Photographs; 553(l), 554(c), Image Club Graphics © 1998 Adobe Systems; 554(tl,tr,br), Bob Daemmrich/HRW Photo; 558, Ross Harrison Koty/Tony Stone Images; 559, Dick Luria/Photo Researchers, Inc.

Chapter Twenty-two Page 562(t), Cindy Roesinger/Photo Researchers, Inc.; 562(b), Visuals Unlimited; 565, Photo Researchers, Inc.; 566, A.T. Willet/The Image Bank; 567(r,l), Leonard Lessing/Photo Researchers, Inc.; 567(c), Michael Fogden and Patricia Fogden/Corbis; 568(l), Robert Wolf; 569(c), Hugh Turvey/Science Photo Library/Photo Researchers, Inc.; 569(r), Blair Seitz/Photo Researchers, Inc.; 569(l), Leonide Principe/Photo Researchers, Inc.; 571(t), Bachmann/Photo Researchers, Inc.; 571(b), The Stock Market; 572, Cameron Davidson/Tony Stone Images; 574, Michael English/Custom Medical Stock Photo; 577, Richard Megna/Fundamental Photographs; 578, Robert Wolf; 579(t), Fundamental Photographs; 581(t), Robert Wolf; 581(b), HRW photo by Stephanie Morris; 583(t), Image copyright 2001 PhotoDisc, Inc.; 583(c), Renee Lynn/Davis/Lynn Images; 583(b), Robert Wolf; 584, Leonard Lessing/Peter Arnold, Inc.; 585, Index Stock Photography; 586, Leonard Lessing/ Photo Researchers, Inc.; 587, Robert Wolf; 589(tr), Charles Winters/Photo Researchers, Inc.; 589(cr), Mark E. Gibson; 589(br), Richard Megna/Fundamental Photographs; 590(t,b), Dr. E.R. Degginger/Color-Pic, Inc.; 591, courtesy of the Raytheon Company.

Chapter Twenty-three Page 592(b), NASA; 592(t), Roger Ressmeyer/Corbis Media WA; 594(b), Harry Rogers/Photo Researchers, Inc.; 594(r), Kindra Clinett/The Picture Cube; 596, HRW Photo by Peter Van Steen; 597, Alan Schein/The Stock Market; 598(tr), Yoav Levy/Phototake; 599(tr), HRW Photo by Stephanie Morris; 600(c), Richard Megna/Fundamental Photographs; 602, 603(b), Robert Wolf, 603(t,c), Dr. E.R. Degginger/Color-Pic, Inc.; 607(l,r), Leonard Lessing/Peter Arnold, Inc.; 612, Don Mason/The Stock Market; 613(l,r), Ken Lax; 616, James L. Amos/National Geographic Society; 618(b), US Patent and Trade Office; 618(t), Private collection of Garrett Morgan Family; 619(b), NASA; 619(t), SuperStock.

LabBook "LabBook Header": "L," Corbis Images, "a," Letraset Phototone, "b" and "B," HRW, "o" and "k," images ©2001 PhotoDisc/HRW; 623(c), HRW photo by Michelle Bridwell; 623(br), Image copyright © 2001 PhotoDisc, Inc.; 624(cl), HRW photo by Victoria Smith; 624(bl), HRW photo by Stephanie Morris; 625(tl), Patti Murray/Animals Animals; 625(tr), HRW photo by Jana Birchum; 625(b), HRW photo by Peter Van Steen; 626, HRW photo by Victoria Smith; 631, NASA; 638, 639(t), HRW Photo by Victoria Smith; 640, Stuart Westmoreland/Tony Stone Images; 644, Gareth Trevor/Tony Stone Images; 649, copyright 2001 Photo Disc/HRW Photo; 653, NASA; 662, HRW photo by Stephanie Morris; 663, Paul Dance/Tony Stone Images; 665(l,r), Robert Wolf; 670, 673, 676, HRW photo by Victoria Smith; 685, Rob Boudreau/Tony Stone Images; 687, 690, 697, HRW photo by Victoria Smith; 701, David Young-Wolf/PhotoEdit; 706, James H. Karales/Peter Arnold Inc., NY; 709(t,c,b), 710, Richard Megna/Fundamental Photographs; 714, HRW Photo.

Appendix Page 727(t), 727(b), 731(b), HRW photo by Sam Dudgeon; 731(t), HRW photo by Peter Van Steen; 748, HRW photo by Sam Dudgeon.

Sam Dudgeon/HRW Photo Page vii(tl,tr,br); xi,(bl); xiv(bl); xv(tr,tl); xvi(cl); xviii-xx; T6(tl,tr); T11(br); T12(bl); T15(tr); 2(cr); 5(b); 8(tl,tr); 9(bl); 12(t,c); 22(cl); 23(t); 30(all); 31(l); 37(bl); 59(b); 61(bl); 64(r); 66; 76(b); 81(tr); 85(tl,tr,c); 87(r); 90(t); 91(cl); 93(t); 94(bl); 96(t,b); 99; 100(b); 101(br); 106(tr); 107; 112(b); 114(b); 116(t); 118(c); 124(bl); 132; 137(b); 157(r); 161; 177(t); 180; 182(b); 187(b); 195(c); 198; 199(bl); 213; 215; 217; 220; 238; 240(t); 244-45; 251; 256; 279; 282-283; 303; 306; 307(c,tl); 308; 311(b); 312(tl,b); 315; 318(t); 336(b); 338; 339(l); 345; 347; 349; 350(bl); 356; 373; 374(b); 378(b); 386(l); 388(t); 393; 397; 408; 411; 431(b); 432; 438(t,bl,bc); 440(b,c); 445(b); 447; 449(b); 454; 455(t); 457; 458; 460; 476-477; 480(b); 481; 482; 484-487; 490; 494-495; 496; 497; 500; 502; 506(c); 509; 518; 527; 533(b); 535(b); 536; 538(r); 541(t); 550(t); 552; 556-557; 563; 568(c); 588; 593; 594(l); 600(b); 611; 620(cl,t,b); 622; 623(b); 624(br,t); 628; 630; 632-633; 634; 636-637; 639(b); 641; 643; 645-648; 650-652; 654-657; 659-661; 664; 675; 676; 677; 678; 681-684; 688; 692-694; 698-700; 702; 703-705; 707-708; 711; 713; 715; 717; 719-720; 723; 727; 731; 748; 723.

John Langford/HRW Photo Page v(cr); vi(tr); x(tl,bl); xii(br); xiii(tr,cl); T7(r); T8(bl); T12(tr); 6(l); 10(tl,c); 20(cl); 21; 22(tr); 28(b); 31(t); 35; 36(t); 37(t); 38-39; 41(b); 42; 52(l); 54(all); 64(l); 91(bl,bc,br); 95(all); 145; 188-189; 191; 193; 195(t); 199(t); 201(t); 205(tr); 206; 207; 208(b); 209(tr); 218(l); 219; 220(b); 223(b); 224; 226; 233(cl,r,bl); 235(cr); 247; 252-255; 257; 258; 260-261; 264; 270; 301; 327-328; 332(r); 336(t); 341; 348(b); 354; 355(c); 362-363; 368(b); 372(t); 377(t); 378(t); 379; 388(bl); 389; 415; 421; 425; 426(tl,tr); 427(t); 431(t); 438(cl); 440(r); 441; 442; 443; 444; 446; 448(b); 449(t); 524(b); 535(t);542; 543(t,bc); 553(r); 568(r); 573; 576; 579(b); 582; 594(inset); 599(b); 600(tl); 601(b); 617; 623(t); 631(t); 665(b); 666; 679; 691; 696.

Scott Van Osdol/HRW Photo Page T17(br); 61(br); 62(all); 63(b); 67(t); 69(b); 71-72; 163; 163: 166; 175(br); 194; 196; 199(br); 351(bl); 384; 385; 386(t); 391; 589; 627; 629.

ANNOTATED TEACHER'S EDITION CREDITS

Front Matter Cover(bkgd), Zigy Kaluzny/Tony Stone Images; T2(l), T3(r), Image ©2001 PhotoDisc; T4(l), NASA; T5(r), Image ©2001 PhotoDisc; T6(l), Stephen Durke/Washington Artists; T6(tl),Sergio Purtell/Foca; T7(r), HRW photo by Sam Dudgeon; T9(r), Image ©2001 PhotoDisc; T10(l), HRW photo by John Langford; T12(t), Brett H. Froomer/The Image Bank; T13(r), HRW photo by Sam Dudgeon; T14(l), Image ©2001 PhotoDisc; T15(r), HRW photo by Sam Dudgeon; T16, John Morrison/Morrison Photography; T17, Image ©2001 PhotoDisc.

Master Materials List Page xxiv(t), HRW photo; xxiv(c,bl,br), xxv(tr,tl), Image ©2001 PhotoDisc; xxv(cr), HRW photo by Scott Van Osdol; xxv(cl), HRW photo by John Langford; xxv(b), HRW photo by Sam Dudgeon; xxvi(t,cl), Image ©2001 PhotoDisc; xxvi(cr), Digital Stock Corporation; xxvi(bl), Image ©2001 PhotoDisc; xxvi(br), HRW photo by Sam Dudgeon; xxvii(tr), Image ©2001 PhotoDisc; xxvii(tl, br), HRW photo by Sam Dudgeon; xxvii(cl,cr), Image ©2001 PhotoDisc; xxvii(br), Image ©2001 PhotoDisc; xxviii(t), Image ©2001 PhotoDisc; xxviii(tc), HRW photo by Sam Dudgeon; xxviii(c), Image ©2001 PhotoDisc; xxviii(bc), EyeWire, Inc.; xxviii(b), xxix(t,tc,bc,b), Image ©2001 PhotoDisc.

Chapter One Background Page 3E(tl) David Lawrence/The Stock Market; 3E(cl, bl), HRW photo by John Langford; 3E (bl), Rainey Kirk/The Neis Group; 3E(br), Brian White; 3F(tl), Keith Locke/Suzanne Craig; 3F(tr), Morgan Cain & Associates; 3F(b), Blake Thornton/Rita Marie.

Chapter Two Background Page 33E(tl), The Granger Collection; 33E(tr), HRW photo by John Langford; 33E(bl), Gary Locke/Suzanne Craig; 33E(br), HRW photo by Michelle Bridwell; 33F(tl), Marty Roper/Planet Rep; 33F(tr), Neal Nishler/Tony Stone Images; 33F(bl), Rob Boudreau/Tony Stone Images; 33F(br), John Morrison/Morrison Photography.

Chapter Three Background Page 57E(t), Dr. Harold E. Edgerton/©The Harold E. Edgerton Trust/ courtesy of Palm Press, Inc.; 57E(b), Stephen Durke/Washington Artists; 57(l), Marty Roper/Planet Rep; 57F(r), David Schleinkofer/Mendola Ltd.

Chapter Four Background Page 79E(t), David Frazier; 79E(b), HRW photo by Sam Dudgeon; 79E(cl), Runk/Shoenburger/Grant Heilman Photography; 79E(c), Richard Megna/Fundamental Photographs; 79E(cr), HRW photo by Sam Dudgeon; 79F(tl), Marty Roper/Planet Rep; 79F(tr), HRW photo by Lance Schriner; 79F(bl,br), Dr. E.R. Degginger/Color-Pic, Inc.

Chapter Five Background Page 105E(t), Doug Henry/American Artists; 105E(b), HRW photo by Michelle Bridwell; 105F(l), Blake Thornton/Rita Marie; 105F(r), NASA.

Chapter Six Background Page 135E(t), Robert Daemmrich/Tony Stone Images; 135E(b), NASA; 135F(l), Marty Roper/Planet Rep.; 135F(tr), Zigy Kaluzny/Tony Stone Images; 135F(b), David Madison.

Chapter Seven Background 159E(cl), HRW photo by Scott Van Osdol; 159E(bl), Stephen Durke/ Washington Artists; 159E(r), Super Stock; 159F(tl), Rainey Kirk/The Neis Group; 159F(c), Larry L. Miller/Photo Researchers; 159F(b), George Hall, Check Six.

Chapter Eight Background Page 185E(l), John White/The Neis Group; 185E(r), Keith Locke/Suzanne Craig; 185F(l), Robert Wolf; 185F(r), HRW photo by John Langford; 185F(b), HRW photo by Scott Van Osdol.

Chapter Nine Background Page 211E(tl,tr), HRW photo by Sam Dudgeon; 211E(bl), Dave Joly; 211F(t), Ted Clutter/Photo Researchers, Inc.; 211F(bl), Dan McGeehan/Koralik Associates; 211F(br), NASA.

Chapter Ten Background 243E(l), Terry Guyer; 243E(br), HRW Photo by Sam Dudgeon; 243F(tl), HRW Photo by John Langford; 243F(cr), Dorling Kindersley, Ltd.; 243F(bl), Dan Stuckenschneider/Uhl Studios Inc.

Chapter Eleven Background Page 277E(tl), William Nawrooki Stock Photography; 277E(tr), Preface, Inc.; 277E(cr), Corbis-Bettman; 277E(bl), Dr. Mitsuo Ohtsuki/Science Photo Library/Photo Researchers, Inc.; 277F(tl), Lawrence Berkeley National Laboratory; 277F(tr), Superstock; 277F(bl), Terry Kovalcik.

Chapter Twelve Background Page 299E(tl), HRW photo by Sam Dudgeon; 299E(tr), Charles D. Winters/Photo Researchers, Inc.; 299E(cr), Michael Jaroszko/American Artists; 299E(b), Richard Megna/Fundamental Photographs; 299F(t), HRW photo by Sam Dudgeon.

Chapter Thirteen Background Page 325E(tl), Stephen Durke/Washington Artists; 325E(bl), Jim Sugar Photography/Corbis; 325E(cr), HRW photo by Peter Van Steen; 325F(l), Keith Locke/Suzanne Craig; 325F(r), HRW photo by Sam Dudgeon.

Chapter Fourteen Background Page 347E(tr), Richard Megna/Fundamental Photographs; 347E(b), Peticolas/Megna/Fundamental Photographs; 347E(b), Richard Megna/Fundamental Photographs; 347F(tr), HRW photo by John Langford; 347F(cr), Tom Stewart/The Stock Market; 347F(bl), Preface, Inc.; 347F(br), Dorling Kindersley, LTD/courtesy of the Science Museum, London.

Chapter Fifteen Background Page 371E(l), HRW photo by Sam Dudgeon; 371E(t), HRW photo by John Langford; 371E(b), Runk/Schoenburger/Grant Heilman Photography, Inc.; 371F(t), Miro Vinton/Stock Boston/PNI; 371F(b), HRW photo by Scott Van Osdol.

Chapter Sixteen Background Page 395E(t), Henry Becquerel/The Granger Collection; 395E(b), Dr. E.R. Degginger; 395E(c) Sygma; 395F(tl), Corbis; 395F(tr) Stephen Durke/Washington Artists; 395F(b), Shone/Liaison International.

Chapter Seventeen Background Page 419E(tl,tr), HRW photo by John Langford; 419E(c), HRW photo by Victoria Smith; 419E(r), HRW photo by Sam Dudgeon; 419F(l), Takeshi Takahara/Photo Researchers, Inc.; 419F(t), Visuals Unlimited; 419F(b), HRW photo by John Langford.

Chapter Eighteen Background Page 451E(tl,bl), HRW photo by Sam Dudgeon; 451E(r), Richard Megna/Fundamental Photographs; 451F(tl), Sidney Jablonski; 451F(bl), Tom Tracy/The Stock Shop; 451F(r), David Fischer.

Chapter Nineteen Background Page 479E(all), HRW photo by Sam Dudgeon; 479F(t), Dr. E.R. Degginger; 479F(bl), Dan Stuckenschneider/Uhl Studios Inc.

Chapter Twenty Background Page 507E(l), AP/Wide World Photos; 507E(cr), Mike Carroll/Steve Edsey and Sons and Will Nelson/Sweet Reps; 507E(b), Erich Schrempp/Photo Researchers, Inc.; 507F(tl), Sidney Jablonski; 507F(tr), Phil Degginger/Color-Pic, Inc.; 507F(bl), Sidney Jablonski; 507F(b), Richard Megna/Fundamental Photographs.

Chapter Twenty-one Background Page 531E(cl,tr), HRW Photo by John Langford; 531E(cl), Gary Ferster (sound waves); 531E(br), Terry Guyer; 531F(cl), Stephen Dalton/Photo Researchers, Inc.; 531F(cl), Gary Ferster (sound waves); 531F(tr), Annie Bissett; 531F(br), HRW Photo by John Langford.

Chapter Twenty-two Background Page 561(tl), Sidney Jablonski; 561E(bl), A.T. Willett/The Image Bank; 561E(cl,cr), Leonard Lessin/Photo Researchers, Inc.; 561F(tl), Leonard Lessin/Peter Arnold, Inc.; 561F(cr), Index Stock Photography, Inc.

Chapter Twenty-three Background Page 591E(l), Dan Stuckenschneider/Uhl Studios Inc.; 591E(tr,b), Robert Wolf; 591F(l), Keith Kasnot; 591F(tr), HRW photo by Sam Dudgeon

Answers to Concept Mapping Questions

The following pages contain sample answers to all of the concept mapping questions that appear in the Chapter Reviews. Because there is more than one way to do a concept map, your students' answers may vary.

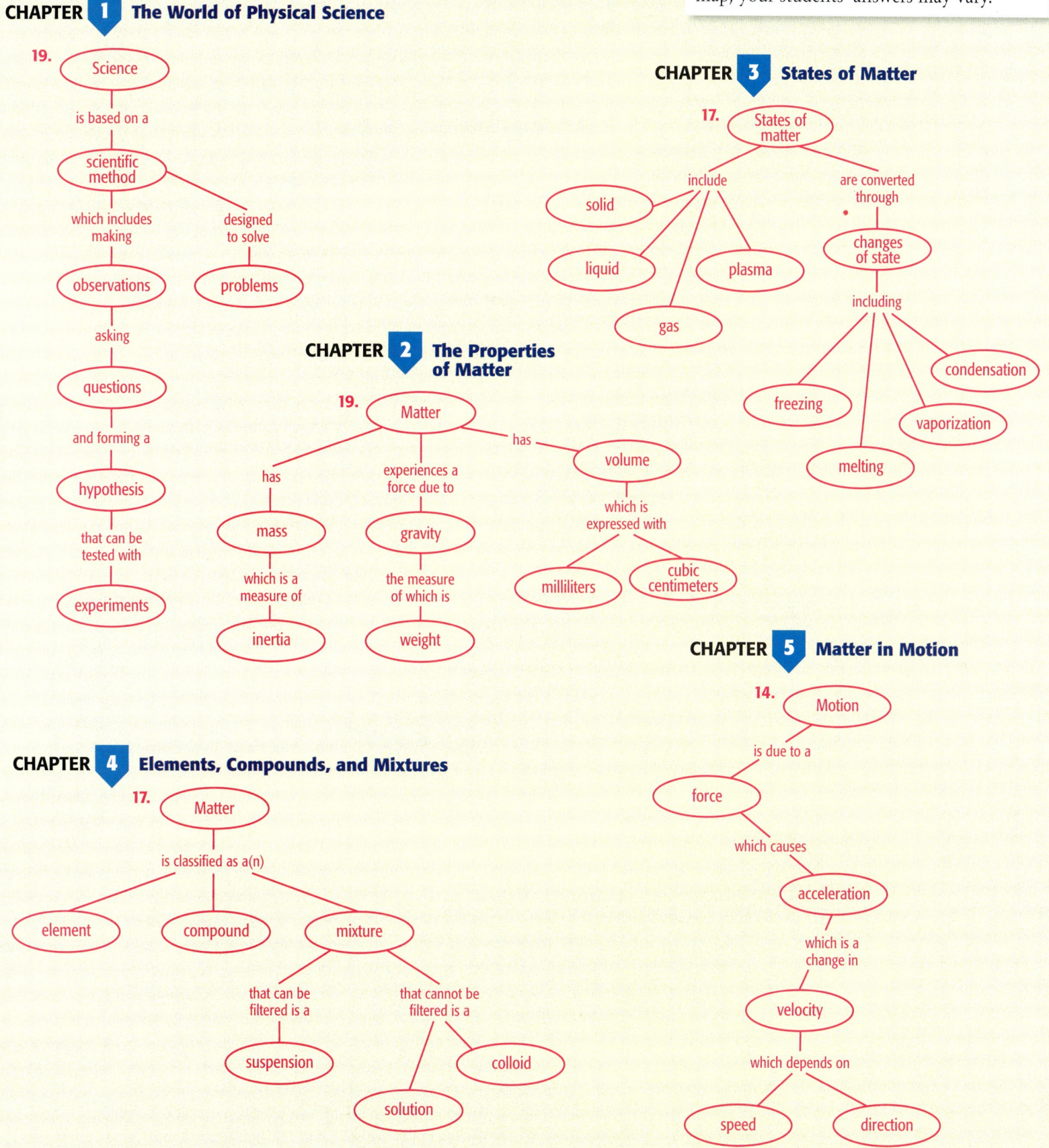

CHAPTER 6 Forces in Motion

15. Gravity
- on an object combines with → air resistance → to determine the object's → terminal velocity
- pulls an object down during → free fall, projectile motion

CHAPTER 7 Forces in Fluids

16. A fluid
- exerts → buoyant force
  - which varies with → density
  - which is caused by differences in → pressure → which increases with → depth

CHAPTER 8 Work and Machines

16. A machine
- makes → work → easier by trading → force, distance → in order to provide → mechanical advantage

CHAPTER 9 Energy and Energy Resources

18. Energy
- has many forms that undergo → energy conversions
  - which always result in → thermal energy → due to → friction
  - that can involve → machines

CHAPTER 10 Heat and Heat Technology

17. Heat
- is a transfer of → thermal energy → by → conduction, convection, radiation → due to a difference in → temperature

780 Concept Mapping Answers

CHAPTER 11 Introduction to Atoms

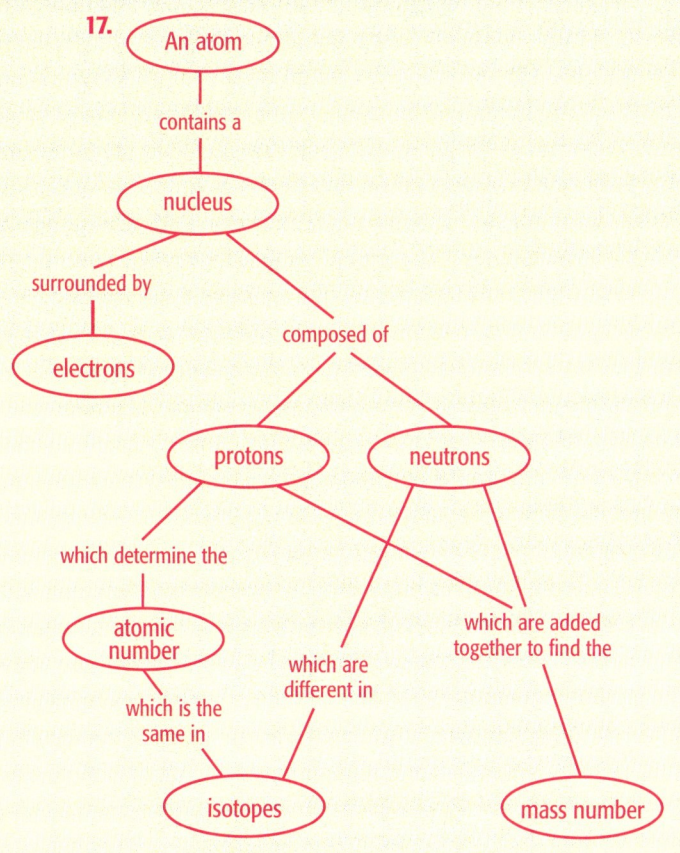

CHAPTER 12 The Periodic Table

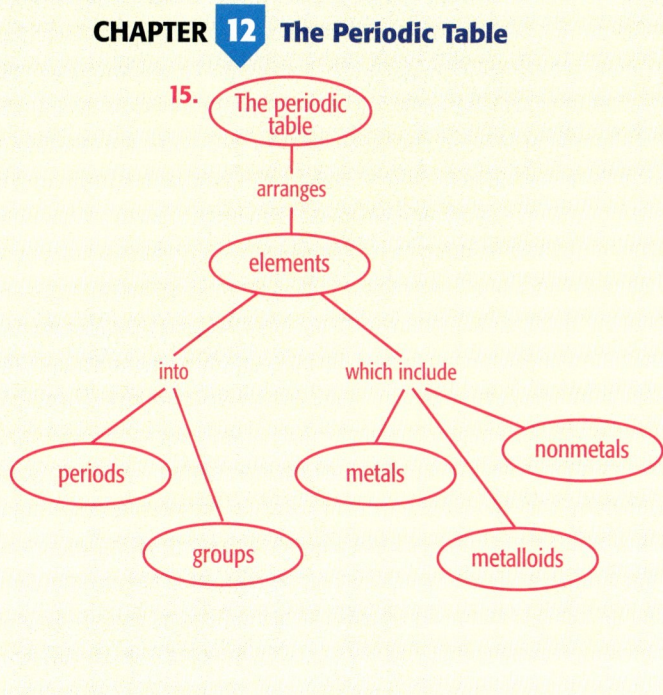

CHAPTER 13 Chemical Bonding

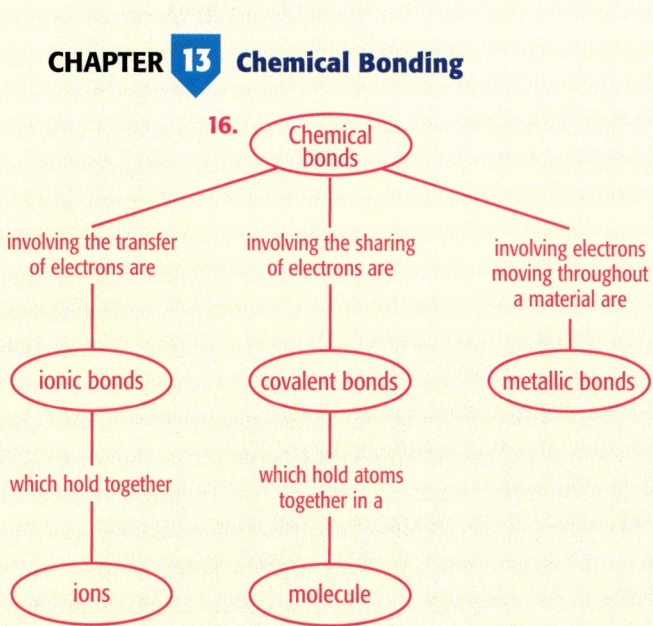

CHAPTER 14 Chemical Reactions

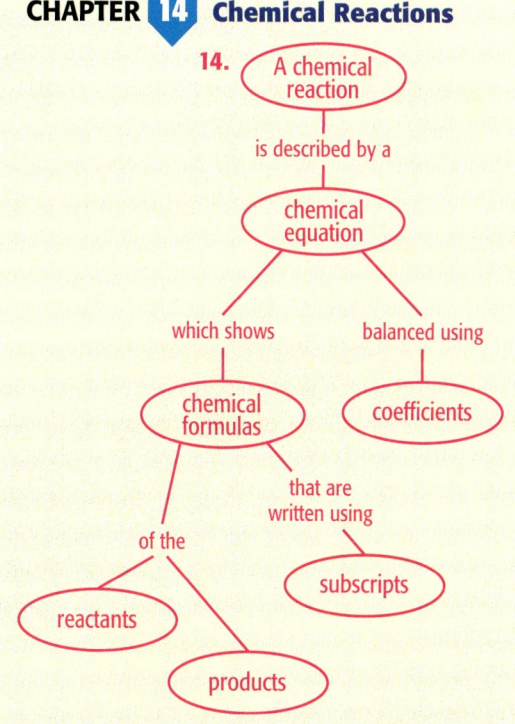

Concept Mapping Answers **781**

CHAPTER 15 Chemical Compounds

16.

- pH
  - less than 7 → acid
  - equal to 7 → neutral
  - greater than 7 → base
- acid and base react together to form water and a salt

CHAPTER 16 Atomic Energy

15.

- Nuclear radiation
  - can be in the form of a(n): alpha particle, beta particle, gamma ray
  - is released during radioactive decay

CHAPTER 17 Introduction to Electricity

16.

- Electric current
  - is produced by a: battery, thermocouple, photocell
  - is a flow of charges
    - that may travel in a circuit
      - which may be a: parallel circuit, series circuit

CHAPTER 18 Electromagnetism

14.

- Electromagnetism
  - is the interaction of electricity and magnetism
    - that can lead to electromagnetic induction
      - which is applied in: generators, transformers

CHAPTER 19 Electronic Technology

19.

- Electronic devices
  - use signals
    - contained in carriers such as: radio waves, electric current
      - to transmit information

782 Concept Mapping Answers

CHAPTER 11 Introduction to Atoms

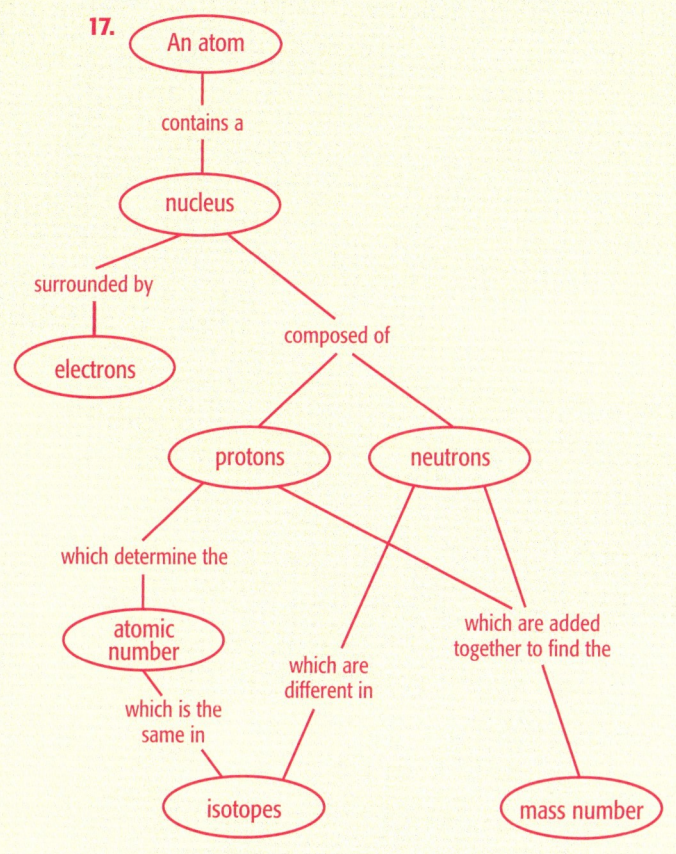

CHAPTER 12 The Periodic Table

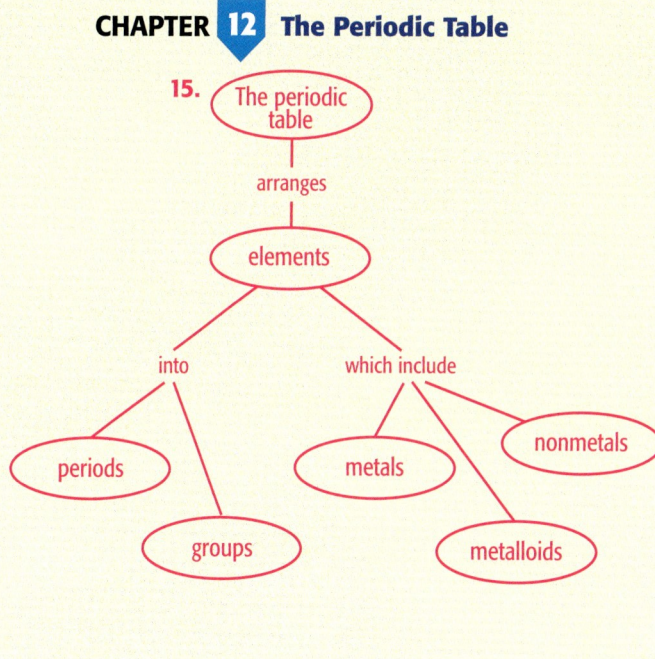

CHAPTER 13 Chemical Bonding

CHAPTER 14 Chemical Reactions

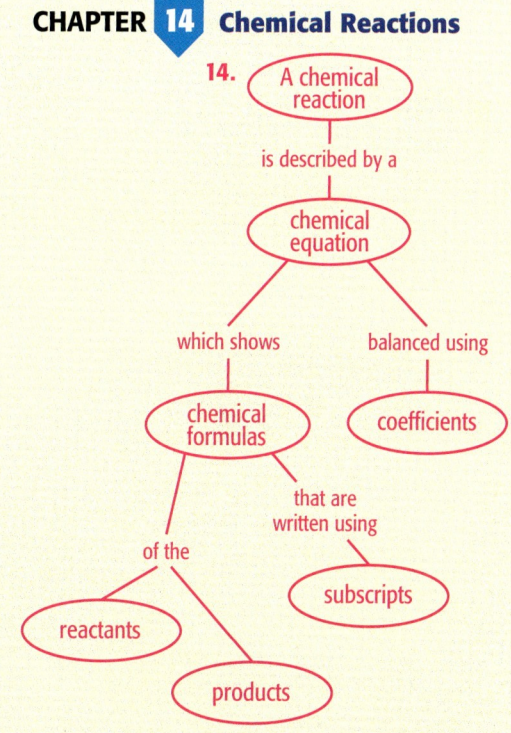

Concept Mapping Answers **781**

CHAPTER 15 Chemical Compounds

16. pH
- less than 7 → acid
- equal to 7 → neutral
- greater than 7 → base

acid and base react together to form water and a salt

CHAPTER 16 Atomic Energy

15. Nuclear radiation
- can be in the form of a(n): alpha particle, beta particle, gamma ray
- is released during: radioactive decay

CHAPTER 17 Introduction to Electricity

16. Electric current
- is produced by a: battery, thermocouple, photocell
- is a flow of charges that may travel in a circuit, which may be a parallel circuit or series circuit

CHAPTER 18 Electromagnetism

14. Electromagnetism
- is the interaction of electricity and magnetism
- that can lead to electromagnetic induction
- which is applied in generators and transformers

CHAPTER 19 Electronic Technology

19. Electronic devices
- use signals
- contained in carriers such as radio waves and electric current
- to transmit information

782   Concept Mapping Answers

CHAPTER 20 The Energy of Waves

18.
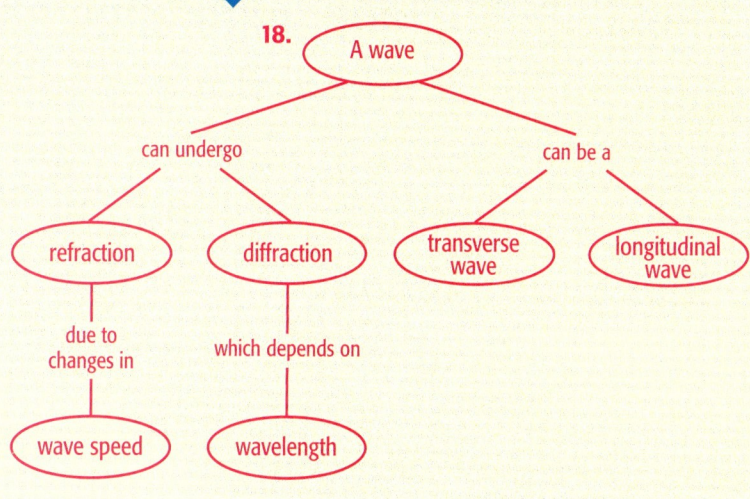

CHAPTER 21 The Nature of Sound

17.
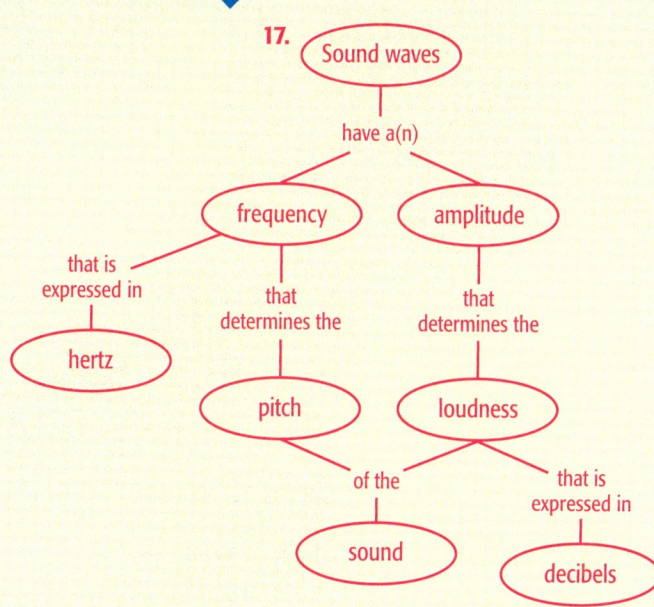

CHAPTER 22 The Nature of Light

18.
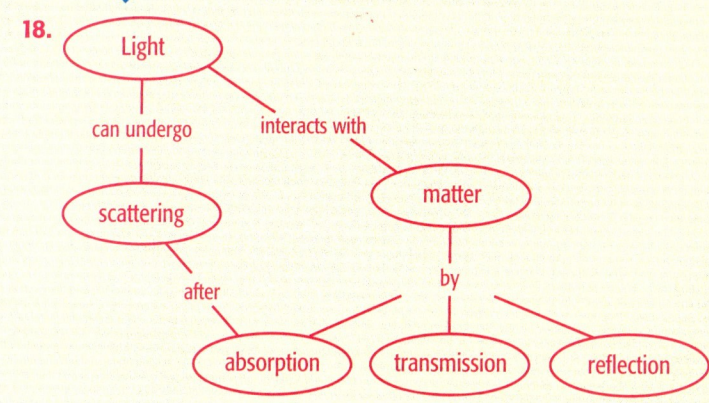

CHAPTER 23 Light and Our World

17.
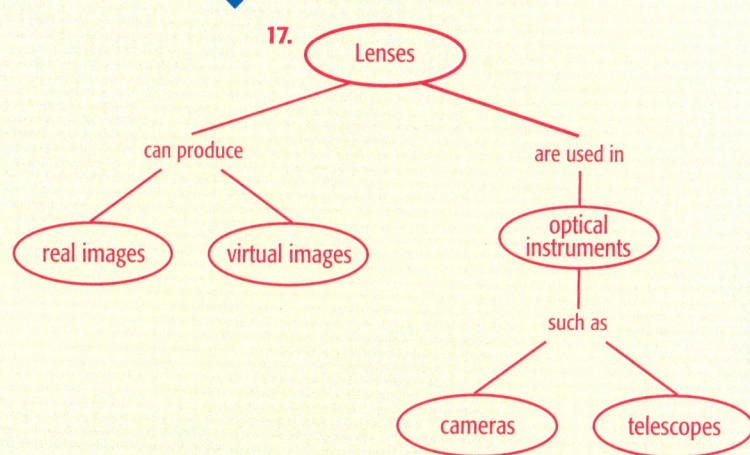